STOKOWSKI

A COUNTERPOINT OF VIEW

Portrait photograph of Leopold Stokowki by Edward Steichen (1927)

STOKOWSKI

A COUNTERPOINT OF VIEW

by Oliver Daniel

Illustrated with photographs

DODD, MEAD & COMPANY • New York

Library of Congress Cataloging in Publication Data

Daniel, Oliver.
  Stokowski: a counterpoint of view.

  Bibliography: p.
  Includes index.
  1. Stokowski, Leopold, 1882–1977.   2. Conductors—
United States—Biography. I. Title.
ML422.S76D3   785'.092'4 [B]   82-2443
ISBN 0-396-07936-9   AACR2

The author is grateful for the permission of the following publishers and authors to quote excerpts
of copyrighted material as follows:

  Agitato, Jerome Toobin, copyright © 1975 by Jerome Toobin. Reprinted by permission of Viking
Penguin Inc.
  Monsieur Croche, The Dillettante Hater, Claude Debussy, translated from the French by B. N.
Langdon-Davies, translation copyright by The Viking Press Inc., renewed 1956 by The Viking Press,
Inc. Reprinted by permission of Viking Penguin Inc.
  Edgard Varèse, Fernand Ouellette, by permission of Viking Penquin Inc.
  A Guide to Recorded Music, New Guide to Recorded Music, and *The New Guide to Recorded
Music—International Edition*, Irving Kolodin, copyright 1941, 1946, 1950 by Irving Kolodin. Re-
printed by permission of Doubleday & Company, Inc.
  Philharmonic: A History of New York's Orchestra, Howard Shanet, copyright © 1975 by Howard
Shanet. Reprinted by permission of Doubleday & Company, Inc.
  Woman to Woman, Gloria Vanderbilt, copyright © 1979 by Gloria Vanderbilt. Reprinted by
permission of Doubleday & Company, Inc.
  5,000 Nights at the Opera, Sir Rudolf Bing, copyright © 1972 by Sir Rudolf Bing. Reprinted by
permission of Doubleday & Company, Inc.
  Toscanini, Harvey Sachs, by permission of Harper & Row Publishers Inc.
  My Husband Gabrilowitsch, Clara Clemens, by permission of Harper & Row Publishers Inc.

Testimony: The Memoir of Dmitri Shostakovich, Solomon Volkov, ed., by permission of Harper & Row Publishers Inc.

The Great Conductors, Harold Schonberg, by permission of Simon and Schuster.

Olin Downes on Music, Irene Downes, ed., by permission of Simon and Schuster.

Barbirolli: Conductor Laureate, Michael Kennedy, by permission of Granada Publishing Limited.

The New Music Lover's Handbook, Elie Siegmeister, copyright 1973 by Elie Siegmeister. Reprinted by permission of Harvey House, Inc.

Bubbles, Beverly Sills, by permission of Warner Books and Meredith Enterprises Ltd.

The Pursuit of Music, Sir Walford Davies, by permission of Thomas Nelson & Sons Limited.

Walford Davies: A Biography, H. C. Colles, by permission of Oxford University Press.

Composers, Conductors and Critics, Claire Reis, by permission of Victoria Bijur (for the estate of Claire Reis) and Oxford University Press.

Musical Discourse, Richard Aldrich, by permission of Oxford University Press.

The Houston Symphony Orchestra 1913–1971, Hubert Roussel, copyright © 1972 by Hubert Roussel. Reprinted by permission of the University of Texas Press.

Johann Sebastian Bach, Volume II, Philipp Spitta, by permission of Dover Publications Inc.

With Strings Attached, Joseph Szigeti, by permission of Alfred A. Knopf, Inc.

Theme and Variations, Bruno Walter, by permission of Alfred A. Knopf Inc.

The Other Side of the Record, Charles O'Connell, by permission of Alfred A. Knopf Inc.

Notes without Music—An Autobiography, Darius Milhaud, by permission of Alfred A. Knopf Inc.

The Guide to Long Playing Records—Orchestral Music and *The Musical Life*, Irving Kolodin, by permission of Alfred A. Knopf Inc.

Themes and Episodes, Igor Stravinsky and Robert Craft, by permission of Alfred A. Knopf, Inc.

The Musical Scene and *The Art of Judging Music*, Virgil Thomson, copyright 1945 and 1948 by Virgil Thomson. Reprinted by permission of Alfred A. Knopf, Inc.

Mrs. Jack, Louise Hall Tharp, by permission of McIntosh and Otis, Inc. and Little, Brown and Company.

Requiem for a Yellow Brick Brewery, John Briggs, by permission of Little, Brown and Company.

An American Musician's Story, Olga Samaroff Stokowski, by permission of W. W. Norton and Company.

Varèse: A Looking Glass Diary, Louise Varèse, by permission of W. W. Norton and Company.

Charles E. Ives—Memos, John Kirkpatrick, ed., by permission of W. W. Norton and Company.

Der Verfolgte Tenor, Sergei Radamsky, by permission of Mary Radamsky and R. Piper et Co. Verlag.

H. L. Mencken on Music, Louis Cheslock, ed., by permission of Schirmer Books.

Those Fabulous Philadelphians: The Life and Times of a Great Orchestra, Herbert Kupferberg, copyright © 1969 by Herbert Kupferberg. Reprinted by permission of Charles Scribner's Sons.

Our Two Lives, Halina Rodzinski, copyright © 1976 by Halina Rodzinski. Reprinted by permission of Charles Scribner's Sons.

The Americanization of Edward Bok, Edward Bok, copyright 1920 by Charles Scribner's Sons; copyright renewed. Reprinted by permission of Charles Scribner's Sons.

Record reviews in the *American Record Guide* by permission of Heldref Publications.

Record reviews in *High Fidelity* by permission of ABC Leisure Magazines Inc. (All Rights Reserved)

Record reviews in *Stereo Review* by permission of Ziff-Davis Publishing Company.

Record reviews in *The New Records*, by permission of H. Royer Smith Company, 2019 Walnut Street, Philadelphia, PA 19103.

Record reviews in *Audio Record Review (Hi-Fi News and Record Review)* by permission of Link House Magazines (Croydon) Ltd.

Record reviews in the *Gramophone* by permission of General Gramophone Publications Ltd.

For Don Ott

Contents

Illustrations

Acknowledgments

I AM particularly grateful to Evangeline Stokowski Merrill, who openly talked of her experiences and relationship with Stokowski, and to their daughters, Lyuba Rhodes and Sadja Greenwood, who supplied valuable information and unique photographs. I'm grateful to Stan and Chris Stokowski for their cooperation.

Sonya Thorbecke, Stokowski's eldest daughter, was a mine of information and was cooperative beyond any expectations. She spent many hours at her home in Sewickley, Pennsylvania, and on the phone with me talking about her divided life as a child between her mother and the household of Evangeline and Stoki. She also recalled her close relationship with her grandmother, Stoki's mother, who lived in England, and his brother, Percy "Jim" Stock, who supplied unique information. I am grateful to all of the Stokowski heirs for permission to quote from his writings and interviews.

There were a number of people whose generosity and kindness extended far beyond the expected.

Unfortunately, a number of those who contributed died before the book was completed: Samuel Barber, Robert Russell Bennett, Orville Bullitt, Carlos Chávez, Avery Claflin, Harvey Fletcher, Ella Grainger, Richard Hammond, Howard Hanson, Richard Huemer, José Iturbi, André Kostelanetz, Olga Koussevitzky, Goddard Lieberson, Norman Lloyd, Anita Loos, Sylvia Marlowe, Ruth O'Neill, Mrs. John DeWitt Peltz, Claire Reis, Francis Robinson, Leighton Rollins, Samuel Rubin,

Victor Seroff, Ruth Steinway, Clara Steuermann, Percy Stock, and Ben Weber.

I am particularly indebted to Charles "Jack" Baumgarten, Stoki's devoted assistant, on whom he relied most heavily during his latter years. Jack became a part of Stoki's adopted family and remained with him in both England and France until the time of his death. He aided me enormously by supplying much information, documents, and pictures and generously examined the manuscript, offering suggestions and corrections.

Natalie "Natasha" Bender likewise was a source of valuable information. She, more than anyone, knew all of the details of his late years. She had been close to Stoki since she was in her teens during the Philadelphia youth concert days in the 1930s. When Stokowski was in his eighties and living alone, she and her friend Faye Chabrow, at the suggestion of his children, moved into his apartment to help take care of him. Natasha was his constant companion until the end.

Edward "Ted" Johnson of London had been most helpful to Stoki, particularly after the latter's move to England. Ted was a font of information, and he prepared the discography of Stoki's records. He also flew to New York and spent days combing through the manuscript to eliminate possible errors and make positive suggestions.

I am most grateful for the help given by my distinguished critic friends: Paul Hume, Harriett Johnson, Irving Kolodin, Herbert Kupferberg, Harold Schonberg, Howard Taubman, Rosemarie Tauris, Heuwell Tircuit, and Bill Zakariasen. Virgil Thomson was most kind in relating experiences, expressing opinions, and letting me examine volumes of his criticisms.

I am also grateful to Wiga Ferrara, who not only translated from the German but meticulously indexed interviews and other material; Val Ott, who translated crucial material from the French and the Czech; Natasha Lutov and Charles Babel, who did the same from the Russian.

Particular thanks to: Belle Schulhof, who was most generous in letting me use correspondence and photos from the 1950s, when her husband, Andrew, was Stokowski's manager; Lawrence Schoenberg and the Arnold Schoenberg Institute, Los Angeles, California, for permission to use the Schoenberg-Stokowski correspondence; Jussi Jalas, for the Sibelius-Stokowski correspondence; Anne B. Shepherd, of the Cincinnati Historical Society; Edwin Heilakka, of the Stokowski Collection at the Curtis Institute of Music in Philadelphia; Kay Dreyfus, of the Grainger Museum at the University of Melbourne, Parkeville, Victoria, Australia; Ann Blatt, of the Greenburgh, New York, Public Library; Wayne Shirley, of the Library of Congress, Washington, D.C.; Mary Boccaccio, of the McKeldin Library's James Felton Collection of Stokowski material at the University of Maryland, College Park, Maryland; Frank Campbell, of the Lincoln Center Research Library of the New York Public Library; Sina Fosdick, of the Nicholas Roerich Museum, New York; the staff of the Philadelphia Free Library; Louis Hood, of the Philadelphia Orchestra Association; and David R. Smith, of the Walt Disney Archives, Burbank, California.

To Alfred Reginald Allen, Don Brodine, James Browning, Tony D'Amato, Robert Gross, Tom Johnson, Sylvan Levin, Merle Montgomery, Preben Opperby, William Lee Pryor, and Gunther Schuller, all of whose help was most substantial, I am deeply indebted.

To the following I extend my thanks. Regrettably, the fund of information far exceeded the extent of this book, and I apologize for the omission of much valuable material that was proffered.

Australia: Kay Dreyfus, Peggy Glanville-Hicks, Denis Vaughan.
Austria: Theodor Berger, Grace Cornell Graff, Gottfried von Einem.
Brazil: Arminda Villa-Lobos.
Canada: Philip Frank, Glenn Gould, Stewart Knussen.
Czechoslovakia: Milena Galuskova.
Denmark: Preben Opperby.
England: Richard Arnell, John Bird, Sir Adrian Boult, Joyce Bright, Tony D'Amato, Edward Heath, Edward Johnson, Yehudi Menuhin, Andrzej Panufnik, Henry Pleasants, André Previn, Stephen Smith, Barry Tuckwell.
Finland: Jussi Jalas.
France: Patricia Brinton, Deanna Durbin, Rolf Liebermann.
Germany: Werner Egk, Carl Orff, Hans Stuckenschmidt.
India: Narayana Menon, Svetoslav Roerich.
Israel: Paul Ben-Haim.
Netherlands: Frans van Rossum.
Norway: Klaus Egge, Øivin Fjeldstad, Kristian Lange, Harald Saeverud.
Soviet Union: Fikret Amirov, Rodion Shchedrin, Maxim Shostakovich.
Switzerland: Pierre Colombo.
United States: CALIFORNIA—Scott Beach, Hall Clovis, William Colvig, Paul Creston, James Dolan, Herschel Gilbert, Albert Goldberg, Ursula Greville, Lou Harrison, Carl Haverlin, Walter Heebner, Elayne Jones,

Philip Kahgan, Raymond Kendall, Ellis Kohs, Henry Koster, Charles Lee, Nan Merriman, Michel Penha, Dane Rudhyar, F. M. Scott III, Nicolas Slonimsky, Leonard Stein. CONNECTICUT—Eugene Cook, Benjamin de Loache, Vivian Perlis. FLORIDA—Jacques Abram, John Bitter, Robert Herman. GEORGIA—Robert Shaw, Martha Gerschefski. ILLINOIS—William Miller. INDIANA—Angeline Battista, Eileen Farrell, Martha Lipton. KENTUCKY—Robert Whitney. LOUISIANA—Clement J. McNasty. MASSACHUSETTS—William Gibson, Ralph Gomberg, Leon Kirchner, Louis Krasner, Malloy Miller, Thomas Perry, Daniel Pinkham, Gunther Schuller, Roger Voisin, George Zazofsky. NEW YORK—Arthur Aaron, Anahid Ajemian, Licia Albanese, Betty Allen, Donna Anderson, Alfredo Antonini, Arthur Austin, Julius Baker, Rose Bampton, Seymour Barab, Greg Benko, Carroll Bratman, Mrs. James Blauvelt, Suzanne Bloch, Robert Bloom, Helen Boatwright, Jorge Bolet, Martin Bookspan, David Brockman, Elizabeth Brockman, Beatrice Brown, Igor Buketoff, Elliott Carter, George Cehanovsky, James Chambers, Schuyler Chapin, Chou Wen-Chung, Arthur Cohn, Harold Coletta, David Cooper, Aaron Copland, Ainslee Cox, Burnett Cross, Jean Dalrymple, Lucia Davidova, Dorothy DeLay, Eugenia Delarova (Mrs. Henri Doll), Paul Dunkel, Joseph Eger, Harold Farberman, Rudolph Firkušný, Harry Fleetwood, Lukas Foss, Malcolm Frager, Urania Giordano, Lillian Gish, Roger Goeb, Morton Gould, John Grady, Gary Graffman, Martha Graham, Felix Greissle, Frank Guarrera, Lily Guest, László Halász, David Hall, Roger Hall, Mrs. William Hammer, Michael Hammond, Helene Hanff, Wendy Hanson, Lynn Harrell, Dorothy Hauser, Philip Hart, Claude Heckscher, Robert Helps, William Hess, Lilette Hindin, Karel Husa, Sophia Yarnall Jacobs, Fritz Jahoda, Theodate Johnson, Ben Johnston, Richard Jones, Mrs. Arthur Judson, David Katz, Ulysses Kay, Arthur Keller, Marcos Klorman, Larry King, Ralph Kirkpatrick, Basil Langton, Ruth Laredo, Harold Lawrence, Lucille Lawrence, Richard Leonard, Jean Leslie, John Lessard, William Lincer, Eugene List, Paul Loewenwarter, Jerome Lowenthal, Otto Luening, Natasha Lutov, Josephine Lyons, Robert McGinn, Stewart Manville, Leonard Marcus, William Masselos, William Mayer, Peter Mennin, Gian Carlo Menotti, Mitch Miller, Tony Miranda, Sharon Moe, Anna Moffo, Richard Mohr, Stewart Mott, Herman Muller, Paul Myers, Jack Ossewaarde, Jerry Pav, Joan Peyser, Adam Pinsker, Fred Plaut, Max Pollikoff, Paul Price, Bruce Prince-Joseph, Nell Rankin, Judith Raskin, Ruggiero Ricci, Filomena Ricciardi, Halina Rodzinski, Ned Rorem, Leonard Rose, Hugh Ross, Cyma Rubin, Julius Rudel, Winthrop Sargeant,

Janos Scholz, Arthur Schuller, William Schuman, Howard Scott, José Serebrier, Rudolf Serkin, Tom Shepard, Alan Shulman, Oscar Shumsky, Elie Siegmeister, Beverly Sills, Gregg Smith, Claudette Sorel, Dorle Jarmel Soria, Eleanor Steber, John Steinway, Isaac Stern, Risë Stevens, Robert Suderburg, Carlos Surinach, Magda Tagliaferro, Ming Tcherepnin, Walter Trampler, Carol Truax, Rosalyn Tureck, Louise Varèse, Ilana Vered, Shirley Verrett, John Owen Ward, Stewart Warkow, Beveridge Webster, Bert Whyte, Earl Wild, Camilla Williams, Alec Wyton, Anita Zahn. OHIO—Matthias Bamert. OREGON—Jacob Avshalomov. PENNSYLVANIA—Samuel L. M. Barlow, Mrs. Curtis Bok, Orville Bullitt, John de Lancie, Max de Schauensee, Ferdinand Del Negro, William Pearson Fischer, Elsa Hilger, Louis Hood, John Krell, Henry P. McIlhenny, David Madison, Samuel Mayes, Leonard Mogill, Francklyn Wynne Paris, Vincent Persichetti, Edna Phillips, Lachlin Pitcairn, Henry Schmidt, Sol Schoenbach, Nancy Shear, Enos Shupp, Jr., Mrs. Adrian Siegel, William Smith, Carl Torello, Marshall Turkin, Mrs. John P. Wheeler, Richard Yardumian, Ruth Yardumian. TEXAS—David Colvig, Wayne Crouse, Jon Embretsen, Leo Ornstein, Albert Tipton. WASHINGTON—William Bergsma, Alan Hovhaness. WEST VIRGINIA—Frances Yeend. WISCONSIN—Lucien Cailliet. WASHINGTON, D.C.—Ralph Backlund, Robert Dumm, Cathy French, Barbara Wolanin.

Foreword

"I WOULD like to go on living for ever and ever, making music all the time," Stokowski once remarked. "In the future, music will become, I'm sure, different, because everything will be gradually different. Instruments will be different. The emotion of the music which will be made will be different. How that will be I cannot foresee, but I'm sure it will come."[1]

With him it was ever thus. He always projected toward the future. His contempt for the past made him indifferent to its documentation. But in view of the constant attention paid by the press and the inordinate curiosity his fans and devotees displayed in reading every scrap of information about him, his comings and goings, his marriages, divorces, and amours were grist for the gossip mills.

He would talk freely and expansively about music, orchestras, travel, diet, philosophy, architecture, painting, and occasionally about his beliefs and religion. He hated dealing with specifics about his past. He preferred to invent stories about his upbringing, his family, and his age. When asked about it he replied, "We as a nation have become enamored of numbers. My desk is sixty-five inches long. It can be measured by quantity but also by quality. But we neglect quality. . . . I never talk about myself, I have friends who do and they are bores."[2]

I asked his daughter Sonya whether she might have any letters that had been exchanged between her mother, Olga Samaroff, and her father. "No," Sonya replied. "I think she was very careful on this. . . . I know that she and Daddy had a very definite agreement that she would write nothing about him in his lifetime nor, frankly, afterwards.[3] That was an agreement that they had. I know that mother destroyed all their letters. . . . This was their agreement. [4] . . . I think this was rather an *idée fixe* of his."[5]

Anyone who tried to delve into his past had a hard time, for Stokowski thoroughly delighted in inventing it. But this is only part of the problem in researching a biography about him, as many have discovered. Victor Seroff, who had written perceptively about Ravel, Debussy, Prokofiev, and later Rachmaninoff, wrote to Stokowski saying that, according to Thomas Carlyle, when Dr. Johnson heard of Boswell's intention to write about his life he said he would prevent it by taking Boswell's. "For some time I have been thinking of writing a book about you, a serious one telling my reader what you stood and stand for in the musical world. . . ."[6]

Stoki fired back a letter saying:

> Do you prefer a sudden or a lingering death? I'm a dead shot with both hands with a revolver and that is a fairly sudden way. I also know some ways of slow poisoning. Please let me know your wishes. I suggest practicing on the harp for the few hours you still have on earth because that is the favorite instrument in heaven. . . .[7]

When Seroff persisted, Stoki replied that "the most interesting things about my life cannot be told. What can be told is less interesting."[8] About that he certainly was correct, but he added encouragingly that they should talk it over.

Stoki outlined in detail various conditions and restrictions and finally stated that the book could only be written if it were to be as he wanted it.[9] Seroff gave up.

Next to try was James Felton, a critic on the *Philadelphia Evening Bulletin*. Felton was not only a most capable writer but a highly trained musician as well. He did a prodigious amount of work in ferreting out details of Stokowski's background. He carefully checked documents and traced the Stokowski family from the arrival of grandfather Leopold in England, through the succession of marriages, births, and deaths leading up to the arrival of Leopold Stokowski himself.

In Philadelphia, Felton spent hours in the basement of the Academy of Music painstakingly going over reviews and all other pertinent material that related to Stokowski's career. He interviewed members of the Philadelphia Orchestra and contacted people who were involved with him on many levels. When he asked Stoki's former managers, the Schulhofs, for aid and information, he was told that he should have saved whatever he had spent on doing his research for a vacation.[10] Felton, too, finally abandoned his project.

Another who devoted his time almost single-mindedly to a story of Stokowski was a Copenhagen English teacher, Preben Opperby. He became a Stokowski fan very young and began to collect his records. When he discovered that Stoki would return to the Philadelphia Orchestra in 1960, he decided to go there and hear him live. In Philadelphia, he was treated with great courtesy and attended several of Stoki's rehearsals.

When Preben told him that he wanted to do a biography, Stoki protested; when after many months he sent a copy of his manuscript, Stoki asked him to desist. Preben persisted, however, and his Stokowski biography was published in England in 1982.[11]

Next to try was Joan Peyser who later did a splendid biography of Pierre Boulez. At the request of the head of the trade division of Macmillan Inc. she visited Stokowski in November 1968. On the afternoon when she arrived for her appointment, "a young woman answered the door," she recalled. "I think it was his secretary. She was wearing a miniskirt and she was very youthful." After keeping Joan waiting for some time, he announced he was ready to speak with her. "Where is your pen and paper?" he asked. She explained that they should first talk about the book and how to approach it. He showed no interest in dwelling on any of the early aspects of his career and announced that he wanted to talk about "the beautiful flower children and the terrible world the adults had given them and why. He wanted to discuss the problems in Israel."

"You really can do that with your secretary and a tape recorder," Joan said. "You don't need me for that." He stood up indicating that the interview was over. "As I was getting up to leave, he said, 'Don't forget your pocketbook! Women are always forgetting their pocketbooks.' "[12] Exit Joan Peyser.

Others made attempts but with no greater success. Interviewers asking about his past invariably ended up with fiction. If he wished to have his past shrouded in fantasy, well and good. It was his way of dissuading anyone from trying to write about the real Stokowski. And if reality were stark against his more colorful visions, why then chill the spirit? "Dad was very inaccurate on these things," said Sonya. "I have always felt that he would have liked to have been the white prince who was washed up on the shore . . . he had great imagination."[13] He once wrote that one should be concerned with "the loveliness of nature, the lovabil-

ity of people, everything that excites us, everything that starts our imagination working, laughter, gaiety, 'pretending' in the way that children
do."[14]

In Boston, on May 21, 1941, I heard Stokowski for the first time when
he conducted his All-American Youth Orchestra. Not long after this I
joined CBS as a producer-director and was in charge of most of the serious
music programs, including the broadcasts of the New York Philharmonic.
There I worked closely with Stokowski, though our relationship was purely
professional at that time.

During the summer, when the Philharmonic vacationed, the CBS
Symphony filled in on Sunday afternoons. At the conclusion of one of
the broadcasts conducted by Alfredo Antonini, the phone rang in the
control booth. It was at that crucial moment when various announcements had to be included at the end of the program, and the atmosphere was tense. (Everything was live then, and timing was critical.) I
picked up a phone and a voice said, "This is Leopold Stokowski. I would
like to speak to the man who is in charge of the meek-ro-phones." I
thought it a very poor time for a practical joke. I said something un-
printable, but a day or two later I received a letter that bore the unmistakable signature. It explained that he had tried to phone but unfortunately could not get through. I never told him that he had.

He lauded us for the fine transmission and wrote in detail about the
balance, resonance, clarity, and the like. He said he would be listening to
the broadcast again on the following Sunday. Everyone was pleased, and
we worked ourselves into a sweat trying to make the broadcast even better.
But the phone did not ring.

A letter arrived a few days later. He criticized the balance, found the
violas too weak, the woodwinds too loud, and had numerous suggestions
for improvement. We were stunned, because without knowing his famous
injunction, "Do better," we had all tried to do exactly that.

Several weeks later another note arrived congratulating everyone on the
great improvements that had been made. I have since wondered whether
he intended merely to keep all of us on our toes. But there was more to
this letter than the discussion of the broadcast. Would I dine with him
and his wife, Gloria Vanderbilt, the following week at 10 Gracie Square
at eight o'clock, "black tie"?

When I arrived at the indicated hour, I was awed. Theirs was one of
the most beautiful penthouses I had ever seen, with very large rooms, high

ceilings, and a magnificent view of the East River and all of midtown and lower Manhattan in the distance. This was the beginning of a close and enduring friendship with Leopold—and one with Gloria, which I deeply regret was less enduring.

During the ensuing years we worked together on many projects, including the Contemporary Music Society, concerts, recordings, broadcasts, and finally the American Symphony Orchestra.

One day in 1976, I had a call from Ruth O'Neill, who had been associated with Stokowski since his first days with the Philadelphia Orchestra. She said that she had been contacted by someone who wanted to interview her about Stokowski, and suggested that we meet instead and do a series of interviews. She wanted to share with me conversations she had had with Arthur Judson and others about Stoki. She urged me to pick up again the biography she knew I had worked on many years before. It was this fortuitous call that resulted in this book. I interviewed members and former members of the Philadelphia Orchestra, his All-American Youth Orchestra, the NBC Symphony, the New York Philharmonic, and the American Symphony, as well as composers, critics, instrumentalists, singers, dancers, engineers, acousticians, friends, and family.

In Jerome Toobin's delightfully irreverent and racy book *Agitato*, he remarked that it was the rare bird whom Stokowski called by his first name. "I can only think of the music publisher Oliver Daniel, whom Stoki called, rather juicily, O-lee-vair."[15]

I always called him Leopold. Almost everyone when talking about him called him Stoki, although but few addressed him that way directly. He himself preferred that spelling and sometimes signed his personal letters that way. In this work, I have referred to him as Leopold in situations of a personal nature, and Stoki most of the time, but not with any sense of irreverence.

Having long been revolted by the sycophantic tone of some biographies of conductors, I vowed not to produce a Stokowski panegyric. Instead, I wanted to present the whole man, seeing his virtues as well as his foibles. "I don't think it would be a true picture of him if it was just all goody-goody, because he was far from that kind of person,"[16] said his daughter Sonya.

There were those who considered him one of the great conductorial geniuses of the time, while others regarded him as a poseur. In his book

Music for All of Us, he seems to be at times most envisioned, expansive, and penetrating. His chapters on certain scientific aspects of music are brilliantly thought out, but at other moments he seems to descend to the level of his talks for children's concerts. It is this type of dichotomy that suggested *Stokowski: A Counterpoint of View* as the title for this book.

STOKOWSKI

A COUNTERPOINT OF VIEW

1

Misterioso

S TOKOWSKI often enjoyed using musical terms for strictly nonmusical situations. When at age 92 he built his stone house in the beautiful French town of St. Paul de Vence, he called it "Con Brio." During his later years, while being driven about in his car, he would amuse himself by giving instructions in musical terms. When he wanted the driver to go faster, he would use such terms as *accelerando, allegro,* or *presto;* for going slower: *andante, lento,* or *più adagio.*

If we were to apply the same little game to his life and career, we might find that it began *andantino semplice* and progressed *con fuoco, grandioso, maestoso,* and often *con amore* and *con fervore.* But mostly it was *misterioso*—an attribute he enjoyed and cultivated assiduously. And as the aura of mystery and awe evolved about him, he became to the public one of the most charismatic figures of his time.

Of Stokowski's background, we have much accurate documentation drawn from official records, which differ substantially from the various apocryphal versions he frequently gave in interviews. He was named Leopold after his grandfather, who had emigrated to London apparently some time after the 1848 political uprisings that wracked central Europe. The London census of 1860 listed him as Leopold Stokowski, country of origin, Poland, living at 9 Oxford Market. At the same address we find a widow, Jessie Jones, listed as a "visitor."

The widow Jones, before her brief marriage, was Jessie Sarah Anderson, the daughter of James Anderson, a Scotsman who was a professional dyer. Jessie had married a confectioner, John Jones, on Christmas day in 1857.

1

Jones died some time before 1860, when we find Jessie living in London, a lively widow of twenty-nine springs.

The house at 9 Oxford Market was apparently the equivalent of a rooming house, with Mr. Roden Cowen, a solicitor's clerk, listed as "Head of the House." In addition to Jessie and Leopold, the motley occupants included a twenty-one-year-old cabinetmaker from Germany listed as a "visitor," a widower bookseller and his twenty-year-old son, who plied the trade of "dressing-case-maker." Added to these there were three young maiden ladies: one a twenty-year-old dressmaker from Reading and two sisters with no listed professions.

Young Leopold and Jessie Jones obviously became attracted to one another. They flaunted tradition in this proper mid-Victorian era and produced a son three years before they found it convenient to marry. Their son, Joseph Boleslaw Kopernik Stokowski was born at 9 Oxford Market on the third of February 1862. The name of the mother is recorded as "Jessie Sarah Stokowski, formerly Anderson." No reference was made of Mr. Jones. The event was registered in the district of Marylebone, subdistrict of All Souls, in the county of Middlesex on March 15, 1862.

Three years and nine months later, Leopold Stokowski, "bachelor," and Jessie Jones, "widow," solemnized their marriage in the Parish Church of St. Marylebone "according to the rites and ceremonies of the Established Church." Witnesses of the event were their landlord, Roden William Cowen, and Anne Donagan. The groom's father is listed as Joseph Stokowski, "collector of taxes." That is all the factual information we have about him. Attempts to trace him in Poland have been inconclusive.

Strangely, Percy Scholes, in the *Oxford Companion to Music*, suggests that Stokowski was either Jewish or partly Jewish. While this is stated in the seventh edition of 1947, it does not appear in subsequent editions. *Time* magazine, on July 13, 1931, reported, "Conductor Leopold Stokowski of the Philadelphia Symphony is a Polish-Jewish British-born artist. . . ." No research has been able to corroborate these statements. And all the evidence we have would seem to point to the contrary.

Curiously, the Poles, who are zealously Roman Catholic, have seldom been drawn to Protestantism. It has never been part of their history. But Polish-born Leopold embraced the Church of England when he married Jessie, and all official documents of births, marriages, and deaths indicate that affiliation for the next two generations.

Just how much we can deduce from the various accounts given by grandson Leopold is moot. On several occasions, perhaps to emphasize his Polish heritage, he denied his early Anglican background and stated that he had been born a Roman Catholic. About his family's place of origin, he said that they came from a place near Lublin, a place called Stoki or Stokki.

In 1925, while visiting Poland, he met Artur Rodzinski, whose widow, Halina, told me that "he asked my husband to go with him to Lublin where he said his family is buried. He wanted to visit the grave of his father or grandfather. So when they came to Lublin, he said to my husband, 'You stay in the hotel and wait for me. I will go alone to the cemetery.' So he went alone, and my husband never saw the grave—and I wonder if anybody else ever saw it!"[1]

At some point he obtained a genealogical chart purporting to trace the family history and background of the Stokowskis. He had ordered it from one of the various genealogical societies that frequently advertise in literary periodicals. From it he selected an ancestor who was a heroic figure in Napoleon's retinue and proceeded to invent stories about him as apparently told to him by his grandfather.

There was much speculation about his origin, his accent, and details of his early life and background. Writers frequently used the word *enigma*. In fact, Irving Kolodin, in writing about him in *Saturday Review*, titled his piece "Variations on an Enigma."

Most of the mystery, misinformation, and fantasy came directly from him. In interviews he continually gave information that was pure fiction. He was doing what nearly every stellar personality of the time was doing: merely embellishing his background for dramatic and publicity purposes. It was all part of the era.

Could anyone blame Olga Samaroff for discarding the utterly unesthetic name Lucie Hickenlooper; Lillian Norton for changing to Lillian Nordica; Jeno Blau to Eugene Ormandy; Bruno Schlesinger to Bruno Walter; or Greta Louvisa Gustaffson to Greta Garbo? Not many musicians would recognize composers Alan Chakmakjian or Joseph Guttoveggio except as Alan Hovhaness and Paul Creston respectively.

Is it any wonder there surfaced an often-quoted statement that Stoki's name was really Leo Stokes, and that for theatrical and artistic purposes he had changed it to Stokowski? This canard has been presented as fact in several reputable sources including that usually reliable font of information *Grove's Dictionary of Music and Musicians* (Fifth Edition, 1954), which erred in stating that "in 1905, after a few years as organist of St.

James's, Piccadilly, where he adopted the name of Stokes . . ." In the recently issued sixth edition (1980), *Grove's* retracted its error. Because of his obsession about being Polish, he particularly resented the whole Stokes story.

His grandfather Leopold came to an early end at the age of forty-nine in Bethlem Hospital on January 13, 1879. The cause of his death was given as "exhaustion and general paralysis." Following his demise, Jessie moved to 111 Titchfield Street with her seventeen-year-old son Kopernik, who by now had discarded his other names: Joseph Boleslaw.

Two years later in the parish church of St. Marylebone, Kopernik and Anne Moore were married, "according to the Rites and Ceremonies of the Established Church." The bride's father, Thomas, stood up for her, and Jessie Stokowski for her son.

Anne (or Annie as she was later called) was born in London on December 28, 1858, at 3 Hollen Street. Her father, Thomas Moore, was a journeyman bootmaker, and her mother was Mary Anne Moore née Corby. Mary Anne was illiterate and signed the birth certificate with an X, "the mark of Mary Anne Moore, the mother."

On the nineteenth of May 1879, shortly after the death of Leopold, who died intestate, Jessie made out a will establishing a small trust to be given son Kopernik when he was twenty-one. In it she named her nephew, Frederick Jaquiery, executor. And indeed at twenty-one, Kopernik Stokowski received his inheritance of approximately 235 pounds, but not before he had made Jessie a proud grandmother. On April 18, 1882, Leopold, named after his grandfather, was born. One year and seven months later, November 25, 1883, Jessie died of a cerebral hemorrhage at the age of sixty-one.

The year 1882 was a significant one and marked numerous events that constitute memorable music history. It was the year that Stravinsky, Grainger, and Szymanowski were born. It was the year Brahms completed his Second Piano Concerto, Wagner introduced *Parsifal,* Rimsky-Korsakov completed his opera *Snow Maiden,* and Rachmaninoff entered the Conservatory in Petrograd. Ralph Vaughan Williams was a lad of ten, Richard Strauss was a young man of eighteen, and Gustav Mahler a promising operatic conductor of twenty-two. And, despite some published accounts to the contrary, 1882 marked the birth of Leopold Stokowski in London during the forty-fifth year of Queen Victoria's reign.

According to the certified copy of an entry of births given at the General Register Office, Somerset House, London, on the eighteenth of

April 1882, at 13 Upper Marylebone Street, Leopold Anthony, a boy, was born to Kopernik Joseph Boleslaw Stokowski and Annie Marion Stokowski, formerly Moore. The birth certificate was registered on the first of June in the registration district of Marylebone, in the subdistrict of All Souls, in the county of Middlesex. This exact documentation is important, since Leopold himself at times gave the date 1887 and the sequence of names as Leopold Boleslawowicz Stanislaw Antoni Stokowski. In an official biographical sketch he approved in the late 1950s, we read that he is of "Polish origin, and is named after his grandfather, Leopold Stokowski, of Lublin and Krakow."

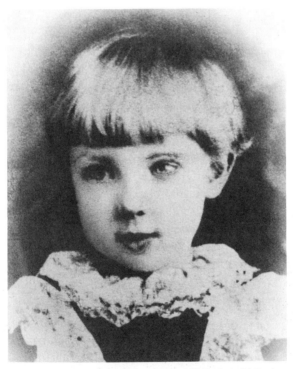

International Leopold Stokowski Society
Leopold Stokowski (c. 1886)

Two more children were born to the Stokowskis—a daughter, Lydia, and a son, Percy. During these years, the Stokowskis lived at 10 Nottingham

Street, still in the district of Marylebone. The street at that time was lined with rows of four-story Queen Anne houses. They were multiple-dwelling structures and often housed various commercial enterprises as well.

Lydia Jessie was born on March 28, 1884, and was named after her aunt, Jessie's younger sister.

Percy John, the Stokowskis' third child, was born on March 31, 1890, also at 10 Nottingham Street, but it was not until April 4, 1900, that he was baptized in the Anglican Holy Trinity Church on Marylebone Road.

Percy hated his name and later in life legally changed it from Stokowski to Stock. Obviously Stock fitted his limousine business better than Stokowski. But Percy had a precedent. His grandfather, the first Leopold Stokowski, also found the name cumbersome for his various business activities, and we find him using the name Stock, too. However, this was only as a business convenience—he never formally changed his name from Stokowski. Records maintained in London indicate that from 1871 to 1879 he advertised as Stock at 34 Castle Street. In 1875, we find his name coupled with that of Edward Charlton, Music Engraver, at the same address.

Percy's and Leopold's cabinet-making father also at times simply found it expedient to be called Stock, for at his death on the tenth of October 1924 (at 14 Elmcroft Crescent, Golders Green U.D.), his certificate reads: "Joseph Boleslau Kopernik Stokowski, otherwise Stock." He was sixty-two years old and his occupation was given as retired furniture manufacturer.

Even after he had officially changed his name to Stock, Percy still chafed at the name Percy, and so his family, friends, and business associates always referred to him as Jim. I met "Jim" for the first time on the day of Leopold's funeral. I later asked him numerous questions about the family and early life in England. Rather than do an interview with me, he preferred to answer in letters. In October 1977, a year before his own death, he wrote me:

> First about our parents. My father's father was a Pole. He was fighting against the Russians when the Poles were beaten, and eventually after marching for days through snow and ice reached England. He later married a Scotch woman named Anderson. So that my father was half Scotch. There was no Polish spoken in our home and I do not think my father knew any Polish. . . . We always called Leo[pold] "Leo" at home—although I called him "Le" and he called me "Dog."
>
> Our family was Church of England, not Catholic, and Leo and I both sang in the choir in the church. . . . You, of course, understand

that I did not see my brother for 50 years until 3 years ago when he got in touch with me. I think he was ashamed at the way he had treated our family, and wanted to get in touch. . . . I have not mentioned my mother. She was born in a small village in Northamptonshire called Corby. This was their family name—and it is now quite a large manufacturing town. My mother's mother married an Irishman named Moore. He turned out a bad lot, from what my mother said, and she was loath to talk about him. From all this, you will see, Leo was a quarter Polish, English, Scotch, and Irish. So I do not know where he got that silly accent from.[2]

Later we shall go into the whys and wherefores of the gradual metamorphosis of an English-born young man whose heritage was three-quarters British, into a Slavic personality—an act that was purposeful and self-conscious. It was all part of the plan and process of molding his career, and it was undoubtedly helpful in evolving the sense of mystery that he so successfully acquired. Later we will trace the steps in this personality mutation and observe how it gradually became manifest. But here let us compare the vital statistics we have established with his own self-created image.

In 1955, in a widely reported confrontation during a radio broadcast, he snatched the announcer's prepared script as it was being read. The script stated that he had been born in 1882 rather than 1887, the date he had by then selected. "All lies!" he shouted at the announcer and stalked off. The broadcast was immediately canceled and a recorded program was heard, instead of the live Miami Symphony, which had been scheduled.

Shortly after he returned to New York, I told him I thought it was perhaps the most inconsiderate thing he ever could have done. Being at CBS at the time, my sympathies were naturally with John Prosser, the Miami announcer. I also observed that if he, Leopold, wanted to see inaccuracies corrected, he should give the authentic version of events. He agreed and asked me to prepare an accurate story of his life. There followed a series of weekly meetings after dinner at my apartment. Wendy Hanson, his secretary at the time, agreed to take the conversations down in shorthand. I quote here a fragment: "I was born in Cracow, Poland, but was taken to Vienna soon after because of political troubles. Then the family went to Paris and from there to London, where my birth was registered. That is how the story of my being born in London occurred."[3]

On a BBC broadcast that originated in London, interviewer Roy Plomley asked, "Although we don't see much of you in London, Mr. Stokowski, this is in fact your native city. You were born here, weren't you?"

"No, I was born in Cracow," he answered, "but I was brought to London when I was five or six weeks old, and my birth was registered here, and I feel it is my home."[4] On another occasion when asked about his parentage, he said his father was a paleontologist and his mother a woman.[5]

Speaking about Stokowski's early beginnings, Gilbert Seldes wrote in an extensive article in the *Boston Evening Transcript* of October 28, 1916: "With the slightest elaboration, the facts of Mr. Stokowski's career can be taken from 'Who's Who,' and they should be left there were not fullness and light so insistently demanded. He was born Leopold Anton Stanislav Stokowski in London, on the eighteenth day of April, 34 years ago. His father Josef Boleslaw Kopernicus, as a young man, had come to London after a political rebellion in which his own father was implicated. While another part of the family went toward the Golden Horn, this branch was making its way to France. A disaster at sea, the presence of a British fleet-unit, and the opportunity of taking on a profitable trade in England, changed Josef's course and brought to his son an Irish mother. Like the hero of a very modern song, Mr. Stokowski confesses that, as a child, he went wild when the band played. He also loved a piano, which, with a violin, were his first instruments. A true prodigy with them, he played, when ten years old, the violin, the viola, and the tuba in orchestra."

Tuba? In no other article or interview have I seen any other mention of Stokowski playing a tuba. At first I thought it quite ludicrous—if not ludicrous, at least incongruous. But in 1977, his brother "Jim" wrote me:

> I have just remembered that when Leo was about 18 years old, he formed a brass band with four other school friends. I remember their names: Ernie Coster, Alf Steed, Arthur Steed, and George Green. Leo played the bombadon [sic]. It was like a very large cornet. They stuck it [out] for about a year; then packed up as the band was not a success.[6]

The bombardon is described in musical dictionaries as a bass-tuba. There were apparently variants of the instrument. This does indeed indicate that he played the tuba, although he never seemed to mention it, and it piques one's curiosity about his playing the violin and viola. Of course he said repeatedly that he studied all of the orchestral instruments in the course of his career. But his story of how he began playing the violin varied considerably from one telling to the next. As part of the "authentic"

version of his early life, he told me: "I used to know a German named
Preis. He was a very fine violinist and he gave me the love of the violin
and I became his pupil. I lived a good deal in Pomerania, north of
Germany, and Preis was there. I studied with him at night. I was seven
years old and had a little violin."[7]

In March 1956, in answer to a set of questions submitted by Gordon
Stafford, he supplied the following version: "When I was about five, I was
taken to the northern part of Germany, in the province called Pomerania,
and I was there all spring, summer, and part of the autumn. And while
I was there on a big kind of estate with many farms around, one day I
heard a man play the violin. His name was Preis. He was not a famous
violinist but a very good one, and I had never heard the violin before. In
fact, I didn't know it existed. I was suddenly inflamed with the sound of
that instrument, and immediately demanded a violin because I wanted to
play it myself.

"It was difficult to find a violin small enough for me, but finally one
was found, and I began to play. Mr. Preis took a little interest in me. He
didn't really give me lessons but he was, I think, amused and noticed what
I was doing and gave me one or two ideas. And so, during all the summer,
besides playing outside with some other boys, I was practicing the violin
inside the house and gradually began to play it a little. Then when I was
taken back afterwards to England, I took that little violin with me and
continued with it."[8]

Basil Moss queried him during a BBC interview in 1969: "But your
family, your parents and your grandfather, were all in London with you.
So I suppose there must have been a great deal of the Polish influence
in your early life."

"There was. There were quite a number of Poles who suffered the same
way from the secret service police of the czar and came to London, and
there were my grandfather and my father [who] used to take me to a club,
and in that club were all men and they used to sing the songs of their
country: Polish, Russian, Czechoslovakian, Rumanian—various countries
—who were for various reasons pushed out of their country and came to
live in England. It was a very free land this way—it's a wonderful country.
So they came here and they used to sing their songs at the top of their
voices—fortissimo—they would shout these songs. But some other songs
which were tender, they sang pianissimo, and I even saw tears coming
down their face sometimes as they were thinking of their homeland that
they could not return to ever again."

"What age would you have been?"

"I know how old I was because one night a man walked into that club with a little something in his hand and began to do this. I said to my father, 'What's that?' He said, 'It's a violin.' And I said to my grandfather, 'I want a violin.' And he said, 'Perhaps.' But he did buy me—what's it called— a quarter-size violin—and so I began at the age of seven playing the violin and that is still my favorite instrument. . . ."9

The first problem we encounter here is that his grandfather had died three years before Leopold was born. Secondly, his brother wrote, "Leo never went to Pomerania or Lublin or anywhere else out of England until he was of age. He did not learn the violin when young, and not at all as far as I know."10

But perhaps Percy might not have remembered correctly, for when Leopold was seven, Percy had not even been born. While it is true that there is fantasy in Stoki's early recollections, particularly about his grandfather, the story of his playing the violin was persistent. Although I have not encountered one person, including members of his various orchestras, who ever saw him play a violin, he did list it as his instrument when he became a member of the Musician's Union in Cincinnati in 1909.

Assuming that he learned to play both the violin and viola, and had piano lessons with Miss Haynes, as Percy confirmed, he apparently discovered the organ, too, when still very young. In the interview with Stafford, Stoki commented: "When I was, I imagine, about eleven—I can't remember exactly—I was very enthusiastic about football. That was not the American kind of football, but what's known as soccer. And I played that every day during a certain winter. . . . I used to like to play in the snow because I became very hot as I was playing, and the cold snow on my face was a delightful sensation.

"One of the boys I was playing with—his father was a priest in the church nearby where I used to go . . . so I asked him one day, would his father let me go and play on the organ in that church. Eventually the priest said I could, and so I began to make some kind of experiments on that organ, but I couldn't reach the distant notes on the pedal. My legs were too short at that time. But I could reach the middle tones of the pedal, and gradually I began to play the organ, and as time went on, I could reach the lower and the extremely high sounds of the pedals, and finally I could play the organ and enjoyed that very much because then I could play the great compositions of Bach."11

In an exchange about musical talent with John Bowen on BBC, he observed: "I think all that is very mysterious and we would have to know more about what are called genes. . . . What goes back, back, back into our ancestry and I don't know enough about it. All I know is that music, when I was a child, was easy to me. I remember the first time I wanted to learn about harmony, and so I had a harmony teacher and he taught me this chord and that chord and gave me the names of the chords. And then I said, 'But I know all those chords already. Please teach me a new chord.' He didn't have any new chords because harmony is, of course, nonsense the way it is taught today. It's too restricted."[12]

True, music did come to him easily. When I asked him about his conducting for the first time when he was still a boy, he said: "When I was twelve in London, I was the piano accompanist for a chorus which had a small orchestra with it. One day the conductor became ill and did not come to the rehearsal. Then they asked me if I could do it. 'Of course I can,' I answered. That is how it all started. I had always wanted to conduct, and this was the first time I ever conducted an orchestra and a chorus. Well, when you are twelve, you think you can do anything."[13]

Not only does one marvel at his precocity, but also at his supreme confidence, a quality that never deserted him.

While we cannot entirely rely on Stoki's recollection of the past, we can only rue what suppression of facts and events has occurred. "I think that one should cultivate memory," he said. "I think that one should also cultivate forgetfulness."[14] This latter cultivation simply enhanced the element of mystery about him and fired the exasperation of anyone trying to chronicle his life.

During his later years in particular, Stokowski talked of Hans Richter as exerting a powerful influence on his personal musical tastes and on the development of his career. Richter was one of the men Stokowski chiefly wanted to emulate.

Richter had built up a tremendous reputation in England. As early as 1877 he appeared in London with Richard Wagner—the two shared the podium for the Wagner Festival being presented that year.

Subsequently he gave numerous series of concerts, which became enormously popular and were dubbed the "Richter Concerts." George Bernard Shaw was one of his ardent admirers and spoke of him perceptively. Shaw observed that "he did not pose and gesticulate like a savage at a war dance."[15] Yet Richter, for all his avoidance of histrionics, seemed to exert an overwhelming power over both his players and his audience.

His repertoire was a rather limited one, however. His principal interests were the music of Beethoven, Brahms, and Wagner. Sir Thomas Beecham once said, rather contemptuously, that Richter could conduct only five works and no more. But the doughty Sir Thomas was always one to relish a clever quip.

The most evident influence of Richter upon Stokowski was in the matter of repertoire, for that of Richter became Stoki's in early programs with both the Cincinnati and Philadelphia orchestras. From Richter, and also Nikisch, he adopted the habit of conducting without a score, but in later years he felt the need of having one before him.

Some critics had found Richter's conducting ponderous and square. Some thought that his Mozart was heavy. But let us forget the little critics and observe the comments of Claude Debussy, who first heard Richter, then sporting a red gold beard and mane, in Bayreuth. Debussy years later wrote: "Now his hair has gone, but behind his gold spectacles his eyes still flash magnificently. They are the eyes of a prophet; and he is in fact a prophet. . . . If Richter looks like a prophet, when he conducts the orchestra he is Almighty God; and you may be sure that God himself would have asked Richter on some hints before embarking on such an adventure."[16]

Leopold at one point proclaimed Richter the greatest conductor he had ever heard and said that he would always be grateful to him, for he had learned so much from hearing him conduct. He was about nine years old or thereabouts when he first heard him, and from that point on he tried to attend all of Richter's concerts whenever the latter appeared in London.

In 1971 when Edward Johnson asked him about Nikisch, whom he also admired, Stoki replied, "Oh yes. But before him was still a greater one. Hans Richter—excellent, wonderful, wonderful man. Subtle, delicate, powerful, everything—wonderful person. The greatest I ever heard."[17] On another occasion he said, "It was like magic what he did, and I was so impressed with that . . . the power that music has to say something that no words could ever say . . . I instinctively went in that direction."[18]

Richter was apparently no slave to the printed page or metronome. "A conductor," Shaw observed, "who takes the time from the metronome and gives it to the music is, for all conducting purposes, a public nuisance; a conductor who takes the time from the music and gives it to the band is, if he take and give it rightly, a good conductor. That is what Richter does." And that is just what Stokowski did during his long career.

②

RCM

O N January 3, 1896, Leopold Stokowski took his entrance examinations at the Royal College of Music and three days later was
admitted as a student. He was just thirteen years old. He was one
of the youngest students ever to have been admitted to the college. Sir
Hubert Parry was then its director, and he was to play a significant role
in advancing the boy's career.

Leopold, however was not a scholarship student, and the cost of his
education was a burden for his cabinet-making father. "My father did
everything for Leo," Percy recalled, "and spent what little money he had
on his music. I am afraid my sister Lydia and I had to suffer, as there was
nothing left for us."[1]

Although I do not remember that he ever spoke to me of his poverty-
bedeviled early years, he did discuss them with others. One was Charles
O'Connell, who became a colleague and close friend of Stoki. Charlie was
the head of Artists and Repertory for RCA Victor and later for Columbia,
and he produced countless Stokowski recordings. He was a gregarious and
affable man who was well liked in the music business and particularly by
Stoki. He was one of the few who maintained a warm social relationship
as well as a close business one.

One day during a taxi ride, Charlie had been discussing the disadvan-
tages of poverty as opposed to the advantages of wealth. Stoki then
remarked wryly, "Charlie, I don't think you want to get rich and I hope
you never do. I like you much better being poor."

"You wouldn't say that if you had ever been poor," Charlie responded.

At this point, Stoki pulled up a trouser leg and, pointing to his ankle, asked whether Charlie might know how that came about.

Charlie responded, "Well, it looks very much to me like the result of malnutrition or rickets."

"That's exactly what it is, so perhaps you will not say again that I don't know what it is to be poor," Stoki replied.[2]

Jerry Toobin, in his book *Agitato*, recounts a conversation that occurred in the mid-1950s, when Stoki's boys were still quite young. "I've led a busy life and I've worked hard. And I think I'm a good musician. And I was poor when I was as old as they are. Were you ever poor? I was poorer than anyone you've ever known. Poorer than anyone."[3] In 1959 John Bowen asked him during a BBC interview whether he had a poor childhood or a rich one. He responded "poor" and immediately changed the subject.[4]

Sir Hubert Parry had more than a purely musical influence on the career of young Leopold, for it was largely due to Parry's efforts that he was able to obtain an Oxford degree. At age ninety, Stoki recalled that "Parry, first of all, was a great sailor. He loved sailing with a boat with sails, not with an engine. He was an extremely masculine man. Parry had a wonderful humor, great kindness, and he'd rather be out in a sailboat than anything —except that he loved music. . . . He was head of the Royal College when I was there." Then recalling a work he had probably not heard since his youth, he asked, "What was that wonderful chorus?"

"Blest Pair of Sirens."

"Ah, yes, 'Blest Pair of Sirens'; wonderful music really. I was going to say aristocratic music."[5]

Although he had heard many of Parry's works at the RCM, Stoki demonstrated little if any interest in his compositions. He did not program any of Parry's works when he directed his choir at St. Bartholomew's, and the only major work of Parry's he ever conducted was his Symphonic Ode *War and Peace,* in Toronto, February 21, 1919, barely five months before Parry's death.

Although his studies at the RCM took up much of his time, Leopold still continued to sing in the choir of the St. Marylebone Church. We find him listed in the *Choir Boys Quarterly Report* of September 29, 1897, under the heading "Alto Cantoris" and he is described as being "very excellent" and "of great service to the Precenter."[6]

His skill as an organist developed quite remarkably and on June 25, 1898, at the age of sixteen, he was elected to membership in the Royal

College of Organists. It was a prestigious honor for one so young. But that was not all. The following year he became an A.R.C.O. (Associate of the Royal College of Organists), and a year later a F.R.C.O. (Fellow of the Royal College of Organists).

In 1900 he formed the choir of St. Mary's Church on Charing Cross Road. One of his former choirboys wrote a nostalgic letter to the BBC's weekly magazine, *Radio Times*, in 1951, following one of Stoki's London broadcasts. He asked whether there was anyone alive who remembered a half century before when Stokowski was a chorister at St. Mary's, Charing Cross Road, where, at the age of seventeen, he trained the choirboys and played the organ. In a subsequent issue, another of his old choirboys answered, but not about being in the choir of St. Mary's. "Over 40 years ago," he wrote, "I was a choir boy under him at St. James's, Piccadilly, and the boys thought it a great treat to be taken by Stokowski to a cafe in Piccadilly for tea and cakes after a special Saturday afternoon practice for an oratorio which was performed in the open air under his direction by a choir and orchestra of over 100 performers."

Then twenty-two years later, following a BBC telecast of a Stokowski concert, another of his former choirboys wrote to him. "Dear Sir," he began deferentially,

> Seeing you on television yesterday (Sunday) and reading of you in the Daily Mirror today, I felt that I must write, as one of your old choir boys. You came to St. Mary's Church, Charing X Rd. in 1900–'01, when the church was rebuilt, (I think from St. Marylebone Church) and formed the choir at St. Mary's, of which I was an alto; after approximately 12 months you went to St. James Church, Piccadilly. I have a photograph of the choir, with yourself, the Rev. G. C. Wilton, and the brothers Stead (tenors) which I greatly cherish. You must then have been around 18 years of age.
>
> One thing I always remember is a man with a fruit barrow, always appearing on Friday nights (full practice night) when you used to purchase a hand of bananas, giving us lads one each, saying that they were good for the throat. In conclusion, I trust that God will give you many more years of life, with good health.
>
> Yours very affectionately
> A. H. Surridge (now 83 y'rs)[7]

Not only did the young Stokowski evince unusual talent, but he worked prodigiously. Although, as we have seen, there are no records of his having had any formal instruction on any stringed instruments, we do know that

Stokowski in St. Mary's Church Choir, Charing Cross Road, London (c. 1900), (front row, seated on right)

he studied piano and organ at the Royal College of Music under the guidance of Stevenson Hoyte. He studied composition with Charles Stanford and counterpoint with Walford Davies.[8] While none of these men made any international impact, they were regarded highly by their British colleagues, and knighthoods were conferred upon Stanford and Davies.

Irish-born Sir Charles Villiers Stanford was a prolific, academic composer. His output included eleven operas, seven of which were produced; seven symphonies and other orchestral works; a lengthy list of trios, quartets, quintets, and other chamber and solo works. He composed many concerted works for various instruments and a massive amount of religious music and songs. His musical sympathies were German, and in the end his music seemed to be watered-down Teutonic imitation. Once in an interview, when asked about Stanford, Stoki's succinct reply was, "Ah, yes—there was Stanford." But despite this apparent lukewarm attitude toward Stanford, Stoki did perform many of his religious works during his years at St. Bartholomew's in New York, and he gave the first American performance of Stanford's *Irish* Symphony during his first year with the Cincinnati Orchestra.

"Walford Davies," Stokowski declared, "was a very sensitive, wonderful man. I learned very much from him." Davies' fame as an organist and composer never traveled much beyond the British Isles, but at home he was regarded with great esteem. In 1882, the year of Stoki's birth, Davies entered the choir of St. George's Chapel in Windsor and in 1890 won a composition scholarship at the RCM; five years later he became a teacher of counterpoint, which position he held until 1903, when he became conductor of London's Bach Choir.

One of the most important events in Davies' career was his appointment as organist and choir director of the Temple Church in 1898, a post in which he was active for the next twenty years. Here he performed the Bach *Passions,* the *Christmas Oratorio,* and cantatas, chorales, and solo organ works throughout the year. It was through Davies that Leopold developed his deep love and preoccupation with the works of Bach, and through him that he had his earliest experiences participating in their performance. When Davies went to the Temple Church, he took Stokowski with him as his assistant for the succeeding two years. Stoki once told Stewart Knussen that the rector preferred his playing to that of Sir Walford because it was a bit more florid.[9]

In his biography of Walford Davies, H. C. Colles related: "His first set of Temple boys were not always little lambs in 'Doctor's' absence; and I remember being present much later at a full practice when the men were driven almost to the point of mutiny by a deputy's exhortation to 'put their hearts into it.' . . . Nevertheless to sit beside him and watch him doing it, whether at the grand piano in the practice room or from the organ loft in the church, was a liberal education for a young musician. Several who now stand high in the musical world profited by it in the early days at Temple. Leopold Stokowski was one of them.

"He was, as he would himself confess and indeed in his letters prove it, the least ruly of Doctor's pupils. They disagreed about everything and most about God, and 'Sto' rebelled truculently against Walford's attempts to subdue him to his own unorthodox orthodoxy. . . . A note written when Stokowski had obtained his first substantial appointment at St. James's Church, Piccadilly, attests the gratitude and affection in which, despite all their differences, he continued to hold the Doctor."

10, Nottingham Street
London, W.
10 March 1902.

Dear Doctor,

I am sure you will be glad to hear that I was appointed to St. James'
Church this morning.

I can never, of course, repay in any way your kindnesses to me, I
can only hope to have an opportunity of passing them on to another.

Your affectionate pupil,
Leopold Stokowski[10]

The distinguished Anglo-American organist Alec Wyton, in a conversation with Stokowski, mentioned that he had been reading a biography of
Walford Davies. Wyton remarked that Davies mentioned Stoki most
affectionately. "Walford Davies was a very good musician," said Stoki,
"and a very great person with a wonderful feeling for humanity. He had
that choir there in Temple Church which he developed to an enormously
high pitch of technique and beauty of phrasing and tone and balance."[11]

Davies was interested in the theory of music and drama combined but
so far as opera was presented then, he found it an "astonishing and
phenomenal enormity. . . . The reality of grand opera as we know it today
is apt to be at its greatest when no speaking or singing problem is raised,
as in the *Götterdämmerung* March,"[12] said Davies, and it was undoubtedly his dictum that inspired Stokowski's efforts in transcribing Wagner
and Mussorgsky.

In 1936, as Stokowski began his movie career, Walford Davies commented, ". . . it is so clear today that the cinematograph and music have
a great future of collaboration before them, and it is good to find their
intimate union beginning to be apprehended, seriously attempted, and
now and then beautifully realized."

Davies apparently regarded Bach as a spiritual-dramatic composer and
he tried to emulate him by composing an extensive body of religious
oratorios, cantatas, and choral works. The deities of the musical pantheon
of the Royal College of Music—as chosen by its reigning trinity: Parry,
Stanford, and Davies—were mainly Purcell, Handel, Bach, Mozart, Beethoven, Elgar, and Wagner.

Davies believed music to be a "universal language." He felt that it had
developed its powers to such a point that it could "depict human life in
its bewildering variety." He believed that there is no known visible object

on earth, or sea or in the heavens, especially in "the sky's unresting cloudland," that music could not tonally interpret.[13] On reading Davies' essays and observing his preferences and prejudices, one may easily appreciate the influence he had on the young Stokowski—and also appreciate the latter's rebellion against him.

About his early studies, Stoki once stated: "I went to the Royal College of Music in England and studied with some very fine musicians there. But I found their ideas very academic and rather stiff and uninspired, compared with the impressions I had from the music of Bach, Mozart, Beethoven, Wagner, Debussy, Chopin, etc., who were then my favorite composers. And I was rebellious and had difficulty with those teachers. They didn't like my attitude and I didn't like theirs."[14]

When he was in his eighties he was asked by Basil Moss of the BBC about his early studies in London. He replied, "I studied at the Royal College—wonderful college—and I go there now sometimes. Sometimes I go and rehearse the orchestra there—the student orchestra."[15] By the time he had reached the autumnal age of ninety, he was asked by the English critic Edward Greenfield, "But your musical education in England—how did you find the Royal College of Music? You went there first, didn't you?"

Stoki answered rather dryly, "Yes. Do you mind not asking that question?" The subject was changed immediately.[16]

"Stokowski's whole approach to music-making is spontaneous, improvisatory, and abhorrent of the metronomic," wrote Edward Johnson. "When he entered the Royal College of Music as a boy of thirteen, he must have memorized the College motto on his very first day: 'The Letter killeth, but the Spirit giveth life.' It has been his credo ever since."[17]

③

St. James's Church, Piccadilly

L ONDON places great stock on tradition and history, and St. James's has both. It is also one of London's architectural masterpieces. It was therefore a singular honor for a young man just starting his career to be engaged as the organist and choir director there. The entire

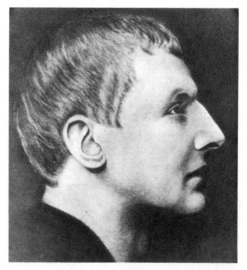

Courtesy Lyuba Stokowski Rhodes
Stokowski portrait drawn on wood by his father, Kopernik Stokowski (c. 1904)

Stokowski family was both proud and elated. Kopernik immediately wrote a letter to Walford Davies. It is a splendid letter by a cultured and cultivated man, and the engraved stationery with the address 10, Nottingham Street belies any suggestion of poverty.

> 10, Nottingham Street,
> London, W.
> Mar 15. 1902

H. Walford Davies Esq
Dear Sir

It is again my pleasurable duty to write to you a letter of thanks; this time for your kind and valuable exertions on Leo's behalf at St. James's.

The "thank you" is so often simply used as an act of politeness and not as a manifestation of gratitude, that it seems quite inadequate, in this case, to express Leo's and my feelings to you.

I feel almost ashamed to reiterate the hope that Leo's association with you will be of lifelong duration, it being manifestly a selfish wish, since up to the present, Leo has been the recipient of all benefits, giving nothing in return.

> With sincere thanks I remain
> Yours faithfully
> K. Stokowski[1]

The church of St. James's is actually somewhat plain. It is of red brick with white trimming. Its interior is rather simple and restrained in a classical sense. Originally its main entrance was from Jermyn Street rather than from Piccadilly. The street is named after Henry Jermyn, Earl of St. Albans, who had obtained permission from Charles II to develop a residential neighborhood in London's St. James's Fields. In 1674 an area on the south side of Portugal Street, now Piccadilly, was set aside for a parish church and churchyard. The architect for the new church was Sir Christopher Wren, and the foundation stone was laid on April 3, 1676, nine years before the births of Bach and Handel.

Wren could afford to be restrained in the building of St. James's, for he was already working on his masterpiece, the magnificent St. Paul's Cathedral, built to replace an early Gothic church destroyed during the great fire of 1666.

St. James's Church, diminutive in comparison, nevertheless drew a fashionable and distinguished congregation, and there are literary allusions to it in the works of Evelyn, Defoe, and others. "I can hardly think it practicable," wrote Sir Christopher, "to make a single room so capacious, with Pews and Galleries, as to hold 2,000 persons, and all to hear the Service, and both to hear distinctly, and see the preacher. I endeavored to effect this in building the Parish Church of St. James's Westminster, which, I presume, is the most capacious, with these Qualifications, that hath yet been built." The two thousand figure was surely conjecture in the mind of Wren, for the church could never have accommodated so large a number. But it was indeed spacious and its acoustics excellent.

One year after St. James's was completed, King James II commissioned the eminent organ builder Renatus Harris to build an organ for his Roman Catholic chapel in the royal palace at Whitehall. But it was not destined to remain there, for in 1691, it was given to St. James's by Queen Mary. The organ case was adorned with elaborate carvings by Grinling Gibbons, the greatest carver of his time, and is a most elaborate affair, with large angels flamboyantly holding long gilded trumpets, while four cherubic angels cavort above them. Gibbons also carved the reredos, or screen, behind the altar and later sculpted the marble baptismal font.

Diarist John Evelyn noted in his journal, December 16, 1684: "I went to see the new church at St. James's, elegantly built. The altar was especially adorned, the white marble enclosure curiously and richly carved, the flowers and garlands about the walls by Mr. Gibbons, in wood; a pelican, with her young at her breast, just over the altar. . . . There was no altar anywhere in England, nor has there been any abroad, more handsomely adorned."

The organ was tested and approved by John Blow and Henry Purcell and was most probably played by Handel, who for many years was a resident in the area. Although it had been extensively altered in 1852, it was the one that Stokowski played to win the hearts of the St. James's parishioners and choir after coming there in 1902. According to all accounts, he was devastatingly handsome and possessed wonderfully winning ways. His boyish looks must have stimulated the mother instinct in the female parishioners, for he was constantly being invited to various homes to dine after services. Half a century later there were still some who were rhapsodizing over their idol. His skill was virtuosic, and listeners were thrilled with his playing of the Bach Toccata and Fugue in D Minor, which, one aged parishioner later recalled, had "shattered" her a half century before.

The parishioner was a Mrs. Hilda Galloway, to whom I was introduced on September 17, 1977, the day after Leopold's interment. I visited St. James's as I wanted to set to rest the canard that when Stokowski played there he had used the name Stokes.

I encountered a sexton in a long cassock busily attending to his churchly duties. When I inquired for the rector, he suggested that I wait until four —about an hour—when the rector was to perform a baptism. I waited. Shortly before four, the sexton beckoned, and I was taken to the sacristy, where I met the Reverend William P. Baddeley.

After I explained my mission, he suggested that I talk to a parishioner who had known Stokowski. He phoned Mrs. Galloway and introduced me. I asked her whether Stoki had ever been known as Stokes when he was at St. James's. "Absolutely not!" she exclaimed emphatically. "And it makes me furious to read in the *Times* that he had. It is absolutely untrue!" she exclaimed. "I ought to know, because I was only seven when he came and he was twenty-one. He knew my father very well, and he knew my sister. He used to come to our house, and I had trouble saying Stokowski. I couldn't say it. So I used to call him Cocky and he loved it. He used to play with me and we had great times at our home. My father loved him and they had long conversations."

Some time later, Preben Opperby of Copenhagen shared with me some correspondence he had had with Mrs. Galloway. She had told me that she was almost blind and that her hand was shaky. To Preben Opperby she wrote:

> I am finding this a very difficult letter to write. . . . re Leo A. Stokowski in his youthful days at St. James's Church. . . . We all made Mr. Stokowski welcome as one of the family. He came and went as he wished. . . .
>
> My memories of the first time I was allowed to stay in church to listen to the whole of the voluntary still remains in my mind, as he was playing the Bach Toccata and Fugue, and I was so entranced that I never hear it without thinking of him. Then the first time I heard a full orchestra, he was conducting Dvorak's New World Symphony. I was able as this small child to go to the piano when I got home and play the simple slow melody in the correct key with the appropriate harmonies.[2]

Young Leopold easily won the affection of his choirboys. He took them on cycling trips, picnics, and excursions to Piccadilly Circus, where he treated them to tea and cakes. At times, after the regular services in the church, he would bring his choir and soloists into the courtyard to give *al fresco* concerts, much to the delight of parishioners and the curious who might be strolling along Piccadilly.

He proclaimed his independence from his family by taking up quarters of his own in a six-story apartment building on Jermyn Street, almost directly across the street from St. James's. In its basement it housed the then-elegant Hammam Turkish Baths, where Edwardian gentlemen voluptuaries steamed away their overindulgences. "Only men and wicked ladies and nobody else lived on this street," he recalled.[3]

Of course, he must have excepted the small but very exclusive Hotel Cavendish, at this time run by Rosa Lewis, who was affectionately dubbed "the Duchess of Jermyn Street." Rosa was a beautiful woman then and as famous for her culinary expertise as she was for her wit, tolerance, and colorful expletives. She had cooked and catered for the grandest of households: for the comte and comtesse de Paris, the Randolph Churchills, the Prince of Wales, and for his cousin Kaiser Wilhelm, who once took her for a spree on his yacht.

Rosa maintained a suite on the ground floor that was entered not by a conventional door, but by way of a floor-to-ceiling, gold-framed mirror that swiveled on a pivot. This was reserved for the Prince of Wales and other of her select clientele. Rosa understood well both privacy and discretion. For the titled and the wealthy she maintained the hotel as a home away from home. And she also seemed to have a fondness for Americans.

But of all the royalty that Rosa admired, she felt closest to the king of chefs, Escoffier, with whom she had developed a close personal friendship and from whom she learned many of her culinary secrets.

While Rosa retained an air of elegance, her speech and comments were hardly of the ladylike variety. She once told novelist Evelyn Waugh to "take your arse out of my chair" as she expelled him. And he took his revenge by writing about Cavendish goings-on in his novel *Vile Bodies.*

St. James's was a mere few steps across the street, and Rosa became a devoted churchgoer. The clergy were fond of her and somewhat incongruously patronized her establishment. Sometimes she would drag one of her guests over to church to hear the music, assuring them that it would do them good as a tonic. One Christmas day the rector went to convey his good wishes to Rosa and found her entertaining her friends in her front parlor. Rosa gallantly passed his hat and made all her guests contribute. She stayed in London throughout the World War II blitz years later, and the Cavendish was narrowly missed by the bombs that hit St. James's.

In 1952, a festive coronation year, I met Rosa Lewis and stayed at her fabled Cavendish Hotel. By then it had an air of faded glory; furnishings were a bit tattered. During the late afternoons she still presided in her front parlor, with guests sitting about her listening to her reminiscences. She sat in a high wooden armchair, feet firmly planted on a footstool, her long skirts barely covering them. I asked her whether she remembered Leopold Stokowski, the young, fair-haired organist who played at St. James's when she had first opened her hotel. She paused for a few moments and then, with a glimmer of recollection, remarked that she did indeed and that "the music was always beautiful then."

It was a gala year, 1902, when Leopold began his stint at St. James's and it marked an almost year-long celebration of the coronation that ushered in the Edwardian era. Some of this period's elegance became part of the young musician's manner, and during his entire life he maintained, at least in public, a sartorial style that fitted his character.

Also in 1902, while fulfilling his duties at St. James's, Stoki entered Queen's College, Oxford. This was arranged by Sir Hubert Parry, who was not only the director of the RCM but also a full professor of music at Oxford. Parry appreciated what an Oxford degree could mean to Leopold, who also recognized this advantage.

Queen's College, on the corner of Queen's Lane, is across from the School Examination Board and the new Examination Schools where Leopold would have taken his examinations. The college itself was founded in 1340 by the chaplain of Queen Philippa, about whom one never hears, and was entirely rebuilt in the early 1700s by a pupil of Wren's named Hawksmoor.

At Oxford, Leopold was not a full member of the college. He did not live there but attended as a part-time student, living in London in his flat on Jermyn Street. Most of his Oxford study was with Parry, and records at Queen's College reveal these details: He took three examinations, the first on November 4 and 5, 1902, when his examiners were Sir Hubert Parry, Joseph C. Bridge, and C. H. Lloyd. His second examination, in 1903, listed as Trinity Term, was given by Parry, Lloyd, and Mr. F. J. Read. His third and final examination on November 3 and 4 was before the same examiners. He passed his examinations brilliantly, and on November 19, 1903, he received his Bachelor of Music degree. Three days earlier he had reentered the RCM, where he continued to study until July 27, 1904. (As a warming footnote to his Oxford experience, the Queen's College appointed him an honorary fellow in 1951.)

During the summer of 1903, Davies wrote to his former pupil a letter expressing some concern about his spiritual life, exhorting him to have faith and admonishing him against conceit. He also sent a new anthem, which he had dedicated to him. Stoki answered him from his parents' home in St. John's Wood:

> 18 Acacia Rd.
> S. John's Wood
> Aug 22. 1903.

Dear Doctor,

It was very kind of you to trouble to write to such an obstinate mule as myself.

My father says he quite agrees with you concerning my conceit: but my mother is quite indignant.

I have known men who, beneath a cloak of seeming modesty and humility, hugged themselves in an ecstasy of self satisfaction. Might not the opposite sometimes exist?

As soon as we settle down to regular work again at St. James's, I will prepare the boys with the new anthem you so kindly sent, with its ironical superscription to me.

You exhort me to "Faith."

I believe that there exists in potentiality an infinite series of things higher and purer than the highest that the best part of one has yet perceived. Is this Faith? I call it Reason.

You speak of Pessimism.

I am driven to it by hard facts. Every true man continually aspires to higher things. By a life of earnest striving he produces, as it were, a beautiful flower, which for a while blooms, then decays and becomes hideous, and finally dies: he collapses in a moment from the pinnacle to the starting point in "the scale of creation."

True, you say, this rise and fall is horrible, but we live for humanity in general not for the individual. This man has aided, to however small degree, in the progress of man.

But I see the same rise and fall in man, in the system of which our sun is the centre, and so on ad infinitum.

But, as you say, this is cold, barren reason; you forget Love, which always comforts and satisfies.

Not so! Love is an appetite which knows no satisfaction.

You are drawn to the person you love but you never "get there."

Take the sum of love of a lifetime. It is simply a number of pleasant sensations. Higher and purer than those of the palate far, but still merely sensation.

To sum up. I find the scheme and conditions of this Universe unsatisfactory. I go on living because other men of infinitely greater intellect than I, have done so. They found a raison d'être; I may.

Dear Doctor, I cannot express my grateful feelings towards you, but I think you understand. Please excuse this absurd growl of a letter.

Your ever indebted,
Sto.[4]

Davies need not have been concerned that his young disciple might lean too far toward unorthodoxy. Even during his early twenties, while he was at St. James's and later in New York at St. Bartholomew's, he experienced growing disenchantment with the crystallized forms of the Anglican Church. His interest in the music that had emerged from both Catholicism and the various Protestant branches never diminished. But his adherence to ritualistic prescription waned. Or perhaps more accurately, he simply rebelled at being told how to govern and plan his life, at being told what to believe. In an interview with John Bowen on the BBC he stated his beliefs succinctly: "I have my own religion . . . it's very simple. Don't harm others. Don't harm yourself. Before you decide to do anything, ask yourself: is it ethical or not. That's all."

"Humanist?"

"If you like—if you like to put a little label on it. That's it."

". . . Where do you get the ethics from?"

"Instinct—where music comes from, where Shakespeare found his poetry, Leonardo found his creative powers. Instinct—and it's a mystery."[5]

During his tenure at St. James's, young Leopold conducted various small orchestral concerts in London. On November 16 and 17, 1904, we find him conducting a theater orchestra in the overture and entr'actes for Jerome K. Jerome's three-act play *Woodbarrow Farm* at a theater in Ealing, West London. The cast was literally peppered with Loftings. Harry Lofting was the stage manager, and playing various roles we find Eric E. Lofting, John Henry Lofting, John B. Lofting, and Hugh J.

AT 9 O'CLOCK.

WOODBARROW FARM

Ĥ Play iŋ Ŧhree Ĥcts,

... BY ...

JEROME K. JEROME.

Allen Rollitt - - -	Mr. ERIC E. LOFTING
Luke Cranbourne -	Mr. JOHN HENRY LOFTING
Mike Stratton - - -	- Mr. J. SAMUELSON
Col. Jack Dexter -	Mr. W. HERBERT MARTIN
Mr. Purtwee - - -	- Mr. JOHN B. LOFTING
The Hon. Tom Gusset - -	Mr. GORDON JACK
Baron von Schnorr -	Mr. HAROLD J. GIBBONS
Richard Hanningford - -	Mr. J. SAMUELSON
Ichabod - - -	Mr. ARNOLD SAUNDERS
Peters - - - -	Mr. ARNOLD SAUNDERS
Piffin - - - -	- Mr. HUGH J. LOFTING
Clara Dexter - - -	Miss MABEL ARLINGTON
Deborah Deacon -	Miss ETHEL WOODHOUSE
Mrs. Rollitt - - -	Miss MARIE HAMILTON
Rachel - - - -	Miss MABEL COLE

Act I. - - - Woodbarrow Farm, Exmoor.

Act II. - - - 13b, St. James's Mansions.

Act III., Scene 1. Library at St. James's Mansions.

Scene 2. - - Woodbarrow Farm.

Time—THE PRESENT.

Stage Manager - - Mr. HARRY LOFTING.

TRINDER & CO., Printers, High Street Ealing.

Programme of Music.

1.—OVERTURE	"La Laitière de Trainon"	-	Wekerlin
2.—ENTR'ACTE OVERTURE	"Merry Wives of Windsor"	-	Nicolai
3.—ENTR'ACTE -	"Salut d'amour" -	- - - -	Elgar
4.—ENTR'ACTE	"Coppelia Valse lente"	- - -	Delibes

CONDUCTOR :—

Mr. LEOPOLD STOKOWSKI, Mus. Bac. Oxon., F.R.C.O.

(Organist of St. James's Church, Piccadilly, W.)

The Floral Decorations have been kindly contributed by Mrs. H. B. Smith, The Broadway, Ealing, W.

The whole of the Antique Furniture has been kindly lent for the occasion by Messrs. Gill & Reigate, of 77, Oxford Street, London, W.

The Costumes and Wigs by W. Clarkson.

The Special Scenery by Messrs. D. S. Hancocks & Co.

The Electric Lighting by Messrs. Seth Bros.

HONORARY SECRETARY :

MR. JOHN HENRY LOFTING,

Mount St. Mary's, Ealing, W.

November 16th and 17th, 1904.

Courtesy Tony Lofting

Woodbarrow Farm program, showing Stokowski listed as conductor, November 16 and 17, 1904

Lofting. While Hugh Lofting never achieved any great fame as an actor, he did win esteem as author of the famous Dr. Dolittle stories, which, with their talking animals, delighted generations of children "all over the world," as Stoki might have said.

During the early summer of 1905, the Reverend Leighton Parks, rector of St. Bartholomew's Church in New York, came to London in search of an organist and choirmaster. He made many inquiries and visited the Royal College of Music, where he discussed his quest with Sir Hubert Parry, Walford Davies and other colleagues. Stokowski was highly recommended. Parks attended services at St. James's and heard Stoki firsthand. He was impressed and sought out the young organist.

Some rather amusing fables grew up about this first meeting between Stokowski and Parks. According to one, Parks, in visiting St. James's, saw a group of choirboys playing in the courtyard and asked them if they could direct him to Mr. Stokowski. Leopold spoke up and said that he was Leopold Stokowski, whereupon Parks is alleged to have asked him to bring him to his father, the organist.

Stoki himself gave me a simplified version of their first meeting: "One day—I was living in a street back of Piccadilly, Jermyn Street—I came back to that place—by that time I was studying in Oxford—and the doorman said there had been a strange American man looking for me. He would be back later in the afternoon. So the man came and he said his name was Dr. Parks and that he was the priest of St. Bartholomew's in New York and had come to England to find an organist, because they thought the best organists and chorus trainers were in England, and so he went to the Royal College, the Royal Academy, and to Oxford and asked for somebody who is not too British. They said take Stokowski. He then asked me if I would be the music director of his church. I said I cannot because I have not finished my doctor's degree, although I would like to accept it as an adventure. He said I could always come back to England and [take a degree] later on. . . . Because I liked the adventure of it, I accepted and came to New York."[6]

4

New York

URING the late summer of 1905, Leopold Stokowski arrived in New York for the first time. He was twenty-three, handsome, tall—six feet, more or less—blue-eyed, and sporting a crewcut. The city was in transition, moving from its romantically flamboyant commercialism to a more vigorous, or rather vulgar, proclamation of it. Skyscrapers became spires of commerce as spires had once adorned the bastions of God. Henry James, on his return to New York at this time, was awed as he sailed up the harbor to find the city looking like a pincushion with extravagant pins overplanted in a hit-and-miss manner. He felt that they were consecrated to no use save the commercial and that they were "the most piercing notes in that concert of the expensively provisional into which your supreme sense of New York resolves itself."[1] The tallest building in the world, the Flatiron Building, was twenty-two stories high.

Although the popular song "In My Merry Oldsmobile" had just appeared, the streets and the avenues were still largely the domain of horses and carriages. *Elegant* is the best adjective for Fifth Avenue. Park Avenue, no rival, was then an open set of railroad tracks that fanned out toward Forty-second Street. Leopold told me that he had found the city fascinating and that he enjoyed admiring the luxurious mansions lining much of Fifth and Madison avenues.

Ever since Mrs. Mary Mason Jones at the age of seventy built a mansion for herself on upper Fifth Avenue, it had become a matter of status to emulate her and thereby achieve social recognition. And so originated the phrase "keeping up with the Joneses." The Vanderbilts were quick to "keep up." William Henry Vanderbilt, possessed of an inheritance of $90 million, built a rectangular brownstone mansion on the northwest corner of Fifty-first Street and Fifth Avenue. Another Vanderbilt, William Kissam, engaged architect Richard Morris to design a château, replete with mansard roof and turrets, a block away on the corner of Fifty-second. Fifth Avenue was soon lined with palaces. On the northeast corner of Fifty-sixth Street sat the marble château of William Waldorf Astor, and adjoining it on the southeast corner of Fifty-seventh Street was the gray stone palace of California rail magnate Collis P. Huntington.[2]

On the other side of Fifth Avenue, a new and most grandiose structure modeled after Fountainebleau rose on the block between Fifty-seventh and Fifty-eighth streets. Regal gates on the Plaza side opened on a shrub-bedecked formal entrance under an intimidating *porte cochère.* The mansion boasted a reception hall larger than that of the Supreme Court of the United States and a ballroom that could be converted into a private theater. It was the palace of Cornelius Vanderbilt, who was one of the pillars of St. Bartholomew's Church. Elegant mansions of Gould, Whitney, Carnegie, Frick, and others added additional luster. And Stanford White's ornate white Metropolitan Club was built at Fifth and Sixtieth Street.

The Four Hundred, as the leading monied and social set was called, behaved like the Medicis and began plundering the art markets of Europe to find treasures for their palaces. They entertained lavishly and engaged distinguished musicians to perform at their private soirées. Paderewski, Sembrich, Farrar, Samaroff, Hofmann, Gabrilowitsch, Bauer, Kreisler, and their kind became part of the social-musical circuit.

Concert life in New York was certainly robust. There were three orchestras vying for patronage: the New York Philharmonic, America's oldest symphony orchestra, founded in 1842; the newer Symphony Society, conducted by Walter Damrosch; and the Russian Symphony, organized in 1904, conducted by Modest Altschuler. The Philharmonic at that time had no regular conductor and depended on a succession of guest conductors. Those engaged for the 1905–06 season included Vassily Safonoff of Moscow, Willem Mengelberg, Max Fiedler, Ernst Kunwald, Fritz Steinbach, and Victor Herbert. Embellishing his popular image rather than his more serious one, Herbert had just composed a less than deathless song called "A Woman Is Only a Woman but a Good Cigar Is a Smoke."

Stoki found America quite different from his preconception. "To be perfectly honest," he said, "I was thinking of Indians and cowboys and a wild, open-air life with horses and ranches; quite idiotic, as I see now, but I must confess that's what I was thinking."[3] One wonders whether he expected cowboys and Indians to be among St. Bartholomew's parishioners.

In London he had been told that St. Bartholomew's, whose organist he was to become, was one of the handsomest churches in the city of New York. It stood on the southeast corner of Madison Avenue and Forty-fourth Street, and though it had begun its days rather modestly, the Vanderbilts changed all that. In 1904, as a memorial to Cornelius Vanderbilt the younger, who had died in 1899, they provided a magnificent new facade with three sets of great, heavily wrought bronze doors. The central set was the work of Daniel Chester French and Andrew O'Connor. Elaborate sculpture was placed above all three sets of doors and two intricate friezes extended between the center portal and the two side doorways. Columns of beautifully veined marble decorated the lower part. The new front was beautiful, if incongruous, but it survived the destruction of the old St. Bart's and now graces the portico of the later basilica on Park Avenue.

"When I arrived here," Stokowski told me, "it was in August and very hot." He had been given a key to the church and organ loft. After finding it on Madison Avenue, he was stopped by a sexton as he entered the church. "I told him who I was and he said he had been told about me. I told him that I wanted to see the organ, so he took me in. It was a magnificent organ in three parts; one on the south side, one on the north, and the other down at the west end of the church."[4]

Compared to the smaller organ of St. James's in London, St. Bartholomew's was a vastly different type of instrument. It was, at the time, the largest in America. It had been built in 1895 by the Boston organ builder George Hutchings and contained 125 ranks over its four manuals. It had an electro-pneumatic action, and the console, which was connected to the organ by a flexible cable, could be moved to any part of the church. The organ contained four divisions (Great, Swell, Solo, and Pedal) in the chancel, and four (Great, Swell, Solo, and Pedal) 130 feet away in the rear gallery.

"If you know how to play one violin, you can play any other," Stoki told me. "You tune it and play it, but the organ is different. Every one is different. Every one is extremely individual, so I had to study and study it. At first the priest was away, but when he came back—he lived by the church—he could not sleep at night because I played and practiced nearly all night long."[5]

Obviously he mastered the intricacies of the instrument quickly. Then, as Leopold Stokovski, he took up his official duties on September 7, 1905. He spelled his name with a v and not a w, to facilitate correct pronunciation. After his name, he added: "Mus. Bac. (OXON) R.R.C.O., Organist and Choir Master."

On Sundays there were two services, one at eleven in the morning and "Even Song" at four. Stoki's forces were impressive. In addition to a vocal quartet, the choir consisted of fifteen sopranos, nine altos, six tenors, nine basses, a harpist, and occasionally a violin. His programs, or should one say services, followed the traditional patterns of those at St. James's. At least in the beginning he obviously did not intend to upset any holy apple carts. And considering the daring he so often showed later in the matter of selecting interesting works to perform, his first months at St. Bart's produced a very bland fare.

On his first Sunday, he began with an organ processional hymn by Webbe; followed by a *Kyrie, Gloria, Sanctus* and offertory anthem by Stainer; a hymn by Hodges; a plainsong *Gloria* and a recessional hymn by Gilbert. The four o'clock "Even Song" began with a processional hymn by Alford; *Psalm 46, Magnificat,* and *Nunc Dimitis* by Stanford; and a recessional hymn by Dykes. With such a beginning, he surely caused no ripples in the music world. But he wanted to start his American career *andante,* just as he once advised me to proceed when I was deciding on a crucial change in my own activities.

His choice of organ solos at the beginning was also on the *andante* side; there was little of the tour de force element about them. Perhaps the simplicity of his early solos points up the fact that he was still trying to adjust to his new instrument. We find him playing such things as the first movement of the Second Organ Sonata of Mendelssohn as well as the Andante from his Violin Concerto, which was performed with violin and organ; a nocturne by Chopin; the first movement of Beethoven's *Moonlight* Sonata; and the Adagio from the *Pathétique* Sonata.

At one point, however, he shook his listeners with a rousing performance of Sousa's "Stars and Stripes Forever."

But more acceptable works soon began to appear on his programs— works of Mozart, Beethoven, Horatio Parker, Gounod, Coleridge-Taylor,

Pergolesi, Purcell, Haydn, and Brahms all surfaced amid an endless stream of conventional anthems.

Then on the morning of January 7, 1906, Stokowski made his American debut as a composer with a processional hymn and on the same day at the "Even Song" service, with a four-verse Christmas carol.

When Christ was born of Mary free,
In Bethlehem, that fair citie,
Angels sang there with mirth and glee,
"In Excelsis Gloria."

The congregation became enchanted with Stokowski, and the choir and soloists seemed to adore him. He had improved the choir. When he first arrived he advertised for singers, auditioned many, and chose his additions with great care. He was not aloof. He often entertained groups of singers, musicians, and friends at his apartment, somewhere in the Thirties, we are told. But if he took his social life lightly, he approached his professional work with the greatest diligence. He became friendly with many of the distinguished parishioners and other important and wealthy New Yorkers. At some point J. P. Morgan seemed to take a fancy to the young man. But none was more drawn to him than Maria Dehon.

Miss Dehon lived with her mother in a brownstone on Fifth Avenue, just below the Waldorf-Astoria, New York's most glamorous hotel, then located between Thirty-third and Thirty-fourth streets. "She was a star member of the St. Bartholomew's where Stoki played the organ," Ruth O'Neill, Stoki's longtime secretary, recalled. In her high-ceilinged drawing room, fitted out in the heavy Victorian manner, Miss Dehon entertained lavishly. She had many private musicales, with some of the day's most distinguished artists. She cultivated celebrities zealously and numbered among her closer friends such stellar personalities as Christine Nilsson, the De Reszke brothers, Marcella Sembrich, Geraldine Farrar, and numerous others. Miss Dehon's newest protégés were Olga Samaroff and Leopold Stokowski, and she planned eventually to bring the two together.

Olga had met Miss Dehon at the time of Olga's celebrated debut as a pianist with Walter Damrosch seven months before Stoki arrived in America. Her success was almost immediate and she made appearances with the Boston Symphony and the Philadelphia Orchestra, followed by solo recitals in London. In short, Olga was already a publicized and successful virtuoso, while Leopold was merely a church organist, albeit one of the rising ones.

Since their lives and careers became so inextricably entwined, let us look at the events that preceded Olga's unprecedented debut and the success of her early career. It is an impressive saga.

5

Olga

We must start at the beginning when little Texas-born Lucie Hickenlooper began to show an interest in music. Her first teacher was her grandmother, an accomplished pianist who had once played a Beethoven concerto with an orchestra in New Orleans. While still in her teens, Lucie was brought to play for MacDowell, de Pachmann, and finally William Steinway. They all advised her to study in Europe, so her grandmother brought her over. The two headed straight for Paris, where Lucie won a scholarship at the Paris Conservatoire de Musique. After Paris, the pair moved on to Berlin, where her progress continued most favorably. Her grandmother began to make preparations for Lucie's Berlin debut into the world of concert pianists.

But it was not to be. Love reared its head, and Lucie married a handsome young Russian engineer named Boris Loutzky, who was "unofficially" attached to the Russian embassy in Berlin. After three years of dividing their time between Berlin and Petrograd, the Loutzkys were divorced, and Lucie returned to New York with every intention of launching a musical career. She may have been naive, but she had the good instinct to go directly to one of the most known and important managers in New York, Henry Wolfsohn.

Lucie walked boldly into the Wolfsohn offices on a September morning in 1904. On hearing that she was a pianist, Wolfsohn immediately asked to see her European reviews, of which she had none. "My dear young lady," he declared, "if you played like Liszt and Rubinstein rolled into one, I could do nothing for you in this country without European prestige.

Now, you go and give some concerts in Europe and if the reviews are good, come back and see me. It isn't what I think of your playing, but what Europe thinks of it that counts."[1] And with that Lucie was summarily dismissed.

Although Wolfsohn showed no interest then, a short time later he accidentally heard her play at the Steinway showrooms on Fourteenth Street and became decidedly intrigued. They renewed their talk about the possibility of Lucie making a debut in New York. The only way she could make a proper splash on the city's musical horizon, he declared, would be to appear with an orchestra. Lucie became fired by the idea, and gradually a plan was worked out whereby she would hire an orchestra and appear in Carnegie Hall. The orchestra, it turned out, was to be the New York Symphony, with Walter Damrosch conducting.

Of course, all of this had to be paid for, and it required a great deal of scurrying around to assemble the funds. The accounts of the various Hickenloopers were tapped. But there was another obstacle that had to be overcome. Wolfsohn balked at presenting a pianist by the unlikely name of Hickenlooper. "It is hard enough at best for a woman to make a successful pianistic career," he said. "With a name like that it is impossible!"[2] In looking for a name, Wolfsohn advised her, there should be nothing that might suggest New England in her background. There should be no Mayflower business whatsoever. If so, reviewers would find her cold. There should be nothing Anglo-Saxon. "Haven't you anything Slavic anywhere?"[3] Wolfsohn pleaded. Something Slavic! After climbing about the family tree and finding nothing really appropriate, she hit upon a distant and long-forgotten relative—real or spurious, it doesn't matter —by the name of Olga Samaroff. Wolfsohn was delighted, and a future celebrity was born.

Olga admitted that she and her mother, who was now managing her career, were babes-in-the-woods when they began: "Neither of us knew anything about the whole business, but within a short time my attractive mother had everybody connected with my career wrapped around her little finger. I attended as well as I could to the piano playing and she did all the rest."[4]

Through Wolfsohn Olga engaged Damrosch and the New York Symphony for the night of January 18, 1905. To appreciate the full extent of her temerity, one must consider that she had never appeared anywhere in a public concert, nor had she ever played a concerto with an orchestra. Furthermore, she had not studied regularly for several years, and her program was taxing. She chose the Schumann Concerto in A Minor and the Liszt E-flat Concerto, along with a group of solo pieces by Chopin, Sgambati, and Tchaikovsky. Damrosch was most considerate. He coached the neophyte pianist beforehand and supplied a sympathetic accompaniment. Wolfsohn, true to his word, practically filled Carnegie Hall.

The gamble paid off. While the reviews were not spectacular, they were sufficiently good so that excerpts could be culled from them for promotion. The critic on the *New York Times* had much praise for her technical skill and precision, but he thought her performance too dry to cope with the brilliance, dash, and *cantabile* required by the Liszt and far from reaching the heart of the Schumann. But is it any wonder? Olga admitted the concert had been a terrible ordeal and that she was so dazed by nervousness it seemed as though someone else had been playing.

While she was still living in Berlin, a great friendship had developed between Olga and Geraldine Farrar, then a leading light in Berlin's operatic firmament. It was well known that Farrar was a great favorite of the Kaiser and an even greater favorite of the Crown Prince. In New York too, she had many fans and admirers, among them the prominent socialite and music lover Maria Dehon. It was a letter of introduction from Farrar that brought Olga to Miss Dehon's attention. Shortly thereafter she engaged Olga to play at her home following a dinner party. It was a very social affair, and as a result Olga was engaged to play in many private musicales at the homes of the wealthy in and around New York. She soon began to make inroads on the debts she had run up for her debut.

Olga had decided charm. She won the friendship and affection of the Steinways, who were to become lifelong friends and aid her greatly in building her career. It was a member of the Steinway firm who brought her to tea at the Paderewskis. There she met a pleasant gray-haired gentleman who took an obvious interest in her. The gentleman turned out to be Charles Ellis, Paderewski's manager and also manager of the Boston Symphony. Ellis, the most powerful and effective manager of his day, was in a sense the Arthur Judson of that period. In addition to the Boston Symphony, he had a relatively small stable of artists, but they were among the most sought after. Kreisler, Melba, and Paderewski were on his roster; he later added Geraldine Farrar and Olga Samaroff.

When Ellis later recalled this first meeting with Olga and her mother, he declared that they were "unlike anything he had ever encountered in the profession." But being both charmed and duly impressed, Ellis offered her an engagement to play in a chamber concert with the Boston Symphony String Quartet. The work was to be the Saint-Saëns C Minor Sonata for Piano and Cello. Ellis was apologetic about the small fee he had to offer.[5]

The concert itself was a modest affair, but in many ways it was as significant as her more impressively elaborate New York debut. Philip Hale, that crusty critic who once advocated placing a sign in Symphony Hall reading "Exit in Case of Brahms," wrote a rave review in the *Boston Herald*. It was so complimentary that Olga put it under her pillow at night and reread it "whenever courage flagged." The success of this first concert in Boston paved the way for an engagement to play with the Boston Symphony Orchestra. Wilhelm Gericke was to be the conductor, and the work that Olga chose to perform was the Grieg Concerto in A Minor.

She played well, having begun to acquire a security and poise that had been sadly lacking at her New York debut. She made a hit not only with the audience but with the critics and, more importantly, with the orchestra players. It was to be only the first of many engagements with the Boston Symphony. Ellis was so pleased that he decided to take the young virtuosa under his management. Her career began to soar.

At the urging of Ellis, Olga and her mother set out for London, where she was to make her debut as a solo recitalist. Again they had to borrow money, but they planned every detail with remarkable care. If, as someone has said, "Genius is the capacity for taking infinite pains," this intrepid pair possessed it. It was particularly true of her mother, who handled all the logistics down to the finest detail.

To make the proper impression, mother Hickenlooper hired a shiny town car and a chauffeur whom Olga found "really quite magnificent." The whole effect, as they made calls and attended soirées and parties, was one of "ducal dignity." To save money they stayed at the Convent of the Holy Sacrament in Brompton Square, which, according to London standards, was a good address.

Her first London concert drew a small but distinguished audience to Steinway Hall. Many of the friends to whom she had had introductions appeared, and one brought a distinguished listener, the English novelist and poet Thomas Hardy. She fared better in her second recital, playing to a much larger audience, which included the painter John Singer Sargent and the poet William Watson. Watson was so impressed that he composed an ode to her playing. The London reviews were very good. Critic Fuller Maitland wrote lyrically about her, and she was soon invited to play in many of the largest and most fashionable drawing rooms.

Though she made no money on the London venture, there was an important *sequitur:* She was engaged to play a concerto with the London Symphony under Nikisch at the start of the following season. She returned to New York in good spirits.

On a crisp November Sunday morning in 1905, Maria Dehon and other music-loving parishioners of New York's St. Bart's listened appreciatively as their young organist concluded the morning service with Bach's "Little" Fugue in G Minor. Olga, whom Miss Dehon had begun to think of as a protégée, was busily working on her own piano transcription of the same fugue for a recital scheduled to take place one week later. Her program was taxing. It included the Schumann *Fantasy* and a *Novelette;* the *Liebestraume, Waldesrauchen* and Fifteenth Hungarian Rhapsody of Liszt; and a Chopin group which included four preludes, four etudes, and a nocturne.

Postrecital reports, though good, were not ecstatic.[6] The critic of the *New York World* wrote: "In complicated passages, instead of burying themes she raises them into hearing [sic] and brings logic into her interpretations. Her technique is good and she has a pretty tone." The *New York Herald* was more direct: "Her playing throughout the entire programme was characterized by intellectual grasp, good taste and refinement, and occasionally by warmth of imagination. It was these latter qualities that stirred the audience to its loudest applause."

Two weeks later she made her first appearance with the Philadelphia Orchestra, playing a new concerto by Eduard Schütt. At that time the orchestra did not rehearse in the Academy of Music, but in a room on North Broad Street. Stokowski encountered the same poor conditions and complained bitterly when he became the conductor of the orchestra seven years later. Olga recalled: "The orchestra completely filled this room. The ceiling was low and there was no space for sound projection. The orchestra could practice notes under these conditions, but no idea of tonal balance could be obtained. At the rehearsal of the Schütt concerto, I played on an upright piano placed in the corner of the room. I could not hear the orchestra as a whole, and the orchestra could not hear me at all. The results may be imagined."[7]

After the usual number of concerts in Philadelphia, Fritz Scheel brought the orchestra—eighty strong—to Carnegie Hall on Monday, December 11, 1905. The *New York Press* reported that "the loud and prolonged expression of approval was well deserved." The *New York*

Evening Post also applauded and observed that "Mme. Samaroff played admirably, with ravishing tone colors, effective phrasing, refreshing animation and ease."

On the previous day at St. Bartholomew's, the congregation had heard their music master perform a nocturne of Chopin, his own organ transcription of Beethoven's *Coriolanus* Overture, and the *Dies Irae* of Mozart.

Maria Dehon, who heard both of the young musicians in their separate performances, began to plan a strategy for bringing them together. What could be more logical?

There are several accounts of how the two artists met. Most agree that it took place at a dinner given by Miss Dehon, but I prefer a much more dramatic account given to me by Ruth O'Neill: "She [Miss Dehon] took Olga down to church one night to hear him play, and after he played, he leaped over the benches to meet her. I wasn't there with them. I just knew this from Olga. She was horrified. She was really quite proper and was of the German tradition."[8]

An almost identical version was told me by Claudette Sorel, one of Olga's finest pupils: "Stoki became so excited when he learned that she wanted to meet the young organist, that he sort of leaped over the pews just to get to her as quickly as possible."[9]

We have countless descriptions of Leopold from various lady admirers portraying him as an Adonis, but we have fewer descriptions of Samaroff. According to an unidentified writer for *Musical America*, "Mme. Samaroff is highly favored. She is rather tall, she is graceful, she is exceedingly fair to look upon; she has dark eyes that sparkle when she talks of her music, and an animated personality that impresses you with the fact that the exigencies of an artistic career have taken nothing from her womanly instincts."[10]

It was not love at first sight, at least not on Olga's part. She may have been somewhat disenchanted by his overexuberance, as well as by his too-correct, punctilious speech—pure English at the time. If she tended to be a bit arrogant, she may have felt she had her reasons. She was, after all, a star in the current firmament of recognized artists.

By comparison, Stokowski was certainly not "big time." Despite his good looks, he did not yet project the aura of an exotic, foreign-born stellar personality. Furthermore, his hair was cropped short, the very opposite of Paderewski's mane. Later on Olga's mother cited some of these same circumstances when the Samaroff-Stokowski relationship became serious. "Her mother warned her not to marry him—she was very adamant about it," said Claudette Sorel.[11]

But if their initial meeting was somewhat cool, things did not remain that way. Miss Dehon saw to that—she frequently invited the two artists to dine with her and her guests. The friendship between the three of them warmed wonderfully. The many mutual interests that they had to explore and discuss added to the growing natural attraction between them.

At the end of Leopold's first season at St. Bart's, he returned to Europe "for further study," a pattern he followed for the three years he was to remain in New York. He afterward repeatedly said that he had studied in Paris, Berlin, and "München," but he never elaborated. The veil of mystery was already creeping in insidiously. One is left to wonder just where he studied and with whom, or was any study for the most part an autodidactic matter of learning primarily by observation? A check of the Conservatoire records in Paris shows nothing. Berlin and Munich, the other two cities he maintained were the places of his studies, yield no clues. One city he never seems to have mentioned was Leipzig, but that may have been the one in which he formally studied.

Paul Donath, a violinist who was with the Philadelphia Orchestra from 1903 to 1917, decided to take a year's leave of absence during the season of 1905 and 1906 in order to attend Arthur Nikisch's master classes at the Leipzig Conservatory (later known as the Staatliche Hochschule für Musik). The school was one of the finest in Europe. According to Donath, in a conversation with Steve Cohen, both Leopold Stokowski and Ossip Gabrilowitsch were there in the same class with him. Donath's wife, who was studying voice in Leipzig, often attended the Nikisch classes, and she confirmed that Stokowski was one of the studying conductors.[12]

Another member of the Philadelphia Orchestra (1906–17), bassoonist William Gruner, also discussed Stokowski with Cohen. He commented on Stoki's fluent German as well as his perfect English, and added that "he studied in Germany, in Leipzig, [with] Nikisch."[13]

Nikisch was the resident conductor of the Leipzig Gewandhaus Orchestra, which was one of the most celebrated in Europe. Many said it was the best.

6

The Organ Loft

R uth O'Neill was perhaps being hyperbolic when she said that Stokowski "was the highest paid organist in the world." Without trying to discover what other organists were paid, we concern ourselves with Stoki. His salary at St. Bartholomew's was $3,500 per year. When he began he had a budget of $13,000, which in the course of three years, despite a depression, he managed to raise to $19,000.

In terms of organists' salaries, Stoki's was probably better than average, but being ambitious, he coveted a more lucrative field in which to work. The congregation of St. Bartholomew's was a very wealthy one, but he saw his income and way of life as meager. And by continuing as an organist and choir director, the possibilities were definitely limited. Ever since childhood, he had wanted to be an orchestral conductor, but the problem of breaking into that foreign terrain was a perplexing one. He talked with some of the church's wealthy patrons. One of these was that blustery tycoon J. P. Morgan, who was much more interested in business than in music. At one of his moments of indecision Stoki practically decided to give up music, according to his brother, Percy: "As you may know, when Leo was organist in New York, he came home for three months—May to July. I think it was during his second year home that he took me down to Soho one day for lunch. As we were eating, he said, 'I'm giving up music, Dog; there is no money in it. I've met a very rich man named Pierpont Morgan and he has offered to take me into his business.' He went on that he thought I would do well there, and that after a year he would send for me. This made me very excited. Leo went off to do some

43

shopping, and I rushed home to tell my mother that Leo was giving up music, and was going to take me to America. My mother was shocked and said my father would not agree to this. That night there were terrible rows and next morning Leo said he was not giving up music because I had not kept my mouth shut. So you see you might never have had the great Leopold—but for me."[1]

Stoki's summer hiatus each year was considerably shorter than Percy remembered. His first season began on September 17, 1905, and ended July 29, 1906. His second season was extended nearly a month and ran from September 23, 1906, to August 25, 1907.

Back in New York, he carried on his duties at St. Bart's assiduously. He inaugurated a series of organ recitals that became enormously popular. Beginning with his first season, he had his chorus and soloists learn various parts of Bach's *St. Matthew Passion*. He finally assembled them and, on April 10 and 17, 1907, gave what was surely one of the earliest American performances of the complete work.

He also explored other great choral works that are usually given with chorus and orchestra. He made his own reduction for the organ, trying to retain the orchestral sonorities. He had his choir perform in piecemeal fragments such works as Brahms' *German Requiem;* Bach's *Christmas Oratorio;* Haydn's *Creation;* Handel oratorios; Mozart's *Requiem;* Mendelssohn's *Elijah.* For his organ solos Stokowski relied heavily on Bach. He played the favorite Toccata and Fugue in D Minor, the "Big" and "Little" Fugues in G Minor; the *St. Anne* Fugue; the Fugue in A Minor, and preludes and fugues from the *Well-Tempered Clavichord.* He played several of Mendelssohn's *Songs without Words,* including the "Spring Song." But in a curious and quite ironic misprint, one is mentioned as coming from the *Lieder ohne Werke,* instead of *Lieder ohne Worte,* in other words, *Songs without Work* instead of *Songs without Words.* Ironic indeed, considering the terrific amount of work he was expending on his musical duties.

As he expanded his series of organ recitals, he felt the need to increase his repertory. This he did, not by learning new organ or piano works, but by learning new transcriptions. When one thinks of a Stokowski transcription, it is usually a Bach-Stokowski, or some other composer-Stokowski transcription for orchestra. But his first transcriptions were the reverse. They were works for orchestra transcribed for the organ. And these no doubt were the result of his intense study of orchestral scores as preparation for his later career, a subject that was constantly on his mind.

He transcribed movements from the Tchaikovsky Fourth and Sixth Symphonies; Schubert's incidental music from *Rosamunde* and the *Unfinished* Symphony; Elgar's Prologue to *The Apostles, Pomp and Circumstance*, the "Funeral March" from *Grania and Diarmid*, the "Imperial March," and a movement from his First Symphony; and most importantly, transcriptions of works by Wagner. He transcribed the "Prize Song" from *Die Meistersinger*, "Funeral March" from *Götterdämmerung;* the Preludes to *Parsifal* and *Lohengrin,* and the "Ride of the Valkyries." He even found time to transcribe parts of Ippolitov-Ivanov's *Caucasian Sketches,* which were later to appear on his debut programs in Paris, London, and Philadelphia.

What a pity we do not have any recordings of his organ playing! With the vast resources of St. Bartholomew's organ he could experiment endlessly, selecting stops to give just the tone colors he demanded.

His organ recitals rarely listed improvisations, but he did improvise frequently. It was something of a fashion at the time, and many recitalists, particularly Paderewski, used to improvise briefly before beginning a recital. Stoki had excelled in Walford Davies' improvisation classes and at various times told me improvisation was one of his great pleasures during his years at St. Bart's. He also enjoyed giving themes to other organists for them to improvise upon and turn into variations. One Stokowski theme was used by the eminent French organist Marcel Dupré when he recorded an improvisation on a player organ roll for the Aeolian Organ Company in 1921.[2]

Stoki did not confine his appearances to New York City. On June 26, 1906, we find him appearing at the First Methodist Church in Stamford, Connecticut, with a baritone named Tom Daniel. His solos included the March from *Le Prophète* by Meyerbeer, *Salut d'Amour* by Elgar, Prelude by Rachmaninoff, Widor's Toccata, and his favorite Toccata and Fugue by Bach. Daniel sang works by Handel, Fauré and Rossini.

Other than music by Palestrina and Pergolesi, Stokowski ignored the Italian repertoire almost completely. On looking through all of his St. Bartholomew's programs, one finds but a single performance of a "Melody" by Puccini, the "Triumphal March" from *Aïda,* and a single bass solo by Rossini. During his second and third seasons, he programmed recitals devoted to the works of Palestrina and Wagner.

Once while discussing how he became a conductor, Stoki recalled that as a boy he was always dreaming about conducting symphonic music. "The nearest I could come to it was by playing on the organ music that was composed for orchestra. This was a necessary compromise because it is extremely difficult for a young man to be permitted to conduct orchestras when his name and abilities are unknown."[3]

Even as his popularity increased and his organ recitals and oratorio concerts began to draw ever larger audiences, the enchantment of the Reverend Leighton Parks with his organist and choirmaster dimmed perceptibly. "We fought all the time, the Reverend Parks and I. I just couldn't do what he wanted." After playing one of his solos, Stoki would sit quietly, like an inspired poet, in full view of the congregation. The audience loved it. Dr. Parks did not!

On one occasion during a wedding ceremony, Stokowski had the bridesmaids, dressed in shepherdess costumes and carrying crooks, march about the church.[4] Dr. Parks was apparently not amused. So by the midpoint of his third season, Stokowski submitted his resignation.

Early in February, he wrote to his dear friend and former teacher, Walford Davies:

> St. Bartholomew's Church
> 16 East 44th Street
> New York
>
> Feb. 1st. 1908.
>
> Dear Doctor,—
>
> I wonder if you remember that I exist.
>
> I am still in America and am happy. I've now acquired an American form of vulgarity which I've richly blended with my English callowness.
>
> You would find me absolutely unbearable now.
>
> I think of you very often but as I am working like a horse and as I know your life is crowded with intense interests, I've not bothered you before by writing.
>
> This time, however, I have a business motive.
>
> Do you remember a fellow-pupil of mine, under you, who also had yellow hair and who ran me close in mawkishness and general futility? I think his name was . . .
>
> Could you spare me a moment to write me his whereabouts, and give me an idea of his development during the last three years?
>
> I think I can be of advantage to him.
>
> Since I've found my native country I've written an oratorio, a number of small things, and for the last nine months have been engaged on an opera.

Dear Doctor, you'd absolutely loathe me but I will always love your memory.

I'm going out to the Woolly West soon, "bustin' bronchos," but I expect to be in London for the second week in September, when I'll do my utmost to track you down.

> Always with affection and
> gratitude,
> Your ugly duckling,
> Sto[5]

This inquiry, a kind and thoughtful one, was obviously an attempt to find a successor to take over St. Bartholomew's after his departure in August. But the reference to the "Woolly West" that he would visit soon must surely translate as Cincinnati.

Stoki's efforts at St. Bartholomew's continued with mounting intensity. He spent increasing amounts of time studying orchestral scores. And as he said, he was working "like a horse." Finally on the eleventh Sunday after Trinity, August 30, 1908, after the last notes of Bach's A Minor Fugue decayed in the incensed air of St. Bartholomew's, he gathered up his scores and left the hallowed halls of "Ecclesia" forever.

7

A Conductor Is Born

*T*HERE was no other path to follow. Conducting was Stokowski's aim and his obsession, and he began to explore the possibilities of obtaining an orchestral post with single-mindedness.

Following the death of Fritz Scheel, the position of conductor in Philadelphia was open. "Orchestral conductors were few in those days," said Frances Wister, and "the board was determined to engage no man but one competent to carry on the work so well begun."[1] Hence they turned down one of the earliest applications received, that of the twenty-five-year-old organist and music director of St. Bartholomew's, "because of his youth and inexperience."[2]

The rejection was not too discouraging. Soon he would have Ohio on his mind. But his next move was to join Olga for a vacation in the Bavarian mountains before proceeding to Paris, where he planned to spend time studying scores and also to make some money accompanying and coaching singers.

Olga had departed on the S.S. *President Lincoln* on April 25, 1908, just ten days after Stoki's memorable performance of the *St. Matthew Passion*. She had been very busy before sailing, for she had given three concerts that week. Her heart beat a little faster as she anticipated one of her greatest ambitions: to play a concerto under the baton of Nikisch in London. "In view of my *Backfisch Schwärmerei* for Nikisch, this was enormously exciting," Olga confessed.[3] (There is no exact translation for the German term, a combination of "schoolgirl crush" and "puppy love.") The concert was an all-Tchaikovsky program, and Olga tore into the B-flat

Minor Concerto. It was a triumph. The critics and the listeners found such "temperamental fire and brilliancy and technical finesse" in her playing that the "large audience gave her an ovation." But a most welcome dollop of praise was added as Nikisch and the members of the orchestra joined in the applause.[4]

Following her performances in London, Olga and her mother set out for Bavaria, a part of the world she particularly loved. She had spent many summers there, several with her dear friend Geraldine Farrar, in the early days of her career. She found a small village in the Algäuer Alps. She called the site her happy valley. To friends in America she wrote:

> The questions which agitate the outside world do not enter here. The church is the center of their village and the old pastor directs their simple lives.
>
> Every morning and evening the "cow motif" is played on a rude horn in the village, and out from the fields and through the main street comes the herd of cows. A band from a neighboring village came here to play one afternoon in the plaza by the church and the cows walked majestically into the band, whose members fled precipitately to the shelter of the neighboring tavern.[5]

During the summer Olga practiced regularly, expanding her repertory and polishing the works she would play soon in Paris and Vienna. Ellis, through his European connections, had arranged for her to play in Paris with the Colonne Orchestra and the eminent doyen, Eduoard Colonne, himself conducting. Olga did not choose to play the Tchaikovsky concerto with which she had triumphed so brilliantly in London but planned instead to play the Grieg concerto.

At the end of the summer, Olga arrived in Paris. Leopold was already there, living in a small room on what he called a "horrible street" in the northern part of Paris.[6] It was probably at this time that Olga and Miss Dehon, who later became Mrs. Polk, visited him. Harriett Johnson, who was associated with Samaroff for many years after her student days at Juilliard, recalled: "I remember that when she told me about her courtship with Stokowski, she and Mrs. Polk went to see him in Paris. She may have been in love with him before; she may have thought he was wonderful. I don't know. But as I remember the story—I'm relying on my memory because I didn't keep a diary, but I'm almost sure it's accurate—as I remember she said, 'Mrs. Polk and I climbed 5 flights to the garret where Stokowski lived.' He was giving them breakfast, brunch or something and she said, 'It was that morning that I capitulated.' And she said, 'One of the things I remember was that at one point, he threw a piece of coal across the court and we asked why he was doing that. And he told us that that was his signal to the maid who was supposed to come over at a certain time every day and do the work.' "[7]

Olga's Paris debut took place in the old Châtelet Theater during the last week of October 1908. The Parisians responded warmly, and the French critics reported that she scored "an emphatic success." An English translation of one review, and a somewhat unidiomatic one at that, was released to the American press. The review was attributed to "one of the most prominent critics of Paris": "Mme. Samaroff's execution is remarkable. Her knowledge of her art is sufficient, and her charm and her nervosity, allied with impeccable precision, give her style a special character and exceptional artistic interest. Her success was very great, and was well deserved."[8]

Following Olga's Paris appearance, she proceeded to Vienna, where she appeared with the Konzert Verein. She then essayed solo recitals in Munich and possibly Dresden. After these European engagements, she returned to America to fulfill the concert obligations that had been booked for her by Charles Ellis.

During the next twelve months, Stokowski worked prodigiously. He later repeatedly stated that he had studied in both Paris and Berlin—this is virtually the only time he could have done so. Could he possibly have gone to Berlin to confer with Nikisch and attend his rehearsals? Nikisch at that time held the conductor's posts of both the Leipzig Gewandhaus and the Berlin Philharmonic. According to Stokowski's own words, Nikisch directly or indirectly played a part in his Paris debut.

Announcements about the revival of the Cincinnati Orchestra had been widely publicized in the press and were carried in considerable detail in various music magazines. Following the annual meeting of the Orchestra Association, it was announced on June 2, 1908, that the orchestra would be revived for the 1909–10 season. Bringing outside orchestras into Cincinnati had proven a financial failure and also a blow to the city's pride.[9]

The Cincinnati Symphony was founded in 1895. From the beginning until its temporary cessation in 1906, it was conducted by Frank Van der Stucken. The hiatus was caused by labor difficulties with the musicians' union. For two seasons the orchestra gave no concerts, but visiting orchestras were brought in. They included the Chicago, Pittsburgh, Boston, and New York orchestras, as well as Altschuler's Russian Symphony. By the spring of 1909, a guarantee of $50,000 had been secured and the board, headed by Mrs. Christian Holmes (née Bettie Fleischmann, of the yeast fortune), was ready to function once again. The search for a new conductor was about to begin.[10]

It was Stokowski's aim to secure that position, and his was one of the first applications received by the orchestra. Bettie Holmes read his letter to the board during their fall meeting in 1908.[11]

Arthur Judson was convinced that it was Olga who had laid the groundwork in Cincinnati, and she was indeed in a position to be able to do so. She had powerful connections in town. One of her cousins was General Andrew Hickenlooper, one of the founders of the Cincinnati Gas and Electric Company and later lieutenant governor of Ohio. Another cousin there was the honorable Judge Smith Hickenlooper of the U. S. District Court. She also knew Cincinnati's first family, the Tafts, as well as Bettie Holmes.

Stoki began bombarding the Orchestra Association with letters. He wrote on January 13, March 2, and March 13, 1909, expressing his willingness to sign a one-year contract and accept a salary of $4,000. He also offered to come to Cincinnati and meet with the board. Because the guarantee fund had not yet been raised, Bettie Holmes cabled Stoki that she "could tell him nothing definite." Yet the auguries seemed good. His competition was not too formidable. Van der Stucken was plugging for Georg Schneevoight; Clara Baur, head of the Conservatory, suggested both Ernst Von Schuh and Ernst Kunwald, who was then director of the Berlin Philharmonic. Kunwald, the most prestigious of those being considered, quickly wrote that he would not be available. Bettie Holmes made other inquiries in New York. Henry Wolfsohn suggested Bruno Walter, but nothing came of that. Maurice Grau, who was then managing director of the Metropolitan Opera, referred to Stoki as "gifted but lacking in experience."[12]

But Stoki had his own proponents. Marcella Sembrich wrote to Wulsin, president of the Baldwin Piano Company and member of the orchestra's Advisory Board, who promptly read the letter at a board meeting held on March 3. Another strong recommendation came from the Welsh tenor Daniel Beddoe, who had made a quite spectacular success singing in the concerts of the May Festival. No one could have discussed Stoki more authoritatively than he. Only a few months before he had sung the tenor part of the *St. Matthew Passion* when Stoki conducted it in New York. He had also sung in all of Stoki's oratorio performances. All told, Beddoe had sung with Stokowski at least a hundred and fifty times, for he had been one of the four soloists in the choir of St. Bartholomew's during the previous three years.

Excitement and curiosity about who would be chosen to lead the new orchestra began growing dramatically. On March 10, Bettie Holmes was interviewed by the *Times Star*. "We wish a man who is young enough to take an interest in building up our new orchestra and to identify himself with the artistic life of our city," she said—one who would be "less solicitous, perhaps, for his own fame than for the good of our organization . . . we do not in any sense desire a celebrity," but prefer a young man "of personal charm and magnetism."[13]

A month later Stokowski arrived in Cincinnati, and he brought all of his personal charm and magnetism with him. "He came all the way from Paris," wrote an indecisive Mrs. Holmes in a letter to the publisher H. W. Gray in New York.

> He came . . . as he felt that a personal discussion of the situation might be advantageous. Everyone he met was very favorably impressed with his personality which is certainly very charming, and he appears to have remarkable force for so young a man, and also seems to have almost an intuitively quick grasp of things under discussion, whatever they may be. But, and it's a very big *but*, he is so young in appearance that I'm wondering how he affects his audience in conducting—would a critical audience be influenced by the magnetism which is certainly apparent to a marked degree in personal contact, as it were. And then too, of course, we can get at little or nothing about his Symphony work—whether his experience has been sufficient to fit him for the necessary routine. . . .[14]

Then just at this point a cable arrived from Wulsin in Paris: "Don't commit yourself. Stokovski lacks reputation and experience, was organist in New York. Think can do better."

To this Mrs. Holmes responded: "Nothing decided. Stokovski. See you in Paris. Letter coming. Holmes."

In her long and informative letter to Wulsin, she described the brief visit by Stokowski. He made a most favorable impression on everyone, she said, and "seems to be a young man of remarkable force and energy, is wonderfully quick to grasp a situation and bears out what was said of him about tact in meeting men, etc."[15]

She assembled as many of the board as were available; numerous members of the Advisory Board; Miss Bauer, the founder of the Cincinnati Conservatory, and members of her staff; the Wurlitzers; and some of the "orchestra husbands." And in addition to these

> . . . others whose influence counts for much in the little narrow musical world of Cincinnati, and whose approval would help much toward making the new orchestra and the new conductor a success . . . and everyone feels that he apparently possesses many of the qualities we deem essential in the man who is to become the conductor of the new orchestra.
>
> Furthermore, he seems to be the only man we can get at quickly —many of those I have investigated were either not available or not desirable—and the general consensus of opinion is opposed to the postponing of the concerts until a year from this coming Fall. Mr. and Mrs. Taft and many others too, believe that interest would lag, should there be another season without concerts. . . . If we do not engage Stokowski we cannot now look further for a conductor and should be obliged to wait until 1910 and risk incurring the displeasure of our staunchest supporters, particularly the Tafts, who are enthusiastically in favor of engaging Stokowski and are emphatically opposed to a delay in beginning.

Perhaps we can discern the fine hand of Olga, for she was well known to the Tafts, and it was no doubt she who created the favorable disposition toward engaging Leopold as the next conductor. "Mme. Samaroff knows him," Bettie Holmes told Wulsin, "and perhaps you can obtain some information as to his ability to conduct and do the necessary routine work of an orchestra from her."[16]

Stoki left Cincinnati on the twenty-fifth of April and proceeded to Paris as quickly as possible. On arriving there he lost no time in contacting Wulsin and had a long and pleasant interview with him. It was a fortunate one. Wulsin was impressed. On May 7 he sent a cable back to the Baldwin Piano Company expressing his pleasure: "Tell Holmes letter received. Had interview—pleasant impression. Best wait hear orchestra players experience with conductor. Report Wednesday."

We may never know just how everything was arranged for Stoki to conduct his debut in Paris; how Litvinne and the tenor Serge Zamkow came to be on the program is not exactly clear. Both Olga and Leopold purposefully covered all of their tracks and released only what they thought would be most advantageous to their careers.

In his own version of his debut concert and the events leading up to it, Stoki explained it like this: "In those days in Paris, many Russians came there in the spring and there was a kind of Russian season in April, May, and June. Félia Litvinne came and was to give a concert with orchestra; Nikisch was to conduct it. Then for some reason he did not come to Paris, and at the last minute they did not know what to do about a conductor. I had a Swedish friend who asked if I could do it, and I said, of course, I could do it. It was to be in the Sarah Bernhardt Theater. We had only two orchestra rehearsals, so I went to Litvinne's studio and played her songs for her on the piano. She was one of those singers who when she sang, one could not imagine that it could be done any other way. One had only to accompany her. That was easy but then I had to conduct other things between her songs to give her a rest. All the music was Russian. I started with something, she sang, we played something between, she sang again, and so on."[17]

Strangely, he made no mention of Olga Samaroff being on the program, nor did he mention her in the composite reviews that were later published in music magazines.[18] Olga in like fashion ignored the fact that he had conducted when she in turn released clips from the Paris reviews.[19]

The Stokowski version is almost painfully oversimplified. On the factual side, we know that the concert was managed by Parisian impresario M. Gutmann. We know that Litvinne had great drawing power in Paris, and during the previous Russian season she had appeared with Chaliapin at the Paris Opera in *Boris.* The tenor Zamkow, who was with the Monte Carlo Opera, was also well known and liked in Paris. We might therefore surmise that the program containing these two stars had been previously planned by Gutmann. Could Nikisch have voluntarily withdrawn so that the young conductor might make his official conducting debut under the right circumstances? If any underwriting were necessary to accomplish this end, it was surely Miss Dehon who supplied this means. Several interviewees suggested it.

We have two different versions of the debut from Olga: one as told to Harriett Johnson and another as related to Adella Prentiss Hughes, that energetic concert manager in Cleveland. (Hughes brought in all of the visiting orchestras and engaged Stoki and also Olga with the Cincinnati and Philadelphia orchestras.)

Harriett Johnson told me the story Olga had related to her: "I don't know about the first conducting appearance but I do remember her telling me this. You know her mother was an amazing lady. I only knew her in late years. Then she was bent over and she had eyes like Madame's, only they were more penetrating. Anyway, Madame, at one of these sessions when we were all talking one night, said: 'You know when we were in Paris that winter or that summer, I said to my mother—can't we do something for Stokowski.' Because her mother was a sort of impresario, I think she did a lot for Madame's career. She was indefatigable when she got an idea . . . and as I remember, that first concert was completely engineered by her mother. Her mother went to managers. I don't know just what she did but she did something to get Stokowski that first date.[20]

Mrs. Hughes, who indulged in a little retrospection, remarked: "It was Olga Samaroff's mother, Mrs. Carlos Hickenlooper, who obtained for him the first opportunity to conduct an orchestra in Europe. Olga Samaroff and the operatic soprano Felicia Litvinne had been engaged by the famous impresario Gutmann. . . . The conductor originally engaged was the Russian, Vinogradsky; however, a few weeks before this concert he had requested his release. Olga Samaroff, hearing that Gutmann was combing Paris for a Russian substitute, persuaded her mother to take Stokowski— who at least had a Slavic name—to call on Mr. Gutmann. He engaged the young man from America at once."[21]

During the rehearsals Leopold had his difficulties. Paris orchestral musicians have always been notoriously difficult. Under Colonne they had to be diligent or be fired. Guest conductors had no such leverage and consequently had to suffer the incivility and crassness of the players. When they found someone so young and inexperienced as Stokowski before them, all of their carelessness blossomed. But they had not reckoned correctly. "I came to the rehearsal," he told me, "and I had the most terrible trouble with the French orchestra. They were completely cynical. Of course, I was very young and they looked at me and thought, 'what does he know' and I took quick tempi and began noticing things and they did not like it. It was one long fight. Then came the place where the timpani had a big passage, and I gave him a sign and he did not play, so I stopped the orchestra and said he had to play there. It was a very important spot. I asked him why he did not play, and said, 'Shall I tell you?' Silence— 'Because you are reading a newspaper.' You see I had noticed him. The orchestra laughed and they started teasing him and that changed the whole course of things. Although I was only a boy, they realized that they could not fool me."[22]

A half century later, when he was in his eighties, Stokowski did an interview for the BBC with Basil Moss: "I came to the first rehearsal and it was simply terrible. The players had their hats on; some were smoking cigarettes, ash was falling on the violins—just awful lack of discipline—frightful." He then repeated the story of the unruly timpanist.[23]

The concert took place as scheduled during the afternoon of May 12, 1909. Mrs. Holmes and the members of the board sent the critic Herman Thuman to join Wulsin and make the final decision on Stokowski. The orchestra preserved its good reputation and gave complete cooperation to the boyish-looking conductor. Wulsin and Thuman were duly impressed. "The programme, meagre though it was, gave Mr. Wulsin and myself the opportunity to observe that Mr. Stokowski possessed the 'conductor's arm' as well as talent," wrote Thuman.[24]

Stoki's own fictional version reads: "We played the concert and the audience was very kind to me and I had worked so hard I was exhausted. I went into the little dressing room and lay on a couch. But two men knocked at the door and came into the room and said that they were from Cincinnati; one was Wulsin and the other's name I forget. Wulsin said he had a music store and the other gentleman was the chief critic of the *Cincinnati Enquirer.* They were on their way to Berlin to find a conductor for the orchestra. . . . By chance they heard the concert and thought I was the man they were looking for. Would I accept? That was just exactly what I wanted so I signed a contract right there. They wrote out a letter contract and later I signed a regular contract and I went to Cincinnati."[25]

Henri de Curzon was one of the critics covering the concert for *Le Guide Musical:* "Mme. Félia Litvinne has just reappeared in Paris, heading the list of artists in a Russian concert organized by M. Gutmann on Wednesday last. Very interesting from the Symphonic point of view, since the Colonne Orchestra performed the picturesque *Caucasian Sketches* by Ippolitow-Ivanow, the *Piano Concerto in B Flat Minor* by Tchaikowsky and the March from the same composer's *Sixth Symphony:* above all, the program underlined the worth of some celebrated pieces of Moussorgsky hitherto unknown to us, and certainly the velvety amplitude of Mme. Litvinne's voice and its astonishing agility in passing from the lower notes to the delicacy and to the ringing flights of the upper notes, were what was required to place these eloquent works, so subtle in feeling, in such incomparable light. . . . The piano concerto was played by Mlle. Olga Samaroff, a tall and lovely young lady, her playing full of life, her gestures lissome. A most remarkable tenor, M. Serge Zamkow, whose voice is of good timbre in the medium, ringing and magnificent at the top, sang an important piece by Moniouszko, an aria from the *Queen of Spades* and another song. Finally, very special praise ought to be bestowed upon the young, very young conductor, M. Leopold Stokowski, for his gestures which are at once full of fire and clarity, rapid and decisive."[26]

With the critic of the *Echo de Paris*, both Olga and Leopold fared better: "The orchestra was directed by a very young chef, L. Stokowski —of Vienna, I think—who proved himself the possessor of remarkable qualities. He is intelligent, a fine musician and above all master of himself.

"As for Olga Samaroff, whom I have very much appreciated when she appeared at the Colonne concerts some months ago, she is a pianist of the first rank who plays with more brilliancy, more warmth, more perfection the *B Flat Minor Concerto* of Tchaikowsky."[27]

Just before the Paris concert, Bettie Holmes cabled Wulsin the consensus of the orchestra board: "Stokowski selected unless your report Wednesday decidedly unfavorable. Holmes."

"Stokowski all right," Wulsin wired back. "Conducted very well. I think your decision good."

Bettie rejoined with a sigh, "Message great relief. Thanks. Holmes."

Thuman wrote a long and enthusiastic report, which was published in the *Enquirer* on May 29, 1909, the very day Stokowski arrived in Cincinnati. "Stokowski," he said, "achieved a most pronounced success, and was accorded an ovation at the conclusion of the concert such as is seldom bestowed upon a conductor in this city." He is "a magnetic conductor, with a firm and incisive beat, who has absolute control over himself and his men, and whose musicianship is never in doubt."[28]

Seven years later, by which time Thuman had come to dislike Stoki thoroughly, he wrote to Gilbert Seldes about the concert. "It was the Russian season in Paris. . . . The concert took place in Bernhardt's Theatre, in the afternoon, and I believe there were about twenty-five people present in the hall. . . ."[29] This was patent mischief on the part of Thuman. No concert given in Paris at that time featuring Félia Litvinne could fail to draw a substantial audience, for she was a reigning queen of the Opéra.[30]

On expressing my frustration in tracking down more information on the concert, I received an informative letter from M. Guy Arnaud, secretary general of the Concerts Colonne. He wrote:

> The last concert of the Colonne's 1908–09 season took place on April 9, 1909. If Stokowski made his debut with the Colonne, as you affirm, on May 12, it was probably within the framework of a special

concert, and we do not, unfortunately, have any trace of it, nor of any others except of Conductor Arthur Nikisch.

The only indication regarding a Russian music concert is the enclosed announcement which was inserted into a program, and of which I send you a photo copy. Madame Litvinne is mentioned therein. (She also featured at the Colonne in various other concerts). We have tried to locate G. Astruc and Company, which organized this presentation, but it has disappeared.[31]

While Gabriel Astruc may have left few or no traces in Paris, his papers and notes are comfortably resting on the shelves of the dance collection in the New York Public Library at Lincoln Center. There is a considerable exchange of letters and telegrams between Astruc and Diaghilev, who was entirely responsible for the annual Russian seasons in Paris.

Unfortunately, neither Leopold nor Olga was able to attend any of the Diaghilev events during this Spring season for on the very day the series began, Stokowski was in London conducting the New Symphony Orchestra in a program featuring American violinist Francis Macmillen. Macmillen, a handsome man who looked very much like the Arrow collar ads of the period, was apparently a very fine violinist desperately trying to carve out a career. He was giving a series of concerts in London and this was to be the third in the series. His reviews were usually very complimentary and he reprinted them extensively in ads that he placed in all the music magazines.

In the *London Times* review we read: "Mr. Macmillen . . . was heard in the Saint-Saens Concerto in B Minor, and in Lalo's 'Symphonie Espagnole.' . . . He was accompanied by the New Symphony Orchestra under M. Leopold Stokowski, who proved to be a conductor with a decided beat and straightforward methods of interpretation, as he showed by his way of taking Beethoven's 'Coriolanus' Overture."[32]

Many other laudatory reviews appeared in other London papers.

During the same week that Stokowski made his debut in London, a Russian concert was performed by the London Symphony Orchestra. The conductor was Serge Koussewitzky (spelled with a *w* rather than a *v.*) It is a curious coincidence that Koussevitzky should have made his Paris debut at the same time that Stoki did, and with the same Colonne Orchestra, and then follow with two concerts in London all during the same month.[33]

One must praise and credit Olga, her mother, and Maria Dehon for their parts in advancing Stokowski's career. But it was Stokowski himself who with his superb confidence and compelling personality pulled off one of the greatest of musical coups. Olga supplied the pattern. Stoki followed it with equally spectacular results. "His engagement by the Cincinnati Symphony Orchestra," wrote Louis Thomas, "was the result of his own dogged determination, and one of the strongest sales promotion campaigns in modern musical history; Stokovski selling Stokovski."[34]

8

Cincinnati

M RS. Holmes and the board lost no time in announcing that the reestablishment of the orchestra was a fait accompli. On May 17, she released the news to the press: "The completion of the annual guarantee of $50,000 for a five year period for the purpose of maintaining the Cincinnati Symphony Orchestra, and the announcement that Leopold Stokovski has been selected as conductor, make the week just ended one of momentous importance," she declared.[1]

Frank Edwards, who had been the orchestra's manager for the previous six years, was reengaged in the same capacity. He explained that in the appointment of Stokowski they had found the ideal man to take over. He described Stoki as a young man, energetic, talented, and experienced— "not a great celebrity, but a man with talent and executive ability which will enable him to form the orchestra and to grow up with it, a man with sufficiently advanced ideas, and one possessed of tact and willingness to become identified with the community."

A succinct and quite factual biographical sketch was given out: "Mr. Stokovski was born in England," it began. "His father was of Polish extraction and his mother was a native of Ireland. Stokovski was educated at Oxford, and his home was in London." Outside of the fact that his mother was not born in Ireland, the rest is unadorned.

Stoki now could tell his old mentor Walford Davies that he was indeed going out to the "Woolly West" and let him share in his success. He lost no time in going there—by the first week in June he had sailed to New York and entrained for Cincinnati. There was a mild flurry of excitement at the station in Cincinnati. Frank Edwards was there to meet him, with a phalanx of photographers and reporters. Stoki began to make news and have his name and photos splashed on the pages of newspapers and magazines before he had even lifted a baton.

He told members of the Cincinnati press that he did not want to talk about himself, but would rather demonstrate by his work than his words. They liked his apparent humility. Then he set about his work with an almost ferocious energy. He began to audition players at once—he had no intention of keeping any deadwood.

After auditioning in Cincinnati for a month, he proceeded to New York to hear and engage other players, and to discuss with New York managers the soloists he would like to have appear with the orchestra. It was also a time to complete his programs for the year and to study new scores. He sent back word that he was "greatly pleased over the excellent musicians who have been secured, and everything augurs for a splendid season."[2]

His list of soloists was a formidable one: It included Sergei Rachmaninoff, Fritz Kreisler, Ferruccio Busoni, Teresa Carreño, and Mischa Elman. Maud Powell, a fine violinist, but not of such international standing, also appeared, as well as the concertmaster Hugo Heermann.

Stokowski completed his programs and sent them on to Cincinnati. They were wonderfully balanced, with an adequate amount of Bach, Beethoven, Mozart, Haydn, Liszt, Tchaikovsky, and Brahms. But he also added many works that were not the usual fare of the old orchestra, by such composers as Sibelius, Debussy, Rachmaninoff, MacDowell, and a Swedish composer, Tor Aulin—all then alive and well.

Stokowski returned to Ohio the first week in October; Bettie Holmes came back from her vacation in Europe; and Frank Edwards continued to scurry about booking the orchestra into various Midwestern cities. Like Charles Ellis in Boston and later Arthur Judson, Edwards not only assumed the management of the orchestra, but booked other artists as well, some of them under his own management.

Interest in the new orchestra and curiosity about the new conductor boosted ticket sales beyond that of any previous season. The board had even arranged an auction of choice seats to bring in additional income. The season was to consist of ten pairs of concerts to be given on Friday afternoons and Saturday evenings. The rehearsals began nearly two weeks before the first concert.

Stoki told me about his first contact with the orchestra: "First of all, the orchestra was completely German. We rehearsed in the German language.

I always spoke German. My nurse was Viennese, so that was not any difficulty. But it seemed strange to rehearse in German in America."[3]

In 1969 on a BBC broadcast, he also recalled his first experiences with the orchestra: "It was rather amusing because Cincinnati at that time was practically a German city. Most people spoke German there and we rehearsed in the German language. And I remember one day we were rehearsing a symphony in which the trombones only play in the last movement and over here was the orchestra and over there was the door and there was a bar there and there was beer in that bar because Germans like beer, you know. So I noticed the trombones went in there and closed the door. So we did the first movement, we did the second movement, we did the third movement. Then I began to think, when the fourth movement comes and they're not there, what shall I say to those Germans. And they were portly Germans like this. And we started the fourth movement, the door opened quietly and they tip-toed in with their trombones and played right in time. It was remarkable how they were listening all the time. It was very amusing how well they did that."[4]

We can indulgently forgive his demifantasy, for he was recalling events that happened a half century before. But the real story is twice as fascinating. The orchestra may have rehearsed in German in Van der Stucken's day, but it was certainly not something that Stoki was to accept. Perhaps he thought it added a bit of glamor to say that they rehearsed in German, but what he did was far more interesting and actually more characteristic.

A reporter from the *Cincinnati Times Star,* attending one of Stoki's first rehearsals, complimented him on one of the first innovations he undertook, "one which cannot be too strongly commended. He employs the language of this country in addressing an orchestra which plays in an English speaking city and is listened to by an English speaking people. . . . The discontinuation of foreign languages, of French, German or Italian, in directing an orchestra of musicians playing in an American city, is a wise and good move in the right direction."[5] He commented on the fact that the musicians were obviously familiar with the scores and then noted the patience and care Stoki used in molding such works as the Beethoven Fifth according to his own conception: "He demands and attains his effect through an appeal to the mentality of the individuals composing the orchestra. To them he explains in clear, concise and well pronounced English, his thought concerning the interpretation of the work in hand. He points out that there is a psychology in playing and that between forte and pianissimo, the degrees are of infinite variety."

The remarkable part of the article is that it emphatically states that Stokowski addressed the orchestra "in clear, concise and well pronounced English."[6] His Slavicization was not to take place until three years later.

He chose his first Cincinnati program with great care. He began with Mozart's Overture to *The Magic Flute*, then Beethoven's Fifth Symphony, a work on which the critics and audience might form their judgments. After intermission, he conducted Weber's Overture to *Die Freischütz*, the "Siegfried Idyll," and the "Ride of the Valkyries," with which he had wowed the parishioners of St. Bartholomew's in his organ transcription.

Courtesy Cincinnati Historical Society

At the piano (c. 1910)

To give music lovers some inkling of what to expect in their new conductor, Herman Thuman of the *Cincinnati Enquirer* presented an extensive article about him. It proclaimed: "He is a man of charming address, is the new leader; simplicity, neatness that is almost painful, a total lack of eccentricity either in dress, speech or manners, mark his demeanor. Neither long, shaggy hair, nor flowing tie, those inevitable attributes of the artist or the musician in the popular picture are affected by him. Slight and slender in physical build with light hair, a clear complexion and light blue eyes, he has a carriage which instantly arrests attention. Composed at all times he had the pleasantest way of avoiding questions which he does not wish to answer, and at the same time an insinuating way of suggesting what he would like you to know. This is diplomacy under another guise, and a successful conductor requires all the diplomacy nature and experience can shower upon him.

"But the most impressive characteristic of the man is his energy. It is not the kind that demonstrates itself in bustle and noise, but of the carefully directed kind which achieves results. It was this energy which made it possible for him to organize the orchestra in spite of the late start and the demand for orchestral players which is just now so keen. . . .

"In his tastes the new leader is equally simple. He likes comfort, though his social aspirations are very circumscribed and he is quietly but firmly enthusiastic about his work. In a letter written to the writer of this a fortnight ago he said, 'As a boy I was soaked in Palestrina and Bach and Beethoven and their contemporaries. I played fiddle in all the great symphonies, overtures and quartets, and when the technical drudgery of the day was done I played Beethoven sonatas for recreation.'

"That was healthy recreation, was it not? The excerpt gives an idea of the man. Later, in a letter he says: 'I have something to say in ideals, in vigor, in mysticism and in savage force.'

"Musical Cincinnati is waiting to hear him. Those who know and have heard his ability are confident and those who are fair will welcome him with an unbiased mind and heart. Verily, the coming of Stokovski is an event."[7]

And verily it was. Expectancy was at fever pitch, and the large audience that packed into the huge auditorium gasped as he strode out before the orchestra. He was greeted by a fanfare of trumpets and rapping of fiddle bows and spontaneous applause from the audience. Thuman, writing in the *Enquirer,* headlined his review in bold capitals with the word "**BRILLIANT**"—and Thuman was the town's most conservative critic: "The concert proved to be unusually interesting from several points of view. . . . The orchestra presented a new appearance, and everywhere there was the subdued air of expectancy. But the unanimity of the verdict in general after the concert was over left no room for doubt. There were differences of opinion expressed, to be sure, as to interpretations but that was to be expected, for the audience included many thorough and capable musicians. As to Stokovski's capabilities, however, there was not a word of doubt and everywhere was most enthusiastic praise.

"When Leopold Stokovski, young and debonair, but earnest and determined, stepped on the stage the orchestra gave him the welcome 'tush.' Most of those in front gasped. A young, tall, simple-looking fellow, with quiet mien, minus all the familiar affectations of the conventional 'musician,' took his place at the stand. He was an unexpected picture to most everybody. But before the program was half over there was not one in the audience but was captivated by his personality, delighted with the graceful manner of his conducting, and immensely pleased with the musical acumen he fervently demonstrated. The ice had been broken. Stokovski had come and had conquered."[8]

"My reason for selecting a program of this style," he said in a preconcert interview, "was to give the audience a full opportunity to measure me by compositions they know and which they have heard before. It is by comparison that judgements are made possible. . . ."[9]

To the critic of the *Cincinnati Times Star:* "The playing of the Beethoven C Minor . . . was taken at a very rapid tempo. The hand of fate which knocks at the door of our new conductor is evidently not one wrinkled with sere and yellow age."

The editor of the New York–based but nationally read *Musical Courier* thought the advent of Stokowski sufficiently important to send out its principal critic, Leonard Liebling, to cover the event. Liebling, soon to become editor in chief of the magazine, was a highly trained musician and a most perceptive critic. He was impressed. He admired the young man's quiet bearing and reposeful manner, and remarked that Stokowski immediately inspired confidence in the audience. He noted, too, that there was no trace of nervousness or trepidation as the young conductor faced the players. "A complete mental and physical grasp of the famous 'Fifth' was evident from the first measure to the last." Liebling felt that Stokowski's conception "embodied many of the best effects made by Nikisch, Mahler and Weingartner, and yet exhibited just the right measure of independence and elasticity . . . to save Stokowski from being called either a slavish imitator or a sensationalist seeking to startle by means of crass innovations." He praised him for evoking the breadth and majesty of the first and last movements and for the full measure of poetry he extracted from the "glorious andante." He added that the audience remained to pay a prolonged tribute "to the conductor who seemed to have conquered them so completely."[10] The local *Courier* correspondent told Liebling she had never heard such a spontaneous ovation in all the years of her concertgoing in Cincinnati.

Stoki had not only won the audience and impressed the critics, he had won the cooperation and affection of the players themselves. Hugo Heermann, the concertmaster, opined, "I am astonished and delighted at the magnificent work of our leader and the way the entire orchestra responded. All the men admire and respect him extremely, both for his musical knowledge and his kindly, courteous treatment of them. They will labor like Trojans to help him make the Cincinnati Symphony the equal of the best bands in the country."[11]

Heermann was undoubtedly the most distinguished member of the orchestra. He was one of the first of Stoki's selections. At the age of ten, he had been brought to play for Rossini, who advised his parents to send him to the Conservatory in Brussels. There, at the end of three years, he won the first prize as a violinist. He then settled in Frankfurt, where he was the first violinist of the famous Frankfurt String Quartet. He migrated to America in 1906 and came to teach in Chicago.

Heermann made numerous international tours and was the first to introduce the Brahms Violin Concerto to Paris and New York. It was that work he was to play later in the season with the new orchestra. He became a close friend and confidant of the young conductor and apparently helped and counseled him about matters of style and tradition. Mischa Elman, who knew Heermann, thought Stokowski was fortunate in having him as his concertmaster.[12]

Olga unfortunately could not share in Leopold's triumph, for she appeared in New York on the twenty-third with the Kneisel Quartet, playing the piano part in the Saint-Saëns Quartet in B-flat. It is a rarely heard work and Samaroff netted rave reviews. Following this performance, she immediately proceeded to Boston to appear with the Symphony for one of its pension fund concerts. She chose the Schumann Concerto. Olin Downes reported that she played it beautifully: "Rarely, indeed, have its simple measures been so simple, so winning, so truly Schumann."[13]

While the Valkyries were riding high in Cincinnati, they were also tearing through the air of Boston's Symphony Hall, for the concert there ended with the same work Stoki had chosen to conclude his.

On his second pair of subscription concerts, Stokowski indulged in a predilection that was to become one of his salient traits. He introduced two contemporary works. One was the set of *Caucasian Sketches* he had played at his Paris concert, and the other was a concerto by the Swedish violinist and composer Tor Aulin. Although soloists too frequently trot out the overplayed warhorses when appearing with orchestras, his soloist, Maud Powell, who had most of the big violin concertos in her repertory, intrepidly suggested this unknown work. But it was just the sort of thing Stokowski enjoyed. The press reported that Powell won an ovation.[14]

Both critics and listeners noted great improvement in the playing of the orchestra. They attributed that to the frequent rehearsals and the discipline acquired during the tour. While not being specific, one critic attributed the betterment of the orchestra to various changes in the seating arrangement of the different instrumentalists.

With each succeeding concert the listeners became more interested in their conductor and in the orchestra. The Cincinnati Musician's Club honored him and the orchestra to show the "high esteem" in which he was held by the most prominent music professionals in the city.[15] The club was made up of the faculties of the musical colleges and conservatories, eminent choral directors, critics, and others active in Cincinnati's musical affairs.

Then, invited by Mr. and Mrs. Charles P. Taft for a soirée in their stately home, one of the town's finest showplaces, Stoki assembled twenty of his key players and entertained a hundred or more of their guests. At the same time in Washington, Mrs. William Howard Taft and her husband—she had been the first president of the Cincinnati Symphony Orchestra— invited Olga to play at the White House.[16] Samaroff offered a potpourri of encorelike pieces, ending with the "Ride of the Valkyries," a work that seemed to please the President. He gave Olga an autographed photo and, on inscribing it, made a remark about "the Ride." This seemingly unimportant gesture was to have an amusing and, in fact, embarrassing aftermath one year later. But we shall come to that in due course.

On January 21, 1910, Stoki had his first direct experience with Rachmaninoff. Their relationship would later develop into a magnificent collaboration. This was Rachmaninoff's first visit to America, and he made his debut at the end of November, playing his recently completed Third Piano Concerto with Walter Damrosch and the New York Symphony. The critics were disappointed with the new work—none of them found it the equal of his Second. They did not feel it possessed the same spirit and originality.[17] Rachmaninoff chose to play his Second for his first appearance with Stokowski. There was an immediate sense of rapport between the two.[18] They could hardly have imagined that two decades later they would make one of the great classic recordings of the work with the Philadelphia Orchestra.

The Cincinnatians knew a good thing when they heard it. Their new conductor was indeed a find. On the first of March the board announced that Stoki had been invited to remain with the orchestra for four more years. The *Times Star* immediately printed an editorial commending the board and lauding Stoki's accomplishments. The critics all praised him; one observed that he was "musically well grounded, and he has been progressive from the beginning."[19] Stoki was very pleased and told everyone that he was very happy with his work and was particularly pleased with the environment. It was a pleasant vindication of the faith that his family in London and his friends here, particularly Olga, her mother, and Miss Dehon, had shown in him.

Cincinnati Orchestra concerts in different Midwestern cities became increasingly popular, and most were completely sold out to standing room only. The orchestra and Stoki were hailed in Cleveland on March 9, 1910, when Marcella Sembrich appeared as soloist. The *Plain Dealer* reported that "Stokowski is, at twenty-four years, and after seven months in America, one of the greatest conductors of the country."[20]

After the concerts of April 1 and 2, Stoki left Cincinnati for New York and then went on to Europe to rest, study new scores, and plan his programs for the coming year. He had a six-month hiatus and was later joined by Olga and her mother, with whom he attended festivals and explored parts of alpine Bavaria.

He sailed for New York, October 18, on the S.S. *Kaiser Wilhelm II* and after a brief stop in New York, proceeded to Cincinnati in time for his first rehearsal on November 15.

There were numerous changes in the orchestra, notably the concertmaster, Hugo Heermann, who had retired after one season to be replaced by his son, Emil. Emil, like his father, not only aided the orchestra but was a superb soloist as well. Other soloists included Ernestine Schumann-Heink, Francis Macmillen, Josef Hofmann, tenor Daniel Beddoe, Olga Samaroff, cellist Boris Hambourg, and Ferruccio Busoni. Two of the concerts were to be without soloists, since it was reasoned that Stokowski's drawing power had grown so remarkably that soloists were not needed.[21]

The seasons had been expanded with the addition of Pop Concerts, which were to be given at the Grand Opera House on Sunday afternoons after the first of the year. Then at the end of the regular series there would be a three-day festival done in conjunction with England's Sheffield Choir and a set of distinguished British soloists.[22] Sir Edward Elgar himself was to be present and conduct a work of his own.

Frank Edwards, too, had been busy. He increased the number of concerts to be played out of town. He had now booked the orchestra for Dayton, Columbus, Indianapolis, Cleveland, Pittsburgh, Detroit, Oberlin, and other towns and college campuses. It was to be a very busy season. The orchestra itself had been strengthened with the addition of eight more string players and replacements in the brass and woodwind sections.[23]

The opening subscription concert featured the well-loved contralto Mme. Schumann-Heink singing music of Saint-Saëns and Wagner. Stoki's major work was the Seventh Symphony of Beethoven. One critic found it "a brilliantly effective reading, one which brought out all its boisterous humor and vigor interrupted by episodes of poetic charm and delicacy."[24]

Francis Macmillen, now back from Europe, where he had paved the way for his career with countless self-produced concerts, set out on an American tour. There was a great splash of paid publicity about him in all the powerful music magazines. His handsome presence graced their covers, and full-page ads quoted excerpts from his European reviews. On the strength of these he secured a number of engagements.

Ohioans were quite naturally interested in his career—he was after all a native of Marietta, Ohio, not far from Cincinnati. His choice for his appearance with Stokowski was the Goldmark Concerto in A Minor. He had played it with Stock and the Chicago Symphony in November, and the critics, while not bowled over, were most cordial. In Cincinnati he fared even better. The enthusiastic applause of his Buckeye listeners brought him back for eight bows and a well-deserved encore. The reunion of soloist and conductor was a happy one, for they had an additional affinity—both were Ohioans now.

The second tour of the season ended the first week of December and was most successful.[25] In Columbus the concert practically became a matter of state importance—it brought out Governor Harmon and his wife, along with a great number of state legislators to add to the overflowing audience. In Akron the orchestra was joined by the Akron Women's Chorus; they performed a real rarity by Elgar called *The Challenge of Thor*. In Indianapolis, the brilliant woman pianist Yolanda Mérö was engaged for an all-Tchaikovsky evening. She chose to play, not the familiar Tchaikovsky First Concerto, but his Second in G Major. The demand for tickets in Dayton was so great that they stayed there to play three concerts.

The music for the first pair of concerts in 1911 was to be all-Russian, so to Cincinnati listeners it would no doubt have seemed appropriate to select a soloist with a name like Olga Samaroff. Though she had played with orchestras in New York, Boston, and Philadelphia, as well as Paris and London, she had not played with the Cincinnati Orchestra before. She may have preferred to play her favorite Tchaikovsky B-flat Minor Concerto, which unfortunately had been played by Carreño the previous season, so she chose instead the Fourth Concerto in D Minor by Anton Rubinstein. By present standards it seems a deplorable piece of virtuosic claptrap, but it had a way of bringing down the house, and Olga scored an immense success. Two months later, on March 9, Olga had her chance. The orchestra was again on tour. This time Leopold invited her to perform her favorite Tchaikovsky piece with the orchestra in Buffalo.

Critics away from the major metropolitan centers often sound naive and sometimes downright embarrassing. But not this time. The concert was reviewed by the distinguished composer Arthur Farwell: "An overwhelming success was scored by Leopold Stokowski. . . . Olga Samaroff, pianist, as soloist shared in the great success of the concert. . . .

"The nature of the attack and accents in the first half dozen bars of the march [*Marche Slave*] made one realize that the orchestra was under control of a force of very unusual nature. The sense of a high vitalization, of almost superhuman keenness of musical consciousness, increased as the interpretation proceeded. Accents and shadings took on new and intenser values, climaxes became strangely powerful and poignant, and when the conductor came to the close the house was in an uproar and recalled him again and again. . . .

"The expectation as to what such a leader would do with the 'Pathétique' Symphony was not disappointed. To hear it under the electrical influence of this astonishing conductor were as if one assisted at the creation of the work in the inspired mind of the composer."[26]

Cleveland was also included on the tour, but here the soloist was the violinist virtuoso Mischa Elman. He apparently was the magnet that drew the huge audience that "filled every seat and left an overflow standing." The reviews for both the conductor and the soloist were exuberant. The critic of the *Press* quoted Elman as saying, "I wish I could think of some word besides wizard to describe [Stokowski's] wonderful virtuosity and artistry, but that is the only thing that fitly expresses his uncanny virtuosity."[27]

The critic of the *Cleveland Plain Dealer* observed that Stokowski "has a magnetic influence, plainly apparent, and the accomplishments of the orchestra must be attributed almost wholly to him. . . . The Cincinnati Orchestra must be reckoned with hereafter, as never before, for this man Stokovski is accomplishing wonders and much may be expected of him."[28] And he was quite right!

The first of the Pop Concerts scheduled for Sunday afternoons began on January 15. The programs were not condescending. They were, in fact, regular symphonic concerts, albeit not heavy, given at popular prices. The "Pop" referred more to the price structure.

Frank Edwards reported that long before the day of the first concert, every seat in the auditorium was sold and over a thousand who came to the box office had to be turned away. During the concert there was thunderous applause, and at the conclusion "the audience broke into a prolonged cheer."[29]

At another Pop Concert Stoki introduced a work by the then-contemporary American composer Rossiter Gleason Cole—it was Cole's setting of a recitation of Longfellow's poem "King Robert of Sicily."

A new critic covered the concert for *Musical America:* "At the seat sale for this concert, as for every preceding concert in this popular series, long lines of people waiting for the sale to open have aroused so much interest that the various newspapers have pictured the scenes as typical features of the popularity of the orchestra at home. These scenes have been repeated before the concerts on Sunday afternoon, when the lobby of the Grand Opera House has been crowded long before the opening of the doors. Time and time again hundreds of people have been turned away after all the available standing room has been sold. . . .

"Leopold Stokovski is himself a great favorite. A conductor of fine stage presence, of magnetic personality, of evident force, he is always hailed with more than perfunctory applause when he steps upon the stage. That his orchestra men feel the same respect as does the audience is shown by the fixed attention which they pay during the performance of any number. I have never seen such unanimity, such an evidence of the director and men being of one mind, outside of New York, and that condition is even rare in some New York concerts."[30]

The name signed by the critic could have caused little stir then, but in retrospect it takes on a significance far beyond its impact at the time. The name of the critic was Arthur Judson, who was to become the manager of the Philadelphia Orchestra, the New York Philharmonic, the founder of CBS, and in general the most powerful manager of musical affairs America would ever know.

Musical America had sent Judson out to Cincinnati to assess the young conductor and the orchestra, who were beginning to make a stir far beyond the confines of the city. It was also in response to the competition. *The Musical Courier, Musical America*'s chief rival, had, after all, sent out its chief critic to cover Stokowski, and *Musical America* was not to be outdone.

Judson reminded Cincinnatians that if the value of the musical culture of any city is to be measured by the popularity of its musical organizations, then Cincinnati must take rank among the first cities of the United States. The citizens of the city were proud indeed.

Judson was admirably equipped to make his judgments. He also knew Ohio. He was born there, in Dayton in 1881, one year before the birth of Stokowski. He had studied the violin extensively and acted as concertmaster for Theodore Thomas in Chicago. At Denison University in Granville, Ohio, he had developed an important music department and conducted the university chorus and orchestra.

"As a young man," he said, "I was for many years a violinist and teacher. I aspired to be a virtuoso. One day when I was professor of music at a midwestern university, I sat down and began to appraise my assets. I soon realized the truth, when I compared my talent with that of the great violinists I knew. There was no use to be pushed on by well meaning relatives and friends. I resolved to get into my present field."[31] It was then, in 1907, that he joined the staff of *Musical America.*

Judson did not leave Cincinnati at once but remained to hear the next subscription concert. It began with the Beethoven *Coriolanus* Overture, a work that Stokowski had frequently played at St. Bartholomew's in his organ transcription. Then came the Mozart Symphony in G Minor; Bohlmann's *Lyric Tone Poem;* and Scharwenka's F Minor Piano Concerto, with the composer as soloist.

Theodor Heinrich Friedrich Bohlmann was as German as his name. He had been born in Osterwieck in 1865 and migrated to Cincinnati in 1890. He was a splendid pianist and taught at the Conservatory. His tone poem was welcomed by the musical community, for he was a great favorite with all the musicians in town.

Judson wrote: "The audience was large and intensely enthusiastic. The orchestra, which is a pliable and responsive instrumental body, succeeded under the magnetic direction of Mr. Stokovski in bringing out every detail of the compositions which they played. The interpretation of the Beethoven overture was one that brought out its tragic points to the fullest extent, while the Mozart, which is popular in this city, to judge from the applause which greeted it, was read with charming and delicate effectiveness. . . ."[32]

Arthur Judson then had long conversations with Stokowski, which became the basis for an extended article in *Musical America.* The article was to have profound consequences for both men. It was on the basis of it that Stoki had Judson engaged as manager of the Philadelphia Orchestra two years later. Judson headlined it "Leopold Stokovski—Thinker, Philosopher and Musician."[33]

"In the last analysis the great man is the man of simplicity," he wrote. He then proceeded to enumerate various other attributes of greatness, applying all of them to Stokowski. He described Stoki's studio, lined with bookcases filled with books and scores—"music of every period and school; books of philosophy, of psychology, novels in many languages and masterpieces of many nations; poetry of every age and every school of thought; and all well thumbed, all companionable with the evidence of frequent use." Judson observed scores piled on tables and orchestral parts in the process of being arranged and double-checked before being used for the next program. Their conversation drifted to a discussion of the previous day's concert and the attributes of a modern conductor.

"In my opinion," said Stokowski, "the orchestral director has two duties, to give impressions and receive impressions. A man can only give out that which he receives, and unless he is receptive he cannot give forth. This is best exemplified in the conducting of accompaniment such as that to the Scharwenka concerto yesterday. Mr. Scharwenka was kind enough to tell me it was the best accompaniment he had yet had in this country and I feel that it was good because of two things. I do not regard accompaniment as a mere piece of hack work and so I study it as I would a symphony, so that I may get into the spirit of the work, and I try to make the accompanying part one with the soloist's conception. . . .

"Strange to say, I find that the greater the artist the easier the accompanying. It must be because the great artist gets close to the real fundamental facts, that he presents the foundation truths, and, for that reason, the thinking director finds that his interpretations and those of the performer largely coincide." He expressed contempt for a "mere virtuoso who plays notes, not ideas. . . .

"And again, one can learn from many sources. In my rehearsals I allow a great liberty. During the preparation of a composition any player is at liberty to advance an idea that he may think important to the correct interpretation of a work and, while I allow nothing to interfere with my direction of affairs, I remain open to suggestions. An orchestra consists of as many individualities as there are men, and the bringing of unity depends on the convincing of these individualities that the one interpretation is the best and frequent discussions of moot points brings about this unity. Furthermore, at the first rehearsal of a work I point out to the men the underlying ideas, historical or critical, of each work so that they may enter more fully into the spirit of the composition. If we play Mozart we talk of Mozart, we get the spirit of the work as he wrote it, and then we can play Mozart, not as we would play a selection from a Wagner opera, but as Mozart would have wanted it.

"And then ensemble is given much attention. I believe most strongly in section rehearsals, and so three or four of the week's rehearsals are given to the various sections separately. In these rehearsals we work out the minutest details, we decide which should be brought out here, which should be subdued there, and at last we find that we have eliminated every passage which might otherwise have been perfunctorily played. While this does not destroy the individuality, the personality, of each player, it brings a splendid oneness of purpose, a unity into play that makes for the best kind of performance. It is nothing more nor less than taking up a work analytically and then synthetically. . . .

"The building of an orchestra is not a matter of one season or two, but a matter of years, and that the public does not realize. First there is the selection of material, the elimination of the unsuitable, and that in itself takes time. Take the Boston Orchestra. That organization has been long in reaching its present stage of perfection, but now it would take many years of bad directing to spoil it. . . . Fortunately, I have had the best support in every way here in Cincinnati and we are well on the way to an organization of supreme merit. I cannot say too much in praise of the women and men who have made this orchestra possible or of the players themselves who have shown the heartiest spirit of cooperation. As far as working conditions go my position here is little short of ideal."

To read the program for the all-Italian concert for the first week in February, one might think it had been chosen by Toscanini rather than

Stokowski, for it is far more characteristic of the former. For Stoki it was an odd program indeed: the Rossini Overture from *The Barber of Seville*, the Sgambati Symphony in D, Sinigaglia's *La Baruffe Chiozzotte*, and arias by Verdi and Puccini. The soloist, however, was not Italian—he was the Welsh tenor Daniel Beddoe.

The season came to an end during the first week of April. On the Wednesday preceding the final Friday and Saturday pair of concerts, the New York Symphony arrived, with Walter Damrosch conducting and Isadora Duncan trailing her draperies. However, concertgoers in Cincinnati had come to realize the treasure they had in their own superb orchestra and were not in a mood to give an ovation to one that was inferior. Damrosch was no match for the young "Lochinvar." Harold Schonberg observed that Walter Damrosch "was never taken very seriously by the critics and by his fellow musicians,"[34] and the Cincinnati audience and press acted accordingly. The curious and rather ironic circumstance of the New York Symphony concert was that it was produced by Herman Thuman, the very man who first recommended Stoki in Paris. He was now in rivalry with the Cincinnati Orchestra, and he was certainly not to emerge the winner. Could the future antagonism between Thuman and the orchestra—particularly that between him and Stokowski—have had its roots in this rivalry? The Cincinnati Orchestra's manager, Frank Edwards, moonlighting as a critic for *Musical America*, dismissed the New York orchestra's concert with a mere acknowledgment, while devoting fifty-eight laudatory lines to Stokowski and the Cincinnati Orchestra.

The ill-feeling between Thuman and the Cincinnati Orchestra may well have resulted from this conflict of interests. The antagonism was to manifest itself in petty sniping, which grew to such proportions during the next season that it became a *cause célèbre*.

But Stoki ended the first season in a veritable blaze of glory. Although surely knowing better, the whole audience burst into applause after the first movement of the Dvořák *New World* Symphony. The critics thought it one of the most eminently successful things Stokowski had done, and some suggested that his affinity for the work might be due to hereditary influences. The season's final soloist was Busoni. On this return engagement he played the Beethoven *Emperor* Concerto and was applauded so vociferously that he had to respond with several encores. As Stoki walked out to conduct the "1812" Overture, which was to close the program, he was greeted with a salvo of applause and a fanfare by the brasses. The orchestra had been augmented to ninety men, and apparently they gave their all. If the Tchaikovsky work was not one to "make a joyful noise," it certainly was one to make a brilliant and wonderful finale with its cannonading racket. Always interested in percussion, Stokowski unleashed a tintinnabulation that must have sounded like all the bells of Moscow put together. As the piece ended in a blaze of glory, the audience broke into wild cheers. It was as if they were Muscovites and had just won the battle.

But it was Stokowski who had won the real battle. He had already been called a genius and magician by the critics from New York, so there was no longer any need for reserve. Cincinnatians hailed their conquering hero, and the board provided a banquet for him and the players immediately after the din had died away. Manager Edwards beamed and said that it was the most successful season the orchestra had ever had. Lucien Wulsin, Bettie Holmes, the Tafts, and all the other members of the board had a right to be well pleased.[35]

Although the symphonic season closed with the end of the regular series, Stoki and Edwards planned a kind of minifestival for the last of April. The Sheffield Choir, which Stoki knew from his London days, was making a tour of Canada and the United States, which would continue on to Australia and South Africa. Their tour was an ambitious one—they would perform nearly one hundred and fifty concerts in seventy cities before returning to England in September.

The choir had an impressive history. It was founded in 1876 by Sir Henry Coward, who conducted it from its inception until 1933. Through the years it performed much of the great choral literature, including Elgar's *Dream of Gerontius*. It was this work that they featured on their tour, and they had Sir Edward Elgar himself to conduct it.

After a resounding success in Montreal, Ottawa, and Toronto, the Sheffield singers journeyed to Cincinnati for three concerts on three successive days. The first half of the concert was all vocal and was conducted by Coward. The choir sang Bach's "Sing Ye to the Lord," and a group of English madrigals and part songs. The audience was so delighted with these that they were added to the choir's later regular program. During the second half of the concert, Sir Edward conducted his *Dream of Gerontius*. [36]

There was great curiosity about the second program, for it would give the audience their first opportunity to hear Stoki conduct a chorus. He chose to do the Beethoven Ninth Symphony, although that was hardly a work to exhibit his prowess with a chorus. The choral part of the work has been regarded by many critics as its weakest part, and, for the soloists more so than the choir, it presents substantial difficulty. Boston critic Philip Hale had once suggested that it would be better "to leave the hall with the memory of the Adagio, than to depart with the vocal hurry-scurry and shouting of the final measures assailing the ears and nerves."

It was fortunate that Hale did not review this particular performance, for according to all accounts, the soloists were totally inadequate and evidently sounded somewhat like "an irritated kennel," to borrow a phrase from Hale. However, the orchestra played superbly, so the overall performance was a success rather than a disaster. The local critic opined that "the rendition of the symphony gave new proof of Mr. Stokovski's genius as a conductor."[37]

The following evening Stoki conducted the Verdi *Requiem* for the first time. Obviously there could not be adequate rehearsals for such a succession of big works in so short a period, and the *Requiem* suffered. Again the soloists were incapable of handling their parts. The critics kindly called the performance "inspiring and creditable." They also praised Stokowski for his ability to overcome the difficulties with which he was confronted.

The reunion with Elgar was a most pleasant one, and there was much conversation about music and about concert life in London. Elgar spoke excitedly about his newest work, his Second Symphony, which he had dedicated to the memory of the late King Edward VII. The first performance would take place in London on May 24 in Queen's Hall, and Stoki immediately asked Elgar for the right to give the first American performance in Cincinnati.

9

Romanza

BOTH Leopold and Olga had gone to great lengths to conceal their interest in one another from the public and from all but their intimate friends. The announcement of their engagement on April 8, 1911, sent shock waves through the hundreds of smitten girls who flocked to Stoki's concerts, or so the newspapers reported. It was made by Olga from her mother's home in St. Louis.

"How had they met?" a reporter asked. Olga replied: "Well, that is no secret. We met socially in New York but we were not in love then. Of course, we admired each other professionally, but so far as sentiment was concerned, there was none. Mr. Stokowski is the greatest conductor in the world and I admired him professionally for a long time. I played with him in Paris two years ago, and this season we appeared together in Cincinnati and Buffalo. I don't know how it all happened but when we were in Buffalo we agreed not to announce our engagement until Mr. Stokowski completed his season. If you must write a romantic story say that he fell in love with my hands, and I in love with his eyes. If you want to tell the truth, just say it was a very ordinary courtship and nothing romantic happened. I am perfectly happy and Mr. Stokowski seems to share my joy. We will be married soon."[1]

Leopold was at no time available for comment, but reporters continued to plague Olga in St. Louis. One reporter trying to get responses about many personal matters, whom Olga was deftly fending off, happened to notice a signed photo of President Taft on the piano. As this seemed a perfectly safe topic, she told about her recent appearance at the White House.

The following day when the interview appeared, her father was one of the first to read it. "Have you lost your mind?" he asked her. She seized the newspaper and to her astonishment read: "President Taft is an admirer of Mme. Samaroff's playing. . . . She says it is a mistaken notion that the President could not appreciate an adventure any more blood-curdling than a game of golf. She says he would be a real daredevil for adventure and fight if he did not keep his primitive impulses under control . . . she has seen him riding wildly in the night in a forest with the tempestuous wind whistling havoc through the branches of the trees and the air rent with demonical cries, as he charged onto a bloody field of battle.

Courtesy Sonya Stokowski Thorbecke

Jewel cabinet made by Stokowski's father as a gift for his son's wedding to Olga Samaroff in 1911

"Of course, Mme. Samaroff did not see the President actually do all this. She saw it psychologically acted out. It was this way . . . 'I selected the *Ride of the Valkyries* to play for the President,' Mme. Samaroff told a *Post-Dispatch* reporter. 'As I played I watched him. And I saw him ride right along with the Valkyries all the way to bring the souls of the dead from the battlefield. His hands, which had dropped easily to his knees, tightened. The genial, pleasant smile vanished as he set out on his ride with the Norse deities. His eyes sparkled. His whole attention was concentrated on the charge, and his face was as true an expression

Photo Hirsch, Munich/Courtesy Mrs. James Blauvelt
With Olga Samaroff Stokowski in Munich (c. 1912)

as if he were actually riding on that imaginary battlefield.' "[2]

She rushed out and wired a friend in Washington to try to explain the interview to Taft. "Word came back that the President was highly amused," she said, "but I did not soon recover from the shock."[3]

The wedding, as planned, was a quiet one held at the home of Olga's parents, Mr. and Mrs. Carlos Hickenlooper. On Leopold's twenty-ninth birthday, April 18, they obtained their marriage license, and their wedding took place on the twenty-fourth. It was duly registered in City Hall, and the marriage certificate states that "the undersigned Minister of the Gospel did at St. Louis in the State of Missouri, on the 24th day of April 1911 unite in marriage the above named persons." It was signed John F.

Cannon. We may infer from this that it was not a Catholic wedding.

Wedding gifts were abundant, but two were unique. Stoki's father sent a beautiful handcrafted cabinet. Decorated with inlays of the most intricate order, it was a remarkable example of the elder Stokowski's art. The other gift, from Maria Dehon, was a villa in Munich.[4]

The young couple sailed for England, where Leopold introduced his bride to his proud parents. They then set out for Munich. During the pre–World War I years, Munich was the sort of magnet that Paris was to become for Americans following the war. Like Paris it was possessed of a spirit of *vie de boheme.* The lively student quarter in Schwabing was filled with cafes and beer halls. It supported a huge student population and played host to the many visitors to the summer music festivals.

"Munich was an ideal summer resort for anyone who wished to combine enjoyment of art and music with excursions to the nearby mountain country," said Olga. And she mused rhetorically whether it was "an emanation from the Isar's grey green glacier water that brought some magic from the mountains to Munich, or did the never ending flow of mellow beer wash away the coldness and oversophistication one finds in most cities?"[5]

They reveled in the comfort of their pleasant villa. (The Germans always referred to their large houses as villas, and the Stokowskis' was obviously one of these.) It was a four-story, three-family, stucco house with wide, expansive windows and spacious rooms with pleasant porches on three floors. It was situated in Herzog Park on Pienzenauer Strasse. Their daughter, Sonya, who first saw it when she was about thirteen or fourteen, did not have the impression that it was very large. "Medium describes it best," she said.[6]

"My small house had a garden," wrote Olga many years later in a fit of mock modesty.[7] There were many elegant villas in Herzog Park, which had an abundance of tall trees. This section of Munich, on the bank of the Isar opposite the English Gardens, had been a ducal hunting preserve. Olga's reminiscence continues: "A terrace off the dining room invited to al fresco meals on warm days. Balconies on each of the upper floors had gay flower boxes without which no Bavarian home is complete. . . . The flowers in the window boxes were luxuriant and varied. Their riot of color gave a finishing touch to the gaiety of the rooms.

"Many things about the house had attracted me, but it was the kitchen that decided me. One of its grilled windows looked out on the quiet Pienzenauer Strasse, where the songs of birds were softly accompanied by

Olga and Leopold lived in the far right of this Munich villa (c. 1912)

the swiftly flowing Isar, just a block away. Another window overlooked a tiny vegetable garden and fruit trees that were spread out on a wall topped with red tiles. Tall poplars flanked the gateway, and a bit of rose garden completed the peaceful picture."[8]

Olga had never really managed a household before. By a stroke of luck a Bavarian maid who had been employed by one of Olga's good friends in Boston, and whom she had known, returned to Munich for the summer and agreed to help the Stokowskis get established in their new home: "First we selected two youngish maids, a cook and a housemaid-waitress from among the attractive and respectful candidates for the privilege of attending to all our wants. Their monthly salary was 20 and 15 dollars respectively.

"The 20-dollar cook, Mathilde, was buxom and rosy as the alpine glow of her native mountains. Her cheerfulness was like a waterfall that has its source in some eternal spring. It tumbled about you with the incessant sound of ready laughter. . . . Tradesmen lingered at the garden gate to enjoy her banter, and the parcel-postman, who occasionally arrived in a horse-drawn, Bavarian blue vehicle with yellow wheels, never failed to play a particularly lusty solo on his horn when he left a package, as Mathilde smiled at him from the kitchen window. I always loved that relic of stage-coach days that had lingered on in Munich, even though the idea of playing a horn solo after leaving a package bore an absurd resemblance to the boastful and ecstatic clucking of a hen that has laid an egg."[9]

During the summer, when most of the other European capitals were drowsing or asleep, the Bavarian *Haupstadt* was teeming with musical activity. Wagnerian operas were being given at the Prince Regent Theater; a Mozart festival was in progress at the Residenz Theater—Richard Strauss himself conducted Mozart's *Marriage of Figaro;* and a Beethoven cycle was drawing full houses. Several American singers were achieving great fame, particularly Sara Cahier, who had triumphed in the role of Brangaene in *Tristan.* She and the Stokowskis developed an especially close friendship.

"My happiest personal recollections of the operatic world are connected with Munich," said Olga. "It was pleasant to wander forth hatless on a bright summer afternoon to the Prinz Regenten Theater where performances began at 4 and ended before 10."[10] There were, of course, intermissions for tea, beer, or dinner during which a great feeling of *Gemütlichkeit* prevailed. Celebrities mingled freely with the burghers. Olga was impressed that Bavarian Prince Ludwig Ferdinand played a violin in the orchestra.

Despite rigorous dedication to their careers and their study and preparation, they led a very social life. Often after performances they dined in the *keller* of the Vier Jahreszeiten Hotel with their close friends Clara and Ossip Gabrilowitsch, who had recently moved into their own Munich home on Aiblinger Strasse "on a happy Spring day." The house had formerly been that of Max von Schillings, whose *Hexenlied* Stoki had presented to Cincinnati. It was situated near the beautiful palace and gardens of the Nymphenburg.

One cannot imagine the Bavarian summers as particularly hot. But for the midsummer months Clara and Ossip rented a house in a little town called Kreuth—a house that belonged to the Archduke Karl Theodore. Bruno Walter and his wife took a house nearby and, Clara relates, "Leopold Stokowski and his wife, Olga Samaroff, came for a short stay at a wee inn beside a little stream, back in the woods. They used to sleep so soundly in that peaceful atmosphere that it took more than pebbles on the window-pane to arouse them in the morning; but you would not have guessed it, once they were up!"[11]

Was it really so hot that summer, or was Stoki trying to emulate some of the bald-pated Bavarians? Whatever it was, Stokowski shaved his head —bald as a billiard ball! It was a dramatic gesture, and photos of the pair appeared in U.S. journals, with Stoki in knickers and knee-length stockings and Olga practicing on an upright piano. She was working at the time on a Saint-Saëns concerto that she was adding to her repertory. Stoki standing behind her looked more like a prototypical Yul Brynner than the typical Stokowski everyone had known. Cincinnati was in for a shock.[12]

Vienna had had Mozart, Beethoven, and Brahms. Later it proudly claimed Bruckner and Mahler. But Munich, too, had a heritage of which it was intensely proud. It had seen the birth of Wagner's *Tristan und Isolde, Die Meistersinger,* and *Das Rheingold;* and now Richard Strauss was writing and conducting his operas there. Thomas Mann had completed his *Death in Venice* in Munich, and leading poets such as Stefan George and Rainer Maria Rilke were writing there. Oswald Spengler had been working on his *Decline of the West,* while the visual arts were represented by Vasily Kandinsky and Paul Klee.

After World War I there was a saying: "When good Americans die they go to Paris." But novelist Thomas Wolfe in his *Web and Rock* said: "How can one speak of Munich but to say it is a kind of German heaven."

The Stokowskis were well aware of Munich's seductive charm, and their honeymoon was an idyllic one. Olga often said that this summer and the next few before the war were among her happiest. They walked daily in the adjacent English Gardens; they drove out into the country and visited King Ludwig's Linderhof Castle, with its strange artificial grotto where Ludwig, seated in a marble boat in a miniature subterranean lake with fake stalactites dripping their frozen cement, heard some of Wagner's works aborning.

They visited the fairy-tale castle of Neuschwanstein and made several trips to Bayreuth, where Cosima Wagner was still in command. The spirits of mad Ludwig and Wagner were still fresh, and they hovered about gently. Another Ludwig was installed in the various royal palaces, but when one said Ludwig, one thought only of the tragic figure who had built those follies that were to become some of Bavaria's most-valued treasures. Memories of the past king and late composer were still fresh and vibrant among Müncheners—Wagner had been dead only twenty-nine years, and Ludwig a mere twenty-six. Wagner's music was still new to many ears. Both Leopold and Olga immersed themselves in it.

In recent years I had the opportunity to talk to Claudette Sorel about the Stokowskis in Munich. Claudette was one of Samaroff's youngest and most favorite pupils. "One day Madame told me that Bavaria was the place where, in all her life, she was the happiest," Claudette told me. "It had such wonderful memories for her and she said that that was where she had been on her honeymoon. She went back many times, and her ashes were thrown there."[13]

I had never heard that before and I asked Sonya for corroboration. She confirmed the report and reminded me that when her mother was studying in Berlin, she had met Geraldine Farrar there, and together they often went to Bavaria on a holiday. "And that's where her great love of southern Germany came. Then later on, of course, she was there with Daddy and they had the Munich house. Then in the early 1930s we started going over every summer. She was very, very fond of that part of the world. When she died, she wished to be cremated and have her ashes distributed in the wind.

"I brought her ashes back [to Grainau] and we distributed them with a small, lovely ceremony high on the village cow pasture up there with a gorgeous view of the mountains."[14]

At the end of summer the musical greats and near greats working in America all began to return. The S.S. *George Washington* was crammed with them, as well as with hordes of summer tourists. It berthed not in Manhattan, but in Hoboken. Critics, reporters, managers, photographers, and the curious were everywhere, and the general atmosphere was like an annex to the Metropolitan, Carnegie Hall, and all the other New York concert halls combined. As the ship disgorged its human cargo, crowds moved from one gangplank to another to get glimpses of their favorites.

"Look there—to the left! It's she! It's Mary Garden!" And it was. The diva, in a floor-length dark suit, was wearing a long ermine stole and an ermine cloche. Reporters described it as looking like "a bird's nest upon which snow had fallen." Mary was always good copy.

Photographers spotted the Stokowskis. Olga was wearing a very broad-brimmed hat, and she smiled radiantly as their picture was taken. Stoki looked dour. His hair, now slowly growing back, made him look more like the close-cropped Rachmaninoff than his usual self. They told reporters about their busy summer and their plans for the coming season. Olga said that she had already accepted some twenty concert dates but would restrict her activities so that she could spend more time in Cincinnati. Stoki spoke of his programs and the new symphony by Elgar that he would introduce to America in the coming months.[15]

In Cincinnati the business of wrapping up loose ends was being pursued vigorously. All details about the season were being carefully worked out with the cooperation of Mrs. Holmes and Frank Edwards. The most eventful occurrence was to be the move at midseason from the overlarge Music Hall to the new specially built Emery Auditorium. Mrs. Thomas Emery had donated $500,000 for a new building for the Ohio Mechanics Institute, which included a twenty-two-hundred-seat auditorium.[16]

Courtesy Dr. William Fischer
Conductor of the Cincinnati Symphony Orchestra (c. 1910)

The orchestra had been enlarged—five new men were added to the string section, bringing the total complement to eighty-two. The number of concerts had also been expanded. Sixty concerts were scheduled: thirty at home and thirty more on the orchestra's tours. Pittsburgh, Detroit, Cleveland, Chicago, Milwaukee, and St. Louis were among the important cities to be visited, and the Samaroff-Stokowski coupling was to be a special attraction for most of them. This included Olga's home town, St. Louis, and a pair of concerts together at home base in Cincinnati.

Herman Thuman announced plans for the next May Festival, the big spring musical event. He also supplied the information that Van der Stucken, who was then conducting the Berlin Philharmonic in a series of concerts, would arrive in Cincinnati in December to begin his chorus training.

However, Thuman had been relieved some time before of his position as press agent for the orchestra—that function was very aptly taken over by Edwards himself. Carrying out his own promotional activities, Edwards also lined up numerous artists for concerts in Cincinnati and other Midwestern cities. His first for the season was a recital by that eminent "Chopinzee" of the piano, Vladimir de Pachmann.

Thuman was certainly not happy with such inroads into his managerial realm. Now as manager of the May Festival he put himself in direct competition with the Cincinnati Orchestra. His ill will was obviously growing, and he let it be known that for the forthcoming festival he would engage the Chicago Symphony rather than the Cincinnati Orchestra to supply the instrumental forces. The orchestra members were shocked, and so were most of the board members.

One significant change was announced, a change affecting Stoki himself. It was perhaps a harbinger of the influence Olga was to have in his life and on his personality. The first sign was the changing of his name back to Stokowski from Stokovski, as he had given it on coming to America. It might have been better to have kept the *v*. He disliked people pronouncing his name as "Sto-cow-ski" and often corrected reporters and others. "Say *cough* not *cow* when pronouncing my name."

10

Sturm und Drang

THE 1911–12 season began with a presubscription concert in Hamilton, Ohio. The official bow took place on a drenching Friday afternoon, November 17. In spite of the weather, the audience was the largest ever assembled in Cincinnati for an opening concert, and all the town's elite were represented. The Friday audience was mainly female, with a small sprinkling of men. In their boxes on the left side were the Fleischmanns and Mrs. Holmes, with Olga in the box of the Tafts.

Immediately after the concert, Olga invited the entire board of the orchestra—which consisted entirely of women, all fifteen of them—to a reception to meet the soloist, Marie Rappold. Members of the Advisory Board attended, too, along with other socialites. "Miss Louise Taft and Mrs. Smith Hickenlooper presided at the tea table, which was dainty with Killarney roses and white carnations," reported one columnist.[1] Olga had worked very hard to make their large Mount Auburn apartment attractive. "It was not easy to be a conductor's wife," she admitted, but she threw herself into the process with much of the same zeal and dedication she had given to her own career. Fortunately she had abundant energy and skill.

The reviews for the concert were as usual heaped with praise. The critic for the *Times-Star* headlined his review: "The Symphony Orchestra Greater Than Ever. First Concert of the Season Proves Its Right to Rank With the Greatest Orchestras of the Country."[2]

What would readers find in the *Enquirer?* Thuman had been quite snipingly critical the previous season. How would he react to the orchestra now that he himself was the manager of a rival institution? Thuman was obviously not enthusiastic—for that matter, probably nobody expected him to be. Even so, the orchestra members reacted to his review almost apoplectically. Their pride had been hurt. In light of the roastings that New York and other metropolitan critics regularly handed conductors and orchestras they did not like, whatever the reasons, Thuman's review was mild. But the players nevertheless felt he was carping and malicious and, above all, that his negative review was undeserved.

Here in part is what Thuman said in his column "Stageland Gossip": "At the beginning of a symphony season it is always interesting to note such differences as might suggest themselves in comparing the present orchestra with the one of last season. The effort has been steadily made by the local association to improve the band from year to year, which tendency makes it necessary to change the personnel considerably. Therefore, we have not as yet reached that point where our orchestra may be called a permanent one. Quite a few changes were made during the past summer, and when the men took their place on Friday afternoon one naturally felt that, to a certain extent, a new element had to be reckoned with. It is, therefore, not quite fair to judge the capacity of an orchestra from its first concert. In the main the changes seem to have been made for good. The string section, especially the second violins, has been improved, though the violas and cellos still remain less adequate. The woodwind choir was always the best in the orchestra, and the single change there has been an improvement. The brasses have been toned down nicely, so that there is better balance than heretofore. Considering the fact that there have been only two weeks of rehearsal, the ensemble was very good, and the rough edges not nearly so prominent as one would expect.

"A word may also be devoted to the conductor, Stokowski. He has gained in poise and surety, and has reduced his gesticulations considerably. There never was any question as to his sincerity and earnestness. His musicianship is ripening as well. . . .

"The C Minor Symphony of Brahms, which was played toward the end of last season, immediately challenged comparison with Stokowski's former performance of it. . . .

"Stokowski paid great attention to every outward means of interpretation. In the main his tempo sounded better than when he played it last year, though the character and rugged spirit of the final allegro was lost in the weak rhythm with which the theme was stated. The performance of this symphony cannot be regarded as one of Stokowski's best achievements. It is not given to every conductor to play Brahms sympathetically, though many, like Stokowski, play him intelligently."[3]

Perhaps the men overreacted, but they drafted a protest signed by every member of the orchestra and sent it to the editor of the *Cincinnati Enquirer*. The editor ignored it, and so did Thuman. But the rival *Times-Star* obtained the document and reprinted it with a small editorial deletion.

> Dear Sir—We, the seventy-nine men of the Cincinnati Symphony Orchestra, are writing to you personally to protest in a body against the incessant prejudice shown our conductor, Mr. Stokowski, and the orchestra by your musical critic. He has consciously striven to belittle and overthrow the work which we with such great care have erected.
>
> Many of us are matured musicians, who have played under the batons of such musical giants as Richard Wagner, Von Bülow, Richard Strauss, Nikisch, Weingartner, Mahler, Toscanini and many others of great renown, and we can with positive knowledge assert that Mr. Stokowski's rendition of the Brahms symphony at our first concert this year was equal to the finest we have ever taken part in. We have endured in silence his animosity, which he has shown in everything he has written in the last two years about us. We protest at last against your critic's unmistakable prejudice. . . .
>
> Must you permit a personal prejudice and persecution here in Cincinnati? Some of us were long associated with Mr. Van der Stucken here, and remember that your criticisms were always fair and friendly. Our present conductor, Mr. Stokowski, whose readings have been (with your exception) unanimously credited with more finesse, exuberance of youthful fire, minute care in phrasing, thorough knowledge of detail and absolute certainty of the ideal intent to be conveyed, is eminently more fitted to enjoy your approval.[4]

The *Times-Star* omitted a paragraph which, according to the *Musical-Leader*, stated that the men of the orchestra had found out that the Theodore Thomas Orchestra had been engaged for the coming May Festival. This they declared to be a public insult to the orchestra.[5]

The men's protest continued:

> We who have learned to know the inmost pleasure of association with Mr. Stokowski, who we feel is divinely gifted, who by the turn of a finger sweeps us all before him, must show in this way your error in declining to accede to him the honors already bestowed, both by

the masses in Cincinnati and elsewhere, and have hereunder attached
our signature.

The letter kicked up quite a storm. It was news. But the most remarkable part was that the men came to the defense of a conductor. Most
orchestras are filled with would-be conductors all thinking they could do
much better than the one who is leading them. Many players are overtly
contemptuous. So for the players in Cincinnati to call their young conductor "divinely gifted" and say that "by the turn of a finger [he] sweeps us
all before him" is positively unique.

The affair was reported in newspapers across the country and in the
music magazines as well. The *Courier* editorialized: "The charge of 'personal prejudice and animosity' is a strong one against a music critic and
should not be made without due cause. J. Herman Thuman, music critic
of the Cincinnati *Enquirer*, has been severe against Leopold Stokowski,
but if the Thuman emanations are the result of true convictions on the
part of that young man, he should at least be given the credit of sincerity
even if real musicians know that he is mistaken in his estimate of the
conductor. . . .

"It is not paramount to the issue for Cincinnati's musical circles to say,
as they are doing, that when Frank Van der Stucken led the orchestra
there was nothing but praise from the music critic of the *Enquirer*.
Outsiders do not know that Mr. Thuman, at Mr. Van der Stucken's
suggestion, was made business manager of the Cincinnati May Festival,
a competing musical institution, and Thuman's name, it is said, appears
with Frank Van der Stucken's in the contract. . . . Mr. Thuman sent much
press matter to Cincinnati last summer about Mr. Van der Stucken while
touring Europe with him. Some reports say that Mr. Thuman has been
endeavoring to have Van der Stucken reappointed conductor of the Symphony Orchestra when Mr. Stokowski's contract expires next year. That
is a legitimate proceeding, but Mr. Thuman should come out into the
open and make his position known, so that his reviews in the *Enquirer* on
the Stokowski concerts could be gauged on their proper value.

"All the present Cincinnati trouble simply grows out of the fact that
Mr. Thuman is a professional music critic and a musical business man at
the same time. The two activities do not mix when viewed from the
ethical side. The *Musical Courier* will never cease to point out that,
generally speaking, no matter how good a music critic a man may be
inherently, his published opinions will have no value if he is known to be

interested financially, or through motives of friendship in the persons, concerts and institutions he criticizes. Were Mr. Stokowski not so gifted, versatile and competent a conductor, the Thuman severities would have passed unnoticed in Cincinnati."[6]

The *Musical Leader* took an entirely different stance. It considered the letter a mean and cowardly attack on Thuman. "Well may Leopold Stokowski pray to be delivered from his friends . . ." wrote the editor. "How much harm has in this way been done the young conductor whose undoubted gifts have placed him in a responsible position cannot now be gauged. Time will show if such action has not placed him in such a predicament that he will perforce shake the dust of Cincinnati from his shoes at the first possible moment."[7] Cassandra couldn't have done better! Who could have imagined then that he would indeed be shaking the dust from his shoes and leaving Cincinnati behind him.

The unknowingly visionary editor thought that the protest held up both the conductor and the orchestra to public scorn and only strengthened Thuman's position. Not so! Thuman was indeed the loser. Several papers commented on the sad news "that Thuman, the young music critic of the *Enquirer* (who like Hanslick, achieved fame through attacking someone greater than himself), is to sever his connection with the newspaper he served while maintaining outside activities as a musical manager and press agent. To friends, Thuman has confided his intention of going to Europe for several years in order to study. Music criticism perhaps?" In other words, Mr. Thuman was apparently sacked. The "sad news" broke on January 17, 1912.[8]

The tempest soon abated and everyone went about their business. Elgar became the new name to occupy the minds of the musically curious. Stoki had brought back from Europe the bulky score of Elgar's Second Symphony and had praised it effusively. So convinced was Stoki of the importance of the Elgar premiere that he had Frank Edwards urge critics from New York and other important cities to come to Cincinnati for the occasion.

Perhaps he pressed the point too much. Henry Krehbiel, critic on the *New York Tribune,* who had once been a critic in Cincinnati, apparently resented the pressure. In a letter to Lucien Wulsin he exclaimed, "His conceit was shown at once by the action of the manager in almost commanding the New York critics to come to Cincinnati to learn what wonders he was doing there and to hear the first performance of the Elgar

Second Symphony, though they would scarcely have had time to hurry back to hear the New York performance."[9]

The critic of the *Times-Star* stated that the American premiere "made of the Symphony concert of Friday afternoon . . . an event of the first musical importance. Sir Edward is the idol of the English music-loving people and is particularly associated with Cincinnati musical affairs through his personal appearances here with the May festivals and with the Sheffield Choir. That he is a personal friend of Mr. Stokowski and of many other Cincinnatians renders the first American performance of his *Second Symphony* here fitting and proper." After a long descriptive discussion of the work in elaborate detail, he came to his final summation. "Sir Edward Elgar has not created a new symphonic school, neither has he followed in the individual pathway of any other symphonist. Nor does he convey the belief that symphonic writing is the most sympathetic medium for his undeniable genius. The composition is pleasant and it is interesting; it is not great, nor in any sense convincing . . . [but] it deserves to be heard by everyone in Cincinnati interested in music."[10]

The second half of the program was devoted entirely to the music of Richard Strauss: the "Dance of the Seven Veils" from *Salome,* the lovely, lyric "Serenade for Thirteen Winds," and *Don Juan.* It was thus an all-contemporary program, and none of the Strauss works were familiar. The serenade, the oldest of the pieces, still almost never appears on a symphonic program, and *Don Juan* was then considered very modern for listeners steeped in Mozart, Beethoven, and *The Merry Widow. Salome* at the time was a mere six years old.

Using her hyphenated name, Olga Samaroff-Stokowski and Leopold in December made their first Cincinnati appearance as a husband-and-wife combination, to the delight of the audience. It was an all-Russian program, and it enabled her to trot out her most successful warhorse, the Tchaikovsky First Concerto. On tour shortly thereafter she played it again, this time in her home city of St. Louis. She was welcomed as a hometown girl and the town folk "marveled." Her well-known parents and friends were jubilant; the local critics were happy to applaud her. "To gild refined gold were as profitable, in the opinion of St. Louis hearers, as to try to improve upon the playing of these visitors. Mr. Stokowski evoked the most spontaneous and pronounced enthusiasm witnessed in this city in many months."[11]

As 1912 arrived people everywhere said farewell to the old year and rang in the new. The orchestra celebrated this rite symbolically by saying farewell to the old, enormous Music Hall during its Friday afternoon concert, January 5, then hail to its new Emery Auditorium quarters the following evening.[12]

While Cincinnati critics wrote conservatively, Stokowski's reviews from other cities were extravagant. In Chicago, Glenn Dillard Gunn wrote in the *Tribune:* "He is first of all one of the most forceful personalities among the young masters of the orchestra. The power of suggestion that compels the participation of players and listeners alike, according to the intention of the conductor, is his in remarkable measure. Its spiritual attributes are fantasy, imagination, and abundant temperament. Its musical manifestations are manifold. The rhythmical sense is so pregnant with impulse that it colors every inflection. Crescendo and diminuendo are achieved not as mechanical contrasts prescribed in the score, but as the result of an irresistible rhythmical intention. Thus there is added to the sensuous beauty of varied and colorful contrast the persuasive eloquence of a vital purposeful movement, inevitable in its logic and in its faultlessly measured progress."[13]

Herman Thuman might have learned something if he had paid any attention to Glenn Dillard Gunn. One of the best-trained and most respected critics of his day, Gunn had studied in Leipzig with Carl Reinecke and later successfully toured Germany as a pianist. He appeared as a soloist with the Chicago Symphony and taught at the Chicago Musical College. He was for four years chief critic on the *Chicago Tribune* and later served on the *Washington Times Herald.* His credentials were certainly more impressive than those of Mr. Thuman.

Paeans and praise became routine in edition after edition of the music magazines. Curiosity and interest were running high in managerial circles. Other orchestras apparently tentatively approached Stoki to consider a position with them.

Although he had not brought the orchestra to New York, critics from New York had already come to Cincinnati and elsewhere to hear him. It is understandable that the nearby City of Brotherly Love, which was no longer having much of a love affair with its conductor Carl Pohlig, developed an increasing interest in Stokowski.

Olga, with her strong sense of publicity as a career builder, saw to it that large ads appeared in the musical trade papers announcing to a national and an international audience Stoki's availability for future engagements. A picture appeared showing him not as the youthful man his previous photos had portrayed, but as a somewhat dour man with a widow's peak that made him look slightly sinister in the manner of a menacing Bela Lugosi.

With all the recognition from critics in Chicago, New York, Detroit, Pittsburgh, and other cities, it was annoying to find members of the board objecting to the orchestra's tours. The atmosphere was becoming unpleasant—various haggles and misunderstandings occurred. The Tafts were particular champions of Stokowski, and because of this Mrs. Holmes seemed to bear some resentment. The tours had been enormously successful in that they brought great prestige to the orchestra, as well as to Stokowski. But they were apparently not a success financially. The Tafts offered to underwrite the tours, but Mrs. Holmes angrily objected. Confrontations took place.

Olga fueled Stoki's ambition and fired his discontent. After their life in Munich, New York, and Paris, Cincinnati did not seem the ideal center for their lives and careers. With promotional expertise, Olga sent copies of the splendid reviews to friends in Boston, New York, Philadelphia, and elsewhere. She was meticulous in maintaining her contacts and must have known from her Philadelphia friends that a change was about to be made there. She began to concentrate intently on the Quaker City.

11

On the Road to Philadelphia

T HE allure that Carl Pohlig had for Philadelphians when he first
appeared with the orchestra on October 18, 1907, seemed substantial. He began his conducting term with a three-year contract. His
first program was drawn from Beethoven and Wagner, and the press
reported that he had won the city, received an ovation, and wearied them
with "two hours of solid music."

But when Pohlig brought the orchestra to New York in November, he
was roasted by the critics. Back in Philadelphia the press reacted with
considerable resentment and printed castigating editorials to assuage local
pride. "It is nothing at all to Philadelphians whether New Yorkers like our
orchestra . . . or anything else that is ours. . . . They may say what they
will, but their manners might be mended. . . ."[1]

Pohlig was a handsome man of the German military style, which was
admired at the time. Some of the players regarded him highly even to the
point of calling him a "genius," but most smarted under his frightfully
arrogant manner. Yet at the termination of his first three-year contract,
it was renewed for a similar span. It was a decision that the board would
soon rue. Frances Wister commented that, while Pohlig's appearance was
elegant and his platform manner excellent, "he was, however, of a difficult
disposition, which made dealings between him and the musicians, and the
Board of Directors, trying and difficult."[2]

Olga, who had played a concerto under Pohlig, thought that he had a
better baton technique than his predecessor, Scheel, but that his conducting was earthbound and uninspired.[3]

Before long after the beginning of his second contract, Pohlig had very much disenchanted the board, and they decided not to renew again. Max Fiedler, the conductor of the Boston Symphony (not to be confused with Arthur Fiedler), was proposed, but important members of the board had different ideas. They had had reports from other cities and had read the superlative reviews of the young conductor in Cincinnati. They wanted just such a man, who could win the combined support of the audience, orchestra, and critics together. They wanted Stokowski. Just how and when the first direct contacts and discussions were held we may never know. Some say as early as January 1912. Several have suggested it was all engineered by Samaroff.

Unfortunately the terminations of the two conductors' contracts were not coincidental. Pohlig's was to end after the 1912–13 season, and Stokowski was contracted until the end of 1913–14. The question of whether Cincinnati might hold Stokowski to his contract was naturally a point of concern in Philadelphia. The orchestra board there made it clear they could in no way enter into any discussions until he would be free of his contract.

Grievances in Cincinnati increased. Frank Edwards, from whom Stoki had so much cooperation, left. A new orchestra manager, Oscar Hatch Hawley, came in, but dissension seemed to continue.

When I asked Stoki about his Cincinnati days, particularly about his resignation, he summarized the events as follows: "I had difficulties. The trouble was the committee. It was mainly composed of women. But if it had not been for the women, I do not think the orchestra would have existed, and they were wonderful. They loved music and they worked hard for the orchestra. But the president and the vice-president were women and they hated each other, so I was always between those two. If I wanted to do some modern symphony, the president said yes; the vice-president said no and vice versa. I had a three-year contract, but after two years I could not stand it any longer and I asked them to release me from it. They asked me why and I said, 'I would rather not say. You know why but I would rather not say.' So finally one man from the committee came to me one day and said, 'Yes, we know, but just the same we would like you to stay, and we will make it better.' I said, 'No. I have had enough. I am going but I wish you would release me from the contract in a friendly way.' The next morning it was in all the Cincinnati papers: 'Stokowski Fired.' Well, it did not deceive anybody in Cincinnati because for weeks before that, there had been questions of why does this man want to leave. They had all kinds of theories and everybody knew they were trying to make me stay."[4]

Like many recollections of his later years the story is oversimplified and as usual rather vague. But there were rumors seeping about during the early part of the year. Just when any overt discussions were held with the Tafts, Mrs. Holmes, or other members of the board, we do not know.

Things began to look more positive when on March 23 Stoki wrote to Lucien Wulsin:

Dear Sir:

During an interview which I had this afternoon with Mrs. Holmes, she made the statement that I had "insulted her more than she had ever been insulted in her life" by approving of Mrs. Taft's offer to finance the outside engagements of the Cincinnati Orchestra. . . .

When I assumed the directorship of the Cincinnati Symphony Orchestra I had hoped of building up a really great institution which would take its rank as a national feature of American music.

The conditions prevailing in this city and the policies of those controlling the orchestra, convince me that this is impossible, and therefore feeling that this disappointment makes it impossible for me to continue my work here with the same enthusiasm which has inspired me for the past three years, I am writing you to beg you to grant my release from my existing contract with you.

When I signed this contract, Mrs. Holmes said to me "of course it is understood that this contract can be dissolved at the end of any season if either side is dissatisfied." I signed the contract with that understanding and should hold myself morally obligated by that understanding should you have requested the cancellation of the contract. I therefore hold you morally obligated by this mutual agreement with the President of your association.

My request to be released is not a sudden decision, but has been one of gradual growth and is both final and sincere.

My true and lasting appreciation of your kindness to me caused me to feel a satisfaction in the knowledge that I leave you an orchestra in excellent condition.

I hasten to place this letter in your hands while your plans for next season are as yet not made and while I know that several excellent conductors are available: Mr. Fiedler is now leaving the Boston Symphony Orchestra and Mr. Gabrilowitsch is having such great success in Europe. . . .

As there will be many important arrangements both for you and

me to make, I beg you to grant me my release at your earliest
convenience. I shall of course finish the season and leave everything
in good condition.

Believe me I shall always remember your personal kindness to me.[5]

Three days after he had dispatched his letter to Wulsin, Stoki announced
his resignation to the press. The news was reported in newspapers
throughout the country, and the magazines devoted columns to discussing
it. It sent seismic tremors through his players and audiences alike. He gave
extensive interviews to explain his reasons. Ironically, the possibility of
becoming conductor of the Philadelphia Orchestra was not one of them.
To be sure that his point of view would be presented accurately, he wrote
out his objections to the *Cincinnati Post:* "The various statements and
rumors which have appeared in the papers oblige me to make a public
statement regarding my desire to sever my connection with the Cincinnati Symphony Orchestra. My difficulties with the Board of Directors I
refuse to make public, especially since they are of a nature which could
be adjusted, and the Board of Directors have expressed their willingness
to adjust them. What cannot be adjusted is the loss of my enthusiasm,
which enthusiasm is absolutely necessary in the constructive work of
building up a great orchestra. This enthusiasm I have lost during the three
seasons of my activity here for many reasons, of which I will give a few:

"The slight on my orchestra concerning the May Festival which I have
mentioned in a recent interview, has deeply hurt me personally and has
done me professional harm in the musical world outside. . . .

"From one of the leading critics of the city I endured a persistent
persecution, manifestly of a personal nature, as he was unable to deny
when publicly accused of it, which also did me great harm outside of
Cincinnati, and it was owing to the indignant protest of my orchestra that
this condition was ameliorated; but again I found no support from public
opinion.

"Putting aside the factions, enmities, and antagonism which I fully
realize exist everywhere, I have been much discouraged by the coldness
of our Symphony audiences as compared with the cordial receptions
tendered the same work by the same orchestra everywhere else. I have
been told that this coldness is a peculiarity of Cincinnati, but I have also
been witness to the fact that Cincinnati is capable of spontaneous enthusiasm, as manifested to outside organizations and artists. . . .

"I am also leaving no work undone, but am leaving the Cincinnati

Orchestra in a condition of such excellence that it cannot fail to prosper under a good conductor—and that there are good conductors at present available is a fact that cannot be denied. . . ."[6]

Another paper reported that "the announcement was received with consternation by the musical people of Cincinnati and they will make a strong protest to induce him to remain."[7]

And so they did. Committee members of the Cincinnati Women's Club Music Department, "representing several hundred lovers of music . . . held a conference on hearing of Mr. Stokowski's contemplated resignation. . . . Discussion of the situation brought out most spontaneous and unanimous expressions of praise and appreciation . . . and hope was expressed on all sides" that he would remain.[8]

"As spontaneously and as naturally as sunshine after the storm the affection of Cincinnatians for their Symphony Orchestra and its brilliant young conductor, Stokowski, has burst forth through the threatened schism and murky clouds of dissatisfaction," editorialized the *Cincinnati Enquirer*.[9]

The *Enquirer* was evidently printing with rose-colored picas. The rest of the press stuck to factual black and white. "I understand a meeting of the board was held Wednesday, but I have not been notified of any action. . . . I am just as determined as ever in my action and I will never change my decision," Stoki told a reporter on the *Commercial Tribune*.[10]

During the rehearsal that same day, the concerned musicians appointed a committee of four to appeal to him to remain. At some point between the strains of the Second Symphony of Brahms, *Till Eulenspiegel*, and Harold Bauer's playing of the Schumann concerto, a longer break than usual took place. After assuring them that if the orchestra would be endangered by his leaving he would remain, Stoki said: "You are all young men and able musicians. There is a demand for you everywhere, and you will have no difficulty in finding positions. Therefore that factor need not enter into the situation. . . .

"The orchestra will go on. It will not be difficult to get a new conductor and a good one, for there are many of them. It has taken three years of hard work to get you all together and to build this organization, and I regret that I am obliged to leave it now. Since I have announced my desire to go, I have had many letters asking me to stay, but it is too late. The record of indifference during the last three years still stands."[11]

The *Times-Star* reported that when he concluded the members of the orchestra were much depressed. They were not alone. The hard-headed businessmen of the Commercial Association urged civic organizations to become involved in the controversy. They believed that the resignation of Stokowski would be a severe loss to the city.[12]

Lucien Wulsin was particularly distressed by all the fuss that had been stirred up. He clipped a sampling of the various articles that had appeared and sent them to his friend Henry Krehbiel in New York. Krehbiel was then critic on the *New York Tribune*. The letter was written on March 29, just two days after the story had broken in the press:

My dear Krehbiel:

It may interest you to get the enclosed cuttings which give some idea of the present condition of Stokowski who, I may add, is a nervous hysterical young fellow with a good deal of native ability and charm, but who has not in him either physically or from the standpoint of the technically skilled conductor the power to do what he has undertaken to do. The most unfortunate thing is that certain personal quality which he has, has carried away a lot of people in Cincinnati, including our dear friends, the Charley Tafts. That this young man has been praised to an extent far beyond his deserts and that he takes all this thing for gospel truth and imagines himself a great man.

Just note his picture accompanying his statement in the Cincinnati *Post* and you will see the neurasthenic boy who at this time, like a naughty child, should have been well spanked and put to bed, carefully fed and rested, to bring him to a certain degree of sanity.

What I am particularly sorry about is the way in which he has been treating the Tafts who have been more to him than mother, father and friend.

All this stuff which he gives to the *Post* came out after his spending two hours with Charley Taft, Schmidlapp, Wilby and myself, where he was spoken to on the assumption that he was a gentleman and the understanding was that, for the time being, nothing would be said as the matter would be carefully considered in all its aspects before the committee reached any conclusion. He goes right from this and gives out this statement.

As I looked at him this afternoon I saw before me a small boy really looking four or five years younger than he appeared in Paris three years ago and my judgement is that he is used up in every way.

I am telling you this in a confidential way simply desiring that you should be posted. It is rather interesting how your own estimate of

him when he was first talked of is being to a great extent borne out.
I must say that in some respects he has surprised me by his ability.
It does not look, however, as though there was the material for any
permanent building. What does one do in such a case as this where
a party comes here and after a year's trial deliberately makes a contract for four years and then proceeds as he is now going on?[13]

Wouldn't Wulsin have been surprised to be told that sixty-five years
later, Stokowski would still be conducting and making records, after having had one of the most spectacular conducting careers of all time.

Two days later, Krehbiel responded with a letter to "Dear Wulsin":

I cannot say that I am at all surprised at your letter concerning
Stokowski. If the Tafts are grieved by the turn affairs have taken they
have only themselves to blame, for it was they who persisted in
believing that the young nincompoop was a great man—believing it
to such an extent that Mrs. Taft fairly insulted me the first time she
saw me after his engagement—and I fancy that the lady will still
think that he will go to Europe and conduct like a star in all the cities
—a second Nikisch. Well, watch and see. . . .[14]

To Stokowski Wulsin sent a very different type of letter. It was both
conciliatory and flattering, but not conclusive. To it Stoki responded:

April 1, 1912

My dear Mr. Wulsin:

Please accept my most sincere thanks for all the kind expressions
in your letter.

While I am absolutely unable to change my decision, I beg you to
accept the assurance of my true appreciation of your friendly interest.

Sincerely yours,
Leopold Stokowski[15]

Taft offered to raise his salary from $7,000 to $10,000 as an inducement
to stay. Speculation continued in the newspapers, but the board met on
the third of April and dispatched this message to Stokowski:

Your letter of March 23, 1912, to the Board of Directors of the
Cincinnati Symphony Orchestra Association asking for a release from
your contract dated March 1, 1910, has been referred to us to act.

After full consideration in all its phases, we have unanimously
concluded not to grant your request. The contract has still two years
to run and we expect you to complete it.[16]

The letter was delivered personally at 4:00 P.M. on April 5. Unaccountably, it appeared in Taft's own *Times-Star* even before it had left Wulsin's hands. At once he wrote an accompanying letter of explanation. Wulsin noted both the time the letter was written and the time that it was dispatched. It read:

April 5th, 1912 3:15 PM

Mr. Leopold Stokowski
Mt. Auburn, City.
My dear Mr. Stokowski:

In accordance with a telegram just received from Mr. Taft, I am sending with this a letter which expresses the conclusion of the committee of the Orchestra Association.

Permit me at the same time to express to you for myself especially and for the other gentlemen of the committee great regret that there should have been any publication concerning this letter and the decision it conveys in this morning's paper.

I cannot understand how such information should have gotten out as the letter now sent you has never been out of my hands since I received it from Mr. Taft day before yesterday, except as I stood by and had it signed by the other two members of the committee.

I am making this explanation to you because I am sure that they as well as I deeply regret that there should have been any apparent lack of courtesy in publishing the matter in advance of the delivery to you of a communication which in some respects concerns only you and ourselves, except as a matter of public interest. It is assumed that the public generally would like to know what is going on.

Believe me,
Very truly yours,
Lucien Wulsin

Delivered April 5th, 4 PM[17]

The news of the board's action appeared prematurely not only in the *Times-Star,* but in other Cincinnati papers as well—the *Enquirer* and the *Post*—although not in quite such complete detail.

The board had not counted on Stoki's intractability. He immediately wrote to them and took to the press as well. He wrote his response the same day, the fifth, but it had not yet reached Wulsin by the seventh, when a reporter from the *Commercial Tribune* spoke to the Advisory Board spokesman. Declared Wulsin: "The various quotations attributed to Conductor Stokowski in the Cincinnati papers are answers to the letter addressed to him by the committee. Yet that body thinks that his reply will come in time and it can then take up the matter with him in detail and find a proper solution. I cannot see how he will consider these statements to the press as having anything to do with the real situation. In fact, I almost know that a letter from him to this committee either has been or will be written."

Written it was:

April 5, 1912

To the Advisory Board of the
Cincinnati Symphony Orchestra
Dear Sir:

I have just received a letter signed by Messrs. Charles P. Taft, J. G. Schmidlapp, Joseph Wilby, and Lucien Wulsin summarily refusing my request for release from my legal contract with the Cincinnati Symphony Orchestra, and ignoring the agreement made in good faith by me with the President of your Association.

In sending you my letter of resignation I most certainly never supposed that men and women of honor would ignore the moral responsibility devolving from the agreement I have with the President of your Association, and to which, in my letter of resignation, I alluded and held you morally bound. Your determination to hold me to the letter of the legal contract can only result from your willingness to ignore moral responsibility, or your doubting my word, as I did not believe it necessary to take the precaution of having witnesses at my business conferences with your President.

In the one case I consider your present action a breach of faith, in the other a gross personal insult.

I shall most certainly sever all personal relations with everyone who countenances such an outrageous breach of faith or such a personal insult to me.

In all my dealings with the present situation I have as a gentleman, refrained from mentioning my difficulties or disagreements with women. However, a woman, if vested with official authority, ought to be just as responsible for her actions as a man. I therefore demand of Mrs. C. R. Holmes, President of the Orchestra Association, a recognition and fulfillment of the compact under which I signed my existing legal contract with the Cincinnati Symphony Orchestra and that she as President of the Orchestra Association, should grant me the full and unqualified release from my legal contract which, in justice, it is my right to demand.

I also state that Mrs. C. R. Holmes affirmed to me that she was fully authorized by the Board of Directors in all her business dealings with me, and in all other matters her power to act has been recognized by the Association. I therefore hold you bound with her.

If you ignore any longer my just claims for release from my contract, I shall make the whole matter public both in Cincinnati and elsewhere.[18]

The board, no doubt somewhat shaken by his response, met on Thursday the tenth to draft a reply. The preliminary versions were milder than the final version.

While the whole board was deliberating, Stoki was busy rehearsing the music for his Friday and Saturday concerts. As if guided by some premonition, he had at the beginning of the season programmed the Beethoven Fifth Symphony for this concluding concert. It was the same work he had conducted for his debut three years earlier. Other works on the program were Goldmark's *Sakuntala* Overture, and Borodin's *In the Steppes of Central Asia*.

The concert was charged with great emotion, and the wildly applauding audience tried to demonstrate again their desire to have him remain. At the conclusion, when the audience had finally departed, Stoki was presented with the letter from the board. If he had any trepidation on opening it he was satisfied with its final conclusion. It was not intended to be polite and it was not. It read:

Dear Sir—

Your letter of April 5, answering that of this committee of the same date, having been considered by the Board of Directors of the Cincinnati Symphony Orchestra Association and their Advisory Board, the undersigned special committee, duly authorized, hereby notify you that your recent behavior and repeated aspersions upon members of the Board of Directors of the Association and your unfounded reflections upon the musical public of Cincinnati, have destroyed your usefulness to the Cincinnati Orchestra Association, and we now notify you that you are released from your contract and the same is hereby cancelled.

Enclosed you will find a check of the treasurer of this association for $875 to your order, which makes, with what you heretofore received, your $7,000 salary for the year ending September 30, 1912, and in full payment of all demands under said contract.[19]

Both Stoki and Olga must have been relieved, for he would now be able to negotiate with the Philadelphia board, although that possibility had never been mentioned in Cincinnati.

The following day the story hit all the papers. The *Times-Star* carried it on the front page, proclaiming that Stoki had been released from his contract. Most of the other papers told it the same way—but not the *Enquirer*, which clearly indicated that Stokowski had been dismissed.

This naturally infuriated him. He immediately fired off telegrams to the press and musical magazines.

> In the letter which the committee representing the Cincinnati Orchestra have published, it will be seen that the Committee is answering my letter of April 5, which was a renewed demand for relief from my contract with the orchestra. The answer to my letter . . . as published by the Association this morning, is a granting of that relief. The futile attempt to convert this granting of relief, which I have insistently demanded for over three weeks, into a dismissal, speaks for itself. It is impossible to dismiss a man who has repeatedly and publicly asked to be relieved.[20]

Then, as if penning an act of contrition, he wrote a letter to the *Times-Star:*

> I was mistaken in my belief that the Cincinnati public did not appreciate my work. I want to acknowledge very cheerfully that I was wrong in my criticism of the attitude of Cincinnati audiences. Especially since my resignation they have shown by every move possible how friendly they are toward me and how warmly they appreciate the work of the orchestra. I feel now that the public is with me. I have received many letters and telephone calls from strangers telling me how sorry they are that I am leaving. But the demonstration by audiences at the last five concerts since my resignation has touched me deeply, and it is with great regret that I leave Cincinnati. I regret to leave not only because of the public but also because of the musicians in the orchestra, to whom I am very much attached. I hope that the orchestra, for which I have worked so hard and for which I have lived for three years, will prosper. I want to express my appreciation for all the kindness shown me by the public.[21]

Some critics, apparently piqued by the whole cantankerous affair, wrote very sharply. One would think their pens had been dipped in Herman Thuman's inkwell. In the *Cleveland Leader*, April 12, 1912, we read: "That comet which trailed its blazing way across the musical firmament these last two years, causing much wonderment and many gapings of mouths in those who know not the difference in value between fixed and wandering stars, has disappeared from the American heavens. . . . Thus ends, for Cincinnati at least, the drum and cymbal career of Leopold Stokowski—née Stokovski—who brilliantly and quickly rose from an inconsequential position in the East to leadership of one of America's greatest orchestras; who made Beethoven dance on his ears; who made Brahms a puling, sickly sentimentalist; who calcimined Strauss in more clashing and fighting colors than Strauss ever knew and who Stokowski-ized each composer whom he took into his directorial hands; who clenched his shaking fists, threshed the air with his arms and distorted his body to secure innocuous and unconvincing effects; and who in violation of all professional ethics caused his pictures to be published far and wide above columns of fulsome matter which had Stokowski for its subject."[22]

The *Commercial Tribune,* which had always been sympathetic, also turned critical: "Cincinnatians have shown their appreciation of the orchestra under the leadership of Mr. Stokowski in the one infallible way Americans have of showing what they really like. We are utilitarian enough to believe that prompt payment of contract salary is more important than the matter of rising en masse as the leader enters the hall."[23]

The remark about rising en masse as the leader enters the hall referred to an announcement placed in the program booklet for one of the last concerts. It was no doubt instigated by the musicians themselves in order to show their loyalty and affection and allow the audience to show theirs as well, probably in consequence of Stoki's complaint about lack of appreciation and coldness on the part of the listeners. The announcement seems rather naive today, but surely it was sincerely motivated.

> It has been suggested that the audience assembled to hear the Cincinnati Symphony Orchestra Saturday evening, March 30, will give Mr. Stokowski, its gifted leader, a visible evidence of their appreciation of the work he has done in the development of the orchestra, as well as of the musical taste and atmosphere of our city.
>
> To this end the friends and loyal adherents of Mr. Stokowski are requested to arise when he comes on the stage and to remain standing until he takes his position as the conductor.[24]

It had, of course, the desired effect. The press reported that he received an overwhelming ovation as he stepped on the stage. "The spontaneity of the tribute which resounded from gallery, balcony, and parquet, evidently deeply affected the brilliant young conductor, who with characteristic loyalty caused his orchestra to share in the demonstration."25

The demonstration was welcome particularly after the rather cool reception his previous concert had been given. That had been an all-English program, without a soloist to help things along.

The saving grace had been the set of *Enigma* Variations by Elgar. On that, all reviews and comments were superlative. But an unfortunate marring took place during the Friday afternoon performance. All went well until the start of the eleventh variation, a troublemaker. Stokowski had to stop twice; on the third try all went well. Even the *Enquirer,* with a rare glint of understanding, said that the slight mishap was of little consequence. But it did observe that no program since Stoki took over "proved to be so unappealing and so commonplace."

Stoki then departed from Cincinnati. "I don't know now just why I took the first train to Boston," he told me. "I wanted to hear the orchestra there. The orchestra was marvelous. It was a wonderful experience."26 But more important was a conference with Charles Ellis, whose colleague in London, Daniel Mayer, was arranging an orchestral concert for Stokowski during the latter part of May. This was all part of Olga's doing, for she was still under Ellis' management. She had been busy in Philadelphia, too.

Working in the Philadelphia office was a young girl fresh out of convent school. Her name was Ruth O'Neill. She told me years later how she happened on a job with the Philadelphia Orchestra as a glorified gal Friday: "One night at a meeting in the home of a minor poet, a girl had us in stitches explaining the job she was holding down for a friend and that she was giving it up. I dreamed about it that night and I called her and I asked whether I might get the job. She said, 'I think we need a mature woman.' 'Well,' I said, 'would it do any harm if I came down and applied for it?' She said, 'Not at all!' So I can see myself now, weighing 118 pounds, tall, skinny and rather naive. But I got the job right away.

"The conductor who was there was a German named Carl Pohlig, and he and the executive secretary, Ella Janssen, a tall Swedish gal, were having an affair. In my naiveté, I saw what was going on in the adjoining room with Carl Pohlig and Ella. . . . Only Philadelphia society could be on the board; they founded it, they kept it theirs. But while there were things that were all right for them to do, they were not necessarily all right for members of the Philadelphia Orchestra."27

So we see that Pohlig's problems were not purely musical. They were moral as well, and the good ladies of Philadelphia obviously resented the arrogant Pohlig's behavior. But apparently nothing was said to him about discussions the board had already had with Stokowski, or rather with Samaroff. At the end of the season Pohlig returned to Europe and proceeded to Munich.

While Stoki was extricating himself from Cincinnati, Olga had been in Philadelphia. "Olga knew everybody who was powerful in any city," Ruth declared. "She even signed Stokowski's Philadelphia Orchestra contract with Andrew Wheeler in the Broad Street station on her way to New York."[28] The whole procedure had been so clandestine that it began to take on the sense of high drama. Secrecy had been so tightly maintained that even members of the office staff were apparently not aware of what was transpiring. Surely no word had gotten to Pohlig's ears before he left. Olga hurried on to New York with the signed contract in her hands, and the following day the Stokowskis embarked for Munich.

Although Pohlig had known that his contract would not be renewed after its expiration, he did not discover that Stokowski had been engaged to succeed him until he had settled down for the summer in Munich. There were other rumors and stories afloat. The fact that Stoki had freed himself a year early was naturally disturbing. Pohlig had had numerous disputes in Philadelphia, and he now worried that the board might find reason to terminate his contract before it would expire. He returned to Philadelphia early in June with a sense of wounded dignity and stormed into the office.

The confrontation Pohlig had with members of the board and the new manager, Harvey Watts, with whom he had never been on good terms, was a stormy one. Various charges and countercharges were aired, including Pohlig's office affair with secretary Ella Janssen. Pohlig was so furious that he physically attacked Watts. One reporter who somehow learned of the fracas reported that Pohlig and Watts "have not been on entirely friendly terms for some time and when they met recently they had a fist fight."[29]

Ruth O'Neill, who was in the office during the confrontation, said simply, "Well, it came to a head, they paid Pohlig off and fired Ella Janssen. And then they asked me to take over the executive secretary job at half her salary. Her salary was $50 so mine was raised to $25."[30]

It was when Pohlig threatened to sue the orchestra, alleging a conspiracy against him, that the board decided to pay him his entire year's salary of $12,000 in exchange for his immediate resignation. In this way face was saved by both Pohlig and the board. In tendering his resignation, Pohlig expressed his desire "to assure the association and its officers of my very deep appreciation of the courtesies and kindnesses which have uniformly been shown me during my connection with the orchestra. With every assurance of my esteem and personal regard, I am very truly yours."

Andrew Wheeler, showing comparable false sentiment, accepted Pohlig's resignation "with full appreciation of the kindly feeling existing between yourself and the Board of Managers . . . and of the distinguished service which you have rendered to it. . . ."[31]

After an exchange of cablegrams between Philadelphia, London and Munich, it was announced that Leopold Stokowski would become the conductor of the Philadelphia Orchestra at the start of the coming season. The management issued a statement that the resignation of Pohlig and the engagement of the new conductor would not, "thanks to the generosity of certain friends of the orchestra, put any extra financial burden upon the guarantors."[32]

No credit was ever given these unnamed contributors, and one wonders whether the generous Miss Dehon may have been one of them. Some months later a short squib appeared in the *Cincinnati Enquirer*. It was a bit of gossip published solely to discredit Stokowski among those disenchanted champions of his who had attempted to keep him in Cincinnati: "An interesting story comes from an inner source of the orchestral situation in Philadelphia, which throws a peculiar light on the engagement of Leopold Stokowski as conductor of that organization. The story has it that the Philadelphia Orchestra was ready to disband at the end of last season and that it had contemplated paying Pohlig, the conductor, his salary for the year his contract still had to run, and then discontinuing the concerts. This was about the time of Stokowski's memorable climax in local orchestral matters. The youthful conductor has a very wealthy patroness in New York, who, hearing of the events both here and in Philadelphia, went to the management of the Philadelphia Orchestra and promised the services of a conductor if they could manage to secure the necessary subvention fund to maintain the expenses of the orchestra exclusive of the conductor's salary. The offer was accepted and Mr. Stokowski signed the contract with the Philadelphia Orchestra before sailing for Europe last spring."[33]

It was a vicious article and an obvious distortion. It is only worth mentioning in that it refers to Stoki's "very wealthy patroness."

The publicity machinery went into full swing and circulars quoting reviews of Stokowski's latest brilliant success, in London, were quickly printed. Extensive coverage of the May London concert was also given by all the music magazines. As further reports and interviews appeared in Philadelphia papers, curiosity and interest mounted. The management happily announced that the subscriptions for the coming season were $6,000 ahead of what they were at the same time the previous year.

(12)

The Gradual En-Slav-ment

"A Pole by birth, a musician by instinct . . ."

The Globe, London, 23 May 1912

"By birth Stokowski is a Pole, and he has his permanent residence in Munich."

The Westminster Gazette, London, 23 May 1912

"The Slav in my husband is never more marked than when he conducts."

Olga Samaroff Stokowski, Philadelphia, 2 October 1912

*I*N the spring of 1912 Arthur Nikisch brought the London Symphony Orchestra on an American tour. It was his first return since his days as conductor of the Boston Symphony between 1889 and 1893. Since then he had attained a worldwide reputation. The trip was remarkably successful, and because of his "legendary" status, he drew great and admiring audiences. Olin Downes observed that he exerted the same remarkable command of his men that he had had in Boston. Nikisch had programmed the Brahms First for his tour, and Downes found it the greatest performance of the work he had ever experienced. On listening to him, he observed, "It was as if one were composing with the composer."[1]

Nikisch and his men returned to London and on Monday, May 20, appeared there before an adoring audience. Leopold and Olga were among them. The following night Nikisch accompanied Elena Gerhardt in a *lieder* recital. Then the next afternoon, in Queen's Hall, Stokowski led the Nikisch forces in what most of his uninformed critics regarded as his official London debut. Olga, with her knowhow and extensive London connections that she had built up for over a decade, helped gather a large and distinguished audience.

Nikisch and Elena Gerhardt attended, as did Sir Edward and Lady Elgar, Sir Charles Villiers Stanford, Sir Walford Davies, Teresa Carreño, Mischa Elman, Joseph Szigeti, and numerous other celebrities who flocked to Queen's Hall.[2] Szigeti recalled: "I had been present at the memorable Stokowski debut in London when the young organist from St. Bartholomew's electrified a Queen's Hall audience. I still remember the already then typically Stokowskian sound of the London Orchestra in the concluding number—Tchaikovsky's *Marche Slave*—and the feline suppleness of the orchestral support that the young conductor gave to Zimbalist's playing of Glazunov's concerto, then still a comparative novelty."[3]

Olga had never forgotten Wolfsohn's advice that she seek out things Slavic and avoid everything that smacked of New England.[4] She now translated New England into old England and urged Stokowski to emphasize only the Polish part of his background. She set about de-Anglicizing him as quickly as possible. It was she who helped Daniel Mayer prepare the biographical material that he supplied to the press.

It must have seemed strange to his colleagues from the Royal College of Music and from St. James's, and to his family, too, to read that Stokowski had been born in Poland. Olga was intent on converting him into a born-again Slav. He was no longer plain Leopold Anthony Stokowski, but henceforth Leopold Antoni Stanislaw Boleslawowicz Stokowski.

There was no mention made of previous appearances in London and only one reviewer seemed to have heard him before. It was, after all, more dramatic that way, and Stokowski's flair for the dramatic was contagious. The concert on Wednesday May 22, 1912, was more than just a concert. It was an event.

The program had been chosen wisely. Zimbalist and Stokowski had performed the Glazunov Violin Concerto a few months before in Cincinnati in a concert which also ended with the *Marche Slave*. The other works—the Brahms First Symphony, the *Die Meistersinger* Overture, and the Debussy *Prélude à l'après-midi d'un faune*—were among those for which he was most praised in Cincinnati and in the various cities where he had brought the orchestra on tour.

London was awash with newspapers. Ten or more covered the concert. Stoki had comments culled from many and put into ads for the American musical magazines. Olga no doubt saw to that. *The Times, Daily Tele-*

graph, Scotsman, Daily Mail, Globe, Standard, and others sent their best music critics, and all wrote enthusiastically. They found his conducting "intensely alive with a big range of expression.[5] "His really splendid interpretations showed the sanity of a thoughtful musician who does not allow his feelings to master his judgement. . . ."[6] The *Scotsman* found him a sympathetic interpreter and his rendering of the *Prélude à l'après-midi d'un faune* "beyond criticism in the perfection of its delicate shading and soft-hued tints."[7]

Others commented: ". . . orchestral playing as fine as it has ever been one's lot to hear. . . . Mr. Stokovski is a musician of brilliant ability."[8] ". . . a product of the present age—the virtuoso conductor. . . ."[9] "I pay him a high compliment when I say that his reading often reminded me of Richter. . . ."[10]

As a tribute to Olga's de-Anglicizing process, we note in the *Westminster Gazette:* "Yet another foreign conductor of note submitted his powers to the judgement of a London audience yesterday afternoon in the person of Herr Leopold Stokowski."[11] Shades of Marylebone!

The critic for the *London Globe* who reviewed the Stokowski concert commented on the large audience that had assembled to hear him, which evidently would be "ready to welcome him again on his next appearance which, it is to be hoped, will not be long delayed."[12] The delay was not long—three weeks. Daniel Mayer booked a concert that was ostensibly to reintroduce vocalist Lillian Nordica, who had been absent from London for some time. He engaged the New Symphony Orchestra with Stokowski as the conductor. It was an all-Wagner program, except for a set of songs Nordica sang with piano accompaniment.

While it was essentially Nordica's concert, the reviews for Stoki were extraordinary. *The Times* reviewer wrote: "In this remarkable performance Mme. Nordica had an admirable colleague in Mr. Leopold Stokowski. . . . He showed great power in dealing with the *Götterdämmerung* scene, and particularly in carrying on the fine conception of the music which Mme. Nordica had placed before us up to an overwhelming climax in the orchestral ending of the opera."[13] The *London Standard* critic went a notch further than most of his colleagues to report that Stokowski "is a young man who promises to be a genius."[14]

Recalling the concert many years later, Stoki told a reporter that on the way to Queen's Hall he realized that he had forgotten to take the scores of the Wagnerian scenes that Nordica was to sing. The orchestral numbers he had intended to do from memory, but not the operatic ones he was to accompany. There was no time to go back so "making a virtue of necessity, he gave the music a 'once-over' in his mind and ere he left the cab was astonished and gratified to find that he could do without the notes."[15]

Air mail did not exist in 1912, and it took two weeks or longer for letters to go between Philadelphia and London. Details of the confrontation between Pohlig and the board of the orchestra had not yet reached Stokowski when a cable arrived on the eleventh of June, two days before the Nordica concert, asking him to take over the Philadelphia Orchestra one year earlier than had been planned. (Some people, of course, expressed their opinion that it had been planned this way from the beginning.) On the following day he cabled his acceptance.[16]

The Stokowskis returned to their home in Munich to plan the programs for the coming season and make arrangements for living quarters in Philadelphia. It was all done by cable. Olga, assuming responsibility for most of the logistical details, rented sight unseen a house at 2117 Locust Street—a four-story, narrow, red brick townhouse that they would abandon immediately after their first season in Philadelphia. One considerable advantage was a studio on the fourth floor where Olga could practice to her heart's and fingers' content. Cables were dispatched to Cincinnati to have the furniture they had stored there sent on to Philadelphia. Arrangements also had to be made to have some things sent from Munich. One plus for the unattractive house was that it was "not very far from the Academy of Music and quite in the heart of the social center, where they will make themselves at home as they have done in their beautiful villa in Herzog Park, Munich, where Mrs. Stokowski has proved to a number of Philadelphians who have seen them there not only to be a fine pianist, but a housewife and hostess of the first rank, in whose household everything moves like clockwork amid the most charming and artistic surroundings." So wrote one of the town's society reporters.[17]

What had for a brief while promised to be a period of ease and comfort, suddenly turned into one of intense study and planning. Each day hours were spent studying new scores and corresponding with the manager, Harvey Watts, about programs and soloists who were to be engaged. Together they visited Strauss in nearby Garmisch and discussed the possibility of presenting the *Alpine* Symphony in its first American performance. Strauss regrettably said that it could not be completed for another year.

Stoki told reporters that the four most important living composers were

Debussy in France, Sibelius in Finland, Elgar in England, and Strauss, whom he regarded as "unquestionably the biggest figure in modern music."[18] He planned to do new works by Debussy, Martucci, Glière, Enesco, and Loeffler. He pored through the past programs of Scheel and Pohlig, and tried to concentrate on areas they had neglected. He worked prodigiously.

In mid-September he and Olga departed for Paris, where they stayed at the newly opened Hotel Lutétia, with its fashionable "art nouveau" decor. On the twenty-second they boarded the boat train for Cherbourg and went on to New York aboard the S.S. *George Washington*. One of their shipmates was Zimbalist and they were photographed together. The picture showed Olga wearing high laced shoes, a big broad-brimmed hat, and a white shirtwaist above her long skirt. (Skirts then came to about a foot from the ground.) Stoki's hair was cropped short and he was sporting a cap.[19]

On arriving in New York after the seven-day crossing, they were met by a host of reporters asking many questions, mostly innocuous ones which were answered politely. The same scene occurred in Philadelphia when they arrived at the Rittenhouse Hotel, where they were to stay until their house was ready. Reporters commented on Stoki's youthful appearance and lack of affectation. One declared that because of his early years in London "he speaks English perfectly." *Nota bene:* no mention of a foreign accent!

"There is not a whit of the exaggerated ego about him," commented a reporter for the *Public Ledger*. "He gets his inspiration from the mountains near Munich, from garden making, from history study. He is deeply interested in the scientific study of acoustics and has worked out and exemplified his own theory of sounding boards. In short, his art rests on a more stable basis than the superficial theatricality of the business of producing sounds. . . . He is willing, if need be, to puzzle his audience a little—never wantonly, but always for the sake of development of musical taste."[20]

He was also willing to puzzle his audience—perhaps a bit wantonly—about his origin and background. Olga once wondered whether, if Paderewski had come from Emporia, Kansas, and "worn his hair cropped short," he would have captivated his adoring audiences.[21] Although Stoki had shaved his head in Munich, Olga persuaded him to let his hair grow again, and it became an aureole of slightly tousled blond hair. He had the appropriate foreign name, and there was obviously "something Slavic" in his background, but what of the mysterious and piquant accent that many people observed and commented on? Ruth O'Neill said that he had it when he first arrived in Philadelphia, but it became more and more pronounced.[22]

I believe it was as a result of the attempt to de-Anglicize his speech and add a continental flavor that he always used the continental pronunciation for European cities. The two exceptions were Paris and Vienna. Other cities were always pronounced in their vernacular, usually with a lingering relish of the foreign sound. Berlin was always "Bair-leeen"; Moscow was "Moskva"; Prague, "Praha"; Warsaw, "Warszawa." It added exoticism and that was fine. But it did seem a little odd to hear him pronounce the name of the Nebraska town of Holdridge with broad emphasis as "Hol-dreh-gah."

He created his own pronunciations for many commonplace words: "tree-angle" *(triangle)*, "or-kesss-tra" *(orchestra)*, "seek-ee-ah-trist" *(psychiatrist)*, "meek-rophone" *(microphone)*, and "Fan-tah-zee-a" *(Fantasia)*. During interviews he would sometimes refer to the "baguette" instead of the baton, thereby mystifying his interviewer. That, I am sure, was one of his pranks and not to be taken seriously.

He cultivated the kind of syntactical Slavic speech pattern that frequently marked the English spoken by Russians and Poles. Koussevitzky's speech was a perfect example. His accent, absolutely bona fide, was at times riotously funny, but it was very real—it was a Russian accent. Stokowski's use of less than the King's English was pure affectation. His attempts at using Slavic-sounding constructions by dropping articles produced some curious results. These are some typical samples from interviews: "He had his timpani tilted this way and on the timpani was a newspaper. . . . I had seen that he was reading newspaper. I took newspaper—threw it on ground."[23]

"And yet in New York is another kind of richness—rich talent in youth."[24]

"It's a strange life that we see today—where all over the world are people killing each other instead of shaking hands in friendship."[25]

Irving Kolodin remarked that "the spoken commentary provided with a 78 rpm recording of the Brahms First Symphony made in 1928 would give an able language student fits."[26]

To me, Stoki did not have an accent. To be sure, he had his own pronunciation of many words and did frequently eliminate articles and use his own sentence structure. He did this more in public pronouncements and interviews than he ever did in private. Perhaps in the early Philadel-phia days it added to the glamor that grew about him. He was being original as always.

Lee Pryor, a professor of English at the University of Houston, told me he had a theory about Stoki's language use: "I personally think it was simply part of the warp and woof of the man. He was always experiment-ing . . . he had an urge, I think, to be original in every way. And I think that he simply chose very deliberately this sort of polyglot accent, because that's the way he wanted to do it.

"It may be that he did it for theatrical effect, etc. . . . but I really think that in so many ways he was always looking for something new, something different, something unusual. I think that people have a rather stupid attitude toward speech. . . . There is nothing more personal than one's voice and I think that he deliberately chose that very personal, very individual way of expressing himself."[27]

Philadelphia critic James Felton wrote, ". . . In 1969, when I last had an interview, he spoke to me in a cultivated English accent."[28] To me it was not like any English accent I had ever encountered. To me it was simply pure Stokowski. I feel that he was playing a role. For Philadelphia the scenario had to be rewritten—it had to accentuate the Slav in him.

13

The Academy of Music

A NDREW Wheeler, who had signed Stokowski's contract, introduced him to the orchestra in the old rehearsal room on Broad
Street.[1] There was an almost immediate rapport between Stoki
and the men. Far from resenting his youth, they seemed eager to cooperate and help him. Unlike the rehearsals of Scheel and Pohlig, which had
been conducted wholly in German, Stoki immediately began his discourse
with the men in English and kept it so. He also instituted something new
in Philadelphia rehearsals: the fifteen-minute rest break. This won more
affection from the men. At first he carefully refrained from complaining
about the impossible rehearsal conditions, but not for long. He won
further respect by conducting entire rehearsals without a score. He knew
what he wanted, and the men admired him for it.

He had told reporters that he was pleased to begin his work with a body
of eighty-five men so thoroughly trained during the last twelve years.[2] He
paid particular tribute to Scheel, the orchestra's first conductor: "The
man who really made the Philadelphia Orchestra from a musical standpoint is Fritz Scheel. I never knew him personally, but he must have had
very high musical ideals. They are evident in everything he did. Also, he
must have had a wonderful faculty for choosing the highest type of artists
for the orchestra; he set a standard then which has been difficult to live
up to musically. Such artists as Rich, Horner, and Schwar, to mention only
a few of the many who are still remaining in the Philadelphia Orchestra
from Fritz Scheel's time, are absolutely in the first rank for their instrument, not only in America but in the whole world."[3]

119

Olga, who had played under both Scheel and Pohlig, briefed him on their styles and attributes. She had found Scheel an earnest and experienced musician. Pohlig she felt was a better technician, but plodding and uninspired.[4]

After twelve years under two German taskmasters, the orchestra had a remarkable sense of discipline, but Stoki found their playing mechanical and stiff.[5] Unlike Pohlig, who behaved like a Prussian officer and treated his men like privates, ignoring them on the streets and in no way fraternizing with them, Stoki immediately won the collaboration of the men by regarding them as friends and colleagues. In interviews he praised them and declared himself proud to head such forces. Together they would accomplish great things, he averred.

The season opened on October 11, 1912, after four days of intense rehearsals, and musical history was made. There was a sense of anticipation and excitement unlike anything that had happened before in the Academy. Every seat was taken, and extra chairs had to be placed within the orchestra rail. The Main Line dowagers and debutantes were agog as the tall, slender figure with a profile that rivaled Barrymore's strode out onto the stage.

This was the true matinee idol conductor, and the Philadelphians were quick to respond. "His looks, when I first saw him, were unbelievable. I've seen handsome men on the stage and elsewhere, but I never saw anyone with that inimitable charm," said Ruth O'Neill. "We called him Aladdin."[6] The critics waxed ecstatic. According to the *Public Ledger:* "There was much enthusiasm, manifesting itself at the beginning in prolonged applause as Stokowski came forward with bowed head. . . . Those who went forth to see a hirsute eccentricity were disappointed. They beheld a surprisingly boyish and thoroughly business-like figure, who was sure of himself, yet free from conceit, who dispensed with the score by virtue of an infallible memory, and held his men and his audience from first note to last firmly in his grasp."[7]

His opening program consisted of the Beethoven *Leonore* Overture No. 3, Brahms' Symphony No. 1, Ippolitov-Ivanov's *Caucasian Sketches*, and Wagner's *Tannhäuser* Overture. Whatever he achieved had to have been done in the matter of four days, since that is all the time he had spent with the orchestra. As the *Ledger* critic stated, "In this brief time the new leader has been surprisingly successful in welding the several choirs into a single coherent entity. They played yesterday with a unity of purpose —particularly among the first violins—not usually attained until midwinter." The same critic likened Stokowski's conducting to that of Ni-kisch, whom "he frankly admires."[8]

Many conductors, including Nikisch and even Pohlig, had conducted without using a score during concerts, but Stokowski made his doing so more dramatic. Just before raising his baton to give a downbeat he would pick up the scores that had been placed on his conductor's stand and, with a broad gesture, toss them onto the floor and push the stand to the side. No wonder Judson years later called Stokowski one of the greatest show-men he had ever known.[9]

The critic for the *Musical Courier* praised the Philadelphia debut: "In not a single measure of any of his readings did Stokowski put into the pages of the music anything but a devotional spirit and a desire to act as an interpretative medium. He has a commanding personality, but he puts it entirely at the service of the composer. . . ."[10]

Arthur Judson, who had written extensively about Stokowski when he was in Cincinnati, also came to Philadelphia to report the debut for his readers: "He raised his baton and the first program was begun with the noble opening of the Beethoven 'Leonore' Overture. The audience lis-tened intently. The overture ended and the applause broke forth spon-taneously. . . . However, whatever that attitude of the audience may have been before the symphony there was no doubt as to its enthusiasm at its completion. . . . The applause was tremendous, the recalls countless.

"Then came the 'Scenes from the Caucasus' and in culmination the glorious 'Tannhäuser' Overture. The audience, now sure of its new con-ductor, could not contain itself and broke in at suitable and sometimes unsuitable intervals with its approval. The reception to Mr. Stokowski was not that of an audience merely glad it had a competent conductor but wildly enthusiastic because it had discovered a genius."[11]

The magnetism that drew his audience and critics for the first concerts continued through the second pair. The scribes noted the "overflow houses" that he drew and mentioned that the "new conductor increased his hold upon the admiration and esteem of local music lovers."[12] They praised his conducting of the *Freischütz* Overture; Beethoven's Fifth; and a new, contemporary work, the Richard Strauss tone poem *Don Juan*. Ernestine Schumann-Heink sang "Erda's Scene" from *Das Rheingold*, and the "Waltraute Scene" from *Die Götterdämmerung*.

George Rogers, the dean of the critical corps of Philadelphia, wrote a long and perceptive review in the *Inquirer*. He concentrated particularly on the Beethoven symphony, saying: "He finely caught the heroic accents which the C Minor is meant to sound. He perfectly apprehended and splendidly communicated, and with an extraordinary fire and force and fervor, the nobility and dignity and gravity of its varied message, and there was never a moment when the suspicion was suggested that he was seeking to do anything else than to play the music as it was written and to express the whole thought of the composer. . . ."[13]

No soloist was needed to draw attention to his third pair of concerts, since by now Stokowski's drawing power was established. He chose an all-Tchaikovsky program: *Marche Slave, Romeo and Juliet,* and the Fifth Symphony.[14] The reviewers praised his "sound musicianship" and reminded music lovers that those who wanted to be "in it" could not afford to miss any of his concerts.[15]

As the season progressed, enthusiasm increased. Everyone knew that Stokowski was a find and that Philadelphia should be sure of keeping him there. Alexander van Rensselaer, president of the orchestra board, announced publicly that he felt Stokowski should not think of his contract being one of four years, but think of it in terms of eight years, and many, many more! Everyone agreed, including the Stokowskis.[16]

The repertory of this opening season was well balanced, with many fascinating new elements introduced to the listeners. But there was no lack of standard fare. Wagner and Beethoven, followed by Tchaikovsky, led numerically.[17] The precedence of Wagner was logical, for 1912 marked his centenary. Nineteen of his works were featured. Beethoven followed with nine major works. There were six by Tchaikovsky. Surprisingly, there were only three works of Brahms. Strauss fared better, with performance of his *Death and Transfiguration,* "Salome's Dance," *Don Juan,* and the "Love Scene" from *Feuersnot.*

There were the predictable works by Schumann, Schubert, Weber, Rimsky-Korsakov, Mendelssohn, and Liszt, but the real surprise was Stoki's devotion to the English school and to music written by his friends. He introduced a new work by Walford Davies, *Parthenia,* which Davies had just conducted in England. Stanford came next with his *Irish* Symphony, and Elgar with three works: *Pomp and Circumstance,* Symphony No. 1, and the *Enigma* Variations. It is interesting to note that Elgar was represented by the same number of works as Schubert, Schumann, and Brahms.

Other distinct novelties were a symphony by Enesco, Glazunov's "Overture Solenelle," Glière's *Sirens,* Rachmaninoff's *Isle of the Dead,*

Loeffler's *La Villanelle du Diable,* and a work that, according to Grove, had its first performance in 1911, Debussy's *Ibéria.*

The repertory Stokowski chose was clearly made up of works calling for rich orchestral color, sweeping romanticism, and arresting orchestral effects. Low in this scheme was the music of the earlier classical school. Of the music of Bach there was one work, the Suite in B Minor. Haydn was represented by the Symphony No. 104 in D ("London") and Mozart by his overture to *The Magic Flute,* Symphony No. 39 in E-flat, and several arias.

Most of the soloists were distinguished. Among the singers we find Schumann-Heink and Nikisch's good friend Elena Gerhardt. The violinists were Mischa Elman, Eugene Ysaÿe, Thaddeus Rich, and Louis Persinger; the pianists were Yolanda Mérö, Rudolph Ganz, Leopold Godowsky, and Ernest Schelling.[18]

In her slender memoir, Elena Gerhardt wrote: "My first engagement with orchestra outside New York was in Cincinnati, with Leopold Stokowski, whom I had already met in London. I do not think there was a season when I did not sing with him, at least as long as he was the conductor of the Philadelphia Orchestra, which he made famous. I enjoyed my concerts with him immensely, for he always took the greatest and sincerest interest in the accompaniments of my songs and arias. During my career I met only a few conductors who gave the vocalist so much time at an orchestral rehearsal."[19]

One of the few was her devoted friend Nikisch, who enjoyed playing her piano accompaniments and always gave her ample time when she appeared with an orchestra. Contemporaries implied that he did so lovingly.

Gerhardt's comments continue: "As a sensitive and serious musician, I often felt very miserable when there were only fifteen minutes left for the vocalist at an orchestral rehearsal, just enough time to skip through the music once. It is not always the fault of the singer if things go wrong, or if the vocalist gives an uninspired performance after such short rehearsals.

"I remember a concert in Philadelphia when I sang Richard Wagner's *Five Songs.* . . . I went to Stokowski's house to go through them with piano accompaniment, and he knew exactly how I sang them when it came to the orchestra rehearsal. That night, we went through scores of Lieder until, to our surprise, we noticed that it was three o'clock in the morning.

A friend who came with me was also fascinated by his interest. This performance of the Wagner songs was such a success in Philadelphia that he made a change in the programme of his New York concert and asked me to sing them there again. I have never forgotten the hothouse atmosphere he obtained from his orchestra in the delicate and difficult *Im Treibhaus.*"

The audience and the critics all seemed happy, but not Stoki. He told me that he found many conditions quite deplorable: "First of all I was never allowed to rehearse in the Academy where the concerts were given. I had to rehearse in a little room where you could not hear anything except a terrific din of sound. The orchestra could not hear each other. There was no question of balance. And that went on for a long time. The orchestra in those days, in my opinion, had about three good players and the rest were not good, but they had a first horn who was wonderful, the timpani was wonderful, and there might have been two or three others, but these stood up like mountains and the rest were valleys."[20]

Among the players he admired were Anton Horner, first horn; Oscar Schwar, timpanist; and Thaddeus Rich, the concertmaster. Rich had joined the orchestra in 1906, when he was twenty-one, and remained with it until 1926. German-born Oscar Schwar was engaged by Scheel in 1903 and continued to play until 1946. By all accounts he was a remarkable performer—on one occasion, after a particularly virtuoso performance, the entire orchestra applauded him. Anton Horner, leader of the horn section and a particular favorite of Stokowski, had been with the orchestra since 1902 and he remained until 1946.[21]

Stoki was not at all satisfied with the orchestra and set about making improvements. The weeding-out process, however, was not to begin until the end of the first season. Changes were gradual at first. About the players in general, he told me: "They had a stiff manner of playing mechanically. It was just terrible so I tried to make that more flexible. But the resistance was very great and the rehearsal conditions were impossible. I begged for better rehearsal conditions and I fought and had awful times with the board. One Saturday night I had a concert and after the concert a man came backstage and said his name was Edward Bok. He had been told that I was having awful fights and asked why. I explained to him and he said I was quite right, that one must rehearse in the same room as the concert. So Bok began to help me. He was Dutch. It happened that the president of the orchestra was also Dutch—Alexander van Rensselaer—a very fine man. When he and Bok came together things began to move, and gradually they gave me one rehearsal a week, then two, then three and finally four rehearsals in the Academy of Music, and then the orchestra began to improve and I began to find better players."[22]

Among the better players that he added were Anton Torello, bass, in 1914; in 1915 the fabulous oboist Marcel Tabuteau and Lucien Cailliet, clarinet, who was later to assist Stokowski with his transcriptions. In 1917 he brought in clarinetist Daniel Bonade, and in 1918 the young, seventeen-year-old trumpeter Saul Caston, who after five years became first trumpet and in 1936 associate conductor. (After leaving the orchestra he became the conductor of the Denver Symphony.) But one of the greatest additions to the ranks of the orchestra did not occur until 1921, when he engaged the spectacular flutist William Kincaid. Kincaid was a most colorful figure—tall, ruddy-faced, and with a shock of platinum white hair that he complemented by playing a platinum flute rather than one of gold or silver. Kincaid was still in the orchestra at the time of Stoki's return in 1960.[23]

In the same way that Stoki began consolidating his position with the players and the board, Olga went about the business of being the ideal conductor's wife. Years before, when she had first played with the Boston Symphony under Gericke, she was deeply impressed by the role Gericke's wife played in Boston and the positive influence she had on his career.[24] Now Olga, a conductor's wife in Philadelphia, plunged into her role with great energy.

She tackled Philadelphia society like a zealot. During their first season she made and received about seven hundred calls. Their house on 2117 Locust Street became a hub of social activity, as did each successive home they were to have in Philadelphia and its environs.[25] "I remember the Friday afternoon teas when the Rittenhouse Square people came and had tea," Ruth O'Neill recalled. "I sent off the invitations."[26] As the season progressed, the Stokowskis became accepted, in fact courted, by Philadelphia society. Stoki never had any problem attracting women; now he succeeded in winning the admiration of men as well.

But his allure and appeal went further. He was to capture the affection of children too. His Children's Concerts were to become enormously popular and really full of fun. It eventually became a matter of having to keep adults out.

Two of his fans were the Yarnall sisters, Sophie and Agnes. Sophie told me: "I was ten years old when he first came to Philadelphia. My parents had a box nearest to the end box on the left-hand side of the balcony at the Academy of Music, and they took me and my sister, who was eight then, to the Friday afternoon concerts every single Friday afternoon. And naturally, we got a frightful crush on this man who was the most beautiful thing that you ever saw, and at the end of the first season, we pooled all of our pennies. I think we must have gotten about four or five dollars

Portrait by Leopold Seyffert (c. 1913)

together, and we went to Battles, which was the good flower shop there, and we bought a laurel wreath that would do credit to any funeral parlor and we sent it to him for the last concert. And we said with love from Agnes and Sophie Yarnall, and we saw it carried up the aisle. In those days for five or ten dollars you could get a really handsome wreath. And it was carried up and put on the stage. And I remember my father saying, "I wonder who in the name of God sent that terrible thing!" We kept our confidence to ourselves. But sure enough, you know, that afternoon Stokowski came around to my parents' house, which was at Seventeenth and Locust streets, just three blocks up from the Academy and he didn't ask to see my parents. He asked to see Miss Sophie and Miss Agnes Yarnall. We came downstairs and he kissed—you know he always liked being adorable with children—he kissed both our hands, and my sister didn't wash her hand for six weeks or something like that."[27]

Artists, too, were intrigued by Stoki. Close friendships developed between him and the young and gifted Leopold Seyffert, and later with the painter Arthur "Artie" Carles. Seyffert became excited about the possibility of doing a portrait of him; after an introduction he timidly invited him to his studio. Stoki was very pleased with what he saw and arranged to take some lessons with Seyffert, studying both etching and painting. And he was delighted to pose for him.

The portrait, when completed, was affectionately dubbed "Whistler's Father" by some and "The Thinker" by the more reverent. Painted in profile in a dark suit against a gray background, Stoki was a striking figure. A dark red curtain added a discreet dash of color, and his blond, somewhat tousled hair is strongly silhouetted against a picture by Goya. It was shown in the 108th Annual Exhibition of the Philadelphia Academy of Fine Arts and easily won the Fellowship Award. The *New York Sun* dispatched its art critic to case the Philadelphia scene, and he dutifully reported "that one of the really distinguished portraits in the exhibition was that of Leopold Stokowski. . . . The subject, a young man with a smooth face and wavy hair, was one to attract any painter with a spark of imagination, and Mr. Seyffert has indicated in terms of substantial but not too literal modeling and of simple colors the essentials of an uncommonly interesting sitter."[28] For a while it was hung in the Academy of Music and later in Stoki's various homes. It was eventually to have been given to the Art Institute, but unfortunately it now lies somewhere on the bottom of the Atlantic. More about that later.

14

Second Season

URING his second season, along with his standard fare, Stokowski
introduced *Légende Symphonique* of Ernest Schelling, an American first. On the same program he gave his listeners two other
works never before performed by the orchestra: Bach's *Brandenburg* Concerto No. 3 and excerpts from Schubert's *Rosamunde.* The critics had
found the Schelling work to be "meritorious but not great."[1]

Another "modern work," which one critic found to be filled with
"weird cacophony" and "nothing but a wild jumble of the most vociferous
noises" was Richard Strauss' *Ein Heldenleben,* then considered ultramodern.[2] Less disturbing to critical ears was another novelty, Hans Pfitzner's
Kätchen von Heilbronn Overture. During November Stokowski gave the
first performance of Florent Schmitt's *Rhapsodie Viennoise* and Fernandez Arbós' *Guajiras* for violin and orchestra, featuring a violinist with
the slightly improbable name of Bonarios Grimson.

But this was not the extent of the new works that he introduced during
the season. Others included Siegmund von Hausegger's *Wieland der
Schmied;* Rabaud's Second Symphony; and Max von Schillings' Symphonic Prologue to Sophocles' *King Oedipus.* All were marked "first time
at these concerts." It is somewhat astonishing to find the performances
of the Brahms Piano Concerto No. 2 and the Sibelius Violin Concerto
also being given for the first time.

When he took the orchestra on tour he included the Paderewski Piano
Concerto, with Katherine Goodson as soloist. A Cleveland critic, Alice
Bradley, who heard him frequently with the Cincinnati Orchestra ob-

served, "The musical and mental growth of Leopold Stokowski is altogether remarkable. It has been a joy to watch this young genius 'in the making.' His boyish exuberance has now disappeared. In its stead has come a poise, a dignity, and a ripe scholarship of the finest quality." She also found his interpretation of the Franck Symphony in D Minor marked by "sobriety, pathos and poetic understanding."[3]

In January 1914 he introduced a new work by American composer Henry Hadley. It was his Symphony No. 4 *(North, East, South, West).* The critics were complimentary. The critic for the *Philadelphia Press* wrote, "Stokowski seems inclined to give the American composer every possible recognition. The conductor made no mistake in his choice of the symphony, as was shown by the delight that each of the numbers afforded . . . the most striking part of the composition is the *South,* for in that section the composer was able to introduce the most character, with the 'ragtime' rhythms and the curious syncopation style, the most typical of purely American music."[4]

Another American "first" was the *Schauspiel* Overture by Erich Wolfgang Korngold, which Stoki presented first in Philadelphia and then on the first tour he made with the orchestra to Boston and other New England cities. But he did not play it in New York.

When Carl Pohlig brought the Philadelphia Orchestra to New York on November 5, 1907, it was a disaster. Now, seven years later and again with a new conductor, the Philadelphia Orchestra returned. There may have been some apprehension, particularly concerning the critic Krehbiel, who had castigated Stokowski for leaving the Cincinnati Orchestra.

The concert was being given as a benefit for the Sisters of the Assumption and the Nursing Sisters of the Poor. It was scheduled for 3:00 on Sunday afternoon, January 21, 1914. The soloist was Alma Gluck, who was to sing a Mozart aria at the beginning of the program.

Apprehension and alarm began to develop shortly before the concert was to begin. Alma Gluck was nowhere to be seen. The players began to take their seats as concert time arrived. There was the usual warming up and tuning, but Stokowski refused to begin until the soloist arrived, since the opening piece was the short overture to Mozart's *Marriage of Figaro.* The audience was graced by the presence of Cardinal Farley and a sea of nuns and various prelates.

Critic Algernon St. John-Brenon wrote a review that is irresistible. He quipped: "I do not quite know why it is so, but a concert with a cardinal is much more interesting than a concert without a cardinal. Perhaps it is because cardinals existed long before concerts, and are much more interesting than most concerts. Then again, the scarlet skull cap of his Eminence gave to the somber background of Carnegie Hall a touch of princely color.

"Just as the concert proceeded with a cardinal it was preceded by a catastrophe. Miss Gluck—a sweet name meaning bountiful and happy— was under the impression that the concert began at 4 o'clock instead of 3. So at 3 o'clock she was sitting quietly at her home, munching a dietetic luncheon, consisting of half a whole meal biscuit, and a vague vision of a glass of water. She was garbed in a wrapper."[5]

At ten minutes past 3:00 a representative of Carnegie Hall rushed to Alma Gluck's apartment and thundered in a tremendous voice, "You are keeping the cardinal, the critics, and Krehbiel waiting." Miss Gluck uttered a strange cry of despair, threw her concert garb into her automobile, and dressed on the way to Carnegie. Better late than not at all, and the concert proceeded amid a small ripple of grumbles.

Henry Krehbiel obviously approached the concert with both doubt and trepidation. In the beginning of his review he hemmed and hawed in rather arch and pontifical fashion: "New Yorkers are beholden to that amiable virtue which, we are told, suffereth long and is kind, envieth not, vaunteth not itself, is not puffed up, for the privilege which they enjoyed yesterday afternoon on hearing a concert of the Philadelphia Orchestra and Mr. Leopold Stokowski." After considerable ambling he came to the meaty part of his review: "There are dreadful memories still alive of a previous visit of the Philadelphia Orchestra when the program was so burdensome that it was impossible for the stoutest heart to endure it all. That was not the case yesterday, Mr. Stokowski was more considerate. . . ." The climax of the concert for Krehbiel was the performance of the Brahms First Symphony: "The symphony had a performance wholly worthy of its sweet, strong, serious beauty. After it the orchestra was no longer on trial."[6]

Philadelphians could be proud. The stigma of the Pohlig affair was completely erased. This, too, was a great personal triumph for Stokowski. He had completely won over the crusty Krehbiel. Henderson in the *Sun* was also deeply impressed. He regarded the performance of the Brahms as one that filled him with great joy.

But the most significant review of all, and incidentally one of the best, appeared in *Musical America*. Critic Arthur Judson wrote: "There is no dearth of good orchestral concerts in New York and the only excuse for an invasion by an orchestra of another city is sheer merit. Such invasions have not often in the past been so successful as to encourage further visits, but the success of Mr. Stokowski and his band evoked a genuine desire to hear them again. . . .

"Mr. Stokowski, since his first ventures in America, has grown tremendously in artistic stature. He is a splendid conductor both musically and practically. . . . His New York debut was an unqualified success."[7]

Stokowski provoked unusual interest in bringing the orchestra to "the home of the bean and the cod." Confident that their orchestra was unquestionably the finest in America, many who attended his Boston debut—and the Philadelphians' first visit there since Richard Strauss had conducted them many years before—had their comfortable assurance somewhat shattered.

The Boston program included the *Schauspiel* Overture of Wolfgang Korngold, written at the age of fourteen, and the Saint-Saëns Third Violin Concerto, with Mischa Elman as soloist. The reviews were quite remarkable. Even that Brahms hater Philip Hale was not turned off by the performance of the Brahms First. About Korngold he was not so kind. Hale wrote: "Mr. Stokowski conducted for the first time in this city. It is said that before he accepted the leadership, a season ago and after the death of Scheel, the orchestra fell from its high estate. If this is true Mr. Stokowski deserves high credit for the present technical proficiency of his men. The performance yesterday was characterized by precision and plasticity. . . ." And about the effort of young Wolfgang, he added, "The Overture deserves an honorable place in the Museum of Infant Prodigies. If Master Korngold could make such noise at 14, what will he not do when he is 28? The thought is appalling."[8]

"The young conductor radiates magnetic fire from the first stroke of his baton," wrote the critic of the *Boston Globe*. "Dispensing with printed score and desk, he is free to look now toward one choir and now another, and projects to his men by an extraordinary transference of energy and spirit the character and the essence of the music as he feels it."[9]

The loquacious H. T. Parker observed in the *Boston Evening Transcript:* "No doubt the assistance of Mischa Elman, the violinist, who has a faithful and exuberant following in Boston, helped to assemble the audience that nearly filled Symphony Hall. . . . Mr. Stokowski and his band had plainly attracted an appreciable part of the audience, and unusual and fortunate are the conductor and the orchestra that can do so in an occasional visit to this town. It sits content with its own conductor [Karl Muck] and its own band, not even seeking the pleasure of flattering comparisons. As the signs went, Mr. Stokowski had quickened its curiosity and by so much he is unique, outside Mr. Toscanini, among the conductors who practice their profession in America. It applauded him heartily when he came to his place; it lingered at the end of a two-hour concert to recall him still more warmly and once it brought the visiting orchestra as well as the visiting conductor to its feet. Out of the musical Nazareth of Philadelphia, as we of Boston and New York are prone to believe it, had come a new and engrossing conductor and an orchestra that was interesting to hear."[10]

The first concert following the tour contained a "Dramatic Overture" by Otto Muller, a member of the first violin section. Stoki let the composer-violinist conduct his own work, while he sat in one of the upper boxes to listen. It was another brilliant stroke that won the affection of his men. The critics were polite—no more—and the piece was never heard of again. But all noticed that he applauded eagerly, and the composer, players, and audience seemed to relish the moment.[11]

He then singled out another Philadelphia composer by the name of Henry A. Lang. The son of German parents, Lang had been born in New Orleans in 1854, studied in Germany, and then taught there for many years. He later settled in Philadelphia and taught in various music schools. He had brought many of his scores to Stokowski, and from them Stoki chose a tone poem called *Fantasies of a Poet.* [12] Today there is no particular attention paid the music of Mr. Lang; even at that time the critics recognized him as a competent composer, but certainly not a great one. The important fact was that Stoki was exploring the whole field of music, and American composers were being presented in major concerts.

He continued to win increasing sympathy and admiration from the players as he programmed compositions written by members of the orchestra. On the following concert he had another one introduced, by Hedda Van den Beemt, another member of the first violin section. Van den Beemt, too, had shown some of his works to Stoki, and together they chose his "Introduction" and "Shepherd Scene" from *Aucassin et Nicolette.* It proved to be the most successful of the three home-grown works, and the critics commented on its pleasing pastoral quality, imagination, and splendid knowledge of instrumentation. He was complimented too on his fine conducting, and at the end he was presented a large laurel wreath by admirers.[13] It was a brilliantly ingratiating move by Stoki.

While the full plans for the twenty-five pairs of concerts to be given the following season were not complete—Stoki would work on them while in Munich—the list of soloists was announced. Among them we find many of his old favorite artists and friends: Alma Gluck, Louise Homer, Efrem Zimbalist, Mme. Schumann-Heink, Harold Bauer, Ossip Gabrilowitsch, Fritz Kreisler, Josef Hofmann, and, we are pleased to note, Olga Samaroff.

Courtesy Reginald Allen

Dr. Alfred Reginald Allen (kneeling); Mrs. Alfred Reginald Allen, Sr.; Stokowski; two unidentified friends; Olga Samaroff; Alfred Hertz, conductor of the San Francisco Symphony Orchestra; and Mrs. Alfred Hertz (seated) aboard the S.S. *George Washington* (1913)

Before sailing on April 21, he told reporters how anxious he and Olga were to get back to their home in Munich—he was most interested in getting back to his garden, which he declared his chief diversion during the summer. He remarked that Olga would have plenty to do preparing for her return to the concert stage in the fall, with over forty dates booked, including those with the Philadelphia Orchestra. During the summer they planned to drive to Switzerland to visit the Paderewskis in their villa in Morges and later to Bayreuth to attend the Wagner festival, where Muck was the principal conductor. "My Munich villa is very pleasantly situated," Stokowski told reporters, "just outside the city but so near the central part of it that I can walk across the river and to the Hoftheater in twenty-five minutes, all the way through gardens and under trees. I am always glad to get back to Munich, but—I am always glad to get back to Philadelphia, too. Now, I am not saying that for effect. I have every reason to like Philadelphia, for I cannot imagine a conductor happier in his work in every respect than I am here."[14]

(15)

Munich 1914

T HE Stokowskis departed for Europe on the twenty-first of April. Before going on to Munich they made brief stops in Paris and in London, where they visited with the Stokowski family and many English friends.

While Leopold remained for a short time in London, Olga and her maid Mathilde went on to Munich to open the house. Shortly after they arrived a quite frightening thing happened. "I awakened in the middle of the night to hear someone fumbling at my door. I had scarcely realized that a burglar had materialized, before I was at the window calling for help in my best chest tones. A night watchman on duty at a handsome villa up the street came running, revolver in hand. As he entered the house by one door, the burglar escaped by another and was seen by the neighbors as he vaulted over a wall across the street and disappeared. My silver and other valuables were in unpacked trunks in my room, so the burglar only got a copious supper in the blue and white kitchen. He must have enjoyed it in leisurely fashion for no less than three empty beer bottles stood on the table beside the remains of his feast."[1]

As a result of this experience Olga decided to hire a manservant for extra protection. She found that she could do so for twenty-five dollars a month and that, instead of the drab clothes of butlers in most other countries, "he would wear a livery of any color I chose, with brass buttons."[2] The color she chose was blue. Quite appropriate for Munich.

That is how Ludwig of the round, china blue eyes became part of the Stokowski household. Olga described him as follows: "His honest face, also very round, always shone as though he had just scrubbed it with some particularly potent soap. He had a finger missing from one hand, but he always wore white gloves when serving. . . . Ludwig was the hardest worker I have ever known. He had a passion for polishing brass and silver. One could not look at the brass knobs of the front door and the doorplate. They were dazzling as the sun. And I found myself secretly wondering how long silver could survive the kind of rubbing Ludwig gave mine. In the morning the blue coat with brass buttons was replaced by a capacious apron, and after eleven o'clock, when the ordinary daily tasks had been accomplished, one usually found Ludwig weeding the vegetable garden, mending the plumbing or roaming the house seeking what he could devour in the way of extra work. I always felt he secretly envied me my piano practice, which obviously had no limit."[3]

Ever since her early experiences with Wilhelm Gericke and the Boston Symphony, and after having witnessed the role Gericke's wife played in promoting his career, Olga had contemplated the role of conductor's wife. She now determined to embrace it with a vengeance. Entertainment was something she regarded as an investment, and in Munich, as in Philadelphia, she took on the role of hostess as a serious preoccupation. And she did it royally. The adverb is not idle—Bavaria, Prussia, Austria, and most of the Germanic states, as well as England, were all dominated by royal houses, and Olga behaved as if she too were entertaining on a royal scale. It was all done with style.

Guests were international. They included many who were drawn by the concerts in Munich, as well as in nearby Bayreuth and Salzburg. Celebrities included Ossip and Clara Gabrilowitsch, the Fritz Kreislers, the Bruno Walters, the Paderewskis, the Ernest Schellings, Harold Bauer, Efrem Zimbalist, Mischa Elman, Josef Hofmann, Mme. Schumann-Heink, Marcella Sembrich, Sara Cahier, and numerous stars of the Munich opera. Maria Dehon was also a frequent houseguest. She had been coming to Europe every year during the summer and at other times as well. In 1938 at the age of eighty-one, she made her hundred and eighth transoceanic crossing, armed with a long ear trumpet to compensate for her increasing deafness.[4]

"Ludwig and cook Mathilde both loved party days," Olga recalled. "The more guests I invited the better they liked it. They thrived on an atmosphere of festivity. On such days . . . while Mathilde prepared a *Rehrücken* [saddle of venison], Ludwig filled little pastry boats with *Prei-*

selbeeren, never losing sight of the right temperature of the Moselle or Rhine wine. Ludwig never forgot anything."[5]

No wonder visiting Philadelphians were impressed. They reported Stoki an ideal host who, "when he throws off the cares of music, enjoys himself like a big, overgrown boy."[6] With all the energy of an "overgrown boy," he tended his garden, which was one of his favorite preoccupations during the summer. He always regretted that someone else had to start it for him in the spring, so that it would be growing by the time he arrived. He guarded his agricultural domain jealously, and only occasionally would he permit Ludwig to assist him.[7]

Olga spent much of her time practicing and preparing for her return to the concert stage. Advertisements appeared in the music magazines announcing her availability and her new management, no longer her former dear friend Charles Ellis but her original manager at her debut, the Wolfsohn Musical Bureau. She also worked very hard adding the Beethoven *Emperor* Concerto to her repertory for one of her appearances with the orchestra later in the season. She planned to give a series of concerts in both Germany and Austria in August with the American contralto Sara Cahier.

Stokowski meanwhile was busy preparing his first Bach transcriptions: the "Pastorale" from the *Christmas Oratorio* and the chorale "Wachet auf" ("Sleepers Awake").

The 1914 musical season in Munich was one of the most brilliant within anyone's memory. Bruno Walter was again conducting both operas and symphonic concerts, drawing huge audiences. The American pianist Edwin Hughes appeared with the Konzertverein Orchestra playing the Schumann concerto. Frederic Lamond, the Scottish pianist who had become renowned in Germany as a Beethoven interpreter, was giving a series of Beethoven sonata recitals with violinist Bronislaw Hubermann. Ossip Gabrilowitsch, a great favorite in Munich both as conductor and pianist, appeared as soloist with the Bohemian Quartet. Sara Cahier on tour in Hamburg won great praise for her Ortrud, in Prague for her Carmen, and for roles she sang in Cassel and Budapest. Praises for her recitals in Frankfurt and Dusseldorf were loud. She then came to Munich, appearing in the opera house and also as soloist with the orchestra.[8]

More musicians, artists, students, and tourists—particularly Americans —converged on Munich during this summer than ever before. Edwin Hughes wrote back to friends in America that there were over two thousand Americans there, many of them residents.[9] Among the latter we find the family of Eugene and Emma Luening, with their two children, a daughter, Helena, and their fourteen-year-old son, Otto, who was then studying flute, piano, and composition at the Royal Academy of Munich.

Otto's recollections of that summer are extremely vivid. "I was just a kid then but I always was very interested in everything that was going on. The very first symphonic and opera music that I heard was all conducted by Bruno Walter. I went to his concerts three or four times a week. It was a great education. He was doing the symphony concerts, as well as being *Generalmusikdirektor* at the opera, and he also did oratorio concerts —the whole thing. He was the big chief in town."[10]

When I asked Otto about Gabrilowitsch, he recalled that he had heard him both as conductor and pianist. "And," he added, "I heard Clara Clemens Gabrilowitsch, too. She was the daughter of Mark Twain. I heard her in Munich . . . it must have been in 1913 or maybe it was the early part of 1914. She was quite a good singer, and he played accompaniments for her—Gabrilowitsch did. It was the usual kind of *lieder* program —probably Schubert, Brahms, and other German *lieder.* That was the way they all came out in those days. I remember I was quite impressed at the time. He was very matter-of-fact in his playing for her, but he was an exceptionally fine accompanist."

Otto was particularly interested in Americans who were succeeding in Munich. "There was an American pianist, Edwin Hughes, who was a Leschetizky student," Otto recalled. "He was the fashionable teacher there—a very handsome young man who gave his occasional concerts twice a year and had a great following. And in the opera there was Edyth Walker, who was quite good, and Madame Cahier."

Richard Strauss was another celebrity whom Otto heard and frequently saw strolling in the Hofgarten or along Odeonplatz. "He was one of my big heroes at the time," Otto recalled, "and I heard him conduct a lot at the opera. In 1914, during his fiftieth-anniversary celebration, which ran for about a year, there was a lot of Strauss being played. I remember him doing *Elektra* and *Salome.* And he did wonderful performances of them. He had complete control over the orchestra and he had a very fine sense of the shape of a piece—its entirety, its overall picture. He didn't always take pieces at exactly the same tempo by any means. If he had a train to make, he would cut off ten minutes of an opera, but within the piece from beginning to end the proportions were always exactly right. The first thing I heard him conduct was *Rosenkavalier* and it was thrilling."[11]

It would have been all but impossible not to encounter Strauss during his fiftieth anniversary, and Munich celebrated it magnificently. With great ceremony they placed a metal plaque on the house where he had been born, and they planned to rename a street in his honor—Richard Strauss Strasse. The Munich Court Opera performed all of his operas during his natal week, and he himself conducted *Elektra*. One interesting departure was a symphonic performance of *Death and Transfiguration* preceding the production of *Salome*. [12]

When I asked Luening if he had ever encountered the Stokowskis in Munich, he reminded me that he could not have heard either of them, for they did not play in Munich. But plans had been made. There was to be a Munich Stokowski concert later in the season. On June 20, a rather terse release was given to the press stating that Leopold Stokowski was to conduct one of the Strauss festival concerts in the Tonhalle. The date was set for August 11. "Olga Samaroff will play, and Mme. Cahier will sing with the orchestra . . . and for this occasion the orchestra will be enlarged to ninety men."[13]

Eight days after the announcement, Gavrilo Princip, a pale young Serbian, fired the shots that assassinated Archduke Franz Ferdinand, heir to the Austrian throne, and his wife, Sophie, the Duchess of Hohenberg. The impact of this event was profoundly felt throughout Austria and Germany. An ominous drift toward war continued throughout July. Although the newspapers emphasized the seriousness of the situation, Olga, immersed in her daily practice, later admitted that she had been too busy to give much attention to the press. She and Sara Cahier were preparing for their series of concerts in Bad Reichenhall, Franzensbad, Marienbad, and Karlsbad at the end of July and the beginning of August.[14]

Bad Reichenhall was a town on the Austrian border, not far from Salzburg. Olga, Leopold, Sara Cahier, and her accompanist arrived early on the afternoon of July 24. All the bands in town were playing the national anthem. While strolling by the Kurhaus they found that three men from the Philadelphia Orchestra were playing in the Kurhaus Orchestra. After that pleasant interlude they proceeded to their hotel, where they discovered posters announcing that Austria had sent an ultimatum to Serbia—if the stated conditions were not met, war would be declared. The public had been told that if they heard six shots from the fortress of Salzburg, it would indicate a declaration of war.[15]

The quartet had tea in one of the pleasant gardens, an ear tuned for the ominous shots from the Hohensalzburg. At six o'clock they heard them. But their concert, sold out weeks in advance, was nevertheless well attended. Olga's new addition to her repertory, the Beethoven Sonata No. 17 in D Minor, sometimes called "The Tempest," made a penetrating impression. "I have never played to such an emotional audience. In the quiet, slow movement of Beethoven's *D Minor Sonata* which I played, a woman began to sob convulsively. Cahier and I could not give enough encores. Nobody wanted to go home. In a sense the evening was—for all of us—a farewell to the old order of things."[16]

At noon on the twenty-seventh, they—Olga, Leopold, Sara, and her accompanist—boarded the train for Franzensbad. The train was filled with Austrian nationals hurriedly returning to take part in the mobilization. There was great commotion at the border, and that night they were kept awake by the cannons, trucks, and military equipment being moved throughout the town. In the morning they discovered that the piano, which had been sent from Prague, was under a pile of military gear in a corner of the station. Then to their dismay they learned that several hundred soldiers had been billeted in the hall where the concert was to take place. The authorities urged them to leave immediately if they wished to get back to Germany. They left at once.[17]

Stokowski had already taken out his first American naturalization papers, but he was technically still a British citizen. There was no time to agonize so they prepared to leave as quickly as possible. Spy hysteria had begun to grip Munich. Olga, returning home after having bought camphor and cheesecloth to pack belongings that were to be left behind, was stopped and questioned by the police and forced to open her packages. She was asked for her whole life history before she was allowed to proceed through a menacing crowd.[18] A few days later another disconcerting event occurred: "A stern-faced soldier on a bicycle rode up to the kitchen window and told us to use no water until notified by the authorities. The water supply, he said, had been poisoned by Serbian spies in nuns' habits. This rumor, which proved to be untrue, was succeeded by many others until one felt the blight of suspicion and fear settling down upon the once cheerful city."[19]

Early in the summer both Olga and Leopold had worked on their vegetable garden. For some reason no one could explain, the only thing that came up were turnips—baskets of them. Just when the products of their garden were most needed, there was nothing but turnips. A friend sent them a case of Asti Spumanti from Italy. "I determined to open a bottle at every meal as long as it lasted," Olga recalled, "just to keep up our spirits. Not only my own household, but several stranded American acquaintances lived for a fortnight largely on turnips and Asti Spumanti."[20]

On July 31 Bruno Walter stepped out from the stage entrance of the Prince Regent Theater into the warm, sunny afternoon. He heard music far different from that which he had been conducting. It was the sound of drums and marching feet. And during the evening, while he was out walking with his wife through the crowded downtown area of Munich, a thin, hysterical man pointing at him began to scream: "A Serbian! A Serbian!" A crowd began to gather and Walter answered, "I am not from Serbia but you are surely from Eglfing." Eglfing was the Bavarian Bedlam, the state insane asylum. But he soon had more serious problems. He worried about his foreign friends, of which he had so many—especially about those who were British, like Stokowski, and Russian, like Gabrilowitsch.[21]

Two days after war had been declared, three German soldiers burst into the Gabrilowitsch house in Kreuth. They insisted on going to their upstairs rooms, demanding to see and go through their papers and correspondence. Unfortunately much of that belonging to Ossip was in Russian. The soldiers seized it all and carted Ossip off to prison in the town of Miesbach. His last words as he was being taken away were, "Greet Bruno for me," which obviously meant that Clara should contact Bruno Walter, who, in his high position in the state-run opera, could be helpful. Fortunately she was able to reach him at the opera house and to blurt out that Ossip had been taken to prison before the connection was broken.[22]

Walter realized at once that the frenzy about foreign spies had caused Ossip's arrest. There had also been rumors that a group of Russians were attempting to smuggle vast quantities of gold out of Germany. Walter immediately began to make inquiries, and he discovered that Gabrilowitsch had been brought from Tegernsee to Munich.[23]

Walter hurried to police headquarters, but he was told that nothing could be done about Gabrilowitsch, for he was being held as a Russian, and possibly a spy. "The Chief of Police, whom I had finally managed to interview, proved a compassionate man. 'Personally,' he said, 'I can't do a thing. These matters are handled by the military authorities, and you won't have any luck there either. If you are really convinced of Herr Gabrilowitsch's innocence and are ready to vouch for him, try your luck with the clerics.' This reminded me that the Catholic Church was still the supreme power in Bavaria. I asked a friend who greatly admired

Gabrilowitsch as an artist and as a man to help me, and we called on Nuncio Pacelli, of whose noble personality and love of music I had heard a good deal. The Nuncio listened to us with sympathy and promised us his help. Ossip was a free man the next day."[24] The helpful Nuncio Pacelli became Pope Pius XII in March 1939.

On the eighth of August Olga and Leopold obtained an interview with the same chief of police, who advised them to leave the country immediately. Since many reports had been circulated that Switzerland would not admit any more refugees, they decided to go by way of Holland. They wired Rotterdam and booked passage on the S.S. *Ryndam,* which was to sail for New York on the twenty-second. The spy panic had now grown to such proportions that it was publicly announced that all English, French, and Russians in Germany were to be interned for the duration of the war. Some subterfuge had to be devised so that Stokowski would not be apprehended as was Gabrilowitsch.

Through one of their influential friends he was able to obtain a military pass from the war minister of Bavaria giving permission to "Mr. Stokowski and his wife of Philadelphia" to proceed to Holland without hindrance. While the document did not state that they were Americans, the phrase "of Philadelphia" and the elaborate official seal that was attached managed to turn the trick. "Personally I was intensely worried," stated Olga, "owing to the fact that my husband was an English subject, although he has no English blood."[25]

Also in Munich at this frightening time was Ruth O'Neill, who was vacationing after her busy season as secretary to Stokowski and general factotum in the Philadelphia Orchestra's office. It was her first trip to Europe. She had landed in Naples and with two girl friends traveled up Italy to Germany. They were at Lake Constance shortly before war was declared. For a while paper money was not being accepted, and she, along with many other foreigners, found herself virtually without money. It was in that state that she phoned the Stokowskis. Olga told her to come see them at once.

" 'Take the trolley car to such and such a place and then another trolley car and there is our villa.' "[26]

It was a very pleasant reunion. Ruth chatted and dined with them and returned to her hotel. Then, for some unremembered reason, she changed hotels but neglected to inform Stokowski. As the time for their departure neared, Stoki made futile attempts to find her but failed. Ruth told me, "I found a nice young man from Dallas, and we would sit in the park and

would go to beer halls and sing "Deutschland über Alles" without knowing what we were doing. So sitting in the park one day, who should come
by but Stokowski, who said, 'We have been looking all over for you.
Where have you been? We are leaving so come out with me at once.' So
I went out and I helped them pack the valuables in closets that were
obscure, and then they said, 'Do you want to come with us? We'll have
to travel third class. We will not be able to get out of the coach. It's too
dangerous.' Ludwig the butler packed enough ice water and food for us
for three days, but it was as uncomfortable a ride as you can imagine."[27]

On August 11, the very day for which their Tonhalle concert had been
scheduled, they planned instead their departure from Munich. Ludwig
begged to go with them. Olga agreed. "His missing finger made it possible
at that time, although he probably guessed that sooner or later the lame,
the halt and the blind would be pressed into service. Ludwig did not want
to fight. No German I knew personally had the slightest desire for war."[28]

With a score of Mahler's Eighth Symphony clutched under his arm,
Leopold, Olga, Ruth O'Neill, and Ludwig were squeezed into a crowded
third-class carriage at the Munich station. For the next three days they
were to stay in their same clothes. They changed cars fourteen or more
times to let various military trains go through.

After thirteen hours they finally arrived at Wurzburg, normally about
three hours away. From there they proceeded to out-of-the-way towns,
sleeping on station platforms at night, not knowing when other trains
would be available. German trains crowded with troops, horses, cannon,
boats for pontoon bridges, and confiscated automobiles covered with
inscriptions and cartoons proclaiming "To Paris and Back" kept passing
them by. Late in the afternoon they arrived at Cassel, had a warm meal
at the station for the first time in days, and waited until nearly four the
next morning for another connection. They continued to avoid towns on
the main routes and, after stopping and changing cars numerous times,
finally arrived at Altenbecken, where they had the luxury of a washroom
and could refresh themselves. As they approached the frontier with their
American flags prominently pinned on them as well as on their luggage,
they became ever more apprehensive.[29]

On Thursday evening at about seven they finally reached the town of
Rheine, but in order to make connections with a train going to Holland
they had to drive seven or more kilometers to the next station. "Finally
at about midnight," Ruth remembered, "we arrived at the Holland border, and the room we were ushered into was maybe three times the size

of this [referring to her Central Park West living room], very dark, with German officers lining the counters. They came to my luggage and went over each item. Then they went over the Stokowskis' papers and luggage, and we all got out and breathed a deep sigh and walked about ten feet into a Dutch train. But earlier they [the Stokowskis] had said, 'Here is a bag of gold pieces. Will you keep it for us?' I said, 'Yes, I'll put it right here in my bosom.' By that time we were all exhausted and we checked into a hotel, where I lay down and went to sleep. Later I was awakened by a terrific thump on the door, and it was Stokowski and the manager of the hotel. He said that they had been trying to wake me for a half an hour and they were just about to break down the door. Well, I got up hurriedly and dressed and couldn't find the gold. I had slept so restlessly that it was underneath the mattress. Finally I was able to hand it over to them."[30]

They arrived in Rotterdam on Friday, August 14, at noon and obtained passage on a Dutch ship sailing at two the next morning. "The trip through the English Channel was most interesting and we saw numberless English cruisers and torpedo boats and one of them stopped us at Dover to warn us of mines ahead," recalled Olga.[31]

At their Rotterdam lodging "there was just one bathroom," said Ruth. "We had to take turns, naturally, but between each bath, water had to be heated. Well, Olga and I went out first in a carriage and drove around Rotterdam." At dinnertime Ruth joined the Stokowskis. "I, who was brought up in a puritanical atmosphere, didn't know what I was doing when he kept pouring a sparkling burgundy into my glass. I couldn't walk out of the dining room. I was so drunk! I was sick all the next day and terribly ashamed. And Olga said, 'You shouldn't have done that, X.' Olga called him 'X' for the unknown."[32]

Stokowski was indeed fortunate in his escape from Germany. Not all British citizens made it out. Sir Ernest MacMillan, who was attending the festival in Bayreuth, was arrested and interned for the duration of the war. Ossip and Clara Gabrilowitsch were finally able to return by way of Switzerland. Fritz Kreisler was not so fortunate. He was a reserve officer in the Austrian army and, although he was in Switzerland when hostilities broke out, he hurried back to Austria to join his regiment.

On the day of the German mobilization, Efrem Zimbalist and his wife, Alma Gluck, were dining with the Paderewskis in Morges, Switzerland. When the news was heard, all of the Paderewski servants but one immediately rushed to the station to return to Germany. The Zimbalists were able to proceed on to Italy and returned to America on the *Espagne*. But hordes of the less fortunate descended on Switzerland. Many made their way to the Paderewski villa—some dear friends and others utter strangers. Among the former were Josef Hofmann and his wife; Mme. Marcella Sembrich; and the composer-pianist Sigismund Stojowski. Forty-four other refugees materialized, and tents were pitched on the villa's lawn to house them.[33]

The gravest problem in both Germany and Switzerland was the difficulty in changing money. Travelers checks, letters of credit, and, in many cases, paper money would not be accepted. Stokowski, we know, had had a cache of gold and consequently did not have that problem to wrestle with, but many of these stranded travelers were temporarily destitute. There were seemingly endless tales of the difficulties and problems that returning travelers had to tell.

Although Italy had not immediately declared her intentions, there was naturally great anxiety there. Gatti-Casazza cabled the *New York Telegraph* September 17, stating, "Should Italy become involved in the European war it would probably mean that Enrico Caruso, the noted tenor, would have to go to the front as a soldier . . . he says that although he would be exempt from service if he applied to the war office, he would join the colors when called. Italians, he says, should place patriotism above everything else."[34] Another good Italian, Arturo Toscanini, did just that. He remained in Italy for the duration of the war and did not return to America until 1921.

In the confusion during the early days of the war many travelers experienced great hardships. Nikisch, who was conducting in Belgium, immediately set out to return to Leipzig by various circuitous routes that took him over thirty-six hours. Most of the time he was without food. Pianist Frederic Lamond, who had lived in Germany for over twenty years and had a German wife, was still a British subject. When he tried to reenter Germany from Switzerland, he was not permitted to do so, although everything he owned was there.[35]

Ernestine Schumann-Heink was appearing in *Parsifal* at Bayreuth, a sentimental act she ritualistically went through each year. When the curtain went down on the first act, a German officer appeared on the stage to announce that war had been declared and that all who were eligible should report to their regiments at once. There was an immediate exodus —the audience dwindled to about two hundred people. Most of the chorus, that is, of the male contingent, as well as many members of the orchestra were liable to service, and it was all but impossible to continue the performance. Karl Muck, who was conducting it, was visibly shaken.

"Leaving Bayreuth after the festival," Schumann-Heink said, "I went to Coburg a short distance away where Mr. Pike, the American consul, was busy giving his own money to stranded Americans. Here, I sent a communication to Secretary of State William Jennings Bryan and as a result a special order for accommodations was issued for myself and son and daughter to transport us safely into Holland. . . . Everywhere the Germans were most courteous to Americans, and I cannot see how it is possible that Americans came back from there with reports of indignities heaped upon them."[36]

Pianist Edwin Hughes was in no hurry to leave. Early in September he wrote back to friends in America, "As I sit in my balcony overlooking the clear, green stream of the Isar, with the towers and red-tiled roofs of Munich stretched out before me in the peaceful late Summer sunshine, it seems impossible to realize that on the French and Russian frontiers the guns are booming and the greatest struggle in the world's history is being fought. . . ." He reported that after the first wave of panic had subsided, the "kinos," as the Germans called the movies, were all reopening, and concert life had been resumed.[37]

The Germans had very good reasons for making a good impression on Americans. They wanted to impress upon them their point of view and, at all costs, help to preserve American neutrality. German propaganda was handled most skillfully inside Germany, and it quite deeply affected many of those who had been living or visiting there.

Olga observed it sagely: "While Germany was being pictured to the world at large as an aggressor nation, bent on conquest, the war was being pictured to the German people by the government that was alone responsible for any aggressive actions, as a war of defence. Germany, surrounded by hostile nations and a faithless ally, had her back to the wall and must fight for her life! This point of view reiterated daily by the press, proclaimed on posted placards, shouted in vociferous speeches and universally believed, sent countless Germans from the most orderly, peaceful and law-abiding life one could find in any part of the world, into the most insane and savage war of all times."[38]

It was estimated that there were as many as five thousand American music students in Berlin.[39] They had converged from all over Germany. Many were in dire financial straits, since they could not exchange their traveler's checks or money orders. Descriptions of the scenes at the American embassy were heart-rending. Embassy personnel in Berlin were harried by huge numbers of Americans impatiently seeking information. Many were in a state of semipanic. One German reporter said that some Americans had told him they received more courteous treatment from German authorities than from their own embassy. In a moment of exasperation, the ambassador exploded at one anxious group, telling them that they were behaving like a pack of idiots, and that he would recall their passports if they did not stop bothering him. The German press played up several similar stories.[40]

Olga and Leopold were astounded at the anti-German feeling that they found in Holland, and even more by the hostile attitude of Americans they encountered on shipboard and on returning to New York.

Ossip and Clara Gabrilowitsch were equally disturbed at the anti-German attitudes that confronted them when they returned. Ossip, Clara said, developed a form of melancholia. "Our friends brought us no comfort, because their convictions were the opposite of ours. We always believed that the Russians started the war. And all the desire in the world could not alter this opinion. So we found ourselves strangers in my own country. Having made a few naive efforts to spread what we considered to be the truth, with no success, we withdrew to a very small group of unfortunates who believed as we did. . . . 'Well, there goes another friend!' —one of us would exclaim after an evening spent among former comrades; for we were a bit slow in learning that silence was the only possible part for us to play."[41]

Shortly before leaving Munich, Olga and Leopold had tried to persuade Mathilde to join them and Ludwig and come to Philadelphia. But three of her brothers and her sweetheart had been drafted, Olga recalled, "and she wanted to be where she could catch a glimpse of them—perhaps nurse them. As I sat with her and tried to comfort her, the hideous reality of what war does to life overcame me, and later when I was surrounded by anti-German propaganda, and by people who firmly believed that the ferocious 'huns' were joyously sharpening their weapons for the extermination of civilization, etc., visions of a blue and white kitchen, of the honest, merry people who had served me, of the peaceful joyous life of Munich and the Bavarian mountains I knew so well made it impossible for me to join in the prevailing hue and cry. These homely things were like an antidote to the poison of hatred that ran through the veins of the world."[42]

16

The New Era

A T the outbreak of the war, anxiety and apprehension ran through the boards of most American orchestras. Since they had leaned so heavily on foreign players and conductors, there was much speculation on whether many of their personnel would be detained in Europe. In Boston and in Cincinnati there was fear that their German conductors, Karl Muck and Ernst Kunwald, might not return. Muck was naturally eager to come back, for he had bought a $30,000 four-story brick house on the Fenway in sight of Mrs. Jack Gardner's famous Fenway Court, and only a short walk from Symphony Hall.

In Cincinnati, Bettie Holmes was relieved to have a cable from Dr. Kunwald saying that he would be able to leave Germany and that he was certain he could arrive on schedule. Before leaving Berlin, however, he was heard regaling a group of listeners in the Tiergarten that he regarded the movements of the seven German armies in their destructive rape of Belgium and France a "Symphony by General von Moltke." Moltke was the German chief of staff. Kunwald elaborated: "The manner in which the military operations were arranged and executed, could only be compared to the construction of one of Beethoven's splendid symphonies," and that, "aside from any patriotic feeling, it has been a purely aesthetic enjoyment to follow the development and the systematic working out of the seven themes musically speaking."[1] (One wonders whether any stomachs turned.) To be certain that his point of view would not be missed, he programmed the "Kaiser March" by Wagner, and the *Eroica* Symphony by Beethoven.

148

Muck, too, opened his season with the *Eroica,* in an all-German program including *Don Juan* of Strauss and the Brahms Variations on a Theme by Haydn.[2]

In Philadelphia the problem of finding replacements for men unable to return was Stokowski's first concern, and he began at once to audition candidates. There were four additions to the orchestra, and they were very significant ones. Roger Britt replaced violinist Otto Muller, who was fighting in the German army; Herman Basse replaced H. C. Le Barbier, principal trumpet, who was with the French forces; and cellist Hans Kindler replaced Hans Rimmer, who wrote to Stokowski, "We will die as did our fathers for God, Kaiser, and the Fatherland."[3] Anton Torello, first bassist, was engaged to replace Paul Rahmig, who was presumed stuck in Germany. Shortly thereafter Rahmig returned, so the line of basses was increased to nine. The additions of both Torello and Kindler proved important for the orchestra.

Shortly before the Philadelphia season began, a letter arrived from the Munich Konzertverein telling Stoki that every member of the orchestra and most of its directors had gone into the army. The letter expressed hope that as soon as the war was over, Stoki would agree to conduct one of their concerts in Munich.[4] The concert which was to have been conducted by Stoki in the Tonhalle in Munich on August 12 was, of course, called off at the beginning of the war.[5] But whatever momentary disappointment he may have had over the Munich cancellation he buried in his preparation for the new season.

Compared to the new music he would introduce in the years to come, the novelties of the 1914–15 season now seem conservative. Stoki scheduled four new symphonies: by Paderewski, Frederick Stock, Mrs. H. H. A. Beach, and Basil Kalinnikow. He also introduced "for the first time at these concerts" Sibelius' *Finlandia* and a Roumanian Rhapsody by Enesco. Two of his novelties were not modern works but ones that would be a new experience to the ears of Philadelphia. They were the Bach chorale "Wachet auf" (or in English "Sleepers Awake") and the "Pastorale, Shepherd's Christmas Music," from the *Christmas Oratorio.* No mention was made that the works had been transcribed by Stokowski.[6]

Ruth O'Neill, who heard these performances, told me that the audience stood up and cheered. "They had never heard Bach before except in the *Brandenburg* Concertos and then they were bored stiff. Nobody played him except maybe in church. He revived Bach; believe it or not. Now people stood up and cheered."[7]

Musicians in general seem to be a rather jealous lot. Few are generous to their colleagues, and this is particularly true of conductors. Stokowski was a rare exception. Perhaps the fact that he was having such unparalleled success and was so idolized helped to give him his supreme confidence. He was happy to perform the Symphony in C Minor of Frederick Stock and announced, "By its profundity of musical thought, its intensity of expression and its elastic and masterly treatment of the orchestra, it is a work which stands out as a remarkable creation."

As an innovation, two weeks were set aside for Pops Concerts. Stoki conducted the opening one; Thaddeus Rich and Stanley Mackey followed. The parquet was floored over and two hundred tables were set up. White-aproned waiters served lemonade and ham and cheese sandwiches, while other waiters in evening dress passed cigars. It was a new experience for Philadelphia. As one member of the audience described it, "There was a box of matches on each table, but for a long time no one lighted a cigar. Then someone struck a match when a very quiet passage had lulled the audience into tomblike silence. Everyone heard that match go off, and in a few minutes there were a hundred scratches, a hundred puffs. Waiters appeared with chocolate sundaes, the women began talking, then the popping of peanut shells added to the hubbub, and the first pop concert (no pun intended) was a success." The admission prices ran from 15 cents to 75 cents.[8]

As the season progressed Stoki continued to refine and improve the orchestra. Early in January he again took it on a tour—to Washington, Baltimore, Cleveland, Indianapolis, Buffalo, and other Midwestern cities. There were glowing reviews and the adjective *genius* became increasingly used whenever he appeared.

Life in the Stokowski household was carefully ordered. Both budgeted their time with care, and Stoki in particular exercised daily. Although they were abstemious, they were hardly spartan. He had a masseur who gave him daily rubdowns.

Olga worked persistently at the piano, appearing twice with the orchestra playing the Tchaikovsky and Beethoven concertos. She also played in chamber concerts with members of the orchestra. With concerts in cities about the country, she needed to have her household run with efficiency —Olga might have thought of it as German efficiency. And that is where the redoubtable Ludwig was to come in.

They had moved from the bleakly modest house on Locust to a far more attractive and spacious town house on Pine Street. It was a good address not far from the Academy. "Everyone who knows anything about neighborhoods in Philadelphia," said Olga, "is aware that those who would take a place in what is called society may not live north of Market Street." She considered it dangerous, socially speaking, "to live west of Twenty-third Street, and the southern border of the desirable residential zone."[9] That

Photo Haeseler, Philadelphia/
Courtesy Dr. William Fischer
Pine Street home in Philadelphia

zone was apparently bordered by the alley back of the houses that faced Pine Street.

The address of the house, 7 Pine Street, was one that she felt could adorn the most exacting visiting card. The front of the house was on Pine, but the back windows, "overlooking the significant borderline alley, were discreetly glazed so that one saw nothing of the socially nonexistent part of the city that lay beyond it."

Generations before the Equal Rights Amendment, Olga had rebelled against the German relegation of women to *"Kinder, Kirche und Küche."* She felt however that her eminently domestic ancestresses had bequeathed her a "distinct leaning towards a well ordered household, a fragrant, dainty linen closet and the like, as well as a still more pronounced aversion to dirt and disorder."

Olga sorely missed her faithful Mathilde, who remained in Munich. She consulted an agency and engaged an English cook. It was a mistake. She had not realized that the woman was deaf, but Ludwig sensed it immediately. He still could speak no English and the cook knew no German. "He laboriously looked up the words he needed in the dictionary and after he found out how deaf she was he began to shout at the top of his lungs." Ludwig apparently thought that the more he shouted the more he would be understood.

"Bridget and Ludwig each believed passionately in their particular way of carving and serving and I learned to know all the differences between Great Britain and Bavaria in such matters." The differences were obviously many. "Bridget was too deaf to hear her own alarm clock in the morning so after many vain attempts to awaken her by knocking, Ludwig adopted the simple plan of pulling her out of bed, a procedure which she bitterly resented."

The tenor of things in the kitchen remained strained. Then on the day of the first Stokowski luncheon party, a very proper social affair, Bridget decided to drown her sorrows and got roaring drunk. "Ludwig, bereft of his brass buttons and looking very mournful in conventional butler's clothes— which he always hated—whispered to me dramatically as he ushered in my guests that I had better go to the kitchen." There Olga found Bridget standing on the kitchen table brandishing a carving knife and defying all comers. When Bridget's rage subsided, Olga and Ludwig managed to subdue her and lock her in her room. Olga phoned a caterer and after an hour's delay the luncheon proceeded. Leopold as always kept calm.

Ludwig had had about enough of the scene and one day came to Olga to tell her that the females in America were too much for him. "He longed to continue to work for me, but he just could not work with them. I understood perfectly and did not try to argue with him." So they found a position for him as a doorman at a bank. "Not only did this post eliminate the women but it restored brass buttons, which I always felt were psychologically indispensable to Ludwig."[10]

Directly across from the Stokowski house on Pine Street lived the Jolines. There were three daughters, all of whom were musically inclined. The second daughter, Geordie (a Scottish nickname for Georgianna), became one of Stoki's early fans. The family regularly attended the Philadelphia Orchestra concerts. Recently I talked to Geordie, who is now Mrs. James Blauvelt, and she told me, "We had long windows in the drawing room downstairs, and my sister, who was six years younger than I, would watch Stokowski as he would leave his house to go to the Academy. We knew what a wonderful-looking Adonis we had in the new orchestral leader. We were a musical family. My older sister went twice to Paris to study piano and my father had a good voice and sang in the Orpheus Club Chorus; altogether we loved music."[11]

It was not long before Mrs. Joline, in proper Philadelphia society fashion, paid a social call on the Stokowskis, and a gradual friendship began to develop between them. Not long thereafter Geordie joined the chorus that Stokowski had organized, and still later she became private secretary and personal friend to both Olga and Leopold. Mrs. Blauvelt reminded me that that was all a very long time ago. "I was quite young when they came to Philadelphia. I'm eighty-five now so you can figure out what I was then [19 or 20]. It's too much for me."

Stoki became an American citizen in 1915. Now they could enjoy a thoroughly American summer as two through-and-through Americans. The question was, where would they spend it?

"I found them a house," said Ruth O'Neill. "Anything they asked me to do, I did. I found a house for them in Vermont."[12] It was not far from the Canadian border and very near Lake Champlain. The Stokowskis persuaded Ossip and Clara Gabrilowitsch to join them, so they, too, found a house there. It was a most relaxing summer. Stoki and Ossip played tennis regularly. A play school was organized for the Gabrilowitsches' little daughter Nina, and each member of the two families in turn assumed the role of instructor.

Stoki played a very special role. "He reincarnated as a perfect lion," recalled Clara, "and becoming roaringly intoxicated with his own power, usually ended the tempestuous scene by carrying the helpless Nina off on his back." One time they were all on a train bound for New York. Ossip and Clara stepped out onto the platform to stretch their legs while the train was standing briefly at one of the intermediate stations. They returned to find Nina "suspended by the belt of her dress from the hat rack high up in the car. She dangled swaying back and forth with a pleased expression on her face as if she quite enjoyed this latest prank of her friend the lion."[13]

Social life in upper Vermont was vastly different from that of Munich, and the Green Mountains were far less dramatic than the soaring mountains beyond the Bavarian city. There were few visitors. But one who came up that summer made a lasting impression. He was Arthur Judson.

Judson had heard that there was to be a change in the management of the Philadelphia Orchestra, and he wanted to apply for the position. Naturally they talked about their previous meetings in Cincinnati and Philadelphia, and Stoki remembered well the interviews that they had done together and the superb reviews that Judson had written. It was not exactly detrimental to Judson's present cause that he had called Stoki a genius on several previous occasions.

On this visit their roles were reversed. Previously it was Judson who had asked the questions. This time it was Stokowski, and he learned much about the six-foot-plus young giant who wanted to work with him. Judson told him that he had wanted to be a violinist—not only a violinist but a virtuoso on the instrument. That was a nice opening wedge, for Stokowski had always said that the violin was his first instrument. But Judson admitted that he was probably not cut out for the virtuoso role.[14]

Judson had arrived in New York in 1907 while Stoki was still at St. Bartholomew's. "I wake up at night," he recalled, "and my mind goes back to the time my wife and son and I came to New York to make my way and the trouble I had was nobody's business. I taught violin, conducted orchestras, and gave musical festivals throughout the country. Finally I decided it was too much. I then went on the staff of *Musical America*. I ended up by being advertising manager, which is a very lucrative job."[15]

Stoki realized that Judson was indeed a remarkable man. He was perceptive, envisioned, powerfully energetic, positive, and *mirabile dictu,* idealistic. He wanted to contribute to music, not merely take from it. And he did both.

Back in Philadelphia, Stoki said to Ruth O'Neill, "That's the man for me."[16] Judson was engaged, and a fantastic collaboration between the two began. It was particularly fortunate that Judson entered the picture at this time, for upcoming was the most important season so far, one that would bring Stokowski and the orchestra into international prominence. The year was indeed to be under the sign of "Leo."

17

The Mahler Mania

STOKOWSKI'S performance of the Eighth Symphony of Mahler was such an exciting and dramatic affair that it made news throughout the country. Not since the days of that great showman Phineas T. Barnum had there been anything like it. Newspapers gave the performance a fantastic amount of space, and local scribes assured Philadelphians that it was a great honor to have the American premiere given by their orchestra.

Mahler himself had conducted the first performance in Munich on September 12, 1910. Both Leopold and Olga had been present. During rehearsals, Stoki recalled, Mahler was "changing and changing; he practically composed it, or recomposed it, in the rehearsals, much to the annoyance of the players in the orchestra. He would stop them and take the part and write it another way and rehearse them in the new way. They didn't like that very much but the results were inspired, and in my opinion it is one of the greatest compositions of the twentieth century."[1]

The symphony's world premiere was promoted and produced by the intrepid organizer Emil Gutmann—the same Gutmann who had presented Olga and Stoki in their Paris concert. He had a flair for publicity —it was he who thought up the name *Symphony of a Thousand*, which piqued the curiosity and interest of the Müncheners as they read the announcements plastered on walls and kiosks all over town. Gutmann promoted the work so noisily, that Mahler himself referred to it as his "Barnum and Bailey performance."[2]

Barnum had his Tom Thumb, Jenny Lind, and "The Greatest Show

156

on Earth." But Judson had Stokowski and the Philadelphia Orchestra, and he knew how to sell his wares fully as well as Barnum or Gutmann—and with a touch of class.

Shocked when Stoki first presented the idea of performing the Mahler symphony, the Philadelphia board finally agreed to it, for Stoki was remarkably persuasive. They appropriated $14,000 for the extra performers he would need. The total number of performers to be used was enough to shock any board—two choruses of 400 each, a children's chorus of 150 (Mahler had used 300), eight soloists, and an augmented orchestra of 110 players. Platforms would have to be built to extend from the Academy stage practically up to the ceiling, and an apron would have to be built extending into the hall to accommodate the additional players. Work on the stage alterations was begun during the summer of 1915. It required a force of men six weeks at a cost of $3,000. The backdrop of the stage concealed the new construction from audiences of early season concerts, and the platform extension was actually not completed until the last minute, so that the full impact of the massed aggregation would not be lost when the actual performance took place.[3]

In the office much of the publicity was handled by Ruth O'Neill, and she did it most skillfully.

"Stokowski's sense of organization was terrific," said Ruth. "He rehearsed four hundred of the thousand singers every week at the Curtis Publishing Company. My sister sang with them—I made her do it. Henry Gordon Thunder, an organist and a good musician, rehearsed the other four hundred; then they would take turns going from one choir to another and in rehearsing the boys. One day Judson said to me, 'My God, Ruth, where are they going to put their clothes—a thousand people in the back of the Academy of Music. I'll have to get coat racks right away.' He did and everything went off smoothly."[4]

Popular interest was so intense that many offered as much as $100 a seat to ticket scalpers. Before the Academy doors were thrown open, there was a long line of lucky holders of general admission tickets who had stood in Locust Street or sat on newspapers spread on the Academy steps for hours. At least one hundred persons were waiting by 3:30 in the afternoon, braving the drizzle for a chance at a good seat.

From seven until eight o'clock, on March 2, 1916, there was a steady stream of automobiles stopping at the Academy doors. All society and all musical Philadelphia streamed into the building. The one thousand chorus members, like sand pouring through the narrow neck of an hourglass, were marshaled through the stage door without a hitch.

Stokowski, the soloists, the chorus, and the orchestra all radiated an intensity that swept through the audience. It reacted explosively. The noise of the applause was so great that the Academy doormen said it could be heard across Broad Street in the foyer of the Walton Hotel. Herbert Kupferberg observed that the *North American* gave more space to the Mahler affair than it did to its coverage of the Battle of Verdun, then raging in France.[5] The *Philadelphia Public Ledger* reported in its extensive review: "Every one of the thousands in the great building was standing whistling, cheering and applauding, when Leopold Stokowski, his collar wilted, and his right arm weary, but smiling his boyish smile, finally turned to the audience in the Academy of Music last night.

"He had scored, so famous musicians agreed, the greatest triumph of his career, the greatest triumph the Philadelphia Orchestra has known in its sixteen years of life and he had done it on a stupendous scale. . . .

"For every one who is any one in musical America was here for the Mahler American premiere last night or will be here when the tremendous work is repeated this afternoon and tomorrow night. The boxes were filled with famous musicians and musical authorities. One and all stood, applauding Mr. Stokowski and the symphony, while the orchestra members blared a 'touche' in honor of their leader.

". . . Fifteen minutes before Mr. Stokowski swung his baton upon his augmented orchestra and upon the chorus, banked 24 tiers high, horns blew a fanfare in the foyer of the Academy of Music, following an ancient custom of Bayreuth. The curtain rose and the audience gasped. The 958 singers filled the great stage from footlights to roof and the orchestra was upon an apron that had been built out into the house. The first twelve rows of singers were women, dressed in white. Above them were twelve rows of men, with a gardenia-like spot of girls, members of the children's chorus, pinned, it seemed in their midst."[6]

Alexander Van Rensselaer presented a wreath "To Leopold Stokowski" and remarked that the evening "marks an epoch in the musical history of Philadelphia to which no other event is comparable."[7]

There was such a demand for tickets that additional personnel had to be engaged to handle the requests. "Philadelphia has gone music mad," Arthur Judson remarked. "There is as much enthusiasm over this work, it seems to me, as one might expect over a championship baseball series. . . . If I had been told that Philadelphia, New York, or Boston would manifest such enthusiasm over any matter of music or art, as I have witnessed in the last three days, I would have laughed."[8] Judson was understandably well pleased, for fifteen hundred disappointed hopefuls were turned down for the last performance, and a total of twenty-five thousand persons in Philadelphia and New York had been "Mahlerized."

"Lots of things happened in putting on a thing of this size," Judson recalled. "We had two hundred choirboys in the back and one night during a muted string part, one boy got up and socked another choirboy square in the eye."[9] Ruth O'Neill did not remember the episode of the angelic little choristers, but she remarked that "after the success of the Mahler symphony, the board of the orchestra presented A. J. [Judson] with a beautiful clock to show their recognition of his role in putting on and managing such a tremendous show."[10]

Mahler's *Symphony of a Thousand*, the Academy of Music, Philadelphia, March 2, 1916

The logistics of bringing the whole, huge aggregation to New York were stupendous. Judson managed it all with enormous skill. At noon on April 9, two private trains totaling eighteen cars transported the twelve hundred people involved in the concert. Accommodations were made available at the McAlpin Hotel, so that they could dress and dine before going to the Metropolitan Opera House several blocks north on Broadway.

The scene in New York was identical to that in Philadelphia. Scalpers were hawking tickets for outrageous prices. Traffic jammed Broadway and musical New York turned out in force. Celebrities jostled for their seats: Paderewski, Pablo Casals, Alma Gluck, Efrem Zimbalist, Henry Hadley,

Courtesy Philadelphia Orchestra Association

Mahler Eighth soloists with Stokowski and Alexander Van Rensselaer, president of the Philadelphia Orchestra Association. Left to right: Margaret Keyes, Susanna Dercum, Inez Barbour, Clarence Whitehill, Stokowski, Van Rensselaer, Florence Hinkle, Reinald Werrenrath, Adelaide Fischer, Lambert Murphy

Ossip Gabrilowitsch, Rubin Goldmark, Harold Bauer, the composer George Chadwick, Mischa Elman, Ernst Kunwald, Arthur Foote, Percy Grainger, Alfred Hertz, Daniel Gregory Mason, Ernest Schelling, Marcella Sembrich, Antonio Scotti, Mme. Schumann-Heink, and countless others.[11] It proved to be one of the greatest musical and social events of the season.

When the great gold curtain of the Met rose revealing the huge performing apparatus there was an audible gasp and then spontaneous applause. Frances Wister, who came along from Philadelphia, remarked that at the end "the audience let itself go in a way never seen in Philadelphia."[12]

After the performances critic W. J. Henderson offered some sage advice to the Philadelphians. "If Philadelphia believes that Mr. Stokowski is essential to her musical development, let her decline to permit him to conduct great concerts in New York. This is a piece of perfectly disinterested advice. The *Sun's* musical chronicler would be delighted to see Mr. Stokowski a New York conductor. He has personality, force, temperament, scholarship and imagination. His conducting of the Mahler symphony was masterly. He would be a valuable factor in the musical life in New York."[13]

Nine performances of the symphony were given in Philadelphia and one in New York; more could have been given to sold-out houses. As a gesture of gratitude not only to Stokowski and the orchestra, but to the choruses and the soloists, in fact to all who had participated, Van Rensselaer hosted a buffet dinner in Horticultural Hall. About twelve hundred guests attended. Following dinner a "Mahler-ia" concert was presented, which included Mozart's "Ein Musikalischer Spass," a "Concerto Brosso (1916) Composer unknown," and a tone poem, *Tausend Kunstler,* by Schreiner (1850–1916), conducted by "actor-conductor" Thaddeus Rich, who was listed as "Riddeus Thatch." It was performed by Oscar Schwar, timpanist, who for the occasion had his name changed to Schwer, which in German means difficult. He performed as a one-man band. "Mr. Schwer will depict thunder claps, echoes, bombardments, combats, cavalry charges, charge accounts, railroad wrecks, and many other scenic effects while performing this work."[14]

From Boston Gilbert Seldes wrote of Stoki and the Mahler performance with an expansive overview: "In the same season he produced Dr. Mason's *Symphony,* played Schoenberg's *Chamber Symphony* and Skriabin's *Divine Poem,* d'Indy's *Istar* and if memory does not fail, Stra-

Studio photograph by N. Coulbourse Brown (1916)

vinsky's *Fireworks*, all new to the orchestra. During the same season he began a fresh series of concerts, took his orchestra on an extended tour through the West, made a special trip to New York for Mahler, and had the satisfaction of knowing that artistically his work was measurably finer than it had been a year before. The difficulties of the choral symphony kept him for a half year tormented, so that it was common talk that he must collapse before the first performance. For a reply he added a series of Sunday concerts."[15]

Seldes was a very perceptive reviewer and had attended some of the rehearsals for the Mahler, which had been scheduled through late fall of 1915. "Those who saw him during the rehearsals of Mahler's symphony last year," he wrote, "know how painstakingly he had gone over the score, how minutely he knew every bar of it." Seldes also made some trenchant observations on Philadelphia and the love relationship between Stoki and the city: "Mr. Stokowski has found himself, within the past two years, in a strange community. Philadelphia was undergoing one of those conscientious crises which affect American cities. It discovered its soul and its subways and was mightily displeased with both. It turned out a reform administration and sent a line longer than a world-series column to buy tickets for Mahler's symphony. . . . The spectacle was arousing and necessarily the orchestra . . . reaped the benefit. . . . The day of Mahler's symphony was, if one cared for that sort of thing, the greatest day of the Philadelphia Orchestra and of its conductor. . . . The circus, the thousand voices, the seventeen part contrapuntal writing, the difficulties of acoustics, the length of the two parts, the musical detail to be mastered, made it a 'stunt.' It could have been all gesture. And yet in the heroic labor of the performance, Mr. Stokowski abandoned the florid phrase. Actually out of the unachieved work of Mahler he brought something perfect, the submission of self. Even the familiar tricks were gone, there was some restraining of the free-flowing motions which habitually he uses in direction. There was no 'pointing' of the musical emphasis, there was control. It was considered a triumph for Mr. Stokowski, but the triumph came before his baton was raised."[16]

Arthur Judson had met Mahler when he first arrived. "He was a queer person. I remember when he came to New York. He was not interested in music. He wanted to walk and look around. He wanted to see the subway. He had a very curious and seeking mind." Ruth O'Neill asked Judson about the hard times that Mahler had had in New York. "Yes," Judson replied, "because he wanted to play what he wanted and the ladies of the Philharmonic Society had other ideas." He recalled that the Eighth Symphony was always referred to as the *Symphony of a Thousand*, but never as the "Great" Mahler symphony "because the music was not great."[17]

Mahler had come to New York in 1907 to conduct at the Met, and it was there that the young organist Stokowski first heard and admired him. (He conducted operas of Wagner and Mozart.) In 1909, just as Stoki was beginning his Cincinnati career, Mahler took over the New York Philharmonic. He immediately began to make changes and improvements in the orchestra. But the Philharmonic, which has been referred to as a "graveyard" for conductors, was to be literally that for Mahler. He was then forty-nine years old. Two years later he would be dead. However, he tackled his chore with a vengeance. He greatly increased the number of Philharmonic concerts. In 1909 they gave eighteen, the following year forty-six, and by the 1910–11 season the number had been increased to sixty-five. But critics observed that his audiences were pitifully small.[18] Mahler also instituted tours. He brought the orchestra to Philadelphia and later on to New England—New Haven, Springfield, Providence, and Boston.

Olga Samaroff made her first appearance with Mahler in New Haven. She had met Mahler beforehand at a dinner party given by the Steinways. Mahler had a reputation for being "irascible and difficult, but he was a great man," Olga observed. Mrs. Steinway, hoping to keep dinner spirits alive and pleasant, seated Mahler next to Olga and told her that she should not expect him to talk during dinner. She even made a five-dollar wager with Olga that she could not involve him in conversation. It was a wager the resourceful Olga won.

Before dinner she had observed that the taciturn Mahler, ignoring the other guests, had taken a copy of *The Brothers Karamazov* from the bookshelves and was perusing it rather intently. When she made her first attempt at conversation, she got from Mahler nothing more than a non-committal "Ja." Then she hit upon a clever ploy. She asked him if he didn't think the Dostoevski was a much overrated book. Mahler jumped to its defense, and for the rest of the evening they pursued a lively conversation about the worth of the opus. Olga had triumphed, and the Steinways gave her six new dollar bills—one extra for good measure.[19]

Olga spoke of their concert in New Haven: "By that time he and I had become good friends, and I had conceived a great liking for his lovely wife who was one of the most beautiful women I have ever seen." Mahler seemed pleased with Olga's performance and suggested that she and Maria Dehon, who had accompanied her to New Haven, dine with him after the concert. But he hadn't reckoned on New Haven. Miss Dehon, fearing that the conversation would be all in German, preferred to return to the hotel suite she and Olga were sharing.

Olga and Mahler set out to find a restaurant, but they could find nothing at that close-to-midnight hour. Knowing it was a university town, Mahler presumed that it would have its share of taverns like the *Bier Stuben* in Heidelburg, with students clanking steins and singing rousing songs. *"Was für eine Stadt!"* he grumbled. The *Gemütlichkeit* he relished in the student quarters of Munich and Vienna was woefully lacking in the chilly New England air. They returned to the hotel and tried to order something there, only to be told that the kitchen was closed and that nothing could be served. Olga then remembered that Miss Dehon always had crackers and other small snacks and milk in case they might become hungry, and that proved to be the dinner the trio had that evening in New Haven. Mahler relaxed, and the conversation went on into the early morning hours. His taciturnity, Olga recalled, "was reserved for strangers and social functions. When he was at his ease with friends he was a brilliant conversationalist with a somewhat mordant wit."

Mahler enjoyed talking with Maria Dehon. Later when he was bedridden in New York's Netherland Hotel, it was Miss Dehon who came to his rescue. He disliked the hotel food—his wife, Alma, told Olga on the occasion of one of Mme. Samaroff's visits that she could not induce him to eat. Olga repeated the story to Miss Dehon, who had her excellent Swedish cook prepare appealing viands for him. "I frequently acted as messenger and brought him these things," Olga said. "They helped to sustain him until he left for Europe, where death overtook him."[20]

Mahler's brief career in New York had been a most unhappy one. He had had difficulties with the orchestra; difficulties with the orchestra's board, which appointed a committee of "four women and two professionals" to oversee the content of his programs; difficulties with the critics, particularly with Henry Krehbiel, who obviously hated him; and difficulties with his audiences. "Finally there was about Mahler's music making an atmosphere and a spirit of almost religious fanaticism; and some of the public were simply not in the same church." So wrote Howard Shanet in his *History of the Philharmonic.*

Krehbiel, in addition to his duties on the *New York Herald*, also wrote the program notes for the Philharmonic concerts. After some scathing reviews of Mahler's own works, Mahler forbade him to write anything about his music in the program notes. That didn't help either. At Mahler's death, when most critics were writing paeans and praises for a departed colleague, Krehbiel chose to write a long and biting denunciation of him. It incensed many of Mahler's admirers, particularly Ossip Gabrilowitsch, who wrote a lengthy open letter to Krehbiel, which was printed in numerous papers across the country and elicited comments pro and con.[21] Stokowski preferred to stay out of the controversy—he paid tribute to Mahler, whom he sincerely admired, by playing his works. He had already expressed his intention of following the Eighth Symphony with the American premiere of *Das Lied von der Erde.*

Immediately after the Mahler affair Stokowski presented two new contemporary works: the Intermezzo and Epilogue from *Goyescas* by Granados. The opera had been presented by the Met in New York on June 28, 1916, in its "world premiere." Granados and his wife had been present, and he had been given an ovation. Parts of the opera were quite familiar, since pianists frequently played the piano pieces upon which the opera was constructed. There was much interest and publicity about the performances at the Met, but very little when the two quite brief miniatures were done in Philadelphia. And no wonder! After the whole Mahler explosion, the audiences and scribes needed time to recover.

There is no record of Granados coming to Philadelphia to hear his works, but he did go to Washington at the invitation of President Wilson to play at the White House. He considered it such a singular honor that he canceled his reservation on the ship on which he was to have sailed directly to Spain and rebooked on the *Sussex.* That ship, tragically, was torpedoed in the English Channel by a German submarine on March 24. Granados and his wife were among those who perished. One possibly apocryphal story has it that Granados, knowing the great difficulty in exchanging paper money in Europe with the war going on, had demanded that he be paid all of his royalties in gold, which he had strapped on him in a money belt. *Sic transit* Granados.

18

After Mahler

B Y this time everyone in Philadelphia and beyond was keenly aware
of Stokowski and the Philadelphia Orchestra. Few other musical
organizations had ever achieved so much publicity and attention.
People who had never even thought about symphonic music were now
aware of it, and the city fathers beamed with pride when they contemplated their precious possession. The Philadelphia Chamber of Commerce in 1917 put out a pamphlet entitled *The Commercial Value of
Music to Philadelphia.* That meant Stoki and the orchestra. The Philadelphia Orchestra was a "commercial asset to the city, rendering it thereby
more attractive to visitors, a better home for its citizens and of greater
value to the nation."[1]

The orchestra was now a major enterprise, but it was still not self-
sustaining. Its deficits were met by a guarantee fund that had to be
replenished annually. The board and Arthur Judson were hell-bent on
obtaining funds as amply and as quickly as possible. They launched a
vigorous campaign to build up financial reserves.

Now a mystery figure came upon the scene who was to become known
to patrons and press as the "Unknown Donor." "A friend of the Philadelphia Orchestra Association, who desires to remain unknown, has offered
to meet any deficit of the orchestra for each of five years, beginning with
the season of 1916–1917." There were three conditions to be fulfilled
before the gift became available. First, the Orchestra Association was to
create an endowment fund of $100,000 yearly for five years. Second, the
contract of Stokowski was to be extended to cover this five-year period.

Finally: "It is earnestly desired that each friend . . . will pledge a generous amount to create this Endowment Fund. Heretofore, all subscriptions to the Philadelphia Orchestra have been spent year by year, to meet the annual deficit. Under this offer the money now contributed will not be so spent but will be invested to insure the permanency of the Orchestra as an institution of Philadelphia."[2] The terms were announced in a notice signed by the Endowment Committee: Alexander Van Rensselaer, Frances Wister, and Edward W. Bok.

The five-year plan the committee had helped to devise was realized; the amount required was raised. From a five-year plan, the committee turned to a seven-year plan, and the result was an accumulated fund of nearly $800,000, which was to grow and multiply until the crash of 1929 and the depression that followed. It was not until 1921 that the identity of the mysterious donor was made known. He was none other than Edward Bok, and by then he had covered deficits of at least $250,000.[3]

The Boks greatly admired Stoki, and an abiding friendship grew up between them. Edward Bok spearheaded a further campaign in 1919 to raise an additional $1,000,000 to celebrate the twentieth anniversary of the orchestra. Great banners were spread across the streets proclaiming "Save the Orchestra." Activity was intense, and Stoki himself made persuasive appeals for contributions. The campaign was a decided success, and the Philadelphia Orchestra became one of the most financially secure orchestras in the country.[4]

Alexander Van Rensselaer had invited Bok to join the board of the orchestra in 1913 shortly after his "conversion" to music. Bok lamented that music had played no part in his early years, but he determined that he would try to provide others what he had lacked. As editor of the *Ladies Home Journal* he published bits of music: Sousa marches, salon pieces by Sullivan, de Koven, Paderewski, Tosti, and others, and even songs by Richard Strauss. He persuaded Josef Hofmann to write a series of piano lessons, and finally engaged him as a regular contributor.[5]

Bok was industrious, frugal, idealistic, and enormously competent. In his autobiographical *The Americanization of Edward Bok* he describes his rise from paperboy to publishing tycoon with a pen dipped in tincture of Horatio Alger. Bok worked for Cyrus Curtis, whose career was also one of rags to riches. Curtis married a Boston girl who had once been secretary to Julia Ward Howe. It was she, using her maiden name Louisa Knapp, who edited the *Journal* from its inception in 1883 until 1889, when she engaged Edward Bok to become its editor. Circulation at the time was

440,000 copies per month. In a short time, Bok married the boss's daughter, Mary Louise Curtis.

Bok's wife tried to interest him in music and occasionally managed to drag him to an opera. Writing of himself in the third person, Bok recalled that "the Philadelphia Orchestra gave a symphony concert each Saturday evening and Bok dreaded the coming of that evening in each week for fear of being taken to hear music which he was convinced was 'over his head.' "6 Bok thought of music as being something feminine. He avoided any contact with the orchestra. But it was Josef Hofmann who changed his mind and gave him an entirely new point of view. Stokowski was finally invited to the Bok home, and the barrier between Bok and the symphony was almost instantly dissipated. Bok attended one of the concerts when Hofmann was soloist: "The symphony, Dvořák's *New World Symphony* amazed Bok by its beauty; he was more astonished that he could so easily grasp any music in symphonic form. He was equally surprised at the simple beauty of the other numbers on the programme. . . . After a busy week," he reported, still in the third person, "he discovered that nothing he had ever experienced served to quiet him so much as those end-of-the-week concerts."7

Hofmann told Bok that Stokowski was a prince of conductors, and that was the start of their friendship. "So, Bok fell in love with Stokowski," said Ruth O'Neill, "and he called him Prince. He said, 'There's nothing you want that I will not get for you.' And from that time onward he never wanted. Stoki was naturally arrogant, although in my early days he was a sweet man."8

Not all were sympathetic toward Bok. Some found him very self-righteous. "I loved Mr. Van and I disliked Edward Bok," said Arthur Judson. "There was something about him that didn't ring true. . . . Mr. Van didn't like him either. Cyrus Curtis was a very canny Yankee, but broad-minded and good."9

But the Boks and Stokowski became inseparable. In 1921, Bok established an award consisting of $10,000 and a medal to be given each year to the man or woman living in Philadelphia who performed an act or contributed a service calculated to advance the best and largest interests of the community. The first award went to Leopold Stokowski.10

As part of the war effort Olga and Leopold manned a booth for the sale of Liberty bonds in Chestnut Street and in two Saturday mornings sold over $114,000 worth.11 Stoki offered his services for a series of concerts for the Red Cross, and in January 1918 Edward Bok and Mr. Van joined him on a trip to Camp Dix, where he conducted the orchestra for an audience of three thousand khaki-clad soldiers.[12]

Together, Stoki and Bok made another patriotic if futile gesture. "Both men disapproved of 'The Star-Spangled Banner' as the national anthem," Mrs. Curtis Bok told me. "They decided to try to get a better one, but they never quite succeeded. It was 'My Own United States.' Stokowski wrote the music and Edward Bok wrote the words. But they didn't win."[13]

Edward Bok did indeed write the words, but the music was from a national song of the Transvaal Republic in South Africa. It may have been of Dutch origin, and that could have been how Bok knew it.[14] Stoki harmonized the melody and orchestrated it. It was introduced at a concert connected with the Philadelphia Forum. Stoki played through the melody, and then the chorus came in, followed by the audience, which had been given copies of the text. When it was over, Stoki pointed to the box where Edward Bok was sitting and the papers reported that he was given an ovation. Theodore Presser published the anthem in 1924, but the country still continued to sing "The Star Spangled Banner."[15]

During the summer of 1919, Judson announced that a salary increase of $30,000 was to be prorated to the members of the orchestra. Stoki's status was also appreciably improved. "I do not care to disclose the exact amount of Mr. Stokowski's salary," Judson stated. "I can only say that it has been considerably increased in order to make it commensurate with his ability and distinction as a conductor of the orchestra."[16]

There was also a new four-year contract. Stoki expressed his appreciation publicly, saying that he was happy with the "beautiful and sensitive instrument to play upon, so that the sublime messages which seem to come from another world and were carried here by the great masters, may be revitalized and adequately presented." He also praised the warm-hearted relations he had struck up with the people of Philadelphia. "Not only from my friends, but also in the streets, on trains, in shops and by letters, strangers almost daily speak to me of their joy in music and of their satisfaction in our concerts." He was not aloof and reveled in the adulation.[17]

During the summer of 1919 the Stokowskis moved to the Philadelphia suburb of Merion. The move, hardly an ideal one, had some compensations. "While living in the old house," said Judson, "Stokowski would often say to me: 'Things are terrible. I am trying to memorize a Tchaikovsky symphony, and what I really do memorize is a Beethoven sonata or a Rachmaninoff prelude which my wife is practicing in the next room.' "18

The new house they rented on Mermaid Lane was larger and had two wings, one for Stokowski and one for Samaroff. Judson saw to it that all of their furniture and belongings were moved while Stoki and Olga were enjoying the clean, cold, clear air of Maine. They were happily vacationing in Seal Harbor.

19

Seal Harbor

M T. Desert Island is a forty-square-mile, rocky island off the coast of Maine. It has numerous granite peaks with bald summits, and the highest mountain on the east coast, Mount Cadillac. The island's great cliffs, eroded by the tides and waves, rise vertically from the sea. Much of it is covered by forests and in the summer it is bathed by clear ocean air and sea breezes.

On Mt. Desert Island are two resort towns: Bar Harbor, which in those years contained vast estates of some of America's great tycoons; and neighboring Seal Harbor, which hosted somewhat more modest habitations, where a most extraordinary collection of musicians congregated during the war summers.

The famous summer residents included: Stokowski, Gabrilowitsch, Carl Friedberg, Carlos Salzedo, Karl Muck, Fritz Kreisler, Leopold Godowsky, Hans Kindler, and Harold Bauer—and all of their respective wives. In nearby Bar Harbor the Frank and Walter Damrosches and the Ernest Schellings had their homes. Then there were countless visitors, among whom were Margarete Matzenauer and Nijinsky.

Summer was for most a time for study and practice, as well as a time for rest and rejuvenation. As many as fifty grand pianos were shipped to the island each summer. The Gabrilowitsches alone had three.[1] Ossip and Olga frequently accompanied one another, playing the solo and orchestral parts of various piano concertos. Finding an edition of Rossini's *La Gazza Ladra* arranged for six hands, Ossip assembled an unusual pianistic trio:

Clara playing the bass part, Olga the treble, and Stokowski sandwiched in between. Ossip conducted.[2]

Acadia National Park, which comprises much of the island, is famous for the remarkable number of wild plants and flowers that flourish there. In the early part of summer there are wonderful drifts of lupine. Leopold and Olga took long walks along the rocky coast and into the forests. So too did Clara and Ossip, and frequently after such jaunts the two couples would meet in a little restaurant on Jordan Pond. The menu offered "lobster, chicken, popovers and chocolate ice cream," Clara recalled.

Courtesy Gregor Benko

Mary Bok's fortieth birthday party, August 6, 1916, Camden, Maine. Edward Bok is costumed as "Mary's Little Lamb." In the back row are Stokowski, Josef Hofmann, Curtis Bok. Olga Samaroff is third from right.

The artists summering at Seal Harbor all cultivated an air of glamor and otherworldliness during the concert season, but in the Maine isolation they were dependent on their own resources. They had to provide their own entertainment. There was no opera, no regal splendor to watch, nor any of the diverting spectacles that had accompanied vacation life in Munich and other European watering holes. Their homespun entertainments took on the element of a curious folk art. They played charades, had numerous fancy dress parties, and invented series of pranks to play on one another. The parties of the Damrosches in Bar Harbor were some of the most elaborate.

Olga summarized the activities. "The Seal Harbor musical colony was more addicted to picnics, mountain climbs and occasional impromptu fancy dress parties, at which we wore improvised homemade costumes, than to formal affairs."[3] At one fancy dress affair Olga devised a costume that would do any Brunhilde proud. It was made of kitchen utensils with a wash-boiler lid as a shield, a pudding mold as a helmet, and a broom with a carving knife attached as a spear.

To celebrate the birthday of Mary Louise Curtis Bok on August 6, 1916, Leopold, Olga, Josef Hofmann, and others got themselves decked out in outlandish costumes. Edward Bok was dressed as Mary's Little Lamb. Olga appeared in a pair of Leopold's knickers and a Bavarian jacket; Leopold came out in white dress, floppy white hat, and long curls à la Mary Pickford; and Josef Hofmann attired himself in a little velvet suit, looking like a cross between Little Lord Fauntleroy and Little Boy Blue.

Early in the summer Ossip stunned his household by arriving home one afternoon with his head shaved and gleaming. No sooner had the initial shock worn off when they were greeted by Stokowski, who tossed his hat in the air to reveal another shorn pate. Then a third arrived, a newly bald Harold Bauer. Like three glabrous satyrs they joined hands and executed a ring dance that Clara described as "a wild dance of exultation." No amount of persuasion, however, could induce the onlooking Kreisler, Hofmann, and Friedberg to follow their example.[4]

During the summer of 1917 America was losing its serenity. The country was at war; the first American forces arrived in France late in June. War hysteria began to mount, reminding Stoki and Olga of their last days in Munich. One manifestation was a repugnance against all things German, even German nomenclature. Sauerkraut, for example, was renamed "liberty cabbage." Some zealots insisted that German music be banned. Naturally that was very troublesome for Stokowski and the other conductors and performers preparing their programs during the Seal Harbor summers. Some people had walked out of the Academy of Music when

Portrait drawing by Leopold Seyffert (1916)

Beethoven or Wagner was played.[5] In New York, the Met banned all German opera.

The matter was disputed hotly in music magazines and in the general press. Some aspects of the controversy took on rather nasty overtones. Artists were booed or boycotted if German music was played. But German music—and that obviously included Austrian music as well—constituted the bulk of the repertory of all of the orchestras and classical music soloists. Stokowski lectured his audiences and pointed out the absurdity of such jingoistic attitudes. Gabrilowitsch wrote letters to the newspapers, protesting them as well.[6]

Finally, as the anti-German hysteria became increasingly serious, Olga and Clara thought up a strategy they believed would be effective. Olga, who, as Ruth O'Neill had often reiterated, "knew everybody worth knowing," knew Colonel House, who was then entertaining President Wilson in his home in Manchester, a beautiful seacoast town north of Boston. The two wives paid a visit to the Houses. So persuasive was Olga in explaining the problem of making up concert programs that she completely convinced the President and returned home armed with his official verdict—it was not necessary to extend current warfare to composers long dead, nor to deprive audiences of hearing great music because of conflict with the country of its origin. The visit was a triumph.[7] Wilson subsequently made his opinions known through the press, and that bit of wartime idiocy abated.

There was growing concern about the possibility of orchestra performers being drafted. In Philadelphia the orchestra proudly expressed its patriotism. Stoki had made a rousing orchestration of "The Star Spangled Banner" and had it played at the beginning of each concert. In December 1917 the Women's Committee, led by the indomitable Frances Wister, presented a flag to Stokowski—"In order to express our loyalty to our country's cause and to the Association which we have fostered so long, and to testify to our belief in the necessity for music as a mighty inspiration, a profound solace during times of stress. . . ."[8]

The patriotic ambience in Boston was more muted. When the season opened in 1917, there were some derogatory remarks made because the American flag was not displayed. Major Henry Lee Higginson, the principal supporter of the Boston Symphony, admitted that this was an oversight. But it was Higginson who felt that "The Star Spangled Banner" had no place on a symphonic concert. He had discussed it with Karl Muck. "What will they say of me at home?" Muck asked when Higginson brought up the matter.[9] Muck was still a protégé of the Kaiser, on loan to Boston.

When on October 30, 1917, the Boston Symphony Orchestra played in Providence, there was a demand that the national anthem be performed. "The Star Spangled Banner" was not yet officially the national anthem, but Higginson objected on esthetic grounds. He should not have, considering the climate of the times. Muck was apparently not aware of the request; the anthem was not performed. All hell broke loose. The situation boiled over into a national scandal. Muck submitted his resignation; Higginson announced that Muck would conduct "The Star Spangled Banner" at the start of each concert for the rest of the season.[10]

During the summer of 1918 Muck was stalked by his Seal Harbor neighbors. He was accused of being a spy. He was caught in a patriotic dilemma. Although he was technically a Swiss citizen, he was considered to be wholly German. While both Olga and Stoki maintained a pleasant relationship with Muck, and Olga continued to play with the Boston orchestra, she remarked that "Muck seems to be filled with contempt for the human race and assumes people are fools unless shown proof to the contrary." And she asked rhetorically "whether such an attitude is born or made?"[11]

Muck was arrested on March 25, 1918, by an overzealous pair of United States marshals who were intent upon seizing him on the stage of Symphony Hall during a Friday afternoon performance of Bach's *St. Matthew Passion*. They were persuaded to wait until the end of the concert but refused to permit him to conduct the performance on the following night.[12]

Muck was interned in Camp Oglethorpe, Georgia, for the next eighteen months of the war, along with his colleague Dr. Ernst Kunwald. There was considerable sympathy for Muck until late in 1919 when the attorney general revealed a set of confidential letters Muck had written to a twenty-year-old debutante. "I am on my way to the concert hall to entertain the crowds of dogs and swine who think that because they pay the entrance fee they have the right to dictate to me my selections," wrote Muck. "I hate to play for this rabble . . . in a very short time our gracious Kaiser will smile upon my request and recall me to Berlin. . . . Our Kaiser will be prevailed upon to see the benefit to the Fatherland of my obtaining a divorce and making you my own."[13]

Coincidentally with the removal of Muck, Major Higginson, who had supported the Boston Symphony single-handedly for several decades, resigned, as did its manager, Charles Ellis. Both Stoki and Olga were

At Seal Harbor, Maine (c. 1917). Standing left to right: Stokowski, Josef Hofmann, Clara Clemens Gabrilowitsch, Olga Samaroff, Ossip Gabrilowitsch. Seated left to right: Dane Rudhyar, Greta Torpadie, Hans Kindler (front), Josefa (back), Nina Gabrilowitsch (front), Marie Eustis (back), Harold Bauer (front), Marie Bauer (back)

distressed at what seemed to be the end of the Boston Symphony Orchestra, but Stoki deeply appreciated his own stable situation and the devotion of the Boks and the indomitable Mr. Van. He continued to preface his concerts with "The Star Spangled Banner," and flags standing like sentries flanked the proscenium of the Academy of Music all through the war.

Much of the summer of 1918 was given over to the rehearsal of the Bach Concerto for Three Pianos. Olga, Bauer, and Gabrilowitsch were the three pianists, with Stoki playing orchestral accompaniment on a fourth piano.[14] They spent many hours practicing and perfecting their ensemble. It was certainly not the once-over-lightly treatment that such combinations are often given. The results justified their diligence. They created a mild sensation when they appeared—not only with the Philadelphia Orchestra during its regular concerts, but also on its tour. Later they appeared together again to celebrate the opening of a new hall for the Detroit Symphony with Gabrilowitsch conducting. It had been a productive summer.

With the ending of the war and the opportunity to travel again in Europe, Seal Harbor's brief time of musical glory all but ended. It had been a beautiful interlude.

20

"X" for the Unknown; "Mad" for Madame

S HORTLY after their marriage in 1911, Olga announced that she would give up her career as pianist and devote her time to being the wife of a conductor. But in 1913 she was lured back as a performer once more by Arthur Judson. The following year she appeared with the Philadelphia Orchestra, and she continued to do so during the succeeding seasons. She appeared as soloist with the orchestra every year from 1914 to 1922 and again in 1925. Judson became her manager and arranged for appearances in other cities as well, both with orchestra and in solo recitals.

"Even though I thus reversed the decision of retiring permanently from the concert stage, I regarded my own career as a secondary matter and always subordinated it to the duties and demands of private life through-out the years from 1913 to 1923," she said.[1] That meant duties toward Stokowski.

The demands that concertizing imposed gradually mounted, and by 1917 Olga suffered from the pressure of constant practice and also from some disharmony between herself and Leopold. There were hints of this from various friends that were bandied about Philadelphia, and some eventually found their way into the newspapers.

Rumors abounded that Olga's practicing irked Stokowski and that there were altercations about it. There were also suggestions that Stoki's roving eye had greatly upset the more puritanical Samaroff. Things came to a kind of head during the first week of February 1917. Olga claimed to have suffered an attack of amnesia and wandered into Roosevelt Hospital in New York after arriving from Philadelphia. Fortunately she had the presence of mind to mention the name of Dr. William M. Polk, the husband of her dearest friend, Maria Dehon, and she was quickly taken to their Park Avenue home.

Courtesy Natasha Bender

Stokowski on skis

When Olga had not appeared at dinner that night, at which she was scheduled to join Leopold, he, after a somewhat frantic search, notified the police of her disappearance. This automatically alerted the press. In the ensuing crisis, the redoubtable Arthur Judson took over. Judson informed the press that Mme. Samaroff had for some time been complaining of headaches and that she had been overwrought with her work, having already filled sixty concert engagements that season. "Mme. Samaroff's railroad tickets to Boston had been purchased," Judson reported, "and were held in our office. She had an appointment to dine with her husband, Mr. Stokowski, after which she planned to leave for Boston. It appears that she had worried considerably over her Boston recital, as her nervous condition had prevented her from preparing her program adequately. . . . Her nervous condition, brought on by overwork, was made more acute, I believe, by certain managerial difficulties that had arisen in Boston in connection with her proposed recital there. As to any reports of a sensational character that may have been spread, I can say authoritatively that there is absolutely no truth in them. It is simply a case of overwrought nerves caused by too diligent application to her concert activities."

Olga's practicing was a definite source of irritation. Arthur Judson remarked to a reporter, "He tried everything. He had the pianos moved about continuously. He put one in the basement at one time, and the other in the attic at another time. But there was no hope. He had heavy curtains and draperies hung, but it did not help. Finally, he had a double wall built and stored his coal and wood in between. Nothing would do."[2]

Although on the surface the Stokowskis always seemed an ideal couple, there were minor altercations that friends observed. Ruth O'Neill, who visited them often, recalled dining with them: "There were none who had the comprehensive intellectualism of those two people. Naturally, I would be the interested auditor as I sat down at dinner with them and there would be an argument about a phrase in a symphony and they would argue it out. But I remember one time on a Saturday evening when I was going to a concert with them, he came to the table in his dress clothes with sapphire and diamond studs in his shirt. Olga said, 'X'—she called him 'X' and he called her 'Mad'—X was for the unknown and Mad was for Madame—'X, are you wearing those good studs to the concert tonight? You know when you get excited they're likely to snap off and roll on the floor. You'll never find them.' So an argument ensued and he pulled them out and . . . threw them across the table at her. And I thought, even at that young age, let him wear them and let him lose them. They're his . . . if he drops them and can't find them, so what!"[3]

Olga was apparently becoming more and more apprehensive about her career. She practiced intently. After her bout with amnesia she was fearful of her memory possibly failing during a concert performance. And suddenly it happened. "She did play well, but, indeed, when she played with Stokowski, she was a different person," said Geordie Joline Blauvelt. "She was freer; she gave a little bit."[4] But it was during a concert with Stokowski that the almost inevitable did occur.

Pianist Beveridge Webster, who was then growing up in Pittsburgh, recalled the incident for me. "It was when Olga Samaroff played the Second Concerto of Saint-Saëns with the Philadelphia Orchestra and Stokowski conducting. As I remember it—I must have been a boy of ten or eleven—and I remember it as being traumatic. I don't remember how many small things happened up to the big trauma when Stoki finally stopped conducting . . . and walked off stage leaving his wife at the piano with her hands folded in her lap. . . . After what seemed a long, long time, she rose with quite a bit of dignity and walked off stage. There was scattered applause from the audience and a few hands clapping in the orchestra. Then, after another long wait, they came back on and finished the piece. I don't even recollect where they picked it up. I don't think they started over again, but I was so impressed by this big drama that I could never forget it."[5]

Olga continued to press herself. On November 2, 1920, she began a series of concerts that were to be amplified by remarks by Stokowski before and during the recitals. Olga elected to perform all of the Beethoven sonatas.[6]

The lecture concerts, given in the ballroom of the Bellevue-Stratford, proved a tremendous success.

Following their 1921 summer together in Europe, Stoki returned alone; Olga remained in London. She was joined there by her mother later in the year. On Christmas Eve, Olga became the mother of a daughter, Sonya Maria Noel Stokowski. The birth, which took place at 29 Lower Seymour Street, was registered on January 19, 1922, in the St. Marylebone Registration District. The father was listed as Leopold Anthony Stokowski, orchestral conductor of Westminster, and the mother, Lucie Mary Olga Agnes Stokowski formerly Hickenlooper. Her address at the time was the Hotel Rubens, Buckingham Palace Road, Westminster.

Olga's mother, being Catholic, insisted that the child be baptized in the faith, so Sonya was christened in Westminster Cathedral, an ugly, pseudo-Byzantine structure that is only exceeded by Sacré Coeur in Paris as an ecclesiastical architectural embarrassment. Sonya slept through most of the ceremony. "But just as the minister came to the part about renouncing Satan, she opened her eyes and winked at him," said Olga.[7]

With Sonya in her arms and her mother in tow, Olga sailed for America on the S.S. *Aquitania* the last week in January. "It was," said Olga, "an abominable passage. Mother was deathly ill and everyone felt it. Everyone but Sonya, that is—she was the only passenger on the boat who wasn't seasick."[8]

When the *Aquitania* docked on February 3, Stokowski was one of the first to bound up the gangplank to greet his wife and child. Olga explained that Noel had been added to Sonya's name because she was born on Christmas Eve; the Maria was for their dear friend Maria Dehon Polk. "She seems not to have very much hair," Stoki observed as he ran his

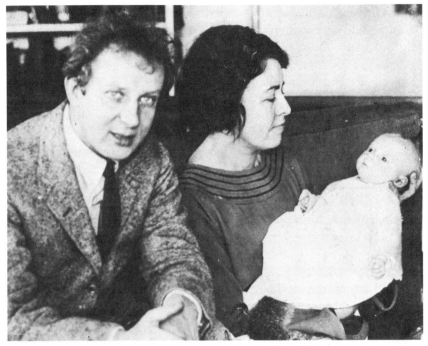

United Press International Photo

Stokowski, Olga Samaroff, and their child, Sonya (1922)

hands over her little head. "She has elaborate papers to prove she's never been in jail and other things," said Olga.[9]

Olga remained in New York to hear the concert of the Philadelphia Orchestra in Carnegie Hall and found it the best orchestra she had heard. A few days later she was driven to Philadelphia and their home on Mermaid Lane. Stoki had preceded her and a royal reception was in order.[10]

Sonya made her debut in a silk-lined bassinet surrounded by a mass of toys and gifts. A hundred guests and friends assembled to welcome her. Mr. Van gave a miniature copy of the Philadelphia Orchestra carved in wooden figures.[11] Even Richard Strauss sent a gift. Maria Dehon Polk was there and talked baby talk to the infant Sonya.

"As I remember it," said Sophie Jacobs, "they had a stage with all the presents on it. There was a little piano and all kinds of little musical instruments for this little two-month-old baby. And Stokowski was sort of amused by it all. . . . Olga saw to it that that birthday party for the baby was a tremendous big do. It was tea, drinks, champagne, and all that. Yes, I think Stokowski was pleased."[12]

Louise Varèse remarked that she knew Sonya as a little girl. "We had Polish friends and Stokowski is supposed to be Polish and half Irish—you know Stokowski and his fairy stories—and so Varèse had a friend of his dress a doll in a Polish costume for Stokowski's little girl, and we sent it to her. Some time later we went over for luncheon at his place near Philadelphia, which was being given for the Polish ambassador. After luncheon we all went up to Stokowski's study where he had his piano. On the piano was this doll, the doll that Varèse had sent to the little girl, and we overheard Stokowski saying, 'You know the people in the village that my family comes from dressed this doll and sent it to my little girl.' "[13]

In October as the new orchestral season began, a new series of musical talks by the Stokowski-Samaroff team was given in the foyer of the Academy of Music. Edward Bok introduced the distinguished pair, and Stoki spoke "in an impromptu though easy and fluent manner, at once establishing cordial and intimate association with his listeners, so that he was able to impart valuable information in a pleasant and interesting manner."[14] It was immediately established that this time it was Stokowski who was to be the star. Olga's role was merely illustrative—she had no thirty-two Beethoven sonatas to perform. To their Philadelphia audience, they were still the ideal musical pair.

With Christmas coming on and carols beginning to fill the air, Stokowski was to participate in a festive celebration planned for Christmas Eve, when a huge choir of more than two hundred voices would sing in five of the city's squares. The carolers were to be escorted by one hundred boy scouts carrying lanterns. The singing was to begin in Franklin Square, and from there the choristers were to proceed to Independence Square, then to Logan Square, winding up in Rittenhouse Square.

Tacked on to the announcement of this joyous festivity was the news that Stokowski would sail for France on January 2 to conduct first in Paris and later in Rome and that he would return on February 1.[15] Three days after his departure, Philadelphians were stunned by the news that Olga and Stokowski had signed a separation agreement. To Philadelphia society matrons who had lionized both Leopold and Olga, this was a social bombshell.

By the terms of the agreement, Olga was to live in the Chestnut Hill house until her concert tour would begin in February. Provision was to be

Photo Kubey Rembrandt Studios, Philadelphia/Courtesy Sonya Stokowski Thorbecke
Stokowski and Sonya (1923)

made for both mother and daughter. Sonya was to spend half of each year with each of the parents. Many of their friends expressed the opinion that the separation was probably only a temporary affair and that they would be reunited soon. Leopold, too, may have been of the same persuasion.[16]

As Stoki so often seemed to do when difficult situations arose, he ignored the present and concentrated on matters that were more distant. In Paris he was given a warm reception by a group of forty composers including Rabaud, Ravel, Roussel, Pierné, Schmitt, and Rhene Baton.[17]

Leopold's concerts with the Pasdeloup Orchestra created a sensation. He won particular praise for including his transcription of parts of Lully's *Triomphe de l'amour.*

In *La Revue Musicale,* Henri Prunières opined: "It required an American orchestra conductor to come to direct the Pasdeloup Orchestra for us to hear, at last, the orchestral music of Lully properly presented. . . . May Monsieur Stokowski be lauded for having had copied, with pious care, those fragments from Lully and for having respected their original orchestration in full measure wherever it was possible, and to substitute modern for bygone instruments. The full and rich sound was delightful. As to the conductor he is certainly one of the most important in the world."[18]

In an almost unique gesture, the Association of Pasdeloup Concerts, represented by its conductor and president Rhene Baton, awarded Stokowski with a bas relief in silver before a cheering Parisian audience.[19]

The following day Stoki departed for Rome, where he conducted concerts with the Symphony Orchestra of the Augusteo, Rome, with equal acclaim.[20] He enjoyed Rome thoroughly, visited the American Academy, and sought out early manuscripts in various libraries. He also contacted several of the Italian composers and brought back new works for his Philadelphians.

The *Mauretania,* on which Stoki returned, was scheduled to arrive in ample time for him to be in Philadelphia to rehearse and conduct concerts of February 2 and 3. The ship, however, was delayed first by fog and later by a violent storm. The loyal ladies in the Academy disappointedly heard the orchestra conducted by Thaddeus Rich.

When the ship docked, Stokowski emerged looking the picture of health, while many of the other fellow passengers still retained their seasick pallor. One reporter commented on his "soft green shirt and pastel gray cravat reminiscent of spring he had just left." Mention was made of his smile and his youthful, unlined countenance, which "rippled into sunshine as memory chased fog."[21]

Stoki remarked that his visit to Rome was a wonderful experience and that he had been very happy there. "It was so peaceful. You see, I'm a Catholic and the whole environment was completely happy for me." He said that he had brought back works of Respighi, Malipiero, Tommasini, and unknown Vivaldi, which he intended to transcribe. He mentioned too that he had bought some fine antique Italian furniture, which turned out to be bogus, much to Stoki's chagrin.[22]

It was not until the first week in May that the furniture arrived. Stoki and his painter friend Arthur Carles helped the draymen unload it on the lawn. At that point a customs inspector arrived. Stoki was untroubled. Since all of the furniture was antique, no duty would need be paid. The inspector immediately questioned the authenticity of many of the pieces. "But see," said Stokowski, "the wood is very old." The unimpressed inspector shook his head. As each succeeding piece was uncrated, he denied that they were legitimate antiques.

"Ah, but Sto," said Artie Carles, "it's wonderful-looking stuff."[23]

Olga had left for New York, leaving Sonya behind with Stokowski in the house on Mermaid Lane. "When it became certain in 1923 that unclouded domesticity was not to be my lot in life," she said, "I decided to take up my winter residence in New York and spend my summers in Seal Harbor."[24]

She punctuated her resolve one day before Stoki's last concert of the season with the orchestra. The papers noted Stoki's little speech to his "cheering" audience, wishing them "every happiness of the glad outdoors and sunshine in their hearts." The same issues contained the information that on the previous day Olga Samaroff Stokowski had sued for divorce in Common Pleas Court.[25]

Leopold did not contest. To the credit of both of them there was no acrimonious exchange in the press, and the whole matter was settled with quiet dignity. Olga had her piano and music sent to New York, and, after moving from one temporary apartment to another, she was invited to share a large Park Avenue apartment which friends in Baltimore kept in New York as a pied-à-terre but seldom used. Olga moved in and shortly thereafter she met with a curious accident. On a morning when her friends were about to return to Baltimore, she went to her host's room intending to say good-bye to her. On leaving she tripped over a small trunk that a maid had inadvertently placed in a hallway beside the door. "I fell over it and twisted my left arm. I picked myself up, conscious that I had hurt my arm but never dreaming how serious the injury would prove to be."[26]

Olga left that night for Chicago, where she gave a recital. There followed others in Memphis and St. Louis. In St. Louis she consulted a family physician, who diagnosed a torn ligament and suggested that she would probably have to keep her arm in a sling for a year. "Thus," she said, "I was thrown out of a profession which at the time had seemed to be the very center of my life." She embraced the idea of becoming a pedagogue and also became the music critic of the *New York Evening Post*, which was owned by her good friends the Boks.[27]

Olga was also approached by John Erskine, who invited her to teach at the Juilliard Graduate School, at the time housed in the Vanderbilt mansion on Fifty-second Street just east of Madison Avenue. She also became the head of the piano department of the Philadelphia Conservatory of Music. She developed a host of young pianistic talents, including Eugene List, Claudette Sorel, Rosalyn Tureck, Jerome Lowenthal, Joseph Battista, and William Kapell.

Frequently Olga mentioned Stokowski and his interpretative techniques to her students. "We were all struck by that," said Eugene List. "He was a kind of obsession with her. She never really got over him at all and she was always talking about him, personally and musically. For instance, if we were playing something she would say, well, Stokowski would phrase it this way or Stokowski would build a climax this way. She was always giving musical examples of how he would do something. We all felt it was a kind of personal tragedy that it hadn't worked out because she was still very much in love with him."[28]

Rosalyn Tureck concurred. "She talked about him mostly in a personal way. She did say that he was a tremendous help to her in musicianship. She said that she used to be very nervous and he said to her: 'Instead of thinking of yourself, think of the music before you walk out onto the stage.' He meant a great deal to her. . . . I think she never lost an iota of her feeling for him."[29]

"Olga had charm and she loved him until her dying breath," said Ruth O'Neill. "She never got him out of her system. The hurt to her was mortal."[30]

In a letter addressed to John Erskine, Olga in a rare moment of revelation wrote:

You will find out as we work together that with all my other faults, there is one that has been knocked out of me—vanity. I think I was born with the average human amount of it, but my experience with Stokowski killed it. When one has worshipped a man and done everything humanly possible to make him happy and then realized that he prefers any inconsequential flapper that comes along, one either becomes bitter or one convinces oneself, as I managed to do, that if one were anything very grand, it just couldn't happen. That is where I learned humility.[31]

One morning while sitting in Sonya's house in Sewickley, Pennsylvania, I asked her about the effect the separation of her parents had had on her. "Well, as you know, my parents were divorced when I was a year old. That made for a more or less chopped-up childhood, if one wants to put it that way. Both of them felt that they were being terribly fair to each other; I have seen this happen in other families. Of course, the person they're not fair to, really, is the child. Each one was going to have 50 percent of that child, and, you see that was going to be frightfully fair. . . . So I lived half of the time with Mother and half of the time with Dad. I couldn't remember the other parent six months later. . . . I had a series of governesses that went back and forth with me. Some did and some didn't because they didn't work with one ménage and the other did."[32]

㉑

AD (After Divorce) 1923

S TOKOWSKI departed for Paris again before the divorce—on general grounds of many vexations and indignities—was made final on June 30, 1923. Shortly before leaving, a lady reporter, Blanche Wolf, trekked to Merion to talk with him. Rugs and pictures were being packed away for the summer and she reported seeing little Sonya running happily through the open French windows. She mentioned the large German police dog that acted as a guard for Sonya when her father was away. She described Stoki as looking "confident yet modest" in a violet shirt.[1]

During the summer the Philadelphia press continued to report his meandering. They described him reveling in an outdoor cafe in Montmartre celebrating Bastille Day; they ran pictures of him exploring the coast of Brittany with a violinist friend—Stoki wearing a wide-brimmed hat and large gloves.[2]

Immediately after his return, he left for what was described as a "camping trip."[3] Judson had been particularly fascinated by the Canadian wilderness and some of his enthusiasm was transferred to Stoki. "There aren't enough words to describe it," said Judson. After many excursions there, he finally acquired a place in an area called Timagami. "It's a forest preserve about one hundred miles square and there must be a thousand lakes on it. The only way to travel was by canoe and portaging the canoe over to the next lake," Judson recalled. "I used to go up there and finally settled down and built a lodge and a lot of cottages. It was a lot of fun."[4]

Shortly after the Canadian jaunt Linton Martin of the *Inquirer* made his way out to "The Poplars," Stoki's house on Mermaid Lane. He was greeted by the somewhat menacing growls of Wolf, Stoki's police dog and the "inscrutable face" of his Swiss male attendant. It was a rather frustrating experience for Martin. Stoki was being his most evasive. When asked whether he had brought back any novelties, he answered, "Quite a few."

"What are they and whose are they?" Martin asked.

"In matters of this kind I've found by experience that it's better to do things and not talk about them. This may not help you. But conducting the orchestra is my business, just as writing for the newspaper is yours."[5]

In a final desperate appeal, Martin pressed on about what new music he would play during the season.

"What good would it do to name it?" Stoki replied. "When I do that, indignant old ladies only make life miserable for me. . . . Or other conductors rush in to play it first . . . there are so many reasons for reticence that it would be unnecessary to name them. But now I must answer my letters."[6] Martin was left to find his way back to the city.

In 1921 Stoki decided to give a series of concerts strictly for children. "I love them . . . and I like the way they think more than the way grown-ups think. For the children have imagination. The grown-ups had it once but educators have beat it out of them, telling them dry facts, killing their imagination. Sonya, my daughter, comes into my studio. She has under one arm a bunny and under the other a moo-cow. And we play by the hour. She has so much imagination, she doesn't need toys. Well, all children are like that."[7]

Stoki began doting more and more on Sonya and at the age of four he let her make her debut with the orchestra in a performance of Haydn's *Toy* Symphony. She had a little rattle and when Stoki would nod to her, she would shake it.[8]

When he presented Saint-Saëns' *Carnival of the Animals*, he did it with Barnumesque flair. He led in three pearl gray elephants, three small ponies, a spindly donkey, and a camel—much to the squealing delight of the small fry.[9]

Author Virgilia Peterson Ross described the event: "When all the children were seated, he told them he was keeping an elephant outside. They smiled at him cynically. 'You do not believe me?' he asked. 'Or perhaps you do not want to see an elephant?' Some of them called to bring him out. The conductor went backstage and reappeared leading a very young elephant by the ear. The children bellowed with delight. One of the musicians rushed to the platform and told Stokowski that there were crowds of elephants outside trying to come in. Three more trotted to the scene. Stokowski and the musicians stood at the door pushing back the imaginary hordes beyond. By this time the children were in a fever of curiosity. The conductor then took up his baton and played the *Carnival* . . . his little audience will probably never forget it."[10]

Miss Peterson did manage to get in one more elephant than the other reporters of the scene had counted.

One young, playful pachyderm began to trumpet quite off-key while the music was being played and Stoki quieted him with a bunch of carrots and a handful of peanuts. The tots were delighted.

On a trip to Europe Stoki had met Charlie Chaplin and he extracted a promise from him that he would make an appearance with the Philadelphia Orchestra for one of the children's concerts. Fully believing that Charlie would appear, Stoki announced it prematurely to his eager audience. Then week after week he had to promise that he would be there for the next concert. Finally, when it became apparent that he was not going to come, Stoki with a flash of inspiration recalled that Adrian Siegel, one of the cellists in the orchestra, had a flair for comedy and was about the same build as Chaplin. He managed to induce him to impersonate him.

Siegel did so brilliantly and the kids were never the wiser. Wearing baggy pants and a little mustache he shuffled onto the stage carrying his cello case. "As planned," Siegel said, "I withdrew the cello and threw the case into the wings where the stagehands broke a piece of glass with a sledgehammer over a steel barrel. What a racket! That part even surprised me."[11] The kiddies squealed. Siegel then played *Trees* with many Chaplinesque flourishes. After the concert the children mobbed the stage door and Siegel had to remain in hiding for over two hours before the last of them had departed.

Sol Schoenbach, formerly first bassoonist with the Philadelphia Orchestra and later executive director of the Settlement Music School in Philadelphia, described another intriguing concert. Stoki had learned that a Philadelphia motor cop was a most expert xylophone player and he proposed that he take part in one of the concerts. With his dramatic flair, Stoki devised a brilliant miniscenario to involve him. "Stokowski was conducting the *Marriage of Figaro* Overture very fast when the motorcycle cop, all in leather, came out with his motorcycle and tapped Stokowski on the shoulder and shouted, 'Stop.' Stokowski turned around and said, 'What is it? What have I done, officer?' 'Speeding,' he replied. 'It was too fast.' He pulled out his big book and took off his leather gloves and said, 'I'm sorry, I have to give you a ticket.' Those kids were just peeing in their pants seeing this guy and his motorcycle. So Stokowski stood there and said to the men, 'How are we going to manage this?' 'Talk to him, talk to him,' they said. So he said to the policeman, 'Is there any way that I could get out of this? I really didn't mean it.' 'Maybe if I could play a piece with your band,' he replied. 'Oh, do you play?' And boom, out comes the xylophone and they played the "Flight of the Bumble Bee." People—now they are grandparents—still remember that concert."[12]

Another element that Stoki added was his use of children as soloists. One of the youngest was the brilliant violinist Oscar Shumsky, who made his debut when he was only eight years old playing a Mozart concerto. The children were fascinated.

Fifty years after that event, I talked with Oscar Shumsky, who remarked that the engagement to play with the Philadelphia Orchestra was the first big step in his career.[13] "I remember more clearly the impression that I had when I played with him later on," he said. "He invited me to play the Brahms concerto with the Philadelphia Orchestra and at that time, I was about fifteen. . . .

"Of all the conductors whose characteristics I recall very well, his seemed to me to be the most natural in terms of contacting an orchestra and playing on them as if they were an instrument. . . . Every move that he made was so natural; it seemed to be so effortless. Of all the people with whom I've played as soloist, I don't recall anyone with that sort of communication. It was an extraordinary experience—like almost a metaphysical experience—working with him. You didn't feel that there was somebody accompanying you. You felt absolutely free to do anything that you wanted to because you felt that, in a sense, he was you and you were he and you were both playing the same thing. He was extraordinarily perceptive and you could feel things happening just before a particular place. They were prepared; they were predestined."[14]

Constantly looking for new ways to enliven the spirits in Philadelphia, Stokowski turned to the idea of developing a band of true symphonic character to be called the "Band of Gold." He had loved the sound of brass ever since his tuba-playing days as a boy in London. The new band, said Arthur Cohn, was made up of "the entire brass section of the orchestra and specially auditioned musicians all in gold uniforms with gold braid and all playing gold instruments. . . . It lasted about two seasons, and what a sound. Can you imagine Stoki conducting a band as no other band director would ever dream of conducting? It sounded like a resplendent Philadelphia Orchestra."[15]

The band made its dramatic debut on May 18, 1924. There had been much anticipation, and as usual for anything that Stokowski essayed there was a huge audience assembled in the Academy. A curtain—great and golden, to be sure—was drawn across the stage. Festooning the boxes and balconies were draperies of blue and gold—"Philadelphia colors." Many of the listeners were a bit surprised when Stoki stepped before the curtain, attired in his usual immaculate black dress suit.

He made some amusing comments on the age of the band—a mere two weeks—and described it as a mewling infant that had to be bottle-fed. He called for the ever-present Marshall Betz, his librarian, sometime masseur, and general factotum. Marshall appeared from the wings with his rugged figure completely clothed in a brilliant gold uniform and saluted Stokowski in good military fashion. "Marshall," Stoki commanded imperiously, "show them my little baby." The curtain was raised on a band of 120 men in gold uniforms, their instruments gleaming brightly. There were cheers, shouts, and stamping of feet by an audience that refused to be silenced. The concert was a sensational triumph even before a note had been played. It was Stokowski at his most skillfully dramatic. The audience loved it.[16]

H. L. Mencken, having heard of the band in Baltimore, came to Philadelphia to hear the next concert and obtained his tickets through the aid of "a friendly bootlegger." Mencken heard the band on Sunday evening. "It was the middle of the week before I was fit for my usual literary and spiritual exercises." He observed that there were numerous very fine bands but he considered Stokowski's infant a brass band of an entirely new sort: "I can only report that the results he achieves are *kolossal*. Here, at last, is a brass band that can play Bach!"[17]

In a lighthearted letter to the critic Lawrence Gilman, Stoki asked, "Did the little rock on which New York is built tremble last Sunday night? If so it was my Gold Band in Philadelphia."[18]

Blanche Wolf, who had interviewed Stokowski shortly before his recent trip to Europe, and her friend Janette Selig had begun music classes in a settlement house in one of the poorest sections of Philadelphia. Mary Louise Curtis Bok became interested in the project, and in memory of her mother, gave funds for a new building that was erected on Queen Street in 1917.[19] By 1923 such an abundance of talent had emerged that Mary

Bok began to discuss with Stokowski and Josef Hofmann the possibility of establishing an institute for advanced music students. It was out of these talks that the idea of the Curtis Institute was born.

Edward Bok bought three houses—the Sibley House on Rittenhouse Square and two adjacent elegant town houses on South Eighteenth Street —to house the institute. To make her initial effort more ceremonial, Mary

Mary Louise Curtis Bok and Edward Bok (1926)

Courtesy Mrs. Cary Bok

Louise Curtis Bok chose April 18, Leopold's birthday, for the signing of the charter of the Curtis Institute in Philadelphia. As the daughter of the wealthy Cyrus Curtis, head of the Curtis Publishing Company, Mary Bok was able to endow the institute lavishly. As the wife of Edward Bok, she and her husband were Stokowski's strongest supporters. Together they planned the structure of the Curtis Institute. A prestigious list of advisors was assembled, including Edward Bok, Ossip Gabrilowitsch, Josef Hofmann, Marcella Sembrich, Leopold Stokowski, and Carl Flesch.

Flesch was a distinguished violinist with an impressive European career behind him. He was to become head of the violin department for a time. A few months earlier, on December 15, 1923, he appeared with the Philadelphia Orchestra playing the Beethoven Violin Concerto. During the first movement he became confused, put down his bow and Stokowski stopped the orchestra. It was one of the rare times that such a thing occurred. After a hurried consultation of the score, they began again and finished to the applause of a sympathetic audience.[20]

Arthur Judson, who managed Flesch as well as the Philadelphia Orchestra, remarked that "Carl Flesch was a purist and he hated everybody." Ruth O'Neill, who also attended the concert, remarked, "Olga Samaroff told a story about Carl Flesch. When his wife presented him with twins, he felt as though he got a double fee for his performance."[21]

Stoki took over the orchestral department, met for the first time on November 14, 1924, and quickly put together an orchestra of unusual quality. Soon it was being heard in Carnegie Hall, Boston's Symphony Hall, and in halls in Baltimore and Washington.[22] He developed here a principle that he was to use in the formation of his Youth Orchestra. He brought into the Curtis the first-chair men from the Philadelphia Orchestra as teachers and in the development of the orchestra had them sit in and play during rehearsals, aiding and instructing their younger charges at the same time. The novelty, however, soon wore off and Stoki absented himself from the Curtis Institute after a mere three years.

Rumors had been circulating that Stokowski was about to resign from the Philadelphia Orchestra and accept a new position in New York. It was also mentioned that Frederick Stock would be leaving Chicago and assuming the Philadelphia post. The rumor disturbed Stock, who issued a statement to the press: "There is absolutely no truth in the report that I intend to leave Chicago and become conductor of the Philadelphia Orchestra. I visited Philadelphia as guest conductor at the invitation of Mr. Stokowski. No proposal was made that I should take Mr. Stokowski's place."[23] Arthur Judson, as manager of both the Philadelphia Orchestra and the New York Philharmonic, denied the report emphatically, and he was certainly in the best position to know. However, in October a new contract was prepared. Stoki's present contract was to run until 1927 and the new one would extend it by seven years, guaranteeing his presence in Philadelphia until 1934.[24] The salary mentioned in the press was $70,000. When he was asked for confirmation, he merely expressed happiness at the extension of the contract, but about the money he made no comment.

Observing that there was no lessening in his constant drive for perfection, Ernest Newman, then with the *New York Evening Post,* wrote: "I'm sorry to say that we have no orchestra in England at present that can compare in quality of material and discipline with the Philadelphia Orchestra."[25]

During Stokowski's mid-winter vacation two special guests appeared with the orchestra. One was Olga Samaroff, who played two concertos: the Mozart Concerto in A Major and the Liszt E-flat Concerto. The concert (January 23, 1925) was conducted by Thaddeus Rich. For the audience in the Academy it was a sentimental occasion and it spared no effort to show its appreciation and affection for her. From all accounts she played brilliantly and there was an ovation for her. The local flower shops did a booming business and bouquet after bouquet was brought to the stage.[26]

The other notable visitor was Igor Stravinsky. He conducted a program of his own works, which included the *Petrouchka* and *Firebird* suites, *Fireworks, Scherzo Fantastique,* and *The Song of the Nightingale.*[27] The 1924–25 season also marked the arrival of Artur Rodzinski. Stoki had discovered him in Poland and encouraged him to come to Philadelphia as his assistant. The board, however, did not accept Stokowski's proposal and Rodzinski had to wait around for a year before his appointment was confirmed. His situation was very precarious. "Then," Halina Rodzinski, Artur's widow, recalled, "Stokowski suddenly out of a blue sky, realizing Artur didn't have any money, gave him money of his own. And he said, 'You can return it to me when you come back so that you can go back to Poland for the summer.' That was a wonderful gesture."[28]

The following October Rodzinski returned to become Stokowski's assistant and thus began his American career.[29] In October there was another returnee: Olga was engaged to appear again and this time with Stoki conducting.[30]

Being very civilized people, one presumes that the reunion of Leopold and Olga was both cordial and pleasant. Their custody arrangement for

Sonya had kept them in contact at least by phone and correspondence. But one must presume, too, that Leopold made no mention of a new love interest. It would also seem doubtful that Maria Dehon Polk, who had maintained her friendship with both of them despite their divorce, would have raised the issue with Olga.

Just as Maria Dehon had brought Olga and Leopold together, she was now to be the catalyst in bringing together Leopold and Evangeline Brewster Johnson. During a conversation in Palm Beach, Evangeline said to me rather abruptly, "Why don't you say to me, 'Why did you marry Stokowski?'" I said I was reluctant to do so but I would like to ask the question. "Why!" she said. "You see I had a box for his concerts in New York; I had a box for Toscanini's concerts. I never wanted to meet either of them. . . . Whenever I was invited to a supper after one of Stokowski's concerts I would ascertain that he would not be there. John Hays Hammond, the brother of Dick Hammond, was a great friend of mine, and he was also a friend of Stokowski's. He always wanted us to meet but as I said, I never wanted to meet Stokowski because I thought he was the greatest musician in the world and I didn't want to know whether he did or did not like spinach and various small less attractive human characteristics that he might have.

"John Hays Hammond asked Mrs. Polk to arrange a supper after one of his New York concerts and invited me to come. I said to him, 'Will you be sure that Stokowski won't be there?' 'Oh, no, no, he won't be there' —planning all the time that he would be.

"I had just returned from a trip to Egypt, where I had been making a study of Coptic music. I am very interested in Egyptian archaeology . . . and I felt perhaps Coptic music would give us some indication about Egyptian music. In so many Egyptian bas reliefs you will see a harp, a sistrum, and various instruments.

"We went to Mrs. Polk's and there, to my horror, was Stokowski and he was seated next to me at the table. 'Oh, I hear you've just come back from Egypt and that you have been making a study of Coptic music,' he said.

"Well, three weeks after that we were married. I was so impressed with him and so serious in my point of view toward life, and I had worked in the Red Cross Ambulance Corps during the war and afterward became chairman of the speakers bureau of the League of Nations Association in New York and I had that Jeanne d'Arc complex that people get in their twenties and I felt that I must do what I could to prevent there ever being another war so. . . . Then I met Stokowski and he introduced me to the idea of the great international spirit of music and I thought to myself, well, what interesting children Stokowski and I could produce. This is a ridiculous reason, I know, for a marriage, but fundamentally it's the best reason."[31]

On Friday, January 9, 1926, rumors were reported by the press that Leopold Stokowski and Evangeline Johnson would wed. Neither the prospective bride nor groom would confirm the story. Reporters eager for information contacted the brother of Evangeline, Robert Wood Johnson, in New Brunswick, who replied that he was not conversant with the facts. When some statements that Stoki had apparently made were quoted to him, his reply was, "How extraordinary! How unusual! How mysterious!"

Mysterious is correct. The press gave a brief outline of Miss Johnson's background, describing her as the daughter of Robert Wood Johnson, founder of the pharmaceutical firm of Johnson & Johnson, and added a few details about her education—that she had attended Miss Spencer's School and made her debut in New York society during the season of 1917.[32]

Such a cloak of secrecy surrounded their plans that Evangeline didn't even confirm to her relatives until Friday night that the rumors were true and that she would be married the following Monday. Even the hour of the ceremony was carefully kept from the press. On Sunday night Leopold stayed at the home of Maria Dehon Polk and the following afternoon, shortly before four o'clock, brought her to Evangeline's apartment a few blocks away. The announcement of the wedding was made in a brief statement by Stoki's secretary, Mary McGinty. It read:

> The ceremony took place at 4:30. It was performed by Supreme Court Justice R. P. Leydon. The guests were as follows: Mrs. William M. Polk, Mr. Robert Wood Johnson, Mr. John Seward Johnson, brothers of the bride, Mr. John Hays Hammond, Jr. . . . Mrs. Bernard Baruch, Miss Belle Baruch, Mrs. Otto Kahn . . . Mrs. Carlos Salzedo and Mr. Artur Rodzinski of Warsaw. . . .
>
> The bride wore a wine-colored velvet, painted in gold. The ceremony was performed against a background of gold.[33]

Reporters noted that "the marriage license was not made public until an hour and a half after the wedding. In it the bride gave her age as twenty-eight and Dr. Stokowski gave his as thirty-eight. He said he was "born in London and his father was an Austrian."[34]

Before departing for their honeymoon in Palm Beach, the newlyweds remained in New York to attend a performance of *Dybbuk* at the Neighborhood Playhouse. All through the day reporters tried to reach and interview them. Their attempts were futile and finally Stoki released a short statement for the Philadelphia reporters: "Please give my love to all my friends in Philadelphia and say I am happy."[35]

Two months later Stoki wrote to his close friend the painter Arthur Carles:

March 6, 1926

Dear Carlsie,

You probably never read the newspaper so have not heard that a few weeks ago something happened to me from which I have not yet recovered,—in fact probably I shall never be the same again.

In any case, I want very much to see you—not about anything particular, but just to have a talk with you. I know you are a very busy man, but all the same I hope you will spare a few moments for me some time.

I saw Sey [Leopold Seyffert] out in Chicago and we spent the whole day doing nothing in particular and had a wonderful time.

I am sending you a little present which I hope you will like, but please do not tell anybody about it—it is a great secret.

Always with affection,
Yours,
Stoki[36]

22

Arvis and Amoris

EOPOLD's marriage to Evangeline was to alter his way of life dramatically; it was to give him prospects and priorities he had not previously entertained. Evangeline was not merely a debutante from New York, as the papers had described her, but she was a person of great intelligence with a broad view of life and an idealistic preoccupation with human betterment. "My address is the Academy of Music," said Stoki. "Evangeline's is the Pennsylvania Railroad."[1] She kept her Park Avenue apartment and repaired there, particularly on weekends when Philadelphia wallowed in its puritanical dullness.

Together Leopold and Evangeline shared a life filled with fantasy as well as reality. They talked of Tibet, India, the South Seas, the Himalayas, and worlds far away. They became immersed in lives and cultures distant from Pennsylvania, and like pilgrims plotting a royal road to romance, decided to explore them. As part of his fantasizing Stoki had said that "he was brought up by a governess because he was the illegitimate child of the Kaiser's sister."[2]

Evangeline was an activist. As early as 1919 she owned and flew her own hand-cranked, single-engine biplane. She first came to Palm Beach in 1914 and joined friends swimming at the Breakers. "It made me so mad to have to wear stockings with my bathing costume. So, I wrote out some articles and flew in my plane, dropping the handbills on the beach, arguing against stockings. And what do you think the outcome was? The story went around that a stocking manufacturer was advertising stockings."[3]

On looking at several photos that had been taken of her, she brought

Courtesy Evangeline Johnson Merrill
Evangeline Johnson perches on her 1919-vintage hand-
cranked, single-engine biplane.

out one in which she was perched on her plane. "I think something like
this is more in character with me," she said. "Notice it's a biplane; it's
a Rolls-Royce motor with a hand crank. You can see the crank hanging
down. That's how I started it. You had to crank the motor."[4]

She mentioned a portrait that had been done of her by Khalil Gibran,
whose book *The Prophet* became a bestseller. "He did a picture of me.
When he did a portrait of someone he always did two heads. He did the
conventional one and then he did a second one that was his idea of your
inner self. . . ."[5]

Evangeline mentioned that she had known Woodrow Wilson while he
was President. "But after his illness . . . he was living in the S Street house
in Washington. I wanted Stokowski to meet him and they liked him very

Courtesy Evangeline Johnson Merrill
Ring made for Evangeline with gold nugget
given to Stokowski by President and Mrs.
Wilson for that purpose

much. We spent a few days with them and Mrs. Wilson gave him a gold
nugget out of which he had made a wedding ring. It was the first gold
nugget ever found in California and Woodrow had his wedding ring made
for her. This is the second Mrs. Wilson I am talking about. She was lovely.
She had a delightful outgoing personality which balanced his ingrown
personality. There was quite a bit of the nugget left over, and I can see
them now. We were all four dining together in his house. He handed this
nugget to Stokowski and said, 'I'm giving you this so you can make a
wedding ring for Evangeline.'

"He took the nugget and he found out how you can hammer gold. He
flattened it out. I had a Chinese ring at the time. Ancient Chinese rings
are interesting because they don't touch together. They end in two separate pieces so they will always fit. Stoki said, 'I'm going to hammer
Amoris.' He would call me Amoris, but only when we were alone. And
he asked me to call him Arvis."[6]

Two events of 1926 dominated the media: the Philadelphia sesquicentennial and the arrival of Queen Marie of Rumania. The former did more
for Philadelphia's architecture and city planning than it did for music.
The concerts of the orchestra were not the fare the visitors of the exposition particularly wanted. The ado about the royal personage was astonish-

ing. The queen did have undeniable charm and the idea of a royal person-age was intriguing, but the amount of attention squandered on her was amazing under any circumstances. Among the elect who were to pay homage were the Stokowskis, although it is doubtful that they did much more than attend the overblown reception at the Ritz-Carlton in New York.[7] More important to them was the imminent arrival of a new Stokowski. On January 2, 1927, a daughter was born.[8]

Naming the new infant became a public matter. She was known as Gloria Amoris Nadya Luba Marzenka Stanislawa Stokowski according to

Stokowski with Lyuba and Sonya (standing) at Santa Barbara (summer 1927)

Courtesy Evangeline Johnson Merrill

the press reports. "But we are open to suggestions," said Stoki. "Our friends are all willing to help us out with names. Maybe we'll change the names around, but I rather think they might stand just as they are." The name Luba did survive, but later on Stoki preferred the spelling Lyuba. It was more exotic.

Sonya, who was then going on five, remarked, "She looks like an angel. Santa Claus brought her. We wanted a boy, but he didn't have any left. Now I'm glad she is a girl and I shall adore playing with her. Why, she knows me already."[9]

During the year Stoki complained frequently of neuritis. He was still using a baton and during concerts it was noticed that he often shifted it from one hand to the other. It will always remain a mystery whether the problems of neuritis were as serious as they seemed or whether it was a partial excuse to obtain a year's leave of absence from the orchestra. An article in the *Ledger* stated that "although all official lips are tightly sealed beyond the formal announcement of the leave of absence, due to the declaration of physicians that Mr. Stokowski must have at least a year's rest, unofficial voices, sufficiently near to the authorities to be respected, give assurance that this physical exigency is the truth and the whole truth at the present moment."[10]

He had been with the orchestra for fifteen years. The challenge was no longer there. The thought of exploring the Orient was now more exciting. The trip began in France, where Lyuba was left with friends while Evangeline and Leopold went eastward.

"We went to India by taking a boat to Jerusalem," Evangeline said, "and from Jerusalem to Damascus to Baghdad. We crossed the Syrian desert in two automobiles. When we came to Baghdad there was some sort of an epidemic there, and we had to be inoculated outside the city. From Baghdad, we got on a funny boat and went down the Euphrates River to a place called Basra. At Basra we took a boat and crossed the Persian Gulf and the Gulf of Oman and docked at Karachi, India . . . and then on to Bombay.

"We went around India by train and on one of the trips—we had to sit up all night on the train—we went to see Gandhi. . . . He was very nice to us and he said that we could ask him any questions we wanted. I noticed that on his lap there was a little hand-weaving machine and he launched into a tirade against the British. You see, at that time England was still importing raw cotton from India to make up fabrics in England. It wanted to keep India as a source of raw material. Gandhi was trying to start a whole cottage weaving industry and he was in favor of people doing this in their homes . . . he was trying to make a cottage industry because he felt strongly that a home was the basis of any social order . . . a kind of attack on the machine. Stoki and I discussed it afterward. How ironic . . . he was talking against the machine . . . yet he had a hand-weaving machine in his lap that he was working on; the English disciple was taking down our questions and answers on a typewriter; and outside the building a metal lathe was going. . . ."

After being typical tourists and visiting the Taj Mahal and other sites, Leopold and Evangeline made their way to southern India to see Annie Besant. "She was head of the Theosophical Society. She had come to Philadelphia and stayed with us, so she invited us to the World Conference of Theosophists even though we weren't theosophists at all. That's where we met Krishnamurti and there was also Bishop Leadbeater, who was the head of the liberal Catholic church in Australia. He said to us, 'Have you ever seen the light that surrounds a spiritually evolved person?' I said 'no.' He said, 'This afternoon Krishnamurti is going to make one of his first appearances before the world group of theosophists and if you will walk between Annie and me, we will each hold your hand and perhaps you will see. . . . I am not going to tell you what color the light around his body is. You're going to tell me because then I'll know whether you really saw it or not or whether you are imagining it.' . . . We went in and when Krishnamurti came out onto the stage, there was a white light all around him—around his whole body."[11]

Both were interested in meeting Sir Jagadis Chandra Bose, the Indian physicist and plant physiologist, in Calcutta. Bose had done considerable research involving percussion instruments. "I knew about him," said Evangeline, "because he was a member of the Intellectual Cooperation of the League of Nations when I was working there in the early 1920s. . . . I had Jesse Bose's book *Plant Autographs,* in which he proved that plants have a nervous system. While we were dining at an English hotel in Calcutta, the head waiter came up to us and said to Stoki that there was a native who had come to see him. Stokowski said, 'That must be Sir Jesse Bose. Please show him in.' And the head waiter said, 'Natives in native dress are not allowed in the dining room.' So Stoki got up and said, 'Then I won't stay in this hotel. Their costume is eminently suited to this terribly hot weather and it's their country.' And he made a big scene.

"We went to Bose's studio; it was a big laboratory and there were flowers and plants on the outside of the door and the man who was with us said that to Indians a scientist is like a god because he knows the inner secrets of nature and that is why people brought him flowers."[12]

Although Evangeline always referred to Bose as "Jesse," Stoki for some curious reason called him Raman. "He resolved for me certain problems regarding the vibration of instruments in the battery section of our orchestra, problems for which I hadn't been able to find an answer in the Western world during several years of effort," he said in an Associated Press interview. "The battery section uses drums, gongs, bells and such. I knew empirically how to produce the sound, but I couldn't discover the reason for certain peculiarities of these instruments. . . . Raman not only answered the questions and solved my problems but he took me into his laboratory and demonstrated them."[13]

From India the Stokowskis sailed to Burma, where they explored and visited the ruins of some magnificent ancient temples before going on to Java. In Djakarta they attended a quintuple wedding ceremony during which five princes were married to five princesses. This royal wedding was a most elaborate affair and seven gamelans, composed of as many as fifty-five men each, performed in the courtyards of the palace. The Stokowskis visited Bali and again relished the wonderful metallic sounds the gamelans produced. In Java and Bali they obtained gongs that they would take back to Philadelphia.[14] A companion on this South Sea jaunt was the composer Henry Eichheim, who memorialized their experience by writing a series of brief tone poems.[15] Two of these, *Java* and *Bali*, Stoki introduced later in Philadelphia. He recorded *Bali* for RCA Victor.

On returning to India, the Stokowskis had hoped to travel by car through Afghanistan and Russia back to Europe. However, the unsettled conditions in Afghanistan made such a trip impossible, and they returned following much of the route by which they had come.[16] Their first concern was Lyuba, who had been taken to Switzerland. The summer was spent partly in Geneva and later in Paris, where they renewed their contacts with music and musicians.

"It is nonsense to say that music is a universal language," Stoki said after his oriental journey. "Japanese, Javanese, Hindus, Persians, Arabs, Egyptians all have music of their own. In Islands of the South Seas there are villages every three miles, and in each village we found different instruments, rhythms, melodic lines—different musical languages."[17] It was curious and regrettable that he did not remember this truism when he wrote his *Music for All of Us*, which begins, "Music is a universal language."[18] Schonberg accused him of "looking a platitude square in the face."[19]

Resettled in their suburban home, Stokowski concentrated all of his attention on the scores he would conduct and began his work with the orchestra with great zest. The men responded and the reviews of the early concerts were as spectacular as any he had ever received. Oscar Thompson in the *Post* wrote that the orchestra was now back on the heights it had occupied before it was taken over by guest conductors. "This meant playing which for sumptuous beauty of tone and unflagging vitality is surpassed nowhere."[20]

Critics and audience were quick to note that Stoki juggled his baton from left to right hand and back, apparently because of the neuritis from which he was still suffering.[21] The 1928–29 season was again to be one from which Stoki would absent himself more and dominate less. Guests were to include Gabrilowitsch, Molinari, Sir Thomas Beecham, and Clemens Krauss.

Evangeline meanwhile busied herself taking care of little Lyuba and also Sonya during the half year she was under the custody of her father. Sonya always called Evangeline "Tanti." "She married Dad when I was about four years old," Sonya recalled.

"Stokowski and I really had an ideal marriage," Evangeline told me, "because we each had our own interests and we had interests we shared in common. We shared the interest of the children in common, of music in common, and my interest in peace was his interest as well. . . ."[22]

It was Evangeline who interested Stoki in health food and "no white bread, nothing fried and raw salads every day for lunch. Stokowski grew stronger and healthier every year . . . he was a very faithful and devoted follower of the healthy life. Stoki was a great believer in Yoga and Yoga exercises and he introduced the idea to me. I was very young and very healthy and I never had worried about taking exercises. When we were married, he showed me some of the exercises that he did—stretching ones and strengthening ones. . . ."[23]

With his substantially reduced conducting schedule in Philadelphia, Stoki preferred to spend most of his time in New York and on the farm. "We called it 'Cloud Walk Farm,' " said Evangeline, "because the clouds in that part of Connecticut seemed to walk over the land. It was about twenty miles from Litchfield, just remote enough and far from all our friends so they couldn't drop in on us at any time. It was very beautiful and Stoki designed the stonework around the walks and the pool."[24] Stoki remarked to a reporter, somewhat facetiously, about their two tame bulls. "Our bulls are named Ophelia and Tristan. We have geese of which I am proudest because they hiss so beautifully. I try out my music on them." And he probably thought about the dowagers.

The last pair of the season's concerts were neatly juxtaposed with the usual Saturday night concert shifted to the preceding Thursday so that Leopold and Evangeline could leave immediately after the Friday afternoon concert for New York and depart the next morning on the S.S. *Bremen* for Europe. After a brief stopover in London, they proceeded to Moscow, where they were welcomed expansively. Stoki was given a dinner with praise-filled speeches by the Union of Composers and he posed for photos with Mikhail Ippolitov-Ivanov and Reinhold Glière in one shot and Nikolai Miaskovsky and Boris Asafiev in another.

On their second night in Moscow, they went to the Bolshoi to hear a performance of *Boris*. In spite of being disturbed by alterations in the score and the dramatic action, Stoki admitted that the Bolshoi Opera House was "simply marvelous. I had never heard opera until I heard this

Stokowski on first trip to Soviet Union with Mikhail Ippolitov-Ivanov (left) and Reinhold Glière (1931)

Courtesy International Leopold Stokowski Society

finished Moscow company sing. The big thing there is the spirit; they are alive and enthusiastic, and they are singers. . . . Not only can they sing exceptionally well, but each one is an actor. . . . The great chorus moves back and forth along the stage and never relaxes a minute, thus giving a perfect picture. Nothing I have ever heard compares with it."[25]

They also attended performances of Mussorgsky's *Khovanshchina* and Janáček's *House of the Dead,* which he said he would produce in Philadelphia. Evangeline's strong interest in education led them to visit Russian schools and even attend a Children's Theater.[26] "These theaters, which receive special government attention," said Evangeline, "are nothing but propaganda centers. In one I saw what were represented as aristocratic Red Cross nurses refusing to give common soldiers anything to drink and letting them die. I was outraged," she told me. "I had been in the Red Cross in World War I and I knew what the Red Cross had done in Russia. . . . They had given a lot of help and supplies." And she asked indignantly, "How can you tell such lies?"

Quite by accident they met Albert Coates, who conducted frequently in Russia. Evangeline remembered that the Russians "put a member of the secret police as a butler in the apartment they had given him. He joked about it and said to us, 'It's very convenient, if you are going to be observed, to be observed by somebody who is of some use to you.' "[27]

Coates had a great advantage, for he spoke Russian fluently. He had been born in Petrograd of an English father and a Russian mother just five days after Leopold's birth in London. The Russians, who seem to have a difficulty for every solution, had not made the best arrangements for the Stokowskis and Coates came to the rescue. He described it in an interview with Linton Martin of the *Philadelphia Inquirer:* "The poor dears. When I took them to lunch Mrs. Stokowski declared that she hadn't eaten like that in a fortnight. And it was just an ordinary lunch for me. . . . And as for the hotel room, I found they had been poked away in some stuffy, dirty hole.

"But you know I don't know where Stoky got the idea that art in Russia, the performances of opera and so forth, are used for the exploitation of propaganda. I can't understand it. Oh, that was Mrs. Stoky, you say? Well, I hadn't read a word. Only know what I was told by Mrs. Otto H. Kahn, who is so pally with both of us, you know."[28]

When Stoki returned to Philadelphia, he began his 1931–32 season with a new title: general music director. His schedule, while not as exhausting as in many previous years, called for him to conduct for sixteen weeks of the

United Press International Photo

Mrs. Leopold Stokowski (Evangeline Johnson) arrives in New York on the *Europa,* June 18, 1931

season and limit his absences to periods of three or four weeks, rather than taking a long mid-winter vacation. Guest conductors included Fritz Reiner, Bernardino Molinari, Alexander Smallens and Toscanini.

Unfortunately, Toscanini suffered a bout with neuritis and had to cancel his two weeks with the orchestra. Judson, who had engineered young Eugene Ormandy's engagement with the Minneapolis, brought him in to substitute for the ailing Toscanini.[29] Who could have presumed that Ormandy would still be conducting the Philadelphia Orchestra over forty years later?

During the weeks when he was not with the orchestra, Stoki hurried to Connecticut to be with Evangeline and his three daughters. "Those were not easy years, growing up with two families," Sonya recalled. "Lyuba is five years younger than I am and Sadja is nine years younger. That's a big gap when you get to nine years and it wasn't easy. . . . Tanti [Evangeline] always reported to Mother when I was there for the six months and they had a very good working relationship although they never saw each other. It was all done on the telephone."

It was Evangeline who saw the absurdity of having Sonya spend exactly six months with each of her parents and suggested greater flexibility. Sonya was particularly pleased and remarked that the original plan didn't "make psychological sense at all. If they were going on a wonderful trip in the summertime—which they did that summer—they would take me along with them."[30]

Sonya had been to Europe with her mother several times. Olga, who had known Stoki's parents, kept in touch with them and visited his mother each time they would be in England. "We always went to see Granny over at Golders Green," said Sonya. "I saw her right up until she was in the nursing home about six months or so before her death." She described her grandmother: "She wasn't of big stature. She was, I would say, a small person. I found her just very warm and very sweet. She was a very kind person."[31]

On a trip to England with her father and Evangeline, Sonya went to a phone and spoke with her grandmother. It was the first time that Evangeline knew of her existence. "You see," said Evangeline, "I never knew any of this. . . . He never mentioned the family at all. He might have been ashamed of the family. . . . It's amazing because he denied to me that he had any relatives in England at all."[32]

"Tanti never realized that my grandmother was my grandmother," said Sonya. "It always amazed me that she would be married to him all those years and didn't know. I think that Daddy started fantasizing a little bit on his own background and at that point maybe his family became an inconvenience. That's an awful thing to say but I think it was just that.[33] . . . He was a complete romantic."[34]

All three Stokowski daughters had attended the Dalton School. Sonya studied dancing briefly with Martha Graham and Doris Humphrey, while the other two studied with Anita Zahn. During the periods Sonya was

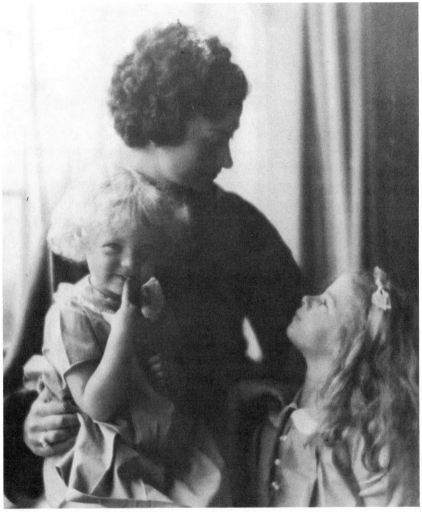

Courtesy Evangeline Johnson Merrill
Evangeline with Lyuba and Sadja in her New York apartment (1933)

with her mother, the house was a sort of musical bedlam. There were several students living there and one was Eugene List. "Eugene List was a brother to me," Sonya recalled. "He was in the house I don't know how many years. When you are sitting back and somebody's saying, 'Will you please get your dirty socks to the laundry!' there is something very brother-like in all this. And Rosalyn Tureck was another dear who was of the family. . . . When Mother decided that each of us should rotate in the kitchen doing the cooking, it was very interesting. I think we had two or three students living in the house then."[35]

Olga once described a typical day in their lives during that period: "I think of a day when a man came to see me on important business. I had just returned from the Juilliard and found him in the hall. I soon realized that every corner of the apartment was occupied. Two pianists were rehearsing in the drawing room, a committee meeting was in progress in the dining room, a debutante pianist was trying on concert dresses in my room, Sonya was having a German lesson in her room, a student who was living with us was working at counterpoint in the guest room and there was nothing left but the hall and the kitchen. I ordered the car and took my caller to the Colony Club."[36]

Evangeline, with her increasing interest in progressive education, and particularly in the education of her daughters, devoted more and more time to the Dalton School, becoming chairman of the Art Department. "There was a remarkable woman—Miss Helen Parker—she created the Dalton plan."[37] The school became famous and the students progressed rapidly. After leaving the Dalton School, Sonya went to Dobbs Ferry. "I had been to Dalton; it was a change from a progressive school to Miss Mah-sters school . . . it was so different."[38]

To be close to the Dalton School, Evangeline took an apartment at 40 East Eighty-eighth Street, where as always she created a fantastic ambience filled with works of art she had collected. "If you think that art is the highest form of evolution and you have a little extra money beyond food, children, clothing, then you must find out about the artists and preferably in the environment where you are," Evangeline remarked. "I didn't think that many years ago when I was collecting Klee, Kandinsky, and Miró in the twenties. I just thought, oh, they're marvelous, they're great, they're wonderful." I asked whether she had collected many of Klee's paintings or drawings. "Two or three but I'll tell you what I have always done when an artist becomes world famous and I have had the joy of it for many years. I either sell it and use the money to buy the works of young artists or I give it to a museum because, as I have said, I don't think you ever own a work of art."[39]

In Philadelphia, Stokowski, too, decided on a more radical change in his life-style. From the large apartment in Chestnut Hill, he moved directly into Philadelphia, just off Rittenhouse Square and within walking distance

Courtesy Philadelphia Inquirer
Stokowski's home in Philadelphia at 1716 Rittenhouse Street (1933)

of the Academy of Music. The old coach house he moved into at 1716 Rittenhouse Street was next to a parking lot just behind the Art Alliance and across the narrow little street from the Barclay Hotel. He was comfortably ensconced there before the beginning of the 1932–33 season.[40]

"Stable? Kennel? Hovel? Speakeasy? All Wrong, It's Stokowski's Town House" headlined an article by Linton Martin. The building was a three-story, red brick affair with a garage door in front proclaiming its carriage-house origin. Martin compared it to a shell-shocked hut from the battle zone of wartime France. "All right then. How about another glimpse from the street. What's that high-boarded backyard effect at the rear of the third floor? Perhaps a dog or cat kennel." That, incidentally, was the boarded enclosure where Stoki took his sunbaths and did his exercises.

"But once inside the scene changes," Martin concluded, "for this is Stokowski's new 'town house,' as utterly original in idea and effect as the maestro of the manse is himself. . . . Navajo rugs and blankets give a picturesque touch to the floors and walls which are finished in a mellow green. . . . Every detail of the exceptional apartment, behind its ramshackle exterior, was devised and developed by [him] . . . from the fenced-in roof at the upper rear where the blond conductor is said to go nudist in daily sun baths . . . to the laboratory-like equipment in the large living room on the second floor, which is also music room and workshop for the pioneering podium personality."[41] This was to become the gathering place for his enthusiastic youth concert group.

On the night of March 1, 1932, the son of Charles and Anne Lindbergh was kidnapped and the shocking news was instantly flashed across the world. It was a mere five years since Lindbergh's epochal solo flight across the Atlantic and he was regarded as one of America's most beloved heroes. It was called the crime of the century. Although a ransom of $50,000 had been paid, the child was not returned, and two months later, on May 12, the body of Charles Augustus Lindbergh, Jr., was found in the woods near the road between Hopewell and Princeton.

Terror spread through homes across the country, particularly those of the wealthy whose children might be taken for ransom. The Stokowskis were constantly before the eyes of the public. There had been recent news articles reporting Stoki's huge income from the Philadelphia Orchestra, radio contracts, and recording royalties.[42] The reports were exaggerated, but he was regarded as a wealthy man. Evangeline was often mentioned as a "wealthy heiress" and this naturally prompted concern. Although less apprehensive about their daughters' safety in New York, Evangeline worried about their long weekends at the farm in Connecticut, and she appealed to the district attorney of Litchfield County for special protection.

The ever-alert press, which always looked for anything newsworthy concerning the Stokowskis, learned of the request and descended on Stoki in Philadelphia. He expressed surprise, saying, "I have not heard of any threats against the children, and I should know if any had been made. . . . I did not know that a guard had been requested."

Similar fears and anxieties plagued other families, too. Pinkerton guards had been hired to protect little Gloria Vanderbilt after an anonymous kidnap threat was received.

A year later an extortionist who called himself Davis wrote to Mrs. Stokowski demanding that $800 be sent to an address on Washington Avenue in the Bronx. Upon checking, the police found no one by that name at that location, and because of the small amount of ransom asked, concluded that it was probably the work of a crank. But shortly thereafter Evangeline received a phone call at the Dalton School from a man demanding that she meet him at Eighty-sixth Street and Park Avenue with an envelope containing $1,000 to prevent her daughters from being abducted. Evangeline agreed. She contacted the police, who arranged for a trap to be set, and she kept the appointment carrying an envelope containing scraps of newspapers. Although she waited three hours, the extortionist did not appear.[43]

Sonya, at the time, was with her mother and together they set out for Haus Hirth in Unter Grainau near Garmisch in Bavaria. Papers printed a photo of Sonya and Olga with the caption: "Flees to Europe with Daughter." They felt entirely free from any threatening dangers there and visited Salzburg, Bamberg, and Nuremberg and took long walks in the country. Olga wrote to John Erskine at Juilliard mentioning that she hated to give up the sense of security that she felt there "in connection with Sonya. I hope and pray we may get it back in America."[44]

23

Mussorgsky's Boris, etc.

HE music of Mussorgsky had always fascinated Stokowski. He had
conducted *Night on Bald Mountain* and excerpts from the operas
Khovanshchina and *The Fair at Sorochinsk,* and now wanted to do
two works that intrigued him more than any others: *Pictures at an Exhibition* and *Boris Godunov.*

While Stokowski knew the version of *Pictures at an Exhibition* done
by Rimsky-Korsakov and his pupil Mikhail Tushmalov, he was never
interested in performing it, though it had considerable popularity in both
Germany and Russia. I heard the Rimsky-Korsakov/Tushmalov arrangement in Berlin long before I heard Koussevitzky conduct Ravel's transcription of it in Boston.

During the summer of 1922, Ravel completed his orchestration while
visiting Roland-Manuel at Lyons-la-Forêt as a Koussevitzky commission.[1]
It was then published in Koussevitzky's own publishing house Edition
Russe and remained his exclusive property for the next seven years. He
conducted the first performance on October 19, 1922, at the Paris Opera
during one of his famous "Concerts Koussevitzky." Then in 1930 he
recorded it with the Boston Symphony for RCA Victor.[2]

Stoki was most eager to perform it and even made a direct request to
Koussevitzky, who adamantly refused. Finally in 1929 it was turned over
to Boosey and Hawks and, on November 22, Stokowski conducted it for
the first time in Philadelphia one week before his presentation of *Boris
Godunov,* which had been in preparation for nearly a year.[3]

One might think that Stokowski, like most conductors, would have

preferred the voluptuous, overblown Rimsky-Korsakov version of *Boris*.
Not so! Stoki was most anxious to produce *Boris* as close to Mussorgsky's
intentions as possible.

He was confronted by the fact that Mussorgsky had actually left two
"original" versions, and with two original versions to choose from, it was
almost impossible to be a purist. Therefore, Stokowski, while offering the
Mussorgsky "original"—it was in fact the first such performance outside
of Russia—did make a compendium of the two versions.[4] He kept the
stark and primitive quality of the first edition and he retained the very
effective Polish scenes, just as Shostakovich did over two decades later,
although they are not part of the first version.

In the preparation of *Boris Godunov*, Stoki was greatly aided by Sylvan
Levin, a young pianist who had come to the Curtis Institute from the
Peabody Conservatory in Baltimore. Levin very quickly showed such
ability that he was asked to join the faculty as a trainer of choruses at the
magnificent sum—so he thought—of $6,000 per season. Stoki wanted to
discuss with him the preparation of the various minor roles and the work
of the choruses.

"We sat down on a couch in Madame Sembrich's studio," Sylvan said,
"and opened the score of *Boris*, and as we talked I found many mistakes in
the horn part of the score right away." Stoki was impressed and he began to
rely heavily on Sylvan's assistance. "He assigned me fourteen roles to train
and let me pick them from the students at Curtis Institute," said Sylvan.
"It made a big shot out of me and from then on we went to town."[5]

Stoki was meticulous in his demands. On November 8 he wrote to
Sylvan giving detailed instructions concerning the scene of the Boyars and
on page after page indicated just where additional voices from the chorus
should be added, and where not. "As you know the five singers in question
so well, I should like to leave it to your judgement how to divide the above
solo parts among them. If anything is not clear about this please telephone
me or come to see me at the Academy and we can talk it over."[6] Four
days later he again wrote to Sylvan Levin instructing him to have Mr.
Groban, one of the Boyars, "sing the officer part beginning on page 106."[7]
Stoki was studying the score constantly.

Sylvan had asked whether he might come to the orchestral rehearsals.
"We have not been able to start rehearsing 'Boris,' " Stoki responded,
"because we have been so busy. As soon as we do I will let you know. I
shall be very happy to have you come. But please come alone, as I never
allow anybody in the rehearsals except for definite purpose of work."[8]

Rehearsals for the soloists and chorus had been going on for months. On the twenty-fifth, Olin Downes, who had heard performances of the "original" *Boris* in Moscow, came to the Curtis Institute and lectured on the various editions of the score while Sylvan Levin accompanied Beniamini Grobani—the former Mr. Groban—in excerpts. Downes called the forthcoming performance one of the most important musical events of the season.[9] Stoki, who attended the lecture, was pleased.

On November 29, 1929, the first of three performances was given in the Academy. Critic Linton Martin echoed Downes and called it "the most monumental achievement in the history of the Philadelphia Orchestra."[10] The concert was truly monumental and ran from 2:30 to 6:00 P.M. with a somewhat depleted audience at the end. Endurance was not always a characteristic of Philadelphia's blue-haired Main Line ladies. The Saturday evening performance fared better.

The impressive cast of vocalists included Richard Crooks as Dimitry and Shuisky, Sophie Braslau as Marina, George Baklanoff as Boris, and Herbert Gould as Pimenn. Among the young Curtis students we find Rose Bampton singing Feodor, Natalie Bodanskaya as Zenia, and among the Boyars Benjamin de Loache, who was appearing with Stoki for the first time. "I had come straight out of South Carolina and at the age of 22 had never heard a great symphony orchestra except on records. I was at the opening concert of that season. . . . Stokowski walked on stage. His swift elegance and the mystery of his power enmeshed me," Ben recalled.[11]

"One morning three months later, when I was working on a Schubert *lied,* Stokowski asked to see me; he was auditioning all the students in the voice department. I ran upstairs three at a time, the Schubert song clasped in my hand. Only an inexperienced child would have chosen Schubert's *Am Meer,* but I did. Of course, the inevitable happened; I did not have enough breath to finish the first phrase. I simply stopped. In my confusion I tried to make apologies. Stokowski merely indicated that he would like me to sit beside him. He then talked of my family and asked me my reasons— and told me his reasons—for loving Schubert *lieder.* He knew precisely the moment I had regained my composure and suggested that I sing again.

"Three months later I made my debut with him. Rose Bampton, Irra Petina, and I were students at the Curtis and he engaged us to sing in *Boris,* which we did."[12]

Rose Bampton, too, recalled her introduction to Stoki: "I was at Chautauqua studying during the summer and I got this call from the school asking me if I would come back because there was a chance that

I could learn something that Stokowski was going to do and that if I came back immediately, they would work with me until I could sing it for him. Well, it was *El amor brujo* and Sylvan Levin worked like crazy with me.

"We went out to his apartment . . . and I sang for him and he finally said, 'Do you know what you're singing about?' And I said, 'No. I've been so busy learning it in these couple of days so that I could sing it for you but now I will get to work on it.' So he proceeded to tell me a story about it that was just hair-raising and when he finished, I must have been quite white and shocked and he said, 'Now I don't care whether you go out and have the experience or whether you really just use your imagination to the point where you know what I'm talking about, but the next time you sing it for me you must sing it as if you knew what it is all about.'

"So that was my introduction to him, and then the following year he again gave me another chance and it was that year we did *Boris*. And I had the part of Feodor in that."[13]

Although Stoki never again conducted a performance of *Boris*, his interest in it never waned and in 1936 he made a Symphonic Synthesis of the work. He conducted the first performance in the Academy on November 6, 1936.[14] It was, he said, based entirely on Mussorgsky's original scores. Stoki leaned heavily on expanded sonorities from percussion instruments, particularly in the coronation scene. Critics noted the remarkable collection of oriental gongs that were placed in the regular percussion section. They were part of the collection that Leopold and Evangeline had obtained when they were in the Orient.[15]

In speaking of the *Boris* transcription, Lou Harrison told me that Stoki used "selected Javanese gongs and Southeast Asian gongs and instruments for the ringing of the great bells in the coronation scene and it was altogether fabulous. I don't think I've ever heard so beautiful a transcription. And it must have been done on an extremely personally supervised basis that took a lot of time and thought and listening . . ."[16]

On November 16, 1936, a little over a week after Stoki gave the premiere of his Symphonic Synthesis of *Boris Godunov*, he recorded it on a set of 78s for RCA Victor.[17] It was later issued on RCA's bargain LP label, Camden, with no credit given to Stoki or the Philadelphia Orchestra. The nonexistent Warwick Symphony Orchestra is credited. It was indeed an example of RCA's loony-bin marketing practices.

In early December 1952 Stoki recorded "highlights" from the Rimsky-Korsakov version of *Boris Godunov* for RCA Victor with the San Francisco Symphony; Nicola Rossi-Lemeni, bass; and the San Francisco Opera Chorus.[18]

Stoki had played both the Ravel and Lucien Cailliet transcriptions of Mussorgsky's *Pictures at an Exhibition* and he now decided to make a version of his own. Linton Martin in the *Inquirer* declared that it was presented to an overflowing and enraptured audience and "came as a revelation of hitherto undisclosed splendor, power, color and quality . . . making its predecessors seem faded in comparison." Stoki had stated that he wanted to preserve and express its Slavic character. "He has done this gorgeously," added Martin, "and he has a great deal more in producing a work well worthy to place beside his masterly 'Boris' transcription, and possessing much of its barbaric splendor, mystical spirit, grotesquerie and strange beauty, with greater diversity of detail made possible by the various 'pictures.' "[19]

Later Stoki did transcriptions of Mussorgsky's *Night on Bald Mountain* and the Entr'acte from *Khovanshchina.* "Mussorgsky composed *Night on Bald Mountain* and later Rimsky-Korsakov changed and added certain passages," wrote Stokowski. "When I was in Russia, soon after the Revolution, I asked to see the original manuscript of Mussorgsky, and only with great difficulty was I able to find it. The authorities permitted me to photograph Mussorgsky's original score which I have in my library. The version we have performed is based on the original of Mussorgsky with certain changes and additions of Rimsky-Korsakov. I have reorchestrated the whole composition because of passages which were out of balance and therefore unclear."[20]

Michel Calvocoressi, who has long been regarded as a foremost authority on Mussorgsky and has written numerous articles about him for various scholarly publications, attended Stokowski's performance of *Boris Godunov.* He had loudly praised both of the original versions of the opera and strongly believed that each should be produced as is and not in any combination: "The one fatal mistake is to attempt to mix the two versions —as was done at the concert performance given four years ago at Philadelphia. This will always mean altering the proportions, impairing the balance, rendering the work too long and less coherent."[21]

Calvocoressi may have been right. His was the view of a purist. But Stokowski, too, was a purist in going back to the original scores, and since it would be entirely impractical to present one version after the other, to be musicologically correct, he instead made the best of both possible choices. He gave his hearers the best of what he felt Mussorgsky had written.

(24)

Repertoire

S TOKOWSKI, from his earliest days, introduced his audiences to the music of their time. He recognized that it was the unfamiliarity with changing musical styles and values that repelled many listeners. He vowed to change that. He was close enough to the times of stormy negative reactions to the music of Strauss, Debussy, Ravel, and Stravinsky to realize that repeated performances of this music would be needed before it could become part of the accepted repertory of the orchestra.

With his introduction of works by Varèse, Schoenberg, Berg, Stravinsky, Cowell, Riegger, and some of the more radical Russians, Stokowski brought the future into the Academy walls and disoriented many of the time-bound listeners whose ears rebelled against the unfamiliar.

During the 1915–16 season Stoki began to culture-shock his audience and force them to grapple with new ideas totally alien to their past experiences. He introduced divergent works that drew hisses and protests from his baffled listeners. Among them were the *Alpine* Symphony of Strauss and Arnold Schoenberg's Chamber Symphony. It was the latter that provided the major shock, and the displeasure of the crowd evoked one of the most noisy demonstrations Stoki had encountered or—might one venture—that he had ever enjoyed! There was no sympathy from the critics and when he brought the Schoenberg work to New York, Richard Aldrich commented: "The *Kammersynfonie* did not yesterday show the prescience of a master, the vision of a seer into unknown realms of beauty. Will our grandchildren see it and smile indulgently at the bewildered listeners of 1915?"[1]

Stoki programmed it in New York again in 1923 and in a letter to Charles Martin Loeffler he mentioned it:

> Last night I played Schoenberg's Kammersymphonie in New York, and was soundly hissed for my pains, but it is all your fault in not finishing your own symphony and letting me play it. I warn you that sometime in August a noisy, dirty Ford will draw up at your door, and I shall bother you again until the symphony is finished. Meantime I am off to Europe quite soon, and want very much to go to Maria-Lachs. Would you do me a great favor?—to give me a letter to some one there who would allow me to penetrate a little into their life and hear their music and see their architecture. I hear always in my mind the combination of notes you played to me of their bells. If you can do this for me I should be most grateful, as I have a great longing to go there and get a little out of this noisy world which seems so cheap sometimes.[2]

After a performance of Scriabin's *Poem of Ecstasy,* his Friday-afternoon audience applauded generously, but on Saturday night the audience, which was usually more progressive, began to bolt even before the work had begun. "Conspicuous use was made of the exit doors," one critic noted. At the conclusion Stokowski turned abruptly, held his baton up to command their attention, and then addressed his listeners tartly: "I consider this poem one of the two best musical compositions written in modern times." Many in the audience who had already donned their hats and coats, moved toward the stage to hear Stoki, "I notice that whenever we present music of a novel sort to the audiences in this city the people here fail to give us a chance to do any justice to the music. It is impossible for any orchestra to do its best work in such an atmosphere of hostility.

"My men go through the hardest kind of drilling each week in order to do proper justice to their work. They have a right to expect that their audiences shall be equally gracious in turn. But it has not always been the case in this city.

"I have a right to expect that people of Philadelphia will do me the justice to believe we are bringing the best kind of music to you and that we have a knowledge of music that is good. But many of my audiences insult me and the orchestra by premature judgement of the music that we present. You have no right to condemn the music that we present after having heard it but once. We of the orchestra know it is good, because we have rehearsed it time and time again and we are cognizant of the beauties that the music contains. I hope in the future there will be no such disregard of the orchestra's efforts as there has been tonight. I want each of you to feel that you are as much a part of the orchestra as the musicians."[3]

Some time later he was overheard discussing Scriabin and other composers. "I was telling a friend of certain tendencies I had observed in some new works I am studying," he said, "and the representative of a magazine who was listening asked me to note them down for him, which I do at random, just as they occur, without any attempt at literary form." The result was a rather brief article that appeared in *Arts and Decoration*, November 1922: "Stravinsky, Schoenberg, Scriabin, Ornstein, Milhaud, Malipiero are all irregular-rhythmic and are all, but in varying degrees, polyphonic. It is useless to speak to many people of Scriabin's *Poème d'Extase*, for example, as they dismiss this remarkable work with a contemptuous muttering of 'decadent' or 'immoral.' It is one of the most highly organized and complex pieces of orchestral polyphony which exists."[4]

During 1921–22 he conducted Schoenberg's Five Pieces for Orchestra and gave American premieres of the Sibelius Fifth Symphony, Falla's *El amor brujo*, and Stravinsky's *Le Sacre du printemps*. While one might have expected *Le Sacre* to tilt the bonnets of some of the Main Line ladies, it ruffled the hair of critics as well. "Paleozoic" one scribe called it. "Without description or program," we read in the *Philadelphia North American*, "the work might have suggested a New Year's Eve rally of moonshine addicts and the simple pastimes of early youth and maidens, circumspectly attired in a fig leaf apiece."[5]

The following season he introduced Stravinsky's Symphonies of Wind Instruments to more sustained sibilation. Writing about Stravinsky in the *Musical Digest* of December 30, 1924, Carlos Salzedo remarked that: "His rhythmic innovations, his increase in the use of percussion, were revolutionary fifteen years ago. Now . . . next to Varèse's Hyperprism, Stravinsky's use of percussion seems mild."[6]

During the summer of 1922, Varèse sent the score of *Amériques* to Stokowski. It was the first work he had written in America and it marked his break with Europeanism. "When I wrote Amériques," said Varèse, "I was still under the spell of my first impressions of New York—not only New York seen, but more especially heard. For the first time with my physical ears I heard a sound that kept recurring in my dreams as a boy —a high whistling C sharp. It came to me as I worked in my Westside apartment where I could hear all the river sounds—the lonely foghorns, the shrill peremptory whistles—the whole wonderful river symphony which moved me more than anything ever had before. . . ."[7]

With his usual promptness, Stoki wrote to Varèse: "I am eager to study it as soon as I am less busy." When no further response was forthcoming, Varèse pressed for an opinion, but Stoki did not answer. In a state of pique Varèse wrote to his wife, Louise, who was then visiting the Carlos Salzedos in Bar Harbor: "Stokowski, the swine, hasn't answered my letter. I don't think I have a chance with him." Then in another letter to her he wrote: "Stokowski is back but takes good care not to answer my letter. Better not say anything. No use pestering him. I myself will ask Stokowski to return the score—and *merde pour lui.*"

Stoki did answer and explained that he had sailed for Europe earlier than he had expected and that he would work on Varèse's score at the earliest possible moment. In November, a final negative answer came: "I fear it will be a long time, before I shall be able to come to your work. . . . Personally I regret this very deeply but the Committee is not able to give me free hand in this matter for financial reasons." Although this seems like a very uncharacteristic dodge, he did conduct the world premiere of *Amériques* "three years and five months" later, Louise Varèse recalled.[8]

The first Varèse work, however, that Stoki performed in Philadelphia was a more modest effort: his shorter though no less cacophonous *Hyperprism.* Varèse attended several rehearsals in Philadelphia and on returning to New York found a letter from Stokowski that read: "We found a very good siren from the fire department which we used Friday and I am going to use it again tonight. You are right; it is much better. . . ." The walls of the Academy had never before heard the screech of sirens from within.

The audience in New York reacted much as it had in Philadelphia. Olin Downes dittoed the critics. "The disciples of the fearsome Varèse were in evidence . . . they applauded long and loudly while the rest of the audience laughed."[9]

Following the concert, a parody by Frank H. Warren appeared in the *New York Evening World:*

> 'Twas the week before Christmas, in Carnegie Hall
> Not a critic was stirring; from every box stall
> Stokowski adherents had lauded the swank
> With which the conductor had led César Franck

And every one heeding the Stokowski rap
Had just settled back for a good Philly nap
When out on the air there arose such a clatter
We sprang from our seats to learn what was the matter
And up from the program—were all going crazy?
Jumped Hyperprism, offspring of Edgar Varèse. . . .[10]

One of Stokowski's shockers during the 1925–26 season was the long-promised performance of Varèse's *Amériques*. The score called for a huge orchestra of 142 players with large brass and woodwind sections and a percussion group that in addition to the usual "kitchenware" added a "lion's roar," whip, sirens, and other noisemakers. It lasted about thirty-five minutes. According to Louise Varèse, there were sixteen rehearsals before the first performance on April 9, 1926. Varèse was on hand for the final rehearsal and the Friday and Saturday concerts. On Friday the good ladies simply lost their "cool" and booed and hissed so vehemently that Stoki spared Varèse the wrath of the sibilants by having him remain backstage.[11]

In Carnegie Hall four days later, Stokowski began his concert with *Amériques*. At the conclusion there was a veritable riot. "The outbreak, moderate at first, swelled gradually to an indescribable turmoil," wrote W. J. Henderson in the *Sun*. "Some men wildly waved their arms and one was seen to raise both hands high above his head with both thumbs turned down, the death sign of the Roman amphitheater. . . . The demonstration lasted more than five minutes, which, as political meeting experts well know, is a long time."[12]

Olga Samaroff was not amused. In her review of the concert in the *Post*, she wrote reproachingly: "Mr. Stokowski, who has a distinguished record in the matter of introducing important new works, could scarcely have done anything more detrimental to the cause of modern music than to produce a composition like *Amériques*."[13]

The next Varèse world premiere was that of *Arcana*, on April 8, 1927. By definition, *Arcana* refers to secrets or mysteries; on a second level, to secret remedies and elixirs. Although *Arcana* is indeed absolute music, part of its inspiration came from writings of Philippus Aureolus Paracelsus, the pseudonym of the sixteenth-century physician and alchemist Theophrastus Bombastus von Hohenheim. The score arrived late and unfortunately there were not enough rehearsals scheduled for so difficult a work. The men in the orchestra hated it, Stoki admitted to critic Paul

Rosenfeld, and they hardly gave their all.[14] But perhaps Stokowski, too, had not given his all, for, suffering from painful bursitis, he had conducted with one arm in a sling.

Stoki so admired Varèse that he recommended him as a teacher of composition for the Curtis Institute. Varèse visited Philadelphia and was eager to accept a post as teacher of advanced composition. I do not know whether there may have been objections from some of the archconservatives, but he was advised that for the time being no decisions would be made. The following season Stoki invited Varèse to take over his conducting class at Curtis. Varèse, however, was reluctant since he had not done any conducting for several years. He wrote to Stokowski and declined the invitation. Stoki replied that he understood his point of view but added: "As you know I am hoping to have the benefit of your cooperation in the Curtis Institute in some form and I feel that in the future this will realize itself."[15]

Stokowski translated his admiration of Varèse with a flair of generosity. Fernand Ouellette recalled in his biography of Varèse: "On October 10, 1928, Varèse left New York with the painter [Joseph] Stella. Before his departure, Stokowski gave him two thousand dollars."[16]

Stoki had also made somewhat similar gestures to Stravinsky and Schoenberg. Stravinsky recalled that Stokowski came to see him in Biarritz in 1922. "He looked like a sleek Russian wolfhound then. . . . He made a handsome cash offer for the first American performance rights to my future works, and he actually paid an installment on the proposed sum. . . ."[17]

Schoenberg, in a letter to Stokowski in 1949, wrote: "I wanted to make you a little present in order to thank you for the generosity when you gave me $1,000 on the occasion of my severe sickness in 1946."[18] He offered to send him a painting—a self-portrait—which he had done. Stokowski was pleased. ". . . Of course, we would like to have a painting from you. We both paint ourselves and so are interested in this art."[19]

Stokowski's intense interest in the progressive movement of these composers was deep-seated. He thoroughly appreciated the fact that Varèse could find musical material in such things as fog horns, sirens, the sounds of traffic, and the like. Stoki agreed that all sound can be music: "Machinery sometimes makes cross-rhythms, accents and frequencies that form a highly complex tapestry of sound."[20]

He formulated his reaction to Schoenberg's procedures. "Music is forever becoming freer. . . . No longer does it circulate around a central tonality, . . . [nor] does it necessarily begin and end in the same key or tonality.

"Just as our ideas of the universe are constantly expanding and becoming freer—giving us a picture of the relativity of everything in the cosmos as opposed to the old ideas of fixed centers—so in music there is a parallel development, and a somewhat similar conception of relativity of sound and key centers. Key centers are like suns around which revolve other tonal centers. Our minds and the imaginative, emotional side of our hearing delight in remote key centers which may be in violent and highly stimulating contrast with an already established key center.

"This tendency has reached a high degree of plasticity with Schoenberg. This composer has liberated himself entirely from the conception of key centers, so that his harmonies flow in any direction with complete freedom. Schoenberg has contributed to music a new conception—and from that conception new resources which at some time in the future may be more widely understood and appreciated than at present."[21]

Schoenberg composed his Variations for Orchestra Opus 31, during 1927 and 1928 and it had its world premiere in Berlin on December 2, 1928, with Furtwängler and the Berlin Philharmonic. Stokowski immediately sent for a score and programmed it the following season, October 18, 1929, for its American premiere. After a frosty reception at home, he brought it to Carnegie Hall. There Olga Samaroff sat between two conservative music lovers and as the piece progressed she looked to her left and observed "a facial expression of such astonished anguish" that she turned to the right and not only on the face of her neighbor but on rows and rows of people she beheld "visible signs of acute distress, utter bewilderment or unmistakable indignation. This geometry in music," she said, "was obviously giving no pleasure to the most sophisticated audience in the most modern of cities."[22]

Shortly after the performance of Variations, Stoki began to study the score of *Gurrelieder* and almost a year before its actual performance began to explore all of the possibilities of a massive performance on the scale of the *Symphony of a Thousand.* Schoenberg had assigned the work to Universal Editions in Vienna, which was represented in the United States by Associated Music Publishers. Stoki had obtained a score and Arthur Judson negotiated the conditions for the first and subsequent performances with AMP.

On November 20, 1931, Stoki received an indignant letter from Schoenberg, who was then residing in Barcelona.

Highly esteemed Mr. Stokowski,

I am still angry with you because you returned my score of "Von Heute auf Morgen," which I had sent you for a four-week study, after a year and a quarter without a line of excuse, without a word. However, I had spent 25 Marks for a telegram in order to answer your question at the time because, according to local standards, it would be impossible for a man of my standing not to answer. . . .

I was just reading that you are scheduling the Gurrelieder in New York or Philadelphia and am very surprised that neither you, nor U.E. [Universal Edition] let me know about it, although I had previously informed you that I reserved with the publisher the right to conduct the premiere myself.

I am inclined to believe that you do not want to cause me harm and that you made arrangements with Director Hertzka which will not hinder the exercise of my rights. . . .[23]

At the bottom of his copy of the letter Schoenberg scrawled: "This letter was answered by Stokowski in a vague manner, dissembling (!) and asserting that the contract was made by the orchestra contrary to the assertion by Hertzka that he made the contract directly with Stokowski."[24]

Obviously, Schoenberg had no understanding of the music business in America. If he had insisted on conducting the American premiere himself, years might have gone by before it would have happened. As it was, years did elapse before another performance took place after the Stokowski one.

But Schoenberg persisted in a series of cables and letters. He wired: "I beg you as a man and artist to cable me truly the complete conditions which Hertzka has got by your society for my right to conduct personally the first performance of Gurrelieder."[25] Stoki apparently cabled that he should take up the matter directly with Hertzka in Vienna, which brought forth this reply:

Highly esteemed Mr. Stokowski,

Neither as a man, nor an artist shall I ask Mr. Hertzka.

My telegram in which I as a man and an artist asked you to tell me the truth regarding the breach of my rights, was sent on the presumption that you as a man and an artist would not cover the likes of Hertzka. . . .

If Hertzka were not committing fraud in dealing with me, there-

fore acting immorally, he would not have forbidden you to tell me
so.

But when you help him commit an immoral act, you become his
accomplice.

Have you thought about this and what the world's opinion is going
to be?[26]

At this point most conductors might have given up the project altogether. But not Stokowski. He wrote to Schoenberg on April 3, 1932:
"Mr. Hertzka has not forbidden me anything nor have I had any communication with him in any form regarding you or Gurrelieder. I have given
six months of intense work to the preparation of Gurrelieder and do not
have time to attend to the business side of the Philadelphia Orchestra.
Mr. Judson does this." Stoki then mentioned that since Associated Music
Publishers had the rights in the United States for Gurrelieder, Mr. Judson
had made a contract directly with them. His letter continued:

> I am sorry you have had a disagreement with Mr. Hertzka but I
> do not know your side of it nor his. Also I have many difficulties and
> problems of my own.
> I should like to be of service to you but I cannot do so in economic
> matters. I am doing my best to serve you with Gurrelieder as I have
> done in the past with Die Glückliche Hand and many other of your
> works which on account of their originality demand many months of
> preparation in each case which I gladly and enthusiastically give
> because of my admiration for you as a composer.[27]

Alas, poor Emil Hertzka, who had been such a champion of Schoen-
berg, Berg, Webern, and other avant-garde composers, died in Vienna on
May 9, 1932, not long after receiving a torrent of abuse from Schoenberg.
The two events, however, were surely not correlative.

Considering the general antipathy to the music of Schoenberg, one
must consider Stokowski's powers of persuasion and superb salesmanship
to convince the board to let him do a performance of Schoenberg's
mammoth Gurrelieder. He assured them that, unlike the asperities of the
Chamber Symphony and the Variations, or the sepulchral gloom of Die
Glückliche Hand, the Gurrelieder was a work of romantic sensuousness.
The score called for four flutes, seven clarinets, ten horns, and a huge
percussion section that included a large iron chain. It called for three male
choruses, a mixed chorus, and five soloists—including Jeannette Vreeland,

Paul Althouse, Rose Bampton, Abrasha Robofsky, and a speaker, Benjamin de Loache. Although not of the magnitude of the Mahler Eighth Symphony, Stokowski did use a total of 532 performers. The Boks were enthusiastic and underwrote the costs.

The first performance of *Gurrelieder* took place on April 8, 1932, not in the Academy but in Philadelphia's Metropolitan Opera House. Two more performances were given on April 9 and 11, followed by a performance at the Met in New York on April 20.

The entire work was recorded live during two of the Philadelphia performances. Although all three of the Philadelphia performances were recorded, no trace of the first remained. The Saturday evening concert was recorded on 33 rpm standard-groove long-playing records, with which Victor was experimenting at the time though few record collectors had the equipment to play them. For the general public the *Gurrelieder* was released on a set of fourteen twelve-inch discs, one of which was devoted to a spoken commentary by Stokowski with piano illustrations by Sylvan Levin.[28] It was the most massive work ever consigned to records and it created a sensation in musical circles.

When the records were withdrawn from the catalog, collectors paid up to $200 for a set.[29] Later there was a reissue on microgroove in 1954 and then to celebrate Stoki's ninety-fifth birthday, there was another reissue in 1977, forty-five years after the initial recording. From that vantage point, the critical reception is even more interesting than a perusal of the first, when the work itself was newer and more surprising.

"The Stokowski miracle goes on," wrote Heuwell Tircuit in the *San Francisco Chronicle:* "In the long run, he may prove to have been the most consequential conductor of the century. And even if you are not willing to allow him that accolade, you have to admit that he has been the most omnipresent. As a man who grew up with Strauss, Mahler and Debussy for contemporaries, that amazing performance has a Romantic beauty of timbre no modern version can hope to duplicate. Then too, subjected to RCA's computer-controlled cleanup process, the mono-only sound is a major documentation of the greatness of the Stokowski-Philadelphia. One wonders, could any modern ensemble make such a performance without retakes or splicing? A treasure!"[30]

Critic Gerald Fox observed that the original recording of *Gurrelieder* was not only a first recording but was to remain an *only* recording for twenty-one years. "Stokowski and the Philadelphia Orchestra were at their peak perfection and popularity. . . . Stokowski's conducting and the orchestra's playing were inspired. The 'old wizard's' drive, sweep and general excitement have yet to be equalled."[31]

A year and a half after the *Gurrelieder* performances, Schoenberg arrived in America and for a brief time became affiliated with the Malkin Conservatory in Boston. "Welcome to our very disturbed country," Stoki greeted him November 2, 1933. "I hope you will find peace here for your work. Have you any new orchestral works that you might care to have performed by us?"[32] Without making any reference to Stokowski's letter, Schoenberg wrote from Boston still complaining about the *Gurrelieder* affair:

> I think you know that I lost my engagement at the Akademie der Musik in Berlin. And further, you know that I am forced to create a new possibility of life, a new musical position in this country.
>
> And also you know that your performance of my Gurrelieder has been a wrong by Hertzka who had broken the contract which had assured me the first performance in America and the fees for it and also my rights of disks!
>
> And further you know that a composer of my rank has no advantage from a performance, for the paid sums are minimally and only for conducting is to get some honorar [sic]. Also in this case the reproducer is better treated than the producer. . . .[33]

Schoenberg then mentioned two works that he had recently completed. They were both arrangements: one was a cello concerto that he had transcribed from a harpsichord concerto by G. M. Monn (1717–50), the other a concerto for string quartet and orchestra based on Handel's *Concerto Grosso* Opus 6 No. 7. He stated that he could not let Stoki have the first performance of either of the works "without a recompensing." "Make me a proposition please, to compensate me and if possible I will see whether I can let you one or both of these performances."[34]

It was in Schoenberg's original works that Stoki was interested, not in his arrangements. Hence he declined the honor of performing either. But he did present the world premiere of Schoenberg's Violin Concerto during his last set of concerts with the orchestra before his final departure in 1940. It was one of his last defiant gestures and it pleased neither the audience, the management, nor the critics.

Soloists who appeared with Stokowski were greeted by an attitude quite unlike that of any other major conductor of the day. Instead of performing the usual warhorses, Stoki would ask what unusual works they had in their repertory. When Walter Gieseking made his debut with the orchestra, it was with Hindemith's Concerto for Piano (*Kammermusik* No. 2). Alfred Cortot performed the American premiere of Germaine Tailleferre's Piano Concerto. Leo Ornstein and Cyril Scott played their own piano concertos. Alfred Wallentein essayed the Cello Concerto of Ibert.

Eleven weeks after Stravinsky conducted the first performance of his Violin Concerto in Berlin with Samuel Dushkin, Stokowski presented it with his Philadelphians with the same soloist on January 5, 1932. When he brought it to New York, it was included in a program that was designed to make ears prickle. It began with *Two Dances* by the Cuban composer Alejandro Caturla followed by *Daphnis and Chloe,* not by Ravel but by Efrem Zimbalist, "the violinist." Next came Milhaud's Percussion Concerto followed by Alexander Mossolov's *Iron Foundry.* All this was prelude to the real sensation of the evening, the first performance in New York of Stravinsky's Violin Concerto. The concert concluded with Mussorgsky's *Pictures at an Exhibition* as orchestrated . . . by Ravel.[35]

Of all contemporary composers, the one to whom Philadelphia audiences seemed most favorably attuned was Sergei Rachmaninoff. Three years before Stokowski's arrival on the scene, Rachmaninoff stepped before the Philadelphia Orchestra and made his conducting debut in America on November 26, 1909.

The relationship between Stokowski and Rachmaninoff began early, with Rachmaninoff appearing as soloist in his Second Concerto with the Cincinnati Orchestra in 1910. Stoki conducted the Second Symphony the same year and the *Isle of the Dead* a year later. In Philadelphia Rachmaninoff was a frequent soloist, performing his own concertos, and in 1920, Stoki introduced *The Bells,* based on a poem of Edgar Allen Poe —a rather dreadful piece that Rachmaninoff considered his favorite work. He dedicated his *Three Russian Songs* to Stokowski, who conducted them on March 18, 1927. Stoki gave the world premiere of the *Rhapsody on a Theme of Paganini* with Rachmaninoff as soloist in Baltimore on November 7, 1934, and the Third Symphony on November 6, 1936.

There were a few clashes between Rachmaninoff and Stokowski. After a performance in 1925, Rachmaninoff wrote expressing some disagreement about tempi. Stoki responded by saying that he was delighted to receive his letter.

> I am sorry I misunderstood the passage in E flat. I tried playing
> it faster at first, but it did not have the kind of yearning expression

that it seemed to me was its nature, so then I drew it out more gradually quickening the tempo later on to the passage where the trombones enter. Next time I play it I will try to enter more into your idea of this part of the work, and am very glad you wrote to me about it so frankly as that will help me in future.[36]

On April 28, 1930, *Time* magazine reported that "at a recent rehearsal he and Pianist Sergei Rachmaninoff almost came to blows over the tempo of a Rachmaninoff concerto concerning which Stokowski felt he knew better than the composer."[37]

Many in Stokowski's audience had little interest in the headlong pursuit of the future. They preferred the rearview-mirror approach. Stoki, to please that contingent, announced that works of the newest composers would be banished from the programs.[38] The gesture was in a sense a trial balloon. Surely Stoki had no intention of abandoning his usual course, but he wanted to arouse his listeners. "I've been selfish," he proclaimed. "But no more. I have reformed, now for the dear people down there," he said, gesticulating toward the Academy from the eminence of his suburban home. "I'll play nothing but what they want. They don't like these new pieces which disturb with their startling strangeness. Well, they won't have to listen to them anymore. For myself, I love these new pieces. But I'll only play them at home this winter . . . for my own pleasure and enjoyment."[39]

It was a clever ploy. There were hundreds of protests. Letters poured in to him directly and to the Judson office. Editorials appeared in the major papers. The whole thing became a civic issue.

One avid subscriber to the orchestra's concerts was Albert Coombs Barnes, locally dubbed "the Argyrol King" for having invented a silver compound derivative used as an antiseptic and from whose sales he rapidly made a vast fortune. His wealth enabled him to collect paintings and eventually assemble one of the greatest private collections in America. He loudly praised Stokowski for his championing of modern works but on one occasion he wrote saying: "I blush for your hackneyed programs . . . for the surfeit of theatrical claptrap like Rachmaninoff's *Bells* or Mahler's spectacular banalities or Wagner's voluptuous debauches or Weber's inanities."[40]

For the opening concert of the twenty-fifth anniversary season (1924–25) Stoki had included a new work by Alfredo Casella that the press called "an extremist work." The piece was Casella's *Elegia Eroica*, written in memory of a soldier who was killed in the war. Just before the beginning of it, Stoki turned toward the audience and explained that his original intention to restrain his own enthusiasm for the modernists had been affected by "an avalanche" of objections. Therefore he wanted to put the matter to a vote. He asked the traditionalists to hiss their distaste for contemporary scores, and the more liberal listeners to applaud. The plaudits won. "Obviously, Mr. Stokowski relished the piquancy of the situation," observed one critic.[41]

Recalcitrantly, Stoki programmed Varèse's *Hyperprism,* Medtner's Piano Concerto (composer as soloist), first U.S. performances of Szymanowski's Violin Concerto and Atterberg's Second Symphony, among other new works.

When, five years later, a similar situation arose, reactions were quite different. During the summer when Stoki was vacationing in Europe, the board met and discussed the declining revenue of the orchestra. One reason, the more pragmatic of them pointed out, was the excessive amount of contemporary music that was being played. Inexplicably, the board released a statement saying that the programs of the coming season would be "almost entirely devoted to acknowledged masterpieces. . . . The Directors feel that in times such as the present, audiences prefer music which they know and love, and that performances of debatable music should be postponed until a more suitable time. With these opinions the conductors fully concur."[42]

Guest conductors who had been engaged to appear during Stoki's absences were all admonished to minimize the amount of new music they would perform and if possible to eliminate it. At a board meeting, so Mr. Van reported, he was delegated to "instruct" Stokowski not to play modern music. The one conductor who did not concur with the board was Stokowski himself; he lashed out at the board and took the matter directly to the press. He emphatically denied that he had ever been consulted and he intended to pay no attention to the dictum. On his opening program he announced that he would perform a new work by Werner Josten called *Jungle.*[43] The work, inspired by the paintings of Henri Rousseau, suggested more wildness and adventure than the music itself, but Stokowski was making a point.

He placed the work at the end of the program and announced that he would play it twice and all who wished to stay could do so. About 80 percent of the audience remained, among them Mary Binney Montgomery, who had circulated a petition that was sent to the members of the board upholding Stoki's stand on contemporary music.[44] Stoki's devoted women's committee also rallied in his defense, as did board member Samuel Rosenbaum.[45]

Stoki spoke to both Friday and Saturday audiences. "There is much misconception of modern music," he told his Friday listeners. "People say: 'That wasn't modern!' They mean it wasn't ear-piercing. Much modern music is as light, as delicate, as gossamer in structure as the Debussy we have just heard [*L'Après-midi d'un faune*].

"There is really no such thing as modern music. It is merely that some composers wish to speak in their own way. A composer may, of course, follow an old pattern—he may like Brahms and write after the manner of Brahms. Then his music will be in good taste—whatever that is. . . . Today, we have great men working. Men such as Sibelius. Sibelius is talking in a great language. He is a great composer.

"It all boils down to this—whether Philadelphia wishes to keep an open mind—whether Philadelphia wishes to hear the best of music—whether Philadelphia wishes to keep an open attitude toward what the world is doing today—or whether Philadelphia, artistically, wishes to stagnate."[46]

While denying any concession to the more conservative tastes of the board, the programs of the 1932–33 season were decidedly milder than those of the preceding seasons. There was nothing of Varèse, Schoenberg, Berg, Webern, and only one work of Stravinsky, an innocuous work for men's voices and orchestra, *The King of the Stars.* Shostakovich, however, was given the full treatment. Stoki gave the first American performance of his Third *(May Day)* Symphony on December 30, 1932, two years after its first hearing in Russia. Abram Chasins' Second Piano Concerto, with the composer as soloist, was given its world premiere, as was a setting of Poe's *The Raven* by Dubensky. It was recited by Benjamin de Loache and recorded. It may have seemed dramatic at the time, but on the record as we hear it today, it is a wonderful example of sonic ham.

Rachmaninoff was not neglected. On March 18, 1933, Stoki wrote a letter that was hand-delivered backstage at the Academy of Music.

> I did not realize that you were playing here this afternoon but just by chance we are playing your "Island of the Dead" tonight at 8:20. Would you care to hear it and if so may I arrange for the tickets for you and how many would you like?
>
> After studying "The Island of the Dead" again for these perfor-

mances I have been so deeply impressed by its unity of style and form. Its psychic power is to me greater than ever but I had never before realized the perfection of its organism. It grows from the roots out to the branches and leaves and flowers and fruits—just as does a tree and just as does the music of Bach.

I hope you will not mind—I have not followed the cuts you made but am playing it in its entirety without cuts. I had someone else conduct it in rehearsal so that I could listen to it and it seemed to me that it was perfect without cuts.

Lately I have not had the pleasure of seeing you but I am always the same in spite of this and my admiration for you and friendship is—if anything—increasing, no matter whether I meet you personally or not.

Sincerely your friend

Leopold Stokowski[47]

While the modern repertory commanded attention, the conventional works that constituted the bulk of Stokowski's programs were not unnoticed. His predilection for works of Wagner, Brahms, Tchaikovsky, and in this romantic context, Bach, loomed mightily in his program making. He told critic Linton Martin that he loved everything Tchaikovsky had written: " 'Not only the large works,' he said, 'but the smaller things. I feel about Tchaikovsky the way I feel about my daughter Sonya—that everything he does is right.' "[48]

It is true that the works of Mozart and Haydn played minor roles in Stokowski's concerts, but he compensated by playing many works of Vivaldi, Frescobaldi, Gluck, and Gabrieli that were otherwise unknown to symphonic audiences. His performances of Beethoven were a staple in his repertory. It is perhaps the Hollywood aura surrounding him during the 1940s that made critics ascribe exaggerations and overcoloring to his interpretations of the conventional repertoire. Those on the scene did not. Olin Downes was, despite his limitations in recognizing the new, a most severe and honest critic. He evaluated Stokowski's conducting of Beethoven sagely: "Mr. Stokowski interpreted Beethoven's Fifth Symphony in dead earnest. There was no thought of the conductor, only of the ruggedness, the sublime heroism and pathos of the music. There was regard for every note and every sign the composer made in his score, and at the same time a flaming conviction which gave white heat to the interpretation. . . . Mr. Stokowski commanded his orchestra despotically; again Beethoven stood four-square to the universe, the most passionate revolutionist of them all, the warrior and prophet of a new era. No orchestra could have excelled, and few equalled, the technical qualities of this performance. For the precision of which this orchestra is capable is equalled by its flexibility and sensitiveness; and, as we have said, Mr. Stokowski stood at the right hand of the composer."[49]

25

On Stage

U NLIKE Toscanini, to whom opera was a very important part of his life and in which medium he achieved his greatest triumphs, Stokowski's ventures into this field were the exceptions to his musical rule. The list of stage works he did conduct is not long, but it is most distinguished. It includes operas, ballets, and even staged oratorios, for he once conducted the Bach *St. Matthew Passion* at the Met in the form of a religious passion play.

Stokowski's first actual experience in combining music with action resulted from his association with Varèse and his International Composers' Guild, which he had organized in 1921.

During the six years of the Guild's existence it presented an impressive list of important new compositions, many for the first time in America. On one of their early programs Varèse planned to present Schoenberg's *Pierrot Lunaire*. Varèse wrote to Schoenberg asking permission to perform the work. Schoenberg responded at once, asking first for the aims of the Guild. After its manifesto was sent to him he answered with what Louise Varèse quite correctly labeled an "indignant and insolent letter." He complained that the Guild, which called itself international, had not played a single German work, that it had announced *Pierrot Lunaire* without knowing whether he would permit it, that in Vienna it had had one hundred rehearsals and questioned how many there would be for this performance, and concluded that if the Guild could satisfy him on these and other points he would permit the performance. After more unpleasant interchange of letters, the rehearsals got under way.[1]

240

Louis Gruenberg, who had attended the rehearsals and performance that Schoenberg had conducted, offered to do it.[2] The one hundred rehearsals that were needed for the first performance were of course out of the question, but Gruenberg, after a series of complaints and threats of postponements, finally came through after twenty-two rehearsals. And he still felt that he had not been given enough. Who knows? He may have been right.

"From the standpoint of the music developed by Bach, Haydn, Mozart and Beethoven," wrote the critic of the *New York Evening Telegram*, "Schoenberg's *Pierrot Lunaire* is mere trash. Judged as music, it is hideous. It is not the sort of thing that an American audience can enjoy."[3]

In the *New York Times*, Richard Aldrich found it merely "a succession of disagreeable noises." Krehbiel in the *Tribune* wrote: "It was a wearisome and futile experiment which some of the hearers were brave enough to smile at. . . . Distinguished musicians who are striving to bring on the millennium in which cacophony will reign were in last night's audience —among them Leopold Stokowski, Alfredo Casella, Georges Enesco, Darius Milhaud and Willem Mengelberg."[4]

Stoki was intrigued with the possibilities of a staged version and the idea stayed in the back of his mind for several years.

At this point, early in the Guild's activity, Claire Reis and her remarkably energetic and able assistant Minna Lederman broke away from the Guild and established a separate society called the League of Composers. In retrospect it may seem to have been merely a tempest in a teapot, but at the time tempers became inflamed, lawyers were called in, and much acrimony was spent by the Varèse camp on one side and the Reis camp on the other. But each prepared to carry on their separate programs.[5]

Varèse appealed to Stokowski and Stoki agreed to help him and the Guild by conducting part of a concert on December 2, 1923. "As soon as it was announced that the glamorous leader of the Philadelphia Orchestra would conduct the first concert," said Louise Varèse, "new subscriptions kept coming in."[6]

Varèse had written to Arthur Judson asking him to inquire whether Stoki would be willing to conduct Stravinsky's *Renard*, which they wanted to perform. Judson responded that he would, provided the instrumentalists of the Philadelphia Orchestra were used.[7] Stoki invited Varèse to his house in St. Martins, and they discussed the program, as well as the ideals of the Guild. Varèse also brought along a number of his scores, which immediately intrigued Stoki. "Stokowski had been charming," said Louise

242 Stokowski

Varèse, "and that famous charm, coupled with Stokowski's warmly pro-
fessed interest in Varèse's score which he was then studying, melted
susceptible Varèse. . . . He also brought back an official letter from
Stokowski stating that he . . . was in complete sympathy with the aims
of the I.C.G."[8]

While Stoki rehearsed the men in Philadelphia, Carlos Salzedo prepared the four singers—the Fox, Cock, Cat, and Goat—in New York.
The concert took place on December 2, 1923, at the Vanderbilt Theater.
The program itself was an odd one. It began with Claudio Arrau playing
piano pieces by Béla Bartók, Lourié, and Hindemith. This was followed
by Schoenberg's *Herzgewächse* (for soprano, harp, harmonium, celesta),
which was conducted by E. Robert Schmitz. At its conclusion the audience was split right down the middle—some hissing and booing, others
applauding wildly and demanding an encore. Schmitz obliged and *Herzgewächse* was repeated. Critics noted that Stokowski was among those
who had demanded the encore.[9]

Quite unlike their reaction to the Schoenberg, the audience was unanimous in its reaction to the Stravinsky work and, as Louise Varèse remarked, they "gave themselves up to uncritical enjoyment like children
at the circus."[10] *Renard* had scored a resounding success.

"After the last bars of the jolly march," wrote one reviewer, "pandemonium broke loose. The walls of the Vanderbilt fairly shook with cries
and entreaties for a repetition. Seemingly a madness was upon some
members of the audience. For them nothing existed except this unique
music of Stravinsky, and they begged and pleaded like people possessed
to hear it one more time. . . . Mr. Stokowski was loath to meet the request.
But finally he had to and, amid jubilant cries, he repeated the entire
score."[11]

Taking advantage of the rehearsals and performance of *Renard* in New
York, Stoki programmed it on one of the subscription series in Philadelphia on April 11 and 12, 1924. It added a bit of tang to an otherwise
conventional program. The critics as well as the audience were amused
but not jubilant. "Since we Quakers must have a moral in everything,"
Stoki remarked, "I have found one for you in *Renard*. Shakespeare said
that all the world's a stage, but Stravinsky says it's a barnyard with some
cocks, some foxes, goats, pigs and donkeys. That is the moral."[12]

Two of the principal sponsors of the International Composers' Guild
were Gertrude Vanderbilt Whitney and Mrs. Christian Holmes—the
same Bettie Holmes who had engaged Stoki as the conductor of the

Cincinnati Symphony and with whom he had feuded over his peremptory resignation. Bettie had abandoned Cincinnati herself and had a spacious apartment on Park Avenue and a large estate on Long Island. She later became one of the sponsors of the New York Philharmonic during Stoki's conducting tenure there.

Mrs. Whitney had her palatial home on Fifth Avenue, an apartment on Eighth Street, and a studio on MacDougal Alley where she plied her skill as a sculptress. She had sponsored many artists and founded the Whitney Club, Whitney Studio Club, Whitney Studio, Whitney Studio Galleries, and finally the Whitney Museum—all to assist American art and artists. She admired Varèse and soon became his patron, "giving him an adequate allowance, which would make it possible for him to go on with his plans."[13]

On the first of March, Stokowski came in like a lion. His program for the Guild concert included four new works: Schoenberg's Serenade, Satie's *Danses de Piège de Méduse*, Eichheim's *Malay Mosaic*, and Varèse's *Intégrales*. The critics had a field day. Olin Downes, after remarking that the Schoenberg Serenade was "excessively ugly and tedious," expressed delight in the Satie opus. "The first of the 'rascal's' pieces knocked the involved, self-important music of Schoenberg on the head with an effect so astonishing and so felicitous in its devastating impudence that the audience first gasped and then roared."[14]

Critic Oscar Thompson remarked that the Guild "gave no refuge for persons of timid or *fogram* tastes"—thereby increasing my vocabulary (the italics are mine). About the Schoenberg he stated candidly that "if it was because he did not understand this music that the reviewer thought it feeble, vacuous, spineless, eviscerated, essentially artificial and unoriginal, of more interest to a psychiatrist than a seeker after beauty, and pathological in such appeal as it apparently exerted, then the reviewer must frankly admit that he did not understand this music." Alas poor, fogram Thompson.

About Varèse, Thompson stated: "*Intégrales* was undoubtedly the salient composition of the evening—for a composition it is, a composition of sounds and timbres, irrespective of whether it contains more than a half dozen bars of what, in a final analysis, may be definitely identified as music. The audience applauded until Mr. Stokowski consented to repeat it, first asking that those who preferred to go home should take the opportunity to do so, thus enabling those who requested the repetition to listen to it in quiet and unanimity."[15]

Critic Henderson wrote facetiously that one hearer knew why there was no earthquake Saturday. "It would have been a fool earthquake that would have . . . brought itself into rivalry with Mr. Varèse's cataclysm."[16]

Private Collection/Courtesy Philadelphia Museum of Art

Arthur Carles when he was in Stokowski's circle of close friends in Philadelphia (c. 1917)

No matter what the critics wrote, the evenings of the Guild were never dull and the audiences were among the most vital and interested of any in New York at the time. And perhaps they realized that history was being made. Stokowski had presented two world premieres that evening: the Varèse and Eicheim's innocuous but pleasing trifle, and in all likelihood the first American performances of the Schoenberg and Satie works.

Bettie Holmes had planned a small, postconcert dinner party for Varèse and Louise and two of her intimate friends. Varèse pointed out that Stokowski would not be returning to Philadelphia that evening and suggested that Mrs. Holmes invite him also, hoping that the chill that had existed between them would happily melt. It might have, had Stokowski not suggested that she also invite his Philadelphia painter friend Arthur "Artie" Carles, who had come with him to attend the concert.

Bettie Holmes, her two friends, and Louise Varèse piled into the Holmes limousine along with the long-legged, gangling Carles. "He was not drunk but not ice-water sober either. The drive up Fifth Avenue was charged with Mrs. Holmes's silent resentment," Louise recalled. After Stoki and Varèse arrived, all were seated around what Louise described as a "gorgeously appointed supper table with much jade in the centerpiece among the flowers, a handsome tablecloth of openwork embroidery, and crystal water goblets and champagne glasses, which had been blown for Mrs. Holmes in Venice."

Champagne flowed abundantly despite prohibition, and Varèse toasted his hostess while Stokowski toasted Varèse. Then, Louise recalled, the sound of shattering glass was heard as Artie Carles broke his champagne goblet while muttering: "Good riddance—a damn bad shape." He held forth in a somewhat drunken harangue on the aesthetics of glassware and then turned his attention to Mrs. Holmes' elaborate tablecloth. " 'It's full of holes,' he said. 'But not enough,' and began lowering his lighted cigarette. Mrs. Holmes gasped, her friends half-rose, but Varèse, again raising his glass, had already diverted Carles' attention with a toast: 'Long live Art!' he cried, leaving unpronounced the ie for Artie." Stoki rose and, walking down to the end of the table where Carles was seated, whispered something in his ear and the two departed.[17] The ice between Stoki and Bettie Holmes was no doubt as chilly as ever.

During his late years Stokowski often referred to three of his friends who had become alcoholics. He mentioned "Artie" Carles, Josef Hofmann, and Jean Sibelius. Arthur Carles, like Stoki, was born in 1882 and his painting career spanned the years between 1910 and 1940. He was one of the painters represented in the famous Armory Show of 1913 and was the recipient of many awards and prizes. His paintings now hang in the Philadelphia Museum of Art, the Hirshhorn Museum, the Metropolitan Museum of Art, the Art Institute of Chicago, the Pennsylvania Academy of Fine Arts, the San Francisco Museum of Art, the Baltimore Museum of Art, and the Museum of Modern Art among others.

Carles painted a splendid portrait of Stoki who in return painted one of Carles. He had a vivid color sense and probably stimulated Stokowski's interest in color and its relation to sound. Carles' late paintings were mainly colorful abstractions, one of which he presented to Stoki who later gave it to the Museum of Modern Art in New York.[18]

In 1941, Carles, while in an inebriate state, fell over the stair-rail as he climbed to his studio and landed on the floor of the stairwell below; this left him partially paralyzed and unable to paint again. His death occurred in 1952.[19]

Next came the matter of Falla's *El Retablo de Maese Pedro (Master Peter's Puppet Show)*. Its premiere had been given in the Paris salon of the Princesse de Polignac on June 25, 1923. So pleased was Falla with the harpsichord part in his orchestration, which had been played by Wanda Landowska, that he immediately wrote a Harpsichord Concerto, which he dedicated to her.

During the 1923–24 concert season Landowska made her American debut playing concertos of Bach and Handel with Stokowski and the Philadelphia Orchestra. She was a marked success and through the years the two artists maintained a strong mutual admiration.

It was Landowska who brought Falla's little puppet opera to Stokowski's attention, naturally with the intention of performing in it herself. Stokowski seemed to be enchanted with the idea. Then with all the absurdity that can be caused by the right hand not knowing what the left hand is doing, an unfortunate contretemps occurred.

Stokowski discussed the work with Varèse, and together they decided that it would be a good piece to include on one of the Guild programs. Landowska, on the other hand, had also discussed it with Claire Reis, and together they decided that it would be just right for a concert sponsored by the League. Claire, whom Louise Varèse described as "having enough energy to split atoms,"[20] made an appointment to discuss the production with Stoki. With foresight and professional acumen she had already cabled Falla's publisher and had secured for the League the right for the first American performance.[21]

On September 30, 1976, I spent a pleasant afternoon with Claire in her Upper East Side apartment, and she shared many recollections about the early days of the League and particularly about the Falla affair. She told me how, at the suggestion of Landowska, she first met Stokowski. It was in the apartment of his dear friend Maria Dehon Polk. "Well, I came in at 4 o'clock one afternoon in the apartment of Mrs. Polk, who was a great social, musical leader and a great friend of his. It was a beautiful apartment with a very Victorian living room," Claire recalled. "And in came Stokowski in a Japanese kimona and sandals and bare feet. I quickly sized up the effect he expected from this and then our discussion began about the Falla. And I said, 'Landowska sent a message to you and she's going to play the harpsichord in it and we're going to have Bufano do the puppets and it's going to be in Town Hall and we are hoping that you will conduct.' 'Well,' said the great Maestro, 'I will be glad to conduct it just as you have described it, but I cannot do it for the League. I have promised Varèse that I would do it with him.' So, not being completely overcome by the costume, I said, 'But we have the rights from England' and he was astonished. 'But,' said Stokowski, 'you will give them to me, won't you?'

Fortunately, I held my ground, and I said, 'No sir. I cannot give them to you. The rights belong to the League of Composers and we hope you will join us.'

"It was a deadlock. When I repeated all of this to Landowska, she was just furious with him. She said, 'We'll leave him alone and we'll get another great conductor'—which we did. We got Mengelberg and he really did a beautiful job, so it came off with great success.

"Then came a pause of about three years when we heard through Smallens, who was doing some assistant conducting for Stokowski, that having heard about our success with the *Retablo,* he would like to do [Stravinsky's] *Les Noces* with us and do it at the Metropolitan Opera House. Immediately it blew up into a great affair. Well, then I had a little problem with members of my own board who couldn't visualize our jumping into the Metropolitan Opera House. But we did. We filled the house—we did *Les Noces.*"22

But Claire never mentioned in her book *Composers, Conductors and Critics* that Stokowski had already conducted the American premiere of *Les Noces* in a concert sponsored by Varèse and the International Composer's Guild in old Aeolian Hall on February 14, 1926. Carlos Salzedo had rehearsed the singers, chorus, and pianists. Stokowski brought his percussion players and a vast bevy of percussion instruments from Philadelphia.

The cast of participants was awesome. The four pianists were Georges Enesco, Alfredo Casella, Germaine Tailleferre, and Salzedo himself. The singers included Mrs. Charles Cahier, with whom Olga had concertized in Europe, Marguerite Ringo, Richard Hale, whose booming voice was later to be captured doing the narration for Koussevitzky's performance of *Peter and the Wolf,* and Colin O'Moore. A chorus of twenty singers from the Oratorio Society completed the ensemble.23

Les Noces received its American premiere that evening and also its second performance, for it was repeated after the intermission.

Much ink was spilled on descriptions, commentaries, and analyses of the score. Stokowski's good friend Richard Hammond had stated extravagantly that "of the whole galaxy of masterpieces written before and after, it is the foremost in invention, freedom and originality."

It was the haunting prospect of a full, staged presentation of *Les Noces* that brought the first cooperative effort of Stokowski, Claire Reis, and the League. It was through Claire that Stoki first met Robert Edmond Jones.24 Stoki and "Bobby," as Jones was always called by his intimates, struck an immediate rapport that was to continue through future collaborations.

In preparing all of the details, Claire invited many of her board members to tea one windy, cold February afternoon, including Norman Bel Geddes, Martha Graham, Theresa Helburn, Doris Humphrey, Charles Weidman, Richard Hammond, Léonide Massine, Agnes De Mille, Donald Oenslager, and Nicholas Roerich. They were all there to hear what Stokowski had on his mind.

Just as the guests arrived, a maid rushed out screaming that the pantry was on fire. Great confusion ensued. Dick Hammond grabbed a fire extinguisher and ran to the kitchen; when he tried to use it, he inadvertently tipped it the wrong way and saturated both himself and Norman Bel Geddes. When the firemen arrived they urged both to remove their clothes quickly or "they'll rot right on you if you don't soak 'em in fresh water quick." Claire's husband provided a change of clothing.

With the fire safely out, the tea meeting took place in candlelight with Stoki presiding as if he were conducting a rehearsal.

When a man from Consolidated Edison arrived to reconnect the lighting, Stoki waved him away with a dramatic gesture telling him to "go away and come back tomorrow!" Claire recalled. But she hurriedly ran after the departing electrician, and lights again filled the room. "We blew out the candles and finished up the tea party with enthusiasm for future plans and a genuine desire by all to cooperate. Stokowski took his departure without ever once having mentioned the fire."[25]

Claire and Minna Lederman worked furiously on all details and achieved remarkable results. The four pianists they recruited were all young emerging composers: Aaron Copland, Marc Blitzstein, Louis Gruenberg, and Frederick Jacobi.

The sets were designed by Serge Soudeikine, who chose colors that were supposed to be typical of Slavic Russian peasant life: the colors of wood, wheat, clay, flax, beer, and honey. Stokowski and Soudeikine clashed at once and arguments about lighting became explosive; but Stokowski's will was indomitable. Soudeikine was left to lick his wounds.[26]

"Rehearsals were always a great heartache," Claire told me. "It cost so much to find places where we could have time and space for anything with stage room. But I found a place up on One Hundred Twenty-fifth Street —the old Harlem YMCA. It had a big hall which we could rent for a very nominal amount for any number of rehearsals.

"My husband, who was always very cooperative about my ventures, said to me, 'Tell Stokowski that you will pick him up at Pennsylvania Station when he comes in from Philadelphia and take him up there.'

"So he wrote and told me what train he would be on and that he wanted four pianos at this first rehearsal in just such a position. And he included a little sketch which I sent up to the janitor. When we got there, the first thing he said was, 'The pianos are not in the right position.' So I said, 'I'll get the janitor at once.' But before I had time to find the janitor and get him to move the pianos, Stokowski had taken off his jacket and, in his famous blue shirt, he was moving the pianos himself. Well, I thought, this is a good sign—a good omen. And I must say the rehearsals went very well. This was our first venture at the Metropolitan and it was packed, sold out weeks in advance."[27]

The name Leopold Stokowski had at this time an awesome power to attract crowds. Surely it was not Stravinsky's *Les Noces* and Monteverdi's one-act opera *Il Combattimento di Tancredi e di Clorinda,* which served as a curtain raiser to fill out the evening. It was the magic of the Stokowski name that drew the audience.

The Monteverdi work was not conducted by Stokowski but by Werner Josten. "We had heard that Werner Josten at Smith College had done a beautiful performance of Monteverdi's *Il Combattimento* and Stokowski was perfectly happy to have Werner come down," said Claire.

After the production Claire went up to Stokowski and said, "The rehearsals were wonderful but this was still greater. 'I knew it would be,' Stoki answered, 'I always know when it's going to be good.' "[28]

So pleased was Stoki with the success of *Les Noces* that he suggested to Claire Reis that they might consider a full, staged production of Stravinsky's *Le Sacre du printemps* at the Met. Claire was delighted and during the early fall of 1929 she visited Arthur Judson to explore the possibility of using the Philadelphia Orchestra for the production.[29] Stoki was in a Russian mood and his programs now leaned heavily on Stravinsky, Scriabin, Rimsky-Korsakov, Rachmaninoff, Liadov, Prokofiev, and Mussorgsky.

26

Stravinsky and
Schoenberg— Double Bill

AVING given the first American performance of *Le Sacre du printemps*, Stokowski wanted to present the first staged performance of it as well. To fill out the program, a companion piece had to be found.

Sylvan Levin, who was constantly on the lookout for new and interesting scores, discovered Schoenberg's *Die Glückliche Hand*, a piece which Schoenberg had called a *"Drama mit Musik."*[1] In English it has been translated variously as *The Hand of Fate, The Hand of Fortune,* and *The Lucky Hand.*

A double bill of *Die Glückliche Hand* and *Le Sacre du printemps*, in stage versions, was exactly what Stoki wanted for his next presentation by the League of Composers. At Stoki's suggestion Claire Reis went to see Arthur Judson in order to discuss the practical arrangements necessary to involve the Philadelphia Orchestra. She had worked out a quite logical and practical plan, which she presented to Judson. The league would take full responsibility for the staging and the program would be given for the regular subscribers with a slight alteration: in Philadelphia the performances would take place in its Metropolitan Opera House instead of the Academy and, similarly in New York, they would use the Metropolitan instead of Carnegie Hall.

Judson, being totally pragmatic, thought the idea more than a bit on the insane side. He argued that the two works by Schoenberg and Stravinsky would be a bomb at the box office and tried to persuade Claire to abandon the whole idea. But Judson was patently wrong. And in a way that was something of a rarity.[2]

Plans for *Die Glückliche Hand* began to take shape. Rouben Mamoulian, who had directed an impressive performance of *Porgy and Bess* as well as several other operas for the American Opera Company, was to be director. Robert Edmond Jones, who had gotten along so famously with Stoki during the production of *Les Noces,* was to do the sets and lighting. Doris Humphrey, Charles Weidman, and Olin Howland were to mime the action.[3] Sylvan Levin was to select and train a chorus drawn from the Curtis Institute, and the single solo vocal role, that of "The Man," which could also be read as "Everyman," was to be sung by the distinguished Russian singer Ivan Ivantzoff.

"It was a very difficult work to stage," Claire told me. "Bobby called me one day and he said, 'Claire, what do you call this?' And I said, 'Well, I suppose it's a pantomime ballet although there is a voice in it.'

"And then Mamoulian would call and say, 'Claire, we've started all over again. We couldn't do what we were trying to do. Now, we are trying for the third time to work out a plan.' It was such difficult music for these men.

"So finally Rouben said, 'We'll call it a whimsy.' And from that time on, we called it a whimsy."[4]

At the performance, the chorus was placed in the orchestra pit and they chanted the gloomy tale of the three characters and the chimera. As the emblem of the chimera, Jones had designed a huge bat which cast eerie shadows on the backdrop.

When the performance of *Die Glückliche Hand* finally took place on April 22, 1930, the audience response was as tepid as that for *Le Sacre* was explosive. The critical response to the Schoenberg was largely negative, although much space was given to a discussion of it. The critics seemed as baffled as Mamoulian and Jones.

But it was *The Rite of Spring* that gripped the audience and stirred up tremendous excitement. It was the work that set the audience to cheering. None of the adverse reaction that had manifested itself when Stoki conducted it in concert form was present now; the vivid stage spectacle captivated the audience.

In his autobiography Stravinsky tells us that in St. Petersburg, while he was finishing his score for *The Firebird,* he had a vision of a prehistoric ritual during which a young girl dances herself to death before a circle of elders, to propitiate the god of spring. Shortly thereafter he told his friend, the painter Nicholas Roerich, who had specialized in painting pagan subjects, about his dream. Roerich immediately offered to collaborate, and when the idea was suggested to Diaghilev in Paris, Stravinsky tells us he was carried away by it.

Stokowski told of an early encounter with Roerich: "He lived in the Himalayas—up in Kulu—one of the highest places in the world. He used to go back to Paris every spring with Diaghilev, and he would go via the Atlantic Ocean. I said to him, 'Why don't you go via the Pacific and on the way, as you go through America, stop at some of those Indian pueblos there and see the way they dance?' He said he would, so he went into New Mexico and Arizona and saw our Indians dance with their costumes, their music, their singing, their drums—particularly their sacred dances. And he was very impressed.

"Then he saw how he could think of primitive dancing in Russia—the Slavic dance, and that was the beginning. He came back and he told it to Stravinsky and Diaghilev, and Stravinsky wrote this music with that idea in mind. That's how it all began. That's Roerich, and I see they don't even mention his name on the score."[5]

During the winter of 1912–13 Stravinsky worked on the score, Roerich planned the scenic effects, and Nijinsky plotted the ballet sequences. The rest is history. The first performance in Paris, at the Théâtre des Champs-Elysées on the night of May 29, 1913, precipitated one of the most scandalous riots ever engendered by a musical performance. It is curious that seventeen years should have elapsed before the ballet would be seen in America. And for that premiere, all thanks are due to Stokowski.

Both Stokowski and Roerich agreed that Martha Graham should dance the role of the sacrificial virgin that climaxes the ballet. At first they wanted Martha to do the complete choreography, but she quickly demurred.

"Stokowski had come with Evangeline to see some things that I did at the Roerich Museum and they were very stark, naturally, because I was in what I call my 'long-winter-underwear period,' very lacking in seduction, you know, charm," Martha told me. "It was at a time when he was contemplating *Sacre* but he said, 'I don't think you have the experience to do the choreography.' I said, 'No, I haven't. I have absolutely no experience to handle groups of people. I'm still searching, still finding things.' "[6]

Both Roerich and Stoki then hit upon the idea of having Léonide

Massine choreograph it, since he had done so most successfully in the 1920 Paris revival. Diaghilev, in preparing for that revival, discovered that no one could accurately remember the original that had been done by Nijinsky. The sets and costumes of Roerich were intact and well preserved since they had only been used eight times in 1913. Massine was asked by Diaghilev to make an entirely new version, which opened in Paris on December 15 with Ansermet conducting.[7]

Martha Graham (center) and other dancers in the American premiere of Stravinsky's *Rite of Spring* (1930). Set and costumes by Nicholas Roerich, almost identical to his design for the original Diaghilev production in Paris (1913)

Interviewed in 1930 prior to the League of Composers production, Stokowski said: "Last spring, when I was in Europe, I had several talks with Stravinsky about this and about the musical side of the work. He has made some important changes in rhythm and orchestration and his publisher is printing a new edition of the work which we are using. Although the creators of this work, Stravinsky and Roerich, are both Russian, we are not aiming to make this production of the work essentially Russian because we felt that the ideas and feelings it expresses are universal. . . ."[8]

Massine had come to the United States in 1928 with his beautiful new wife, the ballerina Eugenia Delarova, and at the time of the *Sacre* performance, he and his company had been performing four times daily and five times on Sundays at the Roxy Theater.[9] They did excerpts from various classical ballets. Roxy (S. L. Rothafel) at the time was offering some of the most elaborate musical and stage entertainment in his movie "palace" that one could find anywhere. He had a symphony orchestra in the pit, a giant organ, a large chorus, and a corps de ballet.

Claire Reis now used all of her energy in trying to pull the various disparate elements together. She went to see Roerich at the Master Institute of Art, then on Riverside Drive at 103rd Street. As she was ushered into his studio, she found him sitting like the Dalai Lama. As an opening gambit, Claire said that she was bringing greetings to him from Stokowski. Roerich seemed pleased and, after hearing about the project, said that he would be very happy to participate in the production and particularly to work with Stokowski.[10]

"And this time," Claire recalled, "we were given a wonderful gymnasium in the Dalton School which had a cork floor. The head of the school at the time was an intimate friend of Stokowski and Evangeline, and we had a perfect place for rehearsing the ballet."[11] Actually, Evangeline, who was always interested in progressive education, and especially the Dalton School, was the chairman of its Art Department, and she was happy to make all the arrangements.

Claire reported that with the first rehearsal a tug of war began. Arguments between Stokowski and Massine erupted over matters of tempo; and with Martha and Massine over matters of style.[12] "She had her own ideas as she always had," said Claire. "Massine wanted it just as it had been done in Paris and they crossed swords and neither one would give in. Stokowski liked what she was trying to do. It was different from Paris, evidently, but Stokowski agreed with her, and Massine turned his back on her when she rehearsed."[13]

"Martha did not like Massine for one minute," said Dick Hammond, who was deeply involved in the production. "But she was a marvelous choice for that particular role. Oddly enough, she had none of the regular ballet training, yet with a thousand people on the stage, it was Martha Graham whom you would watch. You couldn't do otherwise. During rehearsals at the Dalton School, Martha would just freeze and sit on the floor. . . . Massine would try to get her to rehearse. She would not do it. Finally it got to the point when the performance was coming near and Stoki got rather nervous about it. Someone wanted him to meet Tamara Geva, who had been Balanchine's first wife and who was a very accomplished dancer, to replace Martha. And Stoki was playing with the idea. They made an appointment with Stoki and me to go down to the Radio City Theater to meet with Tamara. And I said, 'Stoki, she's a very nice woman and a very good dancer. But before you decide, let it get back to Martha that you have had that appointment.' It came back to Martha and the next thing she was right with it, and she was a *succès fou* because she had just that quality, that magnetism. She didn't need the on-the-point sort of training and she was excellent."[14]

Years have a way of softening memories, and when I questioned Martha about the struggles that reportedly took place she responded most gently. "I'm sorry to disappoint you on that. I had made up my mind that I would follow direction completely, and I did. I never argued with any of them because I felt they were dealing with something which I was not ready to deal with choreographically or musically, and I remember the first time Massine came to my apartment. It was during the depression and I had an apartment that looked over Central Park which I got because nobody else wanted it. . . . I had no furniture. I had an army cot, and a chest of drawers, and a kitchen table, a grand piano, and a Victrola. So Massine came and we played the *Sacre.* He was very nostalgic. He said it was a very different way of hearing it, compared to the last time he had heard it, and it brought back memories which I'm sure didn't encompass a bare living room in the depression facing Central Park with a small Victrola on the floor and no other furniture except the piano.

"But I made up my mind that I would follow his choreography as nearly as I could, and his direction, and I did. There were certain things balletically that I changed a little bit. But my style was beginning to develop at that time and I would do the thing the way I would do it, you see, and usually Massine was very generous and he said, 'We'll keep that.' For instance, a leap or something of that kind. And I remember rehearsing with him at Roseland Studio because there were no studios available— this great big shiny room with all those mirrors. I was very thin in those days and I was in a black dress. And he was very thin and he was in black, kind of Spanish pants that he always had and he looked at us in the mirror. He was teaching and we were alone. He said, 'We look enough alike to be brother and sister.' Well, we did in some strange way.

"Then, half through, he asked me to resign because he said that I would be a failure. And then I said, 'Did Mr. Stokowski say that?' And he said yes. So I said, 'Well, I'll ask him.' And so I went to him and Stokowski said, 'I don't understand you. What are you talking about? Do you want to quit?' I said no. So I stayed and I finished the performance but I did do exactly as he said.

"There was one place I remember I did a pulsation of the body and he told me I had better stand still during that time because the ballerina who had done it in Europe had fainted after every performance, and I said, 'I will not faint.' And I did not. But it was a great turning point in my life, and it moved me into an area which fed me a very great deal. I had no sense of belonging to the ballet world at that time and I was struggling to find a language which was, I felt, a little more true than what I had to do in the follies and in vaudeville when I was there and in Denishawn. . . .

"The passionate Russian thing—whether it's Russian or whether it's primal doesn't matter, but it was a sacrificial rite and it had nothing to

Martha Graham in American premiere of the staged version of Stravinsky's *Rite of Spring* (1930)

do with the idiosyncrasies of ballet style or modern dance. You had to accommodate yourself to it, and the music is very, very powerful, as we all know. We go and hear somebody's new composition just this year and we will say, 'Well, that is just straight out of Stravinsky' because he has a lure for people which is very hard to resist. I met him once. I meant absolutely nothing to him. He was in a wrath at the moment—not at me, but just at the world in general.

"But *Sacre* meant spiritually a great deal to me and still does, and people have hounded me to choreograph it but I've said I couldn't. It's close to me emotionally and it was a turning point in my life. I walked into another room, an entirely different world, and it was a time of great impoverishment. I had no money at all and what I was facing, I didn't know. Somehow one identifies oneself with a central figure; you perform a sacrifice, whatever it is, and whether it's your life or whether it's giving up the extraneous things of your life for a purpose—for the necessity—it's a sacrificial act."[15]

It seems that everyone who was involved in the production commented on the tense and difficult relationship between Martha and Massine. Not so, Martha has told us. And the reaction of Massine bears this out. "I found it very difficult to go back to this early work after so many years," Massine wrote. "However, I was given a large cast of excellent dancers, and found that the facilities at the 'Met' were as good as those in any theater in Europe. As rehearsals progressed I found the ballet again taking shape in my mind. Martha Graham's powerful performance as the Chosen Maiden added considerable strength to the production. I found her a most subtle and responsive dancer to work with, and her small stature and delicate movements gave the role an added poignancy. We were all very relieved when *Le Sacre du printemps* was enthusiastically received. . . ."[16]

May the spirit of Claire Reis rest in peace!

In a curtain speech Stokowski said that Schoenberg and Stravinsky typified directions in which he and certain colleagues were working. He spoke of achieving a synthesis of music, lighting, drama, and dance in the hope of evolving a new and unique American art form.[17]

Both Leopold and Evangeline were deeply moved by Martha, and each of them penned tributes to her in a compilation that Merle Armitage published in 1937 in a handsome, limited edition. " 'She is an avatar' was Uday Shankar's remark when he saw Martha Graham dance," wrote Evangeline. "This proof of the universality of Miss Graham's art adds to

TIME

The Weekly Newsmagazine

Volume XV

LEOPOLD ANTON STANISLAW BOLESLAW STOKOWSKI
His men no longer play baseball.
(See Music)

Number 17

Stokowski portrait by V. Perfilieff on cover of *Time* magazine, April 28, 1930, on occasion of the American premiere of Stravinsky's *Rite of Spring* the conviction that here is a dancer of astonishing force and power whose motivation transcends a local idiom and expresses a planetary idea. . . . That art is essentially attitudinal in its essence and can make us feel and understand more deeply whatever it portrays—this artist demonstrates by her genius. One feels that with the phenomenon of Martha Graham the American dance comes of age."[18]

So impressed was Evangeline that she then began to study with Martha. "She was very beautiful," Martha told me, and photos adequately prove it. "She was eager for something—she was seeking for something. . . ."[19]

Stoki's tribute was succinct: "Martha Graham is unique in her expression of the fundamentals of life through Dance. She is one of the world's great artists."[20]

Long before the Schoenberg-Stravinsky production reached New York, the media was lavish in descriptions, commentary, analysis, projections, and praise. *Time* magazine, moved by the momentum generated, began the preparation of a cover story that was to appear in its issue of April 28, 1930. Stokowski was to be the first conductor ever to appear on the cover of *Time*.

Time observed that, with Boston's Koussevitzky running a close second, Stokowski was the best-groomed conductor in America. "But no amount of posing could have built and maintained for Stokowski the sound prestige which he has everywhere. . . . In matters musical no one can exceed Stokowski's capacity for work. Nor has anyone maintained toward music a more open mind. . . . His interest and energy have made him one of the world's great conductors. He may offend friends and audiences by his increasing arrogance but few have denied his tremendous musical genius."[21]

(27)

Wozzeck

S TOKOWSKI'S interest in perusing new scores was unbounded, and
during the 1930s he frequently asked Sylvan Levin's help in finding
unusual works such as Hindemith's *Neues vom Tage, Mörder, Hoff-
nung der Frauen, Das Nusch-Nuschi, Sancta Susanna,* and *Der Dämon;*
Pizzetti's *Deborah;* and Richard Strauss' *Schlagobers* and *Josephslegende.*
He also inquired about *A Persian Ballet* by Wellesz.[1] Stoki addressed his
letters to Sylvan as "Dear Illustrious Maestro" and signed them "Maestrino."

Sylvan mentioned to Stokowski that Alban Berg's *Wozzeck,* which had
been done in Berlin in 1925, had never been given in America. Somewhat
familiar with the score, Stoki was intrigued and immediately began to
study it. "It is pretty difficult and perhaps people will not be able to learn
it," he told Sylvan. "And it will be very expensive."

"I'll bet you can get the money for it," replied Sylvan.[2] And he did.
Mrs. Bok gave him the money.

Josef Hofmann offered the full cooperation of the Curtis Institute and
Sylvan selected and trained the singers. Rehearsals began early in December 1930. On December 20, Stoki wrote to Henri Elkan, who in the
original Philadelphia program is listed as Assistant Conductor and Chorus
Master (but not in the New York Program):

> I was happy to learn . . . that you and I shall be working together
> again in the production of *Wozzeck.* I am leaving for Mexico, and
> shall be back in about six weeks. During that period I have put all

the preparations of *Wozzeck* in the hands of Sylvan Levin, and have asked him to represent me in these preparations.[3]

The next day he dictated a long memo to Sylvan further outlining his responsibilities:

"Wozzeck"
For the performance of *Wozzeck* and the 3 final stage rehearsals I should like you to assume complete responsibility for everything musical on the stage, and for Mr. von Wymetal to assume responsibility for everything on the stage concerning
lighting
change of scene
and dramatic action
Therefore I would prefer you not to play the piano on the stage, but to keep yourself free to conduct the stage music, and to control everything musical on stage. Therefore will you choose somebody to play the piano and begin to train him or her now?
For the three final rehearsals of *Wozzeck*—which will be on
February 28th   at   10 A.M.
March 7   at   10 A.M.
March 15   at   1:30 P.M.
I should like to have somebody conduct the orchestra so that I can be free to listen and watch everything from about the middle of the house.[4]

The idea of having an English libretto for *Wozzeck* was a matter of considerable importance for Stoki. "You know German, don't you?" he asked board member Reginald Allen. Stoki explained that they needed the libretto to be sold at the performance and asked if he would translate it.

"I had been bilingual in my childhood and I did know German quite well," Reggie told me. "I said yes and I did translate *Wozzeck* and it did come out as the libretto for the performance."[5] No one would have thought then that a few years hence Reggie Allen would be manager of the Philadelphia Orchestra.

The cast of *Wozzeck* was not by any standard star-studded and few of those who appeared have survived memory. Anne Roselle sang the role of Marie, Ivan Ivantzoff that of Wozzeck, but in the role of the Drum Major, Nelson Eddy appeared in the New York production only. It was his first and only opera performance in New York.[6] He did not create much of a stir because it was still years before his successful warbling of the "Indian Love Call" with Jeanette MacDonald. The role of Andres was ably handled by Sergei Radamsky and that of the First Artisan by Abrasha Robofsky. The Second Artisan was Ben de Loache.

Radamsky had a short career as a soloist but he did exert considerable influence as a teacher. One of his pupils was the splendid soprano Patricia Brinton. One evening in Paris she talked to me at length about Radamsky. She showed me a copy of a short autobiographical book he had written called *Der Verfolgte Tenor* or *The Persecuted Tenor*.

Radamsky had met Sol Hurok in Moscow and had helped him get the Isadora Duncan dancers out of Russia. He was under the impression that Hurok was to manage him, and in fact Hurok had promised to obtain a number of concerts for him.

Although these did not materialize, the world began to look brighter again when he received a telegram from Stokowski asking whether he would sing the tenor part in Alban Berg's *Wozzeck*.[7]

Radamsky proceeded to Philadelphia, where five other tenors were waiting to audition for the part. When it came to Radamsky's turn he sang, not one of the usual arias, but one from an opera by Zandonai based on *Gösta Berling*, a play by Selma Lagerlöf. "After the first ten bars, Stokowski stopped the recital, came closer to the stage, took a comfortable seat and asked me to begin anew. When I finished, he called out, 'Bravo! Where did you learn this?' " Radamsky told him that he had heard the opera in 1924 at La Scala, with Toscanini conducting. " 'Would you like to hear another aria?' " Radamsky asked. " 'I have heard enough,' " Stokowski answered. " 'Would you like to sing *Wozzeck* with us?' 'I would indeed,' " answered Radamsky. "Two days later I received a contract, the score of *Wozzeck* and a letter stating that Stokowski's assistant, Sylvan Levin, would come for rehearsals to New York." At the first rehearsal in Radamsky's studio at Seventy-third Street and Broadway, when Ivan Steschenko, Sylvan Levin, and Radamsky began to rehearse, "to our surprise Stokowski appeared . . . with the score under his arm," Radamsky recalled. "He excused himself saying, 'I don't know the score any better than you. I'll sit quietly in the corner and won't bother you.' He acted exactly like a student during a lesson and not like a star conductor as one would suspect. Stokowski's correctness and consideration for his singers was without equal. I was deeply astonished how he, born in London, mastered the German language including the most intricate inflections and nuances. . . . During orchestra rehearsals, he was always on stage an hour early, studying his score, answering questions and correcting parts.

. . . If the rehearsal was set for 10 A.M., he lifted his baton at precisely that minute."[8]

For the *Wozzeck* premiere in Philadelphia on March 19, 1931, critics journeyed south en masse. Critic W. J. Henderson reported that "a special train went hence to convey New Yorkers to the scene of action. Newspapers at both ends of New Jersey printed columns of criticism—pragmatic, dogmatic, ecstatic and lymphatic."

Deems Taylor, whose operas *Peter Ibbetson* and *The King's Henchman* had both been produced by the Met, was conceded to be, perhaps, the most legitimately equipped critic to review it and assess its merits. He led what the Philadelphia reporters labeled as a "laudatory dithyrambic chorus" of the musical scribes. Deems described Stokowski's task as probably the most complex that has ever confronted a conductor in this country. "That task he accomplished with complete success. The performance was smooth and clean-cut, with perfect liaison between the orchestra and the stage. . . . he conducted an orchestral performance that was a tour de force not only of accurate individual and ensemble playing but of delicacy of detail, tonal richness and unflagging vitality. *Wozzeck* may be set down as a triumph of his career."[9]

Discussing the music, Deems wrote: "Good or bad, the music is not to be dismissed with a word—or with many words. It is music that is written by a man who has talent for the theater, who can isolate, as it were, the emotions of a scene and convey it, who has an unerring sense of timing and an almost unfaltering command of climax. Like it or not, *Wozzeck* is a true music drama written by a dramatic artist of the first order."

The production of *Wozzeck* had come under the aegis of the Philadelphia Grand Opera Company, which had been founded by two great opera enthusiasts, Mr. and Mrs. William Hammer.

Mrs. Hammer recalled her first meeting with Stokowski: "He was very polite and he said, 'No! No. Under no circumstances would I conduct any of the old-fashioned operas.' Well, being young at that time, nothing discouraged me. . . . I told him of our dreams and what we had done so far and he suggested that I meet Mrs. Bok and tell her how hard we were working to establish an opera company. I met Mrs. Bok, told her my story, and she. . . . made it financially possible for us . . ."[10]

When Mrs. Bok had agreed to underwrite the costs of the *Wozzeck* production, Stoki agreed to cooperate with the Hammers. Following the Philadelphia performance of *Wozzeck*, the Hammers, stage director Wil-

Mr. Wilhelm von Wymetal, Sylvan Levin, Mrs. William
Hammer, and Alban Berg in Salzburg, summer 1931, after
the American premiere of *Wozzeck* in Philadelphia

helm von Wymetal, and Sylvan Levin all converged on Salzburg during
its music festival. There they met Alban Berg and told him "about the
great success Stokowski had had with Wozzeck."

As the November date for the New York performance neared, Berg
wrote to Sylvan:

27 October 1931

Trauttmansdorffgasse 27
Vienna XIII/1
Austria
Dear Mr. Levin,

    The performances of "Wozzeck" are approaching and I have a
request to make. I would like to possess pertinent mementos pertain-
ing to the Philadelphia "Wozzeck" performance, (and perhaps also
the New York performance) such as programs, program notes, announcements, posters (?), photos of scenes, etc. . . . I would like to
have these souvenirs of the American "Wozzeck" since I am unable
to be present.

    It was a pleasure for me to have met you, Mr. Levin, who had such a great part in the study of my opera, certainly now to be repeated. I also did not forget that you are going to send me your "Wozzeck" score in order for me to inscribe it, which I do with pleasure.

I send you heartfelt greetings and remain yours, devotedly,

Alban Berg

Give my regards to everyone whom I met in Salzburg. Most of all Mr. and Mrs. Hammer, as well as Mr. Wymetal.[11]

When on November 24, 1931, *Wozzeck* finally arrived at the Met in New York, Stoki was confident that it would make as striking effect as it had in its first performance in Philadelphia. Among the distinguished audience, reporters noted the presence of Olga Samaroff (ever faithful), Margarete Matzenauer, Mr. and Mrs. Otto Kahn, the Edward Boks, the Josef Hofmanns, the Fritz Kreislers, the Grand Duchess Marie of Russia, the actor Walter Hampden, Bettina van Wagstaf-Gribble, Ernest Hutcheson, Walter Damrosch, John Erskine, and countless other notables. Koussevitzky, who because of his own orchestral commitments could not come to New York, sent a trusted emissary to report on it.

Stokowski was right. It stirred up an enormous amount of interest and controversy. The press had a field day. Immediately after the performance, opinions were being expressed heatedly, and critics were rushing to their typewriters to express their feelings.

No one seemed indifferent. Walter Damrosch, who on hearing the Philadelphia production told Radamsky that he was not impressed and was surprised that he had liked it, after the New York performance remarked that he thought Berg was a far more talented musician than his teacher Arnold Schoenberg. "This is the second time I have heard *Wozzeck*," said Damrosch, "and as at the first performance I find it very interesting at the start. Later the edge wears off and at the end I'm just bored. Then there are too many diseased people on stage. You don't need pathological cases to make a real tragedy."[12]

Lawrence Gilman, in a philosophical mood, declared: "The evening was one not soon to be forgotten. An original and distinguished work of art, extraordinarily moving and sincere, was placed before us in the fullness of its power, its pity, and its truth—a work which raises in sympathetic minds that haunting question which was asked so long ago by Aeschylus, 'Ah! what is mortal life?' "[13]

In 1961, thirty years after the performance of *Wozzeck*, Stokowski was asked during an interview what it was like for a symphony conductor to move into the opera house. He replied: "It's extremely difficult. I am deeply interested in drama, the drama of all times and all countries. A long time ago I conducted the opera *Wozzeck*. It was the first time it was done in this country. I had the good fortune to do that with Robert Edmond Jones, an extraordinary man. He understood, he made the design of the stage, he made the costumes, and particularly the lighting—like a master. Now lighting is very important, because in opera, your ears hear the music, but your eyes see, and if there is no light, there is no seeing. If you are in a dark house, there is nothing to see. . . .

"Robert Edmond Jones understood the power of darkness, and where to put one little spot of light. There is a scene where Marie is reading the bible and rocking her baby with her hand. And the score described that room, a poor room where she was, and where there was a door and a window and all the rest of it. So we thought about such a room and we designed such a room. It was awful. Finally Jones took a small spotlight, put a piece of asbestos over it so as to hide it. Marie was sitting there, and we took a desk from the orchestra, and we put a telephone book on it, and that scene cost us almost nothing, but was magical in its beauty, and expressed all the drama of *Wozzeck*. [14]

28

Oedipus, Le Pas d'Acier, *and* Pierrot Lunaire

A FTER the success of the *Wozzeck* and the Schoenberg-Stravinsky evenings, another collaboration of Stokowski, the Philadelphia Orchestra, and the League was an obvious sequitur: another double bill, this time Stravinsky and Prokofiev. Less than a month separated the production of the Berg opera and the Stravinsky-Prokofiev pairing, but the indefatigable Stokowski found time between them for another premiere, *Lindbergh's Flight,* by Kurt Weill and Berthold Brecht. The translation of the Brecht text from German into "Americanese" was made by George Antheil and it abounded in colloquialisms. The critics found the score rather monotonous but admired its wide range of style moving from the almost classical to jazz, with plenty of modernistic harmony thrown in.[1]

Stoki met with Claire Reis, Dick Hammond, and other members of the League to discuss Stravinsky's *Oedipus Rex* and Prokofiev's ballet *The Age of Steel (Le Pas d'Acier).* Although both works had been given in concert form by the Boston Symphony, these would be American "firsts" in full production.[2]

The two works were given in Philadelphia and New York in a series of performances beginning on April 10, 1931. In the handsome illustrated program that the League prepared, Stokowski wrote: "When art expresses ideas and emotions that are fundamental, it knows no limit of period or country. The music of Stravinsky's *Oedipus Rex* is in places markedly Russian, as for instance the melodic and rhythmic design of the phrases sung by the shepherd and the messenger after the announcement of the death of Polybus. In other places the feeling of Greek tragedy inspires the

267

music of Stravinsky, as for example the broad sweeping strokes of the melodic line of Creon's speech, or the frenetic agitation of the chorus near the end. But in general the music is detached from natural characteristics —non-realistic, abstract. It is dark, archaic, somber in color, while in form it is one long line of ever increasing ominous tension. In searching for an eloquent visual presentation of *Oedipus Rex*, a type of mobile sculpture has been evolved, in which plastic figures, monumental in height, represent in an impersonal and abstract manner, the conflicting personalities of the tragedy."[3]

Oedipus Rex might be best described as an opera-oratorio. It is based on a libretto by Jean Cocteau, which was originally written in French. For these performances the narrative sections were recited in English by Wayland Rudd while the chorus and soloists sang in Latin. The cast was brilliant. It included Paul Althouse as Oedipus, Margarete Matzenauer as Jocasta, and Sigurd Nilssen as Tiresias. For the Philadelphia performances the Princeton Glee Club was used and for those in New York the Harvard Glee Club. Singing among the basses of the Harvard group were future harpsichordist Ralph Kirkpatrick and painter Rockwell Kent.

Robert Edmond Jones designed the settings, the costumes, and the fifteen-foot figures that celebrated puppeteer Remo Bufano operated. Jones found this production one of the most challenging he had ever attempted, for he considered *Oedipus Rex* one of the great dramas of history. He saw his puppets as "great archaic figures moving half-seen, in a world of dreams: "The Incest-Ridden, The Terrible Mother-Wife, The Soothsayer, The Messenger. . . . Music, mystery, a reminder of the old, forbidden, terrible secret hidden in the depths of our thought . . .

"It is possible that such figures, revealed by changing light and interpreted by music, may be the protagonists in a new kind of theater."[4]

Prokofiev stated that in *Le Pas d'Acier*, or *The Age of Steel* (the title had been the invention of Diaghilev), he had had a radical change in the style of his composition, and that it was "in a large measure diatonic and many of the themes were composed on white keys only."

For the American presentation a scenario was concocted by Lee Simonson, who also did the settings and costumes. He peopled it with personifications of Steel, Iron and Coal; Bucolic Leaders, Labor Leader, Clergyman, Dowagers, Blue Cross Nurses, Flappers, College Professors, a Financier, and Soldiers. The scenario read like a parody. It is all about the revolt of the masses, the revolt against the "devastating monotony of the Ford belt which turns men of forty into human waste."[5]

Although the score is basically diatonic it is one of the more strident of Prokofiev's works and it shares some affinity with Mossolov's *Iron Foundry* and Honegger's *Pacific 231.*

The most important innovation of these productions was Stokowski's decision to have both works filmed with sound. The Pathé division of RKO made the films and, while it was done mainly for experimentation, twelve-minute versions were to be released for public distribution. It was indeed a historic "first."[6]

In an editorial, the *Philadelphia Public Ledger* observed: "With *Wozzeck* a short time ago and Stravinsky's *Oedipus Rex* and Prokofiev's *Age of Steel* for this week's program, the Philadelphia Orchestra and its conductor have swept their audiences into a fourth dimension of music. It is something to know that they are ahead of the world, alone on the ultimate peaks of modernism. And it is somehow encouraging to know that they have gone farther in intellectual liberalism than any other great orchestra in this country or Europe."[7]

Following the New York performance, A. Walter Kramer quipped: "It takes real talent to choose two dodos. . . . Yes, I am all for modern music that has authenticity, not fifth-rate Stravinsky nor tottering Prokofiev."[8]

One Philadelphia scribe pondered: "The persistence of the conductor in putting forth ultra-modern works may be said to be making history for the orchestra, however, as well as serving no doubt to establish his own fame as a master of innovation, and there is reason to believe that the future will bring his vindication, even if in the present lingers some feeling of doubt. The magnitude, the splendor and the artistic quality and completeness of the present production at the Metropolitan at any rate calls for cordial congratulation and praise."[9]

Stoki's interest in the Prokofiev score was based solely on musical considerations. That it was meant to glorify the Soviet way of life probably never entered his mind. About the *Age of Steel* he wrote: "This is music of vitality, and the thrill of speed and power. For a moment the life of thought and tranquility and imagination is put aside in the exalting of motion and strength."[10]

The scenario for the ballet, as created by Lee Simonson, was a satirical, dramatized polemic against the brutally relentless rhythm of manual labor and the triumph of the machine over flesh and blood. It was all corny.

None of the reviewers paid much attention to the ballet. Few of them liked it, but none of the reviews that I have seen indicated that any of them had their patriotic senses affronted. One indignant soul, however, wrote to the press complaining that Stokowski had "introduced a ballet which was Communist propaganda with display of hammer and sickle emblem, waving of red flags, etc." Among his other accusations he fumed: "Stokowski played an *Ode to Lenin* on the anniversary of the Russian revolution. He is on the National Committee of the Department of Cultural Activity of the Communist Workers International Relief and is practically a Communist propagandist in the United States. He is in John Dewey's American Society for Cultural Relations with Russia and was vice president and is now president of the American Institute for Cultural Relations with the Soviet Union, Philadelphia branch."

Then, working on the concept of guilt by association, he lists many Philadelphians who in some way were associated with Stokowski. Among them he cited: ". . . people who have been helping reds, disloyalists and pacifists and who are connected with the American Civil Liberties Union . . . Mary Kelsey of the Philadelphia branch of the American Civil Liberties Union . . . Alexander Fleisher, who is on the Pennsylvania Committee for Total Disarmament with a lot of the American Civil Liberties Union crowd; Wilbur Thomas, extreme pacifist who associates with pinks; Susan M. Kingsbury of Bryn Mawr who also associates with pinks and reds; Gertrude Ely, very active in the Pennsylvania and National League of Women Voters . . ."[11]

When I spoke with Evangeline about Gertrude Ely, she reminded me that "she was a member of the most conservative Philadelphia society and she was considered a great liberal by the Philadelphia that I knew and that she was part of. And those John Birchers! Anybody who was a liberal was called a Communist."[12] Being interested in Russia in the mid-thirties was more than just fashionable. There was, of course, a sense of mystery about it and many Americans, abandoning their once prescribed "grand tour," went off to Russia instead and brought back many intriguing stories about its progress and development.

In New York a group called "We-Have-Been-to-Russia" convened for a dinner under the auspices of the American Russian Institute. Its May-June bulletin included a speech given by Stoki at this dinner. He asked a rhetorical question: "What is it about Russian music that creates such a tension in you?" He then answered: "It is this—that Slavic art, unlike other, covers the whole range of emotions and imagination. The artistic nature of the Slav is without taboos, without limits. The Slav allows his feeling to project itself in any direction. There is no such thing as 'bad form' in Russian art. It expresses to the utmost limit fear, filth, divine wisdom, radiance, all possible feelings and emotions. . . .

"What is there that is new and valuable in the Russian music of the Revolution? That question, so often asked, shows that the questioner doesn't understand art at all. Art does not come to fruition in twenty years. It may require twenty centuries. It is like an oak tree. Do not expect the new spirit in Russia to express itself in music now. But it will some day express itself in music."[13]

The final collaboration of Stokowski and the League was anticlimactic. No one on the board of the League thought that another work of Schoenberg, even with the combination of Stokowski and members of the Philadelphia Orchestra, could draw another sell-out audience at the Met. Wisely they chose Town Hall with its modest seating capacity. Although the League had presented Schoenberg's *Pierrot Lunaire* in a concert version, Stoki was intrigued by the idea of doing it in a staged version.

Robert Edmond Jones did the decor. Stoki chose his players from the Philadelphia Orchestra and Mina Hager mimed and chanted the role of the moonstruck Pierrot.[14] The performance took place on April 16, 1933.

"When Stokowski did *Pierrot Lunaire,*" said Claire Reis, "he made a great issue of having all of the orchestra in the dark. Bobby Jones had designed a kind of half-moon and Mina Hager was in a silvery black costume which Bobby had designed. Then one day Stoki said, 'The music has got to be on black paper' [photostated on black with white notes]. So black paper we had to get for him. Well, we were always pleasing him. After all he was giving us his services. During the intermission of one rehearsal he came out to see me and said, 'Do you think someone could go over to a shop nearby and buy some black cloth?' Well, Stern Brothers was just around the corner from Town Hall and I said, 'Yes, I can send someone over.' 'The white shirt collars show too much of the men,' he said. So I sent for a piece and I watched him as he got someone to tear a piece in half and make a triangle and he tied it around the collar of one of the musicians. We had the lights for the musicians with covers over them so that they were to be in absolute darkness. There was a silver light on Pierrot and, of course, Stokowski's hands were brightly lighted from above."[15]

On reading the far from favorable reviews for the Schoenberg,[16] I was reminded of a remark made by composer Charles Wuorinen on listening to *Pierrot Lunaire,* which, after all, dates back to 1912, just thirty-six years before Charles was born. He remarked that "even at this late date [1971], listening to it occasionally reminds one of attempts to befriend a porcupine."[17]

(29)

Parsifal

*T*HE idea of conducting *Parsifal* had tenanted Stokowski's mind for a very long time, perhaps as far back as his days at St. Bartholomew's when he pleased the parishioners by playing its Prelude. He began to plan a full concert production a year in advance of the performance. He planned to present it during the Easter week of 1933.

He wrote to Sylvan Levin:

May 12, 1932

Caro Maestro Illustre,

Now that you have not a thing to do!!!!! Do you think you would have time to do me a favor and time the whole of *Parsifal* without cuts? I suggest you do this alone and without your orchestra otherwise the tempo might be too fast!!

Also the same afternoon could you look through *Carmen* noting the places that are rich cream, those that are just milk and those that are mainly water? Because we may do next season a very much abridged version of *Carmen*.

I cannot think of anything else to do that afternoon except perhaps you would invite me to tea so as to fill out the time. (Yes lemon meringue pie)

Always

Maestrino[1]

Stoki discussed the matter of the chorus with Sylvan. It was to be a volunteer chorus with students from the Curtis Institute added. He wanted a boys' choir of about twenty-four; a women's chorus of about fifty with half the number from the Curtis; a men's chorus of one hundred with at least twelve from the Curtis. He put all of this into a memo addressed to Sylvan on the first of June, and suggested that the first announcement be released at once and a direct appeal for volunteers be made on September 1.[2]

On August 11 he wrote: "I have just received word from Josef Hofmann that he is willing for us to have some of the students act as leaders in our volunteer chorus for *Parsifal*."[3]

Parsifal was not staged and hence might be thought of as being out of place among the staged works Stoki conducted. Also it was done not in one evening but spread out over three successive concerts. They were done in the Academy of Music for the regular subscription series. On Friday afternoon he began with the Prelude to act 1 and followed with scenes 1 ("In the Domain of the Holy Grail") and 2 ("In the Hall of the Castle of the Holy Grail"). On Saturday evening, he chose music from both acts 2 and 3: Prelude, "In the Keep of Klingsor's Magic Castle," and "In the Garden of the Flowermaidens." This was followed by the Interlude and the Finale ("In the Hall of the Holy Grail"). On the following Monday evening he chose the Prelude and scene 1 ("Landscape in the Domain of the Holy Grail") from act 3, and scene 2 ("In the Hall of the Holy Grail").

The cast was carefully chosen: Robert Steel as Parsifal, Rose Bampton as Kundry, Nelson Eddy as Gurnemanz, and Benjamin de Loache singing a minor role, that of the Second Knight. Among the flowermaidens we find Irra Petina of future musical comedy fame. These were singers with whom Stokowski especially enjoyed performing.

After her beautiful singing in *Gurrelieder*, Stokowski particularly wanted Rose Bampton for *Parsifal*. She told me: "Stokowski engaged me to do Kundry. I remember the shock when I told Mr. Ziegler [Edward Ziegler was assistant to Gatti-Casazza at the Met], 'You know I've already signed my contract with Mr. Stokowski to do the Kundry in *Parsifal*.' 'Kundry! Are you out of your mind? You can't sing Kundry. You don't know what it's all about and this is for a mature person.' I said, 'Well, Mr. Stokowski seems to think I can.' And so did I, but Mr. Ziegler sent me to a very wonderful person to work with who had been a very great Kundry, and I worked very hard on it. Of course, I never sang it [in a full production] until many years later when I did it in Buenos Aires for the first time as an opera.

"But Stokowski was so marvelous with me and worked so carefully with me and had such a faith that it helped me to grow and to believe in myself."[4]

In addition to those who heard *Parsifal* in the Academy, a vast audience was able to hear it in part during two broadcasts, the first one on Friday afternoon and the second on the Saturday evening Philco Radio Hour.

It is curious that for all of his love and interest in Wagner's music, Stokowski was never moved to conduct any complete Wagnerian opera —not even in concert form. Although without cuts, the performances of *Parsifal* really do not qualify since the work was given piecemeal and not in sequence, and the segments were heard by three different audiences. Perhaps he was disenchanted by the insufferable length of the Wagnerian dramas. Even in segmented form, *Parsifal* proved to be trying. As *Musical America* commented: numerous persons in the three audiences "felt that there was a great deal of superfluity, repetition and monotony. . . . The interminable monologues of Gurnemanz, even when so notably presented as Nelson Eddy sang them, were a heavy burden on the average hearer. . . ."[5]

The opera house was never really Stokowski's natural environment. Neither the Metropolitan nor any other major opera house considered engaging him to conduct any of their productions at that time. Nor did any of his various managers push for operatic engagements. It is very possible that during the years when he was tangent to Munich and the Germanic scene he may have been interested in conducting at Bayreuth. Such an idea never protruded in his public conversations. Surely during the years that Toscanini was a prominent figure there he would never have been considered. But later on, when the "Maestro" was no more, he expressed his interest in the possibility of conducting an opera there.

To the Beeks, his European managers, he wrote:

> I have the impression from what I hear that Wagner's grandson has a most profound understanding of the spirit of Wagner's creative genius and that he is most intelligently using all the modern resources of today which his grandfather would use were he living presently. To me the intentions of Wagner are perfectly clear in his music and I would like to conduct "Parsifal" in Bayreuth in the new and freer spirit which is now being created there. The scene of the Flower Maidens has music of great sensuous beauty, so what is on the stage

should have the same spirit. This is also true of "Tannhauser" which I would like to conduct with the Paris version of the "Bacchanale." Nothing could be more sensuous and voluptuous than this music and I think the stage should present a picture with the same spirit with dancers who are nude or as near nude as the law permits. I often see and hear "Parsifal" and "Tannhauser" presented in such a dry, academic, intellectual manner that I feel is exactly the opposite of Wagner's conception so clearly expressed by his music.[6]

"What do you think," asked Stoki in a letter to Capitol Records, "of our some day making recordings of Wagner's Nibelungen Ring and separately perhaps on a small disc could be an analysis of all the themes in which these four music-dramas are extremely rich, sounding the themes with spoken explanation."[7]

The query elicited this response from F. M. Scott III: "I personally am rather high on this idea of recording at Bayreuth and packaging in a two, three or four record set. It is an expensive project, and I really should discuss it with the committee before finalizing. In any event, this is well over a year off."[8]

It was forever off.

30

HP

STOKOWSKI had always been intrigued by Mexico and on December 16, 1930, he announced that he would spend his winter vacation with the Aztec Indians in remote and mountainous parts of Mexico. "I've heard native American Indian music of different types. How far this Mexican Indian music has developed from the primitive Indian I cannot tell. Some of it may be worthwhile from a musical standpoint. I can't tell until I hear it."[1]

"We had a wonderful time in Mexico," Evangeline told me. They visited Yucatán, and from its capital they went to see the ancient ruins of Chichén Itzá and Uxmal. "But in those days there was no motor road from Mérida to Chichén Itzá. There was, instead of a regular train, a sort of steam engine with one car behind it. We spent the night in Chichén Itzá in a building which had been put up for the archeologists from the Archeological Museum in Santa Fe. They're always trying to solve the mystery of what happened to the Mayans," she recalled.[2]

Stoki shared all of Evangeline's enthusiasm about their archeological explorations. "I became very interested because I've always been very interested in archeology and tomorrow and not much in today," she said laughingly.[3] Stoki reiterated the same dictum throughout his career.

Although he had never met Carlos Chávez Stoki became interested in the possibility of conducting his orchestra. Chávez had lived in New York from the end of 1926 to the middle of 1928, when he returned to Mexico and founded the Orquesta Sinfónica de Mexico. "Those were the golden years of the Philadelphia Orchestra as you may remember," said Carlos.

"I was a great admirer of the orchestra under Stoki. Although I would not always agree with his interpretations, the orchestra was a superb instrument and the way he handled it was absolutely phenomenal. One day in 1930 out of a clear sky, as you say in English, I received a wire from Mérida saying, 'I am in Yucatán. I am on my way to Mexico. Would you like me to conduct your orchestra?' Out of a clear sky, absolutely. I had never met him. We had never been in touch. Of course, he already knew of me and knew some of my compositions, so I answered and said I would be delighted."[4]

Leopold and Evangeline boarded the train in Veracruz, which soon began making its slow ascent into the mountains past the magnificent snow-covered Pico de Orizaba and into the valley of Mexico. Since he had not notified Chávez about the exact time of their arrival there was no one at the station to greet them. But after getting settled in their hotel, they went directly to Chávez's home in the Lomas de Chapultepec.

They quickly made plans for his conducting the orchestra. It was a far more innocent world in which schedules and arrangements could be made without upsetting apple carts. Billboards throughout the city proclaimed that Stokowski would conduct the orchestra. That was the only information that was needed. "So he conducted one concert with my orchestra," Chávez recalled. "As a matter of fact he conducted twice. In those days the *Bellas Artes* did not exist, so he conducted one concert in the theater and then we had an open-air concert in Chapultepec Park. He wanted to do the *Leonore* No. 3, and he had the trumpet back among the trees. It was fine. . . ."

Mexican dignitaries vied in paying him honors. He was made *"Huésped de Honor,"* the Mexican equivalent of getting the keys to the city. Stoki responded graciously. He offered to conduct a special concert and broadcast and donate his fee and the proceeds for the relief of victims of a recent earthquake in Oaxaca.[5] Flowers were tossed at his feet by the adoring audience and composer Julián Carrillo presented him with a special citation from the Mexican composers.[6] Stoki further ingratiated himself by playing some of Carrillo's microtonal works.

But his music was not new to him. Four years earlier, Stoki had conducted the world premiere of Carrillo's *Concertino* with the Philadelphia Orchestra, with special instruments for the quarter-, eighth- and sixteenth-tones that Carrillo's score required.[7] It might not have been too difficult for the Mexican orchestra, for I heard it once in a concert—long after the regime of Chávez—try to play *Psyché* by César Franck. The strings were so abysmally out of tune that it sounded as if it had been arranged by Carrillo himself.

The friendship between Stoki and Chávez moved apace. "He used to come to my studio, to my house, and I played some music for him and it was then that he heard me on the piano playing the *HP, Horsepower,* ballet and he said, 'I want to do that in Philadelphia.'"

Carlos explained his concept of *HP.* "It's just a pretext for dances," he said. "The idea is the contrast between the North and the South. He particularly liked that—the South with all its tropical exuberance and the North with the machinery. In those days it was very much in fashion. Although I was never one to follow trends, I liked the idea of the machine."[8]

Through Carlos Chávez the Stokowskis met Diego Rivera, who was living at that time just south of the city. Rivera and his colleague-rival, Orozco, were then painting their murals with a kind of burning fury. Mexico was in the throes of Communism; Rivera expressed his own ethical and political ideology in murals and paintings of brightly colored object lessons.

Rivera and Chávez were close friends and Diego was immediately intrigued by the story of *HP* and agreed to do the sets and costumes for the ballet. In fact he even agreed to do the sets in Philadelphia since he would be working in Rockefeller Center at the time.

Rivera's house was in Villa Obregón, one of the most attractive of Mexico's suburbs; it was situated across from the San Angel Inn which in the late seventeenth century had been a monastery. Here, too, was the house of Leon Trotsky. Nearby was the Pedregal, a great basaltic lava stream that covers approximately fifteen miles. It was quite undeveloped then but the Jardines del Pedregal, one of the most arresting residential developments, was aborning. Both Evangeline and Stoki were fascinated by the Pedregal where excavations had revealed human bones and various artifacts. Working on plans for the new development was the distinguished architect and painter, Juan O'Gorman. The Stokowskis met O'Gorman and Evangeline considered it one of the most interesting experiences they had had in Mexico City. They visited O'Gorman's home and they were fascinated by it.

"Stokowski," said Evangeline, "was always interested in modern music, modern architecture, modern ideas on planning and so on."[9]

His interest in architecture was more than theoretical. He realized the impossibility of doing operatic productions and ballets with the full orchestra in the Academy of Music, although for concerts he felt it was adequate. He also disliked the Philadelphia Metropolitan Opera House; while it was large enough to stage big productions, its orchestral pit was inadequate and uncomfortable and its stage was really primitive, with no modern equipment and technical apparatus. In addition, it was quite an inelegant old barn.

Stoki had discussed the problem with the Boks, and Edward, always interested in aiding his "prince," met with Cyrus Curtis. With the help of a few similar-minded enthusiasts they began to make plans for what Stoki had outlined as a Temple of Music. It was to be situated on the Parkway, Philadelphia's Champs-Élysées, which had come into being after its sesquicentennial celebration in 1926. Stoki had been quite critical of the architecture that lined it and he surely hoped that the Temple of Music would not turn out to be so slavishly conformist.

In April Stokowski addressed a gathering at the Barclay Hotel to launch the Philadelphia Theater Association. Their first project was to be an adaptation of *Lysistrata* by Norman Bel Geddes. After praising the distinctive quality of Bel Geddes' inspirations, he turned his attention to Philadelphia's architecture. He probably had his Temple of Music in mind: "Why can't we rid ourselves of our dependence on Europe in expressing ourselves artistically? When I ride home from the orchestra by way of the Parkway I see a church that reminds me of Michelangelo, a library that reminds me of the Place de la Concorde and a museum that suggests Pompeii. There is nothing, practically nothing that is distinctively original or Philadelphian along the entire stretch of Parkway. I'm not blaming the architects. . . . They plan and work under orders."

He was probably unaware that sitting among the guests was Eli Kirk Price, the man who gave the orders concerning the erection of the buildings on the Parkway. It was not Stokowski's nature to launch such a personal attack on anyone in public. Just as one might refer to a committee or a board, he apparently had not thought of any individual. Mr. Price, it was observed, continued to "inspect the interior of his empty coffee cup, but found nothing."

Stoki continued: "American and Philadelphia architects are among the leaders in their art. We have created our own architecture in America. Nothing in the world is like the picture of New York as seen from the incoming ship. The great building, and we [have] built it here, seems to have sprung from our soil. Perhaps it has roots in Taos. Maybe it is more Aztec than anything else; but, whatever it is, it's our own."[10]

As usual, Stoki's remarks stirred up a heated controversy. Architects, the mayor, and various city councilmen voiced their opinions pro and con. Councilman Charles Hall, who had been active when the Parkway funds were an issue in the City Council, advised Stoki to "stick to his fiddles." And he added, "When it comes to putting up a building I'll take the advice of experts . . . before I'd consider the opinion of a musician."[11]

Paul Benckert, a Philadelphia architect, agreed with Stoki. "There is absolutely nothing representative of American architecture along the Parkway. It's a great pity because we had a great opportunity to express that which is our own. We muffed it."

Mayor Mackey, musing over Stokowski's statements, pointed out that "the Municipal Court Building to be erected on the Parkway will be a reproduction of the Place de la Concorde in Paris. Dr. Stokowski is a great artist and he has his own idiosyncrasies," said the mayor. "All of his remarks regarding the architecture on the Parkway are true . . . but I prefer to regard his remarks as a compliment." Eli Kirk Price, the "father of the Parkway," also declared that everything that Stoki had said was true, and he asked rhetorically, "What of it?"

On the tenth of July the Temple of Music was formally announced to the press with a preliminary design that may have seemed modern then but looks very conventional today.[12] Its facade was symmetrical with columns that, despite being square, did not make it much different from other structures lining the Parkway. The site for the Temple was donated by Cyrus H. K. Curtis at a cost of $2,100,000. Its estimated total cost was to have been in the area of $6,000,000. Edward Bok had pledged $850,000 and a sum in excess of $1,000,000 was already in hand. It was to be operated by a nonprofit corporation headed by Curtis Bok, who was the attorney for the enterprise. The building was to occupy a city block at Nineteenth and Race streets and the Parkway.

"For ten years," Stokowski said, "I have been drawing plans for such a building, as new discoveries in acoustical laws and lighting have been made. Men all over the world have been working for Philadelphia's Temple of Music. I have tried to bring their work to a synthesis." He explained how the stage would revolve and have mobile platforms that could be lifted or shifted and flexible elevators that would permit sections to be lowered. He wanted the orchestra pit very wide with stairs descending from the stage to the pit and continuing beneath the auditorium.

"I have it in mind to produce an Aztec music drama that I have found during my recent trip to Mexico," he said. "This would call for a temple on top of a pyramid. The drama has not yet been presented because the stage requirements are inadequate." He expressed hope that it could be done soon.[13]

Among other plans that Stoki had for his Temple of Music was a main auditorium with a seating capacity ranging from thirty-five hundred to five thousand, a hall for intimate concerts seating about twelve hundred, and a series of small chamber halls for lectures and recitals. On top of the roof he wanted to have an outdoor theater and a restaurant, from which elevators would permit diners to descend to the auditorium. In the corridors he envisioned lighted galleries for exhibits of sculpture, paintings, and arts and crafts. Beneath the structure he had recommended three sublevels for parking space.

Stoki's vision antedated by nearly thirty years the era when the phrases "performing arts" and "edifice complex" became popular. That Stokowski's Temple never materialized was not the fault of any of the protagonists; it was instead the result of the Depression, which was to profoundly affect nearly everyone in those darkening days of the early thirties.

He planned again to spend another winter vacation in Mexico and on January 18, 1932, he left Philadelphia to go first to Havana, where he said he would conduct the orchestra and then proceed to Mexico.[14] In Havana the orchestra was regularly conducted by the Spanish composer-conductor Pedro Sanjuan, who shared Stokowski's concert with him. The program opened with Sanjuan conducting Glinka's *Kamarinskaya* and two excerpts from his own *Liturgia Negra;* Stoki did the *Meistersinger* Prelude and a new work for piano and orchestra, *Hispania* by Cassado, with the American pianist George Copeland as soloist. Copeland, who specialized in Spanish and French music, had a marked success, but the critics concurred that Stokowski was the sensation of the Havana season.[15] All told, Leopold and Evangeline spent a week in Cuba exploring Havana and visiting Cienfuegos and other cities. Then on to Mexico.

Chávez was waiting in Veracruz as a one-man welcoming committee: "Stoki came with Evangeline on the boat to Veracruz, but Evangeline stayed somewhere while Stoki and I went out into the country. I took him to places that were completely unspoiled. There were no planes and the automobile roads were only beginning. We went on the train that goes from Veracruz to Salina Cruz. In those days there was a pullman car but it was one of those old pullman cars with very elaborate decoration. Stoki loved it. We went through the Isthmus of Tehuantepec and went to very wild places and saw the festivities, which in those days were very colorful. He was very much impressed with Oaxaca."

But that was not all that Chávez had shown Leopold. They also went to the state of Michoacán and visited Uruapan, Chapala, Morelia, and Toluca. "Near Uruapan," Chávez recalled, "there is a place where there is the beginning of a river and there is a marvelous garden and Stoki used to say, 'I do not know what the name of this garden is, but this is the Garden of Eden.' "[16]

When he returned to Philadelphia he told his expectant listeners, "I visited no cities in Mexico—only the remotest parts, ancient Mayan settlements or far away villages in the Sierra. It is very interesting. We went mule-back or with horses or occasionally by motor. Sometimes we would get nothing to eat for a day at a time. We visited places where white men seldom go. . . ."[17]

"Chokopul's Travels" was the title *Time* magazine gave to Stoki's trip in Mexico. "From one Mexican village to another this winter," *Time* reported, "a white man traveled, asking for and intently listening to music. A swart Mexican accompanied him, explaining to Aztecs and Tarascans that it was their own native music the stranger wanted to hear, not the imported hodge-podge played in Mexican cities. . . . Indians took to calling the white man Chokopul which means 'one of wandering wits.' "[18]

Much time during the six weeks following his return was spent in preparation for the presentation of Chávez's *HP*. Diego Rivera came to Philadelphia to work on his sets and costumes. From photos they seem less than distinguished. "In Mexico," Evangeline told me, "whenever he painted anything, he painted it by daylight, and in Philadelphia he did it indoors in a big studio and when it was put on the stage at the rehearsal in artificial yellow light on it, Diego kept saying, 'Oh, but that isn't what I painted at all! That isn't the color; those aren't the colors.' I think he did them all over."[19]

Stoki gave a very lucid and succinct synopsis of the ballet, which he said was "to convey the shifting emotional and spiritual experiences that follow climatic changes. The work is in four parts or episodes," he explained. "The first opens on board a steamship leaving New York for Southern waters. The dancers are disclosed in the smug, inhibited climate of a New York winter. Gradually as the ship enters warmer waters, temperamental inhibitions disappear. In the second episode passengers have almost forgotten the steel-edged, jagged life of the North as they approach the tropics, and the third part takes them ashore in a tropical land. The music of the first two episodes is inclined to be abstract. . . . In the third episode the music grows completely languorous and sensuous . . . as if the feeling of sunshine were coursing in the veins. . . . The closing episode takes the passengers back . . . into the North of prohibition and machine civilization. . . ."[20]

The curtain went up on a drop topped by the letters *HP* with a heavy horse on one side and an ordinary electric battery on the other. To express the exuberance of the South, animated pineapples, bunches of bananas, coconuts, coconut trees, and sugar cane pranced about joyously. Mermaids strumming guitars climbed about a ship to beguile an energetic group of sailors. A papier-mâché fish made an appearance. To effect the proper contrast the ship then turned north to the City of Industry with its skyscrapers, machinery, and din. Drab-looking workmen gyrated before a stock ticker, and a set of gasoline pumps, bathtubs, and a ventilator all melded into a materialistic orgy. For his climax Rivera had designed a huge sun, which some thought resembled Diego himself, while others thought it looked like Al Capone.[21]

Critic Oscar Thompson remarked: "As an experience at this first performance anywhere, the horsepower was generated in the pit. Mr. Stokowski was flywheel, crankshaft, piston, lubricating cup and safety valve all in one. What went on above him on the stage was merely the spinning about of lesser cogs whose purpose was illustrative rather than generative."[22]

Critical comment was varied. Some called it an "artless spectacle." One Philadelphia critic commented that the ballet is "characterized by some of the artifices which have been substituted for creative work before in the recent annals of music. It proves again that novelty and forced originality do not constitute a work of art. . . ."[23]

Although the Chávez music was more like the wolf than Little Red Riding Hood, it was a virile and exciting score with some fascinating dances reminiscent of the mariachi bands in Mexico. The important thing was that Stokowski was pleased and intended to program more music by Chávez. When I asked Carlos what other works he had conducted, he replied: "He also gave the premiere of my *Sinfonía India* in this country. I was present. And he also did *Sinfonía Antigona* and I had a very beautiful letter from him about these performances."[24] In 1936, Stoki invited Carlos to conduct the Philadelphia Orchestra, which he called the real beginning of his orchestral conducting career. It was his first engagement with an American symphony.

31

The Audience

M ost orchestras repeat their subscription series two or three times, usually with the same program. In the earlier days, the first concert was referred to as an "open rehearsal." In Berlin, the open rehearsal took place on Sunday morning and the official concert on Monday evening. In Boston the pattern followed with the concerts being on Friday afternoon and Saturday evening. Until World War I, the Friday concert was still called an open rehearsal, which added some confusion when reports were published of Muck being seized by the federal authorities during a rehearsal. In Philadelphia the pair of concerts took place on Friday afternoons and Saturday evenings. Later the concert was repeated on Monday evenings as the subscription concerts were expanded.

The Friday afternoon concert in Philadelphia was essentially a social affair. The audience was almost exclusively female, and according to some of the contemporary attendees, the ladies felt they owned the Academy. They would often come in late and often carry on conversations less than *sotto voce*.

Stoki had begun making little speeches as far back as his Cincinnati days when he would rebuke his audiences for their errant ways. During one Philadelphia concert on November 2, 1928, sneezes erupted while he was conducting a quiet passage in Gluck's Overture to *Alceste*. He stopped abruptly, turned and lectured: "You people down in this section are constantly annoying us. We work hard all week long to give you good music. . . . I do not want you to think I am cross or trying to be

disagreeable with you. It's just you few people who annoy me each week."
As he resumed the overture, several latecomers scrambled down the aisle.
He stopped again, turned his head, glancing at the offenders, and stalked
off the platform. Most of the audience applauded self-righteously and
Stoki, after a few moments, returned and began the overture for the third
time.

While the good ladies of Philadelphia no doubt had impeccable social
manners and knew Emily Post's rules and regulations for good behavior,
the doyennes of etiquette seldom if ever mentioned the etiquette of
concert attendance. It was Stoki who became the social-musical arbiter
in that realm. He lectured them about talking, coughing, knitting, applauding, arriving late, and leaving early.

During one Friday concert on October 10, 1924, he began with the
First Symphony of Brahms and ordered the ushers to prevent any latecomers from entering the Academy before the end of the first movement.
As the movement ended a flurry of latecomers hastily rushed to their seats.
Stoki briefly looked at the audience, registering an attitude of distinct
disapproval and then, standing before the orchestra with his baton pointing to the floor, stood motionless for an unconscionable pause before
resuming the symphony. Following the intermission, perhaps feeling
somewhat contrite, he spoke after playing Stravinsky's new orchestration
of the "Song of the Volga Boatmen." "I see you are completely won by
Stravinsky," he said, and went on to say that he had met a charming lady
who plaintively complained, "But why didn't you tell us before that
Stravinsky wrote the Volga Boat Song?" One of the scribes commented
that "this of course, produced a laugh—at least with those acquainted
with the history of the Volga Boatmen—and happiness reigned again in
an audience somewhat affronted by the conductor's earlier attitude."[1]

While Stoki carried out his disciplinary measure, he met with censure
himself. One critic pointed out, with a tone of rebuke, that since there
will always be tardy listeners, it would be far better if Stoki would program
a short work to begin a concert rather than a long symphony. But the
rebuke did not sink in. Later he began a program with Mendelssohn's
Reformation Symphony and played the entire work without a break,
thereby keeping a goodly number in the foyer until intermission.

He was also particularly annoyed at the fidgety ladies who departed
early in order to get back to their suburbs. "To get there, unless they were
chauffer-driven or driving their own cars, were the famous Paoli local
(making all stops along the Main Line) or the local to Chestnut Hill

(covering the suburbs to the north). The Paoli local was the train those ladies wanted to get," said Henry Pleasants. "They wanted to be home in time for their cocktails and dinner and so forth. They would be looking at their watches and when the time came for them to go to make their train, they would simply get up and go."[2]

Although Stokowski had repeatedly complained and admonished the good ladies, he now decided to make his point more emphatic. On his program of April 16, 1926, he included two works that had never been played in Philadelphia—at least not by the Philadelphia Orchestra: the *Fantaisie Contrapuntique sur un Cramignon Liègeois* by Guillaume Lekeu and Haydn's *Farewell* Symphony. Also on the program were the well-known "Ride of the Valkyries" and "Wotan's Farewell," sung by Reinald Werrenrath, followed by a group of Brahms songs.[3]

The program looked innocent enough. As the time for the concert arrived, the somewhat perplexed audience observed that only two players, one violinist, and one cellist, were on stage. All of the other seats were vacant. Stokowski strode out in his usual brisk fashion and began to conduct the two lone musicians. Then singly, or by twos and threes, other players came on stage as their parts appeared in the score. Stoki had them come in breathlessly imitating some of the late arrivers. Some came in already playing their music and seemed to land in whatever space was available. But it was all planned, and in fact it was how the music itself was to be played. When the small orchestra was finally assembled, they played through without further interruption.

When the piece was over and the ushers opened the doors, the usual numbers of latecomers paraded in. But if they had missed the bit of irony Stoki had presented, they, too, were in for an equally piquant object lesson. The next work, "Ride of the Valkyries," required an expanded orchestra. Stoki raised his baton—he was still using one at that time— and then lowered it as the brasses hurried to their places on stage, with palpable imitation of the hurried manner of the latecomers. Hisses and giggles arose from the audience.

Werrenrath then sang "Wotan's Farewell." But after the first of his Brahms songs, the flutes that were not needed for the later songs hurriedly left the stage. The concert could now proceed with classic serenity. Although some of the audience had known the history of the *Farewell* Symphony, it apparently had not occurred to the audience that Stoki would emulate Haydn literally. But he did! A reporter from the *Sun* described the performance: "The first movement had just got under way when one or two members of the orchestra apparently tired of playing, calmly quit, folded up their music and wandered off the stage. This kept up, to the chagrin of the audience, until, in the last movement, only two violins remained. Through all this Mr. Stokowski maintained a calm composure. . . . Finally, one of the remaining violinists walked off the stage, playing meanwhile. The other arose, walked to the exit, bowed graciously to the director, and the stage was empty except for Mr. Stokowski."[4]

In the audience on that memorable day was a young English conductor, Hugh Ross, who was hearing Stokowski for the first time, and he appreciated the lesson being given. "As the orchestra started leaving," he recalled, "so did large sections of the audience. I sat there and laughed. I thought, goodness, he's giving them a lesson but they're giving him one too. They were furious."[5]

One member of the audience called the concert outrageous. "Very ill-timed," said another. A third remarked, "This isn't Keith's you know. It's the Academy of Music."[6]

Stoki was particularly annoyed by coughing. He called it a disgusting noise, and the ladies carried their supply of cough drops and handkerchiefs and tried desperately to remain silent. But the cold months in Philadelphia did not help and perhaps psychologically coughs were produced by their own tensions. Stokowski had them completely frightened, but they loved him and endured his outbursts.

"One time the coughing got so bad," said bassoonist Ferdinand Del Negro, "he got us all together one morning after one of these concerts and said, 'Boys, we're going to practice coughing.' And he had the whole orchestra cough. But we didn't cough loud enough. So he rehearsed it and we all coughed as loud as we could. When the audience started coughing, he stopped the orchestra and gave us our cue and we coughed at the audience. Those who were guilty were quiet and the other ones laughed and applauded. They got the point."[7] When Stoki left for an extended trip to the Orient in 1927, he bade his ladies farewell and added, "I hope when I come back your colds will be better."[8]

Henry Pleasants remarked, "When we go to concerts today and latecomers are not admitted and there is no applause between movements, I think that Stokowski was very largely responsible for that. He objected to applause. He used to say why do they make all that terrible sound and he scared the audience into not applauding between movements and to coming on time and not leaving before the end of the concert, and that was back in the 1920s."[9]

When the audience burst into spontaneous volleys of applause after the pizzicato movement of the Tchaikovsky Fourth Symphony during a concert on November 8, 1929, Stoki turned, signaled for silence, and explained that his remarks were not intended as a rebuke for their appreciation. "But," he added reflectively, "I have been considering this matter of applause, a relic from the Dark Ages, a survival of customs at some rite or ceremonial dance in primitive times. When the request program blanks are circulated toward the close of the season I may incorporate a questionnaire on the applause topic and ask for your opinion."[10] He then proceeded to conduct the last movement, and as if to show their attitude, the audience again applauded lustily.

Along with a questionnaire sent out by the management soliciting suggestions for an all-request program that Stokowski would conduct as the last concert of the season, there were ballots on the applause question. Over a thousand were returned: the applauders won by a vote of 710 to 199.[11] When Stoki returned he accepted his defeat gracefully. "Thank you for the frankness of your vote," he said. "I lost. Perhaps you were right. The votes were overwhelmingly in your favor. But it's still a question whether these sounds are appropriate, and next season I should like to ask you some other questions and have your frank thoughts."[12]

32

The Orchestra

T HE orchestra that Stoki inherited from Scheel and Pohlig was well trained and contained many fine players. But it was hardly equal to the one he had built in Cincinnati. From the beginning he set out to make it not merely a well-drilled group but a wonderfully pliable one that would eventually be regarded as the finest in the world. The "Stokowski sound" was to become legendary.

Stoki seemed pleased with few of his original players. "I found a rather good orchestra, but not a *very* good one, also very old-fashioned in its attitude toward technical things. . . . Gradually we began to develop their playing according to what I regarded as more modern ideas of technique and of orchestral culture. . . . I didn't wish to change any of the players, or as few as possible, because my idea is you can only build up a great orchestra if you keep the same players and develop all their faculties, all their potentialities, technically and every kind of way. But when one constantly changes players, there is so much disturbance that a great orchestra cannot be built that way."[1]

But slowly he did begin to eradicate dead wood and with canny instinct added some of the most remarkable players found in any symphony. "Strangely enough," said Arthur Judson, "and in spite of his genius, and standing before that orchestra every day, he never woke up to the fact that some of the players were not good, until I got him upstairs in the amphitheater and he got a perspective. . . . He had never gotten off to a distance and heard the orchestra. He fired thirty men that year. That's when we began to build the orchestra. He was so immersed in making these people play that he didn't know the material was bad."[2]

There was no doubt some truth in Judson's story, but the records of the Philadelphia Orchestra do not indicate a mass firing on such a scale, although there was a continuous weeding process that Stoki pursued relentlessly. In 1914 the virtuoso contrabassist Anton Torello was added; then in 1915 Marcel Tabuteau, the distinguished oboist who had played under Toscanini at the Metropolitan Opera. Cellist Hans Kindler and clarinetist Daniel Bonade came in 1917. Saul Caston, then merely seventeen, was added to the trumpet section in 1918. In 1920 Stoki engaged one of his most important performers, the superb flutist William Kincaid. In Hawaii, where Kincaid grew up, he had been a swimming protégé of Olympic champion Duke Kahamamoku, and that may well have given him his superb breath control.[3]

For twenty years, Kincaid played under Stokowski in the Philadelphia Orchestra. "He developed the orchestral sound," said Kincaid. "I think one might say if there had been no Stokowski there would have been no orchestral sound as we know it today. It can be said Stokowski invented the Philadelphia Orchestra."[4]

"A violinist may have a splendid Stradivarius," Stoki remarked, "but a conductor must form his own instrument. He must know how to choose each player, recognizing in him his degree of mastery of the instrument —his flexibility in fitting his part to all the other parts of the orchestra —the beauty and variety of his tone—his understanding of the principles of phrasing—his general musical culture—intelligence—emotional qualities—imagination."[5]

During his summers in particular, Stoki tried playing all of the various instruments in the orchestra. He introduced free bowing—*bogen frei*— and also free breathing for the brass players. "I am completely opposed to standardization, regimentation, uniform bowing, uniform fingering and breathing, and all other conventions which tend to make an orchestra sound mechanical."[6]

"In working with the Philadelphia Orchestra, my dream was, and we partly achieved that dream, to express to the utmost the spirit, the inner spirit, of every kind of music. I say 'every kind' because every composer as an individual, as his life develops, produces—creates different kinds of music. . . . And, of course, the differences between two composers who lived in the same period, like Brahms and Wagner, are like the difference between the North Pole and the equator. . . .

"In order to do all that with the Philadelphia Orchestra, I begged the

Stokowski with Richard Strauss when he conducted the
Philadelphia Orchestra (1921)

players to notice all those differences and I said to them, 'Each one of you must be a poet as well as a great player of your instrument, and through your poetic feeling, you can express every kind of music.' I also said to them, 'Do not permit yourselves to become, as is the tendency in the world today, standardized, so that you all think and feel the same way. Do not crush your real individuality but express your individuality through the music. Give your personality, all your inner feeling, give that expression through the music. Do not be all alike. Be different as you really are different in your natures. No two violins are alike. No two bows are alike. No two hands are alike. No two nervous systems are alike. No two minds are alike. No two emotional characters are alike. You are all different. Be different! Don't standardize yourself. And put all those differences, all that richness of different coloring of personalities into music.' They finally did that and the orchestra became so flexible and so extraordinary!"[7]

When Richard Strauss was invited to conduct the orchestra, he eagerly accepted. "I cabled him," Stoki remembered, " 'Please send me your programs and I will prepare them.' He sent the programs. I rehearsed them all, so that when he came, he just tried a few passages and then he roared with laughter. And he said, 'This is a fabulous orchestra, that is *fabelhaft.*' He couldn't express himself, he was so delighted with the orchestra. *'Fabelhaft* orchestra!' " Strauss conducted three concerts in Philadelphia and four on tour. "I went with him everywhere and enjoyed being with that extraordinary personality."[8]

Sir Adrian Boult told me that his admiration for Stokowski had always been the same since he heard his records in the 1920s and attended one concert in Philadelphia.[9] He had been staying in New York with friends, and when he mentioned Stokowski, they phoned Gertrude Ely, who always had a box for the Friday afternoon concerts.[10] She immediately invited Boult. "I actually visited Philadelphia for a few hours," Boult recalled, "and heard a concert with unforgettable performances of a Haydn symphony, Tchaikovsky's *Nutcracker* Suite and Stravinsky's *Song of the Nightingale*—then quite new to America, and prefaced by a few words from the Conductor.

"As a young man," Boult continued, "I always used to say that there were several places—like Amsterdam, and Manchester (in Harty's time) —that I could always visit for a good lesson. If ever I felt that I was getting to be of some use at my job, an hour listening to those orchestras would act like a tonic and put me in my place again. That day in Philadelphia acted with even more healthy effect: my conceit was knocked out of me for several years!"[11]

People began to speak of the "Stokowski sound," which he modestly called a mystery, an illusion. "It doesn't exist," he said. "When a conductor rehearses an orchestra, who makes the sound? He doesn't make the sound. The players make the sound."

Wendy Hanson said to him somewhat admonishingly, "Yes, but you make an orchestra sound, particularly the strings, so that people can tell it is you conducting. Even if they can't see you, they know it is you."

"It might be," he replied, "I give great attention to relative values, to balance. Sometimes, when I hear an orchestra, practically all one can hear is the brass instruments. They smother everything else. I feel that the strings, the whole string section and the whole woodwind section are extremely important, and equally important. That's why I like to have the strings forward on one side of the stage, and the woodwinds forward on the other side, and don't put the woodwinds back where they are partially submerged. And I like to keep the brasses relatively low so they don't smother the strings and the woodwinds, so there is balance."[12]

With his keen sense of sonorities, Stoki began to experiment with some radical arrangements of the disposition of the players: "The traditional seating of the orchestra came about through custom—almost without thought. Each generation followed this old way of seating the orchestra, without asking, 'Why is it this way?' and 'Is it the best possible?' I have made detailed studies of each instrument in the orchestra, with the idea of discovering in what position for each instrument the tone will sound the best. For example, the string instruments have sound holes in the front part of the instrument on each side of the bridge over which the strings are stretched. The tone is sent out in greater volume from this front part and the sound holes than from the back or sides of the instrument. For this reason, if the first violins sit so that the front of their instruments face down the hall, the tone of the first violins will sound much fuller than the tone of the second violins, if they sit with the back of their instruments facing the hall. In the conventional seating of the orchestras, the second violins sit with the back of their instruments to the audience, and this accounts for the lack of balance that often exists between these two sections."[13]

It was perfectly logical. He then conducted experiments in the use of acoustical shells and baffles. He distinguished between a shell and an acoustical reflector. He explained that "an acoustical reflector is an enclosed space with two side walls, back and ceiling. The two side walls are not parallel but are fan-shaped, with the broad end toward the auditorium."[14]

He placed the strings in back against the reflecting surface, the theory being that their sound would then be reflected out and above the brass and woodwind instruments before them. He soon abandoned this idea, but many performers remember the days when that arrangement was in order. "I've often said," remarked George Zazofsky, who had been a violinist with Stokowski's Youth Orchestra and subsequently a member of the Boston Symphony Orchestra, "that Stokowski in many respects was a man whose vision of what sonority should be was far ahead of his time. His whole concept of how the orchestra should sit was quite revolutionary at that period. For instance, he had violins according to the characteristics of the sonorities sitting in the very back, and I remember learning from Stokowski something which I found to be very true: that the players in the front always hear the back coming up. That's the nature of acoustics. The sound hits; bounces from the back to the front. On the other hand, the players in the back never hear the front. So it was his philosophy and his way of punishing you if you didn't do very well. He would say, 'If you don't do better I'll have you sit way up here.'

"He was an innovative man . . . he was one of the great influences of my life as he was to almost everyone with whom he came in contact when he was a younger man. . . .

"He had two expressions—*noten frei* and *bogen frei*—free of the notes and free of the bow. . . . And these are contradictory to almost every other orchestral situation that I know of. If he saw two people at one stand playing with the same bowing, there would be hell to pay. Because, he said, that's no way to perpetuate sound—if all the bows change at the same time, there must of necessity be some cessation of sonority, and he said the way to overcome that particular problem was to have everybody bowing freely and bowing at different times. He is absolutely correct in this theory.

"The other—*noten frei*—meant that you had to find a way of playing without looking at music. Now that seems to be an illogical kind of proposition to begin with, because if you don't see the music, how can you play. You can't memorize this tremendous repertory. It simply meant that at key points, he needed your eyes when important transitions were coming along—beginnings, retards, and flexibilities in which he needed you. After a while you developed this technique.

At a 1929 party. Top row: Magda Tagliaferro, Stokowski,
Edgar Varèse. Bottom row: Mme. Villa-Lobos, person unknown, Heitor Villa-Lobos, person unknown.

"When I was at Curtis for four or five years I used to go up to the
peanut gallery for fifty cents. We were hypnotized. Everybody was hypnotized by Stoki in those days. . . . He never used a score and never used
a baton and it was the most flexible orchestra I had ever heard in my
life."[15]

The placement of the violins in the back was not one of Stoki's most
successful experiments and he soon reverted to the pattern of having
strings to the left, brass, woodwinds, and percussion to the right. While
Stoki was busy experimenting, the men grumbled about the changes. "He

drove us crazy," said one of the players.[16] Concertmaster Alexander Hilsberg was particularly distressed when the violins were seated in the rear. He remarked to Curtis Bok that Stoki was going to put "the strings in the middle of the stage and the woodwinds on one side and the brasses on the other and what he is going to do with the percussion I don't know. But at any rate we will know Friday morning." During the rehearsal Stoki seemed disappointed with the result, and Hilsberg stood up and said, "Mr. Stokowski, we have been trained to sit in certain positions. Everyone is trained to give you our maximum attention. You have moved us around and we cannot undo our habits as fast as you can move our chairs. I cannot look up at you as rapidly from the center nor can . . ."

Before he could finish, Stoki interrupted him, saying, "Oh! I beg your pardon. I had never thought of that."[17]

The next innovation was a particularly Stokowskian idea. He believed that every one of the violinists was a potential concertmaster. On a rotating principle he had each and every one of the players serve as concertmaster in turn. It struck terror in many of them. There were those who preferred to sit back in their relative anonymity and collect their weekly salary. Now they had to stand the test of exposure. It did much to keep all of the players on their toes. Some said it was a nightmare. When he scheduled *Scheherazade* none of the players knew who would be chosen to play the solos. David Madison, who was to have been the concertmaster one following week approached Stoki and asked whether he would be playing the solos. Stoki merely pointed an extended finger at him and told him to be ready. To see Stoki at that time was not easy. One had to write his secretary for an appointment.[18] There was no easy rapport except for a few of the principals. Madison, by the way, did not play the solos that week. Instead, the chore, if it might be called that, was given to Alexander Hilsberg.

"He made new concertmasters by giving everyone a couple of weeks of playing until he found the one he wanted," said Del Negro, "and that was Hilsberg. He was one of the rank and file. The only ones who did not like it were those whom he put in their place."[19]

Then it was the ear and not the eye that took his attention. He decided that the orchestra should be heard rather than seen. Notices were inserted into the regular programs:

> The conviction has been growing in me that orchestra and conduc-
> tor should be unseen, so that on the part of the listener more atten-

tion will go to the ear and less to the eyes. The experiment of an invisible orchestra is for the moment impossible—so I am trying to reach for a similar result by reducing the light to the minimum necessary for the artists of the orchestra to see their music and the conductor.

Music is by nature remote from the tangible and visible things of life. I am hoping to intensify its mystery and eloquence and beauty.

Leopold Stokowski[20]

Lights in the Academy of Music and in Carnegie Hall were completely extinguished. Tiny lights were attached to the musicians' stands and the only strong and dramatic light was a spotlight focused on Stokowski's head and hands.

Stoki's intention was surely sincere, but the theatricality of it brought down a barrage of critical complaint. "He was so honest," Mrs. Bok told me, "and yet, you see, there were a group of people—and some on the board—who thought he was a charlatan, a poseur absolutely. Well," she added, "maybe he was a little of each."[21]

Letters, pro and con, deluged the music editors. One indignant subscriber suggested that Stokowski should devote all his time to broadcasting and thereby spare the audience the disturbing picture of his head "as a dancing pompon suspended in the air."[22]

The experiment was abandoned by mutual consent, but it had one very positive result. The spotlight of publicity was focused on him sharply and he was, as always, the most talked-about conductor in the nation.[23]

Then came the abandonment of the baton. Sometime during the 1929–30 season, he sprained his right arm and suffered severe neuritis. It was so acute that he conducted some concerts with his right arm in a sling and his baton in his left hand.

"The batons were quite special. He bought those sticks up in Toronto," Ruth O'Neill told me, "because he found someone who weighed them and made them flexible and just exactly right for him. And I would order them for him and then after a while he said, 'I think I could do much better with my hands.' "[24]

During an interview in the late 1960s, Harry Fleetwood asked him, "Did you always conduct without a baton?" Stoki answered, "Oh no. I used the baguette, but once in a concert it broke and I continued with just my hands and I felt a sudden freedom, so from that time on I never used it. But I think that those conductors who feel they can do better with the stick, should do so. And those who feel they are freer without it, should do so."[25]

"I think he felt that the baton was too precise and too mathematical, and without it he could get shadings that he wanted. He felt that the baton was an inhibiting factor," Henry Pleasants told me one day in London. "I think it was probably not so much a matter of showmanship as a decision that he made for something which would help him get the kind of effect from the orchestra that he wanted."[26]

"However," Arthur Cohn remarked, "he realized that he had one of the most gorgeous pair of hands in existence, so he decided to capitalize on it. . . ."[27] Ruth O'Neill agreed: "I never knew exactly how much vanity was in him. I know there was a great deal of pride . . . and his hands were a big item, you know, the most beautiful hands. . . ."[28]

With the opening of the season in October 1930, the *Evening Public Ledger* printed three cartoon sketches of Stoki conducting sans baton with the legend: "Conductor's eloquent hands and agile digits mark tempi, point moods and signal cues as he returns to the Academy of Music and foregoes the director's 'stick' of academic tradition." The caption above the drawings read: "Stokowski Abandons Dynamic Baton." But the review written by Samuel Laciar made no mention of that fact; he spent all of his listening effort on the music itself.[29]

Some detractors thought it was merely a matter of showmanship, others appreciated Stokowski's eloquent molding of the music in a manner "handmade."

While much attention was given to the various external changes that Stokowski effected, the really important changes were not overlooked by the perceptive. The real miracle was the honing of the orchestra's playing into razorlike sharpness. The sumptuousness of the strings, their even legato, the brilliance yet smoothness of the winds were praised extravagantly.

Whenever Stokowski and the Philadelphia Orchestra appeared in New York or on tour to other cities, they generated intense excitement. "Without detracting from the excellence of the other great conductors," wrote a Detroit critic, "it can be said (not without danger of serious argument, but yet with conviction) that Mr. Stokowski is the greatest of them all. He is not behind his rivals in scholarship, and he is a greater poet than any of them, using the word 'poet' in the sense in which Plato used it . . . Mr. Stokowski's coming is marked on the calendar months in advance and the date is as carefully observed as Christmas."[30]

When Ernest Bloch first came to America in 1917 he visited Philadelphia to confer with Hans Kindler about performing his *Schelomo* with the New York Philharmonic. After hearing the *St. Matthew Passion,* he wrote back to his wife in Switzerland: "Stokowski directed splendidly—by heart! like everything he directs. . . . Stokowski is charming, so young, so true, so modest; and a magnificent head, a forehead full of thought, superb eyes; he is a great man, one gets that impression immediately."[31]

The New York Philharmonic concert took place on May 3, and Stoki and Olga came to New York to hear it. Bloch again wrote home describing the event and the numerous celebrities who attended. "Kindler," he said, "played miraculously." Then he added parenthetically, "At my side, in the box, silent Stokowski held my hand, and regarded me with his beautiful eyes of an idealist; he was happy, and his approbation is very precious to me. Just think! this admirable conductor directed, last season, 120 concerts, completely by heart! And how! You can imagine the human being that he is!"[32]

Otto Luening, who had lived out World War I in Germany and Switzerland, returned to America in 1920: "I had heard these fabulous things about the Philadelphia Orchestra and I heard Stokowski in Carnegie Hall. What astonished me, and I was astonished, was the absolute smoothness—what should I say—the silkiness of that orchestral sound and his control over the band. That really got me."

Otto did not meet him at that time but did so some years later when Stoki conducted Schoenberg's *Die Glückliche Hand:* "I had never heard such really fine orchestral playing of a really difficult contemporary score. He made the thing sound like an illegitimate son of *Tristan und Isolde* —just a beautiful orchestral sound that he had gotten."[33]

Rachmaninoff in an Associated Press interview done in Paris and circulated world-wide observed:

"At present New York is undoubtedly the musical center of the world. It has taken the place that Berlin occupied before the war, but it is more brilliant than Berlin ever was. And Philadelphia! Philadelphia has the finest orchestra I have ever heard at any time or any place in my whole life. I don't know that I would be exaggerating if I said that it is the finest orchestra the world has ever heard."[34]

In 1922, while Stoki was taking his mid-season vacation from the orchestra, he invited three composer-conductors to conduct the orchestra: Darius Milhaud, Georges Enesco and Alfredo Casella. No one had bothered to learn whether they had ever conducted an orchestra before. In the case of Milhaud, he had not. He admitted that neither his own manager nor Arthur Judson "had the slightest inkling that I would have the audacity to make my debut as a conductor with his orchestra. I was not too nervous, however; as I had to begin some time, it was all to the good that it should be with the finest symphony orchestra in the world."[35]

Stokowski, with his autocratic manner, struck fear in many of the performers. Some referred to him as being cruel; others commented that he was a hard taskmaster. They watched him like hawks. In the fall of 1928 during the rehearsal of a Mozart symphony, he was displeased with the phrasing of the violin sections and he made each violinist in turn play the part. This infuriated some of the men. And I am told that in the union contracts of some orchestras this practice is strictly prohibited. But at the time Stoki was bound by no such limitation. Two of his leading players announced their resignations: Mischa Mischakoff, who was concertmaster, and David Dubinsky, leader of the second violins who had been with the orchestra since its inception.[36] Mischakoff blurted out that he was leaving because of Stokowski's "rude and unfair treatment." Dubinsky said, "No comment."[37]

But Mischakoff harbored no grudge. He later became concertmaster of the NBC Symphony under Toscanini and was there when Stoki took over. The producer of these broadcasts was a friend and colleague of mine, Richard Leonard, who was doing the NBC broadcasts at the same time I had a similar chore for CBS with the New York Philharmonic. "Mischakoff had played with almost all of the big orchestras," said Leonard, "and once someone asked him who was the easiest conductor to play under and he said, 'Unquestionably Stokowski. You always knew what he wanted—that he knew how to communicate to an orchestra with the least number of words without ever raising his voice.' This of course, is a matter of temperament. He was certainly under control, which the old maestro was not."[38]

Stokowski was just as sensitive to color as he was to sound. He observed that both have similar physical characteristics: "Nearly all musicians feel that different kinds of timbres suggest corresponding kinds of color, and that different degrees of pitch also give the sensation of various colors."[39] Subjectively he had very specific associations between certain tonalities and colors: "Each note of a scale is a definite color to me. F-sharp is a golden brown, G a steely blue, A-flat a dark rich brown, A-natural a brilliant red, C-natural a creamy white and so on." But he emphasized that "colors don't help me to interpret music."[40]

He believed that, in the realm of feeling, music and painting are often akin, as if they were parallel to each other—stemming from the same psychological impulses. To him there was an affinity between the music of Tchaikovsky and the painting of Van Gogh since they shared "the same vivid coloring and almost pathological intensity of emotional expression." He also sensed a similar affinity between the music of Ravel and the painting of Gauguin.[41]

Many of his players commented on his relating of color and tone color. "He had an incredible ear for sonority—just incredible," said George Zazofsky. He wanted endless varieties of sonorities. And he added that he was constantly exploring the possibilities of using different types of mutes. At times he would ask for a red tone, a white tone or refer to various sections of the strings in terms of color.[42]

He announced that when he would next conduct *Prometheus* he would use Scriabin's color notation "which calls for flat tones of color," but some time later he said he wanted to work out his own interpretation. He was very interested in the clavilux, an instrument that threw colors on the screen according to the key that was struck. It was an invention of Thomas Wilfred and was first demonstrated on January 10, 1922. Stoki had been present at the demonstration and admitted that "Wilfred's color forms affect me tremendously and I am anxious to have him work with me when we produce *Prometheus* in the fall."[43] When *Prometheus* was finally performed, the Philadelphia Orchestra, Stokowski, and the clavilux created another sensation.

As the orchestra developed its astonishing flexibility, Stoki was able to achieve the improvisational quality that he so desired. "If he were playing a Mozart symphony and he didn't feel like making a *da capo* in a minuet, he just didn't," said veteran bassoonist Sol Schoenbach. "Or, if he felt that bassoons would help the clarinets in the beginning of the Tchaikovsky symphony, he would just point to us and we were supposed to play even though we didn't have anything in front of us. He was just like a painter who decides he wants to put a little red here, a little blue there and he would do things right on the spot. He couldn't stand anybody who was so rigid and would say, 'I'm sorry I don't have those notes here' or 'I don't have that on my instrument' or 'It can't be done.' "

Sol told me of an instance when, at the beginning of his synthesis of *Boris Godunov*, "he would have the bassoon play this very lugubrious introduction and he would say, 'Do you have another reed?' and I said,

'Yes, I think so.' 'No, that's not the color. Do you have another reed?'
—and go on like that and I would end up with something that I didn't
even anticipate using. 'That's the one.' And by George, I tell you it really
was a different color."[44]

If Stokowski's attitude toward the men in the orchestra seemed autocratic, it began to surface as something quite the opposite in the late 1920s
after the resignations of Mischakoff and Dubinsky. In a most democratic
gesture he announced that since every one of the players was a potential
conductor, he intended to give each one a chance to prove it: "I'm going
to have them conduct at rehearsals. The plan also has other interesting
possibilities. Often the first player of an instrument will wish to conduct.
This will result not only in giving him the experience he desires but in
enabling the second player to play first and the third player to play the
second instrument. Thus all will gain in experience." The anonymous
reporter added that Napoleon said the baton of a field marshal was hidden
in the knapsack of every soldier.[45]

33

The Electronic Era

History was made on October 22, 1917, in the auditorium of the New Office Building, Camden, New Jersey (the Victor Talking Machine Company's recording locale at the time). Leopold Stokowski crossed the Delaware with a contingent of the Philadelphia Orchestra to make its first recordings.[1] For several years he had adamantly refused to record because he thought the techniques were too primitive. Once during an interview with National Public Radio's Bob Wallace, he spoke of those early days. "It was in the year 1917 that we began. We recorded in a church in Camden. It had fine acoustics but the way we recorded was extremely primitive. . . . We had a huge wooden horn and in [front of] that huge horn we crowded as many instruments and players as we could and made records that way. That was, of course, a mechanical [acoustical] method of recording.

"I said at first that I wouldn't do it and then once in the night, I woke up and I thought to myself: how stupid of you! You should record this way although it is bad and you should try to make better methods of recording. So after that, I went to some laboratories to study electronics, particularly the Bell Laboratory in New York and later one in Paris and two in Berlin. Then I tried to find better methods of recording and very slowly they were made better but the first records were made in 1917 and I've forgotten what they were. I'm glad I have because they were awful."[2]

He was not wrong. They are pretty bad but they are historic examples of what early orchestral recordings were like. The first two works were the Brahms Hungarian Dances Nos. 5 and 6. Not only is the sound quite poor, but the orchestra seems more like a brass band than the Philadelphia Orchestra, although he apparently used a contingent of ninety players.[3] The most remarkable aspect of the Fifth Hungarian Dance is the incredibly erratic alternation between a slow dragged tempo and one of frenzied speed. But in these early days, some of the disks he made were obviously among the best that were being recorded at the time. Most notable of these acoustic disks was his recording of Schubert's *Unfinished* Symphony, Stravinsky's complete *Firebird* Suite and *Fireworks,* and two movements of the Rachmaninoff Second Concerto with Rachmaninoff as soloist. The Schubert was recorded on Stokowski's forty-second birthday, April 18, 1924, and the second and third movements of the Rachmaninoff concerto on January 3, 1924.[4] Five years later, during the electronic era, he recorded the concerto again with Rachmaninoff.

Most of the selections Victor chose to have recorded by Stoki and his Philadelphians were slight vignettes. One of the most popular was his version of "Ride of the Valkyries."

With his ever-present interest in sound, Stokowski tackled the problems of recording with complete absorption. He experimented with various placements of the orchestra players—he even had the French horn players sit backward so that the bells of their instruments would be facing the recording horn. He had woodwinds and brasses double some of the strings, particularly in the lower registers; he tried out various baffles to reflect sound. Each recording seemed to be an improvement of the one preceding it.

In 1925 when electrical recording became available, it was Stokowski and the Philadelphia Orchestra that made the first recording: Saint-Saëns' *Danse Macabre.*[5] Later that same year he made the first electrically recorded performance for Victor of a complete symphony: Dvořák's *New World.*

Stokowski's perfectionist compulsion was so exacting that only sixty-six of the 450 acoustic sides made at that time were ever approved by him for release.[6] The new techniques offered great advantages. Tonal range was greatly expanded and instruments that were previously difficult to capture on discs were now heard distinctly. Stoki added impressive works to the now expanding catalog of Victor. He did the *Marche Slave* of Tchaikovsky, which when played on Victor's new "Orthophonic" machines set a new sonic standard. There followed recordings of the Brahms First, the Beethoven Seventh, the César Franck Symphony and finally, on April 6, 1927, the Toccata and Fugue of Bach in Stokowski's mighty transcription. This and the "Shepherd's Christmas Music" from the *Christmas Oratorio* became national bestsellers. The recordings were then being made in the Academy of Music and Stokowski became concerned with every aspect of the process.

Curiously, Stokowski's entry into the field of broadcasting came late. It was a very uncharacteristic hesitation. Judson had attempted to persuade him to enter the field, but Stoki, having listened to many broadcasts, felt that the sound was being too compressed. The New York Philharmonic had been broadcasting educational concerts to a limited number of stations since 1922, and Judson's own radio network, which was about to become CBS, began carrying the Philharmonic concerts on Sunday afternoons throughout the season in 1929. The Boston Symphony, too, was being heard regularly.

Finally Stokowski was persuaded, and he had the distinction of giving the first commercially sponsored symphonic broadcasts in America. Arthur Judson had negotiated the deal with Philco to sponsor the hour-long broadcasts heard at 5:30 on three successive Sunday afternoons beginning on October 6, 1929.[7] They were carried on the network of fifty domestic stations of the National Broadcasting Company. In an article for *The Manufacturer*, Arthur Judson wrote that the sales of records for the past ten years had been splendid and "now make more than $500,000 a year, upcoming broadcasts will reach an even larger audience."[8]

Evangeline was present at one rehearsal and recalled: "He was at the conductor's stand, and off to the side in the wings there was a man sitting at a sort of keyboard with dials. He was called the mixer. Stokowski stopped the orchestra and asked what the man was doing. And they said that the range of sound that they could broadcast was narrower than the range of sound that he could conduct in the Academy of Music and have it clear. He said: 'Then you're paying the wrong man. He's the conductor and I'm not. I don't want this to be broadcast under my name if I'm not controlling the pianissimo, the mezzo forte, and the fortissimo.' "[9]

A reporter from the *Inquirer* reported the scene. He said Stokowski changed places repeatedly with the radio technicians, going from podium to control board to monitor room checking the orchestral sound while Alexander Smallens, the assistant conductor of the orchestra at that time, took over. Stokowski, he reported, crouched at the control board watching the quivering needle that showed volume. He gave much attention to the placement of the mikes. One was mounted on a ladder twenty feet above the fifth row of orchestra seats at the left of stage center. He finally returned to conduct, leaving Evangeline sitting at the control board so that he could have her expert opinion. Finally he said he was satisfied.[10]

The broadcast in the darkened Academy was attended by a small invited audience of about twenty, including members of the press. Stoki, dispensing with his usual sartorial manner, was dressed in a loose sport jacket and golf knickers. He began with a Bach transcription followed by the Mozart G Minor Symphony. After the symphony, he tore off his tie and jacket for greater freedom. Like a one-man band, Stoki not only acted as conductor and engineer, but he had also written the script and acted as the announcer-commentator.[11]

After the first broadcast, Stoki listened to playbacks and felt that the range was too compressed. Just before the second he announced that the broadcast would be given without any control board. Rhoda Cameron in the *New York World* reported that he strolled into the control room and demanded that the galvanometer be moved to the podium, saying that he could then keep the volume down himself without interference by an engineer. When his demand was turned down, he went to his dressing room, where he lay down and proceeded placidly to smoke a cigarette. Frantic pleas left him unperturbed. But after ten minutes or so he was told that his wishes had been granted. He apparently followed the same procedure for the final concert. "All three pick-ups were more perfect than anything which had gone before. . . ."[12]

In December, when he was to begin his winter vacation, he announced over radio that he would devote twelve weeks to the study of radio engineering. "Through his study in radio laboratories, he said he hoped to improve, if not revolutionize, the broadcasting of orchestral music."[13]

With the beginning of the 1930 fall season, the amount of live symphonic music on the air was astonishing. Judson announced that the New York Philharmonic would be heard in a series of forty-two concerts coming from Carnegie Hall on Sunday afternoons. They were to be conducted by Toscanini, Kleiber, and Molinari and aired by CBS.[14] Judson also handled the publicity buildup for the Philadelphia Orchestra's broadcasts, centering attention on Stokowski's experiments. "The secrecy in which Stokowski shrouded his introduction of a new principle in controlling tone in orchestral broadcasts had the desired effect," wrote critic Quaintance Eaton. "Newspaper reporters were keen on the trail, so tantalizingly blockaded against their penetration, and, baffled, wrote columns of speculation. The public read, wondered, and probably listened in droves. . . . The orchestra (composed of only fifty-four players . . .) sounded rich and full. . . . Stokowski stood in a little glass booth and operated his control with the left hand, conducting with the right. In this way he was able to hear the broadcast as it proceeded and to make the necessary adjustments on the spot."[15]

This should put an end to the oft-repeated canard that the engineers had merely supplied Stoki with a fake control panel that had no effect on the broadcast. Effect it had!

"Admitting the failure of the complicated apparatus which managed to throw the first broadcast of the Philadelphia Orchestra completely off the air thirteen times in ten minutes, Stokowski explained a new method, which is nothing more or less than bringing the engineer out of his cage into the orchestra." Instead of working his dials himself, he now resorted to hand signals to the engineer to indicate forthcoming climaxes.[16]

It was Stokowski's refusal to accept the limitations imposed by the engineers that helped stimulate them to conduct experiments that would expand them. Most significant in this matter were the scientists of the Bell Laboratories. The distinguished acoustician Harvey Fletcher was ninety-four when he talked with me from his home in Provo, Utah, about his early experiences with Stokowski and the Philadelphia Orchestra. He told me that he had approached both Koussevitzky and Toscanini about making experiments with their orchestras; neither was interested. He then approached Stokowski in about 1931 "and we made tests of stereophonic sound at the Academy of Music."[17]

It was after visits to the Bell Labs that Stoki agreed to having elaborate equipment installed in the basement of the Academy. In addition to Fletcher, other research engineers were involved, among them Arthur Keller, Harold D. Arnold, and Joseph P. Maxfield. After his visit to Bell Labs in April 1930, Stokowski wrote to Arnold discussing the various timbres of instruments: "I know in my gramophone and radio work how intensely I feel our imperfection in this question of individuality of tone color. We produce too much tone that is thin and metallic and pointed, and our tone leaves much to be desired in the direction of warmth and roundness and depth and soft but firm beauty."[18]

Early in April 1931, after receiving a number of books on acoustics from Arnold, he wrote thanking him and added: ". . . if . . . I or the Philadelphia Orchestra can be of any service to you in any sound experiments we are always at your disposal. These experiments could be made during the rehearsals, so that there would be no expense incurred whatever. We never have anybody at the rehearsals so that the experiments could be private and the results could be kept confidential if you so wish."[19]

Maxfield and Keller had microphones strung on wires across the balcony. Maxfield's experimentation was for live broadcasts and Keller's for future recordings. "Maxfield wanted to be as far back from the orchestra as he could get," Keller told me, "but when I first appeared on the scene, I put some microphones just ahead of his and I did not like what I heard and gradually week after week moved them forward until I was very close to the orchestra and Maxfield was about twenty-five feet behind me . . . this is a kind of subjective thing as to what you get by microphone placement. You can't get too close. You have to determine the size of the orchestra in determining how far out you want to be . . . we made 128 or so records that season. We were interested in getting the widest frequency and volume range."[20]

To listen to the various experiments, huge speakers were set up in the ballroom of the Academy. Here Fletcher was busy in the development of a stereophonic system. Originally he planned to use a great number of microphones. "However, we found that . . . three microphones and three transmitting lines and three loudspeakers were sufficient."[21] Stoki was happy about the stereophonic experiments and wrote the Bell engineers that "listening binaurally gave me more sense of space. . . . I found it better in every way than monaural listening."[22] Stoki, Fletcher, Keller, and their colleagues were a quarter of a century in advance of the first stereo recordings to hit the stands.

Fletcher tried numerous other experiments. "Why do you have twenty-five or forty violins? Why don't you just have one and reproduce it and magnify it? Instead of having ten or fifteen bass viols, have just one and magnify it. For a minute he thought it was fine. But we tried it on one of them and it didn't work. . . . We started with one violin and let him play, and we listened . . . then all of them played. We had the means of making one sound as loud as all of them." Stoki and Fletcher began experimenting first with one, then two, and finally six violins in comparison with the full section. "With six violins against all the violins in the orchestra, you couldn't tell the difference. Now you've got it. You can make your orchestra with a third or a fourth the number of people you have in it," Fletcher continued.

"Ah," said Stoki, "you've got something else to think about. We have a musician's union."[23]

These experiments had no bearing on the future of the orchestra, but they did have a potent effect on Stoki in relation to his later recordings

Courtesy Beatrice Brown
Stokowski with medal from CBS for distinguished contributions to radio art, presented by William Paley, November 2,
1931

with "His" orchestra and also in broadcasts such as the "Twentieth
Century Concert Hall," where he had an orchestra of only thirty musicians. The experiments, too, played an important role in his future broadcasts with the Philadelphia Orchestra. It was Judson who arranged to have

the broadcasts aired over the CBS Network rather than on NBC. The first of the new series of seven concerts began on October 12, 1931, at 8:15 P.M. and lasted an hour and forty-five minutes. They were sponsored by Philco and were carried on a network of seventy-one stations. Pitts Sanborn, music critic of the *New York World-Telegram,* gave verbal program notes and Stoki made his inevitable speech.[24]

The series was most successful and caused considerable excitement and curiosity in the engineering confraternity. On December 9, 1931, Stoki was invited to address the joint meeting of the Institute of Radio Engineers and the Society of Motion-Picture Engineers at the Engineering Club. After describing various experiments he had made with the Bell Lab engineers he added: "The limitations of music are becoming less and less. Eventually all sounds may come under the classification of music. Methods of writing down sound on paper are tremendously imperfect. I believe the composer of the future will create his harmonies directly in tone by means of electrical-musical instruments which will record his idea exactly. Over sound films of the future I believe we will be able to convey emotions higher than ever thought—things subtle and intangible—almost psychic in their being. Radio and television will project them *all over the world.*"[25]

"You might be interested to know," said Fletcher, "that Stokowski and I were given medals by the Audio Engineering Society for this work on stereophonic sound."[26]

Fletcher also devised a series of tests to improve the transmission of music by phone wires. With the entire orchestra assembled in the ballroom of the Academy, they were put on mike and the sounds were transmitted to the stage of the Academy to be heard by an invited audience that filled the hall. Stokowski sat in the center of the balcony controlling the dynamics.[27] "Our machinery was such that he could, by touching certain buttons, make one part of the orchestra come up higher or lower," Fletcher recalled. I specifically asked whether Stoki himself handled the dials. "Yes. He handled them. Nobody but a great musician could do it . . . he could by turning knobs or touching buttons make the violins come way up or any part of the orchestra. He loved that when he found what he could do. . . . He could correct things that he saw ought to be corrected."[28]

"The first public demonstration," said Fletcher, "was given in Washington on April 27, 1933, under the auspices of the National Academy of Science. Stokowski manipulated the controls from the rear balcony of

Stokowski at the controls in one of the Bell Lab experiments transmitting via telephone
lines a Philadelphia Orchestra concert at the Academy of Music to loudspeakers on a stage
in Washington, D.C., April 28, 1933. Harvey Fletcher, standing

Constitution Hall in Washington while the orchestra conducted by
Alexander Smallens was performing on the stage of the Academy in
Philadelphia."[29] Stoki, in his zeal to produce a huge climax, accidentally
twisted off one of the knobs on his dial.

Linton Martin in the *Philadelphia Inquirer* wrote: "For those alive and
alert to the significance of the episode, it took rank as an epochal event
in the history of musical performances." Of the cataclysmic climaxes of
Wagner, he said that they seemed to "split the universe, giving the

destruction of Valhalla the epical emphasis demanded by the imagination, yet with the tone perfectly proportioned as Stokowski, like some modern musical Jove, unleashed his electrical thunderbolts, while swirling orange lights on draperies suggested the consuming conflagration."[30]

A similar demonstration was done at the Hollywood Bowl in 1935 and a final collaboration in Carnegie Hall on April 9, 1940. Harvey Fletcher had been experimenting with recording on film rather than discs. Shortly after Fletcher announced the success of his efforts, Stokowski wrote him: "Is this ready to be used? I should like so much to take advantage of your new method for work I am planning and at the same time to demonstrate to the public—as we have done together in the past."[31]

The result was predictable. Fletcher brought the Bell equipment to Philadelphia and recorded Stoki on film in three-channel stereo. In making the final transfer of the tapes, Stoki manipulated the dials to "enhance" the final version. It was that performance that was demonstrated in Carnegie without Stoki boosting the sounds "live" as he had done in the previous demonstration. Fletcher explained that Stokowski, as he listened, "made volume and tonal changes by electric controls; and simultaneously a new stereophonic record was made of the music as thus 'enhanced.' "[32]

Pietro Yon, organist of St. Patrick's Cathedral, Toscanini, and Rachmaninoff were among the invited guests. Rachmaninoff thought there was "too much 'enhancing,' too much Stokowski."[33]

Fascinated by his experience with the engineers at the Bell Labs, Stoki wanted to explore other possibilities of wedding electricity to music and hence announced that he intended to create an all-electric orchestra. "Some people mistakenly think this new orchestra is iconoclastic," he said, "but it isn't. We have made some marvelous strides in understanding the nature of electricity. It is one of the most supple and powerful agents in the world today. There might be another millennium before anything else is discovered that would be comparable to it. . . . There is still a potentiality in music beyond anything we've found yet."[34]

In 1980, practically a half-century after the recordings were made in the basement of the Academy, the Bell Laboratories released two discs with examples of the performances they had recorded in 1931 and 1932 —with some in stereo.[35] In many respects, they are quite remarkable. The dynamic range is astonishing and the performances are among the best documentations of Stokowski's conducting of the Philadelphia Orchestra at the peak of its perfection. The first disc contains excerpts of works by

Berlioz, Weber, Mendelssohn, Scriabin, Wagner, and Mussorgsky. The second is all Wagner. Some of the examples sound quite dead as a result of too close miking of the players, but the clarity is exceptional. The second disc is more reverberant. At the conclusion of the record there is a short speech by Stokowski made at the close of the last concert of the 1931–32 season (on April 30, 1932)—a time when the orchestra was being severely hurt by the Depression. "Aren't you sorry it's all over?" he asked. The audience responded with a resounding yes and applause. He continued: "When that time comes if it does come, then the Philadelphia Orchestra, like everything else, will have to stand the test of what it means to humanity, to life, to our civilization, to our culture. I think it means, first of all, delight—delight in sound, in the beauty of this thrilling sound —just the delight of it—the essential delight. And what else? Well, that's something still higher—inspiration. Those things cannot be valued in any kinds of evaluation or explanation of it. That's what all this stands for, I think. And that's why we must stand behind the orchestra in any stormy time to come. We'll come through to the sunny days coming up."

(34)

Arthur Judson
and Beyond

F ROM the time of their earliest meeting in Cincinnati, the lives of
Stokowski and Arthur Judson were to be intertwined. To begin with
parallels, both were tall and magnificently imposing men. They were
of the same age—born a year apart—and both had an intense urge to
make music. In Judson's case, the realization was not possible. He had
wanted to be a violinist and did perform the first U.S. performance of the
Strauss Violin Concerto in Granville, Ohio, in 1903 and later conducted
a hundred-piece summer orchestra at Ocean Grove, New Jersey. He
continued to refer to himself throughout life as a "disappointed conductor."[1]

But once he entered the management field rather than that of the
music professional, his ambition was fully as monumental as that of Stoki
himself. The greatest difference between the two was Judson's complete
aversion to public acclaim, while Stoki thrived on being the center of
public attention throughout his life.

Judson's success was impressive and soon he was drawn into the orbits
and affairs of orchestras throughout the country. In 1922, after a quite
spectacular job of saving the concerts of the Lewisohn Stadium in New
York during a strike by New York musicians, he became the manager of
the New York Philharmonic. A year later he took on the management of
the Cincinnati Symphony Orchestra as well.

Judson commuted regularly between Philadelphia and New York with
side trips to Ohio. He soon moved his office for the management of his
artists to New York, where the major source of booking was centered.

Never before, and I am certain never after, would one man be the manager of three major symphony orchestras simultaneously.

Judson moved conductors about with all the skill of a chess grand master. His most audacious plan was to have the two most towering giants exchange podiums. Stokowski would conduct the New York Philharmonic for two weeks while Toscanini would journey to Philadelphia for the same interval. The curiosity and excitement engendered by this arrangement was unprecedented and the box offices were besieged.

On returning from Europe in early July, Stoki was interviewed by the *Philadelphia Bulletin* and as a welcoming gesture remarked: "While I was in Germany, I attended two concerts of the New York Philharmonic-Symphony conducted by Toscanini. They played splendidly, never better, and the audience stayed for thirty-five minutes after the close, applauding and shaking hands with Toscanini."[2]

When Toscanini arrived in Philadelphia he was welcomed warmly. His first act, however, was to reseat the orchestra and insist on uniform bowing of the strings, thus losing some of the sheen that had been a striking feature of the orchestra.

Edna Phillips, the superb harpist and first woman member of the orchestra said, "The contrast between the two conductors was remarkable. The Philadelphia Orchestra had a way of having perfect manners with a guest conductor, and Stokowski was entirely responsible for that."[3]

Bassoonist Ferdinand Del Negro, after a span of more than forty years, recalled the exchange vividly: "It was a disappointment to me when we got him. We never thought there would be an exchange because there was such rivalry. When he came . . . he started in . . . he conducted about a half a page, then he put his stick down, and with his head shaking from side to side, said, 'This is the Stradivarius of all orchestras.'

"A few minutes later he was breaking batons and calling us shoemakers in all languages. . . . Yet he could move you, he was colorful but Stokowski was much more. Stokowski was more poetic. It was beautiful to play with that man."[4]

Edna Phillips concurred: "Toscanini wanted immediate perfection. . . . He would harbor nothing but that and, of course, there was much impatience during rehearsals and pulverizing of batons. . . . We weren't accustomed to that . . . because Stokowski, curiously enough, was very quiet."[5]

Violinist David Madison added: "All these stories about him [Toscanini] were true. He would get mad at the rehearsals and stalk off the stage . . . his son Walter would beg him to come back and start the rehearsal again. He kept us pretty much awestruck."[6]

Toscanini included no Italian works on his programs and the choice of the Bach chorales and Wagner excerpts, which were in a sense Stokowski's particular province, may well have been included to show that the "old man" could give better renditions than his younger colleague. His appearances were decidedly successful and he had every reason to be pleased. His audiences gave him an ovation. "Thunderous acclaim, but no accent of hysteria," wrote critic Craven.[7] Linton Martin observed that his orchestral tone "has more of a surface quality than the dynamic and electrifying effect which Stokowski can so thrillingly command."[8]

In New York Stokowski was shown no reciprocal courtesy by the Philharmonic. He had to face the so-called Toscanini Mafia—that core of devoted Italian players that dominated the orchestra. Gunther Schuller's father, Arthur Schuller, who played in the first stands of violins and also doubled on piano, remembered that during one intermission he heard the name Stokowski and the word *charlatan*. "I figured out what does that mean. Did somebody say that word *charlatan*? I would suspect that Toscanini talked to someone . . . because he didn't like many conductors. He liked Molinari, but he didn't like De Sabata because De Sabata was much better than Toscanini, I can assure you."[9]

We are told that Toscanini in his later years admired Solti "but for the other men of the baton he didn't have much use," reported his biographer, George Marek. "He particularly loathed Stokowski, and would not acknowledge Stokowski's enormous contribution to orchestral development, nor his ability to make music sound with a smooth and luscious, a sheerly beautiful sound."[10]

During the first rehearsal, the Philharmonic players were decidedly hostile. There were some men in the orchestra who had formerly played in the Philadelphia Orchestra and had been dismissed by Stoki. This did not help matters. When he tried to get the double bass players to play certain high notes in Bach's "Little" Fugue, one of them retorted that the passage could not be played on the bass. "I've got nine in Philadelphia who can play it on the bass," Stoki replied.[11]

"I'll tell you about the bass player," said Arthur Schuller. "I guess he was laughing or something, and [Stoki] had him leave the rehearsal immediately. 'You get out!' he said. . . . Then we had a cellist . . . he also laughed or said something funny, and he had to go out for the rehearsal."[12]

"It was not the first or the last time that a conductor who followed Toscanini found himself bedeviled," wrote Howard Taubman.[13] Although Stokowski obviously did not get the results he was able to achieve with his own orchestra, his concerts were a success. Olin Downes observed that "he didn't shrink in the shadow of Toscanini's genius, as most conductors have. Stokowski was himself, his own master, an artist with something of his own to say . . . the Carnegie Hall audience rewarded him handsomely."[14]

For his second series he played the Sibelius First Symphony and the *Rite of Spring*. The Sibelius was being done by the Philharmonic for the first time. The critics lauded him. W. J. Henderson said that he and the orchestra had finally found each other and the entire evening was "one clear revelation of his mastery of the conductor's art."[15]

Back with their respective orchestras, each conductor offered their listeners novelties. Toscanini's was a curious one. He played a Respighi transcription of Bach's Passacaglia and Fugue in C Minor, a work which was closely identified with Stoki.[16] The gesture could only have been one of spite, to prove again with his insufferable arrogance that his way with Bach was better than Stokowski's. The gesture was as meanly childish as his celebrated temper tantrums.

Stoki's novelty was a new Symphonic Poem by the Greek composer Dimitri Levidis for Ondes Martenot, the new electronic instrument invented by the composer-performer Maurice Martenot, who performed the piece.[17] The audiences and players of both orchestras relaxed and breathed more easily again.

That Arthur Judson was showing increasing interest in his New York activities and less with the affairs of Philadelphia was becoming evident. Herein, I believe, lay the cooling of his relationship with Stokowski, although neither mentioned it. For years Stoki had tried to convince the board that he should take the orchestra on a European tour, including especially Russia. One can only imagine his exasperation when Toscanini succeeded in bringing the Philharmonic on an extensive tour in 1930. Philadelphians might also have been somewhat dismayed when the Philharmonic was presented in ninety-minute broadcasts over CBS every Sunday afternoon. Stokowski and his band had no comparable exposure.

All orchestras during the Great Depression had financial difficulties. The Philharmonic was fortunate in having on its board a great many very influential patrons. It benefited too from the broadcasts of the orchestra, for in addition to the amount paid by CBS, though it was not a sponsored program, it derived a considerable amount from contributions made by the growing radio audience. Things in Philadelphia were not so healthy. Edward Bok had died in 1930 and Van Rensselaer three years later. In 1932 the subscriptions had dropped 15 percent.[18] The alarmed board met and actually considered the dissolution of the orchestra.

On May 19, 1933, it was announced that the members of the orchestra had been asked to take a 9-percent salary cut, and that not only had ticket sales decreased but so had the sales of recordings. They reported that they had exhausted every means of reaching an agreement by direct negotiations with the orchestra players and with their union and that the board "has been met with consistent and definite refusal to cooperate in sharing the deficit which cannot be avoided. . . ."[19]

Curtis Bok, who was now the president of the board, was obviously able to negotiate some agreement with the players, and they accepted a cut, as did Stoki, whose fee was reduced "to a reported figure of $1,200 or $1,250 a concert."[20]

At the annual meeting of the board on May 22, 1934, Curtis Bok happily announced that the Association had paid off an accumulated deficit of $55,000, as well as a $20,000 obligation to the players. He reviewed the plans for the coming season and announced that full presentations of operas would be given on the regular concert series. He also mentioned that Stokowski's "salary" would be on the same basis as it was under the ten-year contract that had just expired. "Namely, he will be paid a fee for each concert which he conducts and not a salary for the whole season."

For years the Metropolitan Opera had gone to Philadelphia every three or four weeks, while the Philadelphia Orchestra traveled to Carnegie Hall to supply New Yorkers with some of their most exciting evenings. Due to financial stringencies brought on by the raging Depression, the Met had determined in 1934 that it could no longer continue the Philadelphia performances. Naturally there was an outcry from the Philadelphia opera lovers and it was proposed that the Philadelphia Orchestra should produce an opera season to compensate for the loss of the Met.[21]

Curtis Bok, as the new president of the Philadelphia Orchestra's board, was most interested in the project. Stoki was skeptical, having wanted to explore more experimental ways of producing operas.[22] Furthermore, he had wanted to absent himself from the orchestra for an entire year. He consented, however, to return and conduct all the concerts between

October and December and then take his leave of absence. Judson, as always thinking boldly, favored the project. Curtis Bok, like his father, Edward, and his mother, Mary Louise Curtis Bok, was totally dedicated to Stokowski. His wife told me that before he died, Mr. Van Rensselaer had told Curtis, "I want you to succeed me. I want you to be elected president."

Frankly, Judson was not particularly pleased with the succession. "He and my husband tangled a little bit," Mrs. Bok said. "He and my husband had different ideas about how orchestras should be managed. . . . And Mr. Judson was—well I know I'm really telling you nothing that you don't know—Mr. Judson always worked with the board. May I say that he represented the spirit of bureaucracy. My husband was 100 percent for giving the conductor his way. . . . And Mr. Stokowski that particular winter wanted to produce magnificent operas, and did produce them, but he didn't conduct them."[23]

Although he would not conduct any of the operatic productions, Stokowski chose the works to be performed. They were a distinguished lot. The ten productions included: Wagner's *Tristan und Isolde* and *Die Meistersinger*, Bizet's *Carmen*, Strauss' *Der Rosenkavalier*, a double bill combining Humperdinck's *Hansel and Gretel* and Stravinsky's *Mavra*, Verdi's *Falstaff*, Shostakovich's *Lady Macbeth of Mtzensk*, Gluck's *Iphigenia in Aulis*, Mozart's *The Marriage of Figaro*, and Debussy's *Pelléas et Mélisande*.

On October 19, 1934, the opera season began with an elaborate production of *Tristan und Isolde* in a full, uncut, five-hour version. It was beautifully mounted with sets by Donald Oenslager. Fritz Reiner conducted and the cast, while not star-studded, sang well. But the most compelling aspect about it was the Philadelphia Orchestra in the pit. The audience response was tremendous, and over nine thousand persons crowded into the Academy to hear three performances. To add significance to the occasion, Eleanor Roosevelt came over from Washington to attend the first performance and posed with the tall, handsome Curtis Bok and the dimunitive Fritz Reiner for the newspapers. After the long performance that first evening, one weary devotee was heard to say as he staggered out of the hall, "Is Roosevelt still President?"[24]

The opera season was a financial disaster of major proportions. In all of the operas given during the season new scenery, new costumes, and costly equipment such as the revolving stage had been enormously expensive. The magnitude of the disaster had been foreseen before the final curtain, but the full extent was only realized at the end.

During a conversation in 1972 with Judson and Ruth O'Neill, Sam Rosenbaum said to Judson, "Do you remember the circumstances that led to the opera series in 1934 in Philadelphia? You produced ten operas with three performances for each. This resulted in a loss of $250,000 that came out of the endowment fund." "Now just wait a minute," Judson replied. "That's not so. The circumstances were these: Stokowski took a leave of absence. Therefore we had to do something to keep the public interested. That's the reason I put on the ten operas. And we didn't lose money out of the endowment fund. Nobody ever took a cent out of any Quaker endowment fund in the world. Try it!"[25]

"It is my recollection," said Sam, "that Mrs. Bok was bankrolling the Philadelphia Opera Company and Curtis Bok . . . insisted on your steering the orchestra into this opera venture. I always blamed it on Curtis Bok."

"No, I don't think this was the case at all," Judson replied.

"A.J., excuse me," interrupted Ruth, "but I think Sam is right."

"Listen," A.J. replied, "you don't know me. Nobody ever made me do anything. So, if I did it, there was a reason for it. Bok couldn't make me do anything like that."

Addressing his audience after a concert, Stokowski mentioned that the board had asked him to conduct some of the operas, but he said: "I declined because I wished to have us produce certain operas in new ways, and there was not then time to prepare the new methods. These new methods were partly begun by us in *Wozzeck,* in Schoenberg's *Glückliche Hand* and Stravinsky's *Oedipus,* but since then important new possibilities have been developed."[26]

He had already given several interviews to reporters outlining some of the ideas he had for the ideal presentation of opera. Most of his theories evolved from the experiments he was involved in with the scientists and engineers of Bell Laboratories. What Stokowski envisioned was a "method of direct electrical transcription of the solo singers, the chorus and the orchestra. . . . At the performance neither orchestra nor solo singers will appear and the listeners will behold only the ideal spectacle."[27]

He explained that his first consideration rested in the drama and said that he "looked forward to the time when television would make it possible to carry it from footlights into thousands of homes."[28] He was far ahead of those around him, and more a visionary than any of his conductorial colleagues. It would be four decades before "Live from the Met" or "Live from Lincoln Center" would become a reality.

"One of the principal difficulties in producing opera," Stoki explained, "is to find artists who are equally suitable as singers and actors and whose physical appearance fits the part. Siegfried must be a heroic youth and Tristan should look like a knight of the time of King Arthur. Often an artist has a magnificent voice but does not look right for the role. Sometimes an actor looks well for the role but his voice is unsuitable. Again the voice may be perfect but too small to carry over a modern orchestra. I believe that a way to obviate all this has been found."[29]

"The actors and actresses on the stage will project only the visual," he explained. "They will be mimes chosen for suitability to the role irrespective of voices. Our new method of sound production can amplify, enrich, brighten or dull the timbre of a voice."[30] When he was asked whether it would be possible to make a crooner into a Caruso he answered, "You said that. I didn't!"[31]

Stoki insisted that the sounds heard would not be prerecorded (even though that term was not then in use) but would be live coming from some other area.[32] Sylvan Levin told me about experiments he conducted with banks of speakers lining the entire back of the Academy stage, though hidden from the audience, and the effect of a singer or instrumentalist moving from one area to another was truly realistic.

Here again Stoki and his farsighted engineering colleagues were well in advance of the media. The idea of synchronizing lip movements with sound emanating from another source—lip synching—was hardly discovered by the movies, and as for television, it was literally nonexistent.

To Jean Sibelius Stoki wrote:

> I often think how wonderful could be a modern drama based on one of the Greek dramas of Sophocles or Euripides which would be brief and simple, having the text spoken and not sung, but having a chorus and orchestra back of the stage so that they would be invisible, and having on the visible part of the stage either pantomimists or very large marionettes about six metres high—the decoration on the stage to be extremely simple, and the lighting to play a most important part. The music produced by the invisible orchestra, chorus, and perhaps solo singers not to be continuous, but only to sound at the great moments of the drama.

If it would appeal to you to write such a work, it would be a great artistic pleasure to me to produce it in America, and perhaps also in Europe.

If you would like this idea I should so much like to hear from you.[33]

The letter was dated April 10, 1931.

(35)

The Youth Concerts, 1933-34

L ONG irked by the intransigence of his Friday audiences and their refusal to accept contemporary music, Stoki decided to train and nurture a new and younger audience that would welcome new music with avidity rather than disdain. "Leopold Stokowski, all dressed up in peach pajamas and a woolly, brown dressing gown, elected himself Philadelphia's musical dictator yesterday." Thus began an interview with Elsin Finn on October 18, 1932. "From the modernistic depths of his neo-garage apartment, the Philadelphia Orchestra conductor announced he will perform any contemporary music he deems meritorious. And if the Philadelphia Orchestra Association and audience don't like it—so what," the interview continued.

Stoki explained that he wanted to train a young audience that, when grown up, would not walk out on such music as Josten's *Jungle,* which he had recently performed. Since at most he could reach only an audience of about three thousand at his children's concerts, he planned to broadcast the Friday afternoon concerts directly into the schools and "reach not only the countless thousands of children, but also the farm and country folk whose desire for good music is handicapped by the inaccessibility of the concert hall."

He intended to present contemporary music on each program. "Children," he said, "are much more elastic and receptive. It is easier for them to take in all the new phases of life that are developing today. And in a few years they will form the new generation of music lovers. Most adults,"

324

he continued, "have difficulty in absorbing ideas and impressions . . . they are hopeless."[1]

However, Edwin Broome, the superintendent of schools, remarked: "I am a little surprised that Mr. Stokowski, having evolved a plan concerning 10,000 school teachers and 300,000 pupils, did not consult me before he made his plans public." And he added a bit skeptically that he could not calculate the effect of the virus of modern music upon the younger generation.[2]

Although both Friday and Saturday concerts were being broadcast, the response from the schools proved to be disappointing. Many teachers preferred to stick to their own curriculum and not have Friday afternoon disrupted by a listening session. But Stoki was not to be daunted. He pondered ways to introduce new music to an ever greater young audience.

Twelve years had elapsed since he had begun his tremendously successful Children's Concerts. And now the kiddies were growing up! Envisioning a series of concerts for an audience ranging from thirteen to twenty-five, he announced his plan, saying that he wanted to nurture a more intelligent and tolerant group of listeners by feeding the so-called dissonances of present-day music to young people whose minds and ears had not become so hopelessly stagnant that they could not endure the compositions of contemporary composers. He announced that he wanted to assemble an audience of high school and college students. Adults and children were to be barred.[3]

The initial impetus for the new series seemed to have come from one of the graduates of the Children's Concerts. Ruth Seckelman, who later married the composer Richard Yardumian, told me of meeting an English girl, a Miss Baker, who was a good friend of Stokowski's. She talked to her about her idea of concerts for teenagers. Ruth's enthusiasm and her ideas were immediately conveyed to Stoki through Miss Baker and the result was characteristic. "Stokowski called my home one day," said Ruth, "and he asked if I could come to a concert. I was a senior in high school at the time and I arranged to get off and took a friend with me and went to one of his Friday afternoon concerts. I wrote and thanked him and said how much I had enjoyed it, and he responded with another invitation to attend. I said that I could not possibly get out of school because it was exam time. We agreed, however, to go to his apartment on Rittenhouse Street later on Friday afternoon. He asked me about my ideas and I explained all about my thoughts on these concerts, and we worked out the plan late that afternoon. This was, I believe, in November 1932, and the first concert took place the following March."[4]

He called together a preliminary group of 250 music teachers and students for a meeting and asked them to choose their own evening. They selected Thursday. He also asked them to let him know what pieces they would like to have the orchestra perform. "I want to know what you like in music," he said. "Our tastes differ, you know, for we are of different generations. I will make the program up of one-half familiar music that you want; the other half will be what I may put in."[5]

Many who were in this first meeting became inflamed with the idea and began working with all their energy to make the concerts a success. A veritable bevy of young teenagers, mostly girls, followed Stoki as worshipfully as the groups who later went into ecstasies over Sinatra and Presley, later over the Beatles, and finally—they had acquired the name "groupies" by this time—began trailing after rock stars in the 1960s.

Among those who attended this first meeting were two representatives from two different public schools; they were Natalie Bender and Faye Chabrow. Another was a young socialite, Mary Binney Montgomery. She was a gifted pianist who studied with Moritz Rosenthal at the Curtis Institute and later in Vienna. She also became a gifted dancer and choreographer of her own ballet troupe.

Shortly after this Natalie and Faye joined the Binney Montgomery group. "We all took exotic names for that," said Natalie. She became Natasha. But that was a minor change for, she said: "A counselor at camp began to call me that when I was eight years old. You see Natasha is simply the diminutive of Natalie and since my parents on my mother's side came from Lithuania and Russia, it was natural to call me Natasha. Faye began to use the name Feodora Czabrowska when she was dancing. Her grandparents came from Russia and she took the feminine version of their Russian name."[6]

Mary Binney Montgomery became the first secretary of the Young People's Committee. She told me that Stokowski wanted the young people to participate in all aspects of the concerts—in the choice of pieces programmed, in a request program, and other creative ways. "So since I was the right age, he asked me whether I would help to get it going. We got a committee that would go to schools and talk to them and get them interested. We thought that if that first concert would be sold out, they would all be. So we all worked terribly hard to make it a bang-up success."[7]

Another of the devoted teenagers was Helene Hanff, who later became an important New York–based writer. "I had known Faye very slightly because we went to the same high school. I was a senior. Faye was a freshman or sophomore so I knew her in that very slight way you do someone who is in the same school but not in your class." Helene remarked that Faye and Natasha became Stoki's "favorite children and certainly his most obsessively devoted."[8]

The scale of prices for the concerts reflected the Depression; they ranged from seventy-five cents downstairs, fifty cents in the parquet circle, thirty-five cents in the balcony, and ten cents in the peanut gallery. "Arthur Judson had okayed the prices but poor Mr. Mattson, the assistant manager of the orchestra, just went out of his mind that you could go from ten cents to seventy-five to hear the Philadelphia Orchestra," Ruth Yardumian recalled.[9]

The first of the Youth Concerts took place on the ninth of March 1933. It was an admirable program by any standard. It began with the "Little" Fugue in G Minor of Bach, followed by the *Leonore* Overture No. 3. The remaining works were Bach's chorale "Wachet Auf," Wagner's Prelude to *Lohengrin*, Debussy's *Fêtes*, and the Stravinsky *Firebird* Suite. To round off the evening the howling audience sang "Dixie" as lustily as it had ever been sung.[10]

Three thousand young people had thronged into the Academy and several hundred were turned away. The press proclaimed it a tremendous success. Among Stoki's plans for the series were the presentation of young soloists and compositions by young composers and the inclusion of young people performing in the orchestra. He included several who took their places sitting and playing along with the first desk men of the orchestra. One of these players was Arthur Cohn. He had belonged to a training orchestra in Philadelphia that he later conducted for the last thirty-one years of its life. "One day," Arthur told me, "Stoki called the conductor of the training orchestra and said, 'I want you to pick your three best players and they will play at the concert for youth.' And the three players were Frank Costanzo, Harry Gorodetzer and myself. Incidentally, Costanzo, violinist, and Gorodetzer, cellist, are still in the Philadelphia Orchestra today [1977]. We were fifteen or sixteen years old at that time and we each got letters from Stokowski asking us to appear at a rehearsal at eleven o'clock in the morning. Of course, I shined my boots and was as excited as all get out. And he placed us in the orchestra. I played next to Alec Hilsberg. I don't know where he placed the other two. I remember the opening work as if I had played it yesterday."[11]

During the rehearsal the three young players sat comfortingly among the regular members of the orchestra, but at the concert he told them they were not going to sit in the orchestra. "Stoki had us sitting out on the apron of the stage, almost behind him. Two violins on one side of the stage and the cello on the other and he announced to the audience that here was real youth and so on. Well, I was petrified," Arthur recalled.[12]

"After the first Youth Concert," Mary Binney Montgomery explained, "we were besieged with letters telling us what the young people wanted to hear and begging for another concert this season. We announced a second one for April 20 and three days later we were completely sold out. We could have filled a hall three times the size of the Academy. I never knew there were so many young people in Philadelphia, and I certainly never guessed they were so eager to hear music that was not jazz."[13]

As a spectacle, so contemporary reports tell, the second concert was a joy to behold. Banners of local high schools and colleges, with the most prominent place accorded to the University of Pennsylvania, hung from the balconies and boxes. In one box sat a group of sailors from one of the ships anchored in the Navy Yard. In the first few rows of the parquet there were uniformed lads of the Valley Forge Military Academy, several hundred strong, while in the rear sat the Girl Scouts of Philadelphia. One critic referred to them as a buxom lot.

Stokowski had again selected a group of young players to sit in and play with the orchestra. Four young violinists, three of whom were girls; two cellists, both boys; and four harpists, all girls, were prominently seated at the first desks of their various sections.[14] Two works selected by the audience were the Wagner prelude to *Die Meistersinger* and Ravel's *Boléro*. Stoki chose a brand-new work, *Three Units* by Ernest Brooks, Rimsky-Korsakov's *Russian Easter* Overture, *Bali* by Eichheim, and the third movement from the Tchaikovsky *Pathétique*.[15]

One critic remarked that "He walked off with the hearts of young Philadelphia in his pocket . . ."[16]

The opening season had been a tremendous success and a source of great joy to Stokowski. He was in his element. The young people became immersed in the whole affair. They wrote their own program notes, had the programs printed, and provided ushers with orders to keep out anyone older than twenty-five unless they had ten or more youngsters in tow. Jerry Toobin, who was one of the ushers and age verifiers, said that he had experienced many perils in his time "but nothing compared with going up to some lady (and at thirteen one has a very undeveloped idea of age) and saying, 'Pardon me, Ma'am, but are you over twenty-five?'—especially since I considered twenty-five hardening-of-the-arteries country, and something shameful, like baldness, or being a Republican."[17]

"The idea of bouncers was a great idea, and the young people liked it too. It gave them a feeling of power. Everyone wanted to go," Mary Binney Montgomery told me. "Stoki's special magic and his feeling about young people and his ability to inflame their imagination made the concerts really exciting. He didn't play down to them."[18]

The programs that Stokowski and his young planners made for the second season were more ambitious. Complete symphonies would be given: César Franck's Symphony in D Minor; the Brahms Second, Tchaikovsky's Sixth, and the Beethoven Fifth. While waiting in line before concerts, the standees made up a text for the Beethoven. They chanted a version that would have been a credit to Walter Damrosch:

> *Beethoven's Fifth.*
> *Beethoven's Fifth.*
> *Beethoven's Fifth, Beethoven's Fifth,*
> *Beethoven's Fifth.*
> *Beethoven's Fifth, Beethoven's Fifth,*
> *Beethoven's Fifth.*
> *It gets monotonous;*
> *It gets monotonous;*
> *You know it*
> *Bores*
> *Me*
> *Stiffth.* [19]

During the fourth Youth Concert in January the audience sang the "Marseillaise" with gusto.[20] Stoki then suggested that they learn the words of another national song for the next program. It was the "Internationale," the anthem of the USSR. The audience accepted the idea with equanimity, but when the news reached beyond the walls of the Academy, a terrific brouhaha erupted. Again the Stokowski name and face were splashed across the front pages of every local paper.

The guardians of civic virtue became apoplectic. The American Legion convened a meeting during which the Reverend Robert J. McFetridge, chaplain of the county board, sermonized heatedly that presenting the "Internationale" was "unpatriotic and an attempt to put over Communist propaganda in this city." He suggested that "perhaps Mr. Stokowski feels that in consequence of our recent recognition of Russia the music should be played."

One legionnaire declared that Stoki was a member of the Communist party and was active in its affairs. This was enough for the Legion to vote that a committee of three, including the Reverend McFetridge, visit Stokowski and demand that he remove the offending anthem from his program. Little did they know Stokowski.

Curtis Bok somewhat timidly said, "It was probably just one of those things that popped into Mr. Stokowski's head as he made the suggestion. I doubt if it will be played."[21] Bok should have known better.

The Legion committee recommended that if Stokowski would not remove the Internationale from the program, then Legion members should come to the Academy and prevent the regular audience from attending. They did not know Stokowski's young audience!

"No one need sing unless they wish to," was Stoki's response to the Legion committee. "At the last Youth Concert," he said, "the audience sang the 'Marseillaise' and I asked them if they would like to sing the 'Internationale' at the next concert. They enthusiastically replied 'yes,' so we are planning to sing the 'Star Spangled Banner' and the 'Internationale' at the next concert. Of course, everyone will sing of his or her free will. I explained to the youth audience that we would sing the 'Internationale' as an expression of international good feeling and comradeship. The 'Internationale' was composed by a Frenchman named Degeyter in 1888. The idea back of the work is not a new one. Christ expressed it 20 centuries ago in the Golden Rule, and several centuries before Christ substantially the same idea was expressed by Buddha and Confucius and Lao-tze."[22]

With all the portentousness of such proclamations as "Curfew Shall Not Ring Tonight," the papers blazoned "Red Anthem Will Be Sung Tonight." "I wish to give my personal assurance to the parents and friends of those who attend," Stoki announced, "that they will receive no destructive influence. I have children of my own so that I understand the intense interest every parent has in the children's welfare. But one thing is important to understand. The youth public are not children. Some of them are adolescent, but the majority are from 20 to 25 years old and so are adults. They are completely capable of doing their own thinking and of taking care of themselves. They would be the first to resent my interfering with their opinions in any way, and I should respect them for insisting on their freedom of thought.

"We shall sing only the first verse of the 'Internationale' because that has been our habit with all the songs we sing. We shall sing it in French because I have not been able to find an English translation which does not change the original. . . .

"These concerts are for music. Great music is a thing of beauty. It speaks to us of life—of humanity—of all the deeper things which we think and feel. So although politics should be barred from music, life cannot be. At first this may seem a contradiction, but if anyone will take the trouble to think deeply into this question they will see that the deepest message of music speaks of life in all its possibilities and the highest mission of music is to speak to us with understanding of life in its broadest and deepest sense."[23]

The evening arrived. There was an air of tension both inside and outside the Academy. Extra police were stationed in front and alongside the venerable old building, but no superpatriots arrived to stop the concert or prevent the young audience from entering.

Following the performance of the Richard Strauss Horn Concerto the point in the program's time arrived for the "Internationale."[24] The orchestra played it through first to familiarize the audience with the melody. During the introductory playing between a half-dozen and a dozen in the audience rose to their feet. One girl in the audience stood with her hand poised above her head. A man in the balcony stood behind a box, arms akimbo. Neither was disturbed. As the anthem was sung, about half the audience stood. Many who were seated sang. A reporter from the *Evening Bulletin* observed: "The atmosphere was packed with electricity, with suspense, throughout the performance. It was evidenced by a tumultuous ovation at the close which brought a relief from the tension."

But this was not the end of the anthems. The program closed with "Finlandia" by Sibelius, which contains, Stoki reminded his audience, the national anthem of Finland. He suggested that the melody might be a suitable song for the Youth Concerts, and he invited the listeners to submit texts and also original melodies. "Some may ask," he remarked, "why we should choose a melody from another country. Well, the 'Star Spangled Banner' is an English song, and, I regret to say, a drinking song at that."[25]

The great Red menace came and went. The Liberty Bell developed no new cracks and young Philadelphians survived their subversion. The Austrian anthem and "America, the Beautiful" were sung on the next program.[26] They created no furor.

Frequently groups of his young enthusiasts would go to Stoki's strange little house and serenade him from the adjacent parking lot. They went not only after the Youth Concerts but after the subscription concerts on Saturday nights as well. They often sang songs they had made up while standing in line for rush seats. "Sometimes he would invite us up," Natasha recalled, "and he would be sitting there eating his salad and bowl of soup. And after a while he caught onto the fact that he was going to be serenaded, so there would be just accidentally a lemon meringue pie or a raisin apple pie, which would just happen to be there."27

On one such evening Helene Hanff was among the group serenading under Stokowski's window. "I can hear Faye now—she couldn't have been more than fourteen and she was no taller than she ever was—in the middle of the circle of kids. I couldn't see her; I only heard her voice. . . . After a minute, a living room window opened and he looked out and asked us how many were there." If there were more than six he would come down and talk to the group; if there were merely six he would invite them up. " 'Come round to the front,' he said, 'and I'll press the buzzer.' We went round and he pressed the buzzer and we clambered up the narrow, rickety stairs. He stood at the top in a navy shirt and slacks and counted us with his lips and his fingers. When we had all reached the top and were standing in the hall, he said, 'Which is the sixth?' and we giggled."28

"Sometimes he would invite a few of us to his studio after school," Natasha recalled, "and we would help by checking the music, checking the parts for the next set of rehearsals to make sure that they were all in the folder."29

The 1934–35 season was to be Stokowski's last with the young people —or so they thought at the time. It was the season of turmoil, the season of his resignation and the season when his young audience would rise most vociferously to his defense. The programs were venturesome. He introduced Philip James' *Station WGBZX;* Dawson's *Negro Folk* Symphony (a work he later recorded); the Sibelius *Song of Youth;* Prokofiev's March from the *Love of Three Oranges;* Sigurd Frederiksen's *The Saga of Leif Ericson;* a *Christmas Fantasy* by a young Philadelphia girl, Ann Wyeth, and the Shostakovich Piano Concerto.

The young pianist playing the Shostakovich was Eugene List. He had won the competition Stokowski had originated, the prize being an appearance with the orchestra. Gene was a student of Olga's at the Philadelphia Conservatory of Music. "I tried out the first year and I didn't win. I came in second," Gene told me. "I was very disappointed, but actually it was a stroke of good luck as it turned out. The next year I did win with the

Schumann concerto, and that is what I expected to play. But six weeks before I was to play, Stokowski called me and I went to the Academy and went backstage. He showed me a piece of music. 'I've just received this from the Soviet Union,' he said. It was the First Piano Concerto of Shostakovich. 'Would you like to play it?' Well, I was kind of stunned because I was prepared to play the Schumann and I had very little time to learn this, but, of course, I mumbled and stumbled and said yes. Actually it was the biggest break I ever had because it acted as a springboard. . . . It was a brand new novelty at the time and it did a lot for me."[30] It did indeed, for Gene later appeared playing it with the New York Philharmonic with Stoki conducting.

"I did not know the new concerto myself," said Olga, "and the idea of Eugene's learning a modern concerto, which was sure to be difficult, and playing it with the Philadelphia Orchestra on such short notice, seemed impossible. . . . I knew he could do something very unusual under any circumstances. . . . This meant burning the midnight oil over the Shostakovich concerto myself, for I wanted to give Eugene all the help I could, but I enjoyed it."[31]

Gene described his first visit to Stoki's apartment on Rittenhouse Street. "I went up and there was this hushed atmosphere. Whoever let me in said, 'Quiet.' He was poring over the Bach B Minor Mass because he was going to do it shortly. I was as quiet as a mouse and finally when he finished he turned to me and said, 'Now, would you play for me?' Then I started to play and my foot shook on the pedal uncontrollably. This usually doesn't happen to me; so it shows how overwhelmed I was by this man's presence. I played. It wasn't bad, but I never had that experience before. He was very, very kind to me. He gave me lots of rehearsal. He was constantly encouraging me, and if I made a little blip or something he would pass it over as if it were just the most ordinary thing that happened all the time."[32]

The concert was a tremendous success and Linton Martin, writing in the *Inquirer*, remarked: "Eugene List received a thunderous ovation that threatened to rock the venerable Academy on its foundation. . . ."[33] Stoki was particularly pleased with Gene's success. Olga said it surpassed her wildest hopes. And she was delighted when Arthur Judson said, "I am interested in that boy. I want him to play at one of the Sunday concerts of the orchestra. I want to hear him play a different type of concerto and solos. I will engage him for a spring concert."[34]

36

Co-Conductors

As the 1934–35 season began, Judson's orchestral kingdom was in serious trouble. The Philadelphia's reserves had been entirely wiped out. The Philharmonic, too, in spite of its wealthy patrons, was also in deep financial woe. Judson and the board launched a plan to raise $500,000 for the Philharmonic and radio appeals were a significant part of the strategy. In Philadelphia they had complained that Stokowski's constant programming of contemporary scores had contributed to the decrease in the audiences—much to Stoki's annoyance.

But that was only one of the bedeviling problems that were rife in the Academy. The financial plight was foremost. Both Stoki and Curtis Bok were totally disenchanted with Judson. Without even consulting with the board, Bok appointed Esther Everett Lape as his assistant, possibly intending to promote her as manager at the expiration of Judson's contract at the end of the season. But Judson abruptly resigned. *Musical America* stated that his resignation had been accepted by the board to take effect on June 1, 1935. It reported that the resignation was unofficially due to policy disagreements, including the opera venture, radio contracts, and the question of more power for Stokowski.[1]

The board refused to consider the appointment of Miss Lape for Judson's post and instead appointed Benjamin H. Ludlow, secretary of the board, who was a prominent Philadelphia attorney.[2] It was on the heels of this that Stokowski acted; he released an open letter to the Philadelphia press before even notifying most of the members of the board. Many members of the board first learned of it when they were contacted by reporters. The letter spelling out his various grievances was long but the basic message was short indeed. Stokowski had resigned!

> I am writing this to you as an open letter because I feel that I am speaking not only to the members of your board but also to my colleagues in the orchestra, our concert audiences everywhere, our youth group and our radio listeners.
>
> Last spring my contract with the Philadelphia Orchestra expired and you offered me in your letter of Jan. 24 a new five-year contract. I thanked you, but asked for a year's leave of absence for study. Later you asked me to "help out" by conducting for the three opening months of this season and in this spirit I signed a contract to conduct all of the concerts from Oct. 1 to Dec. 26. You asked me to conduct opera also, but I declined because I wished to have us produce certain operas in new ways, and there was not then time to prepare the new methods. . . .
>
> In October you asked me if I would in principle be willing to sign a further continuing contract to begin September, 1935, with no time limit. . . .
>
> Meanwhile a new element had entered. Mr. Judson had resigned. From that time on, in letters and conversations, I have repeatedly stressed the importance of your selecting and engaging the new executive director (or manager) for next season, so that together this executive director and I could develop the general conception of next season's work, establish the principles upon which we would base our planning, and bring practical execution of the plans to a point where the executive director would be able to carry them on after I leave Philadelphia on Dec. 31 for the other work that I postponed last spring at your request.
>
> You have not been able to find and engage an executive director that is acceptable to the majority of you and to me, and so I have not been able to make the great number of detailed arrangements that would be absolutely essential for the coming season if it were to be carried out as I have conceived it. My plan was so to relate opera and symphony concerts to each other that the whole season would have musical unity. At this date it is impossible to make these arrangements by Dec. 31 and equally impossible for me at this time to defer my departure.
>
> For this reason I cannot now assume the musical responsibility of next season. Even if you found and engaged an executive director tomorrow, there would not be time for adequate preparation between now and Dec. 31. . . .

But from the personal and musical side, I am sad at the thought that I must now leave the orchestra that I have worked so hard to build up. No words can express the affection I feel for all my friends in the orchestra and my unhappiness that I must leave them now. . . .

Because of the loss of time which cannot be made up, I cannot accept the new contract you have offered me for next season. I shall, of course, completely fulfill my present contract and leave my department in good order. I wish to pass over in silence and forget our deep-lying differences of opinion and remember only the beauty and inspiration of the music we have made.

I write this with pain in my heart.

Leopold Stokowski[3]

The very thought of Stokowski leaving Philadelphia was greeted with shock and disbelief. At the first concert after his announcement, a scene took place that was unique in the history of symphony orchestras in America or anywhere else. As Stokowski strode out to conduct with his usual immediate downbeat, he was totally frustrated by the orchestra, which stood up in tribute. The audience burst into a tumult of applause. He turned to the audience several times trying to halt the demonstration, and finally minutes later he was able to begin to conduct the *New World* Symphony. Following it, he was recalled six times by the applauding audience. At the conclusion of the concert, there were cheers of "bravo" and foot stomping mingled with the applause. Finally in this emotionally charged moment he addressed the audience: "I want to thank my colleagues and friends of the orchestra for their marvelous and never-failing cooperation. I can't tell you how wonderful they have always been. . . . You of the audience, and we of the orchestra, have often been united by the magic of music, and unseen by us the vast radio audience was also with us. Somehow—at present I do not know how—I hope we can all be again united through music."[4]

Prior to the concert a petition had been circulated urging Stoki not to resign. It was the work of a lady composer, Frances McCollin, who dubbed the situation as "not only a Philadelphia tragedy, but a world tragedy." The petition circulated read: "Because of the beauty and inspiration of the music you have given us we, the undersigned members of your music-loving public, beg you to reconsider your announced intention of leaving the orchestra." It seemed that the entire audience wanted to sign. Miss McCollin threatened the board: "We will not subscribe to future concerts unless Mr. Stokowski is given a contract to conduct on his own terms next season. I personally will ask every seat-holder to withhold subscriptions for next year unless the directors act at once.

"We must not lose a conductor who, in the opinion of many, is not only the greatest conductor in the world, but the greatest who has ever been seen."[5]

From members of the Women's Committee, loyal friends, and his devoted followers there was a general outcry for the resignation of the board. Curtis Bok presented a plan which he believed would solve all of the problems: "The central point of the plan is the resignation of the present board and the creation of a new board which will be sympathetic to Mr. Stokowski, his philosophy and his musical policy.

"By sympathetic I mean more than acquiescent: I mean an inner understanding and awareness of what he is trying to do.

"My plan contemplates the appointment by me, as president, of a committee to select a new board . . . one which in my judgment will insure placing on the new board people who are sympathetic to Mr. Stokowski in the sense that I have indicated. . . . I cannot compromise this point."[6]

The board listened attentively and then flatly turned down Bok's proposal. Curtis Bok and his mother abruptly resigned.[7]

Other loyal supporters also voiced their dismay. The hubbub and excitement that had permeated the Academy during the subscription concerts was mild compared to that which erupted during the next Youth Concert. It is evident that the young people of Philadelphia adored him. As the young audience filed into the hall, two slips of paper were handed to them. One was a statement from the board of directors: "On the occasion of the last Youth Concert for the present season, we wish to express to Leopold Stokowski and the music-loving youth of Philadelphia our appreciation of their work for and interest in the Youth Concerts."[8]

The other slip contained a poem, not a particularly good one, but one that was sincerely felt. It read:

> Arise, O youth in just indignation
> For all that's true thunders condemnation.
> A better world is now at birth,
> Tradition's chains shall be struck from the earth.
> Too long we followed customs old,
> Youth shall be free from shackle's mold
> To music's call the earth shall rise
> And youth shall lead 'neath peaceful skies.[9]

The poem was sung just after intermission, with Saul Caston conducting the orchestra as Stokowski walked on stage.

At intermission David Hocker, a member of the Executive Committee of the Youth Concerts, proposed a resolution demanding the immediate resignation of the board. "We are in danger of losing Stokowski," Hocker said. "To keep him is uppermost in all our minds. It is essential that his ideas be supported. It has been said that there are deep-lying differences between himself and the orchestra. We do not question that they exist. We of the youth audience know what his aims are: To give the greatest music in Philadelphia to the greatest number of people through the radio. Are we prepared to back him 100 percent in this aim?"

The audience responded with a triple forte, "Yes!"

"It is clear," Hocker continued, "that the present board is not so inclined, or the deep-lying differences would not exist. I move that we demand the immediate resignation of the present board!"

Then in a sensational, dramatic gesture the young child pianist Sol Kaplan, who at one time had been a soloist with the orchestra, leaped up on his seat in one of the first rows and shouted: "It is the only issue— no compromise." Then general pandemonium broke loose, with shouting, cheering, and applause thundering through the house.

During the concert, just before playing the "Marseillaise," Stokowski addressed his young audience: "It is a song of youth, of courage, of impatience with the old order of things and of desire for a new order." And later he complimented them: "You are an audience that responds and understands. There is not another audience like you in the world."[10]

The board was made up of two factions, one fanatically loyal to Stokowski and the other ranging from apathetic to hostile. His greatest supporters were the Boks, Charlton Yarnall, and Henry Ingersoll. One board member and vice-president of the association was Samuel Fels (Fels-Naphtha Soap), who was part owner of the *Philadelphia Record*. Though he did not express his feelings personally, Fels' paper editorialized on what it thought to be Stoki's ingratitude for all that Philadelphia had done for him: "Leopold Stokowski is a genius. No one disputes that.

"Leopold Stokowski has done much for Philadelphia. No one disputes that either.

"But Philadelphia has done a very great deal for Leopold Stokowski. And that seems to be forgotten right now by many people—including Leopold Stokowski. . . .

"Leopold Stokowski has been given financial rewards of the first magnitude. . . . At its peak, for several years, his income through the orchestra was more than $200,000 a year. . . . He has given Philadelphia genius. But Philadelphia paid well for it. . . . He forgets that the directors not only have made him the highest paid conductor in the world—but have given him a greater degree of artistic freedom than is enjoyed by any conductor of any orchestra anywhere. . . .

"The Record hopes Dr. Stokowski will remain with us. So do the directors. They are willing to meet him more than half way. . . . But Dr. Stokowski must also meet the directors half way. . . .

"Many of the present directors are . . . men who gave liberally to make up deficits in the past and who since have contributed generously. . . . Philadelphia owes them a debt, too. And so does Dr. Stokowski.[11]

On Sunday December 16, Edwin Schloss wrote a long article in the *Record* belaboring the fracas. He stated that many of Stokowski's supporters, in their efforts to place him in the public eye as a martyr, "are having difficulty in finding anyone to press the crown of thorns upon his brow. He is hardly being hounded through the streets. In fact, the city is presently ringing with unanimous tributes to his genius. Everyone is praying that he will stay with the orchestra, and the Board of Directors, his supposed persecutors, are leading the chorus of praise. They are begging the maestro to reconsider his resignation and meet with them . . . to adjust those 'deep-lying differences' which the conductor rather vaguely gave as the reasons for his resignation.

"Furthermore, recent disclosures of past financial transactions between Stokowski and the board seem to show that if the maestro has been crucified by the directors, as his adherents claim, it has at least been on a cross of gold."[12]

In response to critics of Stokowski, Mrs. Bok stated that he had "no resemblance whatever to the creature of temperament and vagaries that some spiritually near-sighted folk may claim him to be." She continued in a published statement: "As one of Leopold Stokowski's oldest friends, I am grieved and indignant to read and hear the misstatements that have recently been made about him. . . . He has been an intimate friend of my family for 20 years. . . .

"My son, Curtis Bok, is today, as he has always been, in close sympathy with Stokowski and his most loyal supporter in the present orchestral crisis.

"For Philadelphia to lose Stokowski is unthinkable."[13]

The board, goaded by the sense of urgency, wrote to Stokowski asking him to meet with them as soon as possible. The letter was most conciliatory and attempted to placate him by acceding to practically all of the demands he had made.

Stoki responded with an eight-page letter. He accused the board of being too old and unyielding. He complained about the lack of radio exposure and blamed the board for waiting too long to get a high price from a commercial sponsor. He maintained that having music broadcast was more important than the price obtained for it. He charged that the board had hired inferior guest conductors instead of men like Bruno Walter and Furtwängler, whom he said he had suggested. "Some seasons ago I begged the board to invite Toscanini to conduct our orchestra. Before even trying, I was told it was 'impossible,' " he wrote. "I renewed my request, and because of my insistence he was finally invited and accepted."[14]

Stokowski really never intended to sever himself from the orchestra, but he wanted to reduce the number of concerts he would conduct. He had a precedent. Toscanini conducted the Philharmonic for only a half-season, and there were those who felt that overexposure would have lessened his impact. Furthermore, life in Philadelphia was not satisfactory. Evangeline and their daughters were in New York, where Evangeline devoted much of her time to the Dalton School. Stoki's somewhat ramshackle, Bohemian carriage-house apartment was a far cry from the residences he had formerly enjoyed.

On December 19, 1934, with olive branches spread everywhere, he darted bare-headed from a cab and proceeded into the Girard Trust Company Building for a three-and-a-half-hour meeting of uninterrupted discussion with the eight members of the administration committee of the board. He agreed to return in the fall of 1935 to be a "guest" conductor of the orchestra and nothing more. Another point he insisted on was that he should conduct two performances of the opera *Parsifal* in Philadelphia and one in New York. The committee, which included Frances Wister, Orville Bullitt, and Sam Rosenbaum, agreed.[15]

Since he had relinquished his demand for the engagement of Miss Lape as manager, the board set out to find someone who would not only be capable of fulfilling the demands of the position but one who would also be compatible with Stokowski. The person they found was already a member of the board. He was Alfred Reginald Allen—"Reggie," as he was known to his associates. He and his family were well known to

Stokowski, and Reggie would have been particularly amenable to him. His mother had been one of the founding members of the Women's Committee of the orchestra and most important in the matter of fund raising. "She was very well known in that group," Reggie told me, "and my father, who was an extraordinarily gifted musician himself, although not professional, was known around the city and, of course, they got to know Stoki and Olga fairly well. The earliest moments that I can remember of this acquaintance came about in 1913, when we all went over to Europe on the same boat, the Nord Deutsche Lloyd *George Washington*. Little did he and I know that we were going to get together professionally a great many years later, but with my child's little tin box of watercolor paints, he addressed himself to doing a portrait of me. I was about eight. . . .

"When Stokowski and the orchestra and Judson really got around to clobbering one another and something had to be done, I was one of the people looking around for another manager for the orchestra. . . . Suddenly it became clear that the person the board would rather like to have in that spot was I. And again, this was partly for the reason that I would be acceptable to Stokowski. So that led to my being manager of the orchestra."[16]

Reggie was only twenty-nine when he assumed his new post. I asked him for his recollection about the relationship between Stoki and Judson and about its gradual deterioration: "I think that in the case of a person of Stokowski's makeup he would feel with his own huge success that he increasingly didn't require any help from Arthur Judson and he would also feel in various instances that Judson's real umbrella of power in the whole field of symphonic concert music got in Stokowski's way now and then. I suspect—but I never knew—I was close to both of them, but I never knew of any what you might call real knockdowns. I'm not saying that they were close friends. I'm sure they weren't at that time, but I would simply say that each went his own way but their ways were almost exactly parallel and at the same time extremely top level in their fields.

"I'm sure you don't have to be told, but it was the most fashionable subject in those days to talk about Stokowski, and the rift was the chief subject. . . . It was either with respect to Stokowski or it was with Judson or it was with respect to some social situation in Philadelphia—some young lady—some this—some that. Stoki was a very important subject for loose tongues in social circles to talk about without really, in many instances, the slightest bit of factual background. I'm not gilding him at all. I know plenty of peripheral marks that I wouldn't give. They're dark marks and I wouldn't say he didn't deserve them but it didn't bother him."[17]

In a conversation with Orville Bullitt, who had come on the board in 1931, I asked him about Judson and his rupture with Stokowski. "I will not say anything," said Bullitt. "I don't know what caused it, but I do know he disliked Stokowski intensely."[18]

It was not until the first months of 1935 that Stoki's participation in the orchestra was decided. On January 6, 1935, he accepted the invitation from the board to open the 1935–36 season and remain for the first three months. "I feel," he said, "that all points of disagreement between myself and the board will be satisfactorily solved. In any case, Philadelphia will stand by its magnificent orchestra. It will go on whether I am here permanently or not. But I hope to be here."[19]

The size of the board was reduced from twenty-four to fifteen and Mary Louise Curtis Bok was reinvited to join the board. Sam Rosenbaum, Orville Bullitt, and Miss Frances Wister also remained. In order to involve the subscribers, a questionnaire asking for suggestions was prepared. Among other items, it asked what conductors they would like to have during the next season. Stokowski led, but it was "no landslide." Conductors next in line were Artur Rodzinski, Eugene Ormandy, Otto Klemperer, Bruno Walter, and Wilhelm Furtwängler.[20]

With his wounds healed, Stoki left for Santa Barbara and then off to visit China and Japan. At the end of the summer Reggie Allen announced that Stoki would lead forty concerts. Stokowski replied: "I am planning programs to include outstanding examples of classical, romantic and modern music, and, in addition, a special series of Bach and Wagner programs. . . .

"Words cannot describe how happy I shall be to be again conducting our eloquent and unique orchestra."[21]

As for the next season, Stokowski turned down a contract to resume as director of the orchestra: "For a long time, I have been contemplating research which I hope may be of benefit to the orchestra. Because of this . . . I deeply regret that I shall not be able to accept your kind offer of a new 3-year contract." He also explained that he would be pleased to conduct for a substantial period during the coming season. The board then engaged Eugene Ormandy as permanent conductor, and for the next three years the two conductors would share the concerts of the Philadelphia Orchestra as co-conductors but with Ormandy conducting the lion's share.[22] Stokowski worried little about the arrangement, for it was he who would take the orchestra on its spectacular transcontinental tour in 1936.

While there had often been speculation that Stokowski's real name was Leo Stokes—which we know it was not—Philadelphians didn't seem to know that Ormandy's real name was Jeno Blau until the local press began to publish biographical stories about him. Ormandy worked hard and the relationship between him and Stokowski seemed to be most friendly during the early years.

Ormandy endured. He must have been intensely gratified to read the announcement released by the orchestra on September 29, 1938. It read: "Eugene Ormandy has been appointed musical director of the Philadelphia Orchestra and Leopold Stokowski's participation in the affairs of the orchestra, except for appearances as conductor for some of its concerts, is at an end. The post of music director, formerly held by Stokowski . . . gives Mr. Ormandy full authority over the orchestra's personnel, the content of programs, and the selection of soloists and guest conductors." Stokowski had agreed to conduct eleven concerts beginning in March 1939.[23]

(37)

The Movies

*I*N November 1921 Hedda Van den Beemt—one of the principal violinists of the orchestra—who was then instructor and director of the Eastern State Penitentiary Band, asked Stoki to conduct it. The press referred to it as "probably the most unusual band concert ever held in this city." Stoki conducted the inmates for an audience of nearly two thousand prisoners and guests.

Stokowski was welcomed with a fanfare from the band and then conducted a rather short concert. The inmates, who had been given a half-holiday, responded effusively. No doubt it was Judson's astute sense of publicity that brought in "the movie men," who set up banks of arc lights that lit up the band and illuminated Stoki, who was appropriately dressed in a light gray suit and blue shirt with a soft collar.

"Smiling encouragingly at the musicians, he stepped on the dais and with a masterly wave of the baton electrified every man with a desire to do his best that lasted the entire concert." So reported the *Evening Ledger.* [1] During all of it the cameras "ground away." It was being filmed for newsreels that were shown throughout the country in conjunction with regular films. In those pretelevision days the newsreels were viewed by millions of movie addicts. Many saw Stokowski for the first time in the unlikely scene of a prison, but it was probably more dramatic and certainly more newsworthy that way. So he made his movie debut in the Pennsylvania State Prison on November 3, 1921, sixteen years before *The Big Broadcast of 1937.*

Stoki was always a movie lover and followed them avidly. He made his

344

Courtesy International Leopold Stokowski Society

Stokowski with penitentiary band. Inscribed in his handwriting on the back: "How I look when I think of Sonya" (1921)

movie-theater debut in Philadelphia's Stanley Theater, April 23, 1923. Gloria Swanson in *Prodigal Daughters* was playing on the screen along with a "cultural short" about Einstein's theory of relativity.[2] The Stanley was a huge movie palace and it packed in teeming audiences just for the pictures alone. But with Stokowski and the Philadelphia Orchestra all at no extra cost, it was mobbed. The press reported that over ten thousand were turned away.[3] Stoki conducted the same Wagner program, selections drawn from the *Ring,* just as he had for the regulars in the Academy of Music. Everyone involved was hell-bent for culture.

Stoki's first assault on Hollywood occurred in 1936 during his tour with the Philadelphia Orchestra. RCA was very shrewd when they engaged Merle Armitage to manage the two Los Angeles concerts, for Armitage was a rare combination of entrepreneur, writer, publicist, designer, publisher, and talent cum laude. He was also a meticulous planner. A year in advance he drove up to Santa Barbara, where Stoki was busily working with bricks and mortar, building fireplaces of his own design and steps and terraces for his house high above Santa Barbara. Armitage outlined his plans and Stoki was delighted.

Armitage then purchased an expensive motion picture camera and

Courtesy Reginald Allen
With Reginald Allen, manager of the Philadelphia Orchestra, during the transcontinental tour in 1936

persuaded Stoki to make a special trip from Santa Barbara to pose for him. The result was a portfolio of photos that he sold to RCA; they became part of the national publicity campaign for the whole tour.

So that the concerts could be heard by huge audiences, Armitage leased not a concert hall—Los Angeles didn't have one anyway—but a huge building that had been constructed for ice skating called the Pan Pacific Auditorium. The enormous building was made entirely of wood; it had a dirt floor but no chairs, no stage, and no equipment. Armitage admitted that he had spent a fortune converting it into a concert hall. He had a stage built backed by an acoustic shell that was painted blue. He put in a wooden floor that graduated to a height of twenty feet in the rear, and rented thirteen thousand folding chairs.[4]

Courtesy International Leopold Stokowski Society
Stokowski in front of one of three fireplaces he designed and constructed for his house in Santa Barbara, California (c. 1945)

With a wonderful sense of organization, Armitage established committees in towns all over southern California, some as far as two hundred miles away. He arranged for special trains and buses to bring people for the great event.

Reggie Allen told me that while the orchestra was crossing New Mexico and Arizona he received a telegram: "It was a sample of the wire that had been sent out by the committee to God knows how many hundreds of people in the Hollywood area and the wording of it I will never forget. The opening of it was: 'Will you join with us in lending distinction to . . .' The whole idea of movie actors lending distinction to Leopold Stokowski, and the Philadelphia Orchestra playing their first performance out there was really strictly for the birds," he said laughingly. "But the movie colony certainly turned out."[5]

Joan Crawford and Franchot Tone—they were married at that time—were the heads of the Hollywood committee and acted as hosts for an elaborate party in the ballroom of the Ambassador Hotel for 650 of Hollywood's elite. Joan Crawford played the role of a regal hostess quite magnificently and Stokowski acted the role of Stokowski with equal assurance. He responded with a charming fifteen-minute speech during which he praised Hollywood and its glamorous inhabitants and fervently said how happy he was to be there.[6]

The two Los Angeles concerts were an enormous success. Stoki opened his first program with the Toccata and Fugue of Bach and followed it with four more of his Bach transcriptions. The latter part of the program was devoted to Wagner with the Preludes to *Die Meistersinger* and *Lohengrin* and concluding with the "Love Music" from *Tristan und Isolde*.[7]

Hollywood discovered the real thing. It found a giant, a genius and a personality that radiated all the charisma and glamor that the labored grindings of the studio press agents could never equal. The whole movie industry became Stokowski-conscious. And he too thought that he had found the next phase of his career. It was to be one far more glamorous than that of Philadelphia, and one that would reach out and touch an infinitely greater number of people. Stoki began to envision a career in the cinema that would outshine anything that he had achieved in the past. He was not averse at this point to burning his bridges.

About two weeks before the concerts took place headlines appeared in the Los Angeles papers announcing that Stokowski and the Philadelphia would be featured on the "Kraft Music Hall" hour hosted by Bing Crosby.

James Cagney, Stokowski, Frederic March, Madame Schumann-Heink, Joan Crawford, and Franchot Tone at a reception given by Crawford and Tone in honor of Stokowski (March 10, 1936)

It threw Armitage and many of his committee members into a state of panic since Crosby was suggesting that the audience wait and hear the orchestra for nothing. Armitage immediately protested to RCA and to Stokowski as well. At first Stokowski assured Armitage that there would be no radio broadcast, but as the time grew closer the Crosby announcements continued. Armitage finally reached Stokowski and protested that they were damaging sales of concert tickets. "But Armitage," Stoki replied naively, "that's such a commercial attitude . . . think of all the thousands who can't afford to come to our concerts who will be made happy by hearing the orchestra on the air." And so two days after his second concert he did appear with the orchestra on the Crosby program on April 30, 1936.[8]

The program was a terrible mishmash that critics likened to an unpalatable emulsion like oil and water. In addition to Stoki and the orchestra, Crosby had as other guests Louis Prima and hillbilly Bob Burns. The crooner succeeded in reaching a new low "in dressed up vulgarity," wrote one reviewer. "Mr. Stokowski let himself in for it and probably had to take his medicine. Mr. Stokowski came out of it better than Mr. Crosby."[9]

Stoki wisely turned down an offer to star in the "Life of Wagner," although the idea of conducting Wagner's music for audiences "all over the world" was tempting.[10] Instead he returned to Hollywood as soon as his tour was over and made his film debut in *The Big Broadcast of 1937* with a cast that included Jack Benny, Ray Milland, Larry Adler, Martha Raye, and Benny Goodman. Huge posters used to plug the film showed Stoki on one side and Benny Goodman on the other. When I asked Benny if he had any recollection of their contact, he laughingly retorted, "Hell no! Stoki merely regarded me as a jazz clarinet player and there was really no rapport."

When the film was completed, Stoki wrote an explanatory article for the press: "I want to explain here not why we are now appearing and playing on the screen but why we did not do so before. . . . With my orchestra I pioneered in recording symphony music for the phonograph. I believe our constant willingness to experiment with the scientists of sound aided materially in the great technical improvement in the fidelity of music reproduced from the familiar black disks. Later we plunged into the new field of radio broadcast and learned more about microphones. . . . Naturally such serious study of acoustics made me anticipate the point at which the sound screen would become a fit vehicle for that richest and most subtle of all musical mediums—the full symphony orchestra. That point has arrived.

"But I was determined that our Hollywood debut would wait until all conditions were right. Music has been my life work, so I was not—and am not—willing to conduct frothy or inferior music just because it has the name of being popular or familiar. . . ."

"Stokowski's appearance in 'The Big Broadcast of 1937' is significant for one thing," said George Antheil. "It is extraordinary that audiences lured into a motion picture theater upon the pretense of seeing and hearing the remarkable hat-cha Martha Raye, will likewise swallow a Bach fugue and love it. But this is because the Bach is presented with a technic of showmanship comprehensible to them. Stokowski is entirely equal to the occasion. And since Stokowski remains—for my money at least—the world's greatest orchestral director, so far as I am concerned he can do as he pleases."[11]

The idea for Stoki's next picture grew in the mind of Henry Koster. While still in Germany, Koster began to collect Stokowski recordings. When he arrived in Hollywood in March 1936 and made a fairly successful B-type movie about three pubescent young girls (one was Deanna Durbin) trying to patch up the separation of their parents, he attended some of the rehearsals and recording sessions that Stoki was doing for his "Big Broadcast" film.[12] It triggered Koster's interest at once.

Koster approached the brass at Universal. He proposed doing a picture starring Leopold Stokowski. The studio thought the idea insane. But Koster persisted. I phoned Koster recently at his Pacific Palisades home and we discussed the film. "I asked them at Universal if I could make a movie with Leopold Stokowski," he said, "and they laughed. They didn't think that it was a very good idea. But I insisted and my very fine producer, Joe Pasternak, helped me and we finally got the idea through."

I asked Koster who persuaded Stoki to do it. "At first he had been contacted by the studio, and Stokowski said he would be glad to discuss it. So I went to Philadelphia and talked to him. I went to see him in his apartment on 1716 Rittenhouse Street. I still remember the address. He wanted to know what the story was about and what it was going to be."[13]

The gist of the story was very simple. It was about an appealing young girl with a talent for singing who was to persuade the great Leopold Stokowski to conduct a concert using a group of unemployed musicians and by some miracle save their lives. That did not leave much to go on, but Koster skillfully portrayed Stoki as the star, and the idea of incorporating the Philadelphia Orchestra was enough to convince Stoki. He also would have a chance to perform the kind of music he wanted to introduce to movie audiences.

Koster went back to Hollywood and Stoki philosophized to the press: "It is the birthright of every man and woman to be able to hear inspired music, read great books and live for a time each year close to the earth and the beauty of nature. Because I believe this, I am planning to work in Hollywood each year for three or four months, with the object of doing everything I can to help bring great music to the movies."[14]

Scene from the motion picture *100 Men and a Girl* shows Stokowski directing orchestra of unemployed musicians (1937)

Stoki had great and idealized plans about his potential role in the movie business. He envisioned great scores being composed to be wed to equally great dramas. He wanted nothing academic, stiff, or overintellectual. "What I mean," he continued, "is music that comes from the heart, is warm, emotional, red-blooded, exciting, imaginative, magnetic, inspired."

He felt that it also must be performed with "mastery of the great art of music." Obviously he saw himself as the one to do it. In addition to this he insisted on the finest recording techniques and the most advanced equipment for the theaters where the films would be shown. His vision of the future of movies was idealistic and almost messianic. "There is no limit to motion pictures," he said. And he sincerely believed that there was "nothing in the human heart and mind, no matter how fantastic or wild, or terrifying or inspired, that cannot be expressed by motion pictures." He regarded the cinema as one of man's greatest means of communication. "My ultimate aim is to bring the beauty of music to the greatest number of men, women, and children *all over the world*. Motion pictures are an ideal medium for this. . . . That is why I am planning to work in

Hollywood for a third of each year, and the rest of the time to conduct concerts and radio."[15]

Back in Hollywood Koster and Pasternak assembled an impressive cast that included Adolphe Menjou, Alice Brady, Eugene Pallette, Mischa Auer, Billy Gilbert, Alma Kruger and a thirteen-year-old whom Koster had heard on the Eddie Cantor radio program, Edna Mae Durbin. "She was charming," said Koster, "and we changed her name to Deanna."[16]

In April Koster returned to Philadelphia, bringing with him his recording engineer, an assistant director, Deanna Durbin, her parents, and her singing teacher. All of the music was prerecorded and shots of the musicians playing, particularly on the elaborate staircase, were all superimposed, as was the segment where Stokowski himself plays part of the Bach Toccata and Fugue on the piano. But it was indeed Stokowski who played it.[17]

Stoki and the orchestra recorded the finale of Tchaikovsky's Fifth Symphony, the Prelude to act 3 of Wagner's *Lohengrin,* Berlioz's "Rákóczy March," Liszt's Hungarian Rhapsody No. 2, and accompanied Durbin in Mozart's *Alleluia* and an aria from *La Traviata.*

The film began with a scene of Stoki conducting the orchestra in the Tchaikovsky finale. "I remember that when I did a scene after this first concert number," said Koster, "he had to come down a hallway to his office, where Menjou was waiting to ask him for a job. It was right in the beginning of the film after the Tchaikovsky symphony. And this was, of course, a studio set. He walked down a hallway with some fans following asking for autographs. And there were some doors on the way, one door said 'Administration,' another 'Musicians,' and then the door that said 'Conductor.' That's where he was supposed to go. So we followed him with a camera on a camera track. I said, 'Let's shoot the scene after we rehearse it. We shot it and on the way down he suddenly changed his mind and opened the door marked 'Musicians.' There was nothing behind it but the studio wall. There was no room. He opened the door and said, 'I want to thank you gentlemen for a beautiful performance.' He closed the door and went on."

By this time, Koster was quite perturbed and said, "Mr. Stokowski, we have to know what you are going to do. We have to stick to the rehearsal.' And he said, 'Well, I always thank my musicians after every concert.' I answered, 'Well, if we had known that we would have built a room there and put some musicians in it,' " Koster said laughingly. "I don't know if he was trying to be funny or not. He was a great showman and this was his surprise element."[18]

Courtesy of Universal Pictures
Publicity photo for *100 Men and a Girl* with Adolphe Menjou, Deanna Durbin, and
Mischa Auer (1937)

When the film was released it became an immediate success. Viewers
"all over the world" saw and heard Stokowski and recognized him as one
of the most glamorous and compelling figures of his time. It was, too, a
financial success for Universal and it bailed the studio out of its financial
doldrums. It was also reflected in the sale of Stokowski recordings; a point
that Victor could not ignore. But more important, it created a new star,
Deanna Durbin. Not a star really, for she shone briefly and then disappeared. Durbin was actually a nova.

I contacted Miss Durbin in 1977 in France and asked her about her
early experiences with Stoki. She was most charming and generously
responded from her home in Neauphle-le-Château. "As to the recollection of our work together," she said, "I'm afraid I'll prove most disappointing. *100 Men and a Girl* was my second motion picture. . . . Being

fifteen years old, I had to go to school after each scene, coming back only when everything was ready for the next take. So there was little time for contact between Mr. Stokowski and me, not to mention that when after the day's shooting was over, Henry Koster, the writers, and Mr. Stokowski got together for interesting discussions about music in general and music and its relationship to films and many other fascinating subjects. I had to go home or to one of my studio rehearsals."[19]

She was pleased to learn of Stoki's extraordinary vitality and she asked me to give him her greetings. Stoki's reaction: "Ah yes! She was very pretty."

Hollywood had lured many stars from the concert world: Lily Pons, Gladys Swarthout, José Iturbi, Grace Moore, Nelson Eddy, and many more. Boris Morros was particularly interested in plugging the serious stars who were affiliated with Paramount. At the conclusion of the Hollywood Bowl series at the end of the 1936 summer, he organized a Paramount Night that was to include both serious and pop music played by the orchestra, with stars from the Paramount stable. Stokowski and Gladys Swarthout were to be featured on the serious half. Swarthout was a very popular star at the time and Stoki supplied the accompaniments for three selections from *Carmen*, which had been one of her triumphs. She had a mellow, sultry voice and both the beauty and the temperament to make Carmen credible. Stoki for his part conducted works of Debussy and Wagner.

The concert had been preceded by a considerable amount of ballyhoo, and an immense audience of over twenty thousand assembled. Stoki saw it as another triumph. California seemed to be offering rewards far greater than those he was getting in Philadelphia. And it was far more glamorous.

38

Garbo

O N Stokowski's forty-ninth birthday, April 18, 1931, he lunched
with the then eighty-year-old Alexander Van Rensselaer and they
talked about movies. Stoki admitted that he was a movie buff and
was particularly attracted to the new blonde beauty Greta Garbo.[1] She
had made eleven pictures in America, including her first talkie, *Anna
Christie*, which had been released in March 1930, and a second, *Romance*, which appeared in the fall of that year.

Garbo had become a phenomenon. Some called her the most beautiful
woman in the world. Her pictures had made her world famous. "Never
before has a woman so alluring, with a seductive grace that is far more
potent than mere beauty, appeared on the screen," wrote a critic in the
New York Herald Tribune after viewing *Flesh and the Devil*.[2]

Stoki, too, was struck by the seductiveness of the fabulous star. "Ah,
she is beautiful," he remarked to Mr. Van, "and I would like to meet her.
Perhaps I can if I go to Sweden after my travels in Spain. And Charlie
Chaplin—they are the two movie people I would like to meet."[3] Stoki and
Evangeline sailed for Spain a few days later but did not include Sweden
in their itinerary.

But Stoki did meet both Garbo and Chaplin. The meeting with the
great beauty occurred apparently in 1937, the year *The Big Broadcast of
1937* was released and he was working on *100 Men and a Girl*. Garbo
was then one of the most famous women in the world, and had become,
in the words of Alistair Cooke, "the unapproachable goddess of the most

widespread and remarkable mythology in human history."[4]

In 1937 *Camille* was released; it was hailed as one of her greatest triumphs. She then starred in *Conquest,* playing Countess Walewska to Charles Boyer's Napoleon, which was released November 4, 1937.

Report has it that Stoki and Garbo met at a small dinner party given by Anita Loos, the prominent screenwriter and author of the best-selling *Gentlemen Prefer Blondes.* I asked Anita about their first meeting. "Stokowski had it in mind to have an affair with Garbo and that's why he went to the coast," Miss Loos told me.

"Was it you who introduced them?" I asked.

"I was the one person he knew at MGM and I introduced him—not that I remember it at all. There was a certain group of us out there: Aldous Huxley, Christopher Isherwood—let me think who else—a group of high-powered intellectuals, and, of course, Stokowski belonged to it, and they met at my house at lunch on Sundays and she just happened to meet Stoki. So he joined the group and she belonged to the group. It didn't strike me as a romance because everybody was busy working and he was making film tests concerning sound. And then they ran away to Europe and I never saw them during that time. I guess if you read anything about it, it didn't last more than a few weeks," she said laughingly.[5]

On that score, Miss Loos was quite wrong. It was of much longer duration and, at least on Stoki's part, of considerable seriousness.

I had met Garbo on several occasions. The most memorable was at a party given by her good friend Alan Porter, of the Museum of Modern Art. Alan was color-blind and apparently red was one of the few colors, or perhaps the only color, he could distinguish. Alan's big living room, in a brownstone not far from the museum, was done in bright red and white. The party, if I recall, was in 1950 when Gian Carlo Menotti was working on *The Consul.* The feature of the evening was the appearance of the hypnotist Polgar, who was a fantastic memory expert and worker of quite astonishing tricks of psychic legerdemain. Sam Barber, Gian Carlo, and I shared the expense of engaging Polgar. Garbo arrived with George Schlee. I thought she was indeed the most beautiful woman I had ever seen. She was utterly charming and was fascinated by Polgar, who hypnotized some young subjects he had brought along and did some quite astonishing memory feats—seemingly able to quote the contents of several newspaper pages he had merely scanned.

A scene from Menotti's *Consul* was lifted directly out of that evening.

Gian Carlo had had a contract with one of the main Hollywood studios to do a straight dramatic picture and hoped to persuade Garbo to return to the screen. Nothing came of it however.

Garbo had taken an apartment on Fifty-second Street right at the East River and I had a penthouse a block away. Frequently, I would see her on the street, and occasionally in Gristede's market. But there was no recognition, and I did not try to intrude. One evening when Stoki had had dinner with me and a few friends, I walked with him to First Avenue to help him get a cab. Just as he stepped into the cab, and it began to pull away, a solitary figure approached. It was Garbo. But neither was aware of the other.

On the strength of our few meetings, and the intimate relationship with Stokowski many years ago, I wrote to Garbo to ask whether I might talk with her about her experiences with Stoki. "You'll never hear from her," said Anita Loos.[6] And she was right!

Before beginning his work on *100 Men and a Girl*, Stokowski had been invited to Japan. He and Evangeline had planned to take the trip together, but he preferred to stay and work in Hollywood instead. Evangeline decided to go alone and took both Lyuba and Sadja with her.[7] Lyuba was then ten and Sadja was six. While in Japan she bought some wonderful gongs. One in particular was built like a large soup cauldron mounted on a brilliant red lacquer stand. She wanted it for their Santa Barbara house, and it is still there.

The return from Japan aboard the *Tatsuta Maru* was as leisurely as their tour had been. When it docked in San Francisco on July 7, a group of reporters were at the dock to meet her. But Stoki was not there. Rumors of a possible divorce had been circulated and the scribes at once began to question Evangeline about it. "Just another of those rumors which, like daffodils, bloom every spring," she explained. Reporters observed that "quite undismayed too was the very tall, very slender Mrs. Stokowski at the failure of her famous husband to meet her at the dock. 'Look,' she said, 'I have a telegram from him.' It said something about 'my dear Evangeline . . . terribly sorry not to be able to meet you at the dock . . . shooting pictures every day this week . . . I've got a new car . . . the camp is also ready . . . will be waiting for you at L.A.' And maybe there was more but that told the story of the absent husband. Perhaps few wives have been as much at their ease laughing away divorce rumors as Mrs. Stokowski. Lighting a cigarette and sitting on the edge of a deck chair she enlarged on the Stokowski divorce trouble. 'It's absolutely silly. It's been going on for more than ten years. I was terribly upset once. But it's a joke now. I do often wonder, though, who starts those rumors. But let's not talk about it anymore,' concluded Mrs. Stokowski."[8]

Rumors about Stoki and Garbo frequently hit the press. They were probably subtly leaked by zealous publicists from MGM, Garbo's studio, and Universal, which was producing *100 Men and a Girl*. In August, pictures of both appeared in papers throughout the country. The story was speculative and wondered whether it was their mutual interest in music and cinema that brought them together. "Friends" supposedly pointed out that it could not be romance because Stoki motored a hundred miles to Santa Barbara each weekend to see his wife and children. "No one close to the two," the report continued, "denies any longer that they have been seeing each other, and often. The attitude now is, 'Certainly they see each other, so what?' On that point, the film colony's gossip corner is stumped."[9]

As the rumor mills continued to release stories linking Stoki and Garbo, Evangeline understandably became disturbed, especially because of the children. She told me that one day Lyuba came home from school and asked, "Who is Greta Garbo? Everybody at school says Daddy is having a romance with Greta Garbo."

Evangeline explained that naturally Stoki's interest was in Hollywood at that time and "he was hardly ever in the house in Santa Barbara. When he came home he was tired and irritable."

On one of their Santa Barbara weekends together, Evangeline talked to Stoki seriously: " 'Look, the children are going into adolescence and, in order to make a satisfactory heterosexual adjustment in the future, they've got to have, for at least a few years, a normal home life—a normal sort of family life.' Now, mind you," she told me, "I wasn't complaining, because he and I had agreed when we were first married that we could never be jealous of each other, and I never was jealous of him and he would never be jealous of me, and after all, I was twenty-eight years old and I said, 'I want to lead my own life and you want to lead yours.' But then this thing happened about the children. I said, 'We've got to stay out of the newspapers—we've got to for a few years at least.' And he said, 'I can't do it.' I remember the sentence, and I said, 'All right, honey, then we're going to get a divorce and if I find someone who would be a good stepfather to them and all, I'll marry him, and he'll help me bring up the children.' "[10]

The fall of 1937 was tempestuous. It was a time of unusual changes in the fate of musicians and institutions. Astrologers should have had a field day. But they didn't. The stars, however, if they did exert influence, bestirred things drastically. Stokowski was now co-conductor in Philadelphia, and Ormandy was engaged to conduct the bulk of the season—twenty-two weeks—with Stokowski conducting only six weeks. In New York John Barbirolli succeeded Toscanini as conductor of the New York Philharmonic.

In November Stoki was back in the Academy celebrating the twenty-fifth anniversary of his debut with the orchestra. He was presented with a gold-embossed set of "eulogistic resolutions" that were adopted by the board. Stoki accepted them warmly and remarked: "I am happy the board of directors have made some resolutions." The audience responded with roars of laughter. Aware that there had been much talk about his life in Hollywood and his liaison with Greta Garbo, he said somewhat defensively, "Sometimes, we work all night—the sun is coming up as we finish. Do you do that in Philadelphia?" The audience was utterly fascinated. "My feeling on this occasion is entirely friendly," he said. "The Association and I have had our disagreements and maybe we will in the future, but after all, that is only a matter of opinion. I'm very happy to be here, and I want to say that my interest will always be in Philadelphia. The fact that I spend some time away from you—Hollywood, for example,—does not imply that I have lost interest."[11]

No mention at the time was made of the fact that Mrs. Stokowski had taken up residence at the Boulder City Hotel near Las Vegas.[12] But there was much curiosity in Philadelphia. The editor of the *Inquirer* went so far as to contact her attorney, Roger Marchetti, of Los Angeles, who declined to discuss the reason for her move.[13]

The press continued to pursue Evangeline, but she was clever in avoiding them. On November 16 a dispatch from Reno reported that she was going horseback riding with her sister-in-law, Mrs. J. Seward Johnson, who was about to divorce her brother. It reported further that Evangeline had checked out of the Boulder City Hotel and had gone to Reno, where she would spend several days on a dude ranch.[14]

In Reno at this time was Sophie Yarnall Jacobs, who had known Stoki since she was ten and was also in the process of getting a divorce. "Suddenly there was Evangeline," said Sophie. "She had been in Las Vegas, and she flew up to see me and she told me why she was getting a divorce. . . ." Sophie agreed that her reasons were valid. "They were ready to get a divorce anyway."

Sophie reminisced about earlier days with Stoki. "I had seen him in Maine between his divorce from Olga and his marriage to Evangeline, and I had a lovely time with him up there in Northeast Harbor. I took him on mountains and in canoes, which he had never done. I had to pander to his masculine superiority by letting him think he could do stern paddling. It scared the daylights out of me. I had to do a good deal of cheating on that one. It was a beautiful moonlight night on the sound and he adored that. And that was the same night, I think, that we went up Beach Hill for the dawn and heard the hermit thrushes singing and this was a new experience to him. He loved that sort of thing.

"And then after he married Evangeline, I saw a lot of both of them. I had seen them down in Palm Beach with Lyuba and Sadja—her two children were about the same age as my two children. . . ."[15]

On the first of December Evangeline sued for divorce, alleging "extreme cruelty" as her reason.[16] Stoki did not contest the action but did file a protest denying the charge. According to reports in the press, Evangeline was to have custody of the children. This did distress Stoki, and he said he would like to correct two statements which emanated from Nevada. "When Mrs. Stokowski's legal advisors asked me to sign a property settlement some time ago," he said, "I was willing to sign it only if both she and I had equal joint custody of our children. . . . If her legal advisors have made the divorce contrary to the signed agreement, I shall take steps to make them keep that agreement. The other untrue statement is that I have been guilty of extreme cruelty. I could not be cruel to anyone, so I certainly could not be cruel to my children or their mother. I deeply resent this untrue accusation."

A reporter from the *Philadelphia Evening Bulletin* phoned Evangeline's lawyers in Los Angeles, and Mr. McNamee informed him that both parents would have equal custody of the children for equal parts of the year and that Mr. Stokowski must have been misinformed.[17]

Stoki's final concerts were on December 13 and 14. His program, at least on paper, was a rather odd one. In the first part he offered two new American works: *Music to a Ballet* by Robert McBride and William Grant Still's Symphony in G Minor. The second half was reminiscent of his organ recitals at St. Bart's. Linton Martin summed it up: "Stokowski achieved captivating contrast in the antique music which occupied the second part of the program—Bach's *Prelude and Fugue in E Minor* . . . two ancient liturgical melodies, Palestrina's *Adoramus te,* Byrd's *Pavane and Gigue,* Frescobaldi's *Gagliarda,* Bach's *Mein Jesu* and the lordly and magnificent *Passacaglia,* which closed the concert on a towering note of Gothic grandeur."

At the end of the concert the audience reacted ecstatically. Stokowski was recalled by the eager audience time after time; they were expecting an encore or some sort of farewell speech. But Stoki, who had surprised them for so many years with his observations and comments, had a different surprise for them. He said nothing. The reaction was one of disbelief.[18]

He had said that he was headed for California, but few in Philadelphia knew that he was actually going to Taos in New Mexico to spend ten days over Christmas and the New Year with Evangeline and the children. It is a great tribute to the spirits of both Leopold and Evangeline that they kept up a thoroughly amicable relationship for the rest of their lives.

The hiatus in Taos was pleasant. Evangeline told me once that she and Stoki had visited Taos many times to see their old friends Mabel Dodge Luhan and Tony. They had visited Zuni and the Navajo country as well as the Pueblos along the Rio Grande.[19]

A reporter, Spud Johnson, was inspired to literary heights in his report of the Stokowski doings in the *New Mexico Sentinel.* "Like royalty," he wrote, "the Stokowskis made official visits at the Holy Cross Hospital and sat in Mrs. Astor's box at important first-night performances in the new Taos Theatre; they went to teas and dinners, visited the slums, graced charity bazaars, went shopping, took bows from balconies, and drove through the public squares in open barouches acknowledging the cheers of their public. But, like the Duke of Windsor, H.R.H. Leopold seemed to be primarily interested in 'housing'—adobe construction, to be exact. He thinks he wants to build a mud house—maybe in New Mexico, maybe in Arizona. . . ." Spud Johnson must have been weaned on Lolly Parsons. The *Evening Bulletin* reprinted excerpts for the titillated Stoki followers in Philadelphia on January 25. It also reported that Greta Garbo was in Sweden by the time Leopold had arrived in Taos.[20]

Evangeline, like Edward Bok, often called Stoki "Prince." Now, three days after the previous bit of gossip had been printed, Philadelphians learned that a real prince had entered the scenario. On January 27, in Phoenix, Evangeline married her new husband, the former Prince Alexis Zalstem-Zalessky of Russia. Louella Parsons, the *Philadelphia Inquirer's* Hollywood correspondent, wrote in a special dispatch: "Now that Mrs. Stokowski herself has married, there is nothing to keep Garbo and the orchestra leader apart."[21]

Stokowski's plans were definite. He had booked a reservation on the *Conte di Savoia* as early as the third of January. Reggie Allen was left to conclude and coordinate all the details. The ship was to sail on February 5, and Stoki had wanted to board it the night before to avoid being seen before sailing. That could not be arranged so his ticket was purchased in the name of "Allen." Reggie wrote to Stoki: "The present plan is that you go on board at the rush hour, probably around 10:30. You would be wearing something like tortoise shell glasses and a hat which, together with a heavy overcoat and a muffler would, I feel sure, prevent identification. . . . I would go down, along with your luggage tagged as mine and would go through the ticket inspection formalities at the gang-plank."

Allen was meticulous. He deliberately did not even tell the officers of the Italian Line that Stokowski would actually be on the ship until the last minute, so that there would not be any leak to the press. He arranged for Stoki to be taken from the train at Paoli and driven to New York by Marshall Betz "to the small house of my friends, where there will be complete seclusion not possible in an apartment or hotel. . . . We shall have dinner and do whatever is thought advisable in the evening, and get on the boat the following morning."[22]

The plans worked almost perfectly. A few minutes before the ship was to sail a hatted figure dashed up the gangplank, followed by two porters carrying luggage. He handed his ticket with the name "A. R. Allen" and his own passport. "Are you Stokowski?" the ship's officer asked. "I am Stokowski," he answered.[23]

The *Conte di Savoia* docked in Naples on the twelfth of February and, after his car was unloaded, Stoki drove to the town of Ravello. There he rented the Villa Cimbrone for a month. Garbo arrived in Rome on the twenty-fourth and was driven by Stoki to Ravello the following day. Although they went to great lengths to conceal their identities, they did not succeed. Having to present their passports to the town's mayor, the little man could not contain himself, and soon the whole village was aware of the glamorous visitors. Even in Ravello everyone knew of Garbo. Many, too, had seen *100 Men and a Girl*. Villagers began to crowd around the gates of the villa. Autograph fiends rushed to Ravello from the surrounding towns in any vehicle that was available. When the news reached Naples, the reporters, the paparazzi, and the generally curious also rushed to the scene. Finally four carabinieri and three police dogs were posted at the gate to prevent the enthusiastic mob from breaking into the gardens.

United Press International Photo
Greta Garbo and Charles Boyer in *Conquest* (1937)

The villagers had dubbed Garbo *La Donna Misteriosa* with as much affection as curiosity. At one point Garbo was heard ordering the servants to have a doctor handy "in case someone was hurt." When Stoki went to the Hotel Caruso to accept a long-distance call from Philadelphia, he was cornered by a host of reporters. "I never talk about personal things," he said as they plied him with questions concerning his relationship with Garbo.[24]

But they were news and MGM publicists ground out a continual flow of stories about their romance. It would help to publicize her latest release, *Conquest,* which had, as yet, not made an impressive profit. They brought names of other MGM stars into the act. A story appeared that Wallace Beery had arrived in Naples and hurried to the Villa Cimbrone to discuss the wedding. He was to be the best man. Reports were issued that Garbo and Stoki planned to make a dash for Turin and the altar on March 15. The Rome office of MGM was quoted as saying the marriage would take place at the scenic town of Taormina, almost within the shadow of Mount Etna, on the east coast of Sicily. It even added that the marriage would take place "on the crest of a hill, 650 feet high." In London, Clarence Brown, who directed Garbo in *Conquest* and other earlier pictures, was quoted as saying he was "certain that the wedding bells would ring soon."[25]

Although they were practically prisoners in the villa, they did manage to drive to Sorrento and there take a boat to Capri, where they visited the Blue Grotto and later had tea with the Swedish author Dr. Axel Munthe. Munthe was contacted by the persistent press to know whether his visitor had actually been Garbo. Munthe confirmed that it was Garbo and added that "she was accompanied by a gentleman named Stokowski, whom I do not know but he looked like a Pole."

A cabled report to the *Philadelphia Inquirer* stated that on their return from Capri "the crowd which waited outside their villa to greet them was an Italian version of a Hollywood opening." It observed too that "the pending Anglo-Italian conversations and Adolf Hitler's proposed visit to Rome were completely in the shade (95 degrees) when the news of Garbo's presence spread. . . . All international news was wiped off the front pages of the Italian press by the stories of the Garbo-Stokowski romance."[26]

Finally Stoki and Garbo decided to strike a truce with the photographers and the reporters. In return for a promise to let them live in peace, they agreed to give interviews with the press. They assembled in the library of the old villa. Stoki appeared first and rather curtly denied that they had any plans of marriage, and he made a plea to the curious to let them in peace "so that Miss Garbo can see something of Italy—at least more than I can see from my window." Then he abruptly left the room.

Garbo entered a few moments later dressed in a royal blue gabardine suit, a Norfolk jacket, yellow sweater and blue scarf. She spoke rather wistfully about her holiday in this romantic seacoast retreat with Stokowski and said: "I wanted to see some of the beautiful things of life with my friend Mr. Stokowski who has been very much to me. He has seen so much and knows about the beauty of life and offered to take me and show me these things. I optimistically accepted. I was naive to think we could travel without being discovered. This kills beauty for me." She said she

Stokowski and Garbo in Italy (1938)

was alarmed about the cruel events happening in the world and that she wanted to see things of beauty before they disappeared. She complained bitterly that, because of the curious, she had been able to see so little. "I wish I could be otherwise," she said, "but I cannot." Then after a pause added: "I only want to be let alone."[27]

On the twenty-second of March the couple visited Pompeii en route to Naples, thence to Rome. In Rome they completely succeeded in eluding the press and "all efforts to locate them were fruitless." There were reports that they had gone to Morocco, Tunisia and other North African spots.[28]

They did not burst into the headlines again until the end of June. On the twenty-seventh the UP wires carried the word that both Garbo and Stoki were badly shaken up when their car, driven by Stoki, overturned near Soedertaelje about thirty miles south of Stockholm. Drivers of passing cars stopped and helped Leopold right the car and get it back on the road. Garbo and Stoki had scrambled out of the upturned vehicle, frightened but unhurt.[29] They then proceeded to Garbo's country estate, which she had acquired two years earlier. It was a large, white, rather formal-looking house called Hårby, on Lake Siljan, south of Stockholm. There behind a large sign reading "ABSOLUTELY PRIVATE" they found the isolation they had so eagerly sought.[30]

On their way north, Stoki found time in Paris to have a brief visit with Alexandre Gretchaninoff, who had written to him in the spring telling him that he had just completed his Fifth Symphony. Stoki had responded by cable that he would visit him in May. "He kept his promise," said Gretchaninoff, "and came to see me. I played the score for him, and he took it with him to Sweden. . . . He wrote me from Sweden that he was passing through Paris on his way to America, and gave me an appointment for August 4, 'pour parler encore de votre belle symphonie.' He faithfully kept his appointment, and again expressed his enthusiasm for the work."[31] His enthusiasm for the symphony was genuine and he gave it its world premiere in Philadelphia on April 5, 1939. The composer, unfortunately, was not able to be present.

Either before or after going to Paris, Stoki visited his mother in England. In a *Chicago Tribune* dispatch dated London, August 10, we read: "Leopold Stokowski departed for New York today after a week's secret visit to his mother in England, but the conductor was without Greta Garbo, movie star, who had been his companion almost constantly since February."[32] This was one of the rare times I have come across mention in the press of the existence of his mother. And it is interesting to note that it was described as a "secret" visit.

In mid-July Stoki penned two letters from Gnesta, Sweden. One was to Reggie Allen and another to Sibelius. His letter to Sibelius was virtually a fan letter:

                                                    Gnesta, Sweden
Dear Mr. Sibelius

   I am thinking of you every day and sending you thoughts of
affection—I am often with you in *spirit*—I shall always remember
the day I spent with you—I would go to Helsinki to see you but I
fear to disturb you—please give my greetings to your daughter—I
have had so many wonderful experiences in the world of your music
—such deep revelation
   Sincerely and (may I say it?—) with Friendship

                                             Leopold Stokowski[33]

To Reggie Allen he wrote:

                                                    Gnesta, Sweden
Dear Mr. Allen

   I hope to arrive NY the 15th August on the Normandie—Mr.
Thibaud (son of the violinist) is arranging it for me in Paris—on
arriving in NY I shall see the newspaper men (if they wish) in my
room—but do not wish to have my photograph in the newspapers—
can I leave the ship by an unexpected exit? can I do the customs in
a darkish place so they cannot photograph? and can I leave the dock
by an unexpected exit? will Andrea Berens be in NY then? I hope
I may see her. I shall come alone—and stay 3 days in Philadelphia
—I should like to begin the Walkure music 17 bars earlier—would
you mind asking Mr. Cailliet to copy from the place—

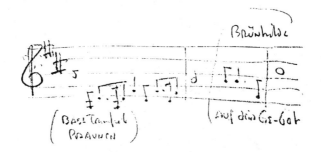

Can you give me this in NY?

                                          With friendliest greetings
                                          Leopold Stokowski[34]

   When the *Normandie* arrived in New York, the reporters were there
in droves. Reggie Allen had gone out by launch and met the boat in

quarantine. At the dock, Henry Pleasants, who had a rather favored status, was first to come to the stateroom, where Allen answered each rap on the door while Stoki stood in the background saying, "No photographers please." Pleasants reported in the *Bulletin* that Stoki answered all questions about Garbo with the stock phrase: "I never discuss my personal affairs."

On other subjects he was more open. He told of visiting Lapland and studying the music of the Lapps. He also said that he had brought back several new scores of Arabian music that he had picked up in Algiers and Morocco.[35]

Stoki and Reggie Allen left for Philadelphia and, in his little studio apartment, they worked out the schedule for Stoki's appearances with the orchestra later in the season and some plans about Garbo's return to California. He then proceeded to New Milford, Connecticut, to see Evangeline, her prince, and Stoki's daughters. As one of New Milford's most famous former citizens, he was invited to conduct a brass band in celebration of New Milford's "Old Home Day." He postponed his departure for a day and led the twenty-five-piece band from nearby Torrington and his fellow New Milford citizens in a rousing performance of the "Star Spangled Banner."[36] Then on to Hollywood.

One reads in a biography of Garbo that after his return he never saw her again.[37] Not so! He remained deeply concerned about her and contrived to make her return to Hollywood as painlessly free from interference as possible. He had discussed it with Allen extensively, and from California he wrote to him: "I have not yet heard when our passenger arrives. I will wire you as soon as I know." He explored the various possibilities of having the "passenger" taken off the train before it arrived in Chicago and boarding again shortly after leaving. "As soon as I hear your opinion about all this," he wrote, "we can make more definite arrangements."[38]

As always, Reggie Allen was meticulous in his arrangements. "All plans are under control," he wrote to Stoki, who was then in his terra-cotta-colored retreat in Beverly Hills. He had arranged with officials of the Swedish-American Line and with customs men so that the visitor could leave by a separate exit. He obtained a cutter pass so that he could board the ship before it docked and had three passes "so that I can take care of Mr. Hammond if he wants me to. . . ." He also made arrangements for the Broadway Limited to be stopped at Gary and for the Chief to be stopped at Joliet so that Garbo could bypass Chicago completely. Not even royalty was given more consideration. "There will be no hitch," he added confidently.[39]

But it was not quite so simple. The Mr. Hammond whom Reggie had mentioned in his letter was Richard Hammond of the famous Hammond family. Dick was a composer, a onetime student of Nadia Boulanger, and, above all, a close friend of Stokowski. Stoki had suggested that Dick join Reggie Allen and together they meet the boat.

"I met Miss Garbo in her stateroom," Reggie recalled, "and after some argument with her, I counseled her strongly not to avoid the press. . . . And she did go up and talk to the press. Then she came down and gave me all her baggage checks . . . a perfectly enormous number. There were so many bags that I had two officials checking them. One man had opened a case that contained nothing but shoes . . . suddenly I heard him say, 'Why this ain't so big!' I turned around and he was holding one of Garbo's shoes in his hand just like Hamlet with the skull in the graveyard scene. But getting her off the pier was quite something because the fans were waiting in chartered taxicabs and we had to devise some ruse. A motion picture newsreel car was down on the lowest level and she was sneaked into it while I and some big shots from the Swedish embassy and some ladies went down the gangplank into a big limousine that belonged to the consul. And then they descended on us! Unfortunately, they also spotted the newsreel car. We tore down the West Side Highway and luckily the consul's car managed to run interference by getting directly behind the newsreel car. When we came to a red light, it stopped, blocking the street. One of the taxicabs simply cut across it and took a fender off . . . and that ended the chase and she got away scot-free. . . ."[40]

Expecting Garbo to be driven uptown in comfort, Dick Hammond had rented a limousine. But instead it was her luggage that was driven up in style to Hammond's spacious apartment on West Fifty-fifth Street. "She stayed a couple of weeks with me there and we would go out to the theater and things like that," Dick recalled. "She had that floppy hat that she pulled down and she would pull her hair back and we would go in after dark. She couldn't make up her mind to go back to California. You know how she is. And so I said, 'Would you like to come up to the country?' And she said, 'Yes, I'd love it.' So we got a drawing room on the *Merchants Limited* and we went up to Gloucester. Nobody knew where she was. Walter Winchell was guessing all over. She stayed in Gloucester about a week and then went back to New York. Poor Reggie Allen was getting a drawing room on every train out of New York. But she couldn't make up her mind to go. Then finally she went back to California and we saw her there."[41]

From Beverly Hills Stoki wrote to Reggie Allen: "Thank you for arranging everything so perfectly. . . . I am deeply indebted to you for all the trouble and thought you have given to this."[42]

He was busily working with Disney on plans for *Fantasia*. He wrote to Sylvan Levin asking him to look for a contralto to sing Schubert's "Ave Maria." He wanted "someone with a large voice—no vibrato and who would be flexible in rhythm in the way that you and I are flexible."[43]

Keenly interested in the connection of electronics and music, he motored up to San Francisco to attend some displays of electronic instruments at the Golden Gate International Exposition. Cornered in the lobby of the Mark Hopkins Hotel, he exasperated reporters by being as vague and secretive as Garbo ever was. Reference was made to an electric orchestra but he refused to elaborate.[44]

"No pictures, no publicity. Please!" he said dramatically. "I will answer two questions. Am I making a picture in Hollywood? Yes. Am I leaving the Philadelphia Symphony? No. That is two—but what more? Ah, Garbo—I never discuss personal matters."[45]

The only time I ever remember Stoki speaking of Garbo was during a 1969 interview over BBC with Basil Moss:

"Was she the enigmatic person that we're led to believe over here?"
"Yes."
"A lot of people said she was really rather dull. Was that true?"
"Oh no—great imagination and great humor."[46]

(39)

Transition

THE 1938–39 season was one of transition. Stokowski was then at the
height of his fame. His escapade with Garbo had given him world-
wide attention. His involvement in the film colony was also a source
of enormous public interest. In January Walt Disney announced that he
had signed him to conduct a forthcoming Disney concert feature.[1] The
feature, of course, was *Fantasia*. Stokowski saw this as the beginning of
an entirely new career. Philadelphia be damned.

Invitations to guest conduct were pouring in. In February he conducted
in San Francisco. Perceptive critic Alfred Frankenstein observed that
"Leopold Stokowski honored San Francisco with the world premiere of
one of his most gorgeous arrangements. . . . It was his recent revision of
Mussorgsky's *Night on Bald Mountain* which henceforth takes on a new
stature and a new significance."[2]

After a fifteen-month absence Stoki returned to Philadelphia for a
mere three weeks with the orchestra. His first concert on March 17,
1939, included works of Bach, Brahms, Wagner, and Shostakovich.
When he stepped out onto the stage both the orchestra and the capacity audience rose in a spontaneous tribute. "Leopold Stokowski came
back to Philadelphia yesterday. And, by the same token, the Philadelphia Orchestra came back yesterday," wrote Linton Martin in the *Inquirer.* Ormandy must have winced at reading this. But there was much
more to come, all in the same vein. "The orchestra has not played with
such splendor and sonority of tone, such voluptuous beauty, glowing

brilliance of colors, shimmering pianissimi, intensity and electrifying effect of inspiration since the symphonic sorcerer departed a year ago . . . to see about the sorcerer's apprentice. But there was no apprentice business about the return trip yesterday. It was the symphonic sorcerer himself."[3]

In New York the reaction was the same. In the *Sun* Oscar Thompson wrote: "The basic sound was sensuous and sumptuous. Here, unmistakably were the well-remembered Stokowski sonorities; neither the conductor nor the orchestra could have been any other in the world." Miles Kastendieck opined: "The musicians responded as of old to his feeling for dramatic intensity with the result that the violins had the peculiar sheen present, it would seem, only when Stokowski is there to draw it forth. . . . For marked orchestral sonority it would be hard to rival."

If these invidious comparisons caused any wounds, salt was deftly added when the management decided to print them in the orchestra's program book.

Ormandy had not only inherited a new title but new headaches as well. On March 30 during Stoki's stint with the orchestra, Reggie Allen suddenly resigned. Unrelated to Allen's resignation came the resignations of two of the best-known members of the orchestra. They were Louis Gabowitz, a thirty-one-year-old first violinist, and Albert Godlis, a twenty-eight-year-old trombonist, who had been a Stokowski protégé.[4] Gabowitz insisted that he resigned because he missed the "great inspiration and high artistic standards of Dr. Stokowski."[5] He added, "I believe that since Stokowski has withdrawn his active participation, the high standards that he set have not been maintained."

Other members of the orchestra were highly critical of Ormandy for having dismissed his first cellist, Isadore Gusikoff, who declared that the real reason for his dismissal was Ormandy's resentment "because he felt that I didn't play for him as well as I played for others."[6] Ormandy said it was because of insubordination.[7]

Members of the orchestra were interviewed backstage and many voiced their resentment. "Things aren't like they used to be," they maintained and added that the morale of the orchestra was "shot." They declared that the dismissal of Gusikoff was an "example of Ormandy's 'pique' and said the personal feelings of the conductor should not have been allowed to interfere with the good of the orchestra."[8]

Stoki did his best to ameliorate the troubled atmosphere and, a few hours after Allen's resignation had been accepted, he addressed his Friday afternoon audience, which had just given him an ovation. He said that he had found it difficult to conduct because of the "disturbing influences," and added that the men of the orchestra probably had the same trouble. He strongly defended Ormandy and the spirit of the orchestra: "I want to tell you that from the very first note of the very first rehearsal I conducted three weeks ago the men played magnificently. This means they have done wonderful work to keep up the high standards of the orchestra. They have never played better than now.

"If Philadelphia is solidly behind them, if certain disturbing and destroying influences stop, the orchestra will reach even higher levels. If I can help, I will be happy to do so."9

Stoki's tribute to Ormandy set off a chain of events. The players met immediately after the concert and drafted a statement prepared by their own committee: "The recent statements by resigned members . . . express their personal opinions only, and in no way reflect the feeling of the orchestra. We deplore deeply the attacks on Mr. Ormandy." The board also issued a statement declaring that it stood beside Mr. Stokowski "in reassuring Philadelphia of the unity of feeling and purpose that exists within the organization. . . ."10

Thanks to Stoki's force and generosity the clouds of doubt were dispersed and Ormandy plodded on for another forty years. There was a move at the time to persuade Stokowski to return and again assume the post of co-conductor with Ormandy, and conduct half the season. "I won't have anything to say about it now," he told the press. "Maybe I'll tell you at the end of the week."11

After lengthy conversations with Allen he signed a contract to return in November. Then after conducting another of his favorite children's concerts he remained in Philadelphia for the next three weeks in order to complete the recording of the score for Fantasia.

At this time of turmoil and distraction for both Stokowski and the Philadelphia Orchestra, a number of recording sessions were scheduled. One of the works selected for a session of April 9, 1939, was a recording of Debussy's Sirènes which was to be used to make up the first complete American recording of his Nocturnes: Nuages, Fêtes, Sirènes.

Gunther Schuller, well-known composer-conductor, was a fifteen-year-old horn player and devotee of Stokowski's Philadelphia Orchestra recordings. When the Debussy recording was released, he was amazed to note during the playing of the *Sirènes* that a couple of short sections for the horns sounded Schoenbergian rather than Debussyan.

This was one of the few times, and perhaps the only time during a recording session, when Stokowski's rehearsal technique failed. Normally he would run through unfamiliar works a number of times without comment and allow players to correct mistakes. Apparently in this instance the horn parts were incorrect and players as well as recording personnel were fearful of informing the Maestro when he didn't pick up the errors himself during the rehearsals. Musicians had been fired for less than that in the past.[12]

Stokowski then set out for Europe. He told Henry Pleasants that he planned to visit England, France, Sweden, and Norway, and possibly Germany and Italy. He said he had plans to conduct in Europe but was slightly vague about them.[13] We do know that he conducted in Stockholm. There was no mention of Garbo's being there at the time. The concert took place on May 25 and an AP release stated that he received homage from a packed concert hall, but Stockholm critics—reputed to be Europe's most rigid—were not so enthusiastic. However, the public was delighted; it included King Gustav V and several other members of the royal family.[14]

Stopping briefly in Philadelphia before going on to California, Stoki took time to discuss some of his European experiences. "European audiences are most extraordinary," he said. "Even in the Scandinavian countries, which I had been told were so cold and reserved, I found them immensely receptive and at the end of the concerts they were explosive. It was the kind of thing one would expect of Italians and Spaniards."[15]

Only ten days had passed since England and France had declared war on Germany. All was very quiet on the eastern front and everyone seemed convinced of the impregnability of the Maginot line. French magazines proudly displayed pictures of *"Nos Grands Chefs"* festooned with their gold braid and their medals. There were photos of endless stacks of bombs in block-long rows many tiers high, and photos of countless land mines that were guaranteed to protect France from any invasion.

When asked to comment on the threatening, still slight rumbles of war from the German side, Stoki disclaimed any knowledge of politics and things military. He did, however, share some of the euphoric confidence that permeated France. He said that he was "immediately conscious of an alert spirit in the citizens, especially in France. There was in the atmosphere there, something so heroic and at the same time so simple and human that I could not help but admire it. They have an attitude of being prepared to face anything, being alive to life and buoyed up to a profound hope that nothing will happen to disturb them.

"I had the most wonderful orchestra in Paris. It is a new organization composed of most talented young players from 18 years upward, and many of them were truly remarkable artists. It is a superb orchestra."

Stoki explained that the concerts in Paris were held in the new Chaillot Hall, and he said that he had built for the stage an acoustical reflector similar to the one which he had designed for the Academy of Music.[16]

In San Francisco Stoki again led the local orchestra in a concert in the California Coliseum. An audience of over ten thousand had gathered. It was all part of the fair, which was dominating San Francisco's life. "It was the sort of playing that boots your emotional temperature higher than a kite, even if, like me, you find the sputterings, ardors and deliriums of Tchaikovsky fairly shallow stuff," wrote Alfred Frankenstein. "This was, beyond question, one of the greatest peaks of virtuoso orchestral playing this or any other community has had the privilege of experiencing."[17]

Then back to Los Angeles, where he gave his services to conduct a mammoth concert for Polish relief. Rose Bampton and Nelson Eddy were among the soloists with a one-hundred piece orchestra.[18] As a tribute to his neighbor Arnold Schoenberg, Stoki programmed a part of the Gurrelieder, the "Song of the Wood Dove." It was a Bampton special. "We had the first rehearsal last night of the Waldtaube," he wrote to Schoenberg. "I was profoundly impressed with the power and imaginative beauty of this great music. It is several years since I last conducted it, and I am absolutely certain it is immortal. It must be a wonderful experience to you to have created something which is beyond question a work of genius."[19]

Stoki invited the Schoenbergs to attend the concert and after initial reluctance they did attend. At the conclusion of the "Wood Dove" the applause was tremendous. But Stoki stopped it and in a little speech asked the audience not to applaud him, Miss Bampton, and the orchestra, but to give their applause to the composer. It was one of the rare times that Schoenberg received a spontaneous ovation. "It was grand of you to speak to the audience to shift the applause you deserved to me. . . ." Schoenberg wrote appreciatively. "Now let me thank you for your great performance. *Wood Dove* came out wonderfully: Rose Bampton's voice is a miracle and how marvelous the sound of the orchestra was. . . ." He then paid Stokowski a beautiful compliment and congratulated him on his orchestration of Debussy's "Clair de Lune." "Frankly—and this seems better than a compliment—I thought it was an original of Debussy and only learned through Mr. Hilsberg, that the orchestration was yours."[20]

During the month of November he brought a few novelties for his programs in Philadelphia. One, however, was a thoughtful gesture. He included "Two Evening Pictures: The Mission and Fiesta" from a suite called *San Juan Capistrano* by the orchestra's new manager, Harl McDonald. But he needed no programmatic surprises. He had an even greater one to throw the orchestra, the audience, and the critics into a state of perturbation. He again rearranged the seating of the orchestra. This time it was the most radical change of all. The woodwinds were grouped directly in front of him flanked by trumpets, trombones, and horns on either side. Massed behind the woodwinds were the strings with double basses, on risers, stretched along the entire back of the stage.[21] Stoki had reasoned that the reflecting surface of the back and sides of the shell would reinforce the weaker instruments while those in front would not benefit from such amplification. One critic called it a "flop" while others were content to listen longer and judge later.[22] It could not have been too far off Stokowski's acoustic target.

During the second week of his three weeks' sojourn, he introduced his transcription of Mussorgsky's *Pictures at an Exhibition*. Linton Martin observed that the audiences had long been familiar with two of the five previous orchestral versions, "those of Maurice Ravel and Lucien Cailliet." It is an important observation since it contradicts assertions made by some that the arrangement had been done by Cailliet and not by Stokowski. The two are very different.[23]

After his last concert with the orchestra Stokowski stopped in Washington, where he made a formal announcement that was carried by the wire services throughout the world. "Leopold Stokowski . . . said today he has accepted an invitation of Latin American republics to conduct an all-American symphony orchestra on tour next spring and summer. The itinerary was not announced."[24]

40

Fantasia

A MONG Stokowski's listeners during his Los Angeles concerts was Walt Disney. He was considerably awed by Stokowski and had in the back of his mind the idea that perhaps they could collaborate on something. The "Silly Symphonies" Disney had produced were a far cry from the symphonies Stoki conducted, but Disney had begun to take himself ever more seriously as an artist and he was beginning to make great plans.

Always interested in the synchronization of cartoons with music, Disney completed his first "Silly Symphony" in 1929. It was called *The Skeleton Dance.* During the next ten years he made over seventy "Sillies." These were followed by such delightful classics as *The Three Little Pigs, The Tortoise and the Hare, The Grasshopper and the Ants* and many more.

While working on his first full-length cartoon film, *Snow White and the Seven Dwarfs,* Walt began to toy with the idea of doing a film using classical music, but one that had an implied story. Someone suggested *The Sorcerer's Apprentice* and Disney became immediately taken with the idea. He also began to think about the possibility of involving Stokowski.[1] Then a fortuitous meeting occurred.

"One night I was in California and I had dinner in a restaurant," Stoki recalled, "and a man walked in and looked at me and came over and said, 'I'm Walt Disney. May I talk with you?' So I said, 'Yes, of course.' And we sat down and talked. He said, 'I have the idea of Dukas' *The Sorcerer's*

Apprentice. I would like to make a short. Would you like to do the music and I'll do the pictorial part?' "[2]

Stoki assured Disney that he would be most happy to collaborate with him, and confirmed as much to Walt's eastern representative, who encountered Stoki on a train while they were speeding back to New York. Disney's man reported that Stoki "is really serious in his offer to do the music for nothing. . . . I found him to be a very charming person and not at all the 'prima donna' that various publicity stories have made him out to be."

Disney was obviously pleased with this information and on October 26, 1937, replied: "I am all steamed up over the idea of Stokowski working with us. . . . I feel that the possibilities of such a combination are so great that we could stretch a point and use his hundred men as well as work out an arrangement to compensate him, personally, for his time—and we could well afford to record the music in any manner Stokowski would want to do it. . . . I am greatly enthused over the idea and believe that the union of Stokowski and his music, together with the best of our medium, would be the means of a great success and should lead to a new style of motion picture presentation."

Stoki was quick to respond: "I am thrilled at the idea of recording *The Sorcerer's Apprentice* with you, because you have no more enthusiastic admirer in the world than I am."

Disney had his animators start work at once and by the middle of November he sent an outline with some visualizations to Stoki saying, "Honestly, I have never been more enthused over anything in my life, and let me say we are anxiously awaiting your arrival here."[3]

I do not know exactly what Stoki expected. He seems to have been jolted slightly by the idea of Mickey Mouse playing the stellar role. After his experience in *100 Men and a Girl* he perhaps saw himself playing the role of Leopold Stokowski but not of second banana, or to put it in more musical terms, second fiddle to the ogling little rodent.

"May I make a suggestion, which perhaps is entirely impractical or does not fit into your other ideas?" wrote Stoki in reply. "What would you think of creating an entirely new personality for this film instead of Mickey? A personality which could represent you and me—in other words, someone that would represent in the mind and heart of everyone seeing the film their own personality, so they would enter into all the drama and emotional changes of the film in a most intense manner. You may have strong reasons for wishing Mickey to be the hero. But it seems to me in looking ahead into the future, there may be many films that you might wish to make with interesting, highly colored, emotional music background and it might be well to create one or more new characters so as to enlarge the range of characterization. It seems to me that one of the most potent factors in the world-wide popularity of films is that the onlooker enters personally into the story and puts himself or herself in the place of the hero or heroine, and by doing so feels every moment of the drama. That is why I feel that if you create a new personality which represents every one of us it might be a valuable factor in the years to come, and enlarge the scope. This is merely a suggestion, which, of course, discard immediately if it does not interest you."[4]

It certainly did not interest Disney and he certainly had no intention of scrapping his favorite little character. The suggestion was merely ignored.

Early in January Stoki returned to California and after some preliminary conferences the first recording session was set up in the big Selznick Studio and a hundred-piece orchestra of top symphony and studio players was assembled. The recording was to be made directly on film and was recorded in six-track stereo.

Bill Garity, who was the chief engineer of the Disney operations, was in charge of the recording session. It began at midnight on January 9 and went on until the early morning hours. The musicians were all highly trained men, but the arrangement of the orchestra, which so completely separated the various sections, made it difficult to keep the orchestra playing together. Garity kept a diary and in it he wrote: "I was very disappointed in the overall results of the session. . . . Due to the isolation of the seven choirs of the orchestra, it was difficult to keep the orchestra playing together . . . at 3:05 (AM) we went into overtime period without having completed the recording of the four sections, nor did we get a complete rehearsal of the entire number."

The music was rerecorded at the RCA studios, but it was the initial takes at the Selznick Studio that were used. When they scheduled a session to film Stokowski conducting, playing in silhouette, the whole session had to be postponed for a week because Stoki's carefully tailored tails had not arrived.

The perfectionist Garity was not satisfied and after the final rerecording of the track on the stage, found the overall "pretty bad." He felt that it was due "to the fact that the six sound tracks were not accurately registered in synchronism to within plus or minus a few thousandths of an inch, and at the moment I don't see how we could synchronize them any more accurately than we have done. . . . Of course," Garity continued, "the easiest way out of it all would be to do the damn thing over again, which I had the temerity to suggest to Walt with the result that my left ear was hanging by a thread."

Stokowski was not distressed. He wisely knew that when the music would be heard in the large space of an auditorium with banks of speakers coming from all directions, it would sound perfectly synchronized. To Disney's relief, Stoki happily okayed it.

When it was finished Disney realized that it had cost three or four times what any previous "Silly Symphony" had cost and there were serious doubts about ever recouping the amount invested. It was at this point that Walt decided to discuss with Stoki the possibility of expanding the idea into a concert project by adding many additional segments. Stoki was naturally enthusiastic and they immediately made plans to turn the modest beginning into a major project which for the time being was called the "Concert Feature."[5]

The idea of drawing Deems Taylor into the picture was made as soon as the idea of making a "Concert Feature" was born. It was logical. At the time Taylor was one of the best-known American composers and a most popular figure on radio, for he supplied the intermission spot on the broadcasts of the New York Philharmonic. His commentaries were witty, informative, and in general most engaging. He also had the unique distinction of being the only American composer to have been commissioned to write an opera for the Metropolitan, not once but twice. The first was *The King's Henchman* based on a libretto by Edna St. Vincent Millay in 1927; the second was based on George Du Maurier's *Peter Ibbetson* and was brought out in 1931.

Early in September Stoki returned to Hollywood with Deems Taylor, and they immediately set up a series of meetings with Walt Disney and a group of his executive aides. The sessions were long, sometimes fruitful, but more often futile and frustrating. It had been decided that Deems would act as a sort of master of ceremonies or, perhaps more rightly, as a one-man Greek chorus to explain the music and other matters—an animated program note.

Meetings began early in September and ran on through the entire month. Much of the time was taken up in playing records of pieces that might be used; the Bach Toccata and Fugue in D Minor and the "Little" Fugue in G Minor were among the first to be given serious attention.

With Walt Disney (c. 1940)

Stoki favored doing the "Little" Fugue because of its brevity. Walt suggested during one meeting that they "cut the tail end of the Toccata and Fugue." Stoki's reply: "Over my dead body!" But the Toccata and Fugue was agreed upon and Walt was happy with it. As he said, ". . . it's going to give a marvelous send-off . . . we can work our abstractions in there. Let the sound form its own pictures and weave them in. . . ."[6]

The next work that was definitely agreed upon was the *Nutcracker* Suite, and it turned out to be one of the most felicitous of choices. Other works discussed and played were the "Ride of the Valkyries" and the "Magic Fire Music" of Wagner; Stravinsky's *Petrouchka, Renard, Firebird,* and finally the *Rite of Spring;* Mussorgsky's *Night on Bald Mountain;* Schubert's "Ave Maria" and "Serenade."

Stoki suggested having a pianist; perhaps Rachmaninoff or Paderewski, "who is the greatest," or Josef Hofmann. They played the Second Piano Concerto of Rachmaninoff and some piano pieces.[7] "In case Rachmaninoff won't do this—he's very peculiar, a very nice man, but a very strange one—we might get Horowitz. He is marvelous," said Stoki. One of the Disney crew remarked that Horowitz was not known to the general public.

"I don't know anything about music," admitted Walt, "but I have heard of Rachmaninoff for a long time."

"He is very peculiar," Stoki reiterated. "He might not want to do it. He is very hard to persuade. If he doesn't want to do something, he doesn't want to do it. Paderewski played over the radio yesterday for the first time in his life. Rachmaninoff has never played over the radio. I've tried over and over again to persuade him, but he won't do it. If Paderewski is already playing over the radio, we might be able to have him play something for our picture. We could record him in Europe."

The idea of using a pianist was rather quickly abandoned. Singers then became the principal topic of discussion. Lawrence Tibbett, who had appeared in several films, and John Charles Thomas were the two in the male contingent. Marian Anderson was suggested for "Deep River." "How about Rose Bampton?" asked Walt.

"She is a marvelous singer," said Stoki, "she has a beautiful voice. If you have two singers, have that girl and then have a man's voice. Bampton has the same type voice as Anderson."[8]

The discussions went on and on. During one of the sessions, Walt said, "I'm looking for a place to use the devil who is supposed to play the violin. You might build a beautiful thing based on the devil's orchestra. We could even bring in the devil's organ, using a sort of 'inferno' idea. . . . We might have a lot of these little devils playing instruments, with the one big devil conducting. . . ."

"We might let Nature be the source of all this music," countered Deems, "boiling cauldrons of volcanos, escaping steam and such things that could be represented musically."

"We might work *Bald Mountain* in with this idea of the devil's orchestra," said Walt. "We could show the devil down below, playing and causing this volcanic eruption, causing the spirits to dance. . . ."

Stoki liked the idea and added, "You could, through your medium, look down into the volcano, and see all these things boiling together down there. You are the only one who could do such a thing. *Bald Mountain* is great music." It was a fait accompli. *Night on Bald Mountain* was definitely in.[9]

Stoki suggested a prelude by Debussy. It was the beautifully evocative "Les sons et les parfums tournent dans l'air du soir." It was based on a poem of Charles Baudelaire. Deems supplied the instant translation "Sounds and Perfumes Turning in the Evening Air." "I have always wanted to put perfume in theaters; have wanted to do it for years," Stoki remarked. "The air will be changed within so many seconds."

"All it takes is a few sprays to blow it out through the audience," added Walt. "We could do that in the *Nutcracker Suite* in the ballet of the flowers. . . ."

"As you change your colors you can change your perfumes," said Stoki. Walt, being eminently practical, remarked, "We couldn't do that. It wouldn't clear out soon enough."

"You mustn't mix your perfumes," Stoki said reflectively. "They would fight each other."

"Get a good flower smell," said Walt. "There you've got something . . . when they are amongst the flowers the audience could smell it. You could get them to name a special perfume for this—create a perfume— you could get write-ups in the papers." Disney with his commercial perception reasoned that they could get all of the perfume they wanted in return for the advertising the manufacturer would get from it. The scent that Stoki was particularly eager to have was "a flower of southern France—jasmine." Stoki had always been responsive to scents. He was most interested in the idea and was being remarkably persuasive. "Let's make some experiments on it," he said. "They now pass the air through water vapor, and instead of that they could wash it with the perfume. Before you came in, Walt, we played *Credo,* and I said that I could almost smell the incense. The sense of smell effects us more than the sense of sound."

Walt replied, "It's a hot idea."[10]

Huxley in his *Brave New World* had projected the "feelies," and Stoki had envisioned the "smellies." Both fortunately died on a point of practicality.

The aroma idea was not one that Stoki took lightly. In his book *Music for All of Us* he expanded on the idea: "The dramatic effect of a battle scene would be greatly increased if we smell the acrid odor of high explosives in addition to seeing the battle and hearing the roar of the guns and the deep sounds of explosions. There are a thousand ways in which our sense of smell can be associated with our senses of seeing and hearing and so heighten our impression of motion picture drama. The technique of doing this has to be developed but we already have its basic principles in the most modern forms of air conditioning through which the blending of perfumes and the timing of their suffusion in an enclosed space like a motion-picture house can be controlled—just as definitely as the duration of harmonies and the blending of timbres in sound."[11]

Was Stokowski the true visionary? Will it happen? Will we in the future be regaled with the odors of garlic, violets, the acrid smell of battle, and roses?

All of the music to be used had been selected and the first recording date in Philadelphia was to be early in April 1939. The final selections included the Bach Toccata and Fugue, Beethoven's *Pastorale* Symphony (somewhat abridged), parts of Stravinsky's *Rite of Spring*, Ponchielli's *Dance of the Hours*, Debussy's "Clair de Lune," some movements from Tchaikovsky's *Nutcracker* Suite, Mussorgsky's *Night on Bald Mountain*, and Schubert's "Ave Maria." Stoki also recorded the Sibelius *Swan of Tuonela*, Rimsky-Korsakov's "Flight of the Bumblebee" and Weber's *Invitation to the Dance* for good measure. These, they hoped, would be used in the next version of *Fantasia*.

Early in April 1939, Disney and a crew that included Bill Garity, staffer Dick Huemer, and many helpers arrived in Philadelphia. Garity was upset that the special limitations of the stage in the Academy would not permit the complete separation of the various instrumental groups. But with thirty-three separate mikes they recorded the entire sound track on nine different channels. They all worked intently. Stoki was most interested to hear the playbacks. Everything was recorded on film, which was sent airmail to Hollywood for processing, and when the films were returned a few days later, Stoki, Disney, and his crew crossed the river to the RCA studios in Camden to listen surrounded by banks of speakers.[12]

During the orchestra rehearsals, Dick Huemer remembered "Stoki didn't get dressed in his coattails. He sat up there with this big, bushy hair and Walt and Joe and I sat in back of the orchestra. Suddenly Walt poked me and said, 'He looks like Harpo Marx.' And he did."[13]

With the Philadelphia recording completed, the Disney troupe returned to Hollywood, where their real work was to begin. Though many sketches had been made, and various characters had been invented, "there

Filming the "live action" part of *Fantasia* with silhouettes of Stokowski and musicians (1940)

wasn't a bit of animation done until we came back with the tracks that had been done in Philadelphia," said Huemer.

I asked Huemer if he had been responsible for the abstractions used with the Toccata and Fugue. "It was someone by the name of Oscar Fischinger," he replied. "He had been doing that sort of thing for many years . . . little geometrical things that bounced up and down or changed shape in time to the music. They were in color too—sometimes red, they would flare out with an accent or be blue, with blue music. He was quite famous for that. Walt hired him to do the Toccata and Fugue, but all he

TIME

THE WEEKLY NEWSMAGAZINE

LEOPOLD STOKOWSKI
He and Mickey Mouse put on a brand-new act.
(*Music*)

Stokowski's second appearance on the cover of *Time*, November 18, 1940, for the opening of *Fantasia*

did were these dinky little things and when Walt saw it, he said, 'This can't be it.' So he was released."[14] Disney took over.

Stokowski's choice of Stravinsky's *Rite of Spring* had been a bold one and Disney tackled his part with equal daring. To give authenticity to the primordial scene that it represented, scientists including Roy Chapman Andrews and Julian Huxley were called in. Instead of the enormous appeal and charm of Donald Duck, Snow White, Mickey Mouse, the Seven Dwarfs, and other well-known Disney characters, the animators now had to wrestle with the problem of recreating such ancient creatures as the giant killer *Tyrannosaurus rex*, the *Eustocenopteron* (who became plain old Eustace), and other dinosaurs by the dozen.

Along with George Balanchine, Stravinsky visited the set, and they were photographed with Disney. He appeared to be looking at a score and pointing to a note, which Walt could not have read had he tried. Stravinsky, he reported, "watched its interpretation with keen interest." Another photo shows Stravinsky and George Balanchine happily admiring one of the ballet models from the "Dance of the Hours." But Stravinsky's mood was a deceptive one. And when one of the animators did a dour-looking sketch of the great Igor, it expressed the Stravinsky mood far more eloquently than the smiling photos.[15]

The "Dance of the Hours" from Ponchielli's *La Gioconda* proved to be one of the funniest satires on classical ballet that has ever been conceived. Its hippos, alligators, elephants and ostriches perform their ballet movements *sur les pointes* with delightful élan.

I asked Dick Huemer whether Balanchine might have advised them about ballet movements when he was there. "He had nothing to do with it," he declared. "It was choreographed by someone named Joyce Coles, and Marjorie Belcher was the chief dancer in it. We had it all acted out."[16]

Elaborate preparations were made to present *Fantasia* in the most spectacular way. Ten units were assembled costing about $27,000 each. As many as 100 to 135 speakers were used surrounding the entire theater. A new word had to be coined to describe the sound system. It was named Fantasound.[17] And that matched nicely with Technicolor.

Fantasia opened in New York at the Broadway Theater Wednesday November 13, 1940, and it was reviewed by both the music and drama critics.

In the *Herald Tribune* Howard Barnes reviewed it from the drama standpoint and Virgil Thomson reviewed the music. Barnes considered the portrayal of the Toccata and Fugue "the purest of abstract pictorial design." Overall he thought it a "brave and beautiful work."[18]

Thomson suggested that "Stokowski Sound" might be a more appropriate description than "Fantasound": . . . . "For Leopold Stokowski, whatever one might think of his musical taste, is unquestionably the man who has best watched over the upbringing of Hollywood's stepchild, musical recording and reproduction.

"Alone among successful symphonic conductors, he has given himself the trouble to find out something about musical reproduction techniques and to adapt these to the problems of orchestral execution. Alone among the famous musicians who have worked in films he has forced the spending of money and serious thought by film producers and their engineers toward achievement of a result in auditive photography comparable in excellence to the results that the expenditure of money and thought have produced in visual photography.

"Musicians will thank him and bless his name. . . ."[19]

During Christmas week in 1940, Stoki revisited *Fantasia* for a matinee performance and wrote his impressions to Walt:

> The beginning of the picture is an absolute stroke of genius. It begins so imperceptibly. The public's attention is gradually attracted and before they know it they are in the picture. It really is a wonderful sensation of gliding into the picture. It has the simplicity that all great things have.

He then made detailed criticisms of each of the segments. He was pleased with the Toccata and Fugue.

> . . . The audience's interest in the Bach and its applause after the Bach was very great. I saw clearly that we did not misjudge the interest that this number can have for an audience and its value as an Overture to the picture.

Stoki was disturbed by a number of changes of direction of the music which had no counterpart on the screen, and felt that they would be confusing to the audience. He pointed out many more points where he felt improvement could be made; he complained that in many places the music was either too loud or too soft.

> After the performance a number of people spoke to me. Those who love music were shocked by the interpretation of the Beethoven. The other group who are inexperienced in music liked the Beethoven.
>
> I noticed that the man in control of the sound telephones to the projectors from a kind of bathroom in the back of the house—where he cannot hear or see the picture—so that the quick changes of level which are necessary to make the music sound well are difficult to make from this place. This man did not know about music and I don't think a man can control music without understanding it. From all the talk I hear in and around New York about "Fantasia," I think if we put in one new number, almost everyone would go to hear the whole picture again. Then a few months later if we put in another new number most of them will go again. All this is in addition to those who have not heard it yet but are planning to go . . .

The letter was simply signed "Stoki."[20]

The backers and bankers of Disney may have been dismayed at the monetary returns after *Fantasia*'s first run, but they were of too little faith. The vision of Stokowski and Disney was far greater than they realized. After World War II, *Fantasia* was revived and it has been playing at intervals ever since. The coffers of the Disney office have been enhanced by millions.

Sonya and I were talking about *Fantasia* one day and she remarked: "My oldest son, who went to the University of Pennsylvania, saw *Fantasia* in Philadelphia. He really had no particular musical background, but I insisted that he go to New York to hear his grandfather's concerts as well as others, and also plays. It really wasn't until he got to college that he suddenly started going out on his own and buying tickets. He went to hear the Philadelphia Orchestra, of course, and went to see *Fantasia*. He said, 'You have no idea what this does to your mind and how many of my fellow students who had never gone to a concert before decided that they'd like to see what a concert was like, after they had seen *Fantasia*.' I think this is probably true. I just hope it will go on doing this for these young people. It's not the all end all—it's the beginning. It just starts the imagination going."[21]

(41)

The All-American
Youth Orchestra

URING the coast-to-coast tour of the Philadelphia Orchestra in
1936, young instrumentalists were encouraged to audition for
members of the orchestra who were connected with the Curtis
Institute. Josef Hofmann had announced that the most talented could
win a free scholarship to the Institute. They were to contact their local
RCA dealers in the cities in which the orchestra was to appear. No one
was more interested than Stokowski, and he personally attended some
of the auditions. He was astonished at the superabundance of talent
he encountered everywhere. The idea of founding a Youth Orchestra
came to him while he was touring the country with the Philadelphia
Orchestra.

The idea of organizing a South American tour was an afterthought and
very probably resulted from talks with Jean Dalrymple. Jean had been to
South America as publicist and manager to José Iturbi. In various Latin
American cities, she had become disturbed by the amount of cultural
propaganda being launched by Germany and Italy and the favorable
reaction their efforts produced. Berlin had sent its famed Philharmonic;
Italy had sent over La Scala. In Chile she found that Germany had sent
over the Staatsoper and the Chileans seemed both sympathetic and impressed.

On her return to America she went to Hollywood and while there she
had a call from Mike Myerberg, who was acting as Stoki's manager at the
time. He asked Jean whether she would like to work for Stokowski.

"Where?" she asked. "And he said, 'Out here. He's making a film—*100 Men and a Girl*. And I said, 'Oh yes, that would be terrific.' "

Myerberg arranged a luncheon engagement for Jean with Stoki. "He had a nice little cottage and a Filipino houseman," Jean recalled, "and we had a wonderful time. I was there from about 12 o'clock until about 4 o'clock and I always remember the luncheon that he served me because it was the first time I had health food and the first time that I had a lecture on health food and health.

"At the end of the time, he said that he really didn't want to have publicity—that this was Michael Myerberg's idea."[1]

Jean, however, wrote a fine description of Stoki's house for the *New York Herald Tribune*: "Distinctly modern in style and deep terracotta in color is the work-studio Leopold Stokowski has just finished building here. It clings to the side of a precipitous mountain near the summit, where there's an airplane view of the town far below and, on a hazeless day, the ocean. It seems a tiny, simple affair, after the rolling opulence of the estates below it, but it was planned by the Maestro himself.

" 'This is how I live when I am working,' he said. 'I have in this place just what I need—nothing unnecessary.' "[2]

It was Jean Dalrymple who first talked to Stoki about conditions in South America, and at that moment the initial idea of taking a youth orchestra south was born. Disappointed that he was never able to tour abroad with the Philadelphia Orchestra, he became intrigued at the idea of tweaking the noses of the orchestra board by succeeding where they failed.

One of Franklin Roosevelt's many imaginative projects was the establishment of a National Youth Administration and he chose Aubrey Williams as its head. From John Bitter, conductor, flutist, and onetime Curtis student, I heard an account of Stoki's first encounter with Williams: "Stokowski had met Aubrey Williams at a dinner party. Stoki said, 'Let us, you and I, form an orchestra of young people and let us travel around the world and really show good will and what we can do and form a true tie among people through youth.' "

Shortly thereafter, John Bitter received a call from Aubrey Williams, who asked him to come to Washington to discuss the feasibility of the project. John, at the time, was the conductor of the Florida WPA Orchestra. Williams suggested that he go to California and discuss the formation of the orchestra with Stokowski: "Needless to say, I was terribly excited with this. At that time my brother-in-law, Walter Abel, the actor, was very much involved in Hollywood and I stayed at his home in Westwood Hills. I called Stokowski and he said, 'Yes. Come right up.' He lived way up in Beverly Hills with a gorgeous view. . . . Stokowski was not there but there was a little Filipino houseboy who said, 'Please come in . . .' and immediately excused himself. He said, 'I have to go home but Mr. Stokowski will be coming back very soon.' So I was all alone in this very unusual house . . . no furniture except low tables and pillows, no chairs, no conventional furniture. Before long the phone rang and a voice said, 'Ha-llo, is Mr. Stokowski there?' And I said, 'No, I'm sorry he isn't. May I take a message? He should be back very soon.' 'No, no matter. Just tell him that Gustafson called.' Of course, I realized then that the love of my life, Greta Garbo, was on the other end of the phone."

Stoki returned about six, and they immediately began to organize their plans. He asked Bitter to play flute in the new orchestra and also to become one of the associate conductors. At about midnight they interrupted their discussion: "He mixed a rum drink which he called the 'alto flute benj.' He spelled it out *b-e-n-j.*" Stokowski then proceeded to prepare a dinner of shellfish and the proverbial salad. They then continued their conversation until three in the morning.

It was a very successful meeting and Stoki with his usual thorough and logical manner had everything worked out in his mind. He also appreciated John's grasp of all of the problems and his faith in being able to help solve them. "First of all," said John, "we decided on committees in various regions of the United States. I would visit them, make plans to audition people, then I would go around for a second audition, and from what later turned out to be ten thousand applicants, we reduced them to one thousand."[3]

Stoki wrote directly to Secretary of State Cordell Hull: "Something entirely new is happening in this country. A generation is arising that is amazingly rich in musical talent. But these young players have no opportunity to play great music in an orchestra which has the same musical standards as the major orchestras in America. It is this opportunity that I wish to create and offer to them. For the All-American Youth Orchestra, I shall only accept players who can measure up to the highest standard of American orchestral performance. But there is such a wealth of talented young players in this country that the only difficulty is that we shall not be able to accept them all."

Cordell Hull responded:

My dear Mr. Stokowski:

In these tragic days, when cultural values are in eclipse in so many parts of the world, there is a special reason for strengthening them in our hemisphere. Music, a universal medium of expression, can perform a very particular role because it transcends the barrier of language which has retarded in many fields the fullest enjoyment of the cultural achievements of the Americas.

President Roosevelt in his proclamation of January 30, last, has proclaimed 1940 to be Travel America Year, during which "our peoples may be drawn ever more closely together in sympathy and understanding." I hope that this orchestral tour will contribute to that objective, in which all of us are so keenly interested, and I wish you full success.[4]

In Washington, Stoki won the total cooperation of the Pan American Union, and arranged meetings with the ambassadors of all of the various countries they would visit. There was a myriad of details that had to be coped with. One, of course, was money. Mike Myerberg, knowing that RCA had underwritten the tour of the Philadelphia Orchestra, approached David Sarnoff to see whether they would underwrite this one. Stokowski was still one of their major recording artists, and it seemed that the arrangement was settled. Myerberg returned to California and brought the good news to Stoki. He reported that Sarnoff and others at RCA were highly enthusiastic.

When Myerberg returned to New York in January 1940, he visited Sarnoff to conclude arrangements with RCA to send the orchestra on its projected tour. He was appalled to learn that Sarnoff had decided to send Toscanini with the NBC Orchestra instead, and that they would immediately precede Stokowski's band. He argued unsuccessfully that the plan would serve no purpose since Toscanini was Italian and the orchestra was predominately composed of foreigners and that the whole purpose was to send something typically American to counter the Nazi and Fascist propaganda in South America. Sarnoff would not be moved.[5]

Toscanini's biographers gloss over this episode with an embarrassing lack of detail. Since Toscanini had never returned to Rio following his debut as a conductor there fifty-four years earlier, he must have been eager to revisit it and this time with an orchestra of his own.[6] He was well aware that Stokowski was planning to take his new orchestra on an almost identical tour and with his pathological envy of Stokowski, he would arrogantly want to show his wares. "When he was told that the tour would be a grand gesture of international friendship, he accepted"—his biographers tell us.[7]

If Toscanini had decided that he wanted to go to South America, Sarnoff certainly would not have opposed it. Lawrence Gilman had remarked that "Toscanini has a single-track mind." He seemed obsessed by Stokowski. He had never been able to achieve a recorded sound that equaled that of Stokowski and the Philadelphia Orchestra, and he behaved toward his colleague like a medieval Tuscan pursuing a vendetta.

"Toscanini loves no one," wrote Charles O'Connell. "On his sleeve he wears not his heart, but his spleen. He is capable of jealousy; he is capable of resentment if one's admiration for him is less than idolatrous. . . . Toscanini is not interested in a union of wills, but only in the imposition of his own. His will he imposes with implacable determination on family, on friends, composers, companions, and corporations; on Beethovens, Sarnoffs, and second violinists; on children, on cooks, on colleagues . . . he burns his energy and torments his soul with little things . . . with vindictiveness, with unreasonableness, with suspicion, and with hate."[8]

We have grown more aware of the "dirty tricks" character of politics. Music, too, has its share and many a savage breast is not lulled by its strains. Frankly, I know of no more viciously reprehensible act than that of the scheduling of the NBC Symphony's tour directly before that of the All-American Youth Orchestra under Stokowski.

For a moment it seemed as if the tour might have to be canceled, but Myerberg approached William Paley, Sarnoff's arch competitor at CBS, and won his backing.[9] It was something of a coup, for it would mean that Stokowski would now be a Columbia recording artist—something he was not about to be with the Philadelphia Orchestra because of its contract with RCA Victor. Stoki appeared to be untouched by the various turns of events and continued to immerse himself in the problem of building his new youthful group.

With the basic underwriting of the tour settled, the cost of assembling and interviewing young performers across the country had to be met, and here Aubrey Williams and the National Youth Administration

welcomed the chance to participate. Auditions were set up throughout
the country and the response was quite overwhelming. While the government had no means of aiding the orchestra on its tour, nor could it
help in any way to compensate the players in the orchestra, it could
underwrite the expenses of travel for Stoki's assistants such as John Bitter, Saul Caston, and others who helped winnow the mass of talented
people, all of whom wanted to be part of the orchestra. It worked expeditiously but suddenly, at a time when the appropriation of $850,000
for the National Youth Administration was being considered by Congress. Congressman Eugene Cox of Georgia suggested an amendment
"to forbid payment of any funds to Mr. Williams." He alleged that Mr.
Williams "consorted with Communists."

Representative Tarver of Georgia countered that Williams was "an
idealist and dreamer" who perhaps needed "to be guided and restrained."
Old, conservative, New York Republican Hamilton Fish shrieked like an
operating exorcist that Williams was "the most dangerous man in the
government." He seems to have gotten his priorities a little confused.

Congressman John Taber (Republican, New York) flatly charged that
both Stoki and Williams had Communist leanings. Congressman Sabath
of Illinois challenged Taber at once and pointed out that none of the
organizations with which Taber accused Stoki of being affiliated "were
Communist."[10] The estimated $1,000,000 cost of the tour, said Taber,
would be put up either by the United States or Soviet government. He
further stated that "the Stokowski venture could not possibly have private
financial backing. It involves too much risk."[11] But Taber never bothered
to discover that it was CBS which was underwriting the tour and with as
much commercial as idealistic intent. Communist! I've never heard of the
USSR welcoming William Paley as a fellow traveler nor CBS as an arm
of Soviet propaganda.

Stoki remained serene and abstained from any argument. The ruffled
feathers of the little witch hunters were smoothed, the appropriation was
passed, and the auditions proceeded apace. While Stoki did not hear all
of the preliminary auditions, he and John Bitter traveled across the country to find the chosen few. They traveled almost entirely by train. "I never
had a more charming, thoughtful, absolutely delightful, considerate companion than Stokowski," said John. "I never felt for a moment that I was
a newcomer in his ken and he could not have been nicer. In the morning
whenever we were at a station, he bought a paper, immediately turned

to the stock pages and made a few notes for a telegram to his broker. But we discussed every subject under the sun."[12]

John also related an episode that occurred in Cleveland while he and Stoki were auditioning two students in the Cleveland Institute. Suddenly a photographer burst in the room and began to snap pictures. "John, get that man," shouted Stoki. John chased across the room as the photographer ran down the stairs. Then, said John, "I took a flying leap off the top of this rather shallow staircase. Luckily it was carpeted and there was another photographer there and he took a picture of me in midair about to land on this photographer." He did retrieve the film.

In Boston, Arthur Fiedler offered to judge the finalists. One of those he selected was violist Harold Coletta. "I was the only one from Connecticut to play in the Youth Orchestra with Stokowski. After playing four or five preliminary auditions I got to play for Fiedler in Boston and then finally for Stokowski."[13]

In Colorado Springs, violinist Robert Gross was teaching at Colorado College and playing an active role in the summer music festivals that were held there. He was active in promoting American music and had given the premier performance of the Roger Sessions Violin Concerto. On hearing about the new youth orchestra, he wrote to Stokowski asking to be auditioned when Stoki would be passing through Denver. "Stoki was very nice to me," Bob Gross said. "The auditions lasted all day. We were complete strangers, naturally. Most of what I had to do was sight-reading, and he was encouraging and said that I would be hearing from him probably fairly soon." But Gross heard nothing from Stoki or anyone else connected with the venture. "One morning in Colorado Springs," said Bob, "I went out to get the morning paper and there was an article on the front page saying that I had been chosen as the only musician from the Rocky Mountain region."[14]

Flutist Albert Tipton, who had just completed his first season with the National Symphony in Washington at that time, told me: "One of my colleagues asked me whether I had heard about the All-American Youth Orchestra, and he said it's an opportunity for young musicians to go with Stokowski to South America. I thought to myself, I'm going to go."[15] Tipton was immediately engaged.

Stokowski appeared at the Curtis Institute, addressed the students, and described the forthcoming tour of his youth orchestra. A young Curtis violin student, George Zazofsky, was in the audience: "It was like magic hearing all the fantastic cities—Rio and Buenos Aires—that he listed on the itinerary. Sitting next to me was a fellow student, Herbert Baumel. He was an excellent violinist. I was lit up with this magic of the Stokowski personality and the prospect of visiting these places." George nudged his friend, told him to follow him and the two proceeded to Stoki's flat. George rang and Stoki answered. They were both invited up and mounted the multicolored stairs to a room with many oriental gongs. After explaining their purpose, Stoki took a mallet, struck one of the gongs, and instructed a servant to "Bring these gentlemen some champagne."[16] Both were hired, and after the tour George went on to become a member of the Boston Symphony.

Another Curtis student who hied to Rittenhouse Street was the seventeen-year-old oboist, Ralph Gomberg. "Everyone knew where that was because that was like a shrine for young musicians in those days." On arriving at Stoki's apartment he was told to wait briefly and then was joined by Stoki in his living room. "He actually had the fireplace going. This was in June in Philadelphia. . . . Philadelphia in June is hot—believe me, it's hot . . . there was the stand with all the music out and I took out my oboe and played. . . ."[17] In spite of his fit of perspiration, Ralph played very well and Stoki engaged him. It was the beginning of a brilliant career. He later became principal oboist of the Boston Symphony. Still another of the young players, who also became a member of the Boston Symphony and later a conductor in his own right, was the bass player, Willis Page.[18]

One young aspirant, who hailed originally from a small town in Kansas called Medicine Lodge, was violinist Dorothy DeLay. She had first encountered Stokowski while she was studying in Michigan. "It was quite a chance encounter. As a matter of fact, it was on the street and I never forgot it because his personality left such an effect on me. I had never really come in contact with anyone who had this power of personality before, at least this was the first time I had been aware of anything of that kind."

When auditions were taking place, Miss DeLay auditioned directly for Stoki without any preliminaries. "I remember," she said, "that I was very tired before the audition. We didn't have specific times to play and when I came in there were several people in front of me so I went to sleep and I remember that he woke me up and said, 'Come and play now'—which was rather embarrassing." Stoki chose her immediately and she remained with the orchestra for its two seasons. Later she was to become one of the most sought-after teachers at the Juilliard School.[19]

Added to the fantastic assembly of young performers, Stoki included a group of young members from the Philadelphia Orchestra to give a sense of security and perhaps discreetly act as unofficial chaperones. One of these was the splendid harpist Edna Phillips. She explained that Stoki wanted to have certain "section leaders"—meaning first-desk men. She mentioned that there were about 28 women, and the rest of the 108 or so were men. "He was an excellent organizer—first class. He was a good housekeeper! He could tell you what kind of water to use for your tea; when to pick up the mop. He knew how to do everything. He could get out in the middle of the Sahara desert and survive. Well, for this tour he decided he would take a nucleus of Philadelphians with him, so everyone who had hair went along!"

All told there were eighteen members of the Philadelphia Orchestra including Samuel Mayes, Sol Schoenbach, Robert McGinnis, Ben and Charles Gusikoff, Mason Jones, David Madison, Manuel Roth, and Emmet Sargeant. Edna added that "it was incredible the way he could take a bunch of mixed nuts (young players), put them together, and create fabulous sound. Well, he worked and worked. They played well!"[20]

By mid-July all of the participants had assembled in Atlantic City and rehearsals began. "We had two weeks of rehearsals," said Robert Gross. "The orchestra as it turned out, was one of the great ones ever put together in this country or anywhere else. . . . We had eight horns, every one of whom was a solo horn player with one of the major symphonies. Mason Jones was first horn. Tony Tomei was assistant first. The third horn was Jimmy Chambers, who at that time was first horn in Pittsburgh and later first horn in the New York Philharmonic. The fourth horn was Helen Kotas, who was first horn in Chicago, and so on. . . ."[21]

"I never saw anything like it," said cellist Sammy Mayes. "It was a fantastic-sounding orchestra he had whipped into shape. . . . It was really amazing what he did with these kids . . . he had a first-class orchestra before we set out."[22]

The first concert took place in Atlantic City's Convention Hall—July 21, 1940—drawing an audience of over five thousand. Stoki used his new seating plan with the strings in the rear and woodwinds and brass up front. The night was hot. "It was 104 degrees for two days in a row," Gross recalled. "The inside of the hall was unbearable. To make it worse, as we began the concert, Stoki insisted that the air conditioning be turned off; it made too much noise."[23]

The program was typical: the "Little" G Minor Fugue, the Brahms

First Symphony and the "Love Music" from *Tristan*. But he also included a Prelude and Toccata by the young American composer Gardner Read. Both the audience and the critical response were excellent. "This is no polyglot orchestra," wrote Arthur Bronson. "What it lacks in experience, it makes up in enthusiasm and discipline, and the net result is beautiful to hear. . . . Undoubtedly, this is all the reflection of Stokowski's wizardry. What many conceived as a stunt originally is a definite reality—a real orchestra."[24]

The next evening they performed in Baltimore. If anything the weather and humidity were even higher. It is difficult to know whether it was the heat or the setting that affected the audience. The review in the *Baltimore Sun* concerned itself almost entirely with descriptions of the audience. "ALL TRADITIONS ARE BROKEN AT YOUTH CONCERT" ran the headline; then in slightly smaller type "Audience in Carnival Mood Loudly Cheers Stokowski." There was a circus air about it. The audience greeted Stoki and the players with "an ovation unrivaled in this city, and every semblance of formality disappeared."

The more expensive seats were in the center with the cheaper ones on risers in the rear and both sides. Suddenly there was a rush from the sides and rear to grab the expensive places "despite efforts of ushers and a battalion of Boy Scouts to keep them back."

Just before Stoki entered he ordered all the electric fans to be turned off. The temperature soared in a matter of minutes. At intermission there was a rush for the bar. "Hundreds of patrons were as wet as the beer and soft drinks they imbibed. Beer and pop bottles were carried by escorts to women who refused to move."

After intermission Stoki conducted the Fifth Symphony of Tchaikovsky and as it ended, "hundreds lost all control. Men and women shouted, even yelled. Staid men stood in their places calling 'bravo.' Women atop chairs waved handkerchiefs frantically. Those on the floor stomped and waved arms. The place was a bedlam. . . . Many of the oldest of the city's music lovers, on leaving the building, assured all within their hearing that Baltimore had never seen anything like it."[25]

The next evening they were spared. The concert, to be held beside the Potomac with the orchestra playing on a barge, was canceled because of rain. In New York there were two concerts set for Lewisohn Stadium—the second was moved indoors. In addition to the traditional part of the program, Stoki paid tribute to New York by programming

Lasalle Spier's *Impressions of the Bowery* and Henry Cowell's *Pastorale and Fiddler's Delight.* Critics again dusted off their superlatives. Aubrey Williams spoke during the intermission and a letter of well-wishing from Cordell Hull was read. As the concert ended, Stoki and his charges sped downtown to board the S.S. *Uruguay,* which was to sail at midnight.[26]

(42)

Saludos Amigos

T HERE were rehearsals every day held in the ship's grand ballroom. "I remember one rehearsal," said James Chambers, "when one of the passengers came to a doorway which was closed but had glass in it. He started taking pictures and Stoki caught a glimpse of him and in a fury he jumped off the podium, dashed right past me—you may remember that in the setup that he was using then the horns were on the front of the stage, so I was right in his line—and he dashed to the door, jerked it open, grabbed the man's camera, called for the Captain and insisted that the film be destroyed. That was our first knowledge that he had this aversion to having his picture taken unless it was prearranged."[1]

Always interested in chamber music, Stokowski asked the players to organize chamber music concerts to be given during the afternoons. At one point when the ship was already in subequatorial waters, Stokowski and Captain William Oakley planned a concert for the passengers to be played in the first-class dining room on Sunday the fourth of August at 10:00 P.M. It was a rather odd program. It began with two marches conducted by Saul Caston: "Under the Double Eagle" by Wagner—not by Richard but by the Austrian composer Joseph Wagner. The second was the "National Emblem" by Bagley.

"As Stoki was about to begin, he raised his hands and then stopped. He cocked his head, listened, and called one of the officers to him and said, 'What's that noise? There's a noise. We can't play with noise.' So the man listened and he said, 'Oh, that must be the air conditioning.' 'Oh,' he said, 'this will never do. We don't play with noise. You must turn

403

it off.' Well, the officer looked over to the Captain, who was watching, and he gave him a nod and he went to the phone and soon the noise stopped.

"Stoki then raised his arms and again stopped. 'But there's still a noise,' he said. There was a low, low hum; that's all we could hear. And the officer said, 'Oh, those are the ship's engines.' 'Well,' said Stoki, 'We can't play with noise. No noise.' And believe it or not they turned off the engines. I don't know if this had ever happened in history before or since, but for an hour and a half that ship sat in one spot in the middle of the South Atlantic while we gave our concert with the engines off." So recalled Robert Gross.[2]

Seeing the name Seymour Barab listed on the program as a pianist puzzled me, for I have known him for years as a splendid cellist. I phoned him to ask him whether the listing was correct. He confirmed it and told me about some of the first rehearsals in Atlantic City during July 1940. "As I remember our first rehearsals consisted of going through South American music because he wanted to play some South American music. We were reading through some things and we found one piece that had a piano cadenza in it. It was then discovered that nobody had thought of hiring a pianist for the orchestra. . . . He asked if there were any pianists in the orchestra. And of course, somebody volunteered my name—some friend! Although I wasn't a pianist, I could play the piano a little, so he stuck me with the piano part for the piece. . . . I sight-read through the cadenza and it was apparently okay because I was engaged to be the orchestra's pianist as well as a cellist.

"Well, somehow we were on a train and he said he was going to do the *Firebird Suite,* and of course, it has a pretty tricky piano part in it. I didn't have a piano to work on and all I could do was look at this thing and it looked horrendously difficult to me so I wanted to get out of it.

"I got word to him that I wanted to talk to him, and we had a little tête-à-tête on two facing seats in his compartment. I remember it clearly. And he snowed me! He said, 'Look out of the window.' And I looked out —the train was moving through the countryside—a lush countryside. And he said, 'Now you see all those trees and all that grass?' And I said, 'Yes.' He said, 'Well, do you see every single blade of grass? Do you see every single leaf on the tree?' I said, 'No.' He patted my knee and said, 'You can do it, my boy.' And I did."[3]

The *Uruguay* arrived in Rio de Janeiro on August 7, the very day of the first concert. "The harbor is so fantastic. It's absolutely the most beautiful harbor in the world and we came late in the afternoon and there was a concert that night at the Teatro Municipal. To get us all out, with our baggage and instruments, and set up in the theater was something," John Bitter recalled.[4] The ship did not tie up directly at the dock and the musicians had to be ferried in small tenders. Edna Phillips described Stoki standing near the prow of the boat looking for all the world like George Washington crossing the Delaware.[5]

John Bitter remembered that Villa-Lobos was on the pier. "That dear man was so helpful and we had trucks and helpers." The players were soon ensconced in hotel rooms, where they had but little time to change their clothes and proceed to the concert hall. "I would say that we had about a two-minute rehearsal, just so Stokowski could tell what the acoustics were like."[6]

On the second night Stoki introduced Villa-Lobos' *Mômoprecóce* for piano and orchestra with the Brazilian pianist Magda Tagliaferro.

After Rio the next stop was São Paulo. The ship proceeded to Santos, its nearest seaport.

Stoki and the orchestra gave two concerts. Magda Tagliaferro repeated the Villa-Lobos *Mômoprecóce* and Villa-Lobos came to hear it. As soon as she arrived in São Paulo she was interviewed by a reporter from *Diario Da Notte*. "Stokowski is a miracle," she said, "a miracle of artistic understanding, of creative spirit, of absolute control of the orchestra. The most curious characteristic of this revolutionary master is that he has dispensed with the traditional baton. He conducts with his hands. And what hands he has! The only thing they don't do is talk!" She then referred to a Brazilian law which stipulated that a Brazilian composition must be played on every program. "To comply with the law," she said, "it was enough for the concert to include any Brazilian composition. However, he wanted to do homage to a great artist of ours. In today's concert, we will hear *Momo Precoce* by Villa-Lobos . . . a lengthy composition whose execution takes close to thirty minutes."[7]

After two pleasant days at São Paulo, all returned to the ship at Santos. Villa-Lobos went along as far as Santos, and on the trip Stoki and he discussed a mammoth concert which the orchestra would give on the way back. It was to be in a huge football stadium. Stoki and Villa-Lobos, with Bob Gross supplying translation when needed, discussed the building of a shell for the orchestra. Villa-Lobos was connected with the Ministry of Fine Arts, which was sponsoring the Brazilian concerts.

Back on the ship they sailed for Buenos Aires with a brief stop—but no concert—in Montevideo. As they proceeded to Buenos Aires, they sailed around the German pocket battleship *Graf Spee*, which had been scuttled by its crew when British destroyers bottled it up in the Río de la Plata. While part of it settled on the bottom, much of it was visible above water.

Courtesy Mme. Arminda Villa-Lobos
With Heitor Villa-Lobos when Stokowski invited him to share the podium for a New York City Symphony concert (1945)

In Buenos Aires they remained for about three weeks giving concerts and making recordings for Columbia. The concerts were given in the Cinema Grand Rex. "It was a beautiful place very much in the tradition of Radio City Music Hall in New York, only this one was bigger . . . for one thing we could get a bigger audience than Toscanini had had."

The first of the Buenos Aires concerts took place on August 14; later

Stoki conducted two concerts in the city of Rosario, northwest of the capital. To keep the orchestra on its toes and to prevent the boredom which eventually must come from repetition, he constantly varied his programs. In Buenos Aires the concerts were scheduled to begin at 9:00 P.M. rather than 8:30, but the audience, lingering at their dinners, never came near the theater by that time. About an hour later they would arrive.[8]

While life seemed casual it was also elegant. When the players were not involved in rehearsals, concerts, or recording sessions, they wandered about the expensive shops and strolled along the Avenida de Mayo and did other sight-seeing.

Recording sessions for the orchestra were held in the Grand Rex, which proved to be a happy choice. Columbia engineers were also busy recording groups of native performers, as they had been doing wherever they could find interesting material. But their principal task was to record the orchestra while it was not only at its peak but together as a unit, something it would be less able to do after returning. As far as Columbia was concerned, this was the payoff.

"In Buenos Aires," said John Bitter, "we gave occasional concerts, but, of course, we spent most of the time recording for Columbia and the experience was just terrific."[9]

"Our three weeks in Buenos Aires," Gross recalled, "were rather full. We recorded for Columbia every morning, but we would have a little spare time early in the afternoons if we did not have a rehearsal. We were rather bleary-eyed most of the time because in addition to following the South American schedule of the late hours, we had to follow the North American schedule for rehearsals and recordings. We never began later than nine in the morning, and most of the local residents didn't know that there was such an hour."

After playing their final concerts, Stoki and his band departed in a ferry that plied between Buenos Aires and Montevideo along the Río de la Plata. They dubbed it the "Albany Night Boat."[10]

Three concerts were scheduled for Montevideo. The first was quite a hectic and dramatic affair. I have heard so many eyewitness reports from numerous members of the group, and they differ so astonishingly, that I would like to give you a composite picture. Some maintained that the concert was to begin at 6:30 P.M. while others were equally certain that it was scheduled for 9:30, so we have some real counterpoints of view.

"I arrived with Stokowski at the hall," said Sol Schoenbach. "You know

Stokowski had a very strange habit of never having any money so would always bum taxicab rides with you and he would always say, 'I have the wrong pisazzes for this country and I'm sorry. Would you pay for it?' "[11] David Madison's recollection differed. "I went to the hall with Stoki in a cab and I remember he didn't have any money. I paid for it and it was in the afternoon."[12]

After arriving at the hall Stoki proceeded to the "green room," where one of the men brought him the program for the evening. The cover of the program announced "Leopoldo Stokowski con la Orquesta Juvenil Americana." So far so good! On opening it he read: "Leopoldo Stokowski nació en Londres el 18 de Abril de 1882, hijo de padre polaco y madre irlandesa. . . . No logró de inmediato estabilizar su situación económica y tuvo que actuar como organista con el apellido asajonado de STOKES. . . ."[13]

In English: "Leopold Stokowski born in London the 18th of April 1882, son of a Polish father and an Irish mother. . . . He was unable to immediately achieve economic stability and was forced to function as an organist with the Anglicized (Saxonized) surname of STOKES. . . ." Since he did not read Spanish fluently he did not even wait for a translation. He spotted his birth date listed as 1882 while he was asserting it was 1887. But the name STOKES, which had been printed in capitals, was enough to set him off. He told John Bitter that he would not conduct and to let the people know that the concert was to be canceled. This was not a simple matter. The President of Uruguay and his party were there as well as the Mayor of Montevideo and members of the American Embassy. Furthermore the program was to be broadcast. "Let Leo Stokes conduct," he is supposed to have said, "Leopold Stokowski is going back to the hotel." John Bitter and Saul Caston, the two assistant conductors, and members of the Embassy staff talked with him and pointed out what a disaster it would be if he did not conduct and that it would hardly promote international goodwill. Finally he said, "If you collect all of the programs, we will do it."

Then the scramble began. Most of the orchestra was already onstage. "So I got some members of the orchestra," John Bitter recalled, "and we went around and we asked people for their programs. If they didn't give them to us, we just took them. There was one young chap, a percussionist, who went to the box of the President and took the program out of the President's hand. The President was outraged. One of the men told me that the President's guards had drawn their revolvers and the lad was almost shot."

When all of the programs were gathered a delegation rushed to the hotel to persuade him to return, which he finally did. Meanwhile the orchestra on stage tuned and retuned. The restive audience began to become rowdy. "The concert started at ten o'clock and the audience wanted to tear the place apart," said John. "They were like a bullfight crowd. They were absolutely furious, but finally he came on and they warmed up and it was a fantastic success."[14]

The concert began with the "Little" Fugue in G Minor. Then an event even more startling was alleged to have taken place. In Montevideo it became a legend. At the time of the concert there was a two-year-old child in Montevideo who later was to become a composer, conductor, and finally assistant to Stokowski. He was José Serebrier. As he was growing up he heard the story from people who were at the concert and according to them this is what happened. "After playing about twenty bars, he heard a camera clicking—someone taking photographs. The audience saw him leave the stage—then they saw him walk to the first tier of boxes, second tier, first mezzanine, second mezzanine . . . until he found the photographer . . . and threw his camera on the floor with a tremendous racket and slapped him on the face. It's incredible, but so many people told me about it that it must be a true story." That is the legend from Montevideo.[15]

From one of the distinguished performers in the orchestra I heard this account. For obvious reasons he shall remain unidentified. After telling me about the program episode, he said the program began "and everything was quiet and everyone was happy . . . and there was such excitement in town because the *Graf Spee* had been bottled up and sunk that day by the British warships outside the harbor. We saw the whole battle and the *Graf Spee* came in and they scuttled it." He then said that shortly after Stoki had begun he left the stage. "I didn't know what to do and I stopped playing—and we all stopped and he disappeared and then appeared up there in a box, fighting with this guy—bang, bang—this guy was taking pictures of him and he was hitting him."

This is a little difficult to believe, for the *Graf Spee* was scuttled in December 1939, eight months before they had arrived in Montevideo. Could the fisticuffs also be true?

When I mentioned this version of the affair to Jim Chambers, he said, "My recollection is slightly different." He remarked that Stoki had a great aversion to having his picture taken. He reminded me about the episode during a rehearsal on shipboard. "So," he said, "in Montevideo this is what happened. During the concert—and the piece was the *Firebird*— he espied in a proscenium box, pretty much at stage level, someone taking pictures of him during the performance. At the end of the movement, he went over to the side door on stage left—his right—had a little difficulty opening the door that got him to the proscenium box area, entered the box, made quite a fuss, and took the man's camera away from him. I don't remember that he punched him in the face, but there was a real scene —Spanish, English and what have you. When that was accomplished, he came back and finished the *Firebird*."[16]

Harold Coletta and I also talked about the episode. His recollection had nothing to do with Stoki's aversion to picture taking. Instead he recalled, "Some idiot was rattling a program and Stoki glared at him until he almost shrank to the floor and stopped wriggling his program. That's all that took place."[17]

Since the President of the Republic was attending the concert, it seems to me that once Stoki had made his point about the programs, he would hardly indulge in a miniature brawl. It simply was against his nature. Also, the concert was being broadcast and, as he was at all times a pro, he would not in any way scuttle a program. "The hall had an unusual feature; high above the stage there was a red neon sign saying '*Silencio*,' Robert Gross remarked. "I could not understand why it was there until we got going. It was a very enthusiastic audience and after each piece, and sometimes in the middle, there would be great applause and stamping of feet and bravos. Stoki couldn't go on. There was always one group trying to quiet another, which would then shout back at them. . . . The only thing that would do any good was the flashing on and off again of this red '*Silencio*,' and eventually people would calm down."

Stoki and his youthful band then began their trip north on the S.S. *Argentina*. With German subs operating in the waters, the ship was brightly lighted at night with American flags painted on both sides. It docked in Santos so the orchestra could give more concerts in São Paulo, from which they proceeded to Rio by train. "That was not a very pleasant trip," recalled Bob Gross. "The railroads were in dreadful shape; the food was terrible. But we got to Rio the next afternoon, and the following afternoon we were to give a concert in the football stadium. This was the one for which Villa-Lobos had been preparing and he had done a beautiful job. He had had a set made—all of tropical hardwoods. It had very extensive wings and was put up at the end of the stadium, which held about forty thousand people. We were to have had a rehearsal in the morning, but we did not know that it was Brazil's Independence Day and there was an enormous parade."

Stokowski was staying with President Vargas in the presidential mansion, which was adjacent to the soccer field. In the morning no one but Stokowski and two violinists showed up. The rest of the orchestra members, who were in downtown hotels, were trapped by the impossible holiday traffic and literally no means of transportation. They finally drifted in along with the patrons.[18]

It was less like a concert than a fiesta. The celebrating Brazilians poured into the soccer field in vast numbers, and although the reflecting shell was no doubt a good one, one wonders how the orchestra could be heard in that vast expanse. But President Vargas was so pleased, he suggested that Brazil would also form a youth orchestra and tour America the following season.

After this gala affair Stokowski and his youthful band started back to New York with stops in Trinidad and Santo Domingo.

(43)

Postlude

N EW YORK, Baltimore, Washington, Philadelphia. In all four cities Stokowski showed off the astonishing virtuosity and cohesion his young orchestra had attained. It was not a matter of propaganda now, and the repertoire was chosen for but one purpose: to exhibit its skill, sensitivity, and ability to evoke sonorities that were "the Stokowski sound." He chose a group of Bach transcriptions and the Shostakovich Fifth Symphony. Included in the Bach was the Prelude from the violin Partita in E Major which had been prepared on shipboard. The violin section played standing.

In New York they appeared in Carnegie Hall. All of the New York papers reported that Stokowski and his players received an ovation. Chotzinoff in the *Post* said that they "generated enthusiasm of flattering volume and intensity. As to the interpretation of all this music," he continued, "Mr. Stokowski's spirit dominated his newest medium of expression as completely as it does the Philadelphia Orchestra. This would go a long way to prove the contention that there are no orchestras, only conductors." During the intermission Mayor La Guardia came onstage to introduce Eleanor Roosevelt, who made a gracious speech of welcome and read a laudatory commendation from Cordell Hull.[1]

In Baltimore in the Fifth Regiment Armory, there was a scene resembling somewhat that of the orchestra's previous appearance. The mood was informal and it seemed to be more of an event than a concert. It was reported to have drawn the largest audiences ever to attend a symphonic concert in the city. Critic Weldon Wallace in the *Sun* remarked:

Stokowski and members of the All-American Youth Orchestra being greeted on their return from South America aboard the S.S. *Argentina* by Mrs. Franklin D. Roosevelt and Franklin, Jr. (September 17, 1940)

"Throughout the evening the tone of the orchestra, molded by the conductor's pliant gestures, was brilliant, invigorating and full-bodied, distinct with the freshness and enthusiasm of youth."[2]

In Washington, Stokowski's reflecting panels countered the dulling effect of the draperies in Constitution Hall, which the DAR ladies so dearly loved and about which Stokowski was to battle later. Glenn Dillard Gunn observed that "it was a distinguished gathering, with many representatives of the Diplomatic Corps in attendance, and all the notable figures in Washington's local musical and social life in the boxes and the main floor seats. . . . Together they cheered Stokowski and the orchestra . . . with an enthusiasm that matched the spirit of the performance."[3]

Gunn then suggested that it was easy to understand how members of the Philadelphia Orchestra, who regarded themselves as belonging especially to Stokowski, had developed an obvious jealousy toward the All-

American Youth Orchestra. This could only have been enhanced by the opinions of the critics everywhere hailing the new group as being the equal of most of the major orchestras.

"Nevertheless," he agreed, "they have achieved an ensemble so much more precise, flexible and responsive than that of the nation's mature orchestras that the value of routine becomes, by inference, matter for debate." Before the final encore Stokowski spoke. He expressed his gratitude to the President and Mrs. Roosevelt and to the Secretary of State for their moral support in this "goodwill" tour of South America. He paid special tribute to Aubrey Williams and the National Youth Administration for their prompt and efficient cooperation.

He then paid his respects to Congress—perhaps respects is not quite the right word. He made a sharp and sarcastic reference to the nation's lack of a department of fine arts, a deficiency which made it impossible for the nation to extend any financial aid to the artistic ambassadors who made up his group of youthful symphonists.

He dwelt on the fact that the tour offered twenty-seven concerts in six nations of the hemisphere as an exhibit of the musical talent and attainment of the youth of our country and yet it could not obtain any financial support from the nation it represented. The audience appeared to relish his remarks as much as it enjoyed the music. But one wonders whether Congressmen John Taber and Hamilton Fish were there to hear it. If at this point they were to have suggested that the tour had been underwritten by the Soviets or for Communist propaganda, they would have been laughed out of their sinecures.

In Philadelphia his sarcasm was equally pointed. "Dramatically, and without warning," wrote Linton Martin, "was the assertion and the accusation which the celebrated platinum-haired maestro hurled in the teeth of the huge audience that hailed him with wild applause, cheers, stamping feet and cries of 'Brava' and 'Encore.' " He said that he was as always happy to be back in Philadelphia after the fulfillment of a dream, that of taking a message of goodwill to our neighbors of South America, but that he was sad because of one thing. "That," he explained, "was because I wanted to make this tour with the Philadelphia Orchestra. But when I suggested it, I was told it was impossible. I can't understand that because we've done it!" he added with emphasis. The excited audience responded with vociferous applause, leaving no doubt concerning their verdict. It was a point that Orville Bullitt and the board certainly could not have missed.

Nor could they have missed the fact that Stokowski still had the affection of Philadelphia's audience, and the critic's admiration.

Martin continued: "The concert itself was a musical marvel. It was the marvel of an infant orchestra lifting its myriad voice with adult authority and inspired eloquence when it gave a concert that was at once Hail and Farewell."[4] It was the final one and the climax of the orchestra's first season.

Everyone felt euphoric. Stoki gave a party for the orchestra, the Columbia engineers, and all involved in the venture at the elegant old Bellevue-Stratford Hotel next to the Academy. "We were going to New York in the morning and we had our various tickets to take us back to our own parts of the country," said Bob Gross, "when Stoki said, 'I think there are a few things that we did not get recorded in Buenos Aires. I want to record them.' And he turned to one of the Columbia engineers and said, 'We could do that tomorrow, couldn't we?' And he answered, 'I'm sure that some studio must be vacant.' These were the days when Columbia was doing most of its recording in the old Liederkranz Hall."[5]

On reading Bob's commentary, I felt that there must be much more detail that he would have, and I phoned him in Laguna Beach and queried him. I mentioned that recently I had read a statement that no recordings were made in South America and that Stoki had come back empty-handed. "That's not true," he responded. "We spent a good many days, in fact, we did more recording in Buenos Aires than we did in New York. This is what we did: the Beethoven Fifth and Sixth, the Tchaikovsky Sixth, the Shostakovich Fifth; then a number of transcriptions. About *Pictures at an Exhibition,* I'm not positive whether we did it in Buenos Aires or New York. . . . I know that in Buenos Aires we did a number of Stokowski's transcriptions: the G Minor Fugue, the Passacaglia and Fugue, and Arioso. We did the *Khovanshchina* Entr'acte and the scenes that he put together from *Boris Godunov.*"

About that single day in New York before disbanding, Bob recounted that they recorded the entire day. "We did the Dvořák *New World* Symphony and the Love Music from *Tristan,* and I think that's when we did the D Minor Toccata and Fugue."

I then learned something that had totally escaped my notice. Columbia was so anxious to have Stokowski added to their catalogue that they had a recording session even before the group embarked for South America. On the very day that they sailed, on the one free afternoon that the orchestra had, Stoki assembled a strong nucleus of the orchestra—he was using reduced strings for the recordings—and recorded the entire afternoon at Liederkranz Hall. The works that they did were the *Boléro*, *The Firebird* and the Brahms Fourth.[6] The Columbia archives confirm that the *Boléro* was recorded on that day. The dates which Columbia indicated for the other recordings are puzzling, for they suggest that most of the recordings were made long after the orchestra disbanded. That would mean that Stoki would have had to assemble a pick-up group, which would have nullified the very idea Columbia was try to promote. The dates may have been those when the records were edited and prepared for release.

One of the best recordings to emerge from this first season was the *New World* Symphony of Dvořák. Comparing it with a previous Stokowski recording with the Philadelphia Orchestra and a more recent one conducted by George Szell and the Czech Philharmonic Orchestra, Irving Kolodin wrote: "Though the new Columbia album directed by Stokowski is slightly more expensive than either of Victor's (including one of five years ago by Stokowski) it is a considerably better value, and thus entitled to the purchaser's preference. It is no less affected by the whims and eccentricities of Stokowski's impression of this work, but the whole conception is far more vital and invigorating than Szell's sober rather stodgy one. In addition, the wonderful quality of the youthful orchestra, its energy and superb discipline are splendidly reproduced."[7]

Columbia was very happy! They now had captured Stokowski on Columbia Masterworks. Then to add a dollop of canned patriotism, they persuaded Stoki to record "God Bless America" and "The Star Spangled Banner" coupled with the "Pledge of Allegiance to the Flag" intoned solemnly by Goddard Lieberson.[8]

The 1940-41 Music Season and the Stokowski Marshall Plan

S TOKOWSKI, with his affinity for grandiloquence, found it difficult to equate the response and public acclaim resulting from a concert in Philadelphia's Academy with his presentation of a concert—such as *Fantasia* had been regarded—in the cinema. He had discussed further collaborations with Disney and fully expected that in the near future there would be continuous offers to do more movies. He now had two houses in California, one in Santa Barbara and the other, his self-designed adobe house, high above Hollywood.

Movies and perhaps the Hollywood Bowl were to be his new outlets. In 1940 the movie climate was auspicious. Hollywood produced an astonishing vintage crop: *Gone with the Wind, The Grapes of Wrath, The Great Dictator* with Charlie Chaplin, Greta Garbo in *Ninotchka, Our Town* with William Holden, and *The Philadelphia Story* with Katharine Hepburn and Cary Grant. And, of course, *Fantasia.*

For three weeks he returned to Philadelphia to fulfill his contract. He did not intend to let the opportunity go by without creating something of an incident. Or perhaps one might say two incidents. They were the premiere performances of the Shostakovich Sixth Symphony and the world premiere of Schoenberg's Violin Concerto. When he introduced the Shostakovich Sixth, the audience seemed to find it quite comprehensible and raised no objections. Critics praised its orchestral fabric, its poetic *largo*, and withal its musical substance.[1] Stokowski seemed very pleased at its acceptance.

Then the blockbuster! It was the Schoenberg Violin Concerto. One reviewer complimented the audience for having written "a few eight to the bar" notes by supplying the rhythm of marching feet. There had indeed been an exodus during the performance. In addition "some 50 or 60 music lovers stood out the Schoenberg opus in the foyer."[2]

"It was like old times at the Academy of Music," wrote Henry Pleasants. The work had aroused the greatest commotion that had been heard for a long while. It was like the good old days after performances of Varèse and some of the more cacophonous Russians. If there was a little applause for Schoenberg, there was a magnificent amount for Louis Krasner for his masterful playing. "But if the concerto offers problems to the violinist and to the orchestra," wrote Pleasants, "it also offers problems to the listener. Mr. Schoenberg may have to wait until audiences come equipped with four ears apiece to have his work understood or enjoyed. And yet for whatever value a first impression may have for the present or for posterity, it shall be stated here that Arnold Schoenberg's Violin Concerto appeared to be a completely cerebral phenomenon, only vaguely related to music in any of the forms in which it has appeared in history of western civilization—and extremely unpleasant."[3]

Henry's colleague Edwin H. Schloss was more caustic. "Yesterday's piece combines the best sound effects of a hen yard at feeding time, a brisk morning in Chinatown and practice hour at a busy music conservatory. The effect on the vast majority of hearers is that of a lecture on the fourth dimension delivered in Chinese."[4]

Louis Krasner related to me some of the events that preceded the Stokowski performance: "I had played the Berg with him and he called me and said that he would like to do the Schoenberg concerto. We set a date and he said, 'Just tell your manager to get in touch with the orchestra.' My manager, Laberge, did, and two or three weeks later Laberge called me and said that he had sent the contract to the Philadelphia Orchestra and it was returned. They said they knew nothing of such a performance and that it was not planned for that season. . . . Well I was disappointed and concerned, and I called Stokowski and said that the manager returned the contract. 'Oh yes,' he said, 'I know they don't want to have it, but tell Mr. Laberge to return the contract again, and it will be all right; it will be signed.'

"Two or three weeks passed and Laberge told me the contract was returned the second time . . . and I called Stokowski. 'Yes,' he said, 'don't worry about it. We are going to play it. . . . Tell him to send it again. You know they are having difficulties about finances. Send it again.' And the third time the contract was returned. . . . When I called Stokowski about it, he said, 'Yes, they have no finances—they don't want to pay for it, but it doesn't matter. I'm going to pay myself for the performance rights and for the soloist fees. We are going to play it. . . .'

"It was the first performance and I had to work very hard on it, and then he told me to come a week before the performance. . . . Again he said to me, 'Don't worry about the fee. The orchestra will not pay it. I'm going to pay it.' Well, we argued for several minutes. I said, under no circumstances would I accept the fee. . . . On the last day he came and said, 'This is your check for the concert.' This was quite a situation because I refused to take it and would not take it and did not take it.

"We had a rehearsal in the morning and when I got back to the hotel they handed me an envelope with a note and a check in it. The check was from Stokowski and the note said, 'If you do not accept this check, please do not come to the concert.' "[5]

About the performance Krasner said, "He did a wonderful performance of it. He knew it very well."

Apprised of the many difficulties attendant to the performance of the concerto, as well as the superb performance by both Krasner and Stokowski, Schoenberg wrote:

December 17, 1940

Dear Mr. Stokowski:

Only a few people wrote me about the performance of my Violin Concerto with Mr. Krasner under your direction. Some seemed embarrassed, but others write more positively about the impression.

But foremostly: *everybody writes enthusiastically about you,* and not only about the perfect manner in which you performed my work, but especially about your brave stand toward my work and against illiterate snobs.

Let me thank you for all that in the most cordial degree. I appreciate highly, what you do for my music and I learned, not only through Mr. Krasner, that you like the work but also, through him and Mr. Engel, that you had also to fight for it in many ways—let me also thank you for that.

With my most cordial greetings,
Yours faithfully,
Arnold Schoenberg[6]

Goddard Lieberson told me that he had gone down to Philadelphia to hear the concerto. "And you can imagine the first performance of the

Schoenberg Violin Concerto in Philadelphia with that afternoon audience there," he said. "They did a very curious thing. They realized the complexity and difficulty of it for the violin, and they applauded Krasner wildly and booed Stokowski when he came out. I think they wanted to show that they were not against the performer, but were against Stokowski for playing the music."[7]

At the end of the concert Stoki made a brief curtain speech saying: "I will say good-bye to you now for a little while. I will be back again in March, God willing . . . and the board of directors willing."[8]

There was an obvious sarcasm in the reference to the board. It had been embarrassing to have the board refuse to pay for the expenses involved in the Schoenberg work. He still chafed at the board's refusal to let him take the orchestra to Europe. Now he learned that Ormandy had just been given a new five-year contract with the title "Conductor and Music Director." But a third argument had developed. Both the board and RCA complained that his records made with the All-American Youth Orchestra for Columbia were in direct competition with those he was making for RCA Victor with the Philadelphia Orchestra. Someone circulated a rumor that Stokowski demanded an increased stipend per concert. This he denied, as did Orville Bullitt.

"I have not asked for an increase," Stoki insisted. "Quite the contrary. My fee is less than it used to be with the Philadelphia Orchestra. It is less than I receive when I conduct in Europe," he continued. "It is much less than I receive in other places in America. And it is less than half what Toscanini receives." According to the *Evening Bulletin* Toscanini was reported to receive $4,000 per concert. "I come to Philadelphia," Stoki added, "not for professional reasons, but because I love to make music with this orchestra and for the wonderful public in Philadelphia. These are the facts."

He submitted a formal letter to the board, and his Philadelphia lawyer, Joseph Sharfsin, spoke to the press stating that Stokowski had not demanded an increase. To help clear up matters, Orville Bullitt said officially that "the compensation requested by Stokowski for next season is exactly the same as that which he requested for this season. The *Bulletin* conjectured that his compensation had been $2,500 for each concert."[9]

Stoki's relation with the board was far different than it had been when Mr. Van, Andrew Wheeler, the Boks, and others were staunch Stokowski supporters. Bullitt was a brilliant man but certainly not one of any soaring imagination. He was practical and pinched the orchestra's pennies gently but firmly. "I was very budget-minded," he told me. "Stokowski got more and more demanding and we just couldn't pin him down. He would say one thing and then the next time we would meet, he would say, we'll do it this way, and we couldn't."[10]

"We continued for a year to negotiate but his demands became impossible," Bullitt said. "We used to meet . . . with lawyers, but it all came to nothing and we had to part company. We were in a strong position, as he only wanted to conduct a few concerts and by that time we had Ormandy as a proven great conductor who was able to carry the whole season and who asked nothing better. It was not always plain sailing about Ormandy, as some of our board wanted to get rid of him and even resigned when we would not. I find many letters from Stokowski with expressions such as, 'The relation between you and me has always been friendly, courteous, and cooperative.' This would be followed a day later by a front-page newspaper blast from him saying the board of the orchestra was impossible."[11]

While the board may have had its disenchanted members, the American public was still more than beguiled, and Stokowski records still outsold those of any other conductor. After the several resignations and reinstatements, Stoki let it be known that this time the impasse was real. Bullitt may have been relieved, for he could now proceed with a conductor who would be less expensive, less demanding, and less prone to stir up controversy. That he was essentially not of Stokowski's stature seemed not to bother the board as long as he could continue to draw his convention-bound audiences, sell records, and enhance the orchestra's reserves. What Bullitt most appreciated in Ormandy was the fact that he "always devoted himself day and night to the good of our orchestra and has always been more than cooperative to deal with."

In spite of their disagreements, Bullitt did not fail to appreciate Stokowski himself. In his memoirs, he wrote: "Stokowski was one of the greatest living musicians. Strikingly handsome, he had an encyclopaedic mind with a far ranging knowledge of art, architecture and other subjects. Abounding with energy, he was a brilliant conversationalist. . . . He had an excellent sense of humor. . . ."[12]

Though the board had agreed to whatever demands and conditions Stoki had proposed and six dates were tentatively agreed upon, he no longer felt that his life or even a part of it was bound to Philadelphia. The All-American Youth Orchestra was being organized once again and he started out on another coast-to-coast hunt for talent.[13] Some of those who were in the first group were not available. Some simply preferred to absent themselves; an American tour to Kansas City, Toledo, Milwaukee, Denver, and even with San Francisco and Hollywood thrown in, did not possess the lure of Rio, Buenos Aires, Montevideo, and other South American cities.

While on his auditioning tour, Stokowski was awakened early in the morning as his train was passing through Chattanooga, headed for Chicago. He announced that he would not return next season as co-conductor with Eugene Ormandy. He dictated a statement, which he gave to the reporters: "I wrote the board of directors about two weeks ago thanking them for offering me a contract for next season, but that in view of the national emergency which is daily growing more serious, I would like for a period to hold myself free and available to serve the Government and our country."[14]

His services to the government consisted in a short stint at Fort McArthur, California, where he gave some dubious suggestions for improvement and deployment of Army bands. The results were inconclusive.[15]

The news release from Chattanooga on March 11 was carried by Associated Press and was apparently the first news of his severance from the Philadelphia Orchestra. The four years that had passed since his first resignation had inured his followers to this inevitable rupture. Linton Martin commented that Stokowski's complete withdrawal from the orchestra for the first time in twenty-nine years was an "incalculable and irreplaceable loss to this city, in which he made unparalleled and important musical history for more than a quarter of a century. Its seriousness and significance are not to be ignored or underestimated, especially if it means the future beyond next season as well . . . and surely every disinterested music lover must fervently hope that some means might be found of restoring symphonic serenity so far as Stokowski's return is concerned."

Martin summarized most of Stoki's remarkable accomplishments in Philadelphia and then observed: "Whether his superb showmanship has been calculated or accidental, instinctive or intentional, may be debatable. But its value as a source of news, and sometimes sensational news, has spoken for itself up to the present." Without Stokowski the Philadelphians would never have so much fun again. At least not until his actual return nearly two decades later. "If he is gone for good—as the expression quaintly has it—it means the end of an unexampled era of music in this city."[16]

Edwin Schloss reported on the Stokowskians' view. "It is pointed out that the orchestra board is dominated by men with no great musical knowledge, taste or ambition, highly competent and successful businessmen, serving selflessly as a public duty to the community and running the orchestra as if they were the trustees of a hospital or the directors of a bank.

"The dominant directors, it is said, are mainly concerned in conserving the orchestra's financial status while ignoring its chief artistic asset. They are, it is claimed, budget balancers in the narrowest sense of the word, more impressed by the symmetry of a trial balance sheet than the greatest symphonic score."

The Stokowskians maintained that every envisioned move that Stoki had suggested during the past years had been thwarted by the budget-minded directors. "This has involved lack of support in the conductor's projected tours of Russia and South America, and has even at times descended to denying him soloists, and the fees wherewith to pay royalties on music he wanted to play. Who then can blame Stokowski for losing patience at long last?"

There were, of course, counterblasts from the camp of the directors. They pointed out that the directors are in a fiduciary capacity; that the orchestra is largely financed from the income of an endowment fund which is a quasi-public trust; that it is their plain duty to conserve this trust fund. "Furthermore, if the Maestro chooses to sulk in his tent it is his own fault. He is always welcome here."[17] But the welcome was obviously on terms to be imposed by the board.

The final termination with the Philadelphia Orchestra was not a really traumatic experience for Stokowski. There were many new invitations beckoning. As early as January 1941 he and Arthur Judson had discussed an appearance or series of appearances with the New York Philharmonic in celebration of its centennial season.[18] He was engaged for at least two weeks, with the possibility of additional weeks being added. Toscanini, too, was engaged, although at that time his appearance was a bit uncertain. There were rumors that he might relinquish his position as head of the NBC Symphony. Doors seemed to be opening everywhere. Meyerberg reported that the cross-country tour of the Youth Orchestra was almost entirely booked, with local groups sponsoring the concerts.

Stokowski's appearances with the Philadelphia Orchestra that began on March 28, 1941, were to be his last. Even in these he was frustrated and angered by the parsimony of the board. He had programmed the *St. Matthew Passion* with the chorus from the Westminster Choir School.

He had wanted to have major singers for the solo roles, but the board balked and he had to do with singers apparently drawn from the chorus. While it was not a disaster, it was not one of the glorious moments in the history of vocal art.

Because of the nature of the piece, its religious character and spiritual nature, he decreed that there was to be no applause at its conclusion. Had the program been otherwise it would undoubtedly have been punctuated by ovations, talks, farewells, and commotion, but here marking the end of his twenty-nine-year tenure with the orchestra, it ended quietly. There was a strange hush that permeated the hall as he departed. It was with the strains of Bach that he made his exit, just as he had done on the last day he played the organ at St. Bartholomew's. But wait! There is a happy epilogue. There was one more concert to come: a children's concert.[19] Here were no melancholy recollections, no emotional farewells. Stoki, enjoying himself immensely, wanted only to have his young audience enjoy the concert, too.

Either late in 1940 or early in 1941, while the war was mounting in Europe, Stokowski, in a burst of patriotic effusion, offered his services to the Army to develop improvements in military bands. The offer was accepted at once. General George C. Marshall, Army chief of staff, authorized him to "experiment" with the army band at Fort MacArthur, California, to see what improvements might be possible.

On the seventeenth of January the wires of the Associated Press announced nationwide that Stokowski would reorganize the band at Fort MacArthur and direct it in a series of concerts. He planned to visit San Pedro three times a week to rehearse with it.[20] The War Department announced that "Stokowski will endeavor to train the musicians with a view to modernizing Army bands, themselves, and utilizing music further in developing espirit de corps."[21]

The nucleus of the band was to include twenty-three members of the 3rd Coast Artillery Band, and twelve regular bandsmen to be provided by the Infantry, Field Artillery, and Coast Artillery training-center bands. To this group he was to add about fifty trainees.[22] To help him in his investigations Stoki brought Saul Caston, Philadelphia's first trumpeter, to assist him.

Stoki's aims were entirely idealistic. "It is a great personal loss leaving the Philadelphia Orchestra," he told one reporter. "I have so many wonderful friends in it. . . . But there is a condition in the world that compels us all to make sacrifices. When I see thousands of young men going into the army and giving up their occupation and living and families and everything, I feel I am not doing any more than they are doing. You see, I want to be completely free so that I can go anywhere and do anything I can to be useful."[23]

To explain his working with the bands, he prepared a rather lengthy article for the press with answers to various questions. To the question "What is wrong with the present Army bands?" he answered: "There is nothing wrong with them; on the contrary, they are excellent. . . . I do not advocate changing them. The regular Army bands are a national institution. But Army training is expanding so rapidly that it will be difficult to keep pace with this expansion when forming additional bands."

About forming new bands he said he aimed for simplicity, speed, and quality. He recommended replacing such difficult instruments as the oboe, clarinet, English horn, bassoon, bass clarinet, and French horn with instruments that are easier to play. In place of the French horns, he suggested "the new type of American melophones or upright alto horns, which are easier to play and can be learned in a relatively short period. These American instruments have great beauty of tone and a richness and fullness of sound which carries a long distance."

To replace the conventional woodwinds he suggested all types of saxophones. For the general composition of the new bands he recommended that they have three principal groups: "one comprised of the most brilliant instruments like trumpets and trombones, contrasted with another of the rich deep-toned saxophones. Between these two groups comes the third made up of the full and mellow sounding fluegelhorns, melophones, baritones, euphoniums and sousaphones."

He ended on a broad and optimistic note. "America," he said, "was made by men and women without maps, who dared to explore, who had the courage and vision to do things that no one had done before, who had the initiative, to whom everything was possible, but defeat. These are the qualities that make America great and which make me proud to be an American and to offer any knowledge or skill I may have to its service."[24]

The new bands, he is reported to have said, should have "one piccolo; one E-flat soprano saxophone; two soprano saxophones in B-flat; two alto saxophones in E-flat; one tenor saxophone in B-flat; one baritone saxophone in E-flat; one bass saxophone in B-flat; two cornets; one high E-flat trumpet; two trumpets in B-flat; three horns, or altos; two baritones; one euphonium; three trombones; one E-flat bombardon; one B-flat tuba and two percussion players to play bass drum, cymbals, snare drum, triangle, marimbaphone and vibraphone."

He is reported to have advised that for "bandsmen on horseback, or in armored cars, I would suggest adding tympani." He claimed that his band would be "modern, easy to handle when required to move with immense swiftness, very brilliant in the open air, both soft and brilliant indoors, capable of playing jazz and jive."

Stoki and his new ideas brewed up a storm. Bandmasters sputtered objections. And then there was Crap. "In my opinion a band can't get along without clarinets," declared Sergeant William B. Crap, marine bandmaster at the Navy Yard. He added that Stokowski was "not even a corporal in the Boy Scouts and therefore has no right to be monkeying around with military music and bands."

It seems highly improbable that Stoki ever seriously suggested putting bands in tanks or armored cars, but his opposition became intensely vocal about it. "What I'd like to have Stokowski explain," said one Army band man, "is how the heck he'd get all those in a tank or an armored car."[25]

When the American Bandmaster's Association held their annual convention in Madison on March 1, the UP reported that they "gave a long unmusical 'raspberry' to Leopold Stokowski's scheme for putting bandsmen in armored cars."[26] Next he found himself being excoriated on the floor of the House by Congressman George H. Bender (Republican, Ohio). He accused Stokowski of squandering the taxpayers' money on experiments. "Picture the possibilities," he exclaimed to his fellow congressmen. "The cries of anguish from the perturbed saxophone players would probably frighten the enemy to a quick and decisive retreat."[27]

Saul Caston came to Stokowski's defense. He had just returned to Philadelphia from Fort MacArthur, where the experiments were held. "The officers and members of the band appeared satisfied with the work of Mr. Stokowski. I can say the experiments were definitely a success. The men were enthusiastic. . . . Mr. Stokowski is chiefly concerned with sound for the army bands," Saul continued. "Anyone has just to consider what he has accomplished in tone quality with the symphony orchestra to realize he knows what he's doing."[28]

But what Stoki would now be "doing" was more preoccupying than his concern with military music. He had the All-American Youth Orchestra tour before him and the New York Philharmonic as well as the NBC Symphony to consider. He also began to plan his book for Simon and Schuster; he had even chosen its title: "Music for All of Us." Even if his private life was not too well ordered at that time, his professional life certainly was.

The Second All-America
Youth Orchestra Tour

P LANS for the second tour began early. Even before he had begun
to hold auditions and recruit his new orchestra, he had decided that
he would play American compositions on every program if possible.
In February 1941 he wrote to Claire Reis from California: "In May, June
and July we are making another tour of the All-American Youth Orchestra, . . . I would like to play as many compositions of American composers
as possible—and I am wondering whether you and the League of Composers would be willing to help me in this?" He explained that he was
particularly interested in shorter works that might be sandwiched among
the longer works on the programs. He concluded his brief note with: "I
shall be happy if we can be working together again as we used to."[1]

Just how the League helped him find works is hard to determine. I
suspect that most of them were ones that he had found on his own. As
he had performed Cowell on the previous tour successfully, he decided
to include him on this tour as well. Other composers whom he chose were
Morton Gould, Roy Harris, Roger Sessions, Natalie Bender, Henry Brant,
Paul Creston, Charles Miller, Victor Young, and William Grant Still.

Natalie Bender, or "Natasha" as Stoki preferred to call her, had continued to be involved in whatever activities she could to be of assistance
to him, just as she had done in her work with the children's and youth
concerts. She helped him prepare scores and check out parts, and helped
him in writing out his various transcriptions. Stoki had performed one of
her works on a Youth Concert and now decided to add one to the
repertory of the All-American Youth Orchestra. "It was really a haba-

428

nera," Natasha told me. "He decided that the title 'Habanera' wasn't interesting, so he suggested *San Luis Rey*. It had to be more exotic. Actually I was very much under the influence of Debussy's *Night in Granada* because I had been helping him copy the orchestration just as Cailliet had helped him with the Bach orchestrations. If you go to the library at Curtis, you will see that half of it is in my handwriting."[2]

As early as 1932 Stoki had played a Cowell work in Philadelphia; it was his *Synchrony*, a work which was originally written for Martha Graham. It began with a horrendously difficult, long trumpet solo, which was followed by a lengthy movement for the whole orchestra. He performed other works including a *Reel* for orchestra. He selected a rather short work, *Ancient Desert Drone*, for the new tour, but out of curiosity wrote to Cowell early in 1941 asking whether there existed any orchestral versions of his early piano pieces. Henry then set about expanding four of his pieces—The *Tides of Manaunaun, Exultation, The Harp of Life*, and *Lilt of the Reel*—as a suite for piano and orchestra, which he called *Tales of Our Countryside*. Stokowski was pleased and invited Cowell to perform it with the Youth Orchestra during parts of the tour.[3]

The invitation to Cowell to perform with the orchestra was a brave and noble gesture. Stokowski and countless other distinguished musicians had been interested in Cowell's plight, for in 1936 he became involved in a homosexual scandal and was sentenced to San Quentin for fifteen years.[4] One of the distinguished celebrities who wrote letters in his behalf was Stokowski.[5] As a result of the efforts of Stoki and many other distinguished musicians and scholars, Cowell was released from prison on May 8, 1940, and was engaged by Percy Grainger, to become his amanuensis and catalogue his music.[6]

Cowell traveled to Atlantic City to rehearse with the new orchestra and made his first appearance with it at its initial program on Sunday May 11, 1941, in the ballroom of Atlantic City's Convention Hall. The program included the Toccata and Fugue in D Minor, the Beethoven Fifth, Cowell's *Tales of Our Countryside*, and the "Love Music" from *Tristan und Isolde*, played "by request."

Like its predecessor, the new orchestra was an excellent one and was even more of a "youth" orchestra. The average age of the players was twenty-two. There were forty-seven new members and fifteen of them were women. The sixteen players from the Philadelphia Orchestra had been reduced to eight. Critics found it more self-sufficient than it had been the previous season.[7]

The tour was managed by Myerberg with great skill. The first week brought it along the east coast from Washington to Boston, then westward and north to Toronto, followed by concerts in the Midwest, and a final series covering the Pacific coast from Seattle to Los Angeles. A projected stop in Tijuana was abandoned. Thirty-five cities had been booked, and with Barnumesque drumbeating, Myerberg was able to insure enormous audiences wherever Stokowski and the Youth Orchestra appeared. He also arranged for interviews in most of the cities en route.

Stoki praised his young musicians extravagantly. "I would not exchange this orchestra for any other orchestra in the world," he stated. "These young people are phenomenal. Technically they are the equals of any musicians. And they have the enthusiasm of youth. They are so sensitive, so quick. With them the playing of music is not just a job. They have a love for it. . . . You see," he said, explaining his own position, "I have a debt to America that I want to repay. America has been wonderful to me. Now I can do something for America, in giving all of these fine youngsters from all over the country a chance to play in a fine symphony. I receive no payment whatsoever for this work. This is not a commercial venture."[8]

In their New York appearance, Olin Downes confirmed Stoki's estimate and called the orchestra astonishing. He praised the remarkable material in the orchestra, and although he considered the performance of the Brahms Third not quite up to par, he found "unforgettable and well-nigh unsurpassable" its playing of Stokowski's transcription of passages from Wagner's *Tristan.*

Like many of his colleagues, Downes was bowled over by the miracle that Stokowski had accomplished in assembling another group of recruits and welding them into a remarkable ensemble.[9]

In Boston the reaction was the same. An enormous throng gathered in the Boston Garden; almost triple the number that ever attended a performance of Boston's own orchestra in Symphony Hall. Then on to Springfield, Buffalo, Toronto, Pittsburgh, Detroit and Chicago. In the "windy city" critic Eugene Stinson, who was then Chicago's most prestigious and perceptive critic, used such adjectives as "perfection" and "spellbinding."[10]

In Milwaukee, critic Edward Halline observed that "even without the peerless help of the Philadelphia Orchestra, Leopold Stokowski proved again . . . that he is still the most dramatic of conductors."[11]

When Stokowski arrived in St. Paul, students from the University of Minnesota were on hand to greet him and present him with a "sheepskin" conferring on him the degree of "Bachelor of Boogie Woogie." They also had composed a special tune for him titled "Stomp 'em Out Stokie." All seemed well until they presented him with a hat bearing the legend "Beat Me Dimitri." Whether the use of Dimitri was merely alliterative or referring to Dimitri Mitropoulos was not clear, but Myerberg stepped in at this point and announced firmly that "we will have no boogie woogie presentation."[12] Mitropoulos was still conductor of the Minneapolis Symphony Orchestra and Stoki would never be party to anything that might seem to ridicule or treat lightly any colleague. His sense of humor did not run in that direction.

The next night in Omaha he included Natalie Bender's *San Luis Rey*, announcing it simply to the audience as *Habanera*. One local critic, Martin W. Bush, found that the work had considerable charm and added that "its ideas seemed to crystallize, it has harmonic feeling, its orchestration is neat and the general effect highly worthwhile."[13]

On June 9 the orchestra played in St. Louis. The large audience that braved a torrential rain to fill the cavernous Convention Hall in the Municipal Auditorium was according to one reporter not an audience of habitual concertgoers. "It was, itself, emphatically an audience of youth."

A new American work by Charles Miller called *Appalachian Mountains* was played for the first time. The local critic liked the work and described its various movements graphically—referring to its "hoedown of Yankee lustihood."[14] Immediately after the concert, Stoki boarded a train and set off for Indianapolis, where he arrived at 6:15 the following morning. The orchestra and all of their baggage and paraphernalia did not arrive until midday.[15]

The reason for Stoki's haste was to confer with Myerberg on an unpleasant matter affecting the finances of the orchestra. The orchestra was placed in temporary receivership due to a complaint made by one Horace Kiser of New York, who alleged that Michael Myerberg owed him $709 in salary and expenses as advance sales manager for the orchestra. Apparently Kiser had worked only two weeks before Myerberg fired him, and he claimed that Myerberg had said that he no longer had any money to pay him. That is the story that went out on the wires of the Associated Press. The matter came to a head and Judge Othniel Hitch appointed Cletus Seibert, deputy county clerk, receiver and ordered that the corporation's share of proceeds of the concert ". . . be turned over to him. . . ."[16]

After the publicity given to the financial problems that had surfaced in Indianapolis, reporters began to inquire into the financing of the orchestra. All seemed impressed that Stokowski received nothing for his services. Myerberg gave numerous interviews and reported that Stoki contributed most of the money to meet the orchestra's deficits. "Stokowski," said Myerberg, "feels a definite sense of obligation to America for the opportunities the country has given to him. And to demonstrate his appreciation, Stokowski is spending his own money—and he is not a rich man—to make America conscious of the greatness of her own native artists and to spread opportunity for young American musicians who otherwise might not have an opportunity to be heard."[17]

Surely, it seems, if CBS and Columbia Records were picking up the tab for the orchestra's tour, Myerberg would have credited their contribution. Although they were to make another series of recordings in Hollywood at the tour's end, I have not found any evidence that they had contributed toward the cost of the tour. Stoki then must have been the sole angel for the new orchestra.

Because of the court issue, Stoki was detained in Indianapolis and arrived in Louisville twelve hours after the orchestra. At the station he was met by a small welcoming group that included Robert Whitney, who was to become the future conductor of the Louisville Orchestra, and, like Stoki, an ardent promoter of American music.[18] Together they proceeded to the State Fair Grounds for a rehearsal for that evening's concert. Rob described the old exhibition hall. "It was an immense thing used for horse shows. They were an annual thing, and I went once or twice when I first came to Louisville. I remember that the roof was glassed over, but a lot of the panes had been broken, so the birds would be chattering up there under the roof. But he had his own shell and, of course, it worked very well."

"I remember he was very irritated after playing the excerpts from *Tristan*," recalled Whitney. "At the quiet end—the Love Death—the people couldn't wait for it to end and started to applaud."[19] The reviewer in the *Louisville Courier-Journal* concurred with the audience: "We remember no more moving reading . . . than the All-American Youth Orchestra gave us. . . . None which drew such magic, such throbbing beauty, which Mr. Stokowski has perfected and sensitized in so short a time."[20]

On June 13, two days after the Louisville concert, the orchestra was heard in Nashville. Here they performed Debussy's *Fêtes*, which "could be heard in all its evanescence in spite of the sound of raucous voices and

automobile horns on the street," the Franck Symphony, and Morton
Gould's *Guaracho*. Between the first and second movements of the Symphony "there was a fantasia performed by a switch-engine on the spur
track on the South side of the baseball park," one critic observed. The
Wagner went without a hitch, but during a final encore, so our critic
reported, "a nearby locomotive started on a concerto of its own, Stokowski
got 'regusted,' and walked away, thus ending the alfresco performance."[21]

The audience had been augmented by hundreds of soldiers from nearby
Camp Forest, at Stokowski's invitation. He had wired to the commanding
officer of the camp: "With General Marshall's approval, we invite any
men from your camp deeply interested in music to attend without charge
our concert in Nashville. We would like to give them a place of honor."[22]
They arrived in bus loads.

On June 15 the All-American Youth Orchestra arrived in Kansas City,
where they "piled out of a special train . . . like a pack of hotel guests
fleeing a fire." Stoki was described as being hatless, shock-haired, and
traveling light. "He carried no luggage and not even a baton. He strode
ahead of a lurching, stumbling horde with his head high, wearing, like a
badge of his individuality, the familiar pink shirt, the narrow green tie,
the gray suit, and curiously contrived tan suede shoes."[23] The concert the
following night was for one of the largest and most varied audiences ever
to hear a symphony orchestra concert in Kansas City. Over eight thousand
were assembled.[24]

The next night was Wichita and then on to Colorado Springs, where
there was a short time for sight-seeing and a break in the tiresome schedule and cramped conditions. The committee members in charge of arrangements were eager to take the young players on sight-seeing trips to
the summit of Cheyenne Mountain, the Garden of the Gods, and Seven
Falls.[25] The announced program contained Interludes from the *Folksong*
Symphony of Roy Harris, who was there on the Colorado College summer
faculty.

There had been considerable concern about having a work of Roy
Harris on the program. As early as the first concert in Atlantic City the
subject had been raised. Harris was not one of the composers whom
Stokowski had ever championed. He left that to Toscanini and Koussevitzky. After looking through many works and trying out some on tour,
he settled on some short segments from the *Folksong* Symphony, which
is basically a choral work with short interludes between each choral setting
of folk songs. It was from these that Stoki fashioned a brief suite using

two of these interludes. The first time he tried it out was in Springfield, where he did it as an encore. "Nobody in the audience knew whether it was over or not," Bob Gross recalled. "And Stoki was not going to help them. He stood with his hands down, his back to them and waited. He could just as easily have been getting ready to go into another movement. . . . It must have been three or four minutes, but it felt like an hour before a few brave souls in the audience clapped very timidly. . . . Stoki just grinned to us and finally walked off."[26]

Wherever it was played the reaction was the same; the orchestra members organized a little pool, wagering on how long it would be before the first person would applaud. With stop watches in hand, they clocked the interval. When it was done in Indianapolis, a critic headlined a paragraph in his review: "Stokowski Enjoys Joke." The program, he wrote, "included an American work, Roy Harris' diverting Interlude for Strings and Percussion from the *Folksong* Symphony. Stokowski and the orchestra enjoyed a little joke at the expense of the audience as they finished this number. The audience didn't know it was ended."[27]

"After all," Bob told his colleagues, "we do know one place where that isn't going to happen, because when we play it in Colorado Springs, Roy will be there and he will lead the applause and that will take care of that situation." But that is not quite what happened. Bob Gross again: "When it came time to play Roy Harris' piece on our Colorado Springs concert, Roy did not recognize the ending anymore than anyone else did. It was one of the longest and most embarrassing waits in the entire tour before someone—I don't think it was Roy—got the idea that the piece was over and started to applaud."[28]

The concert was a great success and the Penrose Stadium adjacent to Colorado Springs' famous Broadmoor Hotel was completely filled. It had been managed by Carol Truax, who expertly handled all details and raised funds to make it possible. "That's what made me an impresario," said Carol. "If it had rained, I never would have bothered with another concert because I had to get underwriting from everyone, you see. Because we had a nice night, it made me a concert manager from then on . . . an impresario."[29]

Natasha had caught up with the orchestra in Colorado and partook of all of the sight-seeing events and social functions. She had set out on a Greyhound bus and hoped to hear her composition when it was played in Wichita but did not arrive on time. Stoki had written to her after its first performance saying: " 'It's beginning to sound wonderful,' " she said.

"I just nearly died with excitement." Natasha met Mrs. Tipton, the mother of Stoki's principal flutist, and with her drove to Seattle while the orchestra proceeded to continue with concerts in Denver and Salt Lake City where Stoki added another American work to his program, Henry Brant's *Decision,* from his ballet *City Portrait.*

In Seattle, Natasha heard her piece for the first time. Just after intermission, Stoki made a short speech outlining the aims of the orchestra. The critic wrote: "A promise of Stokowski's is to play the work of an American composer on every program. Pennsylvanian Natalie Bender's *San Luis Rey,* colorfully tuneful, held the spot last night. The Love Music from *Tristan und Isolde* was an experience for the sated as well as the uninitiated, for it was typically Stokowski." Natasha could be pleased because she was right up there with Wagner.[30]

After Seattle, Stoki brought the Youth Orchestra to Portland and Sacramento and on June 26 arrived in San Francisco for their concert there the following evening. "That amazing and incredible man Leopold Stokowski came back to town yesterday," wrote Alfred Frankenstein in his *Chronicle* review. He wrote that the All-American Youth Orchestra was probably the most important, fruitful, and far-reaching manifestation of the restless search for novelty that has made Stokowski's career "one of the most spectacular in recent musical history."

Then came the clincher. Frankenstein was not only one of the country's finest music critics but also a trained and perceptive reporter. He stated that Stokowski was "financing the whole thing himself. . . . But this tour is not the final answer, and Stokowski cannot go on paying the bills forever." And he added: "One may be sure, however, that this tour will have long-range results, many of them invisible at the present moment."[31]

Obviously for financial reasons, the final spur of the tour taking in San Diego and Tijuana was canceled, and so the grand finale took place in Pasadena's gigantic Rose Bowl under circumstances that were less than ideal. The day was very hot and a blazing sun drenched the players and the audience. A large umbrella was raised over Stoki, but the players sweltered in their shirt sleeves. As always, Stoki was sartorially proper in his tails.

The concert began at 3:00, and as the afternoon progressed the gradually setting sun glared directly into the eyes of the players. Whether these conditions, fatigue, or general letdown at the end of the tour affected them, the orchestra did not rise to its peak. The critics were not thrown into ecstasies.

Many of the players departed for their homes while a nucleus remained to make recordings. On July 3 the first of the recordings took place, and they were to continue until July 11.

One wonders what happened. The overall quality of the records was bad; the conducting in many instances capricious. There seemed to have been considerable postrecording tinkering with dynamics. Reviews were spotty.

In comparing various recordings of the Schubert *Unfinished,* Irving Kolodin mentions "the willful instability of Stokowski [who] every so often fringes on respectability, but the proximity, like a moth at a candle, is too much for him and he veers off into the blackness of self-indulgence."[32]

If the orchestra did not play as perfectly as it might have, we can easily appreciate that for two months they had been playing one-night stands and for the most part sleeping in sleeping cars. But the choice of repertory that Columbia wanted was particularly witless. With so much to choose from, it was folly to duplicate for the most part the identical works Stoki had previously recorded with the Philadelphia Orchestra.

By this time he must have known that his grand plan of taking the orchestra on an even more extensive trip through Mexico and South America would be impractical. If not, Pearl Harbor would soon settle that.

Stokowski eagerly anticipated conducting the New York Philharmonic in October and made out his programs while still in Beverly Hills. The programs of the All-American Youth Orchestra became the basis of Stoki's programs for New York. The 1941–42 season marked the orchestra's centennial season, and Judson engaged a series of distinguished guest conductors to add their respective glamour and lend excitement to the season. He and the board were also casting about for a new permanent conductor. Judson's first choice in the sequence of guest conductors was Stokowski, to be followed by Barbirolli, Bruno Walter, Artur Rodzinski, Dimitri Mitropoulos, Fritz Busch, Eugene Goossens, Serge Koussevitzky, Walter Damrosch, and Arturo Toscanini.

Stoki's engagement was to last two weeks and he was to conduct eight concerts. His opening pair, October 9 and 10, were identical with that of the first concert of the All-American Youth Orchestra on its second tour, but for the addition of a short Andante Sostenuto, from Bach's Sonata for Violin in A Minor, in his own arrangement. Otherwise it consisted of the Toccata and Fugue in D Minor, the Beethoven Symphony No. 5, Henry Cowell's *Tales of Our Countryside,* and Wagner's "Prelude and

Love Death" from *Tristan*. Cowell was again soloist and pounded, thwacked, plucked, and rolled out sonorities that delighted the Philharmonic audience. On his second pair, October 11 and 12, Stoki conducted the Bach-Stokowski Andante Sostenuto, Beethoven's Symphony No. 7, Roy Harris' Folk Dance for Strings and Percussion (this time he listed it as coming from the *Folksong* Symphony) and to conclude, the "Prelude and Love Death."[33]

To avoid any adverse reaction from the players, Stoki had kept the orchestra in its regular seating arrangement rather than follow his own preferred plan. But that did little to mask the latent hostility of the hard-core "Toscanini mafia" and others in the orchestra. The magic that he and his young players had been able to evoke with these same compositions completely escaped the men of the Philharmonic. The lackluster playing of the orchestra during his first evening—and that, of course, was the one that would be reviewed—made the event dull rather than festive. The audience reception was lukewarm; the critical reports were frigid.

The most perceptive and valid assessment of the evening was made not by a New Yorker, but by Philadelphian Henry Pleasants, who covered the concert for the *Evening Bulletin*: "Only one thing was lacking in what might otherwise have been a characteristic Stokowski concert: the Philadelphia Orchestra. And one learned last night to what a degree Mr. Stokowski and the Philadelphia Orchestra were complementary. Conductor and orchestra grew together, and the orchestra knew the conductor, knew his moods, ideas and methods, and responded intuitively.

"Not so the Philharmonic-Symphony. A Philadelphian listening to last night's concert knew very well what Mr. Stokowski wanted and could easily remark how little of it he got. It was very little. Mr. Stokowski's conceptions have more to do with mysticism than with note values and symmetrical dynamics, and the mystical, imaginative element seemed to elude completely an orchestra brought up on the precise stick technique of such as Toscanini, Walter, Busch and Furtwängler. It even caused occasional confusion. . . ."

Henry concluded by remarking that with the All-American Youth Orchestra, he was able to achieve results that approximated the Philadelphia Orchestra. "But the Philharmonic-Symphony is already set in its ways, and its ways are not Mr. Stokowski's."[34]

If the players had planned to sabotage Stokowski, they did not succeed. They sabotaged themselves. All of the critics had remarked about the bad playing of the orchestra and Olin Downes had been severe. He had placed the blame on Stokowski at first. But on reviewing the concerts of the second week, he literally apologized in print. He said that his criticism of Stokowski "did the leader a measure of injustice." He remarked that to his gratification and that of the audience the Philharmonic again played like a first-class orchestra: ". . . when Mr. Stokowski assembled his Youth Orchestra two years ago—an organization, it is true, with a sprinkling of professionals from the Philadelphia Orchestra which Mr. Stokowski had built, but nevertheless a new, if not a green, orchestra—that orchestra played, at its first concerts, considerably better than the Philharmonic-Symphony played at its initial effort, under the same conductor of this season." "Why?" Downes asked rhetorically. And he concluded that "whatever the reason, the orchestra and Mr. Stokowski came into their own last night, to the vast pleasure and approval of the audience."

The war was over. Stokowski had won, and the men, almost as if performing an act of contrition, played for him for the rest of his stay with almost sympathetic cooperation. Downes confirmed his vindication: "We heard again a great orchestra, and the unique Stokowski." His conducting, he said, was "virtuosity incarnate."[35]

46

Bach-Stokowski

No composer's music was more deeply ingrained in Stokowski's ethos than that of Johann Sebastian Bach. As a choirboy he sang Bach chorales and later at the Temple Church he sang in performances of the *St. Matthew Passion*.[1]

At the Royal College of Music he learned music of Bach both for the organ and piano. He knew intimately the preludes and fugues for both instruments, as well as other varied pieces. Almost required reading for students was the English version of Spitta's monumental study of Bach. Spitta viewed Bach's *St. Matthew Passion* in dramatic terms: "Bach, composing a devotional Passion, makes the whole chorus groan out the name of Barabbas. . . . He depicts in the strongest manner the savage feeling of the populace giving them a dramatic identity, and at the same time suggests the sudden horror which seized the believing Christians at their answer . . . .

"The chorus 'Let Him be crucified' . . . after a few bars of recitative, follows this soul-shaking cry. . . ."[2]

Stokowski pointed out these excerpts in Spitta one evening when he spotted the volume in my library.

Sir Walford Davies had suggested doing the *Christmas Oratorio* as a kind of pantomime, but Stoki wanted to go further. He planned a performance of the *St. Matthew Passion* in the Metropolitan Opera for the benefit of the Quakers and sought the cooperation of Robert Shaw, who had trained a superb chorus called the Collegiate Chorale. Stoki regarded

Shaw highly and considered him one of the finest choral conductors he had ever heard.

"In the early Collegiate Chorale," said Bob, "we had something like 205 voices, of which 105 to 110 were men. We had a bass section of about 65 to 70, of which fully a third were very low basses. When he heard this sound and proposed doing the *St. Matthew Passion,* he decided that he would like to have the chorales at least doubled in 8 voices and wherever possible in 12 voices, so that you had an enormously rich texture rather than just the four vocal lines. . . . He responded enormously to texture and to color and he was quick to exploit it. . . ."[3]

Stoki's conception of the work was far more dramatic than that of Bob's, who was then in the grip of a German musicologist. Stoki told me that he wanted parts of it to be "wild like a man who has lost control, and too often those choruses are sung like an oratorio with the kind of tame church singing. I could not make the Shaw Chorale give me that dramatic feeling. I do not know why. There was much that they could not understand; they sang it like a Mendelssohn oratorio. It should be wild, mad. The cruel sound of those vocal phrases 'Let Him be crucified' and that example when Pilot says 'Whom shall I release?' and they shout 'Barabbas' and the effect that Bach made with three notes shows that he meant it to be dramatic. Like so much today, it has been leveled down."[4]

"It wasn't dramatic enough for him, so he made everybody finish with a big hiss, and we yelled it. I think he had something like half the choir yell it at any pitches they wanted and the rest of the choir sing," Bob recalled.[5]

"There are three types of choruses," Stokowski stated. "Those who sympathize with Christ, the choruses expressing the bloodthirsty hatred of a brutal mob and the chorales which are to be sung by everyone."[6]

"Jesus," Bob recalled, "was represented by a vertical shaft of yellow light. Lillian Gish, with her arms outstretched, walked across the stage from place to place."[7]

When I spoke to Miss Gish about the evening she replied: "I was really flattered and pleased to be asked. I thought to myself, oh, it will be wonderful to be on the great stage of the Metropolitan and be on a stage where the floor won't squeak. . . . And of course I had to be barefoot, and the thing that bothered me very much was that here the floor not only squeaked, but there were splinters everywhere."[8]

She was playing the role of Mary Magdalene and symbolically dried the feet of the Savior with her hair at the base of the shaft of light. "So of course I could not be troubled by my own feet," Miss Gish reminded me.

One of the principal soloists was Eleanor Steber. "I had done a lot of oratorios, but as a soloist sitting on the stage with the orchestra in back of me. But here he was putting us in the pit with the orchestra. The chorus was lined up on either side of the old Met stage . . . Jennie Tourel was the contralto."[9]

Time magazine remarked rather snidely that the stage was peopled with "a bevy of hooded mimes, who prowled about like Ku Klux Klansmen at a Konklave." Quipped Olin Downes: "Bach's music . . . stood up surprisingly well under the handicap. . . ."[10] Robert Edmond Jones did the staging, Balanchine the choreography, and Natalie Bender played the organ. The orchestra was drawn from the Juilliard and other student orchestras.

The musicologists were horrified, just as they were about his transcriptions and interpretations of Bach, but the public reveled in it. It became fashionable to deride all of his Bach transcriptions. At a concert when he conducted his Passacaglia and Fugue in C Minor, Winthrop Sargeant referred to it as one of Stokowski's "much denounced Bach transcriptions." He added: "I don't agree with the denouncers. Bach, too, was a romantic composer, and Mr. Stokowski has put this work in a romantic setting that I find majestic and moving. If anyone doesn't like it in this version, there are plenty of tinkling, baroque-organ versions available."[11]

Aesthetically, Stoki thought of Bach in pictorial and emotional terms. "The Toccata and Fugue in D Minor," he wrote, "is like a vast upheaval of Nature. It gives the impression of great white thunderclouds—like those that float so often over the valley of the Seine—or the towering majesty of the Himalayas. The Fugue is set in the frame of the Toccata, which comes before and after. This work is one of Bach's supreme inspirations—the final cadence is like massive Doric columns of white marble."[12]

"Mostly in Bach's music it is a religious feeling," he said. "That kind of feeling is the important thing, whether it is played by pipes in an organ or by pipes like the flute and the trumpet. They're all pipes, those instruments. The important thing is not so much the instrument, although the organ is a very noble instrument, but the feeling that the music expresses."[13]

"Bach's chorale preludes," he wrote, "will live forever in the hearts and souls of all those whose inner nature responds to this profound music. If Bach were alive today, he would undoubtedly write glorious music for the highly evolved modern orchestra—he would find no limits to his expression, but would use every resource of the orchestra today as he used every resource of the organ in his own time. . . .

"When Handel wrote *The Messiah,* he conceived of choruses of heroic dimensions . . . but the orchestra of his time was limited and the instruments were far less evolved than they are today. To play and sing this music today we should, in my opinion, try to conceive of the orchestra as Handel himself would conceive of it, if he had the instrumental potentialities we have today. This is what I have tried to do with some of Bach's music. Naturally those whose minds are concerned with the written and literal aspects of music—who do not fully realize the importance of music as it *sounds*—in our imagination—will not admit the constant evolution of music and the never-ending growth of its expression."[14]

It became fashionable to say "ugh" at the mere mention of a Stokowski Bach transcription. But the same pseudointellectuals made no such gurgle at the mention of those overcolored ones by Respighi or those of Schoenberg or Hamilton Harty. Perhaps because they simply did not know them. Stokowski's "Bach transcriptions were considered monstrosities by most musicians, who in addition were outraged over his free hand with the orchestration of sacred masterpieces. Intellectuals simply laughed at him," wrote Harold Schonberg.[15]

But there were those who didn't laugh. "In the musical sphere," wrote Irving Kolodin, "his wide-eyed wonder that anybody should find the 'spirit of the composer' misrepresented by him might be written off as naïveté if it did not consort with a musical mentality of the highest sophistication and intuition. One cannot mark him down as either a charlatan or a poseur, for his accomplishments are too considerable, his attainments beyond belittling, whatever one may think of this manifestation or that."[16]

When Stokowski programmed a sequence of his Bach transcriptions with the Philadelphia Orchestra in New York, Olin Downes considered them "sheer inspiration."[17] Paul Hume told me: "I can see better now than I used to when I was young and intolerant, the purposes that his transcriptions served. I knew the organ works. Therefore, I didn't think they needed to be transcribed, and in that view I was narrow because I didn't realize that most people never went and heard them played on the organ. . . . I've long since gotten over that. . . . But I would not for anything give up the transcriptions such as 'Mein Jesu! was für Seelenweh,' which just plows me under every time I hear it."[18]

There had been the belief that the transcriptions were done not by Stokowski but by an orchestra member, Lucien Cailliet. I contacted Cailliet in 1978 and received several letters from him. He wrote: "From my first contact with the maître, I always addressed him as 'Maître.' In fact, we only conversed in French which the maître spoke perfectly and, at that time, I did not speak English."

Shortly after World War I, according to Cailliet, Stokowski engaged a soloist who was to sing the "Marseillaise" and he did not like the accompaniment. He asked Cailliet if he could do a revision of the score: "I answered that I would be glad to. . . . He liked my orchestration very much! That started me in doing all his orchestrations. In fact, the next one he asked me [to do] was the C Minor Passacaglia. Of course, *we had some discussions before* as, after all, he was an organist and a famous musician. Later on was the Toccata and Fugue in D Minor, the Fête-Dieu à Seville and so on. . . . The Maestro was very fair and had me well-paid plus my functions as clarinetist, which he also liked. I must confide in you that as the situation developed, Stokowski asked me from the beginning not to mention or speak about it and keep the situation 'entre nous' and adding: 'The people would not understand.' That is how the name of Stokowski appeared on the programs as orchestrator. At that time, all conductors appeared as the orchestrator or composer ([when] in fact they did not!).

"Maestro Stokowski made an orchestra sound better than any orchestra. It was magic!"[19]

On a photo which Stoki sent to Cailliet, he inscribed: "For Lucien Cailliet with deepest appreciation of his collaboration."[20]

One must be fair to both Stokowski and Cailliet. With his many demands with the orchestra, it is inconceivable that Stoki would do the laborious and grinding task of copying the transcriptions. Either Cailliet or someone else would have had to have been assigned that chore. But one must regard seriously Cailliet's remark: "We had some discussions before"—which indicates that Stoki obviously had planned the instrumentation in his own mind and then had Cailliet carry out his indications. Long after 1938, when his association with Cailliet had ended, Stoki continued to produce transcriptions. Shortly before his death, he was planning to do an orchestration of a fugue from Bach's *Well-Tempered Clavier*. It was the Fugue in C-sharp Minor and in the piano score he indicated exactly what instruments were to be used.

Like an organist who presets the stops to produce specific sonic colors,

Stoki knew precisely what instruments he wanted. We can readily see from his scores that after an arrangement had been made, he altered many of them substantially, and, in fact, continued to do so.

David Madison, violinist with the Philadelphia Orchestra, went on the trip to South America with Stoki and the All-American Youth Orchestra. He spoke to me about Cailliet: "He had a reputation of being a very, very good musician and arranger, and it would not be too farfetched to think that Stokowski might have asked him some questions, or shown him a score, or gotten some advice from him. That wouldn't be too farfetched. . . .

"I watched him operate one day on the South American tour. . . . I suggested a work to him. 'Look,' I said, 'there's a marvelous piece, the E Major Prelude of Bach from the last partita.' He said, 'I would love to hear it.' I got the fiddle section and he came into the ballroom, sat down in a chair, and we played it standing up. There was not a kid in that group that didn't know it by memory. . . . He had a music score in front of him and as we went along he filled in. He had it ready the next day for copying. We all got together and copied out all the parts. We rehearsed it and when we got to South America we played it. . . ."[21]

Rosalyn Tureck, now an eminent Bach scholar, once asked Stokowski if he were to do his Bach transcriptions again, would he do them the same way. He answered: "I would do them exactly the same way." When some remarked that the transcriptions were entirely the work of Cailliet and Stokowski didn't have anything to do with them, she replied: "That is really impossible, because no matter how good Cailliet might have been, it certainly would have been Stokowski who directed him to even the registrations and the coloration. I mean the instrumentation, because we must remember that Stokowski was an organist of the romantic school. . . . He played the symphony orchestra as a nineteenth-century organ and his transcriptions show this kind of relationship."[22]

Lilette Hindin, who worked for Stokowski as a copyist for many years, told me that she had done one orchestration for him that was very simple because "he had made very clear exactly what he wanted. It was a Gabrieli work which he transcribed for orchestra, and when he gave me the material, he indicated precisely which instruments were to play what, so that my job was simply to put the notes down for the correct instruments. And I think the only thing I may have had to worry about was the instrument transpositions that I made. Then it suddenly occurred to me that this may very well have been what Cailliet had done."[23]

"If it hadn't been for Stokowski's transcriptions, we would have a

different conception of Bach," said composer Ellis Kohs. "It is generally
regarded now that his transcriptions are not in true eighteenth-century
style, which is neither here nor there. What he did do was to bring out,
in a way that nobody else has, the essential mysticism and the romanticism
of Bach, which is undeniable. And if he had to lean over backwards to
make that manifest, then it was a good thing, and I think we have to thank
him for it."[24]

Following a concert which José Iturbi gave in Pittsburgh during the
early part of April 1937, he was interviewed by a local reporter. Walter
Leuba, an earnest admirer of Stokowski, was quite irked by some of
Iturbi's statements. "As well as I remember," Mr. Leuba informed me,
"he made some claim to having done, or assisted in some of the transcriptions. This struck me as peculiar, since I felt that Stokowski's hand was
clearly evident."[25]

Thereupon Lueba wrote to Stoki about Iturbi's comments and he
expressed his indignation about them. Stoki responded at once. "Thank
you for writing me so frankly about my Bach transcriptions," he wrote.
"I have heard similar rumors as coming from the same person, whom I
have befriended in every possible way. The Bach transcriptions are all
mine, completely so, and nobody else has had any hand in them except
those who copied the orchestral parts. I wish I had more exact proof and
could face this person with his sordid actions."[26]

During a conversation with Iturbi about Stokowski, the subject of
transcriptions never came up. Iturbi mentioned that his debut in America
was with Stoki and the Philadelphia Orchestra. "He was most cordial and
nice," he said. "I can only praise this man for his tremendous personality.
. . . You know, after I made my debut with him, I never played with him
again but I did conduct half of the tour that the Philadelphia Orchestra
made coast to coast [with Ormandy]. And once he played one of my
compositions."[27]

Obviously time changes all things, and particularly points of view.
Marking the centenary of Stokowski's birth a recording of his Bach transcriptions, originally made with the Philadelphia Orchestra in 1927 to
1930, was released in 1982 in England. Now a half century after they were
first recorded we can hear them with fresh ears and regard them with a
counterpoint of view. I know no critic who is more demanding and
intellectually perceptive than Eric Salzman and in *Stereo Review*, March
1982, he wrote: "So much ink has been spilled and so much spleen vented
over the issue of the Stokowski transcriptions that it is worthwhile to recall

a few facts: Stokowski was a great interpreter of Bach and a real pioneer in introducing this music not only to orchestra programs but also to records. In effect, he helped bring a whole generation to Bach, and his arrangements, performances, and recordings were rapturously received even (or especially) by the cognoscenti in a day when Mozart was still considered a cute little fellow in a funny wig. And let us not forget that transcription was considered (as it still should be) a fine branch of the musical art. Schoenberg transcribed Bach, and so did Webern and Stravinsky. So, for that matter did Bach—who also transcribed the music of his contemporaries so relentlessly that scholars are still arguing over who did what and to whom.

"The Stokowski transcriptions offered here are as valid as good modern productions of Shakespeare. What shall I say? That they bring out all the polyphony beautifully? Of course they do. But the real point is that this Bach—Bach/Stokowski, one should say—has magic. And it's not all hoky-Stoky magic either; some of it is quite subdued, internalized, self-effacing. All of it is intense and quite spiritual in a perfectly earthy and sometimes even melodramatic way. This is Bach not yet cut open with the musicological scalpel, but rather a living vision of another age as presented through the good ears and hands of a remarkable and individualistic twentieth-century man and musician who never learned to exchange his soul for a high-power, scientifically acceptable R & D approach.

". . . The playing and the famous sonority of the Stokowski/Philadelphia collaboration are truly overwhelming."[28]

(47)

The NBC
Symphony Orchestra

A T 10:00 P.M. on Christmas Eve in 1937, the NBC Symphony with Toscanini was heard for the first time. Much had been made of the "fact" that NBC had created a completely new orchestra for him, which, of course, was not the case. The nucleus was the house orchestra, which was used in full or in part for any of its regular programs. To a core of thirty-seven men on staff were added sixty-one new, high-caliber players. They had been selected by Artur Rodzinski, and in a series of broadcasts that preceded the official premiere, Pierre Monteux conducted two concerts and Rodzinski three. They originated in Studio 8-H, a boxlike, nonresonant hall that seated an audience of twelve hundred, which further deadened the acoustics. In the studio the sound could be quite overwhelming, but the broadcast quality was decidedly inferior to that of the Philadelphia Orchestra or the New York Philharmonic.

For four years, Toscanini continued to conduct the NBC Symphony in 8-H and made many recordings there which his biographer Harvey Sachs said were damaged by its acoustics. He felt that it was "partly responsible for some of the more atrocious sounding recordings which represent Toscanini to today's listeners."[1] But Toscanini did not object. It seems equally puzzling that during all of that time he apparently was not aware that the orchestra was used for other programs, yet his various biographers imply that such was the case.

The truth surfaced quite dramatically during a rehearsal of the *Missa Solemnis* in Carnegie Hall in December 1940. Thirty-five of the men had to play with Frank Black for a commercial program that was to go on the

447

air at 8:00 P.M. originating in Studio 8-H, almost ten blocks away. The rehearsal had begun at 5:30—a half-hour late—and was continuing well beyond 7:30. The men who had to leave began to do so surreptitiously.

Alan Shulman, one of the cellists in the orchestra, told me: "Maestro knew that he was allocated two and a half hours and he was determined to go on until eight o'clock, so at 7:30 he was going hell-bent for leather because he needed that time to rehearse. Spitalny, the contractor, who was in the wings, beckoned to Carlton Cooley, the principal viola, who snuck out under Maestro's nose. Then, I think that Bill Polisi, the bassoonist, and one or two others left, and suddenly the Old Man became aware of what was going on.

"I think Chotzinoff led him to believe that this orchestra was hand-picked for him, and that it was exclusively his orchestra. . . . He didn't know that half the orchestra had been rehearsing with Frank Black for three and one half hours for the Cities Service program and the others had been with Walter Damrosch for his Music Appreciation Hour. . . . At any rate, that night he stalked out in a huff. He did the *Missa Solemnis,* but he was so furious with NBC that he bowed out. . . . Then they lined up Stokowski."[2]

Rumors about Toscanini leaving NBC circulated for many months. In the early part of September 1941 they were finally confirmed, and Niles Trammell, president of NBC, announced that Leopold Stokowski would be the new conductor of the orchestra.[3] His first broadcasts were to begin in November. It was a sage move on the part of NBC, since it would return Stokowski to Victor and remove him from its rival Columbia.

Requests for tickets for the Stokowski broadcasts were excessive. Over four thousand poured in for the first concert. Since Stoki had balked at playing in 8-H, it was decided to move the broadcast to Mecca Temple, which was then called the Cosmopolitan Opera House and later City Center. It had a seating capacity of 3,300, as opposed to 8-H's capacity of 1,400 persons. Niles Trammell announced that a new policy would be adopted and that a paid-admission policy would be followed. Tickets ranged from 55 cents to $1.65; later it was upped to $2.20 with tax. The income, it was stated, was to pay for the cost of hiring the Opera House. Public interest was enormous.[4]

The first concert took place on Tuesday evening, November 4, 1941, and it began with the Bach-Stokowski Prelude in E-flat Minor, followed by a movement from a Sinfonietta by Philip Warner and the Brahms Third. It was aired nationwide from 9:30 to 10:30. The programs were printed on silk and later on cork to assure that no rustle of sound would be made by paper; a rather silly idea, but it added interest. Later, cardboard was a wartime expediency.

For his second broadcast Stokowski chose Beethoven's Ninth. It was the live audience that was given the full treatment. The performance began promptly at 8:45 in the Cosmopolitan Opera House and the first three movements were played. It was not until 9:30 that the broadcast was begun, and that was given over to the last movement, with the Westminster Choir singing the "Ode to Joy." He gave the listeners at the Cosmopolitan more than their money's worth. In addition to his broadcast program, he would have the audience stay on while he and the orchestra would rehearse some new works. And the executives were surely pleased when he agreed to appear on the air and do a series of promotional interviews speaking about future programs.

After a general introduction aimed at promoting his third program, the NBC announcer continued: "I feel quite sure, Mr. Stokowski, that our audience would rather hear from you than from me regarding the program, for it seems to me a particularly appealing one with its modern Russian and American works and including as it does the Brahms Fourth Symphony . . . would you tell us a little more in detail about your program for this coming week?" Then in his cultivated accent with several articles dropped here and there for Slavic effect, Stoki responded: "Yes, yes. I shall be very happy to tell you about it. First we begin with three parts from Prokofiev's opera *The Love for Three Oranges*. The first we shall play is called the "Infernal Scene" between one of the characters in the opera and Tchelio, who is a magician. This is very agitated kind of music and modern in its sounding and type. Then we play something quite different. . . . It's the scene between the prince and the princess, and here is romantic kind of music with a note of tenderness in it. And if you like, we can play you a little of this, because in the rehearsal yesterday we made a test record of this part of the music. It is merely a test record and so must not be expected to sound like a final record, but it will give you an idea of the music, and if you like, we can play a part of it now. Here it is."[5]

At this point a part of the rehearsal was aired. It was Stoki's custom to listen to all rehearsals and if necessary make adjustments. It was this infinite attention to detail about his broadcasts and recordings that made his performances sound so superior over the air.

Since children were always Stokowski's delight, he wanted to do a

children's concert on his NBC series. The network would have none of
it, and so he planned a concert to follow his regular broadcast and have
it not only for children but for the most part by children. He played short
pieces by Sousa, Tchaikovsky, Mussorgsky, and Prokofiev, and had them
singing songs of Stephen Foster. Then he introduced the most original
part. He had assembled a group of pieces by youngsters and the rest of
the program was to be by them. He addressed them: "We are going to
play some music by young children from various parts of the United
States. The first one is called 'Piper's Song.' It is by a girl aged twelve in
Florida—Palm Beach." And he conducted her short opus. "The next is
called 'Swing Song.' It is by a group. They are aged five. They go to City
and Country School in New York City."[6]

And so it went, with pieces by Charles Rosen, Edward Cobb, Doris
Pines, Robert Helps, Nancy Smith, Suki Terada, and two listed as anonymous. They were actually Stokowski-Stokowski. "The Giraffe" and "Little
Aeroplane" were written by his daughters Sadja and Lyuba and, of course,
orchestrated by their father.

Included in this list were Charles Rosen and Robert Helps, both of
whom developed into brilliant and successful pianists. Helps became a
composer of rare distinction; Stoki would later perform his works. I asked
Bob what he remembered of the event and he responded: "It was about
1941. And what he did was to organize a contest where he wanted kiddies
to send in their little pieces and then they would be orchestrated and he
would do them with the NBC Symphony. And that's what happened.

"I sent one in. I sent in my world-famous 'Dance of the Cinders on
the Hearth.' I was all of about twelve then. It was orchestrated—so at age
eleven or twelve I had a little piece done by Leopold Stokowski and the
NBC Symphony. Quite an event as you can imagine. It was a wonderful
event for us kids."[7]

Among the American composers he performed on the regular broadcasts we find Alan Hovhaness, Herbert Haufrecht, Carlton Cooley, Morton Gould, Edward MacDowell, and Lamar Stringfield.

It seems ironic that as Stokowski began his series with NBC, Toscanini
returned to Philadelphia for the first time in eleven years to conduct a
series of programs that he also presented in Washington and New York.
RCA was determined to record as much as possible of the Toscanini-
Philadelphia concerts. And this they did. But strangely, the famous Philadelphia sound was not captured. Toscanini himself was not pleased and

the records were not then released. The story of this disastrous bungle has been told and retold.

Walter Toscanini, the Maestro's son, brought a package of the first test pressings to David Hall, who had written so perceptively on recordings, and asked him to listen to them. "Alas," David wrote, "the listening results were a disaster. Upper string partials had been wiped out; general playback level was almost below audibility in *pp* passages, with musical content being masked more often than not by a crossfire of clicks and pops against a background of generally heavy surface noise."[8]

Charles O'Connell, who produced the recordings just as he had done for those of Stokowski and the Philadelphia and Koussevitzky with the Boston Symphony, expended great care on the Toscanini recordings. In his book, *The Other Side of the Record*, he relates a whole litany of problems and troubles that beset the sessions. O'Connell admitted to having spent tens of thousands of RCA's money in these recordings, and the performances, he felt, were superb.

When Toscanini heard the first test pressings, he did not approve a "single complete work he recorded with the Philadelphia Orchestra. The Philadelphia Orchestra was, in Toscanini's mind, Stokowski's orchestra, and I wonder if he was determined to show the world in general and Stokowski in particular that he could make this orchestra sound better than Stokowski could. He couldn't, didn't, and can't, for a variety of reasons, only one of which I need cite." Charlie explained Toscanini's disinterest in the process of recording and his stubborn refusal to "understand the possibilities or the limitations of recording and reproduction. He will not adjust himself to the exigencies of recording."

O'Connell observed that the Maestro "does not know, does not care to know, and refuses to learn, how to operate a phonograph. . . . Stokowski, on the other hand, thoroughly understands recording from every point of view, including the commercial."

Toscanini refused to approve any of the records. O'Connell believed that his excessive criticism of them arose mainly because in certain respects they did not compare with the best of Stokowski's or, in fact, with the best of Ormandy's.[9]

After spending countless hours transferring the discs to magnetic tape and painstakingly editing out pops and scratches, the first of them was released in 1963, six years after Toscanini's death. The complete set was finally issued in 1976. It had taken nearly eight hundred hours to prepare the Schubert Symphony in C.[10] The others required similar time consumption.

While Toscanini was recording in Philadelphia, Stokowski was busy making records with the NBC Symphony in New York. Here the results were successful from every angle. Stoki recorded:

> Prokofiev: *The Love for Three Oranges* (Excerpts)
> Bach-Stokowski: Arioso from the Cantata No. 156
> Tchaikovsky: Symphony No. 4
> Tchaikovsky-Stokowski: *Humoresque*
> Stravinsky: *Firebird* Suite
> Rimsky-Korsakov: *Russian Easter* Overture[11]

The Bach and the Prokofiev were reviewed in *The New Records:* "Both of the above discs should enjoy wide popularity. Stokowski's Bach arrangements have been amongst the biggest selling records in the Victor catalogue and the present one should be no exception. . . . Those who like their Bach dressed up for a large orchestra will be mighty enthusiastic about this disc. The selections from Prokofiev's orchestral suite *Love for Three Oranges* . . . are all melodious and Stokowski is at his best in developing music such as this . . . if Stokowski's listeners get as much enjoyment from listening as the Maestro seems to get from playing it, all will be well. The reproduction throughout both of these discs is of the best."[12] The RCA engineering department made no errors here.

In his *New Guide to Recorded Music,* Irving Kolodin compares four different versions of the *Firebird.* Three are by Stokowski: the NBC Symphony on Victor, the All-American Youth Orchestra on Columbia, and an earlier one with the Philadelphia Orchestra also on Victor. The fourth version, on Columbia, was conducted by Stravinsky himself. "I acknowledge a sense of guilt in preferring the gaudy, glassy, and glamorous performance of Stokowski to the competent, continent, and composed (in more than one sense) version by Stravinsky. For there are many points of illumination and stress in the generally slower version by the composer which one does not hear in the newest of the various Stokowski performances. But, taking all the elements together—the recording, which is superb; the orchestral playing, which is first-rate, and the conducting, which is inferior in detail to Stravinsky's but superior to it in sum—it must be recognized that it is the most equitably balanced of all those available. However, if I could afford the indulgence I should own both—one to play for pleasure (the Stokowski-NBC), the other to play for instruction (the Stravinsky)."[13]

On reviewing his recording of the Tchaikovsky Symphony No. 4, Kolodin gave it high praise. Stokowski, he wrote, "has a most interesting and persuasive estimate of this score, one which is personal without being eccentric, vigorous but not erratic. In addition, the NBC orchestra sounds amazingly well, being recorded under acoustical conditions much more favorable to it than is customarily the case in its performances with Toscanini." On comparing it with versions conducted by Koussevitzky and Mitropoulos, he concluded that "the over-all superiority of the Stokowski version is quite plain."[14]

Following his concert on November 25, Stoki departed for his terracotta house in California to rest, study, and enjoy the sunshine. Like most music lovers, he listened regularly to the broadcasts of the New York Philharmonic. A tremendous and loyal audience had been built up for them through the years. Unlike the NBC Symphony, which was shifted to various times and days, the CBS broadcasts had always been at 3:00 on Sundays; at noon in California. The program which Rodzinski had selected for December 7, 1941, was devoted to the First Symphony of Shostakovich and the Brahms B-flat Concerto with Artur Rubinstein. Although in a news flash at 2:26 P.M., President Roosevelt had announced that Pearl Harbor had been attacked, most Philharmonic devotees first learned of it when they tuned in at the regular time, when the newscasters preempted the time for Shostakovich and Brahms. Like all Americans, Stokowski was profoundly shocked.

When he returned to New York to resume his NBC broadcasts, he again agreed to go on the air and do a promotional conversation. The announcer asked him about the place of music in the war-torn world. He answered: "I think . . . we are all so disturbed by the war—the destruction that is going on—the cruelty—the horror that is happening. And we all feel great sympathy for the millions who are suffering so terribly. We cannot forget this. It's constantly in our thoughts and the morale of our nation—the feeling deep in the heart of everyone in our nation is most important for our national defense and for the future of our country, and here is where music can play a part. I know it's only a small part, but it's a very important one because music can bring consolation."[15]

While Stokowski had been vacationing on the coast, Studio 8-H was closed off as engineers and workmen began to reconstruct its interior. In huddles with NBC's chief engineers, Stokowski had outlined the alterations that were to be made. With his acoustical experiments in the Academy of Music and his experience in Hollywood, he had very specific ideas about how the studio should be improved. He recommended that the back wall be covered with convex diffusers that looked a little like a marcelled hairdo, with a slanting roof and side walls arranged to increase the resonance. "We found a way to floodlight sound," he remarked.

It worked. When he returned on March 24 everyone was pleased. "Beethoven's *Pastorale* Symphony never sounded more lush and verdant," reported *Time* magazine. "Studio audience, radio listeners and critics were happy. The reverberations were all they should be; radio's biggest concert hall had at last become musicianly."[16]

As the NBC season ended, Mayor Fiorello LaGuardia persuaded Stokowski to conduct a series of five concerts with the New York WPA Orchestra on behalf of the United States Treasury Department to stimulate the sale of war stamps. Admission was technically free, but it entailed the purchase of stamps ranging from 50¢ to $5.00. The orchestra was made up of unemployed musicians and was considered a grab-bag assortment of players. But he welded them into a splendid performing group. "Mr. Stokowski's talent for making nondescript orchestras sound like nothing else than the Philadelphia Orchestra circa 1933 flourished at its most extraordinary in the New York City WPA Symphony's playing of the Tchaikovsky Fifth Symphony," wrote Irving Kolodin.[17]

At this moment Stokowski was at the center of musical attention not only in New York, just as he had been in Philadelphia, but in the entire country. Toscanini was not making news, and he was determined to return to the spotlight. Obviously, he could not let his archrival dominate the scene. Consequently, he patched up his quarrel with NBC and arranged to return and share the podium with Stokowski for the coming season. The two met and discussed their forthcoming programs. Toscanini wanted to do a Brahms festival and Stokowski agreed to omit Brahms. It was generally agreed that the moderns would be Stokowski's particular purview.

Toscanini, however, crossed the lines. Since the premiere of any new Shostakovich work was sure to generate considerable publicity, and since he had been severely criticized for ignoring contemporary music, Toscanini coveted the right to perform the Seventh Symphony of the popular Russian even though he was aware that Stokowski had urged NBC to acquire the first performance rights as far back as December. When Stokowski discovered Toscanini's intention, he wrote to him immediately.

22 June 1942

Dear Mr. Toscanini:

At our meeting a few weeks ago, you asked me not to broadcast any of the music of Brahms, but said that I should broadcast the modern music. I agreed to do this, although I must confess I was reluctant to give up the music of Brahms, because that is part of our repertoire that I particularly love. I feel strongly that this understanding between us should be kept.

About 10 years ago, when I was in Russia and Shostakovich was comparatively unknown, it was I who perceived his great gifts, believed in him, and against much opposition was the first to play his music in the United States. At that time I became friends with Shostakovich, and since then we have been in correspondence. I have a most tremendous love and enthusiasm for his music. I am of Slavic blood, and for that reason feel more intensely the expression of this music. During all these years, I have been constantly conducting his music and have recorded the major part of his symphonic music.

That is why last December I requested NBC to obtain broadcasting rights for Shostakovich's *Seventh Symphony*. When I was in Russia, I had friendly relations with the department of government which is concerned with music, and culture generally. It was my suggestion that NBC make an agreement directly with this department, which they finally succeeded in doing, and since then, I have been planning with them to broadcast this music.

Now that you know all these facts, I feel confident you will wish me to broadcast this symphony, and that it will be with your approval and in harmony with the agreement we made together. All the more that I understand you will present this symphony for its first public hearing to the New York audience with the Philharmonic Orchestra in October.

May I hear from you at your earliest convenience? Or if you would prefer to discuss this with me, I shall be happy to meet you at any time and place convenient for you.

Sincerely your colleague,
Leopold Stokowski[18]

Toscanini lost no time in replying. The following day he wrote that he would in no way attempt to refute the arguments that Stoki had presented in his letter in order "to prove and claim your right to give the first radio performance of Shostakovich's *Seventh Symphony*." He explained that he had never "urged the honor" of conducting first performances of any composer and admitted that he admired Shostakovich but that he did not "feel such a frenzied love for it like you." He further explained that after seeing the score, he was deeply taken by its beauty and its anti-fascist meanings, and had the greatest desire to perform it. "Don't you think, my dear Stokowski, it would be very interesting for everybody and yourself, too, to hear the old Italian conductor (one of the first artists who strenuously fought against fascism) to play this work of a young Russian anti-nazi composer? I haven't any drop of Slavonic blood in my veins—I am only a true and genuine Latin. . . . Maybe I am not an intense interpreter of this kind of music, but I am sure I can conduct it very simply with love and honesty." And he continued: "Think it over, my dear Stokowski, only a few minutes and you will convince yourself not to give much more importance to the arguments you displayed in your letter. . . ."[19]

Upon receiving the letter, Stokowski responded at once.

24 June 1942

Dear Mr. Toscanini:

First of all, I want to thank you for your letter. I entirely agree with you that it will be very interesting for everyone, including myself, to hear you conduct the Shostakovich symphony. I understand you will conduct this music with the New York Philharmonic on October 14th, and I hope to be in New York that day to hear the performance, because I have always been one of your greatest admirers, and have the highest appreciation of your extraordinary and unique qualities. This performance on October 14th will be the first public presentation of this symphony, because the broadcast will be without audience.

I am glad you are willing for me to make the first radio broadcast. I would like to do everything in friendly cooperation with you during our association together, and this will confirm our previous agreement, that we made when we talked together recently, when you expressed the wish for me to conduct the modern music, but to refrain from conducting any of the music of Brahms on account of your Brahms Festival. I know the choral music of Brahms well, and if I can be of any assistance to you in preparing the chorus, I shall be happy to do so.

> With friendly personal greetings,
> Sincerely your colleague,
> Leopold Stokowski[20]

Toscanini must have been somewhat astonished by this letter and replied: "Your letter of Wednesday troubled me very much because I saw in it the complete result of some misunderstanding—maybe my poor English language has certainly been the cause. . . ." He explained that because of his scanty interest in Shostakovich he had declined to give the first performance of his Fifth Symphony. But on reading the score of the Seventh, he wrote, "I felt the strongest sympathy and emotion for this special work so I *urged the NBC to have it performed the first time by me.*" (Italics added by author.)

Toscanini biographers usually state that it was NBC that wanted him to give the work its American premiere. The duplicity was entirely the Maestro's. He concluded: "Happily, you are much younger than me, and Shostakovich will not stop writing new symphonies. You will certainly have all the opportunities you like to perform them."[21]

Toscanini won. The Shostakovich Seventh was heard during an NBC broadcast on July 19, 1944. Stokowski heard the broadcast in his Hollywood house, where he was studying the score himself, for he fully intended to perform it and in the not too distant future. He expressed some of his feeling for it in the pages of his book *Music for All of Us.* In a chapter on "Architectonics—Form Content" he discusses how, in some symphonies, composers have found ways of linking various movements together. After remarking that such linking of movements is foreshadowed by Beethoven, he adds: "In his *Seventh Symphony,* Shostakovich fades out the end of the third part and merges this with the beginning of the fourth part, which begins in a mysterious, shadowy mood and in another key. The summing up of a symphony is always foreshadowed by Tchaikovsky in his *Fifth Symphony,* where the trumpets play triumphantly in a major key the theme which was melancholy and in the minor key in the first part. Shostakovich develops this unifying growth still further in his *Seventh Symphony.* The theme that begins the symphony passes through many metamorphoses as the symphony unfolds. At the beginning it is heroic and resolute. Later it expresses yearning and reaching up toward an ideal. At the end of the symphony the trombones and trumpets sound it as a clarion of triumph and jubilation."[22]

Five months after the Toscanini premiere, Stokowski gave the work its second broadcast on the same NBC network. In all probability Shostakovich would have preferred the Stokowski performance, for he expressed himself strongly in his memoirs: "I hate Toscanini. I've never heard him in a concert hall, but I've heard enough of his recordings. What he does to music is terrible, in my opinion. . . . Toscanini 'honored' me by conducting my symphonies. I heard those records, too, and they're worthless."[23]

Stokowski, however, he held in high regard. His son, Maxim Shostakovich, in a recent letter to me wrote: "I remember that my father often spoke passionately about Stokowski's interpretations of his compositions, about his excellence in the art of conducting, and that he often expressed his personal 'sympathie' toward Stokowski as a person."[24]

On the Fourth of July, Stoki opened the twenty-first season of the Hollywood Bowl concerts with an all-Russian program. It seemed downright patriotic to play Russian music at that stage of the war when Russia was one of our allies. It seemed even more so to play Shostakovich, since he was so identified with the war, and particularly with the siege of Leningrad, which he used as a programmatic background for his Seventh Symphony. The concert began with Stoki's arrangement of the "Star Spangled Banner" while servicemen presented the colors.

After the concert Stoki addressed the audience: "I have never known the men to play with such enthusiasm and I am happy that under present conditions we are able to offer an all-Russian program, with two numbers written by men still living—Stravinsky and Shostakovich."[25]

48

Stokowski/ Toscanini

*F*OR the next two seasons, beginning in 1942, the two rival maestros shared the NBC podium. During the first, Stokowski conducted thirteen concerts, Toscanini ten; the next year it was twelve each. Their concerts were memorable and the relationship between the two men appeared to be amicable. The men of the orchestra cooperated fully.

"There are those who assert with justice that the NBC Symphony reached its peak of perfection beginning in 1950," wrote David Hall. "But speaking as one who was on the spot through rehearsals and performances alike, I would say that the most spectacular combination of performances and programming were the two Toscanini-Stokowski seasons."[1]

Toscanini conducted the first two concerts. His programs surely made many eyebrows rise and many ears cock. The first, on November 1, 1942, was all-American: Charles Loeffler's *Memories of My Childhood,* Paul Creston's Choric Dance No. 2, Morton Gould's *Lincoln Legend,* and George Gershwin's *Rhapsody in Blue* with Earl Wild and Benny Goodman as soloists. Later in the season (February 7, 1943) another all-American program. This time he did Henry F. Gilbert's *Comedy Overture on Negro Themes,* Kent Kennan's *Night Soliloquy,* Charles T. Griffés' *The White Peacock,* and Ferde Grofé's *Grand Canyon* Suite, part of which had already become overplayed as the theme for the Phillip Morris program. It was almost as if he were atoning for his much-criticized neglect of American works in the past. And in these two programs he played eight of the grand total of eighteen American composers whose works he performed during his entire career![2]

Stoki's return on November 15, 1942, was also all-American: a short, attractive piece, *The Bright Land*, by Harold Triggs, followed by Morton Gould's Spirituals. On his fourth program, he introduced Alan Hovhaness' *Exile* Symphony, and on the succeeding broadcast (December 13, 1942), he performed Shostakovich's Seventh Symphony.

For the next six weeks, while Toscanini was conducting his Brahms festival, Stoki spent his time in California. In San Francisco he made news by conducting the Shostakovich Seventh there.

About the Shostakovich symphony, Alfred Frankenstein observed: "The tremendous ballyhoo it has had as a war piece has not done it any good. To be sure, an ironic attitude toward war expresses itself in the first movement, but even there Shostakovich cannot refrain from making his satiric music beautiful. Shostakovich himself has said that the remaining movements are an answer to the Russian proverb, 'When the cannons roar the muses are silent.' "

Alfred then remarked, "Stokowski was particularly eloquent, lengthy and emphatic in his praise of the San Francisco Symphony and of Pierre Monteux. His praise was borne out in one significant fact—he ended his first rehearsal a half hour before he had to. When Stokowski does that, Stokowski is pleased."[3]

After San Francisco he gave a series of concerts with the Los Angeles Philharmonic and even took it on a mini-tour to Pasadena and San Diego. He introduced Alan Hovhaness' *Exile* Symphony, which was received warmly. The *Los Angeles Daily News* critic called it a "hauntingly moving work ruled by the moods of lament, conflict and triumph. Each of these were typified in beautifully orchestrated outpourings. Stokowski gave the whole a tautly emotional reading."[4]

Back in New York he gave a remarkable succession of contemporary works. There was nothing like it then, and, in fact, there is nothing quite like it now. He programmed Gustav Holst's *The Planets*, Prokofiev's *Alexander Nevsky*, and symphonies by Stravinsky, Hindemith, Vaughan Williams, and Milhaud.

There was splendid critical coverage. In an article for the *Herald Tribune*, Virgil Thomson commented on the performance of the Stravinsky Symphony in C saying that it was notable in every way: "Local musicians and music lovers are grateful primarily to these gentlemen for the work's being done at all. But to have heard it in a rendition marked by such detailed clarity and so much overall comprehension gives double reason for the proffering of public thanks. . . . Mr. Stokowski and the radio people

NBC Photo/*Courtesy International Leopold Stokowski Society*

With William Schuman (c. 1942)

have finally fulfilled a cultural obligation that in former times would have been considered a privilege of the non-commercial agencies."[5]

The following season began with Toscanini conducting the first six concerts, with Stokowski starting his series on December 12, 1943, when he programmed William Schuman's *Prayer in Time of War*. He invited Schuman to come to the rehearsal and the composer recently recalled: "I think it was not the first rehearsal, although it might have been. . . . There was one section where the woodwinds have long, sustained lines, and he took this at an inordinately slow tempo, so much so that the wind players could not possibly hold the notes. . . . At the intermission he said to me,

'Do you have any comments to make?' I said, 'Yes, Maestro. Everything is fine except this section, and you will notice I have written at such and such a metronomic speed and you are playing it so much slower that they can't really follow you.' He replied, 'Thank you very much' and walked away."

After the intermission Stoki addressed the orchestra and said that he would ask the composer to conduct the work; he then abruptly strode into the control room. Bill, who was not an orchestral conductor, asked for the cooperation of the men and said "for heaven's sake don't let me make any mistakes." He pointed out the problematical places in the score and they responded splendidly. "The orchestra was just fantastic because they knew the position I had been placed in. And at the end, Stoki came out and said, 'Thank you very much, I hope you will listen to the broadcast.' I listened, and every single change that I had made he put into the performance. It was absolutely a marvelous, marvelous performance."[6]

He continued with a veritable feast of modernity; works by Vaughan Williams, Roy Harris, Paul Creston, Deems Taylor, Charles Sanford Skilton, Virgil Thomson, Efrem Zimbalist, and symphonies by Howard Hanson and Aaron Copland. There were also world premieres of Daniele Amfiteatrov's *De Profundis Clamavi*, George Antheil's Symphony No. 4, and the Concerto for Piano and Orchestra by Arnold Schoenberg.

Virgil Thomson pointedly observed that "Mr. Stokowski's policy of giving the American public a broad and fair picture of today's musical output is the most loyal gesture I'm acquainted with on the part of any conductor both toward the living public and the living composers of music."[7] One must, however, realize that in spite of the plethora of contemporary works, the programs were exceptionally well balanced with ample amounts of the usual concert choices.

Unquestionably, the work which created the greatest furor and hostility was the Schoenberg Piano Concerto—the saga of which is an odd and fascinating one. Felix Greissle, conductor, musicologist, and son-in-law of Schoenberg, was at that time music editor for G. Schirmer. "Oscar Levant" he recalled, "was at one time a pupil of Schoenberg. He made quite good progress, and Schoenberg was very satisfied with him, and a very friendly communication between the two took place. One day Levant said to Schoenberg, 'Mr. Schoenberg, it is really very remarkable that while you really cannot play the piano, you write so well for it. You should write a piano concerto. Please. I beseech you. Write a piano concerto.'

"Schoenberg did not answer and nothing much was discussed about it

NBC Photo/*Courtesy Beatrice Brown*
With Aaron Copland (c. 1942)

anymore. One day when Levant came to have his lesson, Schoenberg gave him the score of the Piano Concerto and said, 'Mr. Levant, here is your commission. You owe me $5,000.' Levant was frightened. He really had not commissioned the concerto. He had just asked Schoenberg to write one. . . . Well, Levant went to his psychiatrist and I got the score."

After looking it over and perceiving some of its difficulties, Felix said he did what he always did when he was in trouble, he called Stokowski. As soon as Stokowski heard about the work, he replied at once that he would perform it. They chose Edward Steuermann to be the pianist. He was a brilliant technician and had played much of Schoenberg's music.[8]

During the previous June, while Stoki was in California, Schoenberg had invited him to his home. He replied:

7 June 1943

Dear Friend,

I look forward to meeting your children and both of you again. Sunday afternoon is a difficult time for me, but any evening in the week is possible if it will be convenient for you. . . .

I have sketched all my programs for next winter, and your new piano concerto is on them. When will Steuermann be back here? I would like to hear him play it through once so that I can fit the piano part and the orchestral part in my thoughts.

With friendly greetings to you both.

Leopold Stokowski[9]

When Steuermann returned to Los Angeles he contacted Leonard Stein, who is a fine pianist and devotee of Schoenberg and now director of the Schoenberg Institute in Los Angeles. They arranged to try out the work on two pianos, and after a few run-throughs they played it at the home of Mrs. Gus Kahn, the widow of "the famous lyricist, as they called a lyric writer in Hollywood," Leonard Stein recalled. "On that occasion Schoenberg was present, Stokowski, Alma Mahler Werfel, Bronislaw Kaper, and a few other people. We played it for Stokowski, who followed it with a score. He really wanted to get an idea directly from Schoenberg and this seemed to be the best way.

"Schoenberg, of course, made no comments," Stein continued. "Now about the only thing that I remember saying to Stokowski was: 'Do you think it will be a very difficult work?' And he said, 'Very, very tricky.' I think he mentioned something about the rhythms particularly. But he was very perceptive about the problems he would encounter. To Alma Mahler Werfel, it was merely one more historical occasion."[10]

Clara, Steuermann's widow, said that her impression, from stories that Edward had told her about his experiences connected with it, was that "Stokowski used the listening to the two-piano version as a way of familiarizing himself with the work, and he preferred that to simply studying the score. Then from the fall of '43 on, Fritz Jahoda was the second pianist, and they played it on more than one occasion for Stokowski. It seems to me that Fritz Jahoda would have something to contribute about that."[11]

He did indeed. I located Mr. Jahoda and he told me how he and Steuermann played it together for Stokowski in the recording studio of Schirmer's, then on East Forty-third Street. "We played it on three successive Mondays, and each time—by the way, we played it three times—

each time a recording was made. Of course, it was the pretape time, so it was made on acetates." Jahoda remembered Stoki sitting there in the evening with a "beautiful blue shirt against the white hair—very impressive looking."[12]

"Stokowski generously planned on eleven or twelve rehearsals, I think," Felix Greissle recalled. "At any rate it was an enormous amount which we got and we were all very gratified. The rehearsals started, and the first time he went through from beginning to end and repeating occasionally but saying not one word. The same thing happened at the second rehearsal, and afterwards Steuermann got nervous and he said to me, 'Are we always to rehearse without the conductor saying a word?' And so I said to him, 'Well, I think he lets the musicians acquaint themselves with the music, and the time will come when he will start talking to them and making corrections.'

"On repeat rehearsals, Stokowski again and again did not say a word, and finally after the third or fourth, Steuermann said, 'Look, if he doesn't say anything, I cannot play . . . they make the same mistakes over and over. . . .' Then I remembered that Stokowski had asked me a lot of questions about the music and had said to me, 'If you notice something, please write it down and let me have it so that I may take advantage of it when I rehearse the work.' So I invited Steuermann to sit down with me, and we went through the whole work from beginning to end."

Together Felix and Steuermann made up a list that took up about twelve tightly written pages. The next day Felix rather hesitantly told Stoki: "I have here a few sheets and I have put down a few things which we noted." Stoki took the papers and "with one hand opened them like a pack of cards, put them together again, put them into the pocket of his jacket, and turned around without saying one word." Felix regretted that he had said anything and felt that Stokowski was probably offended. But as he began to rehearse, he took out the twelve sheets of corrections and said, " 'Gentlemen, there are a few things which I want you to note.' " And he read the mistakes and corrections from beginning to end. "The result," said Felix, "was a very good, satisfactory performance."[13]

Schoenberg heard the broadcast in his home in Los Angeles. He was obviously pleased and sent a laudatory telegram to Stokowski, who immediately thanked him, adding: "Mr. Steuermann and everyone in the orchestra worked with enthusiasm to try to make the first performance of your concerto adequate, so that music lovers who would be listening might have a clear impression of this wonderful music. I hope to conduct it again soon and do it better next time because now I know it better. Looking forward to the pleasure of seeing you in California."[14]

But before Stoki's letter reached California, Schoenberg had one in the mail.

Arnold Schoenberg
116 N. Rockingham Avenue
Los Angeles, Calif.
February 8, 1944

Mr. Leopold Stokowski
????????????????????
????????????????????
New York, N.Y.
Dear Friend:

> I do not know where you live.
>
> You need not hide—you can come out into the open after the great performance of my piano concerto last Sunday.
>
> I sent you a telegram, addressed to NBC and I hope you get it— or rather I wish you get it.
>
> It would be nice if you would tell me something about the performance; how was it received by the audience; did you hear (friendly) comments upon the music; what was your impression about the orchestration; was it difficult for the orchestra; to which instruments especially?? etc., etc. . . .

The letter then continued with two paragraphs recommending Rudolf Kolisch as concertmaster for the New York City Symphony, which Stokowski was about to organize. Schoenberg then appended: "I hope to hear from you about all those matters and also—what I forgot to ask—how did it sound? Many cordial greetings, yours very faithfully. Arnold Schoenberg."[15]

While Schoenberg would not have been happy reading Downes' review in the *Times*, that of Virgil Thomson's in the *Herald Tribune* was a benison. He carefully analyzed the work without being too technical and made trenchant observations: "There is plenty of melody. . . . It is poetical and reflective. . . . Its inspiration and its communication are lyrical, intimate, thoughtful, sweet, and sometimes witty, like good private talk. . . .

"One cannot be too grateful to Mr. Stokowski for giving himself the trouble to prepare it and for paying his radio listeners the compliment of presuming their interest. It is an honor paid not only to one of the great living masters of music but to the American public as well; and the General Motors Corporation which sponsored the broadcast, should be proud of the event. . . ."[16]

On February 27, 1944, Stokowski conducted his last concert with the NBC Symphony. His contract for the following season was not renewed. Just why evoked much speculation. General Motors continued to sponsor the broadcast until 1946. If they actually preferred to air mostly eighteenth- or nineteenth-century music, they should have been making carriages rather than Cadillacs.

Felix Greissle had heard that when Toscanini discovered Stokowski's intention to perform the Schoenberg concerto, he tried to stop him. "Stokowski was threatened that he would not have the NBC concerts anymore if he would dare to do the Schoenberg concerto, and he did it anyway."[17]

The press became interested, and in a Sunday article entitled "Postmortem: Modernism on the Radio," Virgil Thomson wrote: "The radio, as always, has been copious in its presentation of all sorts of music, ancient and modern, rare and familiar. The most spectacular program gesture in the field of broadcasting was the playing by Leopold Stokowski and the NBC Symphony Orchestra (ordinarily the most conservative outfit in radio) of one or more contemporary works on all but one of his Sunday afternoon hours for 11 weeks running. The aggregate impact of this modernity (some of it the real stuff, too, with no punches pulled) would seem to have brought about a reprimand from institutional executives. There has been constant rumor since that Mr. Stokowski would not be asked to renew his contract another season if he insisted on so much modernism. I have no idea to what length Mr. Stokowski or his employers will carry intransigence in the matter but it seems certainly desirable that a compromise be reached whereby the orchestra's public be not deprived of a valuable and progressive series of programs and the commercial sponsors of these may continue to enjoy both the services of a brilliant musician and the very real intellectual prestige that his modernist policy has brought them."[18]

Not until June 12 was there any official announcement from NBC. On that date, Niles Trammell stated that Stokowski's contract would not be renewed for the following season. At a press conference Trammell declined discussion of the reasons, but Samuel Kaufman, music editor of

NBC, said it was the network's desire to obtain the services of a greater variety of famous conductors that led to the dropping of Stokowski. Among the guest conductors Trammell mentioned were Eugene Ormandy and Malcolm Sargent as Stokowski's replacements.[19] The prepared release given to the press promulgated the theory that it was undesirable for the NBC Symphony to divide its season between two conductors of such widely differing methods. Apparently Toscanini had no objection to the engagement of Eugene Ormandy and Malcolm Sargent, by whom he would not have his eminence challenged.

Time magazine called the shots acidly: "Behind the blow that knocked British-born, Irish-Pole Stokowski over Radio City's ropes was the fine Italian fist of his onetime pal, spry, bantamweight Arturo Toscanini, 77. The blow was the culmination of a friendship that has gone sour.

"Few maestros have held each other in such avowed respect as did Toscanini and Stokowski in the '30s. A frequent attendant at Toscanini's rehearsals, concerts and broadcasts, Stokowski publicly expressed his tremendous admiration for Toscanini. Toscanini, who seldom in his life has had a good word for a competitor who could possibly be considered a rival, recommended Stokowski to replace him when he decided to take a vacation from NBC in 1941."[20]

Time was not quite right in calling Toscanini's absence from NBC a mere vacation. He had angrily resigned, and had even had talks with William Paley to explore the possibility of appearing on CBS. Nothing, however, came of the meeting, we are told.[21] With Toscanini then out of the picture, it was canny David Sarnoff who chose Stokowski as the conductor of the symphony. And at the time many supposed that it would be a permanent post.

But *Time* was quite correct in observing that ". . . the seeds of trouble had already been sown the year before, when Toscanini's South American tour took the bloom off Stokowski's later Good Neighborly trip. . . . The minute Stokowski took over at NBC he began making changes in the broadcasting technique of Toscanini's orchestra. He altered the traditional seating arrangement. He insisted that the stringed instrumentalists bow out of step, to produce the lush, powerful Stokowski tone. He improved broadcasting Studio 8-H with a new ceiling and a set of acoustical gadgets. The improvements left Conductor Toscanini (who had always kicked about the acoustics of Studio 8-H himself) biting his nails."[22]

Since Virgil Thomson had been so close to the situation, I asked him if he would trigger his recollections of the affair, and so we met one afternoon in his very neat though cluttered apartment in the old Chelsea Hotel on West Twenty-third Street. Sitting there beside the glass-covered mahogany bookcases filled with scores and bound volumes of his writings, he talked about the days of the NBC Orchestra nearly forty years before: "Stoki came to me at one time and asked my advice. Actually what he wanted was my help, and I gave it to him. It was when he was fired from NBC . . . for weeks running he had played contemporary works on every program including one of mine, a symphony of George Antheil, something of Schoenberg . . . a contemporary work on every program, and the NBC people weren't having that. And so since Toscanini was technically the musical director, he was the one responsible for the firing, and they gave out a release about how it was no good for the orchestra to have two conductors—no mention was made of modern music.

"Well, he knew that I was always on the warpath about Toscanini and the NBC people and so forth, and he asked me if he could come and get some advice about the situation. So I invited him to a little Sunday-night supper . . . and he told me his side of the situation. He didn't tell me too much, but he was worried about the public image that he was being given, as if he were bad for the orchestra. . . . And so I wrote a Sunday article about it. . . .

"The Old Man had allowed a release to be issued in his name explaining why Stokowski could not be allowed to conduct or continue conducting, and I said this is obviously false. Now, Chotzinoff called me up the next day and he said, 'I bet you know what I'm calling for.' And I said, 'I bet I do too.' He said, 'What would you think of a little apology or correction?' I said that what I wrote is correct. 'If Mr. Toscanini wishes a correction, I'd be delighted to publish anything that he writes.' Of course, he wouldn't write, and the matter was dropped right there."[23]

Was it a premeditated gesture or merely by chance that his last moments with the NBC Orchestra should have been with Bach, as they had been at St. Bartholomew's and with the Philadelphia Orchestra? The program on February 27, 1944, ended with the Passacaglia and Fugue in C Minor. Then exit.

City Center

THE "Little Flower" had vision, bless him. Mayor Fiorello La Guardia developed the idea of converting the old Mecca Temple, which had been acquired by the city, into a center of the performing arts. One of the first persons on the board—which included Newbold Morris as its chairman, Claire Reis, and other prominent New Yorkers—was Jean Dalrymple.

"I was really the only professional there at City Center," Jean told me. ". . . I was the volunteer Director of Public Relations at City Center for twenty-five years, and so when we had already organized the opera, La Guardia said, 'You know, what I would like to see there is a symphony, and we would call it the worker's symphony and give concerts at 5:30 or 6:00 so that before they went home after their work, they could stop in and hear a symphony orchestra. Do you know how we could start such a thing?' And I said, 'Well, somebody should speak to Leopold Stokowski, because he always loves new ideas, and I think that would appeal to him. The last time that I spoke to him he told me that he didn't want to go back to Philadelphia. He wasn't interested in the New York Philharmonic or any of those big organizations. He had had it with big musical organizations, so I think he would probably be very open to suggestions.' Claire Reis said, 'Stokowski is a very good friend of mine. I will propose it to him.' So I didn't say anything about my being a good friend, but I said, 'That would be wonderful, Claire.' So she did, and Mayor La Guardia phoned him, and they had a meeting at City Hall, and the next thing I knew, Stokowski called me and said, 'Now, you remember what I said, don't you?' And I said, 'What do you mean?' He said, 'The Mayor told me that it wasn't Claire who suggested that I form the orchestra. It was you, but let's give Claire the credit because she's older than you are, child.' He always called me 'child.' "[1]

On February 9, 1944, at nine in the morning, according to Stoki's engagement calendar, he and Fiorello met to discuss City Center. They got along splendidly, and Stoki accepted the responsibility of forming the new orchestra. In mid-February he wrote to Sylvan Levin, who was still in Philadelphia.

44
February
16

Dear Sylvan,

When Mayor LaGuardia invited me to form the New York City Symphony, I immediately suggested your name for modern and interesting opera. That was before I heard of your resignation. At present we are forming the orchestra, and it may be some little time before we can organize opera (with the exception of one or two weeks of opera that are going to be given now and which were planned before I was invited to enter the organization). I am giving four concerts in March with the new orchestra. But the real beginning will be next September.
I would love to work with you again and have always felt it would happen. Are you a member of the New York Local? As soon as we begin planning something that might interest you, I will let you know.

Always your friend[2]

Stoki signed the letter "Maestrineto" and added a humorous postscript: "How can you leave Philadelphia to come to a little village like New York? What recklessness!"

Five days later he wrote him again and paternalistically advised: "I think it's a good idea for you to join the New York local just on general principles, because I find the field of music and all the Arts immeasurably freer and wider here than it is in the city of brotherly, sisterly, and otherwise love. . . ."[3]

Sylvan immediately set in motion the process of joining the New York union and wrote to Stoki telling him of this and his eagerness to come to New York and assist him with the new orchestra.

Stoki replied:

> . . . I am glad you are joining the union here. Let's meet next
> September or October and talk over projects for the future.
> The new orchestra is developing wonderfully, although it is terribly
> difficult in war time to start a new orchestra.
> Always your friend[4]

On February 23 Stoki met with Vincent Vanni, who was not only a
tuba player but the contractor of the new orchestra, and they discussed
all of the problems in selecting the players. There were many excellent
musicians on the WPA roles, but the younger ones were scarce because
of the war. Stokowski continued to hold auditions until his departure for
the coast. He left New York on March 15 and arrived in Los Angeles three
days later. During the next week he obtained a Mexican tourist visa,
changed money into pesos, and had his various personal effects and papers
examined to avoid complications at the border on his return. On Sunday
the twenty-sixth he drove to Redlands to look over some orange groves
that he had recently bought. The following day he drove to Phoenix and
on to Laredo, Victoria, and over the forest-covered mountains into the
valley of Mexico. He arrived in Mexico City on Sunday after a week's trip.

He was driving an Oldsmobile at the time, but with whom he was
sharing the trip and the arduously long drive we have no information. On
arriving he went almost at once to the Palacio de Bellas Artes to arrange
all the details covering the series of concerts he was to give there. He
conducted three pairs beginning on April 14 and 16, and for the succeeding two weekends. His repertoire was vintage Stokowski: Bach transcriptions, early Italians, Albéniz, Debussy, Stravinsky's *Firebird*, Shostakovich's Sixth Symphony, Brahms, and Wagner. Not oblivious to the
commercial potential, the programs indicated that all of the works were
recorded on RCA Victor Red Seal discs.

On May 9, he drove to Oaxaca and fell in love with the town. He talked
much about the green-tinted cathedral that he had first seen when he
went there with Carlos Chávez years before. He again revisited the ruins
of Mitla, and when the local Oaxaca musicians invited him to conduct
part of a concert for them, he agreed. The group that was assembled was
at least adequate to perform something as large, instrumentally, as the
"1812" Overture of Tchaikovsky. I remember his recounting the story.
It was all done innocently enough. He had urged a group of locals to ring
the various church bells throughout the city and others to shoot off

fireworks and make whatever noisemaking commotion possible to simulate the Russian victory over Napoleon. He aimed for effect and he got it.

I have heard him tell how the overzealous pyrotechnicians used more than firecrackers. "They used dee-na-meet," he would say, in one of his wonderful, idiosyncratic pronunciations. All went quite well until the moment of victory, when the church bells began to peal and the boys set off their charges. The constabulary was aroused. He apparently scared the wits out of them. In typical fashion they rushed the concert, which was given in one of the town squares, arrested the *campesinos* who rang the bells and set off the charges. They were shots heard round the world, and from New York, *Newsweek* reported that the police "charged the meeting, and arrested all the musicians. Stokowski's explanations finally got them out."[5]

In the end everyone was delighted about the whole affair. There had never been such excitement at a concert in Oaxaca before. The papers in Mexico City had a field day. And with this new blaze of publicity and interest he was invited to conduct the Mexican Symphony in a broadcast commemorating the anniversary of the shelling of the Mexican tanker sunk by Axis submarines in May 1942, which brought Mexico into the war. One of the works which Stoki chose was a song, "La Mort," by Manuel Ponce, the well-loved composer of "Estrellita." It was to be sung by the popular contralto Josefina "Chacha" Aguilar. When "Chacha" and Ponce arrived for the first rehearsal, she tried to explain to Stoki that she did not have a full orchestration but one for six instruments only. Stoki went into one of his rare rages. He had already been irked by the attitude of the players, and an altercation between Stoki and the white-haired Ponce erupted. Tempers flared and there was a partial walkout of the men. Stoki then set about to have two rehearsals on the following day, which was the day of the broadcast, but they were truncated into one. Conditions were even worse than they were before, and Stokowski simply walked out. As far as I can determine, the broadcast was canceled.[6]

The newspapers were quick to denounce him. *La Prensa* averred that "Stokowski is famous not only for undeniable abilities but for bad temper which he ascribes to temperament, but others to ill breeding." Ponce eagerly gave his side of the argument to the press. "I hadn't met Stokowski before," he said, "so I seized the chance to greet and thank him for his kindness. . . . Great was my surprise when instead of a courteous, educated gentleman I found an infuriated individual waving his hands, who shrieked gross reproaches for my not having the complete orchestration ready. I intended to suggest to Stokowski that the matter be solved by letting Chacha sing "La Mort" with piano accompaniment as Heifetz did when he recently appeared on the National Hour, which was certainly not an amateurish or ridiculous performance." Ponce added rather benignly, "Stokowski is a great artist, and I excuse his temperament."

It was more difficult for Stokowski to excuse Ponce's lack of professionalism. But in the end there was a pleasant reconciliation. Mexico's *Excelsior*, however, stated that "Ponce was the innocent victim of Stokowski's violence," and another paper, *Novedades*, remarked: "Ponce chose to withdraw but not before telling the photogenic Stokowski that he was unaccustomed to commercializing his music which belongs to the Mexican people."

Stoki did not take his case to the reporters for them to pass judgment. He bypassed all that. He wrote directly to the President of Mexico, Manuel Ávila Camacho, and expressed his grievances: "Three weeks ago, I was asked to direct the symphonic orchestra for the National Radio Hour's commemoration of the second anniversary of the sinking of the Portrero del Llano. I accepted with pleasure, presenting a list of required instruments and music several days in advance. During the first rehearsal on May 20, I was disagreeably surprised to learn that some of the most important instruments and musicians were not present. . . . I asked for two rehearsals on May 21 with all present. The orchestra requested just one rehearsal for 7:30 A.M. I arrived at the Bellas Artes at 5 past 7 ready to begin at 7:30 according to the agreement, but so many of the musicians were absent that rehearsals were impossible. I waited until 2 past 8 but . . . I was forced to suspend my collaboration.

"In my opinion, Mexican music deserves to be played not under circumstances of deficient preparation due to the absence of important instruments and musicians during rehearsals. I make this protest on behalf of good Mexican music, since I love this country deeply."[7]

For the rest of his stay he decided to devote it to enjoying the scenic delights of Mexico rather than its musical ones. He had his Oldsmobile checked and serviced and set out for Taxco, far from the bustle of the capital.

On the fifteenth of June he started back on the long drive to Beverly Hills, arriving there on the twenty-second. July and August were spent in Beverly Hills visiting or meeting with such friends or colleagues as Dick Hammond, the Antheils, the William Grant Stills, Aldous Huxley ("lunch in the Beverly Wilshire dining room"), Rudy Vallee, Christopher Isherwood, the Basil Rathbones, and even Sol Hurok. But the principal thought that tenanted his mind was New York's City Center. He fully intended to dominate the opera as well as the symphony and began to make plans for both. He spoke to William Grant Still about his opera *Troubled Island* and said that he hoped to produce it in New York.[8]

In mid-July he wrote to Claire Reis:

> It is charming of you to let me call you Claire. Now comes the great and difficult question—what will you call me? In Latin America they called me "Leopi," "Leopoldo," "Stokito," and "Tokoki." They also called me some other names, but I am hoping you will not feel that way about me. . . . Miss Dalrymple was here. . . . I have a good impression of her intelligence and energetic action. . . . I do not know what plans have been formed for opera for next season. But I would like to strongly recommend Sylvan Levin, the young American conductor who has so brilliantly formed and developed the Philadelphia Opera. I have worked with him for years and know his qualifications exactly. He is dependable, honest, energetic, a natural born musician, a fine opera conductor, a good organizer, a musician of imagination and genuine depth of feeling. He would be a great addition to our group at City Center. . . .[9]

He signed his letter "Leopoldo."

On July 20 he wrote to Sylvan saying that he had received word from New York that his suggestion about him had been favorably considered. "All is well so far." Then somewhat philosophically he added, "As in most things in life, there are good and bad things at City Center. I believe we can increase the good and lessen the bad."[10]

Sylvan by this time had made all preparation to move to New York but he did express some trepidation concerning his role in City Center. Stoki wrote back:

> The fact that you are an American will mean nothing at City Center. I am determined to have no racial or any other kind of prejudices there. I had enough of all that in Philadelphia. City Center is going to be clean. If you conduct there, as I am planning for you to do, you will rest entirely on the quality of your work, which is exactly the way I know you will wish it.
>
> Milhaud has asked me to conduct *Bolivar.* He is an old friend of mine from Paris. . . .[11]

He suggested that Sylvan get a score and begin to study it, and he added that he had several other modern operas in mind.[12] One was *Troubled Island* by William Grant Still. In a letter which Still wrote to Sylvan early in August, he mentioned that "Stokowski says definitely that he is going to produce *Troubled Island* in New York and yesterday, when we saw him for the first time since he returned from Mexico, he told us that you are going to work with him on it! Needless to say, that was very good news. . . . He is a wonderful person and he has been a wonderful friend to me."[13]

On Labor Day he returned to New York and in the next few days worked furiously. He met with Claire Reis and the members of the City Center board and also his contractor, Vincent Vanni, and they set up numerous auditions. Among those he auditioned was flutist Julius Baker, and he immediately became a part of the orchestra. It was a fortunate happening. "I quietly went over and took an audition," said Julie, "and then he put things in front of me that I had just finished recording with Kostelanetz—*Peter and the Wolf* and the *Carnival of the Animals*. It wasn't really fair for me to take an audition like that . . . but he offered me the chance to play with him."[14]

What Stoki intended to build was an equivalent of the All-American Youth Orchestra. He wanted a core of superb professionals along with brilliant young aspirants. Many of the professionals would not or could not join him in the new enterprise, and most of the talented poststudent, preprofessional youngsters were being inducted into the armed forces. The All-American Youth Orchestra season was not only short but was at a time when many musicians were enjoying a vacation period. The City Center season was smack in the middle of the musical season, and many of the musicians he had hoped to engage were simply not available.

One stalwart, however, was Bob Gross. "As I understand it now," he said, "this was his way of getting back at NBC. . . . It was perhaps another way of demonstrating that he could put together an orchestra under any circumstances. . . . He wrote to a group of us who had worked with him —including some of his close friends in the Philly Orchestra—asking us to come and play in the new orchestra. The problem was that the new orchestra had no real backing and nobody got a salary. The players in the orchestra got paid per concert and it was union scale. That was little enough, and it was impossible to provide for a family on that kind of basis, which Stoki well knew. Saul Caston was one. Saul refused him and he never forgave Saul. Sylvan Levin came from Philadelphia. The first oboe was Mitch Miller. It was a good orchestra but not like the Youth Orchestra and, of course, not like the Philadelphia. But there were a handful of us that he relied on as leaders of the sections, and he told us that if we came to New York, he would see that we could be supported by playing commercial radio. At that period commercial radio was a very big thing. So I took a leave from college and came to New York."[15]

There were disappointments and frustrations, but Stokowski tackled these problems with equanimity. He envisioned a great art center with himself at its center. He had written to Sylvan during the summer: "I regard my work there as permanent and am determined to make the orchestra as fine as I possibly can and to bring about the highest artistic results as rapidly as possible."[16]

He tried. The New York City Symphony Orchestra made its debut under Stokowski on October 9, 1944. To New Yorkers it was an event. "Personalities from the musical and allied intellectual world were numerous. The house was packed; the applause was solid." So reported Virgil Thomson. All the reviews were good despite some hedging. Thomson perhaps saw it most accurately. "The vagaries of pitch and rhythm and the general insecurity of teamwork manifested last night led one to conclude that even this master trainer cannot produce a high-class result in six rehearsals when his material is inferior. . . . It is to be hoped that Mr. Stokowski will not be discouraged in what he has undertaken."[17]

With each concert the orchestra seemed to improve. As usual Stokowski held auditions almost daily and replaced any musician whom he felt was inferior. The repertoire was challenging and fresh. The concerts were given in pairs, on Monday evenings at 8:30 and Tuesdays at 6:00. The early hour seemed to catch on and the SRO sign was up for nearly every concert. Ticket prices were low, ranging from 60 cents to $1.80. The audiences were warm and enthusiastic. "I have felt a wave of friendliness from the audience which I have never experienced before," he told Quaintance Eaton. "There is an atmosphere of happiness and informality which seems to me unique. These music lovers come solely for the music; they express their enthusiasm by their spontaneous applause—even between movements of symphonies—and they don't rush away immediately afterwards. I believe that the reason for this is that they understand we are trying to build an institution devoted to culture, without any self-seeking."[18]

Stokowski's programs were the most interesting of any symphonic programs being given in New York. On his second set of concerts he included the Barber Violin Concerto superbly played by Roman Totenberg.[19]

In an all-Russian concert (October 23) Stoki conducted a truncated version of the Eighth Symphony of Shostakovich.[20] No one seemed to mind that he had omitted numerous repeats, chiefly in the first overlong and ambling movement. (I, for one, found it a distinct improvement. This was the symphony for which CBS had already paid $10,000 for the right to give its first hearing on the air under Rodzinski. I was at CBS at the time in charge of the Philharmonic broadcasts, and I covered every rehearsal and performance in preparation for the historic occasion. The publicity was enormous throughout the country, and the listening audience on Sunday, October 15, was one of the largest ever recorded for a Philharmonic broadcast.) Stoki's performance of the work was given just eight days later. Although the New York City Symphony played well, it did not have the advantage of the numerous rehearsals and prebroadcast performances of the symphony that Rodzinski and the New York Philharmonic had had. Strangely, the symphony, to my knowledge, was not heard again in New York until, at the invitation of Stokowski, Maxim Shostakovich performed it with the American Symphony Orchestra on January 3 and 5, 1971.

When Shostakovich and his wife Irina came to America in 1973, I hosted a luncheon for him at the Century Club on June 12, the day after his arrival. In addition to such Centurions as Russell Lynes, and Richard Dana, I invited a group of distinguished composers including William Schuman, George Crumb, Otto Luening, Ulysses Kay, Alexander Tcherepnin and others. I described the luncheon to Stoki when we met later in London. He particularly enjoyed my report of the toast I made in Shostakovich's honor. I told Shostakovich that one of the CBS correspondents, Bill Downes, had brought the bulky score out of Russia and that he had brought it directly to my office, and I mentioned the fact that CBS had paid $10,000 for the right to give it its first broadcast performance. As the translators related this to him, he looked rather astonished. I then asked him if he ever received the money, and to this he shook his head and threw up his hands diplomatically.

In September Stoki wrote to Arnold Schoenberg.

16 September 44

Dear Friend

I sent you a telegram for your birthday but Western Union refused to transmit it on account of the war. So now I am sending these words to wish you happiness in the coming year.

All your friends and admirers here are looking forward to your visit
to New York when we shall play your *Second Chamber Symphony*
and others of your compositions.
With sincere admiration and friendship

Leopold Stokowski[21]

True to his word, he programmed the work on November 20. "All
honor to Mr. Stokowski for performing a major work of Schoenberg for
a popular audience," wrote one critic. He praised its "masterly development and magical scoring."[22]

One day at a City Center board meeting, Stoki told Claire Reis that
he had a plan for a Christmas festival and that Robert Edmond Jones
would do the costumes. "He described the whole thing," Claire remembered. "Bobby wanted to give him some of his own beautiful, personal
materials he had collected for the three kings in a Christmas story. Well,
it was to cost $10,000, and every dollar in those days counted, and
Newbold was very firm and said, 'We would love to have it; it sounds
beautiful, but we haven't got the money.' Stokowski persisted and finally
said, 'I'm going to go through with it.' As he got up to leave, he took out
his checkbook and he wrote a check for $10,000 and put it on the desk.
So the Christmas story came off for children for about five or six days of
matinees. It created such a marvelous effect on the children that the
parents wrote letters and telephoned to ask if Stokowski and the group
would please give it one evening so they could see it, and he did. He gave
it on Christmas night. That was one of the nicest things he did in his City
Center era."[23]

Stoki planned the "Children's Christmas Story" as a pageant both for
and with children, the orchestra, and Robert Shaw's Collegiate Chorale.
Robert Edmond Jones immediately suggested that the dancer, Anita
Zahn, should stage it. Anita had been one of the children trained by
Isadora and Elizabeth Duncan. Later in New York she became one of the
most sought-after teachers, and as such, she taught the children of the
Dalton School, which Evangeline so strongly favored. There she taught
the two Stokowski children, Lyuba and Sadja, as well as another youngster,
Gloria Vanderbilt.

One afternoon Anita told me about their early collaboration. " 'I am
now working with Stokowski,' Bobby Jones said, 'and I am going to design
a Christmas story for him and you are going to do it—you have all these
children you teach and you are going to stage it. I will design the costumes,

the sets, the lighting, and Stokowski will do the music.' So then we all had a meeting—Stokowski, Bobby Jones, and I.''

Anita proposed that the youngsters dance to the music of some carols, just as they used to do in Vienna with the Vienna Choir Boys singing. But as soon as the word leaked out that there would be children (some under fourteen) dancing at City Center, the Society for the Prevention of Cruelty to Children stepped in and ruled that no dancing would be permitted. "All they were allowed to do was to raise their arms and drop them again. . . . So Stokowski and I worked very much together. He always greeted me in his apartment in a gorgeous Japanese robe and offered me a cup of yogurt. He was on a strict diet and kept himself very well in those days. . . . He used to call me at the oddest hours, like three or four in the morning. He called me one morning and said, 'A-n-i-t-a, I have just met the head of the Bronx Zoo and we must have an-ee-muls.' And I said, 'Leopoldo, we can't have animals. When there are animals, nobody looks at children. When there are children, nobody looks at the grown-ups. And that's how it goes.' 'Oh yes, we must have an-ee-muls.' So the next day at the rehearsal, up comes an enormous truck with a camel. They tried to get the camel out on Fifty-sixth Street at the stage entrance, but it wouldn't budge. It was too big for the door, so the camel was put back on the truck.''

To fill the part of the narrator, Anita had persuaded Isadora's brother, Augustin Duncan, to take part. He had been a distinguished Shakespearean actor in his time but by now had become old and blind. At one of the final rehearsals, Duncan was in his place on the stage not far from a big klieg light. "Suddenly a ram, a male sheep with horns, came galloping in, right into the klieg light, which fell over on Mr. Duncan, who almost died of fright. . . . So the ram had to be put in a dressing room. And then came the part 'And Mary and Joseph also went unto Bethlehem to be counted. . . .' And Stoki wanted a donkey. 'But Anita,' he said, 'it's a donkey from Sicilia.' The donkey was from the Bronx Zoo. However, the donkey wouldn't go onstage. The stagehands had to push it by its behind to get it up there. Finally Stoki said, 'All right. We will not have the donkey.' So the scene with the shepherds came on. 'And there were in the same country shepherds abiding in the fields keeping watch over their flock, etc.' Well, Bobby Jones had built the stage up to look like a hill. He had this beautiful fire going and the shepherds all around it warming their hands over the fire with the sheep standing there. . . . 'A-n-i-t-a, we are ready. Shall we begin?' 'Yes, yes, Maestro,'

I answered. And as his hands came down the sheep goes baaaah. The Robert Shaw Chorale almost rolled off their steps. The shepherds just looked at the sheep very happily, and Stokowski even had to laugh at that. So finally he said, 'A-n-i-t-a, we will have no an-ee-muls.' Was I ever glad."[24]

The "Children's Christmas Story" was a hit. "The performance, which had the great merit of simplicity, was beautiful, impressive and touching," wrote Noel Strauss in the *Times*.[25] Between each tableau, the orchestra presented interludes of Bach. Stoki had chosen parts of the *Christmas Oratorio*, parts of cantatas, the chorale prelude "Ich ruf' zu dir" and other works. The Chorale sang a round dozen carols from all parts of the world.

As the new year—1945—rolled in, City Center announced a series of five pairs of concerts to be conducted by Stokowski between mid-January and March, as well as a series of three student concerts. The programs continued to be both imaginative and rewarding and constantly drew one of the most eminent of audiences. For the first of the series Stokowski asked Robert Gross to play the Hindemith Violin Concerto, a work rarely heard in New York, or anywhere else for that matter.

Gross scored a marked success. Critics spoke of his opulent sonorities, keen musical insight, noteworthy technical smoothness and polish, purity of intonation, and sympathetic response to the music. "It was a point of significant interest that despite the fact that the essentially cerebral music of this work has not the elemental musical appeal of the standard violin concertos, the audience broke into stormy applause after both the first and second movements and then gave the soloist and conductor an ovation at the end."[26]

The following concert began with the Twenty-first Symphony of Miaskovsky, which Virgil Thomson called "a welcome dish from time to time on any program . . . because it is wholly lacking in the banality of most Soviet music." The program included the Mussorgsky-Stokowski *Boris Godunov* excerpts and Rimsky-Korsakov's *Scheherazade*. "It is a constant source of amazement to this reviewer," Thomson continued, "that Mr. Stokowski can achieve the really delightful concerts that he does with an orchestra of constantly shifting personnel. Certainly it is to be hoped that some arrangement for a more stable financing of these concerts can be worked out, because they have long since proved their excellence and their popularity. They are both a pleasure to attend and a genuine contribution to the cultural life of our city. Last night's audience was large and definitely on the distinguished side."[27]

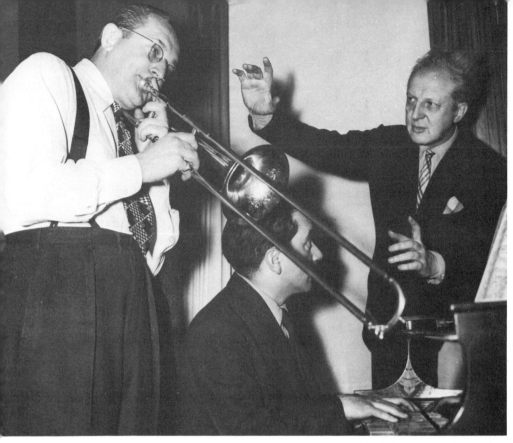

Tommy Dorsey, guest soloist for the New York City Symphony, February 15, 1945; Sylvan Levin, assistant conductor; and Stokowski

On the fifth of February Stokowski met the "Little Flower." La Guardia sympathetically listened to Stoki's plans to enlarge the orchestra and create a chorus that would be adequate to perform large works for chorus and orchestra. He discussed better financing for it and his plans to produce such modern operas as Milhaud's *Bolivar* and Still's *Troubled Island.* The mayor seemed sympathetic.

Although Stokowski intended to increase the number of young peoples' concerts, he scheduled only three for this initial year. As he had done in Philadelphia, he tried to involve young people in every aspect of the series. They were to share in the program making, writing of program notes, and the designs of the program covers. The first was done by daughter Lyuba, who was a student at Barnard College at the time. She was listed as Lyuba Stokowska. The concerts were then called Student Concerts. The audience was asked what compositions they would like to hear, what songs they would like to sing, and whether they would like to write program notes. They were also asked whether they would like to be on the "Make it Known," the "Sell Tickets," or "General Volunteer" committees.

The first student concert began at 2:30 on Tuesday, February 15, 1945, and it introduced William Schuman's carnivallike little overture called "Side Show." It also introduced a soloist who was making his debut with a symphony orchestra, one of the kings of "swing," Tommy Dorsey. He played the world premiere of Nathaniel Shilkret's Concerto for Trombone and Orchestra with gusto. The young, approving audience shouted and applauded the performance vigorously.

Before the season ended, Stoki met with Claire Reis, Gerald Warburg, Newbold Morris, Sylvan Levin and various members of the board, usually at the Lotus Club, and worked out the plans for the next season. They announced to the press that the 1945–46 season would begin on October 8 with Leopold Stokowski conducting in a series of twelve Monday evening concerts and an equal number of "Symphonies at Six." The Student Concerts, expanded to five, were to be called "Symphonies for Young America." The press release concluded: "Mr. Stokowski is now engaged in auditions for next year's soloists before leaving for Hollywood early in April where he will conduct at the Hollywood Bowl for the summer."[28]

50

Gloria

S TOKOWSKI never kept a diary. The closest thing are his date books, which enable one to chart the chronology of his activities. They are fascinating and in many ways quite cryptic. At times his writing is so bad that it probably could be interpreted by no one but himself. And that I am sure is what he wanted. Some times he filled in space with a circle or some other sign. He had private nicknames for many of his friends—particularly his lady friends during the days of his bachelorhood. Once when discussing Stoki's penchant for mystery and concealment of personal affairs, Arthur Judson remarked, "That was typical of Stokowski. He always had something to hide."[1]

In the appointment book we read that on December 13, 1944, he dined with the Saroyans at 2 Sutton Place South. Saroyan had married Carol Marcus, a dear friend of Gloria Vanderbilt—as was her sister, Eleanor, who had been a maid of honor at her wedding to Pat di Cicco in Santa Barbara.[2] This may have been a fateful evening, since Gloria Vanderbilt was one of the invited guests. "Stoki was impressed with her," said Goddard Lieberson, "and, of course, was impressed with the fact that she was a Vanderbilt but would never admit that, and then he said to someone, 'Who was that wonderful girl I met last night? She had a Dutch name.' "[3] The rest is history.

Gloria Morgan Vanderbilt, the mother of the young heiress, recalled the era. In a double autobiographical exposé written in collaboration with her twin sister, Lady Furness, she relates that one day in New York (and that would translate 1944), Gloria called her saying that she would divorce

Pat di Cicco. About two months later she mentioned that she had a telephone call from Mrs. Marcus, the mother of Carol Saroyan, inviting her to a dinner dance. Although she at first declined, Gloria persuaded her mother to attend because she would have a surprise to show her.

Shortly after she arrived, daughter Gloria left her mother's side and dashed off to greet a newly arrived guest. Mother Gloria perceived what she regarded as a rather elderly gentleman whom Gloria introduced: "Mummy, this is it! This is Leopold Stokowski and I am going to marry him." Later when Stokowski confirmed his intention to marry Gloria, her mother said it was in a tone that seemed no more serious than one would use "ordering a new station wagon." Early the following morning Gloria phoned her mother "bubbling like one of the Rhine maidens" to say that she was the happiest woman in the world.[4]

Leopold entrained from Los Angeles for San Francisco on Friday, the thirteenth of April and proceeded to Lake Tahoe to join Gloria and Eleanor Marcus, who was technically their chaperone. Stoki merely indicated the word *bungalow* in his date book for the next four days. As always, there was inordinate curiosity about both of them. Reporters released a story that as Stoki stepped out of the train and was about to enter the secondhand Cadillac that Gloria had just learned to drive, she inadvertently stepped on the gas as Stoki was crossing in front of it, and nearly ran down her future husband. They also reported that Stoki at that crucial time was a victim of the shingles.[5] One doctor reported that he was being treated in a hospital in Reno, but in letters to friends Stoki denied that he had even been in Reno.[6] One wonders!

However, these details are unimportant. On Saturday April 21, 1945, Leopold Stokowski and Gloria Vanderbilt di Cicco were married in the little town of Mexicali. But even that produced more than the usual grist for the press. Leopold had chartered a plane in Reno, and shortly after they were airborne, the pilot had to make a forced landing on a desolate strip of highway in the middle of the Mojave Desert. Fortunately, they were not injured, but the effect was traumatic for Stoki, who for the rest of his life, with but few exceptions, refused to fly.[7] A Hollywood screen writer would have been delighted to have written the scenario. The idea of Gloria Vanderbilt and Leopold Stokowski thumbing a ride from a passing motorist is like a scene with Claudette Colbert and Clark Gable in *It Happened One Night.*

A passing car picked up Gloria and Leopold along with their friend Eleanor Marcus and drove them to the town of El Monte, not far from

Los Angeles. Violinist Philip Kahgan, who was a close friend of Stokowski and the contractor for the Hollywood Bowl concerts, had made all the wedding arrangements. He gave me this version of what transpired next: "They called the manager of the Riverside Inn in Reno, and he and his wife came to El Monte and drove them to Calexico, which is on the California side of the Mexican border." At the time Kahgan also was en route to Calexico. On arriving there he proceeded to see his friend Jimmy Alvarez, the owner of the Café De Oro in Mexicali on the Mexican side of the border. It was Alvarez who made all the legal arrangements.

"Stokowski called me that night and said he could not talk much at that time but I was to expect them some time the next day," Phil added. "They arrived late, and having notified Jimmy Alvarez of their arrival, we went to the Café De Oro, where the judge and his assistants met us. . . . After dinner we all went to the courthouse where the ceremony was performed. This was about 10:00 P.M."[8]

The only attendants at the ceremony were Eleanor Marcus, Mr. and Mrs. Philip Kahgan, Jimmy Alvarez and Mr. and Mrs. Allan, managers of the Riverside Inn in Reno. One dispatch datelined April 24, Mexicali, added these fascinating details: "Stokowski gave his name as Leopold Stokowski Czartorieska, using his mother's maiden surname as his second surname, as law requires in Spanish-speaking countries, his birthplace as London, his nationality North American and his age 58. Gloria Vanderbilt gave her name as Gloria Vanderbilt Morgan, complying with the same legal requirement, her birthplace New York City and her age 21."[9]

What would Annie Moore have thought, being labeled Czartorieska?

"The following morning," said Phil, "we drove them back to Los Angeles."[10] AP reports of their going on a Mexican honeymoon notwithstanding! Back in California, Stoki began immediately to prepare for the Hollywood Bowl concerts, which were to begin on July 10. It was a time, too, to introduce Gloria to many of his longtime friends. The first, as he noted in his calendar, was Richard Hammond. The second was George Antheil. Dick was a next-door neighbor. He told me: "He was on Beverly Crest Drive and I was on Guild Crest. His street formed the base around my property. He had really suggested my coming out there, because one time when we were in Europe and we had a lot of bad weather in New York prior to that, he said, 'You ought to come out to California, Dick. There I can reach out and pick an orange from one tree and a lemon from another.' I began looking around for property, and it was Garbo who said,

'You had better get serious'—because she had looked at something that Loretta Young bought right under her nose. So that frightened me. Our driver said, 'Well, there's some nice property on a hilltop below Ginger Rogers'.' And I got it, and my God, Stoki's house was right there. Lucia Davidova was out there at that time a good deal. . . . Then when he married Gloria they were just below me. They were wonderful neighbors, and they used to come up for Sunday lunches, and it was very cozy and nice. . . . I think they were very much in love."[11]

The name Antheil occurs more frequently in Stoki's date book at this time than almost any other. The meetings were mostly social, since the time was usually seven in the evening—the dinner hour. Their first visit, during which George and his charming wife, Boski, met Gloria for the first time, was on Saturday, April 4. George was a fascinating man who had a personality that made one instinctively feel that something good was about to happen. He was brash, uninhibited, and a most fluent talker on a host of subjects. In addition to being an internationally recognized composer, he also had many other specialties up his sleeve. He wrote several important film scores, and had his opera *Transatlantic* performed in Germany—the first American to achieve that distinction. He wrote articles on infidelity for *Esquire* magazine, "invented a torpedo in collaboration with Hedy Lamarr," ground out a syndicated lonely hearts column, and achieved recognition as a war analyst for the press and radio. Just at that moment he was putting the final touches to his autobiographical book, *Bad Boy of Music*.

In the very last pages, he recounted the first visit of Stoki and Gloria: "At seven-thirty . . . Stokowski and his new bride . . . drove up in back of the house. . . . We, Boski and I, had never seen Gloria before and watched the tall, slender, but utterly beautiful Gloria descend the steps. Whatever else, we agreed, Gloria, the new Mrs. Stokowski, was certainly one of the two most beautiful women we had ever seen, the other being Hedy Lamarr."

George's eight-year-old son and a friend were so curious about Stokowski and Gloria that they crept down and peered into the dining room, where the four of them were dining. George caught them peeking around the dining-room door twice. "At last Stokowski saw them and said: 'Come on in, boys, and take a good look.'" They did and stared at Gloria and blushed as she, too, blushed back. George and Boski also observed Gloria, and he wrote: "She had a youthful, grave beauty, the sensitive face of one who, over a long period, has been hurt and hushed. I could not reconcile the young girl sitting there to her newspaper publicity. . . .

"We both looked at Stokowski. . . . He too, lately, had been hurt and hushed. The antagonistic—and totally incorrect—publicity about the canceled Mexican concerts. The growing difficulties with the new orchestra in New York. The cancellation of his NBC broadcasting contract the year previous. Boski sent me a mental flash: 'These two have found each other because both are being constantly and unreasonably wounded by the world. They are a refuge to each other. For, certainly, any fool can see that they are deeply in love.' "

George recalled the days when as a student he had first heard him in Philadelphia. "He was a hero of mine then, and was scarcely less so now. Here was one of the two greatest orchestral conductors in the world, from many points of view the greatest."[12]

Dick Hammond was on the managerial board of the Hollywood Bowl and worked closely with Stoki. He attended most of the rehearsals and said that "he would have me running up to the top of the Bowl to hear how it was from there and from down below. He was, as always, very interested in sound and the mee-kro-phones, as he called them, and he was concerned with the amplification."[13]

In the past the players for the Hollywood Bowl concerts were always drawn from the Los Angeles Philharmonic, then conducted by Alfred Wallenstein. Stoki planned to change all that. He did choose a core of players from the Philharmonic, but to these he added many of the best players who were attached to the various movie studios. And as a third group, he auditioned young players from the area.[14]

To add a new interest and involve Los Angeles composers in the affairs of the Bowl, he invited fifty-six of them to write fanfares to be played during the concerts. Among those whom he contacted were: Igor Stravinsky, Erich Korngold, Alfred Newman, David Raksin, Ernst Toch, Arnold Schoenberg, Alexander Tansman, Victor Young, Hans Eisler, Miklós Rózsa, Eugene Zador, Nathaniel Shilkret, William Grant Still, Louis Gruenberg, and Italo Montemezzi.[15] Many of the composers came through, but some did not bother to answer the invitation, Stravinsky among them.

Schoenberg was eager to comply. He wrote to Stoki on July 2.

> Just when I had made up my mind in which way I could write a
> fanfare for you, I discovered on your stationery, that the committee

of the Hollywood Bowl is still greatly the same people who systematically excluded me from Los Angeles' public musical life.

I do not want to engage in any connection with these persons and therefore I cannot write something for them. But I decided I will write and dedicate it to you personally on account of our personal friendship.[16]

He also mentioned two possible plans. One was to draw something from the *Moses und Aron* "Tanz um das Goldene Kalb," which he said was a ballet scene of half an hour with two or three fanfares. "I mention them because they are of my latest (12-tone) style." The second suggestion was to use three motifs from *Gurrelieder*. "I would end with the C Major of the sunrise, which does not fit to the hour of the concerts, but to the mood."[17]

Stoki responded:

I understand exactly how you feel about not wanting to give your wonderful music to people who have not treated you well. I think you are quite right and I honor you for your firm determination. . . .

I would not presume to suggest from which of your compositions and themes the fanfare will be created although you so kindly suggest this. I know that with your unerring instinct you will choose exactly what is right.

I greatly look forward to the day when we shall receive the fanfare and play it in the beauty of the night. I hope it will be possible for you and Mrs. Schoenberg to be present. Gloria and I hope you will be our guests in her box."[18]

Schoenberg was having considerable difficulty because of failing eyesight and wrote to Stokowski apologetically about the delay in completing the work.[19] Stoki replied:

It was so kind of you to write me so frankly about everything.

Gloria and I will be very happy to see you and Mrs. Schoenberg whenever convenient for you. . . .

Please do not hurry about the fanfare. Whenever it is ready we will play it and hope you will be able to hear it in the Bowl. . . .[20]

Schoenberg chose to follow his *Gurrelieder* suggestion and arranged motifs for a brass ensemble of trumpets, horns, tuba, and percussion. Late in August Schoenberg sent a score "Dedicated to my friend, Leopold Stokowski."[21] But, strangely, the score was incomplete. On September 1, 1945, Stokowski replied:

Photo Longworth, Warner Brothers/Courtesy International Leopold Stokowski Society
Stokowski with John Garfield and Douglas Fairbanks, Jr. (c. 1942)

Thank you for the three pages of the *Fanfare* which has just
arrived. Whenever it may be convenient for you to finish it we will
play it with the deepest interest.
Thank you also for inviting us for dinner. We would both like to

come very much. We will telephone in a few days to find out what evening is convenient for you.[22]

Schoenberg never did complete the work, and if the fragment sent to Stoki was the original score, it somehow became lost and did not turn up in his library. However, Leonard Stein did have a copy of it and on comparing it with the score of the *Gurrelieder*, he determined the part in the score which Schoenberg had chosen, and he told me that he "just added the final five measures of the *Gurrelieder*. No big problem at all."[23] The now completed *Fanfare* was first performed at the opening of the Schoenberg Institute at the University of Southern California in February 1977.

Like an agile juggler, Stoki concerned himself almost equally with the affairs of both Hollywood and New York. He corresponded regularly with Sylvan and mentioned in one letter that "we shoot airmail letters at each other as rapidly as possible so as to keep everything up to date and make things move quickly."[24]

He wrote to Sylvan about his progress in creating the orchestra for the Bowl:

> There are two groups here, one, the Philharmonic, the other the Bowl. There is a good deal of fighting that goes on between these two groups but I am confident that the plans of the Bowl will lead to great things in the future.
>
> I have been told that Wallenstein, the Conductor of the Philharmonic, is intriguing against me. I do not know whether this is true or not and I am not very interested. So many people have intrigued against me and I have noticed in the long run they do not do me any particular harm. When I conducted the New York Philharmonic, Wallenstein was playing cello in the orchestra so I know exactly what kind of man he is. . . .[25]

In New York the Little Flower had a long meeting with the board of City Center and announced various economies, quite nullifying the progressive plans of Stoki. "Thank you for the clippings about the Mayor," he wrote to Sylvan. "I am doing something about it immediately with Newbold Morris. . . ." And he reported the very good news that "our orchestra is complete for the Bowl season and is composed of wonderful players. The cream of what is here. We have about 25 of the best players from the Los Angeles Philharmonic. . . ."[26]

There was no response to Stoki's letter to Newbold Morris. But in a letter to Sylvan he answers some of his queries:

> . . . I entirely agree with you that the "social tone" you mention is all wrong for City Center. It seems to me that my idea of City Center and the conception the committee has, is quite different. When I return I am going to try hard to make the committee understand my conception and follow it. The old ideas of social prestige are entirely out of place today. . . .
>
> What Mayor LaGuardia said to the directors of City Center at the Lotus Club was a great surprise to me. He said, "sixty-five men make a good orchestra." This depends [upon] *what* is being played, and *where.* In City Center 65 men would be inadequate because the acoustics are so bad. 65 men could not possibly play *Heldenleben* or *Seventh Symphony* of Shostakovich because the strings would be drowned out by the large wind section necessary to the score. For next winter I am asking for two more firsts, two seconds, two viola, two cello and one bass. These nine extra strings will give a better balance. LaGuardia's idea that music must pay for itself shows that he is not thinking clearly. All orchestras and all opera houses need subvention of some kind. . . . Instead of Mayor LaGuardia saying disparaging things about me (although he did not mention my name) he might have thanked me for giving a whole season of work without compensation and for giving up many engagements in United States, Canada, Central and South America, England, Egypt, and Palestine which I declined and which could have brought me a large income as well as the pleasure of traveling in these lands. As people do not seem to understand my ideas of giving my services for idealistic reasons I am not going to do it anymore. People are going to pay me for my services in future just as Hollywood Bowl is doing at present. The only exception to this will be City Center. I promised to give my services there next winter and I will keep my word. . . .[27]

The affairs of City Center continued to perturb Stoki. On July 14 he wrote to Sylvan:

> Every day I see more clearly that my ideals for City Center and Mayor La Guardia's ideals are quite different. This is true also of quite a number of the members of the Board of Directors. The question in my mind is how I can go on working with a group of persons who think so differently from the way I do. It seems to me a waste of time. . . .[28]

Two days later his mind was made up. He wired Newbold Morris tendering his resignation.

On the twentieth of July he wrote to Sylvan explaining the reasons for his resignation and mentioned in the same letter his progress at Hollywood Bowl.

> . . . We have formed an entirely new orchestra of 100 players and it is superb. . . . This is very stimulating to everyone so that we are forming plans for next season on a much larger scale. In a word, we have already achieved here the ideals I had for City Center.[29]

Naturally, Stoki's resignation set off a series of panic tremors in New York. Newbold Morris sent a long though not persuasive wire urging Stoki to continue. He weighed the request calmly and after what he probably thought was a suitable interval, wrote a long and detailed letter to Newbold Morris.

> Thank you for your recent telegram. I must ask your pardon for not having replied sooner. The reason is that I am working day and night at Hollywood Bowl. . . .
>
> Last winter when I donated my services to City Center I was obliged to postpone a tour that was already planned for me in Latin America. I would like to make this tour this coming winter, and in order to do this would like to receive a year's leave of absence from City Center. I shall be happy to conduct the first pair of concerts on October 22nd and 23rd and to help City Center find another conductor, or series of guest conductors for this coming winter.
>
> There is one thing I feel I must frankly tell you. I have definite and unshakable ideals about music. Last winter I was not always able to achieve these ideals because certain essentials were lacking. This forced me to make compromises in musical quality which compromises I am unwilling to make again. I am not criticizing City Center, but my first loyalty is to music.
>
> In order to achieve the quality of performance which I personally believe is what City Center needs, I am convinced that the following are essential—
>
> 1. A really fine orchestra with a larger string section than we had last season, and a good woodwind section with good intonation.
>
> 2. A chorus adequate for the compositions for orchestra and chorus of Bach, Mozart, Beethoven, Brahms, Verdi, Mahler, etc.
>
> 3. An executive director equally experienced and understanding in music and drama. This person must coordinate all artistic activities.

4. The necessary means of producing each season at least one contemporary opera such as Still's *Troubled Island* or Milhaud's *Bolivar.*
5. The whole conception to be carried out in harmony with world conditions of today and the future, and not according to the ideas of the past.

May I hear from you at your convenience whether City Center is willing for me to take a year's leave of absence, whether City Center would like me to conduct the first pair of concerts on October 22nd and 23rd, and whether there is any other way in which I can be of service to City Center.[30]

On August 29 he wrote to Sylvan.

Although I have heard nothing from Newbold Morris, the Associated Press has called me to say that Mayor LaGuardia has granted me a year's leave of absence and nominated Leonard Bernstein in my place as music director.

Newbold Morris did not have the courtesy to reply to my letter in any way so I now know what kind of man he is. . . .[31]

As the weeks passed and still no response came from Morris, Stoki in a fit of indignation sent off a letter to the board.

As I have received no reply to my letter airmailed to Mr. Newbold Morris on August 14th, I imagine he may be out of town so I am writing direct to the members of the Board.

Last October I offered City Center $10,000.00 with which I requested them to begin a music fund to be used for special music performances such as for example, *Troubled Island* by Still, or *Bolivar* of Milhaud. Nothing was done at that time about forming the music fund and on July 21st Mr. Morris wrote, "Just before your telegram arrived I planned to send out the letter to some thirty or forty music lovers who are in a position to make substantial contributions. My letter is drafted and the typing is about to commence."

As this music fund was still not formed at so recent a date as last July 21st, I am requesting by this letter that City Center refund to me the $10,000.00 because I wish to donate it to other creative projects.[32]

Stokowski's donation was never returned.

Meanwhile, the first concert at the Bowl began with three freshly composed fanfares. Fourteen thousand had assembled to greet Stokowski "Under the Stars." Everything seemed "well-nigh perfect," reported the Los Angeles *Times.* [33]

The Bowl concerts ran from the eleventh of July to the second of September, 1945. It was generally conceded that the climax of the season came with the performance of Beethoven's Ninth Symphony with a huge chorus of a thousand drawn from twenty-eight southern California choirs. The biggest turnout came in mid-July for a Gershwin Memorial concert that packed the Bowl, including seven hundred standees for good measure. Jeanette MacDonald, singing arias from *Faust* and *Romeo and Juliet*, drew an assemblage of nineteen thousand. Another immense audience assembled for the "Academy Night" honoring Hollywood's motion picture composers. Stoki conducted parts of scores by twelve of them, including Franz Waxman, Victor Young, Ernst Toch, Alfred Newman, Max Steiner, and others. Frances Langford, Claudette Colbert, and Danny Kaye "did narrations and other decorations." After intermission, Stoki turned over the orchestra to Johnny Green, who devoted his attention to popular song hits (with Frank Sinatra as soloist) and a "comedian's holiday."

In addition to the fanfares, Stoki added much new music for the ears of the Bowl audience. He performed Virgil Thomson's *Plow That Broke the Plains,* Nat Shilkret's Trombone Concerto and a newly commissioned six-minute-long Clarinet Rhapsody by Alexander Steinert. William Grant Still's *Old California* made an excellent impression, as did George Antheil's *Heroes of Today.* Jerome Kern wrote a Fanfare in Memory of W.C. Handy, which was performed in addition to his Portrait for Orchestra. Miklós Rósza had a Pastorale performed.[34] But the sum and substance of the Hollywood composers' output made very little impact and seemed for the most part to be quite tepid stuff.

One special soloist, who appeared early in the series, was Percy Grainger. They had not performed together since 1916, when Percy played the Grieg Piano Concerto. Now nearly thirty years later he was to perform the same work in the Hollywood Bowl. The performance was brilliant and vigorous on the part of Grainger, and the orchestra resounded sonorously. The collaboration was a fortunate one, and it is quite amazing to hear it on an off-the-air recording that is available through the International Piano Archives.

The Bowl had particularly pleasant associations for Percy, who after conducting there on August 9, 1928, was married before an audience of about twenty thousand paying guests. His beautiful, Swedish-born bride, the former Ella Viola Ström, who was a painter, poet, and onetime paramour of Prince Iyemasa Tokugawa of Japan, was dressed in a rose pink gown and sported three camellias in her hair. The ceremony took place at the end of the concert, which had concluded with *To a Nordic Princess,* which Percy had written as a wedding present for Ella.[35]

The reunion of Grainger and Stokowski was a most agreeable one, and Stoki immediately proposed that Grainger return the following season to perform some works of his own. They did, after all, have many things in common: both were of identical age and both were in splendid physical condition. Both were interested in physical culture—though Grainger was far more rigorous about it—and both were intellectually free from any theological complexes.

One April morning in 1977—Ella was eighty-eight at the time—I called on her in the old Grainger house in White Plains. She recalled the performance in the Bowl and mentioned that it was the first time that she had met Leopold and Gloria. "He was adorable, really a great man. I liked meeting Gloria. She was a very sweet woman, and all I can remember was that she was at a dinner party with Stokowski and kindliness was eminent with her. . . . She was a wonderful painter. Oh, I admire her.

"Stokowski I knew quite affectionately. I have a sort of affection towards him for the things he did with Percy and the things he did with Gloria. Percy knew Stokowski rather well. . . . He was a very energetic man in the good sense of the word. He let other people do what they wanted to do and he was very generous."[36]

After the Bowl season ended, Gloria and Leopold set out to drive back to New York.

Since his breakup with Michael Myerberg in 1943, Stoki had not had a manager. Nevertheless, he was aware that in his position of being basically a free-lance artist it was essential for him to have someone to manage his affairs. He discussed it quite freely with Sylvan. He told him that the William Morris Agency had approached him several times during the past year and said that they would like to represent him for everything. But he felt that they would be, perhaps, better for radio than for concerts. Judson, he felt, would be better for concerts, but, he said, "I am not sure how really friendly he is to me. I believe I have seen signs of animosity on his part but it might be that I am mistaken. . . . I feel it is important to have a large responsible organization such as Morris or Judson back of my radio and concert conducting but you may have a better suggestion. . . ."[37]

Shortly after his return from California on October 19, Stoki and

Judson met for lunch at the Lotus Club. The meeting was apparently most amicable. They discussed the situation with the New York Philharmonic, which under Rodzinski was experiencing some rather rocky moments. Halina Rodzinski recalled that her husband had suggested to Judson and the Philharmonic board that Stoki be engaged as guest conductor with the orchestra. "The board was enthusiastic about the idea," she said, "if Judson was not. With the white-maned celebrity contracted to someone else, the agent's percentage would be paid to a Judson competitor and Stoki's fees were high."[38]

Halina was not quite right. Stoki was not affiliated with any other manager. Obviously, that would have been a matter of discussion between him and Judson, but nothing conclusive was agreed upon at that moment. On November 5 Stoki met with the William Morris Agency to probe his representation further. That, too, was inconclusive. But on December 1, he signed with Judson for radio appearances only. Walter Preston, Judson's director of radio at Columbia Concerts, drew up a simple contract, binding on them for one year. Stoki was to pay Columbia 10 percent of any engagements he would conduct during that time excluding, however, the Standard Oil Company of California broadcasts, which had been booked previously in conjunction with the Hollywood Bowl. The following fees were agreed upon: "series of 30-minute broadcasts, $2,500 per broadcast; series of 45-minute broadcasts, $3,000 per broadcast; series of one-hour broadcasts, $3,500 per broadcast."[39]

Far from being hostile, Judson was most agreeable, and he and Stoki met for lunch frequently. Shortly before their midwinter holiday they met at the Hotel Dorset, close to the penthouse Leopold and Gloria had on Fifty-third Street. It was probably at this time that he was invited to return to the New York Philharmonic as guest conductor. It was also at this time that he definitely recognized Judson as his manager, for in a letter to Victor Seroff concerning a query about the Vienna Philharmonic, Stoki answered: "Would you mind asking whoever is the manager of this orchestra to write to Mr. André Mertens of Columbia Concerts, Inc. . . . because Columbia Concerts is my manager. The head of it is Arthur Judson and André Mertens is the head of that department concerning all other countries."[40]

He may not have told Judson about the visit of the Cuban manager Jorge Estradé several months back and his engagement to conduct the Ninth Symphony in Havana. If he had, I believe Judson would have advised him not to accept the engagement. Estradé planned to have the

Havana Philharmonic, which Stoki had conducted in his trip to Cuba with Evangeline back in 1932 and remembered pleasantly. Estradé also spoke highly of the chorus attached to the orchestra. And Havana in those days was a lively carefree city, where the weather in January was close to ideal. Gloria and Leopold had reservations at the Hotel National, which at that time was a most elegant hotel. Their midwinter vacation was to be an extensive one and would include not only Cuba but Mexico as well. It would be a relief to get away from the vexations and quibbles they had experienced in New York. Not being clairvoyant, they could not foresee the real troubles that lay ahead.

(51)

Troubled Islands–
Cuba, Manhattan

T HE happy couple started driving south about mid-January. They stopped briefly at the Williamsburg Inn, where they received a lovely box of goodies from violist and sometime assistant and secretary Beatrice Brown. They opened the gift, so Gloria wrote, while sitting in a pine woods overlooking Chesapeake Bay. And she added jokingly that after eating the whole box neither of them could get into their clothes, and he added his sketch of Gloria and a self-portrait. Leopold's answer was a humorous one.

> Thanks for the irresistible temptations (the only kind
> I like) Please send me to Havana brief lines of interesting
> news from letters etc—like—
> Mayor LaGuardia sends love
> C.C. [City Center] returns your check
> Room 53 has been redecorated
> Your pen works
> Wecker agrees to make Bowl circular
> Phil [Kahgan]   "   "   "   "
> Dick [Hammond] "   "   "   "
> Havemeyer invites you[1]

499

At an unhurried pace they drove through Charleston, Savannah, St. Augustine, and finally Miami. They arrived in Havana by ship on Friday, February 25. After a pleasant week of strolling about the city, Stoki met with Jorge Estradé and learned of various complications that had developed. It seems that Erich Kleiber intended to do a performance of the Ninth Symphony later in the season. There was some talk of Stoki conducting one or more of the regular concerts of the Philharmonic, but he protested that he had signed a contract with Estradé and would not break it. There were meetings between Stoki, Estradé, and the managers of the orchestra and they came to an impasse. The upshot was that Kleiber would not permit a single player of the Havana Philharmonic to play under Stokowski.[2]

Kleiber and Stoki also met, and the intransigence and lack of any spirit of cooperation on Kleiber's part enraged Stoki. Kleiber had the reputation of being a "tough, stubborn, disciplinarian," according to Harold Schonberg. He quotes Kleiber as saying: "A conductor must live in his house like a lion with its claws deep in its prey"; and an intendant of a German opera house as saying, "When Kleiber comes into this theater, there's trouble with a capital T."[3]

Having had two unpleasant, disappointing experiences in New York—
the affair at NBC and the humiliating treatment at City Center, Stoki
was in no mood to be disciplined or to be the prey of Kleiber's claws.
Furthermore, the chorus had been trained for weeks. He managed to find
a nucleus of adequate players, but not enough to play the Beethoven.

Beatrice Brown was one who came to Stokowski's rescue and recalled
that "Kleiber was so furious at Stokowski that he pulled out the whole
orchestra and forbade anyone to play with Stokowski or he would fire
them. So Stokowski went around from cafés to factories—pocketbook
factories, where there were lots of refugees from Europe at that time,
Hitler's refugees—and he knew they were all musicians, so he picked up
a whole orchestra, but he was missing twenty-one musicians and one
tenor."[4]

It was not until February 6 that Stoki made frantic calls to Beatrice
Brown and Laszlo Halasz. At the time, Halasz was the director of the City
Center Opera Company, and he also had had an unpleasant experience
with Jorge Estradé when he conducted two opera performances for him
that were great successes artistically but dreadful financial flops. His stellar
attractions had been Grace Moore and Ezio Pinza.[5]

It was two in the morning when Halasz received his first call from Stoki
saying that he needed twenty-one musicians and one tenor and that they
had to be there in twenty-four hours. Halasz, Bea Brown, and the two
union contractors at City Center began phoning every musician whom
they could contact and miraculously rounded up the required number.
"And among them was Joseph de Pasquale, the violist who became first
violist with the Boston Symphony and then with the Philadelphia," Bea
Brown recalled.

In order to be sure that they would get there on time, it was necessary
to charter a plane, and Laszlo did this expeditiously. He also chose Giulio
Gari, a leading tenor with the City Center Opera Company, who had to
learn his part in the Beethoven in twenty-four hours. "Beatrice Brown,"
said the New York Times, "is in charge of the group."[6]

The first performance in the Proarte Auditorium, which began at
9:00 P.M., was a resounding success. It even drew out the President of
Cuba, Ramón Grau San Martín, members of his cabinet and diplomats,
as well as Army and Navy officials.[7] The work was greeted with tremendous enthusiasm and perhaps much less comprehension. The press had
given the concert tremendous advance publicity, and it seemed that
everyone in Havana wanted to be there except Mr. Kleiber. The concert

was repeated on Saturday night in the square in front of the old cathedral.

On Sunday at 5:30 Leopold and Gloria flew to Miami, picked up their car, and began their trip to Mexico, stopping at Fort Myers, Tampa, Gulfport, and on to Laredo. They entered Mexico on Monday the twentieth and proceeded to Mexico City, where after two days they motored west to San José Purua, one of the most restful and salubrious spots in Mexico. It is a true spa, with medicinal waters pouring from the ground. There are special baths and swimming pools, masseurs, quantities of fresh fruit juices, mineral waters, and everything imaginable to aid and pamper the body. It was just the sort of rest that Stoki needed, and they stayed in San José Purua for nearly two weeks, with a few brief side trips to Morelia and various villages. Nothing could have been more peaceful.

But on returning to Mexico City their tranquility was jarringly shattered. Gloria was suddenly contacted by the Associated Press and other reporters asking questions about her relationship with her mother, who had leaked to the press the fact that Gloria had cut off the $21,000 stipend that she had been receiving annually from the Vanderbilt estate.[8] The papers reported that "Mrs. Stokowski gained control of a $4,363,000 fortune on her twenty-first birthday on February 20, 1945."

Reporters fired questions rapidly and Gloria answered directly and frankly, albeit a bit naively. She had not yet learned Stoki's dictum that when questions are asked about one's private life, the sagest answer is always "No comment."

An Associated Press dispatch datelined Mexico City, March 13, 1946, read: "Mrs. Stokowski, wife of the symphony conductor Leopold Stokowski, said in a statement last night that the money she formerly gave her mother she is now giving 'to blind children and to help feed children who are homeless and starving in many countries.' She has established a foundation for this purpose, she added.

"She issued her statement after Mrs. Vanderbilt had said in New York that Mrs. Stokowski had cut off an allowance awarded her by the courts before her daughter came of age.

"Mrs. Stokowski's statement follows: 'I shall always take care of my grandmother (Mrs. Laura Morgan) and give her everything necessary for a good life, and I shall do the same for my former nurse, who always gave me mother love. When I became of age I decided to discontinue the allowance made by the court to my mother because I am certain she can work as she has done in the past and as I am doing at present. . . .' "[9]

Many reporters were not so objective. One on the distaff side, Julia

McCarthy, wrote snidely: "Her voice betraying an imperious impatience, Gloria Vanderbilt di Cicco Stokowski said yesterday that there is no reason why her 43-year-old, cast-off mother cannot go to work like anyone else.

"Over long distance from Mexico City . . . she said she knew . . . that her mother once ran a dress shop and didn't see why she couldn't do something like that again. . . .

" 'But, of course, she can earn a living,' said the jet-haired multimillionairess petulantly. . . .

"It was apparent that young Gloria, whose personal acquaintance with gainful employment rivals that of an old world princess, was referring to the spectacular unsuccessful venture into business by her mother, the beautiful widowed Gloria Morgan Vanderbilt, and her mother's twin sister, Lady Furness."[10]

To escape the annoyance of reporters who began to hound them, Leopold and Gloria drove to Cuernavaca and then to Taxco, which in 1946 had not yet been turned into a tourist trap. After a few days they decided it was time to end their holiday and start the long drive back to New York, where they arrived on the night of April 1. At about 8:45 they pulled up in front of their apartment on West Fifty-third Street. They locked their car and left most of their luggage behind. Shortly after their arrival three detectives came to their door to inform them that their car had been burgled and the thief with two of their bags had been taken to the station. The detectives helped Stoki bring up the rest of their luggage, which he said contained articles of much greater worth than was contained in the two that were stolen.[11] The fact that the loot belonged to Leopold Stokowski and Gloria Vanderbilt Stokowski was quickly picked up by the press.

Reporters Arthur Noble and Art Smith prepared a story for one of the tabloids. They wrote irreverently: "The best laid plans often go screwy—even when they are plotted by a Vanderbilt heiress and her great music maestro husband. Like last night when Gloria Vanderbilt Stokowski, America's parent-ditching moneybags, and her ever-loving Leopold, the orchestra man, tried to ease quietly into town and failed only because a thief tried to swipe their baggage and Gloria's jewels." They then related the details of the robbery and concluded: "Thus did glamorous Gloria and her Stokie-wokie return last night from Mexico City."[12]

When they were confronted with this and other stories the following morning, Stokowski's rage must have been Herculean. He had received caustic criticism on professional grounds, but never before, even in that publicized romance with Garbo, had he been a subject of ridicule. Gloria, too, being very sensitive, must have been deeply hurt by the sarcasm of the press.

The day after their arrival Stokowski and Judson lunched to discuss how the publicity might affect his forthcoming concerts with the Philharmonic. The same afternoon he and Gloria met with lawyer Malcolm Lovell, and they decided to draft a statement, call a press conference, and hand it out to the reporters.

On Thursday morning Stokowski, accompanied by Lovell, appeared in felony court to testify against the man who had robbed his car. He refused to sign a formal complaint against him and said, "I don't know what prompted this boy to do this thing, and I sympathize with all underprivileged persons." The presiding judge, however, opined that "too much sympathy might cause them to go out and commit other crimes."[13] But Stoki still refused to sign a complaint. As the defendant left the courtroom he turned to Stoki and said, "Thank you very much." When this was reported, it became the best press of the week.[14]

For Gloria's press conference, held in the afternoon, a crowd of reporters assembled. The *New York Herald Tribune* sedately said that "Mrs. Stokowski shook hands with each of the thirty reporters who responded to her appeal for privacy and also posed willingly for pictures. But, on the advice of Malcolm Lovell . . . who described himself as a 'friend of the family,' she refused to answer questions." It then printed, verbatim, the two-paragraph handout that had been prepared. Gloria's statement was simple. It read: "I have a natural filial regard for my mother. Our present difference is not, on my part, one based on money. It is certain that at no time and under no circumstances will my mother suffer privation due to lack of the necessities of life. The extent of my financial aid to my mother, in the future, must necessarily be determined by my own sincere estimate of her proper and reasonable needs.

"My present difference with my mother can and will be resolved, but I respectfully ask the press to refrain from making difficult, and practically impossible, the normal family solutions of problems about which they know little, and which press intervention can only prolong."[15]

Several of the reporters asked why the press conference was called if no questions were to be answered. And to this Lovell replied, "The house has been surrounded by photographers and reporters, making it impossible for her to come and go. I advised her to meet you and give a statement.

Photo Talbot/Courtesy United Press International
Sonya Stokowski at the time she played the leading ingenue role in *The White-haired Boy* (1940)

She is not old enough to parry verbal questions. Other statements will be issued from time to time."[16] The conference ended rather icily. Pictures of Gloria were published profusely and she did look most winsome and beautiful. The tabloids ran them on their front pages.

During the next three weeks before leaving for the coast, both avoided the limelight. They had by this time acquired a place in Greenwich,

Sadja Stokowski at Palm Beach (January 9, 1946)

Connecticut. It was a small, attractive house that had belonged to the singer Hall Clovis, who had a larger house nearby.[17]

Gloria and Leopold spent a few days there each week. Back in Manhattan there were many visits from Sadja and Lyuba, conferences with Judson, and meetings with RCA about recordings that were to be made with the Hollywood Bowl Symphony Orchestra.

After winding up countless details, they departed for California

Sunday, April 28, from Pennsylvania Station. They stopped briefly to visit in San Francisco and Berkeley and arrived in Beverly Hills on the sixth of May. While Gloria was preoccupied with her painting and Leopold was busy preparing for his Hollywood Bowl season, Sonya Stokowski was married to Flight Lieutenant Willem H. Thorbecke of the Royal Netherlands Air Force in St. Bartholomew's Church. Perhaps wisely, in view of the publicity and curiosity that would have been generated by the press, Leopold at the last moment decided not to attend. But the persons participating in this socioreligious ritual were fascinatingly interrelated: two former Stokowski wives and three daughters. The bride was given in marriage by her mother and bridal attendants were her half sisters Lyuba and Sadja Stokowski. Ushers included William Kapell, one of Olga's prize students, Schuyler Chapin, John and Fritz Steinway. The date was June 8, 1946.[18]

"I had known Sonya ever since the age of fourteen," said Schuyler Chapin. "I knew her very well. When she was married, I was an usher at her wedding. By that time Betty and I had been married and I was an in-law of the Steinways. The Steinway family, particularly my mother-in-law, Ruth Steinway, had been Olga Samaroff's closest friend and certainly one of the people Olga depended upon for everything. As you may know, Olga's book, *The Layman's Music Book,* is dedicated to her. Sonya was always in and out of the Steinway house. Both my mother- and father-in-law were almost surrogate parents."[19]

In late March 1977, a little more than a year before Ruth Steinway died at the age of eighty-eight, I met her for the first time at her home on Long Pond near Plymouth, Massachusetts. Situated in a wooded area and originally intended as a summer home, her house was a large rustic wooden affair with a long porch in front overlooking the pond, which elsewhere might have been referred to as a lake. John Steinway greeted us and explained that his mother would be back shortly. In a matter of minutes, a bright red Volkswagen, driven by Ruth, whirled into the driveway.

After the introductions were over she said, "I'm going to call you Oliver; you call me Ruth. Everybody calls me Ruth." She talked a great deal about Olga, about Evangeline and the daughters. Then about Leopold she said: "He had an influence on everybody he met and to my mind, the interesting part of his character was that he did have this influence on people in a very human, natural way. He had a heart somewhere. . . . Sonya has always been fond of Evangeline. Sadja and Lyuba were her bridesmaids."[20]

"They sure were," said John, "and Schuyler, Fritz, and I were ushers. I was the stage manager. . . . It was hot as blazes and we were all done up in cutaways and stripey pants. A telegram from Stoki arrived at the church about twenty minutes before the wedding. Sonya hoped that Daddy would show up, and I got the telegram and handed it to Olga."

Neither John nor Ruth could remember the exact wording of the telegram, but the gist was that he would not be there.[21] Schuyler Chapin also recalled the telegram, but he, too, could not remember just what it had contained. But he recalled that Stoki sent a piece of music that was played by the organist at an appropriate moment. "Sonya came down the long aisle of St. Bartholomew's Church alone, unescorted. She carried a lily, a perfectly beautiful lily, but she was alone."[22]

Angeline Battista, widow of Joseph Battista, one of Olga's favorite pupils, recalled that "when the minister said, 'Who giveth this woman in marriage?'—Madame stood up and walked up to the front of the church and said, 'I do.' It was a very dramatic moment."[23]

After the wedding the Thorbeckes spent their honeymoon at Evangeline's estate in Connecticut.[24]

Out in California meetings with Dick Hammond, Phil Kahgan, and Karl Wecker occupied most of Stokowski's attention during the month of June with all of the matters anent the Hollywood Bowl: engagements of personnel, details of programs, soloists, guest conductors, an improved sound system, and the like. There were meetings, too, with Boris Morros, who was to stage-direct the opening-night performance of *Carmen*. It required an immense amount of preparation. Stoki worked steadily with long daily rehearsals beginning the first of July. He held separate rehearsals for the orchestra, choruses, and soloists and paid close attention to all details of lighting and staging.

At 8:30 on July 9, 1946, before a tremendous audience, he made one of his rare appearances as an opera conductor. It was a gala night marking the Silver Jubilee of the Bowl. Winifred Heidt was Carmen; James Pease, Escamillo; Ramon Vinay, Don José; and Marina Koshetz, Micaëla.

Stoki's meticulous attention to the sound system paid off strikingly. Critic Isabel Morse Jones noted that the "multiple loud-speakers amplified the artists' excellent enunciation, for the work was given in translation, carrying it to the hills of the Bowl. Miss Heidt's opulent voice, the operatic maturity of Mr. Vinay, together with the technically competent work of the orchestra and the solid achievement of the large chorus at the command of Mr. Stokowski, all combined to create a success. All boxes have been sold for the season and the outlook promises financial prosperity."[25]

To Sylvan Levin, Stokowski wrote:

> We gave two performances of *Carmen*, and musically they were a great joy to me. Vinay sang and acted Don José in a manner absolutely first class. Heidt was a fine Carmen. Marina Koshetz sang wonderfully as Micaela. All the other artists were from California and good. We started the rehearsals early so that the ensemble was excellent. The chorus was outstandingly good. Personally I did not like the costumes and scenery very much. But the man who did this was working under certain disadvantages. . . .
>
> The orchestra here this year is just wonderful, so quick, intelligent, friendly and all masters of their instruments. I am enjoying working with them every minute.[26]

True to his earlier promise, Stoki invited Grainger to appear in the Bowl and perform his own music. Percy chose two different suites. The first, *In a Nutshell*, a suite of Australian memories; the second, his *Danish Folk-Music* Suite, on a program that contained music of Lalo, Griffes, Benjamin, and Kodály. *In a Nutshell* is listed as a Suite for Orchestra, Piano and Percussion Instruments. The percussion instruments called for are a marimba or marimbaphone or resonaphone, marimbaphone or marimba-xylophone, Swiss staff bells and nabimba, grouped with the usual xylophone, glockenspiel, and celesta.[27]

With such an array of instruments, it seemed like a charming idea to have Percy's wife, Ella, play the Swiss staff bells along with the regular players.[28] For once the musicians did not object to having a nonunion player in their midst. After all, it was a sort of family affair.

There was an astonishing number of new and unusual works on the Bowl programs. It was a revelation for the Angelenos, for Stoki gave them a chance to hear their own local products, from Stravinsky and Schoenberg to Antheil, Korngold, Toch, Iturbi, Montemezzi, Amfiteatrov, Kanitz, and Rose. Of non-Hollywood Americans he did works of Thomson, Deems Taylor, Copland, Griffes, and Siegmeister. Stoki wanted to avoid many of the overplayed and hackneyed classics. Yet it turned out to be the most successful season in the Bowl's history to date.

On August 13, Nan Merriman joined him in a performance of Falla's *El amor brujo*. It was a stunning performance and it was recorded two days later for RCA Victor. His choice of Merriman for the part was a perfect one. Although she had never sung it before, it was a work that she had admired since her student days. She told me that she heard L'Argentinita do it. That seemed utterly incredible to me, since I had known L'Argentinita only as a Spanish dancer. But on checking I found that she had recorded it with the Ballet Theater Orchestra under Antal Dorati's direction.

Nan recalled: "It was on an old 78 rpm recording and I was *begeisted* by it. I thought it was the most beguiling thing I had ever heard, and it had been in the back of my musical memory bank for a long time. I thought, oh, to be able to do that kind of music, wouldn't that be marvelous. So when Stokowski suggested that I sing it, I got out that recording of Argentinita and I began listening to it again, and I realized that I could do it very well.

"I came for the first rehearsal to his house. He opened the door and there he was, dressed in his usual eccentric fashion. Gloria was there, looking very thin, and very young. All of her paintings—she was painting brilliant colored oils—were strewn around this little house.

"Stokowski said, 'And now will you sing for me?' Not another word. I was terrified. He had the orchestral score on a big coffee table in front of him, and we went through the whole thing. He never spoke a word, and at the end he closed the score and said, 'It is perfect. Have you ever been to Toe-lay-doe?' 'I have never been to Spain,' I said. 'Oh, you must go. You were born to sing this music.' He didn't have a word of criticism. I was on cloud fifty-two. We had a very happy afternoon."

The night of the concert was one of those nights that only the West Coast can have. The sky was still streaked with light as the concert began, but when the time for the Falla piece came it was quite dark. Merriman's entrance was dramatic. "I had spent a great deal of time and thought deciding on precisely the right thing to wear, and when Stokowski came to the dressing room, he took one look at me and said, 'Oh! But it is perfect.' I had acquired a marvelous deep tan, and I had a white lace dress with a big hoop skirt—just nothing but white lace, brown skin, and blue eyes. It was very effective for the Bowl.

"At ten o'clock the next morning, the phone rang. 'I am calling to tell you,' Stokowski said, 'your performance last night was musical perfection.' "[29]

Reviews for the recording were exuberant. Max de Schauensee had particular praise for Nan: "Miss Merriman, with her abandoned style and chest tones, manages to sound really Spanish."[30] Comparing performances, David Hall wrote: "Merriman's vocal style is more authentic, and she has the benefit of superb recording and magnificent playing by the orchestra under Stokowski's direction."[31]

The First Symphony of Brahms, recorded August 1, 1945, received mixed reviews. Being one of the most staple war-horses, for which he had been abundantly praised over so many years, it came in for a drubbing from Irving Kolodin. "Sunkist, rather than sun-lit, might be the word for the Hollywoodish Stokowski performance, which is as faithful to its point of origin as Furtwängler's is to his. Here it appears that Stokowski's latest eccentricity is not to be eccentric at all—what, never? et cetera—the 'et cetera' applying to the finale, in which the chorale is tortured out of rhythmic context, the coda dismally whipped up, retarded, and flung ahead again, like a jockey holding back his mount in order to make a race look close. . . . There is a luxuriance in the sound of the California Orchestra. . . ."[32]

Enos Shupp wrote: "But dear old Stokowski is as irresistible as ever (in his best moments), and there is warmth of feeling and the familiar indescribable quality which compels the listener to be convinced that many facets may be revealed from the same composition by different interpreters."[33]

Hollywood at this time was a symbol of questionable taste, vulgarity, schmaltz, kitsch, exaggeration, pretense, and cheapness. After Stokowski's appearances in a few movies, it led critics to look for signs of Hollywood in everything he did. Affiliating himself with the Hollywood Bowl, after the discreet and prestigious Philadelphia Orchestra, also seemed to be somewhat suspect; something that smacked of self-exploitation, and artificial glamour. I think many reviewers tried to read into his efforts at that time elements that they were conditioned to expect.

However, one ten-inch 78 disc which he recorded in Hollywood did more harm than good. It did nothing to help his image and gave fuel to his critics. He recorded "A Message to Liza," from *Lady in the Dark* by Robert Emmett Dolan. The movie had featured Stoki's neighbor, Ginger Rogers, and that may have had something to do with his selecting it. Or was it RCA's suggestion? It is an innocuous little piece, quite charming in fact, but not something to maintain his image.

Perhaps the best and freshest of all the recordings to have emerged from the Bowl was Virgil Thomson's *The Plow That Broke the Plains*. It was a delightful recording and one which Virgil particularly enjoyed. The sound is sonorous without being overrich. Put in gustatory terms it is as American as apple pie, a well-done hamburger, or corn on the cob. There is nothing that smacks of whipped cream, strudel, sauerbraten, or quiche Lorraine. As Stoki did it, it was a perfect regional masterpiece.

On March 26, 1948, for the second consecutive year, fourteen music critics singled out for recognition the outstanding recordings of the preceding twelve-month period. In the field of program music their choice was Thomson's *The Plow That Broke the Plains*, Leopold Stokowski conducting the Hollywood Bowl Symphony Orchestra.[34]

52

The New York Philharmonic

C ARMEN was not to be the only collaboration of Boris Morros and
Stokowski. Morros had been talking for months about his projected
movie called *Carnegie Hall,* which would involve the New York
Philharmonic and a host of celebrities led off by Stokowski. Other conduc-
tors included Bruno Walter, Artur Rodzinski, Charles Previn, Walter
Damrosch, and Fritz Reiner. Musical celebrities included Lily Pons, Artur
Rubinstein, Jascha Heifetz, Gregor Piatigorsky, Risë Stevens, Jan Peerce,
and Ezio Pinza. Olin Downes made a brief appearance emulating Deems
Taylor.

The story as outlined by Morros was both sentimental and naive. It was
about a charwoman at the hall who brought her son to concert after
concert in the hope that he would become a serious concert pianist. But
sonny didn't exactly take to the classics and in the end, after that expensive parade of talent, we find him on the stage of Carnegie Hall conducting Vaughan Monroe's orchestra with trumpeter Harry James as soloist
performing a non-deathless epic called *57th Street Rhapsody.* Stokowski's
contribution was the slow movement from the Tchaikovsky Fifth, which
he recorded as soon as he returned from California.

Its premiere did not take place until May 1947, and Olin Downes, with
a bit of an ax to grind, praised Morros for "the initiative to prove that
fine music, in and of itself, can be purveyed on a grand scale on the
screen." He regretted that the movie did not catch "all the romance and
glamour that Carnegie Hall means to music and America."[1] Halina Rodzinski called it a "piece of cinematic kitsch."[2]

Rodzinski began the Philharmonic's 105th season on October 3, 1946, and continued with thirty-eight concerts, ending on December 8. After a short interlude between December 12 and December 22, when the concerts were conducted by George Szell, Leopold Stokowski began a series of fourteen concerts—spanning four weekends.

Rodzinski took credit for Stoki's invitation. Halina Rodzinski recalled: "When my husband was there with the New York Philharmonic, he said, 'I want to invite Stokowski. After all I owe him everything.' . . . Once during the war, my husband wrote a letter to Stokowski saying, 'It came to my mind that I owe everything to you and I'm so extremely grateful to you for saving my life.' And Stokowski answered him in a very funny way. He said, 'I don't remember when I saved your life but if you feel that way, it's perfectly all right with me.'

". . . Artur said, 'I want the best conductors for guest conductors so I am going to have Stokowski. Judson will be furious but that's all right.' So at the board of directors' meeting, Artur suggested that it would be great to invite Stokowski. The whole board was very excited about it, especially, I remember, the old Mrs. Steinway. They all adored Stokowski and they wanted him. Judson was mad, but he couldn't say anything and he invited Stokowski. Then they made up, and a few days later, when Stokowski got the invitation, my husband went to the Lotus Club, and what did he see?—Stokowski and Judson having lunch together. And what were they talking about?—about taking the Philharmonic to Europe with Stokowski. That was one of the things that made him so furious with Judson and, of course, with Stokowski."[3]

Having been in New York since the beginning of the season, Stokowski had gone to hear the Philharmonic repeatedly. A gift to Carnegie Hall from Universal, or should we say from Boris Morros, was the pair of elaborate curtains that when pulled back flanked both sides of the proscenium, and the impressive valance above it. It was all part of the decoration for the film *Carnegie Hall.* The back and sides of the stage, too, had been spruced up for the movie with a coat of paint. While Stokowski may have liked the appearance that the additions provided, he realized that the heavy curtains muffled the sound, and when he arrived for his first rehearsal, he had them drawn back as far as possible, placing two plywood sheets in front of them to enliven the sound.

Stokowski's first program, on December 26, 1946, was the 4,410th program of the Philharmonic. It consisted of the Bach chorale prelude, "Wir Glauben all' an einen Gott," the Brahms First Symphony, Sibelius'

Swan of Tuonela, Paul Creston's *Frontiers* and the finale of act 3 from *Parsifal.*

The orchestra was cordial and cooperative. Stokowski was all business and the rehearsals were models of efficiency.

The reviews tell the story—Robert Hague in *New York PM:* "It was an extraordinary concert in many ways. Under Stokowski's guidance the orchestra played with uncommon skill and precision; its tone had a warm and velvety richness that charmed the ear; and though most of the works performed were thrice familiar there was no slackening of this listener's interest during their unfolding."[4]

Louis Biancolli in the *New York World-Telegram* told his story nicely: "Looking fit and dapper as ever, Leopold Stokowski took over the Philharmonic . . . last night. . . . Striding briskly to the podium to an obligato of friendly greeting, the dynamic batonist soon showed that if he was a good conductor once, he is a still better one now. The special Stokowski touch was all over the program last night."[5]

In the *Post,* Harriett Johnson described the baffles that Stoki had ordered looking "as wacky as the 'Looney Loco' engine" that her two-and-a-half-year-old son got for Christmas. But she admitted they prevented the sound of the basses and cellos from being absorbed in the curtains. There was increased depth in the lower string registers, which contributed to the "distinctive organ-like quality that was in evidence. It was an enriching experience to observe the conductor once again concern himself deeply and primarily with the music at hand, minus any of the superficial trappings which accompany a star conductor exhibiting himself before his public," wrote Harriet.[6]

The second set of concerts, during which he programmed the motet *Jesus Dulcis Memoria* of Victoria, the *Don Giovanni* Overture, Hindemith's Symphony in E-flat, the Lalo *Symphonie Espagnole,* with violinist Jacques Thibaud, two movements from Milhaud's *Saudades do Brasil,* and the *Prélude à l'après-midi d'un faune* continued the "love affair" between Stoki, the orchestra, the audience and the critics, and (if that does not put it too strongly) the management. Judson and Zirato both caught parts of of the rehearsals and broadcast from the control room. They were obviously pleased.

To obviate any snide observations that he had tampered with the ending of the Mozart overture, Stoki prepared an explanation of the change he had effected. On December 11 he had written to Dorle Jarmel:

> I enclose a little note from me regarding the Finale of Mozart's *Overture* to *Don Giovanni*. Is there some way in which this could be brought to the attention of the music critics ahead of time so that they will not be surprised when they hear Mozart's Finale instead of Johannes Andre's?[7]

Dorle not only alerted the critics but also had Stokowski's explanation printed in the Carnegie Hall program books. Stoki was also concerned that the radio audience—which, of course, included many critics—be informed, and he wrote another letter to Dorle a week later, asking, "Do the commentators for the Sunday broadcast know about the end of the Don Giovanni Overture?"[8] Miss Jarmel dutifully informed the script writers. Stoki commented thus: "In concert performances, Mozart's Overture to 'Don Giovanni' is usually played with a Finale composed by Johannes Andre, published by Brietkopf and Härtel. Andre's Finale is scholarly, but conventional and uninspired. It would be far better for the Finale to be Mozart's own music. The end of the great scene between the Commendatore and Don Giovanni is musically perfect for this Finale. Not only is this inspired music, but it is appropriate in character and design, because the Overture will then begin and end in the same mood of dramatic intensity, thus unifying the whole composition."[9]

"As for Mr. Stokowski's conducting, it was pure miracle from beginning to end," wrote Virgil Thomson. "Often in the past, critics, the present one included, have protested at errors of taste on this conductor's part. Last night there was none. Everything was played with a wondrous beauty of sound, with the noblest proportions, with the utmost grandeur of expression. The perfection of tonal rendering for which Stokowski and his Philadelphia Orchestra were so long famous were revived last night with the Philharmonic men in a performance of Debussy's *Afternoon of a Faun* that for both beauty and poetry has been unmatched for many years, if ever, in my experience."[10]

The following week it was all-Russian, with the Shostakovich First Piano Concerto as a centerpiece. Eugene List, who had played its American premiere with Stokowski in Philadelphia, was soloist. Gene told me: "I was invited to play with the Philharmonic, and because it was Stokowski, I asked if I could do this concerto. It had a certain sentimental attachment for me. . . . When I got to the first rehearsal, Bruno Zirato, who was standing in the wings, said: 'Now, Gene, don't get upset. Don't get upset.' I said, 'What's there to get upset about?' I really didn't know what he meant. 'It's going to be a little different; it's going to be a little different'—with that fabulous Italian accent.

"When I got out on stage, I realized that the piano was not in the usual place. It was behind the first violins. Don't ask me why. The piano was sort of out in left field. When it was first set up, I couldn't see through the lid, obviously. So I couldn't see his beat, but when we shifted it slightly, it was all right."[11]

The programs for his last week with the orchestra were composed of music by Bach, Beethoven, and Wagner. Along with three of his transcriptions, Stoki also included the Second *Brandenburg* Concerto for Solo Flute, Oboe, Trumpet, Violin, and String Orchestra. It was a sagacious move and one that won affection from the players whom he had singled out.

Stokowski's four sets of concerts with the Philharmonic had been rewarding. Even before they had begun, he was engaged to conduct the orchestra at the close of the season and then take it on a tour of eleven cities. All of this seemed to trouble Rodzinski.

Artur Rodzinski, at that time, was in the process of negotiating a new contract with the Philharmonic. He had been difficult during the preceding months, and various minor arguments had erupted both with Judson and Zirato. Stokowski's success and the extravagant criticisms he received may also have been a matter of minor aggravation. Also his inner rage at the thought of Stoki taking the orchestra on a European tour (which, however, never materialized) made him almost paranoid about all the various people involved. About Stokowski, Halina informs us, "Artur bore Stokie a slight grudge thereafter, but slight compared to his resentment of Judson."

Columbia Concerts, with Judson's blessing, had arranged an impressive tour for Rodzinski in Europe, and his departure was imminent. But because details of his new contract had not been ironed out, Artur feared the worst, according to Halina, and abruptly "canceled the European tour. . . . 'They're waiting until I'm out of the country to fire me.' "

The board was no doubt unaware that the manager of the Chicago Symphony had already approached him with an offer to take over the orchestra there. While there had been some chilling in his relationship with Judson and the board, Judson at the time had no intention of terminating Rodzinski's contract. Instead, he was preparing a new one. But no one was able to assuage Artur's pathological fears and suspicions.

On February 2, immediately after Stoki's last concert, Rodzinski returned to New York and the following day met with the board to discuss his status. On reading the contract that had been prepared, he flew into a rage and, after blasting the contract, called Judson "a dictator who made musical progress impossible."[12]

Steeped in his real and fancied grievances, Rodzinski sent a note to Charles Triller, president of the board. ". . . With great regret I would appreciate your releasing me from all conductorial duties as per October 1947." The board reacted quickly, releasing Rodzinski at once and dropping the legend "Artur Rodzinski, Musical Director," which had graced all of the Carnegie Hall programs.

On the heels of Rodzinski's departure, speculation about his successor was rife. In a special dispatch to the *Philadelphia Inquirer,* it was reported that "Leopold Stokowski was being mentioned tonight as possible conductor of the New York Philharmonic Symphony. . . ."[13]

On February 7, 1947, a dispatch was sent out on the wires of the Associated Press quoting the *New York Herald Tribune* as saying that plans to send the New York Philharmonic on a tour of Europe under Stokowski were under discussion and that André Mertens of Columbia Concerts, who was in charge of booking the tour, would leave for Europe in May to complete details. "It was added that the tour first was proposed by Stokowski as 'a great cultural contribution to war-torn Europe.' "[14] Matters of finance were discussed and it seemed there would be adequate funds. But another far more complicated problem was the matter of transportation and accommodations, particularly in the rubble-strewn bombed cities of Germany. There was a question about whether there would be enough sleeping cars that might serve as hotels where no other space would be available.[15] But after many months the European tour was deemed an impossibility. However, Stokie and Judson began meeting regularly, and both envisioned working together again as they had done in Philadelphia.

Interspersed between the Philharmonic concerts conducted by Charles Munch, Bruno Walter, Efrem Kurtz, and Walter Hendl, Stoki conducted a series of eighteen concerts followed by eleven concerts on tour, in eleven cities on as many days. The remaining concerts, both at Carnegie and on tour, brought forth no surprises. For a mostly French program on March 13, he programmed the *Fête-Dieu à Séville* of Albeniz and Debussy's *Soirée dans Grenade*—both in his own transcriptions. Robert Casadesus co-starred as pianist in the D'Indy *Symphony on a French Mountain Air* and in Franck's *Symphonic* Variations.

Thomson found Stoki's orchestral readings "music making of the first category. Indeed, so impressive an execution of Ravel's *La Valse* has not been heard by this reviewer in many a day. It was terrifying in impact without any ugliness or inexactitude."

The real novelty on the program was the first performance—so the program notes tell us—of Olivier Messiaen's *Hymne pour grand Orchestre.* Thomson found it to be clumsily written. But he conceded: "It is really not very important whether Messiaen's pieces 'come off' or not. Today none of them does. But they are powerful and original music all the same. It is our obligation as listeners, therefore, to get inside them, since they do not easily penetrate our customary concert psychology. If we do not, we are missing a valid musical experience." Stoki completely agreed and continued to explore each new score of Messiaen as he received it.[16]

William Grant Still's "Festive" Overture was given its first New York performance in an otherwise standard program. "I wish you could have been present," Stoki wrote to Still. "The orchestra played it wonderfully and the applause of the audience was equally great for your music as it was for that of Beethoven, Bach and Wagner. I felt that the applause and enthusiasm was completely sincere. What else are you writing for orchestra for the future?"[17]

In the audience attending the Philharmonic concerts at the time was a young violinist, Mehli Mehta, from Bombay, India. He heard concerts conducted by Walter, Mitropoulous, and Rodzinski and sent programs back to his young son, Zubin. After hearing one conducted by Stokowski, he wrote: "I felt as though I were hearing an orchestra for the first time. This man Stokowski is sixty-five and I thank God I was privileged to hear him before he retires from the podium. His strings are silken perfection. They play with such precision, such clarity, and yet with such emotion that one is constantly amazed. I am going to bring back some Stokowski recordings with the Philadelphia Orchestra so you can hear for yourselves."[18]

Following his last Carnegie Hall concert, Stoki and the orchestra left immediately for a concert in Baltimore. From then on it was a concert every night through ten southern cities. One concert on the tour, at the University of Tennessee in Knoxville, drew special attention from the press when a student photgrapher took a photo of Gloria and for ten minutes Stoki refused to go out and conduct until the negative was handed to him.[19]

Each week after the Sunday broadcast, when he was not on tour, Stoki would come to CBS to listen to a playback of the concert. At the time they were made on glass or metal discs sixteen inches in diameter and could only be played on professional equipment. He would come to the office of Jim Fassett, the head of the CBS Music Division at the time, and together we would listen and try to correct flaws that he might detect. None of the other conductors of the Philharmonic ever did the same.

With the Philharmonic season out of the way, Leopold and Gloria sailed for Europe on a small Dutch liner, arriving in Rotterdam nine days later. They visited Den Haag, Haarlem, Volendam, and Marken; they roamed through Delft, admiring the tiles and pottery, stopped at Eindhoven, and in Amsterdam strolled through its great Rijksmuseum. So far they were being tourists. On Friday May 15, Leopold began rehearsals with the Concertgebouw Orchestra for his concert four days later.

From Amsterdam they traveled by train the relatively short distance to Antwerp and from there a sightseeing day in the ancient town of Bruges before proceeding to Brussels. On the twenty-seventh they arrived at the Gare du Nord in Paris and thence to the Ritz on the Place Vendôme. Mertens had made all arrangements for a Paris concert, and Stoki began four days of rehearsals for his appearance in the Théàtre des Champs-Élysées on Sunday June 15. The keystone of his program was Honegger's *Jeanne d' Arc au Bûcher.*

With his professional duties now fulfilled, Leopold and Gloria became tourists again. They visited Mont-St.-Michel and later heard the monks at the Benedictine monastery of Solesmes. On to Switzerland—Zurich, Lugano, the Engadine—followed by Italy—Como, Venice, Locarno— back to Paris.

On July 29 they crossed the channel and stayed at the Grand Hotel in Bournemouth, where his mother was then living in a nursing home. In London they stayed briefly at the Hotel Ritz before visiting Edinburgh and Dublin. They left from Southampton on August 8 arriving in New York on the fourteenth. A reminder scribbled in his calendar for his first day home read: "Call Gilbert, Judson, Zirato, Constance [Hope]."

Judson had been unwilling to have a new Musical Director appointed for the 1947–48 season. He preferred to regard it as an interregnum, and for the time being he and the board appointed Bruno Walter as Musical

Advisor. But the title was simply an umbrella under which Judson and Zirato could act arbitrarily.

Walter was safe. He was not contesting for the position. He had been offered the post as early as 1943 and turned it down then because of his age and the mountainous responsibility it involved. His now somewhat meaningless position was satisfactory to him, and since it enabled him to conduct a less strenuous schedule and devote his talents to conducting his favorite German classics, he was satisfied. The following statement was printed in the program book: "The Philharmonic-Symphony Society of New York announces for its 106th year, the appointment of the distinguished conductor Bruno Walter as Musical Advisor. In this capacity Mr. Walter will supervise the personnel of the orchestra, the choice of fellow-conductors and soloists, and the general over-all planning of programs to insure a balanced and brilliant season. . . ."

In Walter's response he said: ". . . in this situation, as a friend of the Philharmonic-Symphony Society, and in view of many years of association with the orchestra, I feel I have a moral obligation to put my services at the disposal of the Society."[20]

The list of guest conductors included Mitropoulos, Munch, Szell, and Walter. Stokowski, however, inherited the lion's share of thirty-one concerts—fifteen at the opening of the season and sixteen at the close. Numerically, Munch followed with twenty-two; Szell, fifteen; Mitropoulos, fourteen; and Walter, thirteen.

The Stokowski programs were by far the most interesting and provocative. Virgil Thomson, taking a God's eye view, grouped the conductors into two categories: the traditionals and the independents: ". . . The former group is dominated in the United States by Fritz Reiner and Pierre Monteux. The leaders of the other tendency are Leopold Stokowski and Serge Koussevitzky. . . . Managements often refer to tradition minded conductors as 'technicians' and to the independents as 'interpreters.' As a matter of fact, the Stokowskis and Koussevitzkys of this world are no less skillful at attaining their musical ends than are the others.[21]

Stokowski's performance of Elie Siegmeister's Symphony No. 1 was a truly courageous gesture. He had accepted it sight unseen, and it had turned out to be both a longer and more substantial work than he probably anticipated. Not long after he had performed the *Western* Suite in the Hollywood Bowl, Stokowski phoned Elie and in the course of their conversation asked what he was writing. "I have just started a new piece," Elie replied.

"If it is to be a symphony . . . I'll be very happy to perform it," said Stoki.[22]

Elie continued: "I worked furiously for the next four months. The symphony turned out to be a long one (forty-four minutes), but it was ready on time; Stokowski gave it four glowing performances at Carnegie Hall and the audiences responded with warm enthusiasm. I felt at the peak of my powers."[23]

The summer of 1948 was a marked contrast to the previous season's grand European tour. Leopold and Gloria departed for a western jaunt in mid-June, going to Tucson, Phoenix, up to Denver, Colorado Springs, and finally to a dude ranch in Wyoming. From there they proceeded to San Francisco and then to Redlands to look over their orange groves. After that, Beverly Hills until their return to New York on September 1. Conferences with Judson on Philharmonic matters; with Goddard Lieberson regarding recordings for Columbia; with Dick Mohr regarding recordings for RCA Victor; with André Mertens on guest appearances; and endless details concerning their house in Connecticut and their new penthouse apartment at 10 Gracie Square were duly noted in the date book.

Rehearsals with the Philharmonic began on the sixteenth and on Monday the twentieth of September, Stoki and the Philharmonic began a fall tour of thirteen cities: Syracuse, Cleveland, Detroit, Chicago (two concerts), Madison, Milwaukee, East Lansing, Columbus, Buffalo, Utica, Rochester, Boston, and Portland, Maine.

The official opening of the season began on October 7 with Mitropoulos conducting the first of thirty-one consecutive concerts, ending on November 28. These were the only programs he conducted during the season. The lineup was similar to the previous season: Walter was still listed as musical advisor and the guests were Mitropoulos, Munch, Stokowski, and, instead of Szell, Leonard Bernstein. Once more Stokowski conducted the greater number of concerts, and with the spring and fall tours they amounted to fifty-three.

As always he flavored his programs with welcome novelties, among them Otto Luening's Symphonic Interludes. Otto told me that Stoki had phoned him saying: " 'I would like to do the Symphonic Interludes unless you have something new you would like me to look at.' " Otto replied: " '. . . Well, I have a Concertino for Flute, Strings, Harp, and Celesta. Maybe you would like to see that.' 'Yes,' he said, 'I would like the Concertino.'

"And I had a little, short piece called 'Pilgrim's Hymn,' and I sent those to him . . . then he called up and said, 'I will play the Interludes on Thursday and Friday or the "Pilgrim's Hymn" on the Sunday broadcast, whichever you choose.

"I wanted the Sunday broadcast very badly, so I said, 'I'll take the "Pilgrim's Hymn" ' and he did it. . . .

"He was criticized for his Philharmonic programming, but as far as I'm concerned, I think he did some very good programming, and he brought some fresh air into the pretty stifling kind of thing that was going on there."[24]

The broadcasts of the 1948–49 season were sponsored by Standard Oil (New Jersey), and as an intermission feature both CBS and the ad agency came up with a package called "Weekend With Music." I was engaged to produce it. The format seemed simple enough: three bright, young, musical teenagers would be chosen from all parts of the country, brought to New York and exposed to operas, concerts, and musical celebrities, and finally interviewed by Deems Taylor. It turned out to be a terrific strain, and I found myself flying up and down both coasts and zigzagging across the country to find the bright youngsters.

Anything involving young people always intrigued Stoki, and several times during the season groups were invited to his magnificent penthouse at 10 Gracie Square for tea and conversation. The entire top floor of the building was divided into two large apartments: one facing north—looking out over the mayor's Gracie Square Mansion—which belonged to Lily Pons and André Kostelanetz, and the south penthouse of Leopold and Gloria.

"It was a great home for parties," wrote Gloria. "High ceilings, parquet floors, fireplaces, terraces, a roof garden and lots of space. Large rooms, the blaze of light, and the river view with its constantly changing atmosphere gave me new ideas and inspiration. I seemed always to be changing the apartment around, not so much refining as transforming it."[25]

Kostelanetz and Lily Pons also were hosts to some of the youngsters. One of these was a particularly attractive young lady from Birmingham, Alabama, named Joyce Addington. For the final broadcast of the season, which was to take place with Stokowski and the Philharmonic playing in Birmingham, it was decided that Joyce would take the Deems Taylor role and interview me—telling the story of the various weekends that had been talked about during the preceding Sundays.[26]

After the concert, which seemed a bit anticlimactic, we met in Stoki's somewhat dismal hotel suite and heard about the frustrations and difficulties he and Gloria had experienced during the demanding tour. While I departed by plane, Leopold and Gloria prepared for the long train ride back to New York.

Season endings may be letdowns, but the new one offered some exhilaration. No longer was Bruno Walter listed as music advisor. Instead, Leopold Stokowski and Dimitri Mitropoulos were presented as co-conductors. Arthur Judson, who believed that the burden of conducting a whole season, even with guest conductors, was too onerous a burden for one man, suggested the tandem. Each of the conductors would conduct for ten weeks of the season.[27]

Stokowski's programs were to include Prokofiev's Sixth Symphony, Messiaen's *Trois Petites Liturgies de la Présence Divine,* along with works by Ruggles, Copland, Riegger, Revueltas, Britten, Poulenc, Schoenberg, Villa-Lobos, Liebermann, Diamond, and Bloch. He also conducted the first U.S. performance—and most likely the last—of a Russian Overture by Ivanov-Radkevitch.

Mitropoulos scheduled a concert performance of Strauss' *Elektra,* the Sessions Second Symphony, Krenek's Piano Concerto, and scores by Berg, Webern, Bliss, and Vaughan Williams.

On the opening concert, October 13, 1949, Stoki conducted the prelude to *Die Meistersinger,* Copland's suite from *The Red Pony,* La Mer, and Brahms' First Symphony. As with all such openings, it was planned as a gala affair, and Floyd Blair, the orchestra's president, hosted a reception and dinner following the concert for the Stokowskis, members of the board, and special friends.

That quality of magic that Stokowski was known to have possessed seemed strangely absent at the beginning of this season. The players who had given him their total cooperation during the previous season now seemed to respond indifferently. If it escaped the notice of the board, it did not elude the critics.

This was the time when a curious backstage action occurred after every Stokowski concert. It was dubbed irreverently by everyone working behind the scenes as the "Great Escape," or "The Garbage Can Caper." Immediately after taking his last bow, Stoki would leave the stage and instead of going up to his dressing room, he would have someone standing there with his coat, gloves, and whatever paraphernalia he wanted, and they would go directly to the basement and through a passageway lined with garbage cans filled with refuse. From this he and Gloria would exit onto the street, just east of the regular Fifty-sixth Street entrance, to a waiting limousine. They would be gone by the time the first fan, friend, board member, or well-wisher had reached the stage door. Many who had flocked backstage were frustrated and angry that he had departed so abruptly. Some felt cheated.

The audience of the Philharmonic was very different from that of Philadelphia. There Stokowski had a devoted, loyal, and almost adoring public. In New York the affections of the audience had been splintered between Walter, Toscanini, Barbirolli, Mitropoulos, Szell, Rodzinski, and Stokowski himself. The orchestra, too, was not prone to give loyalty to anyone, and Stoki, in his sharing role, did not have the force and authority that he had had so long in his Philadelphia days. The players seemed more interested in their backstage card games than in any aspect of music. They resented the introduction of new works which required more work and concentration than the war-horses they could almost play in their sleep. Hence, Bruno Walter with his standard repertory elicited more coopera-tion than either Stokowski or Mitropoulos.

James Chambers, the orchestra's excellent first horn player, told me: "The orchestra, especially with its Toscanini heritage, did not take well to Stokowski. To most of the people in the orchestra, Stokowski was a fraud, a charlatan. . . . He was certainly a different kind of musician than Toscanini. He didn't have the infallible ear. He didn't know the score as well as Toscanini did. He was after different things in music, but I never felt that he was a charlatan. I think he made a tremendous contribution to orchestral quality in this country and elsewhere. To this day I don't think I've ever played with a conductor who had that ear for color.

"But he never got from the Philharmonic the results he got in Philadel-phia. There wasn't the identification with him."[28]

The following week things were a trifle avian, with Beethoven's *Pas-torale* Symphony, Schoenberg's "Song of the Wood Dove" from the *Gurrelieder*, plus Villa-Lobos' magic bird, *Uirapurú*. Martha Lipton was the soloist in the Schoenberg. "I don't know whether you realize," said Martha, "but he was not happy with the Philharmonic at that point. The men really weren't very nice to him. But he was simply marvelous with me. It was my first appearance with the Philharmonic, and he was so patient and helpful. I had just gotten a new apartment, and he came with flowers and a big steam pot from Hammacher and Schlemmer. He worked with me on the *Gurrelieder* at the piano. He played from the score, and I would say he played well enough—as a conductor would."[29]

"Religious Corn" was the title Virgil Thomson gave to a review of a succeeding concert. He concerned himself primarily with the work of Messiaen, *Three Short Liturgies of the Divine Presence,* which received its first American hearing under Stoki's direction:

"My own opinion is that its author is a case not unlike that of Scriabin. That is to say that he is a skilled harmonist and orchestrator, full of theories and animated by no small afflatus, but that there is a sticky syrup in his product which hinders its flow at concert temperatures.

"In Messiaen's case all the paraphernalia of commercial glamour are mobilized to depict the soul in communion with God—a ladies' chorus, divided strings, piano, harp, celesta, vibraphone, Chinese cymbal, tamtam and an electronic instrument playing vibrato (in this case the Ondes Martenot). The sounds of such an ensemble, however, intelligently composed, cannot transport this listener much farther than Hollywood corn fields. Placing them at the service of religion does not, in his experience, ennoble them; it merely reduces a pietistic conception of some grandeur to the level of the late Aimee Semple McPherson."[30]

The next concert was not designed for the easy ear. He gave his listeners Ruggles' *Organum* (first performance), Prokofiev's Symphony No. 6 (first U.S. performance), Britten's Piano Concerto, with Jacques Abram as soloist, and the Tchaikovsky *Romeo and Juliet* as a sweetener.

Jacques mentioned that he had played the Britten concerto with Mitropoulos a few years earlier: "I was very thrilled to be assigned to playing it again with the great Leopold Stokowski. As a little boy at the Curtis Institute at the age of ten or eleven, they very kindly gave me a box seat to hear the Philadelphia Orchestra . . . and there was Leopold Stokowski in all his glory and magnificence. It was an unforgettable childhood experience that in a sense shaped my artistic and my aspiring life. He was a dream to me as a child, and then later when I was to play with him it was thrilling. He got word to me that he would like me to come to Gracie Square and rehearse the concerto before rehearsing with the orchestra.

"So I went up there, and I remember how excited I was to be going to Stokowski's apartment. I was met at the door by the butler, and I was ushered into his study. It was completely pale blue—pale blue ceiling, pale blue walls, pale blue carpet, pale blue chairs, pale blue everything including Stokowski, who had on pale blue shoes and pale blue trousers and a pale blue shirt. He was almost invisible in this sea of pale blue. The piano was a Steinway upright that had been painted pale blue. It was incredible. It was like being lost in the sky."

Jacques made another sage observation. "When I did the concerto with

him, he was really more a personality than in command of the score.
. . . He was desperately trying to be young during that period and making
a fairly good attempt at it, I must say."[31]

But time had a way of catching up. "Leopold Stokowski Now a Grandfather," ran a headline in the press.[32] "Stokowski's eldest daughter,
Sonya, 27, now Mrs. Willem Thorbecke, gave birth to a 7 pound 1 ounce
girl . . . in Berkeley Saturday morning."[33]

During the first week in December, his concerts, which were the last
in this series, included Wallingford Riegger's Canon and Fugue, the
Brahms Violin Concerto, with Isaac Stern, the Schubert *Unfinished*
Symphony and the "Prelude and Love Death" from *Tristan und Isolde*.
For the Sunday broadcast the program was changed to include a Purcell-
Stokowski suite, the Haydn Violin Concerto, and the Symphony No. 6
of Prokofiev. Mitropoulos took over beginning December 5.

As the old year, 1949, was slipping away, the board of the orchestra met
in Judson's office and discussed the problem of having two conductors
leading the orchestra, and as a result of their deliberations, Charles Triller,
President of the Board, issued a terse statement to the press: "Dimitri
Mitropoulos has been named to conduct the New York Philharmonic-
Symphony Orchestra next season in place of Leopold Stokowski." He
stated further that "Stokowski has made other plans for the 1950–'51
season and cannot appear with the orchestra."[34]

No further amplification was given and Stokowski never alluded to the
matter. We do know, from his date books, that he had lunched with
Judson on December 7, and the following day Bruno Zirato met with him
at 10 Gracie Square. The day before the board met to determine that
Mitropoulos was to be the chosen conductor, Stoki again met with Judson
at the Lotus Club. It was probably then that he told him that he wished
to withdraw from his management.

But there were still two more weeks with the Philharmonic in April.
For these, and perhaps to mark his departure in a spectacular fashion, he
programmed the Mahler *Symphony of a Thousand*, which had brought
him such extravagant attention when he had done it with the Philadelphia
Orchestra thirty-four years before. In addition to the augmented orchestra, he used the forces of the Schola Cantorum of New York, the Westminster Choir of Princeton, and the boy's chorus from Public School
No. 12, Manhattan. To these he added a bevy of excellent soloists,
including Frances Yeend, soprano; Uta Graf, soprano; Camilla Williams,
soprano; Martha Lipton, contralto; Louise Bernhardt, contralto; Eugene

Conley, tenor; Carlos Alexander, baritone; George London, bass.

Stoki spent weeks conferring and rehearsing with the singers and also working with the various choruses. Frances Yeend told me: "We were having rehearsals daily, and we would be there at his house for hours on end."[35]

"I loved singing the Mahler Eighth with him," said Camilla Williams. "He was marvelous to me. I'll never forget it. . . . I learned a lot from Stokowski; he taught me a lot about vocal production. A lot of conductors don't know vocal production, but he did."[36]

Violinist Arthur Schuller, who frequently doubled on celesta for Stoki, received a call from him one morning asking if he could play the mandolin part of the Mahler symphony. Arthur assured him that he could, although he told me he had never played one, but since the fingering was the same as the violin, he felt he could do it. "But you must get the finest Italian instrument for this occasion," Stoki told him. "There was not much of a solo so it really was not that important," Arthur recalled, "but he made it very important." Arthur did not have a mandolin but his butcher did, so he arranged to buy it from him for the magnificent sum of ten dollars. After cleaning and polishing it, he brought it to the first rehearsal. "I had my mandolin there and was sitting right in front of him. I said, 'Maestro, here is this rare Italian mandolin.' It was not a bad instrument, but it was certainly not Italian; it was just any mandolin. So he took it in his hands and said, 'Yes, it looks very good.' So I played my part. I really fooled him there."[37]

In 1916 the performance of the Mahler symphony had been given in the Metropolitan Opera House, where its huge stage could cope with the vast number of persons involved. Carnegie Hall with its limited space posed many problems. The forces literally spilled over the stage, and chorus groups had to be placed along the sides of the hall, as close to the stage as possible. Some groups were put into boxes on both stage right and left. It was a somewhat messy arrangement but very impressive, nevertheless. But it did not achieve anything comparable to the excitement and attention that the earlier performance had been given. Judson may well have had sentimental recollections of the other production. Critics did not hail it as an unquestioned masterpiece.

Thomson found it to be a "glorious experience. . . . Its sculpture of vast tonal masses at the end of each of the two movements was handled by the conductor in so noble a manner that the sound achieved monumentality while remaining musical. The effect was unquestionably grand. . . .

One is grateful to Mr. Stokowski and his assembled forces for letting us hear it. Also for giving it to us with such great care for musical decorum. Such handsome loudness as took place in both perorations one does not encounter often in a lifetime."[38]

It was a magnificent exit. It needed no encore.

53

Two Sides of the Coin

WHETHER Stokowski was relieved or disappointed by the Philharmonic experience is moot. Certainly the orchestra, as a body, was never the helpful, pliant, and sympathetic instrument that his other orchestras had been, and his own handpicked "His" Orchestra was, for him, a rewarding experience. Furthermore, he had come to realize that through recordings he was reaching a much larger audience than he did with the Philharmonic, despite the coast-to-coast broadcasts. The Philharmonic seemed to respond more sympathetically during recording sessions than it did for concert performances.

The reputation for truculence which the Philharmonic had at that time was widespread. When Barbirolli was about to take over the orchestra, Sir Adrian Boult wrote a congratulatory letter: "As I expect many kind people have been quick to tell you, the New York Philharmonic has not too grand a reputation in regard to its treatment of conductors, but I feel sure that you will get the better of them. . . ." Boult was incorrect, alas. Barbirolli's "authorized" biographer, Michael Kennedy, remarked that the players "were known throughout the musical world as 'Murder Incorporated,' the toughest bunch of players under one roof. . . ."[1]

In his case, Stokowski had nothing to say. He made no adverse comment about the orchestra or management. If he had been hurt by Judson's failure to support him, he reflected it merely by dropping Judson as his manager. And this he did not do at once. In view of his multiple professional slaps, it would be hard to find anyone who possessed such resilience as his. His basic philosophy, which kept him forever looking forward to the future, enabled him to place his back firmly against the past: "The past is past. You can learn from it, but never change it. But the future lies in our hands."[2]

He allowed himself no expressions of grief when tragic moments occurred. On May 18, 1948, when he read the news of Olga's death, he accepted it with equanimity. "Stokowski's Ex-Wife Found Dead in Her N.Y. Apartment," read the AP news release. Olga was sixty-five and had apparently died of a heart attack. "Mrs. Stokowski's body was found in the bathroom of her apartment at 24 West 55th Street. Dr. Stanley Brown, Mrs. Stokowski's physician, pronounced her dead."[3]

Her young student, Claudette Sorel, had visited her the day before she died. She told me that Olga—she referred to her as Madame—had had a thyroid operation in April. "For the first time in her life, she was rather despondent. She had a nurse with her after the hospital when she came home. This was very unusual for her because she was extremely independent. She said that we had to be very fortunate if we could hold up three or four fingers on one hand, that meant we had that number of friends —I mean friends really, not acquaintances—those you can rely upon."[4]

One such good friend was Ruth Steinway. "You know in this world," said Ruth, "you know a great many people and you know them casually, but Olga, I really knew intimately. When she died I was in Chicago. They got hold of me right away and I went straight back. I found myself in charge. Who was to arrange for her cremation? Who was to go and see that she was cremated? I did. . . . I would hear her talk about Stoki a great deal . . . you know she loved him until the day of her death."[5]

A simple memorial service was arranged by many of her pupils at the Juilliard.[6] Stoki did not attend.

Until his very late years, preoccupation with death rarely seemed to tenant Stokowski's mind. It was, no doubt, more in consideration of his children that he prepared a new will early in 1950. On January 30, I received the following letter:

> Dear Oliver
>
> I am making a new will and am writing to ask if you would do me the great favor of being one of the executors. The will is not complicated and if you will do me this favor I will promise not to do anything foolish but to go on living to the best of my ability for a long time and never bother you.
>
> The lawyer drawing up the will is William Strong, Smith Building,

Greenwich, Conn. Please be perfectly frank if you would rather not do this for any reason. But I hope you will.

Your friend
Leopold[7]

Needless to say, I was deeply touched by his proposal and I wrote to him at once accepting. This prompted another note, in which he said:

Dear Oliver

Your letter made me very happy. A little later when the will is in final form I would like to discuss it with you.

I was very touched by your writing "should any situation ever arise when I may be of service to you, please feel free to call on me." I will try never to bother you, but if such a situation should arise, I would like to take advantage of your most kind offer.

Sincerely your friend
Leopold[8]

When the will was finally drawn, he called me and together we read through it. He explained that his chief concern was for his three daughters. Suggestions from various people whom I have interviewed that he seemed indifferent to his daughter's lives are quite incorrect. He was deeply concerned, and his various date books show his continued meetings with them.

But now in this important year of 1950, his philoprogenitive instincts were able to soar. Early in August the press announced that Gloria had made a reservation at the New York Lying-in Hospital for later in the month.[9] Maximum secrecy surrounded the forthcoming event. Gloria checked in under the name Mrs. Laura Green. The *New York Journal-American* society columnist, Cholly Knickerbocker, reported that the young mother was guarded at the hospital "with as much secrecy as if she were the formula for the A-bomb." The press further reported that the child weighed six pounds, fourteen ounces and that the father, "white-haired Stokowski," was at the hospital, but this also "was a matter of secrecy."[10]

I had remembered Schuyler Chapin speaking of those days. "I was working at NBC at the time for a man named Ted Cott, whom you probably know." I did. "I was director of publicity for the local television and radio stations. It was 1950. You may also remember it was the three hundredth anniversary of the birth of Bach, and Ted Cott and I talked about doing a series of radio programs with Stokowski about Bach. It was to be a weekly series. Since I was interested in music and married to Betty Steinway, Ted turned this project over to me—the care and feeding of Leopold Stokowski in his new role as a classical disc jockey. Now, it also happened at that time he was married to Gloria Vanderbilt, and she was pregnant. Betty was also pregnant, and we discovered early on in our acquaintanceship that both our wives were due to deliver about the same time. In point of fact, Gloria went to the Lying-in Hospital a week or so before Betty and gave birth to their first son. A week later, Betty went to the hospital and gave birth to twin boys. Stoki and Gloria sent some very exotic flowers in an extremely colorful vase. Little wire butterflies and bees and what have you were intertwined among the plants. And the day after our twins were born, he telephoned me and made a wry remark about the fact that he didn't think anybody was going to beat him at this game but that he had just been beaten."[11]

While the residual effects of his Philharmonic tenure lived on in various memories and press clippings, the tangible evidence of his artistry lives on in the recordings that he made with the orchestra. It was a fortunate time. Columbia had just switched from the old 78-rpm discs to the long-playing, microgroove discs. RCA in a stubborn, internecine struggle continued to produce 78s and tried to convince collectors to convert to machines that would play their large-holed 45-rpm discs. Columbia had a definite advantage, and some of the earliest releases of LP symphonic discs were those by Stokowski and the New York Philharmonic. Some were on now obsolete ten-inch discs. But today they are collector's items.

Fortunately, the Columbia producers and directors completely redeemed themselves after the semidisastrous series of recordings made a decade earlier with the All-American Youth Orchestra. This time they produced a set of sonically magnificent discs.

For me, the real jewel of Stoki's Philharmonic recordings was that of Charles Griffes' *The White Peacock*. It was a fabulous recording and showed off the Philharmonic in all the glory it was capable of, but which, alas, was not always evident. All of the superlatives that had been applied to Stokowski's conducting during his Philadelphia heyday could be dusted off and restated again. It was wonderfully sensitive music making.

Messiaen's *L'Ascension* was another of the outstanding and, in fact, unique recordings he made at the time. Coupled with Vaughan Williams' Sixth Symphony it was one of the prized issues of the year. For those who do not attend Messiaen's church, the work is still intrinsically musical despite somewhat mawkish religiosity. "Leopold Stokowski directs a performance of searching insight and intense feeling and power that reveals the meaning and recreates the substance of Messiaen's music," wrote Enos Shupp.[12]

But the real masterpiece was the Vaughan Williams symphony. Perhaps Stoki's natural Britishness rather than his flaunted Slaviceness gave him his appreciation and insight into the wonders of the symphony. Writing comments for the Columbia liner notes, Stoki opined: "The more I study the Vaughan Williams Symphony in E Minor, the more I have the impression that this is music that will take its place with the greatest creations of the masters. One of the most important characteristics of symphonic music is the relation between form and content. Some music has intense emotional expression, but fails to convey to the listener its full significance, because it is incoherent in form. Other compositions are clear and perfect in form but are cold and cerebral. But the greatest masterpieces are equally balanced in form and content, their emotional expression and their formal structure are perfectly interrelated and perfectly balanced. . . . Vaughan Williams' Symphony in E Minor, although expressing intense and deep feeling, is perfect in form. . . . Every listener will find his own meaning in the unique finale of this symphony—one of the most profound expressions in all music."[13]

After a space of over thirty years, one must agree with Enos Shupp: "It is eloquent, communicative, and masterful in every respect. The reproduction is full and rich, with good resonance and perspective. In every way, this is a first class job."[14]

He recorded the "Song of the Wood Dove" from the *Gurrelieder* of Schoenberg with Martha Lipton. This, too, is now a prized rarity. Of the conventional repertory, he recorded Tchaikovsky's *Romeo and Juliet,* "Siegfried's Rhine Journey" and "Funeral Music" from Wagner's *Die Götterdämmerung,* and Khachaturian's *Masquerade* Suite, along with "In the Village," a movement from Ippolitov-Ivanov's *Caucasion Sketches.*

During this same period he continued to record for RCA Victor. This may have been a very important bone of contention with Judson. There was a great rush everywhere to record as much as possible during the later months of 1947 because of a threatened strike of the musician's union, which did in fact take place early in 1948 and lasted for the rest of the year.

For Victor, Stoki recorded with "His" Symphony Orchestra. He did splendid recordings of Dvořák's *New World* Symphony and Tchaikovsky's *Sleeping Beauty*. In "His" Orchestra he had handpicked the finest players he could find: some were drawn from the Philharmonic, some from the NBC Symphony, and some who were strictly free-lance players. They all gave their utmost and played as if their lives depended on it, which, as far as "His" Symphony was concerned, they certainly did.

"In its first effort to parallel the open, spacious recording which Decca has made famous as *ffrr*, RCA Victor had the good judgement to utilize its alert Stokowski and some of the most gracious, attractive music that Tchaikovsky invented for any of his ballets. . . . Altogether an impressive advance for domestic recording, and one that should be the common standard of the future."[15] So wrote Irving Kolodin about Stoki's recording of a major portion of the complete *Sleeping Beauty* ballet.

On December 11, 1947, he recorded Revueltas' *Sensemaya*, Granados' Intermezzo from *Goyescas*, and the *Swan of Tuonela* by Sibelius.

Mitch Miller told a familiar story of receiving a call from Stokowski and believing it to be a put-on by some friend, since he had never met him. Stoki, who had listened to many of the broadcasts of "Invitation to Music" on CBS, knew of Miller and asked him to play the English horn solo in a recording of the *Swan of Tuonela*. "When I realized it was he, I said I would be delighted. So a few days later we went to Manhattan Center for the recording. It was a magical experience." Mitch described the orchestra as being a combination of all the concertmasters in the string section and some of the finest performers who were "the cream of New York, which meant the cream of the country." Because he was then working for Columbia Records, Mitch told me that when the record was released, they did not even put his name on it. "I just got union scale," he said. "But I was delighted to do it."

Some time later, when speaking about Stokowski with Gloria, she told Mitch: " 'He was an ardent admirer of your playing. He used to listen to 'Invitation to Music' and the CBS Symphony all the time.' "[16] That, Mitch concluded, was how he was chosen.

Stoki did indeed follow the CBS programs avidly. He often made notes in his date book to remind himself to tune in to the late programs on Wednesday evenings. During the summer and early fall before the regular broadcasts of the Philharmonic would begin, the CBS Symphony, with such conductors as Bernard Herrmann, Alfredo Antonini, and Nicolai Berezowsky, would fill in the Philharmonic slot. Stoki would call or frequently write his comments. He wrote me on September 6, 1949:

Last Sunday's concert was wonderful in every way. The program was just right for that day and the intermission fitted in perfectly. It was for everyone, and yet did not sacrifice quality. . . . The conducting of Herrmann was as always a joy to listen to.

A few weeks ago the orchestra sounded metallic and edgy. Yesterday, it sounded full and mellow and warm. I feel you have made a great advance in quality.[17]

At the time the broadcast originated in a converted church on Thirtieth Street, which was Columbia's chief recording studio.

Notes on broadcasts of "Invitation to Music" and other programs continued through the years. He heard Eileen Farrell in a magnificent performance of the "Immolation Scene" from Wagner's *Die Götterdämmerung,* and that led to his engaging her to record the complete set of *Wesendonck Songs* of Wagner.

The *Wesendonck Songs* were the first things Eileen had ever done with Stoki. She told me: "He taught them to me. He taught them word for word and note for note. We worked on them a long time before I recorded them. You remember that was the time when the recording industry went on strike and they wanted to get this in before the strike deadline, and we did it. We had to be through at midnight because that was the deadline. It was the last thing that was done, I think, before the strike. . . .

"I was in great awe of this man, but I loved working with him and he explained things so beautifully to me. . . . I must say, for somebody as young as I was when I recorded those things . . . I think he did one helluva job with me."[18]

Critics agreed. Kolodin wrote: "The honor of being the first soprano to make a complete version of these works with orchestra is one to which the little-known Farrell would hardly seem qualified; but her broad, youthful voice has been shaped by Stokowski to a remarkable realization of the composer's purpose. His feeling for this material is uncommonly acute, and he has transmitted it to both singer and orchestra with masterful certainty."[19]

On February 17, 1949, Stoki gave the first New York performance of the Haydn Symphony No. 53 in D Major (the *Imperial*) with the New York Philharmonic. The idea of performing an unknown Haydn symphony definitely intrigued him. It had been written to celebrate a visit that Empress Maria Theresa paid to Esterhazy in 1773. Strangely, the score was lost. Through the efforts of the German conductor-musicologist

Edvard Fendler, who discovered parts in various European libraries, it was reconstructed, and he presented it in Paris in 1939. Later he made a French recording, which had a brief life before oblivion. Stoki later recorded it with "His" Symphony Orchestra on May 25, 1949, for RCA Victor and not Columbia, as one might have expected. It was the only Haydn symphony that he ever recorded.

The recording was welcomed. A reviewer in the *Gramophone Shop Record Supplement* of May 1950 observed: "The new recording is crystal clear and the orchestra plays with finesse and delicacy. As far as we can trace, this is the first symphony of Haydn that Mr. Stokowski has recorded. More would be welcomed if played with such feeling."[20]

Recording sessions with RCA increased, and during the months following his departure from the Philharmonic he had fourteen recording dates before the end of the year and produced an impressive array of successful discs. The choice of repertory largely determined by RCA pandered somewhat to the commercial: Weber's *Invitation to the Dance*, Tchaikovsky's *Waltz of the Flowers*, and excerpts from *Swan Lake*, *Les Sylphides*, *Sylvia*, and *Giselle* were all chosen for a "Heart of the Ballet" album, for example.

To accommodate RCA and find short pieces for their little 45-rpm discs, Stoki suggested doing a series of works by Percy Grainger.

He wrote to Percy saying that he would like to record six of his pieces if he "would be willing." The six were to be: *Irish Tune from County Derry*, *Molly on the Shore*, *Shepherd's Hey*, *Country Gardens*, *Handel in the Strand* and *Mock Morris*. Under the impression that the orchestrations had been made by someone other than Grainger—though they were not—he asked:

> Would you be willing to orchestrate them *yourself* and make an entirely new version of them . . . that has your great skill in orchestrating? My thought was that each time a theme is repeated, fresh instruments would play. Also, I thought that such instruments as Vibraharps, Marimbaphones, Saxophones, Celestas—in fact all the colorful instruments of the modern orchestra could be employed . . .[21]

Percy and Ella had been vacationing in Europe and on their return he responded:

> My wife and I have just got off the boat from Sweden and the first letter handed to me was your very delightful one. . . . I cannot tell

you how much I rejoice that so great a genius as yourself, and a musician of such exquisite taste and such original thinking should wish to record my pieces. And of course I will be overjoyed to make the special orchestrations for you as soon as I can, but I must warn that I am a slow worker, tho I work long—mostly 16 hours a day.[22]

Percy was slow indeed. Late in August he wrote to Stoki in Connecticut saying that September 3rd would suit him splendidly to discuss the re-orchestrations. Since Stoki had said that they meet either at his house or in White Plains, Percy suggested that they meet there since he had "all the various orchestrations here . . . some of which we might want to consult."[23] From his house on Round Hill Road in Connecticut, Stoki drove to Percy's house on Cromwell Place in White Plains. There they went through the various orchestrations, with Stoki making suggestions for adding additional color.

Grainger took all of Stoki's suggestions very seriously and the arrangements he made were a tour de force. They were finally recorded on May 31, 1950, during a session beginning at 7:30 in which they made six 10-inch sides. Percy was to appear with the group as pianist. "RCAV writes me," Stoki remarked in one of his brief notes, " 'According to union regulations Mr. Grainger will have to be paid union scale for playing the piano parts.' " And he added wryly, "I hope you don't mind!! It won't be very much. We can explode it in some delightful night club in White Plains — or — —!!!" Obviously he did not know White Plains.[24]

The recording was not released until 1952, and it received very favorable reviews. A critic for the *American Record Guide* felt that the six pieces provided a joyful and lilting program for the vernal season of the year. "I have never heard *Country Gardens, Shepherd's Hey* or *Molly on the Shore* played with such a brilliant array of coloration. These performances surely stem from an old friendship between composer and conductor. In *Handel in the Strand,* where Grainger gets the opportunity to show his brilliant prowess as solo pianist, the teamwork has the friendship clasp." As a codetta he observed that Stoki seems "always to obtain the best reproduction from RCA Victor."[25]

Percy liked the recording and said that he was amazed on how marvelously well each and every detail had come out.

"The record certainly is a revelation of recording wisdom no less than of inspired conducting. . . . "I am tempted to say that my ears have never before heard such a coming together of lovely skills and mastery of diversified details in a gramophone record. . . ."[26]

Other RCA Victor releases of that period included: Tchaikovsky's *Nutcracker* Suite, Stravinsky's *Petrouchka*, the Sibelius First Symphony and Schumann's Second Symphony. He recorded two Bach cantata movements, "Sheep May Safely Graze" and "Jesu, Joy of Man's Desiring"; Bach's Suite No. 2 in B Minor for Flute and Strings with Julius Baker; Debussy's Three Nocturnes with the women's voices of Robert Shaw's Chorale in the *Sirènes;* Wagner's *Tannhäuser* Overture and Venusberg Music; and his own "Symphonic Synthesis" of music from *Tristan und Isolde.*

The critics were unanimous in their praise of the Schumann Second Symphony performance Stokowski recorded on July 18 and 21, 1950. Irving Kolodin opined that "when the Stokowski sense of sonority is mated to as valid a conception as he conveys, it is hardly resistible . . . one of his very best contributions to the literature, both as sense and as sound."[27]

The producer of most of the Stokowski recordings for RCA was Richard Mohr. He first began to work for Stoki during the time when he was conducting "His" Symphony Orchestra on Victor. "It was a pickup orchestra. It had marvelous players: Robert Bloom, oboe; Julie Baker, flute; Leonard Rose and Bernie Greenhouse, cellos; Walter Trampler on viola, and, my God, the concertmaster was either Shumsky or Mischakoff for a time. . . . And then we had Vacchiano, who was in his prime as first trumpet, and the whole Philharmonic horn section, which was superb in those days.

"That orchestra! What I think was remarkable about it was that the string strength was 8 [first violins]-6 [second violins]-4 [violas]-4 [cellos]-2 [basses], which is like a Palmer House ensemble. But Stokowski had that unique knack of making it sound as though it were 18-16-14-12-8. We did all those records at Manhattan Center: things like the *Tallis Variations* and the *Verklaerte Nacht.* With Dick Gilbert he did the *Wesendonck Songs* when I was Gilbert's assistant. Eileen Farrell sang them beautifully, but being a healthy Irish girl she sang them sort of virginally—choirboy effect. And he would say, 'Do you know what those words mean? Do you know this is some of the most erotic music ever written?' 'Yes, yes, I know that, Maestro,' she would say, and go out and sing them even more beautifully but not with any Schwarzkopf intensity, because Farrell eroticism wasn't Stokowski eroticism."[28]

Because of the great admiration and interest in the Stokowski recordings, Peter Hugh Reed interviewed him in 1953 for the pages of the

American Record Guide and asked him how these were accomplished. "A good recording is the result of close cooperation between conductor musicians, and several technical key men," he replied. He praised Albert Pulley, Victor's Chief Engineer, and Lou Layton, the recording engineer. "Then there is Dick Mohr who sits quietly at the desk following the score. He times the music and informs me through the intercommunicating system of any variation in timing or any tonal imbalance which he knows to be contrary to what we have planned. Mr. Mohr also instinctively knows what to do. It is wonderful to work with these three men. . . . With such experts as these three cooperating, if we do not make a good recording—the fault is mine."[29]

Reed called Stoki the "godfather" of high fidelity. "Among the great musicians of our time," he wrote, "Dr. Stokowski has been truly unique in his long range concern with reproduced music. Unlike the majority of artists, who leave purely technical aspects of broadcasting or recording to engineers, he has from the earliest association with reproduced music cooperated closely with technicians, and more often than not assisted them with musical advice in regard to the character and quality of reproduction."[30]

During recording sessions Stoki frequently separated the various groups and had them miked separately. Violins and violas would be at his left, cellos and basses to his right, then, separated by about ten feet, he had the woodwinds on the left and the brass farther back to his left. He envisioned multitrack stereo at the time, but it had not yet become commercially available.

"There is a world of difference," he told Reed, "between the early electrical recordings with two-dimensional dynamics—*mezzo-forte* and *forte*—and the modern recordings with their range of dynamics that really gives us a true *pianissimo* and a true *fortissimo*. Naturally, wider range has not only added greatly to realism in sound but also to the music coloration, purer tonal quality and improved dynamics. Today we hear a true *crescendo* and *diminuendo* not possible in the early days of recording and only moderately successful in the first improved dynamic recordings made before and during the war, before a full frequency range was adopted."

And he talked about tradition. "When an artist opposes tradition," he said, "he opens himself to ridicule as well as praise. It is a mistake to allow tradition, as Nietzsche once said, to become holy and inspire awe, for the older it becomes and 'the more remote is its origin, the more confused the origin is. . . .' In the final analysis, it is the artistic results with which the true artist is concerned. It is my firm conviction that no artist need be hampered by the venerability of tradition nor the persistent reverence given it."[31]

Enter Andrew Schulhof

IT was patent that Stokowski and Beecham, the two greatest British-born conductors of their time, should meet and become friends. Just when and how they first met is unclear, but Belle Schulhof, the widow of Beecham's manager, Andrew Schulhof, thought her husband had brought the two together.

There were many parallels in the careers of Stokowski and Beecham, as well as dramatic differences. While Stoki admitted to having been born poor, Beecham had come from a wealthy family whose fortunes derived from patent medicines, chiefly pills, which his grandfather made by hand and peddled in Liverpool, where he worked as a laborer by day and a pill peddler at night. Old Thomas Beecham said that he came about the formula "by dosing a horse."[1]

Grandfather Beecham met and married a maid employed by a chemist. She was totally illiterate. This aspect of the Beecham background is quite similar to that of the grandparental side of Stokowski. Just as Leopold's father had become reasonably successful in his efforts, so did son Joseph Beecham, who amassed the family fortune. Obviously, pharmaceuticals were a more lucrative line than cabinetmaking.

Sir Thomas' father was a baronet, and his son inherited the title at his father's death. Two years earlier, he had been knighted for his services to music. He was a mere three years older than Stokowski.

As a boy, Beecham studied piano and theory, and at Oxford he began to compose. Late in his teens he visited Sir Charles Villiers Stanford at

the Royal College of Music at the same time that young Leopold was
studying with him. On Stanford's advice, Sir Thomas studied for several
years with Stanford's assistant, Charles Wood.[2]

Beecham never attended any music school; he acquired his conducting
expertise autodidactically, just as Stoki had. "A good conductor," Stoki
said, ". . . must devote and concentrate all his life to conducting and to
music. It must mean everything to him. He must have musical intuition
—he must know instinctively the inner invisible powers of music—
through imagination he must be able to reveal remote, yet intensely
stimulating and inspiring, possibilities and moods in music."[3]

Both men possessed these qualifications in abundance. Beecham was
magnificently literate. He possessed a Shavian wit. In fact, the great
G. B. S. once remarked that "Beecham is the most adult conductor I have
ever met."[4] He was highly sophisticated, cultured, urbane, and irrepres-
sible. Like Stokowski, he reveled in making speeches during pauses of his
concerts. A titled millionaire, he had no inhibition about expressing his
opinions. After being, so he thought, unfairly treated by the music critics
of Seattle during his time as conductor of that city's symphony, he was
famous for his characterization of them as having "the literary approach
of a street Arab, the monumental vanity of the high school magazine
editor, the range of knowledge of a stevedore and the vocabulary of a
baboon."[5]

In his conducting he shared one very important characteristic with
Stokowski, for he, too, took an improvisational approach and avoided
stereotyping his interpretations. Like Stoki, he, too, was able to give a
great freshness to his conducting.

In his engagement book, Stokowski noted that the Beechams would
dine at 7:30 on October 30, 1949, and in December he recorded that the
Beechams would arrive in New York on December 15. He and Gloria had
invited them to dine and spend Christmas Eve, and one wonders whether
the doughty Sir Thomas sang his version of the old carol:

> *Hark, the herald angels sing*
> *Beecham's pills are just the thing,*
> *Two for a woman, one for a child*
> *Peace on earth, and mercy mild.*

He may even have remarked, as he did on a similar occasion to Sir
Neville Cardus, that he thought the parody "very eloquently expressed a

sentiment that everyone enjoys when they've had a very good release." He added, "My father wouldn't publish it. Geniuses are never recognized in the family."[6]

Beecham recounted some of his experiences deep in the heart of Texas when he conducted there as a guest in Houston. But more important was a discussion of management, for now that Stoki was finished with Judson, he was definitely in the market for a new manager. Beecham's genial manager, Andrew Schulhof, was a highly cultured man with elegant but not overbearing continental manners.

Andrew was a manager more in the mold of Charles Ellis than that of Judson. He had a relatively small stable of artists, and he was one of the few who specialized in conductors rather than in promoting expensive soloists. In addition to Beecham, he represented Rafael Kubelik, Ernest Ansermet, and would soon add Stokowski.

Since there were still concerts to be conducted with the Philharmonic, Stoki endeavored to maintain amicable relations with both Judson and Bruno Zirato. He then began a series of meetings with Schulhof beginning on February 3 and continuing on February 18, 21, 23, and March 23. In April Siegfried Hearst visited Stoki to see whether NCAC (National Concert & Artists Corporation) could book him for guest appearances, and Stoki agreed provided they would be after the termination of his contract with Judson. Four days later Stoki and Judson met and the matter of his contract with Columbia was discussed without any final determination having been made. Judson nevertheless felt that he would finally decide to remain with him, and some time before the May 1 deadline he sent him a contract. It was to run from May 1, 1950, till April 30, 1953. Stoki never signed. On May 12, 1950, he dispatched to Schulhof the following:

> At our recent conversation we mentioned the possibility of your becoming exclusive representative for me in European countries. I am taking this question up with Mr. Judson. If this can be arranged, I think we should have a simple letter agreement so that there will be no possibility of having any misunderstandings. Would you care to send me your idea of such an agreement? If we can put all this in good order soon, it will avoid delay.[7]

There were several more meetings with Andrew before he departed for Europe, and they were resumed immediately upon his return. On September 14, they met at 10 Gracie Square at 8:00 P.M. and a week later were joined by Sam Rosenbaum for his legal counsel. Through Sam's good offices Stoki was apparently freed from his contract with Judson, and Schulhof took over.

Andrew's ideas were both big and practical. He immediately booked concerts for Houston, Dallas and San Antonio. Together they departed from Penn Station in a double bedroom Pullman suite, arriving in Houston two days later. Newspaper interviews were set up for Tuesday afternoon, November 29, 1950, at his suite in the Warwick, and the next night Stoki dined for the first time at Bayou Bend, the magnificent home of Ima Hogg. The house is a pseudo-Colonial mansion built in 1927, but it is an impressive, unostentatious mansion. It is surrounded by towering pines and live oaks. There are formal as well as wild gardens surrounding the house. Inside, it is filled with excellent antiques, and it is now a part of the Museum of Fine Arts of Houston. It was a very gracious, friendly welcome, and Stoki warmed to it all.

Stoki conducted both sectional and full orchestra rehearsals over a period of four days and presented his concert on Monday, December 4, in a program consisting mostly of works by Wagner, with Charles Ruggles' *Organum* thrown in as an "undigestible" novelty.[8] At least so some Texans believed.

The following day Stoki and Andrew entrained for Dallas, where he rehearsed for eleven hours over a period of four days for a concert on the ninth. Then by car to San Antonio, where he did some conventional sightseeing: the Alamo and a huge Texas ranch. As a novelty in an otherwise conventional program, Stoki introduced a work by Iglesias. "The musical rhubarb," wrote critic Don Pickles, "was the American premiere of Antonio Iglesias' *The First Adventure of Don Quixote*. The piece might be a lament to a dying dog, an ode to an old shoe or a post-mortem for burnt toast."[9]

After several preliminary talks, Schulhof and Sam Rosenbaum met with Stokowski on the thirtieth of December to look over a contract that had been drawn up by Stoki's lawyer. Dated January 1, 1951, it provided that Andrew Schulhof should be the exclusive manager and booking agent for North America and South America, Europe, Australia, and Africa. It was not to cover contracts for recording, motion pictures, radio or television —nor any concerts booked prior to the signing of the contract.

Stokowski agreed to pay Schulhof 15 percent commission on all fees from concerts in the United States and Canada, but 20 percent for all fees collected in any other country. In an amendment to the contract, Stoki spelled out the concerts that were not to be covered by the agreement: Pittsburgh, Denver, and Cleveland.[10] The Cleveland dates had been offered by Siegfried Hearst or NCAC, and the others had presumably been secured by Judson.[11]

The Pittsburgh and Denver concerts took place early in January 1951, and upon his return to New York Stoki immediately concerned himself with recordings for RCA Victor. The first was to be the *"Letter Scene"* from Tchaikovsky's *Eugen Onegin* with Licia Albanese, soprano. He had two rehearsals with Albanese alone, and on the sixth between 7:30 and 10:00 P.M. they recorded: "When Stokowski came he started to rehearse with me and he asked how I learned the Russian," recalled Miss Albanese. "I said, 'Maestro, it's terrible!' 'No,' he said, 'you are fantastic. Who taught you?' " Albanese explained that she had learned it phonetically, first from two young Russians who were staying with her and later with George Cehanovsky of the Met. "I said, 'George, please help me with the Russian.' And he did, and when Stokowski came he said, 'You learned this so well, really. Thank you very much.' You know he was in love with that score. . . . What beautiful music it is!"

Two nights later they recorded the *Bachianas Brasileiras* No. 5 For Soprano and Eight Celli by Villa-Lobos. The *Bachianas* consists of two parts: the "Aria" and a "Danza Martelo." Bidu Sayao had recorded the "Aria" only. "Nobody ever did the 'Danza Martelo,' " said Albanese, "then Stokowski asked me to do it. 'Licia, nobody ever did it. Now we have to do it,' he said. 'This will be the first that will come out.' I think the second one was de los Angeles. But the Brazilian soprano Bidu Sayao told me that she never wanted to do it. She didn't like it. But I adore it. I still sing that beautiful Villa-Lobos piece."

After the first recording session, Stoki gallantly took Albanese home to her apartment at 400 Park Avenue. "He sat in the living room with me and my husband and he wanted to taste all the liqueurs we had. He said, 'Joe, let me taste that. Ah, you have this. I didn't taste that for years. Let me taste it.' He sat down for two or three hours and we talked. It was such a joy to have him."

The evening after the second recording, the Gimmas, Licia Albanese and her husband, dined with Leopold and Gloria. Licia described the evening: "He invited me to his home, which was beautiful . . . a huge apartment, and we had a very good dinner, and Gloria even did the dessert. . . .

"I saw so many beautiful paintings that she did. The colors were so bright, so alive, so striking. Maybe that's what she had in her heart, and it never came out."[12]

On February 15 Stoki recorded *Escales* by Jacques Ibert and the "Dance of the Sylphs" from Berlioz's *Damnation of Faust*. These, along with the Albanese disc, were the only recordings he made for RCA in 1951. Reviews were most complimentary.

James Chambers, who had played horn, remarked that there was a good deal of horn in the *"Letter Scene"*—"always the same little figure repeated. I remember Stokowski beckoned me at the end of that recording date and congratulated me on the quality of the playing and the fact that we had done it so many times and I had not dropped a note. As I remember, that was a very lovely recorded performance."[13]

The *Escales* and "Dance of the Sylphs" were released with a transfer from previously released 78s of the Sibelius *Swan of Tuonela* and Granados' Intermezzo from *Goyescas*. Norwood, in the *American Record Guide*, remarked that "Ibert's impressionistic musical tour of the Mediterranean often has intensity of coloring which Mr. Stokowski exploits very well. The conductor seems to have made some slight changes in the scoring and some alterations in the composer's dynamic markings —in one case making a sweeping run on the harp reminiscent of Debussy in *Festivals*. . . . The beauty of tone achieved in the Sibelius and the exquisite delicacy in the Berlioz are cherishable examples of this conductor's art."[14]

A new series of television programs was in the planning stage late in 1950 and early in 1951. It was to be produced by Arthur Tourtellot for the "March of Time." Tourtellot, an old friend, called me at CBS and asked me to discuss the program with Stokowski and see whether he might be interested in being a part of it. He was interested indeed.

We began immediately to explore its possibilities. We went through ballets; we explored ethnic music; we considered the effect of oriental music on such composers as Lou Harrison and Henry Cowell; we went through choral music from Gregorian chant to the music of Victoria, Palestrina, Bach, and beyond. Baroque music, the Viennese masters, and the moderns were all considered. I met frequently with Tourtellot to report on our progress and to begin to work out plans for recording the music. It was decided to record principally in London during one of Stoki's breaks on his forthcoming tour.

Before his departure Stokowski came to my office at CBS to record discussions on music with Dwight Cooke for a series of programs I was producing called "You and the World." That was on March 19. On the twenty-third I received a note:

Dear Oliver

I enclose a list of compositions, sometimes giving the timing, that I think might be suitable for the ideas we discussed.

Separately we are returning to you, with many thanks for your kindness, the score of Revueltas' *A Federico Garcia Lorca.*

Sincerely,
Leopold[15]

During the next two weeks we worked on plans and details and on the fourth of April, Stoki, Arthur Tourtellot, and I met for lunch at the 21 Club and seemed to agree on nearly all points. That evening Stoki departed from Grand Central for an overnight trip to Montreal, where he conducted two concerts and one in Ottawa, returning to New York just in time to embark on the *Queen Mary,* Saturday, April 14, 1951.

While on shipboard, Stoki and Schulhof discussed the "March of Time" project and decided to elicit my help in clarifying the entire matter with Tourtellot and Time, Inc. Stoki decided to phone. The call came in early on Sunday morning—after a rather late Saturday night. It was my first and only phone call from a ship at sea. Both Stoki and Andrew were on the line. We went over in great detail a résumé of what our discussions and plans had been, and after we had terminated the call, Andrew, meticulous as always, wrote me the following detailed letter:

April 17, 1951

Dear Oliver,

Referring to the transatlantic call between Mr. Stokowski and yourself, as well as with me, I want to put down in writing these conversations, to have as a future reference, and as a guidance, to avoid any misunderstanding.

Mr. Stokowski is willing to enter into an agreement if the following terms can be arranged:

The arrangement will be for 26 (twenty-six) shorts, with 10½–13 minutes music for television and motion picture use only. The motion picture shall be for 35mm as well as for 16mm use; the latter in special view for educational purposes. . . .

Definite arrangements must be made giving Mr. Stokowski assurance that there will be no distortion of the music; no cuts without his written approval; no advertising during the playing of the music.

An explanation of the story some time during the playing, however, seems permissible. You will find a mutually satisfactory way to satisfy his wishes and disperse his worries regarding the visual, pictorial part. . . .

I hope that you have mailed a copy of the list of works which Mr. Stokowski gave you to us to London. Also your reaction to this list, as well as the other gentlemen involved. Please let us know which additional works you would propose. It is of utmost importance that this first venture should be an excellent one in every respect.

I am sure you are pleased with the fast developments.[16]

I answered Andrew on April 25 explaining all that had transpired since the shipboard call:

My dear Andrew:

Arthur Tourtellot was very pleased about all the details we discussed in our transatlantic call. He is now drawing up a contract which will be airmailed to you within a matter of days. I have discussed all the other details with them at considerable length and this is what they would like to do.

They would like to do all the recording in London between the dates of July 18th and 30th. Actually there will be much less music than we had anticipated since many programs would be satisfactorily covered by as little as 8 minutes of music. As I see it, this substantially reduces the amount we would have to do. The total would be somewhat over four hours of music. . . .

Arthur Tourtellot has cabled London asking his office there to reserve Kingsway Hall for as much time as possible during that period. Following the recording, they would like to film the orchestra playing while they listen to a playback of these works. I believe some of this could be done without Mr. Stokowski present. This will save him from some additional wear and tear. All pictures taken of him will be done not only with great care but released only if he approves it. . . .[17]

Even before receiving my letter, Leopold wrote from London.

The Connaught Hotel,
Carlos Place,
London, W.1.,
England.
26th April, 1951

Dear Oliver,

Yesterday Mr. Schulhof sent you a list of my suggestions for the music of the television shorts. In my opinion, many of these are

suitable for dance or ballet. I think we could find splendid dancers
for this in the Sadlers Wells Ballet here, when you arrive.

Some of the music that I have marked "Miscellaneous" presents
some problems which we must discuss when you arrive.

The scenes in Cathedrals I think we could easily do in England.

The music during mass could be best done in Spain, in my opinion.

The sea pictures we could put together from "stock shots," which
we can easily find in London or New York.

In Haydn's Kindersynphonie we could make a charming picture by
having children playing the toy instruments.

We can find "stock shots" for the Marches of Soldiers.

The abstract films we can make best, I think, in New York.

The nature films we can make partly in Europe, partly in America.

As soon as possible, will you send me your suggestions of music so
that I can add them to my list.

All is going well here, the Orchestra is playing beautifully, there
are many wonderful players here, so that I know we will make good
recordings. Soon I will go to Kingsway to observe when Beecham
is recording there, so that I can try to understand the way the engineers work and gain a good idea of the acoustical properties of the
studio.

Always your friend,

On the same day he wrote to his assistant, Lila Phillips, in Connecticut:

The weather here is very beautiful, the Orchestra is playing
wonderfully and everything is going well. I start on the tour
tomorrow. . . .

Thank you for sending me the news about Stan. I am hoping he
will be coming here soon and will bring his mother with him! I am
always happy to receive any news from you about the things which
interest us both. . . .[18]

He signed the letter "Stan's father."

The tour was a taxing one, with nineteen concerts in various English
cities. The first was in Bristol on April 27, marking his first appearance
in England since 1912. He alternated two programs. The first, "Program
A," read thus:

Wagner: Overture and "Venusberg Music" from *Tannhäuser*
Villa-Lobos: "Impressão Moura" from *Descobrimento do Brasil*

Falla: *El amor brujo*
Brahms: Symphony No. 4 in E Minor

This program was heard in Bristol (April 27), Cardiff (April 29), Leicester (May 1), Newcastle (May 7), Oxford (May 17), Southend (May 20), and Croydon (May 28).

The second, "Program B," was as follows:

Berlioz: *Roman Carnival* Overture or
Ruggles: *Organum*
Debussy: *L'Après-midi d'un faune*
Stravinsky: Suite from the *Firebird*
Tchaikovsky: Symphony No. 5

This for the following cities: Bournemouth (April 28), Birmingham (April 30), Hanley (May 2), Nottingham (May 3), Bradford (May 6), Manchester (May 8), Croydon (June 1).

Leopold's second concert was in Bournemouth, where he was able to visit his mother in the nursing home. It would be his last visit, since she died September 23, 1952, at the age of ninety-three.

One of the players in the orchestra was Denis Vaughan. Denis was from Melbourne, Australia, where, as something of a prodigy, he began concertizing as a pianist and organist at the age of ten. At twenty he came to England and studied organ and double bass at the Royal College of Music. He joined the Royal Philharmonic in 1950 and played with it on its American tour that year. He was later to become Beecham's assistant and a distinguished conductor in his own right. Denis was playing in the orchestra when Stoki took over. Denis recalled: "He stopped in the middle of a rehearsal at the Davis Theatre, Croydon, looked up very quietly, and said, 'Gentlemen, do you want to know the secret of living? Have deep principles and then improvise.' There was deathly silence in the orchestra. I've never forgotten the phrase because it is so right.

"He did a musical thing, too, which I remember very well. We did *L'Après-midi* and he said, 'Gentlemen, you know I heard Debussy play the piano, and he did things with the pedal which I've heard no other composer and no other pianist do.' And he proceeded then to prolong quite a number of bass notes beyond the written length in order to get the pedal effects that Debussy had written. As I was playing the double bass it touched on me. It was very original and effective, too. I knew then that he was a master of sound such as there have been few if any at all.[19]

"At the first rehearsal which we did with Stokowski, which, if I remember rightly, was in Abbey Road, he was extremely taken with the sound of the flute (Gerald Jackson) of the Royal Philharmonic and asked to hear a number of passages several times. What the difference was was the size of the flute. It was a large wooden flute, and it had a warmth and a breadth which is very rare to hear now.[20]

"He also insisted that for the whole tour around England in various old cinemas and so on, that the stages be stripped entirely so there were only walls to be seen—no curtains at all of any nature, so that the sound would be as reverberant as possible. He is the only conductor I have ever known who took that much care about preparing the sound beforehand and making sure that he would get a fullness from the orchestra. . . ."

I remarked to Denis that it was my impression that Stoki and Beecham were very compatible and got along very well. "They did indeed," he said. "That's why Sir Thomas invited him to conduct the orchestra."[21]

After his concert in Nottingham, Sir Thomas took over the orchestra for the next two days while Stoki returned to the Connaught Hotel in London. He phoned me from there and expressed his great disappointment that our ideas for the "March of Time" seemed to have been whittled down. He did not want to end up merely doing a set of little pieces that would be distributed throughout the season. I suggested that he write directly to Tourtellot, which he did. I never saw the exchange of correspondence, but the recording sessions in London were canceled. Since the program had not even started, it was perhaps too much to expect that they would turn over a complete program for a single symphonic work or even a major part of any program.

On May 16 he conducted in the Royal Albert Hall. A Reuters dispatch spread far afield the news: "Leopold Stokowski was called back eight times tonight to receive the homage of nearly 6,000 music-lovers packing the Royal Albert Hall for his performance with Sir Thomas Beecham's Royal Philharmonic Orchestra.

"It was Mr. Stokowski's first London appearance in twenty years [actually thirty-nine years] and a memorable experience not only for concert-goers but for millions of radio listeners as well. A storm of applause lasting twelve minutes followed the close of the program.

"The tall, white-haired maestro received the ovation with his usual calm. But his eighth bow was his last. While the applause continued he slipped out the back of the hall and drove to his hotel."[22]

On May 27 he returned again to the Royal Albert Hall with a program that included Berlioz's *Roman Carnival,* Debussy's *L'Après-midi d'un faune,* Prokofiev's *Scythian* Suite, Riegger's Third Symphony, and his transcription of Bach's Passacaglia and Fugue.

Stoki's third appearance in the Royal Albert Hall took place on June 4, and again he offered Londoners an ear-cleaning experience. He began with Ruggles' *Organum* and followed with Schoenberg's Second Chamber Symphony and the Tchaikovsky Fifth Symphony.[23] "I remember very well during the performances of the Tchaikovsky Fifth," said Denis Vaughan, ". . . he achieved remarkable effects of crescendo and diminuendo in the strings at the openings and ends of the movements by starting with only the last desk of each section. As I was the last double bass player, that's why it interested me in particular. But then he just had one desk of each section and not the visible ones. By spacing the players out so far away, it gave a whole new perspective to the sound, so that it really disappeared right into the distance and came from nothing to the full crescendo."[24]

During three separate sessions he made his first English recording for RCA Victor, the *Scheherazade* of Rimsky-Korsakov. He used the Philharmonia Orchestra with Manoug Parikian, solo violin. When it was released it produced some fascinating reactions. In San Francisco, where the sun shines bright and the skies are not cloudy all day, critic R. H. Hagan in the *Chronicle* referred to ". . . the most sensuous, sensual, capricious, luxurious, hedonistic and voluptuous interpretation of 'Scheherazade' that has ever coiled itself around a turntable."[25]

On the East Coast, Peter Hugh Reed praised the British engineers and called the orchestra one of England's finest.[26]

In England, however, the critical climate was less clement. We have the counterpoint of view in the *Gramophone:* "The new H.M.V. is very finely recorded, the orchestra is in magnificent shape, and Manoug Parikian's solo is rather firmer and rounder in tone than that of Pierre Nerini in the French version. But Stokowski's reading is exaggerated, sometimes, to the point of being grotesque. . . ."[27]

On June 9 Stoki made his Royal Festival Hall debut with a typical program of Bach-Stokowski, Beethoven, Barber, and Stravinsky with the BBC Symphony Orchestra and on the following night repeated the program in BBC's Maida Vale Studio for broadcast. Edward Johnson relates that "Robert Simpson, newly arrived at the BBC Music Division, recalls going with Stokowski to the first rehearsal at the newly built Royal Festival

Hall. Stokowski walked in, looked around the auditorium, and without whistling or clapping his hands, turned to Simpson and said, 'What a pity!' "28

Midst all of his frantic activity he found time to concern himself with all sorts of details about the house in Connecticut. He wrote to his assistant, Lila Phillips, asking about the refrigerator. He discussed details about taxes and (as an example of his frugality in some areas) wrote: "I agree with you that the light bill for Innisfree is too high, because we were away most of that period. Is there an error in the bill? It may be that the lights have been left on unnecessarily and the electric current for cooking

Courtesy Belle Schulhof

With Sir Thomas Beecham when Stokowski took Beecham's Royal Philharmonic Orchestra on a tour of England in 1951

has been wastefully used. Can you let me know all about this?" Then he added a floral touch: "I am sending six packets of Aubrieta [rock cress] which is a most beautiful plant with beautiful flowers in many colors. Please ask Walter to plant these now, according to the instructions on the packet. The best place would be in the front part of the perennial border, because this is a low plant."[29]

In a return letter, Miss Phillips wrote about all sorts of small details. One, however, provokes curiosity: "Mr. Schulhof's secretary sent me a check in the amount of $1,500 from Time, Inc. and asked me to deposit it for you. As I do not know what this is for, will you tell me if it is OK to deposit it?" The answer was yes.

Miss Phillips also reported that the washing machine was all hooked up and the refrigerator was working right. Then she added that Mr. Schulhof's secretary had sent her a picture of Sir Thomas handing him a baton. "It is a wonderful picture and I am so glad to see it and to see how well you look (your new suit is beautiful!)—BUT—please send me a new picture WITHOUT a baton because I am afraid Stan will not approve of this one as he is particular about such matters."[30]

Stoki had visited one of London's fine tailors and ordered a blue, pin-striped, serge suit which he would wear for many years to come and always look elegant in. He was meticulous about his clothes even if some of the combinations that he wore were hardly conventional. With his new London suit, he eschewed the traditional white shirt and chose instead dark blue or other complementary colors. In one of his letters to Miss Phillips he wrote:

> Please ask Orlando
> 1. Have my clothes (woolen) moth balls?
> 2. Are all the bags closed?
> 3. Is my car jacked up?[31]

In his personal as well as his professional life, no details were too small to ignore.

On June 9 Gloria arrived in London on Pan American's flight 100 at 9:45 A.M. in ample time to hear Leopold's concert with the BBC Symphony Orchestra in the Royal Festival Hall that night. A broadcast concert was arranged for the following evening. With three free days before his next BBC concert, they decided to visit Oxford as the guest of Stoki's longtime friend Bernard Rose, then organist and fellow at Queen's College, Oxford.

On June 20 Gloria and Leopold arrived in Holland and proceeded to The Hague, where they stayed at the Hotel des Indes, an old converted baronial mansion facing the park and the American embassy. Rehearsals with The Hague Residentie Orchestra—one of Holland's finest—began on the following day for a concert on the twenty-seventh that marked the beginning of the Holland Festival of that season. The novelty on the program was the *Recordare* of Lukas Foss.

His next concert was in Amsterdam with the Concertgebouw on July 5, and following that they departed for Munich and the Vier Jahreszeiten Hotel. Before beginning rehearsals with the Bayerischer Rundfunk Orchestra, Leopold and Gloria made two side trips: one to Ludwig's fairy-tale turreted castle of Neuschwanstein in the Bavarian Alps, and another to Herrenchiemsee, where on a mid-lake island Ludwig left his uncompleted pseudoreplica of Versailles. Gloria wrote back to Miss Phillips that the country was beautiful and that the natives wore wonderful peasant costumes creating an enchanted atmosphere.[32]

The Bayerischer Rundfunk Orchestra, then under the direction of Eugen Jochum, was a superlative orchestra, and Stoki was given four three-hour rehearsals from Tuesday to Friday for a concert-broadcast that was to take place on Monday evening. Taking advantage of the free weekend, they spent it in Salzburg, where they enjoyed two idyllic days in that magically beautiful town. Stoki never spoke of Salzburg in anything but the most affectionate terms.

The Rundfunk concert in Munich included Schoenberg's *Kammersymphonie*, a rarity there in those days. After Munich their movements describe a considerable zigzag. Back to England for two concerts in Liverpool with Beecham's orchestra, during which Stoki introduced a new work by a young British composer, Kenneth Leighton, who, unfortunately, was in Italy at the time and could not hear the concert. The new work was Leighton's *Primavera Romana*. In a letter to Edward Johnson, Leighton remarked, "I had the pleasure of meeting him and dining with him in Oxford during the summer of 1951, in connection with the conferring of an honorary Fellowship by the Queen's College, of which I also was a scholar. He was extremely kind and encouraging, and talked a great deal about folk-song in which he so strongly believed as the basic source of all music. At that time he was very friendly with my tutor, Dr. Bernard Rose, who is now organist of Magdalen College, and became a friend of the family."[33]

Critics found Leighton's piece to be "adroitly written music which has no great depth but is engaging in its verve and glitter."[34]

On August 11 Stokowski opened the Lucerne Festival and then they proceeded to Salzburg again for two concerts. On one he gave the premiere of a short work by the Czech composer František Pícha called *Štěpančikovo*. But he scrapped it the following evening when he repeated the concert and replaced it with Stravinsky's *Pastorale*. Although there was no public mention of it, Stokowski dedicated the August 22 concert to Stan, marking his first birthday. No mention was made either that Gloria was already expecting another addition to the family.

After the Liverpool concerts there was nothing booked until the eighteenth of October, in Lisbon. Gloria and Leopold now set out on an auto trip that would take them to Bayonne, San Sebastian, Bilbao, Santiago de Compostela, Madrid, Escorial, Montserrat, Barcelona, Granada, Jerez, and finally Lisbon on October 10. In his detailed tour schedule, Schulhof indicated "Chorus Concerts" in Spain and Portugal. After each set of rehearsals he indicates "Audicione" rather than concert, which may have indicated that the choral performances were somehow tied in with a type of church service. Although that is not much to go on, we can appreciate his deep interest in the music of Victoria and other early Spanish composers, all stimulated, no doubt, by the abortive "March of Time" project.

Gloria and Leopold returned to New York on October 28, and in November and December he conducted concerts in Pittsburgh and Cleveland. On October 31, three days after their arrival in New York, news was leaked to the press and wired across the country in an AP dispatch: "Conductor Leopold Stokowski, 69, and his 27-year-old wife, the former Gloria Vanderbilt, are expecting their second child in January. They have a son born August 22, 1950. . . ."[35]

On January 31, 1952 Leopold and Gloria became the proud parents of a nine-pound-three-ounce boy.[36] They named him Christopher Chrysostom. William Grant Still wrote that he was sending two small model airplanes, and Stoki replied:

> We shall be so happy to receive the two planes from you. Our big boy Stan is terribly enthusiastic about planes. The little one, Chrysostom, is just a week old today and is interested in nothing yet except sleeping and eating![37]

During one of his Pittsburgh concerts, Stoki gave the world premiere of *Horizontes*, a microtonal work by the Mexican composer Julián Carrillo, who arrived with three specially trained soloists: Nicoline Zedeler-

Mix, violin; Livio Mannucci, cello; and Ann Elizabeth Jones, "arpa-citera."[38] The latter was an instrument constructed by the composer which could produce ninety-seven tones to the octave. Critic Donald Steinfirst found the "tinkling of the harp-zither, something like the light patter of rain. . . ." At the conclusion of *Horizontes*, Stoki asked the audience if they would like to hear the work again. The applause was insistent and he repeated it "not without the loss, however, of some dissidents who retired to the corridors."[39] Subsequently, Stoki conducted the work in Minneapolis and Washington.

Between two of the orchestral concerts in Pittsburgh, he conducted a choral concert in the soaring, Gothic Heinz Chapel on the grounds of the university. His program consisted of four a cappella works of Victoria: *Popule Meus, O Vos Omnes, Vere Languores,* and *Ave Maria.* Prior to the Pittsburgh series, Stoki had written to the manager of the orchestra.

> . . . Amongst many other things, I have been conducting the beautiful and emotional music of Victoria in some of the Spanish cathedrals and Basilicas. The effect of this music is magical in the hearts of the listeners. When I was in the great Gothic cathedrals of Spain I often thought of the Heinz Chapel in Pittsburgh. If you think it is a good idea and if the Heinz family are willing, I would like to conduct some of the Victoria music in this chapel. As there are not many seats could this be done by invitation and could it include some of the students in the university who are interested in 16th Century music? Mrs. Starrett would know which students. Would a small chorus of three sopranos, three contraltos, three tenors and three basses be available? They should all be good musicians and picked voices.
>
> I would like to do this one night about 9 o'clock with no light in the chapel except three large candles on the altar and with the chorus invisible below the altar. A few minutes before the music begins I would like to sound three bells from above and then close the doors to any late-comers. After the first music is finished we could sound three bells again and open the doors again to late-comers. After this the doors would not be opened again until the end.
>
> I would like to do this in a non-professional way, everybody, includ-ing myself, giving their services for the beauty of the chapel and music. . . .[40]

55

Plans and Projects

A T Columbia University a fund established by Alice M. Ditson
enabled the music department to sponsor an annual "mini" music
festival of contemporary American music. Douglas Moore, Otto
Luening, and Normand Lockwood were the prime movers of the enterprise, and as early as 1945 they presented an annual award to conductors
in recognition of their contribution to American music. Howard Hanson
was the first recipient, followed by Leon Barzin, Alfred Wallenstein, Dean
Dixon, Thor Johnson, Izler Solomon, and Robert Whitney. Stokowski
was the eighth to receive Columbia's recognition.

Originally, the concerts were broadcast over NBC, but in 1948 Douglas
Moore and Otto Luening broached the idea of having the concerts broadcast over CBS. They met with James Fassett and me to explore the
possibility, and we were able to work out a plan whereby, for a relatively
small outlay of money for additional musicians, it would be possible to
broadcast the principal orchestral concert on a nationwide hookup. The
CBS house orchestra, numbering thirty-five men, was augmented each
season by additional men who played on the Arthur Godfrey program and
were available when the Godfrey group traveled to Hollywood and originated the program there. These musicians, plus the extra men which the
Ditson Fund would engage, constituted a full orchestra. For several years
the collaboration between CBS and Columbia University resulted in some
outstanding programs.

In 1952 Columbia honored Leopold Stokowski, and to make the event

United Press International Photo
Conducting the CBS American Music Festival of the Air (1952)

really festive, CBS devoted all of its serious music programs that weekend to American compositions.

Stoki's climaxing program consisted of the Concerto for Piano and Orchestra by Alexei Haieff and the Symphony No. 3 by Roger Goeb. Like all the festival concerts, it was to have taken place in Columbia's McMillin Theater, but because of an unrelated strike by kitchen workers, if memory is correct, who picketed all of the university buildings, the orchestra men, good union members all, naturally refused to cross the picket lines, and the concert had to be hastily moved to a quite unrehabilitated theater on Broadway at Sixty-fifth Street. "The theater, a pre-cinema survivor, is a real antique and smells like one," observed Virgil Thomson. "But the CBS Orchestra played beautifully, and the new works that made up the hour length program were very much worth hearing."[1]

Two days later the Goeb symphony was recorded by RCA Victor, with whom Stokowski was under contract. And though the orchestra was actually the augmented CBS Symphony, it was listed as "Leopold Stokowski and his Orchestra." The recording was sponsored by the American Composer's Alliance (ACA), of which I was coordinating manager at the time. To understand some of these developments, and some yet to come, an explanation is needed.

It was through the Ditson Fund concerts that I became friendly with many of the composers whose music was performed. Because of my great interest in American music, Otto Luening and Normand Lockwood, both on the Columbia faculty, invited me to lunch several times at the Faculty Club and told me about ACA and the splendid things they wanted to accomplish through it. It all sounded very interesting, but the "sell" was so soft that I did not realize that they were trying to persuade me to take over the running of the Alliance. Finally I agreed to take it over, and Otto likened my chief function at ACA to the pop "song plugger" but gave it the classier title of "lieder pleader."

I discussed the Alliance with Stoki, and he was eager to cooperate and do all that he could to aid American composers. It was that idealism of his that made him enthusiastic about the idea of recording the Goeb symphony.

Harry Truman's least favorite music critic, Paul Hume, reviewed the work for the Washington Post, March 22, describing it as "an American symphony of imposing dimensions, here recorded for the first time, and in a sumptuous account."[2]

RCA Victor "of little faith" would not record the work unless it was totally subsidized. Hence, ACA had to bring its subsistence coals to RCA's Newcastle.

Roger Goeb, who always seemed to look on the more gloomy side of things, said to me, "I was never overly happy with the actual quality of the sound coming from that recording. But that's neither here nor there. At least it was played and recorded and that's it."[3]

Other composers, however, were eager to be performed by Stokowski and possibly recorded by him. The ACA office had an extensive library of works by its members. There I was able to pore through scores I had never before encountered. I also had the opportunity of meeting a whole group of composers whom I had never known. As I discovered new and interesting works, I would bring them to Stoki's attention, and we began to discuss doing a series of concerts that might be modeled after those he had conducted for the International Composers' Guild and the League of Composers back in the thirties.

He went with me to look at the auditorium of the Museum of Modern Art. We lunched with René d'Harnoncourt, the director, who was most enthusiastic about the possibility of introducing new music in the museum, particularly with Stokowski conducting. ACA was entirely in accord with the idea and in principle agreed to underwrite the cost of a recording, but since their budget was limited, I had to go elsewhere for subsidy for the concerts.

I brought the idea to Carl Haverlin, the enlightened president of BMI, and he agreed to underwrite the cost of a series of concerts at the museum. We hoped, however, to gain a broader base of interest and support. Before Stoki's departure for his European tour, we met with a good friend and CBS colleague, Jack Turner, who at that point was about to become a part of the Ford Foundation. The day before Stoki sailed, Jack and I invited him to join us for lunch at the Brussels, one of Stoki's favorite restaurants. We worked out the first rough plan of drawing together many of the various splinter groups, all of which were interested in promoting contemporary music. This was the beginning of the Contemporary Music Society.

Meanwhile, Andrew Schulhof had booked Stoki for concerts in London with the BBC and in Florence, Zurich, Milan, Hamburg, and Dusseldorf. I joined Stoki and Gloria briefly in Zurich, where we talked further about the establishment of a Contemporary Music Society and of the various groups in New York that might be interested in participating. As always, he envisioned the idea as having national scope with branches in most of the major cities and universities.

Upon his return, Stoki and I met again with René d'Harnoncourt and we set two dates when Stoki would conduct concerts in the museum's auditorium. Its relatively small stage dictated the size of instrumental forces that could be used, and we began to look for works that would not require too many players.

To express his views on the presentation of contemporary music, Stoki prepared a handout for the press. "What the Museum of Modern Art has done for painting and sculpture must be done for music all over the country," he stated. "Societies (some exist already) for contemporary music must be founded in the key cities.

"The membership may be small, but it will be enthusiastic. The first concerts can be for chamber music, because the expense is small, but the principles of modern music are broadly the same for chamber music as for symphonic. Later concerts for chamber orchestra will expand the repertoire. As interest grows in the community and the membership increases, symphony concerts of living American music will eventually be possible, and an ever growing and evolving solution will be reached, covering the whole field of contemporary music.

"Records should be made . . . and radio and television performances will follow when prejudices in some minds are overcome. America can do all of this just as she has achieved similar great results in other fields."

On October 16 I set up a series of interviews at CBS for Stokowski to speak about the forthcoming concerts. One was with Bill Leonard, who had a very popular program called "This Is New York." Among his remarks Stokowski stated: "American music in the future is part of American life in the future—the overall picture that we are trying to foresee now for our children and our grandchildren and all the people who are going to populate this immense country. We have very talented young composers for this, but the outlet of their talents—the possibility of performance of their compositions—could be much, much better than it is now. Those composers should have an opportunity to have their music performed so that they can hear it themselves and see if they've done what they wanted to do when they wrote it down on the paper. . . .

"We may have great masters of music in this country now comparable to the great masters of Europe, only are we giving them enough opportunity? Are we performing their music enough? I think not. And that is why I want to devote much time from now on. In the Museum of Modern Art next week and the week after I'm going to give two concerts with music—solely the music of the young American talented composers which I hope will do the same kind of thing that they have already done there for painting and sculpture."[4]

The first of the museum concerts took place on October 26, with Stokowski conducting the following:

Henry Cowell: Hymn and Fuguing Tune No. 2; Hymn and Fuguing
   Tune No. 5
Ulysses Kay: Suite for Strings
John Lessard: Cantilena for oboe and String Orchestra (Robert
   Bloom, oboe)
Wallingford Riegger: *Study in Sonority*
Alan Hovhaness: *30th Ode of Solomon* (Warren Galjour, Baritone)

The concerts were a remarkable success and drew a large and distinguished audience. There was also a tremendous amount of press coverage
—and all of it good. Downes called Stokowski "the brilliant conductor and
protagonist" of the composers represented. He remarked that Stoki introduced each composer who was present. "Each had his admirers and
partisans in the audience and each was warmly applauded by one or
another contingent, sometimes by everybody. . . ."

The works Downes liked most were the Cowell and Hovhaness, which
he labeled "beautiful, sincere and ancestral." Of Ulysses Kay, he declared
that his suite had some "fine, straight-forward writing in it, with perhaps
a little excess of harmonic pepper. . . ."5

Wallingford Riegger's *Study in Sonority*, which Stoki had conducted
decades before with the Philadelphia Orchestra with a component of forty
violins, was given here with the prescribed ten. It was excitingly effective.
Stoki, in brief comments on the *Study in Sonority* and on contemporary
music in general, told his audience: "The next composition is for ten solo
violins, each playing an individual part—a group of four here, another
group of four here, and two in a central group. And these right- and
left-hand groups play in antiphon, a very ancient, as you know, musical
principle, although the music, in other ways, is completely modern in
idiom.

"We hope to record all or some of this music so that those who live
far from cultural centers all over the United States and Canada can, if
they are interested in progressive, modern music, can hear this music in
their homes—also so that they can be sent all over the world, the records,
because there are those, I know from personal experience, in Europe and
in Asia, who think we are a land of materialism. They do not know that
we have our own culture.

"I was very impressed in studying the five compositions that we play
tonight—how completely different is the style of each composer. And yet
back of that style is, I felt, the modern spirit of freedom.

Downes referred to Riegger as an "indefatigable pursuer of dissonance." The title, *Study in Sonority,* is "innocent sounding enough," he
added, "but Mr. Riegger's designs upon the texture of music are not
innocent, or mild, or bed-time stories for the unsophisticated. They make
you think of the wolf: 'The better to eat you with, my dear!' and the title
is a misnomer, for this is no mere study in sonorities. It is a haunted piece,
with intervals and harmonies wholly of the composer's choice."[6] For
Thomson, it was "dissonant in the grand way."

Both liked John Lessard's *Cantilena:* to Virgil it was a "high-bred piece,
delicate and strong";[7] to Downes, "an amusing piece . . . humorous and
in form astonishingly well knit."[8]

"I remember very vividly about the rehearsal," John told me. "Mr.
Stokowski arrived and just before he started my piece, he turned to me
and said, 'I haven't looked at this piece at all and we're going to start the
rehearsal now and see what kind of a piece it is.' I don't know whether
this is completely true or not." I assured John that that could not have
actually been the case, for I had been with Stoki when he was studying
all of the scores that were to be done at the concert. "Well, anyway," John
continued, "he let me know that it hadn't been rehearsed before, which
it certainly hadn't. . . . But he wanted to let me know that I was right
there from the beginning and going to watch him put it together. . . . Bob
Bloom did his oboe part very, very well, and the musicians were very good
musicians, and it was put together very quickly—amazingly fast. It was
a very fine performance."[9]

The second program, on October 28, was equally varied:

> Lou Harrison: Suite for Violin and Piano with Small Orchestra
>   (Anahid Ajemian, violin; Maro Ajemian, piano)
> Elliott Carter: Eight Etudes and a Fantasy for Woodwind Quintet
> Vladimir Ussachevsky: *Sonic Contours*
> Otto Luening: *Low Speed*
>   *Invention*
>   *Fantasy in Space*
> Ben Weber: Symphony on Poems of William Blake (Warren Gal-
>   jour, baritone)

During our conversations in Zurich, we had decided that on one of the
next programs Stoki would introduce electronic music. It was being considered seriously in both Europe and North America. He was aware of the

experiments being done at Radio Diffusion in Paris and in the studios in Cologne. I told him of some of the experiments that were being done by John Cage, Otto Luening, and Vladimir Ussachevsky. I approached John Cage, but after a considerable time it became evident that he would not be able to complete a work in time for the October concert. I then called Vladimir and Otto and they created works for the Museum of Modern Art. We invented the term *tapesichord*, but the title never stuck.

Otto had first become interested in tape music after hearing some experiments done by Vladimir Ussachevsky in 1951 and the following year invited him to come to the composer's conference in Bennington, Vermont, where both of them made various stabs at composing short pieces on tape. I had heard about their efforts, and I invited them to produce some pieces for the Stokowski concert. They were hesitant at first but finally agreed. Otto recalled that "Henry Cowell invited us to come to his farm at Woodstock, where we built up a sort of homemade studio with borrowed equipment of one kind and another. . . . We began working on these pieces. They were *Low Speed, Invention in Twelve Tones,* and *Fantasy in Space,* where I used the flute as a sound source, and Ussachevsky had one he called *Sonic Contours,* where he used a piano as a sound source, and that was it.

"I remember coming down to the museum; we had to cart all of the equipment and set it up ourselves. The whole house was packed with everybody in town there. It was a very distinguished audience. I was sitting there exhausted from the whole ordeal. Then Stokowski came out and made his introductory speech."[10]

The works were introduced in the usual dramatic, Stokowskian manner. After the playing of the Harrison and Carter works, the museum stage was cleared and two huge speakers were trundled out onto the bare stage.

Seven years later David Randolph wrote: "How many of those present in the auditorium of New York's Museum of Modern Art on October 28, 1952, realized that they were witnessing the beginning of a new era in the annals of music in America? As is the case with so many other important happenings—events that are later invested with a certain aura by the passage of time—this was announced with no special fanfare. In fact, the circumstances were becoming less and less dramatic as the evening progressed. . . . The opening work had involved a small orchestra with piano, the next composition enlisted the services of only a quintet of wind players. . . . Mr. Stokowski spoke briefly. . . ."[11]

From a tape made that evening, I have Stokowski's words: "I am often asked: What is tape music, and how is it made? Tape music is music that is composed directly with sound instead of first being written on paper and later made into sound. Just as the painter paints his pictures directly with colors, so the musician composes his music directly with tone. In classical orchestral music many instruments play different groups of notes which sound together. In tape music several or even many types are superimposed; the tapes sound together the groups of tones that are recorded on them. So, essentially, it is a new way of doing what has been done for centuries by old methods."

With that, Stokowski left the stage, and the audience heard for the first time beeps, gurgles, notes from flutes and piano as no sounds of flute or piano had been heard before. In the light of their own developments, these first pieces of Luening and Ussachevsky were quite primitive, but they were historic.

Time magazine titled its review "The Tapesichordists." The reviewer likened Otto's flute to one that "could growl like a bassoon, or thunder like the trump of doom, as well as chirp like a bird." But he concluded philosophically: "They know their 'tapesichord' will never displace the orchestra."[12] The other works were not slighted. Lou Harrison's wonderfully evocative approximation of a gamelan rang poetically. Composer-critic Robert Evett praised the work's "great clarity and freshness."[13]

On the nights of October 29 and 30, 1952, beginning at midnight, Stoki recorded the Lou Harrison Suite and the Ben Weber Symphony for RCA Victor. Ben had vivid recollections of both the concert and the subsequent recording. Before the first rehearsal, Stoki invited him to Gracie Square, and together they went over the score in great detail: "I had never met him prior to that, but he was very cordial and very nice in his aloof way. We sat down with the score and spent two or three hours. I got there about seven thirty in the evening, and during the course of that meeting, his two children came in to say goodnight. He played with them for a little while and introduced me, and then they were put to bed. Anyway, they left and I began to go through the score with him, and I happened to have with me a very pale blue pencil that I then used to autograph scores for publication. He was always fascinated by interesting things that he had never seen before, and he took the pencil and began making marks according to our conversation about the piece, and he made them in that pale blue pencil, which you could hardly see from a distance. It's meant not to print when it's exposed to blueprint light. However, we got through the whole thing, and we came to some satisfactory notions about how to proceed . . . and then he invited me to the rehearsal. . . .

"I got to the rehearsal a little late, and when I came in very quietly, the orchestra was already playing and I didn't recognize what they were doing because they were doing it at about one-third the tempo, which was his habit in the first rehearsal in order to acquaint the musicians who were reading from their parts. I stood there sort of bewildered. I thought it was somebody else's piece. Then I began to recognize it as it came together."

As for the performance at the concert, Ben had remarkable recall: "I myself had made the parts, and they were very carefully cued so that there wouldn't be any problems. It was one of those scores that was spiral-bound, and once the movement got under way, after about five pages, the rhythm changed from 4/4 to 6/4, and the tempo picked up a little bit. But meanwhile by accident, because of the spiral binding, Stokowski turned about four pages past the change of tempo, which he had evidently forgotten, and as he was standing some feet away, he didn't see his own annotations in pale blue pencil. Gradually the movement fell to pieces and finally at the very end of it—you know the subway runs under the museum there—the first movement ended with a low sustained note, the trombone playing a dissonance, the harp playing *bis-bisiando,* and just at that moment the subway went by. So it sounded really quite mysterious. . . . The musicians gradually dropped out, so it began to sound like a piece by Webern, with somebody going toot here and then somebody going boodle-doodle-do. But the singer kept going on and on and on and he was always right! And Stoki was following the text, since he was prepared to go along with the thing and didn't want to stop. So he just went on. . . . In the audience, there was a poet named Ruthven Todd (pronounced Riven). I think it's a Welsh name. He was a Blake specialist, and he congratulated me saying the first movement, especially, was the best setting of William Blake that he had ever heard."[14]

The recordings of the Lou Harrison Suite and the symphonies by Weber and Goeb were completely underwritten by the American Composers Alliance. Since I negotiated the contracts for all three of these recordings, and knowing Victor's habit of withdrawing works if they were not best-sellers, I insisted on a clause added to the contract that would allow ACA to retrieve all right to the works, including tapes, masters, etc. if the recordings were discontinued. Not long after, they were unavailable and ACA found itself the possessor of three Stokowski recordings with no machinery for handling them. It was out of this acquisition that CRI

(Composer's Recordings, Inc.) was born, and on which label each of these performances were later reissued and given a new and long lease of life.

Record reviewers are often more perceptive than critics of live concerts if only because they are able to hear a work several times before committing themselves. Reviews of the records were extravagant. Alfred Frankenstein waxed lyrical about Ben Weber. "I know of no twelve-tone work by an American that says so much so eloquently as this *Symphony on Poems of William Blake. . . .* It achieves, in short, much the same sort of identification between music and poem that is achieved by Alban Berg in *Wozzeck;* and it is not too much to suggest that with this score Ben Weber becomes the Alban Berg of the American twelve-tone school."[15]

Three concert dates had been set up by Schulhof for November and early December, 1952. The first was at the University of Illinois at Urbana, where Stokowski conducted Wallingford Riegger's Music for Brass Choir, along with Beethoven's Seventh Symphony and Monteverdi's *Vespro della Beata Vergine.* Duane Branigan, dean of the Music School at the time, had made arrangements to record the Monteverdi and hoped to have it released on a major label. The preparation for the work had resulted in great excitement among the chorus and members of the orchestra. Both had been trained carefully: the orchestra by Bernard Goodman and the chorus by Paul Young. The soloists were a splendid lot, particularly the tenor, faculty member William Miller.

On the day Miller was to meet Stoki for his first rehearsal, Paul Young burst into his studio and said, " 'Before you meet this man this afternoon, Mr. Miller, I want to tell you that this fellow Stokowski is an S.O.B.' " Miller became apprehensive, but when they met, he found him to be "a very gracious, kindly man" and so they began the rehearsal. Miller asked Stokowski if he wanted any changes and he responded, " 'Mr. Miller, do exactly what you are doing . . . it's just great what you are doing.' The chorus sang better than it knew how—every soloist did, and we really had a marvelous performance."[16]

I must concur with Mr. Miller, for I have played the recording of the concert with great pleasure. The soloists are all fine and handle their respective parts with élan. They were Miriam Stewart, soprano; Dorothy Clark, contralto; William Miller, tenor; and Bruce Foote, baritone. Stokowski conducted with great restraint but with an admirable grasp of the style of this early Italian music. There was no theatricality, and he played everything with a reverential approach that is so different from that which is used when attacking the ecclesiastical ham in Verdi's *Requiem.* The orchestra, too, played with a kind of absorption of the spirit of the work, and while they may have lacked professional sheen, the piece surely benefited from this treatment.

Unfortunately, the recording was never released by a commercial company but only through the facilities of the university—specifically the University Bookstore. Hence, there was literally no critical attention given to it. But by the strangest coincidence this work, which had never been previously recorded, now appeared on three labels within one year: Period 558, Vox 7902, and L'Oiseau Lyre 50021, with Ephrikian, Grischkat, and Lewis as the respective conductors.[17]

By now Stoki had begun to feel keenly that without an orchestra of his own he was at a distinct disadvantage in both concert performances and recording. He had finally realized that RCA, for example, had contracts with various orchestras as well as conductors, and that he had no such advantage. He had complained bitterly to RCA that he felt he was not being favored.[18]

He had constantly brought up the matter of recording contemporary music, which Victor frowned upon. "It could not be to your own best interest to produce too many records of relatively unknown music and of little sales appeal," George Marek answered. And he proposed that if Stoki wished to do contemporary works which Victor did not care to have recorded, he could do so "for any educational or benevolent group or organization." Marek cited the precedent of the Monteverdi on the label of the University of Illinois.

Stoki had wanted to record Beethoven and Brahms symphonies, to which Marek responded that there were already twelve different recordings of the Fifth, twelve of the *Eroica*, and eleven of the Seventh. He conceded that they would be glad to proceed with one Beethoven and one Brahms symphony. He suggested the *Pastorale* of Beethoven and the Second, Third, or Fourth of Brahms. Stoki had already recorded the First.

Marek added one admonition. "We have one suggestion about these recordings, a suggestion which we hear time and again from our dealers: make them with a 'name' orchestra, not with an 'anonymous' orchestra, no matter how good."[19] One wonders whether at such a time Stokowski may have rued his complete separation from the Philadelphia Orchestra. But ever optimistic, he conceived the idea of forming an orchestra drawn from the best players in the university orchestras throughout the country. The All-American Youth Orchestra was to be the model.

Schulhof was enthusiastic and envisioned himself as the manager of a symphony orchestra, as well as the representative of many major conductors. The assemblage of representatives from many universities was the ideal place to launch his idea. Stoki had talked it over with Duane Branigan before agreeing to conduct the Monteverdi program, and he was assured that the deans of many major schools and universities would be present.

He explained that the Collegiate Orchestra would be a nonprofit, noncompetitive, and nonpolitical organization, and that it was his intention to make the orchestra entirely an educational project. He wanted the orchestra to be drawn entirely from students enrolled at universities and colleges, and that it should be national in scope and should represent the top-flight musical talent. Veterans were to be given special consideration.

Students selected to play in the orchestra, which was to include about 120 to 150 players, were to receive scholarships including all traveling and living expenses in connection with the orchestra. Funds, he explained, were to be solicited from foundations and similar groups, as well as from individuals, for a period of three to four years, after which he hoped it would be self-supporting.[20]

Among those present at Stoki's initial presentation were the heads of the music departments of the universities of Illinois, Indiana, Michigan, Minnesota, Oklahoma, Northwestern, and the Cincinnati Conservatory of Music. Stoki was persuasive, and all agreed in principle that the idea was a fine one, and all promised to cooperate in bringing about the project.

But individual enthusiasm and agreement did not, however, mean that that constituted the official sponsorship of their respective institutions. In February, on the strength of this initial response, Schulhof wrote to the deans of each of the universities, saying that Stokowski had asked him to contact them in reference to the Urbana meeting:

> Mr. Stokowski wishes to incorporate the Collegiate Orchestra of America which would be the first necessary step toward realization of such a project and a legally required procedure before we could approach the different foundations for needed funds.
>
> Your organization was among those who enthusiastically supported and sanctioned the formation of such an organization and expressed willingness to act as one of the sponsors. . . .
>
> We will consider this endorsement as a legal document—signifying your institution's support and sponsorship . . . and it will serve to indicate to Mr. Stokowski your agreement and approval for the formation of this organization.[21]

The letter caused some consternation. Earl Moore, of the University
of Michigan, wrote to Schulhof:

> I am sure that there must be some grave misunderstanding. . . .
> None of us present at the meeting at Urbana . . . was in a position
> to speak in any way officially for the organizations we represented and
> it was further made perfectly clear that in no case could these organi-
> zations officially be sponsors.

Moore felt that the most important matter was to discover whether or
not funds would be available and whether it would not be best to set up
an organization to handle the funds if they would be available.[22]

In spite of something less than total support from the universities
themselves, Stoki and Andrew went on to incorporate the orchestra in
New York State.

Appeals were made to the foundations, as well as to individuals and
educational institutions, but the result was most discouraging. In the end
the Collegiate Orchestra of America, Inc., had its existence only on paper.

After Urbana, Stoki proceeded to Detroit, where on November 20 he
conducted, along with music of Schubert, Wagner, and Tchaikovsky, the
first performance of *The Taking of T'ung Kuan* by Jacob Avshalomov.
The Chinese title was neither incongruous nor accidental, for "Jack," as
Avshalomov is known to his friends, was born in Tsingtao, China, in 1919
of a San Franciscan mother and a Siberian-born father, Aaron Avshalomov, who was a distinguished composer. After the war, Jack came
to New York and became a member of the faculty of Columbia.

"While I was teaching at Columbia," Jack told me, "I decided to write
to Stokowski, invoking the name of my father and asking him if he would
have a look at a work of mine. In fact, I made so bold as to send him
The Taking of T'ung Kuan, which ran only eight minutes, thinking that
one should start with a modest-length piece. Within a few weeks I got
a very efficient-sounding note from his secretary saying that the Maestro
had looked over the score and made some personal notes for himself but
that his programs were made up for the next two years. . . . Two years
later I got a nice note saying that Stokowski had programmed it for
Detroit in November of 1952 and could I be there."

Jack proceeded to Detroit and found his way into the auditorium
during the first rehearsal. Stoki was busy rehearsing the Tchaikovsky Fifth
Symphony. Jack sat quietly in the darkened hall, the only one present. "At
a certain point Stokowski stepped down to say a word to the concertmas-

ter, who was Mischakoff, and out of the corner of his eye he caught a glimpse of me sitting there. They exchanged another word and both sort of peered at me, and Mischakoff was shaking his head, obviously not recognizing me. Stokowski then remounted the podium and from his lordly station asked whether I had permission to be at the rehearsal. So I stood up and said, 'Permission, no, but cause, yes.' And then I said my name. Stokowski broke into a laugh and turned to the orchestra and said, 'Oh, we have the composer.'

"So he sort of waved me down and we shook hands . . . and he announced to me that he had to work on the Tchaikovsky but then would do my piece and I should make notes of what I would like changed and tell him and he would change it. Well, the rehearsal wended its merry way along through the toils of Tchaikovsky until about ten minutes to noon, when the rehearsal was to end. My piece being an eight-minute piece, it didn't seem to me that it left very much time to rehearse it. But he finished the Tchaikovsky and got to my piece, and I was absolutely entranced. In the famous words of our friend Frank Wigglesworth, there's no music like one's own music. . . . Although the first tempo was never really quite as fast as I had hoped it would be, I was able to hear for the first time what my imagined music was like in the hands of profession-als."[23]

Despite its brevity, Jack's piece seemed to add a needed note to the program. The Detroit critic wrote: *"The Taking of T'ung Kuan,* ending as it did in a dissonance of brass, injected a sorely needed bit of spice. . . . It isn't solely dissonance of old harmony that makes the new composi-tion a desirable concert piece. The composer, a young man born and reared in China, has a profound knowledge of the orchestra, and puts it to most effective use. . . ."[24]

San Francisco was always one of Stokowski's favorite cities, and Schul-hof had booked seven concerts with the San Francisco Symphony be-tween December 4 and 20, 1952. It was during the first week that he gave one of his memorable performances when he conducted a selection of scenes from *Boris Godunov.* The number of them was determined by the fact that they were to be recorded for RCA immediately after the last performance. The performance and recording featured the brilliant basso Nicola Rossi-Lemeni, the San Francisco Opera Chorus, and the Sym-phony. For this performance and recording Stoki chose the Rimsky-Korsakov version.

After the hour-long synthesis, the audience "rose, stamped, yelled, and carried on generally to indicate that this was one of the major events in the . . . current season," wrote Alfred Frankenstein. He felt that Stokowski, Rossi-Lemeni, the other vocal soloists, and the huge chorus produced something quite different from that which one experiences in the opera when staged. "For the one thing," he wrote, "Rimsky-Korsakoff's liquid, luxurious orchestration was more often carried to the fore, and for another, the chorus because it was big and was not distracted by stage business, was able at last to fulfill the star role. . . ."[25]

On December 8, two days after the last performance, all of the same forces performed these scenes again for the first RCA session and then completed the recording in a second session on December 10. Peter Hugh Reed had high praise for the results. "The true protagonist of this record is Stokowski and the San Francisco Symphony. The latter is wonderful in sound and rightfully dramatically puissant without stealing the scene when chorus or singer are present. Stokowski is a true man of the theater, and like all such men he knows when to play up a scene and when to underplay one. . . ."[26]

Gabriel Pascal, the noted film producer, had had several conversations with Stokowski about the possibility of turning his version of *Boris* into a TV special. Pascal wrote to Stoki: "I am now making my program for 52 television pictures and would like to incorporate Boris Godunov. . . ." He also discussed finances, suggesting that Stoki should receive 35 percent of all profits and Rossi-Lemeni 15 percent, with 50 percent going to his Italian company. He concluded with "my most affectionate regards to Gloria, to you and *e i due principini*." At the top of the letter Stoki scrawled "wrote delay."[27] Nothing happened.

(56)

Contemporary Music

S YMBOLICALLY, if not officially, the Contemporary Music Society was
born on October 21, 1952, in the wood-paneled boardroom of the
Ford Foundation. Even before the concerts in the Museum of
Modern Art, Stoki had expressed his willingness to offer his services to the
various groups promoting contemporary music in the New York area. Jack
Turner and I, both of us being at CBS at the time, tried to pull together
and relate Stoki's offer to the numerous disparate, competitive rather than
cooperative, groups and societies.

John Coburn Turner had been at Princeton and while still there was
injured in an auto accident that left him paralyzed from the hips down
and kept him confined to a wheelchair. But Jack was a brilliant as well
as a handsome and most personable man; and, too, he was a bona fide
idealist. At CBS he was in the public affairs department, and about this
time he left to work for the Ford Foundation. It was he who arranged the
meeting in the boardroom—the foundation supplying its facilities if not
its support.

Jack and I sent telegrams to the heads of various musical organizations,
composers, and other representative individuals—all in Stokowski's name.
Assembled for the meeting were representatives of ASCAP, BMI, the
Musicians' Union, the National Music Council, the League of Composers
(represented by Claire Reis), the International Society for Contemporary
Music, UNESCO, Columbia University, New York University, Juilliard,
Eastman-Rochester, the Voice of America, the Musician's Trust Fund
(headed by Samuel Rosenbaum), the Society for the Publication of Ameri-

can Music, the American Composers Alliance, composers (Douglas Moore, Otto Luening, William Schuman, Roy Harris, Ulysses Kay, Henry Cowell, Howard Hanson), and a substantial representation by the press.

With Roy Harris, left, and the author (c. 1952)

When Stoki called the meeting to order, he began by asking the group what they thought could be done to advance the cause of contemporary music. Considering the amount of preliminary discussion and the positive aspect of his offer to give his services to the cause, it seemed like a most modest and in fact negative approach. Bill Schuman was the first to respond in a question to Stoki that at the time seemed both rude and critical. But he was actually right. Bill recalled: "I had to question him and say, 'Mr. Stokowski, we were brought here so that we could hear your ideas. Won't you speak of them?' And he remained absolutely silent. In other words, he seemed to be someone who functioned in terms of specifics. While he was a leader of men when they were in an orchestra, he was not a leader of men when they were just sitting before him in a room discussing something. It is not to accuse him of not having those attributes, because many fine musicians and artists do not have them, but yet one would have expected him to because it would have seemed a natural part of his character."[1]

It was at about this point in the proceedings that I asked for the floor and outlined Stoki's proposal as we had so thoroughly discussed it. Carl Haverlin rose and pledged a contribution of $5,000 from BMI and Stokowski offered a personal contribution of one thousand.[2] There was applause, and a ripple of well-being spread about, but not another offer materialized. Then, each of the various insulated groups went about their self-interested ways.

In spite of its somewhat halting start, the Contemporary Music Society became a reality and continued to function even after Stokowski's death. It was to provide him with significant appearances in Carnegie Hall when he conducted Carl Orff's *Carmina Burana* and on another occasion celebrated his fiftieth anniversary as a conductor in America. It was also instrumental in providing funds for the preparation of the score of the Ives Fourth Symphony, which was to be one of Stokowski's late, great conducting triumphs.

His immediate concern was the ACA concert that he would conduct in the Museum of Modern Art on February 22, 1953, and he asked me to bring him scores that would be effective. I again combed the library and brought a great collection for him to examine. One work was the *Unanswered Question* by Charles Ives. Stoki had never programmed an Ives work and, in fact, through the years when he had so assiduously perused new scores, he showed not a whit of interest in Ives. Perhaps some of my own devotion to Ives rubbed off on him. I told him of my own experiences in becoming an Ives afficionado. I told him how I was first brought to Ives' house on Seventy-fourth Street by Clifton Furness, who had introduced Elliott Carter to Ives at an even earlier date. The day we arrived at the house, Ives was feeling too ill to cope with seeing a new person, and I waited downstairs while Ives and Furness conversed on the second floor.

Elliott was more fortunate than I. Furness, who was teaching at the Horace Mann High School in New York, where Elliott was then a student, took him to visit Ives in 1924, at a time when Ives was in far better health, and a friendship developed between young Elliott Carter and Ives that was to last for many years.[3] Goddard Lieberson, another Ives afficionado, had written a very fine article for *Musical America* in 1939,[4] and about that time he and Elliott Carter hit upon the idea of interesting Stoki in his music. "At a certain period right after the war, I felt very much that Ives should be played," Elliott remarked. "It was actually around the time of his seventieth birthday, I believe, and I talked to Goddard and he arranged a luncheon with Stokowski and we talked about it. Stokowski was not terribly interested, as I remember."[5]

I was apparently more persuasive. *The Unanswered Question* was the first work he chose for the succeeding museum concert. The program was as follows:

> Charles Ives: *The Unanswered Question* (1908)
> Halsey Stevens: Suite No. 1 (1945)
> Henry Brant: *Signs and Alarms* (1953) (First Performance)
> Lou Harrison: Canticle No. 3 (1941)
> Peggy Glanville-Hicks: *Letters from Morocco* (1952) (William
>   Hess, Tenor) (First Performance)
> Jacob Avshalomov: *Evocations* (Concerto for Clarinet and Cham-
>   ber Orchestra) (1947) (Herbert Tichman, Clarinet)

A sizable crowd had gathered in the Sunday evening cold on Fifty-third Street even before the last of Garbo's *Camille* had flickered through the projector in the Museum's theater. Being a longer movie than most in the Museum series, there was just enough time for the attendants to sweep away an unusual number of not-too-modern peanut shells, cigarette butts, and a substantial amount of detritus left behind by the polyglot audience that the Museum's movies attract. The musicians—bless them—then began loading the stage with one of the most striking percussion assemblages New Yorkers had ever seen. It ranged from dragon mouths to whiskey cases. Lou Harrison, whose Canticle No. 3 employs these unusual curiosities, declared that the timbre of the Hiram Walker case is superior to that of most popular brands. He had also done considerable research on automobile brake drums and plumber's pipes, which he had included in his percussion group. Instruments of a more conventional nature—Turkish cymbals, Chinese tom-toms, cistras, temple blocks, elephant bells, Chinese wood blocks, water buffalo bells, cow bells, drums, tam-tams and xylophones—littered the stage.[6]

While the program was labeled "contemporary," Ives' touching score was vintage 1908. And Stokowski, instead of describing it to his listeners, preferred to have Ives' own description printed in the program:

The strings play *ppp* throughout, with no change in tempo. They are to represent "The Silences of the Druids" who know, see, and hear nothing. The trumpet intones "The Perennial Question of Existence" and states it in the same tone of voice each time. But the hunt for the "Invisible Answer" undertaken by the flute and other human beings becomes gradually more active, faster and louder through the rough *animando* to a *con fuoco*. The "Fighting Answerers," as time goes on . . . seem to realize a futility, and begin to mock "The Question"—the strife is over for the moment. After they disappear, "The Question" is asked for the last time, and the "Silences" are heard beyond in "Undisturbed Solitude."

Stoki had the strings massed in the center with the four woodwinds to his right; the trumpet was placed at the back of the auditorium. To most in the audience, the Ives work was at that time completely unknown. "The beauty of its sound," quoth Virgil Thomson, "and the integrity of its simple thought so delighted all that the voluntary repetition of this 'Unanswered Question' was a welcome gesture on the conductor's part." It was at that moment, I believe, that Stoki's real interest in Ives began.

Thomson called Harrison's Canticle for flute, guitar and seven percussionists "one of those delicate and delicious symphonies masterfully sustained that are a unique achievement of the composer."[7]

To hear his letters that he had sent from Morocco, Paul Bowles arrived at the concert with a tall Moroccan in full burnoose and Libby Holman in *purdah* by way of dark glasses, while a number of Orientals in turbans and saris lent an additional dash of cosmopolitanism.[8]

Paul's letters were pure poetry, and Peggy Glanville-Hicks set six fragments of them, imaginatively, using a kind of Arabic vocal melisma that seemed most appropriate to the text. One of Paul's letters read:

I have found a new candy,—hashish almond bar.
I shall bring you some.
It's absolutely unbelievable in its effects,
But you have to eat it carefully like Alice nibbling
The mushroom;
Otherwise—the transportation is rather sudden, like gusts
Of golden wind along the vertebrae—and an upward sweep
Into the clouds.

William Hess was the very capable tenor who sang Peggy's settings of Paul's songs. He had rehearsed them with her at the piano, but the orchestral rehearsal was his first experience with Stokowski. "I was so absolutely fascinated with his hands that I could not find the beat. Freddy Klein the horn player was chuckling because he had known this was going to happen and at the first break he came up to me and said, 'What's your trouble, Bill?' I said, 'How do you find the beat? I can't find it.' He said, 'Don't worry. Just look at the concertmaster.' So that's how I solved the problem. . . . And we all got along just fine. And Stoki patted me on the shoulder at his party afterward and said, 'You are a very good musician.' "[9]

The party to which Bill referred was in a sense an elegant quasi disaster. Invitations had been sent out in both Leopold's and Gloria's names. The invitation simply read:

> Mr. and Mrs. Leopold Stokowski
> request the pleasure of your company
> at
> 10 Gracie Square
> on
> February 22nd
> at about 10:30 o'clock
> after the concert

R.S.V.P   Informal

Most receptions following concerts are buffet affairs. I know I was astonished to discover when we arrived at 10 Gracie that Gloria had planned it as a sit-down supper with small tables scattered through various rooms of their huge apartment. When the news of a post-concert party at the Stokowskis was noised about the Museum, it seemed as though everyone there intended to go whether invited or not. After all of the guests were seated, new arrivals began to congregate in the entrance hall like the standee line at Radio City Music Hall at Christmas time. The situation was indeed an awkward one, but the caterer did something akin to the loaves-and-fishes miracle and managed to bring in enough food for all. There were at least three shifts.

After the concert, I wrote an article about it for the *ACA Bulletin* called "Alchemy by Stokowski." It was illustrated with sketches by Carl Malouf, which later Stokowski treasured.[10]

Stoki wrote me a note:

Dear Oliver
    I only this morning found your article on alchemy and must thank you for its humor and deep perception. You have a wonderful under-

standing of the whole situation, of the few who are with us and the
many against, for the liberation of music from outworn concepts; and
you know how to express all this with just enough irony and vision.
I so much enjoy working with you.

Always your friend,
Leopold[11]

Stoki's interest in the Ford Foundation "Omnibus" program, which
was aired on CBS with Alistair Cooke, began even before the first program
had gone on the air. There were many meetings with Jack Turner and
with Robert Saudek to discuss possibilities. In the spring of 1952, Jack
Turner had discussed a series of programs in which Stoki would participate. "We are all delighted," he wrote, "at the prospect of having you play
a prominent role in our series, and we all feel that our discussions thus
far have been most stimulating and fruitful." Turner stated that Stoki's
participation would not be limited to music but would draw upon other
broad areas, such as the dance, painting, sculpture, and other fields of art.
He had planned a series of five films, one on Stokowski himself, another
on "Renaissance man," one on cathedrals and churches, "with organ
music performed by you," one on instruments of the orchestra, and
another one left undecided.

After meeting with Andrew Schulhof and hammering out the various
financial and technical details, Turner wrote: "We recognize fully that
your approach to this series is primarily as a mutual artistic venture and
not solely as a commercial enterprise. And we are gratified that the
financial guarantees you have asked are scaled to our budgetary needs
rather than to your normal range of performance fees."[12]

Turner and his staff outlined their concept of the "Profile of Leopold
Stokowski." They agreed that "it should be in the general nature of a
'New Yorker' Profile, but done with motion picture film. It would com-
prise a story illustrated with films of Mr. Stokowski home with his family
studying a score, entertaining friends, listening to the playback of a recording in the studio control room . . . clips from "100 Men and a Girl,' and
'Fantasia' . . . his paintings, filmed comments about him by players such
as Tabuteau, Kincaid, etc."[13]

Stoki was very interested in doing a telecast using Mussorgsky's *Pictures
at an Exhibition* as a basis. "I am sure it will make an interesting program
to music lovers and others," he wrote to Bob Saudek. "I have recorded

this with Victor and Columbia. Let us obtain both recordings, compare them, and choose the better."[14] He then outlined in detail various phases of the proposed telecast.

Stoki concerned himself with every aspect of the project and was meticulous in his attention to detail. Paul Feigay, who was the assistant producer for "Omnibus," was in charge of this first Stokowski appearance on the series, which took place on December 28, the day that Stoki had selected. The music was taken from his recordings.

Paul told me that for some reason the original Victor Hartmann pictures were not used and that they had engaged artists to make their own realizations of the pictures. John Butler was chosen to choreograph some sequences. Stoki spoke charmingly and the program was a telling success. "We all loved him," Paul remarked.

With all the various suggestions and exchange of ideas in meetings and letters, Stokowski conducted only one "Omnibus" program—on April 12, when he did Haydn's *Toy* Symphony and Britten's *Young Person's Guide to the Orchestra.*

The experience was somewhat traumatic. Mary Ahearn, staff associate for the program, had selected seven attractive youngsters to play the toy instruments: five boys and two girls ranging in age from six to eight years. When Stoki assembled them to play with the orchestra there was chaos. "It's impossible," Stoki shouted. "You have children here who can't read music." Apparently no one had thought about that little detail. "You'll have to do some quick work," he continued. "Find children who can read. It's delightful if it is done right."

While older performers were recruited, Stoki, the indomitable showman, decided to let the musically illiterate youngsters perform one movement, the simplest, and precede the program in a rehearsal. It worked. Stoki encouraged them even when the cuckoo notes went up instead of down.[15] As I recall, the program was not exactly a resounding success. Stoki in his formal Edwardian cutaway seemed out of another and quite distant world.

Ten days after the program, Stoki set sail on the *Queen Elizabeth* for concerts in Rome, Florence, Lugano, Bergen, and Helsinki. "The Florence Festival—the Maggio Musicale—decided to do *Amahl and the Night Visitors,*" Gian Carlo Menotti told me. "Before I could say anything, I was told that Stokowski was going to conduct it with Simionato in the part of the mother and with Balanchine for the choreography. Well, it was quite a wonderful trio, but when I heard that Stokowski was conducting, I threw my head up in the air. I said, 'You can't give *Amahl* to Stokowski. He will absolutely wreck it. It's not his cup of tea. If it had been any of my other operas, but not *Amahl*. . . . I was really so pessimistic about it, but the director of the festival told me that it was too late—Stokowski was signed. I said all right, but I was looking forward to a disaster. Well, there is a wonderful thing about the man. He immediately understood the spirit of the opera and gave, what I believe, was one of the very best performances ever of *Amahl*. He did it with such delicacy, with such simplicity, and with marvelous sound, just as Balanchine did the most delicious, simple choreography . . . they are both great artists and they entered the spirit of a child's imagination. . . . Having worked with Stokowski on *Amahl*, my respect for him grew immensely, because I had never expected this sort of an interpretation from him."[16]

For some curious reason, Menotti had been savaged by the Italian critics for his previous opera performances. *Time*'s Florentine correspondent observed: "Standing in the wings, Menotti felt reasonably confident this time: Leopold Stokowski conducted with a sure hand, a dressy international audience admired the handsome settings, stopped the show after a flashing dance sequence, and cheered up ten curtain calls for the cast at the end. Even the stage electrician admitted he liked it."

But several critics carped. One at Rome's *Il Tempo* sneered: "Music? Zero. Originality? Artistic taste? Zero." But Milan's prestigious *Corriere Della Sera* called it "a vibrant success. . . . Menotti is an artist of tradition, a most Italian artist." Gian Carlo remarked: "Well, the reviews weren't all good. But the good ones were real raves—the first I've gotten in Italy. I must admit it feels wonderful."[17] Stoki, too, was extremely pleased.

In Bergen he conducted works by two Norwegian composers: Harald Saeverud and Fartein Valen. During a visit to the United States some time before, I had arranged a reception for Saeverud, where he met Stokowski. Later I wrote him asking him about Stoki's appearance in Norway. He responded:

> The city of Bergen is rather small but it can boast of having the third or fourth oldest symphony orchestra in the world, dating back to 1765! The great Leopold decided to spread his glory over our bold and risky enterprise, and the day he arrived—oh! we were happy! But he had insisted upon being smuggled into town to avoid the press photographers. On the railway station he therefore was guided to a secret exit, and so nobody could report to the papers if he didn't look quite young any more.

As he had chosen a piece of mine—*The Ballad of Revolt*— on his program, he kindly asked me to discuss with him some of the details. He also gave an exquisite rendition of *The Cemetery by the Sea* by the Norwegian composer Fartein Valen who had died the year before. The concert, which was repeated the next day, was a tremendous success and I believe he really felt happy during his stay in Bergen. . . .[18]

In the Bergen audience was Jon Embretsen. Jon was a part of the Norwegian Information Service in New York, and like a puppeteer he pulled more strings than any other foreign consular officer around. It was he who had suggested to Stoki that he conduct the Valen piece. "It is a beautiful piece and has plenty of mood, and while I knew that Valen was not popular with the concert public in Norway, I felt sure that he could surprise them. I gave him the score and he liked it and he really showed them in Bergen. With his usual flair, he gave the Valen piece a superb rendition—so much so that at the end the audience was stunned, and there was this dead silence of several seconds before a thunderous applause broke out."[19]

Stoki enjoyed Bergen and often recalled going down to the harbor early in the morning to watch the fishermen come in with their fish for the market. He also visited Edvard Grieg's house in Trollhaugen just outside of Bergen, and there he made a sketch of the room in which Grieg had written *Peer Gynt.*[20]

Shortly before the concert, Kristian Lange, of the Norwegian Broadcasting Corporation, did an interview with Stoki that was used during the intermission when the concert was broadcast. Fortunately, the Norwegians have a sense of history and kept a copy of the broadcast in their archives. When I contacted Kristian Lange, whom I had known through the International Music Council of UNESCO, he very kindly sent me a copy of Stoki's talk. From it I culled the following: "I think that Bergen is very fortunate to have so great an orchestra under so great a conductor as Garaguly. This orchestra is full of fine players and Garaguly has brought them to a high state of ensemble. What Bergen needs, though, is a theater with stage suitable for concerts, and opera, and drama, and cinema—and with flexible seating capacity so that a small audience can be there, a medium size, or a very large audience—large enough for the future growth of Bergen, because Bergen will be always greater and greater. And that hall, of course, must have one thing—good acoustics."

In response to Kristian's inquiry about his reasons for selecting Sae-

With Jean Sibelius in 1953 when Stokowski conducted the Helsinki City Symphony.
Stokowski kept this autographed photograph in his score of Sibelius' First Symphony

verud's *Ballad of Revolt* and Valen's *The Cemetery by the Sea*, Stokowski
replied: "I did study many scores of Norwegian music, and I liked most
the two that we are playing tonight because, in my opinion, Saeverud's
music is an expression of the dynamic, vital, powerful qualities of the
Norwegian people and the other music of Valen is an expression of the
deep inner life of the people of Norway."[21]

On arriving in Helsinki, Stoki immediately proceeded to visit Sibelius
in his rustic lakeside retreat. They had a pleasant time together and Stoki
invited the great Finn to attend one of his all-Sibelius concerts with the
Helsinki City Symphony. Sibelius did attend. The program included
Finlandia, Symphony No. 1, music to Maeterlinck's *Pélleas et Mélisande*
and the Seventh Symphony.

I asked conductor Jussi Jalas, who is Sibelius' son-in-law, about Sibelius'
reaction to the concert. "Yes," he answered, "he appreciated it very
much." Then, since Jalas himself was one of the principal conductors of
the orchestra, I queried him about his own reaction to Stoki's conducting

there. "I was impressed by him in Helsinki," he responded, "at the very first rehearsal with the orchestra when he read the First Symphony. I had never heard our orchestra play so well. It was just formidable. But somehow at the concert it was not as good; it was more quiet and highly professional, but it did not have the terrific impact that the rehearsal had.[22] The critic of his concerts was enthusiastic, saying that he got a Philadelphia sound from our orchestra. I still consider him one of the great Maestros of our time."[23]

Following his two Helsinki concerts, Leopold left for Paris, then on to Cherbourg to board the *Queen Elizabeth* for New York on the twenty-fifth of June. On shipboard Stoki penned a handwritten note to Sibelius:

> June 1953
>
> Dear Master
>
> I was *deeply* moved by your truly inspired music. Thank you for such a thrilling and unforgettable experience.
>
> With affection
> Always your friend
> Leopold Stokowski[24]

Stoki was indeed deeply touched by the Sibelius music, and a month after he returned to New York, he wrote a second and longer letter to him:

> 7 August 1953
>
> Dear Friend
>
> I am still so strongly under the impression of your music in Helsinki that I feel I must write to you again. I hope I am not taking too much of your time.
>
> I was so powerfully moved by your 7th Symphony. I think you heard it the first night, but in the larger hall the second night the orchestra played it much better. I am so impressed by the organic growth of its form, and how you have unified all the conventional movements—such as scherzo, slow movement, etc. into one integrated whole. All these different types and tempi and musical textures have relation to each other and make a perfect Symphony, without silence and pause between the different parts, with one continuous stream of musical thought and feeling.
>
> Your Seventh Symphony is on an enormous scale, and the music of "Pelleas et Melisande" is so briefly stated and

emotionally powerful. I am so impressed by your equal mastery of large and small forms. . . .

With affectionate thoughts and deepest admiration,

Leopold Stokowski[25]

The fall of 1953 was a most fecund one. It again brought Stoki back into the New York limelight. Carl Haverlin, who was president of BMI in both the United States and Canada, conceived the idea of presenting a program of all-Canadian music and asked my help in interesting Leopold in the idea. He was interested, to be sure. We met several times and the whole matter was formalized at a meeting at the Netherland Club in Rockefeller Plaza.[26]

The committee to select works for the program consisted of Sir Ernest MacMillan, Claude Champagne, Henry Cowell, Boyd Neel, Wilfred Pelletier, Walter Piston, and William Schuman, and the program they chose was a most interesting one.[27]

Of all the works which Stoki then examined, it was the *Tabuh-Tabuhan* of Colin McPhee that interested him most. He knew Colin and, in fact, Colin prepared a Lucullan Balinese-style feast for him one night at my apartment. Colin was a great gourmet; he had studied at Le Cordon Bleu in Paris and in Bali had learned all of the secrets and niceties of that type of oriental cuisine. He claimed he was the only man who knew seven different ways to prepare bats. What Colin served was varied indeed, but bats were not included.

He was working at the time on his extensive tome on *Music in Bali* and he and Stoki huddled in animated conversation about the music, dance, and various rituals practiced on the island. Colin on one of these occasions gave Stoki a copy of his book *House in Bali* which Stoki told me he had greatly enjoyed.

While studying *Tabuh-Tabuhan* prior to the concert, Stoki wrote to Colin: "I am not sure whether we can form the nuclear gamelan in the front-center of the stage, because we shall have a rather large orchestra and there may not be room. Another possibility would be to put the group at the front to the right of the conductor. Then, we would not disturb the strings. You and I can work this out together at the rehearsals."

Colin's "nuclear gamelan" was a vital part of the work. He used two grand pianos and an exotic array of percussion instruments. "Of course, my tam-tam is at your disposal, but I think Bratman [Carroll Bratman of

Friday Evening, October 16, 1953 at 8:30 o'clock

ARTHUR JUDSON *presents*

CANADIAN MUSIC AT CARNEGIE HALL

A Concert by

LEOPOLD STOKOWSKI

and his Orchestra

Sponsored by

BROADCAST MUSIC, INC.

and

BMI CANADA, LIMITED

Program Notes on Page Six

PROGRAM

NEW YORK PREMIERE OF ALL WORKS

Pantomime .... PIERRE MERCURE
    For Wind Instruments and
    Percussions

Concerto for Solo Violin and
Orchestra .... ALEXANDER BROTT
    Allegro giusto
    Andante
    Allegro vivo
        NOEL BRUNET, *Soloist*

Tabuh-Tabuhan .... COLIN McPHEE
    Ostinatos
    Nocturne
    Finale

INTERMISSION

Antiphonie .... FRANCOIS MOREL

Two Mystical Songs of John Donne
For High Voice and Orchestra .... GODFREY RIDOUT
    1—Thou hast made me. and shall
       thy work decay?
    2—At the round Earth's imagined corners.
        LOIS MARSHALL, *Soloist*

Coronation Suite .... HEALEY WILLAN
    1—Prelude
    2—Ring out, ye crystall sphears (Milton)
    3—Interlude
    4—Come ready lyre
    5—Come thou beloved of Christ

The WESTMINSTER CHOIR
DR. JOHN FINLEY WILLIAMSON, *Director*

Carroll Musical Instruments] has a still better one. We will try both,"
Stoki added.[28]

Before the concert began the event may have looked more like one of
political and diplomatic significance than musical. The hall was draped
with Canadian colors and representatives from practically every delegation to the United Nations were present. Especially chartered planes from
Toronto and Montreal brought down several hundred eager Canadian
enthusiasts. "But the music itself made the evening's real news," wrote
Time magazine.[29] Virgil Thomson thought that Colin McPhee's *Tabuh-
Tabuhan* was "the evening's most brilliant and striking work. . . . It may
be the ending-piece that all conductors are looking for, something to be
used in place of Ravel's *Daphnis et Chloé.*" He also liked Morel's *Antiphonie,* which he called "another lovely piece, an orchestral meditation
on modal melodies of Gregorian cast."[30]

There was extensive coverage in all of the other New York papers, as
well as many in Canada. The reaction was unanimously favorable. Music
periodicals and newsmagazines also gave it ample space. *Newsweek,* after
praising the works of each of the composers and labeling the concert "a
sell out and a rousing success," added this short and pertinent paragraph:
"Stokowski's role as a champion of new music is a long-time one. Aside
from last week's Canadian concert, he is also currently conducting CBS
Radio's new Twentieth Century Concert Hall (Sunday, 1–1:30 P.M.
EST). As produced and directed by Oliver Daniel, Twentieth Century
Concert Hall is doing a rare thing for a radio network, for its repertoire
is two thirds contemporary, a factor which led the American Composers
Alliance, an affiliate of BMI, to join CBS in its presentation. Stokowski's
advice to listeners wary of 'new' music: 'Keep the mind open, keep the
heart open.'"[31]

57

The 20th Century
Concert Hall

O NE of the most inventive, provocative, and generally excellent
series of music programs ever presented on radio was the series
called "Invitation to Music," which was the brainchild of Bernard
Herrmann and James Fassett. It featured the CBS Symphony Orchestra
with Herrmann as the principal conductor. Guests included Alfredo Antonini, Sir Thomas Beecham, Nicolai Berezowsky, Paul Hindemith,
Darius Milhaud, Igor Stravinsky, Fritz Reiner, and, on March 19, 1947,
Leopold Stokowski.

The soloists who appeared were the most prestigious at that time, but
they were not engaged for their reputations or virtuosity but for their
willingness and ability to perform rare and unusual works of all styles and
eras. It was the repertoire that was important.

One new work which was selected as a radio premiere was the *Metamorphosen* of Richard Strauss. Stoki had been a friend and admirer of Strauss
since the early days in Philadelphia. Would he be interested in conducting
Strauss' latest work, his *Metamorphosen?* He would! And although the
work had had public performances by Koussevitzky and the Boston Symphony, this CBS performance would be the first radio broadcast.

It originated in Studio 21 on East Fifty-second Street, and Stoki arrived
for the single rehearsal, which ran from 7:30 to 11:00 P.M., in his usual
immaculate manner. After being greeted by his friend Nicky Berezowsky,
he began the rehearsal. It was a curious one. He began by reading through
the work from beginning to end, and then successively doing the same

on the several sequential readings that made up the entire rehearsal. The end result was a suave, quasi-improvisational performance that lulled rather than excited. It was not a world-shaking evening. But Stokowski, who had been an avid listener to "Invitation to Music" programs, remembered the occasion pleasantly when we discussed it years later.

It was on the pattern of this series that we began to plan a new one. For several seasons I had had a program that was aired on Sunday afternoons called "Serenade for Strings." It was a "no budget" show conducted by Alfredo Antonini. It began as a nondescript, salon-music sort of thing, but gradually we began to slip in new contemporary pieces and classic tidbits.

It was this time slot that I had in mind for the new series of programs about which Leopold and I talked at length on what might be programmed and what forces would be required. Early in 1953 I made a formal proposal to the CBS program board. And it was with some trepidation, because this was a time when the tail was now wagging the dog. Television had passed its prepuberal stage and was now adolescently commanding all attention. For radio programs, neither CBS nor any of the other networks at that time showed much vital interest. I pointed out that ASCAP was currently supporting a series of programs from the Eastman School conducted by Howard Hanson and that there might be some subvention from BMI or its subsidiary, ACA. Since I was at the time the coordinating manager of ACA, I felt quite sure of my ground.

I had talked over this project with BMI President, Carl Haverlin, and he offered to reimburse ACA so that it might contribute to the program for the payment of conductors and soloists. The amount was under $4,000. With that financial ammunition, I pressed forward with the idea. I emphasized that Stokowski would be agreeable to conduct at least six of a series of thirteen broadcasts but would do so only with the proviso that no conductor of lesser stature be engaged to conduct the succeeding concerts. By good fortune, Stoki liked Alfredo Antonini, who was at that time on the staff at CBS. He was entirely agreeable to embrace the project with Alfredo as his successor. Alfredo was a meticulous craftsman imbued with all the Italian warmth needed to kindle melodic lines and make them sing. Stokowski knew well that Alfredo was one of the most gifted technicians on the scene, and he warmly endorsed him as his successor on the proposed series.

Considering the enormous income which CBS was then enjoying, the

arrangement seems almost unbelievable. It provided that ACA pay $250
for each of the programs broadcast and all rights would remain vested in
CBS.

It was duly accepted by Henry Cowell for the American Composers
Alliance and by Adrian Murphy, president of CBS Radio, a Division of
Columbia Broadcasting System, Inc.[1]

To keep him informed, I wrote to Leopold, who was then on tour
conducting in Seattle:

> The program board here at CBS was most enthusiastic about the
> idea of resuming a series of unusual musical programs but they listed
> one point which I believe is quite valid. They pointed out that at the
> present time we could not have a series longer than a few weeks
> before the change to lighter programs for the summer would begin
> . . . they felt it would be far more practical, and certainly more
> appropriate, to begin this project in the fall. They also pointed out
> that we would be able to build up a staunch publicity campaign which
> would prepare the listening audience for a series that would be an
> event of real importance in the present development of radio. . . . It
> has occurred to me that this might also be a great advantage in
> furthering interest in our Contemporary Music Society plans.[2]

Early in September the first announcements of the new series appeared
in the press. But before the series actually began, Stoki conversed with
Dwight Cooke on the initial broadcasts of his own series called "Dwight
Cooke's Guest Book." Stoki explained that he felt that the most exciting
and significant development in the United States was decentralization.
No longer was the serious making of music confined to the major cities
but was emergent everywhere across the country. The "dark side" of the
American music scene, he felt, was the shortage of opportunity for the
American composer to be heard. He blamed both the managers and the
cautious board members with their eyes on the box office. He suggested
a government-sponsored plan to underwrite the production of programs
of American music. If the government would not do so, he suggested that
the burden might be eased by the broadcasting industry, foundations, and
public-spirited citizens. He also suggested an increased use of American
soloists.[3]

On the second broadcast the following evening, Stoki described three
types of listeners: first, those who wanted only modern music; second,
those who wanted only the familiar classics; and third, those who have an
open mind and like both types of music. He then explained that he

believed there were four types of composers. "Well, one type," he said, "they have something to say in music, they have ideas, they have inspiration, they have melodies and harmonies and rhythms which are new and typical of them and are typical of our time and typical of our country, and they also have good techniques. They know how to express that music. That's one type. A second type: they have ideas but they have no technique. Some of them can't even write it down, they can't even write a melody down. They have to bring in somebody else. They sing or whistle a melody to them, somebody else writes it down for them, and a third person puts harmonies to it, and a fourth person orchestrates it.

". . . Now there's another type. They do not really have anything to say in music, but they say it splendidly, because they have wonderful technique. They've studied harmony and counterpoint and orchestration and all the rest of these things in some very good conservatoire, and they know how to do it, but they don't have anything to say.

"And a fourth type are those who have nothing to say. . . . They have a love for music, and they would like to compose great music, and they would like to have the technique to do it, but they just have neither of those things, and they're very unhappy persons."

Dwight asked Stoki whether he had any sage advice for listeners. He remarked that that was a difficult question to answer, but he offered some of his thoughts. "To listen to really great music—music that has inspiration, that really has ideas and is well expressed technically, I think it is best not to listen intellectually, because music speaks to other and perhaps much higher faculties in our minds and in our beings than the mere intellect . . . we should listen very simply and with the heart."

He advised listeners to be honest and if they did not like a modern score to say so, but at least to listen and give it a chance.

His most trenchant point was this. "The great thing about music, both modern and music of the masters, *you must enjoy*. If you don't enjoy, what's the use of it? The same with life. If you don't enjoy life, what's the use of living?" And as if he were making a final summation, he concluded: "Keep the mind open, keep the heart open, and be open to all the feeling that there is in life, and that includes music, modern music and music of the great masters."[4]

At the end of each of the two talks with Dwight Cooke, the announcer put in a plug for the new "20th Century Concert Hall," which was to begin two weeks later. There was much anticipation. There had been more than usual interest shown by the press and we were assured of a vitally interested listening audience. The program for the first broadcast included: Bach-Stokowski: *Siciliano* in C Minor; Berezowsky: Adagio from Sextet Concerto (In Memoriam); and Hovhaness: Concerto for Orchestra. Just before playing the Berezowsky Adagio, Stoki spoke: "May I welcome you to '20th Century Concert Hall'—no, no, no—I rather would say I hope you will welcome us. Let me explain what I mean. In the seventeenth and eighteenth centuries there were very few concert halls. Music was composed to order for some nobleman and was given a private performance right in his own home. I am sure, for example, that the Siciliano which we have just heard was first played and heard in the music room of Bach's employer, who was Prince Leopold, for whom it was written at that time. Only during the last 150 years, or even less, had music really blossomed out for everyone to hear in public concert halls, but the magic of radio makes '20th Century Concert Hall' unique. Unlike most concert halls, it is not located in one central place. '20th Century Concert Hall' is in your living room or your automobile—perhaps even a secluded spot in the woods somewhere. This concert hall comes to you wherever you may be, and that's why I say that I hope you will welcome us.

"Had not fate decided otherwise, the composer of the next work on our program would have been playing in this very orchestra today, for he served for many years as a violinist, violist, and conductor here at CBS. Unfortunately for the future of American music, Berezowsky died a month ago. In his memory, we play the Adagio from his Sextet Concerto for string orchestra. In addition to his work here at CBS, Berezowsky, or Nicky, as we used to call him—practically everybody called him that— was for several years a member of the Coolidge String Quartet. It was for that group and its founder that Nicky wrote his String Sextet in 1940. Then a year or so ago he extended this work into a Sextet Concerto for string orchestra. The Adagio which we play now is the second part of this concerto."

It was a rare thing indeed to have a radio program reviewed by critics as if it were a bona fide concert, particularly when not even a studio audience was present. But the critics tuned in faithfully on Sunday afternoon September 27, 1953, at 1:30 to hear the first of the "20th Century Concert Hall" programs. That is something that even "Invitation to Music" did not achieve.

In the *New York World-Telegram and Sun*, Louis Biancolli observed that the familiar Stokowski touch was on the opening program. "The orchestra," he observed, "carried out his subtlest instructions with fine responsiveness, and at all times the massed tone was good to hear."[5]

Both *Newsweek* and *Time* magazines covered the program. Carter Harman, music critic for *Time*, went with me to Stoki's apartment three days before the broadcast. He spent much time asking Stoki about his ideas and plans; he also quizzed me on the music situation at CBS.

Stoki talked about music and ideas in the same vein he had maintained with Dwight Cooke two weeks earlier. Carter wrote: "CBS came to its new concert series slowly, and not too surely, mostly through the quiet determination of Music Producer Oliver Daniel, 41. Originally trained as a pianist, he joined the network ten years ago, producing such pioneering shows as 'Invitation to Music' and 'School of the Air.' As an enthusiast for contemporary scores, he also sandwiched them into briefer programs along with salon music and show tunes. . . . Old friends Daniel and Stokowski met last winter and agreed that the time was ripe for a more ambitious program. The network played along. . . ."[6]

On succeeding programs Stoki conducted a set of fascinating pieces interspersed with music of Vivaldi, Purcell, William Byrd, Bach, and Cesti—most, if not all, in his own transcriptions.

Mitch Miller was the oboe soloist in Ulysses Kay's *Brief Elegy*, and Ulysses came to the studio for the rehearsal. "I think the thing that struck me about his conception of the piece in performance," Ulysses told me, "was that it sort of floated; he was not metrical and metronomic about it. He just let it float. The music sort of blossomed and flowed and the strings provided this marvelous sheen—a kind of aura—then the oboe came in so you had a contrast. . . . I think the thing that impressed me about it is that there were only maybe twenty players in all and yet he got this marvelous sound with the greatest of ease."[7]

The work which drew the most notice was innocent sounding enough: *Incantation for Tapesichord* by Luening and Ussachevsky. A preview for the press was held in one of the CBS studios, and Stokowski, Otto Luening, and Vladimir Ussachevsky were on hand to comment on the tape music. "The strangest music this side of Paranoia" was the description given by one writer on the *New York World-Telegram and Sun*. "Mr. Stokowski believes *Incantation* is an important piece of music and that the tape recording machine will determine the direction of such music in the future. 'There are thousands of beauties and subtleties which only the composer can feel, and which cannot be written on paper,' he explained. . . . 'In this new process that is coming, there will be no limitations. Of course, many people will say this is not music. But they said that of Bach and Beethoven.' "

The *World-Telegram* staff reporter, who was fortunately not a music critic, advanced his own opinions and reactions to the music in a fresher way than any music critic might have done. "What the piano sounded like," he wrote, "was a harp being slapped like a cello by a hag with fingernails filed like hacksaws. This is music to bring back the time the listener was a little boy, and got sick from the merry-go-round and too much excitement and slightly poison food and dreamed that Mr. Huddleston rode by on his horse and the horse, in a gruff voice, was reading off the names of everybody in the fourth grade."

Then in a more serious frame he added: "If these new sounds are capable of tilting the lid of the subconscious in the sane, then it seems possible that some day sonic experiments may come upon sounds which will reach deep into the recesses of disturbed minds. Eventually there may be standardized dosages of therapeutic sounds."[8]

The series proved to be enormously successful and the mail that flooded in was beyond anything we had expected. There was little difficulty then in having the program continue after its planned demise. Instead of being assisted by the American Composers Alliance, the new thirteen-week series was partially underwritten by the Ditson Fund of Columbia University. The programs were to help celebrate Columbia's bicentennial and the conductors were to be Stokowski, Ansermet, Antonini, the Norwegian conductor Øivin Fjeldstad, and Howard Shanet, a member of the staff of the Columbia University Music Department. The air time was now changed to 4:00 P.M., immediately after the New York Philharmonic broadcasts.

The modern repertoire for the series was to be drawn largely from works by men who had in some measure been associated with the university. Hence works of Avshalomov, Cowell, Luening, and Moore—who were currently on the Columbia faculty—and of former associates such as Bartók, MacDowell, and Mason were included. A committee consisting of Douglas Moore, Otto Luening, and Jack Beeson helped select the programs.

Stokowski conducted three broadcasts in this second series: on February 7, 21, and March 14. On the first he began with a *Largo Cantabile* of Ives; this was the second work of Ives that he conducted. He also gave a moving performance of Vaughan Williams' *Five Variants on Dives and Lazarus* and Bartók's *Romanian Dances*. But it was his second appearance that made the headlines in a quite sensational way. The program contained but two works: the Partita of Paul Creston and Ives' "Washington's Birthday" from the *Symphony: Holidays.*

Although the printed score indicates a Jew's harp was optional, Ives himself was very serious in having one or more of the little instruments used. He explained: "The 'Washington's Birthday' is for a kind of chamber orchestra: strings, 1 horn, 1 flute, a set of bells, and in the chorus a Jew's harp ad lib. I've always been a good Jew's harp player regardless of consequences, but I don't know exactly how to write for it. The notes on the Jew's harp are but some of the partials of a string, and its ability to play a diatonic tune is more apparent than real. And in this piece, from a half dozen to a hundred Jew's harps are necessary—one would hardly be heard. In the old barn dances, about all the men would carry Jew's harps in their vest pockets or in the calf of their boots, and several would stand around the side of the floor and play the harp more as a drum than as an instrument of tones."[9]

To find Jew's-harp players was a bit more difficult than we had imagined. None were listed in the files of the Musicians' Union, which did not recognize it as a legitimate instrument. We decided to make a broad appeal to recruit some players. We combed the music stores and bought every Jew's harp we could find. These we sent to the newspaper columnists and radio and TV commentators with a press release saying that Stokowski was looking for a Jew's harp performer and that auditions would be held in CBS Studio 25 the following week at four in the afternoon.

Alfredo Antonini, Peggy Glanville-Hicks, and I were judges, and although there had been over fifty who had phoned or written requesting an audition, only twenty-four actually showed up.[10] Reporters and photographers appeared, along with members of the CBS news room and curious members of practically every department. Many of the applicants were dismissed quite quickly if they could not read music. But many of the Jew's-harp virtuosi performed most ably.

On the day of the audition, violist Harold Coletta was having lunch with flutist Julie Baker when they heard over the radio the announcement that CBS was looking for a Jew's-harp player. "I looked at Baker and I said, 'I played a Jew's harp when I was a kid' and I was across the street from a music store that sold band instruments and the like, and bought one and came over to the CBS building and took the audition."

The best performer was a man named Eddie Grosso, but we were a little dubious as to his ability to come in at the right time, so we chose as a companion Harold Coletta. "He had a bigger tone," Harold said. Immediately after the audition, I brought Harold to another studio, where we appeared on the six o'clock TV news program, and the world knew that the Stokowski-Ives-Jew's-harp dilemma had been solved. The following morning AP spread the news to practically every paper in the country.

Before Stoki began his rehearsal, which was to start on Sunday at noon, he spied Coletta. "He recognized me right away, and when he saw me, he looked at me and said, 'You're a viola player.' And I had the Jew's harp in my front pocket and I pulled it out and said, 'Not today.' He smiled quietly and said, 'Oh, you're playing the—' and he gave it the German name like a 'mouth drum' [*Maultrommel*]."[11]

Stoki conducted the Ives with great sensitivity. He seemed to catch from the beginning the sense of cold and winter with which Ives had imbued his score. Of "Washington's Birthday," Ives had written: " 'Cold and solitude,' says Thoreau, 'are friends of mine. Now is the time before the wind rises to go forth and see the snow on the trees.' And there is at times a bleakness, without stir but penetrating, in a New England midwinter, which settles down grimly when the day closes over the broken hills."

Ives portrayed the younger generation, which regarded the winter holiday as a time of action, and described their trip afoot or in sleighs through the drifting snow to the barn dance: "The village band of fiddles, fife and horn keep up an unending 'break-down' medley, and the young folks 'salute their partners and balance corners' till midnight; as the party breaks up . . . with the inevitable 'adieu to the ladies,' the 'social' gives way to the grey bleakness of the February night. . . ."[12]

When the barn-dance section began there was a noticeable quickening of attention from the audience. The Jew's harps began their twanging, and all of those who had auditioned, as well as their friends and acquaintances whom they had brought along, paid rapt attention as few audiences ever did. While Coletta and Grosso twanged away, they were on mike, and their amplified sounds cut through the orchestral texture clear and full. If Ives heard it, he would have been pleased. It was well known that he had heard the broadcasts of Bernard Herrmann over CBS, as well as a performance of his Second Symphony by Leonard Bernstein. We all hoped that he would have heard the broadcast; in view of the amount of publicity it had generated, he could hardly have been oblivious.

Stoki was in a particularly happy frame of mind. There was wild applause at the end, and after taking one or more bows, Stoki walked out

from the wings with his little son Stan, who was quite delighted with all
the applause and excitement and began to applaud the audience just as
enthusiastically for their own performance. Stoki by now was a fellow
Ivesian.

All of the works Stoki chose for his final program in the series were by
Americans: Robert Kurka's *Elegy;* Peter Mennin's Fantasy for Strings;
and Walter Piston's Fantasy for English Horn, Harp and Strings. The
latter was a radio premiere. Ross Parmenter wrote a quite noncommital
squib in the *New York Times:* "Two melodious and agreeable works by
American composers were conducted by Leopold Stokowski yesterday
afternoon. . . ." and he singled out the Piston and the Mennin works. But
he did note that the broadcast was a part of the Columbia University
Bicentennial celebration.[13]

The next program was conducted by Øivin Fjeldstad, whom Stokowski
liked. Fjeldstad's program contained works by Telemann, Grieg, and
Harald Saeverud: his Divertimento for Flute and Strings in its American
premiere. Plans were already afoot for a gala all-Norwegian concert in
Carnegie Hall to be conducted jointly by Stokowski and Fjeldstad on April 1.
It had all developed in the fertile mind of Jon Embretsen, director of the
Norwegian government's Information Center. Stoki's all-Canadian concert had sparked the idea: "I was given the green light by the embassy
in Washington and immediately contacted Andrew Schulhof, as I wanted
Stokowski and his orchestra to perform the concert. Stokowski agreed and
a date was set for April 1, 1954. I proposed the program and he accepted.
I also ventured to suggest that a Norwegian conductor be invited to share
the podium with him to give the concert an added Norwegian touch, and
he was receptive to the idea if he could be satisfied as to this conductor's
stature and ability. I had Øivin Fjeldstad in mind, who at that time was
the conductor of the Oslo Philharmonic in radio concerts by the Norwegian Broadcasting Corporation rebroadcast all over Europe. I succeeded
in convincing Andrew—but how to convince Stoki. But then suddenly he
himself solved the problem. He told me that on his visit to Bergen he had
stopped in Oslo to hear an ISCM concert by the Oslo Philharmonic.
There were three conductors on the program—all Norwegian—and he
was impressed by the conductor who conducted the last piece on the
program. He would accept him. Well, that happened to be Fjeldstad."

The program was a long and taxing one. Stoki conducted the two works
he had done in Bergen: the *Cemetery by the Sea* of Valen and Saeverud's
Ballad of Revolt. In addition to these he did the *Carnival in Paris* of

Svendsen, *The Bell* of Edvard Grieg (first performance in America), and an excerpt from *Voluspaa*—Epic Poem for Orchestra and Chorus by David Monrad Johansen. Fjeldstad conducted the Piano Concerto No. 2 by Klaus Egge, with the splendid pianist Robert Riefling, and works by Arne Eggen, Ludwig Irgens Jensen, and Saeverud. Presented by His Excellency Wilhelm Morgenstierne, Norway's ambassador to the United States, it was a command performance for all of the U.N. delegations and other V.I.P.s of the diplomatic set. The turnout was immensely impressive. "Stokowski did more to give Norwegian contemporary music international recognition than any conductor of his time," said Jon Embretsen.[14]

Stokowski was full of plans. I learned in a letter of April 6 that in November he would conduct Orff's *Carmina Burana* in Boston with the chorus and orchestra of Boston University. He asked me to help him find an American composition to precede it. In his brief letter, he wrote:

> You always help me so much with American compositions. I thought
> I knew much about this subject but you always impress and over-
> whelm me by your greater knowledge.[15]

I include this bit of praise with mock reluctance. I found a number of works for him, and from them he chose a new work by Normand Lockwood, *The Prairie*. The concert was planned for the following November.

Stoki was busy now attending to all the details of his forthcoming European tour. He was to make the trip alone, for Gloria was busy with her transition from painter to actress, and was being coached for her appearance in Molnar's *The Swan*.

Stoki departed on the S.S. *Queen Mary* on April 28 for his tour, which began with three programs for the BBC in London. Except for the Beethoven Fifth and the Brahms Second, all of his works were unusual. He conducted Malcolm Arnold's Overture, *Beckus the Dandipratt*, Glière's *Concerto for Coloratura and Orchestra*, Rawsthorne's *Symphonic Studies*, Arnold Bax's *Tintagel*, William Schuman's *Circus Overture*, and Vaughan Williams' *Five Variants on Dives and Lazarus*.

Malcolm Arnold attended the performance of his overture and was obviously pleased. He wrote Stoki a brief note of thanks:

> Dear Sir,
>
>   Thank you very much for the wonderful performance of my over-
> ture "Beckus the Dandipratt."

I am extremely grateful and consider it a great honour that you should conduct a piece of mine.

Thank you very much.

Yours sincerely
Malcolm Arnold[16]

He continued with concerts in Brussels and Paris, and then to Lugano, where he conducted a Concerto for Piano and Orchestra by his good friend the German composer-pianist Kurt Leimer. From here he traveled to Baden-Baden, Germany, where he conducted an all-contemporary program including works by William Schuman, Darius Milhaud, Aaron Copland, Rolf Liebermann, and Boris Blacher.

Following the Paris concert, the Associated Press reported that "Stokowski conducted the Paris Grand Opera Orchestra in his first concert here in five years."[17] Later, Gloria received copies of the Paris reviews, which were ecstatic. I wrote to Leopold, addressing the letter to the Royal Danieli in Venice: "Gloria told me that you had great success in Paris. . . ." I explained that there would not be any possibility of coming to Europe at that time, although we had planned to meet in Italy.[18]

The high point of the European tour was yet to come. Stoki was to conduct three concerts in Venice; one in the Basilica di San Marco and two in the adjacent Palazzo Ducale. He chose works that were particularly appropriate for the ancient basilica. Giovanni Gabrieli's *Canzon Quarti Toni a 15* opened the program and later, after intermission, his *In Ecclesiis Benedicite Domino* with orchestra, organ and choir. Gabrieli had served as organist at San Marco from 1584 until his death in 1612. Another composer also connected with the cathedral was Monteverdi, who in 1613 was elected "maestro di cappella" of San Marco with a salary of 500 ducats, a house, and traveling expenses. He remained there until his death. Stoki did Monteverdi's *Sonata Sopra Santa Maria* for soprano and orchestra. A third composer similarly associated with San Marco was Vivaldi, who was born in Venice and whose father was a violinist in the cathedral. Stoki conducted his *Beatus Vir* (for orchestra, organ and choir).

The Venetians had allotted four days of rehearsal time for the concert, and Stoki used all of it not only to rehearse his forces, but to experiment with various antiphonal effects that had been a tradition at San Marco. He had achieved a sonorous quality from his singers and players that was

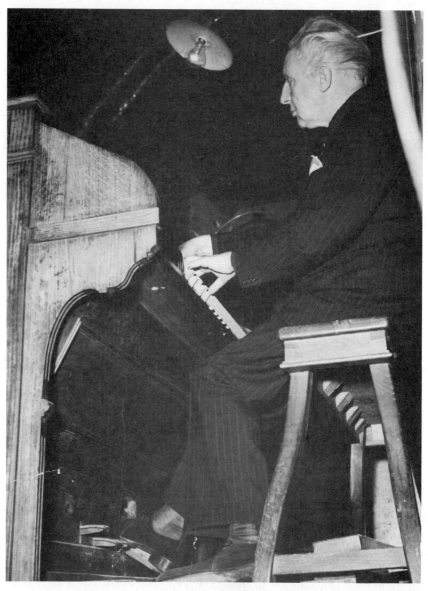

Interfoto, Venice/Courtesy Belle Schulhof

Playing the organ, Venice (1954)

Photo Ferruzzi, Venice/Courtesy International Leopold Stokowski Society
With Cardinal Roncalli of Venice, the future Pope John XXIII, who inscribed the photograph (1954)

Conducting in the Ducal Palace courtyard, Venice, 1954

beyond anything that was then current in the basilica. The result, critics agreed, was unique. No one was more pleased than the Venetian cardinal himself. He was Angelo Guiseppe Roncalli, patriarch of Venice, who was to become Pope John XXIII four years later. He was most enthusiastic, welcomed Stokowski affectionately, and invited him to his private apartment. He posed for pictures with him and expressed his pleasure abundantly. When he died in 1963 and Stoki was told of his death, he remarked that it was sad, for he was such a young man!

After the moving concert in San Marco there were two concerts in the Palazzo Ducale. Here the program was more for the public taste. He performed his transcription of the Bach Toccata and Fugue, Brahms' Symphony No. 2 and the *New World* Symphony.

After the concerts in Venice, those in Rome proved to be somewhat of an anticlimax. The Roman concerts were, however, well attended, with audiences including the American Ambassador, Clare Boothe Luce, and a contingent of Americans.

Two weeks after his return on the S.S. *Liberty,* Stoki set out for Lake George with his two sons while Gloria hied in the opposite direction to the Poconos in Pennsylvania. After a fortnight of rehearsals, she made her stellar debut as an actress in Molnar's *The Swan* in the Pocono Playhouse summer theater at Mountainhome, Pennsylvania, on August 16. The press seemed to want to be sympathetic; critically they were lenient. "As an imperious and lovely princess in a fictitious kingdom, Gloria Vanderbilt (which she uses as her professional name) was completely at home.

"Trained in the best finishing schools and at the age of 17 the most publicized debutante in the world, she quite naturally made every gesture, every enunciation a polished reflection of her own personality."[19]

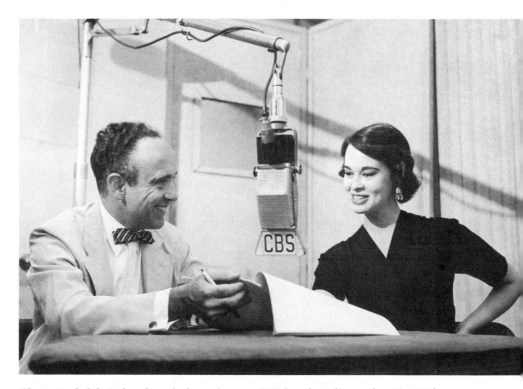

Gloria Vanderbilt Stokowski with the author at a CBS broadcast (September 12, 1954)

That was part of the story sent out on the wires of the International News Service.

She had found an elegant lace gown that looked like a true creation of the mid-1900s. It was as white as the prop swan statute that decorated the scene.

When under stress, Gloria had a tendency to stammer slightly, but she managed to control herself admirably. I confess she looked frightened at first, but that is understandable. Critics rightly observed that in the love scenes there was much that was lacking, and they complained that she lacked fire. But she accomplished what she set out to do.

Early in September, Gloria appeared with me on a CBS program discussing and reading some of her poems, after which Alfredo Antonini conducted the CBS Orchestra as Nell Tangeman sang three which had been set to music by Alan Hovhaness.[20] The work, which Alan characterized as "mysterious music, full of unusual colors and sounds," was a setting of three of Gloria's unpublished poems: "The Mysterious Door," "The Snow," and "Loneliness."[21] The settings were for voice, strings, and woodwinds, and Alan gave the piece the simple title Canticle.

58

NBC Symphony Recordings

*F*OUR days after Stokowski's concert of Norwegian music in Carnegie Hall, Toscanini conducted a broadcast from the same stage with the NBC Symphony. It was to be his last. During the all-Wagner program there was a moment in the *Tannhäuser* Overture that the catastrophe happened. George Marek described it: "Suddenly in the frenzied Bacchanale he seemed no longer in communication with the music. It broke away from him . . . the beat of his right arm became frail, he failed to give cues, and at one moment he pinched his eyes with his fingers of his left hand, like a man who is desperately searching for a lost thought."[1]

The orchestra began to fall apart and for a moment Toscanini stopped conducting. In a moment of panic, Chotzinoff and Cantelli, who were in the control room, cut off the broadcast and switched to a recording. The lapse was brief and the broadcast of Wagner resumed. It was a sad end to a very long and distinguished career.

RCA then announced that the NBC Symphony would be disbanded. What with its imminent demise and the loss of Toscanini as a recording artist, RCA was eager to record the orchestra with Stokowski. He set about the task with his usual enthusiasm, and the results were some of the finest sonic masterpieces of his long recording career.

The first was to be the *Pastorale* Symphony of Beethoven, which was recorded on March 18 and 19. The performance was straightforward. No one could carp about that, and those who would read Hollywood and Disney into the act were quite wrong. It is a very sensitive and deeply felt rendition. Even the snide British critic in the *Gramophone* conceded that it was recorded exceptionally well.

Added to the disc was a sonic dollop that obviously was seen as a good marketing process, but musicians may well have some reservations. As a trailer to the symphony, RCA added a set of sounds that were to evoke the source of Beethoven's inspiration. Stoki was the narrator. "As everyone knows, Beethoven used to love to walk in the woods around Vienna. There he heard the sounds of nature and used some of these sounds as inspiration for his Pastoral Symphony. . . . For example, here is the sound of a brook."

The sound we hear was taken from a recording made in Labrador in the course of a bird-call expedition by the Cornell Laboratory of Ornithology. "And here is Beethoven's impressionistic interpretation." We hear several moments of the *Pastorale* labeled *Scene by the Brookside*. "And here the two are combined." Together the music of the Beethoven and the Labrador brook purled along quite harmoniously. As he continued there were bird songs and thunder.

Reactions to Stokowski's nature-music lesson varied. "Purists may dislike the whole thing roundly," wrote Enos Shupp, "but those who like spoken commentary with illustrations will find this very interesting—and no one is better at it than Stokowski."[2]

The next recording was a set of highlights from *Samson and Delilah* with Risë Stevens, Jan Peerce, Robert Merrill, The Robert Shaw Chorale, and the NBC Symphony. The first rehearsal began on a slightly shaky footing. As always, Stoki was not *on* time but ahead of it. He always wanted to be sure that all of the elements would be falling in place. As three o'clock approached, the orchestra, chorus, and all the soloists but one were there. Robert Merrill was nowhere to be seen. He had been caught in a traffic snarl and arrived five minutes late. He had not thought that it would really matter too much because he knew that most conductors do some warming up with the orchestra first. But not Stokowski! He was quite angry and castigated Merrill in front of the orchestra, chorus, and his colleagues. But at the end both shook hands and Merrill expressed his admiration for Stokowski.[3]

Both Jan Peerce and Risë Stevens also admired Stoki. "I always had a great awe for this man and everything he did," said Risë. And she added: "I didn't have the most pleasant experiences with him, I must truthfully say." She explained that when listening to various play-back tests, she had chosen the one she felt was best. Stoki, however, disagreed and chose one more to his liking. "I wasn't very pleased with the record because I thought the other one was much better. But he had the feeling that he knew about . . . balance between singer and orchestra. I think, though, on the recording I suffered a little bit as a result of that. . . . I've had many people say that the voice sounded like it was very far away."[4]

Critics did not agree. Peter Hugh Reed wrote in the *American Record Guide:* "Admirers of Stokowski's operatic work will welcome this disc, for he had always been a conductor who works easily with singers. His and Miss Stevens' work are the true features of this recording. . . . Miss Stevens sings beautifully throughout, maintaining an ingratiating vocal line. . . . Mr. Stokowski conducts with artistic restraint. . . ."[5]

The next work to be recorded was the Sibelius Second Symphony. Anticipating the recording, he wrote to Sibelius.

> Dear Friend
>
> I am studying afresh your second symphony, which I am going to conduct and record soon, if that will be agreeable to you. I am so deeply impressed by the wonderful themes, and their variety and originality of character and mood. Their range is enormous. Also I intensely admire the architectonics of the whole symphony. It has such a striking and unique form. Another thing I am enjoying so much is the long lines of development, for example in the 2nd movement, from a little after letter F until letter K, and in the 3rd movement from letter F until a little after letter J. Also in the last movement from letter F until letter K and again from letter O to letter S.
>
> The next time I come to Helsinki I would like to conduct this symphony, amongst other things, if that would be all right with you.
>
> > Always with affectionate thoughts
> > Leopold Stokowski[6]

Sibelius answered promptly, but his letter, alas, is another of those that are sogging on the bottom of the Atlantic. Stoki responded with another "Dear Friend" letter on September 21: "I was happy to receive your letter and next Thursday we will complete the recording of your 2nd Symphony. As soon as I have a rough laboratory pressing may I send it to you? Always your admirer and friend."[7]

Sibelius, we gather, was pleased with the recording. "For the most picturesque, evocative, sensuous, and gorgeously tapestried version of the Sibelius *Second Symphony*, Stokowski, as might be expected, walks away with top honors with ease. No other LP of this work compares with this one for imaginative treatment. The members of the NBC Orchestra selected by Stokowski are guided through a reading which demonstrates the virtuoso capacities of the players in a thrilling manner." So wrote the critic of *The New Records*. [8]

Two weeks later Stoki recorded Menotti's *Sebastian* Ballet and *Romeo and Juliet* of Prokofiev. They were both bona fide recording masterpieces. I spoke to Gian Carlo about it and he reminisced. "Curiously enough, when I met Toscanini, we were talking about conductors. . . . Toscanini always called him a *buffone*—a clown. You know Toscanini never said a good word about any other conductor . . . but about Stokowski he always said, 'He is a clown,' but he always added, 'the sound he can get out of an orchestra, not even I can get.' He always recognized that he had a marvelous ear for sound. He had this magic thing about sound. . . . I had proof with the very first recording that he did of my music, which was the *Sebastian* Suite. I think it is one of the very best recordings that I have. . . . I think it is a marvelous record."[9]

This was the beginning of the stereo-tape era, but the stereo-LP-disc era was to be delayed for four years. The ballet, therefore, was released in a mono recording coupled with a previously recorded version of Morton Gould's *Dance* Variations. "Well it's about time that *Sebastian* was brought to LP," wrote James Lyons. "I have always loved this early ballet score above anything else he has done and it is a belated pleasure to welcome it to microgroove. Stokowski's performance is sensitive and loving. . . ."[10] Other reviews were equally praiseworthy. Twenty-four years after the initial release, RCA issued it as a stereo disc for the first time, coupled with Prokofiev's *Romeo and Juliet* Ballet Suite.

The *Romeo and Juliet* Suite was brilliant. The recording contains some of the most sensitive and inspired performances by individual members of the ensemble that I have ever heard recorded. The flute solos of Paul Renzi are an outstanding example.

Perceptive Alfred Frankenstein remarked that the selections which Stoki chose were played with "an absolutely incandescent lyricism, urgency and richness, and the recording is one of the most nearly perfect things ever to issue from Victor's presses. This is far and away the finest version of Prokofiev's *Romeo and Juliet* music that has ever been made, and one of Stokowski's interpretative masterpieces."[11]

Nearly six weeks before he would conduct *Carmina Burana* in Boston, he went up to begin rehearsals with the Boston University chorus and orchestra. He began on October 10 and rehearsed at various times during morning, afternoon, and evening hours. At the end of the week he phoned Olga Koussevitzky and joined her late on Sunday afternoon at the Koussevitzky home.

Before he would return to Boston, Stokowski conducted one more concert to celebrate Columbia University's Bicentennial. After all, he had begun the celebration with the broadcasts on "20th Century Concert Hall." This time it would be a more ambitious undertaking: the New York Philharmonic in Carnegie Hall. All of the works were by composers affiliated with the University. It began with the "Chanticleer" Overture by Daniel Gregory Mason, followed by Otto Luening's Symphonic Fantasia No. 2, Douglas Moore's Second Symphony, and the MacDowell Concerto No. 2 with pianist Gary Graffman. The concert concluded with the Dance Suite by Béla Bartók. For those who raised an eyebrow over that inclusion, Columbia Professor of Musicology Paul Henry Lang explained that "Béla Bartók is rightfully included in this program as an adopted son of Columbia. A man of flaming integrity, he belonged to our research staff rather than to the composers' wing, for he was resolved not to teach composition to anyone. . . ."[12]

On Armistice Day, November 11, 1954, Stoki returned to Boston again to rehearse Normand Lockwood's *Prairie* and Orff's *Carmina Burana*. The concert took place in Symphony Hall on Friday the nineteenth. I joined Stoki before the concert and heard the final rehearsal. While the Lockwood piece was a beautifully effective one, it was no match for the Orff blockbuster.

The concertmaster of the orchestra was faculty member Malloy Miller. "About two weeks before the concert," Malloy told me, "Stokowski was here rehearsing, and I daresay there was little done in the School of Music other than *Carmina Burana*. He had special rehearsals with the soloists —these were student soloists. He had extra rehearsals with the orchestra. He worked with the chorus. The man was tireless. It was an experience! That's a sort of trite word, but it truly was. And I think the students who were here at that time had an experience that they will remember for the rest of their lives."[13]

As the piece ended the audience broke into a fit of applauding, shouting, and foot stamping that seemed wild enough to shake the staid Greek casts that adorned Symphony Hall's upper walls. It was like the cheering that might erupt after a ball game, and I felt convinced that if there had been goal posts in front of the stage, the wildly applauding audience would

have torn them down. It was not a typical Boston audience by any means
—not the one that regularly attended the Boston Symphony, but rather
a youthful one drawn from the University's huge student body.

Naturally, Stoki wanted to bring the whole production to New York.
The University was not willing to assume the responsibility, and this is
where the newly formed Contemporary Music Society was to come in. It
was its first Carnegie Hall presentation. The costs to the Society were
slightly under $4,000, and the box office receipts were close to $2,500. We
were elated that the Society was now really active. Some of the expense
items evoke surprise and economic nostalgia. There were payments for
two meals at $1.00 per meal for 215 members of the chorus and orchestra,
and 10,000 two-page, two-color flyers for $122.80.[14]

Anyone who had heard the performance in Boston would have found
the New York one a somewhat pale carbon copy. Perhaps the New York
weekend did in some of the performers. They seemed tired to me. But
to the New York audience it was still arresting. *Time* magazine called it
"one of the year's most interesting musical evenings." It also recognized
Stokowski's genius in welding raw material into something of outstanding
professional quality. It was the All-American Youth Orchestra all over
again. "Conductor Stokowski, his genius undimmed at 72, had trained the
Boston University Chorus and Orchestra into a unit of highly professional
caliber."[15]

Stoki now set out for Cleveland, where he conducted two pairs of
subscription concerts and, as was his custom, selected unusual fare. For
his first two, he conducted *Fantasia* by Robert Cogan, Henri Barraud's
Homage to a Friend, Stravinsky's *Apollon Musagète,* and the Fourth by
Tchaikowsky. On his next pair he began with a suite of pieces by Purcell
that he had transcribed, Vaughan Williams' *Sinfonia Antartica,* Debussy's Three Nocturnes, and the "Prelude and Love Death" from *Tristan.*

He hurried back to New York to be with his boys for Christmas. On
the twenty-third he wrote a letter to Willy Strecker, who was the head
of B. Schott's Söhne, Orff's publisher in Mainz, Germany. He thanked
Strecker for a cable he had sent congratulating him on his success with
Carmina Burana. "It was one of the greatest experiences of my
life. . . ." he wrote. "If you see Orff please thank him from me and give
him my greetings. I studied in München and know and love that city
greatly. I hope to have the pleasure of meeting him there sometime. Soon
I hope to conduct *Trionfo di Afrodite* in the Hollywood Bowl, and *Catulli*

Carmina in the Pacific Coast Music Festival in Santa Barbara."[16]

The festival was to be one of the happy experiences for Stoki during the coming year. He had asked me to go to Santa Barbara during one of my trips to the Coast and begin working with the people there on the preliminaries. My California trips had been made to talk with Carl Haverlin about coming into BMI. By good fortune I was appointed assistant to the president of Associated Music Publishers, a subsidiary of BMI, and for me the auguries were pleasant; for Stoki they were not. I had discussed my move from CBS before the BMI association had become definite, and he wrote me: "I hope it works out and that you and I will always be associated together in New York and on the Pacific Coast."[17]

59

Sic Transit Gloria Monday

CHRISTMAS had come on Friday. On Monday night, December 27, Gloria left Stokowski at 10 Gracie Square and taking young Stan and Chris with her, checked in at the Ambassador Hotel. She immediately engaged husky guards to post themselves in the hallway outside her suite for fear that Stoki might attempt to take the boys and also to keep away the aggressive hoard of reporters. It was no quiet departure and the press was duly alerted.

Gloria was already rehearsing her role in Saroyan's *The Time of Your Life,* and the break with Stokowski loomed like a magnificent opportunity for publicity. "Her agent, Gloria Safier, confirmed reports of the separation and said that, 'for personal reasons,' the heiress was living at the Ambassador and had nothing to say." From Gloria's barricaded suite came a terse statement the *Mirror* reported: "For personal reasons, I have decided to live at the Ambassador with my children. When I can amplify the situation, I will. But I don't think I can say anything more than that my husband and I have separated. That is the only fair comment to be made at the moment."[1]

But publicity spewed forth. Friends were interviewed and their observations were fed to the press. I went to talk to Stoki early on the morning that the news broke and found a dozen or more reporters and photographers milling about the tunnellike carport that led to the entrance to his apartment. He had at first refused to see any of them. Wendy Hanson and I persuaded him to at least invite them in if for no other reason than to show his goodwill. It was a frigid morning and *Time* magazine reported:

614

"Courtly to the last, her abandoned husband took pity on the newsmen stamping their feet in the cold outside . . . and invited them in for hot coffee, served, a grateful reporter noted, in cups of the finest English bone china."[2]

In characteristic fashion, Stoki refused to have any pictures taken and refused to make any comment other than that he would never say anything against the mother of his children. I also stopped in to see Gloria at the Ambassador, which was just between my CBS office and my apartment on Fifty-second Street. She explained her position and seemed more relieved than distressed. She asked me to accompany her to a party being given by *Life* photographer Gordon Parks in his home in White Plains the following Thursday evening. Gordon Parks had already invited me. At the last minute Gloria called saying that something had come up and that she would see me at the party.

The "something" that had come up was Frank Sinatra, who was appearing at the time at the Copacabana. Frank escorted Gloria to the premiere of the Harold Arlen-Truman Capote production of *House of Flowers.* The *Daily Mirror* had reported that occupants of the Ambassador had said that "it was possible to hear her crying through the walls of her suite." She was reported to be grieving and disconsolate. "There were no signs of streaked mascara as she arrived at the Alvin theater," the *Mirror* reported. Reporters and photographers were alerted about the two celebrities' attendance, and the photos show Gloria at her most poised and Sinatra looking pensive.[3]

"Sinatra seated the svelte brunette before the start of the show, remained for 15 minutes, then dashed to the Copa for his own show. He was back, breathless, by the beginning of the second act." At the end of the production Gloria and Frank were driven in their Carey Cadillac up to White Plains, where they joined us for the epicurean supper the Parks had prepared. Their stay was brief, for Frankie had to rush back to the Copa to do his late-night show. Their pictures, the following day, were splashed about the front pages of tabloids and the insides of the more staid samples of the press. It was splendid publicity for Elsie Mandelspiegel, the character she was learning to play.

Jean Dalrymple, who produced the revival of the Saroyan play, told me: "The part that I cast her in was a very small part, but every small part in *Time of Your Life* is important, as you know. I had asked her if she would like to play it and she said she would. And I always remember, I had to go out to California to do some work for José [Iturbi], and on the way back in the plane, we stopped in Chicago—we used to change planes in Chicago for some reason. I picked up a Chicago paper and the headline said, 'Gloria Divorcing Stoki'—the whole thing. There was a picture of her with Franchot Tone. It said she was to be at City Center playing in *The Time of Your Life.*

"When I got to New York, all the papers called me and said, 'Well, that's another coup in publicity for the Dalrymple office.' I said, 'Good God! I didn't know anything about it.' And they said, 'Come on.' "[4]

With so much that seemed unpleasant and disturbing, I wanted to make some contribution toward a more pleasant time. I organized an almost impromptu New Year's Eve party for Stokowski and friends whom he enjoyed. Kurt and Grace Graff, who brought Vicki Baum; Henry and Sidney Cowell; Peggy Glanville-Hicks; Daniel Pinkham; Barbara and Ulysses Kay, and several other guests.

Stoki seemed to be somewhat diverted from his unhappy plight. I overheard part of a conversation between Vicki Baum and Stoki; the subject was Garbo. I had never before heard him mention her. Vicki talked about her performance in her script for *Grand Hotel.* Several times during the evening Stoki walked to the window facing west. It was a mere four short blocks away that his two boys were ensconced with Gloria.

On the following Monday he departed for the first of a series of engagements. Schulhof had booked concerts which would take Stoki to St. Louis, Dallas, Fort Wayne, New Orleans, Detroit, Oklahoma, and Miami. Schulhof sent on to the managers of each of the symphonies a memorandum containing certain specifications. He sent a precise seating plan for the orchestra and instructions about lighting. "House lights should be dimmed before Mr. Stokowski appears on the podium and they should be maintained so until he takes his final bow at intermission." The second half was to follow the same pattern. "Press Photographers:—Mr. Stokowski never gives interviews to the press because everything he has to say is through music. Also he does not wish to be photographed at any time—either on his arrival or during rehearsals or at the concert. I know that I can trust you to see that his wishes regarding this will be given full consideration."

Another important point in the minds of both Stoki and Schulhof was this. "Biography is enclosed herewith. It is understood that you will use only biographical data and photographs from the material provided by us."[5] This was the joker that was to cause trouble later on. A few other provisos were of less importance.

The biographical material was a booklet prepared by Stoki and Schulhof. On the cover there was a sketch by John Goth, the husband of one of Gloria's dearest friends. It portrays Stoki as an aged adolescent, rather too pretty for words. It is the picture of a simpering movie star rather than that of a great man. The biographical material began: "Leopold-Boleslawowicz-Stanislaw-Antoni-Stokowski is of Polish origin and is named after his grandfather, Leopold Stokowski, of Lublin and Krakow. His father's name was Boleslaw Kopernik Stokowski. He was born in April, 1887."

There was some correct information, but the implication that he was only eighteen when he became the organist at St. Bartholomew's in 1905 smacks of the faintly ridiculous. It was not a very convincing bit of propaganda, although it did include an article by James Collis and two profile photos that presented Stoki with greater dignity.[6]

On Monday the third, he departed on the crack train the Spirit of St. Louis and arrived there the following day. After four days of intensive rehearsals, he conducted two concerts, during which he performed, along with Bach and Wagner, the Seventh Symphony of Roy Harris. This engagement took a week, and on returning he conferred with his lawyer, Alfred Holmes, as he had been doing by phone while away. A modus vivendi had been arrived at with Gloria, and he was allowed to see his boys, though briefly, on Thursday between four and six. The following day, while Gloria was rehearsing her role in *The Time of Your Life*, he took Stan to the Bronx Zoo. But even there he was hounded by at least one photographer, who snapped them as they left the reptile house. The photo appeared in the *Daily News* showing Stoki discreetly holding up his gloves in front of his face.[7]

He then departed for Dallas, arriving on Wednesday, January 19. He proceeded to the Stoneleigh Hotel. In his date book he has cryptically noted "Vendushka Geburtstag" [Vendushka's birthday]. Who of the lights of his life might that have been?*

In Dallas he had programmed the Symphony on G of Lou Harrison.

*About Stokowski and nicknames, Yehudi Menuhin told me an amusing story. "In Lima, Peru, during the war," he said, "I was asked by the Free French if I would attend a reception in my honor in one of the public rooms of the Bolivar Hotel, a very sedate and very dignified hotel with dark leather upholstery and black mahogany walls. Most of the Free French were bearded, old gentlemen talking in very quiet voices. Suddenly a very lightly clad, elegant lady came and stood near the doorway, furtively looked around, and beckoned to me. Out of courtesy and chivalry, I got up, and she led me to a very secret little corner and then whispered in my ear, 'Do you know Stokowski?' I said yes. 'Do you think you will be seeing him when you return to the States?' I said, 'Yes, I may.' And she said, 'Please tell him Strawberry sends her love.'

"A few weeks later in Hollywood, I saw Stoki at the home of Edward G. Robinson and delivered my message. We were sitting around a coffee table—about six of us—and he didn't twitch a hair. No remark at all!" (From a conversation with Yehudi Menuhin on January 16, 1978.)

He had expressed great interest in the work when we had talked about the score. I phoned Lou in California to tell him that it was to be done, and he had it confirmed by the symphony office in turn. Lou recalled the incident: "I took a bus out there hoping to be present only to discover when I got to Dallas that he had changed the program and omitted the piece. . . . I had gotten him a tie in San Francisco's Chinatown and a copy of the *Farmer's Almanac.* I've always loved it, and I gave it as a present quite often. He was glad to see me though a little bit startled, I think, and apologetic about having canceled the symphony, which he said he had done because they didn't have two harps . . . so I went and visited Santa Fe to console myself—I dearly love Santa Fe—and then back home."[8]

Not knowing about the cancellation, I wrote to Stoki at the Stoneleigh in Dallas: "I am filled with curiosity about the performance of Lou's symphony, and I wish you would drop me a note and tell me how it worked out. You can do it with one word—just say 'good' or 'bad' or wherever it might lie in between." I also added somewhat apologetically that "unfortunately, I could not be at the opening of 'Time of Your Life' but I thought you would be interested in the New York reviews which are enclosed."[9] The reviews were complimentary, though none wanted to compare Gloria with Garbo. However, when I did see the play several nights later, I was impressed by the stage presence she had acquired and the confident ease with which she delivered her lines.

The role of Elsie Mandelspiegel fitted Gloria to a T. It was, as Gloria describes her jeans in TV commercials, "*Vanderbilt.*" Saroyan referred to Elsie as a beautiful, dark-haired girl with a sorrowful dreaming face, almost on the verge of tears. "There is an aura of dream about her. She moves softly and gently as if everything around her were unreal and pathetic."

The scene is laid in Nick's honky-tonk, the Pacific Street Saloon, at the foot of the Embarcadero in San Francisco. It was there that Elsie encountered Dudley, whom Saroyan described as "a young man in love." Their scene in the fourth act is a mere vignette at the end of which they leave arm in arm. "We'll go together to a room in a cheap hotel, and dream that the world is beautiful, and that living is full of love and greatness," Elsie says. "Sure, we can, Elsie." They exit.

One streetwalker at the bar bursts out laughing. The audience, I felt, was not even pretending to see Elsie Mandelspiegel; they were more eager to see Gloria Vanderbilt. A second streetwalker says sneeringly: "It's floozies like her that raise hell with our racket."[10] The audience exploded. I do not know whether Saroyan intended the line to be as humorous as it seemed that night, but it did elicit a belly laugh. Stokowski never saw the play.

After his Dallas concerts, he was driven to Fort Worth, where he repeated his program in the Will Rogers Auditorium. From there he proceeded to New Orleans, where he conducted Rimsky-Korsakov's *Dubinushka*, the Shostakovich Symphony No. 10, William Schuman's *Prayer in Time of War*, and the inevitable *Tristan* excerpt.

During the month of January, Wendy Hanson had been extremely busy trying to find an apartment into which Leopold might move. She found one at 1125 Fifth Avenue overlooking Central Park.[11] As to his desirability as a tenant, a Miss Lang of the Albert Ashforth Inc. outfit, which represented the landlord, wrote me asking whether I would recommend Stokowski. Somehow it struck me as being quite funny. I quote my answer to Miss Lang:

> I feel quite honored to be asked to recommend Leopold Stokowski in any capacity whatsoever. I am sure that, if the situations were reversed and I were in the real estate business, I would be equally honored to have a man of such distinction occupying my premises.
>
> It seems to me that anything I could say would be quite a superfluous addition to the name of Leopold Stokowski.[12]

In a rash moment I had written to him that if I could be of any help in moving to the new apartment I would be most glad to do so. I didn't know that I would become the prime mover.

Stoki arrived in time to spend the weekend in New York. On Friday he saw the boys, and had them for dinner at 10 Gracie. Later in the evening he conferred with Holmes. On Saturday we lunched together, and on Sunday, after seeing the boys from 3:00 to 5:00, he joined me at my apartment for dinner after which Andrew Schulhof joined us. The conversation for the entire evening centered on Houston.

Stoki envisioned at this time the idea that he could have his sons in Texas in an environment that would be highly salubrious. He thought of cowboys, wide open spaces, and ranches where his sons could turn to examples of rugged American manhood as models. He was eager to integrate with Texas, and he pressed his lawyer, Holmes, to see that any arrangement in a separation or divorce proceeding would permit him to have the boys with him.

Though Stokowski's first concern was being with his boys, his second preoccupation was his new apartment. Wendy and I packed scores, parts, books, and all. Over two weekends we moved things in my Oldsmobile convertible, which on each trip was loaded like a gypsy van. On the final move, Saturday, March 5, the three of us brought the last remnants of Stoki's belongings and parked in front of the new apartment. As Stoki got out, he opened the door quickly, which was immediately caught by a strong gust of wind and was sprung into a wide-open position and could not be brought back. Both Stoki and I tried our nonmechanical best to close it, but it would not budge. I had then to drive about the neighborhood with the door standing out like a semaphore at a 45-degree angle until I could find a garage where it could be fixed.

Early on Monday morning, Stoki, his two boys, and a nurse-governess set out for Florida. He had been invited by John Bitter, his old friend from the Youth Orchestra days, who was then the conductor of the University of Miami Symphony Orchestra. There were to be two concerts, one in Miami Beach and the second in Miami proper. Schulhof had dutifully sent to John the usual set of instructions and proscriptions, but they were not sent to the local press or radio. Naturally, there was much curious interest in Stokowski apart from his conducting.

"We had a terrible time with the press," John told me. "Someone from the *Miami Herald* had heard that the boys were there, and they wanted to photograph them. But Stokowski wanted no photographs. He was emphatic about it! But under false pretenses a photographer and a young girl reporter got into bathing suits and went out onto the beach, found them, and began taking pictures. When they appeared in the paper, Stokowski called me up and said he would not conduct the concert."

Stoki was always apprehensive about the security of the boys and was haunted by the thought that they might be kidnapped. He also had his phobia about photographers. Furthermore, Gloria was in Florida at that time, and Stoki did not want her to take umbrage at seeing the boys plastered on the pages of the *Miami Herald.*

Stoki demanded that the paper print an apology, and the negotiation of this rather delicate ploy fell upon the shoulders of John Bitter. "I believe I was up all night trying to work something out. At first John Knight, editor and owner of the paper, didn't want to do so. It's hard to get a proud paper to do something like that when they didn't care much whether he conducted the concert or not. But for the university people and the musicians, and with all our tickets sold, it would have been a disaster. We had an apology—enough, at least, so that he accepted it."13

When concert time arrived, the orchestra, having finished tuning, was silently and expectantly awaiting the Maestro's entrance from the wings, but no Stokowski appeared. As the delay lengthened, those in the audience aware of the preceding contretemps became increasingly apprehensive. They did not know that another drama was then unfolding backstage. But millions of radio listeners were stunned.

As was widely reported in the papers, John Prosser was reading from his prepared script: "Leopold Stokowski was born in 1882. . . ." "No, no, no, no, NO! That is not true! I was born in 1887!" Stokowski shouted, with his voice being broadcast far and wide. Reading on, Prosser announced: "He was born of a Polish father and an Irish mother." Another interruption: "My mother was not Irish! This is terrible! Where did you get that stuff?"[14] There were scuffling sounds, then a firm command to cut the broadcast. Standby music peacefully emerged on the air waves. But no symphony concert. Stokowski meanwhile returned to the green room to cool his ruptured feelings. The press was delighted: "Stokowski Cut Off Air in Biography Beef" whirred the Associated Press wires and then in great detail recounted the entire affair.[15]

After a short interval, Stokowski strode on the stage to an ovation and immediately immersed himself in one of his Bach transcriptions. Following the concert, Bitter and his family took Stokowski on a picnic in the Everglades. "That part of Florida is particularly magical, and we had a little fire and we had some fish, which he loved. I tried to get things that he enjoyed very much, and as we were eating there, some raccoons came out—they're notable scavengers—and one of them came right up on the table while we were there, and my children were just delighted with this, and Stokowski made friends with this raccoon. It was just incredible. He enjoyed that so much, and, of course, as you know, the Everglades, they seem to speak with the knowledge of centuries, and this deathly quiet, except for a few little noises, animals, an alligator or a frog or something like that. It was just beautiful and he enjoyed it tremendously."[16]

During the next four busy weeks, Stoki edited his latest set of RCA recordings, applied for a passport—with the wrong birth date, 1887[17]—visited with his boys, conferred with his lawyer, Alfred Holmes, and with Andrew Schulhof about many details concerning his European tour. With his marital life still undecided and his preoccupation with the boys, he wanted to be able to spend more time in New York. To this end, and to Schulhof's distress, he canceled engagements in both Indianapolis and Washington, D.C.

To Fabien Sevitzky in Indianapolis and Howard Mitchell in Washington, he wrote identical letters explaining that "on account of great difficulties which I have in my private life, and which are nothing whatever to do with my musical life, I would deeply appreciate it if you would postpone my conducting of your orchestra until the following season . . . it would greatly help me, in trying to solve personal difficulties, if I could be more in New York the coming season, and less away. I am sure you will understand, and be sympathetic and do your utmost to postpone for one year, by which time I hope to have solved these problems."[18]

The new apartment was still in a bit of a shambles, but Wendy and Stoki haunted Parke Bernet for antiques to fit in among the cold utilitarian shelves that were to house his bulky library. Gongs of all sizes were an added feature of the warehouse-style decor.

While Stoki and Gloria were together, Faye and Natasha were not in the picture at all. But now with things in flux, they reentered Stoki's life and were to become more and more possessive. "They weren't around," said Wendy. "I didn't know who they were. I never heard of them. They weren't in touch. If they were, it was secretive. The first time I remember knowing of them was when I found the co-op apartment which he bought sight unseen. One morning, I walked in and there were whole swatches of material and possible things for curtains and chair coverings, and I couldn't imagine where they had come from, and he said, 'Well, I have these two friends who I used to know in Philadelphia.' That was the first time I knew these two ladies existed."[19]

For several hours over a space of five or more days at RCA, he edited and approved the takes of his last set of pieces.

We met almost every day, and there was much to discuss about the Santa Barbara Festival, which he wanted me to help set up while he was in Europe. He also wanted to discuss his programs for Houston, in which I became deeply involved. We dined on my terrace and at other times made peregrinations to exotic restaurants in Chinatown.

After he had returned to Europe, he thought deeply about his recording future with RCA Victor. From Rome he wrote to Frank M. Folsom of RCA:

28 April 1955

Dear Mr. Folsom

I am in the Holy City, conducting the Santa Cecilia and the Radio Italiana orchestras, and feel I should bring two things to your attention. I am planning to create (Deo volente) a truly great orchestra in Houston, Texas, in collaboration with persons of great vision, and determination and equally great means of carrying out these plans. This will begin next October, and I would like to record for Victor with this orchestra Tchaikovsky's 4th Symphony, Prokofiev's Lieutenant Kije and his Scythian Suite. I am confident all of this music will have a wide public appeal, and we can record it at symphonic rates, after it has been played at concerts. I spoke to Mr. Marek about this, and he expressed favorable reaction.

May I request a definite "yes" or "no" regarding this, because Houston has other recording possibilities, and I do not wish to keep them waiting.

I like to make my plans well ahead because I find it better for everyone concerned. My present contract with Victor expires in March '56 and I would like to request now whether Victor would extend it after that date or not.[20]

Folsom ducked the question and handed the letter to Emmanuel Sacks, vice-president and general manager of RCA Victor. I do not have a copy of Sacks' reply, but it was obviously negative not only about the Houston orchestra but apparently toward Stokowski himself. Stoki replied from Cologne on May 23:

Thank you for your letter of May 10th. I have already foreseen the question of "whether recording the Houston Orchestra on a date basis rather then under a term contract, we will prejudice their effecting an arrangement with another company," and this can definitely be done so that we can record the repertoire that was discussed with Mr. Marek before I left. This was Tchaikovsky's 4th Symphony, Prokofiev's Lieutenant Kije and Prokofiev's Scythian Suite. Of course, this repertoire could be modified by mutual arrangement.

I must say I feel rather sad at the thought that my association with Victor will come to an end because I have been recording for you since October 1917.[21]

It is a sad commentary that the last of the Stokowski recordings under his exclusive contract with Victor were merely bagatelles. His 1955 recordings included "short and long versions" of Strauss' Blue Danube and Tales from the Vienna Woods; the Turkish Marches of Beethoven and Mozart; and Liszt's Hungarian Rhapsodies Nos. 1, 2 and 3. The waltzes and marches were for an album called "In the Lighter Vein," and the Liszt pieces (along with Enesco's Roumanian Rhapsodies) were issued in an album entitled "Rhapsody." RCA cannot take pride in its decisions.

60

Frankfurt

S TOKI dined with his boys on April 12, and before sailing the next
morning, Andrew Schulhof brought them down to the dock to see
their father off. This time he was traveling under the name of
Stanley. The year was 1955.

Schulhof had arranged his tour and attended to the most minute
details: his rail tickets, hotel reservations, cars to bring him to and from
concerts, the scores and parts he would have to bring, the names and
addresses of all the various managers and "intendants" he would need to
know. Concerts were to be given in Rome, Turin, Baden-Baden, Stuttgart, Cologne, Frankfurt am Main, and Vienna. He arrived in Paris on
his seventy-third birthday, which he spent in the Grand Hotel. In Rome,
where he stayed at his favorite Roman hotel, the Hassler, he spent three
days of intensive rehearsals, and on two successive nights, April 23 and 24,
he conducted concerts in the Academia Nazionale di Santa Cecilia. The
program: three Bach chorale preludes and the Beethoven Ninth Symphony. A week later for R.A.I. (Radio Italiana) he conducted what was
presumably the first Italian performance of Orff's *Carmina Burana*, which
he preceded with his transcriptions of Bach's "Ein' feste Burg," "Schafe
koennen sicher weiden," "Ich ruf' zu dir," and the Passacaglia and Fugue
in D Minor—these, too, unfamiliar to Italian listeners.

After two concerts with R.A.I. Torino, Stoki proceeded to Zurich,
where for two days he stayed at the Hotel Storchen in the center of
Zurich. It was a spot where he had stayed with Gloria on earlier and
happier trips. Then Baden-Baden. Programs there were always more inter-

esting than those given in most European cities. His was not run-of-the-mill:

Von Einem: *Meditationen*
Milhaud: Percussion Concerto
Ginastera: *Variaciones Concertantes*
Egk: French Suite
Prokofiev: *Romeo and Juliet* Suite

Andrew Schulhof arrived in Baden-Baden on Saturday, May 14, the day before the concert. It was a pleasant reunion. "Stokowski asked me to dine with him and with a young lady from Zurich," Schulhof said. They discussed an invitation to appear on the BBC doing *Carmina Burana* and a reengagement for Rome the following season. The concert on Sunday was held in the studios of Sudwestfunk for an invited audience of about three hundred. Schulhof recalled: "When Stokowski took a bow after the first number, the radio's official photographer rushed over near the podium and took a picture with flashlight. I rushed to Dr. Strobel, the Music Director, and told him that I did not understand how he could permit such things when he knew so well from the past that Stokowski was completely against being photographed, and, as in the past, we had the understanding that there would not be any. Dr. Strobel was very rude and said he did not care about Stokowski's wishes, but they finally wanted a photograph for their archives. At intermission I reported this at once to Stokowski, who said that he would not go to Baden-Baden again. I urged him to ask Strobel that the photographs either be destroyed or shown to him, and he told me not to do anything further, but that he would speak to Strobel. He did not do this.

"After the concert, Stokowski asked me to take the young girl to the 2:00 A.M. train, which I did reluctantly."

The following day, Stokowski canceled his train reservations and decided to drive to Stuttgart with his friend Kurt Leimer and his wife, leaving Schulhof to go by train with the scores and parts that he needed for the Stuttgart concert. Upon arriving, Schulhof immediately contacted the general music director, Herr Mueller-Kray, and they had a clear understanding that there would be no photographers or reporters allowed at the rehearsals, nor any other outsiders. "Both gentlemen assured me that this was the usual procedure at the radio anyway, and this would be adhered to."

The rehearsal, which began at ten in the morning, started routinely. Schulhof, who was in the control booth, was listening to the orchestral balance when suddenly he heard Stoki shouting. Schulhof rushed out from the control room and saw that a lady was standing there with a camera. "There was a heated exchange of words, and the lady reluctantly gave me the entire film reel from her movie camera. She sobbingly told me that she had spent her hard-earned money in order to take souvenirs of the great artists who came there, and that she had just started the reel of film with the pictures of Stravinsky, who did not object." Schulhof, however, demanded the film, had it developed—there was no picture of Stoki—and returned it to the taker with an additional unexposed film as some recompense. Stoki was apparently not mollified.

Andrew continued: "Stokowski started rehearsing the orchestra again, but after two or three minutes he stopped and, without a word, turned and left to go to his room. Of course, I rushed to him, and he started in a very unpleasant way to shout at me that it was against his contract, and he could not be quieted until about twenty minutes later, despite the efforts of everyone in trying to reason with him. He came out from his room later and asked for the car to go back to the hotel, saying that he would not conduct the concert the following night. After he had resisted the efforts of everyone who wanted to speak to him, I asked him outside the studio to come for a second with me, and when he stepped aside I told him nicely and quietly that we had the film and that I doubted whether it would be any good anyway, that she had only just started to make a picture and it was not a flashlight. I tried to explain the fact that the photography clause, as he knew, was never in any contract, but in a so-called instruction letter which had his full knowledge and approval."[1]

To confirm Schulhof's contention that there was nothing in the actual contract with the Süddeutscher Rundfunk, its legal office sent an official letter of confirmation.

May 20, 1955

Dear Professor Stokowski:

    I make reference to the personal talks yesterday and this morning with our General Music Director Mueller-Kray, at the Park Hotel.
    In compliance with your wishes, we gladly confirm the following:
        I. The contractural points of your guest conducting engagement at the Süddeutscher Rundfunk are contained in the correspondence between Mr. Mueller-

Kray and your agent, Mr. Andrew Schulhof. The entire
correspondence has been made available for your inspection by Mr. Mueller-Kray. Other contracts are not
in existence.

II. As you can yourself ascertain, there are no written
conditions regarding a ban on photographs. And furthermore, there are no conditions to prohibit entry of
strangers to the rehearsals.

We regret the incident on May 19, 1955 to the utmost and do
hope that the talks and this letter served to preserve our good relationship.

Süddeutscher Rundfunk[2]

Without a word to Schulhof, Stoki sent out letters to managers in
London, Rome, and elsewhere announcing that Schulhof was no longer
his manager. Nothing was mentioned during the stay in Cologne, and
Stokowski and the Leimers then drove to Frankfurt, with Schulhof again
proceeding by train. The rehearsals in Frankfurt were "rough going," said
Schulhof. Stoki had programmed *Jeux* by Debussy and insisted that the
score called for a "Contrabasse Sarusophone." None could be found in
Frankfurt and Stokowski insisted that someone be sent to Paris or Geneva,
where he was certain one could be found. None was located, and Stoki
thereupon changed his program and substituted *L'Après-midi d'un faune*.
His difficult program also included a new Cello Concerto by Krenek,
Stravinsky's *Mass*, Karl Amadeus Hartmann's Second Symphony, and the
world premiere of Hans Werner Henze's *Quattro Poemi*, which had been
commissioned specifically for this concert.

"At the concert there was again some excitement," said Schulhof,
"because the doors were closed at 8:00 P.M. sharp. It was a tape recording
and not an actual broadcast, and many people were still in front of the
door when it was closed. Amongst them was Mr. Henze. . . . Despite all
the precautions taken, someone in the first row started to take pictures.
Before Stokowski saw him, I rushed there and we ushered the man out
and I took away the films. He was just a private 'fan' who regretted the
upset."

The critics in general were harsh. The whole imbroglio about photographs seemed both silly and irritating. Photographers appeared increasingly eager to foil him, and they pursued him mercilessly. A reviewer in
the Frankfurt *Abendpost* wrote:

"His dislike of the public goes so far that he did not even grant his

approval of a picture by the resident photographer of the Hessian Rundfunk. A photoreporter at the concert was asked to leave during intermission when Stokowski noted his camera. His film was confiscated. However, this was a fresh film and the one he had used remained in his jacket.

"The 'Maestro' decreed to close the doors to the concert hall and not
to open them until intermission although there were three brief pauses
in the first part of the program; this was done. The result was that 300
people waited with their tickets for one hour in front of closed doors.
Among them were a number of music lovers from out-of-town and from
foreign countries.

"After the premiere of 'Quattro Poemi,' a search took place backstage

Photograph taken without permission at concert in Frankfurt, which resulted in the
dismissal of his manager, Andrew Schulhof (1955)

United Press International Photo

for the composer who was expected to take a bow for the applause. The search was in vain because he, too, stood outside the door and missed his own premiere . . .3"

Schulhof and Leopold arrived in Vienna during the morning of June 2, and they were met at the station by officials of the *Festwochen* committee and the Vienna Philharmonic. The atmosphere seemed to be extremely cordial. Stoki had drawn a picture of an old Bastille in Frankfurt and gave it to Schulhof for his wife, Belle, saying that he hoped she would like it.

Schulhof wrote:

> When we arrived at the first rehearsal on the morning of June 2, despite the signed amendment regarding photographers with the officials of the Festwochen and the Philharmonic, there were not one but scores of photographers waiting to take Stokowski's picture in the hall on the podium; amongst them was a young girl in working dungarees who was introduced as "the official photographer of the Philharmonic." . . . During the first two days I had to circle the hall to make sure that no photographs would be taken at the "peepholes" of the orchestra entrance.[4]

Stoki began rehearsals at once, and the first concert with the Vienna Philharmonic took place on June 5. His program, it seems, was a mistake. It consisted of three Bach-Stokowski chorale preludes, the Mozart Symphony No. 40 in G Minor, and the Brahms Second Symphony. With the exception of the Bach, no other two works were more overplayed in Vienna. And, too, the Viennese felt that they alone had a patent on the interpretation of these.

At the opening of the festival the President of Austria and the Mayor of Vienna were on hand, and the public "greeted this fascinating conductor with virtual jubilation," reported *Weltpresse*. The critic continued on a positive note. "He has the authority of the great conductor . . . his manner . . . is imposing."[5]

Critic Karl Löbl in the *Bild-Telegraf* was not so inclined. He referred to the concert as "Music in Technicolor" and added, "Homicide of Bach." It was an exceptionally sarcastic review. He wrote that because the composers were dead they could not complain.[6]

To mitigate somewhat the spirit of hostility that the press was exhibiting, largely over the photo business, Stoki agreed to give an interview while he was being taken through the refurbished opera house. He also permitted a photograph to be taken of him while he looked upward to the fresco on the ceiling.[7]

Nordisk Pressefoto
Photo Panic, Munich (1951). Half hidden on Stokowski's left is Andrew Schulhof

Months later when he was having all publicity material removed from Schulhof's office, he sent a short note thanking Schulhof's secretary, Miss Wailes, and added a short P.S.: "Thank you for sending the press clippings from Vienna, which I have read and am now returning. I have marked with a 'Y' some that I think are good. Most of them are bad. I think they found me a little too 'unusual.' "[8]

On the day of the last concert in Vienna, Andrew Schulhof received a letter from Mr. Howgill of the BBC telling him that Stokowski had written him from Stuttgart stating that Andrew was no longer his manager. Andrew was most distressed but decided not to mention the matter before the concert: "In the evening after the concert, when I was, as usual, with Stokowski for some time, I asked him for an early appointment the next morning on a very urgent matter. At 9:45 A.M. he telephoned and I went at once to him. I showed him Howgill's letter and his answer was: 'Yes, I was very angry in Stuttgart and I wrote to Mr. Howgill.' I told him how terribly upsetting his action was to me, and how damaging it was to my reputation. I questioned how he could have done such a thing, regardless of his anger. How could he forget the many years of service and friendship I had given him, and I asked especially how he could do such a thing without . . . saying a single word about it to me. . . . At this point Stokowski cut me off, saying that the whole discussion was very unpleasant for him, and that he would think it over and write to me from Munich or Paris. I told him he should not write to me, but urged him to write at once to Howgill, sending me a copy of his letter. Stokowski promised to do this. . . . We parted in the nicest way, and I took him to the car as usual, where we shook hands and exchanged pleasantries."[9]

Following the Vienna affair, Schulhof was still deeply disturbed and still incredulous that a single photographic episode could cause the disruption of his relation with Stokowski. He still felt that Stokowski would change his mind and that they would continue to work in the future as in the past. Stokowski was of a different mind. From New York, he wrote to R. J. F. Howgill, Esq.:

> Before leaving Vienna Mr. Schulhof requested me to write to you to explain why he will no longer be my manager. Upon thinking it over, I would prefer not to do this, because I do not wish in any way to harm Mr. Schulhof's reputation, and I have the greatest admiration for his many good qualities. All I can say is, that my contract with Mr. Schulhof expired on May 1, 1955 and I have reasons for not wishing to renew it. It is my sincere wish to continue the friendly relations I have had with Mr. Schulhof, and I would like, if it is possible, not to make any statements, personal or public, regarding the reasons for this change.

If Mr. Schulhof would like to explain to you those reasons, he is of course perfectly at liberty to do so.[10]

Upon receiving a copy of the letter, Schulhof wrote to Stoki saying that he felt that this letter was even more damaging to his reputation than the first: "But I still want to avoid further unpleasantness, and am convinced, that in a personal meeting we will find a mutually satisfactory solution. Therefore, I suggest, that we postpone further correspondence and publicity on our problems, until we meet. If, beside Miss Hanson and Mr. Howgill, you have written or intend to write upon the same matter to anyone, please, kindly notify me at once and send me copies."[11]

The situation did not improve. Arguments ensued regarding the amount of commission that was due to Schulhof and whether Stokowski would pay any commission on the three-year engagement in Houston. There were also disagreements on whether Schulhof would be entitled to anything resulting from engagements that he had begun to work on in various European and American cities. Schulhof engaged Sam Rosenbaum as his lawyer and Stoki had his own, Alfred Holmes. The two lawyers met and argued and threatened as lawyers frequently do, and after many months, an amicable settlement was reached. But Stoki would never again have anyone as solicitous and skillful as Andrew Schulhof.

Santa Barbara Festival

A T no time was Stokowski's personal life in greater disarray than it was at the beginning of 1955. But on professional and musical grounds there was much to cheer him. Houston was a *fait accompli* and now a new project—one that he took with the greatest interest and enthusiasm—a Pacific Coast festival that would be the equivalent of Tanglewood in the East. The first discussions about it were begun during the summer of 1954. It was spearheaded by a remarkable woman Mrs. Horace Gray, who was active in all sorts of ventures on the Santa Barbara cultural front. Leighton Rollins was to be the director, and he proved to be a most efficient and idealistic person.

On July 29, 1954, Leighton had written that "there remains our determined hope that we might inflame the enthusiasm of one or two patrons who might build us a redwood 'music shed' somewhat in the character of Tanglewood."[1]

Stoki's imagination took fire. He began to envision a festival that would not only rival Tanglewood but perhaps eventually become as renowned as Salzburg. He knew Santa Barbara very well having lived there for several seasons and he was naturally concerned about the location that would be chosen. "Outside of the shed should be extended ground where people can sit out in the open air, and listen to music, particularly after sunset . . . The stage should be large enough for a full symphony orchestra and chorus, because if the Festival is well done it will grow and eventually be a key place on the Pacific Coast."[2]

He concerned himself with endless details and drew many sketches of the ideal setup for such a festival. He asked Leighton: "Can you find out (from those who know) what is the prevailing wind in August? The reason is that if the wind blows into the reflector it will affect the sound waves, whereas if it blows from the stage end all will be well. In open air the question of wind is more important than most people realize."[3]

Knowing that I was planning to be in California, Stoki wrote a letter of introduction to Leighton Rollins.

Shortly thereafter I met Leighton for the first time, and we visited all of the possible sites where the festival might take place. I photographed all of these and brought them back for Stoki to see. I also met many members of the board who were organizing the event. All seemed most eager to develop a festival in Santa Barbara the equal of those in the East. Letters flew back and forth between New York and Santa Barbara. On looking over the tremendous amount of correspondence that ensued, one might think that the final result was to be something of the greatest and most momentous importance. In Stokowski's mind it seemed to be.

What he failed to realize was the fact that unlike the situation at Tanglewood and Saratoga Springs, he did not have a Boston Symphony or Philadelphia Orchestra to bring with him, nor did he have the managerial expertise of these two organizations, nor the organized financial backing such symphonies enjoy.

The best location it seemed was in the courtyard of the Santa Barbara Courthouse in the very center of the city. The setting was most attractive and the sunken garden surrounded on three sides by gleaming white walls of the pseudo-Spanish structure seemed ideal. There was a large tower on one side from which carrillon music could be played which Stoki decided to have preceding each concert. Although the surrounding walls of the courtyard seemed to obviate the need for an elaborate reflecting surface, Stoki continued to sketch plans for an elaborate shell which he decided to call an *Auralium* and later suggested that perhaps a better name would be "*Aurisium,* from the Latin word *auris.* Purists might prefer this, although to my ears auralium sounds a little better."[4]

Brimming with plans for both Houston and Santa Barbara, Stoki set out on his westward trek on Monday, August 15. When his train reached St. Louis, he changed to the Missouri Pacific Eagle, on which he was joined by Paul Hochuli, the amusements editor of the *Houston Press,* for the trip to Houston. Hochuli apparently was an agreeable traveling partner for Stoki. Hochuli wrote: "A more pleasant traveling companion you couldn't find—

except when you ask questions about plans for the coming season.

" 'I'll buy you a drink, but all questions—and I mean all—will be answered at the press conference in Houston when all the music critics will be present,' he said. 'I think that is fair, and I want to do it that way.'

"See what I mean about charm. So we had the drink, and I agreed such questions were off limits. . . . Incidentally, I came out ahead on the drink business. According to agreement, I bought the before-dinner libation (rum for Mr. Stokowski, bourbon for me), and he picked up the tab for the coffee drink—creme de menthe. My check was $1.70, his $2.05."[5]

The following day in his suite in Houston's Rice Hotel, reporters remarked on his attire: a Hollywood-type black shirt and suit and white-figured tie—as he touched on the subjects of women, new personnel for the orchestra and briefly upon his private life. They summed up the gist of his remarks. Ann Holmes reported: "Stokowski showed curiosity about the personality of Houston which he pronounces more like 'Hooston,' and said he expects within a year and a half to have moulded the orchestra to the type of ensemble he had planned.

" 'They are keen musicians here, and I know they will give their best,' he said. On the subject of women in the orchestra he snorted 'of course, we shall have women in the orchestra. We accept women naturally on an equal basis . . . sometimes higher. In music we do not think of whether an artist is a man or a woman.' "

Characteristically, he outlined grandiose plans for production of operas and ballets, the engagement of Léonide Massine as a choreographer to work with local dance groups, broadcasts, and recordings. It all left some of the Texans a bit breathless, but not too much so, since they were used to thinking big.[6]

Stoki had expressed great curiosity about cowboys and horses "so we arranged for him to become an honorary member of the Sheriff's Mounted Posse, a sort of show unit," said Tom Johnson.[7] "Sheriff Leopold (Shoot-'em-Up) Stokowski" is what the press dubbed him. When asked whether he would like to get up on a horse, he shuddered and said, " 'I haven't been on a horse since I was a child. . . . It's bad enough to work with 100 musicians,' he added, 'but when it comes to horses, that's too much.' "

Stoki then spied Hercules, a chubby Shetland pony about three feet tall. He asked photographers to take his picture with the pony to send to his sons. They obliged and the press ran a charming photo of Deputy Parmley, dressed as a real cowboy with chaps, a broad-brimmed hat, and

Photo Richard Pervin/Courtesy Tom Johnson

Inducted as an "honorary Texas cowboy" (1955)

ivory-handled six-shooter; Hercules, in his tousled Shetland horsehair; and Stokowski elegantly attired in "a dudish blue suit, striped polo shirt, polka-dot tie and brown suede shoes."

" 'You've saved my life,' he confided to the posse deputies. 'I told my sons I was coming to Texas and would meet some cowboys. This will prove it to them.' "[8]

After a brief three-day stop in Houston, Stoki boarded a train for Los Angeles, where he proceeded at once to the home of his friend Bernard Herrmann on Blue Bell Avenue in North Hollywood. The house was a rambling affair. The original part was somewhat insubstantial, as many California houses are, but a series of rooms was added, including a guest-house by the pool, which was shaded from the late-afternoon sun by enormously tall eucalyptus trees. Wendy Hanson arrived the following day.

Benny Herrmann was something of a paradox, but so was Stokowski. That these two seemingly disparate individuals should find so much in common could only have perplexed the uninitiated. Benny was outwardly somewhat gauche. He never lost some of his Lower East Side crudity, yet internally and spiritually Benny probably felt like an eighteenth-century gentleman from Bath. When I first met him and had to work with him on various CBS broadcasts, I nearly developed ulcers. But strangely, as one got to know him, one discovered a gentle side that was just as positive as his violent one when rehearsing an orchestra.

But Benny was one of the most enthusiastic and ebullient persons I have ever known. He was an ardent Anglophile and was as much a self-styled authority on English gardens and architecture as he was on music.

After one long discussion between Benny and Stoki during which Benny illustrated certain points by playing some records, Stoki wrote:

Dear Bernardino

I enjoyed immensely your talk about the beauties of Handel. It came particularly well after a performance of a symphony of Beethoven that was completely mechanical, although well done otherwise. It was as if a metronome started off the tempo and from that moment everything was as if a machine were playing. What you said about individual expression and about contributing to the composer, and particularly your choice of language in calling the singers of Handel's period "co-creators" was so just and illuminating. Also what you said about Bach's writing in his decorative phrases, whereas Handel, Gluck and other composers left such elaboration to the player and singer.

You made so clear the idea of collaboration between performer and composer, and what you said is so necessary today, when everything is becoming so materialistic and mechanistic in music. Thank you for having the courage to say it—and the clarity of mind to say it so well.

Your friend
Leopold[9]

On August 30, in the Hollywood Bowl, Stoki conducted Orff's *Carmina Burana*, preceded by "Romeo at the Tomb" from Prokofiev's *Romeo and*

Juliet and Glière's Symphony No. 3 *(Ilya Murometz)*. To Angelenos it may have been just another evening, but to a tourist it was quite magical. The sun still striped the sky with some streamer clouds and the whole atmosphere was perfect for the music that was to follow. Critic Raymond Kendall observed: "In the spirit of tradition, it was particularly appropriate that Leopold Stokowski should return to the podium where he conducted so many concerts in 1945 and 1946.

"Though a noticeably older man mounted the podium last night, the years fell away as he wrestled with the music. . . . Stokowski's own pleasure in the chorus' response brought forth a fervent 'bravo.' "[10]

There was not merely one bravo but thousands as the cheering audience brought Stoki and the soloists back repeatedly for a long sequence of bows. It was the concluding night of the Bowl season and the audience made their salute a thunderous one.

Stoki and Wendy proceeded to the San Ysidro Ranch in Santa Barbara on September 1.[11] There were preliminaries to be discussed and he began his first rehearsal the following day. Rehearsals continued daily and he seemed pleased with the orchestra and the whole ambience of the festival. On Friday the rehearsal took place in the Court House gardens. The stage was covered over with a canvas to protect the players and to prevent wind from blowing away their music. The engineers, who had been engaged by Phil Kahgan, seemed to be very capable and cooperative. Stoki insisted on twelve Altec mikes suspended over the players just under the canvas ceiling. I argued with him, or rather attempted to argue with him, but he said that a young man from Santa Barbara who was a hi-fi expert was helping. I listened as some of the tests were made. It boded disaster. The concertmaster was completely off mike and the last stand of lesser players was highly magnified. The whole arrangement seemed to me to be quite unsatisfactory. Strangely, while Stoki and I had worked so closely together on broadcasts and recordings, he would not hear of any suggestions, and so it proceeded.

Before the first concert, on Saturday, September 10, I gave a lecture at the Lobero Theater on the first two Stokowski programs.[12] The electronic carillon in the Court House tower began its concert as the people milled about before taking their seats. There were newly composed works and early classics. The pleasant tintinnabulations would have pleased Poe himself. Then the trumpeters began their fanfares. It was all very dramatic and festive.

The first program began with a *Concerto Grosso* in D by Handel, four

Bach chorales and a *Serenata Notturna* for Strings and Timpani by Mozart. After intermission the Concerto No. 5 by Hovhaness, the world premiere of Henry Cowell's Hymn and Fuguing Tune No. 10 for Oboe and Strings, and Schoenberg's *Verklaerte Nacht.*

It began beautifully. The unfortunate miking seemed less disparate than it had sounded during the rehearsal, and everyone sat back contentedly listening to music that was designed to soothe the spirit. All went well until shortly after the intermission. As it seemed to do each late afternoon, a gentle breeze began to blow up from the Pacific. It was not strenuous. But it was enough to ripple the canvas cover of the stage a few inches above the twelve Altec mikes that were hanging like stalactites above the orchestra. As the canvas pattered and rippled against the wires and bars that supported it—as well as the mikes—the sound began to be amplified like thunder " 'cross the bay." The engineers, looking visibly distressed, tried to reduce the sound, with the effect of cutting down the sound of the music as well.

For the most part the critics tended to ignore the negative aspect and concentrated on the music and the performance. Patterson Greene of the *Los Angeles Examiner* found only one complaint, and that was the "excessive amplification that frequently caused the music to sound like a rather bad phonograph reproduction of itself." After listening to the *Serenata Notturna,* he regretted that he had never before heard Stokowski conduct Mozart.[13]

Early on Sunday morning, Stoki phoned me and asked me to join him and the engineers to see what could be done to improve the amplification process. I suggested again, as I had done at the beginning, that the mikes be placed on stands and not hung from above. I also suggested cutting down on the number being used. Stoki accepted the idea of using stands but was adamant about his twelve "meek-ro-phones." "Whatever acoustical problems existed during the opening concert had been considerably alleviated by last Sunday afternoon's performance," wrote Henry Seldis in the *Examiner.*[14]

In addition to the presence of the brisk Pacific breezes and the accoustical gremlins, another problem beset Santa Barbara. A serious brush and forest fire broke out south of the town, and the news reports both in the papers and on TV greatly exaggerated the blaze; the music lovers who would have motored up from Los Angeles cautiously stayed away. It very definitely hurt the box office.

Chamber music concerts continued throughout the week. Stoki worked with the chorus for the works to be done on the second weekend. On Friday the jinx settled on the Court House gardens with a vengeance. For dramatic effect, visual rather than aural, Stoki decided to place the large choir for the American choruses in a long line on the balcony that ran along the building in back of the orchestra. I urged him to keep them below, but the suggestion seemed merely to irritate him. I pointed out that it would be virtually impossible to mike them the way they would be spread out above him and that communication between him and the chorus would be very difficult. The chorus, however, was placed on the balcony and mikes were lined up before them.

After the English works by William Lawes, Matthew Locke, Henry Purcell, and John Humphries were played, the protective canopy that sheltered the orchestral musicians was lowered so that the audience would see as well as hear the singers in the early American choruses. Stoki had chosen the *Lamentation Over Boston* by Billings, *How Swift the Moments Fly* by Supply Belcher, and two short works by Jacob Kimball: *Leicester* and *Hark What News the Angels Bring*.

"Amidst the acoustical havoc of Saturday's concert the A Cappella singing of early American masterworks by Billings, Belcher, and Kimball provided one of the festival's highlights," wrote critic Henry Seldis. "This naive and straightforward music was actually enhanced by the amateur choirs singing since more sophisticated vocal groups might well have added unnecessary flourishes."

The real havoc came after intermission. There had been some slight feedback during the playing of the English pieces, which to Seldis "seemed as dull as English cooking."[15] When the canopy was replaced and the orchestra returned to the stage, the engineers brought the mikes forward, in fact beyond the main speakers. During the playing of the Tchaikovsky *Serenade*, on one of the first crescendos, the distressing whine of feedback began. It was shrill and intense. The unfortunate engineer lowered the volume and the string orchestra became almost inaudible at the back of the garden. Throughout the piece, he struggled with his dials, trying to give as much amplification as he might but not succeeding very ably.

After this Stoki called me and asked me to take over the complete management of the audio equipment. The engineers, who were very capable but utterly intimidated by Stokowski, were eager to cooperate.

After fifteen years in radio and producing broadcasts of the Boston Symphony, the CBS Symphony, and the New York Philharmonic, the problems in Santa Barbara were for me neither unique nor monumental. "Amplification problems plagued the Saturday Stokowski concert to such an extent that most of the program was ruined," wrote Seldis. "In contrast," he said, "Sunday's program beyond being extraordinarily well performed, proved that what was needed for the outdoor concerts was not only a shell and an expert sound engineer, but a program which is not restricted to string music."[16]

The program was varied both in content and instrumentation. It read:

Darius Milhaud: Concerto for Percussion and Small Orchestra
Charles Ives: *The Unanswered Question*
Béla Bartók: Music for Strings, Percussion and Celeste
Igor Stravinsky: Mass for Chorus and Double Wind Quintet
Jean Sibelius: Berceuse from *The Tempest*
Ralph Vaughan Williams: *Serenade to Music*

The music was vital and varied, and Stokowski achieved one of those miracles he had been famous for; he made the players sound like the finest ensemble that one could ever encounter. He was at his best during the concert, and the receptive audience responded enthusiastically. It was also the largest that had assembled during the festival, and there was no smoke or fire to deter the flocks of music lovers from Los Angeles from driving up the Coast. The reviews were just this side of being ecstatic.

And so ended the Santa Barbara festival of 1955. I doubt that any other set of concerts ever involved more time, correspondence, and effort than these. But it had been part of another of Stoki's dreams. Leighton told me: "Our deficit for the Pacific Coast Music Festival after the Stokowski concerts was $26,000 . . . and Santa Barbara could not stand that. . . . I think Santa Barbara is the living example of the last small city in America which is holding things with a clenched fist. There are people of vast wealth in Santa Barbara—too many—and they do nothing for Santa Barbara. They always have that beautiful excuse: 'Oh, we come from Chicago, we come from Philadelphia, we come from Boston, and that is where we give our money.' And I wonder whether they do. I rather doubt it. But it was too bad, because it was a beautiful festival and it had distinction."[17]

Concert of the Pacific Coast Music Festival in sunken garden of the Santa Barbara Courthouse (1955)

"Hooston"

THE mother of it all was Ima Hogg. The poor (or rather rich) soul went through life with her ludicrous name and apparently never thought of changing it. By all accounts she was a remarkable woman, and she made a distinct imprint on the cultural life of Houston. To her friends and pupils she was affectionately referred to as "Miss Ima." Her father amassed a huge oil fortune, much of which went into charitable and educational activities. It also helped Miss Ima carry out her various projects, and the symphony was one of them. In 1913 the Houston Symphony was born in the form of a trial concert given between the afternoon and evening shows on a sweltering June day in a vaudeville house called the Majestic. In 1918, along with America's entry into World War I, the orchestra was suspended and did not resume until May 7, 1931.[1] The conductor of the revived orchestra was an Italian named Uriel Nespoli, who had been imported by one of Houston's social bulldozers, Mrs. John Wesley Graham, who was fondly known as "Ma" Graham. In 1930 she met an opera coach in Milan, Mr. Nespoli, and wanted to have him train and conduct a Houston opera enterprise that she envisioned. When he did not arrive at the time he was expected, "Ma" Graham was given an explanation that the Italian immigration quota was filled. This then took on the aspects of a federal case. First she contacted the American consul in Milan, then she moved in on Congress, and finally to the Secretary of State. Ergo, the tardy Mr. Nespoli was put on the next available cattle boat.

Hubert Roussel describes him deliciously. "It was mid-January before

Nespoli finally arrived—tagged and delivered to Mrs. Graham much in the way of a piece of baggage, for he was utterly innocent of English. Nespoli was a stocky, nervous, eruptive little man of 47, myopic and beginning to bald, who peered at the world through round, thick-lensed glasses with the aspect of an unusually emotional salmon."[2] On Nespoli's opening program of the rejuvenated orchestra he introduced the closing scene from Mascagni's opera *Iris*. Though the chorus howled bravely through the creaking relic, the evening was not a howling success.[3] Nespoli was abruptly sacked.

During the 1947–48 season the Houston Symphony Orchestra had no regular conductor and instead relied on a spate of guests. There were thirteen in all during the season, and among them were Abravanel, Buketoff, Chavez, Schwieger, Munch, and Kurtz.[4] Houston was shopping.

But before a new conductor was chosen, the board engaged a new manager, a remarkable, Missouri-born young man, Tom Johnson. He was a highly trained musician with a Bachelor of Music degree. He had attended Southern Methodist University, Southwestern University, and the Juilliard School of Music, where he studied conducting. In 1942 he was inducted into the Army, and during his assignment in Europe he organized and conducted an Army symphony orchestra.

In January 1948 he took over the management of the Houston Symphony Orchestra.[5] Shortly thereafter a new conductor arrived, the suave, elegant Efrem Kurtz, who was to remain until 1954. Tom Johnson had played his first hand.

Following the departure of Kurtz, Houston had a particularly disastrous experience with the Hungarian conductor Ferenc Fricsay, who was engaged for the 1954–55 season. He began auspiciously. But problems soon developed that were more a matter of temperament than of musical ability. "If I come to Houston," he announced in an interview, "I must be second only to God." He was lodged by the orchestra in a luxurious suite in the Warwick Hotel, but he soon let the management know that he expected to have "a house as big as that of Miss Hogg or Mrs. Ledbetter"—those being among the most palatial in Houston. In addition to the house, he expected to have a staff of servants to tend it. All scot-free!

Hubert Roussel summed it up nicely, saying, "The officials who heard this absurdity gave it the name it deserved and then believed that they had not heard it." The board notified him that they would be glad to release him for the second half of the season, to which Fricsay responded with vituperation and acrimony. Then during that lively season of peace on earth and joy to men, Fricsay exited *con brio*.

Perhaps the man most embarrassed by this brief contretemps—Fricsay had conducted a mere eight of its regular concerts—was Andrew Schulhof, his manager.

To Houston's relief, Schulhof came forward with a welcome suggestion: Would they be interested in having Sir Thomas Beecham in their midst? They would indeed, and after a few guest conductors filled in, the redoubtable Sir Thomas arrived in March to finish the season. The Beecham experience was a particularly happy one.[6] As usual, Beecham added a bit of *lagniappe* to his conductorial duties and regaled his audiences with brief and witty comments sometimes during the concerts or immediately after. When he departed at the end of the season, Tom Johnson, the manager of the orchestra, asked him to write his assessment of the orchestra. "The most fortunate thing that could happen to Houston," he wrote, would be the acquisition of a musical director who would take a really serious interest in the artistic life of the community. I regret that both my preoccupations elsewhere and my years are too numerous for me to undertake a task which should be the pride of any younger man of ability to attempt."[7] Beecham then was seventy-five. Stoki was a young man of seventy-three.

Miss Ima decided to do some shopping on her own. Early in February she flew to New York to consult with various managers. The results were disappointing until she finally phoned Andrew Schulhof. She inquired about Stokowski. Schulhof was very receptive and told her that he thought Stoki might be interested in Houston at that particular time. Andrew contacted Stoki at once, and Miss Ima instructed her new manager to pursue the matter as adroitly as possible. Naturally, Tom Johnson was delighted to do so.[8]

On Monday February 14, 1955, Stoki arrived in Detroit. Andrew Schulhof joined him and so did Tom Johnson. Together they developed the idea of Stokowski coming to Houston. Tom recalled that "Schulhof formulated a very appealing argument to Stokowski. In Houston, he could bring up his sons in the great outdoors and in an environment far better than that of New York. I'm convinced that that is the real reason that Stokowski came to Houston. 'It is time that I build another orchestra,' he would say later. But the real motivation was the boys.

"On the train from Detroit to Chicago next day, a negotiations ritual was conducted by Schulhof, with Stokowski at one end of an otherwise empty club car, I at the other end, Schulhof processing sedately back and forth between us carrying out the exchange of terms of all sorts, and eventually administering a laying on of hands in which the three of us gathered in the center of the car to cement our new relationship with a glass of sherry served by Andrew with all the dignity of a friendly bishop.

"We settled on a one-year contract, but by the time we had reached Chicago, Stokowski had become so enthused about the boys being in Texas—'I want them to see how the milk comes from a cow and not a little bottle,' he said—that he suggested that we might extend the contract to three years.

"Two weeks later, we signed the three-year agreement in the Gracie Square apartment, which Stokowski was at the moment evacuating. While Schulhof and I helped to sort out and pack his scores and books, he said I must 'get him a map of Texas.' He was going to 'buy a ranch where the boys could have a real living,' as he put it. He was certain that he would have them in his custody a great part of the time and overjoyed in this anticipation, he was happier than I was ever to see him again. I remember asking him that evening how he felt about women in his orchestra. We had more than the usual number and I was concerned. 'Men, women, monkeys,' he shouted back jovially, 'as long as they can play.' "

Before Stoki set out for Texas, he gave much thought to where he would like to live and how the environment would please the boys. He said to Tom Johnson that he wanted to live on a ranch. "After I told him that no ranches lay within commuting distance, he returned a map with a number of X's marked on the principal roads. One of the locations was marked might do for 'a truck garden,' which he would settle for 'in lieu of a ranch,' he said. When I explained the uneconomical nature of this sort of venture, he reluctantly abandoned his aspirations of being a gentleman in the country, but said he would 'not stay in a hotel.' He now wanted a 'tourist court,' and from the map he determined on precisely which one he wanted. We made the necessary arrangements, but after two weeks of camping out in the rather dismal digs he had chosen for himself, he was not at all reluctant to accept my suggestion that he move into the Warwick, a very nice residential hotel on the park, where he seemed content.[9]

Stokowski arrived in Houston on a sweltering October afternoon. He was met by a welcoming delegation that included Hubert Roussel, who

described him alighting from the train as "the picture of Augustan authority in a unique mold." As he took to Texas, so did the Texans take to him,
even though they were a little nonplussed to hear him pronounce Houston
as "Hooston," like a patriarchal hoot owl.

On Sunday before his first Houston concert, NBC televised part of his
rehearsal on a program "Wide, Wide World." He was rehearsing Alan
Hovhaness' symphony, *Mysterious Mountain.* [10] Watching him on the
TV screen, one could not help noting that he seemed tired and sad,
though he spoke optimistically about the new music life he felt he was
beginning in Houston. The source of his dejection was obvious, for on the
same day an AP dispatch datelined El Paso, Texas, October 30, was
headlined "Files for Divorce from Stokowski." The release read: "Gloria
Vanderbilt Stokowski, 31, petitioned for a divorce from her conductor
husband, Leopold Stokowski, 68, in Juarez, Mexico Saturday." (He was
actually 73.) The charge made by Gloria was "incompatibility of characters." The release continued: "The twice married plaintiff appeared in
Juarez court . . . wearing a black suit, gray coat, white gloves and hat. Her
name has been linked romantically recently with singer Frank Sinatra's
but she did not mention any marriage plans."[11]

The following evening he conducted his first Houston concert, an event
unsurpassed in the annals of Texas music making. The audience in the
Music Hall on that Monday night filled it to its limit and somewhat
beyond. There was a total of 3,154 counted listeners to hear what the
critics called "the most significant orchestral event in the history of
Southwest music."

The principal work which Stokowski had chosen for his opener was
Hovhaness' *Mysterious Mountain,* which he had commissioned. Other
works included Wagner's *Meistersinger* Overture, Ravel's *Daphnis et
Chloé* Suite No. 2, and the Brahms First Symphony—the work he had
also chosen for his Philadelphia debut. The audience was the most brilliant Houston could assemble. Texas has its own royalty, with oil barons,
King ranchers, and merchant princes. The dog was put on and they
arrived with a real Texan-style show of opulence and bravado; they came
in satins, sables, swallowtails, and jewels. There was great excitement on
both sides of the podium, and when Stokowski appeared he was greeted
with one of the most spontaneous and tumultuous welcomes he had ever
received. At the conclusion they burst out like a wild set of sports fans
would. They shouted, stamped, applauded, and bravoed. Stokowski was

in his glory. When I phoned him the following day, he told me how pleased he was and that he knew his stay in "Hooston" was going to be a very happy one.

The critics were jubilant. Ann Holmes in the *Houston Chronicle:* "Houston may have heard its golden chapter of music Monday night."[12]

Roussel in the *Houston Post* headlined his review "Symphony Under Hand of Stokowski Opens Season With Triumph." After an introduction describing the event, he focused on Hovhaness and devoted most of his lengthy review to discussion and praise of the new work.[13]

Cornered during the intermission, Hovhaness was asked about his reaction to hearing a work of his for the first time. "This was a very exciting experience," he said, "especially to hear Mr. Stokowski conduct a piece of mine—he has always interpreted my music better than anyone else. And I thought the orchestra was very, very fine."[14]

His third program presented the world premiere of the Sixth Symphony of Henry Cowell. Not sharing Stokowski's aversion to flying, Henry flew to Houston for the performance. Unfortunately, this symphonic work is not the best of Cowell, and, while the audience paid it respectful homage, it did not stand to cheer.

The fourth concert introduced Howard Hanson's Piano Concerto in G Major, with Rudolf Firkušný as the soloist. When I talked with Firkušný about his Houston performance, he said: "When we played the Hanson concerto, he made the announcement to the audience that after the concert is finished, we will repeat the concerto. Now I'm not quite sure whether we played the whole piece or only some movements, but anyway, we repeated the piece.

"It was really the best performance of the concerto. I played it many times with Hanson, but Stokowski gave it this special kind of Stokowski flair. . . . I don't think many people left . . . practically the majority stayed for the repeat performance."[15]

The fifth concert in the series consisted of three works, all new to Houston: Aram Khachaturian's *Festive Poem* in it's world premiere, Shostakovich's Tenth Symphony, and Wallingford Riegger's sprightly *Dance Rhythms.*

The sixth concert was devoted entirely to the music of Sibelius, during which he gave the American premiere of his *Hymn to the Earth.* The pair of concerts on December 6 was in celebration of Sibelius' ninetieth birthday. Sibelius was born on December 8, 1865, and Stoki wrote a brief greeting to his old friend in Helsinki:

November 30, 1955

Jean Sibelius
Järvenpaa
Helsinki, Finland

Dear Master and Friend:

I wish I could be in Finland for your birthday, but instead I must be in Texas where we shall play Finlandia, The Swan of Tuonela, Berceuse from "Tempest," Hymn to the Earth (first performance in the United States) and your Symphony II, in your honor.
Always with deepest admiration and affection,

Leopold Stokowski[16]

He then packed his bags and entrained for New York and a reunion with his boys.

To celebrate the bicentenary of the birth of Mozart, Harold Spivack, who was then chief of the Music Division of the Library of Congress, invited Stoki to come to Washington to conduct an all-Mozart program on December 17, 1955. The concert was under the aegis of the Gertrude Clark Whittall Foundation, and the program included the *Ave, verum corpus* with the cooperation of a selected choir from the chorus of Howard University and members of the National Symphony. Another major work was a Serenade or as it is sometimes called, Grand Partita for thirteen instruments. This work was of particular interest because the original score was in the collection of the library.

Among the thirteen instruments that this work called for, there were two basset horns. However, the players in the symphony did not have them. The ingenious Spivack contacted the various branches of the services: the Army, Navy, and the Marines.

In a warehouse of one of the services (I no longer remember which), the basset horns were located. They had apparently been there since World War I without having been used.

I met Stoki in New York's old Penn Station, and on the train we talked mostly about Houston and future programs. As always, it was the future that interested him, not the past. But there was much to tell of Houston, for that was the present, and he talked much of the orchestra, the general atmosphere there, and the wonderful hospitality that he had encountered.

When we were passing through Philadelphia, I reminded him of a story that was told—that every time he would pass through Philadelphia on the train he would pull the curtains shut. He laughed at that and pointed out that most trains didn't even have curtains. "Another myth," he said.

In New York on December 28, three weeks after his all-Sibelius concert in Houston, Stokowski was invited to the Park Avenue apartment of Artturi Lehtinen, the consul general of Finland, to be presented with the decoration of Commander of the Order of the White Rose of Finland, one of the country's highest honors.[17] After a brief and fitting tribute paid by Mr. Lehtinen, Stokowski responded by telling of his love of Finland and recounted several happy experiences he had there. Then he launched into a paean of praise for his friend Jean Sibelius.

Leopold regarded this decoration very highly, and I believe it was one of the few decorations of his that he had framed. For many years it hung on a wall next to his work desk.

When Stokowski returned in mid-January 1956, his first premiere was Olivier Messiaen's twittery *The Awakening of the Birds.* The audience seemed to agree with critic Roussel, who felt that it was "strictly for the creatures named in the title." But he followed it in his next program with another Stokowski blockbuster, Orff's *Carmina Burana,* and the audience went wild. It was a dramatic evening, and he used a massive assembly of 150 choristers and a splendid array of soloists.[18] "Wow!" was the expression many of the Texans uttered.

The following day we spoke on the phone, and he told me what a success the evening had been. I decided then that I would send him a little souvenir of the concert. Remembering that in the early days in Philadelphia he had often been presented with elaborate laurel wreaths, I opted for something simpler. I picked up a box of laurel leaves—bay leaves to the culinary experts—and sent them to him in Houston.

"I couldn't make a wreath," I wrote on the note I had attached, and added the line, "May Apollo bless you" and sent it off to the Rice Hotel, where he was then staying.[19] A week later I received one of his characteristically brief notes: "It came. The wreath. It was in some music. I am going to wear it for a time and try to look like Julius Caesar, and after that I am going to use the leaves for cooking, because they give a wonderful flavor (of course I will sterilize them first)." Then after his boldly scrawled "Leopold," he added, "Thanks!"[20]

After only two concerts he again headed for New York to be at home and see his boys. On March 2 he invited a group of friends to celebrate

the first season of his Texas venture. It was a rare evening, for in his ample
but rather Spartan quarters, he almost never entertained.

He planned to return to Houston by a very circuitous route. Stan and
Chris were to be with him for a month and he decided on an auto trip.
His route book gives the itinerary in detail: the trip included Longview
Gardens in Pennsylvania, Nashville, Asheville, Raleigh, Greensboro, Spar-
tanburg. Then on to Florida: Jacksonville, Orlando, Daytona Beach, West
Palm Beach—and a brief visit with Evangeline—Miami, Tampa, St.
Petersburg, and finally Mobile, Alabama, on March 26. From here the
boys and their nurse returned to New York, and Stoki proceeded to
Houston for the two concluding concerts of the season.

For the first of these, he had chosen another work by Orff. Since the
effect of *Carmina Burana* had been so dynamic, he hoped the introduction of his *Triumph of Aphrodite* would elicit a similar response. As he
had done with *Carmina Burana,* he again used large choral forces and gave
his all in presenting it. But the work failed to generate anything like the
enthusiasm that *Carmina* had elicited. The audience applauded limply.

The final program of the season, on April 10, was a very curious
assemblage: Ravel's fanfare for the ballet *L'Éventail de Jeanne,* Camargo
Guanieri's *Danza Negra,* Oscar Esplá's *Don Quixote Verlando las Armas,*
a work by a Texan composer, Paul Holmes, called simply *Fable,* and two
potboilers, Ravel's *Boléro* and the Tchaikovsky Symphony No. 4. Thus
the season closed on a somewhat unresponsive note, for Roussel reported
that "the concert ended with a goodly part of the audience either drowsy
or half way home."[21]

A week later we celebrated his birthday in New York. No one mentioned that it was his seventy-fourth. I gave the party in the Fifty-second
Street penthouse. Among the guests was the colorful Shinichi Yuise, a
young Japanese koto virtuoso. Shin was studying with Henry Cowell at
the time and spent several years in New York. He was a most handsome
person. One might even use the word *beautiful,* for he was just that,
refined and aristocratic.

Shin arrived wearing a magnificent brown and white silk kimono, white
socks, and the traditional shoes held on by a thong. The dinner was
Chinese rather than Japanese. A succulent array of dishes was brought in
by a Chinese caterer and served ceremoniously, and all ate with chop-
sticks. Stoki enjoyed the somewhat pseudoexoticism.

After dinner Shin played many classical Japanese works on the koto and
then added folk music and some compositions of his own—all of which

were very Japanese. Stoki was greatly interested in the instrument, and I believe the evening paved the way for the engagement of Kimio Eto to play the Cowell Koto Concerto a few years later with the Philadelphia Orchestra.

During the course of the evening, discussions revolved around different types of recorded sound. Peggy Glanville-Hicks was championing the dull, dry pressings of MGM recordings against other more resonant ones. It became basically an argument as to the virtues of clarity versus resonance. Always the gallant gentleman, he backed away from the argument, while Peggy with imperious pronouncements tried to make her point. It was a fine evening despite some of its highly charged moments.

As a birthday present I assembled a large collection of various liqueurs of which he was always fond. I also found two illustrated books on Yugoslavia; he was scheduled to conduct there at the end of May. The following morning he dictated a note.

19 April 1956

Dear Oliver

The party last night was a delight, because you had such interesting people, even if we did disagree about certain things! At least you and I entirely agreed.

The food was exceptional and I know how much trouble you must have taken to make it so good.

You overwhelmed me with presents, and it will be fun to open the little bottles and make exotic blends. The two books are not only a delight, but will help me very much to understand that rather big country of many republics called Yugoslavia.

Looking forward to lunch on Monday.

Always
Leopold[22]

63

The Summer of 1956

S
TOKOWSKI'S concerts in Europe during the summer of 1956 took place in Madrid, Zagreb, Belgrade, and Zurich. He had canceled his contracts with the BBC that had been made by Schulhof and now depended upon the Beeks in the Netherlands and Siegfried Hearst in New York. Wendy Hanson acted as anchor person and accepted the title of "Assistant to Mr. Stokowski." Correspondence was voluminous, and Stoki may well have appreciated the tremendous attention to details that Schulhof had maintained.

The Beeks, a husband-and-wife team, operated from The Hague as the Nederlandsche Concertdirectie J. Beek. They had contacted Stoki after learning by the grapevine that Schulhof was no longer to be his manager.

As arrangements developed, he reminded the Beeks that "I do not ever fly because I have been in an accident and frankly I am afraid of planes now." He told them, too, that "the State Department in Washington has a military orchestra playing in Europe from the 7th Army, which they would like to enlarge and have me conduct in Berlin and Vienna. This plan is not quite definite yet, but I feel I should tell you about it so that it will not come in conflict with anything you are doing." He mentioned that he had been invited to conduct in Yugoslavia. These concerts he would manage himself with the efficient help of Wendy Hanson.

Almost as a postscript, he added: "I have a friend here who is also a Manager. He is Siegfried Hearst, a Rheinlander, a most intelligent and fine man. He sometimes works for me in a friendly and non-exclusive way.

I am telling you this in case you might hear that he is in contact with someone in Europe concerning me."[1]

He went to Yugoslavia for both a vacation and an inroad into the musical life of that varied country. There was much interest and curiosity about his appearances. The *Belgrade Borba* informed the citizenry that "a great experience in the lives of music lovers will be the two concerts which will be directed by one of the greatest conductors in the world, Leopold Stokowski. He will first conduct the Zagreb Philharmonic Orchestra on May 25th, and on June 2nd, he will direct a concert of the Belgrade Philharmonic Orchestra."[2]

The programs for both cities were the subject of a staggering amount of correspondence. Stoki had suggested *Ad Lyram* by Alan Hovhaness. This they discarded immediately. It may have been because it required a large chorus; he had suggested using 240 singers. After finally agreeing to a program which included the *Leonore* Overture No. 3, he made a final change, and in the place of the Beethoven he inserted a short work by a young Yugoslav composer by the name of Berce, called *Sunny Fields*. Other works included Three Chorales by Bach-Stokowski, the Brahms Second Symphony, the *Boléro* of Ravel, and his *Tristan* excerpt. The critic of the *Belgrade Politika* reported that "the hall was full of connoisseurs of music and real sympathizers of the musical art. Their appreciation was expressed in their very long and frenzied applause, which not many artists have received from the critical Zagreb public."[3]

"The program of the concert at the Kolarac University [on June 2] reads: a Bach *Chorale Prelude*, Konjovic's *Chestnut-wood* from his opera *Kostana*, Ravel's *Bolero*, and the Tchaikovsky *Fifth Symphony*."[4] The reviews were extraordinarily enthusiastic.

During his stay in Yugoslavia, the country provided Stoki with a guide, a Mrs. Mira Borić, who was apparently a most pleasant and interesting traveling companion. Together they went to Sarajevo and then up the Dalmatian coast with stops in Split and Dubrovnik. When the negotiations for the concerts had been in progress, Stoki insisted that half of his fee be paid in dollars and half in dinars. There was much argument and discussion. However, Veljko Bijedić had written back in March that they were having great difficulties following Stoki's wishes.

> You have rendered us a great service in accepting this time that your fee be paid in dinars, not insisting for a transfer. For this reason, if

this time you would not spend all the dinars, we could take the
balance as a deposit with us for a possible later opportunity, so that
you or your family could use it for a holiday in Dubrovnik or another
tourist center in Yugoslavia.[5]

Stoki had told his Yugoslav friends: "I would like to study the folk
music, dance and costumes of as many places as possible. Also the architecture, particularly everything of the ancient places."[6] After the quasi-
oriental atmosphere of Sarajevo, he went to Split, where he visited the
remains of the ancient palace of Diocletian and roamed through the
narrow streets of the old town. He particularly enjoyed Dubrovnik and
sent a postcard of the old fortress and lower town. On it he wrote:
"Affectionate thoughts from beautiful Yugoslavia. Always, Leopold."[7]

Stoki found the Yugoslavs very attractive and became attached to Mrs.
Borić and her family and also to the young conductor Djura Jaksic, whom
he hoped to invite to conduct in New York and Houston. Not long after
he returned to New York, he received a letter from Mrs. Borić: "First of
all I would like to thank you for your nice letter written from Ljubljana
on the day of your departure," she wrote. "It was a great honor to be
remembered by the greatest man I ever met." She told him that she had
framed the letter and had it in her studio. She concluded explaining that
seventeen years ago when she was married, she bought a refrigerator.
"After so many years, he stopped working and nobody can help because
the refrigerator is just a little too tired." She asked whether Stoki might
find a second-hand one and have it sent to her in Yugoslavia.[8]

Stoki immediately answered.

> I was so happy to receive your letter, and look forward to the next
> time I shall be in Yugoslavia, I hope with the boys.
> Tonight I have to go on a long tour, but while I am away two
> friends of mine will find a good refrigerator and send it to you. We
> shall put in the package that it is "a present," and that it is "not new,"
> because that may make it easier for you with customs.[9]

The two friends, of course, were Natasha and Faye. They dutifully went
about their task and not only found a refrigerator, but worked out all of
the logistics of getting it there. When Leopold returned to New York, he
again wrote, saying that his assistants were looking for a good refrigerator
and that they would send it soon. "All expenses of every kind will be paid
at this end with one exception. The trucking from Riaka to Zagreb you
must pay in dinars. My friend Djura Jaksic will do me the favor of sending

you the dinars (he is kind enough to be my banker as well as my friend)."
  On the same day he wrote to Jaksic:

> Dear Maestro
>
>   Please do me three favors.
>   1. Please reimburse Mrs. Boric in Zagreb for the expenses she will
> have in sending by truck a refrigerator from Riaka to Zagreb. I am
> sending her this as a little Christmas present.
>   2. Please buy a very nice present for Mrs. Boric's son for Christmas.
>   3. Please buy a specially nice Christmas present for Maestro Jaksic
> in Beograd.
>   I shall be deeply grateful to you for these three favors but if you do
> not do the third one I shall be furious with you so please be kind to
> me. Always with affection.
>
> Your friend
Leopold Stokowski

  After Yugoslavia, Stoki went first to Salzburg, where he joined his
friend Kurt Leimer, a thirty-four-year-old composer pianist from Wies-
baden, and they then drove to Zurich. The program for the Zurich
concert was as follows:

Beethoven: *Leonore* Overture No. 3
Mozart: Symphony No. 40 in G Minor
Leimer: Concerto for the Left Hand
Ravel: *Boléro* [10]

  The choice of the program was somewhat comic, or at least musicomic.
Stoki had at first proposed the Hovhaness Prelude and Quadruple Fugue,
a Leimer Piano Concerto, Khachaturian *Gayane* ballet excerpts, and the
Tchaikovsky Symphony No. 5. Stoki described Hovhaness as "a most
talented young American composer" and Leimer as "a young German
composer and pianist, and I am sure his fee would be very reasonable." [11]
  There were immediate objections. A new German composer such
as Leimer might possibly be accepted but an American composer never.
The Swiss were emphatic. Stoki countered and suggested a program of
Bach, Beethoven, Leimer, and Wagner. The Swiss wanted Mozart and
Haydn. "I do not wish to play Haydn and Mozart in Zurich. I love the
music of these two great geniuses, but prefer to conduct other kinds of
music. Also, I do not wish to conduct the *4th* or *6th Symphonies* of

Tchaikovsky, but am willing to conduct the *5th,*" he wrote to Beek.[12]

Beek replied: "After my various telephone calls with them, they have finally agreed . . . with your wish to have Professor Leimer. They will now also agree to Beethoven *No. 7,* but they would very much like you to make one more suggestion for opening the program and please *not* an American work, nor Bach. Wagner is also difficult because it has just been on the program."[13]

About their reaction to Bach, Stoki was rather irate.

> What is wrong with his music? The three compositions I suggested are beautiful as music, with deep mystical qualities. They are seldom heard in the concert hall. Sometimes they are played in Churches, but not all organists can play this profound music with understanding; and even when it is well played, not everyone goes to Church.
>
> If the objection to Bach is on the question of principle that Bach's music should not be played, except in its original form, is not it being overlooked that of all musicians in the whole of history, Bach is the one that made the most transcriptions? Bach would certainly not agree with the prejudice against transcriptions.[14]

In another letter Stoki wrote to Beek: "If the Tonhalle objects to the Leimer concerto on musical grounds, I cannot agree with them. Also have they ever seen the score? If the Tonhalle objects to Leimer because it must pay his fee, I will be glad to pay this fee myself, so that there will be no question of expense regarding Leimer."[15]

Stoki won on the Leimer issue; Zurich on the Mozart.

After the Zurich concert, Stokowski headed for Paris and then for the *Queen Elizabeth* and New York, where he arrived on July 10. He immediately contacted Basil Langton, the executive producer and stage director of the Empire State Music Festival, in Ellenville, where he was to conduct the Orff music for Shakespeare's play *A Midsummer Night's Dream.*

Basil assembled an intriguing cast which included Basil Rathbone as Oberon, Nancy Wickwire as Titania, Alvin Epstein as Puck, and Red Buttons playing Bottom.

"I persuaded Red to do his first Shakespearean role. The idea of being with Stokowski and Basil Rathbone excited Red. It was an extraordinary moment for him."

There were merely nine days between Stoki's return to New York and the Ellenville performance, and the serious rehearsals began immediately. Basil Langton rehearsed his cast and Stokowski worked with the orchestra:

He recalled that "Stokowski would come to the early rehearsals and was fascinated with the way it all went. . . . It was a very complicated show. . . .

"Dear old Red Buttons, who is a marvelous comic and a real burlesque comedian as you know, was full of comic business that he wanted to introduce into the show and he had marvelous ideas . . . Stoki liked these.

"Now in the score, as you may remember, there is a place where Bottom and the double bass player have a little thing together. The bass player comes on the stage and Bottom sings a little song with him. That's in the score. It is the final dress rehearsal and as they're doing this Buttons has a banana and starts to do some comic business with it."[16]

Jerome Toobin, who was there in his role as manager of the Symphony of the Air recalled the incident: "He took the banana the fairies had presented him with and, taking careful aim, threw it toward the open end —the bell—of the tuba. . . . The Bottom-Buttons shot missed the bell of the tuba and ricocheted off the side into the lap of the tuba player. That helpful musician threw the banana back up to Red, and he looked at Stokowski. He was smiling, quietly smiling. . . ."[17] But it did not end there, Buttons continued to toss the banana until Stoki finally erupted.

He abruptly left the stage. Basil recalled: "I waited a moment thinking he might return. When he didn't I went to his dressing room and found him sitting at his dressing table. I looked at him and he said quietly (I never heard him raise his voice, ever): 'You can get another conductor. There are lots of other conductors.' By now Frank Forest and others were in the dressing room and Red Buttons was on his knees apologizing for upsetting him and pleading that he return. I looked at Stokowski in the mirror of his dressing table and said: 'If you won't conduct, maestro, we will cancel the production.' He looked at me in the mirror, I saw a glint of a smile, and he said: 'Let's continue with the rehearsal,' and he went back to the podium. That was it. Why it happened I don't really know and neither does anyone else. The show was a great success and we all parted the best of friends."[18]

Reviews were expansive.

In the *New York Herald Tribune*, Jay Harrison commented on the "competition" between Orff and Mendelssohn. "Whatever fears a listener might have harbored concerning the wiseness of Mr. Orff to do battle with Mr. Mendelssohn were dispelled with the opening fanfare. The composer has written a corking good score and that is all there is to it."[19]

Miles Kastendieck reported: ". . . Stokowski's unfailing sense of theater served him well last night. From the initial fanfare to its final echo he caught the dramatic accents and highlighted the instrumental coloring in his inimitable way. There was no question the music was as much a part of the performance as the spoken lines." Miles also noted that the event drew the largest crowd in the two-year history of the festival, estimated at seven thousand people.[20]

Immediately after Ellenville, the boys began their summer-long stay with their father while mother Gloria pursued her theatrical career appearing at the summer theater in Milburn, New Jersey. Stoki, Stan, and Chris left New York for the West on July 28 and went first to New Mexico, later Arizona, and then on to Hollywood, where Stoki was to conduct a concert in the Hollywood Bowl on August 28. On the same day on the East Coast, Gloria married Sidney Lumet, the brilliant stage, TV, and movie director who had directed her in the play *Picnic* the previous season. As with all of Gloria's various activities, the press, which had been duly alerted by her lawyer Arnold Krakower, was there in force. The reportage in the *New York Times* was brief, that in the *Herald Tribune* more detailed, but the tabloid *Daily News* ran pictures of the bridal couple on its front page with a bold headline " 'Dead End Kid' (Now a Film Wiz) Weds Gloria V." The *Daily News* continued, saying that he would move into her penthouse at 10 Gracie Square.

At this time, Stoki made his first recording with Capitol Records; it was *The Planets* of Holst, which won much acclaim. David Johnson in *High Fidelity* wrote lines that must surely have pleased everyone at Capitol. "This disc is as near perfect a job of conducting as can well be imagined: listen to the immaculate unison passages for the entire string body, the perfectly matched dialogue of solo violin and solo oboe ('Mercury'), the wonderful precision of harp and celesta arpeggios, the weight and balance of the open fifths in the brasses ('Saturn'), and weird harp harmonics. There is not a careless nor an ill-considered measure in the entire performance."[21]

Some of Stoki's initial letters to Capitol's F. M. Scott indicate less than total satisfaction with the test pressings of *The Planets*.[22] Then when these were finally approved, he was justifiably indignant on discovering that in some batches of the commercial mono records the engineers had actually cut off abruptly the ending of the "Venus" movement, which he wanted to fade into nothingness. On September 2, he wrote to Mr. Scott:

We all took immense care to make as fine a record as is humanly possible to us, and it was the composer's wish that the chorus should fade away as if upwards and at a great distance. Then some careless person ruins that ending, and possibly many people buy that particular defective record and blame us for such a crude ending. I am sure you agree with me that we cannot go on that way. There must be some way to trace who was the person by the serial number, so as to protect ourselves, the composer, and the public from a repetition of such brutal stupidity.[23]

The English reviewers were especially cruel; in the *Gramophone* one wrote scathingly: "Stokowski's misinterpretation of *The Planets* needs only a brief description. . . . The 'improvement' of Holst's scoring here and there is perhaps of minor importance: what really matters is the almost total incomprehension by the conductor of what was in Holst's mind."[24]

The English reviewers chauvinistically recommended the more mundane versions of Sir Malcolm Sargent and Sir Adrian Boult.[25] But Sir Adrian in a recent letter remarked:

He conducted the Planets in the Albert Hall about 1963 and I remember being disgusted because the Hall wasn't full; but the performance of the Planets was in most movements splendid, though naturally one or two of them were different and therefore surprising to us here in London—no harm in that! As I get older I understand more and more how widely different performances of fine music can be, without something wrong, or amazing the listener.[26]

Stoki was, however, happy with his new association with Capitol. He found great rapport not only with Glenn Wallichs but also with Richard Jones, Capitol's A & R man (Artists and Repertory) and with F. M. Scott III, album director, whom he quickly began to call "Scotti."

The relationship between them became a close and very cordial one. "I was deeply touched," Stoki wrote to Wallichs, "by your generosity of spirit in personally driving us to the station, because your time must be so crowded, and the decisions you make are so far reaching. Please accept our warmest thanks and the affectionate thoughts of all three of us. The blue-eyed boy and the brown-eyed boy both send you love."[27]

Then for the next succeeding days he dispatched a letter per day. On the fifteenth he wrote to "Scotti" inquiring when he would like to record the Shostakovich (First Symphony) and the Prokofiev (*Scythian* Suite).

He concluded saying: "I greatly enjoyed being with you and your girl friend, and hope we can spend another evening together soon."[28]

Siegfried Hearst was booking Stoki's European tour; the Beeks now seemed to be out of the picture. Wendy Hanson, too, moved on to become a secretary and assistant to Gian Carlo Menotti in Spoleto and then to Brian Epstein and the Beatles. As Stoki's plans for the tour progressed, Capitol became interested in recording in various capitals. Berlin, London, Paris, Leningrad, and other cities were discussed as recording sites. He was delighted to find in Capitol men who shared many of his enthusiasms.

64

The 1956-57 Season

"As a longtime champion of the new and challenging," wrote Irving Kolodin, "Leopold Stokowski was in proper perspective as conductor of a program, under the sponsorship of the Fromm Music Foundation, which opened New York's serious music-making for the winter with unfamiliar scores. . . ."[1] Of the four works on his program, three--*Memorial* by Bernhard Heiden, *Incantation* of Bohuslav Martinu, and an Adagio for Orchestra by Robert Helps—were all world premieres, and the Kirchner Toccata for Strings, Winds and Percussion was heard in New York for the first time.

Some critics felt that the most brilliant piece of the evening was the Martinu work, which had the added advantage of Rudolf Firkušný in the solo part.[2]

Firkušný recalled: "Unfortunately Martinu was not present when we played the first performance of the *Fourth Concerto*. It was called 'Incantation' and it was commissioned by Paul Fromm. Martinu gave me the performance rights for several years. At this particular concert, Stokowski was conducting, very much to my delight."[3]

Miles Kastendieck wrote: "That contemporary music is in a healthy, even lusty state became obvious from the start. These works all held attention, made sense musically and reflected skillful workmanship.

"One wonders, however, if Stokowski magic didn't contribute a great deal because the performances were so dynamic. Surely no other conductor could have set them forth more vividly even though he did so too vociferously for the size of the hall.

"Conducting as though he believed implicitly in the superiority of each work, Stokowski made the listener believe too, at least for the moment. The intensity of that moment belonged to the orchestra and to him."[4]

Harriet Johnson, in the *New York Post*, wrote that "young Helps, who is only 28, scored a signal success with his short atonal *Adagio* which expressed a mystical, reflective quality that indicated promise for his future. There were evidences of immaturity, but the important thing was that he had something to say."[5]

Stokowski's next concert with the Symphony of the Air was scheduled for Carnegie Hall ten days later on October 14. The Sunday music section of the late lamented *New York Herald Tribune* was one of the musical bright spots of the week. Virgil Thomson had made it so and the people he had engaged to write for it all tried to emulate his freshness.

Jay Harrison, a onetime child radio actor on CBS, was then writing for the *Tribune*. On the Sunday of Stoki's concert, Jay did a feature article on him: ". . . Symbols as a rule, however, are either inanimate or of an era passed. Leopold Stokowski is neither. For fifty years he has stood at the peak of his profession, and there is no perceptible diminishing of his activity. Tonight, for example, he is to lead the Symphony of the Air at Carnegie Hall in a concert of contemporary works. His program, of a kind that many a conductor one-third his age would consider too gruelling to undertake, lists Charles Ives' *Robert Browning Overture*, Alan Hovhaness' *Symphony No. 3*, Kurt Leimer's *Piano Concerto No. 4* and Werner Egk's *French Suite*. It promises to be quite an event, the sort of event that has given to the name of Stokowski the brand of magic that has long been his contribution to the world of tone. Why, then, even after one of the most distinguished careers in the modern annals of music making, does the maestro still turn to the dangerously new and untried? His answer is simple:

"I am convinced that music is in a constant state of evolution. Understand, I don't mean progress, for when I hear the word progress I think of the fields of machinery and technology—and that is something entirely different.

"By evolution I refer to the thousand disparate ways in which a composer can develop according to the requirements of his own personality. That fact I am sure of. After all I have been playing modern and American music ever since arriving in this country.

"It is our native-born musicians who need champions for we do not take to our own as quickly as one would like. Look at Charles Ives—in my opinion his extreme originality is comparable to Mussorgsky's. At first, I know, it was difficult for the Russians of the nineteenth century to understand Mussorgsky, but now his music is clearly understood. In the same way it is hard for many Americans to see what Ives meant by his compositions, but the day will come—soon I am sure—in which, he, also, will be clear and understandable to all his own people. In that respect, he is like all American composers; they need time for their very special message to give up its secrets.' "[6]

The Ives, Hovhaness, and Leimer were all world premieres; the *French Suite* of Egk may have been an American first or at least a New York first. The *Robert Browning* Overture, which dates from 1911, was the oldest but in a sense the most modern and current of all the works. It was another ear-opener. No one mentioned it at the time but the 1955–56 season marked the fiftieth anniversary of Stokowski's first season at St. Bartholomew's, the beginning of his musical activities in America.

Stokowski had been a champion of the music of Henry Cowell for many years. Although he had long been interested in the Orient, Cowell had never been west of California, and eagerly looked forward to hearing, in its native surroundings, more of the music that had so moved him and which had become such a natural part of his musical vocabulary.

At the special invitation of the government of Iran, Cowell spent the winter in Tehran, where he spent much of his time at the new Iranian radio station and became fascinated by the music he heard. He, in return, paid tribute to his hosts by composing a number of works not based on any actual ethnic material but written in the style and spirit of Persian music. One was his *Homage to Iran* for violin and piano and another, which he originally thought of as *An American in Iran*, happily became his *Persian Set*.[7]

At the end of November, Henry wrote me from Tehran that he had completed a set of four movements in Persian style that he was scoring for a typical Iranian instrumental group: piccolo, clarinet, tar (mandolin or guitar), strings, percussion and piano. He mentioned that the United States Information Agency (U.S.I.A.) was very anxious to have the work recorded and a tape or disc sent back, as well as a set of score and parts. He suggested, too, that I contact David Cooper, who was chief of the Music Branch of the U.S.I.A.[8]

David liked the idea and discussed it with his colleagues.[9]

I broached the matter to Stokowski but only in the most general terms. I felt certain that the idea would appeal to him, for not only did it touch on the esoteric but was something of international scope—something that aimed at promoting better understanding between two countries.

"Of course I shall be happy to cooperate with you in a recording of Cowell's suite on Persian melodies and with CRI [Composer's Recordings, Inc.]," he wrote by return mail. "I shall have to ask the consent of Capitol Records, and that can be ascertained soon."[10]

As soon as a score had been printed from the transparencies that Cowell had sent, I dispatched a copy to Stoki. He phoned me several days later and urged me to obtain a studio at once and also have the musicians engaged for the recording session.

By good fortune I was able to secure the Columbia studio on Thirtieth Street, a studio which I knew well, since many of the broadcasts of the CBS Symphony originated there. It had once been an Armenian church, and it had a high gabled ceiling and a hardwood floor that made the acoustics particularly brilliant. A second advantage was the availability of Fred Plaut, one of the finest musical engineers in the business. A superb little orchestra was assembled, every member of which was a distinguished virtuoso.

I had asked composer William Bergsma to help me in the control room during the recording session. Not only was Bill a distinguished composer with a good ear for sound in recording, but he was a fellow board member of CRI. He recalled the evening vividly. "I remember sitting in the control booth, shortly before we were to begin, and there was no sign of Stokowski. I was convinced that he had dropped dead on the pavement and that CRI's money was going to go out the window or something of the sort. But at precisely six, he came in.

"I'm convinced that he never laid eyes on the score before. He got that orchestra to sound like the Philadelphia Orchestra in about the first half-hour. They knew exactly what he wanted and they got that suave tone. And I remember that the slow movement—the first take was about four minutes and the final take—you can check the record—he stretched it—spun it out until it was, oh, I believe five or six minutes, giving it a sumptuous sound. He stopped precisely at nine o'clock. There was absolute professionalism about it."[11]

There was a tricky spot in the last movement. Following a custom of many players in native Iranian groups, Cowell called for the players to shout out the syllable *Yah* to punctuate certain rhythmic accents. As we listened to some of the first playbacks before the final take, the *Yahs* sounded rather weak. At that point Stoki suggested that I join with the musicians and add my stentorian *Yahs* to those of the players—at least to all who were not playing wind instruments. I was frankly pleased, for it meant that I would be making my recording debut with Leopold Stokowski as a *"Jasager."* I think Friedrich Nietzsche would have relished that.

When the session was over, we went to Lüchow's, the best typical German restaurant in New York. It is on Fourteenth Street near where the old Academy of Music had stood and also the showrooms of Steinway. Fourteenth Street had been to New York's music life what Fifty-seventh Street was to become, and Lüchow's was once a gathering place for musicians. Stoki knew it well and was fond of the German atmosphere. It reminded him of Munich, he told me.

He entered followed by Wendy Hanson and myself. He was immediately recognized by the maître d' and we proceeded to the checkroom, where we left our coats. A very pretty, gum-chewing check girl protested that they did not check women's coats. Hereupon the maître d' took charge and Wendy's coat was checked in the freshly liberated cloakroom. Wendy recalled to me: "When we sat down at the table Leopold said, 'There is something I want to show you.' And he put his hand in his pocket and said, 'No, it's in my coat.' And you went back and on returning laughingly told us she had asked you for your autograph. So when we left she looked at you again and said, 'Mr. Stokowski, may I have your autograph?' And you wrote very solemnly, imitating Leopold's signature, and he leaned over and said, 'Wouldn't you like mine too?' And she shrugged and said, 'Well, if you want to.' And he wrote 'Oliver Daniel.' "[12]

Shortly after the recording, we had a small bon-voyage party for Stoki at my apartment on May 16, and on the following day he departed on the *Queen Elizabeth II* for Europe, where upon arrival five days later he stopped briefly in Paris and entrained on the Orient Express for Vienna. He stayed at one of his favorite hotels, the Sacher, next to the Vienna Opera.

For some inexplicable reason, the manager of the Vienna Symphony asked Stoki to conduct again the Mozart G Minor Symphony and the Tchaikovsky Fifth. He was not disposed to conduct Mozart in Vienna again. "I conducted a Mozart symphony last year in Vienna," he wrote to Beek, "and everyone hated the way I did it. So next Spring I would like to replace the Mozart symphony with Beethoven's 7th Symphony."[13] In a later letter to Beek he stated:

It seems to me unintelligent to repeat. Also, the public might not wish to come again and listen to the same music from the same conductor. . . . I could include the "Jupiter" Symphony of Mozart and the Third Symphony of Gliere, "Ilya Murometz," if agreeable to Mr. Gansjaeger.[14]

The programs finally accepted were Debussy's *L'Après-midi d'un faune*, Mozart's *Jupiter* Symphony, and the *New World* Symphony of Dvořák for two concerts on May 8 and 9. And for a third concert on June 9 he selected Falla's *Three-Cornered Hat*, Debussy's Three Nocturnes, the Leimer Piano Concerto No. 4, and the *Firebird* Suite.

He was pleased with his reception in Vienna and on May 24 sent a brief handwritten note at the top of a page of review translations:

> Dear Oliver, Austria and Germany delightful—orchestras splendid and friendly—thought you might like to hear about Vienna Always your Leopold[15]

From Vienna Stoki traveled to Berlin, where he conducted the Berlin Philharmonic in two concerts. He admired the orchestra and after hearing it in New York when it was on tour remarked: "It played splendidly. It is first-class and Karajan also conducted in a masterly fashion."[16]

Stoki chose a curiously unbalanced program consisting of Falla's *El amor brujo*, two Stravinsky suites—the *Firebird* and *Petrouchka*—separated by *L'Après-midi d'un faune*. The Stravinsky pieces were programmed because he planned to record them immediately after the concert. Curiously, he avoided including any German works in his concerts with the Berlin Philharmonic in this and two succeeding visits in 1959 and 1961.

Hans Stuckenschmidt, who attended the concert, wrote in a recent letter to me that it was "brilliant and a tremendous success."[17] In the review that he wrote for the *Welt* in Berlin, he was deeply impressed by the impact of the *Firebird*, which "Stokowski turned into a multi-colored Russian fairy-tale using tone effects never before heard, the shimmering color of iridescent insect wings."[18]

When Capitol released the Stravinsky suites reviewers were effusive. "The interaction of the strongminded interpreter and the highspirited orchestra produces a Petrouchka that is one of the best available, dramatically conceived, broadly executed," wrote Irving Kolodin. "As might be expected . . . the Berlin Philharmonic sounds like a 'Stokowski Orchestra.'"[19]

After the recording session, Stoki returned to Vienna from where he wrote me a short, characteristic note, concluding with *"Immer alles Gutes."*

His first concert with the London Symphony Orchestra was on June 26, 1957; the program: Berlioz' *Roman Carnival* Overture, Ravel's *Rapsodie Espagnole*, Debussy's Three Nocturnes, Prokofiev's *Scythian* Suite, and the Stravinsky *Firebird* Suite. One of the important members of the orchestra, horn virtuoso Barry Tuckwell, recalled: "We had done a Hitchcock film with Bernard Herrmann, 'The Man Who Knew Too Much.' In fact, that was the first thing I did with the LSO. Herrmann knew Stoki and said, 'Look, you should get Stokowski to conduct this orchestra.' I was just a playing member of the orchestra at the time and had nothing to do with the administration. But the management asked Stokowski to come and conduct the LSO and he did. It was absolutely extraordinary. It was a concert that transformed the orchestra. It suddenly played 100 times better than it ever had before and this was noticed by the press. It was one of the most exciting concerts I've ever been involved in. It gave us that injection of adrenalin to make us go on. We thought, well, we're not that bad after all. . . . At that time, the orchestra had suffered quite a major internal blow—a revolution—a lot of the players left and that's when I went in. I think Stoki liked a green orchestra—an orchestra that could be improved upon. He was a terrific teacher and this was almost virgin territory."[20] The London *Times* critic welcomed him:

"Mr. Leopold Stokowski is back in London, after an absence of three years. . . . The more solid of the two programs comes on Sunday, with symphonies by Schumann and Vaughan Williams as the main works. Last night, however, he provided an evening of sheer excitement in terms of orchestral colour, miraculously transforming the London Symphony Orchestra into as brilliant a virtuoso body as anyone could ever want to hear."[21]

The London *Times* critic who reviewed Stoki's second concert wrote:

"Vaughan Williams' most recent symphony was presumably new to him, but as it is in some sense an epitome of what had gone before in the composer's *oeuvre* it sounded as though the conductor had always known it; it flowed under his hand and gave the curious but delightful impression that its music was afloat, even in the uproarious finale. Schumann's Second Symphony, which is much less buoyant music, similarly seemed to be off the ground and in the air . . ."[22]

Shortly after these concerts he recorded for Capitol the Debussy *Noc-*

turnes and the Ravel *Rapsodie Espagnole.* When the record was released the comments were both varied and intense.

Rehearsals in Houston began immediately on his return. He had planned to make his opening concert of the 1956–57 season a memorable one and had announced in the prospectus of the years programs that he would introduce the Ives Fourth Symphony. Unfortunately, the editors of Associated Music Publishers (AMP), who could find ample time to produce scores by Etler, Fetler, Pletner or Schimmerling, could find neither the time nor the incentive to produce Ives. To mollify some of the conservative Texans, Stoki devised a miniature Beethoven festival: six of the fourteen concerts he was to conduct during the twenty-week season were "all-Beethoven." The opening concert was dedicated to Ima Hogg, who had just stepped down as president of the society. Stokowski preceded the music by making a charming and witty talk about her.

The program began with the Handel Overture in D Minor, followed by the Brahms Second Symphony, and concluded with the *Tannhäuser* Overture of Wagner. In between came the world premiere of a Concerto for Wind and Percussion Instruments by a local Houston composer, William Rice, in place of the Ives. But the rare work on the program was a performance of *A Solemn Melody* by Stokowski's friend and onetime teacher and colleague H. Walford Davies. It was one of the few times that his name ever found its way onto American orchestral programs. It was composed in 1908 for strings and organ and later arranged for full orchestra. Jack Ossewaarde, the program annotator, described the work. "The composition is all that its title implies—simple, unpretentious and rich in harmonic texture."

On November 27 during an all-Russian program, Fredell Lack performed the Prokofiev Violin Concerto No. 2 in G Minor. All went well until the end of the last movement, when measures of 4/4 and 5/4 are in conflict, and the orchestra finished before the soloist. With true gallantry, conductor and soloist together looked over the score and repeated the coda—this time ending together.[23]

At Christmastime, Stokowski programmed *L'Enfance du Christ* by Berlioz, preceded by Alan Hovhaness' *As on the Night,* which was originally written in 1952 for a series of programs I produced for CBS. After this pre-Christmas concert, on December 19, 1956, he immediately sped to New York.

On New Year's Eve we gathered at my apartment. I had invited guests whom I knew Stoki particularly enjoyed. They included Alan Hovhaness

and his wife, Phyllis, Wallingford Riegger and his daughter Ruth, Wendy
Hanson, Peggy Glanville-Hicks, Carol Truax, and several others, including Avery Claflin and his wife, Patsy, who brought with them their
wonderfully affectionate corgi. I had never realized how fond Stoki was
of dogs. He gave his full attention to him and treated him like a visiting
celebrity. He told us about the big German shepherd named Wolf that
he once had and about other dogs he had had at different times.

Stoki was very fond of Avery from their very first meeting. He had
dropped me a note: "I greatly enjoyed being with you and your friends
last night, and was particularly interested in the opinions expressed by
'Avery.' I would like to meet him again sometime, if he is willing."

In Avery he found a remarkable combination of talents and abilities.
Like Ives, Claflin was both a composer and a businessman. He had just
recently retired as president of the French American Banking Corporation, and was now devoting himself to composition and to helping composers by giving much of his time to the American Composers Alliance
and to CRI, both of which organizations Stoki had also given great
assistance.

On January 20, 1957, Stokowski conducted a gala benefit in Carnegie
Hall for something called UNISOMI. The acronym was rather impres-
sive. It appeared to be an offshoot of the U.N., or perhaps it was
UNESCO. Its aim was "World Peace through World Music."
UNISOMI actually stood for United Nations International Symphony
Orchestra and Music Institute.

The orchestra was the Symphony of the Air, which indulged in a bit
of back-patting by using a full page to explain itself and justify its continued existence. It listed Arturo Toscanini as "Conductor Emeritus" and
went on to explain that it was organized by the members of the former
NBC Symphony and was dedicated to the "traditions established in their
long association with Maestro Arturo Toscanini."

In a characteristic gesture, Stokowski added a special work to his program: the "Funeral March" from *Die Götterdämmerung* as a memorial
to Toscanini, who had died four days earlier.

"The orchestra's attitude toward Stokowski, though, was not very helpful," wrote Jerry Toobin. "The feeling toward him reflected Toscanini's.
. . . But whether it liked Stokowski or not, the orchestra needed him for
his name and his contacts, particularly with recording companies. Recordings were the most lucrative source of income for our personnel. Stokowski
still made records regularly. . . ."[24]

When he returned to Houston, his first program was another all-Beethoven evening, but at his next concert he gave his Texans another world
premiere—a work that had been commissioned by the Houston Symphony, *Ad Lyram* by Alan Hovhaness, based on texts taken from the four
books of *Odes* written by the Roman poet Horace. It was a big work
calling for a double chorus, solo quartet, and full orchestra. It was the
composer's Opus 143. "I think I got one thousand dollars for that, if I
remember rightly," said Alan.[25]

Burt Schorr, of the *Houston Press*, wrote: "In a period that finds many
contemporary composers groping for a syntax on which to hang their
inspiration, Alan Hovhaness stands in refreshing solitude as the possessor
not of syntax alone, but of an entire and unique language. . . . Like strands
of rich Autumn colors, the Latin words honoring the instrument Horace
so admired, filled the air. . . .[26]

Immediately after the performance, Stoki sent me a telegram at my
office with effusive praise for the work, and two days later sent a letter
saying: "I hope that you received my telegram of Ad Lyram. Each word
of it I feel deeply."[27] In response, I wrote back thanking him for his wire
and commenting on the splendid tape Alan had brought back with him.
"It is marvelous to find critics in Houston amenable to new ideas and
excited by them, rather than surfeited and bored."[28]

His next program, on March 18, opened with a very effective Ceremonial and Flourish for Brass Instruments by the English composer Richard
Arnell followed by the world premiere of Soliloquy for Oboe and Orchestra by Natasha Bender. Both Natasha and Faye flew down for the performance. The audience liked the work and critic Roussel described the
composer as being "very glamorous and freighted with ideas."

In his program annotation, Ossewaarde provided the following information:

> Natasha Bender—born in Philadelphia on August 20, 1919, now
> living in New York. Miss Bender is unquestionably a person of great
> creative ability—she not only composes distinctive music, but is a
> dress designer, specializing in sportswear, as well. . . . Although she
> has studied the fundamentals of music . . . she is mostly self-taught.
> . . . Her urge to do creative composing came after studying the scores
> of other composers and listening to phonograph records . . .

Upon Stoki's return to New York, he began rehearsals for a concert in
Ellenville. His program was to be a radical contrast between Stravinsky's

Wendy Hanson, Stan, and Chris in Untermeyer Park, Yonkers, New York (September 1957)

Canticum Sacrum and Orff's simplistic pseudoprimitivism that characterized his *Carmina Burana.* According to *Newsweek* magazine it was hard to tell whether the audience "applauded Igor Stravinsky's *Canticum Sacrum* out of appreciation or from sheer relief of having it over with."[29] But Stoki gave his huge audience—the largest that had assembled that season—a chance to better make up its collective mind. He asked the audience if they would like to hear the rather brief cantata a second time and they docilely indicated that they would. Stoki then repeated all eighteen minutes of it.

Compared with Tanglewood, the Empire State Music Festival at Ellenville was a rather makeshift affair. It was also on shaky financial footing. So far it had been bankrolled almost entirely by Frank Forest, who had already sunk a reputed $350,000 into the venture. He announced that this season would mark the end of his financial help. "More money," he said wistfully, "I just don't have."[30]

Stoki was interested in finding a location that would be more convenient than Ellenville and one that would also be closer to New York City. We looked at places all along the Hudson—one was the old Gould estate, "Lyndhurst," which has since been used for summer concerts. Another likely spot was the elaborate set of gardens—with Greek columns, statuary, and long-dried-up pools with mosaic tile bottoms then

Photograph taken by author of Stokowski with Stan and
Chris in Untermeyer Park with the Hudson River and Palisades in the background

being filled up with refuse—of the once elegant Untermeyer estate.

On Sunday morning, September 29, I picked up Stoki, Wendy, and the
boys and drove to Untermeyer park. The boys immediately discovered a
huge beech tree and began swinging in its lower branches. We walked
down toward the river and I snapped several photos of Stoki and the boys
with the Palisades in the background. After this exploration, we went to
a friend's home, which was atop an old apartment of 1920s vintage, with
high ceilings and a disproportionately tall tower overlooking the Hudson.
The best description of the place might be neo-pseudo-semi-demi-Tudor.
To fortify himself, if necessary, Stoki brought along a flask of Punt e Mes,
much to our amusement. Playing the role of solicitous father, he insisted
that each of the boys take a nap in separate bedrooms. He, too, took his
customary siesta.

At Seventy-five

B Y official reckoning Stokowski was seventy-five; by his own account
he was only seventy, but observing the range of his activities and
plans, one might have regarded him as a man in his forties.

Although he had appeared many times in Chicago with the Cincinnati
Orchestra as far back as 1912 and on later visits with the Philadelphia
Orchestra and still later with the All-American Youth Orchestra, he had
never been invited to conduct the Chicago Symphony. He remarked to
me a little sarcastically that perhaps they wanted to wait until he was
sufficiently mature. He was to conduct four concerts in Chicago and one
in Milwaukee starting January 2, 1958. It was a welcome occasion, for
there were many members of the orchestra who had been with him in the
Youth Orchestra. He gave the Chicagoans an ample serving of his Bach
transcriptions, as well as Brahms, Glière, Tchaikovsky, and Wagner. New
to the city were the excerpts from Prokofiev's *Romeo and Juliet* Suite and
a totally new Toccata by the Polish composer Boleslaw Szabelski which
dated from 1938.

He was described as looking benign and serene when he appeared on
a local telecast. "It's a mystery to me," he said, "but one receives enormously something back from the music. It makes me feel strong. After
a concert I hear music all night. I can't sleep that night. All night I hear
the music, and I hear the bassoons and the oboes and the different
instruments." When asked about his reaction to applause, an old story,
he replied: "What would you suggest as an alternative to applause? Sup-
posing we had no applause? Then what? I can't understand—after one's

heard beautiful music, then you make this noise. But I can't find an alternative."[1]

Shortly after returning to New York, he gave an interview to a reporter for a UP release. He talked about his forthcoming tour of Europe and showed the reporter his looseleaf notebook in which he made notations of all the new scores which he studied. "I am interested in the future," he said. "You can model the future like clay in your hands. This spring I will conduct in France, Yugoslavia, Czechoslovakia and Russia," he stated with slight exaggeration. "I notice wherever you go people are always the same. In the world of politics, there is the frontier, the border, between peoples. But not in music. In each of those countries, my programs will be half American and half the music of that country. . . . It will be all new American music, composed within the last four years. And two of the works were composed in the last four months." When asked how he came to be performing new American works, he replied emphatically: "Because I like it. It's beautiful, dynamic, an expression of life today —because it's good music."[2]

He was particularly buoyed up by his new association with Capitol and thoroughly enjoyed the spirit and enthusiasm of both Dick Jones and F. M. Scott III. He proposed all sorts of works that he wanted to record. It was not to be an endless repetition of the same repertory that he had already done in multiple sessions. He submitted pages of suggestions. He wanted to record works of Boris Blacher, Webern, Jolivet, Riegger, Yardumian, Tippett, Panufnik, Ruggles, Cowell, Hovhaness, Stravinsky, Frank Martin, Martinu, Roy Harris, Villa-Lobos, Peter Mennin, Revueltas, and Ives.[3]

He busied himself listening to test pressings and making suggestions for improvements. In August 1957, Capitol released his first recording: "The Orchestra." It was a pyrotechnical display of Stokowski's conducting and Capitol's engineering expertise. The choice of material was brilliant. It included the Dukas *La Péri: Fanfare,* Barber's Adagio for Strings, the Strauss Gavotte from the Suite in B Flat for Winds, Farberman's *Evolution: Section I,* Vaughan Williams' Scherzo from his Symphony No. 8, Perischetti's March from the Divertimento for Band, and "The Hut on Fowl's Legs" and "The Great Gate at Kiev" in the Ravel orchestration of the Mussorgsky *Pictures at an Exhibition.* Why he did not use his own orchestration seems rather baffling, and one can only conclude that it was Capitol's executives who insisted on the Ravel version. In a letter to "Scotti" he wrote:

In my opinion Ravel's orchestration of 'Pictures at an Exhibition' is most beautiful and masterly, but has a kind of French brilliance and finesse, while Mussorgsky's music has Russian power, dark coloring and sometimes brutal abandon. In my orchestration I have tried to preserve these Slavic characteristics. Would you like to consider recording it some day?[4]

Philip Geraci commented in *High Fidelity:* "Stokowski shines in endeavors such as this; he is completely in his element. . . . The tonal beauty of the record lies mainly in its carefully preserved sonic perspective. In the *Peri* fanfare the brasses are sharp and big sounding, but clean in every detail, without fuzziness. The strings in Barber's Adagio are—there is only one word for it—breathtaking. . . . Section I of Farberman's Evolution with gongs, xylophones, bells, cymbals, and drums alternating for attention—is the most striking section of the entire record."[5]

Probably because of the contractual complications, there is no mention of the fact that the players for this segment of the record were members of the Boston Symphony, of which Farberman himself was a member. He described his first meeting with Stokowski: "We went through the score very carefully and we set up a recording date and we used the members of the Boston Symphony percussion section who had played the work many times before. . . . The procedure we used was this: I rehearsed it first and then he did a take, in his way, then I rehearsed it and he did a take, and so on. . . . He had brought his kids along and was as much concerned about the children having a good time seeing all the percussion stuff going on as he was in the piece. . . ."[6]

Stokowski began his 1957–58 Houston season on October 28 with a program that was bound to please: Three Chorales and the Fugue in G Minor of Bach, Sibelius' Seventh Symphony, and music from Wagner's *Die Götterdämmerung.* Sibelius had died the previous month—September 20, 1957—and the symphony which Stokowski had introduced in America was being played "In Memoriam."

On his second concert he introduced José Serebrier's Sinfonía No. 1 in its world premiere. Stokowski, again, had intended to perform the Ives' Symphony No. 4, but Associated Publishers' slow-crawling editors still could not get it ready on time. Serebrier had just won a BMI award and his winning work was this symphony. Since I handled the contest through my office, I met José and admired his score. As usual, I sent the winning orchestral works to Stokowski. I asked José about his first encounter with Stokowski and he replied: "I was a student at Curtis. I was 17, and I had a telephone message from the operator of the Curtis Institute saying, 'Stokowski called. Please call Operator 80 in Houston, Texas.' I was sure that it was a joke because we were constantly leaving each other jokes like that. . . . I left messages for other people saying that Bernstein called or that Arthur Judson called and other people said that Marilyn Monroe called, so I tore it up. Then another one came and another and finally a telegram saying please call immediately. I called him and my first conversation with him was about ten seconds long. He never said hello, how are you, or how do you do. He said literally: 'This week I play your symphony—Ives Fourth not possible—please bring music.' So he needed a world premiere, and since he had already announced the Ives Fourth, this was it. It was quite exciting, and the Houston office contacted *Time, Life*, and *Newsweek* and I was interviewed, but nothing ever appeared because that same week, exactly the day after my piece was played, the first sputnik went up!

"I didn't have any money to go to Houston, so Mrs. Curtis Zimbalist gave me a $100 check to help me buy a ticket. And then there were no parts for my piece, so all the students at Curtis, all my friends—people who are now quite famous—sat up all night copying parts, so I was able to go down with the music. . . .

"The performance of my symphony was an incredible revelation of conducting . . . he made the piece sound better than I could imagine, but it was in the concert that he made it come alive. Some magic took place during the concert that had not happened before, and I've realized since that no other conductor that I've seen has ever had it. They're wonderful in rehearsals and in concerts they're maybe a little bit better, but not a million percent better like Stokowski could be."[7]

The next program was a blockbuster for the Texans. It contained Orff's *Nänie und Dithyrambe* (first performance in America); Vaughan Williams' Symphony No. 8 (first performance in Houston); Krenek's Concerto for Cello and Orchestra (first time in Houston); and Panufnik's *Sinfonia Elegiaca* (world premiere). Houston was not quite ready for it and Roussel referred to the Krenek concerto as "a case of aggressive atonalism; the work affected the hall like an east wind seeping under the doors."[8]

After the concert, Stokowski cabled Panufnik.

> Tonight we performed your powerful and profoundly moving Sinfonia Elegiaca. Audience's and orchestra's reaction deeply emotional and enthusiastic. Shall repeat tomorrow. Thank you for unforgettable experience.[9]

His following program was Russian, starting with an American premiere of Rodion Shchedrin's ballet *The Humpbacked Horse*. It may well have been both the first and the last performance in America.

The choice of the Shchedrin was another instance of Stokowski's interest in the young; Shchedrin was only twenty-five at the time, but he was becoming one of the most talked about of the young hopefuls.

I had met him in Moscow when the International Music Council convened there in 1970 and later, in 1978 when he was in Washington, we had a conversation about Stokowski. He told me that he had written him very enthusiastically after the performance of *The Humpbacked Horse* in Houston. "He was a legendary figure to our musical people," he told me. "I met with him in Moskva and Kiev also. And, of course, I was at his concerts in the Moscow Conservatory and Tchaikovsky Hall. He had enormous success in our country."[10]

After his all-Russian program, Stokowski bade farewell to Houston while Villa-Lobos, Stravinsky, and Walter Susskind filled in. He did not return until March 17, for four more concerts. The new works then included Barber's agreeably old-fashioned Intermezzo from *Vanessa*, Revueltas' *Janitzio*, Peter Mennin's Symphony No. 6, and the Shostakovich Symphony No. 11 in its American premiere. For good measure, he added another rousing performance of *Carmina Burana*.

Capitol recorded both the Orff and the Shostakovich, and R. D. Darrell said nicely in *High Fidelity*: "From the first ominously brooding bars of this Eleventh Symphony one might think that Shostakovich had written solely to furnish Stokowski with one of the most dramatic showpieces the latter has ever reveled in . . . I must admit that—with Stokowski giving it his all—it is a potent sonic intoxicant."[11]

"I should tell you what I am thinking," Stoki wrote to F. M. Scott prior to the recording. "This music is very dramatic and exciting. It needs an extremely extended dynamic range and powerful lows. If we were recording a Mozart symphony, one of our chief aims should be, in my opinion, beauty of tone, but this Symphony needs much more than that. Unless we give it a full dynamic range and powerful lows, its sometimes overwhelming impetuosity will not be immaculate. I hope the committee in Hollywood will keep this in mind and will not restrain us to a less extended dynamic range than some of our competitors are using."[12]

In Stoki's luggage when he sailed on April 30 were tapes and dubs of the work which he intended to give to Shostakovich as soon as he arrived in Moscow.[13] Faye and Natasha were with him in his stateroom when I arrived to bid him farewell. He was in excellent spirits and we all departed before 3:00 and the ship's debarking. He arrived in Paris, where he stayed at the Plaza Athénée. His concert with the French National Radio Orchestra (L'Orchestre National de la Radiodiffusion-Télévision Française) took place in the Théâtre des Champs-Élysées on May 12. He had to bow to French objection to American music and instead gave his listeners Bach-Stokowski and the Brahms First. The three French works—Ibert's *Escales,* Ravel's *Alborado del Gracioso,* and Debussy's *Ibéria*—were all to be recorded for Capitol.

As always Stoki was meticulous in his attention to every detail in the production of his recordings. He devoted hours to work with the engineers when the tapes were being edited and transfers were made onto discs. As an example of his fastidiousness, here is a copy of a memo which he wrote to Richard Jones about the Paris recordings:

17 July 58

R. J. from L. S.

I think we can improve Iberia from a purely musical standpoint by the following:

Movement #1

No. 19 trombones much stronger
3rd and 4th bars after No. 32 more dim. in violins and violas

Movement #2

No. 41 the pp. softer
3 bars before No. 43 the pp. of woodwinds softer
2 bars before No. 45 slightly less volume
2 bars after No. 49 more dim, at end of bar
2 bars before No. 51 softer like an echo of the previous bars
No. 51 Piano of woodwinds much softer
4th and 6th bar after No. 51 much softer like an echo of the previous bars
3 bars before No. 52 the pp. softer
1st and 2nd bars after No. 52 softer
3rd, 4th and 5th bars after No. 52 more dim. into the 3rd Movement

Movement #3

First four bars softer as if from a great distance
No. 53 softer
No. 54 start softly and then with gradual cres.
No. 56 Subito pp. with cres. in 3rd bar
One bar before No. 57 the utmost cres. possible in the woodwinds.
It cannot be too much.
3 bars before No. 60 more dim.
3 bars after No. 61 the utmost cres. in woodwinds
5 bars after No. 64 the sudden pp. as soft as possible with cres. about
3 bars later.

Ibert—Escales

Movement #1

No. 3 the violins sound metallic. I suggest reducing highs so as to
make the tone more velvety.
One bar before No. 8 much more dim. like an echo of the previous
bar.
2 bars before No. 14 less forte and then cres.
1 bar before No. 27 start softer and then utmost cres. possible
No. 27 violins more velvety
2nd bar after No. 30 sf. stronger

Movement #2

3 bars before No. 41 much dim. until pp. one bar before No. 41

Movement #3

No. 53 cellos much stronger
No. 55 cellos much stronger
10 bars before No. 58 more cres. into sf. 2 bars later
5 bars after No. 62 violins only mezzoforte at start with cres. afterwards

The reviews were as usual pleasantly mixed. Writing in the *American
Record Guide,* critic Alfred Kaine remarked: "Stokowski proves all over
again that he is in a class by himself as an orchestral colorist. The languor-

ous musical mist and the distant bells that break the reverie in *Les parfums de la nuit* are incomparably atmospheric. . . ." He praised the "gorgeous lushness of the strings" and the "ingeniously evoked snake-charmer effects" in *Escales*. But of the recording itself, he was rough. "The orchestra sounds as if it had been recorded in a subway. Imbalanced, out of focus, and absurdly reverberant. . . ."[14]

By contrast Colin Wilson, in England's *Record Review*, found: "The recording throughout is excellent. . . . Everything on this record is polished till it glitters."[15]

Twenty years after the recording had been made it was rereleased in Britain. The English reviewers were probably younger and did not read "Hollywood" into every Stokowski reading. "Such pieces invite, and from Stokowski receive, performances of full-blooded exuberance that is most engaging," wrote Max Harrison. "This animated, even vivacious, reading is the best I know, with the conductor quite clearly revelling in the luxuriant textures. His sense of colour is sharp, indeed sometimes almost obsessive, and occasionally a detail is unduly heightened. . . . Stokowski's feeling for atmosphere is remarkable. . . . A pity he did not record more such music."[16]

On Sunday morning, May 18, 1958, Stoki took the Orient Express passing through Prague and then to Warsaw, where he broke up the long trip to Russia with an overnight stop at Paderewski's Hotel Bristol. Then on to Moscow for a brief stop before proceeding to Kiev. By fortuitous coincidence Eugene Ormandy and the Philadelphia Orchestra arrived in Kiev at the same time. In that far-off Ukrainian city, Stokowski heard the orchestra for the first time in seventeen years.[17] Ormandy sagely programmed the Mussorgsky-Ravel *Pictures at an Exhibition* and the piece had a particular relevance to the city, for it ends with the brilliant "Great Gate of Kiev."

One could only wonder that Stokowski, sitting there and applauding, must have envied Ormandy, who was doing what he himself had so ardently wanted to do in his own Philadelphia days. He, too, might have wondered whether his more characteristic and, in a sense, bombastic rendition of the "Great Gate" might have resulted in an even more tumultuous ovation than it received.

For his own concert in Kiev with the Ukrainian State Orchestra he also had a work to inflame their patriotic as well as their musical sensibilities. He programmed the new Eleventh Symphony of Shostakovich.

On the same day as the Ormandy concert, Stoki was already in the second day of his rehearsals with the orchestra. He discussed music with many of the younger composers—Rodion Shchedrin among them. It seems that they and others were eager to hear American music; Stoki sent me a cable that read:

RUSSIA ENTHUSIASTIC RECORD AMERICAN MUSIC PLEASE AIRMAIL MY EXPENSE SCORE PARTS COW-BELLS PERSIAN CAT RIEGGERS NEW DANCE URGENT THANKS LEOPOLD ADDRESS HOTEL SAVOY MOSKVA[18]

What he wanted was Henry Cowell's *Persian Set* and no cowbells or Persian cat. Through David Cooper and the good offices of the State Department, the music was sent by diplomatic pouch to the Embassy in Moscow and arrived without delay.[19]

In Moscow Stoki went to the embassy, where the music had arrived, and wrote a note: "Thanks for the music received safely. Orchestras good, public marvelous."[20] The word *marvelous* was thrice underlined.

To the Russian music lovers, Stoki was indeed a legend. They had known him only through his recordings, and these seem to have been well known in Russia. For one of his concerts, he said: "They stood in queue all night in order to buy tickets. . . ."[21]

The spontaneous ovation that he won at the close of his first concert sent correspondents rushing to cable their report on the international wire services. The reporter for the Associated Press cabled that he "had won a roaring chorus of cheers and bravos." He had concluded his program with the Shostakovich Eleventh Symphony and the composer came on stage to share the ovation—the audience "chanting 'Stokowski, Stokowski, Stokowski.' "[22]

As an encore, Stoki repeated Samuel Barber's Adagio for Strings, which he had included in the program. At the conclusion the audience was still insistent on more and Stoki obliged by again repeating the Adagio. "After the concert," he wrote, "the whole audience was in the street around the stage door, thanking me for coming to Russia, for the music, begging me to come back again, and asking unending questions about America."[23]

In all he conducted five concerts in Moscow, during which he performed symphonies of Tchaikovsky, Shostakovich, and Prokofiev. Not only had he been the first American conductor to be invited to conduct

Applauding Shostakovich in Moscow after performance of his Eleventh Symphony (1958)

in Russia, but was also the first to be invited to record. He waxed the Prokofiev Symphony No. 5 with the USSR State Radio Orchestra in Moscow and it was released immediately for the Recording Society of the Soviet Union.[24]

A group of students collectively sent a telegram to his hotel:

Dear Sir Leopold Stokowski:

Greatest thanks to you for the bright moments of delight which you gave us by your wonderful performances.

Your concerts will remain in our memories for the rest of our lives! Come back again to us.

In the Soviet Union there are millions of people to whom you are very near and dear.

From the bottom of our hearts we wish you everlasting artistic powers, successes and health.

We strongly shake your wonderful, intelligent hands—hands of the musician.

Moscow. Group of Students.[25]

Music lovers in Leningrad were perhaps even more demonstrative than those in Moscow. When he arrived at his hotel, he could hear noise and laughter outside of his window. Thinking that it was possibly an outdoor cafe, he was surprised at what he saw. "Across the street was the stage door of the concert hall of the Conservatory of Music where I was to give four concerts. Near the stage door there was another door, and the noise was coming from there, where a line of people, all the way down the street, were standing. . . ." The standees apparently remained there all night until the box office opened at 10:30 the following morning. When he went to his morning rehearsal, "The line was all the way down the street. There must have been about two-thousand persons there. . . . When I came out of the rehearsal at one o'clock, although the box office had closed earlier, as all seats had been immediately sold for all four concerts, nearly all the people were still there. We shook hands and I tried to answer all their questions about our musical life in America. There were some quite young children; in fact, every age was represented.

"After each of the concerts, practically the whole audience came to the stage door, and it took me about half an hour to walk across the street to the hotel because there were so many people to shake hands with."[26]

For his first program he pulled out all of the famous Stokowski stops. He gave them the Toccata and Fugue in D Minor, the *Tristan* "Love Death," and the Shostakovich Eleventh. His success was again given worldwide attention by the wire services.[27]

Before giving his final symphonic concert on the thirtieth of June, Stoki was somehow induced to conduct a balalaika orchestra. That he obviously enjoyed and must have done it with rare good humor. His final concert was reported by Moscow radio as being "brilliantly conducted."[28]

Just before leaving Leningrad, he sent two postcards. On one: "Much to tell you. Has been thrilling experience. Public hungry for music. Let's celebrate!"[29] On a second: "Arrive July 15 late afternoon. Will call you or meet at boat if you have time. Shall go see boys." He then signed it in the Cyrillic alphabet.[30]

Even before his return we had been working on a major project of the Contemporary Music Society: a symphonic concert in Carnegie Hall to mark Stoki's fiftieth year as a conductor. The choice of fifty was based on the 1908 date that at that time was always given as the year he made his debut in Paris. We know now, of course, that it was actually 1909; but one way or another the concert was to be a milestone. We had engaged Carnegie Hall for September 25, 1958, and we had three months to raise the money for the whole affair and be sure that we would have a large and distinguished audience.

The crux of the program was to be the Shostakovich Eleventh Symphony—all sixty-one minutes of it. To precede it Stoki chose a Toccata by Paul Creston, *Mysterious Mountain* by Alan Hovhaness, and the *New*

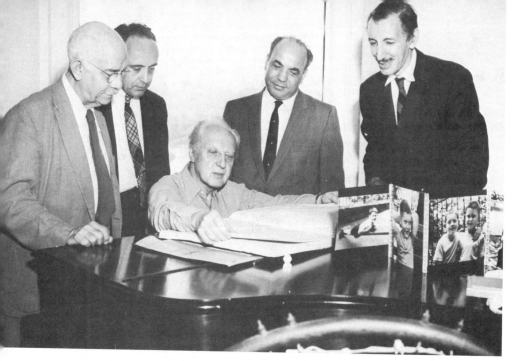

With Wallingford Riegger, author, Paul Creston, and Alan Hovhaness discussing scores to be performed for concert in September 1958 at Carnegie Hall celebrating the fiftieth anniversary of Stokowski's conducting debut in Paris in May 1909

Dance of Wallingford Riegger. To add to the festive air of the concert, Stoki sent an invitation to Shostakovich to attend the concert personally.[31] He was scheduled to come to the United States later with a contingent of Russian composers, but the lack of elasticity in Russian bureaucracy did not provide for an earlier visit.

Meanwhile, on August 26, Stoki's old friend Ralph Vaughan Williams died in London. In tribute, Stoki decided to perform his new Symphony No. 9 for the first time in America. The length of the Vaughan Williams being considerably shorter than the Shostakovich, Stoki added the *Obertura Festiva* of Juan Orrego-Salas to open the program.

At the time I was presenting a series of hour-long radio programs on WNYC devoted entirely to contemporary music. On the Sunday before the concert, I interviewed Stoki on one of those programs. He spoke first about Vaughan Williams: "When I was a student at the Royal College in London, he was teaching, so I knew him then as a teacher. But later I learned to know him more intimately and found him to be a remarkable man—very profound, very warm."

Photo United States Information Service/Courtesy Mrs. Ralph Vaughan Williams
With Ralph Vaughan Williams, 1957

I mentioned that the *New York Times* in an editorial stated that
Vaughan Williams was a composer who created music in the immortal
tradition, which led me to ask whether Stoki felt that music was being
created today that equals the great music of the past. "Nobody can answer
that question because I think it takes several centuries to really evaluate
any artist, musician, dramatist, or poet, no matter what. It is time that
enables people to finally decide what is to be remembered and what is to
be forgotten. That may not be the ideal way of doing it but that is the
way it happens. That is a realistic attitude toward it."[32]

On my remarking about the disproportionate attention given to the
music of the past in our symphonic programs, he answered: "It is really
tragic that so many gifted young composers of today—in this country and
in other countries too—so seldom can have a performance." After making
an ardent plea for the inclusion of more contemporary music in our
concert life, he remarked: "Music, in my life, has always been the greatest
interest. When I was a little child, six or seven years old, I always knew
I would be a musician. . . . I have many hobbies. . . . *But the great thing*

is music."33 It was this last phrase that Evelyn Hinrichsen, President of C. F. Peters, had made into a voiceprint.

In the *New York Herald Tribune,* Jay Harrison ran a long article on Alan Hovhaness, concentrating on his *Mysterious Mountain,* which Stokowski was to perform on the concert. The most important coverage of the anniversary program was to be a telecast. That, however, was to run at noon on Bill Leonard's program "Eye on New York." The papers announced that Stokowski would reminisce about his distinguished musical career and talk about the future of music on the eve of his fiftieth anniversary as a conductor.

Stoki talked about music in general but devoted most of his time discussing the Thursday-night program. Naturally, he hoped that it would help to draw an even larger audience than that we had calculated. It did indeed, but not as planned. At noon on Sunday, Stoki, his two boys, Faye and Natasha gathered before their TV screen to watch. I had invited Wendy Hanson and several other friends to my apartment for the same purpose. Noon arrived. Bill Leonard as the genial host appeared, but what followed was not the interview with Stokowski but, inadvertently, a replay of the ballet program that had been aired the previous Sunday.

The Stokowski wrath, which was usually carefully reined, was mighty. He phoned the station and attempted without success to reach William Paley by phone. He then sent him a strongly worded telegram insisting that the program be aired in some other slot before Thursday evening's concert. The ploy produced immediate results. If no heads rolled they were at least ruffled. The papers took up the flap enthusiastically. Val Adams in the *New York Times* the following day reported that she had contacted CBS and "a station spokesman" told her that someone grabbed the wrong tape and put it in the machine. She also contacted Stokowski, who told her that "the only right thing to do is to put the program on the air before Thursday. It certainly should be rescheduled."34

Rescheduled it was. Sam Cook Digges, general manager of WCBS-TV, announced that the station would cancel the very popular prime-time situation comedy "Our Miss Brooks" in order to run the Stokowski tape. It was an unprecedented move, for it meant the cancellation of several lucrative commercials. Digges was reported to have said that he and "other station executives had met yesterday morning and rescheduled the program of their own volition." He also sent a note of apology to Stoki. Persistent Ms. Adams called Stokowski, who with obvious self-satisfaction declared: "Everything is in order."35

Not only was everything in order, but far beyond that. The evening
audience that watched the program was vastly larger than the one that
might have caught it Sunday noon, and the interest it engendered provided a welcome spurt to the box office sales. The concert was off to an
auspicious start. Although CBS had not taken a box for the concert, its
subsidiary Columbia Records had, and Goddard Lieberson was there
applauding along with his colleagues.

The title of the first piece, "Festive" Overture, was prophetic of the
entire evening. Stoki was in top form; the handpicked orchestra was the
equal of any major symphony. At midpoint James Fassett, CBS-Philhar-
monic commentator, read a telegram from President Eisenhower:

> ... THE NAME STOKOWSKI BRINGS TO MIND THE VERY
> FINEST IN MUSIC. WITH COURAGE, IMAGINATION
> AND ZEAL MR. STOKOWSKI HAS OPENED THE MUSI-
> CAL TREASURY OF MANKIND AND MADE US RICHER
> THROUGH THE POWER OF HIS ART. MY PERSONAL
> CONGRATULATIONS TO THIS DISTINGUISHED CON-
> DUCTOR AND BEST WISHES TO ALL JOINED IN HIS
> HONOR.
>
> DWIGHT D.
> EISENHOWER[36]

Mayor Wagner, who introduced himself as a frustrated violinist, presented Stokowski with a plaque from the city of New York and a citation
that hailed him as an "outstanding interpreter of music whose fresh
insights and vigorous imagination bring life to both the untried works of
contemporary composers and the world's great orchestral literature." It
also cited him as a pioneer and a world citizen.[37]

Stoki responded by inviting Wagner to play in the orchestra. Wagner
protested, saying that he had left his fiddle home. Stoki continued with
a bit of banter about how much he admired the music of his father
Richard. He then spoke about the Contemporary Music Society and his
own efforts to encourage contemporary composers. Somehow the evening
generated an aura of good feeling and affection toward Stokowski that
seemed unlike the ambience of any other concert of his that I had ever
attended. In one box, Evangeline, then Princess Zalstem-Zalessky, applauded vigorously. Daughter Sonya had flown in for the concert and in
another box, along with Faye and Natasha, were his two sons Stan and
Chris.

Before the concert, Stoki had talked to Scott Beach, who had been one of the bright youngsters brought to New York to be interviewed by Deems Taylor during the intermission of the Philharmonic. He was later to become a distinguished actor and TV personality. At a break during the final rehearsal, Scott recalled "He completely abandoned all of the people standing around him with scores in their hands waiting to ask him questions, and he focused on me and about ways and means of making sure that his children were well provided for and well guarded. He was afraid at the time of kidnapping. He was scared to death that without some macho guy in the box the kids might be harmed. I was husky enough, I suppose, but the size of the whole undertaking seemed outrageous to me because I expected Dutch Schultz to jump out from behind a building. I had heard all these stories about New York. I can't remember the exact words he said to me, but he fixed upon me like a hypnotist—you will do this—you will do that. He was orchestrating the way I would do this.

"As it turned out, I arrived at Carnegie, went to the box where the governess and the youngsters were, and after the intermission she took them home. I never even saw them after the intermission. But I was scared to death to go backstage after the concert because Stokowski might see me and wonder what had happened. But I made sure the next day that they had gotten home safely."38

There was a general consensus that the program, minus the razzmatazz that the Shostakovich symphony was to have supplied, was too conventional. From the critics' point of view, the opinion was valid, but from the audience reaction, the choices could not have been better.

"No other living conductor has done so much or is doing as much for the music of our time," wrote Miles Kastendieck. "Stokowski achieved singular success as usual. . . . Both composers and audience should be most grateful." He singled out the Vaughan Williams work as having the most substance. "To these ears," he continued, "Wallingford Riegger's *New Dance* sounded the most youthfully alive and also the best proportioned. . . . The lovely texture and personal quality of Hovhaness' impressionism can hardly fail to be ingratiating."39

A member of the audience that night, who also shared great admiration for the symphony, was Percy Grainger. Percy was pleased, and to Ursula Vaughan Williams he wrote:

My wife and I went to hear your husband's 9th Symphony in New York last night, conducted by Stokowski.

The performance seemed a perfect one in every way and the exquisite beauty and cosmic quality of this immortal work struck me as being ideally realized.[40]

Stoki expressed his admiration of the symphony in a cable:

LAST NIGHT IN CARNEGIE HALL WE PERFORMED IN MEMORIAM YOUR HUSBANDS NOBLE AND POWERFUL NINTH SYMPHONY. ORCHESTRA AND PUBLIC WERE DEEPLY MOVED BY ITS BEAUTY.[41]

Mrs. Vaughan Williams answered at once and told of her endeavor to catalog all of his manuscripts. Stokowski replied:

I can understand the immense amount of work that will be necessary to put in perfect order for posterity the enormous amount of music created by your husband, and of course you are the only person who can do it.

It was so right that he was buried in Westminster Abbey with all the other great creative artists of the past and the future.

I can imagine how beautiful it was in Dorset, which is a county I particularly love, and also in Salisbury Cathedral with the light streaming through the mystical windows there.[42]

Another letter, which he wrote the morning after the concert, is one that I cherish:

Dear Oliver

I never can express to you my gratitude for the simply *colossal* amount of work you have done for the concert last night, and all the heartbreaking difficulties you overcame. The result was without exaggeration a miracle, because we know only too clearly how few people are really interested in contemporary music. And yet how great is the need for performances and *good* performances. After we have recovered from last night, let's look to the future and further plans.

Always your friend
Leopold

There was an interesting and unexpected coda to that evening—invitations came from both the Philadelphia Orchestra and the New York Philharmonic to reappear with them during the following 1959–60 season. A press release issued by the Philadelphia Orchestra stated that Stokowski had been engaged as guest conductor "at the invitation of Eugene Ormandy."[43] Several of my Philadelphia friends have assured me that the idea certainly did not originate in Ormandy's mind. "It was absolutely the reverse. Contrary to any ideas in any books," said composer Richard Yardumian, "Ormandy did not want Stoki in Philadelphia. It was the board that wanted him."[44]

Season 1958-59

Dᴜʀɪɴɢ the 1958–59 Houston season, Stokowski again conducted four pairs of concerts to begin and another four to conclude it. The programs were varied and obviously chosen with great care, for there were very few alterations or substitutions. The opening program again contained a new work by Hovhaness—this time his *Meditation on Orpheus.* There was an SRO audience. And a writer in the *Houston Press* reported that the opening concert "had all the excitement of a Broadway opening night."[1]

A Russian program came next on which he introduced Prokofiev's magically beautiful music from the ballet *Romeo and Juliet* and Khachaturian's blatant Symphony No. 2. It also provided two little sonic tidbits: Stoki's own arrangement of Rachmaninoff's Prelude in C-sharp Minor and Tchaikovsky's fragile *Solitude.* On his third program he gave the world premiere of Serge de Gastyne's *Atala,* following it a week later with Paul Creston's Toccata and Vaughan Williams' Symphony No. 9 along with Tchaikovsky and Strauss.

By November Stoki was headed north and did not return to Houston until it was time to rehearse for his pair of concerts on March 16 and 17. His new works included Amirov's *Azerbaijan Mugam* and Scriabin's *Poème d'extase.* The following week the novelty was Menotti's Piano Concerto played by one of the youngest soloists ever to appear with the orchestra. She was Francesca Bernasconi, a chubby youngster affectionately known to her friends and to the Maestro as Kiki. Stokowski had visited the Bernasconis in Naples, and, always being interested in the very young, he invited ten-year-old Kiki to appear with the orchestra in Houston. She played beautifully and delighted the Texans.

Strangely, the new works that Stokowski introduced in Houston were actually not very advanced; in fact, most were on the conservative side. But it is obvious that musical sophistication in Houston was not very high. Come to think of it, is it any higher among symphony subscribers anywhere else?

Tom Johnson concurred: "There's no need to dwell on the content of Stokowski's programs during the seasons he was with us. They accorded to his established pattern. He was careful at first to provide only a sprinkling of contemporary works, but as time went on these developed into quite a downpour. It got to the point where the multiplicity of asterisks in the program—'first time in Houston' (one asterisk), 'first time in the U.S.' (two asterisks), 'first time in the world' (three asterisks)—served only to signal an alarm of dissidence to the conditioned public. Soon the Sol Hurok Goldwynism—'If they don't want to come, nothing will stop them' —began to take effect. Despite their admiration for Stokowski, the public's reception of his contemporary items regressed from that of reluctant tolerance, to indifference, to rejection. There was much walking out after these works, and, of course, L. S. knew it and I was sorry for it—but more so for myself, I suppose, because it indicated a decline in renewed subscriptions. A conductor stands or fails by his programs, and I was not inclined to volunteer suggestions in this area, but when L. S. asked me what I thought Houston might want to hear, I told him that Houston, like other cities, was pretty much of a roast beef town. Another time when he asked for specific suggestions, I proposed a Beethoven cycle. L. S. gave Houston a superb Beethoven cycle and served up great repasts of roast beef.

"Now, what I've said about the public's disaffection for contemporary music does not mean that Stokowski's and Houston's lot was not a happy one. He proposed new projects and Houston responded with support. He felt that a contemporary music society should be established. We found the proper leaders in the community, sympathetic to such a venture, and a contemporary music society was established. He proposed cooperation with the University of Houston and the University Chorus was invited to participate in choral presentations."[2]

Through his old friend Sam Rosenbaum, Stoki was also able to obtain the cooperation of the Musicians Trust Fund, which at that time Sam controlled. The first program of the Contemporary Music Society of

Houston was an unusually long one, but it is fascinating to see what Stoki gave to his contemporary fans:

> Varèse: *Octandre*—for solo flute, clarinet, oboe, bassoon, horn, trumpet, trombone, and contrabass
> Harrison: *Nokturno*—for violins, violas, and cellos
> Farberman: Theme and Variations for Piano and Percussion
> Lutoslawski: *Musique Funèbre* for Strings
> Villa-Lobos: *Chôros* No. 3—for men's voices, and solo clarinet, saxophone, bassoon, three horns, and trombone
> Barber: *Dover Beach*—for baritone, violins, viola, and cello
> Carrillo: *Meditacion* for Strings with quarter tones
> Hovhaness: *Meditation on Demeter*, Opus 170—for solo piccolo, English horn, alto saxophone, fluegel horn, tuba, and percussion
> Surinach: *Tientos*—for solo harp, English horn and timpani
> Arthur Hall: *Mobiles*

At this time, Stoki talked a great deal about oriental music and the possible fusion of East-West influences. For over a year he had studied a score of the Turkish composer Ahmed Adnam Saygun. There had been numerous conversations with Turkish officials in the New York consulate and with members of the Turkish delegation in the U.N. On November 25, 1958, the Turks engaged him to conduct a concert in the hall of the General Assembly honoring the United Nations and their own distinguished composer as well. The main thrust of the evening was the dramatic oratorio *Yunus Emre* of Saygun, which was performed by the Symphony of the Air, four vocal soloists, and a 110-voice choir from the Crane Chorus of the Potsdam, New York, Teachers College.[3]

It was the sort of event that Stoki particularly enjoyed. It was conceived as an adjunct to a reception given by Dr. Charles Malik, president of the General Assembly, and by Dag Hammarskjold, secretary general of the United Nations.

Steeped even more deeply in a wash of exotica, Stoki conducted a concert on December 2, 1958, in the Metropolitan Museum consisting of Egyptian, Japanese, Chinese, Israeli, and American composers; it was his own East-West encounter. Instrumental requirements, too, were exotic; the scores called for such unusual instruments as the tar and derabucca. It opened with the *Fantasia-Tahmeel* for derabucca and strings by the Egyptian-American composer Halim El-Dabh. The derabucca is a small hand-held pottery drum with a taut drumhead which is played by the palms and fingers. Its contribution was insufferably dull. Then came Cowell's *Persian Set,* Odeon Partos's *Yiskor,* and Shukichi Mitsukuri's *Ten Haikus* based on the classic short poems of the Japanese poet Basho. There was a world premiere of Colin McPhee's Balinese-influenced Nocturne and Chou Wen-Chung's *To a Wayfarer* for clarinet, strings, harp and percussion, which "made the deepest impression" on the ears of Ross Parmenter of the *New York Times.* [4] There were also percussion pieces of Malloy Miller and Hovhaness, as well as Walter Piston's Divertimento for Nine Instruments, which seemed as out of place as a diplomat in a diaper.

Dances of India, Japan, and Burma were performed in native costume by children from the United Nations International School during a children's concert with the Symphony of the Air sponsored by the Parents League of New York. It was the young audiences that continued to intrigue him. He gave them tastes of Bizet, Shostakovich, Humperdinck, and others. A group of ten youngsters from the Diller-Quaile School of Music tootled, rattled, and drummed their miniature instruments in Haydn's *Toy* Symphony. He compared a fugue to a game of follow the leader, and when he played the "Little" Fugue in G Minor of Bach, he asked the young audience to identify each instrument as it came. There were some ear-splitting volleys of shouted guesses. The children loved it. [5]

A little later, Stoki, clad in a striped navy blue and white polo shirt and gray slacks, was sitting at his window overlooking Central Park. As the late-afternoon sun streamed in, he talked about children with Fern Marja of the *New York Post.* He did not want to talk about his own children but about everybody's children. And he remarked that in most of the children's concerts he gave, the youngsters seemed to enjoy most a fugue of Bach. " 'It is the least thing you would expect them to like and it all shows how little we understand children. What is going on inside of them is a mystery to us. If we are just quiet and notice how they react to everything in life, and don't expect them to react as we do, then it is clear.' "

Ms. Marja used her fourth-estate privilege to make an editorial comment: "Leopold Stokowski did not mention his ex-wife nor the millions she had inherited. He did not mention the way of life she was providing for his sons. He did not have to." [6]

Ever since the divorce from Gloria, there had been arguments about the matter of their custody. At the time he said that "if Gloria leaves me, there will be a custody fight for our boys that will make the court battle her mother and aunt waged over her 20 years ago look like a picnic story."[7]

For some time Leopold had wanted the boys for a longer period. Under an agreement executed in 1955 before the divorce, Gloria and Leopold shared custody—with him having the boys between January 1 and March 1. He wanted to have the period extended until June 15 and have the right to take the children to Europe with him.[8] He had discussed it all at great length with his attorneys, and on May 5 Gloria said she was served with a show-cause order on the street—why the visitation rights should not be revised more to his satisfaction. "He then departed for Europe, leaving the time bomb to explode in my face and the faces of my children."[9]

It was just twenty-four years earlier that Gloria herself was a pawn in one of the most acrid and sensational custody suits on record in American jurisprudence. The papers reviewed many of the charges and counter-charges of that suit when Gloria's mother was declared unfit and Gloria was put in the custody of her aunt Gertrude Vanderbilt Whitney. Gloria's mother had been denounced by her own mother, and she was accused of being a playgirl who paid no attention to her daughter's welfare and kept late hours, slept late, gave a continual round of cocktail parties, and spent her money recklessly. It was ironic that Gloria had to defend herself against Stoki's allegation that "she is a stay-up-late who sleeps in the mornings."[10]

There were announcements to the press daily presenting Gloria's side of the picture. In custody papers filed in the New York Supreme Court on Wednesday, May 13, Gloria declared that Stokowski has " 'an old world, 19th century folklore superstition' about children and hovers over their two sons 'like an overanxious, harassing and harassed great-grandmother . . . his practice is to create neurotic explosions over minutiae. Why, pandemonium could result if one of the boys so much as sniffled.' . . . He's 'compulsive and nomadic . . . doesn't want a home . . . believes in yogi exercises' and 'roughhouses with the boys until they are exhausted.' "[11]

Stoki's counsel, William Mulligan, charged that the affidavit filed for Gloria was "utterly scurrilous and defamatory." So reported the *Daily News*. One point of contention was the result of the 1955 agreement banning plane travel for the boys. "This anachronism in this space age was inspired over my protest," Gloria said in her affidavit. "Mr. Stokowski insists on its observance. The trips he has taken and those he contemplates for the boys are either by train or by automobile. I believe that statistics will sustain my contention that travel by automobile is at least as hazardous as plane travel. And this is particularly true when the driver is a man of 85. Certainly his reflexes, stamina and sight cannot conceivably be deemed to be adequate to the requirements of a long journey."[12]

On reading the account in the *Daily News,* Stoki cabled the city editor:

> MY BIRTH LONDON 18 APRIL 1887 ALL THESE COMPLETELY UNTRUE AND ABSURD ACCUSATIONS ARE MADE TO HIDE REAL AND BASIC QUESTION WHICH IS PRESENT AND FUTURE PHYSICAL AND MENTAL WELFARE AND SENSE OF SECURITY OF OUR TWO SONS WHO SHOULD HAVE MOTHER AND FATHER SOLIDLY BEHIND THEM IN FRIENDLY SPIRIT OF COOPERATION BECAUSE BOTH PARENTS ARE EQUALLY RESPONSIBLE FOR THE SECURITY OF TWO OTHERWISE HELPLESS BOYS.
>
> THANKS
> LEOPOLD STOKOWSKI[13]

As she represented it in a further affidavit filed by her attorney, Arnold R. Krakower, Gloria averred: "Mr. Stokowski, dressed in a Japanese silk black kimono and wearing either bathing trunks or absolutely nothing underneath, took the children and these two friends of his to a crowded restaurant. The five of them sat there for about an hour. This scene was reported to me by an observer."

Although she did not identify them, the two friends were Faye and Natasha, and she charged: ". . . They have played an increasing role in his life. He takes them on trips with the boys to restaurants. . . . He appears in all public places with them and the children. . . .

"It would be hard to imagine two women less qualified to provide a proper influence over the children. They are present at his home almost constantly when the boys were either visiting there or living there. They cannot continue to be subjected to this type of influence.

"As he grows older and older, he lives more in fear of loneliness. I can understand but I will not permit him to draw the children into this desperation. He is devoted exclusively and frantically to his own needs and seeks to draw the boys into fulfilling them."[14]

Gloria permitted the release of excerpts from her affidavit and the *New York Mirror* reported:

" '. . . Tyrant, despot, hypocrite, dictator'—these and many more [words] went to make up her portrait of her ex-husband. . . . Gloria described his petition as a 'vicious act of cruelty' and said: 'By it he expected me to crumble.' But, said Gloria, she is one cookie who won't crumble. She declared: 'He seeks to be restored to the tyrannical and despotic power he asserted over me when we were married and which he obviously feels deprived of by the divorce and my remarriage. . . .' "

Another *Mirror* quote was taken from one of Gloria's letters to Stoki that were also included in the affidavit. " '. . . Understand this: You will never, never take my boys from me, no matter how underhanded the methods you use. The longer you persist in your machinations, your ludicrous 19th century plotting, the more you will prove to me that it is your right and control over my boys that should be cut down.' "[15]

On May 17, the *New York Journal-American* ran a headline that spanned five columns: "Text of New Letters to Stokowski."[16] They were in a similar vein, but one could only question what purpose such personal revelations could possibly serve. Stoki, on the other hand, had no part of his own affidavit fed to the press. Two days after these latest revelations, Justice Nathan "ordered that all future court proceedings be held behind closed doors," reported the *New York Post,* and one of its reporters placed a call to Stoki in Warsaw. The paper reported: "Stokowski in Warsaw, told the *Post* by telephone that his answers to Gloria's charges 'will be made in the court to the Judge,' he said. 'All I am asking for is the best conditions for the boys, both mental and physical, both now and in the future.'

"Stokowski's attorney . . . agreed to the sealing of the papers and closing of the case yesterday, but protested that Gloria had made a lot of public charges that had to be answered privately. Stokowski's answering papers make no counterattacks on the mother of the two boys,' Mulligan said.

" 'I'm the one that asked that the papers be sealed originally,' Mulligan explained. 'We were unsuccessful in the beginning. Then all the charges were made in an affidavit released to the press. For five days there was publication defamatory to the father, his character and his personality, and even in the quality of his love for his sons.' "[17]

Even before leaving Houston, Stoki had confided in Tom Johnson that he dreaded the legal proceedings which might or might not result in more time with his sons. Now that the suit was in progress, he contacted Tom and General Hirsch, who had just succeeded Ima Hogg as president of the Houston Orchestra. "So we made the trip to New York," said Tom, "and did our best. This was not good enough, and, unfortunately, Stokowski's attorney did not seem to us to be as aggressive an advocate as the 'fighting Irishman' he had described himself to be. In any event, the decision did not favor L. S. and I believe that from that day, he lost his ardor for Houston, not musically, of course. He worked as diligently as ever, but he was a lonely man."[18]

During a transatlantic call he asked if I would testify for him. I assured him I would be most happy to do so and on June 1 I met with Mulligan and after lunch was sworn in to testify about his qualities as a father.

But all this time Stoki was in Europe. The trip had begun well, and for a week he stayed at the Bernasconi villa in Posilipo, one of the most spectacularly beautiful villas on the Bay of Naples. The concerts which he had planned to conduct with the Scarlatti Orchestra of Naples were canceled, and he had an entire week to rest and enjoy the beauty of his surroundings. His next stop was Poland; he arrived in Warsaw on May 17 and after four days of rehearsals conducted two concerts with unusual success. Next came Leipzig, where on June 1, 1959, he sagely avoided the German repertory and gave them some less familiar fare: Ravel's *Rapsodie Espagnole*, Debussy's *Trois Nocturnes*, and the Shostakovich Symphony No. 5.

A Reuters dispatch from Leipzig was reprinted in the *New York Post*, as well as in other papers throughout the world. It was dated June 2, and the headline read "Stokowski Wows East Germans": "Leipzig music lovers went wild last night after the second and final appearance of Leopold Stokowski with the 200-year-old Gewandhaus Orchestra here.

"Applause for the program . . . lasted ten minutes. Several hundred of the 1,600 member audience crowded down the central aisle to applaud the conductor and the orchestra. . . ."[19]

In Berlin he repeated the program to an equally receptive audience. After this concert on June 7, he was scheduled to do another, a radio broadcast for RIAS, the American-run radio station. While in East Germany Stoki had given several interviews and was accused by a spokesman for RIAS of having "welcomed Communist party boss Walter Ulbricht's idea of inviting U.S., British and French Foreign Ministers to visit East Germany." In retrospect it seems like a perfectly sensible idea, but at the time it was an explosive suggestion. "We therefore did not consider it a good thing at the present time to broadcast a concert of Mr. Stokowski," a spokesman said.[20]

Stoki was actually pleased, because he wanted to return to New York as quickly as possible, and he did an unprecedented thing. He boarded a Pan Am plane in Berlin and landed in New York in the late afternoon of the tenth. He was met by William Mulligan. Photographers and reporters were also waiting. He showed no apparent reluctance to being photographed and talked guardedly with the scribes. "I came here to see my boys," he said as he left the plane. "I don't know where they are and I don't know when I can see them. But I am here to see the boys." He explained that he had interrupted his European concert tour and would go back to resume it if Judge Nathan agreed. He showed photos of the two boys and when one reporter commented that the boys were handsome, he responded: "They have a handsome mother."[21]

The *New York Daily News* headlined: "Stoky Arrives for Custody Concerto." For his appearance in court the following morning, the press reported: "So exclusive is the maestro's performance that two small windows in the doors of the courtroom of Justice Edgar J. Nathan were papered over late yesterday."[22] Heretofore, they had been the only communication of newsmen with the censored court proceedings. They could see Gloria testifying, but could not hear her. Now they wouldn't even be permitted to see the white-haired music man. His testimony was not extensive, and he returned to London in time to conduct his postponed concert and broadcast for the BBC. In New York the month-long litigation ended on June 25. Neither Leopold nor Gloria was present when Judge Nathan rendered his verdict. "The court does not find that either parent is unfit," he stated. He then tartly added this observation. "It is a sad commentary that an entire month of the court's time and energy has been devoted almost exclusively to the resolution of problems which mature, intelligent parents should be able to work out themselves for the sake of their children. . . . No conduct on the part of either is found to be such as would warrant depriving either of a right of visitation or limited custody," he said.[23]

Stoki had lost. Instead of increasing the amount of time his sons would be with him, it was reduced from the previous five months to one month in the summer and every weekend when he would be in New York.

Five days later, Stoki conducted the London Symphony Orchestra in a concert in Royal Festival Hall which was later to be broadcast by the BBC on July 8. Stoki had gone to London for this single concert and returned to fill his American engagements.

The first was the opening of the Empire State Music Festival. It had found a new location: the Anthony Wayne Recreation Area of the Bear Mountain-Harriman State Park, a mere one hour's distance from the city. Frank Forest was still in charge and the orchestra and audience were seated under a new aqua, cerulean blue, and gold tent.

As an American premiere, Stokowski introduced a big sprawling cantata called *Ode to Joy* by Aram Khachaturian, which also received a curt critical brush-off, and the concert ended with the epochal *Alexander Nevsky* of Prokofiev.

If the opening concert of Stokowski seemed inauspicious to the reviewers, they changed their tune remarkably when he returned a month later. On Saturday evening, July 25, he conducted a concert of more stable fare than that of the previous one. He began, not with the Passacaglia and Fugue in C Minor as programmed, but with a movement from Ernest Bloch's *Trois Poèmes Juifs, Cortège Funèbre.* It was played in memoriam, for Bloch had died on July 15. The audience was deeply stirred by the music of Bloch and by the absorption and intensity of Stoki's conducting.

Then, following the Bach, he conducted the Third Symphony of Brahms and *Oedipus Rex* of Stravinsky. Three decades had passed since he had conducted the work in a staged version with giant puppets suggesting the ancient Greek drama. Now, without the trappings of a stage performance, he concentrated on the seemingly simple means that Stravinsky had employed and the delicate blending of the soloists and chorus and the orchestra. Hugh Ross had prepared the chorus and the orchestra was the Symphony of the Air.

67

The New York City Opera

To Stokowski, the *Oedipus* performance at the Empire State Music Festival was a preview of his New York performances later in the season. Julius Rudel, director of the New York City Opera, had begun discussions with him more than a year earlier. Strangely, Stokowski had never been invited by any of the regimes at the Metropolitan Opera, and I congratulated Julius on his perception in engaging Stoki to conduct an opera at City Center.

"Stoki had always been my idol," said Julius. "As a young boy I had two: one was Toscanini and the other was Stokowski. That was still in my Viennese days. The recordings of these two men really were the ear-openers for me, and I loved the contrast—one side Toscanini and the other side Stokowski. Then, of course, when I came to this country, I became a bit friendly in a way with Stokowski. . . . I knew that he did the American premiere of *Wozzeck*. I knew that he did the American premiere of *Gurrelieder*."

"And the *Glückliche Hand*," I added.

"Yes, various things, and I figured that there must be a way of somehow involving him, and when I got together with John Butler, we talked about doing *Carmina Burana* on the stage. It seemed a logical thing to ask Stoki whether he would come in by that door, so to speak. . . . First, I had to find another piece to go with it. I thought *Oedipus Rex* was such a monumental contrast that we could put it together with *Carmina Burana*. When I presented the idea to Stoki, he literally jumped at it. . . . He said to me, 'As far as money is concerned, my fee is either $2,500 or nothing

703

and since evidently you can't pay, it's nothing. So he never took a penny. Did you know that?"[1]

Dates for the presentation of the double bill were worked out for the end of September and one additional performance was scheduled for Philadelphia. When asked if he would like to conduct a performance there, Stoki was delighted.

As soon as the announcement appeared in the papers in Philadelphia, a musical hell broke loose. Ormandy had scheduled a performance of *Carmina Burana* with the Philadelphia Orchestra at a later date and was furious that Stoki would precede him with a staged version. Outgoing manager Donald Engle, whose termination was to take place on July 1, drafted a statement that appeared in the Orchestra's monthly newsletter, which was sent to members of the Philadelphia Orchestra Association. Its tone was sharply reproachful. He complained that Stokowski would be making an appearance in Philadelphia prior to his return engagement with the Philadelphia Orchestra and that he was about to conduct *Carmina Burana*, which Ormandy had scheduled later in the 1959–60 season. "All of this," Engle's letter complained, "only confirms once again my conviction that the concept of ethics, as you and I know it, simply doesn't exist in the egocentric world in which conductors operate, or if it does, it is often warped and twisted to satisfy the whim of the moment."

Stokowski was shocked at the tone of Engle's letter and when contacted by the press said that he didn't see how the two performances conflicted. "They are in two different categories," he said and stated emphatically that his commitment was made "before we knew anything about" the Philadelphia performance. "I was asked many months ago to conduct for the opera and I accepted. I was asked, 'Have you any objection to going to Philadelphia,' and I said no."

C. Wanton Balis, Jr., president of the association, issued a statement disassociating it from Engle's newsletter. Balis was quoted: "While we do regret the duplication [in programming *Carmina*], the sentiments expressed by Mr. Engle are strictly his own and in no way represent the position of the Philadelphia Orchestra Association."[2]

Stoki certainly had no intention of offending Ormandy, members of the Association, nor any of the music confraternity in the City of Brotherly Love. He replied when queried by a reporter of the *Inquirer:* "If the Board of Directors of the Philadelphia Orchestra and the Philadelphia public wish me to forego these stage performances on September 29, I am perfectly willing to request the Philadelphia Lyric Opera and the New

York City Center Opera to cancel our agreement for Philadelphia.

"I shall do this with regret because I remember well the enthusiastic reception in the past of Philadelphia lovers of music and drama to our stage performances of 'Wozzeck' and 'Oedipus.'

"In any case, I look forward with extreme pleasure to making music again with the artists of the splendid Philadelphia Orchestra next February."[3]

He phoned Julius Rudel and they discussed the matter. Stoki then refused to conduct the works in Philadelphia rather than cause discord. Ironically, the performances did take place, not conducted by Stokowski but by Rudel, Mr. Engle notwithstanding.

In New York, the idea of having Stokowski as an opera conductor created great curiosity. On Sunday, September 20, five days before the opening at City Center, Jay Harrison visited Stoki for an interview: Jay asked why he had absented himself from opera for so long, and Stoki paused, looked out of the window over the lake in Central Park and said that the reasons were really very simple: "They involve the terrible difficulties that face someone who is looking for singers who are good actors and actors who are good singers. That, mainly, is what has kept me away."

His reason for returning were the two works of Orff and Stravinsky: "They both have much to say to everybody, to *jedermann.*"

Stoki interrupted the interview and walked over to his bar in the corner, on which he always had an array of glasses and very special silver goblets, of which he was very fond. He had, too, an array of varicolored liqueurs, including a purple concoction made by Bols of Holland; and he would blend very "mysterious" specialties. He handed Jay a silver cup and raised one himself saying: "Here is vodka, Polish vodka. To ask a man how he prepares his vodka is a discourtesy, it is prying into a secret gained through a lifetime of experience. Try it." Jay exclaimed that it went down like molten glass.

Stoki believed that a great era of American opera could be possible if we were to develop our own themes in our librettos. "What is the Revolutionary War? Drama. And the Civil War? Drama. Think what Shakespeare did with the wars and kings of his country. Think too, what a great librettist—and one shall appear—can do with our history. What material for a composer of opera to work with! Our history: yes, in every era, in every year, there is great drama somewhere."[4]

Stokowski rehearsed his forces strenuously. "I remember the first time he came to the orchestra rehearsal," said Julius Rudel, "the orchestra was scared stiff because he had the reputation of being nasty and sarcastic. And he was like a lamb with them . . . they ate out of his hand. It was marvelous—really marvelous."[5]

Critics agreed. "Philosophic reflections are not commonly the product of an evening's entertainment in the opera house or concert hall," wrote Irving Kolodin, "but in juxtaposing Stravinsky's 'Oedipus Rex' and Orff's 'Carmina Burana' for the opening bill of its new season . . . the New York Opera Company has permitted an immediate contrast between two major art movements of the day, as well as providing one of the liveliest evenings in its history. To make the auditor's evening complete, the company turned over its musical resources to Leopold Stokowski." After discussing in detail both works, Kolodin concluded: "Taken together 'Oedipus' and 'Carmina Burana' represent a kind of musical theater too seldom presented hereabouts and practically never on the level projected by Stokowski. No one with a broad interest in the subject should pass it by."[6]

So successful was the double bill that Rudel invited Stokowski to conduct them again in a series of performances the following season. Stoki declined and herein, perhaps, lies the reason that he never seriously went into opera. While he was interested in the challenge of doing something new, he was not interested in the devitalizing aspects of repetition. "On the other hand," Julius recalled, "he was willing to do something else, so I asked him to do another double bill: Monteverdi's *Orfeo* and Dallapiccola's *Il Prigioniero.* "What intrigued me, and I think him also, was the juxtaposition of one of the earliest operas and one of the very latest. There was a three-hundred-year difference between the two composers."[7]

Preparations for the productions were meticulous. Stoki and Rudel worked painstakingly to reduce the length of *Orfeo;* uncut it would have exceeded two hours. It is doubtful that today's audiences could have been beguiled by the Monteverdian modalities and archaisms for such a span. As presented it seemed of adequate length, though some critics carped at the excisions. For both productions, Donald Oenslager designed magnificent sets and costumes and made a strong contrast between the baroque setting for *Orfeo* and the dour and tragic setting for *The Prisoner.*

Instead of evoking a pseudoclassic style for *Orfeo,* Oenslager set it in the baroque style of Mantua in 1607, where the opera was first performed. It was brilliant and flamboyant; hell seemed a lively place, quite unlike Dante's grim inferno. "Pluto not only resembled a professorial Santa Claus," said Harriet Johnson, "but he was, of all rare things, a reasonable man . . . the stunning costumes in baroque style charmingly stretched the imagination."[8] Orfeo, sung by Gerard Souzay, was crowned with a tall plumed helmet, and protected by a burnished breastplate. Director Christopher West conceived the proceedings in the manner of an Elizabethan masque and even had Apollo descend on a cloud.

To achieve something of the sound Monteverdi had envisioned, Stokowski added numerous rare and antique instruments, including recorders, viola da gamba, small portative organs, and other little-used instruments. "The difficult aggregation . . . was handled with exemplary skill, and the little orchestral interludes as well as the charming vocal madrigals were delightful," stated Paul Henry Lang.[9]

The critics who commented on the qualities of the singers all singled out Souzay as an exceptional artist; Judith Raskin, as Euridice, and Regina Safarty, as the Messenger, won equal praise for their substantially shorter roles.

Months before the season began Miss Raskin had been engaged to sing in both *Orfeo* and *Der Rosenkavalier*. "Both were new to me and *Orfeo* was a big premiere. When I got the contract, I discovered that my fee had been cut. I was getting a big $150 for *Rosenkavalier* and it was cut to $125 for *Orfeo*. Then I said, 'Why are you doing that?' And they said, 'It's not a very big part.' I got very angry and I said, 'Look, $150 is my fee and . . . I want $150.' And the management got angry and said, 'We'll take it away from you then.' I said, 'Fine. I don't need to do *Orfeo*.'

"I started to rehearse *Rosenkavalier* and I got a frantic call from the management. 'Mr. Stokowski doesn't like the girl we engaged for Euridice. You've got to learn the part and sing it for him.' I said, 'I know it's not very long but how can I . . .' 'We will give you special coaching.' And I said to them, 'Are you still going to pay me $125?' They said, 'Judy, you don't understand. This is a great maestro. You must do it for us.' I realized they were in a bind and I quickly learned the part, and then I sang for Stoki. I sang it rather correctly and he turned to me and said in front of the management: 'If you have a girl like this in your company, why did you give me an Aïda. . . . This is what I was waiting for.'

"They called me aside and said, 'Look, Judy, do us a favor. He wants you very much. Sing the premiere.' And I said, 'Okay, if you don't take the *Rosenkavalier* away from me, I'll do this for you.' And so I agreed.

"Then I got a call from management and they said, 'Judy, you've got to do the second performance—just get us through the second performance.' And I said to them, 'Okay, but you've got to promise me that you will give the third performance to the other girl, because I have to do

Rosenkavalier. And they said, 'Just get us through the second performance.' So I did and Stoki was really very happy.

"The third performance was coming up and I was very suspicious that
they weren't rehearsing the other girl and I was killing myself to get
Rosenkavalier ready, and sure enough, in that good old City Center
fashion, they did not plan the other girl in time. But because I had forced
them, they brought her to rehearsal and she sang it for Stoki, and he said,
'I don't want her. I want Raskin.' She had learned the notes. But he said,
'She can't do it. . . .' They said to me, 'Judy, you have to do the third
performance.' I said, 'No!' That's the first time in my life I had ever been
temperamental. They said, 'Come to the opera house and you tell him.'
Well, that's no way to run an opera company, but I came to the opera
house. I got all dressed in costume and I said to them, 'What am I
supposed to do?' They said, 'You go in now and tell Maestro you can't
sing.' Well you know that's a terrible thing to do to an artist, and I went
in and I said in a whisper 'Maestro, I can't sing. I have laryngitis.' I never
in my life have done that. I was in costume already. I was an idiot not
to go on, because he turned to me and said, 'Miss Raskin, you are a great
artist. You should have taken care of yourself. You should never have
allowed yourself to get sick.' And he never hired me after that. . . . And
it was so ironic that of all people, I should have been the one chosen to
sing for his ninetieth birthday. Apparently he was angry, but he never
forgot that he liked me so. . . ."[10]

Dallapiccola's work was indeed a contrast, with its angular song-speech
and twelve-tone dissonances—yet there was something peculiarly Italian
about it.

The score of *The Prisoner* calls for an off-stage chorus, but in old City
Center there was no room for one backstage. "So we put them in the
basement under the stage," Julius recalled. "We had to amplify it, and
I remember how much time he took to get the amplification just right.
He kept saying he wanted a 'meek-ro-phone' here and a 'meek-ro-phone'
over there. He really spent a great deal of time perfecting that marvelous
effect when the chorus came in."[11]

Capitol-United Artists-Everest

D URING this very busy time, both professionally and personally, Stoki continued to make an unusual number of recordings. He had been particularly happy with Capitol and enjoyed the men with whom he worked, and although his contract called for only two releases per year, he would have preferred a hundred. Capitol, however, did extend their resources and recorded a number of additional records, but their release was vexingly slow.

Stoki was also distressed to read in an issue of *High Fidelity* a column, "Notes from Abroad," that had an announcement by a Capitol representative with the pulchritudinous name of Patricia Pretty. In her press release, Miss Pretty reported that "a classical schedule based chiefly on the Pittsburgh Symphony under Steinberg . . ." was to be launched by Capitol. Stoki wondered why no mention was made of the records he made in England and also of the concerts he conducted in London in the Royal Festival Hall and in Oxford.

> While I have the greatest respect for Steinberg, I am not willing to be second to any conductor in the world, and still worse not to be mentioned at all. If Capitol's plans are to "base their classical repertoire chiefly with Pittsburgh and Steinberg," I feel they should have told me so frankly before I signed the contract with them, in which case, I would not of course have signed.[1]

When other companies approached him about recordings, especially if they were willing and interested in doing some of the things he particu-

709

larly wanted to do, he was naturally eager to do so, and he had discussions with both United Artists Records and Everest Records during the fall of 1958.

He had discussed the matter with Glenn Wallichs, who wrote expressing his sorrow that Stoki would want to record with a company other than Capitol. Stoki answered:

> I am glad you wrote me so frankly how you feel about my recording with other companies. I feel just as sorry about it as you do because I had hoped to have a happy cooperation with you and Scotti but it turned out to be otherwise than the way I had expected. I give a great amount of thought and work and effort into making a record, and afterwards within a reasonable length of time I would like it to be made available to music lovers all over the civilized world. . . .
>
> Also, within a reasonable length of time I like to receive the financial return of my effort, because that is the way I make my living, and because I have responsibilities which require a certain amount of financial ability.

He complained about recordings he had made over a year earlier which had not been released:

> I cannot understand this. I presume Capitol Records invested a fairly large amount of money in making those records in London, but by this delay the company still has no income from those expenses. Even from the standpoint of pure business, this does not seem to me to make sense.
>
> Some time ago I received an offer from another company to record but I did not accept it. Later a second company made me an offer and again I did not accept it. But recently a third and a fourth company have made me offers, and I do not feel I can reject them, but must ask Capitol Records according to my contract whether or not they are willing to record the music suggested by these two companies. . . .
>
> United Artists Recording would like me to record with them the following:
>
> Beethoven: Symphony No. 7
> Brahms: Symphony No. 3
> Mozart: Jupiter Symphony
>
> Would Capitol Records like to record these in the near future?
>
> As I like working with you and Scotti so much it is painful for me to write you all of this, but I feel it is only right that I tell you exactly how I regard everything.[2]

Stoki therewith signed a contract with Everest Records (Belock Instrument Corporation) on September 26, 1958, and on December 12, he signed with United Artists Records. Bert Whyte, an ebullient giant of a man, was one of the founders of Everest; he was also a superb engineer and the A & R man for the company. "Harry Belock and I founded Everest Records," Bert told me. "Everest was our brainchild."[3]

By September 22, 1958, Bert Whyte confirmed that they intended to record the Shostakovich Fifth Symphony as well as Falla's *El amor brujo* and the Albéniz *Feast Day in Seville,* along with the "Dance" from *La Vida breve.*[4]

The Shostakovich was recorded with the Stadium Symphony Orchestra of New York. Bert confirmed that "it was really the New York Philharmonic, but we couldn't call it that, so it was called the Stadium Symphony."[5] In all, Stoki recorded eleven records for Everest in a two-year period (1958–59). Six of these were recorded with the Stadium Symphony and the remaining five with the Houston Symphony Orchestra.

On January 6, 1959, Stoki wrote to Harry Belock:

> In my opinion, your equipment is great and progressive. But I think that your ideas and mine about recording are different. You naturally see recording from the standpoint of mathematics, engineering equipment and recording techniques. I naturally see it from the standpoint of music. I feel very strongly that we must only make the finest records in the world. I also feel strongly that we must convey the composer's ideas and their intentions to the listeners. I hope we can reach millions of listeners all over the world, and the majority of listeners will wish to enjoy the *music,* and recording techniques will only be secondary in their minds.

To ameliorate any sharpness his remarks might have conveyed, he added: "Thank you for the delightful supper the other night and our conversation."[6]

After listening to test pressings of the Shostakovich on "a good Stromberg Carlson reproducer and an equally good RCA" one, Stoki summed up his observations in another letter to Belock three days later:

> 1. There is not enough dynamic range between the loudest and the softest parts of the music.
> 2. The lows are weak where the music demands they be powerful.
> 3. The balance between the strings, winds and percussion is not what the music requires.

All these three deficiencies could be put right at the same time by skillful transfer while reducing the recording from three channels to two and one.

As you are unwilling to make these musically necessary changes during transfer, and as the pickup during the recording session did not fully record these three deficiencies, I definitely cannot approve these records, and I request you not to release them in their present state. If you are willing to put right these deficiencies during transfer either by someone else or myself, these records can be made suitable for release, and can be something of which Everest can be proud.[7]

On January 20, he complained about the monaural test pressing of the Fifth:

I have been listening to Shostakovich's Symphony No. 5 on new stereophonic equipment which gives very good reproduction. When I listened recently to this music on monaural the reproduction was less good. It is possible that for the next year or two many persons may be listening to the recordings of the Shostakovich Fifth Symphony, Tchaikovsky's Francesca and Hamlet on monaural. For this reason I strongly urge you to wait until you have new equipment by which we can make a transfer from tape to disc, and during that transfer improve the balance on certain places, give more lows at a few moments where lows are needed by the music, and also make certain places softer in relation to the loudest places. By doing these things we can greatly improve the records and make them more exciting and emotional. I shall be glad to cooperate with you in this. Let us only offer the public the *highest quality of which we are capable.* [8]

In spite of the diligence of the engineers in following Stoki's suggestions, he never seemed to be satisfied. The Shostakovich symphony was finally released, however, and the reviews ranged from so-so to excellent.

Alfred Frankenstein, who had followed Stoki through the years, had this to say: "Stokowski's old 78 rpm records of Shostakovich's First, Fifth and Sixth Symphonies were primarily responsible for establishing the reputation of that composer in this country. They had a tension, a breadth, drama, richness, and drive that no other interpretation has ever quite equaled, and to hear Stokowski's performance of the Fifth again is like home-coming. . . . Ladies and gentlemen, the old master is back, and better than ever."[9]

Stoki's Tchaikovsky album won particular praise. Deryck Cooke felt that both *Francesca da Rimini* and the *Hamlet* Overture suited Stoki "down to the ground." He observed that the liner notes, or sleeve notes as the British call them, announced Stokowski conducting Tchaikovsky. For once, he said slyly, it is true. It is Tchaikovsky, not Tchaikovsky arranged by Stokowski. "Having often gunned for Stokowski in my time, . . . I'm glad to be able to say that these performances are really, as he would no doubt put it, 'stoopendous.' These are performances in a million; to hear these rarely-played and much-disparaged works played like this is to realize that Tchaikovsky was one of the very great, who could meet Dante and Shakespeare on their own level."[10]

Stoki agreed and as he said later, when he would arrive in heaven, he would seek out Tchaikovsky and shake his hand.

One of the most spectacular of his Everest recordings was his version of the Villa-Lobos *Uirapurú* and the *Modinha* movement from the *Bachianas Brasileiras No. 1*. These were coupled with a suite from Prokofiev's *Cinderella*. "The only thing wrong with this album is that there isn't more of it," wrote Alfred Kaine.[11]

Stokowski recordings began to be pirated. In a letter written to Bernard Solomon of Everest Enterprises, Inc., he said: "A friend has just given me a record with a 'tiara' label of Wagner's Parsifal which I recorded with the Houston Symphony for Everest Records. On the Tiara label is my name as conductor and the name of the Houston Symphony . . . as I have a contract with Everest, but none with Tiara I do not understand how this can be possible. What does your company know about this, and what can be done to protect our mutual interest?"[12]

He received a reply from Mr. Solomon requesting him to send a copy of the record to Everest in Hollywood and suggested that it was probably a bootleg record.[13] But Stokowski made another discovery; he found a record apparently marketed by Everest of Prokofiev's *Ugly Duckling* and his *Cinderella* Ballet Suite. "This record also contains three compositions of Debussy which were so badly recorded that I was forced to refuse . . . my approval for release."[14]

As the Everest recordings were hitting the market, so were those of both Capitol and United Artists. Stoki's contract with United Artists was a rather loose affair and provided that selections to be recorded were to be chosen by mutual agreement. It was agreed, too, that all records were to be released the first month after recording. That was obviously a thrust at Capitol, which was very late in its recording release schedule. No records were to be withdrawn from sale except by mutual agreement. As in most of his other contracts, Stoki was to receive "five percent (5%), with no deductions, of the retail list price of every record sold."

Early in 1959 he wrote stating that on February 16 he would conduct a concert in Carnegie Hall for the United Jewish Relief which would include Ernest Bloch's *Schelomo* and Ben-Haim's Suite, *From Israel.* "This music will have three rehearsals and one concert, and so would be completely prepared for recording one or two days after the concert. Would United Artists like to record it? If so, I would like to do it with you. If not, I will offer it to another company. The timing is perfect for two sides of one LP."[15]

This proposal met with eager response. The orchestra that was to be used was the Symphony of the Air and manager Jerry Toobin engaged Gunther Schuller to be the A & R Director of the new series of symphonic works to be recorded with United Artists.

Gunther recalled: "We recorded in the Manhattan Center up on Broadway. The first recording was the *Second Symphony* by Khachaturian, which I thought Stokowski did magnificently. A very exciting recording. We had quite a fabulous orchestra and the acoustics of the Manhattan Center were very conducive to this piece. Also it was the kind of piece that Stokowski had a great feel for. Its intellectual quotient may not be terribly high, but like all Khachaturian, it's really captivating and easily accessible music. It gets to you—on a sort of not very discriminating gut level.

"Anyway, we made that recording and it went pretty smoothly. Stokowski and I didn't know each other all that well and I guess he was sort of testing me out in a variety of ways. I remember the first real trouble— although I didn't let it become an issue, because I simply gave in. But when we were editing that Khachaturian record, he sat down at the board with all of those knobs and dials, and started doing the most *incredible* things in terms of balances. He was practically recomposing Khachaturian's piece. Mind you, the orchestra had played it as written with all the correct dynamics. Strangely enough Stokowski had not monkeyed around with the dynamics—as was often his wont. It was pretty straight conducting. But when we got into the mixing studio—my Lord—flutes became twice as loud as brass sections; he was bringing out the viola's inner parts *over* the melody in the violins and other strange distortions.

"And yet in that piece, looking at it charitably, he gave the final product a kind of raw, animalistic excitement. He made the music bigger than life-size. He also distorted it, but what's new about that? Stokowski was always fond of putting in the extra tam-tam note or gong, always souping up and reorchestrating and recomposing. I didn't take that too seriously, knowing his inclinations.

"But I remember another more serious point of contention. This came in the first movement, a sonata form with an exposition, second subject, development section, and a recapitulation. Now a certain passage occurred three times in exactly the same instrumentation and the same tempo. My idea on how we should mix and edit these passages was to make those three repetitions as exactly identical as possible. But Stokowski sat down at the console and started fooling around with these repetitions, trying to make them *totally* different. I said, 'But you know this is a recapitulation; we really should make it sound the same as the first time.' He said, 'My young man, *never* make it sound the same.' As he was talking, I realized he didn't even believe his own words. But because he always had to be right, he was lecturing me on how same things should never be the same. I realized that it was useless to argue with him. I let it go; and because I gave in, it didn't develop into a serious thing between us. I just sat there dutifully listening to the master pontificating.

"We did *Schelomo* just a few weeks later and that also went very well. Stokowski had chosen George Neikrug to be the soloist on this recording. Stokowski had already recorded it once with Feuermann and the Philadelphia Orchestra—to me still the most beautiful recording of that piece. Anyhow, our *Schelomo* recording sessions went very well, and I remember Stokowski telling Jerry Toobin—so that I could hear it—how well I had run that particular session: very economically done, and how he loved the sound when he heard the playbacks, and all that. A compliment from Stokowski, as you know, is a very rare thing. So I was feeling pretty good.

"Now, that same night as an extra filler for the record Stokowski had decided to record a piece by Ben-Haim, Suite, *From Israel.* The way we. were set up in the Manhattan Center, the orchestra was down on the main floor while I, with the recording engineer and equipment, was way up on the fifth floor. I could be in communication with Stokowski only through a microphone. I could hear everything that he was saying and doing, but I had difficulty in communicating with him at that distance and of course had no eye contact with him. I either had to interrupt him by talking over the microphone, or else run all the way down five flights to talk to him face to face. Anyway, he started rehearsing and I was following the score. I didn't think it was a particularly great or important piece, but it had been decided to record it, and naturally I felt that we must do a perfect job,

"We were going along rather well, but suddenly there came a section for cellos *divisi à 4,* and strange, painful dissonances came to my ears over the microphones. Ben-Haim's music has a sort of mild atonality at best. I looked at the score and in an instant saw what was wrong: two of the four divisi lines of cellos had wrong clefs. They were correct in the score but wrong in the parts, so that the cellos were playing a fifth below what they *should* be playing.

"Very often in something other than really familiar music—Beethoven or Mozart or Tchaikovsky, let's say—musicians will play through a section like that and not even know that it's wrong or if they know it's wrong, they don't know *how* to correct it—particularly in the last frantic minutes of a record date, when they're probably already thinking about going home.

"So they played through this passage. I didn't say anything the first time. I figured Stokowski would sooner or later catch the mistake. But we got to that spot again and the same thing happened. He *didn't* stop and now I realized that he hadn't heard it. Now what was I going to do? Some survival instinct told me not to speak to him about this over the microphone in front of the whole orchestra.

"When he went through it a third time and *still* didn't hear it, and no one in the cello section seemed to react, at least verbally, I really was beginning to panic. It was getting very close to the end of the recording session, and I knew we could not go into overtime. We had about fifteen minutes left to record this movement. I figured if I go down five flights of stairs and whisper into his ear, and back up again, I'm going to waste at least three or four minutes; and obviously we didn't have that kind of time to waste. So finally I decided to stop him. I said something over the microphone to the effect that 'there seems to be an error in the parts. I think some of the cello clefs are wrong.' I did it as obsequiously as I could, so as not to irritate him. He muttered something I couldn't understand, some annoyed thank you, perhaps. The cellists corrected their parts. But I knew, I could just sense, that he was *really* furious with me.

"We were very short of time now, and very worried as to whether we were going to get that piece recorded in time. Because of union rules there had to be another break for the orchestra. Now, this is what happened. During this five-minute break, I went downstairs and sort of hung around him a little bit, because I wanted to find out how he was taking all this. Finally I said something like, 'I'm glad we—*we* caught that mistake. It would have been terrible to have that wrong on the tape.' No reaction. He just turned away from me, completely ignoring me. I slunk away with my tail between my legs.

"Everybody in the orchestra were friends and colleagues of mine. So I went over to one of the percussionists when, just at that point, the contractor called everybody back again and Stokowski got on the podium ready to continue. You know how impatient and quick he was—the downbeat *immediately!* I was hastily talking to this percussionist, trying to correct something in his part. It was a small thing which I didn't feel I wanted to bother Stokowski about—something I could quickly correct myself. But when he started to rehearse again, I naturally started to run up the five flights of stairs to get back to my booth. But as I walked away from the percussionist saying something like, 'Okay, now don't forget'— that's when Stokowski exploded and fired me that instant. Everybody thinks he fired me because I corrected him in public—which, of course, *is* the real truth—but what really capped it was my talking to the percussionist. He nailed me with his eyes and said, 'Sir, leave these premises immediately.' I didn't even finish the date. The fact that I was not in my booth and that I was—so he probably thought—surreptitiously doing something with this percussionist behind his back—he was a *very* suspicious man—that was the real capper. Getting fired by Stokowski happened to many people, but I was fired right then and there on the spot.

"Well, for years after that incident, I gather he would not mention my name. As with many others, he simply cut me out of his life. When Jerry Toobin tried to bring up my name several times, Stokowski would say, 'Who?'—with a sort of disdainful look, as if I didn't even exist.

"The interesting thing is that during those weeks when we made those records, every evening after the recording date, he and Jerry Toobin and I went to Reuben's for sandwiches or a late snack.

"Those were wonderful times because Jerry got Stokowski to talk about the past, and I wish I had had a tape recorder there, because he talked about his years in Philadelphia—he even began to talk about Gloria a little bit and about his alleged love affair with Greta Garbo. I admired Jerry's nerve in even asking those questions. Here the man was sitting with us, very relaxed, with a sardine sandwich or whatever it was and talking about the past in a way that I don't think many people ever heard from him.

"I felt I was in the presence of a great man and felt very honored to be sitting there—me, a mere horn player, sitting there with this famous man and hearing him talk about his fantastic past. But when this firing occurred, it really hurt me, because it was so unwarranted. I was only trying to help him in ways that he couldn't even comprehend. And after those weeks of working closely with him and getting to know him enough so that we could be at ease with each other—which was never easy with Stokowski—this was such a sudden reversal. I felt I had acted absolutely correctly. But I knew that this kind of thing had happened to dozens of other people before me. I was in pretty good company."

Although Gunther faulted Stoki for not spotting occasional errors that had crept into certain orchestral parts, he did continue to maintain his regard for his conductorial genius: "My admiration for Stokowski really dates back, as it does for so many Americans, to his recordings which I started collecting when I was 12 or 13—those first impressions of mine of Stokowski were really almost mesmerizing ones. The man was part genius and part charlatan. But still, if pressed on the point, I would always put the genius part first—the fact that he created a whole new kind of orchestral sound—which he did with the Philadelphia Orchestra—cannot be taken away. And incidentally about that sound: I saw him do that on any number of occasions with other orchestras or even pick-up orchestras. The mystery, of course, is how Stokowski did this. I doubt that anyone really knows the answer. He didn't do anything in any way extraordinary and yet within three minutes of his starting a rehearsal, the sound of an orchestra, any orchestra, was transformed. I don't know anyone who knows how he did it. I certainly don't, and I have watched him closely, playing with him often."[16]

Ben-Haim wrote to me recently and recalled that he had met Stoki personally only once in April 1959 when he was in New York to hear a performance of his symphony conducted by Lenny Bernstein with the N.Y. Philharmonic:

> In one of the rehearsals a man approached me saying that Stokowski wishes to see me and speak with me about problems of the recording of my Suite, "From Israel." The next day I went to Carnegie Hall, where at 3 P.M. he conducted a Youth Concert. During the interval I went to the Artist's Room, where Maestro waited for me and received me very friendly. I was so impressed by his powerful personality during the concert and during the meeting; I must say it was one of the unforgettable events of my life![17]

Stoki made only five records for United Artists. These were released at the same time as recordings he had made for Capitol and Everest. Reviews for all of the things he did at that time were almost uniformly good.

Alfred Frankenstein observed that Stokowski was retraversing works that he had done with such sensational success with the Philadelphia Orchestra. "His mastery of these works has not changed in the slightest, but the art of recording has changed enormously for the better. . . ."[18]

In the short space of three years Stokowski made some of his finest recordings on Capitol, Everest, and United Artists. Then each of the projects folded. Capitol survived the longest and Stoki recorded fourteen discs. But the relationship was not always harmonious in spite of his warm relationship with Richard Jones, F. M. Scott III, and Glenn Wallichs. It must be remembered that at this time stereo was just beginning to take hold. Recording companies were releasing both mono and stereo discs as well as mono and stereo tapes. Frequently, two reviews of the same work by two different critics would appear simultaneously, one reviewing the mono version and another the stereo. The industry was experiencing problems. "I see from the last statement I received from Capitol Records," wrote Stoki, "that the expenses have exceeded the income to the amount of $81,000. This means that any income for me will be long delayed. That is another reason why it will be to my advantage to have the records I have conducted put in final good order and released with as little delay as possible." He complained that one recording which he had made in June 1957 was still not out a year and five months later. Even the *transfer* of the record had not been put in final order. "I am no worshipper of the golden calf," he added, "but I earn my living by music, and I have rather heavy responsibilities, in addition to my own personal expenses. I am by no means complaining, but I would like to put before you my situation, and how I feel about it. It seems to me that to be $81,000 in debt is a serious matter. Never in my life have I been even nearly so deeply in debt."[19]

The perspective of a man past his mid-seventies and that of his colleagues thirty or more years his junior was traumatically different. No matter how Stoki tried to ignore time, he must have inevitably felt its presence. He wanted to record as much as possible and quickly record the most interesting repertory available. No wonder he pressed Capitol. Scott took issue with Stoki's hurry-up attitude and said that at Capitol they were of a different opinion.

If at this point Stoki placed his hopes on Everest and United Artists, he was soon to be jolted by the happenings at Everest. I once remarked to Bert Whyte that I thought Everest's recordings were marvelous. "Those were my babies," he told me, "I put a lot of work into them and it was just heartbreaking that the Board of Directors pulled the plug on it just as we were starting to roll. They claimed that Harry had spent too much money. Harry had foolishly diluted his interest in the company. I guess he figured since he had founded it he didn't need more than 22 percent. But he found that 22 is not 51 and they just pulled the rug from under us. . . ."[20]

Everest recording with Stoki came to a quick end as did United Artists, which ceased its serious recording not long after the five discs he made for that company. Although Capitol had reduced its schedule to almost nothing, they continued to release stereo versions of their earlier mono releases. Some stereo recordings had to wait a decade or more before they were finally released in England.

⟨69⟩

Exit Houston

E VEN before he began his 1959–60 season in Houston, Stoki had expressed disenchantment with the whole Texas affair. Other options were so much more appealing: invitations from Philadelphia, from the New York Philharmonic, City Center, and major orchestras in Europe were all crowding in. Although he felt that Houston was both provincial and far away, he tackled his chore with complete dedication. His programs were heavily laden with Brahms, and his new works were ample and discreet. He had looked at a score of Henry Cowell that I had brought him, the Variations for Orchestra, and he planned to give it its world premiere; Henry decided to go to Houston for the performance.

Another work which Stoki had scheduled was the Symphony for Strings and Percussion by Harold Farberman. He had recorded Farberman's *Evolution* fragment for Capitol and it was a sensational sonic bash. He was delighted with it and eager to perform another work of his. Harold flew down to Houston, arriving just as Stoki was finishing rehearsing the Cowell Variations. When Stoki asked Cowell if he had any suggestions to offer, Henry said that it was just the way he wanted it and that it was absolutely marvelous.

Stoki then began to rehearse the Farberman work. "I had a pencil and a piece of paper, and as he was going along, I was jotting down frantically —this tempo is not correct, this is not right, this is very good and this is not so good," Harold recalled. At the end he expressed his thoughts to Stokowski, who did everything that he had suggested. "Everything he did was terrific, and so I thanked him and thanked the orchestra."

Just before the concert, Tom Johnson suggested that Harold go back-stage and thank Stokowski and wish him well for the concert. This he did, and when Stoki asked him if there were any last-minute suggestions he would want to make about the work, Harold suggested that he take the scherzo a little slower and Stoki made a mental note. When he came to that movement, he began conducting in three instead of one to the measure, which made the movement three times slower than they had rehearsed it. "Then came the third movement, which is a slam-banger. And Stoki ripped into it. There was one extra page of manuscript bound into the score. As fate would have it, when he came to it he turned two pages at once. . . . Because there were many meter changes, first the violins stopped playing, then the second violins stopped, then the cellos. . . . And Stoki was madly trying to figure out what's going on because he obviously thought he was right and nobody seemed to understand him. Finally everyone stopped playing and then Dave Wuliger, who is the timpanist, had a big solo, and that gathered everyone up and Stoki found his palce and everyone finished in what was a blaze of glory."[1]

There was much applause and Stoki motioned to Farberman, who took a bow from his seat in the hall. Stoki left and quickly returned as the applause continued. He motioned to the composer to take another bow, and he then turned and gave a downbeat to begin the Cowell Variations. He had forgotten that the rest of the orchestra was still backstage, and after a few moments while players were frantically trying to come onstage, Stoki ground the straggling orchestra to a halt with much applause and merriment supplied by the audience. "Two or three minutes later, all music on the racks, all musicians in place, smilingly, he began again—and finished strong," wrote critic Ann Holmes.[2]

After the concert Stoki explained: "Mr. Farberman, not every perform-ance can be wonderful, but tomorrow it will be wonderful." They then were driven to a party being given by some members of the orchestra. In the car, after an embarrassingly long silence, Stoki asked, "Have you seen any good movies lately?" Harold had just been in Boston with Leon Kirchner and saw *Some Like It Hot* with Marilyn Monroe, and he said instinctively, "Yes, I saw a wonderful movie with Marilyn Monroe." Stoki's response: "Ah, what I would give to have that woman."[3]

Guest conductors filled in while Stoki was back in New York for his midwinter respite, and among them was Sir John Barbirolli, who was on leave from his Hallé Orchestra in Manchester, England.

Since the rapport between Stokowski and Houston had cooled noticeably, it was inevitable that the Texans would welcome a change in leadership. New York, not Houston, spelled home to Stoki, and his attitude about being in Houston became strictly that of a visitor. When Barbirolli arrived for his guest appearance, he was hailed as a possible conductorial messiah.

Tom Johnson became very interested in Barbirolli as a candidate, and three weeks later he met him in Atlanta to explore the possibility of having him in Houston. Barbirolli was interested but noncommital. Although the matter was really exploratory, the story was leaked to the press and so came to Stoki's attention.[4]

This compounded his disillusionment with Texas. His mind was more preoccupied with the forthcoming events in New York and Philadelphia, as well as with the increasing interest in his work in Europe. When he returned to Houston in mid-March, he conducted a mostly modern concert with Thomas Canning's *Fantasy on a Hymn Tune by Justin Morgan* and Henry Cowell's Symphony No. 12 in its world premiere.[5] Unfortunately, the Cowell symphony was not one of the composer's best efforts, and it was received apathetically. The work which received the most attention was the *Fantasy on a Hymn Tune by Justin Morgan*. Whether the Texans realized that Morgan the composer was also Morgan the horse breeder, who produced the Morgan horse, is moot. Since the Morgan Horse Society is nationwide and Morgan horses are not uncommon in Texas, it is probable that the horsey set found a double interest.

The Canning piece is a stunning work for double string quartet and string orchestra much in the mold of Vaughan Williams' *Variants on Dives and Lazarus* and the *Fantasia on a Theme by Thomas Tallis*. Stoki recorded the Canning *Fantasy* splendidly along with three Chopin transcriptions: the Mazurka in A Minor, the Prelude in D Minor and the Waltz in C Sharp Minor.[6] The Chopin performances are questionable. In the middle of the Mazurka there is a dynamic sweep rising to a shrieking crescendo double forte that is a virtual travesty. It is the sort of thing that anti-Stokowski critics might latch on to. It also might be cited as an example of his tampering with dynamics in the control room, but its release was apparently without Stoki's sanction. In a memo to Everest Records, he wrote: "Chopin—most of this is so bad that I feel we should record it again. In any case we should not offer it to the public in its present form."[7] He was absolutely right!

The Canning work appeared on an illegal, pirated pressing released by the Great International Corporation, Bloomfield, New Jersey. The title is changed to read "Fantasy for Double String Quartet and String Orchestra." The conductor is listed as Sir Malcolm Sutherland and the orchestra is labeled the London Stadium Orchestra. The recordings are identical.

The last concert of the season was devoted to the Brahms *German Requiem,* and before beginning its haunting strains, he turned to the audience and in a most dramatic gesture announced that his next season in Houston was to be his last. At the time he had no idea that he would not even complete it.

Some time before his break with Houston he told me about his growing disenchantment with conditions in Texas. He discussed his desire to do a performance of *Gurrelieder,* and it was perhaps out of sheer deviltry that he wanted to use a black chorus as part of his vocal forces. It had created a mild hubbub.

Quite by accident I ran across a letter he had written to the composer Mary Howe way back in 1934. I have no idea of the contents of her letter, but in Stokowski's brief answer he wrote:

27 November 1934

Dear Mrs. Howe,

Yes, that is exactly what I have always wanted to do—conduct a chorus of unsophisticated negroes. Their response would be thrilling. . . .[8]

Since he was being frustrated in his plans to present the *Gurrelieder,* a certain resentment lingered in his mind and he gave the story to the press that Houston was reluctant to let him use a black chorus. Tom Johnson recalled the incident.

Regrettably, Stokowski seemed to have a penchant for departing on a Charger. He made an inflated issue out of an artistic divergence. . . . For whatever personal reason he might have had, he insisted that we utilize a chorus from a Negro university for the Gurrelieder. Our Chorale director insisted that the chorus which Stoki wanted was not capable of performing the work. Stoki became adamant; the director Alfred Urbach was also my No. 1 man (Operations Manager) and very conscientious. He had, in the past, delighted such conductors as Sir Thomas Beecham and Sir Malcolm Sargent and others with his first rate choral preparation, none more so than Stokowski (for Orff's *Carmina Burana, Aphrodite,* etc.). He felt that Stoki wanted to use that particular chorus for other than musical reasons.

I stuck by my man, Stoki seemed to forget it, went ahead with the programming and all went well, until, I believe he conceived of this closed issue as the Charger upon which he could exit the Houston scene. He told the General and me toward the end of his Fall spell that he had to be "near the boys" and felt that he should not return in the Spring. This left me with the challenge of filling in for him in the Spring but it was not the first time that I had faced this sort of thing.

Stokowski departed; we saw him off correctly and all was personally pleasant, if a bit strained, for he had by then made an "issue" and you can well imagine the treatment of certain elements of the Press toward the Society.[9]

Not only did Stoki want to use a black chorus, but he wanted to use black soloists as well. He had heard of a young black singer, Shirley Verrett, and he asked her to audition for him, but there were objections. When I mentioned this to David Colvig, who had been flutist for the orchestra for over thirty years, he replied: "Oh, I'm sure that's right; even Marian Anderson wasn't allowed to sing there. . . . Houston was extremely lily-white at the time. The blacks who bought tickets to the symphony had to sit in the upper right-hand corner of the balcony and we never had black soloists—never used black people in the choir. But that's all gone, of course . . . the old South has gone away, thank God."[10]

Shirley recalled going to Stoki's New York apartment for her audition. "I remember his big book that he used to write in. I would be very, very interested to find out what he did write in that book about me." I suggested that perhaps some day we might be able to look through it. But neither of us could have known at the time that the book and all of his carefully written estimates and criticisms would finally end up at the bottom of the Atlantic.

For her audition, Shirley chose Brahms: "I sang some or maybe all of the *Vier Ernste Gesänge,* and he was very much taken with my voice, and he told me that we were going to do some things together, but I didn't know what. I was very flattered, and right after that came the offer to sing Waldtaube in the Schoenberg *Gurrelieder* that he was to perform in Houston. . . . I was not able to do it because at that time, in 1960—as late as that—Houston was not open to blacks. And the message came back to me."

Shirley took the news stoically. "Well, it didn't matter." And truly it didn't, for he called her back to audition Falla's *El amor brujo.* "I looked at it and I said yes. I learned it and sang it for him. He said, 'It's exactly what I want.' And that's how it happened."[11]

What had happened was that Shirley would be the soloist when Stokowski returned to Philadelphia for his first concert in nineteen years. The loss of Houston was immaterial.

I talked to Wayne Crouse, violist in the Houston Symphony, about some of these events and he interrupted me to ask if anyone had mentioned Lee Pryor to me. I assured him that no one had and in fact, I did not know his name at all. "William Lee Pryor," Wayne told me, "is a professor of English at the University of Houston here, and he had at one time been a singer and musician and had worked with Dohnányi in Florida, and when Stoki came, Lee Pryor had a television program on the educational channel on which he interviewed people, and, of course, he had Stoki on several times and they became good friends. I would say that he really was the closest person to Stoki here in Houston as far as seeing him on a regular basis and having him to his home for dinner. He might be able to tell you some things that would be of interest."[12]

I followed Wayne's suggestion and phoned Pryor. He had a warm, deep, resonant voice, and he was most happy to reminisce about Stokowski. I queried him particularly about the last part of his stay in Houston and broached the subject of the *Gurrelieder.* He confirmed what Tom Johnson had told me: he had resigned a year before the question about the *Gurrelieder* matter had come up. Pryor recalled that he had mentioned his sons, and "for personal reasons he had decided that he would live in New York City."

When Stoki returned for the next fall season, he told Pryor that he was told by the management that he could not have blacks appearing in his concerts. "Just before conducting his final pair of concerts before the Christmas holidays, he invited me to dinner on a Saturday evening, and we went to a little restaurant called 'La Louisianne,' and during dinner he said, 'I want you to read something,' and he took out of his pocket a letter which turned out to be his letter of immediate resignation in which he said he could no longer serve a city which had this kind of racial bias. After dinner, he said, 'Would you mind taking me to General Hirsch's house?' So I drove him there; he went up to the door, rang the bell—there was no response—and I saw him put the letter in the mail slot. The following Monday and Tuesday he conducted the concerts, which ended, by the way, with a brilliant performance of

the Shostakovich Fifth Symphony for which he got a standing
ovation. . . ."[13]

During the summer of 1978, I was talking to Isaac Stern, who was the
soloist on that program, and I asked him if he recalled it.

"I remember our playing in Houston because I remember going down
in the elevator with him and discussing the opening of the Brahms. He
looked at me very quietly and said, 'Isaac, what are you talking about?
We're playing the Beethoven.' So I gulped and said, 'Okay.' And we went
down to the rehearsal and played Beethoven. I had just confused one
concerto with another. Both are in D Major. Somehow we managed to
do it and by the time I was through rehearsing and several hours of furious
practicing up until the performance, we had an enjoyable concert. From
that night on we also became very good friends."[14]

The program began with the Toccata and Fugue in D Minor. The
audience applauded with true Texan gusto. Isaac played the concerto
superbly and the audience went wild. The Shostakovich Fifth Symphony,
which is always arousing, was performed with a fire and a youthful spirit
that amazed the audience and the critics alike. They cheered and bravoed;
they were particularly eager to give their maestro a rousing cheer—perhaps in the nature of a pre-Christmas present. And they did. No one in
the hall, nor in the office of the Symphony, knew that this would be the
last concert Stokowski would conduct in Houston. And in fact at that
moment, neither did he. "Stokowski's marriage to the Houston orchestra
had been one of convenience," wrote Roussel. "That being the case, both
parties got from the union everything it was possible to get."[15] They were
never to be joined again.

Stoki had scheduled four more concerts for later in the season and
I believe that he initially planned to conduct them. But the isolation
of Houston was becoming more than he could bear. He had met
with General Hirsch and expressed his desire for a cancellation of his
contract. At a special meeting called by the general on November 21,
1960, that matter was decided. In the minutes of that meeting we
read:

> Further consideration was given to the request by Maestro Leo-
> pold Stokowski to be released from his contractual obligation to
> direct the final four concerts of the Houston Symphony Society
> Orchestra for its 1960–61 season. After further extended discussion,
> the President individually polled each of the members present for a

personal expression of attitude toward the request and each person in turn actually expressed approval of granting of Maestro Stokowski's request. . . .

On motion then made, seconded and unanimously carried, it was resolved that Maestro Leopold Stokowski be offered the opportunity of presenting, as guest conductor, the composition "Gurrelieder" at one of the concerts during the 1961–62 season . . . provided that satisfactory arrangements could be made for adequate choruses necessary for such performance. . . .[16]

Quite apart from Houston, there were increasing overtures to conduct in New York and other cities less distant. On November 29, the Met announced that he would conduct *Turandot* in February. Due to the illness of Reiner, he would conduct the Chicago Symphony in a pair of concerts toward the end of December. Compared with these events, the prospects of concerts in Houston seemed less appealing. Also, since the orchestra had announced the engagement of Barbirolli for the coming season, Stokowski could only view his career in Houston with sadness. But he had won his fight in breaking the color barrier; General Hirsch and the board capitulated, agreeing to allow him to use the black chorus from Texas Southern University along with the other two.

Having made his point with the board, he definitely planned to accept the invitation tendered by General Hirsch and present a performance of the *Gurrelieder* in Houston, and on December 21, 1960, eight days before his unfortunate hip fracture, he wrote to Barbirolli:

Dear Maestro

General Hirsch, President of the Houston Symphony, has arranged for me to conduct Schoenberg's Gurrelieder next season for one pair of concerts in Houston, Texas, and as you will be chief conductor for next season, I am writing to ask in which week it would be convenient for you that I make these performances? I can understand how difficult it is for you, with all your commitments in Europe, to plan such an extensive tour in the United States, but if you could let me know at what period your European commitments will permit you to come to the United States, it will help me to plan my engagements for next season. I am very happy that you will conduct so many concerts with the Houston Symphony next season, and I hope you will enjoy working with the orchestra, and that your visit to Houston will in every way be agreeable to you.

Houston is very fortunate to have such a highly gifted and experienced conductor as yourself and I am sure the orchestra will enjoy
making music with you.

> Sincerely your admirer and
> colleague[17]

Stoki was obviously happy that he had won the sympathetic approval
of General Hirsch and members of the board. He had not, however, won
the same from the two white choruses. Hirsch, at a January 11, 1961,
meeting of the Executive Committee, discussed the problems. He said
that both the Houston Chorale's Board of Directors and the University
of Houston's dean of the College of Arts and Sciences declined with regret
for their groups to participate. "Due to these facts" it was moved and
seconded that "Mr. Stokowski be advised that the Houston Symphony
Society was obliged to withdraw the invitation to conduct the 'Gurrelieder' so far as the 1961–62 season is concerned."[18]

Apparently, on notifying Stokowski, the reasons for the withdrawal of
the invitation were not spelled out. We can realize the extent of his anger
on reading his February 4, 1961, letter to Lee Pryor.

> I have just sent a letter (copy of which I enclose) to the Houston
> Post, Press, and Chronicle, expressing my disappointment in not
> performing the *Gurrelieder* for the music lovers of Houston, and
> saying why I think it has been cancelled and the orchestra's invitation
> to me for the next season withdrawn. . . .[19]

He addressed his letter "To the Music Lovers of Houston":

> I have requested the privilege of telling you how disappointed I am
> that I shall not be able to conduct the beautiful, romantic and
> dramatic music of Schoenberg's *Gurrelieder* for you as I had pro-
> mised, and as it was promised to me for next season.
>
> In my opinion, this masterpiece should be offered to the public as
> a musical experience of cultural importance. I do not fully understand
> the reasons that were given me why it cannot be done.
>
> In addition to women's voices, *Gurrelieder* needs three separate
> choruses of men's voices. Fortunately, we have three fine choruses in
> Houston. Mr. Urbach's Chorale is one. The University of Houston
> has another, which cooperated so splendidly with the orchestra in
> Brahms' *Requiem*, and the Texas Southern University has a third. In
> my opinion, the true reason why the planned performances have been

cancelled is that some, possibly only a few persons are opposed to having a colored chorus be part of the performance. In fact, I was told that "if we did (use this chorus), we would lose such financial support that the very future of the orchestra would be at stake" and "the entire future of the orchestra would be put in jeopardy."

I would like to thank all the subscribers to the orchestra and all my personal friends in Houston for so many kindnesses to me. Also, I would like to thank all members of the Contemporary Music Society for their interest in Twentieth Century music, and their openmind-edness and progressive approach.

Particularly, I would like to thank the orchestra for their wonderful devotedness to music, and the great efforts they always made toward a high standard of performance. . . .

I shall always be deeply interested in the future of the orchestra, and in the cultural growth of the greatly expanding city of Houston. I know this cultural growth is the intense interest of so many citizens. But, as a principle, that a masterpiece in any form of art should be denied the public because of racial prejudice of any kind is, in my opinion, profoundly wrong.

Believe me, with deep regret but no hurt feelings, and only wishing a great cultural future for Houston.[20]

On April 20, 1961, he again wrote to Pryor: "As none of the three newspapers in Houston printed my letter in full, and only one of them printed a part of the letter out of context so as to give a false impression, I think I had better forget Houston. Particularly as I am greatly enjoying my musical work in and near New York."[21]

Lee Pryor has a definite theatrical flair and can imitate Stoki most convincingly. He catches the right inflections and the perceptible accent. On one trip to New York City he called him and Stoki, then over eighty, answered the phone himself:

"Ahh-lo," said Pryor, imitating Stoki.

"Ahh-lo," Stoki said in his characteristic manner.

"Do you know who this is, Maestro?"

"Yes, you're the man who used to conduct the orchestra in Hooston and you should have left much sooner!"[22]

70

Philadelphia Return

XCITEMENT began building in musical circles as soon as the first
mention of Stokowski's imminent return early in January 1959.
"The simple announcement that Leopold Stokowski will be one of
the guest conductors of the Philadelphia Orchestra next season," wrote
Delos Smith, "should tug at the sentimental strings of your heart. Time
heals, as they say, and there can be a happy ending to almost any tragedy
if enough time is mixed into it."[1]

When Max de Schauensee asked him whether he was pleased to come
back to Philadelphia, he replied with a touch of irony: "Yes, I am very
pleased. But it took a long time, didn't it?"[2]

A week before going to Philadelphia, Stokowski appeared on the intermission broadcast of the "Metropolitan Opera Quiz." The subject of his
return was brought up and he replied: "I worked so hard there. I have so
many friends amongst the artists of the orchestra, and other friends too.
And I have so many wonderful memories of my life in Philadelphia.
When I left there I went all over the world. I went to Asia and Africa
and Europe and behind the iron curtain. . . . And I never thought I was
going back to Philadelphia but suddenly Maestro Ormandy and the Board
of Directors invited me to come back, so next week the biggest thrill of
my life, musically speaking, will happen."[3]

Stokowski had chosen his program carefully, and it was designed to
explore and highlight all of the most virtuosic capabilities of the orchestra.
He began with Mozart's overture to *The Marriage of Figaro* and followed
with Falla's *El amor brujo*, Respighi's *The Pines of Rome*, and Shos-

takovich's Fifth Symphony. In typical Stokowski fashion, he chose as his soloist Shirley Verrett-Carter (she summarily dropped the Carter), whom he had wanted to engage to sing the *Gurrelieder* in Houston. The choice proved to be an ideal one.

As Stoki stepped onto the stage of the Academy, the audience and the players lept to their feet and burst into such rapturous applause that the walls shook. Many in the audience had attended his youth or children's concerts; some were merely old-timers. But to many of the younger listeners he was a living legend.

The program was to be broadcast, and listeners who were not lucky enough to be in the hall heard William Smith, the assistant music director of the orchestra, acting as commentator. Over a background of strings and other instruments tuning, he described the scene below him. He reported that Stokowski had completely reseated the orchestra. The heavy strings, the cellos, and the basses were ranked in the back of the stage; the violins and violas were massed from the center to his left. An organ, piano, celeste, and all the winds, the battery, and the brass were massed to his right. He had even brought up from the cellar the old aluminum and blue podium that had been designed for him. Smith told me that he is now the proud possessor of the famous relic.[4]

When the concert was over, the standing audience applauded him wildly—finally breaking into the rhythmic clapping that the Russians often do to express their pleasure. It built to a tremendous crescendo, and after several recalls to the stage, Stokowski, with the kind of gesture he used to indicate a diminuendo to his players, finally hushed the audience and said: "I speak to you a moment. As I was saying about nineteen years ago—" At this point the audience exploded with laughter and more applause. "It's a thrilling pleasure to make music with this magnificent orchestra and for such a sensitive public—listeners—as you are. I want to thank Mr. Ormandy and the Board of Directors for inviting me to come back home in the Academy with the beautiful new ceiling [much laughter]—it was always there, but it was so nice and dirty before [more laughter]—and to tell you it's an unbelievable thrill to make music with masters of their instruments so that every technical thing that the music demands they can give with ease. But much more than that, they can express the spirit and the soul and the deep message that is in great music. What a thrill!"

So great had been the demand for tickets that people were offering $50 and more to subscribers for their seats. But there were none to be had.

Immediately after the concert, a reception for Stoki, given by the Board of Directors, was held at the Cosmopolitan Club. Without taking the time to change from his concert clothes "the glamorous conductor" was whisked away to a waiting Jaguar. With a police escort and sirens screeching, they then completed the three-minute ride. Here he was greeted by Orville H. Bullitt, chairman of the orchestra's Board of Directors; Stuart Louchheim, president of the Academy, and their wives. There, too, in a wheelchair, was ninety-six-year-old Mrs. Arnett, who was a member of the board that had engaged Stokowski in 1912.

When the reception was over, Stoki and Shirley Verrett were driven to Bryn Mawr to the home of one of his dearest and staunchest admirers during his long Philadelphia tenure, Miss Gertrude Ely. And there, so it was reported, they enjoyed a quiet dinner.[5]

The Philadelphia critics were jubilant. The perceptive Max de Schauensee with a neat turn of phrase said: "Mr. Stokowski has acquired the advantages and benisons of age rather than its infirmities. Still alert and springy of step, he radiates a new-found dignity, an intellectual grasp of the music which is informed with authority and serenity."[6]

The orchestra which he faced was hardly a strange one to him, for no less than thirty-six were his old Philadelphia players and among the new additions some had come from the Curtis Institute and others from his Youth Orchestra. It was a joyful reunion and players and conductor gave their all. The result was spellbinding.

When Stokowski and the orchestra arrived in New York, the atmosphere seemed to have been almost as highly charged as it had been in Philadelphia. Even his famous podium had been brought along. The audience was ecstatic and so were the critics.

Miles Kastendieck in the *New York Journal-American* led off with a bold headline, "There Is Only One Stokowski": "His innate sense of drama has guided him infallibly for over half a century. Mr. Stokowski can mesmerize listeners as well as musicians: he succeeded in doing both last night. . . ."[7]

In the *New York World Telegram* critic Louis Biancolli wrote: "It was a proud night for Leopold Stokowski. . . . The prolonged ovation that greeted the brisk, graceful figure was hearty testimonial to an old friend and a tribute to Mr. Stokowski's four decades and more of stalwart service to the allied cause of American and world music.

"One had only to hear him conduct Mozart's 'Marriage of Figaro' overture to recognize the knowing hand of mastery as it wove magic of the divine chatter that keeps this music—and those who play it—unalterably young.[8]

In the *Saturday Review* Irving Kolodin reported: "Rapture abounded in Carnegie Hall as Leopold Stokowski and the Philadelphia Orchestra performed there together. . . . And why not? Each brings out something in the other that nothing else can, and together they achieve results that performing groups elsewhere can only envy. "In a subtle way, this remains his orchestra. . . . In addition to 'handling' beautifully, it veered and turned, slowed and accelerated at the slightest touch from the bridge (a remarkable aluminum-covered affair).[9]

One wonders whether either Ormandy or the board could have foreseen the sensational response of the public and the orchestra itself to the reunion. But the management reacted quickly. Roger Hall had come to the Philadelphia Orchestra as its manager in 1959. I asked him the inevitable question of whether it was he who had been behind the invitation. He told me that he was not: "By the time I got there Stokowski had been engaged to make his great return. I was fortunate enough to be the manager when that event occurred and I'll never forget that. It was magical."[10]

A week after the New York concert he returned again to Philadelphia to do one for the Pension Fund. He chose three Chorale Preludes of Bach, the Brahms First Symphony and the "Love Music" from acts 2 and 3 of Wagner's *Tristan und Isolde*. During the intermission he was presented with a Pension Fund scroll by William Kincaid, the wonderfully ruddy-faced flutist whose splendid playing had enhanced the perfection of the orchestra. Kincaid was a little arch about it all and referred to Stoki as "Mr. Music" and "Mr. Philadelphia Orchestra." Stoki offered a pleasant rejoinder and called Mr. Kincaid "Mr. Pan." He thanked everyone who had made it possible for him to make music again with "this unique orchestra," and reminded the audience that the orchestra was its "sacred trust." He then launched into two encores, *The Afternoon of a Faun* and a Prelude from *Lohengrin* which "shone with white glory." He was enjoying himself immensely, as was his ovation-minded audience. "Good-bye until next year," he said, "when we will meet with the 'Gurrelieder.' "

Max de Schauensee had observed that "the orchestra played as though Stokowski had never left it. His imprint was as distinctive, as clear as day."[11] And it seemed manifest that his impact on the audience and his mesmeric way with the music was as vital as it had been two, three, and four decades before.

They were not to wait until the next season to welcome him again. By April the news was out that he would conduct a concert in Robin Hood Dell on July 21. It was his first appearance in the Dell in twenty-seven years. "Music-lovers will hang from the trees that night," said one of the ladies on the women's committee.[12] Mr. Fredric Mann, city representative and president of the Dell, held a press conference the day before the concert in Stoki's suite in the Barclay. He stated that the ticket demand for the concert had been the biggest in the Dell's history. "You'll have close to 30,000," he said. And he remarked that they usually distributed 20,000 tickets, but for this special event an additional 5,000 had been printed.[13]

When trains, planes, locusts, katydids, and a single complaining bullfrog added their sounds or noises to the orchestral timbres, Stoki did not stalk off in a huff as he had done years earlier when an incessantly coughing, throat-troubled audience disturbed the Academy's sacred silence. Apparently without irritation and with good humor he yielded to the passing trains and competing planes and merely stopped the music until they went away. At the conclusion of the concert he mentioned the noise and implored the audience to do something about it. But very little could be done.[14]

Fredric Mann pleaded with him to give more time to the Dell—one week, two weeks perhaps. He pleaded with him to consider it, but Stoki cautiously said that although he wanted to he could not do so without contacting his manager, Siegfried Hearst, who was then ill, in order to know what dates he had booked for him. It was clever fending, because he was now eager for rest and change.[15]

During the early Stoki days RCA Victor was the company that had always recorded the Philadelphians. But now it was Columbia. Fortunately, it was headed at that time by two men of remarkable perception —Goddard Lieberson who was then president, and Schuyler Chapin, then director of the Masterworks Division. Goddard had at one time been a composer, not of world-shaking importance, but he was above all a man of taste. Stoki always called him "Go-dahr"! Together Goddard and Schuyler proposed that Columbia should record the performance of Stokowski and the Philadelphia Orchestra commemorating the historic reunion. Schuyler told me: "Stoki and the Philadelphia Orchestra in stereo was something that everybody was looking forward to. We had decided that we would take repertoire from the several concerts that he was going to do, specifically the *Tristan und Isolde* synthesis, *El amor brujo,* and some

Bach suites. . . . And, of course, it was very tricky with Ormandy . . . but eventually he graciously agreed and the trustees of the orchestra agreed and we were all set. There came, of course, the matter of the Maestro's fee, and he telephoned me one morning and we reacquainted ourselves on the phone and talked about our respective children. . . .

"And I then said to him that we were delighted to capture this important event on records and what we offered him—I've forgotten exactly how much—was clearly not enough. The advance payment was perfectly reasonable, but it was the royalty question that bothered him. He said he never did anything for less than 5 percent royalty. Well, I wasn't in a position to be able to pay him 5 percent royalty, because our arrangements with the Philadelphia Orchestra at that time were to pay them and they in turn had a separate contract with Eugene Ormandy, and I believe Ormandy received 2.5 percent of the royalties of his catalog. And that was really all I could offer Stoki. Our conversations went on for several days, and he got extremely haughty on the subject and I had to get rather haughty back again, saying that I really wasn't in a position of altering the normal Philadelphia arrangements.

"So at one point I said to him on the phone that I was terribly sorry, but if we couldn't come to an understanding on this subject, I was afraid that the whole project would have to be canceled. Two or three days before he actually went down to Philadelphia he called and said that he would accept the offer that we had made although he did not approve of it and felt that he was being badly treated. We ended up in a very friendly but distant agreement on this subject.

"I went to Philadelphia and it was a rather special occasion when he walked out on that stage again. There was an ovation. It was very moving and I thought he carried it all off with enormous drama. The whole thing was terrific.

"Now, I should have known better than to be complacent about settling what he considered onerous and less than honorable, terms for his services. . . .

"In 1960, '61, the musician's union contracts for recording recognized symphonic organizations was different than those for free-lance sessions. You had to pay every member of the symphony orchestra a full fee for the first two hours of a session, after which you cut down the number of players to fit the repertoire that you were actually doing. Naturally, one always began such recording sessions with the larger works, and in this case it happened to be the *Tristan*.

"About 10:05 the morning of Stoki's recording session, the phone rang and Howard Scott, who was in Philadelphia producing the record, called me up and said, 'We have a problem.' I said, 'What is it?' He said, 'Stoki wants to begin with the Bach.' And I said, 'Well, that's out of the question. You can't do that. You're going to have everyone sitting around for two hours being paid for nothing and then go into expensive overtime when we reach the heavy repertoire.' Scott said, 'He wants to do the Bach and if he doesn't do the Bach, he is not going to record.' So I sat on the edge of my seat thinking—he knows exactly what the rules are and he is getting back at me because of the royalty arrangement. And I told Scott to go and tell him that we had to begin with the *Tristan* and ten minutes later the phone rang again and Stoki said, 'No, no. Either we begin with the Bach or we don't do anything.' I did a rough calculation as to what it would cost us to pay everybody for the two hours and not record anything, and then a rough calculation as to what it would cost if we did the Bach and programmed the session the way he wanted. I realized that either way the company was going to be out a pretty penny. So I told Scott to go ahead and play it Stoki's way, which he did, and he began with the Bach. The two LPs were the most expensive records of the Philadelphia Orchestra's entire recording year, so I figured that Stoki had now had his revenge.

"Some two or three weeks later he arrived in my office to edit his tapes. I took him upstairs, introduced him to the chief engineer, and went into the console cubicle to see him get started. The engineer doing his tape-editing sessions was a man named Graham, who knew Stoki from the past, from the days when Columbia recorded the All-American Youth Orchestra, so they greeted each other affectionately and Stoki said, 'I will sit at the console. You know I'm a member of the union.' He started and the opening measures of the Prelude to *Tristan* began, and within five minutes the door of the cubicle opened and the chief engineer of Columbia Records came in for a moment, followed by another engineer. They did a quick double take and saw that Stokowski was at the controls and quickly went out the door and closed it. I didn't think very much about it. I stayed another five or ten minutes and then went back to my office. I had not been there more than ten minutes before the phone rang, and it was the chief engineer, who said to me, 'Get up here, but fast.' And I went upstairs, and there were all the engineers standing outside of their respective cubicles with the chief engineer. I said, 'What's the matter?' He answered, 'You go in and tell Stokowski to get away from those controls.

Until he does, no engineer will go anywhere near the consoles in the other cubicles. He is breaking every union rule. . . .' But I said, 'He says he's an honorary member of the union.' The chief engineer replied, 'I don't give a damn if he's an honorary member of five hundred unions. Get him out of there!' Now, that morning, in other cubicles, George Szell was editing some tapes, Bruno Walter was editing some tapes; everybody was there except Bernstein. So I went inside. *Tristan* was wafting over the speakers and Stoki was pushing up the swell buttons and having a grand time. I went up to him and I said, 'Maestro, I'm sorry. You must get out from behind that desk because every Columbia engineer is outside in the hall protesting. A strike has been called. You are not allowed to be at that console and we cannot close down Columbia Records.' He looked at me and said, 'I'm a member of the union.' I said, 'I don't care whether you are a member of the union or not. You must get out of there.' So finally he rose—slowly and majestically—and Graham went and sat down quickly and he turned to Graham and said, 'Do you mind if I put my hand on yours so that we can move these things?' And Graham said, 'No.' I went outside and got the chief engineer, who came back and saw that Stoki was standing and Graham was at his console. A couple of other engineers came in and saw this and then everybody went back to work. By the time we got through with the only LPs that Stoki made for Columbia with the Philadelphia Orchestra, they had cost more than a full-scale opera. He knew perfectly well what he was doing. He knew he was throwing a spanner into the works with each moment because I wouldn't give him his 5 percent royalty. Well, the upshot of all that was that the record did come out and was quite lovely. It sold well, but to this day I don't think it ever made back its total costs."[16]

Critical reaction to the recording was splendid, with hardly a sour-note comment being made. Irving Kolodin observed that the recording "affirms, for those who were not able to share the experience 'live,' that they remain a matchless combination."[17]

Before his second seasonal return, he was asked to conduct another gala, festive Pension Foundation concert on November 28, his first in the 1960–61 season. He chose an all-orchestral concert, which he repeated on successive nights in Newark and Baltimore. His program included the Beethoven Fifth, his transcription of parts of Mussorgsky's *Boris,* music from Prokofiev's *Romeo and Juliet* and Rimsky-Korsakov's *Capriccio Espagnol.*[18]

Stokowski's drawing power in Philadelphia at this time was tremendous, and the business-minded members of the board were well aware of it. One has only to read the superlatives of the critics and their constant reporting of the vivid ovations he received, and no wonder. After two decades of paying complacent homage, it was exciting to have something to cheer about.

On March 7, 1961, eleven days after his sensational debut conducting *Turandot* at the Metropolitan Opera and a little more than nine weeks after he had broken his hip, Stokowski conducted the first series of performances of Schoenberg's *Gurrelieder*—a remarkable achievement for a man who was about to become seventy-nine on April 18.

It had been thirty years since he had introduced the work in Philadelphia. He performed it then with all the vast resources that the overblown score called for. The orchestra had been augmented to 123 players, there were three male choruses, a mixed chorus, five soloists, and a speaker, making a grand total of 532 participants. While it had been a great critical success, it had also been a financial disaster.[19]

Stokowski had, of course, taken for granted that in this new performance he would be able to have a similar aggregation, but he had not reckoned on the resistance he would encounter from the new management. Roger Hall, who was the new manager of the orchestra, had indeed a counterpoint of view. "He got annoyed with me because obviously," Roger recalled, "Gurrelieder is a very large undertaking and we were willing to go along to a certain extent, but not as far as he wished to go in what he felt the forces should be and the extent of rehearsal time. Of course, in those situations it's always a matter of compromise, because very often the music director, or the conductor in this case, is absolutely right. He should have those forces and he should have those rehearsals. That, of course, must be played against the problem of the budget and the monies at hand and the cost of subsidizing the orchestra. And somewhere in between is a compromise, and we made a compromise."

Instead of the huge forces the original score had required, Stokowski used a thinned out and reduced version that had been prepared by Edwin Stein at Schoenberg's request. One of the principal fears of Roger Hall was that they might become involved in the payment of overtime for rehearsals. But Stokowski was meticulous. When I asked Roger whether he had run into overtime, he remarked that he did not. Then he made a very perceptive observation: "You know that there is a word that we bandy about all the time—the word *pro*. He was a pro—a real pro. . . . One of the things that impresses one was the organization, the efficiency of Stokowski. There was no baloney. He knew exactly what he wanted; it was all thought out prior to rehearsals. He made little notes on small pieces of paper that would remind him to talk to some of the first-chair men before the rehearsals and before the concert. There was a maximum of efficiency and a minimum of conversation."[20]

On March 7, 1961, he brought the work to New York to a solidly packed Carnegie Hall. New Yorkers, too, seemed to have developed a new affection for him, for it was a mere eleven days since his spectacular debut at the Met. "When the orchestra, chorus and soloists had taken their places," wrote Louis Biancolli, "there was a moment's silence and then a roar of applause as the beloved maestro began his slow, cautious way to the podium on crutches . . . one more testimonial to Mr. Stokowski's indomitable and ageless spirit."[21]

All paid high tribute to Stokowski. Harriett Johnson summed it up succinctly: "Leopold Stokowski may be nearing 80 but he, rather than the score he conducted last night . . . provided the youthful spirit. . . . His quantitative conducting record this week is the miracle: two performances of 'Turandot' at the Metropolitan Opera and four of 'Gurrelieder' here or in Philadelphia within seven days."[22]

On January 20, 1962, the venerable Academy of Music reached the notable age of 105. It had opened with great fanfare in 1857, and now to celebrate the grande dame's birthday, Roger Hall, in managerial full-swing, proposed an intriguing affair. Roger happily told me about it: "Following Stokowski's great return . . . the board and everyone thought it would be a very good idea to engage Stokowski to conduct the Academy Anniversary Concert that year. And he agreed to do so. . . . and it was up to me to produce that concert. Since Mr. Stokowski was the conductor, obviously I worked very closely with him as to programming and soloists."

Their choices were soprano Birgit Nilsson and baritone George London, both at the height of their Met fame. The program was foolproof.

But there was a special intermission feature. Harpo Marx appeared to conduct the Toy Symphony of Haydn and perform on his favorite instrument, the harp. Roger told me how it had all come about. He had called Stokowski one day and said: " 'Maestro, I've just read that Harpo Marx has done some benefit concerts with symphony orchestras on the West Coast and they've come off very successfully. Would you mind if I got in touch with him to see whether he would be on this program?' And Stoki said, 'Well, I wouldn't mind, but just as long as whatever Harpo does and I do are not concurrent.' I remember his saying to me: 'You know, clowns and comedians are usually very serious people. They're usually intellectuals, and I admire what he has done, it's just that that's not for me. So if it can be separated from my portion of the concert, that's fine.'

"So I just assumed that Stokowski, who had been in and out of Hollywood during the course of his career, and Harpo Marx must have met. . . . Harpo was no sooner ensconced in his room with his wife and boy when he said to me, 'I've never met Stokowski. Where is he staying? Is he here?' And I said, 'Yes, he's in this hotel.' 'Well, I'd like to see him. Let's call him up.'

"I had some trepidation because I had already been through that conversation with Stoki and he felt that 'everything is fine but just don't involve me.' But there I was and Harpo was my guest, so I picked up the hotel phone and dialed Stokowski's room. 'Maestro?'

" 'Yes.'

" 'Harpo Marx and his family have just arrived and he is very interested to meet you; he admires you greatly and would like to come to see you and I wonder if this is an inappropriate time?'

" 'No, no. This is fine. Would you like to come now?'

" 'Yes, this would be a good time.' So we proceeded to Stokowski's room, which was on another floor . . . I presented Harpo to Maestro Stokowski, who was very gracious but rather cool. Harpo did the talking and he said: 'Well, it sure is nice to meet you Mr. Stokowski. You know I have a feeling you and I got a lot of friends in common out in Hollywood. Incidentally, you know what I would have loved to do if if I had known it was so easy to come and see you. I'd have prepared the way with an act. I would have just walked in the door—I got a great act where I have a clarinet and I fix it up beforehand so that when you open the door, I'm playin' the clarinet except music's not comin' out—water's comin' out— jet stream from the whole clarinet and I think you would have been amused by that.' I was very amused. I laughed and Mrs. Marx laughed and Bill Marx laughed and Stoki's face was just absolutely stone cold. There was no reaction one way or another—so then all of a sudden things calmed down and there was one of those rather awkward silences and Harpo stepped right in and said, 'Well, I just wanted to meet you. You know I don't pretend to be a musician,' and there was some banter about the harp and then we turned around and walked out."[23]

The next Stokowski appearance at the regular subscription concerts occurred in mid-March 1962 with a program that included Webern's Passacaglia. Thirty years had passed since he introduced Webern's short

Symphony for Small Orchestra, at which time the Main Line ladies hissed so vociferously that he stopped before he had finished the piece, stalked off the stage, and then after a sobering interval returned and repeated it.[24] This time the Passacaglia evoked no such outburst. When the concert was repeated in New York, the critics reacted warmly. Early in March 1962 the board had decided to again invite Stokowski for the coming season. Roger Hall, doing a bit of simple calculation, quickly realized that the beginning of the 1962 season would mark the fiftieth anniversary of Stoki's debut with the orchestra. In a letter of March 12, 1962, Ormandy expressed his hope that Stokowski would be able to conduct the orchestra again with concerts in Philadelphia, Washington, and Baltimore. "Mr. Hall made an excellent suggestion that perhaps you would conduct the same program that you performed at your opening concerts fifty years ago. I think this would be most appropriate for the occasion, but if you would prefer to make a different program will you please send me some other suggestions?" In a postscript Ormandy said that he hoped he would accept an invitation to conduct the Anniversary Concert again next season on January 26.[25]

In his response to Ormandy, Stokowski wrote thanking him for his invitation to conduct the orchestra in the cities he had mentioned and also for the Anniversary Concert, but made no mention of the programs.[26] The anniversary, which was the Academy's 106th, called for a program which would equal or surpass that of the previous season, and Stoki and Roger Hall planned a brilliant one with the fabulous Joan Sutherland and Franco Corelli as the principal soloists, and young Susan Starr, who played Rachmaninoff's *Rhapsody on a Theme of Paganini.* [27]

There were a few, but very few, members of the audience who had been present when Stoki made his Philadelphia debut, but on February 8, 1962, he repeated the same program he had performed during his initial season in 1912. A facsimile of the original program with its exhortation to women-patrons that they remove their hats was reproduced and included with the usual program notes. Four of the players who were in the orchestra when he made his debut were now present a half-century later: Anton Horner, French horn; William Gruner, bassoon; and two violinists, Emil Kresse and Walter Pfeifer.[28]

The event was one that evoked a deeply felt sense of nostalgia and sentiment. Critic Edwin Schloss observed that time had taken its toll: "Though Stokowski is amazingly vigorous and alert for an artist of his years, the golden aureole has been supplanted by a long, lank, silver thatch, but the maestro's grace in action is unimpaired. Any physical resemblance today between Stokowski and Apollo is purely honorary. But clouds of glory still cling to him."[29]

At the conclusion of the concert Stoki introduced Anton Horner and William Gruner, he spoke of his predecessors Fritz Scheel and Karl Pohlig, and paid tribute to those who meant so much to him in his early days: Alexander Van Rensselaer, Edward Bok, Miss Frances Wister, and others. "And here we are now," he said. "We cannot change the past but we can shape the future."[30]

Ripples of the event spread far beyond the Academy walls, and from Washington there came a telegram from President and Mrs. Kennedy. It read:

> On the occasion of this 50th anniversary concert in commemoration of your debut with the Orchestra at the Academy of Music, it is with great pleasure that we extend to you our warmest congratulations and best wishes.
>
> Music has been said to be the speech of the angels, and through your great talent you have transported audiences throughout the world to many delightful hours of heavenly sound.
>
> We hope you will continue to share your wonderful gift with music lovers everywhere for many years to come.[31]

Then came concerts in Washington, Baltimore, Richmond, Allentown, Pennsylvania, and Bowling Green, Ohio. Finally on May 8, 1963, we find him in Detroit, and the critic of the *Windsor Star*, one John Gardiner, called him the "fabulous doyen of orchestral maestri."[32] I think Stoki must have appreciated that one.

In mid-January 1964, Ormandy wrote to Stokowski telling him how happy "we all are that you will conduct the Philadelphia Orchestra again next season." He particularly asked that he avoid programming Beethoven, since he himself was conducting a Beethoven cycle. "Also, the Brahms 2nd and 4th Symphonies have already been picked."[33] Stoki therefore suggested a program beginning with the Smetana *Sarka* and Dvořák's Seventh Symphony, and then the Martin Concerto for Seven Wind Instruments, Timpani, Percussion and Strings, and Wagner's prelude to act 3 and "Dance of the Apprentices" from *Die Meistersinger.*[34]

But the content of the program was to change dramatically. Henry Cowell had visited Tokyo in 1957 while on a world tour, and the Japanese experience resulted in a series of most characteristic works strongly conditioned by the Japanese idiom. One was an orchestral work called *Ongaku*, followed by concertos for harmonica and later by two concertos for koto and orchestra. Stoki was intrigued with the idea of a koto concerto, but it was not until the arrival of the blind Japanese koto virtuoso Kimio Eto that his interest really flamed. He wrote to Ormandy saying that he would like to replace the Martin concerto with the Koto Concerto of Henry Cowell. Ormandy replied that he was interested in having him give the world premiere of the work with Eto performing: "Mr. Eto played for me when he first came to this country, but at the time there was no work written for his instrument and orchestra. Of course, it will be a pleasure to replace the Martin concerto with Henry Cowell's new work."[35]

For those unfamiliar with the koto, it might be described as a cross between a giant zither and a table harp. It consists of a six-foot-long slab of paulownia wood over which are stretched thirteen taut strings, each with its own movable bridge. The player sits on the floor behind the instrument and plucks it with plectras that look like the elongated fingernails of Dr. Fu Manchu.

Stoki had placed the concerto after intermission and the audience was anticipant. A crimson padding had been placed on the floor of the stage on which the koto rested. Behind it was a large, red silk cushion on which the blind Eto would kneel. With his arm firmly resting on Stoki, Eto, in a large, abundant kimono of black and ivory silk, walked majestically onto the stage and assumed his position on the floor behind the instrument. Every eye in the Academy was riveted on him. Being a very willful artist as well as a magnificent ham, Eto was determined to make a vivid impression. He made his solo entrance after the orchestral introduction with grand gestures. Although the tempi had been carefully rehearsed, he began in a tempo all his own. This was one case when the soloist would have the conductor follow him at all times, since he could take no visual direction. He also added an elaborate cadenza of his own that gave him a good chance to show off his fleetness but added nothing to the musical content. Yet the overall effect was delightfully colorful and the audiences were entranced at every performance. Irving Lowens commented in the *Washington Star* on Cowell's "knowledge of the world's musics and whose insatiable curiosity about them is a constant wonder. . . . Eto did a fine job with the work—so fine that one almost wished that Cowell, who is just recovering from a serious illness, or another composer so young in heart and so adventurous would double the koto concerto repertory."[36]

Photo Adrian Siegel

With Henry Cowell and Kimio Eto after the performance of Cowell's Concerto for Koto and Orchestra with the Philadelphia Orchestra and Eto as soloist (1965)

In midsummer—June 29, 1964, to be exact—Stokowski made a special trip to Philadelphia to conduct the orchestra as part of a celebration during which a bronze plaque honoring the late President John Kennedy was to be unveiled in the plaza before Independence Hall. Stoki had a particular affection for the Kennedys and was attracted to their youth and charm. The event was to commemorate the President's visit there on July 4, 1962.

His seventy-three-year-old mother, Rose Kennedy, dressed in white, with a white hat to shield her from the eighty-degree heat in the sun-drenched plaza, spoke, saying that the late President had come there to declare the interdependence of nations, because he realized "that what was true of the 13 colonies is true of the western world: 'United we stand; divided we fall.' "

Stoki then led the Robin Hood Dell Orchestra in Bach's *Come Sweet Death* and the slow—"Goin' Home"—movement from the *New World Symphony*. It was a deeply moving moment. At the conclusion, Rose Kennedy and Stokowski signed the "Scroll of Freedom," to be followed by the participants and the audience as well. The scroll now rests in the Kennedy Memorial Library in Boston.[37]

On returning to Hyannis Port, Mrs. Kennedy wrote to Stoki to thank him for coming to Philadelphia and conducting the orchestra. "All the members of the family and I were deeply appreciative of the esteem and the admiration which were expressed by the citizens of Philadelphia for him. The fact that you and the Orchestra contributed to the programme in his honor made the day an especially memorable one for us."[38]

Late in October 1964, Ormandy wrote inviting Stokowski to conduct some of the summer concerts in Saratoga Springs,[39] but Stokowski had other plans. He answered, saying: "Next summer I shall be conducting in Japan and Tanglewood, so much to my regret I shall not be able to accept your kind invitation for Saratoga."[40] His concerts in Japan and later in Hawaii would again involve Eto and the koto concerto. The summer of 1965 would mark the first time he would be able to take his sons to the Orient, and that was a subject of great anticipation.

Though he had to refuse the invitation to conduct in Saratoga, he did agree to conduct the orchestra in both Philadelphia and New York in the fall. After his New York concert on November 23, Alan Rich lamented that there had to be a program, for the real news of the evening was "the sounds the orchestra made under Leopold Stokowski. Thirty years ago, when this was "Stokie's Orchestra" and no questions asked, this was the greatest sound human ears could hope to hear in a concert hall: sensuous, wheedling, richly roaring at one moment, throttled in the next down to a pianissimo below the level of audibility. Nobody worried much about whether these were the sounds the composer had in mind; in most cases they weren't but this made no difference.

"Have things changed? Not at all. Last night this fantastic old wizard drew the old repertory of sounds out of the orchestra all over again. . . .

It was a special kind of evening, therefore. Needless to say, it was pure Stokowski. And, since this man remains one of the most amazingly endowed of all conductors, that was interest enough. After all, music you can always hear."[41]

During the 1950s the Philadelphia Orchestra had been bedeviled repeatedly by strikes, and finally in 1966 one which extended over two months silenced the orchestra, canceling thirty-five concerts at the beginning of the season. It provoked a great deal of bitterness, and in the usually conservative *Bulletin* Max de Schauensee rebuked the players, stating that over the past fifteen years the orchestra had "one of the worst strike records" of any major symphony orchestra in the country.

Ormandy cautiously absented himself from the fray and fled to Europe. "I feel so helpless,"[42] he proclaimed. And so he was. But not Stokowski! When he was approached by some of the players to conduct a benefit for the strikers he immediately accepted, and as he stepped onto the stage at Convention Hall, the entire orchestra rose and greeted him with rousing cheers. When the rehearsal was over a broadly smiling Stokowski told them that it was a "wonderful, wonderful rehearsal. You'll even be better at the concert, if that's possible." The orchestra then made another spontaneous and impulsive gesture: they stood and cheered and applauded him as the violinists joined in striking their instruments with their bows. Stoki was deeply touched.

Queried by a reporter about his reason for conducting the concert for the benefit of the musicians, he paused and said: "I don't know why. I do these things on impulse. Sometimes I make a mistake. But this was no mistake. It was just a happy impulse."[43] But to the management and the board the impulse was not a particularly happy one. "He broke his contract," said Orville Bullitt. He explained that in the contract between Stoki and the orchestra there was a stipulation that he would not conduct any other concert in Philadelphia before his appearance in the Academy. "So I called him up," Bullitt recalled, "and I said, 'Look, what about this?' Well, there was a great to-do about it and he apologized and was sorry. . . ."[44]

The huge throng of over nine thousand gathered in Convention Hall greeted Stoki with salvos of applause. He began with David Diamond's Overture to *The Tempest* and continued with Beethoven's Seventh Symphony, the Prelude to Khovanshchina, and Stravinsky's *Petrouchka*. At the concert's end he made one of his Stokowskian speeches. He asked one and all to do everything in their "power to bring an end to this most unhappy condition and see that this great orchestra's future is assured. . . ." Then in his own mock humorous and winning way, he asked the listeners if they would like to go home now. A resounding "No!" rang out. Then he added four encores, including a rousing performance of the popular *Sabre Dance* of Khachaturian, a Prelude in E-flat Minor of Bach, a Haydn transcription, and the *Tannhäuser* Overture. "There would have been many more," wrote James Felton in the *Bulletin*, "if the cheering crowd that gave the maestro one standing ovation after another had had its way. But the evening came to a glorious end. Stokowski seemed not only a father but a god to the thousands of Philadelphians who came out to salute him and the orchestra which breathed a new life through him."[45] Proceeds of the concert topped $17,500 for the strikers.

The strike that had begun on September 19 ended on November 15, canceling all of the concerts between those dates, Stokowski's among them. He was to have conducted four times—three times in Philadelphia and once in New York. No animosity, however, lingered after the concert for the striking men, and Stoki was invited to join the orchestra on its tour of the West Coast and conduct five concerts in California beginning June 12, 1967, and also conduct concerts in Philadelphia and New York later in the season. The California tour he regretfully had to refuse, explaining that "I shall be in Austria and other parts of Europe in the spring and summer of '67."

Stokowski was invited to conduct another Pension Fund concert on February 13, 1969. His program was pure Stokowski—Palestrina's *Adoramus te,* Victoria's *Jesu dulcis Memoria,* the Bach *Chaconne,* the Prelude to act 1 and "Love Death" from *Tristan,* his own symphonic synthesis from Mussorgsky's *Boris,* and the *Petrouchka* Suite. The players tried to surpass themselves, the audience luxuriated, and the critics poured out their superlatives. None could have known then that this was to be the last time that the Maestro and the orchestra he had brought to such perfection would ever make music again. It was at this point that he decided to move to England, from where he would never return.

To mark the sixtieth anniversary of his debut in Philadelphia, he had been invited to return for still another Pension Fund affair. He was pleased when he was contacted many months before and began making plans to return. Machinery was set in motion and the public responded. A vast number of subscriptions were sold, but at the last moment Stoki suffered a fall and was unable to make the transatlantic trip. "So we had to cancel and return all that money," said Louis Hood, the orchestra's director of public relations, "something we are always loathe to do."

The reunion with the Philadelphia Orchestra had been a happy one for Stokowski as well as the management, the players, and his devoted listeners. Between February 15, 1960, and February 13, 1969, he had conducted the orchestra fifty times, not counting his appearances with the Robin Hood Dell. His age span ran from seventy-eight to eighty-six years. But the old master had given the Philadelphians a shot of aesthetic adrenaline. And they loved him for it.

Turandot—Tragedy and Triumph

I T was just before Stoki's last concert in Houston, scheduled for November 7, 1960, that the tragic news was flashed across the country. Dimitri Mitropoulos had died of a heart attack while conducting a rehearsal of Mahler's Third Symphony with the La Scala Orchestra in Milan.

Mitropoulos had first come to the Met during the 1954–55 season. "A little to his own surprise," stated Rudolf Bing, "he found that he loved working in an opera house, and he was happy at the Metropolitan."[1] He had eagerly looked forward to conducting Puccini's *Turandot*, which was being revived for the first time since 1930. It was to be an elaborate production: Cecil Beaton was to do the sets and costumes, and Yoshio Aoyama was engaged as stage director. There was to be a stellar cast headed by Birgit Nilsson and Franco Corelli.

When the shock waves generated by Mitropoulos' death abated somewhat, Rudolf Bing invited Stokowski to conduct in his stead, and he accepted at once. The first public confirmation came in articles appearing in New York papers on November 29: "Leopold Stokowski will conduct the Metropolitan's new production of Puccini's *Turandot* which will be first performed on Friday night, February 24, as a benefit sponsored by the Metropolitan Opera Guild."[2]

The idea of conducting *Turandot* appealed to Stoki. It had the drama, passion, exoticism, and sensuosity that particularly appealed to him. He had turned Bing down on earlier occasions when he had invited him to appear at the Met. The first came late in 1959 when Bing proposed that he conduct Gluck's *Alceste* with Eileen Farrell, whom he greatly admired.

Stoki wrote thanking Bing for his offer and "for the pleasure of meeting
. . . again." He said that he had studied the score thoroughly and "in my
opinion, it is beautiful music of a classical nature, but it is not *dramatic*
music. . . . I think that Gluck composed very beautiful music in *Alceste*,
but I do not think he has 'theater blood,' so I do not feel that I would
be the right conductor for these performances. I would be very happy to
cooperate with you in some other performances, of music that is truly for
the theater, with the kind of dramatic dynamic that in my opinion is
essential for good opera."[3]

Knowing Stokowski's great fondness for Wagner, Bing immediately
countered with another suggestion, a work which it would seem had all
the elements Stoki had described as being essential. But the reaction was
again negative:

> Thank you for suggesting Tannhäuser which of course is a great
> masterpiece. What I would prefer to do with you, is opera in the
> contemporary spirit of the 20th century, such as Prokofiev's "War
> and Peace" and possibly Berg's "Lulu," or Bartok's "Bluebeard," or
> Milhaud's "Christopher Columbus."[4]

Stokowski began to study the *Turandot* score immediately after his
return from Houston, and became completely absorbed in it. He was
meticulous in planning the production and he immersed himself in every
detail. On December 8 he wrote to Bing stating that he would like to
organize certain details so that no time, money or effort would be lost. He
had noticed discrepancies between the vocal and orchestral scores and
asked to have the librarian check, and then bring the score and parts back
to him "so that everything is definite."

He outlined specific plans for the sequence of his rehearsals and suggested that the Met install television equipment so the conductor backstage could see the conductor in the pit. He had already investigated the
matter and had all the prices worked out. "Perhaps we could find a donor
who would give us such equipment, which could later be moved to the
new hall in Lincoln Center."

He asked for the addresses of the stage director Yoshio Aoyama in
Tokyo and Cecil Beaton in London so that he could discuss with them
their respective ideas about staging and decor. He made suggestions about
possible amplification and pointed out various details concerning the

chorus and the standbys, who might be called upon to replace the principals should they become indisposed.[5]

Bing was completely cooperative and was reassuring on all points except the matter of a closed-circuit TV. He explained that the idea had been discussed for several years but it was impractical chiefly because of the unions. "It appears," he said, "that installation of such equipment would require the permanent engagement of two extra electricians and this is impossible."[6]

On the twentieth, he wrote to Cecil Beaton. "Mr. Bing has asked me to conduct *Turandot* and I look forward with pleasure to cooperating with you. As soon as you arrive in New York, may I meet you so that we can discuss any problems you may have in mind? One of these is to make sure that the scenery is hung forward enough toward the footlights so that there is plenty of room for the chorus and stage band behind the scenes and that they have enough light. Sometimes these conditions are overlooked."[7]

Beaton was quick to respond. "How very exciting to hear you are going to conduct *Turandot*!" he wrote. "This is most good news, especially as it will give me an opportunity of meeting you." Beaton explained that the sets were already being constructed but suggested that Stoki look at the plans. He assured him that the sets were not deep and would not create a problem for either the backstage chorus or band. He concluded with "kindest wishes and looking forward to meeting you with much anticipation."[8]

Stoki wrote to Aoyama and a considerable correspondence followed, which, alas, was quite futile.[9] Bing wrote a note saying that Aoyama was today suddenly taken ill and was operated on. "I hear all seemed to have gone well. What next!?"[10]

Stokowski's study of *Turandot* was interrupted by a call from John Edwards, the manager of the Chicago Symphony Orchestra, stating that Fritz Reiner had been suddenly taken ill and wondered whether Stokowski would be able to conduct a pair of concerts beginning on December 15, 1960.[11] He accepted at once, for he admired the orchestra and enjoyed conducting it. And, in addition, he had always enjoyed a warm relationship with Reiner since the early days in Philadelphia.

His program this time consisted of Smetana's Overture to the Bartered Bride, the Suite from *Háry János* of Kodály, the First Piano Concerto of Prokofiev with Malcolm Frager, pianist, and the Fifth Symphony of Shostakovich.

"He accompanied very, very well," Frager told me. "I don't know if he had ever accompanied that concerto before. It seemed to me at the time that he did not know the piece. He had a little trouble with one of the accelerandi in the last movement, but we stayed together. You know," he added, "I don't think he was terribly interested in that particular piece, and I can't blame him, because it's really not one of the greatest pieces of piano literature."

After the dress rehearsal of the concerto, Malcolm stayed on to listen to Stoki rehearse the Shostakovich. "I remember very distinctly that he rehearsed a few bars of the first movement, possibly two minutes. Then he skipped to something in the next movement. He did approximately two minutes of each movement and then he stopped and said, 'Gentlemen, that's it.' And he cut the rehearsal short by more than an hour and sent everyone home. I remember that that evening they really played beautifully. I really believe that there was something very special in his understanding of the fact that it is perilous to overrehearse."[12]

Back in New York he again immersed himself in the Puccini score and took time off to prepare for Christmas and his daily visits from his boys. His interest in them was literally all-consuming, and he played games with them with all the ardor of a twenty-year-old new father. He tried perhaps too much to deny the evidence of the calendar, and while playing football (he referred to it as soccer) in his apartment he slipped on an uncarpeted floor and suffered a broken hip two days before the beginning of another new year.

The first person to be notified was Stewart Warkow who was associated with the Symphony of the Air. He recalled: "I was going about my business when I got a call. Stoki had suffered an accident. And the first words out of my mouth were: 'Is he alive?' At that age you think, my God, who knows what happened. I really couldn't get any more out of anybody, so I tried calling the apartment, and the girls were there but I couldn't get a straight answer out of them . . . so I hopped in a cab and went right to the apartment. Stoki was in one of the boys' rooms laying out racked with pain. You could see it written all over him. He was doing calisthenics —he was doing pushups so that he wouldn't stiffen. In the meantime, an ambulance was coming and the girls were running around absolutely frantic. He looked as if he was really on the verge of saying bye-bye, but the ambulance operators who bundled him off and put him in this chair were calling him 'gramps.' 'Take care gramps; don't worry.' You could see that this, in addition to the pain, was just driving Stoki up the wall, but he couldn't do anything about it. The girls went with him to the Hospital for Special Surgery to make sure that the proper surgeon and doctor were arranged for. Stoki's surgery was rather complicated—a combination of age and the particular injury. Rather than try to have the bone knit, as they would do in some cases . . . because of postoperative complications and age, they opted for putting a stainless steel joint into the hip socket, which would probably mean a speedier recovery. . . . After the operation, I got a call from the girls. 'Come to the hospital.' And I said, 'My God, what happened now?' 'Stoki is calling for you.' So I went to the hospital, and he was in his room coming out of the anesthesia and rambling on and saying things that only a person who had been close to him for any period of time would really understand. He was lying in bed and just reaching out and saying, 'Spoon, spoon, spoons.' Well, I knew what he meant because he had a little collection of spoons. He would say that this is Queen Anne's spoon and this was somebody else's spoon. So I understood that this was something personal to him—the little spoons. So we tried to humor him and then he said, 'Pencils, pencils, pencils.' I happened to have always carried a set—an extra set of marking pencils. These were thick crayon pencils that had black and red lead that he would use to mark things in his score. It just so happened that I had a set with me and I gave it to him then and he reached up and started twisting them like he always used to do. It was like marking a score of *Turandot* that wasn't there."

When I mentioned going to the hospital, too, Stewart asked, "Did you notice the name on the door?"

"No, I didn't."

"It was not Leopold Stokowski," Stewart added gleefully. "It was Anthony Boles. When he was admitted into the hospital, Faye used his middle name. In other words, they tried to keep it from the press and especially from Gloria. So he was registered in the hospital under the name of Anthony Boles, which were really his middle names, Anthony Boleslawowicz, but they couldn't get the Boleslawowicz out, so it became Anthony Boles and not Leopold Stokowski."[13]

I visited Anthony Boles the second or third day after his surgery. His room faced the East River with a window, which gave just the right illumination for him to study. With his leg in traction, he had a special metal table which held the bulky *Turandot* score. In his hand he had one of the pencils Stewart Warkow had provided.

Even before he had returned home I assembled a collection of the rarest wines and liqueurs I could find and had them delivered to his hospital room. Carl Haverlin had found a particularly special Madeira and this too was sent up.

Punctilious as always and with the scores of *Turandot* and *Gurrelieder* before him, he found time to dictate his usual short notes. He thanked me for "the five entrancing-looking bottles which I am going to enjoy in leisure, and hope you will assist me. Please come by some time and play with the boys and me. Also there is a little package under the tree waiting for your attention."[14]

As the *Turandot* date neared, Stokowski was thoroughly prepared. He had separate rehearsals with the soloists, chorus, and orchestra. "He was really fantastic at rehearsals," said Anna Moffo, who sang the role of Liù in the first performance. "I don't think he ever did much Italian opera in his life, but he had a great gift of knowing every style—everything, and he had such a great sensitivity for rhythm and tempi."[15]

In later performances, two other sopranos also sang the role of Liù: Licia Albanese and Leontyne Price. But they did not have the advantage of the rehearsals that preceded the premiere. Albanese described her experience excitedly. The evening of her first performance she said to herself, "My God, I didn't even rehearse it with him." So she went to see Stoki, who was resting on a cot in his dressing room. " 'Maestro,' she said, 'in a few minutes we have to go onstage. What do you want me to do?' He said to me, 'You sing and then I accompany you. Don't worry.' Those are the words of a great conductor."[16]

For Stokowski, the physical obstacles were immense. He had to be carried out of his car and then transferred to a wheelchair. At other times he depended on crutches. He was still suffering much discomfort and the long rehearsals were arduous indeed.

George Cehanovsky, who sang the role of the Mandarin in the original performance of *Turandot* at the Met in 1926 with Jeritza as Turandot, and who was to take the same role in several of the performances that Stokowski conducted, made some perceptive observations. "Certainly nobody can take anything from Stokowski; he was the number-one conductor and that is all. His knowledge, especially of Beethoven, was something absolutely overwhelming. But when he came to the Met he was not hearing too well."

About this I could take issue with Cehanovsky, for I found that his hearing acuity up to the time of his death was remarkable. His vision was not. One problem besetting rehearsals was due to a stand-in substituting for Nilsson, and her voice simply did not have the carrying power to soar over the orchestra. "But when the real Turandot, Nilsson, appeared and had a real voice for Turandot," Cehanovsky continued, "it was all different because then there was enough volume. Stokowski did not speak Italian but he knew the opera from A to Z. He could give the words to people. But he was not himself. I wonder if it was his accident which disturbed him?"[17]

It was not until the full stage rehearsals were in progress that utter chaos began to rule. First of all, Aoyama was replaced by Nathaniel Merrill, who seemed to have a penchant for having nearly everyone in constant motion.

It was this business which particularly disturbed and distracted Stokowski, and he registered his annoyance emphatically. To further ruffle the atmosphere, Bing, who was known to be an intolerable autocrat at times, had met a man of equally monumental ego. The air was charged. Although Bing admitted that it was his decision to engage Stokowski, he quickly came to regard it as a decision "he would soon regret."

I sat through the final dress rehearsal with considerable dismay. But the situation was one not usually encountered by Stokowski during his long career and he desperately tried to control it. Stage directions were being given right and left, ballet members were scampering about in rather aimless fashion, and the principals seemed to meander in a somewhat ghostly stupor. There were constant interruptions. Stokowski felt that all of the stage activity should have been rehearsed separately and not at the expense of the orchestra. Finally he called a halt.

A rapid backstage conference took place and the rehearsal once again continued. There were no more interruptions and a Stokowskian order was resumed. But the welding together of all the elements was an act of phenomenal will, and Stokowski achieved it.

So much excitement had been generated by the combination of Stokowski and the stellar cast Bing had assembled that the rush of standees broke a new record. At 6:15 in the morning the first brave soul prepared to wait outside in the February cold until 7:00 P.M., when standing room would go on sale. As the morning wore on, the first standee was joined by more and more enthusiasts, and gradually the line snaked around the building from Broadway into Thirty-ninth Street. In a rare charitable move, the management, realizing that the number of standees assembled vastly exceeded the total number of 224 standing-room tickets, opened the box office and sold the coveted places. A new record had been set of standee participation.[18]

The cast for the opening night read thus:

Turandot	Birgit Nilsson
Emperor Altoum	Alessio De Paolis
Timur	Bonaldo Giaiotti
Calaf	Franco Corelli
Liù	Anna Moffo
Ping	Frank Guarrera
Pang	Robert Nagy
Pong	Charles Anthony
Servants	Thomas Russell
	Craig Crosson
	Robert Bishop
A Mandarin	Calvin Marsh
The Prince of Persia	Edilio Ferraro

Time magazine's critic wrote with enthusiasm. Of *Turandot* he said, "Leopold Stokowski was its master. . . . Having always been a theatrical conductor in the concert hall, he seemed completely at home in the theater, drawing all the score's turbulence from the orchestra without trying to make it the star of the show at the singers' expense."[19]

Ovations indeed were the order of the evening. The house went wild after each act. The final demonstration was cyclonic. It burst into a roar when finally Stoki appeared onstage supported by his crutches. Instead of taking a bow, he brought his crutches in front of him and applauded the audience with them, clapping them together. "He looked like a whooping crane doing a mating dance," one observer happily remarked.

Rudolf Bing's second in command at the time was Robert Herman, assistant manager and artistic administrator at the Met. I asked him to trigger his memory, and his recollections of Stoki and *Turandot* were vivid after two decades. That Stokowski wanted and got a spotlight on the floor which would shine up on his hands seems a natural demand, since that was his basic means of communication. Herman continued: "The main thing that I can remember about him was the way he marked his opera scores. There were great big slashing marks with colored crayons because he couldn't really see to read the music. He had every change of tempo and every major cue marked in a different colored crayon or pencil so that he could see from a distance. His scores were fantastic to look at!"

I remarked to Herman that I had been at the final dress rehearsal and was appalled at the hectic confusion that existed and wondered whether all dress rehearsals were so frantic and seemingly disorganized. "I remember what happened," he recalled. "It was a very unusual situation. Cecil

Beaton, the designer, had an assistant execute the working drawings and the sets were built to these specifications. Then when they got onstage something wasn't right. It didn't satisfy and it didn't please. We went through the preliminary rehearsals really thinking, well, it's going to come together—it will look better when he finishes with the lighting or when he finishes with this or that. Then, on the day of the first dress rehearsal, he realized that it was the way the staircase had been redrawn in the working drawings that made it look heavy, like a lump on the stage, rather than having the graceful sweep of the original design. We decided at that point to have them reconstruct the entire staircase between the predress and the opening night. For that reason there was great chaos. Parts of the new pieces were perhaps done, part were not done. It just wasn't finished at that point—the only time I can remember that ever happening at the Met."

Discussing minor alterations to the score, I asked Herman what his own reaction had been and he replied: "There were very few real alterations. No, certainly the Met couldn't go along with something if it were really unfaithful to the composer. . . .[20] But it was not Stokowski who made alterations; it was the Met itself. In an indignant letter to Rudolf Bing, Stoki wrote: "It is inconceivable to me that the staff of the Metropolitan Opera, one of the greatest in the world, would plan an opera by Puccini, one of the greatest composers of music drama, without reading the piano score in which Puccini's indications are expressed in Italian and English. Or, if they read the score, they then arbitrarily changed his indications."[21]

When I talked about *Turandot* with Paul Hume in Washington, he said: "I had been waiting for certain things to happen there which I thought Nilsson would only do with the right conductor. And they happened with Stokowski. The Met bad-mouthed him, especially Bing who disliked him, I think, throughout. But I thought there were some marvelous things which Stokowski did. There are certain passages in that opera that need to be stretched and they can be stretched if you have the right chorus, the right orchestra, and the right soprano. Then everything else will fall into place. And it happened then. I did not hear Nilsson do it that way any other time; not in either of her recordings although I think the Leinsdorf is quite fine. After that she just got so that she wanted to make it a singing match with Corelli, which was why she did the second recording. But I thought the performance with Stokowski had something quite extraordinary."[22]

During the summer, Nathaniel Merrill wrote to Stokowski saying that he heard it rumored that Bing had invited him to conduct Cilea's *Adriana Lecouvreur,* and that he hoped he would accept. He told him that Cecil Beaton would design the settings and costumes, Danilova would be the choreographer, and he would stage it.[23]

Though Stoki was pleased with the invitation, he still smarted at the arbitrary handling of the scenic matters in *Turandot.* "I would like to do anything you wish," he wrote him, "but I do not feel that I am the right conductor for this opera. Some time, at your convenience, could we discuss *Turandot* from the standpoint of Puccini's directions in the score?"[24] No one has ever been more persistent.

72

Orchestras

T HE return to the New York Philharmonic on March 4, 1960, was a far cry from Stoki's return to the Philadelphia. His program was not the most felicitous from a critical standpoint but it did please the audience. He programmed the Handel *Water Music* in his own amplified arrangement, Mozart's Symphony No. 40, Fikret Amirov's Symphonic Suite *Azerbaijan,* and the Shostakovich Fifth Symphony. I remember the concert well, for it had nothing of the sense of magic excitement that his recent appearances with the Philadelphia had had.

"Mr. Stokowski is a very great conductor, endowed with phenomenal gifts and a facility which is famous and which created one of the world's greatest orchestras," wrote Paul Henry Lang. "Moreover," he continued, "he still possesses them today, but one cannot help thinking that these have been squandered here on a program that falls between two stools." Being a musicologist first and a critic second, Lang naturally attacked the arrangement of Handel's *Water Music* and likened the performance of the Mozart G Minor Symphony to a "Rococo charmer with beauty patches, rouge and powder."[1]

Harold Schonberg took a different point of view, and tweaking the noses of musicologists was a predilection: "Not that Mr. Stokowski has wreaked great violence with Handel. . . . But it definitely is a romantic piece of work and it received a romantic reading. It is the kind of thing that musicologists regard with the hysteria of an old maid who sees a mouse in the living room. . . .

"He led a quite restrained, songful Mozart, using a reduced orchestra.

His approach was relaxed, the tempos were on the sensible side, the balances came through clearly. . . ."[2]

Orchestras outside of New York were the ones that gave Stoki their greatest cooperation and hence, for him, proved his most pleasurable musical experience. He had had enough of the uncooperative elements in the Philharmonic, he had had his fill of antagonism from the old NBC Orchestra and its now disintegrating Symphony of the Air. Apart from his tours he had begun to toy with the idea of forming a new orchestra with players of his own choice. Meanwhile, he continued to accept European engagements and in May 1960 we find him giving concerts in Poland, where he conducted the excellent orchestras of Katowice and Bydgoszcz in concerts and broadcasts. The Poles showed a particular adulation that bordered at moments on a mild hysteria.

In London after his Polish visit, he conducted the London Symphony Orchestra. Here the players responded to him with spirit. Leader of the second violins was Neville Marriner, later the brilliant conductor of St. Martin-in-the-Fields Academy Orchestra and Music Director of the Minnesota Orchestra—a post once held by Eugene Ormandy and later Dimitri Mitropoulos.

Marriner discussed and praised Stoki's use of free bowing and he felt that it made a richer sound and actually a "completely different texture. He also used to build the sound up from the bottom. The most important sonority for him were the double basses so that he would get this bass resonance going. He got an enormous fat sound from the bottom and it was just one of those infectious things; if you get a heavy bass sound then the cellos respond, their instruments sound better and and the middle sounds better. I would say that Stokowski's sonority was about 20 decibels above anybody else's just purely because he gave people this freedom." Marriner felt that Stokowski made "an enormous contribution to symphonic style. He was someone who gave us a completely new aspect of what a symphony orchestra could sound like and actually the luxury of the sound itself was exciting . . ."[3]

The London Times, which referred to him as "the legendary Dr. Leopold Stokowski," prefaced its review with double headlines: "Dr. Stokowski Supreme" and "Sonority at Festival Hall": ". . . orchestral sonority was in fact the great delight of the evening. Dr. Stokowski has a much finer regard for colour than for design and even his most questionable licence with regard to tempo and rubato was always mitigated by the sheer quality of the sound produced in flagrante delicto."[4]

Photo CTK/Courtesy Edward Johnson
Conducting the Czech Philharmonic Orchestra in Prague,
1961

In the spring of 1961 following his remarkable recuperation from his
fall, his triumphs at both the City Center Opera and the Metropolitan,
as well as his taxing *Gurrelieder* performances and others with the Philadelphia Orchestra, he set out for Europe on the *Christophero Colombo*,
arriving in Naples on May 4. He immediately was driven to Rome, where
he began his rehearsals with the Santa Cecilia Orchestra for his concert
on May 7.

From Rome he went to visit Jean Tennyson, now Mrs. Ernest Bois-

sevain, at her palatial Florentine Villa della Rose. On May 14 he arrived
in Vienna to make arrangements for his rehearsals and concert on June 2.
With the preliminaries disposed of, he entrained for Prague, where he
spent five days devoted to rehearsals and visits about the city. Although
this was the first time that Stokowski had conducted in Prague, he had
long been known through his recordings, and both players and critics
repeatedly referred to him as a "living legend." He was welcomed with
great cordiality and warmth and the Czechs vied in taking him about to
see their beautiful city. He visited the St. Vitus Cathedral and the famed
Hradčany Castle, where he posed agreeably for photographers. He visited
the Tyl Theater, where Mozart's *Don Giovanni* was heard for the first
time.

After his pleasant Prague interlude, he returned to Vienna to conduct
a concert of the London Symphony Orchestra in its first visit to the
Austrian capital. With his penchant for always presenting something new,
he programmed Walton's Second Symphony along with Strauss' *Death
and Transfiguration* and the Shostakovich Fifth. The musically insular
Viennese typically felt little sympathy for a new English symphony, but
the response to the orchestra under Stokowski was positive.

Next Berlin, where he conducted two concerts with the Philharmonic.
Two of the reviewers headlined their critiques: "Tone-Magician Stokowski" and "Sorcerer of the Orchestra." Erwin Kroll writing in *Der Tag*
remarked that "although physically somewhat handicapped . . . the 79-
year-old conductor is still a sorcerer of the orchestra who, by means of a
minimum of gestures, attains a maximum of enchanting sonorities."[5]

Another writer observed that the orchestra played "with engraved
precision, with a whirling brilliance in the strings, as the Philharmonic is
apt to play in their best, most inspired moments. How Stokowski 'does
it' is his secret. . . . His style is perfect and a definite personal statement,
a virtuosity in the best sense, nobility, spirit and tightly reined-in temperament combined, induced the public to break into wild applause. . . ."[6]

Following his triumph in Berlin, he hurried to London, where he
enjoyed another. Stokowski was no everyday event in London and the
press was eager to cover every aspect of his visit. A reporter from the
London Daily Express attended one of the rehearsals: "He perches on the
rostrum like an aged stork, his hands waving languidly in the slow movements or clenching and punching the air above him when the tempo
speeds up . . . this is Leopold Stokowski at work making an orchestra of
100 musicians obey his every command."

During an intermission break, Stoki responded to various questions. "I would love to farm if I had the time," he said. "I love to plant trees myself to feel that anything that I've had anything to do with grew up. I know a lot about the land." Responding to queries on how he keeps fit, he said rather tartly: "There was a lot of talk about it all being due to me doing yoga daily. Rubbish! Yoga is a religion, a way of life. I have my religion; I am a Roman Catholic."

Critical response to his concert was vivid. About the Royal Festival Hall itself Stoki had sharp comments. "The acoustics are all wrong," he told one reporter. "The sound waves get crushed. There is not enough air in here."[7]

Two days later he revisited his old school, the Royal College of Music, and conducted a rehearsal with the student orchestra. He thoroughly enjoyed working with young people there and on one occasion he encountered Sir Adrian Boult, who described the event: "Stokowski had come to the Royal College of Music to see Sir Hugh Allen—I cannot remember whether he came to lunch but I think so. Anyhow he and I were with H. P. A. in his rooms, and Allen invited L. S. to come to the orchestral concert which was to be held a few days later. I pitied the poor man who had to sit through this concert of the student orchestra. They weren't bad, of course, but it was a student's orchestra! And so I suddenly said, 'Couldn't Mr. Stokowski conduct something?' Well the show finished with the Meistersinger Overture. So we hatched the plot; it was to be kept a deadly secret and after the penultimate piece I turned around and made the sensational announcement! It was of course a terrific performance— a real thrill for the orchestra and audience."[8]

Stoki had little time to savor his triumph, for he departed on the *Queen Mary* on June 25 for a mere ten-day stay, during which he conducted the Philadelphia Orchestra in the Dell for another cheering audience of thirty thousand.[9] On Thursday, July 6, 1961, Stoki and his two sons left New York for Europe aboard the *Queen Elizabeth*. "We went first to Paris," he wrote. "The thing that interested the boys most was the Tour Eiffel. We had dinner up on the top lift. Then we went to Geneve, Switzerland, right on the French border where we had wonderful experiences and the boys heard much French language."[10] They stayed with his daughter Lyuba and her husband Homi Devitre at their villa in Fossard just outside of Geneva. This was Stoki's first visit with Lyuba and it set a pattern for the next decade. Hers was a large country house called Campagne Gouy and shortly after their arrival, Sadja arrived with her husband, Dr. Robert

Courtesy Lyuba Stokowski Rhodes

With Chris, Stan, and Lyuba's and Sadja's families in Switzerland, 1961. Back row: Stokowski; Lyuba's husband, Dr. Homi Devitre; Sadja's husband, Dr. Robert Goldsmith. Middle: Chris, Ricky Devitre, Stan. Front: Lyuba's older daughter, Diana; Lyuba holding daughter Laila; Sadja holding elder son, Jason

Goldsmith, and their six-month-old son, Jason. Here they made many trips along the lake and visited many beautiful Swiss towns and enjoyed splendid restaurants, such as the Père Bise at Talloires, which they all particularly enjoyed.[11]

On August 9, Stoki and his boys departed for London, where he showed them his natal city before going on to Edinburgh. Stoki was very concerned about where the boys could stay in Edinburgh. He knew that he would be preoccupied much of his time there with rehearsals and he wanted to be sure that they could be somewhere where they could have a certain amount of freedom and not be confined to a hotel room. "Is there a place in Edinburgh," he wrote Lord Harewood, "where I could live with the boys and where there is space so that they can play out in the open?"[12] Two decades later, Stan recalled that he had liked Edinburgh very much. "It was really nice," he said. "We stayed in a castle-hotel. It was great. I remember they had bread that had full kernels of wheat in it; it was kind of rustic. It went with the castle."[13]

When Lord Harewood first broached the idea of Stokowski opening the Festival for its 1961 season, Stoki declined the invitation. He explained that he would probably be conducting in the Soviet Union but he would have a concert in London on June 18 with the Philharmonia Orchestra. "Would your Lordship consider the Philharmonia, because I shall have the Philharmonia already rehearsed in my rather unorthodox methods! This might be in Edinburgh after June 18," he replied. He suggested that he would be eager to conduct Schoenberg's *Moses and Aaron* if it could be arranged, and mentioned that he would be conducting the *Gurrelieder* in Philadelphia, New York, and Houston and that he would very much like to conduct it in both Edinburgh and London.[14]

The idea of having the *Gurrelieder* as the opening work of the Festival was a most happy one for Lord Harewood. He answered immediately and suggested that Stoki conduct the *Gurrelieder* but explained that the time could only be on August 20, when the Festival began. He was most persuasive in his arguments and assured Stoki that there was probably no organization in Europe other than the board of the Edinburgh Festival that would "contemplate the rehearsals and other expenses of this complicated work."[15]

The idea was so tempting that Stoki immediately set about rearranging his schedules and accepted Harewood's invitation. He wrote to him, saying: "I hope the atmosphere of the festival will be intensely Scottish, with plenty of bagpipes and kilts and Drambui and tartans!! Do you think the Duke of Edinburgh would open the festival and could Gurrelieder be a command performance from the Queen? It would be wonderful if the festival could attract a large international public from all the European countries and the Americas."[16]

The musical forces in Edinburgh were splendid: The London Symphony Orchestra and the Edinburgh Royal Choral Union with Nell Rankin and James McCracken singing the roles of Tove and Waldemar.

On the evening of the Festival's opening, Lord Harewood sent a chauffeured limousine to collect Nell Rankin, McCracken, and the Maestro and bring them to the hall. "A young guard positively refused to deposit us at the stage door, stating that we were all trying to attend the concert without tickets," Nell Rankin remembered. "Mr. Stokowski quietly reminded him that there would be no opening of the Festival if he insisted on holding him and the soloists 'at bay.' Finally when the guard insisted that not only would we not be allowed to attend the concert, but that we must drive away immediately, Mr. Stokowski asked for a changing of the guard and sent the young man to alert the Festival officials of his momentous decision. In a short time officials came pouring out of the stage door to the rescue."[17]

"Scotland went mad about 'Gurrelieder' and I thought what a pity Texas cannot hear it," wrote Stoki to his Houston friend, William Lee Pryor.[18]

Two nights later at the Edinburgh Festival on August 22 Stokowski conducted an all-orchestral concert with Gabrieli's *Sonata pian' e forte*, Michael Tippett's Concerto for Double String Orchestra, the Liszt *Mephisto Waltz* and the Fifth Symphony of Shostakovich. Immediately after this second concert, Stoki and his two boys returned to New York.

Back in the United States again he opened the 1961–62 season with the Chicago Symphony Orchestra on October 12. He chose a work by Alexander Tcherepnin, who for many years had been living in Chicago; it was his *Georgiana*, Suite for Orchestra.

Early in January he was again back in Chicago. "It was quite a night in Orchestra Hall," wrote Claudia Cassidy. "Leopold Stokowski came back to the Chicago Symphony Orchestra with an apocalyptical 'Götterdämmerung' finale that soared to Valhalla in a blaze of burnished brass ... it doesn't really matter if there were nine horns or 19. The important thing was that at the helm stood a man who is a giant among conductors. ... It was Wagner incarnate."[19]

There was then a reengagement with the New York Philharmonic, but not one initially planned by its management. The invitation came when ailing Fritz Reiner could not appear. The concerts—there were three—were given on March 1, 2, and 4. He began with a short Epilogue to *Julius Caesar*, by the late Robert Kurka, followed by the Vaughan Williams *Tallis Fantasia*, Scenes from Parsifal, and the Shostakovich Fifth. "A white-haired man of noble bearing, striding gallantly to the podium with the help of a cane, was given a rousing reception at the Philharmonic concert in Carnegie Hall yesterday afternoon," wrote Louis Biancolli.[20]

During this period there occurred a marked change in the attitude of the members of the Philharmonic. To the men, Stoki, fighting his battle to continue in spite of his serious accident, made him appear as a truly gallant figure. In his conducting there seemed to have grown a greater seriousness and immersion into the music at hand. At no previous time had the players given him such cooperation and manifested such sincere goodwill. Miles Kastendieck observed that "the orchestra played glowingly under his positive direction."[21]

All of the critics devoted considerable space to a discussion of his seating arrangement and all admitted that it did indeed enhance the quality of the sound. In the *New York Herald Tribune*, Ronald Eyer explained to his readers: "Basic to his thinking is that the strings should be massed together with their f-holes facing the audience. This is to insure solid ensemble and maximum audibility. The cellos are strung out in a line across the back of the stage and they sit on a high platform well above the heads of their colleagues. . . .

"The first and second violins and the violas are bunched on the left, as the audience sees them, and the woodwinds, brass and percussion are bunched on the right, so the main divisions of the orchestra sit facing each other like two contending armies.

"It looks all wrong, but in sound, somehow, it comes out fine. The tone of the woodwinds, no longer buried in the middle of the orchestra pipes up sharper and cleaner, the strings seem richer, and there is no cleavage, no loss of ensemble between the two sides."[22]

To me it is utterly astonishing that, while critics, musicians, and audience alike constantly speak of the remarkable tone quality Stokowski was able to get out of an orchestra, slavish academicians continue to insist on the old, less logical seating plan of the German tradition, and shun free bowing as if it were a plague. But Stokowski continued to coax fabulous sounds out of each orchestra he conducted and the critics continued to pay heed.

Immediately after his concerts with the New York Philharmonic, he traveled to Cleveland for his first concert there in seven years. Composer-critic Herbert Elwell wrote: "A tall, slender man with long white hair moved slowly to the podium of Severance Hall stage last night. He was, as you may know, Leopold Stokowski, giant among conductors, and of almost legendary fame . . . time has slightly altered his appearance. . . . But from the moment he stretched out his arms to the Cleveland Orchestra, he was magically transformed into the Stokowski we knew 30 years ago. . . . The orchestra seemed to acquire a new spirit, to breathe freely in a new atmosphere. It even took on a new sound, which of course could be explained partly by Stokowski's special seating arrangement. . . ."[23]

From Cleveland Stoki returned to Philadelphia, where he began his series of concerts with his seventeenth appearance in the Academy since his return there two seasons before. When he brought the band to New York, Miles Kastendieck remarked: "The texture of sound he commands from musicians never ceases to be as mesmerizing as it is individual."[24]

Encore Turandot

W HILE Bing may have been somewhat disenchanted, he obviously realized that Stokowski could be as valuable a commercial asset to the Met as an artistic one. Hence he contacted him and inquired whether he would be available to conduct another series of *Turandot*s. Stoki may well have been bored by the repetitive task by that time, but he accepted. The Met was plagued by a series of union troubles during that 1961 summer, and rumors were bandied about that possibly it would not be able to open for its fall season.

Many performing organizations were in serious trouble. Early in August 1961 the Met regretfully announced that the forthcoming season would have to be canceled due to the intransigent stand of many of the unions involved in its operation. The principal one was the Musicians' Union.

On August 8, Bing wrote to Stokowski:

> You will have heard about the tragic developments. This is merely a short personal note to accompany the official one, and to tell you how happy I am that at least I have had the pleasure of having had you here at the Metropolitan and how much I hope that a year hence we may be functioning again and you may be with us again. In the meantime, thank you for the past season, and best wishes.[1]

Bing's attitude was indeed most cordial.

Bing then cannily plotted a strategy to solve the impasse, and intermediaries Leontyne Price and Risë Stevens flew to Washington and appealed directly to President Kennedy, who was very sympathetic. He turned to a member of his Cabinet, Secretary of Labor Arthur Goldberg. Goldberg knew exactly how to deal with unions, for he had once been counsel to the CIO. He immediately met with various union officials and in a short time unruffled the troubled waters, and plans for the opening of the fall season were announced.[2]

With the Met back in business and the performances of *Turandot* assured, Stoki again reexamined and restudied the score. Conductor Denis Vaughan had had a long battle with the house of Ricordi in Milan over errors in Verdi and Puccini scores. He had discussed the matter with Stoki, who was most sympathetic, and explained Ricordi's reluctance to provide him with copies of the original scores. They went over the *Turandot* score together and Stoki pointed out several parts that he thought were questionable. He then decided to approach Ricordi directly and a series of letters were exchanged. Stoki gave copies of the correspondence to Denis, who in turn gave them to *L'Espresso* in Rome. It created something of an international incident.

"Gentlemen," wrote Stokowski in his opening letter dated November 16, 1961, "for my personal study, would it be possible to obtain a microfilm of the first act of the original *Turandot* score which has not been changed in any way by anyone? As soon as you quote me the cost of the microfilm, I will send you the amount either in Italian lire or in dollars."

On December 5 Stoki received a letter from Eugenio Clausetti, the administrator of Casa Ricordi, who explained the delay of his answer to the fact that he had to consult with Signora Rita Puccini, the widow of the composer's only son, Antonio, and heiress to the Puccini estate. "Many years ago," the letter continued, "shortly after the world premiere of *Turandot*, Antonio Puccini gave us specific instructions that no reproduction of the original *Turandot* score may be published until 50 years after the first performance. This period will terminate on 29 November 1974."

But Signora Puccini maintained that she had no authority to reverse her late husband's stipulation and Casa Ricordi in turn regretted it could not grant Stoki's request: ". . . Should you come to Italy, Signora Puccini and we ourselves shall be happy to put the manuscript at your disposal for your strict personal study."[3]

Considering Stokowski's eminence, his age, his position with the Metropolitan Opera, and physical condition, the intransigence of Ricordi seems to have been myopic and crassly inconsiderate. But Stoki was persistent.

He replied by return mail on December 8, 1961:

Thank you for your letter of 5 December. I am sure that Antonio Puccini, son of one of Italy's greatest musical geniuses, did well to stipulate that no reproduction of the original *Turandot* score should be issued until 50 years have elapsed from its first performance. I, however, a great admirer of the Maestro and above all of *Turandot* —in my opinion, his finest opera—must protest this decision. . . . Hence, I am renewing my request for a microfilm of the first act and ask you to let me know what the cost will be so that I can reimburse you.[4]

Stubbornly, Ricordi reiterated its previous refusal and expressed their own deep regrets as well as those of Signora Puccini. Giacomo could have set them to music as an aria tragica. But they renewed their invitation to have him come to Milan and examine freely the original manuscript of *Turandot.*

Stokowski could be just as obstinate as Ricordi and he persisted. On January 26, 1962, he wrote again to the Casa Ricordi.

I can understand that Signora Puccini does not wish to alter her husband's decision concerning his father's music. As I have written before, in view of my commitments in other countries, I cannot come to Milan in the near future. Even if this were possible, however, I should need many hours of study on the original *Turandot* score, in fact, an unlimited period of extensive work to examine it. This I could do in my New York study during the intervals between my various tours. I wish to do this work without compensation, only for the satisfaction of serving the great Maestro Puccini. I do not know who orchestrated *Turandot,* but whoever it was has not shown much sensitivity for the enormous differences between the orchestration accompanying the singers and those passages which only express the drama enacted on the stage.

In *Tosca* and *Butterfly* we clearly see Puccini's skill in orchestrating the music accompanying the singers. Puccini supports the voice and increases the intensity of the orchestra as the voice rises to the highest notes; when, however, it drops to the low range and a *piano,* his orchestration is always transparent, so that the voice easily comes through.

He never obliges the singer to force his voice, which could harm it. His orchestration is always sensitive to the problem of making the voice heard throughout the opera house.

In my opinion, *Turandot* is the most complete expression of Puccini's genius. It is our duty to him and to opera lovers all over the world to make known his original intentions directly from the original manuscript, and to find the way to present them exactly as Puccini would have done himself if he were alive and if he himself had orchestrated the final part of *Turandot*.

I put myself at Puccini's service and yours, as his publishers, and I hope that you will permit me to have a microfilm of the first act of *Turandot* so that I can work on it whenever I have time.[5]

Ricordi wouldn't budge.

On August 28 Stoki received a telegram from Bing stating that at the personal request of President Kennedy he was attempting a revival of the 1961–62 season and asked whether the dates that had initially been agreed upon were still possible.[6]

Stoki answered at once, saying, "I am deeply sympathetic for the difficulties everyone is having, and I hope that the season can be revived as far as possible to everyone's satisfaction." He also reminded Bing that if he were to conduct *Turandot* he wanted it produced "according to the directions of Puccini, as clearly indicated in the score." He was observing the dictum "as written" even more intensely than Toscanini, who, his adherents claimed, had a monopoly on the phrase. He also stated that after the cancellation of the initial agreement, he had accepted certain other engagements but would still be free to conduct five of the original dates.[7]

"I am delighted that you can be available for at least five *Turandot* performances and distressed that you seem to be obliged to miss one or the other," Bing responded. "The general situation is so disastrous now that I have to be selfish and must attempt to get you free if at all humanly possible. Please cooperate if you can." Bing was indeed under great pressure and told Stoki that "we will be glad if we can get the curtain up and there is not the ghost of a chance of any substantial change."[8]

Stoki responded that he would cooperate in every possible way but he felt that he had "a moral obligation to Puccini and to the public to perform this masterpiece exactly as the composer indicated. . . . But the fact that the public considered *Turandot* a great success does not necessarily mean that we gave the best performance possible, and they naturally do not know in how many ways the composer's intentions were not followed. In the long line of Italian dramatic composers beginning with Monteverdi, Puccini was one of the greatest masters of stagecraft. I have given deep study to this score, and I feel strongly obligated to protect and defend Puccini's ideas. . . . But if, as you write, 'there is not the ghost of a chance of any substantial change' and the changes which would bring the performance into accordance with Puccini's directions are not possible now, I definitely cannot continue to conduct this masterpiece as part of a production which does not completely fulfill Puccini's dramatic conception."[9]

Bing responded. "Forgive me," he wrote, "if in a very desperate situation I try once again to appeal to you." He explained that the production of *Turandot* had been in the planning stages long before Stokowski had been brought in to replace Mitropoulos, and recognized that he had complained about effects that were not as he would like. "No doubt," he continued, "you know better than I that you yourself introduced a few musical changes here and there, all of which we felt improved the overall effect of the work, and I well remember your own statement when you told us that Puccini had never seen this work on the stage and, if he had, he would have made many changes himself." He reiterated that the Met was in the midst of its most serious crisis and it was impossible at this time "to find time for anything beyond the barest necessity of getting the curtain up."[10]

With only a modicum of conciliation, Stoki dispatched a set of eleven questions to Nathaniel Merrill, stating that everything would depend on his answers and that they would determine whether or not he would conduct *Turandot* in any further performances.

He asked the names of the singers, the size of the chorus, and then listed questions about lighting. "At the opening of Act I, can the whole stage be 'bathed in golden light' and can we replace the present backdrop with one suggesting the 'distant spires of Peiping?' . . . In Act I at No. 17, at the point where the chorus sings 'Perche tarda la luna?' can the crowd be 'watching the sky which has already darkened.' . . . 13 bars after No. 18, as the chorus makes a great crescendo, can the moon markedly rise, and can the stage be bathed in silver light? . . . Where the funeral march begins, can the light remain silver? . . . Can Turandot appear 'illumined by the moon's rays like a vision?' . . . (May I suggest that this effect might be easier to achieve if she wore, instead of the golden costume and crown, a simple silver costume and crown? This would also make her appearance in the golden costume in Act II more effective.) In Act I, 2 bars before No. 25, can the light be 'dim in the deserted square?' . . . At No. 38, can we retain the 'shadows of those who die for Turandot flitting to and fro on the ramparts?' This was very well done . . . can the silver light of the moon become still more intense as the dramatic action becomes more intense? . . . In Act III, at No. 1, the heralds sing with full voice; at No. 2 they sing farther off; at No. 3 they should sing still more distantly. I conducted *Turandot* for the Metropolitan eight or nine times, but only once was this magical effect of distance achieved, although I strongly requested it before each performance. Can something be worked out so that this effect is achieved at every performance, if I conduct *Turandot* again?"

In complimentary fashion he told Merrill that he had enjoyed working with him last year and that he admired his control of the complex grouping of the crowds on the stage.[11]

Merrill responded to all of Stoki's queries, indicating that he would attempt to carry out all of his suggestions.[12] But this was not enough for the Maestro. He wrote Merrill again, stating that he would conduct *Turandot* only if all of his suggestions were incorporated. He objected to the rehearsal schedule, stating that he felt strongly that "the orchestra reading at 10:00 and the stage rehearsal to begin at twelve is a completely unacceptable arrangement. Most of the orchestration of *Turandot* is quite obviously not Puccini's. It is much too heavy for solo voices and chorus. We need a rehearsal of three hours to reduce all the dynamics of the orchestration. If the orchestra plays the accompaniments as printed, the solo voices and chorus will not be heard."

He also offered to join Merrill, sitting back in the auditorium to observe the "re-lighting of Act I" even if there would be no cast on the stage, and he tried to pin Merrill down to an exact time for them to do so. As an amelioratory postscript he wrote: "I feel that the success of *Turandot* is greatly owing to the beautiful and imaginative decor and costumes of Beaton, of whom I am a great admirer."[13]

But he continued to prod. He wrote to Robert Herman demanding to know why in the planning stage "Puccini's directions regarding a glorious sunset over the roofs of Peiping were not carried out."[14] He phoned Tony Bliss, president of the Met, and poured out to him his complaints.

It was time for Bing to again step into the controversy. He wrote Stoki a most tactful and diplomatic letter placating him thoroughly, but still Stoki was not to be deterred from his demands.[15] He had, however, to drop two of his demands and expected the nine remaining ones to be met, and with that in mind instructed his manager to sign a contract for two performances only.[16]

Stoki finally acquiesced and, after considerable fussing about details, pulled the performance together and conducted the first one of the revivals as scheduled. The cast included Nilsson as before, but with Richard Tucker replacing Franco Corelli, and Ezio Flagello singing the part of Timur. Lucine Amara did the part of Liù, the fourth singer to appear in that role.

Courtesy Wendy Hanson
Stan, author, Stokowski, and Chris at the author's home in Westchester, New York (November 1961)

The magic of the preceding season was lacking. The performance was ragged and the critics were not oblivious. Stoki found the performances of both Nilsson and Tucker "splendid vocally and dramatically," he told Bing, "but some other parts of the performance were far from good. He explained that he needed another full dress rehearsal preceded by several preparatory piano rehearsals. He complained that in the first act when the girls sing "Silencio," the prompter's voice was distinctly heard. "The stage band was extremely ragged in some spots," he complained and suggested that they rehearse in his dressing room before the next performance. He complained too that the Mandarin made many noticeable mistakes and should have additional piano rehearsals.[17]

After the two performances for which he had signed a contract, Stoki resigned. The news was given to the press by the Met and some rather critical comments appeared, to which he replied in an open letter to the *New York Times*, December 17, 1961.

> I have seen what was printed in the *Times* about my not conducting the remaining performances of *Turandot* at the Metropolitan. May I tell you my thoughts about it?
>
> I have enjoyed making music with Nilsson, Tucker, Guarrera and the others, and we are all conscious of the difficulties under which the Metropolitan is performing. I agreed to conduct the first two performances of *Turandot* this season because I knew how difficult it was to open the season at all.
>
> It is true that the Metropolitan, at my request, had one light rehearsal this season to bring the lighting of the first act into conformity with Puccini's directions. We were forced to present *Turandot* with only one full stage rehearsal.
>
> Everybody tried his utmost under these difficult conditions but the performances did not attain the artistic level I insist on for myself, due solely to lack of rehearsal time. As additional stage rehearsals were not possible, I felt obliged to decline to conduct further performances. This was nobody's fault, as my manager, at my request, did not express any dissatisfaction with the quality of the performances.
>
> We all look forward to opera at Lincoln Center, and I am confident that the difficulties of insufficient rehearsal can be overcome there, if some form of subsidy can be arranged from the national government, in addition to support from opera lovers, the city government, the state government, the many foundations and from union funds. If all these six sources were to contribute a share, I am sure the present difficulties could be overcome.
>
> Leopold Stokowski
> New York[18]

Bing seethed. He lost no time in coming to the defense of the Met and in challenging Stokowski. In a letter to the *Times* music editor he wrote:

> I read Leopold Stokowski's letter in your issue of December 17 with great interest. I could not disagree with him more. I do not know how Maestro Stokowski in his few weeks at the Metropolitan gained such a profound insight into the workings of our house.
>
> The fact, however, is that the shortage of rehearsals is not at all due to financial reasons. It is for the same reason that theaters like

Vienna and La Scala which have ample means at their disposal, do not in general rehearse one hour more than we do. . . .

Turandot was last performed during the 1960–61 season on May 30 in Toronto during the Spring tour. It was revived on the second week of this season on November 4 with one orchestra reading, two stage-piano rehearsals and one full-dress rehearsal. With the exception of the tenor, it was the same cast, the same chorus and the same orchestra that had done sixteen performances last season. It was amply rehearsed. . . .

I regret to say that the discrepancies between the orchestra and the chorus and solo singers about which the press justifiably complained were equally apparent in last season's *Turandot* performance, which had more than sufficient rehearsal. The reason for these discrepancies was not lack of rehearsal time.[19]

Irving Kolodin told me that he was awed at how "the amazing stamina of this man asserted itself." Irving told me some of his personal recollections of the original opening night.

"At intermission I went upstairs with my wife to Sherry's and along the way we encountered Rudolf Bing. I made some complimentary remarks and congratulated him on the outcome of the near debacle and to my surprise, he was anything but responsive. In fact he started attacking Stokowski, saying that he was no opera conductor and that he had given him all kinds of trouble during the rehearsals.

"I learned subsequently that a lot of irritation was derived from Stokowski's impatience with the method of rehearsal, which gave priority—even over the music and the people involved—to lighting considerations. The orchestra would be sitting in its place for half an hour doing nothing while someone was arranging the lights. He thought this was amateurish and cursed everybody in sight and soon developed a fine state of animosity toward the production.

"The countercomplaint from the side of management—and what they put him down for—was that he did not give enough cues to the chorus and that his whole attention was focused on the orchestra. Obviously there was no reference to his annoyance at being required to sit there and do nothing for an hour at a time."[20]

It was Stoki who expressed the final word. "I do not think the orchestration is by Puccini; it is by another hand. Whoever made it did not understand the difference between accompanying voices and solo orchestration. At performances, I have as far as I could, held down the volume of sound when the orchestra accompanied solo voices or the chorus. It has been very difficult, because the orchestration is much too thick. Sometimes, one voice is singing on the stage and sixty or seventy instruments in the orchestra are playing the accompaniment. Even if they play pianissimo, their volume and density of sound is too great for one voice. And in *Turandot* the reverse happens. When the orchestra is playing alone, it is too thin; it lacks dramatic power. That has been one great difficulty of conducting *Turandot.*"

Stoki did not find this same difficulty in other Puccini scores. "He never covered solo voices, never covered the chorus. But," he added, "in Puccini's lifetime he could be present whenever his operas were performed and make adjustments. Unfortunately, he died before he finished *Turandot.* . . . I have asked to see Puccini's own handwriting. Then I will see what he wrote, and the difference between him and whoever made the orchestration afterward. . . . I am willing to spend hundreds of hours to try to put that score right, because I feel it is Puccini's greatest opera, a masterpiece."

Stoki was not certain whether it was Alfano or someone else who worked on the orchestration, but in regard to the conclusion, which was indeed the work of Alfano, he said, "There is much less difference between Alfano and Puccini than some people think. Alfano was sensitive; in the last part he mainly used the thematic material of Puccini already heard, and I think he did it very well."[21]

(74)

The American
Symphony Orchestra

S TOKOWSKI was not insensitive to the adulation that he was receiving
so abundantly conducting orchestras during the 1961–62 season. He
did, however, tire of the endless trips he was making. He traveled
alone, and as he approached eighty he began to plan more and more for
ways to remain in New York. For some months we met in small groups
discussing the organization of a new symphony orchestra that would be
Stokowski's own. His manager Siegfried Hearst brought in a porcine
character named Gregory Roberts. Roberts was apparently a man of
considerable wealth—or so some thought—and he indicated that he
would help subsidize the aborning orchestra. He was also reported to be
affiliated with various international concert agencies, particularly in South
America. He invented something called Artists Associates of the Americas, which was supposedly linked with representatives in Buenos Aires,
Santiago, Lima, Quito, Mexico City, Caracas, São Paulo, Montevideo,
and other Latin-American cities. It was under this aegis that the new
symphony was announced.

In the Penthouse Club overlooking Central Park, a large and prestigious press conference was called on April 26, 1962. It was there that
Stokowski laid out his plans. It was to be called the American Symphony
Orchestra and six concerts had been booked in Carnegie Hall for the
1962–63 season. Ticket prices were to be kept low. The American Symphony Orchestra, a nonprofit organization, was being underwritten by a
group of public-spirited citizens "who, for the present, prefer to remain
anonymous," and according to a spokesman for the organization, "the

779

Announcing formation of the American Symphony Orchestra at the Penthouse Club restaurant in New York (1962)

money is already in the bank."[1] That spokesman was obviously Mr. Roberts. Everyone was filled with unquestioning belief in the future of the new organization. Stoki announced that a host of new American scores would be performed and that he planned to have young conductors work with him in apprentice fashion. On May 18, 1962, the incorporation papers for the orchestra were duly signed by Gregory Roberts, Siegfried Hearst, Oliver Daniel, Sophia Yarnall Jacobs, and D. D. Brockman. With all of this heady news, we all went off to our various pursuits while Gregory Roberts and Siegfried Hearst remained to tend the store.

Stoki began to audition young hopefuls at once. Crowds of them gathered in his apartment every day. A group of nervous and anticipant players would assemble in a small room waiting to be called for their audition. There was one young man from Katowice, Poland, who was one of the first to audition, and Stoki engaged him immediately. A twenty-year-old from Graz, Austria, was another to play for him.[2] The first woman chosen was Martha Gerschefski, cellist, who was the daughter of the American composer Edwin Gerschefski. Martha played the first movement of the Dvořák Cello Concerto and sight-read part of *Don Juan*, the *Marriage of Figaro*, and Beethoven's Fifth. "The Maestro is very patient," she said. "I did find reading the manuscript notes a little hard, but he gave me lots of time."[3]

Stoki also contacted old favorites of his, such as violinist Beatrice Brown and other seasoned players who had been with him earlier. "He would audition from morning to night," said Stewart Warkow. "I think he got a kick out of it. It revitalized him. . . . I think it was one of those things that kept him going."[4]

Jean Leslie, who was Stoki's secretarial assistant, recalled those auditions. "Sometimes it would be very funny because we would have a clarinetist in Chris' room, a trombonist in Stan's, and a violinist in the guest room. We had people warming up even in the dining room. The cacophony was great. When they came for their auditions, Maestro would ask them questions about their playing and their instruments. He didn't care about their backgrounds; what he wanted was fresh, new talent that he could mold."[5]

Auditioning Martha Gerschefski. Stokowski designed one-handed wall clock in background (1962)

Courtesy Martha Gerschefski

United Press International Photo
With a Greek royal guard on the Acropolis (1962)

Memos on an almost daily basis were sent to Roberts covering everything from posters placed in shop windows, sponsors and contributors, subsidy for the orchestra, to details about the formation of a chorus to go with it. He outlined his plan for a seminar for student conductors: "Instruction in principle of ensemble, phrasing, orchestral bowing, technique for strings, orchestral breathing technique for wind instruments, balance of dynamics, attack, release, articulation and sforzando."[6] He gave much thought to the establishment of an advisory committee—honorary, of course—which would include Mayor and Mrs. Robert Wagner, Senator and Mrs. Jacob Javits, Ralph Bunche, Adlai Stevenson, Jackie Kennedy, Eleanor Roosevelt, Avery Claflin, and numerous others. He felt confident that everything was progressing in good order, and with that he set out for his annual visit to Europe.

Stoki and his two boys went first to Geneva to stay with Lyuba, and from there they traveled to Venice and then to Athens, where they were joined by Faye and Natasha. Lyuba arrived later just before Stoki's concert in the Herod Atticus Theatre below the Acropolis.[7] They explored the Acropolis and the other Athenian antiquities; Stoki was photographed with a towering evzone. They rented a car and set out for Delphi, stopping overnight at the monastery of Osios Loukas, which is adjacent to a magnificent Byzantine church on the slopes of Mount Phocis. Stan remembered that it was "very mysterious." In spite of being on crutches, Stoki did manage to scramble up part of the steep hill to the Temple of Apollo in Delphi. From there the travelers wound their way to Corinth, where they began a two-day boat trip visiting Delos, Mykonos, and other Greek islands.

After their brief tour they stayed at the very modern tourist hotel, Hotel Mont Parnes, thirty-five miles north of Athens on the side of the mountain. He sent a large picture postcard of the hotel with the message: "Affectionate greetings from beautiful Greece. Home soon." It was signed "Leopold, Stan and Chris." Their next stop was Rome, where he conducted the Santa Cecilia Orchestra with great success. It was in Rome that he received disturbing news concerning Mr. Roberts. Until then he had been spared information about distressing developments involving the American Symphony Orchestra.

At some point in midsummer, Gregory Roberts did a disappearing act as complete as that of any prestidigitator. However, to the annoyance of Stokowski and everyone connected with the infant American Symphony his flimflams surfaced. Without any authorization, Roberts opened several bank accounts in his name and that of the American Symphony Orchestra. Technically, the official name was the American Symphony Orchestra, Inc. The *Inc.* is a very important point. The official account required that two signatures be necessary to issue a check. Roberts had received various sums from people he pretended to represent. In Kansas City, he had conductor Hans Schwieger cash a check for him in the amount of $2,000 and in Chicago he paid a hotel bill of $460 with a check: both checks bounced.[8] Bills from various restaurants continued to come in. Money sent by subscribers seemed to wind up in Mr. Roberts' accounts. One irate sponsor, who had sent a check for $1,000 and was to receive box seats for all of the six planned concerts, complained that she had never received the tickets she had ordered. A photostat of the canceled check revealed that it had been deposited in Roberts' defunct account.

Through NBC's International Facilities, it was learned that Roberts had booked the American Symphony Orchestra with Stokowski for a series of three concerts for Radio Caracas. Fortunately, no money had been exchanged.[9]

Before Stoki's return, we had a series of meetings with all of the board members who were available during the summer to try to straighten out some of the mess. Roberts had engaged a young assistant, a volatile young Cuban, who refused to produce any of the books or accounts that Roberts had left behind. At one meeting he fell to his knees, with his arms outstretched like Christ in the Andes, proclaiming his loyalty to Roberts. But the books for the time being were carefully hidden.

Before returning from Europe, Stoki contacted Stewart Warkow, asking him to become the new manager of the orchestra; upon his return, he and the board elected attorney Leonard Carson to become president of the board. It was a fortunate move, and Carson handled the vexing problems with great skill and contacted the district attorney of New York County, Frank S. Hogan, explaining the whole intricate con game that had been perpetrated.[10]

Stewart Warkow recalled that during the summer while he was "in beautiful downtown Orkney Springs, Virginia," where the American Symphony Orchestra League was conducting a managerial conference, he received a cable from Stokowski asking him to meet him when his boat was docked—which Stewart did. "We tried to piece things together and discovered that Roberts had disappeared with what everybody thought were the funds, but there really wasn't much money that he had taken. He had bounced some bad checks and made an awful lot of promises that were embarrassing to Stoki, who was now faced with a decision—whether he would conduct the series in Carnegie Hall, which had been committed and advertised, or not. Tickets were being sold and the orchestra, for all intents and purposes, had been engaged. . . . I drew up a budget and arrived at a reasonable amount that would have to be raised. It turned out that Stoki felt honor bound to do it . . . in the end he coughed up fifty or fifty-five thousand dollars himself."[11]

The most urgent need was to develop a committee of patrons and sponsors, and Stoki asked the assistance of David and Elizabeth Brockman, who lived in the same building a few floors below him. "After that first period when Roberts did his mischief and ran off," said David, "Stoki asked us whether we would help in getting people who could afford to substantially provide the funds necessary for the establishment of the symphony. We told him that we would certainly try, and two of our very close friends were Mr. and Mrs. Samuel Rubin."[12]

This contact with the Rubins was to become one of the most significant in the development of the orchestra. An impressive list of sponsors and patrons was assembled, including ASCAP, BMI, CBS President Frank Stanton, Mr. and Mrs. O. Roy Chalk, Clairol, Inc., Mr. and Mrs. Hans Hoffmann, Charles Revson, the Rubins, Countess Sonia P. Seherr-Thoss, and Princess Alexis Zalstem-Zalessky. These were on a partial list that was assembled for one of the earliest mailings to prospective sponsors.

In spite of all of the various problems, the orchestra did come into being. The first American Symphony Orchestra concert took place on the evening of October 15, 1962, in Carnegie Hall. The atmosphere was festive and the hall was completely filled. The program included works by Gabrieli, Bach, Beethoven, and Shostakovich. In addition to the New York music lovers who turned out, there was a large contingent from Philadelphia. The soloist for the evening was the young Philadelphia-born pianist Susan Starr, who had been one of the prize winners in Moscow's Tchaikovsky Competition. The *Philadelphia Evening Bulletin* sent up its critic, James Felton, who described the event. "Leopold Stokowski, one of the all-time great conductors, and one of the few remaining musical giants of his own generation, presented his newly formed American Symphony Orchestra . . . for the first time last night . . . the event was a landmark in the history of music in America."

Felton wrote that at the conclusion of the concert "hundreds of admirers thronged backstage through police lines to pay homage to the frosty-maned idol of the musical world. Without a trace of his famous temperament, Stokowski responded by greeting them with the calm and simplicity of a man who knows he has done his work well and successfully —and for a very long time. But even in a long lifetime of trail-blazing victories, without a doubt last night provided Stokowski with one of his finest hours. . . ."[13]

It became evident that the new American Symphony Orchestra had caught on for another sell-out audience congregated for its second concert. It began with the Fifteenth Symphony *("Thesis")* of Henry Cowell and concluded with Hindemith's *Mathis der Maler* with Wagner and Tchaikovsky in between. "The magician of sound," wrote Louis Biancolli, "was back on the Carnegie Hall podium. . . . A huge audience, fascinated by conductor, orchestra and program alike, gave the performance of the four listed numbers a rousing reception. Stokowski and his brand of music-making are higher than ever in concert-goers affections. . . . So powerfully was the tension maintained last night, so shrewdly timed every stroke of rhythm and dynamics, that many in the crowd began applauding and cheering before the performance ended."[14]

Miles Kastendieck was equally ecstatic:

"Music as an emotional force surged through Carnegie Hall last night. The American Symphony Orchestra became the medium of its expression. The audience will cherish the memory of its exhilaration. . . . It takes the magic of a Stokowski to produce such miracles of performance.

"The electrifying effect of the conductor became as interesting to watch as to hear. The new orchestra has responded to his technical resourcefulness and follows his leadership in hawk-like fashion. As he draws out the music in them, the performances radiate all the ardor within him.

"These American Symphony Orchestra concerts may steal the whole musical show this season if the remainder can match the vibrant quality of this second event."[15]

"Have Baton, Will Travel" was Winthrop Sargeant's headline in *The New Yorker.* "He exerts a unique personal force," he wrote, "and a feeling of indomitable authority communicates itself to an orchestra in such a manner that the musicians are swept along into doing things that one would hardly think possible. Just how it all happens is hard to say. Perhaps the secret lies in his dramatic, insistent gestures, perhaps in some sort of hypnotic power. At any rate, of all the conductors now before the public he most deserves the appellation 'virtuoso.' "[16]

On Stoki's third program he made a great exception in his practice of playing transcriptions. Other than his own, he almost never did them. For this program he included Ernest Ansermet's superbly beautiful arrangements of Debussy's *Six Épigraphes Antiques,* and by good fortune Ansermet himself was in the audience. Stoki also included Frank Martin's *Petite Symphonie Concertante* with Sylvia Marlow playing the harpsichord.

After the performance of the *Épigraphes,* Stoki turned to the audience, saying, "We would like to thank Maestro Ansermet for his beautiful and creative orchestrations." He then pointed to the first tier box, where Ansermet rose to accept the sincere applause that a deeply moved audience gave him.[17]

The orchestra was now getting more than local interest as articles about it began appearing in the London press, as well as on the pages of the various international magazines. *Time* magazine called Stokowski's reading of the Debussy *Six Epigraphs* "haunting and evocative," the Brahms Second Symphony "relaxed and singing," and the *Petite Symphonie Concertante* "beautifully articulated. . . . Stokowski led his 95 musicians with surgically precise gestures of the hand, the long, scythelike sweeps of the arm that are as familiar to concertgoers as the white-maned profile." Questioned on how he could obtain such a high professional gloss with such a new orchestra Stoki replied: "It's a misunderstanding that an orchestra must be together for a long time; some orchestras have been together for a century and still cannot play well."[18]

On March 11, 1963, Stokowski conducted a performance of the *St. Matthew Passion* that was memorable if only because he had as his soprano soloist a young singer, Beverly Sills. He had auditioned her earlier when he was planning to do *Carmina Burana.* "I was very pregnant at the time. I wanted to sing for him because the baby was supposed to be born on July 25 and I thought we would have plenty of time. So when I went to sing for Mr. Stokowski, I was rather large already and he had just heard an awful lot of sopranos—all of whom he turned down. I remember him telling me about the lady who had just left. He had said to her: 'Can you sing a high D pianissimo?' And the woman said to him, 'Mr. Stokowski, I couldn't sing a high D pianissimo for God!' " Beverly said laughingly. "And he persisted, saying, 'Can you sing it for me?' I won't tell you the woman's name because she's really quite well known. . . . And as I walked in he stared at me and said, 'Do you practice breathing exercises?' And I thought he had said 'breeding exercises' and I looked at him and stared at my stomach and said, 'Obviously!' He looked at me and laughed and said, 'No, my dear, breathing—breathing. It's good for the baby.' So that was my introduction to him. . . . I didn't do it with him but he remembered the audition and some time later he called me to sing with him and the American Symphony Orchestra. It was a Bach piece, none of which I can remember now or which Bach piece it was." And at this point in our phone conversation I could hear her ask her husband,

Rehearsing with the BBC Symphony Orchestra, London (1963)

"What Bach piece was it?" And she returned saying: "The St. Matthew Passion—just that little piece." There was more wonderful Sills laughter. "He made drastic cuts in it and I said the public would be very upset. And he wrote back saying he didn't think the public would know. Then I wrote him that I thought God would be very upset and he said that he thought God would forgive him. And then I wrote him that I thought Bach would be very upset.[19] 'From your delightful letter,' he wrote, 'I fear you are not satisfied with these inspired pieces of music by Bach. When I meet him in heaven, I will tell him about your 'frustration' and I am sure he will be deeply sorry, because he is such a naive man (although a genius). I hope you will pardon him and me.' "[20]

Apart from the regular announced series of concerts, Stokowski collaborated with the Fédération Internationale des Jeunesses Musicales, which was being sponsored by the Carnegie Hall Corporation. He introduced two young soloists who have since become major performing artists: Ruth Laredo and Lynn Harrell. Both young artists acquitted themselves magnificently; Miss Laredo did the First Piano Concerto of Mendelssohn, and Harrell the Boccherini Cello Concerto in B-flat.

"I was very, very young and naturally I had heard about him all my life and it was quite a thrill just to be in the same room with him," Ruth recalled. During one of the rehearsals when she was playing with great concentration, she remembered that after quite a long stretch of playing on her own she realized that he had stopped the orchestra without her realizing it. "I stopped playing, feeling a little embarrassed, and he made an announcement in his inimitable fashion, terribly courteous and aristocratic. He said, 'That, ladies and gentlemen, is concentration.' "[21]

On April 15, the season ended on a deeply emotional note. President Kennedy sent greetings, which were delivered by August Heckscher, the White House consultant on the arts. Heckscher described the ensemble as a "young symphony that has added new luster to these old walls." And when he added: "May the sound of its music be here for many years to come," the audience burst into applause and cheers. Stoki too expressed appreciation at the conclusion of its moving performance of Brahms' Fourth Symphony, saying to the audience: "We hope you will continue to be with us next season. And now we would like to express our thanks in music." Thereupon he led the orchestra in Bach's "Little" Fugue in G Minor.

The mayor's congratulations were conveyed by Robert Dowling, the city's cultural officer. He also presented the city's Handel Medal to

Stokowski.[22] "It would be more appropriate to call it the Ives Medal," Stoki remarked to me later.

In the back of the printed program it was announced that Stokowski would include symphonies such as Beethoven's Seventh, Mahler's Tenth, Shostakovich's Fifth, Sibelius' Second, Haydn's *Miracle,* Tchaikovsky's Fourth, Brahms' First, and the Sinfonia Concertante in E-flat of Mozart. Prokofiev's *Alexander Nevsky* and music by Barber, Bartók, Britten, Ives, Kodály, Schoenberg, Stravinsky, Vaughan Williams, and other contemporary composers would also be included.

Board meetings after the end of the season were not postmortems but very active planning sessions. Cyma Rubin was added to the board and she quickly became a driving force. The deficit for this first season amounted to a mere $13,389.40. The Rubins were tireless in planning events to dramatize the orchestra and win new patrons.

Sam was intrigued that Stoki at the age of eighty would embark on a project as vast as starting a new symphony orchestra and at first doubted that it could be done. Isaac Stern cautioned that it would take ten years to do so, but at the end of the first season he thought otherwise. "So I started some nominal contribution for the second year," Sam recalled. The contribution was more than nominal. It amounted to $100,000 each year for the next decade and this did not include the numerous lavish events and parties that the Rubins funded. "It may sound important to you," said Sam, "but actually the dollars that we invested in the Symphony don't loom that important to us because we were more interested in what he would produce in the music world. . . . I feel that having provided the platform for Stoki where he had an orchestra that he alone built may well have added better than ten or fifteen years to his life."[23]

The new season, 1963–64, was expanded to eight concerts, and at the outset the skill of Cyma Rubin as an entrepreneur was most evident. The opening concert on October 7 was arranged as a tribute to the United Nations and 112 flags colorfully decorated the stage.

The pattern had been set, and the opening of each succeeding season was a colorful U.N. salute. New and wealthy sponsors became interested and the orchestra came to be regarded as a permanent addition to New York's musical life. Cyma ambitiously tried to expand the activities of the orchestra beyond its regular season. With a burst of imagination, she proposed that the orchestra initiate a series of free concerts to be given for New York's schoolchildren.[24]

Photo Whitestone/Courtesy International Leopold Stokowski Society
Sam and Cyma Rubin, American Symphony Orchestra backers, welcoming UN delegates
after concert in tribute to the United Nations. Author in background (c. 1963)

Anything to do with children always delighted Stokowski, and he was
happy to go along with the idea. It was also of interest in that his young

apprentice conductors might have a chance to conduct the orchestra and be heard in New York. His carefully chosen group rotated, and it included young men who later became distinguished conductors. They were David Katz, José Serebrier, Ainslee Cox, Joseph Eger, and Matthias Bamert.

"I was the associate conductor from the beginning," said David Katz. "I helped him with all of the auditions and getting personnel together at the beginning. In addition, I was not only associate conductor, I was the personnel manager from the inception in 1962. After I became the associate conductor, he decided to add another one and then still another."[25]

Stokowski knew José Serebrier as a composer and he welcomed him as one of his associates. "I was only 21 when I began to work with him. He would always call us 'Maestro.' I think he may have done this for several reasons: so he wouldn't have to remember our names, or to make us develop self-respect and self-importance, or perhaps to make up for the lack of salary. . . . I think he reasoned that if he wasn't receiving any salary . . . we shouldn't either.

With animals used for a children's concert by the American Symphony Orchestra (c. 1965)

Photo Whitestone

"When he organized his teenage concerts, he decided to conduct the first and last numbers, and each of us would conduct all the middle works. I had always used a baton. During one of the concerts I had an accident. I hurt myself with the baton and Stokowski said, 'I told you so.' But in any case, I learned enormously; I learned how he could be such a great artist in the nineteenth-century sense—complete with élan and imagination—and also be the most businesslike conductor in rehearsals."[26]

Joseph Eger was an expert horn player and had worked under Stokowski numerous times. "Maybe the most important thing he had was a sense of drama and of sound. . . . He had a depth, a kind of sensuality that somehow conveyed itself to the orchestra, which achieved a velvety, rich, dark Stokowski sound."[27]

Ainslee Cox was twenty-six when he arrived in New York in 1962 from Austin, Texas, and attended the first concert of the American Symphony Orchestra: "It was a kind of revelation for me because, first off, I wasn't sure he was still alive. I had grown up with *Fantasia*. I had known about his activities in Houston, but I really didn't know what had happened to him. Suddenly there he was giving an absolutely magnificent concert.

"In the printed program was a message saying that the American Symphony Orchestra had been founded to give opportunities to young players and young conductors. The next day I wrote him a note addressed to Carnegie Hall and said, in effect, that I was a conductor newly arrived in New York, and asked just what he intended to do. The next day or so there came a letter signed by Jean Leslie which said, 'Dear Mr. Cox, please phone this number.' I didn't know any Jean Leslie at all. So I called and said, 'This is Ainslee Cox,' and I heard her say, 'Maestro,' and a voice said, 'Ah-llo.' It was only then that I realized who it had to be."

After a short conversation Stoki invited Ainslee to visit him, which he did. Stoki was impressed by the young man and called to Stewart Warkow, whose office was the Stokowski dining room at the time, and introduced him to Ainslee, saying that he would come to his rehearsals to watch and listen. "He did try to do what he could for young conductors. He set up a kind of seminar where we could come and meet each other and talk. . . . There were about four or five of us. . . . But at these sessions Stokowski avoided all questions that were about music specifics. If someone said, 'I'm going to do the *Freischutz* Overture—how do you do this spot in it?' he would say, 'How do you do it?' and they were forced to tell him what *they* would do. Ultimately it came down to: 'If that is the way it works for you, that's the way to do it.'"

From this pool of young aspirants, Stoki selected those he considered most gifted and they would remain a few years as assistant conductors with the American Symphony Orchestra. He preferred to rotate them, and by the time Ainslee was appointed, Serebrier, Katz, and Eger had all moved to orchestras of their own. "Of the newer ones," said Ainslee, "there were two whom I thought were really quite outstanding. One was Judith Somogi and the other was Matthias Bamert."[28]

Swiss-born Matthias Bamert had won a scholarship to work with George Szell in Cleveland. He and his wife sailed in the fall of 1969 on the *Queen Elizabeth* to start a new life in the States. He described the trip as boring, but on looking over the passenger list, he noted the name Stokowski. Before the trip was over, they had met, and a year later he became one of Stoki's assistants.

"I only knew him as an old man," Bamert responded when I asked him how he regarded Stokowski. "There were moments of greatness and moments when he just was an old man. But the moments of greatness were so great that anything that was not always great could easily be forgotten."[29]

It was during the second season of the American Symphony Orchestra that Stoki was approached by the president of Bryn Mawr College to speak on the making of orchestras. He was pleased by the invitation and on February 4, 1963, he set out for Philadelphia. On the train, in what seemed an entirely fortuitous meeting, he encountered his longtime and dear friend Sophie Jacobs. Surprised at seeing her on the train, he was equally surprised and pleased when he learned that she was coming to Bryn Mawr to hear him speak. What he did not know at the moment was that Sophie was actually, by prearrangement, to introduce him before his lecture.

At Bryn Mawr, Sophie told the assembled group that she was one of the few women who belonged to his past "in an innocent way." She told of episodes that had occurred fifty years earlier, when as a child, she and her sister had played cops and robbers with him in Rittenhouse Square. She also told about visiting him in the hospital immediately after he had broken his hip when he was studying the score of *Turandot* and heard with incredulity that he would conduct it some six weeks later. "But he did," she said, "and these two stories tell you a great deal about this man: one, that he was sensitive and aware and tender, and the other, that he had a devotion to his work and a discipline of himself that has made him what he is today—Mr. Stokowski."[30]

Stoki responded graciously. "I was asked by the president of this college to speak about the making of orchestras. Fortunately, it's a very simple subject. All you need are one hundred really good players, a really good conductor, a really good hall in which to play the concerts and rehearsals, and a great city back of the orchestra which is proud of it and supports it. That's the end of the lecture."

After considerable laughter, Stokowski continued saying that those four things were often difficult to achieve. He spoke of the requisites of a conductor, that he must be able not only to read a score and beat time but that he must have a quality which he called X. He said it was something both psychological and partly physical but which he felt could not be analyzed.

"The spirit of the music is the important thing—not the mere physical notes. . . . So we are going into a period where the performance level may go down, anyway for a time. You will, I think, notice if you remember what I am now saying that during the next ten years there will be greater deficits, more performances, and to some extent fatigue on the part of the players, and to some extent mechanical perfection without that inner spiritual message which is the essential and deep thing of music—mystery, imagination, impulsiveness—all the things that . . . you value and regard as . . . the most important part of musical experience. . . ."[31] When asked about *musique concrète* and electronic music he opined: "Every form of music, of painting, of sculpture, of drama, of all the arts should be cultivated and those who are interested in those forms should express themselves and create in those forms. Then, in the long run, it is for humanity to decide. Do they find it interesting? Does it say something to them or does it not? They will make the final answer. . . ."[32]

One audience member asked: "What direction would you like to see contemporary music go?" He replied that it should express our feelings of life today—"something which is universal, which is of all time and all space. It should go in many directions. It depends on the composer, on his sense of creation, of his feeling about music and life. There should be no restrictions. Nobody should tell him what to do or what not to do. He should be free. Just as we have freedom of thought, freedom of speech —so we should have freedom of composition."[33]

To the final question, which was whether there was one city about which he could feel that he would rather conduct there than any other place, he replied with gusto: "Yes. Philadelphia!" There was much laughter and applause. He then added: "May I ask a question? Which is the best tavern in Bryn Mawr?"[34]

(75)

The Ives
Fourth Symphony

*I*N 1955 BMI received a request from the Southwest German Radio for the score and parts of the complete Fourth Symphony of Charles Ives. Elliott Carter had talked to Hans Rosbaud, who wanted to conduct it with his orchestra. As early as 1954 I had acquired the second movement, which Cowell had published in his New Music Edition, for BMI's subsidiary, Associated Music Publishers, and later the first and fourth, which were controlled by the American Composer's Alliance. The third movement, the fugue, had been published by Peer International as part of the First String Quartet. On looking through the copies of the fourth movement, which had been placed with the American Composer's Alliance, several pages appeared to be missing. Lou Harrison and Henry Cowell, who had reconstructed part of the *Robert Browning* Overture, began exploring ways of conjecturally restoring the missing pages.[1] Later it was claimed that the originals were all safely resting in Redding, but no one came forth with that information at the time. By sheer accident, copies of the missing pages were discovered among some loose miscellaneous pages and the work of decoding the almost illegible manuscript began.[2]

The editors at Associated Music Publishers were not enthusiastic at the time, and I might correctly say that they were almost hostile; they pointed out that it would be a very expensive project and the publishing budget could not afford it. I discussed all of this with Leopold, and at a meeting of the Contemporary Music Society we elected to make a donation toward the expenses of preparation. Theodore Seder, curator of the Fleisher

Collection of the Free Library of Philadelphia, had taken over the problem of deciphering and editing the last movement, and it was to him our contribution of $2,000 was made.

Having programmed the Fourth Symphony twice before, and having been foiled by the lack of a completed score and parts, Stoki discussed the idea of doing it during the 1964–65 season. "Thank you for your kindness in sending the tape of Ives' Robert Browning Overture," he wrote. "Now we must try to put Ives' Fourth Symphony in order, rehearse it and perform it. . . ."[3]

I sent a copy of Stoki's letter along with a memo to Leonard Feist, who was then managing head of Associated Music Publishers, urging him to "please keep at this project so that something eventually can be done. In November it will have been with AMP a mere nine years."[4] My sarcasm helped light a little fire. Kurt Stone, then editor in chief of Associated Music Publishers, wrote an explanatory note to Feist on the status of the publication. About the first movement he wrote that "production of a legible score from the manuscript will begin under Ted Seder's direction in about 3 weeks." My only observation was that it should have begun nine years earlier. The second and third movements were completed and parts extracted. Of the fourth movement Stone wrote: "Ted Seder tells me that shortly after he, Henry Cowell, and I had made decisions about the last remaining problems of the score, Stokowski asked for a copy. . . . He offered to make some practical suggestions for the best possible method of notating the parts. A couple of years went by. Then Stokowski sent the score back without suggestions because he had simply not been able to find time to do the work. . . ."[5]

Ted Seder and his able assistant, Romulus Franceschini, in conjunction with Ronald Herder, who had taken over as editor for Associated Music Publishers, managed to have all the materials ready in ample time before the rehearsals were to begin.[6] It was evident that in order to perform the difficult work many extra rehearsals would be necessary, and the American Symphony Orchestra budget simply had no provision for such an expenditure. Norman Lloyd, another Ives fancier, was with the Rockefeller Foundation and listened to my request for aid with welcome sympathy. They announced on February 20 in the *New York Times* that the Rockefeller Foundation would underwrite the expense of six extra rehearsals.[7] This and other stories that appeared began to arouse great curiosity among the public. There seemed something almost mystical about the first performance of a masterwork that had lain unplayed for nearly half a century.

Theodore Seder, Stokowski, Henry Cowell, and author at press conference in Voisin restaurant before the world premiere of the Ives Fourth Symphony with American Symphony Orchestra (1965)

Rehearsals began as far back as February for the forthcoming premiere on April 26, 1965. There was such great interest among musicians, critics, in fact, all of the musical confraternity, that Stoki decided to open the rehearsals to them. The news spread by a sort of grapevine process. There was no public announcement, but the floor of Carnegie was like a *Who's Who* in music.

In the Carnegie Hall program books for all of the concerts preceding the Ives premiere, there appeared an essay on it by Stokowski himself. He had given much time to its preparation and was very pleased with the result. In it he said: "Ives' music is a self-portrait in sound, revealing his complex personality, and the many facets of his mind and imagination. It is sometimes based on New England folk and religious music, but foremost is his vision of the evolution of music so far ahead of his time and environment. . . .

"Ives' musical philosophy is complex, but is in no sense rhythmic or harmonic anarchy. In all his music there is a basic rhythmic pulsation, and a controlling tonality.

"His Fourth Symphony is the most uncompromising expression of his revolutionary ideas in complex counterpoint, flexible melodic lines, polyrhythm and polytonality. . . .

"The universality of Ives' mind regarding music was eloquently expressed when he wrote: 'The future of music may not lie entirely with music itself, but rather in the way in which music makes itself a part with —in the way it encourages and extends, rather than limits, the aspirations and the ideals of the people—the finer things that humanity does and dreams of.' "[8]

To prompt the press and give the critics some idea of the complications of the score and the various involvements of its preparation, a press conference was called for 5:00 P.M. on April 12 at the Voisin, one of New York's most exclusive and elegant restaurants. In Stoki's invitation telegram, he said he would like to have the opportunity to talk about the unique technical difficulties of the Ives Fourth.[9] I chaired the conference, and in addition to Stokowski's very impressive talk, remarks were made by Henry Cowell, Ted Seder, and others involved in the preparation of the score.

The public interest in Ives and Stokowski's performance of the Fourth Symphony was enormous. Reports from the box office were that it would be a complete sellout. On the day of the concert, I was entertaining a group of representatives from various foreign licensing agencies which controlled composer's and publisher's performance rights. I was taking them through BMI and showing the methods used in logging performances and ultimately paying both the composers and publishers. After giving them what I called "the 25-cent tour" we arranged for a number of limousines to take them to the Columbia-Princeton Electronic Center. We drove from our office on Fifth Avenue over to Sixth Avenue and turned left on 57th Street. We noticed immediately that a long line extended from the entrance of Carnegie Hall all the way to Sixth Avenue and around the corner. It was an exciting sight and I explained that the line was made up of people who wanted to hear Stokowski conduct the Ives Symphony. While all were interested in Stokowski, I don't think any of them had ever heard of Ives. Naturally all wanted to attend the concert and we had to find ways to squeeze them in. What I had not known was that the line was not to hear Ives, but to hear Horowitz, whose recital was to take place on May 9, and tickets went on sale that morning.

There was an air of excitement in Carnegie Hall the night of the concert. It was packed to capacity, and although not apparent if one looked at the rather dressy audience in the boxes and on the main floor, there was an outpouring of long-haired and bearded young hippie types and young girls in sweaters and jeans. They, too, were there to discover Ives and applaud Stokowski.

The program began with Wagner's *Flying Dutchman* Overture, followed by the Sibelius "Swan of Tuonela." Then the Ives. I do not remember any more rapt audience. They seemed to want to follow Ives' dictum: "The aesthetic program of the work is that of the searching questions of 'What?' and 'Why?' which the spirit of man asks of life."[10] Stoki achieved a sense of mysticism in the impressionistic Prelude, which softly introduced a small chorus singing "Watchman Tell Us of the Night." David Katz was placed at the back of the orchestra, from where he conducted the chorus and other odd rhythmic sections. José Serebrier was at Stoki's side to perform a similar function when sections played entirely different rhythmic lines.

In the second movement all hell broke loose in one of the most glorious swirls of cacophony, with ordered and disordered confusion, that ever rocked the walls of Carnegie. It was a feast of polyrhythms, polytonality, and as critic Harriett Johnson observed, other "polys" as well. "Yankee Doodle," "Columbia the Gem of the Ocean," "Nearer, My God to Thee," "Marching through Georgia," and other tunes were piled up one above the other.[11]

Ives had described the second movement not as a scherzo but rather as a comedy "in which an exciting, easy, and wordly progress through life is contrasted with the trials of the Pilgrims in their journey through the swamp. The occasional slow episodes—Pilgrim's hymns—are constantly crowded out and overwhelmed by the former. The dream, or fantasy, ends with an interruption of reality—the Fourth of July in Concord—brass bands, drum corps, etc."

At the conclusion of the movement, a few joyous whoops and shouts erupted from the balconies like Mexicans shouting an appreciative "Olé" in the bullring.

Ives had described the third movement, a short hymnlike fugue, as the second answer to the first movement and "an expression of the reaction of life into formalism and ritualism." The last movement, marked "Very Slowly, *Largo Maestoso*," was, so Ives explained "an apotheosis of the preceding content, in terms that have something to do with the reality of existence and its religious experience."[12] It was that sense which

Stokowski so nobly achieved, and something which I have found lacking in nearly all of the subsequent performances I have heard by other conductors. It was Stokowski's holistic approach that gave it its sense of expansion and grandeur.

At the conclusion of the work there were wild bursts of applause and cheers. A surge of young people rushed down the aisles toward the stage. Stokowski at eighty-three was experiencing one of the greatest ovations of his entire career, and it was indeed one of the most deeply felt. After the first round of applause, he turned to speak to the audience. He began by saying that "tonight we are honoring one of America's greatest artists." He proceeded to describe the difficulties involved in performance and praised the efforts of all who had been involved in the preparation of the score. As he called upon Ted Seder to take a bow, there was a rasping sneeze coming from the balcony. "That's not in the score," Stoki said tartly. There was an immediate burst of friendly laughter and applause. Then, after thanking the orchestra, he announced that the symphony would soon be recorded by Columbia Records.[13]

The following morning Stoki received a note from Ives' business partner Julian Myrick. "I just wanted to write you a note to say how much I appreciated and enjoyed the performance last night of Charles Ives' Fourth Symphony. . . . I even participated to the extent of the *sneeze* which was mentioned by yourself and also in the New York Times this morning . . ."[14]

Critics were exultant. "Above everything," wrote Miles Kastendieck, "towered Mr. Stokowski, as individual a conductor as Ives a composer. His creative spark kindled the orchestra to spirited performance. Together they made the evening significant as well as historical."[15]

One of the longest and most penetratingly perceptive reviews was that of Glenn Gould in *High Fidelity/Musical America.* After disclaiming his less than proper qualifications as an Ivesian, he proceeded to analyze and dissect the symphony with consummate expertise. He praised Ives' "precognitive ability—an ability to intercept the psychic transmissions of his age and to crystallize in this art something of the turbulent metamorphosis which was taking place just before World War I." After his lengthy discussion he turned his attention to the conductor. "Leopold Stokowski's performance was a marvel of identification with the score. He is surely made for such music, or it for him, as the case may be, and one can recall again the debt which we owe to this superb artist, who has so often led us into an encounter with the great and/or problematic works of our age."[16]

Stoki read the review with great interest and wrote to Gould.

> Thank you for your brilliant, penetrating, and witty article about the Ives Fourth Symphony. I wish I had your talents for finding *le mot juste*. I have so much difficulty trying to find words which describe some subtle aspects of Music. I sometimes suspect that the words for which I am looking are not even in the biggest Dictionary. As words gradually became in use from Cavemen until Civilization (!) it might be that only the things, ideas, and emotions for which most people have created words—that these words will find their way into Dictionaries. But as the most mysterious and elusive elements in the Arts are only discerned by a small minority, no words are created to express these rare perceptions.[17]

The concert was sponsored by Mr. and Mrs. Pierre Schlumberger, and following the program they gave an elaborate champagne reception for Stokowski in their Sutton Place apartment. The *New York Herald Tribune* sent a society reporter who dutifully listed names of the guests, including Mr. Sigismund von Braun, the German ambassador to the United Nations, French ambassador Herve Alphand and Mrs. Alphand, Mme. Lucia Davidova, Mme. Eugenia Delarova, Mrs. Sophia Yarnall Jacobs, Carol Truax, Mr. and Mrs. Leonard Bernstein, and Mr. Igor Stravinsky.[18] It was usually meticulously correct, so one does not question the old *Herald Tribune*. But that Stravinsky was there seems questionable. That he did hear the Fourth of Ives we know, but whether he was at this performance seems unlikely, for someone else would surely have observed him. I certainly did not see him. But Stravinsky was aware. He sagely wrote: "Few conductors can have done as much as Stokowski to gain a hearing for new music, and now, in his eighties, he has crowned his achievements by his patient preparation and performance of that astounding work, the Fourth Symphony of Ives. No conductor has been as good an orchestra-builder, either, and from basic sticks and stones to chromium plate. For better or worse, the tricks he taught still survive (along with the popular image of conducting as a kind of legerdemain) as, for example, the way cello sections stagger their bowing in the *Tristan* Prelude to produce a smooth and consistent *crescendo*."[19]

One of the comments that Stoki prized most was a letter from John Kirkpatrick.

As an old friend of Ives, may I thank you from the bottom of my heart for your magnificent performance of the 4th Symphony. The Cowells brought me to the party of the Schlumbergers', but I didn't get a chance to tell you what a wonderful clarification you brought to Ives's music. He was a deeply loyal and appreciative person, and those of us who knew him literally cannot thank you enough to make up for the way he would have wanted to thank you. . . .

John then added an apology for not having identified one of the hymns that Ives had used, particularly in the clarinet phrase before the end of the fugue. It was a quote from the chorus of the old revival hymn "I Hear Thy Welcome Voice." John wrote further:

It's a hymn Ives was very fond of. He told me: "You won't find it in many hymnals—it's too good."

Having long been at Cornell University, way up; in upstate New York, it has been far too many years since I've heard you conduct, and you may be amused at my strongest impression—that, besides being a great artist, you're really a teacher. You do everything in such a way as to help them,—simply, clearly, precisely, directly, inspiringly.[20]

It was written in the West Side Airlines Terminal as John was waiting to return to Ithaca.

The recording of the Ives was done immediately after the performance. And thereby hangs a curious tale—one of imperception and one of perception. Early in December of 1964 on a plane trip to Washington, I talked to Goddard Lieberson about the Ives work and tried to interest him in recording it. Goddard, I knew, had been one of the early Ives enthusiasts. I wrote to Goddard in mid-February 1965 pointing out the advantage of $10,000 worth of rehearsals and a polished performance that would be impossible to achieve at a later time.[21] He responded, thanking me for calling it to his attention and added that "John McClure tells me that he has been interested in this for some time and is in touch with the publishers. I assume, then, that it is under consideration and that, if things come out right, something can be done about it."[22]

Columbia, at a time when William Paley was announcing to his stockholders millions of dollars in corporate profits, was not inclined to pay for the recording of the Ives masterpiece without subsidy. I turned then to the Naumberg Foundation, which has done so much noble work in aiding music projects. I knew most of the members of the board, and some were good friends and colleagues, but they demurred. They suggested that the matter be tabled until a later date. The imperception of that decision was, to me, so shortsighted that I decided to look elsewhere. I spoke to Sam Rubin. He agreed to sponsor the recording, and on each disc credit is given to the Samuel Rubin Foundation. As I recalled, the amount he advanced was in the neighborhood of $22,000, and when I asked Sam about the sum he replied: "Whatever was required at the time. I don't remember." When I again repeated the figure, he said: "I shouldn't be surprised, but then, as you know, in consideration for that we had the honor of seeing our name on the label of the record. We were very pleased to have had the privilege to participate in it because it was an historic thing. . . . Generally there is always a catalyst for anything that's done. In creating the new symphony orchestra, Stoki was the catalyst. With the Ives recording, we were the catalyst in having encouraged more Ives music to be played during that period and thereafter."[23]

Like the live audience, the record listeners showed an equal curiosity and interest. The record immediately went on the top of the lists compiled by *Billboard* and other commercial record publications. Critics were as enthusiastic for the recorded version as they had been for its concert performance.

An interesting counterpoint developed in the opinion of two English reviewers. "Of all Ives's remarkable and almost aggressively original works, perhaps none is more extraordinary than this fourth symphony," wrote Robert Henderson in London's *Audio Record Review*. "Here at last, however, is a vivid and exciting performance which seems to come as near as is at present possible to faithfully realizing Ives's intentions. . . . The engineers have done a superb job in capturing the full range and intricate detail of Stokowski's invigorating account of the work."[24]

Critic Malcolm MacDonald in the *Gramophone* took a different stance: "Many American critics have also hailed it as great music; and no doubt there will be English critics who share this view. I am not, alas, among them; but I am very glad to have had the opportunity of hearing and enjoying such a glorious technicolored feast of hokum. . . . The recording is splendid, especially in stereo; and it is good to see one further act of justice done towards a composer who has been so shockingly neglected in the past."[25]

Stokowski has been accused of giving more first performances than any other conductor but fewer seconds. The allegation is not accurate, for he continued to perform works that seemed to meet his personal test of time, as he did with the Ives Fourth. He repeated the difficult work again in two concerts in December 1965 and in two others in December 1967. In each case there was a capacity audience. And there we have another instance of the immense power he exerted in altering certain trends in American musical mores; albeit quite unintentionally.

The music of Ives had been there all along, but no conductors—except the few such as Bernard Herrmann, Nicolas Slonimsky, and later Antal Dorati—ever waved a baton to perform him. At the time when Ives became a member of the American Composer's Alliance shortly before his death, I released each year a survey of the repertory of all symphony orchestras in the United States. No works of Ives surfaced in the report. Two decades later there was an Ives Centennial Festival Conference held in New York and New Haven (October 17–21, 1974), and delegates wore yellow dollar-size lapel pins proclaiming "Ives Thrives." The BMI Orchestral Survey which was then released indicated that American symphony orchestras played a total of 467 Ives works, surpassing all of his compatriots and most of the international elite—Bartók, Hindemith, Prokofiev, and Shostakovich as well.[26]

The music of Ives has arrived in both recognition and recompense: the earnings of royalties from BMI, from the various publishers and recording companies became an awesome figure. What the public in general did not realize was that none of the monies reverted to the Ives estate but instead were paid to the Academy of Arts and Letters, an arrangement which was effected by Otto Luening and myself in conferences with Ives' son-in-law, George Tyler. But none of that could have happened were it not for Stokowski.

76

The Boston
Symphony Orchestra

FROM his early organ-playing days at St. Bartholomew's, Stoki had heard and admired the Boston Symphony. It, too, was one of the most important influences in Olga Samaroff's career. While still in Cincinnati during the trying period when he was arguing with the board about his desire to cancel his contract, he described the situation to me years later, saying that after leaving there he made a special trip to Boston just to hear the orchestra.[1] Later, after he and Olga were ensconced in Philadelphia, they rarely missed the concerts of the BSO when Muck brought the orchestra there on tour, and they frequently entertained Muck on those occasions.

It was in the fall of 1924 that Koussevitzky began his career in Boston. Stokowski and the Philadelphians had been together for twelve years, and his reputation at the time was formidable. It seems that the first approach between the two men was instituted by Koussevitzky, for in the spring of his initial season Stoki wrote to him:

> Madame Samaroff has told me of your conversation with her, and I am very distressed about the letter which you wrote me, which I never received.
>
> I am hoping to have the pleasure of meeting you personally some time, and also of hearing you conduct. I often thought this winter I would write to you a friendly message as from one colleague to another, even although we do not know each other personally, but then I imagined you were overwhelmed with work and correspondence just as I am, and so I did not intrude upon your time.

With deepest regret for my seeming discourtesy in not answering your letter, and with most friendly greetings, believe me

Sincerely your colleague,
Leopold Stokowski[2]

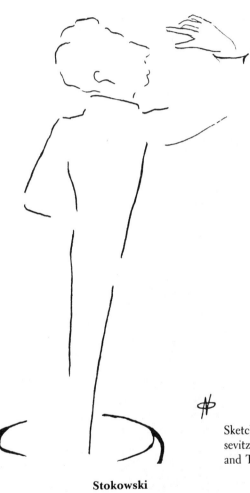

Stokowski

Sketches by Olga Naumoff Koussevitzky of Stokowski, Koussevitzky, and Toscanini

Always considerate of his colleagues, Stoki wrote to Koussevitzky on September 26, 1925, mentioning that Artur Rodzinski, who for many years had been conductor of the opera in Warsaw, would be coming to America in October. "As you probably know, he is a very fine conductor," he wrote, ". . . And as we are friends I am trying to help him all I can while in America. Do you think there will be any chance for him to conduct some concerts for you in Boston? I can promise you that you will not be disappointed if you take him. . . ."[3] Although Koussevitzky did not respond to the suggestion, he did write, saying that he thought it advantageous if they would continue to exchange opinions about artists, conductors, and composers. Stoki replied that the idea was excellent and added: "I shall always be happy to cooperate with you in this."[4] The rivalry which was being perceived between the two men did not erupt into any

Koussevitzky

acrimony between them. Perhaps both had read headlines that appeared in the *New York Times Magazine:* "A New Musical War Opens Brilliantly—Koussevitzky and Stokowski Strive to Win Favor of New York with Their Batons."[5]

Toscanini

Two years before the celebrated exchange of podiums between Stokowski and Toscanini took place, a similar idea was being discussed directly between Stokowski and Koussevitzky. In a letter to Koussevitzky on November 11, 1928, Leopold wrote:

> I have spoken to my Committee here about your delightful idea of exchanging a pair of concerts next season. They fear there might be difficulty on account of your orchestra not being union and mine union. They suggest that we exchange a pair of concerts both with

orchestra and conductor; if this idea appeals to you and is possible
for your administration we can talk it over later and make the arrangement.

Our President sends you affectionate greetings and says you are
entirely in the right about everything and I am entirely in the wrong![6]

The reference to "our President" probably means Evangeline, for she
and Stoki were planning to form a corporation whose primary aim was
educational—with "special attention to the musical development of children."[7] She was to be listed as president and Stoki as treasurer.

"As to the delightful idea of exchanging conductors," Koussevitzky
replied, "(which, by the way, does, unfortunately, not belong to us—the
honor of its discovery being due to your wife, Mrs. Stokowski) this idea
meets with great obstacles. My trustees do not ever wish to hear anything
of my conducting another orchestra, though, I personally may invite a
guest conductor. But to exchange both orchestra and conductor would be
very well, indeed."[8]

"I am glad you and your Committee like the suggestion of exchanging
both orchestra and conductor," Stoki replied. "What part of the next
season would be agreeable to you for this exchange? Perhaps it is too soon
for you to say yet, but when the time comes and you can suggest a definite
date please let me know so I can make arrangements at this end."[9]

Amiable correspondence flowed back and forth between the two maestros and Koussevitzky made numerous suggestions regarding new works
that he had chosen to publish. He warmly recommended a new symphony
by Dukelsky [Vernon Duke], as well as works by Prokofiev and other
Russian composers.[10] They discussed the idea of simultaneous performances of new works so that both could be credited for their premiere
performance.

Koussevitzky also brought up the matter of engaging various soloists:

> Knowing that Prokofiev is writing a new Piano Concerto (the
> Fourth), I believe it very interesting if we give him an appearance
> with our orchestras, and include in our next season's repertory this
> concerto, performed by Prokofiev himself, for he not only is one of
> the most outstanding composers nowadays, but a first-rate pianist,
> too.[11]

Apropos Prokofiev, Stoki wrote on November 24, 1928:

> Yes, I should like to cooperate with you regarding engaging Proko-
> fiev to play his new piano concerto. I will ask our President for
> suggestions of how we both can play it—you in Boston and I in
> Philadelphia—on the same date!!!
>
> Our President sends you friendliest greetings in which I cordially
> join.[12]

The three exclamation points were inked in by Stoki. Was it intended to be humorous, satirical, or a slightly reproachful slap at Koussevitzky for his suggestions of simultaneous performances? In any case, poor Prokofiev would have had to be like Saint Isadoro, who, tradition has it, performed one of the earliest "bilocation" acts and preached in Madrid and Mexico on the same Sunday back in the 1500s.

"As to Prokofiev," Koussevitzky replied, "could not our President solve the question: Could she not draw lots in order to tell us where he is going to appear first?? But to tell the truth, you and I have so many first performances, that it has no importance which of us will perform Prokofiev's work first. If you wish, I shall cede him to you if you play first his new Concerto, then I shall play first his new symphony, and inversely. It will be very easy to arrange the matter."[13]

Another example of the impracticality of the plan to give simultaneous performances was that of the first American performance of the Second Symphony of Prokofiev, which Koussevitzky insisted on giving. On August 31, 1929, Stokowski wrote:

> First of all may I offer you my warmest congratulations on your
> Doctorate from Harvard University. In honoring you, the University
> very much honors itself, and I was most happy when I heard about
> it.
>
> I shall, of course, do what you ask regarding the Second Symphony
> of Prokofiev, although I feel genuine regret that it is not in accord-
> ance with your splendid idea of playing certain new works on the
> same date. If you ever feel like going back to that idea, I hope you
> will let me know because I should so much like to carry out that idea
> with you.[14]

Koussevitzky replied from Paris. The letter had a slightly reproachful tone, and one perhaps wholly deserved.

> I am always ready, with pleasure, to cooperate with you. Coopera-
> tion on artistic ground is of great value both to art itself and to the
> mass for which we work. But, my dear colleague, how do you wish

me to cooperate with you, when you pay so little attention to my
letters and propositions! For instance: this year Prokofiev will come
to America; the interest in his compositions is very great among the
public, and our duty is to do all we can, for Prokofiev is one of the
most brilliant talents of our epoch. So, last year, I informed you of
his arrival and you received the news with joy, telling me that you
would like to cooperate with me regarding his engagement. I immediately advised Prokofiev about it. After that, I wrote to you, to your
manager, without getting any answer. The same happened with the
plan of performing simultaneously Prokofiev's Second Symphony last
season.

   You will understand that I am discouraged in this direction. I am
ready to cooperate with you, with the greatest pleasure, but cooperation has its meaning only in the reciprocal fulfillment of one's duties.

   I shall, perhaps, make records in Philadelphia at the end of this
month and will, of course, try to see you.[15]

Stoki blithely ignored the critical aspects of Koussevitzky's letter and
answered, saying that he was glad that he would be passing through
Philadelphia soon "so that we can talk about everything." He assured him,
too, that he would arrange his schedule "so as to be sure to have time
placed at your disposal."[16]

Few guest conductors appeared with the Boston Symphony Orchestra,
and Koussevitzky was careful to engage lesser-known figures than any who
might challenge his supremacy with the orchestra. He engaged the unknown Dimitri Mitropoulos, who created such a sensation in Boston that
after three engagements he was not invited again. In an interview Koussevitzky explained: "I prefer that we may not have one like Toscanini, or
Beecham, or Walter, but that Burgin, our own concertmaster, conduct.
For he goes my way. I feel that my orchestra retains its same artistic
discipline."[17]

It was at some point during this period that Stokowski and Koussevitzky
met in Paris. "Koussevitzky had a very lovely home in Paris," Olga Koussevitzky recalled. "Stokowski conducted in Paris at that time and he and
Evangeline came over and they had dinner. The cook had prepared a
special dessert with burnt sugar which made a sort of golden crest around
the ice cream and when Evangeline admired it, Serge bent over to her
and said, 'Stokowski hair.' She enjoyed the joke enormously."[18]

It was RCA Victor that sponsored Stokowski's 1936 tour with the
Philadelphia Orchestra that brought him to Boston. The reception was

Photo Popsie

With author and Olga Koussevitzky at reception following BMI Student Composer's Awards (1970)

clamorous. Stoki conducted four encores and concluded with a very nice, politic speech praising Koussevitzky and the Boston Symphony, "from which I learned so much when I first came to the United States."[19]

"This is how it was in the early period," said Olga, "but later on, when he was married to Gloria, he came over to conduct [with the New York Philharmonic] and after the concert Serge and I went to the room where he was after the concert. Serge was intending to greet him. The door never opened. It was a disappointment for Serge, of course." I raised the question whether he had already left the hall. "No, he was still there and Gloria was at his side constantly at that time. I'm just reporting things as they happened."[20]

Early in 1963 I recall talking with Todd Perry, then manager of the Boston Symphony, about Stokowski and how peculiar I thought it was that he had never been invited as a guest conductor. Todd expressed surprise and very shortly thereafter spoke to Charles Munch, who, said Todd, "thought highly of him. Charles Munch brought two people to the orchestra—Stokowski for the first time and Monteux who hadn't conducted since before Koussevitzky came."[21]

Stokowski's debut with the orchestra took place on Friday afternoon March 6, 1964, with a repeat on Saturday evening. This was the program:

Gabrieli: *Canzon Quarti a 15*
Vivaldi: *Concerto Grosso* in D Minor
Mozart: *Sinfonia Concertante* in E-flat
Hovhaness: Prelude and Quadruple Fugue
Rorem: *Eagles*
Stravinsky: *Petrouchka* Suite

"It seems almost incredible that Leopold Stokowski—at the age of 82 with an extraordinarily distinguished career behind him—could have just made his debut as a guest conductor of the Boston Symphony," wrote Harold Rogers. "Yet he has. And it is far less incredible that his debut was extraordinarily successful. His appearance at Symphony Hall . . . was an event of the first order, no matter how you look at it: his program, his performance of it, its impact on the listeners—all were infused with musical interest and emotional excitement. The old maestro is still filled with the old magic." He added too that "everything was rapturously applauded."[22]

Michael Steinberg, by far the most demanding of the critics of that time, wrote that "*Petrouchka* really blazed, the orchestral men even smiled as they gave out those wonderful tunes, and those 15 minutes were by far the most excited and exciting music-making I have heard at Symphony since arriving here."[23]

All of the critics had high praise for both the Rorem and the Hovhaness works. Harold Rogers called *Eagles* a powerful piece of writing. The Hovhaness work, he averred "could have been written by an old master as far as its technical complexities are concerned . . . the prelude could almost have been a page out of Rimsky-Korsakov; the fugue, however, is a marvel of interweaving lines, the like of which Rimsky never dared to fabricate. Mr. Hovhaness, formerly of Boston, was on hand to accept the rapturous applause."[24]

"I would say that his performance of my . . . *Eagles,*" said Ned Rorem, "is the best performance I'll ever have of any piece ever. I can't imagine another piece or another conductor understanding the music and playing it with more energy and playing it with more force and comprehension."[25]

There were many of the players in the Boston Symphony who had been students at Curtis, and some who had been in his All-American Youth Orchestra. There were pleasant little reunions. George Zazofsky had once told Stoki that he had become a member of the Boston Symphony and remarked that he asked Stoki why he never came to conduct in Boston: " 'Oh they won't invite me.' And I said, 'Well, why not?' And he said, 'When you talk about the Boston Symphony'—and he made a little sign of the cross on his chest—'that's something very holy and special.' But he said it with tongue in cheek.

"Stoki and Koussie, although in very different ways, were the greatest influence on my life. . . ."[26]

Oboist Ralph Gomberg, one of the soloists in the Mozart *Sinfonia Concertante,* had been on the famous trip to South America. At the start of Stokowski's first Boston rehearsal, Ralph went over to welcome him: " 'I remember you,' said Stoki. 'I remember what a troublemaker you were in São Paolo.' " Ralph admitted laughingly that it was all part of Stoki's sense of humor. Then in a more serious vein added: "Stokowski was definitely one of the giants. . . . I don't know why it is, but there aren't as many really great giants as there were in those days. There were Koussevitzky, Toscanini, Stokowski, Fritz Reiner, Bruno Walter, and there was Furtwängler. Stokowski was a great personality. He put his stamp on music. . . ."[27]

Todd Perry immediately invited Stoki to conduct the orchestra again during the final week of the Tanglewood season in late August. Stoki altered the program he had given in Symphony Hall and replaced Gabrieli and Vivaldi works with Strauss' *Death and Transfiguration,* which would fill the vast expanse of the Shed far better than the more delicate early Italian works.

Stokowski was very happy about the vivid response he had received from both the orchestra and the audience, not to mention the critics, and felt that he had added Boston to Philadelphia, Cleveland, and London— cities in which he was experiencing some of the great triumphs of his long career.

Earlier, on July 10, 1964, he had sailed for a vacation in Europe. He visited Koblenz and Strasbourg and then motored to Basel. He described the scenery as being "most beautiful." By July 23 we find him in Geneva for a visit with Lyuba. He found time to call the Chaplins at their home, Manoir de Ban, Corsier sur Vevey, not far from Geneva. The cryptic notation in his day book reads: "Spoke to Chaplins. Seer. He does not wish [?]. She or he will write me."

After writing to Oona Chaplin explaining that I was interested in any information she might have about the contacts the two men might have had in Hollywood or perhaps even in Switzerland, I received a very nice and polite letter from her secretary. "Lady Chaplin has asked me to thank you for your letter . . . concerning the book that you are writing about Leopold Stokowski. She has asked me to tell you that when they were in California they often met Leopold Stokowski socially, but that unfortunately, she cannot think of any special anecdote to pass on to you."[28] Dead end!

Chatting with Sam Barber shortly before his death, Sam recalled dining with Stoki and Gloria at their house in Connecticut. "It was a very hot summer night, and he was obviously feeling ready to enjoy himself," said Sam. Stoki then told Sam and Gian Carlo Menotti that one of the other guests was a composer but he would not say who.

"That didn't cheer us up because composers are dreadful company most of the time and it would have been more fun to talk to him and Gloria. He played some of the composer's music; it was light music orchestrated by someone else. It was not a real composer's music. Then he played another piece by this composer. All of our guesses were wrong. Then suddenly I had a vision of a small, dapper man walking in a funny way and I thought I knew who it was. . . . Just at that moment the door opened and in came Charlie Chaplin followed by his wife who was a great friend of Gloria's.

"It was a wonderful evening mainly because Charlie Chaplin did improvisations at dinner and those were some of the greatest things. . . . Stoki loved things like that. He loved surprises. He loved tricks."[29]

Twelve days after his Tanglewood concert on August 21, 1964, we find him again en route to Europe, this time to conduct two London concerts and record Rimsky-Korsakov's *Scheherazade,* his first session for London-Decca.

His concert with the BBC Orchestra on September 15, 1964, was a Promenade Concert in the Royal Albert Hall. He played the Vaughan

Williams Eighth Symphony, Falla's *El amor brujo,* and the Sibelius Second Symphony. An unidentified critic on the *London Times* wrote: "That legendary lion, Mr. Leopold Stokowski, has returned to London. . . . Vaughan Williams was in his 84th year when he threw aside all past restraint and flirted shamelessly with instrumental colour in his Eighth Symphony. Mr. Stokowski is only in his own eighty-third year, but he could meet the composer on common ground because all his life he himself has made sonority one of his big loves. . . .

"Sibelius's Second Symphony . . . won still more appreciative applause from the audience, probably because it was so astonishing to hear orchestral playing of such melodic warmth and tonal brightness issuing from such economical gestures on the rostrum. . . . But here he was rather less closely attuned to the composer's own northerly latitude. Not only the tone colours sounded saturated, but changes of tempo always came a bit too soon and were a bit overdone, so that the music emerged Mediterranean blue rather than Arctic grey."[30]

Someone should have reminded him that Sibelius began writing the Second Symphony in Rapallo along the shores of the blue Mediterranean and spent the winter working on it far from the "Arctic grey."

The second program, this time with the London Symphony in the Royal Albert Hall, was made up of works by Mussorgsky, Nováček, Tchaikovsky, and Shostakovich, and it drew strong and rather carping criticism, which, however, ended with laudatory codas. He was chided for using a giant tam-tam in the Shostakovich and also of doubling some of the horn parts.[31] He was accused of excising parts of the *Bald Mountain* score "even if it could be argued that some at least of the excised passages were tautologous."[32] The *Daily Telegraph* critic summed things up, saying: "For all that there was no want of the magic touch and average listeners in their thousands warmly rewarded Mr. Stokowski's solicitude for their musical well being."[33] In other words, no one but the public liked it.

Another invitation to return to Boston came early in 1965 and Stoki entrained northward for a pair of concerts on March 12 and 13. His program for this second visit was more conventional than his previous one had been. He programmed his version of the Bach Passacaglia and Fugue in C Minor, the *Unfinished* Symphony of Schubert, and the Shostakovich Fifth. He was to repeat the same program for the Berkshire Festival in Tanglewood in August.

Never one to mention comments by reviewers, he may well have savored, if ever so slightly, a comment of critic Harold Rogers in the

Christian Science Monitor saying that his transcription of the Bach Pass-acaglia and Fugue elicited great organ tones from the orchestra (in keeping with the Bach original) in which "he proved his version to surpass by far the one by Respighi. . . ." The Respighi being the one Toscanini commissioned to denigrate that of Stokowski. "Small wonder his listeners responded with rounds and rounds of bravos."[34]

Robert Taylor of the *Boston Herald* was apparently in a choleric mood and could find nothing worthy in the entire program.[35]

Before beginning the second half after the intermission, Stokowski turned to the audience and announced: "We of the orchestra would like to play, in memory of the Reverend James Rieb, Gluck's *Music of the Blessed Spirits* from *Orpheus.*"[36] He did this act of homage for the Boston clergyman who was killed in Alabama by white segregationists.

A hiatus of three years elapsed before Stoki and the Boston Symphony were to be united again, but this time he would conduct it not only in Boston but in Providence and Philadelphia as well. The program was routine: Mozart, Beethoven, and Mussorgsky, plus a slight rarity, the *Hamlet Fantasy* Overture of Tchaikovsky. Of the Philadelphia concert, Max de Schaunsee wrote: "In the old days, I always thought that there was more than an artistic semblance between Stokowski and John Barrymore. Last night's Hamlet brought this once more to mind. The conductor brought out all the drama and turgid passion of this neglected piece with its strange yet magical ending. . . .

"Though he will be 86 in a couple of months, Mr. Stokowski continues to give the lie to this fact. His music has a freshness that seems inextinguishable. The effect he has on Philadelphia music lovers is still, at this late date, that engendered by a timeless necromancer."[37]

(77)

Summer Concerts —
Tokyo, Paris, and London

E VER since crash-landing in the desert with Gloria en route to Mexico for their marriage, Leopold had an almost pathological fear of flying. Because of it the Houston Orchestra was unable to arrange a South American tour; because of it his conducting engagements became increasingly limited. But in the summer of 1965, he made a remarkable exception.

He had been invited to conduct in Japan, and he was eager to take Stan and Chris on their first trip to the Orient. There was no way to do so other than by air. On June 24, 1965, they flew from New York to San Francisco, where they spent one night at the Fairmont Hotel and on the following afternoon departed for Tokyo. There they stayed in the Frank Lloyd Wright Hotel Imperial. "It was quite beautiful," Stan recalled, "with gardens inside. The floors were a little wavy from earthquakes." They visited the Imperial Palace and made a side trip to Kyoto, where, Stan said, they "stayed at a traditional hotel and slept on the floor."[1]

They visited Nara, its temples and deer park; they motored to Osaka and made an excursion to Mount Fuji. Stoki arranged to introduce the boys to the Kabuki dancers, exhibitions of judo, and performances of the Noh dramas. He had apparently given much more thought to the touristic aspects of the trip than the musical ones, at least on the managerial level. He himself had made all the arrangements for the concerts he was to conduct. He had promised both the Nippon Yomiuri and the Japan Philharmonic that he would conduct each orchestra. When the Japan Philharmonic turned up with a contract for his appearance, the Nippon

Yomiuri protested vigorously, maintaining that it had obtained a prior verbal agreement with Stoki. The legality of the contract was not in question, but the Oriental concept of dignity, of "face-saving" was. The matter became one of international scope, and the orchestras finally turned to the American Embassy, which tried its best to settle the affair amicably. But it was Stoki who was the clever diplomat and suggested that he conduct both of the orchestras, which he did.[2]

The first Tokyo concert on July 8 with the Japan Philharmonic Symphony took place in the Tokyo Metropolitan Festival Hall. Mixed with Bach-Stokowski and Tchaikovsky were two works new to the Japanese. The first was Ives' *The Unanswered Question* and the other was a *Sinfonia* by a little-known young Japanese composer, Minao Shibata. Two days later in the same hall he conducted the Nippon Yomiuri Orchestra in an elaborate videotaped concert, satisfying completely the sensitive feelings of the TV-oriented group.

Stoki's second concert with the Philharmonic in Tokyo's huge Nippon Budokan Auditorium featured Kimio Eto playing the Cowell Koto Concerto. It created a sensation, for the Japanese had never before heard their favorite native instrument in a full-fledged symphonic work, and the fact that it incorporated both occidental and oriental influences made the work particularly intriguing. About Japanese musical life, Stoki observed: "What is surprising and unique is that they have our kind of music, their kind of music, and a third kind of music. Some Japanese composers are now taking their ancient instruments, their ancient ideas of what we would call scale, harmony, and rhythm and so forth and developing new kinds of music of their kind.

"So they are playing Stravinsky or Shostakovich—our kind of music— on our instruments. They play their kind of music also—their ancient music—and they are developing a new kind of Japanese music. Not only that but the orchestras there are splendid. Their sense of rhythm and of concentration! Their self-control! You ask something—sometimes by a gesture, by a look—and they give immediately. They are very sensitive. It's a wonderful nation."[3]

Stoki persuaded Kimio Eto to join him in Honolulu for a concert with the Honolulu Symphony Orchestra. The manager there was Marshall Turkin. "I heard that he was coming to Hawaii, and I took advantage of it. I asked him if he would conduct the orchestra," said Marshall, "and, by golly, he agreed." Stoki planned to spend three weeks in Hawaii and, said Marshall, "he rented a beautiful apartment right on the ocean very near the Waikiki Shell, and during the whole month [three weeks] we became chums because I had sons—I have four sons actually—and he definitely enjoyed the idea of being with another father who also had sons."[4]

During one long weekend Stoki with Stan and Chris and Marshall with two of his boys went to the island of Kauai. Contrary to all of his protestations about flying, Stoki wanted to take a helicopter sight-seeing trip with the boys. "It was pretty amazing," said Stan, "because you would come right into the cliffs; it looked like you were going right into them and all of a sudden you would go up and there would be very high plains where you could see wild boars running along."

When I commented on Stoki's fear of flying, Stan replied: "He enjoyed the flight very much. I think he decided that if he were flying, he was going to enjoy it. He didn't have a hard time at all."[5]

The concert with the Honolulu Symphony took place in the Waikiki Shell on a starlit night. Jet planes swooping down overhead stopped the concert several times, but the audience reception was boisterous. Eto, as usual, made a colorful impression, but by this time, it was more visual than musical. Henry Cowell had complained about the interpolations that Eto had added at the very first performance. He had also slowed down the tempo so that he could add more elaborate improvisational flourishes. Since he could not take any direction from Stokowski, he set his own tempi and savored each extended phrase of his own like an auditory lollipop.[6] What the audience was hearing was almost as much the product of Mr. Eto as that of Cowell.

The climax of the concert came with an encore. Stoki conducted Sousa's "Stars and Stripes Forever" with the orchestra augmented by flutists from various high schools and brass players from the Pearl Harbor, Schofield, Kaneohe, and Hickam military bands. "It was terrific," said Stan. Critic Allen Trubitt called it rousing: "Shades of Louis Jullien, who a century ago conducted orchestras of 400 players or more and was known, when the climax of a work arrived, to pull a piccolo out of his pocket and play along! Such Barnum-like antics are sure fire.

"I counted ten piccolos myself and although they sounded more like howling furies than Sousa, I had to jump up and yell bravo. I wasn't alone, there were thousands of others who felt the same way, and we all left the concert with a smile.

"I'll bet Stokowski did, too."[7]

After a brief stopover in Los Angeles, Stoki and the boys were back at

With William Lee Pryor, Stan, and Chris at "Trivi," Stokowski's home in Purchase, New York (1966)

his house in Westchester, New York, "Trivi," on August 7 for a week's
rest before his rehearsals and concert in Tanglewood. He now meticulously concerned himself with every detail of his next trip—this time to
Europe. He met with representatives of the BBC, of London Records, and
wrote a reminder to himself to have his stage clothes cleaned and ready
for his appearances in London.

On August 25 he departed on the *Queen Elizabeth II* for Cherbourg
and after a night in Paris at the Hotel Pont Royal, he left via the Gare
Austerlitz for Bayonne to visit Sam and Cyma Rubin. "We had bought
a château in France in the Basque country," said Cyma. "It was a sixteenth-century château built in 1543 and it had been, as the French say,
abandonné. I was restoring it, which was a great deal of fun for me and
I loved the whole thing. I was working like mad on it and I invited Stoki
to come for a holiday not realizing that it wouldn't be ready.

"It was in August and I was walking around with two sweaters and a
jacket and heavy pants in that damn house because it was so damp and
cold. And there was Stokowski walking around in a cotton, Japanese robe

naked as a jaybird underneath—totally naked. We had painters in the house and they were painting the ceilings of what was called the 'grand hall.' They brought in a tremendous scaffold that went all the way up, perhaps twenty-five feet. There were at least eight painters up on the scaffold.

"Basque men sing beautifully. They're very musical—not the women —the men. Stokowski's French was not bad and he talked with the painters and asked them many questions. They all knew who he was and suddenly they burst out in a song. They sang beautifully and there was Stoki down below in his Japanese kimono conducting these eight or ten men up on this crazy scaffold. It was marvelous.

"Before he came the girls and Stewart sent me a list of what he was to eat, his various habits, and the fact that he slept on a little Japanese neck roll. I ran around the countryside like a madwoman trying to find the only things he would eat. Of course, they were not available. When we dined [out] he ate as if it were the end of the world. He ordered the spiciest dishes and sauces. He drank all the wine. He loved it. It was unbelievable!

"The magnetism of his personality was enormous and I had such fun with him. This was the only time he was ever really intimate with me in terms of revealing intimate things about himself and his life and the pain he felt because of the divorce. This was a totally different Stokowski.

"Before he left, he said to me: 'Work until you die because if you stop working you are already dead.'"[8]

From France, Stoki left for England, where he was met by Wendy Hanson and after a few days went to visit the Panufniks in their beautiful Thames-side home in Twickenham. He did a series of broadcasts and recorded with London Phase 4 Records in Kingsway Hall excerpts from Tchaikovsky's *Sleeping Beauty* and *Swan Lake* ballets, Mussorgsky's *Pictures at an Exhibition,* and other shorter works during September.

As soon as the Rubins arrived back in New York, Cyma, with consummate skill, set about planning the opening of the American Symphony Orchestra's season. She was indefatigable. Flags of the ninety countries represented in the United Nations fluttered from the boxes on both of the horseshoe-shaped tiers. In addition to the ambassadors, secretaries, or chargés d'affaires who were invited, Cyma contacted the Midtown International Center and asked a number of residents to attend dressed in their native costumes.[9] It all added color and excitement. Sam Rubin, who by this fourth season had become president, made a short and dignified speech to welcome the international delegates, guests, and Stokowski as well. He announced that during the program Bach's "Ein' Feste Burg" would be played in memory of Adlai Stevenson.

The program Stoki chose for his polyglot audience began with Aaron Copland's acerbic Variations and then Virgil Thomson's evocative *The Seine at Night,* Robert Russell Bennett's symphonic arrangement of parts of *Porgy and Bess,* and in conclusion, the Fourth Symphony of Brahms.

"The old wizard came back to Carnegie Hall last night and had the stars dancing their familiar dance," wrote Alan Rich. ". . . One heard plenty of the authentic, Stokowski sound: the rich, plangent string tone (a little TOO rich, perhaps for Brahms), the deep, mellow brass sonority, the slightly soft-spined wind. The blend was magnificently achieved, by a man whose orchestral ear is one of the seven wonders of the musical world."

Alan then made an observation with which many of his scrivener colleagues concurred. "Times were," he wrote, "when all of us intellectuals used to sneer at Stokowski's way with the German classics: too juicy, too much for the moment, too inclined to slacken at crucial points. Lately the conductor seems to have rethought his position. His Brahms . . . has been taut, brilliantly controlled, spirited and linear. And so it was on this occasion."[10]

By the 1965–66 season the number of concerts had jumped from six given in the first season to twenty: eight pairs on Sunday afternoons and Monday evenings and four Monday evening concerts. The operating budget by this time had risen to over $300,000.

Stokowski during this period was quite a changed person both emotionally and musically. He had mellowed in a way that seemed to confound his critics. There were no spotlights; there were none of the dramatic and exaggerated gestures that had turned off some of his critics during the 1940s. Then, too, there was a new and younger generation of critics who were discovering Stokowski live for the first time and were making up their own minds. Those of us who had watched and listened to concerts over several decades could easily recognize the care and attention to detail that he was applying. There was no longer any need to dramatize more than was necessary to make the music come alive. He had his own orchestra. He was totally absorbed in finding new and eager performers. He continued to look through new scores and there were endless calls and notes asking for new works—American, European, South American, and Japanese. It was for him a happy time for it was one of total involvement in the thing he loved most: music. For him it was a joy—not work: "Music isn't work. Let's find another name. I just love making music. That isn't work to me," he said.[11] It was also a time-consuming substitute for the family life he could not then enjoy. Other than visits of the boys and the almost daily visits of Natasha and Faye, Stoki was leading a lonely existence.

The critical response was of a new order.

"Almost the oldest active maestro of the world podium, Leopold Stokowski is still the youngest of them all in heart," wrote Louis Biancolli. "The hall was sold out. Why shouldn't it be?" he commented. "All one had to hear, really, was the performance of the Second Symphony of Beethoven. That alone established the three-year-old orchestra as one of the major ensembles in the business. Along with that, it confirmed Stokowski's rank in the hierarchy of Beethoven interpreters. Are there more than two or three conductors alive who could give the symphony that exquisite grace and spiritual depth?"[12]

"There used to be an old idea about Music as Magic," wrote Eric Salzman. "Not just the 'weave-a-spell' bit but a really serious notion that a great musician could transform mere sound into something more than the sum of its parts—an illusion of tangibility, so to speak, a kind of shared revelation and no questions asked. Now there's only one of those wizards left and his name is Leopold Stokowski . . ."[13]

Following a concert during which Stoki programmed Webern's Six Pieces for Orchestra, Biancolli was in rare form: "I was evidently in the mood for one of the founding fathers of atonalism. The pieces were refreshingly spare and went before they came. . . .

"Then I had a shock. I hadn't opened the program. Because of a mistaken recollection of the week-end listings, I was expecting a flute concerto. I rested my head on the back of the seat and closed my eyes. Flow gently, sweet Afton!

"Some flute concerto! It was 'The Dance of the Seven Veils.' The jolt of surprise was almost physical. I was ready to shout 'Foul! but, instead, found myself again transfixed by that wild slut. I can't escape her.

"The performance was the sexiest of the season. You might say it left little unsaid and nothing unseen. One sensed more than ever the lasting power of passion in Stokowski. He was baring his heart and Salome's body."[14]

Stoki was delighted with the review and dictated a note to Biancolli.

It is difficult to be serious and witty at the same time, but you so often achieve this apparent contradiction.

May I thank you for your knowledge and understanding of the limitless possibilities of Music, and for your eloquent command of language. I always enjoy your humor, and particularly liked your last sentence when you wrote that the conductor was "baring his heart and Salome's body."[15]

In Chicago's *Sun-Times* (January 20, 1966) Robert Marsh wrote a "Critic At-Large" article about the greatness of conductors. "The miracle, we now see, is the vigor and skill with which Leopold Stokowski remains a musical force of first magnitude. Indeed, it is now clear that of the eminent conductors of 30 years ago, it is Stokowski who has made the greatest contribution to the cause of music in this country. Toscanini could challenge him in the area of absolute musicianship but his influence has proved less over the years. . . .

"Georg Solti observed that it was the messianic quality of Stokowski that could overcome all prejudice to a demanding new work [the Ives Fourth Symphony] to secure such a success. . . .

"Stokowski is not only our most important direct link to a great era of orchestral performance in the Eastern United States, he is the living embodiment of the great tradition in his art."[16]

The musical season with all of the complex and vexing details that he had had should have been enough for any man, but Stokowski pushed himself inordinately. And he was merely in his middle eighties. During the summer of 1967, he sailed alone (May 28) on the *United States* for Southampton and thence to London. On June 18 he arrived in Paris and began to rehearse the Premiere Prix Orchestra, which was drawn from the students of the Conservatoire. He conducted two concerts with them (June 3 and 5) and the critic of *Le Figaro,* having heard the first, told his listeners that he envied all who were yet to hear him during the second.[17]

After Paris, Stokowski returned to London for a fortnight, during which he conducted the London Symphony Orchestra in Royal Festival Hall on June 15.

"Panting Time, with his scythe, has apparently given up as a bad job," wrote Neville Cardus as he observed Stoki the octogenarian. "The more the years envelope him, the more he remains the same Stokowski, able to take charge of any orchestra and make it sound own brother to the one in Philadelphia which he directed decades ago. . . . Throughout the playing of the LSO was evidence of Stokowski's extraordinary power to

In mock serious banter with the author at a Plaza Hotel Luncheon (April 1968). Guests, left to right: Roger Hall, William Schuman, Alberto Ginastera, Carlos Surinach (half hidden), Oleg Kovalenko, and Norman Dello Joio

stamp on instrumentalists his own ideas as to how music, or an orchestra, should sound. . . . How does he get his effects? . . . Whatever his influence and the make-up of his arts, there is no denying the impact he achieves, on players and audience alike—without excess of gestures.[18]

On June 21, 1967, he sailed for New York, where after a week with the boys at "Trivi," the three of them embarked for Europe. They proceeded to Geneva and to Lyuba's home in Vandoeuvres. After a pleasant two weeks in Switzerland Stoki took the boys to the French Riviera. They went to Monaco, where Stoki conducted the Monte Carlo Opera Orchestra. Then to Copenhagen, where he conducted Nielsen's Second Symphony on August 4, and from there to Stockholm for another concert.

They then returned to New York, and after a brief stay Stoki returned to London for a concert and recording in the Royal Festival Hall (September 19 and 20).

Beethoven's Ninth Symphony brought the concert to a close. Neville Cardus remarked that "the Ninth Symphony, conducted by Stokowski, is an exciting experience. His audience at this concert obviously felt the impact. The deaf Beethoven himself might have felt it."[19]

During the summer of 1968 the pattern was much the same, but one unusual event was a concert in London on June 18 with the New Philharmonia during which he included a work that rarely appeared on his programs, the Berlioz *Symphonie Fantastique*. Following the concert it was recorded for London-Decca. Stoki had never recorded it before and rarely played it in concert. The reviews for the concert were adulatory.

"Hardy perennial Leopold Stokowski . . . again exercised his old wizardry, producing the familiar Stokowski tone, a shining precision of instrumentation which sometimes falls as a fascinating curtain on the orchestra, half-concealing the composer behind it.

"He phrased the Berlioz masterpiece most admirably, giving to the melodic lines the proper emphasis, never missing the presence, no matter how disguised, of the 'idée fixe.' The performance brought out more than most the extraordinary genius and originality of the work; it sounds, though more than a hundred and thirty years old, much more 'modern' in its fundamental thinking processes than the latest atonal coodling. . . ."[20]

So wrote Neville Cardus.

But the prize of all was a brief review by Felix Aprahamian in the Sunday *Times:* "Stokowski again obtained that rich, glowing sound which, quite apart from 'improvements' to the scoring of the Masters, belongs to him rather than any orchestra: this time from the New Philharmonia, in a programme of full-blooded romanticism,—Wagner's 'Rienzi' Overture and Berlioz's 'Fantastique' framing the orgiastic convolutions of Scriabin's Poem of Ecstasy—surely the *most* Complete Musical Fornicator."[21]

The summer of 1969 was even more taxing. Stokowski arrived in London for a concert in the Royal Albert Hall on June 15 arranged by Tony D'Amato that would result in a Phase 4 recording for London-Decca. The program was all-Russian and was intended to be spectacular; the participants were the John Alldis Chorus, the Welsh National Opera Chorale, the Band of the Grenadier Guards (with special sound effects), and the Royal Philharmonic Orchestra. The principal works were the "1812" Overture, Borodin's *Polovtsian Dances,* Mussorgsky's *Night on Bald Mountain,* and Scriabin's *Poem of Ecstasy.* The concert was broadcast by the BBC and in its periodical, *The Listener,* we read a review by Ronald Stevenson. "The old sorcerer Leopold Stokowski worked his magic again. . . . The batonless hands of the wandless wizard had the orchestral sparks flying in the first seconds and there was no let-up in the pyrotechnics till the last note was extinguished. He confounds criticism. The only comment is an exclamation of astonishment. And perhaps the only exclamation to match is the orchestral crash of the 34-letter word in *Finnegan's Wake:* "Ishallassoboundbewilsothoutoosezit."[22]

On June 18 he arrived in Paris for concerts with the Orchestre de Paris. These were given in Fontainebleau at the Théâtre Municipal de Fontainebleau and in Paris at the Théâtre des Champs-Élysées. Byron Janis performed the Piano Concerto No. 1 of Brahms: the rest was Beethoven, Tchaikovsky, and Stravinsky.

From Paris Stoki and the boys went to Geneva for their customary visit with Lyuba, who, having left her husband, Homi Devitre, was now Mrs. Richard Rhodes. After two weeks we find the trio in Paris again and thence to Saarbrücken, where Stoki conducted. Next, an extended visit with Kurt Leimer in Liechtenstein.

Stoki returned Stan and Chris to New York via the *Queen Elizabeth II* on August 27 and on the same night boarded a plane for a return trip to Europe; this time to St. Moritz for the International Festival of Youth Orchestras. On September 8, he was back in England for a concert with the London Philharmonic Orchestra in Croydon. The Beethoven Fifth and the Shubert *Unfinished* were on the program and two days later were recorded by Tony D'Amato. Then quickly back to New York for the American Symphony Orchestra season.

78

Dollar Chords
of Happiness

DURING the course of an American Symphony Orchestra board meeting, Stewart Warkow announced that he had received confidential information that the Ford Foundation would release in a matter of days the news that it would make grants to major and metropolitan symphony orchestras totaling about $85 million. Individual grants were to range from $600,000 to $2.5 million. Warkow and Sam Rubin lost no time and they made an application for a grant in December 1965. There was, however, delay on the part of the foundation. Sam and Stewart later prepared an elaborate presentation, filled out a questionnaire that had been submitted, and proposed a budget on a ten-year basis, assuming that a grant of $2 million would be made to the orchestra.

"A loud $-major chord of happiness resounded through the world of the American symphony orchestra with yesterday's announcement of the Ford Foundation's $85 million grant,"[1] wrote Harold Schonberg after attending the press conference at the foundation offices on Madison Avenue. Along with fifty-odd other orchestras, Stoki's American Symphony was listed as one of those considered eligible for assistance.

The largess of the Ford Foundation stimulated government subvention both on the state and national level. It forced symphonic boards into a tizzy in their attempts to think up ways to match the amounts which the Foundation would award. In some cases certain smaller orchestras had considerable difficulty in matching their grants. Some simply defaulted.

There was a flurry of activity within the office and board of the American Symphony Orchestra and all attention was given to the problem of fund raising. Cyma Rubin was tireless and she planned a whole series of affairs and events to swell the orchestra's coffers.

Her most imaginative coup was an evening which she dubbed "Salud Casals." It was to honor the ninety-three-year-old cellist-conductor-composer in a concert mainly led by Stokowski, who was a mere five years younger. The basic idea, however, was a money-raising event for the benefit of the orchestra. To give a broader appeal to the charitable instincts of donors, the evening was to benefit not only the ASO (for its free concerts for children) but the U.N. International School as well.

In addition to Casals, there were two soloists, both of whom had large followings in New York: Beverly Sills and Rudolf Serkin. The Barnumesque touch was to be Casals conducting his short, six-minute *Sardana* played by 100 cellists drawn from all over America and as far overseas as Denmark and Japan.[2]

The program in Philharmonic Hall opened with a spirited performance of the Third *Leonore* Overture of Beethoven followed by three frothy arias by Bellini, Rossini, and Donizetti floridly sung by Beverly Sills. After intermission and the Toccata and Fugue, Serkin played a splendid performance of the *Emperor* Concerto of Beethoven. That was followed by Casals' *O Vos Omnes,* which Stokowski had arranged for brass instruments. The stage was now being set for the appearance of Casals himself.

Arthur Aaron was involved in the complicated logistics of getting a full orchestra on and off the stage and finding a way to seat 100 cellists—he said there were actually 101—and have it all run smoothly. He recalled that "maneuvering between Maestro Stokowski and Casals as to who was to open and close the program and the last-minute switches between the printed program were very difficult. Maestro Stokowski seemed to want to take a back seat but was always upstaging Maestro Casals."[3]

After Stoki had conducted Casals' *O Vos Omnes,* he left the podium and went to the stage door where Casals was about to appear and then led him out for the applause of the standing audience. At no time did there seem to be any tension among any of the participants. "It was one of those evenings where everybody loved everybody else," observed Harold Schonberg.[4]

The gross income from the Salud Casals amounted to $155,490. This netted $18,969 for the United Nations School and $80,132 for the American Symphony Orchestra. But in spite of this the deficit for the 1969–70 season amounted to over $90,000. The conditions of the Ford grant were these: the million figure had to be matched by the orchestra and $500,000 was clear and could be used for the expenses of the orchestra over a five-year period. The financial situation was alarming and enormous effort was made merely to cope with the orchestra's mounting deficit without even considering the matching million-dollar amount. Unfortunately, the orchestra was never able to match the Ford grant and the million dollars was lost by default.

The financial problems did not seem to fade away; they merely multiplied, in spite of grants from the State Arts Council, the National Endowment, the Billy Rose Foundation, and loans from the Rubin Foundation and Stewart Mott.

Both Sam and Cyma, realizing that the sum they had invested in the symphony would be wasted if the orchestra were to die, began to think of someone to replace Stokowski. "We were suspicious through the whole period that during his lifetime or at least during his activity with the American Symphony, he would never tolerate anyone replacing him while he was still around. He couldn't make that adjustment," said Sam. "One day I was sitting in London with the beautiful Carlo Maria Giulini, who knew Stoki well and was a guest [with the ASO]. He was torn between saying yes to a proposal to take over at a given time as musical director of the American Symphony and turning it down because . . . he considered it an historic tribute to follow in Stoki's footsteps, and at one point, tears came to his eyes when he began talking about the greatness of this man Stokowski. He just worshiped him. And here were two beautiful personalities—Giulini in his own right, really quiet, modest, and here Stoki, in his right, the biggest egotist in the world though he wouldn't show it; but always onstage with no element of modesty ever. . . . He was always playing a role."5

During the 1966–67 season there were more than the usual number of guest conductors, each conducting a pair of concerts. The first was Karl Böhm, who conservatively stuck to Mozart, Hindemith, and Schubert. Early in December 1966 Yehudi Menuhin made his New York conducting debut playing concertos of Bach and Mozart along with Bartók's Divertimento for Strings and the Schumann Fourth Symphony.

David Katz and Paul Kletzki then filled in while Stokowski was in Europe conducting concerts in Bucharest and Budapest. In both of the cities, Stoki's program was the same: Bach's Toccata and Fugue, the Beethoven Seventh Symphony, the Entr'acte from Mussorgsky's *Khovanshchina,* and the *Petrouchka* Suite. He was welcomed rapturously. "A packed Budapest Opera House gave Leopold Stokowski a standing ovation

Photo Vámos Lászlo/Courtesy International Leopold Stokowski Society
With Zoltan Kodály and Cimbalom player in Budapest (January 1967)

at the concert marking his first visit to Hungary since World War II,"
cabled the Associated Press on February 4, 1967. "It was the 85-year-old
conductor's only concert during his two-week stay. The audience included
cultural leaders, government officials and diplomats." The critics praised
his "complete mastery" and added that he interpreted the music in "an
intriguing and highly individual style."[6]

During his stay he spent some time with Zoltan Kodály, and for the
BBC he recorded the *Háry János* Suite with the composer present. The
three-hour session was conducted in Magyar Radio's capacious Studio 6
and aired by the BBC on December 16, 1967.

During an interview Stokowski spoke of Kodály: "I have been conducting his music for many years, but this is the first time I met him and I
found in him a wonderful human being with warm personality, with true

inborn musicianship. He is a born composer. . . . I noticed the extraordinary mind that he has—that he is cognizant of what is happening all over the world. . . . He thinks simply and directly to the center of every subject. . . . He has, like all great persons, great simplicity. I have had the honor and privilege to meet many great persons in all countries. They are always simple. It is the smaller minds which are complicated and like in a string —knots—they tie knots."

Stoki invited Kodály to be present in his recording session. " 'Please come and please assist me and please be 100 percent frank with me if I do anything which you do not like.' But he was kind enough to say he liked everything we did."[7]

From Budapest he sent a picture postcard:

> Greetings from Hungary! Houses of Parliament Blue Danube in front (Not very blue!) Hope you are well (I am!) Affectionate thoughts
>
> Leopold[8]

Later in the season, Stoki invited Henry Lewis to conduct and another American conductor, not to conduct but to be a listener, the conductor-composer Leonard Bernstein. When Stoki first contacted Lenny back in January 1966, saying that he would like to conduct one of his works, Lenny replied:

> Dear Maestrissimo:
>
> I was pleased and flattered beyond description at your wish to perform my music. It is a rare conductor indeed who ever seems to think of this idea, and I am particularly touched that it is you who have thought of it. As you requested, my secretary will be in touch with yours. May I put in a special plea for my very first symphony, Jeremiah?
>
> > Warmest greetings, and
> > gratefully,
> > Leonard Bernstein
> > 11 Jan 66[9]

When the concert took place on April 3, 1967, it began with music of Villa-Lobos: first the barbaric *Uirapurú*, followed by the same composer's *Canção do Carreiro* and the *Bachianas Brasilieras* No. 5 with a remarkable young mezzo-soprano, Maria Lucia Godoy. She had been recommended by Ruth O'Neill many months before. After the Villa-Lobos,

Miss Godoy essayed the soulful vocal lines of the *Jeremiah* Symphony. Leonard Bernstein was present to hear Miss Godoy in his Symphony, and between the two of them plus Stokowski, "a good-sized ovation was generated."[10]

With Philippe Entremont as his soloist, Stokowski chose Bernstein's Symphony No. 2 *(Age of Anxiety)* as the centerpiece of his programs of April 28 and 29, 1968. The relationship between the two colleagues was most cordial and resulted in two more professional encounters. They appeared together on Sunday afternoon, October 20, 1968, conducting a concert called "Musicians for O'Dwyer for Senator of New York." Stokowski opened the program with the prelude to act 3 of *Lohengrin* and closed with Ravel's *Boléro*. Bernstein conducted the Saint-Saëns Variations on a Theme of Beethoven with Lorin Hollander as soloist. The orchestra was, of course, the American Symphony and the whole affair had "been cooked up by the Rubins," said Ainslee Cox. The Rubins were ardent supporters of O'Dwyer and so, too, apparently was Lenny Bernstein.

The following season Lenny invited Stoki to appear on one of his "Young People's Concerts," which were televised on CBS. The music of Bach was the subject of the program and while Stoki conducted it, Bernstein tried to show the relationship of Bach to modern music. Stokowski had pioneered in the field of children's and young people's concerts and relished both conducting and speaking to his young audiences. Bernstein assumed the explanatory role, and as the program progressed the aged maestro and the younger one seemed in some measure to represent two different worlds. Yet it was one of the most memorable shows in the series.

When the name of Otto Klemperer was suggested, Stoki was pleased and agreed that he should be engaged for a single pair of concerts, but in a meeting between Stewart Warkow and Sam Rubin they decided to extend it. When it came to the attention of Stokowski, he became irate and a memo was subsequently dispatched to Stewart Warkow:

> When the contract with Klemperer was signed on May 13, 1967, for four concerts and ten rehearsals, instead of the one concert I had approved, I was told nothing about it, although I was in New York until May 24, and conducted concerts of ASO on May 7–8, and May 21–22, '67. When the contract was broken on August 1, '67, our orchestra put itself in the position of an organization that may or may not keep its contracts. This is known to the managers of Europe, and

may make it difficult for us to engage guest conductors and soloists in future. The reason given for breaking the contract was "circumstances beyond our control." The real truth was that the circumstances were completely within our control. As Music Director and Founder of the Orchestra, I have serious responsibilities to the Board of Directors and all the young talented players in the Orchestra. For all these reasons, from now on I would like to receive prompt memoranda in writing of everything that in any way concerns the musical side of ASO. So that there will never be anything hidden. . . .

I would like to see and initial all contracts before they are signed. No future contracts concerning music should be legal until I have approved them.

From my lifetime of experience with orchestras all over the world, I know that the only successful method of administering an orchestra is perfect and complete cooperation. It cannot be successful by making and breaking contracts.[11]

In addition to his assistant conductors, Stokowski had engaged such celebrities as Jussi Jalas, Akeo Watanabe, Eugen Jochum, Hans Schmidt-Isserstedt, Maxim Shostakovich, André Previn, Igor Markevitch, Karl Böhm, Charles Munch, Øivin Fjeldstad, Georges Prêtre, Paul Paray, Paul Kletzki, Vladimir Golschmann, Kazuyoshi Akiyama, Izler Solomon, and Jascha Horenstein. Composer conductors included Hans Werner Henze, Luciano Berio, Gunther Schuller, and Aram Khachaturian.

Stokowski had become intrigued by the possibility of conducting and recording Khachaturian's huge Third Symphony with its overblown orchestration—ten trumpets, organ, the works—as a sound spectacular at the suggestion of RCA's A & R chief, Roger Hall: "I went to Stokowski and I said, 'Maestro, would this interest you?'

" 'I've always enjoyed Khachaturian's music. Get me the score.'

"So we did and he called me one day and said, 'This is a very good work and we must do it.'

" 'Why don't we do it in Chicago?'

" 'Excellent idea.' "

Khachaturian was to be in America at the time and wanted to supervise the recording and also have the right to approve the tape. Stokowski refused and told Roger to assure Khachaturian that he would make a fine recording that he would be proud of. Time and schedules solved the problem, for Khachaturian could not be in Chicago at the time of the recording. The recording was duly made. "A sound spectacular, yes! It was very noisy but really not a good work and it neither set the record world on its ear . . . nor did it impress the musical fraternity as an important work."

Some time later, after a concert Khachaturian had conducted with the American Symphony in Carnegie Hall, Roger and Skitch Henderson went back to greet the distinguished composer: "I walked in the door and an Armenian lady pianist . . . was acting as interpreter. She very graciously said, 'May I present Roger Hall?' Well, in front of God and everybody the place exploded and in what ever dialect he speaks in the Soviet Union, apparently he called me every conceivable name and the man got apoplectic. People didn't know what to do. Skitch looked around and said, 'How do we get out of here?' . . . Everything came to a standstill and, of course, the accusation was that we had done this [the recording of the Third Symphony] in secret and that it had come out without his approval. Everybody got it; Stokowski got it; the orchestra got it; I got it. He just wiped the floor with us."[12]

The work had been officially denounced by the Central Committee and was only restored to favor in the Soviet Union shortly before the recording. "I'm not sure that this sleeping dog should not have been allowed to lie. It's a pretty obvious and vulgar splurge . . ." wrote David Hall.[13] "What's more to the point," wrote R. D. Darrell, "is that music of this sort is succulent red meat for Stokowski, and that the warm, spacious acoustics of the Medinah Temple provide a perfect ambience for the superb performance and the well-nigh ideally transparent, luminous stereo recording."[14]

79

Save the Met

THE "great gold curtain"—as Milton Cross, the announcer of the Met's radio broadcasts, used to say so unctuously—had not dropped permanently on Stokowski. For the gala wake that marked the end of the old house (April 16, 1966), he was to begin the ritual and conduct first the "Star Spangled Banner" and then the opening chorus from the Wartburg scene in *Tannhäuser*, the "Entrance of the Guests."

John Briggs, in his *Requiem for a Yellow Brick Brewery*, has written a splendid chronicle of that last night. Many arrived early to dine at Sherry's for the last time. Briggs spotted Mrs. August Belmont and Gene Tunney, who, incongruously it would seem to some, had been a member of the Metropolitan Opera Club since the year he beat Jack Dempsey. There were Princess Marina of Greece, Katherine Cornell, Ethel Merman, and "a boxful of Mellons, in from Pittsburgh for the occasion."[1] There were Vanderbilts, Whitneys, Rockefellers, Kahns, Sarnoffs, Knopfs, and Doubledays, and on and on.

Outside, pickets with placards proclaiming Save the Met were circling before the entrance and chanting their protestations. Reporters were milling about, and flashbulbs were aimed at tiara-topped ladies as well as the plainly dressed pickets.

To begin the nostalgia, Bing stepped before the gold curtain and said, "This is a farewell, and every farewell hurts, however long one may have been looking forward to it. Fortunately, it is a good-bye to brick and mortar only, and not to friends. A building is replaceable. Friends are not. . . ." The curtain parted on an empty stage littered with empty chairs.

Leading audience in singing the national anthem at the Gala Farewell Concert at the old Metropolitan Opera House, New York, April 14, 1966, before its demolition

Then one by one, in alphabetical order, former greats of the Met were ushered in by members of the ballet. Marian Anderson led the procession. Then came a parade of singers, some still remembered and some almost forgotten. Among them were Rose Bampton, whom Stoki greatly admired, John Brownlee, and Marjorie Lawrence in her wheelchair, now stricken with polio. Then came Lotte Lehmann, Martha Lipton, Lily Pons, Elizabeth Rethberg, Stella Roman, and Risë Stevens. Farrar and Ponselle sent regrets, as did Traubel and Melchior. But one wonders about Eileen Farrell and Maria Callas. They were absent.

It was now Stokowski's turn. After he conducted the chorus from *Tannhäuser*, "Happily We Salute the Noble Hall," he turned and addressed the audience. And he made the headlines. The *New York World-Telegram* chronicled the moment: "Hail and farewell: Leopold Stokowski brought down the house on Saturday night at the Met. Ironically, the white-maned patriarch of the podium was making an impassioned plea to do just the opposite. There was warm applause when he completed 'The Entrance of the Guests' from *Tannhäuser* which began the 4½-hour-long swan song to Manhattan's oldest temple of the muses. But it swelled, in cheering crescendo, when Stoki turned to the VIP-packed audience and announced with spontaneous emotion: 'What a beautiful house. What splendid acoustics! I hope you're going to help us save this magnificent building.' "[2]

The gasping intake of breath in some quarters was like a punctured tire in reverse. Spontaneous applause broke out elsewhere, particularly in the gallery, where one inspired listener shouted loudly, "Save the Met." Bing blanched.

"Had Stokowski removed his pants," observed John Briggs, "he could hardly have created greater consternation. Whether he had planned it as such, or whether it was simply a spontaneous gesture, it was Stokowski's revenge. Bing didn't miss it. When a reporter encountered him during one of the intermissions, Bing snapped, "It was rude. He was invited here to conduct, not to make a speech."[3]

"It was a shock to everybody and it just really was an abuse of hospitality," echoed Francis Robinson of the Met. "A chill went through the house. Even those who were in favor of saving the old place were appalled. Really it was an act of mischief the like of which I have seldom encountered." But he added reflectively, "He was an old magician. There are no two ways about it."[4]

One of the least surprised and offended was Reggie Allen, who was the Met's business manager at the time. He remembered the days in Philadelphia when Stoki was "constantly being a hazard . . . trying to develop spectacular words he could deliver from the Academy stage that would make headlines and deeply upset the orchestra Board of Directors."[5]

What followed was a marvelous olio of operatic excerpts involving every star the management could cajole into performing free. They all did it willingly and, for many, quite sentimentally. After Licia Albanese had sung "Un bel di," she kissed her fingers and reverently touched the floor. Her husband, Joseph Gimma, who was a partner in the brokerage firm of Hornblower & Weeks and chairman of the New York State Racing Commission among other things, was to spearhead the attempt to "Save the Met."

When "the great gold curtain" closed at 1:15 A.M., it was drawn up again in a matter of seconds and there assembled was the entire company:

chorus, conductors—including Stokowski—and the elegantly coifed and gowned divas, along with the appropriately tailored tenors and basses. Linking their arms together they trumpeted "Auld Lang Syne" with the four thousand opera lovers joining in. What a wonderful wake![6]

Two days after the Met gala Stoki celebrated his eighty-fourth birthday. It was a Monday, the night of an American Symphony performance which had included works of Piston, Schumann, Ravel, Debussy, and Wagner. Evangeline—now Princess Zalstem-Zalessky—despite their years of separation, threw a party celebrating both of their birthdays. The orchestra had been frustrated when they tried to play "Happy Birthday" —an act which Stoki prevented by leading the concertmaster out with him before he could give the cue. But at the party, with twin birthday cakes without the appropriate number of candles, Stoki conducted an impromptu performance of the birthday tune with all the solemnity he might have reserved for Bach and Wagner.

After a polite and affectionate toast to Evangeline, he proposed another to that venerable lady the Old Met. "Would we tear down Notre Dame because it is out of date?" he asked. "The Met is not mere bricks and mortar," he said. "It is a shrine." His shibboleth now was "Save the Met."[7]

Less than a month later Stoki led a delegation to Albany to appeal to the legislature to save the old Met from destruction.

The amount needed to buy and put the old Met into full operation was calculated to be in the neighborhood of $26,000,000. The appeal for help was urgent indeed, but the money simply did not materialize. No doubt the competitive bids for it, the expenses of the huge new Lincoln Center complex, Carnegie Hall (which Stoki had also helped to save), and numerous other worthy projects were more than the spirit of philanthropy could endure. So for the old Met: curtains!

There was a codetta to be added to Stoki's association with the Met. In fact, it was one of Stoki's late appearances that I had entirely forgotten. Critic Bill Zakariasen told me about it. The concert took place in October 1969: "This was, of course, the time of the four-month lockout which kept the house closed until the first of the year. The locked-out artists put on a fund-raising concert in Avery Fisher (then Philharmonic) Hall. . . . Several big vocal stars contributed their services, the chorus sang *Va Pensiero* from *Nabucco*, Lenny Bernstein guested with the *Leonore No. 3* and Stoki did the *Rienzi* Overture. Stoki's performance was really hair-raising that night, and as was his wont during that period, he encored the last section in response to tumultuous applause.

"What struck me most, though, was that by 1969, he was really show-ing his age. He looked very, very tiny and extremely weak, while his skin actually made him look transparent. He was helped to the door going to the stage—I think by that female secretary of long standing, he shuffled, not walked. However, as soon as he passed through the door, he seemed to gain a foot in height, while an amazing spring took over his feet. Twenty or thirty years were shed in an instant. When he came back through the door backstage, he suddenly turned into the little old man again.

"Actually," Zakariasen remarked, "though the old Met was indeed demolished, Stoki was vindicated, if only because La Scala and the Vienna State Opera were unable to stage operas here because of the lack of an adequate auditorium."[8]

Church Concerts

S TOKOWSKI always thought young. Having once knocked five years off by shifting his date of birth from 1882 to 1887 like a movable feast, he accepted age reluctantly but with grace. "Senior Musician of the Year" was not an award he most eagerly coveted. To confer this honor the Senior Musicians Association of the Musicians Union (Local 802) gave a testimonial luncheon in New York's Roosevelt Hotel on May 10, 1968.[1] I was asked to be chairman of the affair and present him with a plaque.

After my brief tribute to him, I made the presentation and read the inscription: "Leopold Stokowski, senior musician of the year . . . in recognition of his lifetime of service to the musical culture of our community, and our country, and especially his achievement in establishing the American Symphony Orchestra."

When the applause abated and he took the award, he gave what is unquestionably the shortest acceptance speech ever given. He paused for a moment and then said, "Not guilty," and ceremoniously sat down. There was much laughter and applause, and as if he were giving an encore he rose again and said: "We live, we senior citizens, in a time of immense change. Every day, every week, every month, every year, life is different all over the world. And yet, we senior citizens began in another age. We were educated in music schools with old ideas. Consider, for example, counterpoint—that medieval method we were taught. It is not alive today —that method. The composers of the twentieth century have developed entirely new conceptions of counterpoint. The question in our minds should be, shall we accept the new and live in it, or shall we fight against the new? The future development and evolution of music depends on how, not only we, but all persons in all countries all over the world are willing to look life straight in the face; life as it is, so changed—or to reject it."

He then talked about a program he had conducted the previous evening with an orchestra of 90 and a chorus of 120: all high school students. It was labeled "American Youth Performs." For this special concert he chose a contemporary work, Kodály's *Te Deum*. He praised the youngsters and observed that "we have a generation of extraordinary talent willing to make great effort—willing to concentrate mentally with great intensity, because that's what they did."

This was the time of the Vietnam war and the time of the flower children, the long-haired hippies, and the young protesters who were much in evidence. He watched them with interest and concern. "They do not bathe very often," he remarked, and he observed that many were asking little from life and had as their motto "let me alone" or just "let me dream." But, ever optimistic, he remarked that while some aspects of our lives here were going down, others were going up powerfully. He concluded by urging the senior musicians to accept the new conditions of life and to continue their lives with the joy of living.[2]

Stoki followed his own injunction and regarded these flower children with kind regard and quiet tolerance. He was less tolerant of much of the ugly and brutal tactics that the spirit of revolt was generating. But he was never aloof from the disquieting events that were seething through the 1960s. He even interested himself in some of the music this generation espoused and he expressed admiration for the Beatles. He watched with interest the enthusiasm of his sons Stan and Chris for new music and their playing of percussion instruments along with electric guitars, pianos, and the like. They rocked and they rolled joyously.

The new postadolescent generation was creating its own life-style, effecting messy dress, long unkempt hair, and Afros. It was the time of the hippies and yippies. Stoki's sons were moving along in their teens and he observed in them, too, their antagonism to many of the accepted mores. Above all he dreaded that they might become embroiled in the war. After the election of Nixon and the constant crescendo of the conflict, he bombarded the oval office with his pleas and protests. The only effect was that he undoubtedly made the President's "enemy list."

As he had done during the two previous wars he now decided to give a series of concerts in various veteran's hospitals. "Nothing is too good for these men and women who have given so much," he said. "If we can give them an hour of pleasure through good music, then we are happy." Members of the American Symphony Orchestra volunteered their services but union regulations required that they be paid. Rather than spend time seeking outside support, Stoki picked up the tab for the concerts himself. "Stokowski Plays and Pays for Vets," read the headline in the *New York Journal Tribune*. [3]

On April 4, 1968, the news of Martin Luther King's assassination was flashed across the nation by every television and radio network in the country. Stoki was deeply moved and angered. He went into action immediately; he summoned Arthur Aaron, personnel manager of the American Symphony Orchestra, to alert the orchestra. He contacted George Lynn, the director of the Westminster Choir in Princeton, and Abraham Kaplan, director of the Camerata Singers, and together they planned a memorial program to coincide with the King funeral on April 9. The King story was given fantastic coverage by the media and the memorial which Stokowski would conduct in Central Park was liberally publicized. There was an immense crowd and it was a deeply emotional one. [4]

Following the "Star Spangled Banner," Stoki led parts of the Brahms *Requiem*, followed by two Bach chorales from the *St. Matthew Passion* and its final chorus, "Here at Thy Grave Sit We All Weeping." In addition to their singing with the orchestra, the choruses sang three Negro spirituals: "Nobody Knows the Trouble I've Seen," "Swing Low Sweet Chariot," and "Go Down Moses." For the finale of the program Stoki chose the "Ode to Joy" from Beethoven's Ninth Symphony.

So total was the response to the music and so thorough was the pent-up rage and grief of the thousands gathered there that the singers and the members of the orchestra almost spontaneously began to sing "We Shall Overcome." Stoki was as deeply moved as any of the thousands who were there. Television cameras ground away and viewers across the nation and abroad witnessed the remarkable spectacle of the King memorial in Central Park conducted by a conductor who was a mere eighty-six years old. But he did not spare himself, for two days later on April 11 and 12, 1968, he conducted the New York Philharmonic in a program consisting of Rimsky-Korsakov's *Russian Easter* Overture, Shostakovich's Symphony No. 6, Thomson's *Ship Wreck and Love Scene from Byron's Don Juan*, and his own "Symphonic Synthesis" from act 3 of Wagner's *Parsifal*.

Stoki now began to speak about giving concerts in churches, and I'm sure he felt that his music could be as spiritually uplifting as any of the countless sermons given there. It was his compelling urge to promote peace that underlined his penchant for finding the right ecclesiastical background. He planned to perform a work by his admired friend Andrzej Panufnik, whose setting of Alexander Pope's "Universal Prayer" had deeply touched him. Like all English school boys, he had learned the poem in his youth:

> *Father of All! in every Age,*
> *In every Clime ador'd,*
> *By Saint, by Savage, and by Sage,*
> *Jehovah, Jove, or Lord!*

The lines appealed to his inherent sense of pantheism. The prayer contains thirteen quatrains ending thus:

> *To Thee, whose Temple is all Space,*
> *Whose Altar, Earth, Sea, Skies;*
> *One Chorus let all Being raise!*
> *All Nature's Incense rise!*

He wanted to perform the *Universal Prayer* in St. Patrick's Cathedral and instituted a series of letters and calls to the rectory. They continued for a space of two years but there was no positive response.[5]

Before he could make any other overtures another tragedy struck during a protest of the Vietnam war. It was the brutal shooting of students at Kent State. He had seen it on the TV news and was horrified and thoroughly enraged. "It is horrible," he fumed. "What can we do for these children?" He asked the orchestra whether they would donate the services for a memorial to the students of Kent State. The reaction was unanimous. Carnegie Hall donated its space and the concert was held on May 8, 1970. There was little time to publicize the event although there were some TV announcements on the network news programs. The orchestra had had leaflets distributed, and shortly before noon trumpeters took to the streets to play fanfares and attract crowds of office workers. For anyone who had not been there it might be difficult to realize how

Photo Bill Bossert
In the living room of his Fifth Avenue, New York, apartment, 1970, before the Seyffert 1913 portrait

intense and supercharged was the emotional complexion of that time.

The program contained Barber's Adagio for Strings, a Bach chaconne, a Scriabin étude, and ended with the Bach chorale *Come Sweet Death*. To this he added his own arrangement of the Casals' *O Vos Omnes* and the Chopin *Funeral March*. After the Barber Adagio, Stokowski spoke slowly about his feelings concerning the massacre of the young students of Kent. Then after each number he would let members of the orchestra express their feelings. "I remember Pia Lindstrom coming out of a box with tears in her eyes," Arthur Aaron recalled.[6]

Photo Popsie

With author and Otto Luening at reception after BMI Student Composer's Awards (1970)

Since there had been no response from St. Patrick's, Stokowski, still set on performing the *Universal Prayer*, looked toward the Cathedral of St. John the Divine, the most magnificent Gothic cathedral in America. Stoki phoned Alec Wyton, its music director. "He said that he would like me to see the Panufnik score," Alec told me, "and he would like to do it at the cathedral. Could he come up to see me? I answered, 'Maestro, may I not come to see you?' 'No,' he replied, 'I want to see you in the cathedral.' So he came up and he showed me the score. I was captivated by it because it had an unusual kind of sonic background. It was for a large choir and there was a big organ part which was quasi-improvisational, four soloists, and any multiple of harps. That I found intriguing."

The world premiere took place on May 24, 1970, when over four thousand filled the long, six-hundred-foot nave of the great church. The *Prayer* made a deep impression and after an interval during which Alec Wyton conducted a work by Richard Felciano called *Sic Transit* for boy's voices, organ and electronic tape, Stoki repeated the last part of the *Prayer.*

". . . The grandest, most awesome kind of music," reported the *New York Times.* At the end of the first performance the audience had burst into spontaneous applause. "No, you must not break the theme," Stoki said, addressing his vast audience. "We are going to do the last part of it again." And he repeated the second half "because he wanted it to die away in silence," Wyton recalled.[7]

Just at this time a new organist was engaged for St. Patrick's Cathedral. He was John Grady. One of his conditions of taking the new post was that he would be able to produce a series of concerts entirely separate from the regular services. His initial approach was to Stokowski. Stoki was pleased and at their first meeting he proposed that he conduct the *Universal Prayer.* Grady agreed. Stoki then suggested that Grady play something for organ and orchestra, and he opted for the Poulenc Concerto for Organ, Timpani and Strings, which Stoki had never conducted. The program was also to include the *Sinfonia* from the 29th Cantata of Bach. Stoki wanted the chorus to be truly ecumenical, consisting of all possible religious groups, including Catholics and Protestants, Muslims as well as Jews, Hindus and Buddhists. Confident that his message of peace would surely get across, he decided that the atmosphere should be more relaxed than that in the Cathedral of St. John the Divine and the listeners were invited to applaud whenever they considered it appropriate.[8]

In the *New York Times,* Donal Henahan made some trenchant observations quite apart from the music: "Cardinal Cooke and other church dignitaries, seated at the left, on the audience level, leaned forward like everyone else to get a better view of Mr. Stokowski as the famous hands drew massive sonorities out of his orchestral and choral forces. Cameramen prowled about the edges of the orchestra, recording the event. Long haired youths held hands in the pews, or wrapped arms about one another as they might at a Central Park concert. Matrons smiled indulgently, or aimed admonitory glances at latecomers whose heels clicked disturbingly on the stone floors."

After the Poulenc concerto, the "cheering listeners" called for an encore. It was a scene unprecedented in the annals of St. Patrick's. Stoki obliged with Albinoni's Adagio for Strings and Organ. But they still demanded more, and having run out of rehearsed material, he repeated the Albinoni.[9]

The following day when I went to see him, I commented on the fine review that Henahan had written for the *Times,* and he said to me, "Just look at this," and he pointed to a UP news story that followed directly after the review. It reported that Representative William R. Anderson, the Tennessee Democrat, visited with the Reverend Philip Berrigan and his brother, the Reverend Daniel Berrigan, in their cells at the Danbury Federal Correctional Institution. The priests were serving prison terms for destroying draft records in Cambridge, Maryland, in 1968. Stoki was indignant and talked heatedly about the fact that in America one could be jailed for protesting the evil and illegal war. "Even priests!" he exclaimed.

During the spring and early summer of 1971 there was a continual escalation of the war and protests were increasing in intensity. One protesting group of the young and disenchanted longhairs rallied in a protest at City Hall, only to be attacked by hard-hat, Nixonite workers. Many of the youngsters, who had much less brawn, were badly beaten and eventually made their way to St. Paul's Chapel and Trinity Church, where some required first aid and medical attention. "My own personal horror at the atrocities taking place in Indochina were shared by the staff and the congregation of Trinity Church," said Larry King, Trinity's organist and choir director. To give form to his indignation, he and an organization called "Music for Peace" outlined a proposal for an all-day musical plea to end the war in Vietnam. "We considered Trinity to be an ideal location for this all-day concert because of its concern about the war, its prominent history, and its location in the heart of the powerful financial community." He set the date for April 30, 1971.

One of King's first moves was to call Stokowski "because of his known commitment to peace and brotherhood" and he asked him to conduct an orchestra of volunteers from the various music schools. Stoki was most enthusiastic and suggested he could probably bring a good part of the American Symphony if a donation could be made for its endowment fund.

Dr. John Butler, rector of Trinity Parish, donated a thousand dollars and Stoki called back, saying that the entire American Symphony had volunteered. He then joined King and others who were busy framing a statement of purpose which placed the concert under the mantle of "musicians joining together to offer an all-day statement for peace and unity in the hope of creating an awareness about the war and its effect in the United States of America."

Following the noon Mass for peace, Stokowski conducted the last movement of Beethoven's Ninth Symphony "because of its message of brotherhood." Hundreds of singers had volunteered from various schools and church choirs augmenting that of Trinity. The performance brought a standing ovation from an SRO audience. Other groups and solo performers continued the concert until seven o'clock in the evening. A program of the day's events with a covering letter was sent to President Nixon. I was most curious to know his response. "Never a word," said King.[10]

Stokowski was singularly honored by Yale University on November 23, 1971. It had been instigated largely by Ben de Loache, who as a singer had appeared with him over thirty-five times when Stoki was conducting the Philadelphia Orchestra. "I worked for five years trying to get him an honorary degree at Yale," said Ben. "I just don't know why it was not done. . . . So when Philip Nelson became dean, and after I knew him better, I mentioned it to him." Nelson accepted the idea at once and suggested that they award him the Howland Prize, which was the highest award the music school could give. "Stokowski came up here and spent three days with us conducting the Yale Symphony and talking to the students," Ben recalled. "It was a tremendous success. I was in England but Yale flew me back for these three days."[11]

Stoki came with Natasha and Jack Baumgarten. He seemed very pleased with everything; they were housed in a Victorian house on the edge of the campus. The presentation of the Henry Elias Howland Memorial Prize took place in Woolsey Hall, and after the award was conferred, Stoki rehearsed two Yale orchestras: the Collegium Orchestra in the Beethoven Seventh and the Yale Symphony Orchestra in the Bach Passacaglia and Fugue in C Minor.

"We begin with the Beethoven," Stokowski said at the beginning of what was labeled an open rehearsal. One of the players was oboist Jerry Pav, who was later to become affiliated with many important orchestras.

He recalled that as they began rehearsing the Beethoven, "he stopped the orchestra and he called out to me that my playing was too loud at one point. He resumed and, of course, I tried to play more piano, but it still wasn't good enough for him so he stopped and started and stopped and started and it still wasn't exactly to his liking. This went on over a period of at least seven minutes until he told me to go home and practice playing softer. . . . This was the only time I played with him."[12]

He was so pleased with the whole musical atmosphere that he invited the Yale Glee Club to appear with the American Symphony Orchestra in the Beethoven Ninth Symphony during the spring season.

Young and eager people always stimulated Stokowski and he was pleased to be talking with the students, teachers, composers and even newsmen and answering questions and dispensing the wisdom of his 89 years. He said he was more interested in hearing something new than in retiring. What about women conductors, he was asked? "Why not? Take ballet, for example. Or in opera, the soprano is just as important as the tenor or the baritone," he said. "So why should there not be women conductors? Perhaps at the beginning there will be prejudice against them. But if she is a good conductor the public will come to accept her."[13]

He had already appointed a young conductor Judith Somogi as one of his assistant conductors and had strongly encouraged Beatrice Brown in her career as a conductor. He even guest-conducted one concert with her orchestra in Scranton, Pennsylvania.

Would he retire, he was asked? "I've never thought of it. It's not a strain. Conducting great music is a wonderful experience," he answered.[14]

Although he had toyed with the idea for some time, it was during this New Haven episode that Stokowski made his decision to leave the United States and return to England. Natasha remembers his saying that she should look at these young people: "Look at their eagerness, look how wonderful they are, look how marvelous it is being here with them. Why can't my life be like this? Why does it have to be in New York . . . always raising money. . . . I want to go to Europe, where a musician doesn't have to live that way."[15]

Several times he told me that he was about to resign, and he was particularly annoyed when he discovered that some people were referring to the American Symphony as Sam Rubin's orchestra. He realized that both Cyma and Sam were becoming more interested in the Broadway scene than the orchestra. For Cyma the theater was natural. Wasn't her grandmother a circus performer, as she proudly recounted?

Early in 1969 Cyma met a sometime successful Broadway producer, Harry Rigby. Together they talked about and explored various possibilities of a nostalgic revival and they finally hit on the idea of *No, No, Nanette*. For the next year this project began to grow and loom larger each day while the ASO seemed to be mired in its financial woes.

Although they began working harmoniously at first, Cyma eventually dominated the project and by the time it finally hit Broadway, she had dissolved the partnership with Rigby and they were in the middle of an acrimonious litigation.

After tryouts in Boston, Toronto, Philadelphia, and Baltimore, *No, No, Nanette* opened in New York on the night of January 19, 1971. Stoki attended and, as I recall, enjoyed its good fun. Sam and Cyma threw an elaborate party at the Hotel Pierre when it was over and everyone waited for the reviews. When they arrived there was jubilation. *Nanette* was a smashing success. New Yorkers began to sing "I Want to Be Happy" and "Tea for Two" just as they had done in the twenties. "The next morning, on the heels of ecstatic reviews in the newspapers and on radio and television, a block-long line of ticket buyers stretched out from the theater box office, while two models dressed as maids served hot tea to ward off the January cold, and Irving Caesar [the show's lyricist] tramped joyfully up and down, singing 'Tea for Two' for his captive audience."[16]

The new ambience in the Rubin household was becoming Broadway and Hollywood Boulevard rather than the locale of Carnegie Hall and Fifty-seventh Street. They had given much but they also received much in the expansion of their social activities and their position as musical leaders. Stoki and a large and distinguished following appreciated the elaborate functions that Cyma produced so abundantly. The Rubins were sincerely fond of "the old man," as Cyma often referred to him.

"I must admit he enriched my life personally to a measurable degree," said Sam. "Not always do you have the special privilege of rubbing shoulders with people of that stature."[17]

"This was the great showman," said Cyma. "I loved his energy and everything was 'do better'—he was never settled. . . . He was very difficult to work with, as you know. At times I feel he was unreasonable." Then Cyma continued reflectively: ". . . was he kind, was he unkind, was he sincere, was he insincere. He was many things and you either accepted that madness or not. I would say that he was probably one of the greatest showmen who ever lived."[18]

With its staggering deficit, the ASO had lost its most generous backer. That there would be a clash between Stoki and the Rubins, particularly Cyma, was inevitable. Both she and Stoki had monumental wills and gargantuan egos. "She wanted to run the symphony," said Jack Baumgarten, ". . . she tried to tell Stokowski what to do and he got tired of it."[19]

Some months later the very able Stewart Warkow had resigned and the management was taken over by Jack Baumgarten, with Cathy French playing the role of a glorified Gal Friday. But Jack was becoming more and more indispensable to Stoki, who began to rely on him completely in the matter of keeping musical things straight. He prepared his scores, kept his library in order, and with his sense of organization saw to it that whatever Stoki would need, he would have. Jack was meticulous. Stoki soon persuaded the board that Jack Baumgarten should be his assistant, and at that juncture, the board appointed Cathy French executive director.[20]

(81)

1970-71

STOKOWSKI's annual summer trips to Europe provided a respite from the pressures that seemed omnipresent in New York. Tony D'Amato, with perceptive publicity sense, planned to couple concerts with his Decca recordings affording both the excitement and ego fuel so necessary to Stoki's well-being. If it were too exhausting, as Natasha maintained, it nevertheless added a tincture of drama to his eighty-eight years.

He arrived in London early in June 1970 to rest and relax before his concert and recording with the London Symphony Orchestra. The program was entirely of the twentieth century. It included Messiaen's *L'Ascension*, the Ives Second Orchestral Set, *La Mer*, and the *Daphnis et Chloé* Suite No. 2. "Leopold Stokowski in his eighties is a sobered showman," wrote Colin Mason, "but the results he gets are as spectacular as ever."[1]

At the close of the concert Stoki added an encore; it was Berlioz's *Dance of the Sylphs*. The audience accepted this bonus without realizing that it, as well as the Ives and Messiaen, were all being readied for the recording sessions on June 22 and 23.

I received a cable from Stoki asking me to secure the rights if possible for the new Symphony No. 14 of Shostakovich.[2] After a bit of sleuthing, I regretfully had to reply: "I wish that I could tell you that you have the performance rights of the 14th Symphony of Shostakovich but unfortunately, this is not the case. The conditions on which it was assigned were a payment of $3,500 for the first performance, with the provision that it be recorded within 48 hours. I grieve to tell you that RCA and the

Philadelphia Orchestra have teamed up and it will be done by them."[3]

After the London recording session, Stoki and the boys left to visit Kurt Leimer in Vaduz, Liechtenstein. There was a broadcast set up in Saarbrücken and another in Hilversum, Holland. The invitation to come to Hilversum had been given the previous year, and when he arrived, "they did it up in grand style," Tony D'Amato recalled. Stoki's program for the broadcasts and recording included Ravel's quiddity, little Fanfare from *L'Éventail de Jeanne,* the Franck Symphony in D Minor, and Prokofiev's *Alexander Nevsky* with Dutch soprano Sophie van Sante. "The Ravel," said Tony, "is a gorgeous piece . . . a little piece to wake up everyone."[4]

Stoki spent eighteen days in Hilversum and worked with the orchestra intently. One young producer who was present at the rehearsals described them to me one day in Paris. Frans Van Rossum was only twenty-six when he first saw Stokowski live. He was merely a child when he had seen him in a revival of *100 Men and a Girl:* "I wanted to see him once in my life. And I thought he was very old. . . . I did not meet him personally, but I was upstairs in the control room and I heard him talking and I saw him rehearsing the orchestra and explaining the difficulties of the Franck Symphony . . . then he started to change the parts because he wanted to add some special effects. I remember the bassoons and the oboes. He didn't like their playing . . . so he started an experiment with the English horn and with the contrabassoon, to double the parts. The orchestra was very cross, though they didn't show it immediately. But afterwards they asked 'what is this man doing?' "

"The men asked Stokowski to explain why he was doing it. And he told this story, saying that he 'didn't expect César Franck to agree with what he did but once he heard it he would have agreed,' " said Frans. And as the rehearsals progressed, "everyone was so incredibly impressed by his ears and his memory. . . . I think after a few days, the whole orchestra adored this man."[5]

Stoki appeared with the orchestra in both Amsterdam and Rotterdam, but the recording was made in the studio in Hilversum. While in Amsterdam, Stoki took Chris and Stan to see the Van Goghs, and they explored the sights of the city.

To express his appreciation of the fine cooperation the orchestra had given him, he wrote: "To All the Artists in the Radio Filharmonisch Orkest":

Thank you for the brilliant, powerful, sensitive and flexible concerts you played in Amsterdam and Rotterdam.

I have begged whoever is responsible for it, not to transmit the very bad television that was made with our first rehearsal with Chorus. Obviously the television should have been made at the last rehearsal with Chorus so as to show to the television public the Orchestra, Chorus and Soloist in similar quality to the performance that you have achieved in the two concerts.

With heartfelt thanks for your great playing.

Leopold Stokowski[6]

Tony D'Amato recalled that the National Television Company of Holland filmed the *Nevsky* rehearsals plus the performance and Stokowski "refused to have it shown, absolutely refused. . . . I think that he later regretted it when he heard it played back. They gave him a grand performance, but he was unhappy with it. I don't know why, but you never knew why Stoki was unhappy with something."[7]

After Hilversum he made his annual pilgrimage to visit Lyuba in Switzerland, but the visit was short and he left for London, where he recorded Panufnik's *Universal Prayer* for Unicorn Records.

Stoki opened the 1970–71 American Symphony Orchestra season in flag-bedecked Carnegie Hall with a brief speech saying that although the program stated that the opening work, his arrangement of a Handel overture, was being played in memory of George Szell and Sir John Barbirolli, he wanted it also to be a tribute to Jonel Perlea, who, along with the other two, had died three days apart.

The program included the world premiere of Gian Carlo Menotti's Triple Concerto a Tre, the Paderewski Piano Concerto in A Minor with Earl Wild as soloist, and the Schumann Second Symphony. The Menotti work was one of three which had been commissioned by the Rubin Foundation.

The Menotti Triple Concerto at this opening concert was rough going. The work was modeled on the idea of the Baroque *concerto grosso*. It utilized three solo groups with three players each: oboe, clarinet, bassoon; violin, viola, cello; and piano, harp, percussion. The score that Stokowski used was a reproduction of Gian Carlo's original manuscript and was very difficult to read. It also contained many time changes and because of his great vanity, Stoki never used glasses. He had difficulty with the score but the performance squeaked by.

"You know," said Gian Carlo, "he went through a period when his memory was not so good—his eyesight, too, but especially memory. He could not memorize the score and really had trouble with a very tricky part in 5/8 and 3/8 and so on. He got terribly mixed up."[8]

Earl Wild scored a jubilant success with the Paderewski concerto. Some time before the performance Stoki contacted Earl and asked him to come to his studio to talk about it. Earl arrived, ready to play it for him, and as he entered the apartment he found that Stokowski was having an interview with someone from the *New York Times:* "A big black man arrived to photograph him and while he was photographing him he asked a couple of questions. He said to him, 'Maestro, where were you born?' Stokowski stood up and struck an attitude and put his hand on his heart and said, 'Poland.' Then the photographer said to Stokowski, 'Maestro, put those baby blue eyes in my lens.' I thought he was going to throw him out but he never let on that anything was unusual or different and went right along and was photographed."

Earl then joined Stoki at his desk to go over the score: "He said to me, 'What can we do? What about the tempo?' I didn't know what to say to him, because, after all, he was a big conductor, so I said, 'Not too fast and not too slow.' And then he looked at the second movement and said, 'What can I do to make it sound more romantic?' So I just said to him, 'In four. If you took it in two it would be too fast.' Then he thumbed through the last movement and didn't say anything about that. Then he stood up. So I said, 'Can I play it for you now?' He said, 'Oh, it's not necessary. Thank you so much for coming.' So I was ushered out and that was all—all that distance for that baloney. I got out on the street and I had to laugh. I had put myself out to drive about three hundred miles— I was in the middle of Pennsylvania near Altoona at the Pennsylvania State University.

"I forgot to mention one other thing. He said, 'I played this piece once in Poland with a Polish pianist who came from Russia—who drank a lot.' And then I tried to think of all these names and then it dawned on me. I said, 'You don't mean Josef Hofmann, do you?' He said, 'That was the name.' "[9]

How Stoki chose William Mayer's *Octagon* for a world premiere with the orchestra illustrates one of Stoki's peculiarities and his penchant for wanting to be the first to do new works of new composers. William Masselos had been engaged to appear with the orchestra and I had strongly recommended that he do the Brahms First Concerto, which I had heard him do with Mitropoulos some years before. But Stoki did not concur. "Let's not do the Brahms," he said to Masselos. "What modern works do you have?" Bill mentioned the concerto of Ben Weber, which he had played with Bernstein, and the Robert Helps concerto. But since both of these had been performed, Stoki rejected them. Bill then suggested the *Octagon* of Mayer. "He said, 'Has it ever been played?' I said, 'No.' He said, 'Well, that's it.' "[10]

Bill Mayer told me that he had never met nor talked to Stokowski: "One day there was a phone call . . . and I heard the Russian-sounding name and I thought it was our piano tuner. I said, 'Thank you very much Mr. Kuchinsky, but we've just had our pianos tuned.' There was a pause and the voice said, 'Stokowski speaking.' "

Stoki invited Mayer to come to his studio and they went through the score very carefully. The score had many meter changes, so he asked him to indicate the changes in gigantic red numbers. Apparently Mayer fulfilled this requirement nobly, for Stokowski not only knew where he was in the score, but performed *Octagon* brilliantly.[11]

"One of my friends," Bill Masselos recalled, "said that she was never nearer a heart attack than being in Carnegie, sitting in the first row watching what was like a wild Westerner. . . . He turned two or three pages at once . . . but it never sounded better."[12]

While the last concert of the season was being conducted by Luciano Berio, Stokowski was in Cleveland to conduct the orchestra there in a program of war-horses. Artistically, it was a celebration but personally it was a veritable disaster. Because of his aversion to flying, Stoki tried to take the Amtrak train to Cleveland, only to discover that the passenger traffic to Cleveland had been eliminated. The alternative was to book passage to Canton, Ohio, and then motor sixty miles to Cleveland. But the train did not ordinarily stop in Canton in the early morning hours, so he had to arrange to have it make an exception. Stoki and Natasha arrived in Canton at 4:00 A.M. and were met by a limousine for the drive into Cleveland.[13]

I flew into Cleveland to hear the concert. It was a festive evening, and to see it in retrospect we can turn to critic Robert Finn: "It is not just a concert that is closing out the Cleveland Orchestra season. . . . It is an Event, almost a musical papal audience. . . .

"He is a Presence, a patriarch, a walking, living, breathing chapter from the musical history books. . . .

"He took the Szell-trained Cleveland Orchestra we are all used to, waved those famous hands over it and transformed it into what so many record labels have described as 'Leopold Stokowski and His Orchestra.' "[14]

Lynn Harrell was the principal cellist with the Cleveland Orchestra during Stoki's visit. "It was staggering," said Lynn. "There was a change in the sound of the orchestra. . . . Of course, there was much titter and talk in the orchestra about his rearranging the seating of the orchestra so dramatically. . . .

"At intermission I came up and introduced myself to him reminding him that we had played together in Carnegie Hall years before. 'Oh yes,' he said, 'I remember. . . . The cello sound was very good. . . . What kind of cello do you have?' I said, 'It's a Montagnana.' He said, 'Let me see it.' I brought the cello up to the podium and he looked at it, plucked the strings very forcefully, turned the cello around and started tapping the back with his knuckle, seeing if it had resonance. . . . That was fascinating to me because, first of all, no conductor that I knew except Stokowski was so in tune with the instrument's role in the sound production.[1]

The major work on the Cleveland concert was Glière's *Ilya Murometz*. "He stood up and conducted through this magnificent, sprawling symphony," Lynn recalled, "and it was electrifying, and of course, how he must have been as a young man, with a lot more energy and muscular and physical verve, is impossible for me to conceive."[15]

After the concert Stokowski and Natasha joined me and some Cleveland friends briefly at a private club, but he was tired from the long and strenuous concert and after a brief stay returned to his hotel. Before flying back to New York, I urged him to fly rather than depend on trains, but he was adamant: he would not fly. Hence, he and Natasha departed by train and by the time they arrived in Albany, they were forced to leave it because of a wildcat strike by railroad workers that had just been called. Stoki and Natasha had to transfer to a Greyhound bus for the rest of the way into the city.

On June 11, 1971, he left on the *Queen Elizabeth II* and checked in at the Hotel Stafford just off St. James Place six days later. His first project after arriving in London was to conduct Panufnik's *Universal Prayer*. What made it very special was that the concert was to be in the Parish Church in Twickenham on the Thames, where Alexander Pope, on whose poem it was based, lies buried. Also in close proximity is the Panufniks' home, where Stoki enjoyed examining the splendid collection of ancient musical instruments. It included a huge mechanical organ that worked on the same principle as the hand organ, requiring the player to emulate the stance of the organ-grinder.

Stokowski's appearance in the charming little town caused a flutter of excitement. The BBC sent down a mass of TV equipment and videotaped the concert for a delayed telecast. Edward Johnson remembered driving down from London with Stoki and John Goldsmith, of Unicorn Records, for the afternoon rehearsal: "The performance was to be televised, and during rehearsal the BBC engineers were rigging up cameras on scaffolding up and down the church. You know what the music was like—very modern indeed! When we returned after the afternoon rehearsal, there was a large BBC van parked outside the church with four engineers sitting in the back playing poker. Stoki got out of the car, walked over to watch these men for a minute, and then one of them looked up and said in a very cockney accent, 'Allo Leo, do you fancy a game?' Stoki said, 'What happens if I win?' To which the engineer replied, 'Well, whoever loses can come and listen to your bleedin' music!' Stoki moved off very sedately with a big grin on his face. I think he probably sympathized with the man's viewpoint."[16]

After Twickenham Stoki returned to his hotel and immersed himself in the music he was to conduct in a series of concerts and recordings that Tony D'Amato had arranged. Three days after the concert he complained of feeling ill and collapsed in his hotel room with an apparent heart attack. "We put him into Westminster Hospital just opposite the Decca offices," said Tony. "Joyce Bright's doctor had him entered there. When I went to see him he looked ever so frail under those covers and yet he was issuing orders in a very slow, easy kind of way, saying, 'What is the name of the LSO conductor?' We told him André Previn and he said, 'Would Mr. Previn take the first rehearsal?' He had four rehearsals scheduled, so presumably he was determined to get better for the second rehearsal. He didn't realize how ill he was."[17]

Daily dispatches on his condition were sent out via the various international wire services. A Reuters dispatch on June 24, 1971, reported him being hospitalized and the story was picked up by the U.S. papers.[18] The following day the Associated Press reported that it was "a slight heart attack" and that he would remain in the hospital for several days.[19] In Philadelphia, the papers quoted London: " 'He's very cheerful and he's not in any pain,' said a spokesman for Stokowski's record company. 'He's just taking it easy, that's all.' "[20]

Natasha had been visiting in Florence and arrived in London not knowing anything about it. She immediately went to the hospital: "He was in a ward. I think there were about eight men in the room. It was a special-care unit for heart people and he was getting excellent care. The family was very distressed that he wasn't in a private room, and finally when a private room was available and the doctor asked whether he would like to be moved to one he said, 'Certainly not. This is interesting. There are people around me here. I see a slice of life that I would never see anywhere else.' There was a cockney in one bed, somebody from another part of London in another."[21]

Stoki's family rallied. Sadja, Lyuba, Chris, and Stan all converged on London. André Kostelanetz, who was conducting concerts in London at the time, visited the hospital. "I walked in the ward and there sat Stokowski in bed, completely erect, dressed in a beautiful silk robe. He said that he was in perfect health. 'The doctors made a mistake.' "[22]

It was decided that Stoki would go to Geneva and be with Lyuba during his recuperation. Although everyone urged him to fly, he adamantly refused and instead insisted on going there by car. Tony D'Amato offered to drive, and so Stoki, Chris, Natasha, and Joyce Bright, with Tony at the wheel, set out for Switzerland: "I remember driving an automatic Ford to Southampton and getting on a hydrofoil that skims the surface of the water over to Calais."

In France they switched to a Peugeot, and as they drove along Stoki would admonish Tony to " 'allow the wheels to roll to a stop—allow the wheels to roll away from the stop.' In other words, he didn't want any jerking and jumping around. . . . I couldn't make time. . . . I was doing forty miles an hour on the auto route, the inside lane. And every time that I could see through the rearview mirror that he had dozed off, I would simply go 70 to make up time."[23]

When they arrived in Geneva, Stoki retired and with a wave of his hand dismissed Joyce Bright and Tony. One wonders whether members of any other recording company ever did as much and extended themselves as thoroughly as these two members of Decca had.

The concerts which Tony had set up in London, as well as the recording sessions, had to be canceled and the rest of the summer was devoted to recuperation. "I was very anxious about him then," said daughter Sadja, who was herself a doctor. "He completely recovered."[24]

On July 10, 1971, a letter from the Western White House, San Clemente, arrived:

July 10, 1971

Dear Mr. Stokowski:

It has just come to my attention that you have had to set some time aside for a rest, and knowing the rugged pace you usually set for yourself, I can understand the disappointment you must feel at having to cancel your summer engagements.

Together with your countless admirers throughout the world, Mrs. Nixon and I want to add our warm wishes that you will soon be feeling better, and we look forward to the news that you have returned to the podium once again.

Sincerely,
Richard Nixon[25]

82

American Finale

B Y March, or at the latest early in April, most symphony orchestras have their forthcoming season well planned. Near the end of April 1971 there had not been a decision about how many concerts were to be given during the coming 1971–72 ASO season. As yet no soloists had been booked and Stoki was exasperated by the delay largely caused by Sam Rubin, who after all was the main backer. Sam had been considerably irritated when he heard that some board members, in shirking responsibilities, had maintained that Sam did it anyway.

Highly disturbed by the state of indecision, Stoki called Sam and a meeting of the executive board was convened in his apartment on April 20. Sam agreed that if the 1971–72 season were to be planned around a series at Carnegie Hall, valuable time had been lost. He explained that the symphony faced a great financial crisis and although the subscription and box office income was higher than in previous years, it was insufficient to meet the financial requirements.

He mentioned that he and Stoki had discussed the idea of a series of educational concerts in Town Hall. He said that he had come to the conclusion that only by divorcing itself from the mainstream of orchestral activity in the city could the ASO capture a unique identity and find hope of financial support. He proposed, therefore, that all American Symphony concerts be free and that they be given in churches rather than in Carnegie or Philharmonic Hall. He suggested that barrels be placed at the doors of the churches to encourage voluntary contributions and he maintained that the pressure for advance planning would be eliminated if the subscription series were canceled. "We would not be obliged to commit ourselves to artists, conductors, or the public. A reduced staff of about two people could operate such a plan."

At this point, Stoki reminded Sam that he had come to him earlier and had suggested that they give eight pairs of concerts in Carnegie Hall next season and had later made the proposal about the churches. Sam countered, saying that he could not be held responsible for simple suggestions and that his proposal for church concerts was offered as a substitution for, not an addition to, the Carnegie suggestion. He said frankly that the Rubin Foundation seeks to assist innovative programs and that it would not fund the American Symphony Orchestra subscription concerts in the future and that the subscription concept in the eyes of the foundation was outmoded and no longer a valid means of operation.[1]

Stewart Mott, one of the members of the executive committee, voiced what I believe represented the attitude of all who attended the meeting. He said it left him "shocked, stunned, and speechless." Having gone to a dinner party immediately after the ASO meeting, he returned home past midnight and sat down and drafted a note—a long one—to Sam Rubin. He took up seventeen points that he questioned. He brought out items that were not discussed and accused Sam of not giving positive arguments in favor of a church setting—of not being interested in discussing the economies of church-operating costs. "Your concern seemed more with the elusive political impact of a dramatic press release," he stated. And he added that "new packaging may sell more tomato soup, but a really good product is marketable no matter what the packaging. . . . Since when," he asked, "can or should a foundation deliver a virtual ultimatum to its 50% + supported organization that no longer will the general support funds be given [except] on a restricted project basis? What kind of eleemosynary ethics are involved here? . . . The announcement tonight was a bombshell. What's innovation?" he asked. "A plastic bottle for soup or a new recipe for soup? Who sez subscriptions are old hat? . . . Concerts should be free? Why not *No, No, Nanette?*"

But the clincher was Stewart's final statement: "Are you really trying to say obliquely that you, Rubin Foundation, want out altogether? If so, please say so. Why present an impossible alternative and attendant horrendous hassles? All of us on the ASO board love you and respect you and want to help ASO succeed but the scene tonight was perplexing beyond belief."[2]

The board rejected the Rubin plan and eight pairs of concerts were scheduled—all to be given in Carnegie Hall. Only one outside guest conductor, Antonio de Almeida, was engaged: Stoki conducted six pairs and Ainslee Cox, one. In addition to these there were to be four concerts in Town Hall, for which Sam Rubin offered assistance.

Flags bloomed as usual for the opening concert in Carnegie despite the lack of aid from the Rubins, and Jorge Bolet tore the piano apart in the Prokofiev Piano Concerto No. 3; Stoki conducted memorably Rimsky-Korsakov's Prelude to act 3 of *Ivan the Terrible*, and the Brahms Fourth Symphony.

Perhaps all of the various controversies and troubles that were besetting the orchestra caused Stoki to have a short lapse of awareness during the performance, or possibly it may have been a matter of sheer exhaustion. But Jorge Bolet mentioned that during the first of the two concerts such a lapse did occur: ". . . the last movement of the concerto has a middle section which is briefly introduced by the orchestra and then the piano takes it alone; it's a rather extended section—rather lyric, poetic, and it must be probably forty-five or fifty bars of music where the piano plays completely alone and then, without interruption or break, the orchestra comes in with a bassoon solo using the same theme as the piano had announced before. Well, I got to that spot and there was no bassoon. What does one do in a case like that? . . . So I played about two or three bars and went back to make the connection again to see if the bassoon would come in. Stokowski was completely on the moon. I don't know whether he was so entranced with the beauty of the music or what. I presume he forgot where he was or that he was conducting. He was probably just listening. It was a terrible moment. I never exactly found out how he finally reacted, whether it was some member of the orchestra that made some motion to him but he finally [came to]. Everything else went like clockwork."[3]

A special moment that Stoki particularly relished was the appearance of two of his favorite performers, Elayne Jones and Anthony Miranda, in the Bernard Rogers Fantasia for Horn, Timpani and Strings. The concert also featured a *Fanfare* by Sharon Moe, the beautiful blond horn player who was one of the most decorative additions to the orchestra. At this point, Sharon was Mrs. Tony Miranda.

Stoki had heard that Sharon composed and he asked her about her works. She said that she would like to write something special, so she began to write a suite. "About a month later, he asked, 'Do you have anything finished? I would like to see it.' At the next rehearsal Stoki said,

With associate conductor Ainslee Cox and Elayne Jones, timpanist, at a rehearsal of the American Symphony Orchestra

'I think you should hurry!' " Tony realized that Stoki was probably going to leave the orchestra and insisted that Sharon give him what she had written.[4] Stoki was pleased with the *Fanfare* and used it as an opening work on the same program on which Tony and Elayne Jones were featured.

Elayne was one of the orchestra members for whom he had a special affection. He told Robert Sherman before an audience at New York University: "We have now, in the American Symphony, a timpanist—a young black girl, but what a wonderful player, what imagination. If you would look at the piece of paper on which timpani parts are printed and other percussion instruments are printed, you would see something completely dull and uninteresting. She knows how to bring life into that, with imagination. . . . She is one of the greatest artists in the world. She's a girl. She's black."[5]

The four concerts in Town Hall verged on disaster. Gerhard Samuel, Matthias Bamert, and Ainslee Cox each conducted one concert—the fourth was conducted by Stokowski. All were beautifully played and the programs were interesting. The problem was that there was no audience. There had been no publicity, no promotion, and it was sad to find Stokowski conducting in Town Hall to a half-empty house. His program contained works of Ulysses Kay, Ned Rorem, and Alan Hovhaness. Ulysses' piece was his *Brief Elegy* for oboe and strings. "Instead of doing it as a piece for string orchestra with oboe solo," said Ulysses, "he apportioned the solo bits of the oboe part with other woodwinds. I think he used a flute and a clarinet and a high bassoon, so that the piece had a different timbre. . . . I was quite surprised because I hadn't gone to a rehearsal—and yet I was pleased."[6] At the conclusion of the piece Stoki gestured toward the audience for Ulysses to take a bow.

After playing Alan Hovhaness' Alleluia and Fugue, he had Alan rise and accept the plaudits of the audience. But after playing *Pilgrims* by Ned Rorem, no one rose in response to Stokowski's gesture. At that very moment Ned had gone alone to see the movie *A Clockwork Orange*, feeling slightly guilty: "Now Stokowski is a great man, an idol of my childhood, and more than once he's played my music. But I don't like *Pilgrims* anymore. My contention: the worse a piece is the worse it will sound the better it's played, like a wart on a well-focused photo. Apparently the Maestro gestured for me to rise, but I was invisible, so he shrugged and went on to the next work. (I know about this from the newspaper. No one invited me either to a rehearsal or to the program.)"[7]

Alas, poor Ned. His "wart" received but mild applause.

At the conclusion of the concert, Stoki added an encore. It was a Reverie that he had conducted from time to time, attributing it to a composer by the name of Slavichi. He finally admitted that it was composed by himself when he was a student. It was attractive and had a distinctly Slavic character.[8]

Early in 1972 Stoki phoned Jack Ossewaarde, organist and choirmaster of St. Bartholomew's Church, telling him that he had composed a *Pianissimo Amen* and wondered whether he might come down and have some time with the choir to see how it sounded. It was quickly arranged, and again at St. Bartholomew's, as he had first done sixty-seven years before, he conducted its choir. From this brief reunion with Ossewaarde, who had been a member of the Houston Symphony Orchestra under Stoki, came the suggestion that he conduct a concert in the new Cathedral-sized church on Park Avenue—the earlier St. Bartholomew's in which he had played the organ had stood a few blocks away on Madison Avenue.[9]

The concert took place on Sunday, April 16, just two days before his ninetieth birthday. As in the other church concerts, the place was completely filled.[10]

The program began with two motets that he himself had conducted when he was choirmaster of the church (1905–8): Palestrina's *Adoramus te*, Victoria's *Jesu, Dulcis Memoria*, and Mozart's *Ave Verum Corpus*. Then came an Adagio and Fugue in C Minor of Mozart and the *Magnificat* of Alan Hovhaness. The conclusion was his *Pianissimo Amen*. It was a profoundly touching moment and the audience was deeply moved.

It would have been nice and, in fact, quite dramatic if this had been his final concert in America. It would have been his alpha and omega in St. Bartholomew's, but it was not quite so, for he had two more concerts to conduct with the American Symphony Orchestra.

Although he always said that birthdays were for children, he celebrated his ninetieth with gusto. He was at his television set by 8:30 to watch the "Today" show on NBC. He had pretaped an interview with Barbara Walters and he was curious to see how it had turned out. "I'm not like some who do what they do not like in order not to starve," he said. "That is how life is today. I hope that some day we shall make a better life so that men and women can enjoy their lives and not have to do what is uninteresting to them, and even boring and even annoying to them."

Walters read a quote of a statement Stoki had once made: "I have learned much more from my failures than my successes. Success can poison you." Walters then asked somewhat facetiously how he kept from being poisoned. Stoki chuckled and responded: "It is an interesting question. And I don't know the answer. . . . I think from failures one learns more because usually when one fails one did something and should do the opposite of that, so one learns from the failure." When Barbara Walters asked whether he thought that our century has created music that is on a level with the great music of the past, he responded very intently. "What you are really asking," he said, "is do we know the future? And we do not. We don't know what will happen tomorrow—tomorrow morning what will happen. We don't know. We can guess, but we don't know. So I cannot tell you what will be the results in the future of music that is being created today. . . . But what will be the result of 10 years from now, 50 years from now, 100 years from now of the music that is being created today, we do not know."

"Can you guess?"

"I never indulge in guessing. I like facts."[11]

After watching the telecast, he departed for his rehearsal in Carnegie

Hall and one of the rare occurrences in his career; he arrived at his rehearsal about ten minutes late. He apologized to the players and launched into a three-hour rehearsal of the Ninth Symphony of Beethoven.

Photo Popsie

Receiving a first edition of Beethoven's Ninth Symphony score presented by Ulysses Kay for BMI at ninetieth birthday party

To spare him extra travel and simplify the rest of his day, he had engaged a suite at the Plaza Hotel in which he could rest before the festivities of his birthday party. At five he came into the ballroom. Jack Baumgarten was at his side. He stood at the entrance and then walked straight to the dais, counting the number of steps he would have to take. He rehearsed the entrance as thoroughly as he might have rehearsed the beginning of an overture.

Over three hundred friends and admirers gathered to make the evening a gala occasion. Each had paid $100 for the privilege. The tab also included cocktails before the banquet, and in order to summon the revelers to their tables, Ainslee Cox conducted three fanfares. Other fanfares —there were seven in all—were to be interspersed throughout the evening. The pieces had been commissioned for the International Music Council's convocation, which had been held in New York a few years before. They were by Richard Arnell (England), Klaus Egge (Norway), Carlos Surinach (Spain), Josef Tal (Israel), and three Americans: Ross Lee Finney, Ulysses Kay, and Donald Lybbert.

It all began splendidly. The sequence of things had been carefully plotted and Norman Cousins acted as the able master of ceremonies. A fanfare sounded to welcome the guest of honor and Stokowski carefully strode to the dais and took his place among his children, grandchildren, and his former wife, Evangeline. Gloria, however, chose not to attend.

Things began to vary from the carefully planned schedule. Mayor Lindsay arrived suddenly and Ainslee quickly greeted him with a fanfare. The players, enjoying the free-flowing wine at their table, began to read notes that none of the composers had ever dreamed of putting on paper. The audience, quite unaware, merely regarded them as increasingly modern expressions.

There were tributes from many organizations: Ulysses Kay representing BMI presented him with a first edition of the Ninth Symphony dated 1826. There were greetings from most of the musical organizations in the city, and one special gift that I had assembled was a collection of tributes, mostly musical, from sixty-three different composers, including Shostakovich, Kabalevsky, Frank Martin, Carl Orff, Darius Milhaud, Leonard Bernstein, Ulysses Kay, William Schuman, Alan Hovhaness, Ernst Krenek, Gunther Schuller, and fifty-two more. Lou Harrison wrote a *Jahla in the Form of a Ductia to Pleasure Leopold Stokowski on His Ninetieth Birthday.* It was for harp and percussion, beautifully illuminated in Lou's superb calligraphy.

Norman Cousins had a sheaf of letters and telegrams from various dignitaries who were not able to be present. He began to read. The first was from Richard Nixon:

Dear Mr. Stokowski:

I take special satisfaction in adding my compliments to those of your friends whose special pleasure it is to honor you on your ninetieth birthday.

Few have been given your extraordinary measure of talent; and fewer still have remained so dedicated to their calling. Your gifted leadership of the American Symphony Orchestra and your devotion to talented young citizens have earned you my deepest personal respect and that of men and women everywhere.

I regret that I cannot be with you on this happy occasion, but I want you to know that my thoughts will be there as will my best wishes that every joy and satisfaction may be yours in the years ahead.

Sincerely,
Richard Nixon[12]

Before Cousins could proceed and read greetings from Nelson Rockefeller and others, Stokowski stood, and with his right arm extended as if he were conducting, said that he had had enough. He wanted no more tributes and we should get on with the music. Jorge Bolet obliged with a ballade of Chopin. Later Judith Raskin sang and William Masselos played parts of Schumann's *Davidsbündlertänze*. A part of *Fantasia* was shown. Quite unplanned and unscheduled was a tribute made by timpanist Elayne Jones. She stepped up to the lectern and made a spontaneous tribute to Stokowski in the name of the orchestra members. It was one of the brightest moments of the entire evening.

A fanfare introduced the birthday cake and everyone sang "Happy Birthday" as Stoki rose and conducted. Surrounded by his children and grandchildren, he seemed to be very happy. "For me there are two great things in life," he said in response. "They are friendship and music."

A day or so after his birthday, a letter arrived from Jacqueline Onassis:

April 19, 1972

Dear Maestro

I have just returned from Europe and write you this note to say that if ever you could come to tea with the children and me —we would be so happy—

I realize how very busy you are, so that it will really be a miracle if it ever happens!

Most Sincerely,
Jacqueline Onassis[13]

Two weeks later on May 1, a board meeting of the American Symphony was held and Stoki was scheduled to attend. Shortly before the meeting was to begin, Jack Baumgarten, Stoki's assistant, brought me two letters. One was addressed to the "Board of Directors" and the second to the

Photo Popsie
With author and Sadja's son Jason at ninetieth birthday
party at the Plaza Hotel (April 18, 1972)

"Members of the Corporation of the American Symphony Orchestra."
Both notes were in his usual way, terse. In the first he wrote:

> Thank you for all you have done to assist in maintaining the
> American Symphony Orchestra for the past 10 years. I wish to thank
> Mrs. Tishman and Oliver Daniel and their committee for making the
> benefit of the ASO a success.
>
> Because of the impossibility of recording in the United States, it
> is necessary for me to now record in Europe. For this reason, I shall
> only be able to conduct the first pair of concerts for the 1972–'73
> season. Since I am leaving next week for Europe and will return only
> for these concerts, it is necessary for me to resign as Music Director
> and Vice-President. . . . I sincerely regret this decision and wish you
> every success in the future.[14]

The second letter was a simple one-liner: "I submit my resignation as
a member of the corporation because increased duties elsewhere make it
impossible for me to continue."[15]

For several years he had no exclusive recording contract and had made "ad hoc" recordings with Capitol, Everest, Vanguard, CRI, Columbia, and others. His recent concerts in England had been very rewarding and he did not have to struggle building and rebuilding the orchestras as he had been doing with the ASO. Since 1964 he had made a most satisfying series of recordings for London-Decca, and now Tony D'Amato, director of the Phase-4 project at Decca, urged him to come to London and promised to set up an elaborate series of concerts and recordings.

The prospect was most intriguing for Stokowski. He enjoyed England more on each successive visit and now definitely wanted to return. For about a year he had been looking through copies of the English magazine *Country Life*, which carries elaborate ads for houses and estates throughout Britain, and he was eager to visit some of these properties.

Shortly before leaving for England, he and a few friends joined me for a small dinner party at my house in Westchester. It had been an old mill dating back to 1784. There is still a millstream that cascades beside the house and on that evening we walked out to the little bridge that spans the stream. "I want to have a place like this with a stream," he told me. And that is what he found. Right from the pages of *Country Life* he chose a place in the town of Nether Wallop. The several-hundred-year-old house was on a one-and-three-quarter acre plot, with a little vegetable garden and a running stream at its foot.

The Move to England

NOT for a moment did Stoki envision the demise of the American Symphony. He and Jack Baumgarten had worked on plans for the 1972–73 season for many months and he announced that he would be happy to return and conduct the opening concert in the fall. Some conductors had been contacted—among them Jascha Horenstein and Karel Ančerl.[1] Even details of programs were being considered. Economics dictated otherwise. The morning after the birthday party, Cathy French, without consulting the board, utilized all the money that had accrued and used it to pay salaries that were owed to the players without paying the bill at the Plaza.

Having shelled out $100 apiece for the fund-raising party, sponsors were in no mood to repeat the process in order to pay the Plaza. The board was confronted with an appalling debt. Largely because of his personal admiration for Elayne Jones, Stoki had bought a set of timpani for the orchestra. "These were over $4,000," said Arthur Aaron. "They were used by the orchestra, but when the orchestra got into difficulty, they were sold to pay off some of the debts."[2]

When Stoki and Natasha embarked on the *Queen Elizabeth II* in mid-May they anticipated a quiet and peaceful crossing. It was not to be. Three days out, a bomb threat was telephoned to the offices of the Cunard Line. The caller demanded a $350,000 ransom. A royal demolition crew was flown from Britain and dropped alongside the sixty-five-thousand-ton ship about five hundred miles northwest of the Azores. Searchers inspected the luggage as well as the ship itself, but no bomb was found. In

Home at Nether Wallop, Hampshire, England (1977)

reporting the incident, the Associated Press informed its readers: "The liner left New York Monday with 1550 passengers, including 90-year-old conductor Leopold Stokowski and about 800 crewmen." His name was the only one mentioned among the more than two thousand who were on board.[3]

Joyce Bright was at dockside when Stoki and Natasha disembarked in Southampton. She drove them to see friends in Sussex and from there they began to explore leads they had come upon through the pages of *Country Life,* the magazine that Edward Johnson had been sending over for more than a year. While exploring the area not far from Salisbury, Stoki and Natasha discovered a house which Stoki seemed to think ideal: "It was a rainy day and I saw this advertisement in *Country Life,* so I called the owner. The description of the house sounded very nice, so we hired a taxi and went and looked at it. I think he just fell in love with it as soon as we arrived. It was very old. The floor in the entrance hall was made of old flagstones and there were cows across the road. Even in the downpour it was beautiful."[4]

Natasha explained that the deed of the house went back to 1270 but the house itself was "only" about five hundred years old. "We did a great deal to it. . . . It had one and three-quarters acres and a little vegetable garden. It was a very peaceful, lovely life in a quiet early village. . . ."[5]

After finding the house in Nether Wallop, the next item of importance was the planning of the concert to celebrate the sixtieth anniversary of his first appearance with the London Symphony Orchestra in 1912. Tony D'Amato and Harold Lawrence, the manager of the orchestra, had the matter well in hand. The initial idea for the affair had germinated in the mind of Edward Johnson, who was doing some research into Stoki's early days in London.[6] Stoki was to repeat the identical program that he had conducted on that earlier date: Wagner's Prelude to *Die Meistersinger*, Debussy's Prelude to the *Afternoon of a Faun*, the Glazunov Violin Concerto, and the First Symphony of Brahms. The date was June 14, 1972, and almost as soon as the concert was announced there was a complete sellout. After a hasty conference it was decided to repeat the concert the following night in London's much larger Albert Hall. Tony planned to record in both locations.

Efrem Zimbalist had been the soloist during the first concert and for this recreation the soloist was to be a young and very beautiful Rumanian virtuoso named Silvia Marcovici, who was a mere seventy years younger than the Maestro. For some not entirely explained reason Miss Marcovici was detained in Rumania—a circumstance that greatly disturbed Stoki. He phoned me at my hotel and discussed commandeering some other violinist to appear in her stead. For the first rehearsal an appeal was sent out to various London music schools: the Royal Academy, Royal College, the Menuhin School, and others asking a young violinist to fill in until the tardy Miss Marcovici would arrive. "The piece has just gone right out of fashion," reported the *Guardian*, "no student could claim to play it. Stokowski, who likes to encourage young musicians like this, will have to re-arrange his rehearsal schedule after all."[7]

When Miss Marcovici finally did arrive, she took her place on the rehearsal stage dressed in the most abbreviated miniskirt and leather laced-up boots that were practically knee-length. She was a stunning creature—a fact that did not elude Stokowski.

The concert was one of the more exciting musical and social events of the season. It was not only recorded but telecast as well. "The thing was done in style," reported the *Times*. "Television lights blazed, the audience bounced up and down like scalded grasshoppers. . . ."[8]

"Stokowski's legendary hands," wrote Peter Stadlen, "are without exception put to the strictest functional use. His angular, almost ungainly movements are the simple tools for some of the most masterly conducting the century has witnessed . . . by what seemingly incongruous flicks of the wrist did he promote the fabulously sensitive woodwind solos in Debussy's *L'Après-midi d'un faune?* In Brahms's *First Symphony*, Stokowski made his points not hysterically but forcefully, without compelling us to live on our nerves and often suggesting the terraced, cumulative effect of an organist's lines. Never has lifelong global fame rested on more solid foundations."[9]

There was one item missing from the concert to make it conform to the original one. After the wildly exuberant applause following the Brahms, Stoki asked his eager audience whether they would like to hear the missing item. They shouted that they would and with the applause still ringing, he turned and with a slash of his hands unleashed all of the color, sound, and brazen inspiration of Tchaikovsky's *Marche Slave*.

The repeat program was as successful as the first. In addition to the *Marche Slave* he added five extra encores: Byrd Pavane and Gigue, Schubert *Moment Musicale*, Clarke (Purcell) *Trumpet Voluntary*, Tchaikovsky *Song without Words*, and the Scriabin Etude in C-sharp Minor.

Decca's recording of the concert suggests that it was taken solely from the performance in Festival Hall. Edward Johnson adds additional information: "The 'Phase 4' recording on Decca/London records has the Wagner Overture and part of the Debussy from the Festival Hall performance; the second half of the Debussy finds the sound 'opening out' and this comes from the Albert Hall performance. The first minute of the Glazunov is Festival Hall, then the rest is Albert Hall; the Brahms and speech and Tchaikovsky are all Albert Hall."[10]

Tony D'Amato's next concert-cum-recording was to take place in Prague and the recording was to be a joint effort of Decca and the Czech company, Supraphon, with releases on both sides of the Iron Curtain. There were to be two concerts—both in the Dvořák Hall of Prague's House of Artists—on September 7 and 8. There was much interest in these concerts and Stoki's son Chris and Edward Johnson set out by plane from London while Ainslee Cox flew in from the States. Stoki, Natasha, and Joyce Bright crossed the Channel and set off by train for Prague. Tony

D'Amato and the recording crew drove. All were to meet in Prague's Hotel Esplanade.

"We all arrived at the hotel," said Ainslee, "and there was no Stokowski. He was supposed to have arrived two days before but he was not there. . . . So here we all were having tea at the Esplanade Hotel for hours and hours waiting for Stokowski to appear. . . . The next day was the first rehearsal but still he didn't appear. But we all went to the hall where the orchestra's assistant conductor took the rehearsal. . . . Stokowski's music had just arrived by mail."[11]

No one in Prague was contacted. There were no phone calls nor telegrams. There was a sort of mild panic spreading about and some of the orchestra members had doubts that he would ever arrive. Meanwhile, Stoki had been proceeding by train when he sustained a serious fall. "I traveled with him to Prague on that fateful trip when he fell," Natasha recalled, "I had gone ahead to see to the luggage and Joyce Bright was with him. We were stopping, I think, at Metz. We were very concerned that somebody might steal our luggage and walk off the train with it. We had been in the dining car, so I dashed ahead just to stay with the luggage and a youngster who was trying to get his suitcase off quickly kicked it in front of Stoki. He didn't see it and he tripped and fell. That's how it happened; he was in great pain. So we took him off the train at Frankfurt and got him to a little Catholic hospital. It was a beautiful jewel of a hospital—St. Elizabeth's. They treated him marvelously. I said his name was Anthony Boleslawowicz and he was there for two nights. They didn't want him to travel but he said, 'I have to. I have to work in Prague.'

"The surgeon in the hospital said that the fact that he had an artificial hip is what saved him. He fell on that side, and while he was severely bruised and in considerable pain, he didn't break anything . . . it was just a miracle."[12]

Joyce Bright, with fine presence of mind, phoned London and told Tony D'Amato about the turn of events. Tony flew to Frankfurt and there he hired a van. He could not fit all the luggage into any conventional car —"Joyce Bright had so many boxes with hats in them."[13]

"As we were leaving," Natasha recalled, "there was one Sister who spoke English and she said to me, 'Please tell me. I know that he's somebody. He's not an ordinary person. Who is he?' So I said, 'Well, you won't let on. We're concerned about the press finding out about this.' She said, 'No. You know I wouldn't tell.' And she never did."[14]

"We picked Stoki up at the hospital," said Tony, "and he hobbled along on crutches. I had bought a cane for him from London; he wanted one especially from Harrods. We had this rather fascinating trip in a Volkswagen minivan. We stopped at Rothenburg, at the Kaiserhof, and I had to carry him into the hotel. It was very difficult for him. One of the things he was so finicky about was being helped in and out of cars or up and down stairs. . . . He really was uncomfortable but he knew it was necessary. There was no other way that he could get up the stairs.

"We sat down and had a drink. He was really quite happy in spite of his ailment. . . . To him, it was almost as if he were angry with his body. It was a machine that was breaking down and he didn't like it because his brain was intact, his instinct was intact, and his bloody body was failing him. He resented that.

"He hated being taken to the toilet. He hated being helped to be undressed. I had a sense of that, but he had no choice. Something very close developed as a result of that.

"We had all sorts of adventures on the way to Prague. We were stopped by the Czech police. I ran a red light—Natalie was yapping about directions and 'isn't this beautiful and isn't that beautiful' and 'look at this, Maestro.' He had his leg stretched out on the seat and just wanted to rest and sleep. Joyce, as always, was very tactful."[15]

On the following morning Tony and his precious contingent drove up before the Esplanade. "We were horrified!" said Ainslee. "He was in pain. There was no question about that. But he was, as always, determined to go right ahead and he did. . . . He was in a wheelchair, but we got him in and out of the buildings all right. We would wheel the chair to the edge of the stage and get him up, and he would use his crutches to get onto the stage."[16]

Jaroslav Holeček, a musicologist, celesta player, and librarian for the Czech Philharmonic Orchestra, related that the entire orchestra had looked forward to Stokowski's arrival with great anticipation. But when he did not arrive and there seemed to be no explanation, the musicians became alarmed. When he appeared on the platform of Dvořák Hall, supported by his assistant, Holeček observed that "it was evident that he had not yet recovered from his accident and that he had to gather all of his strength to conduct the rehearsal. In spite of that he started with the most difficult work: Scriabin's *Poem of Ecstasy.* The Czech Philharmonic had played this work under Jan Krenz, the Polish conductor, the previous spring, so we knew it well. But in Mr. Stokowski's reading, the tempo, expression, and conception were altogether different. The first run-through was rather confused. The conductor's gestures were weak and indistinct, he had difficulties in reading the score and he often made mistakes even in beating the changes of time. . . .

"There was great anxiety as to whether the conductor would be able to conduct the two concerts in such a demanding program without damage to his good name as well as the orchestra's. After the rehearsal the Artistic Council of the orchestra met to consider whether it wouldn't be better to cancel the concerts due to the conductor's ill health. Fortunately, it was decided to await the next rehearsal.

"And then, to the great surprise of everyone, Mr. Stokowski was totally changed. He had recovered so well that he was able not only to play the works through without stopping, but to rehearse them properly. . . . The orchestra played and felt better, of course.

"Now there were no more doubts; the concerts would take place. Their atmosphere was very festive. Everybody felt that they were present at an extraordinary artistic event, not only because of the age of the conductor, but because of his merits, personal charm, and last but not least, his great art. . . . Unforgettable were his words at the end of the rehearsal when he said, smiling kindly, 'It's marvelous how you play.' "[17]

"Then came the performances," said Ainslee. "He still had to use his crutches, so I had to help him onto the stage. I sat on a little chair just under the podium to be there to help him up and down, because he literally couldn't do it alone."[18]

Tony, Ainslee, and all who were there agreed that the orchestra "adored" him. "When he walked on stage," Tony recalled, "you could see that he was a marvelous actor—and I mean that in the best sense of the word."

The Bach transcriptions and the *Enigma* Variations were entirely new to the orchestra, and Stokowski was able to impose his own conceptions rather than fight the traditional approach that comes after an orchestra has been playing and replaying certain works for a thousand times.[19]

"They played for him with incredible attention," said Ainslee, "with a kind of concentration that you rarely see in any orchestra anywhere in the world. . . . They played with a style and unanimity of tone which struck me as being very much like what the Philadelphia Orchestra must have done in the early days of the heyday."

The entire concerts were recorded, including the encores that he added. They were not merely capricious additions but well-planned additions to the recording package: the Rachmaninoff Prelude in C-sharp Minor, a Tchaikovsky *Song without Words* and the Dvořák Slavonic Dance in E Minor.

When the recording session was over, Tony D'Amato and the Decca crew flew back to London. Everyone tried to persuade Stoki to fly also, but he refused. It was suggested that Ainslee drive the Volkswagen mini-van, but he declined, since he did not have an international driver's license and was reluctant to take the responsibility of transporting such a precious cargo through unknown roads and territories. It was decided then that Stoki, Natasha, and Chris would proceed by train.

"Of course," said Ainslee, "in Prague it was necessary to spend as much of the money as possible because you couldn't take it out of the country. So Natasha had gone to a lot of shops and bought lots of things, including a kitchen cabinet. . . . Of course, their train was stopped at the border and was examined and searched for hours. It evidently turned into an extremely uncomfortable, disagreeable trip. . . ."[20]

"It was on the way back that he became ill," Natasha remembered. "He caught a very bad cold on the trip back . . . we were in Frankfurt station and it was bitter cold when we came in at ten at night and there were no taxis or anything and poor Chris was looking for a taxi and Stoki was on his crutches. . . . Finally we got a taxi and got to the hotel and then he complained that he wasn't feeling well and I was very concerned and I called doctors in London. Stoki finally said, 'I think perhaps we had better fly back.' He should have flown from Prague with Tony D'Amato."[21]

When Leopold, Chris, and Natasha finally reached Nether Wallop, he was still suffering from the torn ligament in his leg as well as from the cold and exposure he had endured during the trip. Natasha was rightfully concerned, and on the advice of his physician, she urged him to cancel his forthcoming concert with the Philadelphia Orchestra. It had been the management's plan to celebrate not only his four-score-and-tenth anniversary but to also mark the sixtieth anniversary of his first appearance with the Philadelphia Orchestra. He was to have conducted the identical program that he had led at his debut with the orchestra.[22]

The decision to cancel was made after Boris Sokoloff, the Philadelphia Orchestra's manager, received a cable from Stokowski:

MR. SOKOLOFF, MR. EUGENE ORMANDY AND ALL THE ARTISTS OF THE PHILADELPHIA ORCHESTRA:

BECAUSE OF THE INJURY TO MY LEG MY PHYSICIANS
HAVE ADVISED ME AGAINST AN OCEAN VOYAGE AT
THIS TIME AND HAVE ORDERED ME TO TAKE A COM-
PLETE REST FOR THE NEXT THREE MONTHS SO RE-
GRETTABLY I AM FORCED TO CANCEL THE PENSION
FUND CONCERT ON OCTOBER 11.
WITH WARM GREETINGS TO ALL MY FRIENDS IN
PHILADELPHIA.

LEOPOLD STOKOWSKI[23]

In addition to the disappointment he keenly felt on canceling his
appearance with the Philadelphia Orchestra, he was equally distressed
when he discovered that his beloved American Symphony Orchestra was
being temporarily disbanded. He had given so much of himself to it—the
endless auditions and rehearsals that he had shepherded for the past
decade and the other assistance he had given in the matter of finances.
During the entire period he had never received a penny from the orchestra
and, as we know, had aided it financially from time to time. Now, even
after his resignation, he still felt obligated and concerned about the plight
of its devoted players.

During the summer he had contributed $30,000 to the orchestra on a
matching-fund basis with checks of $10,000 remitted on July 11, July 25,
and August 22. He also added about $4,000 to help amortize other debts
that the orchestra had incurred. He renewed his offer to conduct an
opening concert if the orchestra were to be reactivated. The feelings of
many of the players were the same as that expressed by harpist Lise
Nardeau: "We're all hoping Maestro Stokowski will change his mind and
come back from England to lead us again."[24]

Tony and his colleague Raymond Few had been working for many
months preparing a television documentary on Stokowski to be called "A
Portrait of Greatness." Few had been the manager of the Royal Philharmonic and subsequently, when becoming affiliated with London-Decca
and the Phase-4 operation, was the producer of Stoki's last recordings.
Tony D'Amato and Raymond Few formed their own production team
and worked jointly with a Dutch TV company known as Nederlandse
Omroep Stichting.

They planned a fifty-six-minute telecast in color that was to be filmed
during a three-week journey from his home in Nether Wallop to Israel,
where to commemorate the twenty-fifth anniversary of the founding of
the state of Israel, he would conduct the Israel Philharmonic Orchestra

in a series of concerts. Film and recording crews were to be flown to Israel from England and Holland. Stoki, Natasha, Tony, and the Dutch producer, Wilhelmina Hoedeman, were to travel by ship and auto across the Channel and through various French villages where Stoki would be received and honored, and finally to Marseilles.[25]

From here the party was to proceed by ship stopping at Genoa, Malta, Cyprus, and finally Haifa. Tony planned to conclude the telecast with a visit by Stoki into old Jerusalem: "At ninety, in the dead of winter, so arduous a journey for so fragile a bodily machine has all the semblance of a pilgrimage, a personal pilgrimage. It is this quality, this journey, this purpose, attended by deep and meaningful and, often, humorous thoughts and ideas on all subjects . . . will make this filmed 'Portrait' unique."[26]

The pilgrimage to Israel was to begin on February 8, 1973, in Nether Wallop, proceed to Southampton, on to Le Havre, and arrive at Caudebec-en-Caux at seven-thirty in the evening. The next day and the days thereafter were all meticulously planned in exhausting detail. Perhaps *exhausting* was the correct adjective to describe the project, since it was Natasha who perceived, and correctly, that the "bodily machine" of Stokowski was not up to it. She convinced Stoki that such a tour at that time would be impossible, and she was certainly right, for Stokowski was not in any physical condition to undertake such an arduous trip.

Other options were also being reexamined. Tony D'Amato had long maintained that the physical effort of a concert so stimulated Stokowski that recordings either on the spot or immediately after were preferable. Natasha and Jack Baumgarten disagreed. For a long period both Tony and Raymond Few had acted as official and unofficial managers, booking Stokowski with various orchestras with recordings to follow.

Tony buttressed his arguments for recording in concert halls persuasively. He felt that that was how one could get the best out of Stokowski. "That's where the energy was and at his advanced age, studio work was just too dull and too technical and, in a sense, too antiseptic. A live-recorded situation was the best possible situation for him. That was my opinion."[27]

A concert with the New Philharmonia Orchestra was set up by Tony in the Royal Albert Hall on January 11, 1973, followed by two recording sessions in Kingsway Hall. The concert program included the *Egmont* Overture and Seventh Symphony of Beethoven, Rimsky-Korsakov's *Capriccio Espagnol,* and Elgar's *Enigma* Variations. All but the Elgar appeared on London-Decca's Phase-4 series. The *Capriccio Espagnol* was added as a filler to complete the recording which Stoki had done of Scriabin's *Poem of Ecstasy* with the Czech Philharmonic.

No exceptions were made by the critics in deference to his age. "Leopold Stokowski proved last night that he is still probably the most dynamic and imaginative of all conductors in spite of his 90 years," wrote Frank Granville Barker in the *London Daily Express*. [28]

The reception of the Stokowski Beethoven Seventh was splendid and offered ample opportunity for comparison. One wonders whether any aspect of the entertainment business was ever more unimaginative and closed-minded than the recording industry. Four other new recordings of the symphony were released almost simultaneously. They were by Casals, Böhm, Carlos Kleiber, and Solti. But these were not the only ones competing for the collector's dollar. A quick look at a Schwann catalog listing other versions of the same work available in June 1973 included: Abbado, Ansermet, Bernstein, Boult, Cantelli, Gielen, Giulini, Jochum, Karajan, Klemperer, and Reiner. The British classical record catalog, *Gramophone* (the Schwann equivalent), listed twenty-one different versions of the Beethoven Seventh available in its June 1973 edition. One must be appalled at this seemingly senseless duplication. Is it any wonder that the bottom began to fall out of the recording business?

After the Beethoven recording there was relatively little that was in the offing now that the trip to Israel was no longer viable. A Youth Orchestra concert had been set up as well as a concert in Croydon.

Since the whole purpose of moving to London had been largely motivated by the opportunity of making many recordings, Stoki decided that he should no longer be bound by an exclusive contract with Decca. And to that point he engaged Marty Wargo, who had previously been with Decca, as a personal manager who would not only book concerts but arrange recording dates with other companies. This obviously came as a shock to Tony D'Amato, who had devoted ten years to Stoki with Decca. Since Stoki wanted to be free of the exclusivity restriction that his contract with Decca imposed, Tony went a step further and canceled the contract completely; there would be no more recordings for Decca.

For the final confrontation, Tony did it with a flair. "I decided if I'm going to get edged out, I'm going to do it in style. So I put on my best suit and tie and I got a chauffeur with a cap and Skip Muller drove with me from London down to Nether Wallop." Stoki appeared to be quite upset and remained only a short while and left Tony, Skip Muller, Marty Wargo, and Natasha to argue the matter. Before leaving, Stoki mentioned "that business of the universality of music and how he had to work for all companies, and that music is the universal language and all the rest of that nonsense," Tony concluded. But without any bitterness, he added that "it's just part of the business and if Stoki wants to go that way, bless him. He's ninety-five and a giant. . . . What happened is that he has worked now for many companies and there has been no diversity of repertoire. . . . I think it is singularly unfair to that old man who dreams of Mahler not to let him do the whole cycle. What the hell is he doing with Bizet's *Carmen* and the *L'Arlésienne Suites?*"[29]

During his decade with Decca Phase-4, Stoki had made many splendid discs and the repertoire was distinguished. He had done the Second Orchestral Set of Ives, Messiaen's *L'Ascension*, Berlioz's *Symphonie Fantastique*, the Fifth, Seventh and Ninth symphonies of Beethoven, Mussorgsky's *Pictures at an Exhibition* and *Night on Bald Mountain*, Elgar's *Enigma* Variations, Debussy's *La Mer*, Ravel's *Daphnis et Chloé* Suite No. 2, Scriabin's *Poem of Ecstasy*, and Vivaldi's *Four Seasons*.

One of the last major works planned for the Decca series was to be the Rachmaninoff Rhapsody on a Theme of Paganini. Stoki had conducted it in its world premiere with Rachmaninoff as the soloist in Philadelphia on November 7, 1934, and they subsequently recorded it for RCA Victor. Now, thirty-nine years later, Stoki was eager to record it again and this time he wanted to do it with Horowitz. But when he realized that because of various contractual complications it would not be possible, he mentioned to Tony D'Amato that he had only done it with Rachmaninoff and that if he could not have Horowitz he would like some brilliant youngster to play the piano part. "I had a pianist that I was very much interested in—a young girl called Ilana Vered," Tony told me. Stoki quickly had her play for him and was most eager to make the recording. Although nearly forty years had elapsed, Stoki remarked that he could remember almost note for note the details of Rachmaninoff's playing.

The concert with Ilana Vered and the London Symphony took place in the Royal Albert Hall on April 25, 1973. "He was superb," Ilana recalled. "He balanced so well with me and the orchestra . . . many times with other conductors you have to fight for your life; you have to play louder in order to be heard. But with Stokowski there was no such question. He balanced the orchestra to suit the piano.

"He was already getting on in his years and he asked me at one point during the rehearsal, 'Where are we?' I told him we were in Albert Hall, so that seemed to satisfy him.

"I certainly was frightened by that, and I said, my God, if he doesn't know where we are, how can we play it tonight?"

During the concert there was apparently a brief memory lapse. "After variation number eighteen he got very tired and I could see his head going down toward the music stand. I thought, oh my God, either he is drunking out on me or he's going to have a little snooze." The lapse was only momentary and "all of a sudden we were in business again and his head came up and he heard me playing and he recognized where he was . . . and we were going at an incredible speed, which is amazing because I've played with some other old conductors who just got slower as they got older. It wasn't a question that he got slower, he just would lose contact from time to time."[30]

The critics observed none of the aberrations Miss Vered had described. They listened attentively and even exercised some of their ready superlatives. Edward Greenfield reviewed the concert in the *Guardian:* "Just what chemical ingredients go to making a Stokowski concert into a great occasion is something which eludes precise analysis. It always helps of course to have a packed Albert Hall, an audience expectant, an audience aware that this hunched seemingly fragile figure has been conjuring up great occasions for well over 60 years.

"But that is only the start of the precipitation process. If one wanted to analyze the magic in this latest concert . . . it was more than usually evident just how much Stokowski, like others in the tradition of greatness, leads to the inspiration of the moment. That was particularly true of the performance of a work which he helped to see into the world almost 40 years ago, Rachmaninoff's Rhapsody on a Theme of Paganini."

He had high praise for Vered and felt that she matched Stokowski's imagination remarkably well. While he did not think that the performance of the orchestra was one of the tidiest, he did remark that "the pointing was still so delicate that it was one of the wittiest. . . . It was also one of the most beautiful, with each variation even the luscious eighteenth striking one afresh in the refinement and originality of the instrumental colouring."[31]

The recording was made. Vered appeared as the fleet-fingered soloist but the conductor was Hans Vonk. A semi-official story was circulated that the substitution of Vonk was because of Stoki's health. It was instead the state of his contractual health with Decca.

The concert had taken place one week after his ninety-first birthday. During the same week he conducted the second half of a concert in

Fairfield Hall, Croydon. Sir Arthur Bliss, Master of the Queen's Musick, had been commissioned to compose a set of Variations for Orchestra for the Croydon Festival and it was conducted by Vernon Handley. After intermission Stoki conducted a performance of Tchaikovsky's *Pathétique* Symphony that exuded "enough Slavonic grief to drown the whole of Croydon in a sea of tears."[32]

Marty Wargo now arranged a resumption of Stokowski recordings with RCA. The first sessions were scheduled for July 2 and 4, 1973, in the Walthamstow Town Hall. The work to be recorded was the Dvořák Symphony No. 9 (*New World*). It was hardly a daring choice but it was to enjoy a somewhat imaginative packaging. In a two-record set it would be coupled with the 1927 Philadelphia Orchestra recording of the same work with Stoki's spoken "outline of themes."

Just as he had done for London-Decca, Stoki conducted a concert for the BBC featuring the *New World* Symphony with the New Philharmonia Orchestra before making the recording. The BBC concert was given almost a month before the studio recording date, but it was not to be aired by BBC until October 5. The program began with the *Egmont* Overture of Beethoven followed by the Symphony No. 28 of Havergal Brian.

One of Brian's scores had been taken to Stokowski by Edward Johnson as early as 1967. Brian, who was born in 1879, was one of the most neglected of British composers. He composed twenty-seven symphonies between the ages of seventy and ninety-two, but unfortunately did not live to hear Stokowski's performance of his symphony. The work which Edward Johnson had originally suggested was his *Sinfonia Tragica*, but since a score was not immediately available, the BBC sent a number of other unperformed symphonies to Stokowski instead. Stoki chose the Symphony No. 28 in C Minor, written when Brian was a mere ninety-one. It was a noisy work requiring eleven percussionists, and "did nothing either for this neglected composer nor for Stoki, who despite having chosen it from several scores, clearly didn't like the piece once it had been 'read through' at the first rehearsal," Edward Johnson said ruefully.[33] However, it was to be the last in a long list of world premieres that Stoki conducted.

It is difficult to see how RCA could have benefited from the rehearsals and performance of the *New World* Symphony a month in advance. Stoki had difficulties with the New Philharmonia which he had not encountered with the London Symphony. Unable to get the precision and quality he wanted from the brass, he delivered a sharp rebuke and suggested that when they returned home they practice. "The sensitive brass dissolved into hoots of derision and the Grand Old Man, waiting until the mirth had died said shortly: 'I have no sense of humor.' " Visibly furious, he strode from the hall and went to the control room to listen to tapes of the rehearsal. After a space of at least thirty minutes he returned to finish the recording "confronted by a chastened orchestra."[34]

Courtesy Mrs. Percy Stock
With brother, Percy (Jim) Stock, at Nether Wallop

The packaged pair of discs was attractive, with photos of Stokowski in his young days looking across toward a rather pathetic photo of him at ninety-one. Both critically and commercially it was a success and RCA could be happy to have one of its stars back—one whose career with the company spanned fifty-six years. "Here," said one reviewer, "is a collectors item in the making—a set that will be in very great demand as soon as RCA deletes it from its catalog. Don't say we didn't warn you!"[35]

After the fateful trip to Prague, Stokowski had had several bouts of illness and exhaustion, and during the inclement winter months had taken several trips to the Riviera to escape the damp and cold that often tenanted the slate-floored house in Nether Wallop. Word of his slow but perceptible decline had been circulated, though at very low key.

Ainslee Cox, who had heard such rumors, returned to London for an early summer vacation: "I was very uncomfortable about going to see him in '74 because I had not seen him in well over a year. I had heard . . . real horror stories about his memory having gone; about his not recognizing people—not recognizing his daughters when they came to visit and things like that and I didn't want to see him in that state.

"I resented very much the fact that the house that they bought to live in England was so far away from London and that he was cut off from people whom I knew he found stimulating. And I knew that people who were very fond of him and whom he liked very much simply didn't get to visit him often because they felt that was so far away and that they were somehow not welcome. I felt that I could not be in England without making the effort but I didn't want to see him in the condition that I had been told he was in because of all my memories of him—so full of sparkle and vitality."

Overcoming his reluctance, Ainslee, along with Greg Benko of the International Piano Archives and Edward Johnson, took a train to Salisbury, where after visiting the cathedral, they took a taxi to Nether Wallop. Natasha had told them to arrive in midafternoon, when Stoki would be asleep and they could visit before he joined them.

"When we got there," said Ainslee, "it hadn't been more than two minutes before he was up, out of bed after his nap, fully dressed, and beaming from ear to ear and coming out of his bedroom saying, 'Let's have tea.' I really thought he wouldn't remember me. . . . I had just recently been appointed Music Director of the Oklahoma City Symphony and he immediately asked, 'Are there any Indians there?' I reminded him that he had conducted the Oklahoma Symphony himself not too many years before."

Adjacent to the main house there is a shed with a thatched roof. The thatchers had just been there the week before Ainslee's visit and had put in new thatch two feet thick. Stoki had watched the operation intently "all day long every day and, I daresay, told them how to do it," said Ainslee. "He was very proud of that newly thatched roof and told us all about how it was done and he said: 'You know thatching is a dying art. There are just not many people around any more who know how to do it and I don't know what we are going to do when this has to be done again thirty years from now.' And Natasha replied: 'Oh, Maestro, don't worry about it. We'll just have the same people come and do it again.' "[36]

Stoki would have been a mere 122!

Courtesy Skip Muller
Jack Baumgarten and Natasha Bender at Nether Wallop

Stoki insisted that he and Natasha drive their three guests to the station for their return to London. On the following day at "about three in the morning, he got pains in his chest and I called the doctor," Natasha recalled. "I thought he was having a heart attack and that he was going any minute. He couldn't breathe and he had terrible pains in the left side of his chest. The doctor came and listened to his heart and said his heart was perfectly all right, so he gave me something to give him to quiet the pain. The next morning the cardiologist came and said, 'I think I know what it is but I want to have a chest X-ray.' So they got the man there with his machine and the diagnosis was pleurisy which turned into pneumonia. . . .

"At the same time we were remodeling the house. We had a house full of workmen and there was all sorts of noise going on while he was in bed with pneumonia. But you know I think in a way it helped to save him because he was interested in it. He liked to meet the workmen and talk with them and watch them working. He would sit for hours and watch them at their work. He was fascinated when they did the kitchen. It had to be scraped, cleaned, and sandblasted off of the bricks. There was this thick plaster and paint. We had it all stripped off. . . . The beams were scraped and cleaned. This all went on while he was recuperating and he loved it."[37]

Tony D'Amato had a counterpoint of view. He remarked that the house in Nether Wallop was very beautiful. "I haven't been there for years, mind you. But when I was there, the workmen were chipping away. Oh, Natalie does some crazy things, really, and they were so detrimental to the old man's health. She had those workers there. . . . She could have waited until he had gone to France to do the stupid job. It was just absolutely ridiculous. The whole place was like a scene out of Bergman."[38]

The next Albert Hall concert showed all the possibilities of a minidisaster. Because of his lifelong interest in youngsters he responded favorably when he received a letter from Lionel Bryer, chairman of the International Festival of Youth Orchestras. His good friend Edward Heath was its president and that surely motivated his decision. For four years the festival had taken place in Switzerland, but in 1973 it was moved to Aberdeen, Scotland, because, as Mr. Bryer put it: "We had never been able to raise any money in Switzerland."

"I must give Leopold Stokowski his due," said Bryer. "When we first asked him to conduct at our festival, we had absolutely no idea of forming an international orchestra. Out of the blue, a letter arrived from the great Maestro. He said he was prepared to conduct our international orchestra. Now this floored us because we thought . . . what are we going to do? . . . But we worked and auditioned all the best musicians attending the festival."

One hundred fifty players were chosen from the thousand participants from ten different countries. "During the first week and all of the second of the festival, Leopold Stokowski took over and welded them and created a fine orchestra. . . .

"There was a great shock in these young faces as he started to work with them because there were no holds barred. He didn't mince any words. He wanted their very best and they had to concentrate . . . he really kept them on their toes and we did have a few breakdowns, a few tears. . . . But he never nursed them along. He worked them hard."[39]

After the rehearsal, Stoki talked to Alan Haydock: "It's always been my idea that [of] the great things of life, music is the one I'm interested in. [It] should be international in every way, and it should be something which brings the whole world together in the clasp of friendship of two hands shaking hands. . . ."

"I did hear that some of the children were rather terrified of you at first," Haydock remarked.

"Terrified! Well, if they are artists, they are sensitive. A person who is not sensitive can never be an artist no matter how much he or she try. It's impossible. They must be sensitive about everything in life including, naturally, music. . . . It's not of any importance how old they are. The important thing is do they feel the music?"[40]

The first half of the concert was conducted by Zdeněk Košler of the Czech Philharmonic, the second half by Stokowski, conducting the Tchaikovsky Fifth Symphony. As always, the critics were amazed at the Stokowski ability to make such raw material sound. "And what a sound the massed cellos made when they took up the main theme in the slow movement. Stokowski rallied them as though it was a vintage Philadelphia concert of the 1920s," reported the *Guardian.* [41]

Along with the Proms audience that crowded into Albert Hall, there were over eight hundred other young musicians applauding their colleagues on. There was camera equipment and a battery of lights which seemed to somewhat consternate Stokowski. Recording equipment, too, had been abundantly installed to tape the event for future release as well as broadcast. The rehearsal as well as the performance had been photographed and taped, and on a Saturday afternoon in his suite in the Savoy Hotel, the TV-film crew set up their equipment in Stoki's large drawing room.

I had stopped off in London, particularly to see him, before going on to attend conferences in Geneva and Warsaw. Shortly after I arrived at the Savoy, the engineers began to show the film. Stoki asked a number of them why he was seeing the film and if he had approved it, he didn't have to see it again. It caused some dismay among the engineers, but they suggested that he see the film once more. Natasha was disturbed that they had shown Stoki coming onto the stage with the aid of a cane. Stoki in the telecast seemed noticeably older and during the rehearsal scenes seemed remarkably testy. There was one part when he had an argument with a very young bassoon player who could not seem to play soft enough for him. On the recording of the performance of the Fifth as well as the rehearsal, we hear part of that scene, but on the record it seems very mild. On the video tape, however, the fear and distress registered by the boy was truly pathetic. He was a young bassoon player and Stokowski addressed him by the name of the instrument played, as he often would do when he did not know the name of the player. But in this instance Stoki used the German word *Fagott* rather than *bassoon.* "No, no, no! *Fagott* you! Third bar, *Fagott,* I signed for you to play softly. Will you do it or not?" shouted Stokowski.

The youngster cringed and was on the verge of tears. Jack Baumgarten was shown trying to placate Stoki, who was behaving toward the boy as sternly as he would have to one of the musicians of the London Symphony.

We had a little time to talk before the film had started, and throughout the showing I sat on a sofa five or more feet from Stoki. When the lights had all been turned on in the room and the equipment hurriedly removed, Stoki said rather plaintively, "Why did Oliver leave?" I went over to assure him that I was still there, and after a few pleasantries, he announced that he was going to rest. He retreated to his bedroom and I tried to catch up on all that was happening in London with regard to concerts and records. Jack Baumgarten, as always, was most helpful, and while we were talking Stoki reappeared and we visited for perhaps a half-hour. I was dismayed at the obvious lessening of vigor and the feeling that he was not fully aware of what was transpiring about him.

84

The End of the Concert Season

S EVEN days after quietly ushering in the New Year (1974) in Nether Wallop, Stokowski appeared in the Royal Albert Hall with the London Symphony Orchestra conducting three of his Bach transcriptions, Tchaikovsky's Serenade for Strings, and *Francesca da Rimini.* If, as it would seem, the concert had been intended as a preliminary to a recording session, it did not prove to be so, at least at that time. RCA showed no interest in recording the Tchaikovsky, although it did plan to record a complete disc of his Bach transcriptions later in St. Giles Church, Cripplegate.

Anent the Tchaikovsky pieces, it was left to Marty Wargo to find a solution, which he did on a rather long-range basis. They were finally recorded by Philips the following October. After the concert on which they were played, Martin Cooper reported that Stokowski had "strung out 21 cellos and basses behind, and feet above, the rest of the players. He obtained a breathtaking balance and beauty of tone by this unusual disposition of his forces and his still unsurpassed handling of familiar Tchaikovsky scores."[1]

One cannot fault RCA in its decision to record Stokowski conducting the *Eroica,* the Brahms Symphony No. 4, the *Academic Festival* Overture, and the Mahler Symphony No. 2 *(Resurrection).*

On February 10 he conducted an all-Beethoven concert in Albert Hall. He began with the *Coriolan* Overture, followed by the Eighth Symphony and the Symphony No. 3 *(Eroica).* In view of the reports concerning his forgetfulness, it was heartening to read Hugo Cole in the *Guardian:* "At all points he showed himself to be still in command of the situation. Only the most watchful direction could ensure such good balance and refined pianissimos in a difficult hall."[2]

RCA's recording sessions were scheduled for March 25, 27, and 28 in Walthamstow Town Hall. Strangely, it was the first time in his long career that he had ever recorded either the *Coriolan* Overture or the *Eroica* Symphony. In the earlier days such plums were routinely given to Toscanini, particularly during the time when George Marek was RCA's Artists & Repertoire man.

Thomas Heinetz, writing in *Records & Recordings*, was quite in error when he stated that Stokowski had "chosen to wait till he was past 90 before putting on disc a performance of the *Eroica*." Stokowski had wanted to do so for years. It was the recording companies that balked and selected what they deemed to be more commercial. "All things considered," added Heinetz, "I find this an *Eroica* of considerable stature, as well as one exuding a vitality astonishing in a man his age."[3]

"I have it on good authority," wrote Richard Osborne in the *Gramophone*, "that one of the great admirers of Stokowski's Beethoven conducting was the late Otto Klemperer. Perhaps the admiration was reciprocal for Stokowski's performance has many things in common with Klemperer's famous 1956 EMI recording of the Symphony. There is a virtually identical pace in the first movement and a comparable style and authority: dark textures and a rock-steady pulse, humanely alive. Where the Stokowski inevitably scores over the Klemperer is in the sheer impact of the recording, each line of the texture decisively there."[4]

By coincidence, Stoki's next concert with the New Philharmonia Orchestra coincided with Klemperer's birthday, and since Klemperer had been honorary president of it, the management suggested that Stokowski include one of Klemperer's compositions on the program. The chief *raison d'être* for the concert, however, was the playing of the Brahms Fourth Symphony, which he had not recorded for RCA since his early days with the Philadelphia Orchestra.

Stoki was entirely amenable to playing something written by his colleague and Klemperer's widow promptly sent a number of scores. "He chose a piece called *A Merry Waltz*," said Ainslee Cox. "I'm sure he chose it for its title, because he would do things like that. . . . Well, the music came and he studied it for some time and then a peculiar thing began to happen. He would say, 'We have on this program a piece called *A Merry*

Waltz by Klemperer. Now Klemperer is going to conduct this, isn't he?'
And everyone would go very blank and say, oh my God, he has forgotten
. . . and they would finally say, 'You know Maestro Klemperer died a few
years ago.' A few days later he would say, 'We have a piece on the program
by Klemperer. Isn't that the conductor Klemperer?' And they would say,
'Yes.' He would answer, 'Oh, well, let's invite him to do it. . . .'

"I thought that kind of stuff sounded just enough like the old Stoki
humor for it to be questionable. So when I was at his house, I walked past
his desk and there was a stack of the music that was coming up for this
concert and on top of the stack was the piece by Klemperer. As we were
talking about the concert, he said, 'Oh, this is on the program,' and he
added, '*A Merry Waltz* by Klemperer. He will conduct it, won't he?'

"And I looked at him and I said, 'That's for you to conduct.' And a
twinkle came in his eyes immediately because he knew that I knew that
he knew that this was the scene, and that he had been doing that number
on everyone who came by. And there hadn't been anyone who was willing
to say, 'Oh, come off it!' "[5]

The concert was in most respects highly successful. "Immortal, or
merely a miracle?" wrote Gillian Widdicombe. "Even at 92, no legend
can compete with the real Stokowski. Nor post-mortems describe in brief
why those who heard last night's performance of the Brahms Fourth
Symphony . . . will remember it as an incredible occasion. . . .

"The joy of watching Stokowski is simply that his economy and eloquence continue to represent the perfect baton technique (though he
conducts without one, of course); and even now one could read the entire
performance from watching his hands at work."[6]

But insinuated in the favorable reviews were somewhat ominous comments. They all had to do with the matter of tempi. Stokowski's tendency
to speed up various works was evident months earlier when he performed
the *Eroica*, a mere six minutes shorter—or faster—than he had done it
previously with the American Symphony. This time it was the Brahms.
"Last night his tempos for the Brahms Fourth were sometimes so fast that
one chuckled at the sheer nerve of the performance," observed Gillian
Widdicombe.[7]

"The slowest imaginable performance of Vaughan Williams's Tallis
Fantasia, one of the fastest ever of the Brahms Fourth Symphony: who
else could have adopted such willfully individual methods to produce
results both apt and unforgettable but Leopold Stokowski?" wrote the

usually sympathetic Edward Greenfield.[8] The fast pace of the Brahms, however, wasn't one that he found objectionable, but rather remarkable. So too did the audience.

While great fluctuations of tempo could be controlled in some measure in the recording studios, they were not so accommodating in the concert hall. Having been present at some of Stoki's last recording sessions, I realize how variant some of his first run-throughs could be. He would at times start out in a tempo far in excess of that which he would finally choose. It was perhaps this realization that caused those around him to urge that he confine himself to the recording studio. The concert with Klemperer's *Merry Waltz* and the Brahms Fourth was the last public concert he conducted in England.

The recording of the Fourth retained some of the rapid tempi he had followed in the concert. Richard Osborne reviewed the recording for the Gramophone: " 'Grant me an old man's frenzy,' wrote W. B. Yeats in one of his late poems. And as Leopold Stokowski sweeps through the coda of Brahms's first movement one can imagine he too has made the same request and had it granted. . . . The scherzo is passionate and precise, the finale full of passion and energy, as Brahms directs, boiling towards another of Stokowski's impetuous, racing codas."[9]

Richard Mohr, who produced the last ten records that Stoki did for RCA, commented about the excessive speed Stoki sometimes employed during some of the last recording sessions: "Jack and Natalie were always needling him, [saying] 'It's too slow.' And he worried about that—that he was getting old and slowing down. So occasionally I would say, 'Don't tell him its too slow because he overcompensates and it just becomes ridiculously fast and then there is nothing for me to splice between. One session would have one tempo and another a different tempo."[10]

That Leopold had failed since his ninety-second birthday was evident and Natasha, Jack, Marty Wargo, and Skip Muller all agreed that a trip to the south of France would be beneficial. On May 19, 1974, Stoki, Jack, and Natasha left London for Dover. They arrived there at midnight only to discover that the usual arrangement of having the train board a ship for the Channel crossing was not in effect. "We had to get up in the middle of the night. Stoki was bright and alert. He dressed in a hurry and we crossed the docks to a little old boat where they found him a stateroom with a place to stay. Everyone else had to sit up all night. But he was in great shape when we finally got to Paris," said Jack.

The three stayed at the George V overnight and the following evening

set out for Antibes, where they arrived at five o'clock in the morning. "We
went to the Château du Domaine St. Martin in Vence and Stoki had a
villa there. . . . He looked out over Vence and the mountains and the sea
and said: 'I want to live here. I want a house here.' And that was when
the decision was made to get a house there.

"We could not find one, so later he decided to build one. That's when
the decision was made to get a house in France—on May 22, 1974."

The last major recording with RCA, just fifty-seven years after his first
disc, which he made in Camden in 1917, was Mahler's *Resurrection*
Symphony. There were two sets of recording sessions—one at the end of
July and the second at the beginning of August. Jack and Natasha were
with Stoki during all of the sessions and according to Jack's carefully kept
diary, the second and third movements were taped on July 19, and at the
time Jack noted that Stoki was not feeling well. On July 22 the first
movement was done; playback on July 23, and more recording on July 25,
27 and 29. It was during this last recording session that there was some
time left, and it was decided that he would do another recording of the
Toccata and Fugue in D Minor.[11] "Stokowski knew the Mahler well, but
he knew that Toccata and Fugue like crazy, and during the last forty
minutes he started conducting as though he were eighteen years old
again," Dick Mohr recalled. "A lot of the Mahler he would do sitting
down and he would rise for climaxes and things like that. But during the
recording of the Toccata and Fugue he had a fainting spell and slumped
forward on the podium. They had to give him smelling salts."[12]

"He wasn't well," said Jack, "and I talked him into coming home and
resting and not going on." In comparing the performance of the Mahler
Second on this new recording with the one Stoki had conducted in Albert
Hall in 1963, Jack remarked that the 1963 performance was "much finer."
He spoke of some conversations he had with Stoki about the work in 1974:
"He had become very strange about this whole thing. There was gloom
and darkness to the symphony that he hadn't seen before, and it comes
out on the recording. It was a different approach because he saw it from
a different side. He said that he never wanted to conduct Mahler again.
. . . He said the music was unhealthy and sick and that he didn't want
to conduct Mahler any more."[13]

And he didn't.

A friend and Stoki admirer from Philadelphia, Dr. William Fischer,
was in London at the time of the Mahler recording: "They had just
discovered hypoglycemia and the doctor, like most British doctors, didn't

explain anything. He told them that if he ate too much sugar, insulin would be secreted and would drive his sugar down farther, so that the only treatment was not to take sugar. He was in the habit of having many, many cups of tea with two, three, and four sugars in them each day. He was to stop that. This immediate drastic reduction in sugar intake, especially in a man of his age, was responsible for an intolerably low level of blood sugar, and that is why he collapsed. I gave him a diet and he apparently had no trouble after that."[14]

"Have you heard about his acupuncture treatments?" Dick Mohr inquired. "He goes to an acupuncturist, a Dr. Siow, a Chinese person in London, at least once a week or the doctor comes to him. . . . He says it helps to keep his head clear. I went to Dr. Siow myself because I had sinus in London. . . . I didn't have it again for two years."[15]

While those closest to him could sadly observe the frail, failing man that he was, others more removed were touched by the vision, spirit, and uncanny mastery of sound that still carried a magical impact. Those who heard the release of the Mahler Second heard nothing faint of heart. Eric Salzman indulged in a bit of reminiscence before wading into the matter of the *Resurrection.* He recalled that he had had standing room in Carnegie Hall when Stoki conducted the Eighth Symphony, and "as Stokowski turned, lifted up those hands, and brought in the balcony brass all around, it was definitely pearly-gates time; I may never again be that close to paradise.

"It is extraordinary that in all these years he never made a Mahler recording," Eric observed. "Now that Stokowski's Mahler has finally arrived, it's obvious that this is a perfect combination. Stokowski is the master of the kind of orchestral sound and musical expression of which Mahler, as a conductor and as a composer, was perhaps the greatest exponent. Glorious sound, passion, stark tragedy, irony and exaltation are Stokowski trademarks. . . .

"Stokowski is a master, not just of phrase, but of the inner or large rhythm of the music. This is really what makes his climaxes so damned exciting; they are built on the dynamics of long-range rhythmic tension."

In summation Salzman called the performance "passionate, apocalyptic, human, and terrifically well performed by a group of outstanding singers and instrumentalists who obviously rise to the old Stokowski magic. I know I did."[16]

After completing each of his recording sessions, he, Natalie, and Jack would head for the Riviera. He selected a spot on a hill overlooking St.

Courtesy Natasha Bender

At St. Paul de Vence (c. 1975)

Paul de Vence where he planned to build his house. From there he could see the sea. He busied himself about its design and plans for construction. Both Jack and Natasha were gifted and knowledgeable about design and decoration. Stoki, too, had plans for the landscaping. Perhaps the situation reminded him of Santa Barbara.

Sadja visited during the summer of 1975. "It was about a third to a half finished, so we saw the outside and the landscaping going on and a lot of plans for how it would be. It's going to be a place with an incredible view."[17]

Nancy Shear, who had known Stoki since she was in her teens and had
worked for him part-time as a librarian, visited him in France during a
Christmas vacation: "He was just building the house at that time and we
would get in the car and drive out there every day and he was perfectly
content to sit and watch the workmen working on it for hours at a time.
It was almost like people who would sit and watch a movie. He would
occasionally go out and talk with the workmen and discuss the house with
them."[18]

At playback session for recording of Rachmaninoff Third Symphony, with musicologist
Edward Johnson in background, with glasses (1975)

Photo David Francis

Another visitor during this construction period was Lilette Hindin, who recalled that when she saw the house for the first time, it was little more than a shell. "There were no stairs . . . we climbed up by an outside ladder to see the second floor." She described how Stoki was hoisted up sitting on a chair which was strapped to a crane in order to explore the construction himself. "He went up to see it twice a day. He was absolutely enthralled with the whole idea and loved watching it being built."[19]

Josephine Lyons, a lifelong friend of Sonya's—they had shared an apartment in New York before Sonya's marriage—spoke of the house: "When he couldn't get the windows put in—he wanted to have these big picture windows—Natasha said, 'Oh, we've talked to the laborers and they can't do it for two or three months.' He said, 'I do remember I was decorated several times by the French government and I've never asked them for anything.' So apparently he put in a long-distance call to Paris and he got to the minister of interior or whatever and he said, 'This is Leopold Stokowski. I don't know whether you remember me or not but I did get a decoration or two from you and I am building a house in Vence because I love France very much and I'm having a terrible time because of the masons. I can't get the windows built properly and they say it will take me six months to a year and I can't wait that long. I'm ninety-three years old.' Within two weeks they had people down there and in four weeks they had the windows built. Nobody in the south of France has ever had it done so quickly."[20]

It was during this period of construction that Stoki was visited by a young American record producer who had yet to produce a record. His name was Marcos Klorman. He had met both Marty Wargo and Jack Baumgarten, whom he impressed by his plans, sincerity, and intentions, and they were eager to help him. Now that Stoki was out of the grooves of RCA, the new record company—Desmar by name—seemed to offer a chance to do some repertory that he had wanted to conduct: "I went to visit him in St. Paul de Vence and I spent an afternoon with him on the Riviera. We had a very nice, long lunch and went for a walk. It was quite a fascinating afternoon. While we were seated in the restaurant, which was called L'Auberge Colombe d'Or—a very old place with all kinds of original art, including some things by Calder and Picasso—Stoki complained that somebody was whistling something out of tune. I couldn't hear a thing. I thought he was having hallucinations. But a few minutes later, I got up to get my coat, which was on the other side of the restaurant, and I heard a man in the kitchen whistling a Rossini overture. That was it. I realized his hearing was still absolutely there and beyond.

"We discussed the Third Symphony of Rachmaninoff; he had given its premiere in Philadelphia [November 6, 1936], but he had never managed to record it. . . ."

In addition to the Rachmaninoff, Klorman proposed that Stoki conduct the Vaughan Williams *Tallis* Variations and his transcription of Purcell's *Dido's Lament*. Together they also chose Rachmaninoff's *Vocalise* and the Dvořák Serenade for Strings as companions. The choices were all good and the Rachmaninoff was made in the West Ham Central Mission ten days after his ninety-third birthday; the Vaughan Williams and Dvořák coupling four months later.[21]

Thirty-nine years had elapsed since Rachmaninoff had brought his new Third Symphony to Stokowski for him to perform with his favorite orchestra. "Let me say a few words about my new symphony," Rachmaninoff wrote to a Russian friend, Vladimir R. Vilshau, on June 7, 1937. "I was at the first two performances. It was played wonderfully (the Philadelphia Orchestra about which I have written you, Stokowski conducting). The reception by the public and the critics was . . . sour . . . I personally am firmly convinced that the composition is good."[22]

Critics circa forty years later all tended to agree, more or less, with the composer rather than the early critics. Byron Belt called the recording "dazzling" and added that "for sheer, gorgeous orchestral sound, the Rachmaninoff offers master chef Stokowski ingredients of rare beauty, and the maestro transforms the somewhat amorphous music into a veritable feast of glorious sounds. He brings dignity and powerful drama to the somewhat prolix work, implanting his signature in such a manner that Rachmaninoff's music soars to life as never before."[23]

Stoki and his surrounding aides were all sympathetic toward Klorman. "When I released the Rachmaninoff, Marty sent me a cable congratulating me. . . . To me, it was one of the great experiences of my life. I never had that kind of cooperation on that scale with so many people involved. . . . If I had been on the other side, I would have killed the person who was trying to produce the records," he said laughingly.[24]

But all knew that Klorman's ability to provide for more and larger instrumental recordings was limited, and Marty arranged a contract with Pye Records, for whom Stoki made two discs. While they were quite spectacular sonically, they were of tidbits—the sort of thing the British always refer to as lollipops. Beecham seemed to like the appellation. The first of the Pye Records consisted of ten "encores" by Berlioz, Brahms, Chabrier, Haydn, Tchaikovsky, Ippolitov-Ivanov, Mussorgsky, Saint-Saëns, Sousa, and Johann Strauss. It was released as a "Stokowski Spectacular." The second disc was a bit more appropriate. There were four overtures: Berlioz, *Roman Carnival;* Rossini, *William Tell;* Schubert, *Rosamunde;* and the Beethoven *Leonore* Overture No. 3. Neither of the two discs added anything to the Stokowski stature.

The house in France was nearing completion, and after a quiet Christmas and New Year's celebration in Nether Wallop, Stoki, Natasha, and Jack flew to Nice. All of the trips to and from France were made by air after the first uncomfortable one. "I was wrong about flying," Stoki told Jack. "Now, I have changed my mind."

On January 30, 1976, the trio arrived at the Hôtel Le Mas D'Artigny in St. Paul de Vence. The house was supposed to have been ready but was still incomplete. The first floor was unfinished when they moved into it on February 9. Three bedrooms were done, as well as a temporary kitchen, but the pleasure of being in his own Mediterranean home outweighed any inconveniences. The name of the house was *Con Brio.*

Stoki was entranced with the Riviera ambience—the profusion of flowers, the warm fresh air, the view of the sea and the mountains with their rock faces that caught the changing colors of the day, and the orange-barked pines that lined much of the coast. He got to know his neighbor, Marc Chagall, who at eighty-eight had built a house in St. Paul de Vence that would eliminate the climbing of stairs, which his studio in the town of Vence required. "At my age," Chagall confessed, "I'm absolutely mad to build this house."

Stoki, at ninety-three, seemed to have no such misgivings. He was not attached to the calendar. At one point, when André Kostelanetz was conducting in Israel, he contacted Stoki by phone. Stoki did not inquire about his health but asked, "How is the orchestra?" At the end of their conversation Stoki added: "Please stop on the way when you return home and let's all meet Chagall, whom I know very well."[25]

Stoki enjoyed visiting the Foundation Maeght and observed with interest and admiration that splendid collection of art works which were assembled there. Although Picasso lived nearby in Mougins, the two ancients never met. Stoki, with a touch of the voluptuary, relished lunches in Antibes at the Eden Roc and happily visited perfume and pottery centers nearby sampling their wares. Monte Carlo, too, was another point of interest and on one occasion he went there to receive the Villa-Lobos

Gold Medal, which was presented to him by Madame Villa-Lobos. Natasha remembered that the ambassador of Brazil was there and that it was therefore convenient to make the presentation in Monaco.[26]

Recently, I wrote to Mme. Villa-Lobos about the event and she answered, apologizing for her limited English. But the letter has such a charming character and sincerity that I quote from it verbatim:

> Rio, 22 September 1980
>
> Dear Mr. Daniel:
>
> I am so happy to give you my cooperation about our dear friend Leopold Stokowski.
>
> The first time Villa-Lobos met him was in Paris. In that occasion Stokowski attend the performance of Villa-Lobos' Choros 8 for two pianos and orchestra. . . . Stokowski went to Philadelphia and in 1929 he conducted this Choros. . . . It was wonderful especially because that and so many times Stokowski showed his friendship and admiration to Villa-Lobos. Then, in 1977, the Museum Villa-Lobos of the Ministry of Education and Culture that I am the Director decided to offer to Stokowski a Gold Medal for the [promotion] he did, during years and years about Villa-Lobos' works. Our friend Stokowski was so happy when he received from me the Medal in Monte Carlo. . . .
>
> Always,
> Arminda A. Villa-Lobos[27]

"It was delightful to be with you once more," wrote Stoki to Mme Villa-Lobos on March 3, 1975. "I hope we shall be together again soon. It was so kind of you to give me the Villa-Lobos Gold Medal, which reminds me of his beautiful music."[28]

Frequently, Stoki visited the chapel in Vence, which had been completely decorated by Matisse. He admired the stained-glass windows and the simple murals that his elderly colleague had drawn. He appreciated, too, the fact that Vence had named one of its prominent streets in honor of Matisse.

When he was invited to participate in the Festival of Vence, he happily accepted. The concerts were spread over a six-day or rather six-evening span. They were organized by the violinist Ivry Gitlis, and on Tuesday, July 22, 1975, the sixth of the concerts was conducted by Stoki. The concert was held in the beautiful town square of Vence, "la place de la Mairie." Natasha, Stan, and his friend Brenda were with Stoki.[29] A reporter on the *Nice-Matin* was there. "I saw him arrive . . . a man, half bent, leaning on his stick, supported by two people," he wrote. "He moved painfully, step by step. . . . When he came out into the square where the musicians and the crowded people of Vence were waiting for him, he became another man. He sighted the music as a navigator in distress sights land on the horizon."

Stoki conducted five Bach transcriptions for strings: Prelude in E, Air on the G String, Prelude in B Minor, *Siciliano,* and the "Little" Fugue in G Minor. To get all the players to give their all, Stoki had them stand —all except the cellists.[30] They played like a band of soloists and the result was magnificently impressive.

It was with these works of Bach that Stokowski conducted publicly for the last time. Did he plan it that way? Did he intend to end his conducting life with the strains of Bach, as he had done at St. Bartholomew's and on his official departure from the Philadelphia Orchestra conducting Bach's *St. Matthew Passion?* But in that calm dark night in the square of Vence, Stokowski heard his last public applause.

The concluding piece on the concert was the Fugue in G Minor, which he had transcribed for full orchestra; therefore, he needed a special arrangement for this concert and he transcribed the work for strings alone. Natasha copied out the parts. This was his last transcription.

To celebrate his ninety-fourth birthday, the board and players of the newly revived American Symphony played the "Little" Fugue in G Minor as a birthday tribute. It was on Easter Sunday and it was exceedingly hot. The temperature had soared up into the high nineties and the Easter paraders had begun deserting New York as fast as they could once their parade was over. The streets seemed almost deserted, particularly in front of Carnegie Hall. But when the doors opened, crowds began to trickle in.

I had not heard the orchestra since Stokowski had left it, and I was most eager to hear Akiyama with the revived orchestra. There were a few familiar faces among the players, but the orchestra was not seated according to the usual Stokowski plan but rather in the old conventional seating. Akiyama began with the "Little" Fugue. It was a travesty, sounding like a Sunday-afternoon band concert along a Swiss lake.

Immediately after the playing of the "Little" Fugue, Stewart Warkow came on stage and announced that a response from London had been recorded by Stokowski: "Greetings to all the artists and friends of the American Symphony Orchestra at this concert in Carnegie Hall. Thank you for honoring me by playing the inspired music of Bach's Fugue in G Minor in my orchestration.

"My best wishes for the continued success of the orchestra I founded thirteen years ago. I hope in the future to see you all again and thank you personally."[31]

Life Begins
at Ninety-four

S OMEWHERE I read that Voltaire at the age of eighty had planted an
apple orchard from seed. That impressed me no end. Then on May 25,
1976, a news item appeared in the *International Herald Tribune*
Paris and London editions that did Voltaire one better: "It is with
great pride and pleasure that we announce recording sessions with Leopold Stokowski. The 94-year-old maestro is signing an exclusive contract
with CBS to run for the next six years, for a series of several recordings."[1]

On this same day I attended the first of his CBS recording sessions in
London. Paul Myers, his CBS producer, told me that in the record
industry you usually sign a five-year contract, but since he was ninety-four
Paul asked, "Could we please make it a six-year contract, because it would
be a shame to stop at 99."[2]

The session was held in the West Ham Pentecostal Mission. It is a
large, truly ugly, undistinguished church. The shape is square with a
slightly domed roof and a balcony running around three sides. Pews were
piled up in corners and side areas and were under a layer of dust that made
some look as if they were covered with felt. The orchestra, seated toward
the back, occupied about half of the floor space, and a small forest of
thirteen or more mikes was suspended above the players. The famous
Stokowski seating plan was gone and the usual, conventional seating was
used: violins and violas on the left; cellos and basses to the right; and brass
and percussion in the center.

The work recorded was music from *The Sleeping Beauty* ballet by
Tchaikovsky—to be commercially packaged as "Aurora's Wedding." It

was Serge Diaghilev who chose the sequence of the movements when he truncated the ballet into a single act.

Wearing a straw hat with a wide, down-turned brim and a vivid multicolored hatband, Stokowski arrived punctually at 2:15 sitting in the front seat of a rented Daimler limousine. With him were his eldest daughter, Sonya; the ever-faithful Natasha Bender; and Jack Baumgarten. It had been three years since I had seen Stoki in London and although I realized he had failed in that time, he still radiated a patrician dignity.

As he stepped from the car he turned to Sonya and asked, "Is that Oliver?" His vision had failed tragically and his eyes seemed to look out into nothingness. When he was assured it was I, he held out his arms and gave me a warm embrace. Then with one arm on Jack's shoulder and another on mine, he let us help him into the church. With his superabundant vanity still in force, he refused to wear eyeglasses despite his failing eyesight. Natasha mentioned his visual difficulty and said that he could hardly see out of one eye and had no side vision but could see objects directly ahead. Yet he was still able to read the scores on the stand before him.

The session began promptly at 2:30. Stoki walked slowly to the podium —one hand on Jack's shoulder while grasping a sturdy cane in the other. The proud, erect, regal figure was gone. He was bent and appeared tired, with a look that was never beamed backwards but seemingly directed toward infinity.

Yet once the music began, he became transformed. He no longer sat but stood, conducting with the old and familiar gestures; his right hand with his long fingers pointing upward, as he had done from the day he first discarded the baton. Rhythm was precise; tempi, vigorous. Little by little the miracle occurred: sonority, shading, pace, balance, and every musical subtlety and nuance fell into place. His capacity to make music seemed utterly undimmed.

Paul Myers, then vice-president of CBS Records and producer of the session, declared: "The moment he stepped on the podium—and it's no exaggeration—the years literally dropped away. I found him quite extraordinary because his hearing was outstandingly good. He heard things that very often the producers, myself and Roy Emerson, or the engineer didn't pick up. He heard notes that he disapproved of. He asked for certain balances and he was always right in asking for them; it was like recording a conductor in his prime, at the age of fifty, say. The only thing that I think should be mentioned and it's very important: it's been suggested that in those final years, the orchestra was absolutely dedicated to him and they played almost without him—that he was just standing up there in front of them. That wasn't true for one moment and you only have to listen to any one of the last few recordings he made. There are certain rubati and controlled accelerandi that only a conductor can achieve, and he knew exactly what he was going for and exactly how to get it.

"I have rarely seen an orchestra with such dedication. As you know, the orchestra he conducted was not one of the standard London orchestras. It was a special orchestra made for recording purposes called the National Philharmonic, which has done a lot of recording. That orchestra made up as it is of independent musicians from various different orchestras is very good and well-disciplined, but it shows that certain independence that players have when a conductor comes in to record them. It's the only orchestra I've ever seen, either in the United States or in Europe, which would stand silently as he got on the podium. It was a beautiful token of their respect."[3]

When the session was over, we sat together talking and Stoki asked me about my eyesight. I assured him that I had to wear glasses. Then, looking about—most of the players had departed by that time—he asked quite plaintively, "Where are we?"

We joined him the day after this session in his suite at the Stafford near St. James's Palace. We brought him a present, a bottle of Bristol Cream Sherry, which Natasha reminded me he always enjoyed.

He seemed to be pleased and we toasted the new recording contract and his plans for more and newer recordings. He was particularly interested in hearing about the new works that had been presented in Paris at the International Rostrum of UNESCO, where I had been the previous week as the U.S. delegate. One new work in which he expressed particular interest was the Symphony No. 2 by Oliver Knussen, the son of one of his oldest and dearest British friends, Stewart Knussen, the bassist of the London Symphony Orchestra. He wanted to hear other works that had been submitted by the BBC and was also curious to hear a Danish work, *The Rainbow Snake*, by Erik Norby, which had been highly recommended by the judges of the Rostrum.

During the course of our conversation I made some rather elaborate but sincere comments about his genius as a conductor. He stopped me with a wave of his hand as if he were indicating a diminuendo and said, "No, no, Oliver. You must remember that I am a very modest man." At this there was a slight ripple of laughter and I reminded him of a saying of

Goethe that modesty is the virtue of him who has no other. "You are not modest, Leopold. You are egocentric and have been all your life." Then he said rather slyly, "Then I probably should say I'm an egocentric." We all agreed.

The following day he completed the recording session. The final tape was a beauty. The verve and ebullience were that of a very young man. A very young ninety-four!

"His vitality is unimpaired," wrote a critic in the *Gramophone* of January 1978, "and there is some splendidly lively playing, plus some moments of magic, too, in the lyrical pages of the score."[4]

His recording sessions on July 12, 13, and 16, 1976, at the West Ham Mission were devoted to ten of his transcriptions of pieces by Albéniz, Debussy, Tchaikovsky, Rimsky-Korsakov, Nováček, and Chopin. One of the Debussy works was "Clair de Lune," a work he had not recorded since 1947. Paul Myers recalled: "I once made the foolish mistake of suggesting that a take he had done of *Clair de Lune* was a little on the fast side. He managed to get through it in about three-and-a-half minutes, and I went out and whispered very quietly, 'Do you think that was just a little bit fast?' And he did a great theatrical double take, stood back, and said, 'What! You're telling me how to conduct? You should conduct this orchestra!' I had to stand there and be hauled up on the carpet, which I didn't mind, and the orchestra found it amusing because they had seen it happen to a number of producers . . . he gave me a very rough ride for suggesting that I could have anything to do with the interpretation of the piece. I remember it with affection—not with rancor—and it was an amusing event. At the time, my face was very red."[5]

The brisk pace of the first run-through was something I had noted, too, during the recording of "Aurora's Wedding," when he would play each section at first quite quickly. Then after listening, his sense of timing and pace settled into what seemed to be an unalterably right tempo.

CBS News was interested in filming Stokowski for a TV profile. After numerous letters, transatlantic calls, and discussions had softened Stoki's initial reluctance, producer Paul Loewenwarter flew to London and proceeded to West Ham Mission to film the first rehearsal and taping of the Sibelius First Symphony. He had never met Stoki before, so Paul Myers brought him back to the little room where Stoki was listening to playbacks of the first takes. Paul Loewenwarter described that initial meeting: "I was wearing a blazer and gray slacks; looking very conventional. As I stood in front of him, he looked up and said, 'Young man, you're looking very polite.' I said, 'I have to be, Maestro, because I'm here on bended knee. After all I'm here to ask a favor.' And he looked down at my legs and said, 'I don't see any crease in your slacks.' And I said, 'I was only speaking figuratively, not literally.' And he looked up at me and said, 'Young man, do you sometimes tell the truth?' . . . He certainly made me very wary of him very quickly."

Details about bringing camera crews into the studio for the recording session were worked out, and there was also the matter of lights, which Loewenwarter discussed with Jack Baumgarten and Natasha. They were particularly apprehensive about strong lights which might tend to blind him or prevent the musicians from seeing him clearly. Loewenwarter said: "With that in mind, we put all of our lights quite high up in the air. That way the lights were out of his line of sight as he looked at the musicians and that was the only stricture on us at all. There was one question: Would he wear a microphone pinned on his clothes? . . . The answer was no, so we simply tacked a microphone on the podium. . . . We filmed two rehearsals . . . the complete symphony from the beginning to the end."

The CBS crew then moved on to Stoki's admirable, old house in Nether Wallop, where nearly an hour-long conversation with Dan Rather was filmed. Various difficulties were encountered there which made the video-taping a problem. Loewenwarter explained: "The British Army chose to have helicopter maneuvers overhead, so a lot of the footage had to be thrown out because of bad audio. . . . I was out in the kitchen talking to some WAAF major and she was trying to get the maneuvers called off while we did the interview with the Maestro."[6]

On prime time, the evening of January 4, 1977, CBS presented the Stokowski special on a program called "Who's Who." Dan Rather began: "You've heard that old lament. The age of the giants is over. There are no Churchills, no Einsteins, no Picassos anymore—men who stood head and shoulders over their peers. Well, the lamenters are wrong by at least the count of one. If you're fifty, this is how you remember him—a matinee idol."

The camera focused on a glamorous photo of Stoki in his prime, then opened on a scene of him conducting a rehearsal for the recording of the Sibelius First Symphony.

After an excerpt of Stoki conducting Sibelius, the scene shifted to Nether Wallop. "I always wanted to be first," Stoki remarked. "I'm what is known as egocentric. It's a disease—a mental disease. I'm egocentric."

"We all have some of that though," countered Dan Rather.

"You have some?" Stoki said.

Dan replied, "Yes, I think we all have. Is that part of what has kept your aspirations high?"

"No," Stoki answered, "it's because I tried the opposite and it's boring."

Dan Rather continued: "There was a reverential awe as we watched the aging Maestro at work, but in the hard reality of the commercial music world, is Stokowski still a first-rate conductor at ninety-four? We asked first a fellow conductor."

Here the scene shifts briefly to the penthouse of André Kostelanetz at Gracie Square in New York, high above the East River. André admitted that he was completely baffled at how, at this time of life, Stokowski could conduct like a youngster. It is "because he has no age," he added. At the conclusion, back with Stokowski at Nether Wallop, Rather asked: "I know that you have never taken a composer's work absolutely literally, have you?"

"I don't know what you mean by literally," Stokowski countered.

"Note for note—just play the notes."

"Oh no," Stoki replied, "Oh, that's not enough. You must play the correct notes in the right time—*ein, zwei, drei—ein, zwei, drei*—in two or in three or in four—but you must feel it also. Emotion is a great part. If your father had no emotion, you wouldn't exist now. [You're here] because he loved your mother. So it's simple. It's plain; no emotion, death. Emotion, life—while life lasts."[7]

$$\widehat{86}$$

1977

A FORTNIGHT before his ninety-fifth birthday, Stoki began the first of three recording sessions for CBS—April 4, 5, and 9, 1977— in the EMI Studio 1 on London's Abbey Road with the National Philharmonic; the repertory: Brahms's Symphony No. 2 and the *Tragic* Overture. Stokowski, who was the first conductor to record all of the Brahms symphonies during his Philadelphia days, had now finally remade all of them in long-playing stereo. The recording of the *Tragic* Overture was his first.

During one of the sessions, a reporter from the Associated Press asked whether he intended to continue to conduct. Explaining why he could not leave the podium, he answered: "It is the music, the music." He then paused briefly and added: "Brahms, he has been in the grave a very long time. But his music lives. That is why I am here today."[1]

He was in much better form than when he had recorded the Brahms Fourth for RCA. In this recording there is none of the exaggerated speed that marred the former disc. When the record was released three years later, Richard Freed regarded it affectionately: "While some of his other valedictory recordings are so highly charged that one might suspect he was determined to show his age had not slowed him down, this one has a soft radiance and a pervasive mellowness that suit the score well and make it seem an especially apt choice for what proved to be the conductor's farewell . . . a warm-hearted leavetaking, utterly free of gratuitous gestures, on the part of one of the most remarkable practitioners of the conductor's art."[2]

Mr. Freed was not quite accurate; although this was the last record to be released, it was not Stokowski's last. CBS had already set up sessions during which he was to do symphonies of Mendelssohn, Bizet and Rachmaninoff.

In both London and New York, there were celebrations to mark his ninety-fifth birthday. Robert Sherman on New York's WQXR had a two-hour program with guests reminiscing about the Maestro. Wendy Hanson, Stewart Warkow, Arthur Aaron, and I all added some personal recollections, and recordings of Scriabin, Bach, Wagner, Prokofiev, and Ives were played.[3] In London the BBC presented its own special tribute.

Early in May I wrote to Stoki telling him that I would be covering the meetings of the International Rostrum of Composers of UNESCO and that I would arrive in Paris on May 23. I asked whether we might meet in St. Paul de Vence or Nether Wallop.[4] A cable came back at once saying that he would be in London at the Royal Garden Hotel after May 29 and added the dates and times of his recording schedules.[5]

It was in the EMI studios on Abbey Road that we met on May 31 and Stoki was to begin his recording sessions. He was to record the Mendelssohn *Italian* Symphony and the Bizet Symphony in C. Like so many studios, this one was a sort of antiseptic cigar box with institutional lighting that gave everything a slightly sepulchral hue. Stoki was seated at a small table with his score before him. Natalie was about with a thermos of tea. Jack was there checking various details. Although Stoki looked very tired, he seemed somehow more alert and composed than he had the year before.

Promptly at three, Stoki began the Mendelssohn. He played through the first movement and then conferred with CBS producer Roy Emerson and began again. This time he played through the entire four movements of the symphony. The pace was somewhat brisk but it seemed flawless. After listening to the playback in the control booth, he repeated the first movement and did a few small segments from the others which he felt needed work. It was all done in one session.

During the break Natasha asked whether I had seen the *Herald Tribune* that morning. Since I had not, she brought out her copy, which reported the death of Goddard Lieberson, of whom Stoki was very fond. It was decided that it would be better to say nothing about it during these recording sessions, but a cable was sent to Vera Zorina, Goddard's widow. Stoki was to learn of it much later.

The following day I had tea with Stoki in his suite at the Royal Garden

Hotel overlooking Kensington Palace and with a magnificent view of the full length of Hyde Park—with the House of Commons and Westminster Abbey in the far distance. Natasha had ordered a veritable mound of sandwiches and Stoki ate with obvious relish and drank numerous cups of tea. We talked about the biography I was planning to write and I suggested that we might do some taping when I returned to Europe for a conference in Prague. That triggered recollections of his various visits there—no mention, however, of his accident during his last visit. He talked affectionately about his house in France and mentioned that they had just put in a large swimming pool. But he shortly decided that he would like to rest and then study the Bizet symphony, which he was to record the following day. Natasha interjected that he had been studying it for weeks. "But I want to study it more," he replied.

The following day the procedure in the studio was much as it had been on the previous one. He conducted the entire symphony without taking a break. Again the tempi were brisk and his approach seemed much more literal than was his wont. He seemed to be more interested in litheness and clarity than in sumptuous sound. And he did achieve it.

Critics were quick to observe this, all but one—and the contrast is amusing. A thick-headed review by one Karen Monson appeared in *High Fidelity:* "Leopold Stokowski's Italian on Columbia is so full and fat that it wants to fall asleep."[6]

To James Harding's keener ears, the strings in the Italian Symphony have "a glittering burnish on them, and the strands of the texture are outlined with glowing clarity." He found the Bizet "brimming over with exuberance. The brass is especially crisp and crunchy, and the lovely oboe solo against pizzicato violas in the Adagio has a pellucid freshness."[7]

The finale of the Bizet, wrote Edward Greenfield, "brings just the sort of spark of Stokowskian naughtiness to have one cheering the old man's last marvelous record, a tempo so fast you would never believe that any players, even those of the National Philharmonic, could cope with it. Yet they do so without any feeling of being rushed. . . . In principle this may be too fast a speed . . . but it makes just the superlative full close one would have wanted for the most perennially youthful conductor on record."[8]

To Enos Shupp "the Stokowski disc is pure delight . . . the "Italian" is brisk but not raced, with fine detail, no fussiness, and a total impact that makes it one of the best . . . the same for the Bizet . . . given just due by Stokowski; the orchestra plays with style and deftness . . . just about a perfect disc in every way."[9]

Conducting the National Philharmonic Orchestra, London, in Bizet's Symphony in C, Stokowski's last recording session on June 4, 1977. Perhaps the only time he ever wore glasses in public

Does that sound like something "so full and fat that it wants to fall asleep"?

During much of the summer, Stoki enjoyed the balmy weather of the Riviera and late in August he returned to Nether Wallop to prepare for his recording sessions. He was ardently studying the Rachmaninoff Second Symphony. Curiously, it was not a work that figured in his concert programs, although it would seem to have been one that he would have relished. As the date for his recording approached, he did not feel well and the September 13 session was postponed. Both Jack and Natalie were apprehensive. It was they who were in constant attendance and cared most for his well-being. Sonya remarked that "Daddy would not have done what he did the last ten years if it hadn't been for both Jack and Natasha."[10] Oddly, on that day, while both were in the village of Nether Wallop, Stoki, quietly resting in his studio, passed away.

The news spread rapidly. Radio and television news programs broadcast the story widely and newspapers "all over the world" produced obituaries. The *New York Times* called him "possibly the best known symphonic conductor of all time," and again had him on the front page. In addition to the regular obituary, Harold Schonberg penned a special tribute. "There was a kind of alertness, of dynamism and imagination that made Stokowski in his prime one of the greatest conductors in history," he wrote. "Everything about the man was glamorous. . . . His accent which was always a mystery—nobody seemed to know where it came from—was part of the glamour. So was his private life, which included a liaison with one of the most beautiful and mysterious Hollywood actresses. . . . Stokowski had a personal radiance that, in his time, could be matched only by Serge Koussevitzky and Arturo Toscanini. With these two conductors he molded musical taste for two generations of Americans. Each brought something unforgettable to music. In Stokowski's case, it was pure brilliance, with a touch of Lisztian charlatanism, plus a quality of adventure in programming and orchestral textures, that made him a unique figure. And, in his way, a genius."[11]

In Philadelphia, Eugene Ormandy proclaimed that he was "deeply shocked and saddened at the news of Leopold Stokowski's death. . . . I inherited a very great Philadelphia Orchestra, and during my own tenure as music director, I have been extremely grateful for the kind of dynamic leadership that my predecessor possessed in such abundance. . . ."[12]

In Washington Paul Hume devoted an entire page of the *Washington Post* to an article that was syndicated throughout the country. He called him "a conductor of supreme genius, unforgettably possessed of true charisma long before that word became overused. He was a genius whose greatest talents exploded in front of an orchestra. . . . In a profession whose most famous practitioners have always had a strong aura of glamour, Leopold Stokowski exuded far more than the amounts collected by even the most renowned conductors. . . . 'Stokie' was unique . . . there will not be another like him."[13]

Time magazine in its pithy fashion remarked that "his hands became a legend, and he kept them in the spotlight, even when his players were in penumbral gloom. In his mind's ear he heard orchestral sounds never made before—and proceeded to make them. . . . He also turned conducting into a spectator sport, giving the role of conductor a panache that has not yet been surpassed . . . he made people feel, with justice, that it was a stimulating experience to have Leopold Stokowski in their midst during the years of his long life."[14]

In London the *Times* repeated that tiresome old canard that he had once been known as Leo Stokes, but added in summation: "Stokowski's music did not merely sound splendid; it was splendid. . . ."[15]

All five of Stoki's children had converged on London. Sonya flew in from Pittsburgh, Sadja from San Francisco, both Chris and Stan from New York, and Lyuba with her husband, Richard Rhodes, and their young daughter, as well as Lyuba's son, Ricky—tall, handsome, and dark, resembling somewhat his Hindu father, Homi Devitre, Lyuba's first husband.

I flew in from New York and proceeded to the Marylebone Cemetery, which is some distance from the heart of London in the town of Finchley. The chapel that had been chosen was that of Marylebone Crematorium, which presumably had the best available organ. With the late-afternoon sun streaming into the severe brick chapel, Leopold's younger brother, Percy, and his wife, Sonya, Sadja, Stan, Chris, Natasha, and Lyuba with her children sat in the foremost pews. Others who were present included his very good friend Stewart Knussen and his wife, Alan Margoles, Joyce Bright, Edward Johnson, Jack Baumgarten, Skip Muller, Marty Wargo, and CBS producer Roy Emerson.

After an improvised prelude, six pallbearers brought in Stoki's last remains in a blond wooden casket, which seems to be traditional in England. The organist then led on with *Jesu, Joy of Man's Desiring* and Purcell's *When I Am Laid in Earth*. It was at this point that a white-haired gentleman rose—I had presumed he was a minister—and began a deeply moving eulogy. I suddenly realized that he was the distinguished former Prime Minister of Britain, Edward Heath, who had flown back from a meeting in Brussels to attend the funeral. Following his personal tribute, he read quotations from *Music for All of Us* which Sadja and Lyuba had selected. He began with Leopold's concept of the root of inspiration: ". . . I believe it is a passionately strong feeling for the *poetry* of life—for the beautiful, the mysterious, the romantic, the ecstatic—the loveliness of nature, the lovability of people, everything that excites us, everything that starts our imagination working, laughter, gaiety, strength, heroism, love, tenderness, every time we see—however dimly—the god-like that is in everyone—and want to kneel in reverence. . . .[16]

"In Nature the Supreme Artist has created with never-ending variety marvels of form, color, motion, sound, drama, poetry—never repeating—always creating new developments of basic motives. The unending variety of the design of flowers, the beauty of their form and color, are some of the highest creations of the Supreme Artist. Mountains and arroyos . . . are Nature's sculpture on a vast scale . . . The mysterious light of the moon and the stars is pure poetry. The burning heat of the sun is life-giving inspiration. The great geological changes of the earth are like an immense drama, spreading over centuries. . . .[17]

"Music is dynamic—ever evolving—flowing like a river . . . it has the impulsive heartbeat and surge of life—never sounds twice alike—never becomes hard and inflexible and stagnant—but is always breathing and pulsating. Music is untamable—like the impulse within us that rebels against the prosaic and confining. Music sets us free—sings in our souls —overflows in our hearts—leaps with joy. . . . Music . . . drives us mad with longing—then soothes us with the loving touch of a Divine Mother.[18]

"I believe that music can be an inspirational force in all our lives—that its eloquence and the depth of its meaning are all-important, and that all personal considerations concerning musicians and public are relatively unimportant—that music comes from the heart and returns to the heart . . . that music can be one element to help us build a new conception of life in which the madness and cruelty of wars will be replaced by a simple understanding of the brotherhood of man. . . .

"It is like a great dynamic sun in the center of a solar system which sends out its rays and inspiration in every direction of the three dimensions of space and the fourth dimension of time. . . .[19]

"Everything that is great, beautiful, inspiring in the past must be preserved. To these great cultural riches which we have inherited . . . we must constantly add new things that are great, beautiful, and inspiring. In this way the past will unfold with continuous growth into the future . . . beauty and inspiration are beyond time. They are forever, and they are for all men . . . in all centuries to come. . . . For some of us this inner life—the life of dreams, of imagination, of visions—is the *real* life—the life we touch intimately.

"Through music we see a vision. . . . In our hearts we know we are in touch with some of life's highest potentialities—we understand only dimly, but our inner voice tells us that in the greatest music we are vibrating in tune with beauty that is eternal. When we reach its ultimate essence, music is the voice of the All—the divine melody—the cosmic rhythm—the universal harmony."[20]

Following Edward Heath's eulogy, the organist played "A Mighty Fortress Is Our God," at which point Stokowski's body was removed and driven to the grave site, followed by the little band of mourners. Here, Skip Muller delivered a brief tribute and Stokowski's body was lowered into the ground.

As the casket was being lowered sprays of flowers were placed around the grave. Then, in a touching moment, Sonya took one of them, handed it to Leopold's brother, and together they placed it on the grave of his mother, father, and sister Lydia, which was directly across from Leopold's own.

A simple granite tombstone was erected bearing the inscription:

LEOPOLD STOKOWSKI
18 April 1882–13 September 1977
Music is the Voice of the All

Two days after the funeral, a memorial service was held in St. Bartholomew's Church in New York. Jack Ossewaarde thoughtfully led the chorus in two Stokowski compositions, his *Benedicite, omnia opera Domini* and his 1968 *Pianissimo Amen.* He also included an *Orison Hymn* by Stoki's friend and teacher Walford Davies and a chorus from the Brahms *Requiem.* Some time later John Grady arranged a concert in St. Patrick's in honor of both Toscanini and Stokowski.[21] Acting on a proposal advanced by Councilman Joseph L. Zazyczny, the Council of the City of Philadelphia issued a formal resolution, which read in part: "Relative to the death of conductor Leopold Stokowski, one of the marvels of twentieth century symphonic music. . . .

"WHEREAS, Although he left the Philadelphia Orchestra his style lingers on tangibly, the standards he set for the Philadelphia Orchestra have never been surpassed, and on his long journey through life the Philadelphia Orchestra remains his supreme achievement. . . ."[22]

In both Philadelphia and New York, conductors Ormandy and Akiyama led their orchestras' opening concerts in dutiful homage with Bach's *Come, Sweet Death.*

The Women's Committee and Auxilliary of the orchestra set up a Stokowski Memorial Fund to provide Conducting Fellowships for young conductors. They were to be selected by a panel of judges of which Ormandy was the honorary chairman. The young winners were to receive $1,000 and be invited to conduct part of a Senior Student Concert.[23] That was a way I think Stokowski would like to have been remembered.

The Curtis Institute in Philadelphia held a memorial service on September 23; John de Lancie, its director, began by saying: "Leopold Stokowski, a name that evokes so many thoughts, emotions, and memories —an incredible career that has spanned as much of the twentieth century that the world has known and includes practically every composer and performer." He spoke of his relationship with the Curtis Institute and then turned to music: a Bach-Stokowski transcription of *I Call to Thee, Lord Jesus Christ* which was recorded in 1928, a 1927 recording of the *Prelude to the Afternoon of a Faun,* and a Chopin mazurka that had been recorded in 1937.

Photo Preben Opperby

Gravestone in Marylebone Cemetery

A touching tribute was made by Sylvan Levin, who concluded by saying: "I really loved this man. . . . As far as I'm concerned, Stokowski doesn't die. He will live for me forever and this is something that I feel very strongly . . . and if I say any more, you will see a grown man shedding tears. . . ."[24]

It was to the Curtis that Stokowski's library was given; it is housed there in a special room where it can be studied. Jack Baumgarten had carefully packed and sent the scores from Nether Wallop and later helped to assemble and display them in their Philadelphia home.

The houses in both St. Paul de Vence and Nether Wallop were sold and much of the furniture; paintings of Stoki including the famous "Whistler's Father" portrait by Leopold Seyffert, many drawings and paintings that Stokowski himself had done, notebooks, photographs, correspondence, silverware, carpets, souvenirs, talismen, mementos, and many personal items that he had acquired during his long life were loaded into a huge container and sent to America. During a severe Atlantic storm, the container, which had been strapped on deck along with several others, was washed overboard. I think he would have liked it that way; he might have felt that it added to the sense of mystery that he always enjoyed.

The legacy that he wanted to leave was the music he had recorded. Therein were his thoughts, his affections, and spirit. "Prolific and Pulsating Legacy of Stokowski Remains on Disk," proclaimed the *New York Times*. "Such was his wizardry . . . that even the sonic limitations of acoustical records hardly seemed to get in his way. . . . Few conductors made an orchestra, even an inferior one, glow, pulsate and explode with color the way Stokowski could . . . everything he recorded, including innumerable disks no longer in print, are the work of an inimitable musician whose impact on the musical life of three generations has not yet been adequately assessed."[25]

Stokowski left a simple will. His estate was divided equally between his five children, with ample provision for Natasha, who had devoted most of her life to him and remained with him to the end. The will was probated in White Plains, New York, not far from his Westchester home, which by this time had been sold; but his last official address was 250 Garth Road, Scarsdale. He had always planned to return.

Chapter Notes

Foreword

1. BBC-Radio Memorial Tribute with Yehudi Menuhin and Bernard Keefe, September 13, 1977.
2. *New York Herald Tribune,* 12 May 1963.
3. Sonya Thorbecke, conversation, February 26, 1979.
4. Sonya Thorbecke, conversation, September 12, 1979.
5. Sonya Thorbecke, conversation, February 26, 1979.
6. Victor Seroff to Stokowski, January 19, 1945.
7. Stokowski to Victor Seroff, January 20, 1945.
8. Stokowski to Victor Seroff, January 24, 1945.
9. Stokowski to Victor Seroff, May 21, 1945.
10. James Felton to the author, February 15, 1971.
11. Preben Opperby, conversation, May 28, 1977.
12. Joan Peyser, conversation, June 4, 1979.
13. Sonya Thorbecke, conversation, June 13, 1978.
14. Stokowski, *Music for All of Us,* p. 6.
15. Jerome Toobin, *Agitato,* p. 54.
16. Sonya Thorbecke, conversation, February 26, 1979.

Chapter 1

1. Halina Rodzinski, conversation, November 22, 1976.
2. Percy Stock to the author, October 13, 1977.
3. Stokowski, conversation, 1955.

4. BBC Radio interview with Stokowski by Roy Plomley, 1957.
5. BBC Radio interview with Stokowski by John Bowen, 1959.
6. Percy Stock to the author, October 13, 1977.
7. Stokowski, conversation, 1955.
8. Stokowski interviewed by Gordon Stafford, March 1956.
9. BBC Radio interview with Stokowski by Basil Moss, 1969.
10. Percy Stock to the author, October 13, 1977.
11. Stokowski interviewed by Gordon Stafford, March 1956.
12. BBC Radio interview with Stokowski by John Bowen, 1959.
13. Stokowski, conversation, 1955.
14. BBC Radio interview with Stokowski by John Bowen, 1959.
15. Harold Schonberg, *The Great Conductors*, p. 180.
16. Claude Debussy, *Monsieur Croche, the Dilettante Hater* (New York: Viking Press, 1928), pp. 168–70.
17. Stokowski interviewed by Edward Johnson, April 1971.
18. Stokowski interviewed by Edward Greenfield, 1972.

Chapter 2

1. Percy Stock to the author, October 13, 1977.
2. Charles O'Connell, *The Other Side of the Record*, p. 279.
3. Jerome Toobin, *Agitato*, p. 52.
4. BBC Radio interview with Stokowski by John Bowen, 1959.
5. Stokowski interviewed by Edward Greenfield, 1972.
6. P. F. Coventry to Edward Johnson, May 3, 1974.
7. A. H. Surridge to Stokowski, October 1, 1973.
8. Rollin Smith, "Leopold Stokowski, Organist 1882–1977," *Music/The AGO-RCCO Magazine*, November 1977, p. 56.
9. Steve Cohen, "The Stokowski Story," WUHY-FM Radio (Philadelphia) Series, c. 1967.
10. H. C. Colles, *Walford Davies: A Biography*, p. 49.
11. Alec Wyton, "Leopold Stokowski," *Music/The AGO-RCCO Magazine*, July 1970, p. 27.
12. Walford Davies, *The Pursuit of Music* (New York: Thomas Nelson & Sons, 1936), p. 394.
13. Ibid., pp. 8, 9.
14. Stokowski interviewed by Gordon Stafford, March 1956.
15. BBC Radio interview with Stokowski by Basil Moss, 1969.
16. Stokowski interviewed by Edward Greenfield, 1972.
17. Edward Johnson, ed., *Stokowski*, p. 45.

Chapter 3

1. Kopernik Stokowski to Sir Walford Davies, March 15, 1902.
2. Hilda B. Galloway to Preben Opperby, undated.
3. Rollin Smith, "Leopold Stokowski, Organist 1882–1977," *Music/The AGO-RCCO Magazine,* November 1977, p. 56.
4. Stokowski to Sir Walford Davies, August 22, 1903.
5. BBC Radio interview with Stokowski by John Bowen, 1959.
6. Stokowski, conversation, 1955.

Chapter 4

1. Henry James, *The Art of Travel* (New York: Anchor Books, 1962), p. 406.
2. Lloyd Morris, *Incredible New York* (New York: Random House, 1951), p. 141.
3. Stokowski interviewed by Gordon Stafford, March 1956.
4. Stokowski, conversation, 1955.
5. Ibid.

Chapter 5

1. Olga Samaroff Stokowski, *An American Musician's Story,* p. 30.
2. Ibid., p. 34.
3. Ibid., p. 36.
4. Ibid., p. 39.
5. Ibid., p. 51.
6. *Musical America,* 25 November 1905, p. 5.
7. Olga Samaroff Stokowski, *An American Musician's Story,* p. 93.
8. Ruth O'Neill, conversation, February 20, 1976.
9. Claudette Sorel, conversation, April 5, 1978.
10. *Musical America,* 17 February 1906, p. 4.
11. Claudette Sorel, conversation, April 5, 1978.
12. Steve Cohen, "The Stokowski Story," WUHY-FM Radio (Philadelphia) Series, c. 1967.
13. Ibid.

Chapter 6

1. Percy Stock to the author, October 13, 1977.
2. Rollin Smith, "Leopold Stokowski, Organist 1882–1977," *Music/The AGO-RCCO Magazine,* November 1977, p. 57.

3. Stokowski interviewed by Eugene Cook, November 21, 1961.
4. Steve Cohen, "The Stokowski Story," WUHY-FM Radio (Philadelphia) Series, c. 1967.
5. Stokowski to Sir Walford Davies, February 1, 1908.

Chapter 7

1. Frances Wister, *Twenty-five Years of the Philadelphia Orchestra*, p. 89.
2. *Philadelphia Inquirer*, 15 November 1925.
3. Olga Samaroff Stokowski, *An American Musician's Story*, p. 55.
4. *Musical America*, 6 June 1908, p. 1.
5. *Musical America*, 12 October 1907, p. 15.
6. Stokowski interviewed by Edward Johnson, April 1971.
7. Harriet Johnson, conversation, July 13, 1977.
8. *Musical America*, November 1908.
9. *Musical America*, 6 June 1908, p. 1.
10. *Musical America*, 22 May 1909, p. 1.
11. Louis R. Thomas, *A History of the Cincinnati Orchestra to 1931*, p. 306.
12. Ibid., p. 306–10.
13. Ibid., p. 310.
14. Bettie Fleischmann Holmes to H. W. Gray (Novello Publishing Company), April 12, 1909.
15. Bettie Fleischmann Holmes to Lucien Wulsin, April 25, 1909.
16. Ibid.
17. Stokowski, conversation, 1955.
18. *Musical Courier*, 2 June 1909.
19. Ibid.
20. Harriett Johnson, conversation, July 13, 1977.
21. Adella Prentiss Hughes, *Music Is My Life*, p. 125.
22. Stokowski, conversation, 1955.
23. BBC Radio interview with Stokowski by Basil Moss, 1969.
24. *Boston Evening Transcript*, 28 October 1916.
25. Stokowski, conversation, 1955.
26. *Le Guide Musical*, 16 May 1909, p. 416 (translated by Michael Aspinwall).
27. *Musical Courier*, June 1909.
28. Louis Thomas, *A History of the Cincinnati Orchestra to 1931*, p. 316.
29. *Boston Evening Transcript*, 28 October 1916.
30. Richard Buckle, *Diaghilev* (New York: Atheneum, 1979), p. 151.
31. Guy Arnaud to the author, January 27, 1978.
32. *Times* (London), 19 May 1909.

33. Moses Smith, *Koussevitzky*, p. 43.
34. Louis Thomas, *A History of the Cincinnati Orchestra to 1931*, pp. 305, 306.

Chapter 8

1. *Musical America*, May 1909.
2. *Musical America*, 24 July 1909, p. 2.
3. Stokowski, conversation, 1955.
4. BBC-Radio interview with Stokowski by Basil Moss, 1969.
5. *Cincinnati Times Star*, 17 November 1909.
6. Ibid.
7. *Cincinnati Enquirer*, 10 October 1909.
8. *Cincinnati Enquirer*, 27 November 1909.
9. *Cincinnati Enquirer*, 5 October 1909.
10. *Musical Courier*, November 1909.
11. Ibid.
12. Steve Cohen, "The Stokowski Story," WUHY-FM Radio (Philadelphia) Series, c. 1967.
13. *Musical America*, 4 December 1909, p. 33.
14. *Musical America*, 18 December 1909, p. 5.
15. *Musical America*, 22 January 1910.
16. *Musical America*, 26 February 1910, p. 23.
17. Victor Seroff, *Rachmaninoff*, p. 112.
18. *Cincinnati Enquirer*, 22 January 1910.
19. *Musical America*, 5 March 1910.
20. Adella Prentiss Hughes, *Music Is My Life*, p. 126.
21. *Musical America*, 8 October 1910, p. 29.
22. Ibid.
23. Ibid.
24. *Musical America*, 3 December 1910.
25. *Musical America*, 10 December 1910, p. 26.
26. *Musical America*, 18 March 1911, p. 3.
27. *Cleveland Press*, 10 March 1911.
28. *Cleveland Plain Dealer*, 9 March 1911.
29. *Musical America*, 21 January 1911.
30. *Musical America*, 18 February 1911.
31. *Etude*, January 1940.
32. *Musical America*, 25 February 1911.
33. *Musical America*, 4 March 1911, p. 6.
34. Harold Schonberg, *The Great Conductors*, p. 345.
35. *Musical America*, 8 April 1911, p. 36.

36. *Musical America,* 29 April 1911.
37. Ibid.

Chapter 9

1. *St. Louis Post-Dispatch,* 19 April 1911.
2. *St. Louis Post-Dispatch,* 9 April 1911.
3. Olga Samaroff Stokowski, *An American Musician's Story,* pp. 225, 226.
4. Ruth O'Neill, conversation, February 20, 1976.
5. Olga Samaroff Stokowski, "Kitchens and Cooks" (unpublished memoir), p. 17.
6. Sonya Thorbecke, conversation, March 9, 1979.
7. Olga Samaroff Stokowski, "Kitchens and Cooks" (unpublished memoir), p. 18.
8. Ibid.
9. Ibid., pp. 19, 20.
10. Olga Samaroff Stokowski, *An American Musician's Story,* p. 137.
11. Clara Clemens, *My Husband Gabrilowitsch,* p. 62.
12. *Musical America,* 30 September 1911, p. 2.
13. Claudette Sorel, conversation, April 5, 1978.
14. Sonya Thorbecke, conversation, March 9, 1979.
15. *Musical America,* 1911.
16. *Musical America,* October 1911.

Chapter 10

1. *Cincinnati Times-Star,* 18 November 1911.
2. Ibid.
3. *Cincinnati Enquirer,* 19 November 1911.
4. *Cincinnati Times-Star,* 4 December 1911.
5. *Musical Leader,* 7 December 1911.
6. *Musical Courier,* 13 December 1911.
7. *Musical Leader,* 7 December 1911.
8. Unidentified clipping (Felton Collection), 17 January 1912.
9. Henry Krehbiel to Lucien Wulsin, March 31, 1912.
10. *Cincinnati Times-Star,* 25 November 1911.
11. *Musical America,* 23 December 1911, p. 37.
12. *Cincinnati Commercial Tribune,* 6 January 1912.
13. *Cincinnati Times-Star,* February 1912.

Chapter 11

1. Philadelphia newspaper clipping (unidentified), 7 November 1907.
2. Frances Wister, *Twenty-five Years of the Philadelphia Orchestra*, p. 94.
3. Olga Samaroff Stokowski, *An American Musician's Story*, p. 94.
4. Stokowski, conversation, 1955.
5. Stokowski to Lucien Wulsin, March 23, 1912.
6. *Cincinnati Post*, 27 March 1912.
7. *Columbus Dispatch*, 27 March 1912.
8. *Cincinnati Times-Star*, 27 March 1912.
9. *Cincinnati Enquirer*, 27 March 1912.
10. *Cincinnati Commerical Tribune*, 28 March 1912.
11. *Cincinnati Times-Star*, 28 March 1912.
12. *Cincinnati Post*, 28 March 1912.
13. Lucien Wulsin to Henry Krehbiel, March 29, 1912.
14. Henry Krehbiel to Lucien Wulsin, March 31, 1912.
15. Stokowski to Lucien Wulsin, April 1, 1912.
16. Charles P. Taft, J. G. Schmidlapp, Joseph Wilby, and Lucien Wulsin to Stokowski, April 3, 1912.
17. Lucien Wulsin to Stokowski, April 5, 1912.
18. Stokowski to the Advisory Board of the Cincinnati Symphony Orchestra, April 5, 1912.
19. *Cincinnati Enquirer*, 15 April 1912.
20. *Musical America*, 20 April 1912.
21. *Cincinnati Times-Star*, 15 April 1912.
22. *Cleveland Leader*, 28 April 1912.
23. *Cincinnati Commercial Tribune*, 15 April 1912.
24. *Musical America*, 6 April 1912.
25. *Cincinnati Times-Star*, 30 March 1912.
26. Stokowski, conversation, 1955.
27. Ruth O'Neill, conversation, February 20, 1976.
28. Ruth O'Neill, conversation, July 8, 1977.
29. *Cincinnati Enquirer*, 13 June 1912.
30. Ruth O'Neill, conversation, February 20, 1976.
31. *Musical America*, 15 June 1912.
32. *Musical America*, 29 June 1912.
33. *Cincinnati Enquirer*, 29 September 1912.

Chapter 12

1. *Musical America*, April 1912.
2. *Musical Courier*, 5 June 1912.

3.   Joseph Szigeti, *With Strings Attached,* p. 244.
4.   Olga Samaroff Stokowski, *An American Musician's Story,* p. 36.
5.   *Times* (London), 23 May 1912.
6.   *London Daily Telegraph,* 23 May 1912.
7.   *Scotsman,* 24 May 1912.
8.   *London Daily Mail,* 23 May 1912.
9.   *London Standard,* 23 May 1912.
10. *Birmingham Post,* 23 May 1912.
11. *Westminster Gazette,* 23 May 1912.
12. *London Globe,* 23 May 1912.
13. *Times* (London), 15 June 1912.
14. *London Standard,* 15 June 1912.
15. *Outlook,* 29 March 1922, p. 499.
16. *Musical America,* 20 July 1912.
17. *Musical Courier,* 25 September 1912.
18. *North American* (Philadelphia), 30 September 1912.
19. *Musical America,* 19 October 1912.
20. *Philadelphia Public Ledger,* 1 October 1912.
21. Olga Samaroff Stokowski, *An American Musician's Story,* p. 18.
22. Ruth O'Neill, conversation, February 20, 1976.
23. BBC-Radio interview with Stokowski by Basil Moss, 1969.
24. Stokowski interviewed by David Frost, 1971.
25. Ibid.
26. Irving Kolodin, *The Musical Life,* p. 201.
27. William Lee Pryor, conversation, January 15, 1978.
28. *Philadelphia Evening Bulletin,* September 1977.

Chapter 13

1.   *Philadelphia Public Ledger,* 8 October 1912.
2.   *Musical America,* 12 October 1912.
3.   Frances Wister, *Twenty-five Years of the Philadelphia Orchestra,* p. 85.
4.   Olga Samaroff Stokowski, *An American Musician's Story,* pp. 93, 94.
5.   Stokowski, conversation, 1955.
6.   Ruth O'Neill, conversation, February 20, 1976.
7.   *Philadelphia Public Ledger,* 12 October 1912.
8.   Ibid.
9.   Arthur Judson, conversation with Ruth O'Neill and Samuel Rosenbaum, January 6, 1972.
10. *Musical Courier,* 16 October 1912.
11. *Musical America,* 26 October 1912.
12. *Musical America,* 26 October 1912, p. 6.

13. *Philadelphia Inquirer,* 12 October 1912.
14. *Philadelphia Inquirer,* 26 October 1912.
15. *Musical America,* 2 November 1912.
16. Herbert Kupferberg, *Those Fabulous Philadelphians,* p. 37.
17. Philadelphia Orchestra Program Bulletin, Prospectus of the 1912–1913 Season.
18. *Musical America,* 12 October 1912.
19. Elena Gerhardt, *Recital,* pp. 60, 61.
20. Stokowski, conversation, 1955.
21. Herbert Kupferberg, *Those Fabulous Philadelphians,* pp. 38, 39.
22. Stokowski, conversation, 1955.
23. Herbert Kupferberg, *Those Fabulous Philadelphians,* p. 39.
24. Olga Samaroff Stokowski, *An American Musician's Story,* p. 88.
25. Herbert Kupferberg, *Those Fabulous Philadelphians,* p. 37.
26. Ruth O'Neill, conversation, February 20, 1976.
27. Sophia Yarnall Jacobs, conversation, March 5, 1976.
28. *Musical America,* 15 February 1913; unidentified clipping ("Prize Stokowski Portrait"), 1913.

Chapter 14

1.   *Musical America,* 8 November 1913, p. 27.
2.   *Musical America,* 15 November 1913, p. 25.
3.   *Musical America,* 20 December 1913, p. 37.
4.   *Musical America,* 24 January 1914, p. 10.
5.   *New York Morning Telegraph,* 22 January 1914.
6.   *Musical America,* 28 February 1914, p. 20.
7.   *Musical America,* 31 January 1914, p. 49.
8.   *Boston Herald,* 16 February 1914.
9.   *Boston Globe,* 16 February 1914.
10. *Boston Evening Transcript,* 16 February 1914.
11. *Musical America,* 28 February 1914, p. 8.
12. *Musical America,* 14 March 1914, p. 30.
13. *Musical America,* 11 April 1914, p. 39.
14. *Musical America,* 18 April 1914, p. 9.

Chapter 15

1.   Olga Samaroff Stokowski, "Kitchens and Cooks" (unpublished memoir), p. 23.
2.   Ibid., pp. 23, 24.
3.   Ibid.

4. *Daily Herald,* 6 July 1938.
5. Olga Samaroff Stokowski, "Kitchens and Cooks" (unpublished memoir), p. 24.
6. *Musical Courier,* 25 September 1912.
7. *Musical America,* 18 April 1914, p. 9.
8. *Musical America,* 11 April 1914, p. 9.
9. *Musical America,* 10 October 1914, p. 10.
10. Otto Luening, conversation, September 22, 1978.
11. Otto Luening, conversation, April 7, 1979.
12. *Musical America,* 11 July 1914, p. 20.
13. Ibid.
14. Olga Samaroff Stokowski, *An American Musician's Story,* p. 141.
15. *Musical America,* 5 September 1914, p. 21.
16. Olga Samaroff Stokowski, *An American Musician's Story,* pp. 141, 142.
17. *Musical America,* 5 September 1914, p. 21.
18. Ibid.
19. Olga Samaroff Stokowski, "Kitchens and Cooks" (unpublished memoir), p. 26.
20. Ibid.
21. Bruno Walter, *Theme and Variations* (New York: Alfred A. Knopf, 1947), p. 220.
22. Clara Clemens, *My Husband Gabrilowitsch,* pp. 64, 65.
23. Bruno Walter, *Theme and Variations,* p. 220.
24. Ibid., p. 221.
25. *Musical America,* 5 September 1914, p. 21.
26. Ruth O'Neill, conversation, February 20, 1976.
27. Ibid.
28. Olga Samaroff Stokowski, "Kitchens and Cooks" (unpublished memoir), p. 26.
29. *Musical America,* 5 September 1914, p. 22.
30. Ruth O'Neill, conversation, February 20, 1976.
31. *Musical America,* 5 September 1914, p. 22.
32. Ruth O'Neill, conversation, February 20, 1976.
33. *Musical America,* 12 September 1914, pp. 2, 3.
34. *Musical America,* 26 September 1914, p. 3.
35. *Musical America,* 12 September 1914, p. 2.
36. Ibid., p. 3.
37. *Musical America,* 10 October 1914, p. 10.
38. Olga Samaroff Stokowski, "Kitchens and Cooks" (unpublished memoir), pp. 26, 27.
39. *Musical America,* 12 September 1914, p. 2.
40. Ibid., p. 1.

41. Clara Clemens, *My Husband Gabrilowitsch*, pp. 84, 85.
42. Olga Samaroff Stokowski, "Kitchens and Cooks" (unpublished memoir), p. 27.

Chapter 16

1. *Musical America*, 10 October 1914, pp. 1, 2.
2. *Musical America*, 24 October 1914, p. 8.
3. *Musical America*, 19 September 1914, p. 32.
4. *Musical America*, 26 September 1914, p. 2.
5. Ibid., p. 6.
6. *Musical America*, 17 October 1914, p. 35.
7. Ruth O'Neill, conversation, February 20, 1976.
8. Louis Hood, *The Spirit of '75*, p. 23.
9. Olga Samaroff Stokowski, "Kitchens and Cooks" (unpublished memoir), p. 28.
10. Ibid., pp. 29, 30.
11. Mrs. James Blauvelt, conversation, April 15, 1977.
12. Ruth O'Neill, conversation, February 20, 1976.
13. Clara Clemens, *My Husband Gabrilowitsch*, p. 86.
14. *Etude*, January 1940.
15. Arthur Judson, conversation with Ruth O'Neill and Samuel Rosenbaum, January 6, 1972.
16. Ibid.

Chapter 17

1. BBC-Radio interview with Stokowski by Deryck Cooke, September 1965.
2. Henry-Louis de La Grange, jacket notes for Mahler Symphony No. 8 recording on Epic SC 6004.
3. Louis Hood, *The Spirit of '75*, p. 24.
4. Ruth O'Neill, conversation, February 20, 1976.
5. Herbert Kupferberg, *Those Fabulous Philadelphians*, p. 42.
6. *Philadelphia Public Ledger*, 3 March 1916.
7. Frances Wister, *Twenty-five Years of the Philadelphia Orchestra*, p. 105.
8. Louis Hood, *The Spirit of '75*, p. 27.
9. Arthur Judson, conversation with Ruth O'Neill and Samuel Rosenbaum, March 8, 1972.
10. Ibid.
11. Frances Wister, *Twenty-five Years of the Philadelphia Orchestra*, pp. 108, 109.

12. Ibid., p. 108.
13. *New York Sun,* 10 April 1916.
14. Frances Wister, *Twenty-five Years of the Philadelphia Orchestra,* pp. 110, 112.
15. *Boston Evening Transcript,* 28 October 1916.
16. Ibid.
17. Arthur Judson, conversation with Ruth O'Neill, Samuel Rosenbaum, and Jack Buckley, March 8, 1972.
18. Howard Shanet, *Philharmonic: A History of New York's Orchestra,* p. 218.
19. Olga Samaroff Stokowski, *An American Musician's Story,* pp. 159, 160.
20. Ibid., pp. 160–62.
21. Howard Shanet, *Philharmonic: A History of New York's Orchestra,* p. 214.

Chapter 18

1. *Musical Courier,* 30 March 1916.
2. Frances Wister, *Twenty-five Years of the Philadelphia Orchestra,* pp. 113, 114.
3. Herbert Kupferberg, *Those Fabulous Philadelphians,* p. 50.
4. Louis Hood, *The Spirit of '75,* pp. 26, 29.
5. Edward Bok, *The Americanization of Edward Bok,* p. 263.
6. Ibid., p. 264.
7. Ibid., pp. 266, 267.
8. Ruth O'Neill, conversation, February 20, 1976.
9. Arthur Judson, conversation with Ruth O'Neill and Samuel Rosenbaum, January 6, 1972.
10. Edward Bok, *The Americanization of Edward Bok,* p. 326.
11. Louis Hood, *The Spirit of '75,* p. 29.
12. *Philadelphia Public Ledger,* 3 January 1918.
13. Mrs. Curtis Bok, conversation, June 12, 1979.
14. Edward Bok (words) and Stokowski (music arranged and orchestrated from the original melody by C. F. van Rees), *Our United States* (Philadelphia: Theodore Presser Company, 1924).
15. Unidentified clipping (Philadelphia Orchestra Archives), 18 December 1924.
16. *Philadelphia Public Ledger,* 19 June 1919.
17. Ibid.
18. *Musical America,* 30 August 1919.

Chapter 19

1. Olga Samaroff Stokowski, *An American Musician's Story*, p. 146.
2. Clara Clemens, *My Husband Gabrilowitsch*, p. 89.
3. Olga Samaroff Stokowski, *An American Musician's Story*, p. 147.
4. Clara Clemens, *My Husband Gabrilowitsch*, pp. 90, 91.
5. Olga Samaroff Stokowski, *An American Musician's Story*, p. 155.
6. Clara Clemens, *My Husband Gabrilowitsch*, pp. 95–98.
7. Olga Samaroff Stokowski, *An American Musician's Story*, p. 156.
8. Frances Wister, *Twenty-five Years of the Philadelphia Orchestra*, p. 117.
9. Louise Hall Tharp, *Mrs. Jack* (Boston: Little, Brown & Company, 1965), p. 302.
10. Philip Hart, *Orpheus in the New World*, pp. 64, 65.
11. Olga Samaroff Stokowski, *An American Musician's Story*, p. 139.
12. Louise Hall Tharp, *Mrs. Jack*, p. 303.
13. Ibid., p. 305.
14. Olga Samaroff Stokowski, *An American Musician's Story*, p. 149.

Chapter 20

1. Olga Samaroff Stokowski, *An American Musician's Story*, p. 170.
2. *Philadelphia Public Ledger*, 19 August 1919.
3. Ruth O'Neill, conversation, February 20, 1976.
4. Mrs. James Blauvelt, conversation, April 15, 1977.
5. Beveridge Webster, conversation, November 6, 1977.
6. Unidentified clipping, 2 November 1920.
7. Unidentified clipping (Philadelphia Orchestra Archives), 3 February 1922.
8. Ibid.
9. Ibid.
10. *Philadelphia Public Ledger*, 10 February 1922.
11. *Philadelphia Evening Bulletin*, 13 February 1922.
12. Sophia Yarnall Jacobs, conversation, March 5, 1976.
13. Louise Varèse, conversation, July 16, 1976.
14. *Philadelphia Evening Bulletin*, 25 October 1922.
15. *Philadelphia Evening Bulletin*, 19 December 1922.
16. Unidentified clipping, 27 May 1923.
17. Unidentified clipping (Philadelphia Orchestra Archives), 12 January 1923.
18. *La Revue Musicale*, 1923.
19. *Philadelphia Public Ledger*, 15 January 1923.
20. *La Tribuna* (Rome), 23 January 1923.

21. Unidentified clipping (Philadelphia Orchestra Archives), 2 February 1923.
22. Ibid.
23. *Philadelphia Public Ledger*, 7 May 1923.
24. Olga Samaroff Stokowski, *An American Musician's Story*, p. 170.
25. *North American* (Philadelphia), 28 April 1923.
26. Olga Samaroff Stokowski, *An American Musician's Story*, p. 211.
27. Ibid., p. 212.
28. Eugene List, conversation, September 10, 1976.
29. Rosalyn Tureck, conversation, April 3, 1979.
30. Ruth O'Neill, conversation, February 20, 1976.
31. Olga Samaroff Stokowski to John Erskine, June 8, 1931.
32. Sonya Thorbecke, conversation, June 13, 1978.

Chapter 21

1. Unidentified clipping (Philadelphia Orchestra Archives), June 10, 1923.
2. Unidentified clipping (Philadelphia Orchestra Archives), August 1923.
3. Unidentified clipping (Philadelphia Orchestra Archives), August 25, 1923.
4. Arthur Judson, conversation with Ruth O'Neill and Samuel Rosenbaum, c. April 1972.
5. *Philadelphia Inquirer*, 11 October 1923.
6. Ibid.
7. *Philadelphia Public Ledger*, 20 October 1924.
8. Steve Cohen, "The Stokowski Story," WUHY-FM Radio (Philadelphia) Series, c. 1967.
9. Unidentified clipping (Philadelphia Orchestra Archives), 10 April 1923.
10. *Literary Digest*, 24 May 1930, pp. 19, 20.
11. Adrian Siegel interviewed by James Felton.
12. Sol Schoenbach, conversation, November 27, 1976.
13. Oscar Shumsky, conversation, December 7, 1977.
14. Ibid.
15. Arthur Cohn, conversation, March 11, 1976.
16. *Philadelphia Evening Bulletin*, 19 May 1924.
17. *Baltimore Evening Sun*, 25 May 1925.
18. Stokowski to Lawrence Gilman, May 22, 1924.
19. *Overtones*, 1 October 1974.
20. Unidentified clipping (Philadelphia Orchestra Archives), 15 December 1923.
21. Ruth O'Neill, conversation with Arthur Judson and Samuel Rosenbaum, c. April 1972.

22. *Overtones,* 1 October 1974.
23. *Philadelphia Evening Bulletin,* 25 January 1924.
24. *Philadelphia Evening Bulletin,* 30 October 1924.
25. *New York Evening Post,* 22 October 1924.
26. Unidentified clipping (Philadelphia Orchestra Archives), 24 January 1925.
27. *North American* (Philadelphia), 31 January 1925.
28. Halina Rodzinski, conversation, November 22, 1976.
29. *Philadelphia Inquirer,* 14 October 1925.
30. *Baltimore Daily Post,* 29 October 1925.
31. Evangeline Johnson Merrill, conversation, January 31, 1978.
32. *Philadelphia Evening Bulletin,* 9 January 1926.
33. *Philadelphia Evening Bulletin,* 12 January 1926.
34. Ibid.
35. *Philadelphia Evening Bulletin,* 13 January 1926.
36. Stokowski to Arthur Carles, March 6, 1926.

Chapter 22

1. Evangeline Johnson Merrill, conversation, November 21, 1977.
2. Evangeline Johnson Merrill, conversation, January 31, 1978.
3. *Palm Beach Daily News,* 19 December 1973.
4. Evangeline Johnson Merrill, conversation, January 31, 1978.
5. Ibid.
6. Ibid.
7. *New York Times,* 21 October 1926.
8. *Philadelphia Evening Bulletin,* 3 January 1927.
9. *Philadelphia Evening Bulletin,* 12 February 1927.
10. Philadelphia Public Ledger, 13 April 1927.
10. *Philadelphia Public Ledger,* 13 April 1927.
11. Evangeline Johnson Merrill, conversation, September 13, 1978.
12. Ibid.
13. *Philadelphia Record,* 2 June 1928.
14. Unidentified clippings (Felton Collection), 7 September 1928.
15. Evangeline Johnson Merrill, conversation, September 13, 1978.
16. Unidentified clippings (Felton Collection), 7 September 1928.
17. Unidentified clipping (Philadelphia Orchestra Archives), 9 December 1928.
18. Stokowski, *Music for All of Us,* p. 1.
19. Harold Schonberg, *The Great Conductors,* p. 313.
20. *New York Evening Post,* October 1928.

21. Unidentified clipping (Philadelphia Orchestra Archives), 5 October 1928.
22. Evangeline Johnson Merrill, conversation, January 31, 1978.
23. Ibid.
24. Ibid.
25. *Time*, 13 July 1931.
26. Unidentified clippings (Philadelphia Orchestra Archives), 5 July 1931.
27. Evangeline Johnson Merrill, conversation, January 31, 1978.
28. *Philadelphia Inquirer*, 4 August 1931.
29. Herbert Kupferberg, *Those Fabulous Philadelphians*, pp. 87, 88; *Musical America*, 10 November 1931.
30. Sonya Thorbecke, conversation, June 13, 1978.
31. Sonya Thorbecke, conversation, September 11, 1978.
32. Evangeline Johnson Merrill, conversation, January 31, 1978.
33. Sonya Thorbecke, conversation, September 12, 1979.
34. Sonya Thorbecke, conversation, February 26, 1979.
35. Sonya Thorbecke, conversation, June 13, 1978.
36. Olga Samaroff Stokowski, *An American Musician's Story*, pp. 202, 203.
37. Evangeline Johnson Merrill, conversation, January 31, 1978.
38. Sonya Thorbecke, conversation, June 13, 1978.
39. Evangeline Johnson Merrill, conversation, January 31, 1978.
40. *Philadelphia Public Ledger*, 4 October 1932.
41. *Philadelphia Inquirer*, 13 January 1933.
42. *Philadelphia Record*, 17 April 1932.
43. *Philadelphia Evening Bulletin*, 19 May 1933.
44. Olga Samaroff Stokowski to John Erskine, August 9, 1933.

Chapter 23

1. Victor Seroff, *Maurice Ravel* (New York: Henry Holt & Company, 1953), p. 231.
2. Arbie Ornstein, *Ravel: Man and Musician* (New York: Columbia University Press, 1975), pp. 86, 269.
3. Unidentified clipping (Philadelphia Orchestra Archives), 23 November 1929.
4. *Musical America*, 10 December 1929, p. 5.
5. Sylvan Levin, conversation, January 29, 1977.
6. Stokowski to Sylvan Levin, November 8, 1929.
7. Stokowski to Sylvan Levin, November 12, 1929.
8. Ibid.
9. *Philadelphia Record*, 26 November 1929.
10. *Philadelphia Inquirer*, 30 November 1929.

11. Edward Johnson, ed., *Stokowski*, p. 29.
12. Benjamin de Loache, conversation, July 26, 1978.
13. Rose Bampton, conversation, April 19, 1977.
14. *Philadelphia Evening Bulletin*, 7 November 1936.
15. Evangeline Johnson Merrill, conversation, November 21, 1977.
16. Lou Harrison, conversation, July 1976.
17. Edward Johnson, ed., *Stokowski*, p. 92.
18. Ibid., p. 102.
19. *Philadelphia Inquirer*, November 1939.
20. Stokowski, jacket notes for Mussorgsky *Night on Bald Mountain* recording on London SPC 21206.
21. *Musical America*, 25 December 1934, pp. 5, 17.

Chapter 24

1. Richard Aldrich, *Musical Discourse*, p. 477.
2. Stokowski to Charles Martin Loeffler, April 4, 1923.
3. *Musical America*, 22 February 1919.
4. *Arts and Decoration*, November 1922.
5. *North American* (Philadelphia), 4 March 1922.
6. *Musical Digest*, 30 December 1924.
7. Edgar Varèse, jacket notes for Varèse *Amériques* recording on Vanguard VRS 1156.
8. Louise Varèse, *Varèse: A Looking-Glass Diary*, pp. 195, 196.
9. Ibid. p. 223.
10. Louis Hood, *The Spirit of '75*, p. 30.
11. Louise Varèse, *Varèse: A Looking-Glass Diary*, pp. 245, 246.
12. *New York Sun*, 14 April 1926.
13. Louise Varèse, *Varèse: A Looking-Glass Diary*, p. 246.
14. *Twice a Year*, Autumn-Winter 1941.
15. Louise Varèse, *Varèse: A Looking-Glass Diary*, pp. 247, 248.
16. Fernand Ouellette, *Edgard Varèse*, p. 97.
17. Igor Stravinsky and Robert Craft, *Themes and Episodes*, p. 154.
18. Arnold Schoenberg to Stokowski, 1949.
19. Stokowski to Arnold Schoenberg, September 7, 1949.
20. Stokowski, *Music for All of Us*, pp. 48, 49.
21. Ibid., p. 120–23.
22. Olga Samaroff Stokowski, *The Layman's Music Book*, pp. 250, 251.
23. Arnold Schoenberg to Stokowski, November 20, 1931.
24. Arnold Schoenberg (note on his file copy of the above letter to Stokowski), November 20, 1931.
25. Arnold Schoenberg to Stokowski, 1932.

26. Arnold Schoenberg to Stokowski, March 16, 1932.
27. Stokowski to Arnold Schoenberg, April 3, 1932.
28. *American Record Guide*, August 1977, p. 6.
29. Arnold Schoenberg to Stokowski, 1949.
30. *San Francisco Chronicle*, 1977.
31. *American Record Guide*, August 1977, p. 5.
32. Stokowski to Arnold Schoenberg, November 2, 1933.
33. Arnold Schoenberg to Stokowski, November 14, 1933.
34. Ibid.
35. Irene Downes, ed., *Olin Downes on Music*, p. 171.
36. Stokowski to Sergei Rachmaninoff, April 21, 1925.
37. *Time*, 28 April 1930.
38. *Musical America*, 18 October 1924.
39. *Philadelphia Inquirer*, 28 September 1924.
40. *Saturday Evening Post*, 4 April 1942.
41. *Musical America*, 18 October 1924.
42. *Philadelphia Evening Bulletin*, 28 September 1932.
43. Ibid.
44. *Philadelphia Evening Bulletin*, 30 September 1932.
45. *Philadelphia Evening Bulletin*, 29 September 1932.
46. *Philadelphia Public Ledger*, 9 October 1932.
47. Stokowski to Sergei Rachmaninoff, March 18, 1933.
48. *Philadelphia Inquirer*, undated clipping.
49. Irene Downes, ed., *Olin Downes on Music*, p. 110.

Chapter 25

1. Louise Varèse, *Varèse: A Looking-Glass Diary*, p. 186.
2. Ibid.
3. *New York Evening Telegram*, 5 February 1923.
4. Nicholas Slonimsky, *Lexicon of Musical Inventive*, p. 160.
5. Louise Varèse, *Varèse: A Looking-Glass Diary*, pp. 188–91.
6. Ibid., p. 208.
7. Ibid., p. 204.
8. Ibid., p. 205.
9. Ibid., p. 208.
10. Ibid., p. 209.
11. *Musical America*, 8 December 1923.
12. Unidentified clipping (Philadelphia Orchestra Archives), 12 April 1924.
13. Louise Varèse, *Varèse: A Looking-Glass Diary*, p. 155.
14. Ibid., p. 227.
15. *Musical America*, 7 March 1925, p. 13.

16. Louise Varèse, *Varèse: A Looking-Glass Diary*, p. 230.
17. Ibid., pp. 231, 232.
18. Barbara Wolanin, *Arthur B. Carles, 1882–1952: Philadelphia Modernist*, pp. 79, 80.
19. Henry G. Gardiner, "Arthur B. Charles: A Critical and Biographical Study," *Philadelphia Museum of Art Bulletin*, 1970.
20. Louise Varèse, *Varèse: A Looking-Glass Diary*, p. 188.
21. Claire Reis, *Composers, Conductors and Critics*, p. 83.
22. Claire Reis, conversation, September 30, 1976.
23. Louise Varèse, *Varèse: A Looking-Glass Diary*, p. 244; *Musical America*, 20 February 1926, pp. 4, 9.
24. Claire Reis, *Composers, Conductors and Critics*, p. 87.
25. Ibid. pp. 141–43.
26. Ibid. pp. 88, 90.
27. Claire Reis, conversation, September 30, 1976.
28. Ibid.
29. Claire Reis, *Composers, Conductors and Critics*, p. 92.

Chapter 26

1. Sylvan Levin, conversation, January 6, 1978.
2. Claire Reis, *Composers, Conductors and Critics*, pp. 92, 93.
3. Ibid., p. 95.
4. Claire Reis, conversation, September 30, 1976.
5. Stokowski interviewed by Eugene Cook, November 13, 1961.
6. Martha Graham, conversation, April 19, 1977.
7. Richard Buckle, *Diaghilev* (New York: Atheneum, 1979), pp. 366, 368.
8. *Musical Leader*, 20 March 1930.
9. Léonide Massine, *My Life in Ballet*, pp. 172, 178; Mrs. Henri Doll (Eugenia Delarova), conversation, April 17, 1978.
10. Claire Reis, *Composers, Conductors and Critics*, p. 96; Claire Reis, conversation, September 30, 1976.
11. Claire Reis, conversation, September 30, 1976.
12. Claire Reis, *Composers, Conductors and Critics*, p. 97.
13. Claire Reis, conversation, September 30, 1976.
14. Richard Hammond, conversation, March 15, 1978.
15. Martha Graham, conversation, April 19, 1977.
16. Léonide Massine, *My Life in Ballet*, pp. 178, 179.
17. *New York Times*, 23 April 1930.
18. Merle Armitage, ed., *Martha Graham*, p. 34.
19. Martha Graham, conversation, April 19, 1977.

20. Merle Armitage, ed., *Martha Graham*, Preface.
21. *Time*, 28 April 1930.

Chapter 27

1. Stokowski to Sylvan Levin, March 30, 1931; Mildred Geiger (assistant to Stokowski) to Sylvan Levin, December 7, 1931.
2. Sylvan Levin, conversation, January 29, 1977.
3. Stokowski to Henri Elkan, December 20, 1930.
4. Stokowski to Sylvan Levin, December 21, 1930.
5. Reginald Allen, conversation, August 6, 1976.
6. Steve Cohen, "The Stokowski Story," WUHY-FM Radio (Philadelphia) Series, c. 1967.
7. Sergei Radamsky, *Der Verfolgte Tenor*, pp. 177–79.
8. Ibid.
9. *Philadelphia Evening Bulletin*, 20 March 1931.
10. Mrs. William C. Hammer, conversation, September 3, 1979.
11. Alban Berg to Sylvan Levin, October 27, 1931.
12. *Philadelphia Evening Bulletin*, 25 November 1931.
13. Ibid.
14. Stokowski interviewed by Eugene Cook, November 13, 1961.

Chapter 28

1. *Musical America*, 25 April 1931, p. 42.
2. Claire Reis, *Composers, Conductors and Critics*, p. 132.
3. Souvenir Program Booklet for Stravinsky's *Oedipus Rex* and Prokofiev's *Le Pas d'Acier* (New York: League of Composers, 1931), p. 3.
4. Ibid., p. 4.
5. Ibid., p. 10.
6. *New York Times*, 6 April 1931.
7. *Philadelphia Public Ledger*, 11 April 1931.
8. *Musical America*, 10 May 1931, p. 9.
9. *Philadelphia Evening Bulletin*, 11 April 1931.
10. Souvenir Program Booklet for Stravinsky's *Oedipus Rex* and Prokofiev's *Le Pas d'Acier*, p. 3.
11. Francis Ralston Welsh to the press, April 16, 1931.
12. Evangeline Johnson Merrill, conversation, September 1, 1979.
13. *American Russian Institute Bulletin*, May-June 1931.
14. *Musical America*, 10 April 1933, p. 15.
15. Claire Reis, conversation, September 30, 1976.
16. *Musical America*, 25 April 1933, p. 13.

17. Charles Wuorinen, jacket notes for Schoenberg's *Pierrot Lunaire* recording on Nonesuch H 71251.

Chapter 29

1. Stokowski to Sylvan Levin, May 12, 1932.
2. Stokowski to Sylvan Levin, June 1, 1932.
3. Stokowski to Sylvan Levin, August 11, 1932.
4. Rose Bampton, conversation, April 19, 1977.
5. *Musical America*, 25 April 1933, p. 14.
6. Stokowski to J. Beek, September 5, 1956.
7. Stokowski to F. M. Scott III, September 21, 1957.
8. F. M. Scott III to Stokowski, October 11, 1957.

Chapter 30

1. Unidentified clipping (Philadelphia Orchestra Archives), 16 December 1930.
2. Evangeline Johnson Merrill, conversation, September 27, 1978.
3. Ibid.
4. Carlos Chávez, conversation, September 14, 1976.
5. *Philadelphia Evening Bulletin*, 24 January 1931.
6. *Philadelphia Public Ledger*, 5 February 1931.
7. *Musical America*, 12 March 1927.
8. Carlos Chávez, conversation, September 14, 1976.
9. Evangeline Johnson Merrill, conversation, September 27, 1978.
10. Unidentified clipping (Philadelphia Orchestra Archives), 17 April 1930.
11. *Philadelphia Public Ledger*, 16 April 1930.
12. *Musical America*, July 1930, p. 11.
13. *Philadelphia Public Ledger*, 19 February 1931.
14. *Philadelphia Evening Bulletin*, 18 January 1932.
15. *Musical America*, 25 February 1932, p. 30.
16. Carlos Chávez, conversation, September 14, 1976.
17. *Philadelphia Evening Bulletin*, January 18, 1932.
18. *Time*, 11 April 1932.
19. Evangeline Johnson, conversation, February 27, 1978.
20. *Musical America*, 25 January 1932, p. 6.
21. *Philadelphia Evening Bulletin*, 1 April 1932.
22. *Musical America*, 10 April 1932, pp. 3, 7.
23. *Philadelphia Evening Bulletin*, 1 April 1932.
24. Carlos Chávez, conversation, September 14, 1976.

Chapter 31

1. Unidentified clipping (Philadelphia Public Library Collection), 10 October 1924.
2. Henry Pleasants, conversation, May 29, 1976.
3. *Musical America,* April 1926.
4. *New York Sun,* 17 April 1926.
5. Hugh Ross, conversation, November 15, 1977.
6. *New York Sun,* 17 April 1926.
7. Ferdinand Del Negro, conversation, December 4, 1977.
8. Herbert Kupferberg, *Those Fabulous Philadelphians,* p. 56.
9. Henry Pleasants, conversation, May 29, 1976.
10. *Musical America,* 25 November 1929, p. 14.
11. Herbert Kupferberg, *Those Fabulous Philadelphians,* p. 78.
12. *Philadelphia Evening Bulletin,* 22 April 1930.

Chapter 32

1. Stokowski interviewed by Gordon Stafford, March 1956.
2. Arthur Judson, conversation with Ruth O'Neill and Samuel Rosenbaum, January 6, 1972.
3. Herbert Kupferberg, *Those Fabulous Philadelphians,* p. 81.
4. John Krell, *Kincaidiana,* p. 96.
5. Stokowski, *Music for All of Us,* pp. 215, 216.
6. Ibid., p. 195.
7. Stokowski interviewed by Gordon Stafford, March 1956.
8. Ibid.
9. Sir Adrian Boult to the author, July 18, 1978.
10. Sir Adrian Boult interviewed by John Bird, May 22, 1967.
11. Edward Johnson, ed., *Stokowski,* pp. 15, 16.
12. Stokowski interviewed by Eugene Cook, November 13, 1961.
13. Stokowski, *Music for All of Us,* p. 180.
14. Ibid., p. 183.
15. George Zazofsky, conversation, August 14, 1976.
16. *Hi/Fi Stereo,* February 1960, p. 42.
17. Mrs. Curtis Bok, conversation, June 12, 1979.
18. David Madison, conversation, November 27, 1979.
19. Ferdinand Del Negro, conversation, December 4, 1977.
20. *Musical America,* 30 October 1926.
21. Mrs. Curtis Bok, conversation, June 12, 1979.
22. *New York Times,* 24 October 1926.
23. *New York Times,* 28 October 1926.

24. Ruth O'Neill, conversation, February 20, 1976.
25. NBC-Radio interview with Stokowski by Harry Fleetwood, c. 1968.
26. Henry Pleasants, conversation, May 29, 1976.
27. Arthur Cohn, conversation, March 11, 1976.
28. Ruth O'Neill, conversation, February 20, 1976.
29. *Philadelphia Public Ledger,* 4 October 1930.
30. *Detroit News,* 24 November 1916.
31. Ernest Bloch to Marguerite Bloch, March 29, 1917.
32. Ernest Bloch to Marguerite Bloch, May 4, 1917.
33. Otto Luening, conversation, September 20, 1976.
34. *Associated Press* dispatch, 12 January 1929.
35. Darius Milhaud, *Notes without Music: An Autobiography,* p. 133.
36. Herbert Kupferberg, *Those Fabulous Philadelphians,* p. 80.
37. Unidentified clipping (Philadelphia Public Library Collection), c. 1928.
38. Richard Leonard, conversation, April 24, 1978.
39. Stokowski, *Music for All of Us,* p. 53.
40. *Philadelphia Public Ledger,* 16 April 1922.
41. Stokowski, *Music for All of Us,* p. 54.
42. George Zazofsky, conversation, August 14, 1976.
43. *Philadelphia Public Ledger,* 16 April 1922.
44. Sol Schoenbach, conversation, November 27, 1976.
45. Unidentified clipping (Philadelphia Public Library Collection), c. 1928.

Chapter 33

1. Stephen G. Smith, jacket notes for "Leopold Stokowski: The Early Years" recording LS 3.
2. National Public Radio interview with Stokowski by Bob Wallace, c. 1965.
3. Stephen G. Smith, jacket notes for "Leopold Stokowski: The Early Years," recording LS 3.
4. Edward Johnson, ed., *Stokowski,* pp. 87, 88.
5. Ibid., p. 88.
6. Stephen G. Smith, jacket notes for "Leopold Stokowski: The Early Years," recording LS 3.
7. *Musical America,* August 1929, p. 14.
8. *Manufacturer,* October 1929.
9. 'Evangeline Johnson Merrill, conversation, January 31, 1978.
10. *Philadelphia Inquirer,* 6 October 1929.
11. *Musical America,* 10 October 1929, p. 13.
12. *New York World,* 15 December 1929.
13. *San Francisco Chronicle* (AP), 9 December 1929.

14. *Musical America*, September 1930, p. 4.
15. *Musical America*, 25 October 1930, p. 29.
16. *Musical America*, 10 December 1930, p. 35.
17. Harvey Fletcher, conversation, May 9, 1979.
18. Robert E. McGinn, "Stokowski and the Bell Laboratories: Collaboration in the Development of High Fidelity Sound Reproduction, 1939–1940." Revised version of a paper presented at the annual meeting of the History of Science Society, New York, December 29, 1979, p. 10.
19. Ibid., p. 11.
20. Arthur Keller, conversation, May 3, 1979.
21. Harvey Fletcher, conversation, May 9, 1979.
22. Robert E. McGinn, "Stokowski and the Bell Laboratories," p. 13.
23. Harvey Fletcher, conversation, May 9, 1979.
24. *Musical America*, 10 October 1931, p. 39.
25. *Musical America*, 25 December 1931, p. 39.
26. Harvey Fletcher, conversation, May 9, 1979.
27. *Baltimore Post*, 13 April 1933.
28. Harvey Fletcher, conversation, May 9, 1979.
29. Steve Cohen, "The Stokowski Story," WUHY-FM Radio (Philadelphia) Series, c. 1967.
30. Robert E. McGinn, "Stokowski and the Bell Laboratories," p. 24.
31. Ibid., p. 29.
32. Ibid., p. 30.
33. *New York Times*, 10 April 1940.
34. Unidentified clipping (International Leopold Stokowski Society Archives), November 1939.
35. H. Ward Marston IV, jacket notes for "Early Hi-Fi: Wide Range and Stereo Recordings Made by Bell Telephone Laboratories in the 1930s," recordings BTL 7901 and BTL 8001; Bert Whyte, "The Roots of High Fidelity Sound." *Audio*, June 1981; *Gramophone*, July 1980, p. 180.

Chapter 34

1. *New York Times*, 29 January 1975.
2. *Philadelphia Evening Bulletin*, 3 July 1930.
3. Edna Phillips, conversation, September 3, 1976.
4. Ferdinand Del Negro, conversation, December 4, 1977.
5. Edna Phillips, conversation, September 3, 1976.
6. David Madison, conversation, November 27, 1979.
7. Unidentified clipping (Philadelphia Orchestra Archives), 29 November 1930.

8. *Philadelphia Inquirer,* 29 November 1930.
9. Arthur Schuller, conversation, September 8, 1978.
10. George Marek, *Toscanini,* p. 110.
11. Herbert Kupferberg, *Those Fabulous Philadelphians,* p. 83.
12. Arthur Schuller, conversation, September 8, 1978.
13. Howard Taubman, *The Maestro: The Life of Arturo Toscanini,* p. 186.
14. *New York Times,* 28 November 1930.
15. *New York Sun,* 5 December 1930.
16. *Musical America,* 25 December 1930, p. 6.
17. Ibid.
18. Edward Arian, *Bach, Beethoven, and Bureaucracy,* p. 14.
19. *Musical America,* 25 May 1933, p. 46.
20. *Philadelphia Evening Bulletin,* 24 October 1934.
21. Herbert Kupferberg, *Those Fabulous Philadelphians,* p. 94.
22. *Philadelphia Evening Bulletin,* 7 December 1934.
23. Mrs. Curtis Bok, conversation, June 12, 1979.
24. Herbert Kupferberg, *Those Fabulous Philadelphians,* pp. 95, 96.
25. Arthur Judson, conversation with Ruth O'Neill and Samuel
    Rosenbaum, c. April 1972.
26. *Philadelphia Evening Bulletin,* 7 December 1934.
27. *Philadelphia Public Ledger,* 31 May 1932.
28. *Philadelphia Public Ledger,* 4 October 1932.
29. *Philadelphia Public Ledger,* 31 May 1932.
30. *Philadelphia Evening Bulletin,* 4 October 1932.
31. *Philadelphia Public Ledger,* 4 October 1932.
32. *Philadelphia Evening Bulletin,* 4 October 1932.
33. Stokowski to Jean Sibelius, April 10, 1931.

Chapter 35

1. *Philadelphia Record,* 18 October 1932.
2. *Philadelphia Public Ledger,* 19 October 1932.
3. Unidentified clipping (Philadelphia Public Library Collection), April
   1933.
4. Ruth Yardumian, conversation, December 31, 1977.
5. Unidentified clipping (Philadelphia Public Library Collection), April
   1933.
6. Natasha Bender, conversation, September 19, 1979.
7. Mrs. John P. Wheeler, conversation, January 22, 1979.
8. Helene Hanff, conversation, December 5, 1978.
9. Ruth Yardumian, conversation, December 31, 1977.
10. *Musical America,* 25 March 1933, p. 27.

11. Arthur Cohn, conversation, March 11, 1976.
12. Ibid.
13. Unidentified clipping (Philadelphia Public Library Collection), April 1933.
14. Ibid.
15. *Musical America*, 10 May 1933, p. 20.
16. Unidentified clipping (Philadelphia Public Library Collection), April 1933.
17. Jerome Toobin, *Agitato*, pp. 36, 37.
18. Mrs. John P. Wheeler, conversation, January 22, 1979.
19. *New Yorker*, 9 December 1961.
20. *Musical America*, 25 January 1934, p. 18.
21. *Philadelphia Evening Bulletin*, 24 January 1934.
22. *Philadelphia Evening Bulletin*, 25 January 1934.
23. *Philadelphia Public Ledger*, 22 March 1934.
24. *Musical America*, 10 April 1934, p. 32.
25. *Philadelphia Evening Bulletin*, 23 March 1934.
26. *Musical America*, 25 April 1934, p. 18.
27. Natasha Bender, conversation, September 19, 1979.
28. *New Yorker*, 9 December 1961.
29. Natasha Bender, conversation, September 19, 1979.
30. Eugene List, conversation, September 10, 1976.
31. Olga Samaroff Stokowski, *An American Musician's Story*, pp. 198, 199.
32. Eugene List, conversation, September 10, 1976.
33. *Philadelphia Inquirer*, 13 December 1934.
34. Olga Samaroff Stokowski, *An American Musician's Story*, p. 199.

Chapter 36

1. *Musical America*, 25 October 1934, p. 3.
2. *Musical America*, 10 December 1934, p. 3.
3. Ibid.
4. *Philadelphia Evening Bulletin*, 8 December 1934.
5. Ibid.
6. *Philadelphia Inquirer*, 12 December 1934.
7. Ibid.
8. *Philadelphia Evening Bulletin*, 13 December 1934.
9. Ibid.
10. Ibid.
11. *Philadelphia Record*, 13 December 1934.
12. *Philadelphia Record*, 16 December 1934.
13. *Philadelphia Evening Bulletin*, 10 December 1934.

14. *Philadelphia Record*, 19 December 1934.
15. *Philadelphia Inquirer*, 20 December 1934.
16. Reginald Allen, conversation, August 6, 1976.
17. Ibid.
18. Orville Bullitt, conversation, November 9, 1978.
19. *Philadelphia Record*, 6 January 1935.
20. *Philadelphia Evening Bulletin*, 21 January 1935.
21. *Philadelphia Evening Bulletin*, 15 April 1935.
22. *Philadelphia Evening Bulletin*, 2 January 1936.
23. *Musical America*, October 1938.

Chapter 37

1. *Philadelphia Public Ledger*, 3 November 1921.
2. *Philadelphia Public Ledger*, 24 April 1923.
3. Unidentified clipping (Philadelphia Orchestra Archives), 26 April 1923.
4. Merle Armitage, *Accent on America*, pp. 84–86.
5. Reginald Allen, conversation, October 7, 1977.
6. Merle Armitage, *Accent on America*, p. 87.
7. *San Francisco Chronicle*, 28 April 1936.
8. Merle Armitage, *Accent on America*, pp. 87, 88.
9. *Musical America*, 10 May 1936, p. 27.
10. Steve Cohen, "The Stokowski Story," WUHY-FM Radio (Philadelphia) Series, c. 1967.
11. *Modern Music*, November-December 1936, p. 49.
12. *New York Times*, 10 June 1977.
13. Henry Koster, conversation, February 16, 1978.
14. *Philadelphia Public Ledger*, 6 July 1937.
15. Ibid.
16. *New York Times*, 10 June 1977.
17. Henry Koster, conversation, February 16, 1978.
18. Ibid.
19. Deanna Durbin to the author, January 23, 1977.

Chapter 38

1. *Philadelphia Public Ledger*, 18 April 1931.
2. Frederick Sands and Sven Broman, *The Divine Garbo*, p. 88.
3. *Philadelphia Public Ledger*, 18 April 1931.
4. John Bainbridge, *Garbo*, p. 187.
5. Anita Loos, conversation, September 11, 1978.
6. Ibid.

7. Evangeline Johnson Merrill, conversation, September 13, 1978.
8. *San Francisco Chronicle*, 8 July 1937.
9. Unidentified clipping (International Leopold Stokowski Society Archives), 13 August 1937.
10. Evangeline Johnson Merrill, conversation, November 21, 1977.
11. *Philadelphia Evening Bulletin*, 5 November 1937.
12. *Philadelphia Public Ledger*, 19 October 1937.
13. *Philadelphia Inquirer*, 19 October 1937.
14. *Philadelphia Evening Bulletin*, 16 November 1937.
15. Sophia Yarnall Jacobs, conversation, March 5, 1976.
16. *Philadelphia Evening Bulletin*, 2 December 1937.
17. *Philadelphia Evening Bulletin*, 3 December 1937.
18. *Philadelphia Inquirer*, 14 December 1937.
19. Evangeline Johnson Merrill, conversation, September 27, 1978.
20. *Philadelphia Evening Bulletin*, 25 January 1938.
21. *Philadelphia Inquirer*, 28 January 1938.
22. Reginald Allen to Stokowski, January 17, 1938.
23. *Philadelphia Public Ledger*, 5 February 1938.
24. *Time*, 14 March 1938.
25. *Philadelphia Record*, 7 March 1938.
26. *Philadelphia Inquirer*, 2 March 1938.
27. John Bainbridge, *Garbo*, p. 198; *Philadelphia Evening Bulletin*, 17 March 1938; *New York Herald Tribune*, 18 March 1938.
28. *San Francisco Chronicle*, 22 March 1938.
29. *Philadelphia Public Ledger*, 27 June 1938.
30. John Bainbridge, *Garbo*, p. 200; Frederick Sands and Sven Broman, *The Divine Garbo*, p. 190.
31. Alexandre Gretchaninoff, *My Life*, p. 152.
32. *San Francisco Chronicle*, 11 August 1938.
33. Stokowski to Jean Sibelius, July 1938.
34. Stokowski to Reginald Allen, July 1938.
35. *Philadelphia Evening Bulletin*, 15 August 1938.
36. *Philadelphia Evening Bulletin*, 20 August 1938.
37. Frederick Sands and Sven Broman, *The Divine Garbo*, p. 190.
38. Stokowski to Reginald Allen, September 6, 1938.
39. Reginald Allen to Stokowski, September 28, 1938.
40. Reginald Allen, conversation, August 6, 1976.
41. Richard Hammond, conversation, March 15, 1978.
42. Stokowski to Reginald Allen, October 4, 1938.
43. Stokowski to Sylvan Levin, December 22, 1938.
44. *San Francisco Chronicle*, 21 December 1938.
45. *San Francisco Chronicle*, 20 December 1938.

46. BBC-Radio interview with Stokowski by Basil Moss, September 2, 1969.

Chapter 39

1. *San Francisco Chronicle*, 25 January 1939.
2. *San Francisco Chronicle*, 18 February 1939.
3. *Philadelphia Inquirer*, 18 March 1939.
4. *Philadelphia Inquirer*, 31 March 1939.
5. *Philadelphia Public Ledger*, 30 March 1939.
6. *Philadelphia Evening Bulletin*, 30 March 1939.
7. *Philadelphia Public Ledger*, 30 March 1939.
8. *Philadelphia Inquirer*, 31 March 1939.
9. *Philadelphia Evening Bulletin*, 31 March 1939.
10. *Philadelphia Evening Bulletin*, 1 April 1939.
11. *Philadelphia Public Ledger*, 4 April 1939.
12. Gunther Schuller, conversation, April 6, 1976.
13. *Philadelphia Evening Bulletin*, 10 March 1939.
14. *San Francisco Chronicle*, 26 May 1939.
15. *Philadelphia Public Ledger*, 16 September 1939.
16. *Philadelphia Public Ledger*, 16 September 1939.
17. *San Francisco Chronicle*, 24 September 1939.
18. *San Francisco Chronicle*, 19 October 1939.
19. Stokowski to Arnold Schoenberg, October 18, 1939.
20. Arnold Schoenberg to Stokowski, October 20, 1939.
21. *Philadelphia Evening Bulletin*, 11 November 1939.
22. Unidentified clipping (International Leopold Stokowski Society Archives), 18 November 1939.
23. *Philadelphia Inquirer*, 18 November 1939.
24. *San Francisco Chronicle*, 30 November 1939.

Chapter 40

1. *Millimeter*, February 1976.
2. BBC-Radio interview with Stokowski by John Bowen, 1959.
3. *Millimeter*, February 1976.
4. Ibid.
5. Ibid.
6. Stokowski and Walt Disney, meeting notes on *Fantasia*, September 30, 1938.
7. Stokowski and Walt Disney, meeting notes on *Fantasia*, September 14, 1938.

8. Stokowski and Walt Disney, meeting notes on *Fantasia*, September 26, 1938.
9. Stokowski and Walt Disney, meeting notes on *Fantasia*, September 10, 1938.
10. Stokowski and Walt Disney, meeting notes on *Fantasia*, September 14, 1938.
11. Stokowski, *Music for All of Us*, p. 245.
12. Steve Cohen, "The Stokowski Story," WUHY-FM Radio (Philadelphia) Series, c. 1967.
13. Dick Huemer, conversation, November 10, 1976.
14. Ibid.
15. *Fantasia* Program Booklet (Walt Disney Productions, 1940), pp. 19, 20, 24.
16. Dick Huemer, conversation, November 10, 1976.
17. Steve Cohen, "The Stokowski Story," WUHY-FM Radio (Philadelphia) Series, c. 1967.
18. *New York Herald Tribune*, 14 November 1940.
19. Ibid.
20. Stokowski to Walt Disney, December 27, 1940.
21. Sonya Thorbecke, conversation, June 13, 1978.

Chapter 41

1. Jean Dalrymple, conversation, July 27, 1978.
2. Unidentified clipping (New York Public Library Collection), 1937.
3. John Bitter, conversation, August 4, 1976.
4. All-American Youth Orchestra Program Booklet, Latin-American Tour, Summer 1940, pp. 2, 8.
5. Steve Cohen, "The Stokowski Story," WUHY-FM Radio (Philadelphia) Series, c. 1967.
6. *Time*, 10 June 1940.
7. Harvey Sachs, *Toscanini*, p. 273.
8. Charles O'Connell, *The Other Side of the Record*, pp. 103, 104.
9. Steve Cohen, "The Stokowski Story," WUHY-FM Radio (Philadelphia) Series, c. 1967.
10. Associated Press, March 26, 1940.
11. Unidentified clipping (New York Public Library Collection), 1940.
12. John Bitter, conversation, August 4, 1976.
13. Harold Coletta, conversation, October 13, 1977.
14. Robert Gross, reminiscences, November 1976.
15. Albert Tipton, conversation, December 14, 1976.
16. George Zazofsky, conversation, August 14, 1976.

17. Ralph Gomberg, conversation, August 14, 1976.
18. Unidentified clipping (New York Public Library Collection), 14 June 1940.
19. Dorothy DeLay, conversation, April 13, 1977.
20. Edna Phillips, conversation, September 3, 1976.
21. Robert Gross, reminiscences, November 1976.
22. Samuel Mayes, conversation, November 27, 1976.
23. Robert Gross, reminiscences, November 1976.
24. Unidentified clipping (Philadelphia Public Library Collection), 22 July 1940.
25. *Baltimore Sun,* 23 July 1940.
26. *New York Times,* 27 July 1940.

Chapter 42

1. James Chambers, conversation, November 17, 1979.
2. Robert Gross, reminiscences, November 1976.
3. Seymour Barab, conversation, December 25, 1979.
4. John Bitter, conversation, August 4, 1976.
5. Steve Cohen, "The Stokowski Story," WUHY-FM Radio (Philadelphia) Series, c. 1967.
6. John Bitter, conversation, August 4, 1976.
7. *Diario da Notte* (Rio de Janeiro), August 9, 1940.
8. Robert Gross, reminiscences, November 1976.
9. John Bitter, conversation, August 4, 1976.
10. Robert Gross, reminiscences, November 1976.
11. Sol Schoenbach, conversation, November 27, 1976.
12. David Madison, conversation, November 27, 1979.
13. Estudio Auditorio del S.O.D.R.E., Montevideo, program, August 17, 1940.
14. John Bitter, conversation, August 4, 1976.
15. José Serebrier, conversation, October 18, 1976.
16. James Chambers, conversation, November 17, 1979.
17. Harold Coletta, conversation, October 13, 1977.
18. Robert Gross, reminiscences, November 1976.

Chapter 43

1. *New York Post,* 19 September 1940.
2. *Baltimore Sun,* 20 September 1940.
3. *Washington Times-Herald,* 21 September 1940.
4. *Philadelphia Inquirer,* 22 September 1940.

5. Robert Gross, reminiscences, November 1976.
6. Robert Gross, conversation, December 27, 1979.
7. Irving Kolodin, *A Guide to Recorded Music*, p. 134.
8. Edward Johnson, ed., *Stokowski*, p. 95.

Chapter 44

1. *Musical America*, December 1940.
2. *Philadelphia Evening Bulletin*, 6 December 1940.
3. *Philadelphia Evening Bulletin*, 7 December 1940.
4. *Philadelphia Record*, 7 December 1940.
5. Louis Krasner, conversation, October 25, 1976.
6. Arnold Schoenberg to Stokowski, December 17, 1940.
7. Goddard Lieberson, conversation, October 28, 1976.
8. *Philadelphia Evening Bulletin*, 7 December 1940.
9. *Philadelphia Evening Bulletin*, 12 December 1940.
10. Orville Bullitt, conversation, November 9, 1978.
11. Susan B. Bullitt and Orville Bullitt, *From Candlelight to Satellite*, p. 115.
12. Ibid., pp. 112, 113.
13. *Minneapolis Tribune*, 14 March 1941; *San Francisco Chronicle*, 8 March 1941.
14. *San Francisco Chronicle* (AP), 12 March 1941.
15. *Philadelphia Public Ledger*, 24 February 1941.
16. *Philadelphia Inquirer*, 16 March 1941.
17. *Philadelphia Record*, 23 March 1941.
18. *New York Times*, 31 January 1941.
19. *Philadelphia Evening Bulletin*, 29 March 1941.
20. *New York Post* (AP), 17 January 1941.
21. *New York Post*, 25 January 1941.
22. Unidentified clipping (Felton Collection), 25 January 1941.
23. *New York World-Telegram*, 5 April 1941.
24. Unidentified clipping (Felton Collection), 6 April 1941.
25. *Philadelphia Public Ledger*, 24 February 1941.
26. *San Francisco Chronicle* (UP), 2 March 1941.
27. Unidentified clipping (Felton Collection), 18 March 1941.
28. *Philadelphia Public Ledger*, 18 March 1941.

Chapter 45

1. Stokowski to Claire Reis, February 26, 1941.
2. Natasha Bender, conversation, February 11, 1980.

3. Joscelyn Godwin, *The Music of Henry Cowell* (Ann Arbor, Michigan: University Microfilms, 1969), p. 536.
4. Ibid., p. 14.
5. Lou Harrison, conversation, February 23, 1980.
6. Joscelyn Godwin, *The Music of Henry Cowell*, p. 16.
7. *New York Times*, 17 May 1941.
8. *Milwaukee Journal*, 4 June 1941.
9. *New York Times*, 17 May 1941.
10. *Chicago Daily News*, 3 June 1941.
11. *Milwaukee Sentinel*, 5 June 1941.
12. *St. Paul Pioneer Press*, 6 June 1941.
13. *Omaha Morning World-Herald*, 7 June 1941.
14. *St. Louis Globe-Democrat*, 10 June 1941.
15. *Indianapolis Star*, 10 June 1941.
16. *Louisville Courier-Journal*, 11 June 1941.
17. *Denver Post*, 20 June 1941.
18. *Louisville Courier-Journal*, 12 June 1941.
19. Robert Whitney, conversation, February 19, 1980.
20. *Louisville Courier-Journal*, 12 June 1941.
21. *Nashville Tennessean*, 14 June 1941.
22. *Nashville Tennessean*, 13 June 1941.
23. *Kansas City Times*, 16 June 1941.
24. *Kansas City Times*, 17 June 1941.
25. *Colorado Springs Evening Telegraph*, 18 June 1941.
26. Robert Gross, reminiscences, November 1976.
27. *Indianapolis Star*, 11 June 1941.
28. Robert Gross, reminiscences, November 1976.
29. Carol Truax, conversation, February 22, 1980.
30. *Seattle Post-Intelligencer*, 24 June 1941.
31. *San Francisco Chronicle*, 28 June 1941.
32. Irving Kolodin, *New Guide to Recorded Music*, pp. 264, 265.
33. John Erskine, *The Philharmonic-Symphony Society of New York: Its First Hundred Years*, p. 163.
34. *Philadelphia Evening Bulletin*, 10 October 1941.
35. *New York Times*, 17 October 1941.

Chapter 46

1. H. C. Colles, *Walford Davies: A Biography*, pp. 55, 58.
2. Philipp Spitta, *Johann Sebastian Bach*, volume 2 (New York: Dover, 1951), p. 546.
3. Robert Shaw, conversation, December 1, 1977.

4. Stokowski, conversation, 1955.
5. Robert Shaw, conversation, December 1, 1977.
6. Stokowski, program notes for "Miracle Play Based on Bach's *St. Matthew Passion* Music," April 1943, p. 10.
7. Robert Shaw, conversation, December 1, 1977.
8. Lillian Gish, conversation, February 24, 1977.
9. Eleanor Steber, conversation, May 10, 1978.
10. *Time*, 19 April 1943.
11. *New Yorker*, 5 April 1969.
12. Stokowski to Reginald Allen, November 14, 1928.
13. Stokowski, lecture at Bryn Mawr College, "The Making of an Orchestra," February 4, 1963.
14. Stokowski, *Music for All of Us*, pp. 146, 147, 208.
15. Harold Schonberg, *The Great Conductors*, p. 313.
16. Irving Kolodin, *The Musical Life*, p. 207.
17. *New York Times*, 6 November 1935.
18. Paul Hume, conversation, October 17, 1978.
19. Lucien Cailliet to the author, June 1, 1978.
20. *Kenosha News*, 16 September 1977.
21. David Madison, conversation, November 27, 1979.
22. Rosalyn Tureck, conversation, April 3, 1979.
23. Lilette Hindin, conversation, January 24, 1979.
24. Ellis Kohs, conversation, June 30, 1976.
25. Walter Leuba to author, August 1979.
26. Stokowski to Walter Leuba, April 20, 1937.
27. José Iturbi, conversation, April 2, 1977.
28. *Stereo Review*, March 1982, p. 84.

Chapter 47

1. Harvey Sachs, *Toscanini*, pp. 262, 264.
2. Alan Shulman, conversation, March 4, 1980.
3. *San Francisco Chronicle*, 10 September 1941.
4. *New York Times*, 24 October 1941.
5. NBC-Radio interview with Stokowski, November 1941.
6. Ibid.
7. Robert Helps, conversation, October 10, 1977.
8. David Hall, jacket notes for the Toscanini-Philadelphia Orchestra recordings RCA CRM5-1900.
9. Charles O'Connell, *The Other Side of the Record*, pp. 123–25.
10. David Hall, jacket notes for the Toscanini-Philadelphia Orchestra recordings RCA CRM5-1900.

11. Edward Johnson, ed., *Stokowski*, p. 94.
12. *New Records*, March 1942, p. 5.
13. Irving Kolodin, *New Guide to Recorded Music*, p. 304.
14. Ibid., p. 313.
15. NBC-Radio interview with Stokowski, 1942.
16. *Time*, 6 April 1942.
17. Unidentified clipping, 4 May 1942.
18. Stokowski to Arturo Toscanini, June 22, 1942.
19. Arturo Toscanini to Stokowski, June 23, 1942.
20. Stokowski to Arturo Toscanini, June 24, 1942.
21. Arturo Toscanini to Stokowski, June 25, 1942.
22. Stokowski, *Music for All of Us*, p. 110.
23. Solomon Volkov, ed. *Testimony: The Memoir of Dmitri Shostakovich* (New York: Harper & Row, 1979), p. 24.
24. Maxim Shostakovich to the author, September 1978.
25. *Los Angeles Times*, 5 July 1942.

Chapter 48

1. David Hall, jacket notes for the Toscanini-Philadelphia Orchestra recordings RCA CRM5-1900.
2. Harvey Sachs, *Toscanini*, p. 280.
3. *San Francisco Chronicle*, 5 January 1943.
4. *Los Angeles Daily News*, 22 January 1943.
5. *New York Herald Tribune*, 28 February 1943.
6. William Schuman, conversation, September 22, 1976.
7. *New York Herald Tribune*, 10 January 1944.
8. Felix Greissle, conversation, August 1977.
9. Stokowski to Arnold Schoenberg, June 7, 1943.
10. Leonard Stein, reminiscences, January 20, 1977.
11. Clara Steuermann, reminiscences, January 20, 1977.
12. Fritz Jahoda, conversation, November 12, 1977.
13. Felix Greissle, conversation, August 1977.
14. Stokowski to Arnold Schoenberg, February 9, 1944.
15. Arnold Schoenberg to Stokowski, February 8, 1944.
16. *New York Herald Tribune*, 7 February 1944.
17. Felix Greissle, conversation, August 1977.
18. *New York Herald Tribune*, 14 May 1944.
19. *New York Herald Tribune*, June 1944.
20. *Time*, 19 June 1944.
21. Harvey Sachs, *Toscanini*, p. 276.

22. *Time,* 19 June 1944.
23. Virgil Thomson, conversation, October 1, 1976.

Chapter 49

1. Jean Dalrymple, conversation, July 27, 1978.
2. Stokowski to Sylvan Levin, February 16, 1944.
3. Stokowski to Sylvan Levin, February 22, 1944.
4. Stokowski to Sylvan Levin, March 5, 1944.
5. *Newsweek,* 5 June 1944.
6. *Time,* 5 June 1944.
7. *Newsweek,* 5 June 1944.
8. William Grant Still to Sylvan Levin, August 9, 1944.
9. Stokowski to Claire Reis, July 10, 1944.
10. Stokowski to Sylvan Levin, July 20, 1944.
11. Stokowski to Sylvan Levin, July 28, 1944.
12. Stokowski to Sylvan Lenin, July 20, 1944.
13. William Grant Still to Sylvan Levin, August 9, 1944; William Grant Still to Sylvan Levin, July 17, 1944.
14. Julius Baker, conversation, March 10, 1977.
15. Robert Gross, reminiscences, November 1976.
16. Stokowski to Sylvan Levin, August 26, 1944.
17. *New York Herald Tribune,* 10 October 1944.
18. *Musical America,* 10 November 1944.
19. *New York Times,* November 1944.
20. *Musical America,* 10 November 1944.
21. Stokowski to Arnold Schoenberg, September 16, 1944.
22. *Musical America,* 10 December 1944.
23. Claire Reis, conversation, September 30, 1976.
24. Anita Zahn, conversation, December 27, 1976.
25. New York Times, 22 December 1944.
26. *Musical America,* January 1945.
27. *New York Herald Tribune,* 30 January 1945.
28. *Musical America,* 13 April 1945.

Chapter 50

1. Arthur Judson, conversation with Ruth O'Neill and Samuel Rosenbaum, c. April 1972.
2. Unidentified clipping (International Leopold Stokowski Society Archives), Associated Press, 14 April 1945.

3. Goddard Lieberson, conversation, October 28, 1976.
4. Gloria Vanderbilt and Thelma Lady Furness, *Double Exposure*, pp. 346, 349.
5. *Time*, 23 April 1945.
6. Stokowski to William Grant Still, May 18, 1945.
7. *New York Herald Tribune*, 23 April 1945.
8. Philip Kahgan to the author, April 29, 1980.
9. *Philadelphia Evening Bulletin*, 24 April 1945.
10. Philip Kahgan to the author, April 29, 1980.
11. Richard Hammond, conversation, March 15, 1978.
12. George Antheil, *Bad Boy of Music*, pp. 363, 364.
13. Richard Hammond, conversation, March 15, 1978.
14. Unidentified clipping (Felton Collection) 1945.
15. Ibid.
16. Arnold Schoenberg to Stokowski, July 2, 1945.
17. Ibid.
18. Stokowski to Arnold Schoenberg, July 7, 1945.
19. Arnold Schoenberg to Stokowski, July 18, 1945.
20. Stokowski to Arnold Schoenberg, July 20, 1945.
21. Leonard Stein, reminiscences, January 20, 1977.
22. Stokowski to Arnold Schoenberg, September 1, 1945.
23. Leonard Stein, reminiscences, January 20, 1977.
24. Stokowski to Sylvan Levin, June 4, 1945.
25. Stokowski to Sylvan Levin, May 25, 1945.
26. Stokowski to Sylvan Levin, July 4, 1945.
27. Ibid.
28. Stokowski to Sylvan Levin, July 14, 1945.
29. Stokowski to Sylvan Levin, July 20, 1945.
30. Stokowski to Newbold Morris, August 14, 1945.
31. Stokowski to Sylvan Levin, August 29, 1945.
32. Stokowski to the Board of Directors, City Center, September 5, 1945.
33. *Los Angeles Times*, 11 July 1945.
34. *Musical America*, September 1945.
35. John Bird, *Percy Grainger*, pp. 195, 199.
36. Ella Grainger, conversation, April 26, 1977.
37. Stokowski to Sylvan Levin, September 20, 1945.
38. Halina Rodzinski, *Our Two Lives*, p. 281.
39. Walter Preston to Stokowski, December 1, 1945.
40. Stokowski to Victor Seroff, 1945.

Chapter 51

1. Stokowski and Gloria Vanderbilt Stokowski to Beatrice Brown, January 14, 1946.
2. *New York Times*, 8 February 1946.
3. Harold Schonberg, *The Great Conductors*, p. 320.
4. Beatrice Brown, conversation, October 1, 1979.
5. *Havana Bohemia*, 17 February 1946.
6. *New York Times*, 8 February 1946.
7. *Musical America*, February 1946.
8. Unidentified clipping (Philadelphia Public Library Collection), 14 March 1946.
9. Unidentified clipping (Philadelphia Public Library Collection), Associated Press, 13 March 1946.
10. Unidentified clipping (Philadelphia Public Library Collection), 14 March 1946.
11. Unidentified clipping (Philadelphia Public Library Collection), 2 April 1946.
12. Ibid.
13. *New York Journal-American*, 4 April 1946.
14. Unidentified clipping (Felton Collection), Chicago Tribune Press Service, 5 April 1946.
15. *New York Herald Tribune*, 4 April 1946.
16. *New York PM*, 4 April 1946.
17. Hall Clovis, conversation, November 8, 1976.
18. *New York Times*, 9 June 1946.
19. Schuyler Chapin, conversation, February 7, 1977.
20. Ruth Steinway, conversation, March 27, 1977.
21. John Steinway, conversation, March 27, 1977.
22. Schuyler Chapin, conversation, February 7, 1977.
23. Angeline Battista, conversation, December 6, 1977.
24. Schuyler Chapin, conversation, February 7, 1977.
25. *Musical America*, July 1946.
26. Stokowski to Sylvan Levin, July 23, 1946.
27. John Bird, jacket notes for Grainger's *In a Nutshell* Suite recording on HMV ASD 3651.
28. Ella Grainger, conversation, April 26, 1977.
29. Nan Merriman, conversation, October 19, 1978.
30. *New Records*, March 1947, p. 3.
31. David Hall, *The Record Book. International Edition*, p. 556.
32. Irving Kolodin, *The New Guide to Recorded Music. International Edition*, pp. 81, 82.

33. *New Records,* June 1946, p. 2.
34. David Ewen, ed., *The Year in American Music* (New York: Allen, Towne & Heath, 1948), pp. 174, 175.

Chapter 52

1. Richard Schickel, *The World of Carnegie Hall,* pp. 352, 353.
2. Halina Rodzinski, *Our Two Lives,* p. 276
3. Halina Rodzinski, conversation, November 22, 1976.
4. *New York PM,* 29 December 1946.
5. *New York World-Telegram,* 27 December 1946.
6. *New York Post,* 27 December 1946.
7. Stokowski to Dorle Jarmel, December 11, 1946.
8. Stokowski to Dorle Jarmel, December 18, 1946.
9. Carnegie Hall Program, 2 January 1947.
10. Virgil Thomson, *The Art of Judging Music,* p. 70.
11. Eugene List, conversation, September 10, 1976.
12. Halina Rodzinski, *Our Two Lives,* pp. 281, 286, 289.
13. *Philadelphia Inquirer,* 5 February 1947.
14. Unidentified clipping (Felton Collection), Associated Press, 7 February 1947.
15. Unidentified clipping (Felton Collection), February 1947.
16. *New York Herald Tribune,* 14 March 1947.
17. Stokowski to William Grant Still, April 11, 1947.
18. Martin Bookspan and Ross Yockey, *Zubin: The Zubin Mehta Story,* pp. 7, 8.
19. *Philadelphia Evening Bulletin,* 23 April 1947.
20. Howard Shanet, *Philharmonic: A History of New York's Orchestra,* p. 305.
21. Virgil Thomson, *Music Right and Left,* p. 178.
22. Elie Siegmeister, conversation, May 24, 1978.
23. Elie Siegmeister, *The New Music Lover's Handbook,* p. 564.
24. Otto Luening, conversation, September 20, 1976.
25. Gloria Vanderbilt, *Woman to Woman* (New York: Doubleday, 1979), pp. 123, 124.
26. *Birmingham News Age Herald,* 24 April 1949.
27. *New York Times,* 9 October 1949.
28. James Chambers, conversation, November 17, 1979.
29. Martha Lipton, conversation, October 20, 1977.
30. Virgil Thomson, *Music Right and Left,* p. 84.
31. Jacques Abram, conversation, January 14, 1978.
32. Unidentified clipping, 28 November 1949.

33. Unidentified clipping, 29 November 1949.
34. Unidentified clipping (Felton Collection), Associated Press, 30 December 1949.
35. Frances Yeend, conversation, January 15, 1978.
36. Camilla Williams, conversation, March 7, 1977.
37. Arthur Schuller, conversation, May 26, 1978.
38. *New York Herald Tribune*, 7 April 1950.

Chapter 53

1. Michael Kennedy, *Barbirolli: Conductor Laureate*, pp. 104, 106.
2. *Philadelphia Evening Bulletin*, 9 February 1963.
3. *San Francisco Chronicle*, 18 May 1948.
4. Claudette Sorel, conversation, April 5, 1978.
5. Ruth Steinway, conversation, March 27, 1977.
6. *St. Louis Post-Dispatch*, 19 May 1948.
7. Stokowski to author, January 30, 1950.
8. Stokowski to author, February 4, 1950.
9. *San Francisco Chronicle*, 9 August 1950.
10. Unidentified clipping (Felton Collection), 23 August 1950.
11. Schuyler Chapin, conversation, February 7, 1977.
12. *New Records*, April 1950, p. 2.
13. Stokowski, jacket notes for Vaughan Williams Symphony No. 6 recording on Columbia ML 4214.
14. *New Records*, August 1949, p. 1.
15. Irving Kolodin, *The New Guide to Recorded Music. International Edition*, p. 426.
16. Mitchell Miller, conversation, January 9, 1978.
17. Stokowski to author, September 6, 1949.
18. Eileen Farrell, conversation, October 1, 1977.
19. Irving Kolodin, *The New Guide to Recorded Music. International Edition*, p. 484.
20. *Gramophone Shop Record Supplement*, May 1950, p. 6.
21. Stokowski to Percy Grainger, January 17, 1949.
22. Percy Grainger to Stokowski, January 31, 1949.
23. Percy Grainger to Stokowski, August 29, 1949.
24. Stokowski to Percy Grainger, January 18, 1950.
25. *American Record Guide*, June 1952, p. 305.
26. Percy Grainger to Stokowski, May 16, 1952.
27. Irving Kolodin, *The Guide to Long-Playing Records: Orchestral Music*, p. 196.
28. Richard Mohr, conversation, November 23, 1976.

29. *American Record Guide,* February 1953, pp. 173, 174.
30. *American Record Guide,* January 1953, p. 137.
31. *American Record Guide,* February 1953, pp. 171, 172.

Chapter 54

1. *Le Grand Baton,* December 1975, pp. 3, 4.
2. Sir Thomas Beecham, *A Mingled Chime* (New York: G. P. Putnam's Sons, 1943), p. 64.
3. Stokowski, *Music for All of Us,* p. 219.
4. Harold Schonberg, *The Great Conductors,* p. 289.
5. *Le Grand Baton,* September 1978, p. 3.
6. *Le Grand Baton,* March/June 1979, p. 9.
7. Stokowski to Andrew Schulhof, May 12, 1950.
8. Hubert Roussel, *The Houston Symphony Orchestra,* p. 133.
9. *San Antonio Light,* 17 December 1950.
10. Stokowski to Andrew Schulhof, January 6, 1951.
11. Siegfried Hearst to Stokowski, December 20, 1950.
12. Licia Albanese, conversation, December 7, 1977.
13. James Chambers, conversation, November 17, 1979.
14. *American Record Guide,* May 1952, p. 270.
15. Stokowski to author, March 23, 1951.
16. Andrew Schulhof to author, April 17, 1951.
17. Author to Andrew Schulhof, April 25, 1951.
18. Stokowski to Lila Phillips, April 26, 1951.
19. Denis Vaughan, conversation, April 30, 1977.
20. Denis Vaughan, conversation, December 29, 1980.
21. Denis Vaughan, conversation, April 30, 1977.
22. Reuters dispatch, 17 May 1951.
23. *New York Times,* 29 May 1951.
24. Denis Vaughan, conversation, December 29, 1980.
25. *San Francisco Chronicle,* 3 May 1953.
26. *American Record Guide,* May 1953, p. 286.
27. *Gramophone,* March 1956, p. 383.
28. *Leopold Stokowski Society Bulletin,* May 1979, p. 5.
29. Stokowski to Lila Phillips, May 29, 1951.
30. Lila Phillips to Stokowski, June 1, 1951.
31. Stokowski to Lila Phillips, June 1951.
32. Gloria Vanderbilt Stokowski to Lila Phillips, July 1951.
33. Kenneth Leighton to Edward Johnson, October 24, 1971.
34. *Guardian* (London), 8 August 1951.
35. *San Francisco Chronicle,* 1 November 1951.

36. *San Francisco Chronicle,* 2 February 1952.
37. Stokowski to William Grant Still, February 7, 1952.
38. Julián Carrillo to Stokowski, February 26, 1951.
39. *Pittsburgh Post Gazette,* 1 December 1951.
40. Stokowski to Edward Specter, November 1, 1951.

Chapter 55

1. *New York Herald Tribune,* 28 April 1952.
2. *Washington Post,* 22 March 1953.
3. Roger Goeb, conversation, December 6, 1977.
4. CBS Radio interview with Stokowski by Bill Leonard, October 16, 1952.
5. *ACA Bulletin,* Winter 1952–53, pp. 3, 4.
6. Ibid.
7. *New York Herald Tribune,* 27 October 1952.
8. *ACA Bulletin,* Winter 1952–53, pp. 3, 4.
9. John Lessard, conversation, November 17, 1977.
10. Otto Luening, conversation, September 20, 1976.
11. Otto Luening, "The Beginning of Electronic Music in the United States," in Herbert Russcol, ed., *The Liberation of Sound,* p. 96.
12. *Time,* 10 November 1952.
13. *New Republic,* 10 November 1952.
14. Ben Weber, conversation, October 1, 1977.
15. *High Fidelity,* May 1958, p. 51.
16. William Miller, conversation, October 23, 1978.
17. *American Record Guide,* April 1954, p. 272.
18. Stokowski to George Marek, February 19, 1953.
19. George Marek to Stokowski, May 6, 1953.
20. Collegiate Orchestra of America, Inc., "General Aims of the Organization," 1953.
21. Andrew Schulhof to Paul Oberg, Earl Moore, George Howerton, Harrison Kerr, Wilfred Bain, and Duane Branigan, February 12, 1953.
22. Earl Moore to Andrew Schulhof, February 24, 1953.
23. Jacob Avshalomov, reminiscences, July 28, 1976.
24. *Detroit Free Press,* 21 November 1952.
25. *San Francisco Chronicle,* 6 December 1952.
26. *American Record Guide,* December 1953, pp. 116, 117.
27. Gabriel Pascal to Stokowski, March 2, 1953.

Chapter 56

1. William Schuman, conversation, September 22, 1976.
2. Stokowski to Carl Haverlin, April 21, 1953.
3. *Parnassus,* Summer 1975, p. 1.
4. *Musical America,* 10 February 1939.
5. Elliott Carter, conversation, December 8, 1977.
6. *ACA Bulletin,* Spring 1953, p. 6.
7. *New York Herald Tribune,* 23 February 1953.
8. *ACA Bulletin,* Spring, 1953, p. 6.
9. William Hess, conversation, July 15, 1978.
10. *ACA Bulletin,* Spring 1953, pp. 6. 7.
11. Stokowski to author, September 19, 1953.
12. John Turner to Stokowski, May 9, 1952.
13. Ford Foundation TV Film Project Memorandum, May 1952.
14. Stokowski to Robert Saudek, November 26, 1952.
15. *New York Times,* 12 April 1953.
16. Gian Carlo Menotti, conversation, September 10, 1976.
17. *Time,* 25 May 1953.
18. Harald Saeverud to author, July 19, 1978.
19. Jon Embretsen, conversation, April 22, 1978.
20. NRK (Norwegian Broadcasting Corporation) Radio interview with Stokowski by Torstein Gunnarson, August 15, 1967.
21. NRK Radio interview with Stokowski by Kristian Lange, June 9, 1953.
22. Jussi Jalas, conversation, November 16, 1977.
23. Jussi Jalas to author, August 2, 1977.
24. Stokowski to Jean Sibelius, June 1953.
25. Stokowski to Jean Sibelius, August 7, 1953.
26. Carl Haverlin to Stokowski, July 6, 1953.
27. BMI (Broadcast Music, Inc.) Special Projects Department Press Release, July 1, 1953.
28. Stokowski to Colin McPhee, September 30, 1953.
29. *Time,* 26 October 1953.
30. *New York Herald Tribune,* 17 October 1953.
31. *Newsweek,* 26 October 1953.

Chapter 57

1. Adrian Murphy to Henry Cowell (Letter-Agreement to American Composers Alliance), September 11, 1953.
2. Author to Stokowski, March 11, 1953.

3. CBS Radio interview with Stokowski by Dwight Cooke, September 14, 1953.
4. Ibid.
5. *New York World-Telegram and Sun,* 28 September 1953.
6. *Time,* 5 October 1953.
7. Ulysses Kay, conversation, November 29, 1976.
8. *New York World-Telegram and Sun,* 24 October 1953.
9. John Kirkpatrick, ed., *Charles E. Ives—Memos* (New York: W. W. Norton & Company, 1972), p. 96.
10. *New York Times,* 17 February 1954.
11. Harold Coletta, conversation, October 13, 1977.
12. John Kirkpatrick, ed., *Charles E. Ives—Memos,* pp. 96, 97.
13. *New York Times,* 15 March 1954.
14. Jon Embretsen, conversation, April 22, 1978.
15. Stokowski to author, April 6, 1954.
16. Malcolm Arnold to Stokowski, May 4, 1954.
17. *San Francisco Chronicle,* 22 May 1954.
18. Author to Stokowski, June 1, 1954.
19. Unidentified clipping (Philadelphia Public Library Collection), International News Service, 17 August 1954.
20. *Musical Courier,* October 1954.
21. *New York Herald Tribune,* 12 September 1954.

Chapter 58

1. George Marek, *Toscanini,* p. 281.
2. *New Records,* January 1955, p. 3.
3. Steve Cohen, "The Stokowski Story," WUHY-FM Radio (Philadelphia) Series, c. 1967.
4. Risë Stevens, conversation, July 12, 1978.
5. *American Record Guide,* February 1955, p. 183.
6. Stokowski to Jean Sibelius, August 30, 1954.
7. Stokowski to Jean Sibelius, September 21, 1954.
8. *New Records,* April 1955, p. 3.
9. Gian Carlo Menotti, conversation, September 10, 1976.
10. *American Record Guide,* May 1955, p. 298.
11. *High Fidelity,* November 1957, p. 74.
12. Carnegie Hall Program (Columbia University Bicentennial Concert), 26 October 1954.
13. Malloy Miller, conversation, April 6, 1976.
14. Paul Preus to Andrew Schulhof, December 29, 1954.
15. *Time,* 6 December 1954.

16. Stokowski to Willy Strecker (B. Schott's Söhne), December 23, 1954.
17. Stokowski to author, November 9, 1954.

Chapter 59

1. *New York Daily Mirror*, 31 December 1954.
2. *Time*, 10 January 1955.
3. *New York Daily Mirror*, 31 December 1954.
4. Jean Dalrymple, conversation, July 27, 1978.
5. Andrew Schulhof to orchestra managers (form letter), February 7, 1954.
6. "Leopold Stokowski" brochure (authorized biographical material), c. 1951.
7. *New York Daily News*, January 1955.
8. Lou Harrison, reminiscences, July 1976.
9. Author to Stokowski, January 21, 1955.
10. William Saroyan, "The Time of Your Life," in John Gassner, ed., *Best Plays of the Modern American Theater* (New York: Crown, 1947), p. 69.
11. Wendy Hanson, conversation, January 16, 1979.
12. Author to Edith Lang, February 2, 1955.
13. John Bitter, conversation, August 4, 1976.
14. *Time*, 28 March 1955.
15. *San Francisco Chronicle* (AP), 15 March 1955.
16. John Bitter, conversation, August 4, 1976.
17. Andrew Schulhof, memorandum for Schulhof file, May 27, 1955.
18. Stokowski to Fabien Sevitzky and Howard Mitchell, April 12, 1955.
19. Wendy Hanson, conversation, January 16, 1979.
20. Stokowski to Frank M. Folsom, April 28, 1955.
21. Stokowski to Emmanuel Sacks, May 23, 1955.

Chapter 60

1. Andrew Schulhof, memorandum of European trip with Stokowski, 1955.
2. Süddeutscher Rundfunk (Neufischer) to Stokowski, May 20, 1955.
3. *Abendpost* (Frankfurt), 1 June 1955.
4. Andrew Schulhof, memorandum of European trip with Stokowski, 1955.
5. *Weltpresse* (Vienna), 6 June 1955.
6. *Bild-Telegraf* (Vienna), 6 June 1955.
7. *Weltpresse*, (Vienna), 13 June 1955.
8. Stokowski to Anne Wailes, July 16, 1955.

9. Andrew Schulhof, memorandum of European trip with Stokowski, 1955.
10. Stokowski to R. J. F. Howgill, June 22, 1955.
11. Andrew Schulhof to Stokowski, June 29, 1955.

Chapter 61

1. Leighton Rollins to Stokowski, July 29, 1954.
2. Stokowski to Leighton Rollins, July 31, 1954.
3. Stokowski to Leighton Rollins, August 12, 1954.
4. Stokowski to Leighton Rollins, January 14, 1955.
5. *Houston Press,* 17 August 1955.
6. *Houston Chronicle,* 18 August 1955.
7. Tom Johnson, reminiscences, January 1977.
8. *Houston Post,* 20 August 1955.
9. Stokowski to Bernard Herrmann, April 2, 1955.
10. *Los Angeles Mirror-News,* 31 August 1955.
11. Wendy Hanson, conversation, January 16, 1979.
12. *Santa Barbara News-Press,* 11 September 1955.
13. *Los Angeles Examiner,* 12 September 1955.
14. *Los Angeles Examiner,* 16 September 1955.
15. *Los Angeles Examiner,* September 1955.
16. Ibid.
17. Leighton Rollins, conversation, December 14, 1976.

Chapter 62

1. Hubert Roussel, *The Houston Symphony Orchestra,* pp. 17, 26, 39.
2. Ibid., pp. 30–32.
3. Ibid., p. 40
4. Ibid., p. 121.
5. Ibid., p. 123.
6. Ibid., pp. 146, 149, 150.
7. Ibid., p. 153.
8. Ibid., p. 151
9. Tom Johnson, reminiscences, January 1977.
10. Hubert Roussel, *The Houston Symphony Orchestra,* pp. 155, 157.
11. *Milwaukee Journal,* 30 October 1955.
12. *Houston Chronicle,* 1 November 1955.
13. *Houston Post,* 1 November 1955.

14. Ibid.
15. Rudolf Firkušný, conversation, November 15, 1977.
16. Stokowski to Jean Sibelius, November 30, 1955.
17. Tatu Tuohikorpi to author, December 16, 1977.
18. Hubert Roussel, *The Houston Symphony Orchestra*, p. 162.
19. Author to Stokowski, January 17, 1956.
20. Stokowski to author, February 9, 1956.
21. Hubert Roussel, *The Houston Symphony Orchestra*, pp. 162, 163.
22. Stokowski to author, April 19, 1956.

Chapter 63

1. Stokowski to J. Beek, February 16, 1956.
2. *Belgrade Borba*, 21 May 1956.
3. *Belgrade Politika*, 30 May 1956.
4. *Belgrade Vecernje Novosti*, 2 June 1956.
5. Veljko Bijedić to Stokowski, March 29, 1956.
6. Stokowski to Veljko Bijedić, February 22, 1956.
7. Stokowski to author, June 14, 1956.
8. Mira Borić to Stokowski, October 3, 1956.
9. Stokowski to Mira Borić, October 23, 1956.
10. J. Beek to Stokowski, March 23, 1956.
11. Stokowski to J. Beek, February 1956.
12. Stokowski to J. Beek, March 3, 1956.
13. J. Beek to Stokowski, March 9, 1956.
14. Stokowski to J. Beek, March 13, 1956.
15. Stokowski to J. Beek, February 25, 1956.
16. Basil Langton, conversation, October 24, 1978.
17. Jerome Toobin, *Agitato*, p. 59.
18. Basil Langton, conversation, October 24, 1978.
19. *New York Herald Tribune*, 20 July 1956.
20. *New York Journal-American*, 20 July 1956.
21. *High Fidelity*, November 1957, p. 68.
22. Stokowski to F. M. Scott III, October 19, 1956.
23. Stokowski to F. M. Scott III, September 21, 1957.
24. *Gramophone*, December 1957.
25. Ibid.; *Gramophone Record Review*, January 1958, p. 243; *Gramophone Record Review*, October 1958, p. 969.
26. Sir Adrian Boult to author, July 18, 1978.
27. Stokowski to Glenn E. Wallichs, September 12, 1956.
28. Stokowski to F. M. Scott III, September 15, 1956.

Chapter 64

1. *Saturday Review,* 20 October 1956.
2. *New York Times,* 5 October 1956.
3. Rudolf Firkušný, conversation, November 15, 1977.
4. *New York Journal-American,* 5 October 1956.
5. *New York Post,* 5 October 1956.
6. *New York Herald Tribune,* 14 October 1956.
7. *Stereo Review,* December 1974, p. 81.
8. Henry Cowell to author, November 28, 1956.
9. David Cooper to author, February 20, 1957.
10. Stokowski to author, March 15, 1957.
11. William Bergsma, conversation, October 18, 1978.
12. Wendy Hanson, conversation, October 19, 1978.
13. Stokowski to J. Beek, August 18, 1956.
14. Stokowski to J. Beek, November 9, 1956.
15. Stokowski to author, May 24, 1957.
16. Stokowski to J. Beek, October 13, 1956.
17. H. H. Stuckenschmidt to author, April 29, 1978.
18. *Welt* (Berlin), 16 May 1957.
19. *Saturday Review,* 22 February 1958, p. 50.
20. Barry Tuckwell, conversation, November 4, 1978.
21. *Times* (London), 27 June 1957.
22. *Times* (London) 1 July 1957.
23. Hubert Roussel, *The Houston Symphony Orchestra,* p. 164.
24. Jerome Toobin, *Agitato,* p. 40.
25. Alan Hovhaness, conversation, September 28, 1977.
26. *Houston Press,* 13 March 1957.
27. Stokowski to author, March 15, 1957.
28. Author to Stokowski, March 18, 1957.
29. *Newsweek,* 29 July 1957, p. 77.
30. Ibid.

Chapter 65

1. *Time,* 20 January 1958.
2. *San Francisco Chronicle* (UP), 30 January 1958.
3. Stokowski to Richard Jones, September 16, 1957.
4. Stokowski to F. M. Scott III, April 8, 1957
5. *High Fidelity,* September 1957, p. 86.
6. Harold Farberman, conversation, November 5, 1977.
7. José Serebrier, conversation, October 18, 1976.

8. Hubert Roussel, *The Houston Symphony Orchestra*, p. 166.
9. Stokowski to Andrzej Panufnik, November 11, 1957.
10. Rodion Shchedrin, conversation, September 19, 1978.
11. *High Fidelity*, August 1958, p. 74.
12. Stokowski to F. M. Scott III, April 12, 1958.
13. Stokowski to Ralph O'Connor, April 24, 1958.
14. *American Record Guide*, July 1959, p. 787.
15. *Gramophone Record Review*, January 1960, p. 165.
16. *Gramophone*, October 1978, p. 682.
17. *New York Times* (UP), 27 May 1958.
18. Stokowski to author, 26 May 1958.
19. Author to Stokowski, 29 May 1958.
20. Stokowski to author, June 1958.
21. Stokowski, recollections of the tour in the Soviet Union, July 1958.
22. *San Francisco Chronicle* (AP), June 8, 1958.
23. Stokowski, recollections of the tour in the Soviet Union, July 1958.
24. *New York Journal-American*, 22 July 1958.
25. Moscow students to Stokowski, June 1958.
26. Stokowski, recollections of the tour in the Soviet Union, July 1958.
27. Unidentified clipping (Felton Collection), Associated Press, 24 June 1958.
28. Unidentified clipping (Felton Collection), Associated Press, 1 July 1958.
29. Stokowski to author, July 1958.
30. Stokowski to author, July 7, 1958.
31. *New York Daily News*, 15 August 1958; Zaostrovtsev to author, September 25, 1958.
32. WNYC Radio, interview with Stokowski by the author, September 23, 1958.
33. Ibid.
34. *New York Times*, 22 September 1958.
35. *New York Times*, 23 September 1958.
36. Dwight D. Eisenhower to Sponsor's Committee, Contemporary Music Society, September 25, 1958.
37. *New York Times*, 26 September 1958.
38. Scott Beach, conversation, November 4, 1976.
39. *New York Journal-American*, 26 September 1958.
40. Percy Grainger to Mrs. Ralph Vaughan Williams, September 26, 1958.
41. Stokowski to Mrs. Ralph Vaughan Williams, September 26, 1958.
42. Stokowski to Mrs. Ralph Vaughan Williams, September 29, 1958.
43. Philadelphia Orchestra Press Release, 10 December 1958.
44. Richard Yardumian, conversation, December 31, 1977.

Chapter 66

1. *Houston Press*, 21 October 1958.
2. Tom Johnson, reminiscences, January 1977.
3. *New York Times*, 26 November 1958.
4. *New York Times*, 4 December 1958.
5. *New York Times*, 26 April 1959.
6. *New York Post*, 4 August 1959.
7. *New York Daily News*, 31 December 1954.
8. *New York Mirror*, 12 May 1959.
9. *New York Mirror*, 16 May 1959.
10. *New York Daily News*, 15 May 1959.
11. *New York World-Telegram and Sun*, 13 May 1959.
12. *New York Daily News*, 15 May 1959.
13. Stokowski to city editor, *New York Daily News*, May 1959.
14. *New York Mirror*, 15 May 1959.
15. *New York Mirror*, 16 May 1959.
16. *New York Journal-American*, 17 May 1959.
17. *New York Post*, 20 May 1959.
18. Tom Johnson, reminiscences, January 1977.
19. *New York Post* (Reuters), 2 June 1959.
20. *San Francisco Chronicle* (UPI), 12 June 1959.
21. *New York Daily News*, 11 June 1959.
22. *New York Journal-American*, 11 June 1959.
23. *New York Daily News*, 25 June 1959.

Chapter 67

1. Julius Rudel, conversation, July 10, 1978.
2. Unidentified clipping (Felton Collection), 19 March 1959.
3. *Philadelphia Inquirer*, 3 April 1959.
4. *New York Herald Tribune*, 20 September 1959.
5. Julius Rudel, conversation, July 10, 1978.
6. *Saturday Review*, 10 October 1959, pp. 34, 35.
7. Julius Rudel, conversation, July 10, 1978.
8. *New York Post*, 30 September 1960.
9. *New York Herald Tribune*, 30 September 1960.
10. Judith Raskin, conversation, October 4, 1978.
11. Julius Rudel, conversation, July 10, 1978.

Chapter 68

1. Stokowski to F. M. Scott III, September 3, 1957.
2. Stokowski to Glenn Wallichs, October 11, 1958.
3. Bert Whyte, conversation, November 9, 1979.
4. Bert Whyte to Stokowski, September 22, 1958.
5. Bert Whyte, conversation, November 9, 1979.
6. Stokowski to Harry Belock, January 6, 1959.
7. Stokowski to Harry Belock, January 9, 1959.
8. Stokowski to Harry Belock, January 20, 1959.
9. *High Fidelity*, April 1959, p. 72.
10. *Gramophone*, February 1960.
11. *American Record Guide*, July 1960, p. 920.
12. Stokowski to Bernard Solomon, April 15, 1963.
13. Bernard Solomon to Stokowski, April 22, 1963.
14. Stokowski to Bernard Solomon, June 12, 1963.
15. Stokowski to Kay Norton, February 4, 1959.
16. Gunther Schuller, conversation, April 6, 1976.
17. Paul Ben-Haim to author, July 5, 1978.
18. *High Fidelity*, July 1959, p. 58.
19. Stokowski to F. M. Scott III, 28 November 1958.
20. Bert Whyte, conversation, November 9, 1979.

Chapter 69

1. Harold Farberman, conversation, November 5, 1977.
2. *Houston Chronicle*, 3 November 1959.
3. Harold Farberman, conversation, November 5, 1977.
4. Hubert Roussel, *The Houston Symphony Orchestra*, pp. 171, 172.
5. *Houston Post*, 29 March 1960.
6. *Hi Fi/Stereo Review*, March 1963, p. 100.
7. Stokowski to Mr. Polyakin, September 17, 1960.
8. Stokowski to Mary Howe, November 27, 1934.
9. Tom Johnson to author, November 15, 1977.
10. David Colvig, conversation, November 12, 1977.
11. Shirley Verrett, conversation, March 1, 1977.
12. Wayne Crouse, conversation, December 7, 1977.
13. William Lee Pryor, conversation, February 3, 1980.
14. Isaac Stern, conversation, July 2, 1978.
15. Hubert Roussel, *The Houston Symphony Orchestra*, p. 175.
16. Minutes of Executive Committee Meeting, Board of Directors, Houston Symphony Society, November 21, 1960.

17. Stokowski to Sir John Barbirolli, December 21, 1960.
18. Minutes of the Executive Committee Meeting, Board of Directors, Houston Symphony Society, January 11, 1961.
19. Stokowski to William Lee Pryor, February 4, 1961.
20. Stokowski to *Houston Press, Houston Post,* and *Houston Chronicle,* February 4, 1961.
21. Stokowski to William Lee Pryor, April 20, 1961.
22. William Lee Pryor, conversation, January 15, 1978.

Chapter 70

1. *Philadelphia Inquirer,* 4 January 1959.
2. Herbert Kupferberg, *Those Fabulous Philadelphians,* p. 166.
3. Stokowski, Metropolitan Opera Quiz Interview, February 6, 1960.
4. William Smith, conversation, November 9, 1978.
5. Unidentified clipping (Felton Collection), 14 February 1960.
6. *Philadelphia Evening Bulletin,* 13 February 1960.
7. *New York Journal-American,* 17 February 1960.
8. *New York World Telegram and Sun,* 17 February 1960.
9. *Saturday Review,* 5 March 1960.
10. Roger Hall, conversation, August 26, 1976.
11. *Philadelphia Evening Bulletin,* 24 February 1960.
12. Unidentified clipping (Felton Collection), 15 April 1960.
13. Unidentified clipping (Felton Collection), 20 July 1960.
14. Unidentified clipping (Felton Collection), 23 July 1960.
15. Unidentified clipping (Felton Collection), 20 July 1960.
16. Schuyler Chapin, conversation, February 7, 1977.
17. *Saturday Review,* 29 October 1960, p. 38.
18. *Philadelphia Evening Bulletin,* 29 November 1960.
19. Herbert Kupferberg, *Those Fabulous Philadelphians,* p. 88.
20. Roger Hall, conversation, August 26, 1976.
21. *New York World Telegram and Sun,* 8 March 1961.
22. *New York Post,* 8 March 1961.
23. Roger Hall, conversation, August 26, 1976.
24. Herbert Kupferberg, *Those Fabulous Philadelphians,* p. 87.
25. Eugene Ormandy to Stokowski, March 12, 1962.
26. Stokowski to Eugene Ormandy, March 27, 1962.
27. *Philadelphia Inquirer,* 26 January 1963.
28. *Philadelphia Inquirer,* 9 February 1963.
29. Ibid.
30. *Philadelphia Evening Bulletin,* 9 February 1963.
31. *Philadelphia Evening Bulletin,* 10 February 1963.

32. *Windsor Star,* 9 May 1963.
33. Eugene Ormandy to Stokowski, January 15, 1964.
34. Stokowski to Mary Krouse, January 15, 1964; Stokowski to Eugene Ormandy, January 17, 1964.
35. Eugene Ormandy to Stokowski, June 23, 1964.
36. *Washington Star,* 29 December 1964.
37. *Philadelphia Evening Bulletin,* 29 June 1964.
38. Rose Kennedy to Stokowski, July 6, 1964.
39. Eugene Ormandy to Stokowski, October 27, 1964.
40. Stokowski to Eugene Ormandy, October 29, 1964.
41. *New York Herald Tribune,* 24 November 1965.
42. Herbert Kupferberg, *Those Fabulous Philadelphians,* p. 175.
43. *Philadelphia Evening Bulletin,* 12 October 1966.
44. Orville Bullitt, conversation, November 9, 1978.
45. *Philadelphia Evening Bulletin,* 15 October 1966.

Chapter 71

1. Rudolf Bing, *5,000 Nights at the Opera,* p. 177.
2. *New York Herald Tribune,* 29 November 1960.
3. Stokowski to Rudolf Bing, February 1, 1960.
4. Stokowski to Rudolf Bing, February 4, 1960.
5. Stokowski to Rudolf Bing, December 8, 1960.
6. Rudolf Bing to Stokowski, December 12, 1960.
7. Stokowski to Cecil Beaton, December 20, 1960.
8. Cecil Beaton to Stokowski, December 28, 1960.
9. Stokowski to Yoshio Aoyama, December 20, 1960.
10. Rudolf Bing to Stokowski, January 25, 1961.
11. *Chicago Tribune,* 11 December 1960.
12. Malcolm Frager, conversation, May 5, 1978.
13. Stewart Warkow, conversation, March 2, 1976.
14. Stokowski to author, January 28, 1961.
15. Anna Moffo, conversation, February 24, 1978.
16. Licia Albanese, conversation, December 7, 1977.
17. George Cehanovsky, conversation, November 22, 1977.
18. *New York Times,* 25 February 1961.
19. *Time,* 3 March 1961. p. 54.
20. Robert Herman, conversation, May 19, 1978.
21. Stokowski to Rudolf Bing, April 1, 1961.
22. Paul Hume, conversation, October 17, 1978.
23. Nathaniel Merrill to Stokowski, May 12, 1961.
24. Stokowski to Nathaniel Merrill, July 1, 1961.

Chapter 72

1. *New York Herald Tribune,* 5 March 1960.
2. *New York Times,* 5 March 1960.
3. BBC Radio interview with Neville Marriner by John Amis, July 1, 1978.
4. *Times* (London), 29 June 1960.
5. *Der Tag* (Berlin), 12 June 1961.
6. Unidentified clipping (Berlin), 12 June 1961.
7. *London Daily Express,* 19 June 1961.
8. Sir Adrian Boult to author, July 18, 1978.
9. Unidentified clipping (Fischer Collection), 22 June 1961.
10. Stokowski to William Lee Pryor, September 8, 1961.
11. Lyuba Rhodes to author, July 1, 1978.
12. Stokowski to Earl of Harewood, October 7, 1960.
13. Stan Stokowski, conversation, October 19, 1980.
14. Stokowski to Earl of Harewood, February 15, 1960.
15. Earl of Harewood to Stokowski, February 27, 1960.
16. Stokowski to Earl of Harewood, September 2, 1960.
17. Nell Rankin, conversation, November 18, 1980.
18. Stokowski to William Lee Pryor, September 8, 1961.
19. *Chicago Daily Tribune,* 5 January 1962.
20. *New York World Telegram and Sun,* 3 March 1962.
21. *New York Journal-American,* 3 March 1962.
22. *New York Herald Tribune,* 3 March 1962.
23. *Cleveland Plain Dealer,* 9 March 1962.
24. *New York Journal-American,* 21 March 1962.

Chapter 73

1. Rudolf Bing to Stokowski, August 8, 1961.
2. Rudolf Bing, *5,000 Nights at the Opera,* p. 268.
3. *L'Espresso* (Rome), 4 March 1962.
4. Ibid.
5. Ibid.
6. Rudolf Bing to Stokowski, August 28, 1961.
7. Stokowski to Rudolf Bing, August 30, 1961.
8. Rudolf Bing to Stokowski, September 1, 1961.
9. Stokowski to Rudolf Bing, September 4, 1961.
10. Rudolf Bing to Stokowski, September 7, 1961.
11. Stokowski to Nathaniel Merrill, September 9, 1961.
12. Nathaniel Merrill to Stokowski, September 19, 1961.

13. Stokowski to Nathaniel Merrill, September 28, 1961.
14. Stokowski to Robert Herman, October 3, 1961.
15. Rudolf Bing to Stokowski, October 4, 1961.
16. Stokowski to Rudolf Bing, October 7, 1961.
17. Stokowski to Rudolf Bing, November 6, 1961.
18. *New York Times*, 17 December 1961.
19. *New York Times*, 31 December 1961.
20. Irving Kolodin, conversation, March 4, 1977.
21. *Opera News*, 24 February 1962, pp. 46, 47.

Chapter 74

1. *New York Herald Tribune*, 26 April 1962.
2. *New York Times*, 3 June 1962.
3. *Coatesville Record* (Pennsylvania), 28 June 1962.
4. Stewart Warkow, conversation, March 2, 1976.
5. Jean Leslie, conversation, June 17, 1978.
6. Stokowski to Gregory Roberts, June 13, 1962.
7. Lyuba Rhodes to author, July 1, 1978.
8. Leonard Carson to Frank S. Hogan (copy to Stokowski), September 25, 1962.
9. Richard L. Berman to Stokowski, November 5, 1962.
10. Leonard Carson to Frank S. Hogan (copy to Stokowski), September 25, 1962.
11. Stewart Warkow, conversation, March 2, 1976.
12. David Brockman, conversation, October 21, 1976.
13. *Philadelphia Evening Bulletin*, 16 October 1962.
14. *New York World Telegram and Sun*, 6 November 1962.
15. *New York Journal-American*, 6 November 1962.
16. *New Yorker*, 17 November 1962.
17. *New York Times*, 4 December 1962.
18. *Time*, 14 December 1962.
19. Beverly Sills, conversation, September 9, 1978.
20. Beverly Sills, *Bubbles*, p. 95.
21. Ruth Laredo, conversation, November 26, 1980.
22. *New York Times*, 16 April 1963.
23. Samuel Rubin, conversation, April 7, 1977.
24. Cyma Rubin, conversation, March 10, 1976.
25. David Katz, conversation, October 4, 1978.
26. José Serebrier, conversation, October 18, 1976.
27. Joseph Eger, conversation, July 28, 1978.
28. Ainslee Cox, conversation, August 27, 1976.

29. Matthias Bamert, conversation, November 18, 1977.
30. Sophia Yarnall Jacobs, introduction to Stokowski's Bryn Mawr lecture on "The Making of an Orchestra," February 4, 1963.
31. Stokowski, lecture at Bryn Mawr College on "The Making of an Orchestra," February 4, 1963.
32. Ibid.
33. Ibid.
34. Ibid.

Chapter 75

1. John Kirkpatrick, Preface to the score of the Ives Fourth Symphony (New York: Associated Music Publishers, 1965), p. x.
2. Author to Stokowski, February 23, 1965.
3. Stokowski to author, June 11, 1963.
4. Author to Leonard Feist, June 13, 1963.
5. Kurt Stone to author, June 24, 1963.
6. John Kirkpatrick, Preface to the score of the Ives Fourth Symphony, p. x.
7. *New York Times,* 20 February 1965.
8. Carnegie Hall Program, 5 April 1965.
9. Stokowski to author, April 7, 1965.
10. John Kirkpatrick, Preface to the score of the Ives Fourth Symphony, p. viii.
11. *New York Post,* 27 April 1965.
12. John Kirkpatrick, Preface to the score of the Ives Fourth Symphony, p. viii.
13. *New York Times,* 27 April 1965.
14. Julian Myrick to Stokowski, April 27, 1965.
15. *New York Journal-American,* 27 April 1965.
16. *High Fidelity/Musical America,* July 1965, pp. 96, 97.
17. Stokowski to Glenn Gould, June 22, 1965.
18. *New York Herald Tribune,* 27 April 1965.
19. Igor Stravinsky and Robert Craft, *Themes and Episodes,* pp. 154, 155.
20. John Kirkpatrick to Stokowski, April 27, 1965.
21. Author to Goddard Lieberson, February 17, 1965.
22. Goddard Lieberson to author, March 1, 1965.
23. Samuel Rubin, conversation, April 7, 1977.
24. *Audio Record Review,* June 1966, p. 32.
25. *Gramophone,* July 1966, pp. 58, 59.
26. *The Many Worlds of Music* (BMI), December 1974.

Chapter 76

1. Stokowski, conversation, 1955.
2. Stokowski to Serge Koussevitzky, April 21, 1925.
3. Stokowski to Serge Koussevitzky, September 26, 1925.
4. Stokowski to Serge Koussevitzky, October 5, 1925.
5. *New York Times*, 28 November 1924.
6. Stokowski to Serge Koussevitzky, November 11, 1928.
7. *New York Times*, 13 November 1932.
8. Serge Koussevitzky to Stokowski, November 20, 1928.
9. Stokowski to Serge Koussevitzky, November 24, 1928.
10. Serge Koussevitzky to Stokowski, June 2, 1928.
11. Serge Koussevitzky to Stokowski, November 20, 1928.
12. Stokowski to Serge Koussevitzky, November 24, 1928.
13. Serge Koussevitzky to Stokowski, December 1, 1928.
14. Stokowski to Serge Koussevitzky, August 31, 1929.
15. Serge Koussevitzky to Stokowski, September 12, 1929.
16. Stokowski to Serge Koussevitzky, September 28, 1929.
17. Harold Schonberg, *The Great Conductors*, p. 302.
18. Olga Koussevitzky, conversation, October 21, 1976.
19. *Time*, 27 April 1936.
20. Olga Koussevitzky, conversation, October 21, 1976.
21. Thomas Perry, conversation, August 14, 1976.
22. *Christian Science Monitor*, 7 March 1964.
23. *Boston Globe*, 7 March 1964.
24. *Christian Science Monitor*, 7 March 1964.
25. Ned Rorem, conversation, May 14, 1979.
26. George Zazofsky, conversation, August 14, 1976.
27. Ralph Gomberg, conversation, August 14, 1976.
28. M. H. de Montel to author, September 19, 1978.
29. Samuel Barber, conversation, March 20, 1979.
30. *Times* (London), 16 September 1964.
31. *London Financial Times*, 18 September 1964.
32. *Times* (London), 18 September 1964.
33. *London Daily Telegraph*, 18 September 1964.
34. *Christian Science Monitor*, 16 August 1965.
35. *Boston Herald*, 16 August 1965.
36. *Christian Science Monitor*, 16 August 1965.
37. *Philadelphia Evening Bulletin*, 31 January 1968.

Chapter 77

1. Stan Stokowski, conversation, October 19, 1980.
2. *New York Times*, 10 July 1965.
3. New York University interview with Stokowski by Robert Sherman, April 7, 1972.
4. Marshall Turkin, conversation, February 6, 1980.
5. Stan Stokowski, conversation, October 19, 1980.
6. *Honolulu Advertiser*, 2 August 1965.
7. Ibid.
8. Cyma Rubin, conversation, March 10, 1976.
9. *Jersey Journal* (Jersey City, N. J.), 5 October 1965.
10. *New York Herald Tribune*, 5 October 1965.
11. BBC Radio interview with Stokowski by Reginald Jacques, 1959.
12. *New York World Telegram and Sun*, 26 October 1965.
13. New York Herald Tribune, 26 October 1965.
14. *New York World Telegram and Sun*, 25 January 1966.
15. Stokowski to Louis Biancolli, January 31, 1966.
16. *Chicago Sun-Times*, 20 January 1966.
17. *Le Figaro* (Paris), 5 June 1967.
18. *Guardian* (London), 16 June 1967.
19. *Guardian* (London), 20 September 1967.
20. *Guardian* (London), 19 June 1968.
21. *Times* (London), 23 June 1968.
22. *Listener* (BBC-London), 26 June 1969.

Chapter 78

1. *New York Times*, 22 October 1965.
2. *New York Times*, 16 April 1970.
3. Arthur Aaron, conversation, February 17, 1977.
4. *New York Times*, 16 April 1970.
5. Samuel Rubin, conversation, April 7, 1977.
6. *San Francisco Chronicle* (AP), 4 February 1967.
7. Hungarian Radio and television interview with Stokowski, 1967 (included on the Kodály *Hary Janos Suite* recording on Leopold Stokowski Society LS 2).
8. Stokowski to author, January 1967.
9. Leonard Bernstein to Stokowski, January 11, 1966.
10. *New York Times*, 4 April 1967.
11. Stokowski to Stewart Warkow, October 24, 1967.
12. Roger Hall, conversation, August 26, 1976.

13. *Stereo Review,* August 1969, p. 84.
14. *High Fidelity,* July 1969, p. 75.

Chapter 79

1. John Briggs, *Requiem for a Yellow Brick Brewery,* pp. 328, 331, 332.
2. *New York World Telegram and Sun,* 18 April 1966.
3. John Briggs, *Requiem for a Yellow Brick Brewery,* pp. 335, 336.
4. Francis Robinson, conversation, September 7, 1978.
5. Reginald Allen, conversation, August 17, 1976.
6. John Briggs, *Requiem for a Yellow Brick Brewery,* pp. 336, 339, 340.
7. *New York World Telegram and Sun,* 19 April 1966.
8. Bill Zakariasen to author, November 5, 1979.

Chapter 80

1. *New York Times,* 11 May 1968.
2. Stokowski, speech at Senior Musician's Award banquet, May 10, 1968.
3. *New York World Journal Tribune,* 6 April 1967.
4. Arthur Aaron, conversation, June 6, 1979.
5. John Grady, conversation, June 7, 1979.
6. Arthur Aaron, conversation, June 6, 1979.
7. Alec Wyton, conversation, June 3, 1978.
8. John Grady, conversation, June 7, 1979.
9. *New York Times,* 30 November 1970.
10. Larry King, conversation, June 8, 1978.
11. Benjamin de Loache, conversation, September 14, 1977.
12. Jerry Pav, conversation, September 5, 1976.
13. *San Francisco Chronicle* (AP), 24 November 1971.
14. Ibid.
15. Natasha Bender, conversation, June 5, 1979.
16. Don Dunn, *The Making of No, No, Nanette* (New York: Citadel Press, 1972), pp. 313, 319.
17. Samuel Rubin, conversation, April 7, 1977.
18. Cyma Rubin, conversation, March 10, 1976.
19. Charles (Jack) Baumgarten, conversation, January 2, 1981.
20. *New York Times,* 5 March 1970.

Chapter 81

1. *London Daily Telegram,* 19 June 1970.
2. Stokowski to author, June 15, 1970.

3. Author to Stokowski, June 22, 1970.
4. Tony D'Amato, conversation, May 2, 1977.
5. Frans Van Rossum, conversation, May 25, 1977.
6. Stokowski to Hilversum Radio Philharmonic Orchestra, August 23, 1970.
7. Tony D'Amato, conversation, May 2, 1977.
8. Gian Carlo Menotti, conversation, September 10, 1976.
9. Earl Wild, conversation, January 19, 1978.
10. William Masselos, conversation, April 24, 1979.
11. William Mayer, conversation, April 20, 1979.
12. William Masselos, conversation, April 24, 1979.
13. *New York Times*, 7 May 1971.
14. *Cleveland Plain Dealer*, 14 May 1971.
15. Lynn Harrell, conversation, November 29, 1980.
16. Edward Johnson to author, August 14, 1978.
17. Tony D'Amato, conversation, May 2, 1977.
18. *San Francisco Chronicle* (Reuters), 24 June 1971.
19. Unidentified clipping, Associated Press, 25 June 1971.
20. *Philadelphia Inquirer*, 25 June 1971.
21. Natasha Bender, conversation, November 28, 1979.
22. André Kostelanetz, conversation, July 8, 1976.
23. Tony D'Amato, conversation, May 2, 1977.
24. Sadja Greenwood, conversation, May 3, 1976.
25. Richard Nixon to Stokowski, July 10, 1971.

Chapter 82

1. Samuel Rubin, minutes of American Symphony Orchestra Executive Board Meeting, April 20, 1971.
2. Stewart Mott to Samuel Rubin, April 20, 1971.
3. Jorge Bolet, conversation, December 14, 1976.
4. Anthony Miranda, conversation, June 10, 1978.
5. New York University interview with Stokowski by Robert Sherman, April 7, 1972.
6. Ulysses Kay, conversation, November 29, 1976.
7. Ned Rorem, *The Final Diary*, p. 390.
8. *New York Times*, 3 March 1972.
9. Jack Ossewaarde, conversation, September 21, 1977.
10. *New York Times*, 17 April 1972.
11. NBC-Television interview with Stokowski by Barbara Walters, April 18, 1972.
12. Richard Nixon to Stokowski, April 12, 1972.

13. Jacqueline Onassis to Stokowski, April 19, 1972.
14. Stokowski to the Board of Directors, American Symphony Orchestra, May 1, 1972.
15. Stokowski to Members of the Corporation, American Symphony Orchestra, May 1, 1972.

Chapter 83

1. Stokowski, notes on 1972–73 American Symphony Orchestra guest conductors and one Stokowski concert for a prospectus, April 1972.
2. Arthur Aaron, conversation, February 17, 1977.
3. Unidentified clipping, Associated Press, May 1972.
4. Natasha Bender, conversation, May 22, 1979.
5. Ibid.
6. Edward Johnson to author, December 1, 1977; Harold Lawrence to Edward Johnson, September 10, 1968.
7. *Guardian* (London), June 1972.
8. *Times* (London), 15 June 1972.
9. *London Daily Telegraph*, 15 June 1972.
10. Edward Johnson to author, December 1, 1977.
11. Ainslee Cox, conversation, August 27, 1976.
12. Natasha Bender, conversation, September 19, 1979.
13. Tony D'Amato, conversation, May 2, 1977.
14. Natasha Bender, conversation, September 19, 1979.
15. Tony D'Amato, conversation, May 2, 1977.
16. Ainslee Cox, conversation, August 27, 1976.
17. Jaroslav Holeček, reminiscences of Stokowski in Prague, 1972 (Milena Galuskova to author, November 20, 1977).
18. Ainslee Cox, conversation, August 27, 1976.
19. Tony D'Amato, conversation, May 2, 1977.
20. Ainslee Cox, conversation, August 27, 1976.
21. Natasha Bender, conversation, September 19, 1979.
22. *Philadelphia Evening Bulletin*, 22 September 1972.
23. Philadelphia Orchestra News Release, 8 October 1972.
24. *Philadelphia Evening Bulletin*, 3 October 1972.
25. Wilhelmina Hoedeman to Tony D'Amato, November 24, 1972.
26. Tony D'Amato, outline for television film, "A Portrait of Greatness: Leopold Stokowski," June 1972.
27. Tony D'Amato, conversation, May 2, 1977.
28. *London Daily Express*, 12 January 1972.
29. Tony D'Amato, conversation, May 2, 1977.
30. Ilana Vered, conversation, September 20, 1977.

31. *Guardian* (London), 26 April 1973.
32. *London Financial Times,* 23 April 1973.
33. Edward Johnson to author, December 15, 1977.
34. *London Daily Mail,* 6 July 1973.
35. *New Records,* June 1974, p. 4.
36. Ainslee Cox, conversation, August 27, 1976.
37. Natasha Bender, conversation, September 19, 1979.
38. Tony D'Amato, conversation, May 2, 1977.
39. BBC-Radio interview with Lionel Bryer by Alan Haydock, August 6, 1973.
40. BBC-Radio interview with Stokowski by Alan Haydock, August 6, 1973.
41. *Guardian* (London), 20 August 1973.

Chapter 84

1. *London Daily Telegraph,* 8 January 1974.
2. *Guardian* (London), 11 February, 1974.
3. *Records & Recording,* September 1975, p. 30.
4. *Gramophone,* October 1975, p. 602.
5. Ainslee Cox, conversation, August 27, 1976.
6. *London Financial Times,* 14 May 1974.
7. Ibid.
8. *Guardian* (London), 14 May 1974.
9. *Gramophone,* December 1975, p. 1031.
10. Richard Mohr, conversation, November 23, 1976.
11. Charles (Jack) Baumgarten, conversation, January 18, 1981.
12. Richard Mohr, conversation, November 23, 1976.
13. Charles (Jack) Baumgarten, conversation, January 18, 1981.
14. Dr. William Pearson Fischer, conversation, December 9, 1978.
15. Richard Mohr, conversation, November 23, 1976.
16. *Stereo Review,* April 1976, p. 113.
17. Sadja Greenwood, conversation, May 3, 1976.
18. Nancy Shear, conversation, September 19, 1979.
19. Lilette Hindin, conversation, October 7, 1976.
20. Josephine Lyons, conversation, April 17, 1977.
21. Marcos Klorman, conversation, February 4, 1981.
22. Victor Seroff, *Rachmaninoff,* p. 196.
23. *Long Island Press,* 21 December 1975.
24. Marcos Klorman, conversation, February 4, 1981.
25. André Kostelanetz, conversation, July 8, 1976.
26. Natasha Bender, conversation, February 21, 1980.
27. Mme. Arminda A. Villa-Lobos to author, September 22, 1980.

28. Stokowski to Mme. Arminda A. Villa-Lobos, March 3, 1975.
29. Natasha Bender, conversation, February 21, 1980.
30. *Nice-Matin*, 24 July 1975 (translated by Michael Aspinwall).
31. Stokowski, speech played on cassette at the American Symphony Orchestra concert honoring him on his ninety-fourth birthday, April 18, 1976.

Chapter 85

1. *International Herald Tribune* (Paris), 25 May 1976.
2. Paul Myers, conversation, December 19, 1977.
3. Ibid.
4. *Gramophone*, January 1978, p. 1308.
5. Paul Myers, conversation, December 19, 1977.
6. Paul Loewenwarter, conversation, April 16, 1977.
7. CBS-Television interview with Stokowski by Dan Rather, November 1976.

Chapter 86

1. *Los Angeles Times*, 12 April 1977.
2. *Washington Post*, 16 November 1980.
3. Robert Sherman, WQXR Radio ninety-fifth birthday tribute to Stokowski with guests Arthur Aaron, Wendy Hanson, Stewart Warkow, and the author, April 18, 1977.
4. Author to Stokowski, May 8, 1977.
5. Stokowski to author, May 17, 1977.
6. *High Fidelity*, October 1978, p. 99.
7. *Records & Recording*, September 1978, p. 62.
8. *Gramophone*, September 1978, p. 470.
9. *New Records*, June 1978, p. 2.
10. Sonya Thorbecke, conversation, March 9, 1979.
11. *New York Times*, 14 September 1977.
12. *Philadelphia Orchestra Program* September 1977.
13. *Washington Post*, 14 September 1977.
14. *Time*, 26 September 1977.
15. *Times* (London), 14 September 1977.
16. Stokowski, *Music for All of Us*, p. 6.
17. Ibid., pp. 7, 8.
18. Ibid., p. 11.
19. Ibid., p. 318.
20. Ibid., pp. 318, 319, 321, 322.

21. *New York Times*, 24 November 1977.
22. Council of the City of Philadelphia Resolution No. 234, September 21, 1977.
23. Philadelphia Orchestra News Release, 30 November 1977.
24. John de Lancie and Sylvan Levin, speeches at memorial for Stokowski at the Curtis Institute of Music, Philadelphia, September 23, 1977.
25. *New York Times*, 19 September 1977.

Selected Bibliography

Aldrich, Richard. *Musical Discourse.* New York: Oxford University Press, 1928.

Antheil, George. *Bad Boy of Music.* Garden City, N.Y.: Doubleday, Doran & Company, 1945.

Arian, Edward. *Bach, Beethoven, and Bureaucracy.* University, Ala.: University of Alabama Press, 1971.

Armitage, Merle. *Accent on America.* New York: E. Weyhe, 1944.

Armitage, Merle, ed. *Martha Graham.* Merle Armitage Limited Edition, 1937.

Bainbridge, John. *Garbo.* Garden City, N.Y.: Doubleday & Company, 1955.

Bing, Sir Rudolf. *5,000 Nights at the Opera.* New York: Doubleday & Company, Popular Library, 1972.

Bird, John. *Percy Grainger.* London: Paul Elek, 1976.

Bok, Edward. *The Americanization of Edward Bok.* New York: Charles Scribner's Sons, 1920; Pocket Books, 1965.

Bookspan, Martin and Ross Yockey. *André Previn: A Biography.* New York: Doubleday & Company, 1981.

Bookspan, Martin and Ross Yockey. *Zubin: The Zubin Mehta Story.* New York: Harper & Row, 1978.

Briggs, John. *Requiem for a Yellow Brick Brewery: A History of the Metropolitan Opera.* Boston: Little Brown & Company, 1969.

Bullitt, Susan B. and Orville Bullitt. *From Candlelight to Satellite.* Privately Printed, 1978.

Burian, K. V. *Leopold Stokowski.* Prague: Editio Supraphon, 1976.

Chapin, Schuyler. *Musical Chairs: A Life in the Arts.* New York: G. P. Putnam's Sons, 1977.

Chasins, Abram. *Leopold Stokowski: A Profile.* New York: Hawthorn Books, 1979.

Cheslock, Louis, ed. *H. L. Mencken on Music.* New York: Alfred A. Knopf, 1916; Schirmer Books, 1975.

Clemens, Clara. *My Husband Gabrilowitsch.* New York: Harper & Brothers, 1938.

Colles, H. C. *Walford Davies: A Biography.* London: Oxford University Press, 1947.

Downes, Irene, ed. *Olin Downes on Music: A Selection from His Writings during the Half-Century 1906 to 1955.* New York: Simon and Schuster, 1957.

Erskine, John. *The Philharmonic-Symphony Society of New York: Its First Hundred Years.* New York: Macmillan Company, 1943.

Gelatt, Roland. *The Fabulous Phonograph,* 2d rev. ed. New York: Macmillan Publishing Company, 1954; Collier Books, 1977.

Gerhardt, Elena. *Recital.* London: Methuen & Company, 1953.

Gerson, Robert A. *Music in Philadelphia.* Philadelphia: Theodore Presser Company, 1940.

Goldsmith, Barbara. *Little Gloria—Happy at Last.* New York: Alfred A. Knopf, 1980.

Gretchaninoff, Alexandre. *My Life.* New York: Coleman-Ross Company, 1952.

Hall, David. *The Record Book.* International Edition. New York: Oliver Durrell, 1948.

Hart, Philip. *Orpheus in the New World: The Symphony Orchestra as an American Cultural Institution.* New York: W. W. Norton & Company, 1973.

Hood, Louis. *The Spirit of '75.* Philadelphia: Philadelphia Orchestra Association, 1975.

Hughes, Adella Prentiss. *Music Is My Life.* Cleveland: World Publishing Company, 1947.

Johnson, Edward, ed. *Stokowski: Essays in the Analysis of His Art.* London: Triad Press, 1973.

Kennedy, Michael. *Barbirolli: Conductor Laureate.* London: Hart-Davis, Mac-Gibbon, 1971.

Kolodin, Irving. *A Guide to Recorded Music.* Garden City, N. Y.: Doubleday, Doran & Company, 1941.

Kolodin, Irving. *New Guide to Recorded Music.* Garden City, N. Y.: Doubleday & Company, 1947.

Kolodin, Irving. *The Guide to Long Playing Records: Orchestral Music.* New York: Alfred A. Knopf, 1955.

Kolodin, Irving. *The Musical Life.* New York: Alfred A. Knopf, 1958.

Kolodin, Irving. *The New Guide to Recorded Music. International Edition.* Garden City, N. Y.: Doubleday & Company, 1950.

Krell, John. *Kincaidiana: A Flute Player's Notebook*. Culver City, Calif.: Trio Associates, 1973.

Kupferberg, Herbert. *Those Fabulous Philadelphians*. New York: Charles Scribner's Sons, 1969.

Leinsdorf, Erich. *Cadenza: A Musical Career*. Boston: Houghton Mifflin Company, 1976.

Levant, Oscar. *A Smattering of Ignorance*. Garden City, N. Y.: Garden City Publishing Company, 1942.

Luening, Otto. *The Odyssey of an American Composer*. New York: Charles Scribner's Sons, 1980.

Maisel, Edward M. *Charles T. Griffes: The Life of an American Composer*. New York: Alfred A. Knopf, 1943.

Marek, George R. *Toscanini*. New York: Atheneum, 1975.

Mason, Daniel Gregory. *Music in My Time*. New York: Macmillan Company, 1938.

Massine, Léonide. *My Life in Ballet*. New York: Macmillan Company, 1968.

Milhaud, Darius. *Notes without Music: An Autobiography*. New York: Alfred A. Knopf, 1953.

Mueller, John H. *The American Symphony Orchestra: A Social History of Musical Taste*. Bloomington, Ind.: Indiana University Press, 1951.

O'Connell, Charles. *The Other Side of the Record*. New York: Alfred A. Knopf, 1947.

Opperby, Preben. *Stokowski*. London: Midas Books, 1982.

Ouellette, Fernand. *Edgard Varèse*. New York: Orion Press, 1966.

Radamsky, Sergei. *Der Verfolgte Tenor*. Munich: Piper Verlag, 1972.

Reis, Claire. *Composers, Conductors and Critics*. New York: Oxford University Press, 1955.

Robinson, Paul. *Stokowski*. Toronto: Vanguard Press, 1977.

Rodzinski, Halina. *Our Two Lives*. New York: Charles Scribner's Sons, 1976.

Rorem, Ned. *The Final Diary*. New York: Holt, Rinehart & Winston, 1974.

Russcol, Herbert. *The Liberation of Sound*. Englewood Cliffs, N. J.: Prentice-Hall, 1972.

Roussel, Hubert. *The Houston Symphony Orchestra, 1913–1971*. Austin, Tex.: University of Texas Press, 1972.

Sachs, Harvey. *Toscanini*. New York: J. B. Lippincott Company, 1978.

Sands, Frederick and Sven Broman. *The Divine Garbo*. New York: Grosset & Dunlap, 1979.

Schickel, Richard. *The Disney Version*. New York: Simon & Schuster, 1968.

Schickel, Richard. *The World of Carnegie Hall*. New York: Julian Messner, 1960.

Schonberg, Harold. *The Great Conductors*. New York: Simon & Schuster, 1967.

Seroff, Victor. *Rachmaninoff*. London: Cassell & Company, 1951.

Shanet, Howard. *Philharmonic: A History of New York's Orchestra.* New York: Doubleday & Company, 1975.

Siegmeister, Elie. *The New Music Lover's Handbook.* New York: Harvey House, 1973.

Sills, Beverly. *Bubbles: A Self-Portrait.* New York: Bobbs-Merrill, 1976; Warner Books, 1978.

Slonimsky, Nicolas. *Lexicon of Musical Invective.* New York: Coleman-Ross Company, 1965.

Slonimsky, Nicolas. *Music Since 1900.* New York: Coleman-Ross Company, 1949.

Smith, Moses. *Koussevitzky.* New York: Allen, Towne & Heath, 1947.

Stokowski, Leopold. *Music for All of Us.* New York: Simon & Schuster, 1943.

Stokowski, Olga Samaroff. *An American Musician's Story.* New York: W. W. Norton & Company, 1939.

Stokowski, Olga Samaroff. *The Layman's Music Book.* New York: W. W. Norton & Company, 1935.

Stravinsky, Igor and Robert Craft. *Expositions and Developments.* Garden City, N. Y.: Doubleday & Company, 1962.

Stravinsky, Igor and Robert Craft. *Themes and Episodes.* New York: Alfred A. Knopf, 1966.

Stravinsky, Vera and Robert Craft. *Stravinsky in Pictures and Documents.* New York: Simon & Schuster, 1978.

Szigeti, Joseph. *With Strings Attached.* New York: Alfred A. Knopf, 1947.

Taubman, Howard. *The Maestro: The Life of Arturo Toscanini.* New York: Simon & Schuster, 1951.

Thomas, Louis R. *A History of the Cincinnati Symphony Orchestra to 1931.* Ann Arbor, Michigan: University Microfilms, 1972.

Thomson, Virgil. *The Art of Judging Music.* New York: Alfred A. Knopf, 1948.

Thomson, Virgil. *Music Right and Left.* New York: Henry Holt, 1951.

Thomson, Virgil. *The Musical Scene.* New York: Alfred A. Knopf, 1945.

Toobin, Jerome. *Agitato.* New York: Viking Press, 1975.

Vanderbilt, Gloria and Thelma Lady Furness. *Double Exposure: A Twin Autobiography.* New York: David McKay Company, 1958.

Varèse, Louise. *Varèse: A Looking-Glass Diary.* New York: W. W. Norton & Company, 1972.

Wister, Frances. *Twenty-five Years of the Philadelphia Orchestra, 1900–1925.* Philadelphia: Edward Stern & Company, 1925.

Wolanin, Barbara. *Arthur B. Carles, 1882–1952: Philadelphia Modernist.* Ann Arbor, Michigan: University Microfilms, 1981.

Wooldridge, David. *Conductor's World.* New York: Praeger Publishers, 1970.

Stokowski's Recorded Repertoire

Compiled by Edward Johnson

The following listing is not intended as a specialized discography: such a project would need to provide full details of matrix numbers, take numbers and takes issued, exact recording dates and locations, worldwide catalogue numbers, and so on. Limitations of space preclude such an undertaking, which would, in any case, be of interest only to specialized record collectors.

What the listing shows is Stokowski's vast published recorded repertoire, alphabetically by composer, giving the orchestra, year of recording (or, in a few cases, of publication), principal catalogue numbers (for the U.S.A. and U.K. only), and principal reissue numbers.

Where a 78-rpm disc occupied part of a set or album, only the album number is shown, in preference to the single-disc number. For acoustic recordings that were issued in both single-sided and double-sided format, only the double-sided catalogue number is shown. Where records were issued in several concurrent formats (i.e., 78 rpm, 45 rpm and 33 ⅓ rpm) during the change-overs in speeds during the late 1940s, only the LP number is given. Where LP records were issued in both mono and stereo simultaneously, only the stereo number is shown.

For further details, the appropriate record company catalogues should be consulted. It should be noted, however, that some Stokowski performances that have appeared on disc have not been made commercially available to the general public. These records have been designated "Limited Issue."

Acknowledgment is duly made to other Stokowski discographers who have provided assistance. They include Charles Baumgarten, Jim Cartwright, Robert Gatewood, David Kendig, and Ivan Lund.

Record Companies and Catalogue Number Prefixes

78rpm Records:

Columbia single discs—Col.
Columbia Masterworks Albums—Col. M, MM, and X
His Master's Voice (UK)—DA and E (10″); D and DB (12″)
RCA Victor single discs—Vic.
RCA Victor Masterworks Albums—DM and M

Long-Playing Records:

Audio-Visual Enterprises (Geneva)—AVE
Bell Telephone Laboratories, Inc.—BTL (Limited Issues) (Experimental recordings made
    during rehearsals and concerts)
Bruno Records—BR
Bruno Walter Society—BWS
Brunswick (UK)—SXA
Buena-Vista Records (UK) ("Disneyland")—BVS
Camden (USA)—CAL (pseudonymic reissues)
Camden Classics (UK)—CCV
Cameo Classics (UK)—GOCLP
Capitol—SP; SPBO; SPBR; SSAL
CBS (UK)—SBRG
Classics for Pleasure (UK)—CFP
Columbia (UK)—33CX; 33C
Columbia (USA)—BM; M; MS; ML; P
Composer's Recordings Inc.—CRI
Decca (USA)—DL
dell'Arte (UK)—DA
Desmar—DSM
Disneyland (USA)—WDX
Everest—SDBR
EMI/HMV—SXLP
His Master's Voice (UK)—ALP; BLP; CSLP
International Piano Archive—IPA
International Piano Library—IPL
Leopold Stokowski Society—LS
Melodya (USSR)—MK
Music for Pleasure—SMFP
Niemann-Marcus (Dallas, Texas)—DMM4; DPM4

"Phase-Four" Decca (UK)—OPFS; PFS; SPA
"Phase-Four" London (USA)—SPC
Odyssey (Columbia) (USA)—Y
Philips (UK)—VSL
Pye—PCNHX
Quintessence (USA)—PMC
RCA Victor (UK)—GL; LSB; SB; SRS; VCM; VIC
RCA Victor (USA)—ANL1; ARL1; ARL2; ARM3; AVM2; LCT; LM; LSC; VRL1;
    VCM; ERA (45 rpm)
Seraphim—S
United Artists—UAS; USLP
Vanguard—SRV; VSD; BGS
Varèse-Sarabande—VC
World Record Club (UK)—WRC

Other companies are shown in full in the listing (including "pirate" labels).

Orchestras—Abbreviations

AAO   — All-American Orchestra
AAYO   — All-American Youth Orchestra
ASO   — American Symphony Orchestra
BPO   — Berlin Philharmonic Orchestra
CPO   — Czech Philharmonic Orchestra
CSO   — Chicago Symphony Orchestra
DRO   — Danish Radio Orchestra
FNRO   — French National Radio Orchestra
HBSO   — Hollywood Bowl Symphony Orchestra ("Star Symphony" on Camden
         reissues)
HRPO   — Hilversum Radio Philharmonic Orchestra
HSO   — Houston Symphony Orchestra
IFYO   — International Festival Youth Orchestra
LAPO   — Los Angeles Philharmonic Orchestra
LPO   — London Philharmonic Orchestra
LSO   — London Symphony Orchestra
NatPO — National Philharmonic Orchestra*
NBC   — NBC Symphony Orchestra ("Members of" for 1954–55 recordings)
NPO   — New Philharmonia Orchestra
NSO   — New Symphony Orchestra of London*

NYCSO — New York City Symphony Orchestra ("Sutton Symphony" on Camden reissues)
NYPO — New York Philharmonic Symphony Orchestra
NYSSO — New York Stadium Symphony Orchestra (pseudonym for New York Philharmonic)
PO   — Philadelphia Orchestra ("Warwick Symphony" on Camden reissues)
RCASO — RCA Victor Symphony Orchestra*
RPO   — Royal Philharmonic Orchestra
SFSO — San Franciisco Symphony Orchestra
SO   — Leopold Stokowski and his Symphony Orchestra*
SOA   — Symphony of the Air (formerly the NBC Symphony Orchestra)
SRO   — Suisse Romande Orchestra

*—specially constituted recording ensembles

Other orchestras are shown in full in the listing
Note: works recorded "live" during public performances are indicated (pp).

Stokowski's Recorded Repertoire

Anonymous (or "Traditional")

1. "Deep River"
   NSO (1961) (with the Norman Luboff Choir) LSC 2593
2. "Doxology" ("Praise God from Whom All Blessings Flow")
   NSO (1961) (with the Norman Luboff Choir) LSC 2593
3. *Etenraku*—Eighth-Century Japanese Ceremonial Prelude (orch. Kunoye)
   PO (1934) Vic. 14142
4. "Russian Christmas Music" (orch. Stokowski)
   a) PO (1934) Vic. 1692
   b) SO (1947) Vic. 11-9837
5. "Two Ancient Liturgical Melodies" (orch. Stokowski)
   "Veni Creator Spiritus" and "Veni Emanuel"
   PO (1934) Vic. 1789; DA 1551

Adolphe Adam (1803–1856, France)

Giselle Ballet excerpts
SO (1950) LM 1083; ALP 1133; VIC 1020

Isaac Albeniz (1860–1909, Spain)

"Fête Dieu à Seville" from *Iberia* (orch. Stokowski)
   a) PO (1928) Vic. 7158; D 1888
   b) NatPO (1976) M 34543; CBS 73589

Fikret Amirov (b. 1922, USSR)

Azerbaijan Mugam
HSO (1959) SDBR 3032

Johann Sebastian Bach (1685–1750, Germany)

1. *Brandenburg* Concerto No. 2
   PO (1928) Vic. M.59; D 1702-3; DA9001

2. *Brandenburg* Concerto No. 5
   PO (1960) MS 6313; Y 33228; CBS Harmony 30061

3. Suite No. 2 for Flute and Strings
   SO (1950) (with Julius Baker, flute) LM 1176

Transcribed for Orchestra by Stokowski (except where stated otherwise):

4. Chorale "Jesus Cristus, Gottes Sohn" from the "Easter Cantata"
   a) PO (1937) Vic. M-401
   b) SO (1950) LM 1176
   c) NYPO (1947) NYP 821/2 (pp): labeled "Christ lag in todesbanden"
   d) CPO (1972) SPC 21096; PFS 4278 (pp)

5. "Jesu Joy of Man's Desiring" from Cantata "Herz und Mund"
   a) SO (1950) LM 1176; HMV 7ER 5004
   b) NSO (1961) (arr. Luboff) (with the Norman Luboff Choir) LSC 2593
   c) SO (1967) (arr. Schickele) BGS 70696

6. "Arioso"—"Sinfonia" from Cantata "Ich steh mit einem Fuss im Grabe"
   a) NBC (1941) Vic. 18498; DB 6150
   b) AAO (1941) Col. M-541
   c) LSO (1974) ARL1-1880; GL 42921

7. "Sheep may safely graze" from the "Birthday Cantata"
   a) SO (1950) LM 1176
   b) NSO (1961) (with the Norman Luboff Choir) LSC 2593
   c) SO (1967) BGS 70696

8. Chorale "Ein Feste Burg" (after Luther)
   a) PO (1933) Vic. 1692; DB 2453 (abridged)
   b) AAO (1941) Col. X-219

     c) SO (1958) SP 8489; S-60235

     d) LSO (1974) ARL1-0880; GL 42921

9. "Shepherd's Christmas Music" from the "Christmas Oratorio"
     a) PO (1929) Vic. 7142; D 1741
     b) SO (1958) SP 8489; S-60235
     c) SO (1967) BGS 70696

10. "Es ist vollbracht" from the *St. John Passion*
     a) PO (1934) Vic. 8764; DB 2762
     b) PO (1940) Vic. M-963

11. "My Soul Is Athirst" from the *St. Matthew Passion*
     PO (1936) Vic. M-401; DB 3405

12. Song "Komm süsser Tod"
     a) PO (1933) Vic. M-243; DB 2274
     b) AAO (1941) Col. X-220
     c) SO (1950) LM 1176; BLP 1074
     d) SO (1958) SP 8489; S-60235
     e) LSO (1974) ARL1-0880; GL 42921

13. Song "Mein Jesu was für seelenweh"
     a) PO (1936) Vic. M-401; DB 3405
     b) AAYO (1941) Col. 19004-D
     c) SO (1950) LM 1133
     d) SO (1957) SP 8415
     e) CPO (1972) SPC 21096; PFS 4278 (pp)

14. Chorale Prelude "Aus der Tiefe rufe Ich"
     PO (1930) Vic. 7553; DB 1789; DA 9001

15. Chorale Prelude "Christ lag in Todesbanden"
     PO (1931) Vic. 7437; DB 1952

16. Chorale Prelude "Ich ruf zu dir, Herr Jesu Christ"
     a) PO (1927) Vic. 6786; D 1464; DMM4-0341; DA 9001
     b) PO (1939) Vic. M-963
     c) NYPO (1949) NYP 821/2 (pp)
     d) PO (1960) MS 6313; Y 33228; CBS Harmony 30061

17. Chorale Prelude "Nun komm der Heiden Heiland"
     a) PO (1934) Vic. M-243; DB 2274
     b) PO (1960) MS 6313; Y 33228; CBS Harmony 30061

18. Chorale Prelude "Wachet Auf, ruft uns die Stimme"
     LSO (1974) ARL1-0880; GL 42921

19. Chorale Prelude "Wir Glauben all' an einen Gott" ("Giant Fugue")
    a) PO (1929) Vic. M-59; D 1710; DA 9001
    b) NYPO (1949) NYP 821/2 (pp)
    c) SO (1950) LM 1176; HMV 7ER 5004
    d) PO (1960) MS 6313; Y 33228; CBS Harmony 30061
    e) CPO (1972) SPC 21096; PFS 4278 (pp)

20. Toccata and Fugue in D Minor
    a) PO (1927) Vic. 6751; D 1428; VCM-7101; DMM4-0341;
       DA 9001
    b) PO (1934) Vic. 8697; DB 2572
    c) PO (1939) WDX 101; BVS 101 (*Fantasia* soundtrack)
    d) AAO (1941) Col. X-219
    e) SO (1947) LM 2042; BLP 1074
    f) SO (1957) SP 8399; SMFP 2145; S-60235
    g) CPO (1972) SPC 21096; PFS 4278 (pp)
    (This transcription has also been recorded by Arthur Fiedler and the Boston Pops
    Orchestra on Deutsche Grammophon 2584 001)

21. Passacaglia and Fugue in C Minor
    a) PO (1929) Vic. M-59; D 1702-3; VCM-7101; DA 9001
    b) PO (1936) Vic. M-401; DB 3252-3
    c) AAO (1941) Col. X-216
    d) SO (1950) LM 1133; BLP 1074
    e) SO (1958) SP 8489; S-60235
    f) IFYO (1969) AVE 30696
    g) CPO (1972) SPC 21096; PFS 4278 (pp)

22. Prelude and Fugue No. 3 in E Minor
    PO (1937) Vic. M-963

23. "Great" Fugue in G Minor
    PO (1934) Vic. 1728

24. "Little" Fugue in G Minor
    a) PO (1931) Vic. 7437; DB 1952
    b) AAO (1940) Col. M-451 and 11992-D
    c) SO (1950) LM 1176; HMV 7ER 5004
    d) SO (1958) SP 8489; S-60235
    e) LSO (1974) ARL1-0880; GL 42921

25. Adagio from Toccata, Adagio and Fugue in C Major
    PO (1933) Vic. M-243; DB 2335

26. First Movement of the Trio-Sonata No. 1 in E-flat
    PO (1939) Vic. M-963; DB 6260

27. Sarabande from Violin Partita No. 1 in B Minor
    a) PO (1936) Vic. M-401
    b) SO (1958) SP 8489; S-60235

28. Andante Sostenuto from Violin Sonata No. 2 in A Minor
    AAO (1941) Col. M-541

29. Chaconne from Violin Partita No. 2 in D Minor
    a) PO (1934) Vic. M-243; DB 2451-3
    b) SO (1950) LM 1133
    c) LSO (1974) ARL1-0880; GL 42921

30. Preludio from Violin Partita No. 3 in E Major
    a) AAO (1941) Col. 11983-D (arr. for strings and winds)
    b) SO (1957) SP 8415 (arr. for strings only)
    c) LSO (1974) ARL1-0880; GL 42921 (arr. for strings and winds)

31. Bourrée from English Suite No. 2 in A Minor
    a) PO (1936) DMM4-0341 (Catalogued as HMV DA 1639 but not issued)
    b) SO (1950) LM 1133
    c) SO (1958) SP 8489

32. Sarabande from English Suite No. 3 in G Minor
    PO (1934) Vic. M-243

33. Siciliano from Sonata No. 4 in C Minor for Violin and Clavier
    a) PO (1934) Vic. M-243; DB 2275
    b) SO (1950) LM 1133

34. Fugue in C Minor from Book 1, *Well-Tempered Clavier*
    PO (1934) Vic. 1985; DB 2453; CAL 120

35. Prelude in E-flat Minor from Book 1, *Well-Tempered Clavier*
    a) PO (1927) Vio. 6786; D 1464; DA 9001
    b) AAO (1941) Col. M-541
    c) CPO (1972) SP 21096; PFS 4278 (pp)

36. Prelude in B Minor from Book 1, *Well-Tempered Clavier*
    a) PO (1929) Vic. 7316; D 1938 and D 1995; DA 9001
    b) SO (1950) LM 2042

37. Aria from Orchestral Suite No. 3 in D Major
    a) PO (1936) Vic. M-401; DA 1605
    b) AAO (1941) Col. X-220

c) SO (1958) SP 8458; SXLP 30174

d) LSO (1974) ARL1-0880; GL 42921

Addendum: a selection of Bach-Stokowski transcriptions has been recorded by the Sydney Symphony Orchestra conducted by Robert Pikler on Australian RCA VRLI-0315 and Chandos Records ABR 1055 (Published 1980).

Samuel Barber (1910–1981 U.S.A.)

Adagio for Strings from String Quartet Op. 11 (arr. composer)
SO (1956) SSAL 8385; SXLP 30174

Bela Bartok (1881–1945, Hungary)

1. Concerto for Orchestra
   HSO (1960) SDBR 3069; WRC SCM 36

2. Music for Strings, Percussion and Celeste
   SO (1957) SP 8507; WRC SCM 69

3. Sonata for Two Pianos and Percussion
   Gerson Yessin and Raymond Viola, pianists;
   Elayne Jones and Alfred Howard, percussion
   (1952) LM 1727

Ludwig van Beethoven (1770–1827, Germany)

1. Symphony No. 2
   CSO (1962) LS 4 (pp)

2. Symphony No. 3 (Eroica)
   LSO (1974) ARL1-0600

3. Symphony No. 5
   a) PO (1931) Vic. L 7001; DPM4-0210
   b) AAO (1941) Col. M-451
   c) LPO (1969) SPC 21042; PFS 4197; DPA 599-600

4. Symphony No. 6 (Pastoral)
   a) PO (1939) WDX 101; BVS 101 (abridged Fantasia soundtrack)
   b) NYCSO (1945) Vic. M-1032; CAL 187
   c) NBC (1954) (with Stokowski's talk "Sounds of Nature") LM 1830; ALP 1268

5. Symphony No. 7
   a) PO (1927) (with Stokowski's "Outline of Themes") Vic. M-17; CAL 212; Parnassus 5; DMM4-0341

b) SOA (1958) UAS 8003; PMC 7110

c) NPO (1973) SPC 21139; PFS 4342

6. Symphony No. 8: Allegretto only
PO (1920) Vic. 74661; DB 385; LS 3

7. Symphony No. 9 *(Choral)*
a) PO (1934) (with Agnes Davis, Ruth Cathcart, Robert Betts, Eugene Lowenthal
and Chorus. Finale in English) Vic. M-236; DB 2327-2335
b) LSO (1967) (with Heather Harper, Helen Watts, Alexander Young, Donald
McIntyre, and LSO Chorus. Finale in German) SPC 21043; PFS 4183; DPA
599-600

8. Piano Concerto No. 5 *(Emperor)*
ASO (1966) (with Glenn Gould, piano) MS 6888; CBS 72403

9. *Coriolan* Overture
LSO (1974) ARL1-0600

10. *Egmont* Overture
NPO (1973) SPC 21139; PFS 4342

11. *Leonore* No. 3 Overture
NatPO (1976) PCNHX 6; DA 9003

12. "The Heavens Are Telling" (Die Ehre Gottes, Op. 48 No. 4)
NSO (1961) (with the Norman Luboff Choir) LSC 2593

13. "Turkish March" from *The Ruins of Athens*
SO (1955) LM 2042

Paul Ben-Haim (b. 1897, Germany)

"From Israel"—Suite for Orchestra
SOA (1958) UAS 8005

Theodor Berger (b. 1905, Austria)

Rondino Giocoso for Strings
SO (1958) SP 8485

Irving Berlin (b. 1888, Russia/U.S.A.)

"God Bless America"
AAO (1940) Col. 17204-D

Hector Berlioz (1803–1869, France)

1. *Symphonie Fantastique*
NPO (1968) SPC 21031; PFS 4160; SDD 465

2. *The Damnation of Faust*—
    "Dance of the Sylphs"
    a) SO (1951) LM 9029
    b) LSO (1970) SPC 21059; PFS 4220

    "Hungarian March" ("Rakoczy March")
    a) PO (1927) Vic. 6823; D 1807; VCM-7101

    b) NatPO (1975) Pye 12132; PCNHX 4
3. *Roman Carnival* Overture
    a) PO (1931) BTL-7901
    b) NatPO (1976) PCNHX 6; DA 9003

Georges Bizet (1838–1875, France)

1. Symphony in C
    a) SO (1952) LM 1706; ALP 1181; VIC 1008
    b) NatPO (1977) M 34567; CBS 76673
2. *Carmen*—Orchestral Suites—
    Prelude to Act 1
    PO (1919) Vic. 796

    Prelude to Act 1 and Entracte Act 4
    PO (1927) Vic. 1356; E 531

    "Soldiers Changing Guard" and "Smugglers March"
    a) PO (1923) Vic. 1017
    b) PO (1927) Vic. 6874; D 1816

    Intermezzo Act 3, "Les Dragons d'Alcala" and "Gypsy Dance"
    PO (1927) Vic. 6873; D 1618

    Selections (including a Minuet and the Andantino, labeled
    "Farandole," from the "Pastorale" in *L'Arlésienne*)
    NYCSO (1945) LM 1069; DB 9505-8

    Selections from Suites 1 and 2
    NatPO (1976) M 34503; CBS 76587
3. *L'Arlésienne*—Orchestral Suites—
    "Spanish Dance" (Andantino from "Pastorale," Suite 2)
    PO (1922) Vic. 1113

    Suite 1 and the Andantino (labeled "Danse Provencale")
    from "Pastorale" (Suite 2)
    PO (1929) Vic. M-62; D 1801-3

Suites 1 and 2
SO (1952) LM 1706; ALP 1181; VIC 1008

Suite 1; Andantino ("Pastorale"), Minuet, and Farandole (Suite 2)
NatPO (1976) M 34503; CBS 76587

Ernest Bloch (1880–1959, Switzerland)

1) *America*—An Epic Rhapsody
SOA (1960) (with the American Concert Choir)
VSD 2056; VSL 11020; SRV 346 SD

2) *Schelomo*—A Hebrew Rhapsody
a) PO (1940) (with Emmanuel Feuermann, cello) Vic. M-698; DB 5816-8s; CAL
254; DMM4-0341
b) SOA (1959) (with George Neikrug, cello) UAS 8005; USLP 0009

Luigi Boccherini (1743–1805, Italy)

Minuet from String Quintet in E Major (arr. Stokowski)
a) PO (1922) Vic. 798
b) PO (1929) Vic. 7256; D 1864; CAL 120
c) SO (1958) SP 8458; SXLP 30174

Alexander Borodin (1833–1887, Russia)

1) *In the Steppes of Central Asia*
SO (1953) LM 1816; PMC 7026

2) Nocturne from String Quartet in D Major (arr. Sargent)
SO (1957) SP 8415; SXLP 30174

3) *Prince Igor*—
"Polovetzki Dance"
PO (1925) Vic. 6514

"Dances of the Polovetzki Maidens" (arr. Stokowski)
a) PO (1937) Vic. M-499; DB 3232-3; CAL 203
b) SO (1950) (with Women's Chorus) LM 1054; VIC 1043; CDM 1071

Polovtsian Dances (orch. Rimsky-Korsakov and Glazunov)
RPO (1969) (with John Alldis Chorus and Welsh National Opera Chorale)
SPC 21041; PFS 4189

Johannes Brahms (1833–1879, Germany)

1. Symphony No. 1

a) PO (1927) (with Stokowski's "Outline of Themes") Vic. M-15; D 1499-1503; GOCLP 9009(H)

b) PO (1935) Vic. M-301; DB 2874-8; CAL 105

c) HBSO (1945) LM 1070

d) LSO (1972) SPC 21090-1; OPFS 3-4; SPC 21131; PFS 4305 (pp)

2. Symphony No. 2
   a) PO (1929/30) Vic. M-82; D 1877-82
   b) NatPO (1977) M 35129; CBS 76667

3. Symphony No. 3
   a) PO (1928) Vic. M-42; D 1769-73; CAL 164; LS 1
   b) HSO (1959) SDBR 3030; WRC ST 102

   Poco Allegretto only
   PO (1921) Vic. 6242

4. Symphony No. 4
   a) PO (1931) Vic. M-108 (unissued); DPM4-0210
   b) PO (1933) Vic. M-185
   c) AAYO (1941) Col. M-452
   d) NPO (1974) ARL1-0719

5. Serenade No. 1 in D Major
   SOA (1961) DL 710031; VC 81050

   Minuet only
   PO (1934) Vic. 1720; DA 1462

6. *Academic Festival* Overture
   NPO (1974) ARL1-0719

7. *Tragic* Overture
   NatPO (1977) M 35129; CBS 76667

8. Hungarian Dance No. 1 (orch. Stokowski)
   a) PO (1920) Vic. 1113
   b) PO (1934) Vic. 1675; DA 1398; CAL 123
   c) HBSO (1946) Vic. 10-1302
   d) NatPO (1975) Pye 12132; PCNHX 4

9. Hungarian Dance No. 5 in G Minor
   PO (1917) Vic. 797; LS 3

10. Hungarian Dance No. 6 in D Major
    PO (1917) Vic 797; LS 3

11. Variations on a Theme by Haydn
     CSO (1962) LS4

Havergal Brian (1876–1972, England)

Symphony No. 28 in C Minor
NPO (1973) Aries LP-1607 (from BBC Studio Broadcast. Issued under the pseudonym of "The Hamburg Philharmonic Orchestra conducted by Horst Werner." The coupling, Brian's Violin Concerto, features Ralph Holmes with the NPO conducted by Stanley Pope—BBC Studio Broadcast of 1969).

William Byrd (1543–1623, England)

Pavane from *The Marquis of Salisbury* and Gigue from *The Fitzwilliam Virginal Book* (orch. Stokowski)
     a) PO (1937) Vic. 1943; DA 1637
     b) LSO (1972) SPC 21130; PFS 4351 (pp)

Thomas Canning (b. 1911, U.S.A.)

"Fantasy on a Hymn Tune by Justin Morgan"
for Double String Quartet and String Orchestra
HSO (1960) SDBR 3070

Joseph Canteloube (1879–1957, France)

"Songs of the Auvergne"
ASO (1964) (with Anna Moffo, soprano) LSC 2795; LSB 4114

Marc Antonio Cesti (1618–1699, Italy)

"Tu mancavi a tormentarmi crudelissima speranza" (transc. Stokowski)
     a) SO (1952) LM 1721 and LM 1875; ALP 1387
     b) SOA (1958) UAS 8001

Emmanuel Chabrier (1841–1894, France)

España Rapsodie
     a) PO (1919) Vic. 6241
     b) NatPO (1975) Pye 12132; PCNHX 4

Frederic Chopin (1810–1849, Poland)

1. *Les Sylphides*—Ballet excerpts—
    Prelude No. 7 in A; Waltz in G-flat Op. 70 No. 1; Mazurka in C Op. 67 No. 3;
    Grande Valse Brillante No. 1 in E-flat Op.18
    SO (1950) LM 1083; ALP 1133; VIC 1020

2. Mazurka No. 13 in A Minor Op. 17 No. 4 (transc. Stokowski)
    a) PO (1937) Vic. 1855
    b) HSO (1960) SDBR 3070
    c) LSO (1972) SPC 21130; PFS 4351
3. Mazurka No. 17 in B-flat Minor Op. 24 No. 4 (transc. Stokowski)
    a) PO (1937) Vic. M-841
    b) NatPO (1976) M 34543; CBS 73589
4. Prelude No. 4 in E Minor Op. 28 No. 4 (transc. Stokowski)
    a) PO (1922) Vic. 1111
    b) SO (1950) LM 1238
5. Prelude No. 24 in D Minor Op. 28 No. 24 (transc. Stokowski)
    a) PO (1937) Vic. 1998; DA 1639
    b) SO (1950) LM 1238
    c) HSO (1960) SDBR 3070
    d) NatPO (1976) M 34543; CBS 73589
6. Waltz No. 7 in C-sharp Minor Op. 64 No. 2 (transc. Stokowski)
    HSO (1960) SDBR 3070

Jeremiah Clarke (1673/4–1707, England)

"Trumpet Voluntary" (arr. Stokowski)
    a) HBSO (1946) (attrib. Purcell) Vic. 11-9419; DB 6737; CAL 153
    b) LSO (1972) (with Howard Snell, trumpet) SPC 21130; PFS 4351 (pp)

Aaron Copland (b. 1900, U.S.A.)

Billy the Kid Ballet Music—
"Prairie Night" and "Celebration Dance" only
NYPO (1947) ML 2167

Arcangelo Corelli (1653–1713, Italy)

Concerto Grosso in G Minor (*Christmas*) Ccerto
SO (1967) BGS 70696

Henry Cowell (1897–1965, U.S.A.)

1) *Persian Set* for Chamber Orchestra
    SO (1957) CRI SD 114
2) *Tales of Our Countryside* for Piano and Orchestra
    AAO (1941) (with composer as soloist) Col. X-235

Paul Creston (b. 1906, U.S.A.)
Symphony Op. 20—Scherzo only
AAO (1941) Col. 11713-D

Luigi Dallapiccola (1904–1975, Italy)
Il Prigionero (Opera in Prologue and Four Scenes)
New York City Center Opera (1960) (with Ann McKnight, Norman Treigle,
Richard Cassilly) Private Edition—MR 2009 (in English)
(2-LP Set with Busoni's Turandot conducted by Otto Ackermann)

William Dawson (b. 1898, USA)
Negro Folk Symphony
ASO (1963) DL 710077; SXA 4520; VC 81056

Claude Debussy (1862–1918, France)
1. Children's Corner Suite (orch. Caplet)
   a) SO (1949) LM 9023; ANL1-2604(e)
   b) Three excerpts ("Jumbo's Lullaby," "Little Shepherd," "Golliwog's Cakewalk")
      NYSSO (1959) SDBR 3108
2. "Clair de Lune" from Suite Bergamasque (orch. Stokowski)
   a) PO (1937) Vic. 1812; DA 1634; CAL 123
   b) SO (1947) LM 1154; HMV 7ER 5011
   c) SO (1957) SP 8399; SMFP 2145
   d) NatPO (1976) M 34543; CBS 73589
3. Danses Sacrée et Profane
   PO (1931) (with Edna Phillips, harp) Vic. M-116; DB 1642-3
4. "The Engulfed Cathedral" (Prelude No. 10) (orch. Stokowski)
   a) PO (1930) Vic. M-116; DMM4-0341
   b) NPO (1965) SPC 21006; PFS 4095
5. "Ibéria" from Images for Orchestra
   FNRO (1958) SP 8463; S-60102; SXLP 30263
6. La Mer—Three Symphonic Sketches
   LSO (1970) SPC 21059; PFS 4220
7. Nocturnes—
   "Nuages"

a) PO (1929) Vic. M-116; DB 1614; DMM4-0341
b) PO (1937) Vic. M-630; DB 3596; CAL 140

"Fêtes"
a) PO (1927) Vic. 1309; E 507; DMM4-0341
b) PO (1937/9) Vic. M-630; DA 1742; CAL 140

"Sirènes"
PO (1939) (with Women's Choir) Vic. M-630; DB 3981-2s; CAL 140
Complete
a) SO (1950) (with Women's Voices of the Robert Shaw Chorale) LM 1154
b) LSO (1957) (with BBC Women's Chorus) SP 8520; S-60104

8. *Prélude à l'après midi d'un faune*
   a) PO (1924) Vic. 6481; DB 840
   b) PO (1927) Vic. 6696; D 1768; DMM4-0341
   c) PO (1940) Vic. 17700
   d) SO (1949) (with Julius Baker, flute) LM 1154; DB 21297
   e) SO (1957) (with Julius Baker, flute) SP 8399; SMFP 2145
   f) LSO (1972) SPC 21091-2; OPFS 3-4 (pp)

9. "La Soirée dans Grenade" from *Estampes* (orch. Stokowski)
   a) PO (1940) (Unissued on 78 rpm) DMM4-0341
   b) NatPO (1976) M 34543; CBS 73589

Leo Delibes (1836–1891, France)
Sylvia Ballet Music—
Valse lente and Pizzicati only
SO (1950) LM 1083; ALP 1133; VIC 1020

Robert Emmett Dolan (1908–1972, U.S.A.)
"A Message for Lisa" from the 1944 film *Lady in the Dark*
HBSO (1946) Vic. 10-1302

Arcady Dubensky (1890–1966, Russia/U.S.A.)
The Raven—Melodrama for Speaker and Orchestra (from the poem by Edgar Allen Poe)
PO (1932) (with Benjamin de Loache, speaker)
Victor Picture Records—2000-1

Paul Dukas (1865–1935, France)
1) *La Peri*—Fanfare
   SO (1956) SSAL 8385

2)   "The Sorcerer's Apprentice"
      a) PO (1937) Vic. M-717; DB 6038-9; CAL 118
      b) Disney Studio Orchestra (1938) (attributed to the Philadelphia Orchestra) WDX
      101; BVS 101 (*Fantasia* soundtrack)

Henri Duparc (1848–1933, France)
Song "Extase" (orch. Stokowski)
LSO (1972) (with David Gray, solo horn) SPC 21130; PFS 4351

Antonin Dvořák (1841–1904, Bohemia)
1.   Symphony No. 9 *(From the New World)*
      a) PO (1925) Vic. 6565-9
      b) PO (1927) (with Stokowski's "Outline of Themes") Vic M-1; D 1893-7; ARL2-
      0334
      c) PO (1934) Vic. M-273; DB 2543-7; CAL 104; CDN 1008
      d) AAYO (1940) Col. M-416
      e) SO (1947) LM 1013
      f) NPO (1973) ARL2-0334

      Largo only
      PO (1920) Vic. 6236
2.   "Serenade for Strings" in E Major
      RPO (1975) DSM-1011
3.   Slavonic Dance No. 10 in E Minor
      CPO (1972) SPC 21117; PFS 4333 (pp)

Henry Eichheim (1870–1942, U.S.A.)
1.   Japanese Nocturne
      PO (1929) Vic. 7260; D 1936
2.   *Bali*—Symphonic Variations
      PO (1934) Vic. 14141-2

Sir Edward Elgar (1857–1934, England)
Enigma Variations
      CPO (1972) SPC 21136; PFS 4338 (pp)
      (coupled with Elgar's "Serenade for Strings" and "Elegy for Strings":
      RPO conducted by Ainslee Cox, rec. 1975)

Georges Enesco (1881–1955, Rumania)

1. Rumanian Rhapsody No. 1 in A
   a) SO (1947) Vic. 12-0067; DB 6828
   b) SO (1953) LM 1878; PMC 7023
   c) RCA SO (1961) LSC 2471; SB 2130
2. Rumanian Rhapsody No. 2 in D
   SO (1953) LM 1878; PMC 7023

Manuel de Falla (1876–1946, Spain)

1. *"El amor brujo"*
   a) HBSO (1946) (with Nan Merriman, mezzo-soprano) LM 1054; VIC 1043; CDM 1071
   b) PO (1960) (with Shirley Verrett, mezzo-soprano) MS 6147; Y 32368; CBS 61288

   "Ritual Fire Dance" only
   AAYO (1941) Col. 11879-D
2. "Spanish Dance" from *La Vida breve*
   PO (1928) Vic. M-46; DB 1949
3. *Nights in the Gardens of Spain*
   NYPO (1949) (with William Kapell, piano) Opus MLG 71 (pp)
   (coupled with Shostakovich's 1st Piano Concerto: William Kapell with Eugene Ormandy conducting); NYP 821/2 entitled NYPO/WQXR 1982 Radiothon Special Edition—Historic Recordings Vol. II (pp)

Harold Farberman (b. 1929, U.S.A.)

Evolution—Section One
SO (1956) SSAL 8385

César Franck (1822–1890, Belgium)

1. Symphony in D Minor
   a) PO (1927) (with Stokowski's "Outline of Themes") Vic. M-22; D 1404-8
   b) PO (1935) Vic. M-300; DB 3226-31s
   c) HRPO (1970) SPC 21061; PFS 4218
2. Andante from *Grand pièce symphonique* for Organ (orch. O'Connell)
   PO (1937) Vic. 14947
3. *Panis Angelicus* (orch. Stokowski)
   PO (1936) Vic. M-300; DB 3318

Girolamo Frescobaldi (1583–1643, Italy)

"Gagliarda" from Five Gagliards, Book 2 (arr. Stokowski)
- a) PO (1934) Vic. 1985; DA 1606
- b) SO (1952) LM 1721 and LM 1875; ALP 1387
- c) SOA (1958) UAS 8001; PMC 7110

Giovanni Gabrieli (1557–1612, Italy)

1. Canzon Quarti Toni a 15
   Brass Choir (1952) LM 1721

2. "In Ecclesiis Benedicite Domino"
   A Cappella Chorus (1952) (with Brass Choir and Charles Courboin, organ)
   LM 1721

3. Sonata Pian e Forte (transc. Fritz Stein)
   SOA (1958) UAS 8001

Alexander Glazunov (1865–1936, Russia)

1. Violin Concerto in A Minor
   LSO (1972) (with Silvia Marcovici, violin)
   SPC 21090-1; OPFS 3-4 (pp)

2. "Danse Orientale" from *Scènes de ballet*
   PO (1927) Vic. 1335; E 521

Reinhold Glière (1875–1956, Russia)

1. Symphony No. 3 *(Ilya Mourometz)* (ed. Stokowski)
   a) PO (1940) Vic. M-841; LCT 1106
   b) HSO (1956) SP 8402; S-60089

2. "Sailor's Dance" ("Yablochko") from *The Red Poppy*
   a) PO (1934) Vic. 1675; DA 1398
   b) SO (1953) LM 1816; PMC 7026

Christoph Willibald Gluck (1714–1787, Germany)

1. "Dance of the Blessed Spirits" from *Orfeo ed Euridice*
   a) PO (1917) Vic. 6238; LS 3
   b) SO (1958) (arranged for strings and labeled "Reigen") SP 8458

"O Saviour Hear Me" (arr. Norman Luboff, orch. Walter Stott)
NSO (1961) (with the Norman Luboff Choir) LSC 2593

2. Musette and Sicilienne from *Armide*
    SO (1957) SP 8415

3. Lento from *Iphigenie in Aulis*
    SO (1957) SP 8415

Roger Goeb (b. 1914, U.S.A.)

Symphony No. 3
SO (1952) LM 1727; CRI 120

Morton Gould (b. 1913, U.S.A.)

1. "Guaracha" from *Latin-American Symphonette* No. 4
    AAO (1941) Col. 11713-D

2. "Dance Variations"
    SFSO (1953) (with Whittemore and Lowe, duo-pianists) LM 1858

Charles Gounod (1818–1893, France)

"Kermesse Waltz" from *Faust*
PO (1923) Vic. 944; DA 562; LS 3

Percy Grainger (1882–1961, Australia)

"Country Gardens," "Mock Morris," "Shepherds Hey," "Molly on the Shore,"
"Early One Morning," "Irish Tune from County Derry," "Handel in the Strand"
SO (1950) (with Percy Grainger at the piano) LM 1238; 7ER 5046; VRLI-
0168

Enrique Granados (1867–1916, Spain)

Intermezzo from *Goyescas*
SO (1947) LM 9029; DB 6915

Edvard Grieg (1843–1907, Norway)

1. Piano Concerto in A Minor
    HBSO (1945) (with Percy Grainger, piano) IPA 508 (pp)

2. "Anitra's Dance" from *Peer Gynt* Suite No. 1
    PO (1917) Vic. 799; LS 3

Charles Griffes (1884–1920, U.S.A.)

"The White Peacock" from *Roman Sketches*
NYPO (1947) ML 2167

George Frederic Handel (1685–1759, Germany)

1. Messiah—Selections
    LSO (1966) (with Sheila Armstrong, Norma Proctor, Kenneth Bowen,
    John Cameron and LSO Chorus) SPC 21014; PFS 4113; SPA 284

    Pastoral Symphony (arr. Stokowski)
    a) PO (1930) Vic. 7316; D 1938; CAL 120
    b) SO (1947) Vic. 11-9837
2. "Water Music" Excerpts
    a) arr. Harty and Stokowski PO (1934) Vic 8550-1; DB 2528-9
    b) arr. Stokowski RCA SO (1961) LSC 2612; SB 6522; VICS 1513;
       CCV 5002
3. "Music for the Royal Fireworks" (arr. Stokowski)
    RCA SO (1961) LSC 2612; SB 6522; VICS 1513; CCV 5002
4. Overture in D Minor (arr. Stokowski from Concerto Grosso Op. 3 No. 5)
    PO (1935) Vic 1798; DA 1556
5. Concerto in B-flat for Harpsichord and Orchestra Op. 4, No. 6
    NYPO (1949) (with Wanda Landowska, soloist) BWS-720 (pp); NYP 821/2 entitled
    NYPO/WQXR 1982 Radiothon Special Edition—Historic Recordings Vol. II (pp)
6. Largo from Serse
    NSO (1961) (with the Norman Luboff Choir) LSC 2593
7. Tamburino from Alcina
    SO (1958) SP 8458

Lou Harrison (b. 1917, U.S.A.)

Suite for Violin, Piano and Small Orchestra
SO (1952) (with Anahid Ajemian, violin and Maro Ajemian, piano)
LM 1785; CRI SD 114

Franz Joseph Haydn (1732–1809, Austria)

1. Symphony No. 53 (Imperial)
    SO (1949) LM 1073
2. attrib. Haydn
    Andante Cantabile from String Quartet in F Op. 3 No. 5 (arr. Stokowski)
    a) PO (1929) Vic. 7256; D 1864; D 1995 (as "18th Century Dance")
    b) HBSO (1946) Vic. 11-9419; DB 6737; CAL 120 (as "18th Century Dance")
    c) NatPO (1975) Pye 12132; PCNHX 4

Gustav Holst (1874–1934, England)

The Planets Suite
LAPO (1956) (with Women's Voices of the Roger Wagner Chorale)
SP 8389; SMFP 2134; S-60175

Engelbert Humperdinck (1854–1921, Germany)

Hansel and Gretel—
Prelude
SO (1949) LM 2042; DB 21256
"Evening Prayer" (arr. Norman Luboff, orch. Walter Stott)
NSO (1961) (with the Norman Luboff Choir) LSC 2593

Herman Hupfeld (1894–1951, U.S.A.)

"When Yuba Plays the Rhumba on the Tuba Down in Cuba"
NYPO (1949) NYP821/2 (pp) (Young People's Concert)

Jacques Ibert (1890–1962, France)

Escales (Ports of Call)
    a) SO (1951) LM 9029
    b) FNRO (1958) SP 8463; S-60102; SXLP 30263

Mikhail Ippolitov-Ivanov (1859–1935, Russia)

Caucasian Sketches—
    "In the Village"
    a) PO (1925) Vic. 6514
    b) NYPO (1947) Col. MM-729

    "Procession of the Sardar"
    a) PO (1922) Vic. 796
    b) PO (1927) Vic. 1335; E 531; CAL 123; VCM-7101
    c) NatPO (1975) Pye 12132; PCNHX 4

Charles Ives (1874–1954, U.S.A.)

1. Symphony No. 4
    ASO (1965) (with Associate Conductors David Katz and José Serebrier,
    and Members of the Schola Cantorum of New York, Hugh Ross, Director)
    MS 6775; SBRG 72403
2. Four Songs for Chorus and Orchestra—
    "They are There," "Majority (or The Masses)," "An Election,"

"Lincoln, the Great Commoner"
ASO (1967) (with the Gregg Smith Singers and Ithaca College Concert Choir)
Columbia Set M4 32504 ("Charles Ives: The 100th Anniversary")

3. Orchestral Set No. 2
    LSO (1970) (with LSO Chorus) SPC 21060; PFS 4203

4. *Robert Browning* Overture
    ASO (1965) MS 7015; SBRG 72646

Werner Josten (1885–1963, Germany)

1. Concerto *Sacro* I-II
    ASO (1965) (with David del Tredici, piano) CRI SD 200

2. Symphonic Poem *Jungle*
    ASO (1971) CRI SD 267

3. *Canzona Seria* for Flute, Oboe, Clarinet, Bassoon and Piano
    Members of the ASO (1971) (recording supervised by Stokowski)
    CRI SD 267

Francis Scott Key (1779–1843, U.S.A.)

"The Star-Spangled Banner" (arr. Stokowski)
AAYO (1940) Col. 17204-D
Preceded by "Pledge of Allegiance to the Flag"—
Recitation by Goddard Lieberson

Aram Khachaturian (1903–1978, Armenia)

1. Symphony No. 2 *(The Bell)*
    SOA (1958) UAS 8002

2. Symphony No. 3
    CSO (1968) LSC 3067; SB 6804

3. *Masquerade* Suite
    NYPO (1947) ML 4071; P 14137

Zoltan Kodály (1882–1967, Hungary)

1. *Háry János* Suite
    Hungarian State Radio Symphony Orchestra (1967) LS2

2. *Te Deum*
    The American Youth Performs Chorus and Orchestra (1968)
    (with Joyce Mathis, Ivanka Myhal, Arthur Williams and Alan Ord)

Audio Recording EC 68006 (pp) (limited issue)
(Souvenir record sponsored by American Airlines and featuring other conductors and soloists)

Edouard Victor Lalo (1823–1892, France)

Symphonie Espagnole (Movements 1, 2, 4, and 5)
NYPO (1947) (with Jacques Thibaud, violin) BWS 1G1-339 (pp)

Kurt Leimer (1922–c. 1974, Germany)

Piano Concerto No. 4
SOA (1959) (with composer as soloist)
German Electrola C 063-29030

Anatol Liadov (1885–1914, Russia)

1. "Dance of the Amazon"
   PO (1924) Vic. 1112; LS 3
2. "Eight Russian Folk Dances"
   PO (1934) Vic. 8491 and 1681; DB 2443 and DA 1415

Franz Liszt (1811–1886, Hungary)

1. Hungarian Rhapsody No. 1 in F Minor
   NBC (1955) LM 1878; PMC 7023
2. Hungarian Rhapsody No. 2 in C-sharp Minor
   a) PO (1920) Vic. 6236
   b) PO (1926/7) Vic. 6652; D 1296; VCM-7101
   c) PO (1936) (arr. Muller) Vic. 14422; DB 3086
   d) AAO (1941) (arr. Stokowski) Col. 11646-D
   e) NBC (1955) LM 1878; PMC 7023
   f) RCA SO (1961) LSC 2471; SB 2130
3. Hungarian Rhapsody No. 3 in D-flat
   NBC (1955) LM 1878; PMC 7023
4. *Les Preludes*—Symphonic Poem No. 3
   SO (1947) LM 1073

Charles Loeffler (1861–1935, Alsace)

A Pagan Poem
SO (1959) SP 8433; S-60080

Jean Baptiste Lully (1632–1687, France)

1. Prelude from *Alceste*
   PO (1930) Vic. 7424; DB 1587
2. Nocturne from *Le Triomphe de l'amour*
   a) PO (1930) Vic. 7424; DB 1587
   b) SO (1952) LM 1721 and LM 1875
3. Marche from *Thesée*
   a) PO (1930) Vic. 7424; DB 1587
   b) SO (1952) LM 1721 and LM 1875

Gustav Mahler (1860–1911, Bohemia)

1. Symphony No. 2 *(Resurrection)*
   a) LSO (1963) (with Rae Woodland, Janet Baker, BBC Chorus, BBC Choral Society, Goldsmiths' Choral Union and Harrow Choral Society)
   Penzance Records PR 19N (pp)
   b) LSO (1974) (with Margaret Price, Brigitte Fassbaender and LSO Chorus)
   ARL2-0852
2. Symphony No. 8 *(Symphony of a Thousand)*
   NYPO (1950) (with Carlos Alexander, Eugene Conley, Frances Yeend, Martha Lipton, George London, Uta Graf, Camilla Williams, Louise Bernhardt, Westminster Choir, Schola Cantorum and Boys' Chorus from Public School No. 12, Manhattan) Penzance Records PR 19N (pp)

Frank Martin (1890–1974, Switzerland)

Petite Symphonie Concertante
SO (1957) (with Gloria Agostini, harp; Albert Fuller, harpsichord; Mitchell Andrews, piano) SP 8597; WRC SCM 69

Harl McDonald (1899–1955, U.S.A.)

1. Symphony No. 2: Rhumba only
   PO (1935) Vic. 8919; DB 2913; CAL 238
2. Concerto for Two Pianos and Orchestra
   PO (1937) (with Jeanne Behrend and Alexander Kelberine, pianos)
   Vic. M-557; DB 5700-2
3. "Dance of the Workers" from *Festival of the Workers* Suite
   PO (1935) Vic. 8919; DB 2913

4. "Legend of the Arkansas Traveller"
PO (1940) Vic. 18069

Felix Mendelssohn (1809–1847, Germany)

1. Symphony No. 4 *(Italian)*
NatPO (1977) M 34567; CBS 76673
2. Scherzo from *A Midsummer Night's Dream*
a) PO (1917) Vic. 6238
b) PO (1931) BTL-7901
c) AAO (1941) Col. 11983-D

Gian Carlo Menotti (b. 1911, Italy)

Sebastian Ballet Suite
NBC (1954) LM 1858; ARLI-2715

Olivier Messiaen (b. 1908, France)

L'Ascension (Four Symphonic Meditations)
a) NYPO (1947/9) Col. MM-893; ML 4214
b) LSO (1970) SPC 21060; PFS 4203

Claudio Monteverdi (1567–1643, Italy)

Vespro della beata Vergine—excerpts
Illinois University Chorus, Soloists and Orchestra (1952)
Illinois Bookshop Records LP CRS 1 (pp) (Limited Issue)

Wolfgang Amadeus Mozart (1756–1791, Austria)

1. Symphony No. 40: Menuetto only
PO (1919) Vic. 6243; DB 385; LS 3
2. Piano Concerto No. 20
IFYO (1969) (with Maria Isabella di Carli, piano) AVE 30696
3. Piano Concerto No. 21
NYPO (1949) (with Dame Myra Hess, piano) MJA Records 1967-1B (pp) (coupled
with Beethoven's 3rd Piano Concerto: Dame Myra Hess, with Toscanini conducting)
4. Sinfonie Concertante in E-flat, K. Anh. 9
PO (1940) (with Marcel Tabuteau, oboe; Bernard Portnoy, clarinet;
Sol Schoenbach, bassoon; Mason Jones, horn)
Vic. M-760; DB 10118-21; CAL 213
5. Serenade in B-flat for Thirteen Wind Instruments
ASO Wind Players (1966) VSD 71158; WRC ST 898

6. *Don Giovanni* Overture (concert ending by Stokowski)
    NatPO (1976) PCNHX 6
7. Deutsche Tanze No. 3 *(The Sleighride)*
    SO (1949) LM 1238
8. "Turkish March" ("Rondo alla Turca") from Piano Sonata No. 11 in A
    (orch. Stokowski)
    SO (1955) LM 2042

Modeste Mussorgsky (1839–1881, Russia)

1. *Boris Godunov*—Highlights
    SFSO (1952) (with Nicola Rossi-Lemeni and San Francisco Opera Chorus)
    LM 1764; DA 9002

    "Symphonic Synthesis" (arr. Stokowski)
    a) PO (1936) Vic. M-391; DB 3244-6; CAL 140
    b) AAO (1941) Col. M-516
    c) SRO (1968) SPC 21032; PFS 4181
2. "Night on Bare Mountain" (orch. Rimsky-Korsakov and Stokowski)
    a) PO (1939) WDX 101; BVS 101 *(Fantasia* soundtrack)
    b) PO (1940) Vic. 17900; DB 5900; CAL 118; VCM-7101
    c) SO (1953) LM 1816; PMC 7026
    d) LSO (1967) SPC 21026; PFS 4139
3. *Pictures at an Exhibition* (orch. Stokowski)
    ("Tuileries" and "Market Place at Limoges" are omitted)
    a) PO (1939) Vic. M-706; DB 5827-30
    b) AAO (1941) Col. M-511
    c) NPO (1965) SPC 21006; PFS 4095

    orch. Ravel:
    d) PO (1932) Excerpts in stereo and mono—BTL-7901
    e) "The Hut on Fowl's Legs" and "The Great Gate of Kiev" only
       SO (1956) SSAL 8385
4. *Khovantshchina*—
    Entracte Act 4 (Orch. Stokowski)
    a) PO (1922) Vic. 6366; DB 599
    b) PO (1927) Vic. M-53; D 1427
    c) NatPO (1975) Pye 12132; PCNHX 4

    Prelude Act 1, "Dance of the Persian Slaves," Entracte Act 4
    SO (1953) LM 1816; PMC 7026

Carl Nielsen (1865–1931, Denmark)

Symphony No. 2
DRO (1967) (in preparation)

Ottakar Novacek (1866–1900, Hungary)

"Perpetuum Mobile" ("Moto Perpetuo") Op. 5 No. 4 (transc. Stokowski)
  a) PO (1940) Vic. 18069; CAL 123
  b) AAO (1941) Col. 11879-D
  c) NatPO (1976) M 34543; CBS 73589

Jacques Offenbach (1819–1880, Germany)

Barcarolle from *The Tales of Hoffmann* (transc. Stokowski)
HBSO (1945) Vic. 11-9174; DB 10130; CAL 153

Carl Orff (1895–1982, Germany)

Carmina Burana
HSO (1958) (with Virginia Babikian, Clyde Hager, Guy Gardner, the Houston Chorale
and the Houston Youth Symphony Boys Choir)
SP 8470; WRC ST 793; S-60236; CFP 40311

Niccolo Paganini (1782–1840, Italy)

"Moto Perpetuo" Op. 11 (arr. for strings)
SO (1957) SP 8415; SXLP 30174

Giovanni Palestrina (1524–1594, Italy)

1. *Adoramus te* (transc. Stokowski)
   a) PO (1934) Vic. M-963; DA 1606 and DB 6260
   b) SOA (1958) UAS 8001; PMC 7110
   Choral version:
   A Capella Chorus (1952) LM 1721
2. "O Bone Jesu"
   A Capella Chorus (1952) LM 1721

Andrzej Panufnik (b. 1914, Poland)

Universal Prayer
(1970) (with April Cantelo, Helen Watts, John Mitchinson, Roger Stalman; the Louis
Halsey Singers; Nicholas Kynaston, organ; David Watkins, Maria Kochinska and Tina
Bonafacio, harps)
Unicorn RHS 305

Vincent Persichetti (b. 1915, U.S.A.)

March from *Divertimento for Band*
SO (1956) SSAL 8385

Amilcare Ponchielli (1834–1886, Italy)

"The Dance of the Hours" from *La Gioconda*
PO (1939) WDX 101; BVS 101 (*Fantasia* soundtrack)

Francis Poulenc (1899–1963, France)

Concerto *Champêtre*
NYPO (1949) (with Wanda Landowska, harpsichord)
IPL 106-7; Desmar IPA 106-7 (pp)

Serge Prokoviev (1891–1953, Russia)

1. Symphony No. 5
    USSR State Radio Orchestra (1958) MK 1551; BR 14050
2. Symphony No. 6
    NYPO (1949) (previously unissued) First issued on NYP 821/2 entitled NY-PO/WQXR 1982 Radiothon Special Edition—Historic Recordings Vol. II (pp)
3. *Cinderella* Ballet Suite
    NYSSO (1958) SDBR 3016; WRC ST 173
4. *The Love of Three Oranges*—
    "Scene Infernale," "Marche," and "Le Prince et la Princesse"
    NBC (1941) Vic. 18479; DB 6151 and DB 11130
4. *Peter and the Wolf*
    a) AAO (1941) (with Basil Rathbone, narrator) Col. M-477; ML 4038; CL 671
    b) NYSSO (1959) (with Bob Keeshan, narrator)—reverse features "Orchestral Suite" (the music without the narration) SDBR 3043
5. *Romeo and Juliet*—Excerpts from Suites 1, 2, and 3
    NBC (1954) LM 1858; ARL1-2715
6. *The Ugly Duckling*
    NYSSO (1959) (with Regina Resnik, mezzo-soprano)
    SDBR 3108; WRC ST 173

Giacomo Puccini (1858–1924, Italy)

Turandot

New York Metropolitan Opera (1961) (with Birgit Nilsson, Franco Corelli and Anna Moffo) Historical Recordings Enterprises HRE 299-3 (pp)

Henry Purcell (1658–1695, England)

1. "When I Am Laid in Earth" from *Dido and Aeneas* (transc. Stokowski)
   a) SO (1950) LM 1875; ALP 1387
   b) RPO (1975) DSM-1011
2. "Hornpipe" from *King Arthur Suite*
   SO (1958) SP 8458
3. "Trumpet Prelude" (or "Trumpet Voluntary")
   see Jeremiah Clarke

Serge Rachmaninoff (1873–1943, Russia)

1. Symphony No. 3
   NatPO (1975) DSM-1007
2. Piano Concerto No. 2
   a) Second and third movements only
      PO (1924) (with composer as soloist) Vic. 8064-6; DB 747-9; ARM3-0260 (LP transfer including part of unpublished first movement)
   b) PO (1929) (with composer as soloist) Vic. M-58; DB 1333-7; LCT 1014; CSLP 517; ALP 1630; LSB 4011; ARM 3-0296
3. Rhapsody on a Theme of Paganini
   PO (1934) (with composer as soloist) Vic. M-250; DB 2426-8;
   LCT 1118; CSLP 509; LSB 4013; ARM 3-0296
4. "Vocalise"
   a) SO (1953) (orch. composer) LM 2042
   b) SO (1957) (string arrangement) SP 8415; SXLP 30174
   c) ASO (1964) (with Anna Moffo, soprano) (arr. Dubensky) LSC 2795; LSB 4114
   d) NatPO (1975) (orch. composer) DSM-1007
5. Prelude in C-sharp Minor (transc. Stokowski)
   CPO (1972) SPC 21130; PFS 4351 (pp)

Maurice Ravel (1875–1937, France)

1. "Alborado del Gracioso"
   FNRO (1958) SP 8463; S-60102; SXLP 30263
2. *Boléro*
   AAYO (1940) Col. X-174

3. *Daphnis et Chloé* Suite No. 2
    LSO (1970) (with LSO Chorus) SPC 21059; PFS 4220
4. "Fanfare" from *L'Eventail de Jeanne*
    HRPO (1970) SPC 21061; PFS 4218
5. *Rapsodie Espagnole*
    a) PO (1934) Vic. 8282-3; DB 2367-8; CAL 118; DMM4-0341
    b) LSO (1957) SP 8520; S-60104

Ottorino Respighi (1879–1936, Italy)

The Pines of Rome
SOA (1958) UAS 8001; USLP 0005

Silvestre Revueltas (1899–1940, Mexico)

Sensemaya
SO (1947) Vic. 12-0470; DB 6915

Nicolas Rimsky-Korsakov (1844–1908, Russia)

1. *Scheherezade* Symphonic Suite
    a) PO (1927) Vic. M-23; D 1436-40; DMM4-0341
    b) PO (1934) Vic. M-269; DB 2522-7
    c) Philharmonia Orchestra (1951) LM 1732; ALP 1399
    d) LSO (1964) SPC 21005; PFS 4062
    e) RPO (1975) ARL1-1182

    "The Young Prince and Young Princess" (third movement, abridged)
    PO (1921) Vic. 6246

    "Festival at Bagdad" (fourth movement, abridged)
    PO (1919) Vic. 6246
2. *Russian Easter Festival* Overture
    a) PO (1929) Vic. 7018-9; D 1676-7; VCM-7101
    b) NBC (1942) (with Nicolo Moscona, bass) Vic. M-937; DB 6173-4
    c) SO (1953) (with Nicolo Moscona, bass) LM 1816; PMC 7026
    d) CSO (1968) LSC 3067; SB 6804
3. *Capriccio Espagnole*
    NPO (1973) SPC 21117; PFS 4333
4. "Dance of the Tumblers" from *The Snow Maiden*
    PO (1923) Vic. 6431; LS 3
5. "Flight of the Bumble-Bee" from *The Tale of Tsar Sultan*

   a) AAO (1941) Col. 19005-D
   b) NatPO (1976) M 34543; CBS 73589
6. *Ivan the Terrible*—Prelude to Act 3 (concert ending by Stokowski)
   a) PO (1939) Vic. M-717; DB 6039
   b) NatPO (1976) M 34543; CBS 73589

Gioacchino Rossini (1792–1868, Italy)

William Tell Overture
NatPO (1976) PCNHX 6; DA 9003

Camille Saint-Saëns (1835–1921, France)

1. *Carnival of the Animals*
   a) PO (1929) (with M. Montgomery and O. Barabini, pianists) Vic. M-71; D 1992-4
   b) PO (1939) (with Jeanne Behrend and Sylvan Levin, pianists; and Benar Heifetz, cello) Vic. M-785; DB 5942-4; CAL 100 (On side 3 of this set, Saul Caston substituted for Stokowski, and Joseph Levine substituted for Sylvan Levin)
2. "Danse Macabre"
   a) PO (1925) Vic. 6505; D 1121; DMM4-0341
   b) PO (1936) (with Alexander Hilsberg, violin) Vic. 14162; DB 3077; CAL 254; VCM-7101
   c) NatPO (1975) (with Sidney Sax, violin) Pye 12132; PCNHX 4
3. *Samson and Delilah*—Highlights
   NBC (1954) (with Risë Stevens, Jan Peerce, Robert Merrill and the Robert Shaw Chorale) LM 1848; ALP 1308 (The 45 rpm set ERB 49 featured an extra choral number not included on the LP version)

   Bacchanale only
   a) PO (1920) Vic. 6241
   b) PO (1927) Vic 6823; D 1807; VCM-7101

Erik Satie (1866–1925, France)

Gymnopédies (orch. Debussy)
PO (1937) Vic. 1965; DA 1688

Ahmed Saygun (b. 1907, Turkey)

Yunus Emre, an oratorio
SOA (1958) (with the Crane Choir and Potsdam State University Choir)
RW 3967-8 (pp) (limited issue)
(Souvenir record sponsored by the Turkish Embassy's New York Office of Tourism and Information)

Arnold Schoenberg (1874–1951, Austria)

1. *Gurrelieder*
   PO (1932) (with Jeanette Vreeland, Rose Bampton, Paul Althouse, Robert Betts, Abrasha Robofsky, Benjamin de Loache, the Princeton Glee Club, Fortnightly Club and Mendelssohn Club; and with Stokowski's "Outline of Themes") Vic. M-127; DB 1769-82; LCT 6012; AVM2-2017 (pp) (Another performance plus an extended "Outline of Themes" was issued on early LP set LM 127)

   'Song of the Wood-Dove" only
   NYPO (1949) (with Martha Lipton, soprano) ML 2140

2. *Verklärte Nacht (Transfigured Night)*
   a) SO (1952) LM 1739; ALP 1205
   b) SO (1957) SP 8433; S-60080

Franz Schubert (1797–1828, Austria)

1. Symphony No. 8 *(Unfinished)*
   a) PO (1924) Vic. 6459-61; DB 792-4
   b) PO (1927) Vic. M-16; D 1779-81; Parnassus 5; DMM4-0341
   c) AAO (1941) Col. M-485
   d) LPO (1969) SPC 21042; PFS 4197

2. *Rosamunde*—Incidental Music—
   Ballet Music in G Major
   PO (1927) Vic. 1312; CAL 123
   (Another 1927 recording, unissued on 78 rpm, appears in DMM4-0341)

   Overture, Entracte in B-flat Major, and Ballet Music in G Major
   SO (1952) LM 1730; ALP 1193

   Overture only
   NatPO (1976) PCNHX 6; DA 9003

3. "Moment Musicale" Op. 94 No. 3 (orch. Stokowski)
   a) PO (1922) Vic. 799
   b) PO (1927) Vic. 1312; CAL 123; DMM4-0341
   c) HBSO (1945) Vic. 11-9174; DB 10130
   d) LSO (1972) SPC 21130; PFS 4351 (pp)

4. *Tyrolean Dances* (orchestral arrangements)
   (from 16 Deutsche Tanze, Op. 33, and 2 Ecossaises)
   a) PO (1922) (labeled "Viennese Dances") Vic. 74814
   b) SO (1949) LM 1238; HMV 7ER 5043

5. "Ave Maria"
    PO (1939) (with Juliet Novis, soprano, and chorus)
    WDX 101; BVS 101 (*Fantasia* soundtrack)

Robert Schumann (1810–1856, Germany)

1. Symphony No. 2
    SO (1950) LM 1194
2. "Traumerie" (orch. Stokowski)
    AAO (1941) Col. 11982-D

Thomas Scott (1912–1961, U.S.A.)

"From the Sacred Harp"
NYPO (1949) V-Disc 896 (pp) (Limited issue)

Alexander Scriabin (1872–1915, Russia)

1. *Poem of Ecstasy*
    a) PO (1932) Vic. M-125; DB 1706-7
    b) HSO (1959) SDBR 3032
    c) CPO (1972) SPC 21117; PFS 4333 (pp)
2. *Prometheus (The Poem of Fire)*
    a) PO (1932) (with Sylvan Levin, piano, and the Curtis Institute Chorus)
        Vic. M-125; DB 1708-9
        b) PO (1932) Excerpts in stereo—BTL-7901
3. Etude in C-sharp Minor Op. 2 No. 1 (transc. Stokowski)
    ASO (1971) VCS 10095

Dmitri Shostakovich (1906–1975, Russia)

1. Symphony No. 1
    a) PO (1933) Vic. M-192; DB 3847-51s
    b) SOA (1958) UAS 8004
2. Symphony No. 5
    a) PO (1939) Vic. M-619; DB 3991-6
    b) NYSSO (1958) SDBR 3010; WRC ST 281
3. Symphony No. 6
    a) PO (1940) Vic. M-867
    b) CSO (1968) LSC 3133; SB 6839
4. Symphony No. 11 *(The Year 1905)*

HSO (1958) SPBR 8448; SPBO 8700; WRC ST 776-7; Everest 3310-2; S-60228

5. *The Age of Gold* Ballet Suite
   CSO (1968) LSC 3133; SB 6839

6. Prelude No. 14 in E-flat Minor (transc. Stokowski)
   a) PO (1935) Vic. M-192 and M-291; DB 2884
   b) AAO (1940) Col. M-446 and 12903-D
   c) SOA (1958) UAS 8004
   d) NatPO (1976) M 34543; CBS 73589

7. Entracte from *Lady Macbeth of Mtsensk*
   SOA (1958) UAS 8004

Jean Sibelius (1865–1957, Finland)

1. Symphony No. 1
   a) SO (1950) LM 1125; ALP 1210
   b) NatPO (1976) M 34548; CBS 76666

2. Symphony No. 2
   NBC (1954) LM 1854; ALP 1440; DA 9004

3. Symphony No. 4
   PO (1932) Vic. M-160; SRS 3001

4. "Berceuse" from *The Tempest*
   a) PO (1937) Vic. 14726; DB 6009; CAL 123
   b) SO (1950) LM 1238; DB 21334

5. *Finlandia*
   a) PO (1921) Vic. 6366; DB 599
   b) PO (1930) Vic. 7412; DB 1584; CAL 120; VCM-7101
   c) SO (1957) SP 8399; SMFP 2145

6. "The Girl with Roses" from *Swanwhite*
   NYPO (1947) Col. M-806

7. *Swan of Tuonela*
   a) PO (1929) Vic. 7380; D 1997; VCM-7101
   b) SO (1947) (with Mitchell Miller, cor anglais) LM 9029; DB 21555
   c) SO (1957) (with Robert Bloom, cor anglais) SP 8399; SMFP 2145
   d) NatPO (1976) (with Michael Winfield, cor anglais) M 34548; CBS 76666

8. "Valse Triste" from *Kuolema*
   a) PO (1937) Vic. 14726; DB 6009; CAL 123
   b) SO (1949) LM 1238; DB 21334

Bedrich Smetana (1824–1884, Bohemia)

1. *The Bartered Bride* Overture
   RCA SO (1961) LSC 2471; SB 2130
2. "The Moldau" ("Vltava") from *Ma Vlast*
   RCA SO (1961) LSC 2471; SB 2130

John Philip Sousa (1854–1932, U.S.A.)

1. "The Stars and Stripes Forever"
   a) PO (1929) Vic. 1441; E 556
   b) NatPO (1975) (orch. Stokowski) Pye 12132; PCNHX 4
2. "El Capitan"
   PO (1930) Vic. 1441; E 556

William Grant Still (1895–1978, U.S.A.)

Afro-American Symphony: Scherzo only
AAO (1940) Col. 11992-D

Johann Strauss II (1825–1899, Austria)

1. Waltzes from *Die Fledermaus* (transc. Stokowski)
   HBSO (1946) Vic. 10-1310 and ERA 67
2. *Blue Danube* Waltz
   a) PO (1919) Vic. 6237
   b) PO (1926) Vic. 6584; D 1218
   c) PO (1939) (arr. Stokowski) Vic. 15425; DB 3821
   d) SO (1949) Vic. 12-1160; DB 21346
   e) NBC (1955) Vic. 45 rpm ERA 259 (extended version; also on LM 2042
      as "SO." An abridged version, also as "SO," issued on 45 rpm
      447-0780)
   f) SO (1957) (complete) SP 8399; SMFP 2145
3. *Tales from the Vienna Woods*
   a) PO (1926) Vic. 6584; D 1218
   b) PO (1939) (arr. Stokowski) Vic. 15425; DB 3821; CAL 153
   c) SO (1949) Vic. 12-1160; DB 21346
   d) NBC (1955) Vic. 45 rpm ERA 259 (extended version; also on LM 2042
      as "SO." An abridged version, also as "SO," issued on 45 rpm
      447-0780)
   e) NatPO (1975) (complete) Pye 12132; PCNHX 4

Richard Strauss (1864–1949, Germany)

1. "Dance of the Seven Veils" from *Salome*
   a) PO (1921) Vic. 6240; DB 383
   b) PO (1929) Vic. 7259-60; D 1935-6; CAL 254
   c) NYSSO (1958) SDBR 3023; WRC ST 108

2. *Don Juan*
   NYSSO (1958) SDBR 3023; WRC ST 108

3. Gavotte from Suite in B-flat for Wind Instruments
   SO (1956) SSAL 8385

4. *Till Eulenspiegels lustige Streiche*
   NYSSO (1958) SDBR 3023; WRC ST 1088

5. *Tod und Verklärung*
   a) PO (1934) Vic. M-217; DB 2324-6
   b) AAO (1941) Col. M-492
   c) NYCSO (1944) Vic. M-1006; CAL 189; DB 6320-2; LS 5

Igor Stravinsky (1882–1972, Russia)

1. *Firebird* Suite
   a) PO (1924) Vic. 6492-3; DB 841-2
   b) PO (1927) Vic. M-53; one disc (7047) from set issued in UK: D 1427; (Special edition entitled "Centennial Celebration") DPM2-0534 (Limited issue)
   c) PO (1935) Vic. M-291; DB 2882-4
   d) AAO (1941) Col. M-446
   e) NBC (1942) Vic. M-933
   f) SO (1950) LM 9029
   g) BPO (1957) SP 8407; CFP 134; S-60229
   h) LSO (1967) SPC 21032; PFS 4139

2. "Fireworks"
   PO (1922) Vic. 1112; LS 3

3. *L'Histoire du Soldat (The Soldier's Tale)*
   Instrumental Ensemble (1966) (with Madeleine Milhaud, Jean-Pierre Aumont and Martial Singher)—2 versions: in French on VSD 71165, English on VSD 71166 (2-LP Set). French version only issued in UK on WRC ST 859.

   Orchestral Suite from the above (without narration) issued in VSD 707-8

4. "Pastorale" (orch. Stokowski)
   a) PO (1934) Vic. 1998
   b) RPO (1969) SPC 21041; PFS 4189

5. *Petrouchka* Ballet
    a) PO (1937) Vic. M-574; DB 3511-4; CAL 203; (special edition entitled "Centennial Celebration") DPM 2-0534 (Limited issue)
    b) SO (1950) LM 1175; ALP 1240

    Suite only
    a) BPO (1957) SP 8407; CFP 134; S-60229
    b) Budapest Symphony Orchestra (1967). Includes an interview with Stokowski— LS 2 (pp)
6. *The Rite of Spring (Le Sacre du printemps)*
    a) PO (1929/30) Vic. M-74; D 1919-22; (special edition entitled "Centennial Celebration") DPM2-0534 (Limited issue); DA 9005
    b) PO (1939) WDX 101; BVS 101 (abridged: *Fantasia* soundtrack)

Peter Ilyich Tchaikovsky (1840–1893, Russia)

1. Symphony No. 4
    a) PO (1928) Vic. M-48; DB 1793-7
    b) NBC (1941) Vic. M-880
    c) ASO (1971) VCS 10095

    Scherzo only
    SO (1956) SSAL 8385
2. Symphony No. 5
    a) PO (1934) Vic. M-253; DB 2548-53; CAL 201
    b) SO (1953) LM 1780
    c) NPO (1966) SPC 20107; PFS 4219
    d) IFYO (1973) (2-LP set with extracts from final rehearsal) GOCLP 9007

    Andante Cantabile (second movement) only:
    e) PO (1923) Vic. 6430-1
    f) SO (1947) ("Themes," arr. Stokowski, for film *Carnegie Hall*) Vic. 11-9574
3. Symphony No. 6 *(Pathétique)*
    a) AAO (1940) Col. M-432
    b) HBSO (1945) Vic. M-1105; CAL 152
    c) LSO (1973) ARLI-0426

    March-Scherzo (third movement) only:
    PO (1921) Vic. 6242

4. *1812* Overture
    a) PO (1930) Vic. 7499-7500; DB 1663-4
    b) RPO (1969) (with the John Alldis Chorus, Welsh National Opera Chorale and the Band of the Grenadier Guards) SPC 21041; PFS 4189
5. *Francesca da Rimini*
    a) NYPO (1947) ML 4071 and 4381; 33CX 1030; P 14137
    b) NYSSO (1958) SDBR 3011; WRC ST 98
    c) LSO (1974) Philips 6500 921
6. *Hamlet* Fantasy Overture
    NYSSO (1958) SDBR 3011; WRC ST 98
7. *Capriccio Italien*
    a) PO (1929) Vic. 6949-50; DB 6005-6
    b) LPO (1973) Philips 6500 766
8. *Marche Slave*
    a) PO (1925) Vic. 6513; D 1046
    b) HBSO (1945) Vic. 11-9388; CAL 153
    c) LSO (1967) SPC 21026; PFS 4139
    d) LSO (1972) SPC 21090-1; OPFS 3-4 (pp)
9. *Romeo and Juliet* Fantasy Overture
    a) PO (1928) Vic. M-46; DB 1947-9
    b) NYPO (1949) ML 4273 and 4381; 33CX 1030
    c) SRO (1968) SPC 21032; PFS 4181
    (A recording of *Romeo and Juliet* on Everest SDBR 3463 attributed to Stokowski, is in fact spurious.)
10. Serenade for Strings in C Major
    LSO (1974) Philips 6500 921

    Waltz only
    NYPO (1949) Col. MM-898
11. *Nutcracker* Suite
    a) PO (1926) Vic. M-3; D 1214-6
    b) PO (1934) Vic. M-265; DB 2540-2; CAL 100
    c) PO (1939) WDX 101; BVS 101 (abridged: *Fantasia* soundtrack)
    d) SO (1950) LM 9023; ALP 1193; ANL1-2604(e)
    e) LPO (1973) Philips 6500 766

    "Dance of the Flutes"
    PO (1922) Vic. 789

"Dance of the Sugar-Plum Fairy"
SO (1949) Vic. 10-1487

12. *Sleeping Beauty*—Ballet Excerpts
a) SO (1947) LM 1010; ALP 1002
b) NPO (1965) SPC 21008; PFS 4085

"Aurora's Wedding" (Selections—edited by Diaghilev)
c) SO (1953) LM 1774
d) NatPO (1976) M 34560; CBS 76665

13. *Swan Lake*—Ballet Excerpts
"Dance of the Swan Queen" and "Dance of the Little Swans"
SO (1950) LM 1083; ALP 1133; VIC 1020

Acts 2 and 3
NBC (1954/5) LM 1894; ALP 1443; PMC 7007
Selections
NPO (1965) SPC 21008; PFS 4085

14. *Eugene Onegin*—
Polonaise
a) SO (1953) LM 2042
b) LPO (1973) Philips 6500 766

Waltz
LPO (1973) Philips 6500 766

"Tatiana's Letter Scene"
SO (1951) (with Licia Albanese, soprano) LM 142; BLP 1075

15. Andante Cantabile from String Quartet No. 1 (arr. Stokowski)
SO (1958) SP 8458; SXLP 30174

16. "Chant sans Paroles" Op. 40 No. 6 (orch. Stokowski)
a) PO (1924) Vic. 1111
b) PO (1928) Vic. M-71; D 1994
c) LSO (1972) SPC 21130; PFS 4351 (pp)

17. "Humoresque" Op. 10, No. 2 (orch. Stokowski)
a) AAO (1941) Col. 19005-D
b) NBC (1942) Vic. M-933
c) HBSO (1945) Vic. 11-9187; CAL 153
d) SO (1953) LM 1774
e) NatPO (1976) M 34543; CBS 73589

18. "Solitude" ("Again, as before, alone") Op. 73, No. 6 (transc. Stokowski)
    a) PO (1937) Vic. 14947; DB 3255
    b) AAO (1941) Col. 11982-D
    c) HBSO (1945) Vic. 11-9187; CAL 153
    d) SO (1953) LM 1774
    e) NatPO (1975) Pye 12132; PCNHX 4
19. "Pater Noster"
    NSO (1961) (with the Norman Luboff Choir) LSC 2593

Ambroise Thomas (1811–1896, France)
Gavotte from *Mignon*
    a) PO (1923) Vic. 944
    b) PO (1929) Vic. M-116; DB 1643

Virgil Thomson (b. 1896, U.S.A.)
1. *The Plow That Broke the Plains* (Film Music Suite)
    a) HBSO (1946) Vic. M-1116
    b) SOA (1961) VSD 2095 and VSD 707-8
2. *The River* (Film Music Suite)
    SOA (1961) VSD 2095
3. *The Mother of Us All* Suite
    NYPO (1950) (previously unissued)
    First issued on NYP 821/2 entitled NYPO/WQXR 1982 Radiothon Special Edition
    —Historic Recordings Vol. II (pp)

Joaquin Turina (1882–1949, Spain)
La Oracion del Torero (arranged for string orchestra)
SO (1958) SP 8458; SXLP 30174

Ralph Vaughan Williams (1872–1958, England)
1. Symphony No. 6 (original version)
    NYPO (1949) ML 4214; CBS 61432
2. Symphony No. 8: Scherzo only
    SO (1956) SSAL 8385
3. Fantasia on *Greensleeves*
    NYPO (1949) Col. MM-838; BM 13
4. Fantasia on a Theme of Thomas Tallis

a) SO (1952) LM 1739; ALP 1205
b) RPO (1975) DSM-1011
(A recording of Vaughan Williams's *Wasps* Overture on Everest SDBR 3327, attributed to Stokowski, is in fact spurious.)

Heitor Villa-Lobos (1887–1959, Brazil)

1. *Bachianas Brasileiras* No. 1: "Modinha" only
   NYSSO (1958) SDBR 3016; WRC ST 173

2. *Bachianas Brasileiras* No. 5
   a) SO (1951) (with Licia Albanese, soprano) LM 142; BLP 1075
   b) ASO (1964) (with Anna Moffo, soprano) LSC 2795; LSB 4114

3. Symphonic Poem *Uirapurú*
   NYSSO (1958) SDBR 3016

Antonio Vivaldi (1675–1741, Italy)

1. Concerto Grosso No. 11 in D Minor (orch. Stokowski)
   a) PO (1934) Vic. 14113-4; DB 6047-8
   b) SO (1952) LM 1721
   Original Instrumentation:
   c) SO (1967) BGS 70696 and VSD 707-8

2. *The Four Seasons*
   NPO (1966) (with Hugh Bean, violin) SPC 21015; PFS 4124

Richard Wagner (1813–1883, Germany)

Music from *The Ring of the Nibelungen:*

1. *Das Rheingold*—Excerpts (arr. Stokowski)
   PO (1933) Vic. M-179; DB 1976-8

   "Entrance of the Gods into Valhalla"
   a) SOA (1960) (with Chorus) LSC 2555; SB 2148; VICS 1301
   b) LSO (1966) SPC 21016; PFS 4116

2. *Die Walküre*—Excerpts (arr. Stokowski)
   PO (1934) (with Lawrence Tibbett, baritone) Vic. M-248; DB 2470-3

   "The Ride of the Valkyries"
   a) PO (1921) Vic. 6245; DB 387
   b) PO (1932) Partially in stereo—BTL8001
   c) SOA (1960) (with Martina Arroyo, Carlotta Ordassy, Doris Yarick,
      Betty Allen, Doris Okerson, Regina Sarfaty, Shirley Verrett,

Louise Parker) LSC 2555; SB 2148; VICS 1301
d) LSO (1966) SPC 21016; PFS 4116

"Wotan's Farewell and Magic Fire Music"
a) PO (1921) Vic. 6245; DB 387
b) PO (1932) 90-second gap near beginning—partially in stereo—BTL8001
c) NYPO (1947) ML 2153; 33C 1026
d) HSO (1960) SDBR 3070; WRC TP 79

"Magic Fire Music"
a) PO (1939) Vic. 15800; DB 3942 and DB 6024; CAL 120; VCM-7101
b) RPO (1973) ARL1-0498

3. *Siegfried*—Excerpts
PO (1936) (with Frederick Jagel and Agnes Davis) Vic. M-441; DB 3678-80s

"Forest Murmurs" ("Waldweben")
a) PO (1932) BTL8001
b) HBSO (1946) Vic. 11-9418; DB 21238; CAL 153
c) LSO (1966) SPC 21016; PFS 4116

4. *Götterdämmerung*—Excerpts
"Siegfried's Rhine Journey, Death and Funeral Music; Brunnhilde's Immolation"
PO (1933) (with Agnes Davis, soprano) Vic. M-188; DB 2126-30

"Siegfried's Rhine Journey and Funeral Music"
a) NYPO (1949) ML 4273
b) LSO (1966) SPC 21016; PFS 4116
c) LSO (1974) ARL1-1317

"Siegfried's Funeral Music"
PO (1932) BTL 8001

"Immolation Scene" (orchestral version by Stokowski)
a) PO (1932) Includes an excerpt of a speech by Stokowski to the audience—
   BTL 8001
b) LSO (1974) ARL1-1317

"Closing Scene"
PO (1927) Vic. 6625; D 1227

Other Works:

5. *Flying Dutchman* Overture
NYPO (1949) (previously unissued) First issued on Columbia LP BM 39

entitled "New York Philharmonic: A Tradition of Greatness"
(Special Festival Edition, 1980) (Limited issue)

6. *Lohengrin*
   Prelude to Act 1
   a) PO (1924) Vic. 6490; DB 839
   b) PO (1927) Vic. 6791; D 1463; CAL 120
   Prelude to Act 3
   PO (1940) Vic. M-731; DB 5853 and DB 6041

7. *Die Meistersingers von Nürnberg*
   Prelude to Act 1
   a) PO (1936) Vic. M-731; DB 5852-3 and DB 6040-1
   b) LSO (1972) SPC 21090-1; OPFS 3-4 (pp)

   Prelude to Act 3
   PO (1931) Vic. 1584; DA 1291
   Prelude to Act 3, "Dance of the Apprentices," "Entry of the Masters"
   RPO (1973) ARL1-0498

8. *Parsifal*
   Prelude to Act 1
   PO (1936) Vic. M-421; DB 3269-72; CAL 163

   "Symphonic Synthesis" of Act 3 (arr. Stokowski)
   a) PO (1934) Vic. 8617-8; DB 2272-3
   b) SO (1952) LM 1730; LS 5
   c) HSO (1959) SDBR 3031; WRC TP 79

   "Good Friday Music"
   a) PO (1936) Vic. M-421; DB 3269-72; CAL 163
   b) SO (1952) LM 1730 (erroneously labeled "Prelude to Act 1"); LS 5
   c) HSO (1959) SDBR 3031; WRC TP 79

   Excerpts from the first U.S. broadcast of *Parsifal*
   PO (1933) (with Nelson Eddy, Rose Bampton, Robert Steel, etc.)
   Unique Opera Records UORC-280-C/D (Limited issue in very poor sound) (pp)

9. *Rienzi* Overture
   a) PO (1919) Vic. 6239; DB 382
   b) PO (1927) Vic. 6624-5; D 1226-7; GOCLP 9009(H)
   c) NYPO (1947) ML 2153; 33C 1026
   d) RPO (1973) ARL1-0498

10. *Tannhäuser*
    Overture
    PO (1921) Vic. 6244 and 6478; LS3

    Overture and Venusberg Music
    a) PO (1929/30) Vic. M.78; D 1905–7
    b) PO (1937) (with Chorus) Vic. M-530; DB 3775-7
    c) SO (1950) (with Chorus) LM 1066
    d) SOA (1960/61) (with Chorus) LSC 2555; SB 2148; VICS 1301

    "Fest March" Act 2
    PO (1924) Vic. 6478; LS3

    Prelude to Act 3
    a) PO (1936) Vic. M-530; DB 3254-5
    b) SO (1950) Vic. DM-1383

    "Pilgrim's Chorus" (arr. Norman Luboff, orch. Walter Stott)
    NSO (1961) (with the Norman Luboff Choir) LSC 2593

11. *Tristan and Isolde*
    Prelude, "Liebesnacht" and "Liebestod" ("Symphonic Synthesis")
    a) PO (1932) Vic. M-154; DB 1911-4
    b) PO (1935/7) Vic. M-508; sides 4-9 only issued in UK: DB 3087-9 (This set
    originally ended with the Act 2 finale after the "Liebestod" but in 1939 the
    more conventional Act 3 ending was recorded and substituted.)
    c) SO (1950) LM 1174

    Prelude and "Liebestod" (conventional concert version)
    RPO (1973) ARL1-0498

    "Love Music from Acts 2 and 3"
    ("Liebesnacht, Liebestod" and Act 3 Finale) (arr. Stokowski)
    a) AAO (1940) Col. M-427
    b) PO (1960) MS 6147; CBS 61288

    Prelude to Act 3
    SOA (1961) (with Henry Schuman, cor anglais)
    LSC 2555; SB 2148; VICS 1301

    "Liebestod" only
    PO (1931) BTL-7901

12. *Wesendonck Lieder*
    a) "Im Treibhaus," "Schmerzen" and "Traume" only ("Three Deathless Songs")
       PO (1940) (with Helen Traubel, soprano) Vic. M-872; DMM4-0341

b) Complete—Five Songs
SO (1947) (with Eileen Farrell, soprano) LM 1066; AVM1-1413

Ben Weber (1916–1979, U.S.A.)

Symphony on Poems of William Blake
SO (1950) (with Warren Galjour, baritone) LM 1785; CRI 120

Carl Maria von Weber (1786–1826, Germany)

Invitation to the Dance (orch. Berlioz and Stokowski)
    a) PO (1919) (orch. Weingartner) Vic. 6237; LS 3
    b) PO (1927) Vic. 6643; D 1285; LS 1
    c) PO (1931) BTL-7901
    d) PO (1937) Vic. 15189; DB 3699; CAL 123
    e) AAO (1940) Col. 11481-D
    f) SO (1950) LM 1083; ALP 1133; VIC 1020

Miscellaneous:

Native Brazilian Music
    Volume 1—Columbia Set C-83
    Volume 2—Columbia Set C-84
    By Brazilian Artists, recorded under the personal supervision of Stokowski.

Pablo Casals (1876–1973, Spain)

O Vos Omnes (transcribed for Brass Ensemble by Leopold Stokowski)
Recorded 1979 by the Philip Jones Brass Ensemble on Argo ZRG 912

Edward Johnson
London
June 1982

Various First
Performances

Abbreviations:

WP	World Premiere
US	First performance in the United States
UK	First performance in the United Kingdom
AAYO	All-American Youth Orchestra
ASO	American Symphony Orchestra
HSO	Houston Symphony Orchestra
NBC	NBC Symphony Orchestra
PO	Philadelphia Orchestra
NYPO	New York Philharmonic
SO	Leopold Stokowski and His Symphony Orchestra
SOA	Symphony of the Air

AMIROV, Fikret
 Azerbaijan Mugam (US)—HSO—16 March 1959
 Azerbaijan, Symphonic Suite (US)—NYPO—3 March 1960
AMFITEATROV, Daniele
 De Profundis Clamavi (WP)—NBC—20 February 1944
ANTHEIL, George
 Heroes of Today (WP)—Hollywood Bowl Symphony Orchestra—15 July 1945
 Symphony No. 4 (WP)—NBC—13 February 1944

1040

ARBÓS, Enrique Fernández
Guajiras (US)—PO—28 November 1913

ATTERBERG, Kurt
Symphony No. 2 (US)—PO—5 December 1924
Symphony No. 4 (US)—PO—11 March 1927

AUBERT, Louis
Offrande (US)—NYPO—17 November 1949

AVSHALOMOV, Jacob
The Taking of T'ung Kuan (WP)—Detroit Symphony Orchestra—20 November 1952

BARLOW, Samuel L. M.
Babar (WP)—PO—23 November 1936

BARTH, Hans
Quartertone Piano Concerto (WP)—PO; composer at piano—28 March 1930

BAUER, Marion
"Sun Splendor" (revised version) (WP)—NYPO—25 October 1947

BENDER, Natasha
"San Luis Rey" (WP)—AAYO—4 June 1941
"Soliloquy" for Oboe and Orchestra (WP)—HSO—18 March 1957

BEN-HAIM, Paul
Piano Concerto (US)—ASO; Amiram Rigai, piano—11 November 1963

BENNETT, Robert Russell
Abraham Lincoln Symphony (WP)—PO—24 October 1931

BERG, Alban
Wozzeck (US)—PO—19 March 1931

BERGER, Theodor
Malinconia (US)—Pacific Coast Music Festival Orchestra—11 September 1955

BLISS, Sir Arthur
Introduction and Allegro (US)—PO—19 October 1928
Melée Fantasque (US)—PO—27 February 1925

BRAUNFELS, Walter
Fantastic Variations (US)—PO—14 October 1921

BRIAN, Havergal
Symphony No. 28 (WP)—New Philharmonia Orchestra—5 October 1973

BROOKS, Ernest
Three Units (WP)—PO—20 April 1933

BRUCH, Max
  Concerto for Two Pianos and Orchestra (WP)—PO; Rose and Ottilie Sutro, duo-pianists—29 December 1916

BUSONI, Ferruccio
  Indian Fantasy (US)—PO; composer at piano—19 February 1915

CARPENTER, John
  Carmel Concerto (WP)—NYPO—20 November 1949
  A Pilgrim Vision (WP)—PO—26 November 1920

CARRILLO, Julián
  Concertino (WP)—PO—4 March 1927
  Horizontes (WP)—Pittsburgh Symphony Orchestra—30 November 1951
  Sonido 13 (WP)—Mexico City—2 January 1931

CHASINS, Abram
  Piano Concerto No. 2 (WP)—PO; composer at piano—3 March 1933

CHÁVEZ, Carlos
  HP (Horsepower) (staged) (US)—PO—31 March 1932

CHOU, Wen-chung
  "To a Wayfarer" (WP)—SO—3 December 1958

COPLAND, Aaron
  Dance Symphony (WP)—PO—15 April 1931

COPPOLA, Piero
  Burlesque (US)—PO—25 April 1930

COWELL, Henry
  Concerto for Koto and Orchestra (WP)—PO; Kimio Eto, koto—18 December 1964
  Hymn and Fuguing Tune No. 10 (WP)—Pacific Coast Music Festival Orchestra—10 September 1955
  Pastoral and Fiddler's Delight (WP)—AAYO—26 July 1940
  Symphony No. 6 (WP)—HSO—14 November 1955
  Symphony No. 12 (WP)—HSO—28 March 1960
  Synchrony (US)—PO—1 April 1932
  Tales of Our Countryside (WP)—AAYO; composer at piano—11 May 1941
  Variations for Orchestra (WP)—HSO—2 November 1959

DAVIES, Sir Henry Walford
  Parthenia Suite (US)—PO—1 November 1912
  A Solemn Melody (US)—PO—13 February 1920

DAWSON, William
Negro Folk Symphony (WP)—PO—16 November 1934

DUBENSKY, Arcady
Concerto Grosso (WP)—NYPO—3 November 1949
Fugue for 18 Violins (WP)—PO—1 April 1932
The Raven (WP)—PO; Benjamin de Loache, speaker—9 December 1932
Tom Sawyer Overture (WP)—PO—29 November 1935

EICHHEIM, Henry
Bali (WP)—PO—20 April 1933

EL-DABH, Halim
Fantasia-Tahmeel (WP)—SO—3 December 1958

ELGAR, Sir Edward
Symphony No. 2 (US)—Cincinnati Symphony Orchestra—24 November 1911

ENESCO, Georges
Second Orchestral Suite (US)—PO—19 February 1926

ESPLÁ, Oscar
Don Quijote velando las armas (US)—HSO—10 April 1956

FALLA, Manuel de
El amor brujo (US)—PO—15 April 1922

FITCH, Theodore
Terra Nova (WP)—NYPO—31 March 1949

FITELBERG, Gregor
Polish Rhapsody (US)—PO—4 November 1921

FULEIHAN, Anis
Concerto for Theremin (WP)—New York City Symphony Orchestra—26 February 1945

GASTYNE, Serge de
Atala (WP)—HSO—3 November 1958

GLANVILLE-HICKS, Peggy
Letters from Morocco (WP)—SO; William Hess, tenor—22 February 1953

GLIÈRE, Reinhold
Symphonic Poem, *Sirenen* (US)—Cincinnati Symphony Orchestra—31 January 1910

GOEB, Roger
Symphony No. 3 (WP)—CBS Symphony Orchestra—27 April 1952

GOULD, Morton
Chorale and Fugue in Jazz (WP)—PO—2 January 1936

GRETCHANINOFF, Alexander
  Symphony No. 5 (WP)—PO—5 April 1939
GRIEG, Edvard
  The Bell (US)—SO—1 April 1954
GRIFFES, Charles Tomlinson
  "Bacchanale" (WP)—PO—19 December 1919
  "Clouds" (WP)—PO—19 December 1919
  "Notturno" (WP)—PO—19 December 1919
  "The White Peacock" (WP)—PO—19 December 1919
GUTCHË, Gene
  Genghis Khan (WP)—ASO—23 March 1969
HAIEFF, Alexei
  Concerto for Piano (WP)—CBS Symphony Orchestra; Leo Smit, piano—
    27 April 1952
HARRISON, Lou
  Suite for Violin, Piano and Small Orchestra (US)—SO; Anahid Ajemian, violin, and
    Maro Ajemian, piano—28 October 1952
HAUSEGGER, Siegmund von
  Symphonic Poem, *Wieland der Schmied* (US)—PO—17 October 1913
HEIDEN, Bernhard
  Memorial (WP)—SOA—4 October 1956
HELPS, Robert
  Adagio for Orchestra (WP)—SOA—4 October 1956
HENZE, Hans Werner
  Quattro Poemi (WP)—Frankfurt Radio Symphony Orchestra—31 May 1955
HINDEMITH, Paul
  Nusch-Nuschi Tanze (US)—PO—14 November 1924
HOLMES, Paul
  Fable (WP)—HSO—10 April 1956
HOVHANESS, Alan
  Ad Lyram (WP)—HSO—12 March 1957
  Meditation on Orpheus (WP)—HSO—20 October 1958
  Meditation on Zeami (WP)—ASO—5 October 1964
  Mysterious Mountain (WP)—HSO—31 October 1955
  Praise the Lord with Psaltery (WP)—ASO—22 December 1968

Symphony No. 3 (WP)—SOA—14 October 1956
Vision from High Rock (WP)—Detroit Symphony Orchestra—17 February 1955

IGLESIAS, Antonio
The First Adventure of Don Quixote (US)—San Antonio Symphony Orchestra—
16 December 1950

ILLIASHENKO, Andre
Suite de Danses Antiques (US)—PO—16 April 1927

IVANOV-RADKEVITCH, Nicolay
Russian Overture (US)—NYPO—13 November 1949

IVES, Charles
Orchestral Set No. 2 (UK)—London Symphony Orchestra—18 June 1970
Robert Browning Overture (WP)—SOA—14 October 1956
Symphony No. 4 (WP)—ASO—26 April 1965

JOHANSEN, David Monrad
Voluspaa (Excerpt)—Epic Poem for Orchestra and Chorus (US)—SO—1 April 1954

KHACHATURIAN, Aram
Festive Poem (WP)—HSO—28 November 1955
Russian Fantasy (US)—NYPO—1 April 1948
Symphony No. 3 (US)—Chicago Symphony Orchestra—15 February 1968

KHRENNIKOV, Tikhon
Symphony No. 1 (US)—PO—20 November 1936

KIRCHNER, Leon
Toccata for Strings, Winds, and Percussion (WP)—SOA—4 October 1956

LEIGHTON, Kenneth
Primavera Romana (WP)—Royal Philharmonic Orchestra—4 August 1951

LEIMER, Kurt
Piano Concerto No. 4 (WP)—SOA; composer at piano—14 October 1956

LIEBERMANN, Rolf
Furioso (WP)—Dallas Symphony Orchestra—9 December 1950
Suite on Swiss Folk Melodies (US)—NYPO—16 October 1949

LEVIDIS, Dimitri
Poème Symphonique pour solo d'Ondes Musicales (Martenot) et Orchestre (US)—PO
—12 December 1930

LOURIÉ, Arthur
Sinfonia Dialectica (WP)—PO—17 April 1931

MAHLER, Gustav
Das Lied von der Erde (US)—PO; Tilly Koenen, contralto; Johannes Sembach, tenor—
15 December 1916
Symphony No. 8 (US)—PO—2 March 1916

MALIPIERO, Gian-Francesco
Pause del silenzio (WP)—PO—1 April 1927

MARTINU, Bohuslav
Piano Concerto No. 4 (Incantation) (WP)—SOA; Rudolf Firkušný, piano—
4 October 1956

MASON, Daniel Gregory
Symphony No. 1 (WP)—PO—18 February 1916

MAYER, William
Octagon (WP)—ASO; William Masselos, piano—21 March 1971

McDONALD, Harl
Concerto for Two Pianos (WP)—PO; Jeanne Behrend and Alexander Kelberine, duo-
pianists—2 April 1937
Symphony No. 1 (Santa Fe Trail) (WP)—PO—16 November 1934
Symphony No. 2 (Rhumba Symphony) (WP)—PO—4 October 1935
Festival of the Workers (WP)—PO—26 April 1934

McPHEE, Colin
Nocturne (WP)—SO—3 December 1958

MEDTNER, Nikolai
Piano Concerto No. 1 (US)—PO; composer at piano—31 October 1924

MENGELBERG, Kurt Rudolf
Scherzo Sinfonico (US)—PO—16 April 1927

MENOTTI, Gian Carlo
Triple Concerto (WP)—ASO—6 September 1970

MESSIAEN, Oliver
Awakening of the Birds (US)—HSO—23 January 1956
Hymne pour grand Orchestre (WP)—NYPO—13 March 1947
Trois Petites Liturgies de la Présence Divine (US)—NYPO—17 November 1949

MIASKOVSKY, Nikolai
Slavic Rhapsody (US)—NYPO—20 October 1949
Symphony No. 5 (US)—PO—2 January 1926
Symphony No. 6 (US)—PO—26 November 1926
Symphony No. 10 (US)—PO—4 April 1930

MOE, Sharon
"Fanfare" (WP)—ASO—26 March 1972

MOERAN, Ernest
In the Mountain Country (US)—NYPO—27 January 1949

MONTEMEZZI, Italo
My Italy (US)—Hollywood Bowl Symphony Orchestra—30 July 1946

NORDOFF, Paul
Fugue (WP)—PO—9 April 1937

ORFF, Carl
A Midsummer Night's Dream (staged) (US)—SOA—19 July 1956
Nänie und Dithyrambe (US)—HSO—11 November 1957
Trionfo di Afrodite (US)—HSO—2 April 1956

ORNSTEIN, Leo
Piano Concerto No. 2 (WP)—PO; composer at piano—13 February 1925

PADEREWSKI, Ignace Jan
Symphony in B Minor (US)—PO—15 January 1915

PANUFNIK, Andrzej
Epitaph for the Victims of Katyn (US)—ASO—17 November 1968
Sinfonia Elegiaca (US)—HSO—21 January 1957
Symphony for Peace (US)—Detroit Symphony Orchestra—17 February 1955
Universal Prayer (WP)—New York—24 May 1970

PONCE, Manuel
Chapultepec (US)—PO—16 November 1934

PORRINO, Ennio
Symphonic Poem, *Sardegna* (US)—NYPO—5 November 1949

PROKOFIEV, Sergei
Alexander Nevsky (US)—NBC—7 March 1943
Le Pas d'Acier (staged) (US)—PO—10 April 1931
Symphony No. 6 (US)—NYPO—24 November 1949

RABAUD, Henri
Symphony No. 2 (US)—PO—24 October 1913

RACHMANINOFF, Sergei
Piano Concerto No. 4 (WP)—PO; composer at piano—18 March 1927
Rhapsody on a Theme of Paganini (WP)—PO; composer at piano—7 November 1934
Symphony No. 3 (WP)—PO—6 November 1936

The Bells (US)—PO—6 February 1920

Three Russian Folk Songs (dedicated to Stokowski) (WP)—PO—18 March 1927

RAVEL, Maurice

Concerto in G for Piano and Orchestra (US; presented simultaneously by the Boston Symphony Orchestra and Jesús María Sanromá, pianist, with Serge Koussevitzky conducting)—PO; Sylvan Levin, pianist—4 November 1932

RICE, William

Concerto for Winds and Percussion (WP)—HSO—30 October 1956

RIEGGER, Wallingford

Study in Sonority (WP)—PO—30 October 1929

Symphony No. 3 (UK)—Royal Philharmonic Orchestra—27 May 1951

RIMSKY-KORSAKOV, Nikolai

Invisible City of Kitezh (Excerpts) (US)—PO—26 October 1923

ROUSSEL, Albert

Evocation No. 2 (US)—PO—2 January 1914

RUGGLES, Carl

Organum (WP)—NYPO—24 November 1949

SAINT-SAËNS, Camille

"Marche héroïque" (US)—PO—24 March 1920

SAYGUN, Ahmed Adnan

Yunus Emre, an oratorio (US)—SOA—25 November 1958

SCHELLING, Ernest

A Victory Ball (WP)—PO—23 February 1923

SCHMITT, Florent

Rapsodie Viennoise (US)—PO—28 November 1913

SCHOENBERG, Arnold

Die Glückliche Hand (staged) (US)—PO—11 April 1930

Gurrelieder (US)—PO—8 April 1932

Kammersymphonie (US)—PO—5 November 1915

Piano Concerto (WP)—NBC; Eduard Steuermann, piano—6 February 1944

Variations for Orchestra (US)—PO—18 October 1929

Violin Concerto (WP)—PO; Louis Krasner, violin—6 December 1940

SCOTT, Cyril

Piano Concerto (US)—PO; composer at piano—5 November 1920

SCRIABIN, Alexander

Symphony No. 3 *(Divine Poem)* (US)—PO—19 November 1915

SEREBRIER, José
Poema Elegiaco (WP)—ASO—7 October 1963
Sinfonia No. 1 (WP)—HSO—4 November 1957

SHCHEDRIN, Rodion
Suite from *The Humpback Horse* (US)—HSO—18 November 1957

SHILKRET, Nathaniel
Concerto for Trombone and Orchestra (WP)—New York City Symphony Orchestra;
Tommy Dorsey, trombone—15 February 1945

SHOSTAKOVICH, Dmitri
Piano Concerto No. 1 (US)—PO; Eugene List, piano—12 December 1934
Symphony No. 1 (US)—PO—2 November 1928
Symphony No. 3 (US)—PO—30 December 1932
Symphony No. 6 (US)—PO—29 November 1940
Symphony No. 11 (US)—HSO—7 April 1958

SIBELIUS, Jean
Song of the Earth (US)—HSO—6 December 1955
Symphony No. 5 (US)—PO—21 October 1921
Symphony No. 6 (US)—PO—23 April 1926
Symphony No. 7 (US)—PO—3 April 1926

SIEGMEISTER, Elie
Prairie Legend (WP)—NYPO—18 January 1947
Symphony No. 1 (WP)—NYPO—30 October 1947

STEINERT, Alexander
Rhapsody for Clarinet and Orchestra (WP)—Hollywood Bowl Symphony Orchestra—
22 July 1945

STILL, William Grant
Symphony in G Minor (WP)—PO—10 December 1937

STRAUSS, Richard
Alpine Symphony (US)—PO—28 April 1916 (sneak preview with the Cincinnati
Symphony Orchestra conducted by Ernst Kunwald on 27 April 1916)

STRAVINSKY, Igor
Le Sacre du printemps (US)—PO—3 March 1922
Le Sacre du printemps (staged) (US)—PO—11 April 1930
Les Noces (US)—New York—14 February 1926
Les Noces (staged) (US)—New York—25 April 1929
Oedipus Rex (staged) (US)—PO—10 April 1931

Song of the Nightingale (US)—PO—19 October 1923
Symphonies of Wind Instruments (US)—PO—23 November 1923

SZYMANOWSKI, Karol
Symphony No. 3 (Song of the Night) (US)—PO—19 November 1926
Violin Concerto No. 1 (US)—PO; Angel Reyes, violin—18 November 1924

TANSMAN, Alexander
Ouverture symphonique (US)—PO—12 April 1929

THOMSON, Virgil
Shipwreck and Love Scene from Byron's Don Juan (WP)—NYPO—11 April 1968

TIPPETT, Michael
"Ritual Dances" from *The Midsummer Marriage* (US)—HSO—5 November 1956

VARÈSE, Edgar
Amériques (WP)—PO—9 April 1926
Arcana (WP)—PO—8 April 1927

VAUGHAN WILLIAMS, Ralph
Symphony No. 9 (US)—SO—25 September 1958

VILLA-LOBOS, Heitor
Dansas Caracteristicas de Indios Africanos (US)—PO—23 November 1928

WEBER, Ben
Symphony on Poems of William Blake (WP)—SO; Warren Galjour, baritone—
28 October 1952

WEBERN, Anton von
Passacaglia (US)—PO—4 March 1927

WEIGL, Karl
Symphony No. 5 (WP)—ASO—27 October 1968

WEILL, Kurt
Lindbergh's Flight (US)—PO—4 April 1931

WIDOR, Charles-Marie
Symphony No. 6 (US)—PO—27 March 1919

ZEMACHSON, Arnold
Chorale and Fugue in D Minor (WP)—PO—21 November 1930

Acknowledgment is made to others who have compiled information on premieres: Herbert
Kupferberg, Edward Johnson, Preben Opperby, Howard Shanet, Nancy Shear, and
Nicolas Slonimsky.

Leopold Stokowski Orchestral Transcriptions

ALBENIZ	"Fête Dieu à Seville" (March 1925)
BACH, J. S.	Adagio from the Toccata and Fugue in C Major (28 April 1933)
	Andante Sostenuto from the Sonata No. 3 in A Minor for Violin
	Aria from the Overture-Suite in D Major (30 November 1923)
	Arioso from Concerto for Harpsichord in F Minor (22 November 1940)
	"Aus der Tiefe rufe ich," Chorale Prelude (28 March 1924)
	"Aus Tiefer Not," Chorale Prelude
	Bourrée from the English Suite in A Minor (10 January 1936)
	Chaconne in D Minor from the Partita for Violin (19 December 1930)
	Chorale from the Easter Cantata
	"Christ lag in Todesbanden," Chorale Prelude (15 March 1931)
	"Ein' feste Burg ist unser Gott," Chorale Prelude (6 October 1933)
	"Es ist Vollbracht" from *Saint John Passion* (13 November 1914)
	Fantasia and Fugue in G Minor

Fugue in C Minor *Well-Tempered Clavier* (7 October 1932)

Fugue in G Minor (The Greater) (30 December 1926)

Fugue in G Minor (The Lesser) (12 December 1930)

"Ich hatte viel Bekummernis" Cantata No. 21

"Ich ruf' zu dir" Cantata No. 177 (30 December 1926)

"Jesus Joy of Man's Desiring" Cantata No. 147

"Komm süsser Tod" (3 March 1933) Schemelli's *Gesang Buch*

"Mein Jesu" from Schemelli's *Gesang Buch* (16 April 1937)

"My Soul is Athirst" from *St. Matthew Passion* (16 April 1937)

"Nun komm, der Heiden Heilland" Cantata No. 62 (9 October 1931)

Passacaglia and Fugue in C Minor (10 February 1922)

Prelude in B Minor, *Well-Tempered Clavier* (April 8 1927)

Prelude in E-flat Minor, *Well-Tempered Clavier* (8 April 1927)

Prelude and Fugue in E Minor, *Well-Tempered Clavier* (10 December 1937)

Prelude from the Partita in E Major

Sarabande from the Partita in B Minor

Sarabande in C Minor from Partita No. 1

Sarabande in G Minor, English Suite No. 3

"Sheep May Safely Graze" from the *Birthday Cantata*

"Shepherds Christmas Music" from the *Christmas Oratorio*

"Wachet auf" ("Sleepers Awake"), Cantata No. 140 (22 November 1940)

Wir glauben all' an einen Gott, Chorale Prelude (28 March 1924)

BEETHOVEN	*Moonlight* Sonata (first movement)
BIZET	"Spanish Dance"
BOCCHERINI	Minuet (String Quintet in E Major)
BORODIN	"Dances of the Polovetzki Maidens" from *Prince Igor*
	Requiem
BRAHMS	Hungarian Dances No. 1 in A Minor
	Songs: "Die Mainacht," "Feldeinsamkeit," "Immer Leiser

	wird mein Schlummer," "Kommt dir Manchmal in den Sinn," "Lerchengesang," "Liebstreu," "Nicht mehr zu dir zu gehen"
BUXTEHUDE	Sarabande and Courante
BYRD	Pavane and Gigue from the *Fitzwilliam Virginal Book*
CESTI	*Tu mancavi a tormentarmi crudelissima speranza*
CHARPENTIER	Passacaille from *Medee*
CHOPIN	Mazurkas: No. 13 in A Minor; No. 17 in B-flat Minor
	Preludes: No. 4 in E Minor; No. 24 in D Minor
	Valse Op. 64 No. 2 in C-sharp Minor
CORELLI	Adagio from Sonata No. 5
DEBUSSY	"La Cathedrale Engloutie"
	"Claire de Lune" (November 1937)
	"La Soirée dans Grenade" (November 1940)
	"Romance"
DUPARC	"Extase" (October 1920)
DVOŘÁK	Slavonic Dance No. 10 in E Minor
FRANCK	*Panis Angelicus*
FRESCOBALDI	Gagliarda
GABRIELLI	Canzon Quatri Toni a 15
	In Ecclesiis
	Sonata pian e forte
GLUCK	Sicilienne from *Armide*
HANDEL	Dead March from *Saul*
	Concerto Grosso in B Op. 3 No.1
	Fireworks Music
	Overture in D Minor from Concerto Grosso Op.3 No.5
	"Pastoral Symphony" from *Messiah*
	Water Music
HAYDN	Andante Cantabile from String Quartet Op.3 No.5
LISZT	Hungarian Rhapsody No. 2
	"Wanderer's Night Song"
	Die Drei Zigeuner
LULLY	*Atys*, Act 1, Scene 4
	"Air de Arcaine" from *Armide*
	Prelude from *Alceste*
	Nocturne from *Le Triomphe de l'amour*
	March from *Thesée*

MATTHESON	Air
MOZART	Quartet in F Major, K. 370 (April 1920)
	"Turkish March" from the Piano Sonata in A Major
MUSSORGSKY	*Boris Godunov:* Symphonic Synthesis (November 1936)
	Khovanshchina: Entr'acte, Act IV, Scene 2
	Night on Bald Mountain (December 1940)
	Pictures at an Exhibition (November 1939)
NOVACEK	"Perpetuum Mobile" (Op. 5 No 4)
PALESTRINA	*Adoramus te* (October 1934)
PURCELL	Suite from *The Faery Queen* and *Dido and Aneas*
	Trumpet Voluntary (Clarke, attrib. Purcell) (December 1924)
RACHMANINOFF	Prelude in C-sharp Minor
RAMEAU	*Castor and Pollux* Overture
RIMSKY-KORSAKOV	Dance from *Snegourotchka*
	Andante and Prelude from *The Battle of Kitesch*
	Prelude to Act 3 of *Ivan the Terrible*
SCHUBERT	Deutsche Tanze Op. 33
	Dances and Eccossaise ("Tyrolean Dances")
	"Moment Musicale" No. 3
	Songs: "Der Leiermann," "Du bist die Ruhe," "Erlkonig," "Gute Nacht," "Serenade"
SCHUMANN	"Traumerie"
	"Bride's Songs" Nos. 1 and 2
SCRIABIN	Etude in C-sharp Minor
SHOSTAKOVICH	Entr'acte from *Lady Macbeth of Mtsensk* (April 1936)
	Prelude in E-flat Minor
	United Nations March
SOUSA	"El Capitan"
	"Stars and Stripes Forever"
STRAUSS, J.	*Blue Danube* Waltz
	Waltzes from *Die Fledermaus*
	Waltzes from *Tales from the Vienna Woods*
STRAVINSKY	Pastorale
TCHAIKOVSKY	Andante Cantabile
	"At the Ball"
	Berceuse
	"Chant sans Paroles"
	"Cherubim Song"

	"He Truly Loves Me"
	"Humoresque"
	"Solitude"
VITTORIA	*Jesus Dulcis Memoria*
VIVALDI	Concerto Grosso in D Minor
WAGNER	Excerpts from *Götterdämmerung, Parsifal, Das Rheingold,*
	Siegfried, Tristan und Isolde, and *Die Walküre*
WEBER	*Invitation to the Dance*
TRADITIONAL	Two Ancient Liturgical Melodies
	Slavonic (Russian) Christmas Music

Original Stokowski Compositions

CHORAL

Benedicite Omnia Opera (1907, revised 1947)
Carol "When Christ Was Born of Mary Free" (1907, revised 1954)
Pianissimo Amen (1968)

INSTRUMENTAL

Dithyramb for flute, 'cello, and harp
Processional Hymn
"Reverie" for String Orchestra
Symphony
Vision for Orchestra
"Vocal Rhapsody" ("Negro Rhapsody")
Themes and Sketches:
  "The War God" for voice and piano
  "Tristesse" for Keyboard
  Two Tennyson Songs: "Milkmaid's Song" and "The Lute Song"

For the research done on these compilations of Stokowski's transcriptions and original compositions I am indebted to Peter Dobson of London; Dr. Edwin E. Heilakka, curator of the Stokowski Collection in the Curtis Institute of Music, Philadelphia; Jack Baumgarten; and staff members of the Philadelphia Orchestra Association.

Index

Note: page numbers in italics refer to illustrations.